FEDERAL ADMINISTRATIVE LAW

Eighth Edition

■ ■ ■

Gary Lawson

Philip S. Beck Professor of Law
Boston University School of Law

AMERICAN CASEBOOK SERIES®

WEST
ACADEMIC
PUBLISHING

American Casebook Series is a trademark registered in the U.S. Patent and Trademark Office.

© West, a Thomson business, 1998, 2001, 2004, 2007
© 2009, 2013 Thomson Reuters
© 2016 LEG, Inc. d/b/a West Academic
© 2019 LEG, Inc. d/b/a West Academic
    444 Cedar Street, Suite 700
    St. Paul, MN 55101
    1-877-888-1330

West, West Academic Publishing, and West Academic are trademarks of West Publishing Corporation, used under license.

Printed in the United States of America

ISBN: 978-1-64020-149-1

To Patty, Nathaniel, and Noah

PREFACE

When I wrote the first edition of this book in 1998, I perceived a need for a casebook that concentrated on the doctrinal fundamentals and historical development of federal administrative law. Seven editions later, I am even more smugly confident of the value of that approach. The doctrinal and historical emphasis of this book has not changed, and it never will.

This edition contains the usual amount of updating, revising, and organizational tweaking, in part to accommodate the fact that Administrative Law is increasingly becoming a first-year course. Materials that traditionally were part of a Legislation course, especially materials concerning techniques of statutory interpretation, are rapidly becoming the province of this course, and I have accordingly continued to revise and expand Chapter 1 to include a significant discussion of statutory interpretation for those who want or need to pursue the topic. But I have not altered the philosophy, structure, or primary materials from the previous editions. The "vision thing" that drove this book remains constant.

That "vision thing" is a deliberate set of choices about Administrative Law pedagogy that reflects a distinct and (I hope) coherent approach to a difficult subject—and Administrative Law is widely and justly regarded as one of the most difficult subjects in the law school curriculum. It is a hard course to take and a hard course to teach.

The good news is that there is widespread agreement about which features of American administrative law are primarily responsible for these difficulties: (1) the sheer scope of the subject, (2) the technical complexity of many of the doctrines and of the factual contexts in which the doctrines are often applied, (3) the difficulties of drawing useful generalizations across agencies that have different statutory authorizations, histories, and relationships with other legal actors, (4) the uneasy coexistence of doctrines that were developed at different periods of time under different assumptions about the legal and political status of agencies, and (5) the intimate connections among many aspects of administrative law that make it impossible fully to understand individual branches of doctrine without a grasp of the larger picture. The bad news is that there is far less agreement about the appropriate solutions to these problems. This casebook reflects one set of integrated solutions—a set that I hope will allow both students and teachers to realize the enormous potential offered by a course on administrative law.

(1) The first problem facing any student or teacher of administrative law is the seemingly limitless scope of the subject matter. In principle,

administrative law encompasses virtually everything that today goes under the banner of public law. Although the primary focus of administrative law is the operation of the executive arm of government (which itself encompasses everything from policymaking on the frontiers of science to the management of prisons to the administration of benefits programs to the regulation of public utilities), a study of administrative law very quickly shades into a study of the legislative process, with additional rapid detours into constitutional law, civil procedure, federal jurisdiction, jurisprudence, and a host of more specialized subjects such as labor law, securities regulation, food and drug law, environmental law, and health law. That way lies madness.

This book adopts three strategies to reduce the Administrative Law course to a manageable set of materials. First, and most importantly, the book deliberately concentrates on *federal* administrative law, to the near-total exclusion of *state* administrative law (except to the extent that procedural due process implicates state agencies). This is a controversial strategy. Most real-world administrative law problems arise at the state or local level. It is therefore not surprising that many people believe, with Professor Arthur Bonfield, that by "failing to integrate state law into their administrative law courses, law schools are * * * remiss in their intellectual obligations to students and in their duties to the bar and the public at large." Arthur Bonfield, *State Law in the Teaching of Administrative Law: A Critical Analysis of the Status Quo*, 61 Tex. L. Rev. 95, 95–96 (1982). To which one can only respond, "Yes, but . . ."

There is no such thing as "state administrative law." There are fifty systems of state administrative law, plus some much larger number of local variations. There are *commonalities* among those systems, but those commonalities are in large measure shared by the federal system and can be taught effectively through a focused examination of federal administrative law. In order to learn and understand the *differences* among the various state systems, one must first establish a doctrinal baseline against which comparisons can be made—and that is a task that quickly consumes the entire course. If one knows that most of one's students will practice in a specific state, then there is good reason to include material on that state's administrative law in a basic course. But that is something that a nationally marketed casebook must leave to the discretion of individual instructors. Accordingly, this book's straightforward organization readily invites supplementation with comparisons between federal administrative law and individual state systems. The book itself, however, is true to its name: it is a tool for the study of federal administrative law and the unique forces that have shaped it.

Moreover, the consequences of a federal focus are not as dire as Professor Bonfield fears. Although the federal and state systems often provide different answers to many of the questions posed by administrative law, the questions are largely the same. Once one understands the questions, it is not that difficult to translate from federal law to the law of any specific jurisdiction.

Second, this book concentrates on administrative *law*. There is much to be said for a course that focuses instead on techniques of administrative policymaking and the role of the lawyer in shaping agency decisions outside of formal legal channels. I believe, however, that this material is best handled through advanced courses or seminars, presumably with smaller enrollments and more opportunities to engage in role-playing, problem-solving, and negotiating exercises. If one tries to give significant coverage to the "nonlegal" world of administrative law in an introductory course, it must come at the expense of basic elements of doctrine. Such a tradeoff is defensible but, I think, ultimately unwise. Thus, this casebook is self-consciously *doctrinal*, focusing on the formal legal doctrines that establish the framework within which policymakers, lobbyists, and lawyers can ply their trades.

Third, this book deliberately sacrifices breadth for depth. Even if one limits oneself to a doctrinal study of federal administrative law, the volume of material is overwhelming. Accordingly, this book strongly emphasizes what I regard as the four fundamental branches of administrative law: the constitutional foundations of the administrative state, the law (both constitutional and statutory) governing agency rulemaking and adjudicatory procedures, the law governing the scope of judicial review of agency action, and the law governing the timing and availability of judicial review. Each of these topics is treated with some attention to detail in order to promote a deep *understanding* of administrative law. But to pursue these topics in depth, others must be left behind. Thus, this book does not cover such important subjects as agency collection and disclosure of information, public participation in and initiation of agency proceedings, or the law governing private rights of action. These subjects can usefully be taught in advanced courses, but there simply isn't room for them in the basic course.

(2) & (3) Administrative law is difficult in large measure because it is difficult. Much of the doctrine is very complex. Moreover, the factual settings that one encounters in a study of administrative law range over a wide variety of specialized subjects. A fair degree of technical competence in these subjects is often required in order to place material in its proper context. Students and teachers—and even casebook editors—cannot be expected to rise to the challenge in all circumstances.

My answer to the problem of doctrinal complexity is: don't hide the ball. The organization of this book is straightforward and even mechanistic; this is not a course in which it pays to be fancy or clever. Furthermore, the book is uncommonly didactic in tone. The book consists almost entirely of principal cases and textual notes. There are very few "note cases" that are not woven into a textual elaboration and even fewer (nonrhetorical) questions for which the book does not at least suggest an answer. In my experience, it is impossible to be too explicit with students about the meaning or relevance of the material in this course. Socrates never had to teach Administrative Law.

The problem of technical complexity is much trickier to handle. One popular solution is to focus the course on a detailed study of one or two agencies. Not only does this make it easier for the students and teachers to have an adequate mastery of the underlying substantive law, it also avoids the problems that come from attempts to generalize across a large number of agencies. One can argue that just as there is no "state administrative law," but instead fifty different state systems, so there is no "federal administrative law," but instead a materially different body of law that governs every (or at least every major) federal agency.

I respectfully but firmly reject this approach—and some of the major premises on which it is founded. First, as an empirical matter, it is easy to overstate the problems of generalizing doctrine across federal agencies. I suspect that skepticism about the existence of a unitary "federal administrative law" partially, or even largely, reflects a deeper skepticism about the possibility and value of traditional doctrinal analysis. (One encounters this skepticism most frequently in connection with scope-of-review doctrine.) As an unrepentant traditional doctrinalist, I do not share this skepticism: there *really is* a federal administrative law, in the sense of a robust set of principles and doctrines that have general application in a wide range of settings. In my judgment, an introductory course in Administrative Law should focus on this general doctrine, leaving it to specialized courses to work out how these principles get adapted to the circumstances of individual agencies. Second, a book that focuses on general principles makes it possible to supplement the basic course with additional material, either state or federal, that is of special interest to the instructor. It is much harder to supplement a book that focuses on a small number of agencies. Third, an agency-specific focus is better suited to courses that emphasize the "nonlegal" aspects of agency decisionmaking. If one wants to learn about the day-to-day functioning of agencies in the real world, there is much to be said for the case-study approach. It is a less useful approach, however, for a course with a doctrinal focus.

There still remains, however, the problem of acquiring an adequate grasp of the many specialized subjects that are encountered in a "generalist" administrative law course. To my mind, there is simply no solution to this problem that is not worse than the problem itself. Technical complexity is a real feature of modern administrative law, and one simply needs to ride it out. Hopefully, this book's straightforward organization and style will minimize the problem—if only by not muddying the waters any further.

(4) Administrative law has gone through several identifiable stages of development—most notably the Founding Era (which in this context spans roughly the country's first century), the Progressive era, the New Deal era, the "capture theory" era from the mid-1960s to the early 1980s, and the as yet unnamed period from the early 1980s to the present. Each era was driven by distinctive understandings of the roles and functions of agencies, courts, administrative lawyers, and government in general, and those different understandings often lead to very different doctrinal conclusions. Modern administrative law consists of doctrine drawn from all five eras. In order to understand the structure of modern doctrine, one must understand the mix of forces that spawned it.

This book therefore places very heavy emphasis on tracing the historical evolution of modern doctrine. Even when "old" cases are no longer "good law," it is often necessary to study the old cases in order to understand contemporary law. Administrative law makes a great deal of sense if one knows the context from which particular elements of doctrine emerged; it makes very little sense if one simply takes a slice-of-time look at a series of statutes and court decisions. How, for example, can one teach *Vermont Yankee* or the hard look doctrine without giving students a clear understanding of the legal developments—and the myriad reasons for those developments—in the D.C. Circuit in the decade preceding 1978? Indeed, a major impetus for the production of this book was my dissatisfaction with the treatment of history in contemporary casebooks. A good historical sense is also important as a way of understanding change. Federal administrative law has been, in many respects, remarkably stable since the burst of activity in the 1970s. *See* Aaron L. Nielson, *Visualizing Change in Administrative Law*, 49 Ga. L. Rev. 757 (2015). If that stability starts to erode, either through legislative or judicial action, knowing where that change comes from will be very helpful for seeing to where that change is going.

(5) In many respects, administrative law presents students with a Catch-22 situation: in order to understand the procedural law governing agencies, one must understand scope-of-review and timing doctrines, but in order to understand scope-of-review and timing doctrines, one must first understand the basic procedural categories of action and their legal consequences. When all of the pieces are in place, the story of modern federal administrative law is remarkably coherent and understandable. Until all of the pieces are in place, however, one often experiences the frustrations that accompany any uncompleted puzzle. There is, unfortunately, no way to begin at the end.

This feature of administrative law is inescapable. I have tried to mitigate its effects through frequent references to prior—and, where feasible, subsequent—materials. I have also tried to maintain a sense of "flow" throughout the book, so that students can see how the material builds over the course of the year. The underlying (though often nonobvious) coherence of administrative law doctrine contributes to the subject's difficulty, but it also accounts for a good measure of the subject's ultimate intellectual satisfaction.

Learning administrative law is like reading a story; each chapter reveals a bit more about the plot. This book is designed to tell the story of modern federal administrative law in a straightforward yet sophisticated fashion. I will be deeply gratified if I can help users of this book find that story as rewarding and enjoyable as I have.

A note on form: Textual omissions from quoted materials are indicated by three asterisks, but citations and footnotes are generally omitted from quoted material without indication. I have also, on some occasions, omitted subheadings from quoted material without indication. Where I have retained footnotes from quoted material, I have also retained the original numbering, with one exception: The excerpt on pages 595–604 contains so many footnotes that I simply let them number consecutively within the excerpt. Editor's footnotes, including editor's footnotes inserted into quoted material, are numbered consecutively in each chapter. Editor's footnotes that appear in quoted material are clearly identified and are marked in brackets.

GARY LAWSON

November 2018

ACKNOWLEDGMENTS

I have come to rely on users—both faculty and students—for suggestions on everything from organization to case selection to grammar. I am especially grateful to Professors Mike Abramowicz, Adam Babich, Patrick Brennan, Robert Butkin, Eric Claeys, John Duffy, Stephen Gilles, Linda Jellum (and her student Lindsay Wilson), Bill Kelley, Erika Lietzan, Tom Merrill, Peter Phipps, Philip Pucillo, Mike Rappaport, Jim Speta, Rena Steinzor, and Amy Widman for their thoughtful suggestions over the years. I am also forever indebted to Lesliediana Jones in the Northwestern University Law Library and two anonymous WESTLAW employees for crucial help in downloading material for the first edition, to the William M. Trumbull Fund and the Julius Rosenthal Fund at Northwestern University School of Law for support in the production of the first edition, to Boston University School of Law and the Abraham and Lillian Benton Fund and the Michaels Faculty Fund for support in the production of subsequent editions, and to Barbara H. Granger and Kathy Ellis (now Bruyn), without whom the second and third editions probably would still be unfinished. Most of all, I am grateful to Patricia B. G. Lawson—editor, critic, consultant, and inspiration.

I acknowledge with appreciation the following authors, publishers, and journals who have granted permission to reprint excerpts from their copyrighted publications:

Administrative Law Review: Gary Lawson & Stephen Kam, *Making Law Out of Nothing at All: The Origins of the* Chevron *Doctrine*, 65 Admin. L. Rev. 1 (2013).

The Brookings Institute: Roger G. Noll, Reforming Regulation (1971).

Chicago-Kent College of Law, Illinois Institute of Technology: Gary S. Lawson, *Reconceptualizing* Chevron *and Discretion: A Comment on Levin and Rubin*, 72 Chi.-Kent L.Rev. 1377 (1997).

Connecticut Law Review: Jack M. Beermann, *End the Failed* Chevron *Experiment Now: How* Chevron *Has Failed and Why It Can and Should Be Overruled*, 42 Conn. L. Rev. 779 (2010).

Cornell University: Peter B. McCutchen, *Mistakes, Precedent, and the Rise of the Administrative State: Toward a Constitutional Theory of the Second Best*, 80 Cornell L. Rev. 1 (1994).

Cornell University: Peter L. Strauss, *Formal and Functional Approaches to Separation-of-Powers Questions—A Foolish Inconsistency?*, 72 Cornell L. Rev. 488 (1987).

Duke Law Journal: Antonin Scalia, *Judicial Deference to Administrative Interpretations of Statutes*, 1989 Duke L.J. 511.

Harvard Law Review: Ralph F. Fuchs, *Procedure in Administrative Rule-Making*, 52 Harv. L. Rev. 259 (1938).

Harvard Law Review: Gary Lawson, *The Rise and Rise of the Administrative State*, 107 Harv. L. Rev. 1231 (1994).

Harvard University Press: John Dickinson, Administrative Justice and the Supremacy of Law in the United States (1927).

Notre Dame Law Review: Gary Lawson, Katharine Ferguson & Guillermo Montero, *"Oh Lord, Please Don't Let Me Be Misunderstood!": Rediscovering the* Mathews v. Eldridge *and* Penn Central *Frameworks*, 81 Notre Dame L. Rev. 1 (2005).

Oxford University Press: Jerry L. Mashaw, *Prodelegation: Why Administrators Should Make Political Decisions*, 1 J.L. Econ. & Org. 81 (1985).

Pace Law Review: Arnold I. Burns & Stephen J. Markman, *Understanding Separation of Powers*, 7 Pace L. Rev. 575 (1987).

Princeton University Press: Marver H. Bernstein, Regulating Business by Independent Commission (1955).

Rutgers Law Review: Gary Lawson, *Outcome, Procedure, and Process: Agency Duties of Explanation for Legal Conclusions*, 48 Rutgers L. Rev. 313 (1996).

St. Louis University Law Review: Gary Lawson, *Prolegomenon to Any Future Administrative Law Course: Separation of Powers and the Transcendental Deduction*, 49 St. Louis U.L. Rev. 885 (2005).

Vanderbilt Law Review: Richard J. Pierce, Jr., Chevron *and Its Aftermath: Judicial Review of Agency Interpretations of Statutory Provisions*, 41 Vand. L. Rev. 301 (1988).

James Q. Wilson: James Q. Wilson, The Politics of Regulation (Basic Books 1980).

Yale Law Journal: Thomas W. Merrill, *Judicial Deference to Executive Precedent*, 101 Yale L.J. 969 (1992).

Yale Law Journal: William F. Pedersen, Jr., *Formal Records and Informal Rulemaking*, 85 Yale L.J. 38 (1975).

Yale University Press: James M. Landis, The Administrative Process (1938).

SUMMARY OF CONTENTS

TABLE OF CONTENTS

TABLE OF CASES

The principal cases are in bold type.

FEDERAL
ADMINISTRATIVE LAW
Eighth Edition

CHAPTER 1

INTRODUCTION

■ ■ ■

A. AGENCIES: THEIR ORIGINS, FORMS, AND FUNCTIONS

1. WHAT IS AN AGENCY?

The basic unit of analysis of administrative law is the government *agency*. Indeed, a good working definition of administrative law is "the law governing the forms, functions, and activities of government agencies."

There is no explicit and precise definition of an agency that is applicable in all legal contexts. There are, however, explicit—even if far from precise—definitions prescribed by various statutes that apply in most contexts relevant to the federal administrative law system. The most important, though by no means the only, federal statutory definition of an agency is contained in the Administrative Procedure Act (or "APA"), which is a statute that regulates many of the operations of federal administrative agencies. Much of this course involves a careful study of the APA as it has been interpreted and applied since its passage in 1946. The APA provides the following definition of an agency, which is applicable in most (though not quite all) contexts likely to be encountered by a lawyer navigating the federal regulatory world:

"[A]gency" means each authority of the Government of the United States, whether or not it is within or subject to review by another agency, but does not include—

(A) the Congress;

(B) the courts of the United States;

(C) the governments of the territories or possessions of the United States;

(D) the government of the District of Columbia;

or, except as to the requirements of section 552 of this title—

(E) agencies composed of representatives of the parties or of representatives of organizations of the parties to the disputes determined by them;

(F) courts martial and military commissions;

(G) military authority exercised in the field in time of war or in occupied territory; or

(H) functions conferred by sections 1738, 1739, 1743, and 1744 of title 12; chapter 2 of title 41; or sections 1622, 1884, 1891–1902, and former section 1641(b)(2), of title 50, appendix * * *.

5 U.S.C. § 551(1) (2012). Ignore the strange-sounding subsections (E) and (H), which the administrative lawyer is unlikely to encounter today. Ignore also the reference to "section 552 of this title" following subsection (D), which is a reference to the Freedom of Information Act (or "FOIA")—an important statute requiring public access to most documents and data held by federal agencies.[1] What remains as the definition of an agency is any "authority" of the United States government except Congress, the federal courts, territorial governments, and certain military entities. Note that an "authority" can be an agency under this statute even if it is "within or subject to review by" another agency.

So what is an "authority" of the United States government? The statute does not tell us, so we must reason it out for ourselves. Surely, for example, the Department of Justice, one of the most important units of administration in the United States government,[2] constitutes such an

---

[1] With *considerable* reluctance, this book does not cover the many crucial questions facing administrative lawyers posed by the FOIA. The FOIA contains its own definition of an agency that is understood to be slightly broader than the definition under discussion here. For purposes of the FOIA, "the term 'agency' * * * includes any executive department, military department, Government corporation, Government controlled corporation, or other establishment in the executive branch of the Government (including the Executive Office of the President), or any independent regulatory agency." 5 U.S.C. § 552(f) (2012). Many litigated disputes about the definition of an agency actually concern this FOIA definition rather than the more generally applicable APA definition. For some interesting cases exploring some of the recurring problems under the FOIA definition of an agency, see *Citizens for Responsibility and Ethics in Washington v. Office of Administration*, 566 F.3d 219 (D.C.Cir.2009) (holding that the Office of Administration within the Executive Office of the President is not an agency under the FOIA because it has no independent decisional authority); *Armstrong v. Executive Office of the President*, 90 F.3d 553 (D.C.Cir.1996) (holding, in a 2–1 decision, that the National Security Council is not an agency for purposes of the FOIA); *Meyer v. Bush*, 981 F.2d 1288 (D.C.Cir.1993) (holding, in a 2–1 decision, that the first President Bush's Task Force on Regulatory Relief was not an agency for purposes of the FOIA).

Other statutes also sometimes contain their own definitions of an agency. For example, a statute concerning the management of federal records defines a "Federal agency" to mean "any executive agency or any establishment in the legislative or judicial branch of the Government (except the Supreme Court, the Senate, the House of Representatives, and the Architect of the Capitol and any activities under the direction of the Architect of the Capitol) * * *." 44 U.S.C. § 901(14) (2012). This definition of an agency, unlike the definition in the APA, includes the lower federal courts.

[2] The Department of Justice is one of fifteen federal agencies labeled as "departments" by statute, whose heads belong to the President's so-called Cabinet. The Cabinet is not a formal legal entity. It exists by custom and tradition and provides a means by which the President can regularly get advice from his or her most important subordinates. The composition of the Cabinet changes over time. In 1996, the Cabinet consisted of the Vice President and the heads of the then-fourteen departments—the Departments of Agriculture, Commerce, Defense, Education, Energy, Health and Human Services, Housing and Urban Development, Interior, Justice, Labor, State, Transportation, Treasury, and Veterans Affairs—plus the President's Chief of Staff, the Chairman of the Council of Economic Advisers, the Director of the Office of Management and Budget

"authority." The same is true of many formal sub-units of the Justice Department—for example, the Antitrust Division, the Solicitor General's Office, or the Federal Bureau of Investigation. Each of these units is a sub-unit of the larger Department of Justice, and therefore "within or subject to review by another agency," but each surely has enough distinctive identity and final decisionmaking responsibility to come within the meaning of "authority" under the APA definition.

What about an informal working group within the Justice Department, consisting of a small number of employees from several different units brought together temporarily to study some discrete problem? Is such a group an "authority," and therefore an "agency"? There is no way to give a general answer without knowing the legal effect, either within or without the government, of the group's activities. The status of a federal governmental unit as an "authority," and therefore an "agency," depends ultimately on its powers and responsibilities. Conceivably, a single person could be an "agency" if that person has sufficient responsibilities to make him or her an "authority." For example, Cabinet-level officers such as the Attorney General (the head of the Department of Justice) or the Secretary of Labor (the head of the Department of Labor) are important enough figures to meet the APA's definition of an agency. Even lesser officials can be agencies if they have sufficient decisionmaking responsibilities. As a legislative report issued prior to the passage of the APA explained:

> It is necessary to define agency as "authority" rather than by name or form, because of the present system of including one agency within another or of authorizing internal boards or "divisions" to have final authority. "Authority" means any officer or board, whether within another agency or not, which by law has authority to take final and binding action with or without appeal

---

("OMB"), the Administrator of the Environmental Protection Agency ("EPA"), the Permanent Representative to the United Nations, and the United States Trade Representative. *See* United States Government Manual 1995/1996, at 91. In 2000, by the end of President Clinton's second term, the list also included the Director of the Central Intelligence Agency, the Counselor to the President, the Director of the Federal Emergency Management Agency, the Director of the Office of National Drug Control Policy, and the Administrator of the Small Business Administration. *See* United States Government Manual 2000–2001, at 87. During the administration of the second President Bush, the Department of Homeland Security was added as a fifteenth Cabinet department, and the list of Cabinet members besides the heads of those fifteen departments and the Vice President was down to the President's Chief of Staff, the EPA Administrator, the OMB Director, the Director of the Office of National Drug Policy, and the United States Trade Representative. *See* United States Government Manual 2008–2009, at 87. By 2012, under President Obama, the Director of the Office of National Drug Policy had been dropped and the Chair of the Council of Economic Advisers and the Permanent Representative to the United Nations were back—essentially restoring the Cabinet to its composition as of 1996 (with the addition of the Department of Homeland Security). *See* United States Government Manual 2011–2012, at 81. Under President Trump, the Cabinet has added back the Director of the Central Intelligence Agency and the Administrator of the Small Business Administration and has included the Director of National Intelligence. *See* https://www.whitehouse.gov/the-trump-administration/the-cabinet/.

to some superior administrative authority. Thus, "divisions" of the Interstate Commerce Commission and the judicial officers of the Department of Agriculture would be "agencies" within this definition.

Sen. Doc. No. 248, 79th Cong., 2d Sess. 13 (1945).

Is the President of the United States an "agency" under this statutory definition? Hold that thought for a few pages.

Definitions of an agency provided by Congress, in the APA or elsewhere, are not conclusive for all legal purposes. Congress cannot determine, through statutory labels, whether entities are subject to the Constitution. For example, in *Lebron v. National R.R. Passenger Corp.*, 513 U.S. 374, 115 S.Ct. 961, 130 L.Ed.2d 902 (1995), an artist (successfully) sought to apply the First Amendment's freedom of speech clause to Amtrak, a government-sponsored corporation. The First Amendment applies only to acts of government, not to acts of private entities. Amtrak's statute specified that the organization "will not be an agency or establishment of the United States Government." 45 U.S.C. § 541 (1994). (The statute has been recodified, with minor amendments, at 49 U.S.C. § 24301 (2012).) The Supreme Court held that this statute

> is assuredly dispositive of Amtrak's status as a Government entity for purposes of matters that are within Congress' control—for example, whether it is subject to statutes that impose obligations or confer powers upon Government entities, such as the Administrative Procedure Act, the Federal Advisory Committee Act, and the laws governing Government procurement * * *. But it is not for Congress to make the final determination of Amtrak's status as a government entity for purposes of determining the constitutional rights of citizens affected by its actions. If Amtrak is, by its very nature, what the Constitution regards as the Government, congressional pronouncement that it is not such can no more relieve it of its First Amendment restrictions than a similar pronouncement could exempt the Federal Bureau of Investigation from the Fourth Amendment.

513 U.S. at 392, 115 S.Ct. at 971. The Court concluded that Amtrak is an "agency" for purposes of the Constitution and is therefore subject to the First Amendment.

2. WHERE DO AGENCIES COME FROM?

The basic institutions of the United States government are created by the Constitution. The Constitution creates the national legislature, consisting of the Senate and the House of Representatives, *see* U.S. Const. art. I, § 1, the offices of the President and Vice President, *see id.* art. II, § 1, and the Supreme Court, *see id,* art. III, § 1. The Constitution does not create, or explicitly require the creation of, any other offices or institutions.[3] The Constitution anticipates that there will be, inter alia, "officers of the United States," "ambassadors," "public ministers and consuls," "judges * * * of the * * * inferior courts," and "heads of departments," but it does not of its own force create any of those positions. Similarly, the Constitution anticipates that there will be executive "departments," and specifically a "treasury of the United States," but it does not of its own force create any administrative institutions. Instead, Congress is given power "[t]o make all Laws which shall be necessary and proper for carrying into Execution" the powers vested by the Constitution in Congress, the President, the Vice President, and the federal courts, *see id.* art. I, § 8, cl. 18, which includes the power to create positions in the government.

All units of the national government except the President, Vice President, Supreme Court, and Congress are thus created by congressional *statute* or by presidential allocation of resources placed at his or her disposal by congressional statute. The entire machinery of the executive arm of the United States government below the level of the President[4] is the result of congressional action. None of the many federal agencies with which we are all familiar has to exist—or has to exist in its present form. Accordingly, behind every federal agency (apart from a few created through statutorily authorized executive reorganizations of existing authorities, *see infra* page 192 n.24) lies a legislative act, called an *organic act*, which creates, empowers, defines, and limits that agency.

But while the Constitution does not directly create most of the institutions of the national government, it does place limits on the manner in which Congress can create and structure those institutions. Chapter 2 is largely concerned with identifying those limits.

3. THE STRUCTURE OF FEDERAL AGENCIES

Federal agencies come in all different shapes and sizes, from the United States Department of Defense to the late (and by your editor deeply lamented) federal Board of Tea Appeals, which until its abolition in 1996 adjudicated the claims of tea importers whose products were denied entry into the United States by federal tea-tasters. For most real-world purposes, the concrete differences among agencies are far more important than any formal similarities that one might find. Although overlapping jurisdiction among federal (and between federal and state) agencies is the norm in the

---

[3] The Constitution authorizes the House and Senate to select their officers, including, respectively, a Speaker and a President pro tempore. *See* U.S.Const. art. I, § 2, cl. 5; *id.* art. I, § 3, cl. 5. Because these provisions declare that the houses of Congress "shall" select their officers, they could be read to require the creation of at least the named legislative offices.

[4] The Vice President, unless acting as President, has no specific constitutional role in the executive arena. The Vice President's only constitutionally prescribed power is to serve as president of the Senate and to break ties in that body. *See id.* art. I, § 3, cl. 4.

modern world,[5] lawyers are seldom called upon to deal with "agencies" in general. When a lawyer is brought into the picture, it is usually to deal with a discrete problem (whether present or anticipated) involving a specific agency or a small number of specific agencies. Because most dealings with agencies take place outside of formal legal channels, the lawyer in such a case will need to know the unique internal and external power structures of the relevant agencies. In other words, "agency structure" for most practical purposes means the agency's actual decisionmaking process, which is likely to be more a function of personalities, politics, and informal relationships than of formal legal organization.

Nonetheless, the study of agency structure in this book will be almost exclusively confined to an examination of the formal organization of agencies at the highest level of their internal chains of command. This focus seriously distorts our study of agencies, but, in the words of the Bard, "though this be madness, yet there is method in't." *Hamlet*, Act II, Scene II, line 205. While most agencies conduct very little of their business at the upper levels of the command structure, the formal organization at the agency's head is at least one important aspect of the agency's overall decisionmaking structure, gives rise to some important constitutional issues, and, most importantly, is the only facet of this subject that lends itself to useful generalizations.

There are two such useful generalizations, which reflect the two ways in which one can differentiate among the formal command structures of federal agencies. First, all agencies are either *single-headed* or *multi-member*, meaning simply that there is either a single person at the top of the organizational chart or more than one person sharing (at least in theory) ultimate decisional authority.[6] All Cabinet-level agencies are single-headed, while most, though by no means all, of the alphabet-soup agencies that broadly regulate economic activity are multi-member boards or commissions.[7]

---

[5] A nuclear power plant, for example, must be licensed for construction and operation by the federal Nuclear Regulatory Commission. Construction of the plant requires approval from local land-use commissions, and perhaps also from federal environmental agencies if, for example, the site involves protected wetlands or animal species. Operation of the plant also requires licenses from a number of state and federal environmental agencies. And the operation of any business involves compliance with the directives of a vast range of federal and state agencies that cover subjects from pricing practices to labor conditions.

[6] As a matter of terminology, multi-member federal agencies are almost always called *commissions* or *boards*. Single-headed federal agencies go by a bevy of different names; a sample includes the Environmental Protection *Agency*, the *Department* of Justice, the *Office* of Management and Budget, the Federal Aviation *Administration*, the Internal Revenue *Service*, and the *Bureau* of Standards. The choice of label has no legal significance.

[7] Prominent multi-member agencies include the Federal Reserve Board, the Federal Trade Commission, the Federal Energy Regulatory Commission, the National Labor Relations Board, the Consumer Product Safety Commission, the Nuclear Regulatory Commission, and the Securities and Exchange Commission. A sample of single-headed agencies with broad regulatory authority includes the Environmental Protection Agency, the Occupational Safety and Health

The second structural distinction among agencies concerns the manner in which the head or heads of an agency can be removed from office by the President. (As we will see in Chapter 2, all agency officials can in theory be removed from office by Congress through the constitutional impeachment process, though that almost never happens in the real world.) Some agency heads serve entirely at the pleasure of the President, who can fire them at any time for any reason or even for no reason at all. Agencies whose heads are subject to unlimited presidential removal authority are generally referred to as *executive agencies*. Other agency heads are, by statute, given some form of tenure of office. This typically consists of a term of years (such as five or seven years) along with provisions authorizing earlier removal by the President for "misconduct" or "cause." Sometimes such "for cause" removal provisions are implied by courts from statutes that create offices with fixed terms but specify no conditions for removal. "Cause" or "misconduct" in these contexts typically encompasses things like criminal dishonesty or gross incompetence but is *not* ordinarily understood to include making policy decisions with which the President disagrees.[8] Agencies headed by persons who the President cannot remove at will are generally called *independent agencies*.

Be very careful with this understanding of the executive/independent distinction. It is not the only way in which the terms "executive agency" and "independent agency" are used in administrative law,[9] though it is the most important way from a legal standpoint. Moreover, the term "independent" in this context means *only* that the agency head(s) enjoys some form of job security. It does *not* mean that such agencies are functionally independent of other institutions—certainly not of Congress, *see FCC v. Fox Television Stations, Inc.,* 556 U.S. 502, 523, 129 S.Ct. 1800, 1815, 173 L.Ed.2d 738 (2009) ("[t]he independent agencies are sheltered not from politics but from the President, and it has often been observed that their freedom from presidential oversight (and protection) has simply been replaced by increased subservience to congressional direction"), and

---

Administration (which is part of the Department of Labor), the Food and Drug Administration (which is part of the Department of Health and Human Services), the National Highway Traffic Safety Administration (which is part of the Department of Transportation), the Internal Revenue Service (which is part of the Department of the Treasury), and the Federal Bureau of Investigation (which is part of the Department of Justice).

8   Because these limitations on the President's removal power are statutory, their contours are determined by the particular statutes at issue. For example, the term "misconduct" can have one meaning in one statute and an entirely different meaning in another. There are serious constitutional questions about the permissible scope of congressional restrictions on the President's removal power. *See infra* pages 241–276.

9   For example, the *United States Government Manual* calls every federal agency except the Cabinet departments and the units within the Executive Office of the President an "independent establishment." A major 1941 book similarly noted that while "[t]he term 'independence' is sometimes used to refer to this immunity of a commission from the President's discretionary removal power * * * [,] [i]t is used here rather to denote a location in the governmental system outside the [at that time] ten executive departments." Robert E. Cushman, The Independent Regulatory Commissions (1941).

possibly not of the President either. Although the whole point of limiting the President's power to remove agency personnel is to insulate the agencies from presidential control, political scientists vigorously debate how effectively it really does so.

There is a substantial correspondence between the single-headed/multi-member and executive/independent axes. All of the major multi-member boards and commissions are independent, and almost all of the single-headed agencies are executive.[10] This is not accidental. The theory behind these particular combinations has long been that single-headedness and executiveness both promote accountability (because you can blame a single administrator for the agency's mistakes and then blame the President for retaining the administrator), while multi-memberness and independence both promote disinterested professionalism (because a group of tenured officials will presumably be less vulnerable to special-interest and presidential influence). Thus, according to this theory, if your aim is scientific governmental management, you will tend to create independent multi-member commissions, while if your aim is political accountability, you will tend to create single-member executive agencies.

Whether or not the theory is valid, it has been around at least since the beginnings of the Progressive Era, near the end of the nineteenth century. For roughly the first one hundred years of the nation's history, all federal agencies of note were single-headed executive agencies. Indeed, there were serious doubts during that time whether any other arrangement could be constitutional. The first multi-member independent commission, the Interstate Commerce Commission, was created in 1887. As the Progressive vision of government by impartial experts gained strength, such commissions began proliferating: the Federal Reserve Board in 1913, the Federal Trade Commission in 1914, and the Federal Radio Commission in 1927. When the New Deal came along in the 1930's, distrust of overweening presidential power was added to progressivism as a reason to make agencies multi-member and independent. The enduring New Deal regulatory agencies, such as the Securities and Exchange Commission, the National Labor Relations Board, and the Federal Communications Commission, typically take this multi-member independent form.

In the 1960's and 1970's, single-headed executive agencies came back into vogue, as the Progressive vision of impartial professional administration gave way to a very different perception of agencies as pawns of the regulated industries. Thus, when Congress began empowering the modern breed of agencies to deal with health, safety, and

---

[10] There are a few odd exceptions. The now-defunct Office of the Special Prosecutor, which you will encounter a bit later in the course, was a single-headed independent agency, located within the more conventional single-headed executive Department of Justice. An off-the-wall example of a multi-member executive agency is the American Battle Monuments Commission, which maintains overseas American war memorials.

environmental concerns—for example, the National Highway Traffic Safety Administration in 1966 and both the Occupational Safety and Health Administration and the Environmental Protection Agency in 1970—the conventional wisdom was that political accountability, of both the agency heads and the President, was a necessary structural response to the inevitable industry pressure on agencies.[11]

In subsequent years through the early 1990s, the pendulum swung back towards independence, as seemingly entrenched Democratic congressmen tried to keep authority out of the hands of seemingly entrenched Republican presidents. The elections of 1992 and 1994 demonstrated graphically, however, that political entrenchment is a temporary phenomenon for both major parties. No doubt the pendulum will continue to swing—perhaps in unforeseeable ways.

4. INTERLUDE: AN INTRODUCTION TO STATUTORY INTERPRETATION

Recall the APA's definition of an agency as any "authority" of the United States government. If, as was previously noted, a single person, such as a Department of Agriculture adjudicator, can sometimes be an "agency" under the APA definition, is the President of the United States an agency for purposes of that statute?

At first glance, the answer seems to be rather obviously yes. If the President is not an "authority," it is hard to imagine who or what would fit that description. Moreover, the APA definition of an agency specifically exempts Congress, the federal courts, and even territorial governments but contains no exemption for the President. The conclusion that the President is an agency under the APA seems inescapable.

If interpreting statutes was as simple as reading their language in the context of their structure, then it would indeed be inescapable that the President is an agency under the APA—and this course would be much shorter and easier than it is. As it happens, the Supreme Court has held, on two occasions, that the President is *not* an agency under the APA. *See Franklin v. Massachusetts*, 505 U.S. 788, 801, 112 S.Ct. 2767, 2776, 120 L.Ed.2d 636 (1992); *Dalton v. Specter*, 511 U.S. 462, 476, 114 S.Ct. 1719, 1728, 128 L.Ed.2d 497 (1994). How did the Court (and the President) escape the inescapable? How can the APA's definition of an agency possibly fail to include the President?

---

[11] There was a substantive response as well. If one believes that scientific, nonpolitical agency administration is a myth, one is also likely (though by no means obliged) to believe that conferring unlimited discretion on unelected administrators is a bad idea. Accordingly, the single-headed executive agencies created in the 1960's and 1970's were given somewhat more specific statutory mandates than were the Progressive Era and New Deal agencies, though that difference is easy to overstate, as we will see in Chapter 2.

These questions are an entrée into a topic—the interpretation of statutes—that is properly the subject of a separate course (and often is the subject of a separate course) but which plays such a central role in administrative law that it warrants a brief discussion here. Administrative agencies are empowered and limited by statutes, so every administrative law case at least indirectly involves the interpretation of one or more statutes. A good number of such cases turn entirely on the interpretation of statutes. And, of course, statutory interpretation is central to many subjects besides administrative law, such as criminal law. Knowing how to interpret statutes is one of the most important skills that a lawyer can possess.

It is therefore somewhat surprising—one might even say embarrassing—that our legal system has no single governing theory of statutory interpretation. The statement is important enough to bear repetition: Our legal system has no single governing theory of statutory interpretation. Various people, both on and off the bench, will tell you that any or all or some combination of the following sources are admissible[12] in discerning the meaning of statutory provisions:

the language of the statutory provision,

the language of accompanying statutory provisions,

the linguistic context of the statutory language,

the statutory provision's relation to the entire act of which the statute is a part,

the statutory provision's relation to the entire universe of legislation,

the expressed purpose of the statute,

the implicit or inferred purpose of the statute,

the background, or social context, of the statute,

the statute's legislative history,

canons of construction,

the consequences of different interpretations, and

good social policy.

---

[12] The term "admissible" should not be taken to suggest that the formal rules of evidence apply to the proof of statutory meaning. They do not; the traditional rules of evidence apply only to certain conventionally labelled factual questions, not to questions of law or legal meaning. And, as we shall later see, the traditional rules of evidence generally do not apply even to fact-finding in administrative law. But any inquiry, including an inquiry into statutory meaning, must necessarily count some things and discount or exclude others, and "admissibility," in a non-technical sense, seems like a descriptive term for that process of inclusion and exclusion. For those interested in how the idea of proof can apply to something like legal meaning, see Gary Lawson, Evidence of the Law: Proving Legal Claims (2017).

The list is obviously partial, even on its own terms. For instance, in considering statutory language, in any of its variations, one might look for either the language's original meaning or its present meaning. Similarly, the "meaning" might refer to the meaning as understood by the general public, the legislature, or some small group of technical experts. Such meanings might be gleaned from dictionaries or other evidence of common literal meaning or from inquiries that look to ways in which meaning is conveyed indirectly or by implication (sometimes called "pragmatics"). The phrases "legislative history" and "canons of construction" also conceal enormous possible variations in what is considered admissible to prove statutory meaning. For example, as we will see in more detail shortly, legislative history can consist of hearing transcripts, floor statements, committee reports, conference committee reports, and presidential signing statements. Those individual categories of legislative history can be further subdivided: floor statements, for instance, might be viewed differently depending on whether they are statements by proponents or opponents of the legislation, statements by the legislation's sponsor(s), or statements that can reliably be known to have been actually made rather than inserted into the *Congressional Record* after the fact. There is similar dissensus about the appropriate canons of construction to employ and when they are applicable. In sum, there is simply no consensus in our legal system about which of these (and other) considerations are admissible evidence of statutory meaning.

Even more pointedly, once one determines which considerations are relevant, there is the additional problem of determining their relative weight or significance. Two people could, for example, agree entirely that all of the considerations listed above are legitimate but strongly disagree about the hierarchy of importance of the various considerations—such as whether legislative history trumps canons of construction, whether either of those considerations can trump any of the various admissible forms of statutory language, or whether considerations of policy can trump any or all of the above. There is no consensus in our legal system about the appropriate weight or significance to be given to the many considerations that can plausibly be thought relevant to statutory interpretation.

Can a legal system in which statutory interpretation is a fundamental operation really get by if people cannot agree on something as basic as what counts towards statutory meaning and how much it counts? That is a question that will loom large for the rest of this course.

For graphic illustrations of the depth and breadth of disagreement concerning issues of statutory interpretation, as well as exemplars of many of the most commonly employed techniques of interpretation, consider the following cases. The first case, one should note, implicates a doctrine, known as the "*Chevron* doctrine," that will consume a good percentage of this course in Chapter 4. That doctrine gives agencies a large measure of freedom to interpret statutes whose meanings are not clear, so in many administrative law cases courts are looking for "clear" meanings of statutes, and if none is to be found then for "reasonable" meanings, rather than for *correct* ones. Do not worry about that doctrine quite yet; just concentrate for now on the tools that the various opinions employ to discern statutory meaning.

ZUNI PUBLIC SCHOOL DIST. NO. 89 V. DEPARTMENT OF EDUCATION

Supreme Court of the United States, 2007.
550 U.S. 81, 127 S.Ct. 1534, 167 L.Ed.2d 449.

JUSTICE BREYER delivered the opinion of the Court.

A federal statute sets forth a method that the Secretary of Education is to use when determining whether a State's public school funding program "equalizes expenditures" throughout the State. The statute instructs the Secretary to calculate the disparity in per-pupil expenditures among local school districts in the State. But, when doing so, the Secretary is to "disregard" school districts *with per-pupil expenditures . . . above the 95th percentile or below the 5th percentile of such expenditures . . . in the State.*" 20 U.S.C. § 7709(b)(2)(B)(i) (emphasis added).

The question before us is whether the emphasized statutory language permits the Secretary to identify the school districts that should be "disregard[ed]" by looking to the *number of the district's pupils* as well as to the size of the district's expenditures per pupil. We conclude that it does.

I

A

The federal Impact Aid Act provides financial assistance to local school districts whose ability to finance public school education is adversely affected by a federal presence. Federal aid is available to districts, for example, where a significant amount of federal land is exempt from local property taxes, or where the federal presence is responsible for an increase in school-age children (say, of armed forces personnel) whom local schools must educate. The statute typically prohibits a State from offsetting this federal aid by reducing its own state aid to the local district. If applied without exceptions, however, this prohibition might unreasonably interfere with a state program that seeks to equalize per-pupil expenditures throughout the State, for instance, by preventing the state program from taking account of a significant source of federal funding that some local school districts receive. The statute consequently contains an exception that permits a State to compensate for federal impact aid where "the Secretary [of Education] determine[s] and certifies . . . that the State has in effect a program of State aid that *equalizes* expenditures for free public education among local [school districts] in the State."

The statute sets out a formula that the Secretary of Education must use to determine whether a state aid program satisfies the federal "equaliz[ation]" requirement. The formula instructs the Secretary to compare the local school district with the greatest per-pupil expenditures to the school district with the smallest per-pupil expenditures to see whether the former exceeds the latter by more than 25 percent. So long as it does not, the state aid program qualifies as a program that "equalizes expenditures." More specifically the statute provides that "a program of state aid" qualifies, *i.e.,* it "equalizes expenditures" among local school districts if,

> "in the second fiscal year preceding the fiscal year for which the determination is made, the amount of per-pupil expenditures made by [the local school district] with the highest such per-pupil expenditures . . . did not exceed the amount of such per-pupil expenditures made by [the local school district] with the lowest such expenditures . . . by more than 25 percent." § 7709(b)(2)(A).

The statutory provision goes on to set forth what we shall call the "disregard" instruction. It states that, when "making" this "determination," the *"Secretary shall . . . disregard [school districts] with per-pupil expenditures . . . above the 95th percentile or below the 5th percentile of such expenditures."* § 7709(b)(2)(B)(i) (emphasis added). It adds that the Secretary shall further:

> "take into account the extent to which [the state program reflects the special additional costs that some school districts must bear when they are] geographically isolated [or when they provide education for] particular types of students, such as children with disabilities." § 7709(b)(2)(B)(ii).

B

This case requires us to decide whether the Secretary's present calculation method is consistent with the federal statute's "disregard" instruction. The method at issue is contained in a set of regulations that the Secretary first promulgated 30 years ago. Those regulations essentially state the following:

When determining whether a state aid program "equalizes expenditures" (thereby permitting the State to reduce its own local funding on account of federal impact aid), the Secretary will first create a list of school districts ranked in order of per-pupil expenditure. The Secretary will then identify the relevant percentile cutoff point on that list on the basis of a specific (95th or 5th) percentile of *student population*—essentially identifying those districts whose students account for the 5 percent of the

State's total student population that lies at both the high and low ends of the spending distribution. Finally the Secretary will compare the highest spending and lowest spending school districts of those that remain to see whether they satisfy the statute's requirement that the disparity between them not exceed 25 percent.

The regulations set forth this calculation method as follows:

"[D]eterminations of disparity in current expenditures . . . per-pupil are made by—

"(i) Ranking all [of the State's school districts] on the basis of current expenditures . . . per pupil [in the relevant statutorily determined year];

"(ii) Identifying those [school districts] that fall at the 95th and 5th percentiles of the total number of pupils in attendance [at all the State's school districts taken together]; and

"(iii) Subtracting the lower current expenditure . . . per pupil figure from the higher for those [school districts] identified in paragraph (ii) and dividing the difference by the lower figure." 34 CFR pt. 222, subpt. K, App., ¶ 1 (2006) (emphasis deleted).

The regulations also provide an illustration of how to perform the calculation:

"In State X, after ranking all [school districts] in order of the expenditures per pupil for the [statutorily determined] fiscal year in question, it is ascertained by counting the number of pupils in attendance in those [school districts] in ascending order of expenditure that the 5th percentile of student population is reached at [school district A] with a per pupil expenditure of $820, and that the 95th percentile of student population is reached at [school district B] with a per pupil expenditure of $1,000. The percentage disparity between the 95th percentile and the 5th percentile [school districts] is 22 percent ($1000−$820 = $180/$820)." *Ibid.*

Because 22 percent is less than the statutory "25 percent" requirement, the state program in the example qualifies as a program that "equalizes expenditures."

C

This case concerns the Department of Education's application of the Secretary's regulations to New Mexico's local district aid program in respect to fiscal year 2000. As the regulations require, Department officials listed each of New Mexico's 89 local school districts in order of per-pupil spending for fiscal year 1998. (The calculation in New Mexico's case was performed, as the statute allows, on the basis of per-pupil *revenues,* rather than per-pupil *expenditures*. See 20 U.S.C. § 7709(b)(2)(A). For ease of reference we nevertheless refer, in respect to New Mexico's figures and throughout the opinion, only to "per-pupil expenditures.") After ranking the districts, Department officials excluded 17 school districts at the top of the list because those districts contained (cumulatively) less than 5 percent of the student population; for the same reason, they excluded an additional 6 school districts at the bottom of the list.

The remaining 66 districts accounted for approximately 90 percent of the State's student population. Of those, the highest ranked district spent $3,259 per student; the lowest ranked district spent $2,848 per student. The difference, $411, was less than 25 percent of the lowest per-pupil figure, namely $2,848. Hence, the officials found that New Mexico's local aid program qualifies as a program that "equalizes expenditures." New Mexico was therefore free to offset federal impact aid to individual districts by reducing state aid to those districts.

Two of New Mexico's public school districts, Zuni Public School District and Gallup-McKinley County Public School District (whom we shall collectively call Zuni), sought further agency review of these findings. Zuni conceded that the Department's calculations were correct in terms of the Department's own regulations. Zuni argued, however, that the regulations themselves are inconsistent with the authorizing statute. That statute, in its view, requires the Department to calculate the 95th and 5th percentile cutoffs solely on the basis of the number of school districts (ranked by their per-pupil expenditures), without any consideration of the number of pupils in those districts. If calculated as Zuni urges, only 10 districts (accounting for less than 2 percent of all students) would have been identified as the outliers that the statute instructs the Secretary to disregard. The difference, as a result, between the highest and lowest per-pupil expenditures of the remaining districts (26.9 percent) would exceed 25 percent. Consequently, the statute would forbid New Mexico to take account of federal impact aid as it decides how to equalize school funding across the State.

A Department of Education Administrative Law Judge rejected Zuni's challenge to the regulations. The Secretary of Education did the same. Zuni sought review of the Secretary's decision in the Court of Appeals for the Tenth Circuit. Initially, a Tenth Circuit panel affirmed the Secretary's determination by a split vote (2 to 1). Subsequently, the full Court of Appeals vacated the panel's decision and heard the matter en banc. The 12-member en banc court affirmed the Secretary but by an evenly divided court (6 to 6). Zuni sought certiorari. We agreed to decide the matter.

II

A

Zuni's strongest argument rests upon the literal language of the statute. Zuni concedes, as it must, that if the language of the statute is open or ambiguous—that is, if Congress left a "gap" for the agency to fill—then we must [under the *Chevron* doctrine] uphold the Secretary's interpretation as long as it is reasonable * * *.

Considerations other than language provide us with unusually strong indications that Congress intended to leave the Secretary free to use the calculation method before us and that the Secretary's chosen method is a reasonable one. For one thing, the matter at issue—*i.e.,* the calculation method for determining whether a state aid program "equalizes expenditures"—is the kind of highly technical, specialized interstitial matter that Congress often does not decide itself, but delegates to specialized agencies to decide.

For another thing, the history of the statute strongly supports the Secretary. Congress first enacted an impact aid "equalization" exception in 1974 * * *. Soon thereafter, in 1976, the Secretary promulgated the regulation here at issue defining the term "equalizing expenditures" in the manner now before us. As far as we can tell, no Member of Congress has ever criticized the method the 1976 regulation sets forth nor suggested at any time that it be revised or reconsidered.

The present statutory language originated in draft legislation that the Secretary himself sent to Congress in 1994. With one minor change (irrelevant to the present calculation controversy), Congress adopted that language without comment or clarification. No one at the time—no Member of Congress, no Department of Education official, no school district or State—expressed the view that this statutory language (which, after all, was supplied by the Secretary) was intended to require, or did require, the Secretary to change the Department's system of calculation, a system that the Department and school districts across the Nation had followed for nearly 20 years, without (as far as we are told) any adverse effect.

Finally, viewed in terms of the purpose of the statute's disregard instruction, the Secretary's calculation method is reasonable, while the reasonableness of a method based upon the number of districts alone (Zuni's proposed method) is more doubtful. When the Secretary (then Commissioner) of Education considered the matter in 1976, he explained why that is so.

* * *

The Secretary added that under the regulation's calculation system the "percentiles" would be "determined on the basis of numbers of pupils and not on the basis of numbers of districts." He said that to base "an exclusion on numbers of districts" alone "would act to apply the disparity standard in an unfair and inconsistent manner among States." He then elaborated upon his concerns:

"The purpose of the exclusion is to eliminate those anomalous characteristics of a distribution of expenditures. In States with a small number of large districts, an exclusion based on percentage of school districts might exclude from the measure of disparity a substantial percentage of the pupil population in those States. Conversely, in States with large numbers of small districts, such an approach might exclude only an insignificant fraction of the pupil population and would not exclude anomalous characteristics."

To understand the Secretary's first problem, consider an exaggerated example, say a State with 80 school districts of unequal size. Suppose 8 of the districts include urban areas and together account for 70 percent of the State's students, while the remaining 72 districts include primarily rural areas and together account for 30 percent of the State's students. If the State's greatest funding disparities are among the 8 urban districts, Zuni's calculation method (which looks only at the number of districts and ignores their size) would require the Secretary to disregard the system's 8 largest districts (*i.e.,* 10 percent of the number 80) even though those 8 districts (because they together contain 70 percent of the State's pupils) are typical of, indeed characterize, the State's public school system. It would require the Secretary instead to measure the system's expenditure equality by looking only to noncharacteristic districts that are not representative of the system as a whole, indeed districts accounting for only 30 percent of the State's pupils. Thus, according to Zuni's method, the Secretary would have to certify a state aid program as one that "equalizes expenditures" even if there were gross disparities in per-pupil expenditures among urban districts accounting for 70 percent of the State's students. By way of contrast, the Secretary's method, by taking into account a district's size as well as its expenditures, would avoid a calculation that would produce results so contrary to the statute's objective.

To understand the Secretary's second problem consider this very case. New Mexico's 89 school districts vary significantly in respect to the number of pupils each contains. Zuni's calculation system nonetheless forbids the Secretary to discount more than 10 districts—10 percent of the total number of districts (rounded up). But these districts taken together account for only 1.8 percent of the State's pupils. To eliminate only those districts, instead of eliminating districts that together account for 10 percent of the State's pupils, risks resting the "disregard" calculation upon a few particularly extreme noncharacteristic districts, yet again contrary to the statute's intent.

Thus, the history and purpose of the disregard instruction indicate that the Secretary's calculation formula is a reasonable method that carries out Congress' likely intent in enacting the statutory provision before us.

B

But what of the provision's literal language? The matter is important, for normally neither the legislative history nor the reasonableness of the Secretary's method would be determinative if the plain language of the statute unambiguously indicated that Congress sought to foreclose the Secretary's interpretation. And Zuni argues that the Secretary's formula could not possibly effectuate Congress' intent since the statute's language literally forbids the Secretary to use such a method. Under this Court's precedents, if the intent of Congress is clear and unambiguously expressed by the statutory language at issue, that would be the end of our analysis. A customs statute that imposes a tariff on "clothing" does not impose a tariff on automobiles, no matter how strong the policy arguments for treating the two kinds of goods alike. But we disagree with Zuni's conclusion, for we believe that the Secretary's method falls within the scope of the statute's plain language.

That language says that, when the Secretary compares (for a specified fiscal year) "the amount of per-pupil expenditures made by" (1) the highest-per-pupil-expenditure district and (2) the lowest-per-pupil-expenditure district, "the Secretary shall . . . disregard" local school districts "with per-pupil expenditures . . . above the 95th percentile or below the 5th percentile of such expenditures in the State." 20 U.S.C. § 7709(b)(2)(B)(i). The word "such" refers to "per-pupil expenditures" (or more precisely to "per-pupil expenditures" in the test year specified by the statute). The question then is whether the phrase *"above the 95th percentile . . . of . . . [per pupil] expenditures"* permits the Secretary to calculate percentiles by (1) ranking local districts, (2) noting the student population of each district, and (3) determining the cutoff point on the basis of districts containing 95 percent (or 5 percent) of the State's students.

Our answer is that this phrase, taken with absolute literalness, limits the Secretary to calculation methods that involve "per-pupil expenditures." But it does not tell the Secretary which of several different possible methods the Department must use. Nor does it rule out the present formula, which distributes districts in accordance with per-pupil expenditures, while essentially weighting each district to reflect the number of pupils it contains.

Because the statute uses technical language (*e.g.,* "percentile") and seeks a technical purpose (eliminating uncharacteristic, or outlier, districts), we have examined dictionary definitions of the term "percentile." Those definitions make clear that "percentile" refers to a division of a distribution of *some* population into 100 parts. Thus, Webster's Third New

International Dictionary 1675 (1961) (Webster's Third) defines "percentile" as "the value of the statistical variable that marks the boundary between any two consecutive intervals in a distribution of 100 intervals each containing one percent of the total population." A standard economics dictionary gives a similar definition for "percentiles" * * *. The American Heritage Science Dictionary 468 (2005) explains that a percentile is "[a]ny of the 100 equal parts into which the range of the values of a set of data can be divided in order to show the distribution of those values" * * *.

These definitions, mainstream and technical, all indicate that, in order to identify the relevant percentile cutoffs, the Secretary must construct a distribution of values. That distribution will consist of a "population" ranked according to a characteristic. That characteristic takes on a "value" for each member of the relevant population. The statute's instruction to identify the 95th and 5th "percentile of such expenditures" makes clear that the relevant *characteristic* for ranking purposes is per-pupil expenditure during a particular year. But the statute does not specify precisely what *population* is to be "distributed" (*i.e.,* ranked according to the population's corresponding values for the relevant characteristic). Nor does it set forth various details as to how precisely the distribution is to be constructed (as long as it is ranked according to the specified characteristic).

But why is Congress' silence in respect to these matters significant? Are there several *different* populations, relevant here, that one might rank according to "per-pupil expenditures" (and thereby determine in several *different* ways a cutoff point such that "*n* percent of [that] population" falls, say below the percentile cutoff)? We are not experts in statistics, but a statistician is not needed to see what the dictionary does not say. No dictionary definition we have found suggests that there is any *single* logical, mathematical, or statistical link between, on the one hand, the characterizing data (used for ranking purposes) and, on the other hand, the nature of the relevant population or how that population might be weighted for purposes of determining a percentile cutoff.

Here, the Secretary has distributed districts, ranked them according to per-pupil expenditure, but compared only those that account for 90 percent of the State's pupils. Thus, the Secretary has used—as his predecessors had done for a quarter century before him—the State's *students* as the relevant population for calculating the specified percentiles. Another Secretary might have distributed districts, ranked them by per-pupil expenditure, and made no reference to the number of pupils (a method that satisfies the statute's *language* but threatens the problems the Secretary long ago identified). A third Secretary might have distributed districts, ranked them by per-pupil expenditure, but compared only those that account for 90 percent of total pupil expenditures in the State. A fourth Secretary might have distributed districts, ranked them by per-pupil expenditure, but calculated the 95th and 5th percentile cutoffs using the per-pupil expenditures of all the individual *schools* in the State. A fifth Secretary might have distributed districts, ranked them by per-pupil expenditure, but accounted in his disparity calculation for the sometimes significant differences in per-pupil spending at different grade levels.

Each of these methods amounts to a different way of determining which districts fall between the 5th and 95th "percentile of per-pupil expenditures." For purposes of that calculation, they each adopt different populations-students, districts, schools, and grade levels. Yet, linguistically speaking, one may attribute the characteristic of per-pupil expenditure to each member of any such population (though the values of that characteristic may be more or less readily available depending on the chosen population). Hence, the statute's literal language covers any or all of these methods. That language alone does not tell us (or the Secretary of Education), however, which method to use.

JUSTICE SCALIA'S claim that this interpretation "defies any semblance of normal English" depends upon its own definition of the word "per." That word, according to the dissent, "connotes . . . a single average figure assigned to a unit the composite members of which are individual pupils." In fact, the word "per" simply means "[f]or each" or "for every." Thus, nothing in the English language forbids the Secretary from considering expenditures *for each* individual pupil in a district when instructed to look at a district's "per-pupil expenditures." The remainder of the dissent's argument, colorful language to the side, rests upon a reading of the statutory language that ignores its basic purpose and history.

* * *

Finally, we draw reassurance from the fact that no group of statisticians, nor any individual statistician, has told us directly in briefs, or indirectly through citation, that the language before us cannot be read as we have read it. This circumstance is significant, for the statutory language is technical, and we are not statisticians. And the views of experts (or their absence) might help us understand (though not control our determination of) what Congress had in mind.

* * *

The judgment of the Tenth Circuit is affirmed.

It is so ordered.

* * *

JUSTICE STEVENS, concurring.

In his oft-cited opinion for the Court in *Griffin v. Oceanic Contractors, Inc.*, 458 U.S. 564, 571 (1982), then-Justice Rehnquist wisely acknowledged that "in rare cases the literal application of a statute will produce a result demonstrably at odds with the intentions of its drafters, and those intentions must be controlling." And in *United States v. Ron Pair Enterprises, Inc.*, 489 U.S. 235, 242 (1989), the Court began its analysis of the question of statutory construction by restating the proposition that "[i]n such cases, the intention of the drafters, rather than the strict language, controls." JUSTICE SCALIA provided the decisive fifth vote for the majority in that case.

Today he correctly observes that a judicial decision that departs from statutory text may represent "policy-driven interpretation." As long as that driving policy is faithful to the intent of Congress (or, as in this case, aims only to give effect to such intent)—which it must be if it is to override a strict interpretation of the text—the decision is also a correct performance of the judicial function. JUSTICE SCALIA'S argument today rests on the incorrect premise that every policy-driven interpretation implements a judge's personal view of sound policy, rather than a faithful attempt to carry out the will of the legislature. Quite the contrary is true of the work of the judges with whom I have worked for many years. If we presume that our judges are intellectually honest—as I do—there is no reason to fear "policy-driven interpretation[s]" of Acts of Congress.

* * *

Analysis of legislative history is, of course, a traditional tool of statutory construction. There is no reason why we must confine ourselves to, or begin our analysis with, the statutory text if other tools of statutory construction provide better evidence of congressional intent with respect to the precise point at issue.

As the Court's opinion demonstrates, this is a quintessential example of a case in which the statutory text was obviously enacted to adopt the rule that the Secretary administered both before and after the enactment of the rather confusing language found in 20 U.S.C. § 7709(b)(2)(B)(i). That text is sufficiently ambiguous to justify the Court's exegesis, but my own vote is the product of a more direct route to the Court's patently correct conclusion. This happens to be a case in which the legislative history is pellucidly clear and the statutory text is difficult to fathom. Moreover, it is a case in which I cannot imagine anyone accusing any Member of the Court of voting one way or the other because of that Justice's own policy preferences.

Given the clarity of the evidence of Congress' "intention on the precise question at issue," I would affirm the judgment of the Court of Appeals even if I thought that petitioners' literal reading of the statutory text was correct. [See *Church of the Holy Trinity v. United States*, 143 U.S. 457, 459 (1892) ("It is a familiar rule, that a thing may be within the letter of the statute and yet not within the statute, because not within its spirit, nor within the intention of its makers").] The only "policy" by which I have been driven is that which this Court has endorsed on repeated occasions regarding the importance of remaining faithful to Congress' intent.

JUSTICE KENNEDY, with whom JUSTICE ALITO joins, concurring [omitted].

JUSTICE SCALIA, with whom THE CHIEF JUSTICE and JUSTICE THOMAS join, and with whom JUSTICE SOUTER joins as to Part I, dissenting.

In *Church of the Holy Trinity v. United States*, 143 U.S. 457 (1892), this Court conceded that a church's act of contracting with a prospective rector fell within the plain meaning of a federal labor statute, but nevertheless did not apply the statute to the church: "It is a familiar rule," the Court pronounced, "that a thing may be within the letter of the statute and yet not within the statute, because not within its spirit, nor within the intention of its makers." That is a judge-empowering proposition if there ever was one, and in the century since, the Court has wisely retreated from it, in words if not always in actions. But today *Church of the Holy Trinity* arises, Phoenix-like, from the ashes. The Court's contrary assertions aside, today's decision is nothing other than the elevation of judge-supposed legislative intent over clear statutory text. The plain language of the federal Impact Aid statute clearly and unambiguously forecloses the Secretary of Education's preferred methodology for determining whether a State's school-funding system is equalized. Her selection of that methodology is therefore entitled to zero deference under *Chevron*.

I

The very structure of the Court's opinion provides an obvious clue as to what is afoot. The opinion purports to place a premium on the plain text of the Impact Aid statute, but it first takes us instead on a roundabout tour of "[c]onsiderations *other* than language"—page after page of unenacted congressional intent and judicially perceived statutory purpose Only after we are shown "why Zuni concentrates its argument upon language alone" (impliedly a shameful practice, or at least indication of a feeble case), are we informed how the statute's plain text does not unambiguously *preclude* the interpretation the Court thinks best. This is a most suspicious order of proceeding * * *.

We must begin, as we always do, with the text. Under the federal Impact Aid program, States distributing state aid to local school districts (referred to in the statute as "local educational agencies," or "LEAs") may not take into account the amount of federal Impact Aid that its LEAs receive. But the statute makes an exception if the Secretary of Education certifies that a State "has in effect a program of State aid that equalizes expenditures for free public education among local educational agencies in the State." Congress has specified a formula for the Secretary to use when making this equalization determination:

"[A] program of State aid equalizes expenditures among local educational agencies if . . . the amount of per-pupil expenditures made by, or per-pupil revenues available to, the local educational agency in the State with the highest such per-pupil expenditures or revenues did not exceed the amount of such per-pupil expenditures made by, or per-pupil revenues available to, the local educational agency in the State with the lowest such expenditures or revenues by more than 25 percent."

The Secretary is further instructed, however, that when making this determination, she shall "disregard local educational agencies with per-pupil expenditures or revenues above the 95th percentile or below the 5th percentile of such expenditures or revenues in the State." It is this latter subsection which concerns us here.

The casual observer will notice that the Secretary's implementing regulations do not look much like the statute. The regulations first require the Secretary to rank all of the LEAs in a State (New Mexico has 89) according to their per-pupil expenditures or revenues. So far so good. But critically here, the Secretary must then "[i]dentif[y] those LEAs . . . that fall at the 95th and 5th percentiles *of the total number of pupils in attendance* in the schools of those LEAs." Finally, the Secretary compares the per-pupil figures of *those two* LEAs for the purpose of assessing whether a State exceeds the 25% disparity measure. The majority concludes that this method of calculation, with its focus on student population, is a permissible interpretation of the statute.

It most assuredly is not. To understand why, one first must look beyond the smokescreen that the Court lays down with its repeated apologies for inexperience in statistics, and its endless recitation of technical mathematical definitions of the word "percentile." This case is not a scary math problem; it is a straightforward matter of statutory interpretation. And we do not need the Court's hypothetical cadre of number-crunching *amici* to guide our way.

There is no dispute that for purposes relevant here " 'percentile' refers to a division of a distribution of *some* population into 100 parts.' " *Ante,* at 1543. And there is further no dispute that the statute concerns the percentile of "per-pupil expenditures or revenues," for that is what the word "such" refers to. See 20 U.S.C. § 7709(b)(2)(B)(i) (Secretary shall "disregard local educational agencies with *per-pupil expenditures or revenues* above the 95th percentile or below the 5th percentile of *such* expenditures or revenues in the State" (emphasis added)). The question is: Whose per-pupil expenditures or revenues? Or, in the Court's terminology, what "population" is assigned the "characteristic" "per-pupil expenditure or revenue"? At first blush, second blush, or twenty-second blush, the answer is abundantly clear: local educational agencies. The statute requires the

Secretary to "disregard local educational agencies with" certain per-pupil figures above or below specified percentiles of those per-pupil figures. The attribute "per-pupil expenditur[e] or revenu[e]" is assigned to LEAs—there is no mention of student population whatsoever. And thus under the statute, "per-pupil expenditures or revenues" are to be arrayed using a population consisting of LEAs, so that percentiles are determined from a list of (in New Mexico) 89 per-pupil expenditures or revenues representing the 89 LEAs in the State. It is just that simple.

The Court makes little effort to defend the regulations as they are written. Instead, relying on a made-for-litigation theory that bears almost no relationship to the regulations themselves, the Court believes it has found a way to shoehorn those regulations into the statute. The Impact Aid statute is ambiguous, the Court says, because it "does not specify precisely what *population* is to be 'distributed' (*i.e.*, ranked according to the population's corresponding values for the relevant characteristic)." *Ante,* at 1544. Thus the Court finds that it is permissible for the Secretary to attribute the characteristic "per-pupil expenditure or revenue" to pupils, with the result that the Secretary may "us[e] . . . the State's *students* as the relevant population for calculating the specified percentiles." *Ante,* at 1544. Under that interpretation, as the State manages to explain with a straight face, "[i]n New Mexico, during the time at issue, there were approximately 317,777 pupils in the [S]tate and thus there were 317,777 per-pupil revenues in the [S]tate." Brief for Respondent New Mexico Public Education Department 37; see also *id.,* at 36 ("Each and every student in an LEA and in a[S]tate may be treated as having his or her own 'per-pupil' expenditure or revenue amount"). The Court consequently concludes that "linguistically speaking, one may attribute the characteristic of per-pupil expenditure to each [student]." *Ante,* at 1545.

The sheer applesauce of this statutory interpretation should be obvious. It is of course true that every student in New Mexico causes an expenditure or produces a revenue that his LEA either enjoys (in the case of revenues) or is responsible for (in the case of expenditures). But it simply defies any semblance of normal English usage to say that every pupil has a *"per-pupil* expenditure or revenue." The word "per" *connotes* that the expenditure or revenue is a single average figure assigned to a unit the *composite members of which* are individual pupils. And the only such unit mentioned in the statute is the local educational agency. It is simply irrelevant that "[n]o dictionary definition . . . suggests that there is any *single* logical, mathematical, or statistical link between [per-pupil expenditures or revenues] and . . . the nature of the relevant population." *Ante,* at 1544–1545. Of course there is not. It is the *text* at issue which must identify the relevant population, and it does so here quite unambiguously: "*local educational agencies* with per-pupil expenditures or revenues." (emphasis added). That same phrase shows the utter irrelevance of the

Court's excursus upon the meaning of the word "per." It does indeed mean " 'for each or 'for every' "—and when it is contained in a clause that reads "local educational agencies with per-pupil expenditures or revenues" it refers to (and can only refer to) the average expenditure or revenue "for each" or "for every" student out of the total expenditures or revenues of the LEA.

The violence done to this statute would be severe enough if the Secretary *used* the actual expenditure or revenue for each individual pupil. But in fact the Secretary determines the per-pupil expenditure or revenue for each individual student by (guess what) *computing the per-pupil expenditure or revenue of each LEA!* As the New Mexico brief explains:

> "[A] per-pupil expenditure or revenue is an average number. It is not the amount actually spent on any given pupil, an amount which would be impossible to calculate in any meaningful way. It is roughly the total amount expended by an LEA divided by the number of pupils in that LEA." Brief for Respondent New Mexico Public Education Department 36.

The Secretary thus assigns an artificial number to each student that corresponds exactly to *his LEA's* per-pupil expenditure or revenue. In other words, at the end of the day the Secretary herself acknowledges that "per-pupil expenditures or revenues" pertains to LEAs, and not students. And she is interpreting "per-pupil expenditure or revenue" *not* as the Court suggests (an amount attributable to each student), but rather *as I suggest* (an average amount for the pupils in a particular LEA). But she then proceeds to take a step not at all permitted by the statutory formula—in effect applying "per-pupil expenditure or revenue" a *second* time (this time according to the Court's fanciful interpretation of "per-pupil") in order to reach the result she desires. Of course, if the Secretary did apply the "per-pupil expenditure or revenue" only once, arraying students by their actual expenditures or revenues, her entire system would collapse. Students from the same LEA, rather than appearing on the list with the same per-pupil figure, would be located at various points on the spectrum. And so long as an LEA had at least one student above the 95th or below the 5th percentile of pupil "per-pupil expenditures or revenues," that LEA would have to be excluded from the disparity analysis. The result would be a serious distortion of the disparity determination, excluding many more LEAs (in fact, perhaps all of them) from the disparity calculation * * * *.

The Court makes one final attempt to rescue the Secretary's interpretation, appealing to "statutory context." "Context here tells us," it says, "that the instruction to identify school districts with 'per-pupil expenditures' above the 95th percentile 'of such expenditures' is . . . ambiguous, because both students and school districts are of concern to the statute." *Ante,* at 1546. This is a complete non sequitur. Of course students are a concern to a statute dealing with school funding. But that does not create any ambiguity with respect to whether, under this statute, pupils can reasonably be said to have their own "per-pupil expenditures or revenues." It is simply irrational to say that the clear dispositions of a statute with regard to the entities that it regulates (here LEAs) are rendered ambiguous when those entities contain sub-units that are the ultimate beneficiaries of the regulation (here students) * * *.

The Court's reliance on statutory context is all the more puzzling since the context obviously favors petitioners * * *. [T]he provisions at issue here make not the slightest mention of students. That is both sensible and predictable, since the Impact Aid program's equalization formula is designed to address funding disparities between *LEAs,* not between *students* * * *.

In sum, the plain language of the Impact Aid statute compels the conclusion that the Secretary's method of calculation is ultra vires. Employing the formula that the statute requires, New Mexico is not equalized.

II

How then, if the text is so clear, are respondents managing to win this case? The answer can only be the return of that miraculous redeemer of lost causes, *Church of the Holy Trinity.* In order to contort the statute's language beyond recognition, the Court must believe Congress's intent so crystalline, the spirit of its legislation so glowingly bright, that the statutory text should simply not be read to say what it says. JUSTICE STEVENS is quite candid on the point: He is willing to contradict the text. But JUSTICE STEVENS' candor should not make his philosophy seem unassuming. He maintains that it is "a correct performance of the judicial function" to "override a strict interpretation of the text" so long as policy-driven interpretation "is faithful to the intent of Congress." *Ante,* at 1549. But once one departs from "strict interpretation of the text" (by which JUSTICE STEVENS means the actual meaning of the text) fidelity to the intent of Congress is a chancy thing. The only thing we know for certain both Houses of Congress (and the President, if he signed the legislation) agreed upon is the text. Legislative history can never produce a "pellucidly clear" picture, *ante,* at 1550 (STEVENS, J., concurring), of what a law was "intended" to mean, for the simple reason that it is never voted upon-or ordinarily even seen or heard-by the "intending" lawgiving entity, which consists of both Houses of Congress and the President (if he did not veto the bill). Thus, what judges believe Congress "meant" (apart from the text) has a disturbing but entirely unsurprising tendency to be whatever judges think Congress *must* have meant, *i.e., should* have meant. In *Church of the Holy Trinity,* every Justice on this Court disregarded the plain language of a statute that forbade the hiring of a clergyman from abroad because, after all (they thought), "this is a Christian nation," 143 U.S., at 471, so Congress could not have meant what it said. Is there any reason to believe that those Justices were lacking that "intellectua[l] honest[y]" that JUSTICE STEVENS "presume[s]" all our judges possess, *ante,* at 1550? Intellectual honesty does not exclude a blinding intellectual bias. And even if it did, the system of judicial amendatory veto over texts duly adopted by Congress bears no resemblance to the system of lawmaking set forth in our Constitution.

JUSTICE STEVENS takes comfort in the fact that this is a case in which he "cannot imagine anyone accusing any Member of the Court of voting one way or the other because of that Justice's own policy preferences." *Ante,* at 1550. I can readily imagine it, given that the Court's opinion begins with a lengthy description of why the system its judgment approves is the *better* one. But even assuming that, in this rare case, the Justices' departure from the enacted law has nothing to do with their policy view that it is a bad law, nothing in JUSTICE STEVENS' separate opinion limits his approach to such rarities. Why should we suppose that in matters more likely to arouse the judicial libido—voting rights, antidiscrimination laws, or environmental protection, to name only a few—a judge in the School of Textual Subversion would not find it convenient (yea, *righteous!*) to assume that Congress *must* have meant, not what it said, but what he knows to be best?

* * *

Contrary to the Court and JUSTICE STEVENS, I do not believe that what we are sure the Legislature *meant* to say can trump what it *did* say. Citizens arrange their affairs not on the basis of their legislators' unexpressed intent, but on the basis of the law as it is written and promulgated. I think it terribly unfair to expect that the two rural school districts who are petitioners here should have pored over some 30 years of regulatory history to divine Congress's "real" objective (and with it the "real" intent that a majority of Justices would find honest and true). To be governed by legislated text rather than legislators' intentions is what it means to be "a Government of laws, not of men" * * *.

* * *

Finally, the Court expresses its belief that Congress must have intended to adopt the Secretary's pre-1994 disparity test because that test is the more reasonable one, better able to account for States with small numbers of large LEAs, or large numbers of small ones. See *ante,* at 1541–1543. This, to tell the truth, is the core of the opinion. As I have suggested, it is no accident that the countertextual legislative intent judges perceive *invariably* accords with what judges think best. It seems to me, however, that this Court is no more capable of saying with certainty what is best in this area than it is of saying with certainty (apart from the text) what Congress intended. There is good reason to be concerned—in the implementation of a statute that makes a limited exception for States that have "in effect a program of State aid that equalizes expenditures for free public education *among local educational agencies*"—that the Secretary's methodology eliminates from the disparity calculation *too many LEAs*. In the certification at issue in this very case, the Secretary excluded 23 of New Mexico's 89 LEAs, approximately 26%. Is this Court such an expert in school finance that it can affirm the desirability of excluding one in four of New Mexico's LEAs from consideration?

* * *

The only sure indication of what Congress intended is what Congress enacted; and even if there is a difference between the two, the rule of law demands that the latter prevail. This case will live with *Church of the Holy Trinity* as an exemplar of judicial disregard of crystal-clear text. We must interpret the law as Congress has written it, not as we would wish it to be. I would reverse the judgment of the Court of Appeals.

JUSTICE SOUTER, dissenting.

I agree with the Court that Congress probably intended, or at least understood, that the Secretary would continue to follow the methodology devised prior to passage of the current statute in 1994. But for reasons set out in JUSTICE SCALIA's dissent, I find the statutory language unambiguous and inapt to authorize that methodology, and I therefore join Part I of his dissenting opinion.

YATES v. UNITED STATES
Supreme Court of the United States, 2015.
576 U.S. ___, 135 S.Ct. 1074, 191 L.Ed.2d 64.

JUSTICE GINSBURG announced the judgment of the Court and delivered an opinion, in which THE CHIEF JUSTICE, JUSTICE BREYER, and JUSTICE SOTOMAYOR join.

John Yates, a commercial fisherman, caught undersized red grouper in federal waters in the Gulf of Mexico. To prevent federal authorities from confirming that he had harvested undersized fish, Yates ordered a crew member to toss the suspect catch into the sea. For this offense, he was charged with, and convicted of, violating 18 U.S.C. § 1519, which provides:

> "Whoever knowingly alters, destroys, mutilates, conceals, covers up, falsifies, or makes a false entry in any record, document, or tangible object with the intent to impede, obstruct, or influence the investigation or proper administration of any matter within the jurisdiction of any department or agency of the United States or any case filed under title 11, or in relation to or contemplation of any such matter or case, shall be fined under this title, imprisoned not more than 20 years, or both."

* * *

Yates * * * maintains that fish are not trapped within the term "tangible object," as that term is used in § 1519.

Section 1519 was enacted as part of the Sarbanes-Oxley Act of 2002, 116 Stat. 745, legislation designed to protect investors and restore trust in financial markets following the collapse of Enron Corporation. A fish is no doubt an object that is tangible; fish can be seen, caught, and handled, and a catch, as this case illustrates, is vulnerable to destruction. But it would cut § 1519 loose from its financial-fraud mooring to hold that it encompasses any and all objects, whatever their size or significance, destroyed with obstructive intent. Mindful that in Sarbanes-Oxley, Congress trained its attention on corporate and accounting deception and cover-ups, we conclude that a matching construction of § 1519 is in order: A tangible object captured by § 1519, we hold, must be one used to record or preserve information.

I

On August 23, 2007, the *Miss Katie*, a commercial fishing boat, was six days into an expedition in the Gulf of Mexico. Her crew numbered three, including Yates, the captain. Engaged in a routine offshore patrol to inspect both recreational and commercial vessels, Officer John Jones * * * decided to board the *Miss Katie* to check on the vessel's compliance with fishing rules * * *.

Upon boarding the *Miss Katie*, Officer Jones noticed three red grouper that appeared to be undersized hanging from a hook on the deck. At the time, federal conservation regulations required immediate release of red grouper less than 20 inches long. 50 CFR § 622.37(d)(2)(ii) (effective April 2, 2007). Violation of those regulations is a civil offense punishable by a fine or fishing license suspension. See 16 U.S.C. §§ 1857(1)(A), (G), 1858(a), (g).

Suspecting that other undersized fish might be on board, Officer Jones proceeded to inspect the ship's catch, setting aside and measuring only fish that appeared to him to be shorter than 20 inches. Officer Jones ultimately determined that 72 fish fell short of the 20-inch mark * * *. After separating the fish measuring below 20 inches from the rest of the catch by placing them in wooden crates, Officer Jones directed Yates to leave the fish, thus segregated, in the crates until the *Miss Katie* returned to port. Before departing, Officer Jones issued Yates a citation for possession of undersized fish.

Four days later * * *, Officer Jones measured the fish contained in the wooden crates * * *. [T]he measured fish * * * slightly exceeded the lengths recorded on board. Jones surmised that the fish brought to port were not the same as those he had detected during his initial inspection. Under questioning, one of the crew members admitted that, at Yates's direction, he had thrown overboard the fish Officer Jones had measured at sea, and that he and Yates had replaced the tossed grouper with fish from the rest of the catch.

* * * Yates * * * was indicted [and convicted] * * * for destroying, concealing, and covering up undersized fish to impede a federal investigation, in violation of § 1519 * * *.

II

The Sarbanes-Oxley Act, all agree, was prompted by the exposure of Enron's massive accounting fraud and revelations that the company's outside auditor, Arthur Andersen LLP, had systematically destroyed potentially incriminating documents. The Government acknowledges that § 1519 was intended to prohibit, in particular, corporate document-shredding to hide evidence of financial wrong-doing. Prior law made it an offense to "intimidat[e], threate[n], or corruptly persuad[e] *another person*" to shred documents. § 1512(b) (emphasis added). Section 1519 cured a conspicuous omission by imposing liability on a person who destroys records himself * * *.

In the Government's view, § 1519 extends beyond the principal evil motivating its passage. The words of § 1519, the Government argues, support reading the provision as a general ban on the spoliation of evidence, covering all physical items that might be relevant to any matter under federal investigation.

Yates urges a contextual reading of § 1519, tying "tangible object" to the surrounding words, the placement of the provision within the Sarbanes-Oxley Act, and related provisions enacted at the same time, in particular § 1520 and § 1512(c)(1). Section 1519, he maintains, targets not all manner of evidence, but records, documents, and tangible objects used to preserve them, *e.g.*, computers, servers, and other media on which information is stored.

We agree with Yates and reject the Government's unrestrained reading. "Tangible object" in § 1519, we conclude, is better read to cover only objects one can use to record or preserve information, not all objects in the physical world.

A

The ordinary meaning of an "object" that is "tangible," as stated in dictionary definitions, is "a discrete . . . thing," Webster's Third New International Dictionary 1555 (2002), that "possess[es] physical form," Black's Law Dictionary 1683 (10th ed. 2014). From this premise, the Government concludes that "tangible object," as that term appears in § 1519, covers the waterfront, including fish from the sea.

Whether a statutory term is unambiguous, however, does not turn solely on dictionary definitions of its component words. Rather, "[t]he plainness or ambiguity of statutory language is determined [not only] by reference to the language itself, [but as well by] the specific context in which that language is used, and the broader context of the statute as a whole." *Robinson* v. *Shell Oil Co.*, 519 U.S. 337, 341 (1997). See also *Deal* v. *United States*, 508 U.S. 129, 132 (1993) (it is a "fundamental principle of statutory construction (and, indeed, of language itself) that the meaning of a word cannot be determined in isolation, but must be drawn from the context in which it is used"). Ordinarily, a word's usage accords with its dictionary definition. In law as in life, however, the same words, placed in different contexts, sometimes mean different things.

We have several times affirmed that identical language may convey varying content when used in different statutes, sometimes even in different provisions of the same statute. As the Court observed in *Atlantic Cleaners & Dyers*, 286 U.S., at 433:

> "Most words have different shades of meaning and consequently may be variously construed . . . . Where the subject matter to which the words refer is not the same in the several places where [the words] are used, or the conditions are different, or the scope of the legislative power exercised in one case is broader than that exercised in another, the meaning well may vary to meet the purposes of the law, to be arrived at by a consideration of the language in which those purposes are expressed, and of the circumstances under which the language was employed."

In short, although dictionary definitions of the words "tangible" and "object" bear consideration, they are not dispositive of the meaning of "tangible object" in § 1519.

* * *

B

Familiar interpretive guides aid our construction of the words "tangible object" as they appear in § 1519.

We note first § 1519's caption: "Destruction, alteration, or falsification of records in Federal investigations and bankruptcy." That heading conveys no suggestion that the section prohibits spoliation of any and all physical evidence, however remote from records. Neither does the title of the section of the Sarbanes-Oxley Act in which § 1519 was placed, § 802: "Criminal penalties for altering documents." 116 Stat. 800. Furthermore, § 1520, the only other provision passed as part of § 802, is titled "Destruction of corporate audit records" and addresses only that specific subset of records and documents. While these headings are not commanding, they supply cues that Congress did not intend "tangible object" in § 1519 to sweep within its reach physical objects of every kind, including things no one would describe as records, documents, or devices closely associated with them. See *Almendarez-Torres* v. *United States*, 523 U.S. 224, 234 (1998) ("[T]he title of a statute and the heading of a section are tools available for the resolution of a doubt about the meaning of a statute." (internal quotation marks omitted)). If Congress indeed meant to make § 1519 an all-encompassing ban on the spoliation of evidence, as the dissent believes Congress did, one would have expected a clearer indication of that intent.

* * *

The contemporaneous passage of § 1512(c)(1), which was contained in a section of the Sarbanes-Oxley Act discrete from the section embracing § 1519 and § 1520, is also instructive. Section 1512(c)(1) provides:

> "(c)   Whoever corruptly—

> "(1) alters, destroys, mutilates, or conceals a record, document, or other object, or attempts to do so, with the intent to impair the object's integrity or availability for use in an official proceeding

> . . .

> "shall be fined under this title or imprisoned not more than 20 years, or both."

The legislative history reveals that § 1512(c)(1) was drafted and proposed after § 1519. See 148 Cong. Rec. 12518, 13088–13089 (2002). The Government argues, and Yates does not dispute, that § 1512(c)(1)'s reference to "other object" includes any and every physical object. But if § 1519's reference to "tangible object" already included all physical objects, as the Government and the dissent contend, then Congress had no reason to enact § 1512(c)(1): Virtually any act that would violate § 1512(c)(1) no doubt would violate § 1519 as well, for § 1519 applies to "the investigation or proper administration of any matter within the jurisdiction of any department or agency of the United States . . . or in relation to or contemplation of any such matter," not just to "an official proceeding."

The Government acknowledges that, under its reading, § 1519 and § 1512(c)(1) "significantly overlap." Brief for United States 49. Nowhere does the Government explain what independent function § 1512(c)(1) would serve if the Government is right about the sweeping scope of § 1519. We resist a reading of § 1519 that would render superfluous an entire provision passed in proximity as part of the same Act. See *Marx* v. *General Revenue Corp.*, 568 U.S. ___, ___ (2013) (slip op., at 14) ("[T]he canon against surplusage is strongest when an interpretation would render superfluous another part of the same statutory scheme.").

The words immediately surrounding "tangible object" in § 1519—"falsifies, or makes a false entry in any record [or] document"—also cabin the contextual meaning of that term. As explained in *Gustafson* v. *Alloyd Co.*, 513 U.S. 561, 575 (1995), we rely on the principle of *noscitur a sociis*—a word is known by the company it keeps—to "avoid ascribing to one word a meaning so broad that it is inconsistent with its accompanying words, thus giving unintended breadth to the Acts of Congress." (internal quotation marks omitted). See also *United States* v. *Williams*, 553 U.S. 285, 294 (2008) ("a word is given more precise content by the neighboring words with which it is associated"). In *Gustafson*, we interpreted the word "communication" in § 2(10) of the Securities Act of 1933 to refer to a public communication, rather than any communication, because the word appeared in a list with other words, notably "notice, circular, [and] advertisement," making it "apparent that the list refer[red] to documents of wide dissemination." 513 U.S., at 575–576. And we did so even though the list began with the word "any."

The *noscitur a sociis* canon operates in a similar manner here. "Tangible object" is the last in a list of terms that begins "any record [or] document." The term is therefore appropriately read to refer, not to any tangible object, but specifically to the subset of tangible objects involving records and documents, *i.e.,* objects used to record or preserve information.

This moderate interpretation of "tangible object" accords with the list of actions § 1519 proscribes. The section applies to anyone who "alters, destroys, mutilates, conceals, covers up, *falsifies*, or *makes a false entry in* any record, document, or tangible object" with the requisite obstructive intent. (Emphasis added.) The last two verbs, "falsif[y]" and "mak[e] a false entry in," typically take as grammatical objects records, documents, or things used to record or preserve information, such as logbooks or hard drives. It would be unnatural, for example, to describe a killer's act of wiping his fingerprints from a gun as "falsifying" the murder weapon. But it would not be strange to refer to "falsifying" data stored on a hard drive as simply "falsifying" a hard drive * * *.

A canon related to *noscitur a sociis, ejusdem generis,* counsels: "Where general words follow specific words in a statutory enumeration, the general words are [usually] construed to embrace only objects similar in nature to those objects enumerated by the preceding specific words." *Washington State Dept. of Social and Health Servs.* v. *Guardianship Estate of Keffeler,* 537 U.S. 371, 384 (2003) (internal quotation marks omitted). In *Begay* v. *United States,* 553 U.S. 137, 142–143 (2008), for example, we relied on this principle to determine what crimes were covered by the statutory phrase "any crime . . . that . . . is burglary, arson, or extortion, involves use of explosives, or otherwise involves conduct that presents a serious potential risk of physical injury to another," 18 U.S.C. § 924(e)(2)(B)(ii). The enumeration of specific crimes, we explained, indicates that the "otherwise involves" provision covers "only *similar* crimes, rather than *every* crime that 'presents a serious potential risk of physical injury to another.'" 553 U.S., at 142. Had Congress intended the latter "all encompassing" meaning, we observed, "it is hard to see why it would have needed to include the examples at all." *Ibid.* Just so here. Had Congress intended "tangible object" in § 1519 to be interpreted so generically as to capture physical objects as dissimilar as documents and fish, Congress would have had no reason to refer specifically to "record" or "document." The Government's unbounded reading of "tangible object" would render those words misleading surplusage.

Having used traditional tools of statutory interpretation to examine markers of congressional intent within the Sarbanes-Oxley Act and § 1519 itself, we are persuaded that an aggressive interpretation of "tangible object" must be rejected. It is highly improbable that Congress would have buried a general spoliation statute covering objects of any and every kind in a provision targeting fraud in financial record-keeping.

* * *

C

Finally, if our recourse to traditional tools of statutory construction leaves any doubt about the meaning of "tangible object," as that term is used in § 1519, we would invoke the rule that "ambiguity concerning the ambit of criminal statutes should be resolved in favor of lenity." *Cleveland* v. *United States*, 531 U.S. 12, 25 (2000) (quoting *Rewis* v. *United States*, 401 U.S. 808, 812 (1971)). That interpretative principle is relevant here, where the Government urges a reading of § 1519 that exposes individuals to 20-year prison sentences for tampering with *any* physical object that *might* have evidentiary value in *any* federal investigation into *any* offense, no matter whether the investigation is pending or merely contemplated, or whether the offense subject to investigation is criminal or civil. In determining the meaning of "tangible object" in § 1519, "it is appropriate, before we choose the harsher alternative, to require that Congress should have spoken in language that is clear and definite." See *Cleveland*, 531 U.S., at 25 (quoting *United States* v. *Universal C. I. T. Credit Corp.*, 344 U.S. 218, 222 (1952)).

For the reasons stated, we resist reading § 1519 expansively to create a coverall spoliation of evidence statute, advisable as such a measure might be. Leaving that important decision to Congress, we hold that a "tangible object" within § 1519's compass is one used to record or preserve information * * *.

JUSTICE ALITO, concurring in the judgment.

This case can and should be resolved on narrow grounds. And though the question is close, traditional tools of statutory construction confirm that

John Yates has the better of the argument. Three features of 18 U.S.C. § 1519 stand out to me: the statute's list of nouns, its list of verbs, and its title. Although perhaps none of these features by itself would tip the case in favor of Yates, the three combined do so.

Start with the nouns. Section 1519 refers to "any record, document, or tangible object." The *noscitur a sociis* canon instructs that when a statute contains a list, each word in that list presumptively has a "similar" meaning. A related canon, *ejusdem generis* teaches that general words following a list of specific words should usually be read in light of those specific words to mean something "similar." Applying these canons to § 1519's list of nouns, the term "tangible object" should refer to something similar to records or documents. A fish does not spring to mind—nor does an antelope, a colonial farmhouse, a hydrofoil, or an oil derrick. All are "objects" that are "tangible." But who wouldn't raise an eyebrow if a neighbor, when asked to identify something similar to a "record" or "document," said "crocodile"?

This reading, of course, has its shortcomings. For instance, this is an imperfect *ejusdem generis* case because "record" and "document" are themselves quite general. And there is a risk that "tangible object" may be made superfluous—what is similar to a "record" or "document" but yet is not one? An e-mail, however, could be such a thing. An e-mail, after all, might not be a "document" if, as was "traditionally" so, a document was a "piece of paper with information on it," not "information stored on a computer, electronic storage device, or any other medium." Black's Law Dictionary 587–588 (10th ed. 2014). E-mails might also not be "records" if records are limited to "minutes" or other formal writings "designed to memorialize [past] events." *Id.,* at 1465. A hard drive, however, is tangible and can contain files that are precisely akin to even these narrow definitions. Both "record" and "document" can be read more expansively, but adding "tangible object" to § 1519 would ensure beyond question that electronic files are included. To be sure, "tangible object" presumably can capture more than just e-mails; Congress enacts "catchall[s]" for "known unknowns." *Republic of Iraq v. Beaty,* 556 U.S. 848, 860 (2009). But where *noscitur a sociis* and *ejusdem generis* apply, "known unknowns" should be similar to known knowns, *i.e.,* here, records and documents. This is especially true because reading "tangible object" too broadly could render "record" and "document" superfluous.

Next, consider § 1519's list of verbs: "alters, destroys, mutilates, conceals, covers up, falsifies, or makes a false entry in." Although many of those verbs could apply to nouns as far-flung as salamanders, satellites, or sand dunes, the last phrase in the list—"makes a false entry in"—makes no sense outside of filekeeping. How does one make a false entry in a fish? "Alters" and especially "falsifies" are also closely associated with filekeeping. Not one of the verbs, moreover, *cannot* be applied to filekeeping—certainly not in the way that "makes a false entry in" is always inconsistent with the aquatic.

Again, the Government is not without a response. One can imagine Congress trying to write a law so broadly that not every verb lines up with every noun. But failure to "line up" may suggest that something has gone awry in one's interpretation of a text. Where, as here, each of a statute's verbs applies to a certain category of nouns, there is some reason to think that Congress had that category in mind. Categories, of course, are often underinclusive or overinclusive—§ 1519, for instance, applies to a bomb-threatening letter but not a bomb. But this does not mean that categories are not useful or that Congress does not enact them * * *.

Finally, my analysis is influenced by § 1519's title: "Destruction, alteration, or falsification of *records* in Federal investigations and bankruptcy." (Emphasis added.) This too points toward filekeeping, not fish * * *. The title is especially valuable here because it reinforces what the text's nouns and verbs independently suggest—that no matter how other statutes might be read, this particular one does not cover every noun in the universe with tangible form.

* * *

JUSTICE KAGAN, with whom JUSTICE SCALIA, JUSTICE KENNEDY, and JUSTICE THOMAS join, dissenting.

A criminal law, 18 U.S.C. § 1519, prohibits tampering with "any record, document, or tangible object" in an attempt to obstruct a federal investigation. This case raises the question whether the term "tangible object" means the same thing in § 1519 as it means in everyday language— any object capable of being touched. The answer should be easy: Yes. The term "tangible object" is broad, but clear. Throughout the U. S. Code and many States' laws, it invariably covers physical objects of all kinds. And in § 1519, context confirms what bare text says: All the words surrounding "tangible object" show that Congress meant the term to have a wide range. That fits with Congress's evident purpose in enacting § 1519: to punish those who alter or destroy physical evidence—*any* physical evidence—with the intent of thwarting federal law enforcement.

The plurality instead interprets "tangible object" to cover "only objects one can use to record or preserve information." The concurring opinion similarly, if more vaguely, contends that "tangible object" should refer to "something similar to records or documents"—and shouldn't include colonial farmhouses, crocodiles, or fish. In my view, conventional tools of statutory construction all lead to a more conventional result: A "tangible object" is an object that's tangible. I would apply the statute that Congress enacted and affirm the judgment below.

I

While the plurality starts its analysis with § 1519's heading ("We note first § 1519's caption"), I would begin with § 1519's text. When Congress has not supplied a definition, we generally give a statutory term its ordinary meaning. As the plurality must acknowledge, the ordinary meaning of "tangible object" is "a discrete thing that possesses physical form." A fish is, of course, a discrete thing that possesses physical form. See generally Dr. Seuss, One Fish Two Fish Red Fish Blue Fish (1960). So the ordinary meaning of the term "tangible object" in § 1519, as no one here disputes, covers fish (including too-small red grouper).

That interpretation accords with endless uses of the term in statute and rule books as construed by courts. Dozens of federal laws and rules of procedure (and hundreds of state enactments) include the term "tangible object" or its first cousin "tangible thing"—some in association with documents, others not. See, *e.g.*, 7 U.S.C. § 8302(2) (referring to "any material or tangible object that could harbor a pest or disease"); 15 U.S.C. § 57b–1(c) (authorizing investigative demands for "documentary material or tangible things"); 18 U.S.C. § 668(a)(1)(D) (defining "museum" as entity that owns "tangible objects that are exhibited to the public"); 28 U. S. C. § 2507(b) (allowing discovery of "relevant facts, books, papers, documents or tangible things") * * *. No surprise, then, that—until today—courts have uniformly applied the term "tangible object" in § 1519 in the same way. See, *e.g.*, *United States* v. *McRae*, 702 F.3d 806, 834–838 (CA5 2012) (corpse); *United States* v. *Maury*, 695 F.3d 227, 243–244 (CA3 2012) (cement mixer).

That is not necessarily the end of the matter; I agree with the plurality (really, who does not?) that context matters in interpreting statutes * * *. And sometimes that means, as the plurality says, that the dictionary definition of a disputed term cannot control. But this is not such an occasion, for here the text and its context point the same way * * *. Stepping back from the words "tangible object" provides only further evidence that Congress said what it meant and meant what it said.

Begin with the way the surrounding words in § 1519 reinforce the breadth of the term at issue. Section 1519 refers to "any" tangible object, thus indicating (in line with *that* word's plain meaning) a tangible object "of whatever kind." Webster's Third New International Dictionary 97 (2002). This Court has time and again recognized that "any" has "an expansive meaning," bringing within a statute's reach *all* types of the item (here, "tangible object") to which the law refers. And the adjacent laundry list of verbs in § 1519 ("alters, destroys, mutilates, conceals, covers up, falsifies, or makes a false entry") further shows that Congress wrote a statute with a wide scope. Those words are supposed to ensure—just as "tangible object" is meant to—that § 1519 covers the whole world of evidence-tampering, in all its prodigious variety.

Still more, "tangible object" appears as part of a three-noun phrase (including also "records" and "documents") common to evidence-tampering laws and always understood to embrace things of all kinds * * *. The Model Penal Code's evidence-tampering section, drafted more than 50 years ago, similarly prohibits a person from "alter[ing], destroy[ing], conceal[ing] or remov[ing] any *record, document or thing*" in an effort to thwart an official investigation or proceeding. ALI, Model Penal Code § 241.7(1),p. 175 (1962) (emphasis added) * * *. [C]ourts in the more than 15 States that have laws based on the Model Code's tampering provision apply them to all tangible objects, including drugs, guns, vehicles and . . . yes, animals. See, *e.g.*, *State* v. *Majors*, 318 S.W.3d 850, 859–861 (Tenn. 2010) (cocaine); *Puckett* v. *State*, 328 Ark. 355, 357–360, 944 S.W.2d 111, 113–114 (1997) (gun); *State* v. *Bruno*, 236 Conn. 514, 519–520, 673 A.2d 1117, 1122–1123 (1996) (bicycle, skeleton, blood stains); *State* v. *Crites*, 2007 Mont. Dist. LEXIS 615, *5–*7 (Dec. 21, 2007) (deer antlers). Not a one has limited the phrase's scope to objects that record or preserve information.

* * *

And legislative history, for those who care about it, puts extra icing on a cake already frosted. Section 1519, as the plurality notes, was enacted after the Enron Corporation's collapse, as part of the Sarbanes-Oxley Act of 2002, 116 Stat. 745. But the provision began its life in a separate bill, and the drafters emphasized that Enron was "only a case study exposing the shortcomings in our current laws" relating to both "corporate and criminal" fraud. S. Rep. No. 107–146, pp. 2, 11 (2002). The primary "loophole[ ]" Congress identified, see *id.*, at 14, arose from limits in the part of § 1512 just described: That provision, as uniformly construed, prohibited a person from inducing another to destroy "record[s], document[s], or other object[s]"—of every type—but not from doing so himself. § 1512(b)(2); see *supra*, at 5. Congress (as even the plurality agrees) enacted § 1519 to close that yawning gap. But § 1519 could fully achieve that goal only if it covered all the records, documents, and objects § 1512 did, as well as all the means of tampering with them. And so § 1519 was written to do exactly that—"to apply broadly to any acts to destroy or fabricate physical evidence," as long as performed with the requisite intent * * *.

As Congress recognized in using a broad term, giving immunity to those who destroy non-documentary evidence has no sensible basis in penal policy. A person who hides a murder victim's body is no less culpable than one who burns the victim's diary. A fisherman, like John Yates, who dumps undersized fish to avoid a fine is no less blameworthy than one who shreds his vessel's catch log for the same reason * * *.

II

A

The plurality searches far and wide for anything—*anything*—to support its interpretation of § 1519. But its fishing expedition comes up empty.

The plurality's analysis starts with § 1519's title: "Destruction, alteration, or falsification of records in Federal investigations and bankruptcy." That's already a sign something is amiss. I know of no other case in which we have *begun* our interpretation of a statute with the title, or relied on a title to override the law's clear terms. Instead, we have followed "the wise rule that the title of a statute and the heading of a section cannot limit the plain meaning of the text." *Trainmen* v. *Baltimore & Ohio R. Co.*, 331 U.S. 519, 528–529 (1947).

The reason for that "wise rule" is easy to see: A title is, almost necessarily, an abridgment. Attempting to mention every term in a statute "would often be ungainly as well as useless"; accordingly, "matters in the text . . . are frequently unreflected in the headings" * * *.

* * *

* * * Says the plurality: If read naturally, § 1519 "would render superfluous" § 1512(c)(1), which Congress passed "as part of the same act." But that is not so: Although the two provisions significantly overlap, each applies to conduct the other does not. The key difference between the two is that § 1519 protects the integrity of "matter[s] within the jurisdiction of any [federal] department or agency" whereas § 1512(c)(1) safeguards "official proceeding[s]" as defined in § 1515(a)(1)(A). Section 1519's language often applies more broadly than § 1512(c)(1)'s, as the plurality notes.

* * *

Getting nowhere with surplusage, the plurality switches canons, hoping that *noscitur a sociis* and *ejusdem generis* will save it. The first of those related canons advises that words grouped in a list be given similar meanings. The second counsels that a general term following specific words embraces only things of a similar kind. According to the plurality, those Latin maxims change the English meaning of "tangible object" to only things, like records and documents, "used to record or preserve information." But understood as this Court always has, the canons have no such transformative effect on the workaday language Congress chose.

As an initial matter, this Court uses *noscitur a sociis* and *ejusdem generis* to resolve ambiguity, not create it. Those principles are "useful rule[s] of construction where words are of obscure or doubtful meaning." *Russell Motor Car Co.* v. *United States*, 261 U.S. 514, 520 (1923). But when words have a clear definition, and all other contextual clues support that meaning, the canons cannot properly defeat Congress's decision to draft broad legislation.

Anyway, assigning "tangible object" its ordinary meaning comports with *noscitur a sociis* and *ejusdem generis* when applied, as they should be, with attention to § 1519's subject and purpose. Those canons require identifying a common trait that links all the words in a statutory phrase. In responding to that demand, the plurality characterizes records and documents as things that preserve information—and so they are. But just as much, they are things that provide information, and thus potentially serve as evidence relevant to matters under review. And in a statute pertaining to obstruction of federal investigations, that evidentiary function comes to the fore. The destruction of records and documents prevents law enforcement agents from gathering facts relevant to official inquiries. And so too does the destruction of tangible objects—of whatever kind. Whether the item is a fisherman's ledger or an undersized fish, throwing it overboard has the identical effect on the administration of justice. For purposes of § 1519, records, documents, and (all) tangible objects are therefore alike.

* * *

And the plurality's invocation of § 1519's verbs does nothing to buttress its canon-based argument. The plurality observes that § 1519 prohibits "falsif[ying]" or "mak[ing] a false entry in" a tangible object, and no one can do those things to, say, a murder weapon (or a fish). But of course someone can alter, destroy, mutilate, conceal, or cover up such a tangible object, and § 1519 prohibits those actions too. The Court has never before suggested that all the verbs in a statute need to match up with all the nouns. And for good reason. It is exactly when Congress sets out to draft a statute broadly—to include every imaginable variation on a theme—that such mismatches will arise. To respond by narrowing the law, as the plurality does, is thus to flout both what Congress wrote and what Congress wanted.

Finally, when all else fails, the plurality invokes the rule of lenity. But even in its most robust form, that rule only kicks in when, "after all legitimate tools of interpretation have been exhausted, 'a reasonable doubt persists' regarding whether Congress has made the defendant's conduct a federal crime." *Abramski* v. *United States*, 573 U.S. ___, ___ (2014) (SCALIA, J., dissenting) (slip op., at 12) (quoting *Moskal* v. *United States*, 498 U.S. 103, 108 (1990)). No such doubt lingers here. The plurality points to the breadth of § 1519, as though breadth were equivalent to ambiguity. It is not. Section 1519 *is* very broad. It is also very clear * * *.

B

The concurring opinion is a shorter, vaguer version of the plurality's. It relies primarily on the *noscitur a sociis* and *ejusdem generis* canons, tries to bolster them with § 1519's "list of verbs," and concludes with the section's title * * *.

But § 1519's meaning should not hinge on the odd game of Mad Libs the concurrence proposes. No one reading § 1519 needs to fill in a blank after the words "records" and "documents." That is because Congress, quite helpfully, already did so—adding the term "tangible object." The issue in this case is what that term means. So if the concurrence wishes to ask its neighbor a question, I'd recommend a more pertinent one: Do you think a fish (or, if the concurrence prefers, a crocodile) is a "tangible object"? As to that query, "who wouldn't raise an eyebrow" if the neighbor said "no"? In insisting on its different question, the concurrence neglects the proper function of catchall phrases like "or tangible object." The reason Congress uses such terms is precisely to reach things that, in the concurrence's words, "do[ ] not spring to mind"—to my mind, to my neighbor's, or (most important) to Congress's * * *.

* * *

* * * [W]hatever the wisdom or folly of § 1519, this Court does not get to rewrite the law * * *. If judges disagree with Congress's choice, we are perfectly entitled to say so—in lectures, in law review articles, and even in dicta. But we are not entitled to replace the statute Congress enacted with an alternative of our own design.

I respectfully dissent.

NOTES

Since Justice Stevens' departure from the Court in 2010, his strong intentionalism—the view that statutory interpretation is a search for the concrete thoughts and expectations in the heads of specific legislative actors—has been unrepresented on the Supreme Court, though it may still find favor with some lower court judges. The major battles seem to involve the interplay among text, context, and purpose—and those are battles enough to keep lawyers busy for quite some time.

Indeed, in *Ivy Tech Community College of Indiana,* 853 F.3d 339 (7th Cir.2017) (en banc), the Seventh Circuit Court of Appeals exhibited a multi-directional split on interpretative methodology in holding that discrimination on the basis of sexual orientation is prohibited by Title VII of the Civil Rights Act of 1964, which covers discrimination based on "race, color, religion, sex, or national origin." 42 U.S.C. § 2000e–2(a) (2012). A majority opinion, two concurring opinions, and one dissenting opinion canvassed a broad range of interpretative principles in holding that discrimination based on sexual orientation amounts to discrimination based on "sex" within the meaning of that statute. Interestingly, only one judge out of eleven openly argued for interpretation based on a modern rather than an original meaning of the statute; the majority opinion and two other concurring judges maintained that their conclusion that Title VII prohibits sexual orientation discrimination simply drew out meaning that had been present, even if unrecognized, in the statute from 1964 onwards. In the end, however, the case may have turned on the proper interpretation, not of a statute, but of previous Supreme Court opinions applying the statute. That was plainly true of another case involving exactly the same issue under exactly the same statute. *See Zarda v. Altitude Express, Inc.,* 883 F.3d 100 (2d Cir.2018) (en banc). This is characteristic of many cases of statutory interpretation; oftentimes, they are not cases of first impression but take place against a long backdrop of prior court decisions applying the statute in question. Should those prior decisions be included in the list of tools of interpretation, or are they side-constraints on the interpretative process? However one answers that question, much of the time what looks like statutory analysis will really be conventional "common-law" analysis because the decisive consideration will be how to read prior court opinions construing the statute.

One long-standing battle that appears to have faded a bit (though perhaps less than some would like to think) in recent years concerns the use of legislative history. The details of the legislative process are a subject for a separate course, but a few aspects of that process are critical for administrative law.

Legislation is the end result of an often-lengthy process. Proposed legislation, introduced in draft form as a bill by one or more members of Congress, is generally referred to the appropriate committees (and subcommittees) in each house—and a dozen or more such committees may review one bill, depending on the breadth and subject matter of the legislation. Some of those committees may hold hearings on the bill (and on other bills relating to the same subject matter), sometimes over a period of years. Those hearings are generally transcribed.

If the bill continues to have support, it may come to a vote before the full House or Senate. By that time, however, the bill is likely to have undergone substantial revisions in the various committees. Often, those committees will prepare documents, known as committee reports, describing the bill, its evolution, and its avowed purposes.[13] Because of the overlapping jurisdiction of many congressional committees, there can easily be more than one report in each house on any given bill. In addition to describing the bill, these reports will often express the committees' views, which might well be conflicting views, of the *meaning* of potentially ambiguous terms in the bill. The reports may thus self-consciously seek to influence the way that agencies and courts will subsequently interpret and apply the bills once they are enacted into law.

---

[13] The avowed purposes are not necessarily the real ones. One is most unlikely to find a committee report declaring: "The purpose of this legislation is to transfer wealth from the unsuspecting public at large to a favored constituency of the committee's chairperson."

If a bill comes up for a vote on the floor of either house, there may be a substantial oral debate over the bill. Those debates are reported on a daily basis in the Congressional Record. In addition to discussing the policy implications of proposed legislation, members of Congress can also make speeches in which they describe their understandings of a bill's meaning. The bill's sponsor or sponsors may be especially likely to express views on the bill's intended meaning. Members of Congress may also have remarks inserted into the Congressional Record *after* the debate is completed (and indeed after legislation is enacted) expressing their views on a bill's meaning. In principle, remarks that were never actually made publicly on the floor of Congress are supposed to be specially marked in the Congressional Record; in practice, there have been serious questions about the reliability of the marking system.[14]

In order for a bill to go to the President for signature or veto, the House and Senate must pass bills with exactly the same language. If each house passes a proposal in a different form (and the differences can be minor matters of wording or enormous differences in substance), the matter is referred to a joint committee of the House and Senate, known as a conference committee. That committee is then charged with coming up with a version of the bill that is acceptable to each house of Congress. The committee version can be a compromise between the House and Senate versions, full adoption of one of the two versions, or even an entirely different proposal. The conference committee will often prepare a committee report on its recommendation that may also offer views on the meaning of the bill.

Finally, if both the House and Senate enact an identical bill, it goes to the President for signature or veto. It has become increasingly common since the 1980s for presidents, upon signing legislation, to issue statements indicating the President's view of the meaning of the legislation that is being enacted. Messages accompanying vetoes can also be based on presidential interpretations of the language of bills. *See* Alvan Balent, Jr., *Statutory Interpretation and the Presidency: The Hierarchy of "Executive History,"* 30 J. L. & Pol. 341 (2015). Use of such presidential "signing statements" has been controversial, though much of the controversy has involved the use of signing statements to signal a presidential intention to disregard laws which the President considers unconstitutional rather than the use of signing statements as legislative history analogous to congressional committee reports. The real issue in that constitutionally-charged context is the substance of the underlying presidential intention (nonenforcement of allegedly unconstitutional laws) rather than the form (signing statements) in which that intention is expressed. Confining ourselves only to signing statements that seek to take their place in the pantheon of legislative history as aids to discerning statutory meaning: Advocates of the use of signing statements point to the President's formal role in the enactment of laws (at least if they are not enacted over a veto) in support of the relevance of presidential opinions on meaning, while opponents argue that giving credence to signing statements

---

[14] A suit to compel Congress to enforce its marking rules was dismissed without a determination on the merits. *See* Gregg v. Barrett, 771 F.2d 539 (D.C.Cir.1985).

threatens to dilute the status of Congress as the paramount lawmaking institution. Whatever the merits of the various arguments may be, casual empiricism suggests that signing statements have not, at least thus far, had much of an impact on courts as tools of statutory interpretation. *See* Paul T. Stepnowsky, *Deference to Presidential Signing Statements in Administrative Law*, 78 Geo. Wash. L.J. 1086, 1096 (2010).

Thus, by the time a bill becomes a law, there will often be an extensive paper trail, perhaps spanning years, that includes: draft versions of the bill; hearing transcripts; committee reports from the House, the Senate, or both; statements on the floor of the House and/or Senate from individual members of Congress; a conference committee report; and a presidential signing (or veto) statement. These documents are generally referred to as the statute's *legislative history*. Sometimes the term is used more broadly to include also general understandings of a statute's purpose and context that are not specifically recorded in any official document. But the most common usage refers to the paper trail left by Congress and the President.

There is an informal hierarchy of importance among the documents, with conference committee reports generally being viewed as the most authoritative forms of legislative history and individual statements of legislators (or presidential signing statements if one does not favor them) generally placed at the bottom of the heap. George A. Costello, *Average Voting Members and Other "Benign Fictions": The Relative Reliability of Committee Reports, Floor Debates, and Other Sources of Legislative History*, 1990 Duke L.J. 39, 41–42. Modern scholars have grave doubts about the merits of this hierarchy, *see* Victoria A. Nourse, *A Decision Theory of Statutory Interpretation: Legislative History by the Rules*, 122 Yale L.J. 70, 109–110 (2012), but it is a standard fixture in judicial decisions. *See, e.g., Council for Urological Interests v. Burwell*, 790 F.3d 212, 231 (D.C.Cir.2015) (Henderson, J., dissenting in part).

As we will later see, *see infra* pages 180–181, legislative history, including statements of individual legislators, is important to agencies, and therefore to lawyers dealing with agencies, whether or not courts give it any heed. For the moment, however, consider only how legislative history affects courts decisions.

The proper role that legislative history should have in court deliberations about the meaning of statutes has long been a very hot topic, both on and off the bench. It is not too much to say that any lawyer arguing a statutory case in court during the 1970s or 1980s who was not fully conversant with the relevant statute's legislative history, and whose brief did not contain a substantial discussion of that legislative history, was behaving unprofessionally—and was quite possibly committing malpractice. This was true even if the language of the statute clearly supported the lawyer's position. Courts would routinely scrutinize the legislative history even when the statute was, by the courts' own lights, entirely clear. And if by some chance the statute said "dog" and the legislative history said "cat," there was at least a non-zero chance that the court would construe the statute to mean "cat."

Since that time, a small but vocal and determined group of judges, most notably the late Justice Scalia, has crusaded against the use of legislative history as an authoritative tool of statutory interpretation. Part of the critique is theoretical: If statutes are public acts, their meaning is *public* meaning rather than the private meaning of representatives or committees. Part of the critique is practical: Even as evidence of legislatively intended meaning, legislative history is unreliable, and canvassing it is a royal pain for judges and lawyers alike and simply introduces one more source of uncertainty into the interpretative process. Such judges, and the scholars who agree with them, *see, e.g.,* John F. Manning, *Textualism as a Nondelegation Doctrine*, 97 Colum. L. Rev. 673, 684–89 (1997), generally do not object to more modest uses of legislative history, such as to indicate the general social context in which legislation was enacted and the set of problems to which it was most likely addressed. Legislative history, in this limited sense, carries little more (but no less) authority than newspaper columns, which could in principle provide the same information. They do object to treating legislative history as something that can trump statutory language or even shed light on the particularistic meaning of statutory terms.

This crusade does seem to have had some significant effect on judicial practice, especially in the Supreme Court, though such changes are hard to document with precision. Note the tepid and qualified use of legislative history materials in the *Zuni* and *Yates* cases. And in *NLRB v. SW General, Inc.*, 137 S.Ct. 929, 941–42, 197 L.Ed.2d 263 (2017), six Justices said: "The Board contends that legislative history, purpose, and post-enactment practice uniformly show that subsection (b)(1) [of the Federal Vacancies Reform Act of 1998] applies only to first assistants [rather than, as the Court ultimately holds, to all persons serving as acting agency officials under the statute]. The text is clear, so we need not consider this extra-textual evidence." *Id.* at 941–42. Although the Court then went on at some length to consider that extra-textual evidence anyway, noting that "[i]n any event, the Board's evidence is not compelling," *id.* at 942, the Court's explicit focus on plain statutory meaning has become commonplace. Indeed, almost never has legislative history played a decisive role in Supreme Court cases in recent years, and that manifestly would not have been true just a few decades ago. *See, e.g., Wisconsin Public Intervenor v. Mortier,* 501 U.S. 597, 610 n.4, 111 S.Ct. 2476, 115 L.Ed.2d 532 (1991).

But that does not mean that legislative history, or controversy about its use, is entirely absent from Supreme Court opinions. In *Digital Realty Trust, Inc. v. Somers*, 138 S.Ct. 767, 200 L.Ed.2d 15 (2018), the Court unanimously determined that a statute protecting corporate whistleblowers from retaliation for reporting malfeasance, *see* 15 U.S.C. § 78u–6(h)(1)(A)(iii) (2012), only applied to people who reported the alleged violation to the Securities and Exchange Commission. (Somers had reported suspected violations to senior management in his company but not to the SEC; he was fired and then unsuccessfully sought the protection of the whistleblower statute.). The Court relied primarily on the plain language of the statutory provision, which defines a protected whistleblower as someone "who provides * * * information relating to a violation of the securities laws to the Commission," and on the relationship of that language to related statutory provisions. The Court then added, in a brief section, that the "purpose and design," 138 S.Ct. at 777, of the larger statutory scheme "corroborate our comprehension," *id.* of the statute's meaning. As evidence of that "purpose and design," the Court cited a Senate report indicating a desire "to motivate people who know of securities law violations to tell the SEC." S. Rep. No. 111–176, at 38 (2010). That passing mention of legislative history prompted three Justices to write a separate opinion:

THOMAS, J., with whom ALITO, J., and GORSUCH, J., join, concurring in part and concurring in the judgment.

I join the Court's opinion only to the extent it relies on the text of the Dodd-Frank Wall Street Reform and Consumer Protection Act (Dodd-Frank), 124 Stat. 1376. The question in this case is whether the term "whistleblower" in Dodd-Frank's antiretaliation provision, 15 U.S.C. § 78u–6(h)(1), includes a person who does not report information to the Securities and Exchange Commission. The answer is in the definitions section of the statute, which states that the term "whistleblower" means a person who provides "information relating to a violation of the securities laws to the Commission." § 78u–6(a)(6). As the Court observes, this statutory definition "resolves the question before us." *Ante,* at 777. The Court goes on, however, to discuss the supposed "purpose" of the statute, which it primarily derives from a single Senate Report. Even assuming a majority of Congress read the Senate Report, agreed with it, and voted for Dodd-Frank with the same intent, "we are a government of laws, not of men, and are governed by what Congress enacted rather than by what it intended." *Lawson v. FMR LLC,* 571 U.S. 429, ___, 134 S.Ct. 1158, 1176, 188 L.Ed.2d 158 (2014) (Scalia, J., concurring in part and concurring in judgment). And "it would be a strange canon of statutory construction that would require Congress to state in committee reports . . . that which is obvious on the face of a statute." *Harrison v. PPG Industries, Inc.,* 446 U.S. 578, 592, 100 S.Ct. 1889, 64 L.Ed.2d 525 (1980). For these reasons, I am unable to join the portions of the Court's opinion that venture beyond the statutory text.

138 S.Ct. at 783–84. Two Justices responded:

SOTOMAYOR, J., with whom BREYER, J., joins, concurring.

I join the Court's opinion in full. I write separately only to note my disagreement with the suggestion in my colleague's concurrence that a Senate Report is not an appropriate source for this Court to consider when interpreting a statute.

Legislative history is of course not the law, but that does not mean it cannot aid us in our understanding of a law. Just as courts are capable of assessing the reliability and utility of evidence generally, they are capable of assessing the reliability and utility of legislative-history materials.

Committee reports, like the Senate Report the Court discusses here, are a particularly reliable source to which we can look to ensure our fidelity to Congress' intended meaning. Bills presented to Congress for consideration are generally accompanied by a committee report. Such reports are typically circulated at least two days before a bill is to be considered on the floor and provide Members of Congress and their staffs with information about "a bill's context, purposes, policy implications, and details," along with information on its supporters and opponents. R. Katzmann, Judging Statutes 20, and n. 62 (2014) (citing A. LaRue, Senate Manual Containing the Standing Rules, Orders, Laws, and Resolutions Affecting the Business of the United States Senate, S. Doc. No. 107–1, p. 17 (2001)). These materials "have long been important means of informing the whole chamber about proposed legislation," Katzmann, Judging Statutes, at 19, a point Members themselves have emphasized over the years. It is thus no surprise that legislative staffers view committee and conference reports as the most reliable type of legislative history. See Gluck & Bressman, *Statutory Interpretation From the Inside—An Empirical Study of Congressional Drafting, Delegation and the Canons: Part I,* 65 Stan. L. Rev. 901, 977 (2013).

Legislative history can be particularly helpful when a statute is ambiguous or deals with especially complex matters. But even when, as here, a statute's meaning can clearly be discerned from its text, consulting reliable legislative history can still be useful, as it enables us to corroborate and fortify our understanding of the text. Moreover, confirming our construction of a statute by considering reliable legislative history shows respect for and promotes comity with a coequal branch of Government. See Katzmann, Judging Statutes, at 35–36.

For these reasons, I do not think it wise for judges to close their eyes to reliable legislative history—and the realities of how Members of Congress create and enact laws—when it is available.

Id. at 782–83. And the beat goes on. One possible drummer of note is Justice Brett Kavanaugh, who has written: "As a formal matter, committee reports and floor statements are not the law enacted by Congress. And as a functional matter, committee reports and floor statements too often reflect an effort by a subgroup in Congress—or, worse, outside of it—to affect how the statute will subsequently be interpreted and implemented, in ways that Congress and the President may not have intended." Brett M. Kavanaugh, *Book Review,* 129 Harv. L. Rev. 2118, 2149 (2016).

Whatever its status on the Supreme Court, legislative history continues to play an important role in many lower-court decisions. In a survey of forty two federal court of appeals judges, encompassing nearly one-fourth of the active appellate bench, all but one respondent indicated that they used legislative history. *See* Abbe R. Gluck & Richard A. Posner, *Statutory Interpretation on the Bench: A Survey of Forty-Two Judges on the Federal Courts of Appeals,* 131 Harv. L. Rev. 1298, 1324 (2018). Whether or not judicial use of legislative history is a good idea, it is not going to disappear any time soon. Accordingly, while your editor is sympathetic to some of the critiques of legislative history, it is still his view that it remains unprofessional for an administrative lawyer not to be intimately familiar with the legislative history of any statute with which he or she is dealing in court.

And if the reader is still wondering why the President is not an agency for purposes of the APA, the answer does not lie in the statute's text, structure, or legislative history. The answer lies in the canons of interpretation.

Canons of interpretation, many of which were on display in *Yates*, can serve two distinct functions. One function is to resolve ambiguities that are generated by other sources of meaning, such as text or structure. If one is not sure what is meant by a "tangible object," perhaps one can alleviate that uncertainty by reference to canons about how to integrate terms with surrounding language or other terms with which they are found in a list. Such principles of interpretation, such as the *noscitur a sociis* and *ejusdem generis* canons employed by the *Yates* plurality, *see supra* pages 33–34, are sometimes called *semantic canons*.

Some of those semantic canons, as *Yates* illustrates, concern how to deal with lists of terms. If, for example, there is a list of terms in a statute followed by some kind of modifier—such as a provision requiring enhanced criminal sentences for prior convictions involving "aggravated sexual abuse, sexual abuse, or abusive sexual conduct involving a minor or ward," 18 U.S.C. § 2252(b)(2) (2012)—does the modifier ("involving a minor or ward" in this example) apply to all of the terms in the series or just the last? Would "aggravated sexual abuse" that did not involve a minor or ward fall within this provision? Sometimes, the latter construction, in which the qualifier applies only to the very last term in the series (in this case "abusive sexual conduct"), seems clearly right:

> For example, imagine you are the general manager of the Yankees and you are rounding out your 2016 roster. You tell your scouts to find a defensive catcher, a quick-footed shortstop, or a pitcher from last year's World Champion Kansas City Royals. It would be natural for your scouts to confine their search for a pitcher to last year's championship team, but to look more broadly for catchers and shortstops.

Lockhart v. U.S., 136 S.Ct. 958, 963, 194 L.Ed.2d 48 (2016). This principle of interpretation is often called "the rule of the last antecedent," because it applies the modifier only to the immediately preceding term in the prior list. If applied in the context of our criminal sentencing statute, sentence enhancement would be proper for *any* prior aggravated sexual abuse or sexual abuse but *only* for abusive sexual conduct involving a minor. On the other hand, sometimes modifiers apply more broadly to terms in a series:

> Imagine a friend told you that she hoped to meet "an actor, director, or producer involved with the new Star Wars movie." You would know immediately that she wanted to meet an actor from the Star Wars cast—not an actor in, for example, the latest Zoolander. Suppose a real estate agent promised to find a client "a house, condo, or apartment in New York." Wouldn't the potential buyer be annoyed if the agent sent him information about condos in Maryland or California? And consider a law imposing a penalty for the "violation of any statute, rule, or regulation relating to insider trading." Surely a person would have cause to protest if punished under that provision for violating a traffic statute. The reason in all three cases is the same: Everyone understands that the modifying phrase—"involved with the new Star Wars movie," "in New York," "relating to insider trading"—applies to each term in the preceding list, not just the last.

Id. at 969 (Kagan, J., dissenting). If this construction was applied in our criminal context, sentence enhancements would be permissible only when the prior sexual abuse convictions—whether classified as "aggravated sexual abuse," "sexual abuse," or "abusive sexual conduct"—involved minors or wards. So which principle of interpretation governs this particular sentence-enhancement statute? The Supreme Court in *Lockhart* split 6–2 on that question, with the majority going with the rule of the last antecedent, so whatever answer you give finds support in the views of some very smart people. The answer, as both the majority and dissenting opinions recognized, probably depends on the larger context in which the list of terms appears.

The moral of the story is that semantic canons of construction can sometimes help discern meaning, but they cannot be applied automatically or mechanistically. *See* Linda D. Jellum, Mastering Statutory Interpretation 123 (2d ed. 2013) ("These canons are not hard and fast rules, but rather guides or presumptions").

Semantic canons have received considerable scholarly attention in recent years, most notably because of a prominent book—co-written by a late Supreme Court Justice and the editor of *Black's Law Dictionary*—which identifies, and defends, no fewer than thirty two canons that deal with language and punctuation. *See* Antonin Scalia & Bryan A. Garner, Reading Law: The Interpretation of Legal Texts (2012). Much of the ensuing scholarship is sharply critical of the plausibility of those canons as actual guides to intended meaning. Semantic canons are designed to identify informed and sensible uses of language, but "there is empirical evidence suggesting that reasonable readers do not read statutes as if they were drafted according to the rules of sensible language use." Cory R. Liu, *Textualism and the Presumption of Reasonable Drafting*, 38 Harv. J.L. & Pub. Pol'y 711, 717–19 (2015). More specifically, there is good reason to doubt whether the actual drafters of legislation make much effort to conform to the rules represented by canons of interpretation. *See* Lisa Schultz Bressman & Abbe R. Gluck, *Statutory Interpretation from the Inside—An Empirical Study of Congressional Drafting, Delegation, and the Canons: Part I*, 65 Stan. L. Rev. 901 (2013); Lisa Schultz Bressman & Abbe R. Gluck, *Statutory Interpretation from the Inside—An Empirical Study of Congressional Drafting, Delegation, and the Canons: Part II*, 66 Stan. L. Rev. 725 (2014). Nor is it clear that even the most popular canons actually reflect sensible language use. *See* Brett M. Kavanaugh, *Book Review*, 129 Harv. L. Rev. 2118, 2159–62 (2016) (criticizing several canons, including *ejusdem generis* and the "anti-redundancy" canon that tries to give independent effect to every word of a statute, as unlikely to reflect actual communicative intentions). Nonetheless, semantic canons have assumed an increasingly important role in statutory interpretation, including interpretation in administrative law cases.

A second function of canons, quite distinct from the first, is to *create* ambiguity that otherwise would not exist. Some canons are designed to shape meaning rather than to help discern it. The rule of lenity invoked by the plurality in *Yates*, for example, tells courts to resolve ambiguities in criminal laws against the government—not because that is the best way to decode the communicative signals contained in statutes but, as a matter of policy, to protect citizens from unanticipated criminal liability and to encourage Congress to draft criminal statutes with an eye towards clarity. These kinds of ambiguity-generating, or meaning-shaping, canons are sometimes called *substantive canons*, because they purport to serve goals other than the accurate discernment of communicative signals.

One of the most prominent substantive canons is known as the *doctrine of constitutional avoidance*. The basic precept is to instruct courts to make an effort to interpret statutes to avoid raising constitutional problems. That is, if interpretation A would obviously be constitutional while interpretation B would at least make one think about a constitutional problem in a serious way, the avoidance canon directs judges to adopt interpretation A, even if one thinks, without reference to the canon, that B is the better answer and even if one would probably conclude that the law is constitutional if one went with B. The avoidance canon is designed to avoid constitutional *inquiry* and not merely constitutional *invalidation*. In its less modest forms, the avoidance canon encourages courts to prefer relatively far-fetched interpretations of statutes over more seemingly plausible ones if the plausible ones would then require constitutional analysis.

Such a canon drove the Supreme Court decisions that exempted the President from the definition of an agency under the APA. As we will see in great detail later in the course, one consequence of being an "agency" under the APA is to be subject to various forms of judicial control. It is a potentially thorny constitutional question whether Congress has the power to subject at least certain presidential decisions to those judicial controls. The Supreme Court has said that it will not conclude that Congress has tried to test those limits without a very clear statement from Congress that it intends such a result: "Out of respect for the separation of powers and the unique constitutional position of the President, we find that textual silence is not enough to subject the President to the provisions of the APA." *Franklin v. Massachusetts,* 505 U.S. 788, 801, 112 S.Ct. 2767, 2776, 120 L.Ed.2d 636 (1992).

The legitimacy and wisdom of at least some substantive canons is certainly open to question, *see* Amy Coney Barrett, *Substantive Canons and Faithful Agency,* 90 B.U.L. Rev. 109 (2010); Lisa Heinzerling, *The Power Canons,* 58 Wm. & Mary L. Rev. 1933 (2017), but, as with semantic canons, their use is a standard part of the interpretative process in the administrative law world.

One might take from all of this that statutory interpretation is more art than science, *see* Linda D. Jellum, Mastering Statutory Interpretation 22 (2d ed. 2013), and that much turns on the interpretative theory of the decisionmaker. Arguments that will convince a judge who reasons like Justice Breyer might have little traction with a judge whose interpretative theory more closely resembles that of Justice Gorsuch. And a great many decisionmakers do not have or apply theories of statutory interpretation that fit neatly into any categories or that appear to be consistent. Indeed, Abbe Gluck and Richard Posner have shed much light on this feature of the legal world by doing something simultaneously simple and brilliant: They asked federal court of appeals judges how those judges reasoned about statutory interpretation questions. The responses indicate that judges, or at least lower-court judges, do not generally sort themselves onto one or the other side of scholarly divides about interpretative theory. As Professor Gluck and Judge Posner report: "The approach that emerged most clearly from our interviews is not a single approach at all but rather what might be described as intentional eclecticism * * *. [M]ost of the judges * * * consider many different kinds of material [and] * * * told us * * * that they eschewed an 'ecclesiastical' ideology." Abbe R. Gluck & Richard A. Posner, *Statutory Interpretation on the Bench: A Survey of Forty-Two Judges on the Federal Courts of Appeals,* 131 Harv. L. Rev. 1298, 1302 (2018). That result is consistent with your editor's anecdotal sense gathered over more than three decades.

Recall how this section of the book began: Our legal system has no single governing theory of statutory interpretation. This course will afford ample opportunities for you to make your own judgments about which theories of statutory interpretation (if any) seem to make the most sense and which (if any) best describe the actual operation of the legal system.

5. AGENCY FUNCTIONS: THE DISTINCTION BETWEEN RULEMAKING AND ADJUDICATION

a. Nonbinding Agency Action

Action by agencies falls into two categories: action that has formal legal effects on people and action that does not. The second category occupies by far the greater proportion of most agencies' time. Agencies typically spend most of their energy analyzing, investigating, synthesizing, deliberating, planning, and studying. None of these activities directly affects the legal rights and relations of private parties,[15] though they are often preludes to action that does have legal consequences, and they can have an effect on parties' practical affairs that is as great as the effect of formal legal action. Suppose, for example, that it becomes known that the Federal Trade Commission (FTC) is considering initiating an investigation into certain practices of the funeral home industry. The imminence, or even the commencement, of the investigation does not affect the legal status of funeral home operators; the operators are not legally bound to do or refrain from doing anything simply because the FTC is thinking about regulating their industry. As a practical matter, however, funeral home operators may find it necessary to hire lawyers and lobbyists to represent their interests in the regulatory process or to hire public relations consultants to fend off adverse publicity from the investigation—all at great expense. Moreover, operators or potential operators who are seeking financing may find that lenders are reluctant to commit resources in the face of uncertainty about the industry's future. A marginal operator can thereby be pushed into bankruptcy by agency action that technically has no legal consequences.

A good case can be made that a course on administrative law should focus on this enormous body of agency activity that has no immediate legal consequences. Most courses, however, including this one, instead concentrate on the small percentage of agency activity that is intended to be legally binding on outside parties. The reason for this focus is simple: while administrative lawyers spend most of their time dealing with agencies engaged in nonbinding activity,[16] it is very hard to make useful generalizations about that activity. On the other hand, there is a great deal that can be said about the "legalistic" aspects of administrative law. Moreover, in order to deal intelligently with an agency on nonbinding matters, one must have some familiarity with the formal legal doctrines that lurk in the background. Agency activity, even when it is not immediately legally binding, always takes place in the shadow of the law.

b.   Rulemaking and Adjudication

When legislatures affect the rights and obligations of people, they do so through the enactment of legislation. When courts affect the rights and obligations of people, they do so through the issuance of judgments in particular cases. When agencies affect the rights and obligations of people, they do so through one of two modes of activity: *rulemaking* or *adjudication*.

---

[15] Some of these activities, of course, may *indirectly* have legal consequences—for example, if the agency tries to coerce information out of a party unwilling to provide it.

[16] For an excellent brief description of this aspect of the work of an administrative lawyer, see James DeLong, *How to Convince an Agency*, Regulation, Sept./Oct. 1982, at 27.

When an agency engages in rulemaking, it does something that looks very much like a legislature passing a law. A properly conducted rulemaking results in something called a *rule* (or *regulation*), which functions in most ways like a statute. If you violate a rule, you can be heavily fined, punished in other ways, or even sent to jail under appropriate circumstances. Note that in the *Yates* case, *see supra* page 29, before Mr. Yates tossed his too-small groupers overboard and thus made himself liable for evidence-tampering, he faced a fine and loss of a license simply for holding onto the undersized fish (which is why he wanted to be rid of them before he got to port). No statute fixed the minimum size of groupers at twenty inches. That was accomplished through an agency *rule*, and the relevant statute simply punished violations of the agency's rules. *See* 16 U.S.C. § 1857(1)(A) (2012) ("It is unlawful—for any person—to violate any provision of this chapter *or any regulation* or permit issued pursuant to this chapter") (emphasis added). The rule—the administrative action—was the primary determinant of forbidden and permitted conduct. That is often the case; agency rules frequently outdo congressional statutes in importance in the legal world. At the end of 2012, the number of pages in the Code of Federal Regulations, the set of volumes that codifies the most important agency rules, exceeded by a factor of four the number of pages in the United States Code, which codifies congressional statutes. *See* Tom Cummins, *Code Words*, 5 J. Legal Metrics 89, 98 (2015). Furthermore, it is well established that agency rules can even preempt otherwise valid state laws, *see, e.g., Geier v. American Honda Motor Co., Inc.,* 529 U.S. 861, 120 S.Ct. 1913, 146 L.Ed.2d 914 (2000), though the theoretical basis for that doctrine is somewhat obscure. *See* David S. Rubenstein, *The Paradox of Administrative Preemption,* 38 Harv. J.L. & Pub. Pol'y 267 (2015). A properly conducted agency rulemaking is a formidable legal entity.

When an agency engages in adjudication, it does something that looks very much like a court deciding a case. A properly conducted adjudication results in something called an *order*, which functions in most ways like a court judgment. If you violate an agency order, the order can be legally enforced. Agency orders can even have res judicata and collateral estoppel effect in subsequent court proceedings. *See B & B Hardware, Inc. v. Hargin Industries, Inc.,* 576 U.S. ___, 135 S.Ct. 1293, 1303, 191 L.Ed.2d 222 (2015) ("issue preclusion is not limited to those situations in which the same issue is before two *courts*. Rather, where a single issue is before a court and an administrative agency, preclusion also often applies"). A properly conducted agency adjudication, like a properly conducted agency rulemaking, can be a formidable legal entity.

It can make a great deal of difference to the law whether an agency action is appropriately characterized as rulemaking or adjudication. Indeed, much of this course explores the different legal consequences that attach to the labels "rulemaking" and "adjudication" (and much of the rest of the course explores what it means for a rulemaking or adjudication to be properly conducted). The following materials address this critical distinction—perhaps the most critical distinction in all of administrative law—between rulemaking and adjudication.

JOHN DICKINSON, ADMINISTRATIVE JUSTICE AND THE SUPREMACY OF LAW IN THE UNITED STATES

(Harvard University Press, 1927) pp. 16–21.
Reprinted by permission of the publisher from Administrative Justice and the Supremacy of Law in the United States by John Dickinson, Harvard Studies in Administrative Law, 2, pp. 16–21, Cambridge, Mass.: Harvard University Press.

* * * Our constitutional distinction between "legislative," "executive" and "judicial" powers draws the courts frequently into discussions in which the "legislative" or "executive" aspect of an administrative act is generally emphasized at the expense of the "judicial." Thus, for example, the act of a public-utilities commission in fixing a rate has been held to be "legislative" for constitutional purposes. From one aspect of juristic analysis, legislative it no doubt is—that is, from the aspect of its future operation and its applicability to a whole class of cases. But the writ of mandamus is future in its operation, and yet is not for that reason regarded as legislative; and if we examine rate-fixing from the standpoint of the general applicability of the resulting rate to an indefinite number of future cases as a class, we observe the significant peculiarity that, while the rate applies indifferently, indeed, as against all future shippers, it applies only to the particular carrier or carriers who were parties to the hearing and other proceedings before the commission, and for whom, as the outcome of those proceedings, the rate is prescribed. From the standpoint of shippers, therefore, the rate may no doubt be regarded as legislation, but from the standpoint of the carriers it seems quite as truly adjudication. Even with respect to the shippers, however, it may be likened to the procedure whereby an injunction is obtained against a group of persons designated by a class-description and not named personally in the bill. If the latter procedure is judicial, there is certainly an element of adjudication in administrative rate-fixing; and that is all I wish to insist on here. There is no intention to deny that rate-fixing involves as one of its elements the exercise of a function which may as well as not be called "legislative." The whole discussion should go to demonstrate the futility of trying to classify a particular exercise of administrative power as either wholly legislative or wholly judicial. The tendency of the administrative procedure is to foreshorten both functions into a continuous governmental act.

* * * The essential difference between legislation and adjudication is not that one looks to the future and the other to the past—there is nothing inherent in the judicial process which requires that it should look wholly backward * * *. What distinguishes legislation from adjudication is that the former affects the rights of individuals in the abstract and must be applied in a further proceeding before the legal position of any particular individual will be definitely touched by it; while adjudication operates concretely upon individuals in their individual capacity.

RALPH F. FUCHS, PROCEDURE IN ADMINISTRATIVE RULE-MAKING

52 Harv. L. Rev. 259, 260–65 (1938).

It has been said that rule-making operates as to the future whereas other mandatory governmental acts affect present or past situations. However, almost all governmental orders have the characteristic of prescribing or forbidding future conduct. A judgment for money damages, an order for the abatement of a nuisance, and a decree compelling an employer to bargain collectively with a union must be executed in the future, no less than a statute requiring the payment of taxes or an administrative regulation which orders the submission of specified data by public utilities to the government * * *.

* * *

It is clear that mere futurity of operation, which is common to most official acts, cannot serve to distinguish rule-making from other governmental functions. It sometimes is said with respect to legislation, however, that the considerations which enter into it relate to the future and that adjudication is distinguishable because its basis lies in past facts and existing rules of law * * *.

* * *

Legislation and adjudication cannot, however, be kept true to these ideas * * *. [I]t cannot be said truthfully that adjudication is wholly determined by past facts and existing rules or that legislation is enacted with an eye single to future welfare.

When the attempt is made to carry this distinction between "legislation" and "adjudication" into the functions of the executive branch of the government, and to identify rule-making by means of it, additional difficulties are encountered. Many acts of the executive are supposed to be determined by considerations of future advantage, indicated more or less definitely in the controlling statute. In other words, they are discretionary acts. Regulations governing some of the practices of banks and insurance companies, safety regulations, and regulations prescribing the conduct of public services fall within this category. So do certificates of convenience and necessity, licenses to persons of good moral character, rate orders, and the abatement of nuisances upon the general ground that they are threats to comfort or decency. If rule-making were defined as official action based upon considerations of future benefit, all of the foregoing types of administrative acts would be included within it, for it would embrace all discretionary activity. So sweeping and varied a category would hardly possess utility and certainly would depart far from accepted concepts.

The most obvious definition of rule-making and the one most often employed in the literature of administrative law asserts simply that it is the function of laying down general regulations as distinguished from orders that apply to named persons or to specific situations. Most acts of legislatures, though by no means all, establish rights and duties with respect either to people generally or to classes of people or situations that are defined but not enumerated. Conversely, the judgments of courts usually are addressed to particular individuals or to situations that are definitely specified. Similarly, administrative action can be classified into general regulations, including determinations whose effect is to bring general regulations into operation, and orders or acts of specific application.

Difficulties present themselves in relation to this distinction also. Classes of people or situations may be so narrowly defined that the identity of the component units virtually is specified. Thus a law or regulation forbidding the discharge of industrial waste into the waters of a stream would not differ in effect, at least immediately, from an order directed to the only mill-owner engaged in the practice. Conversely, an order establishing specified freight rates on a named railroad affects a host of shippers as well as the respondent and applies to a multitude of transactions. When an order, such as a labor injunction, applies to a vague group of people of whom only a few are named, it takes on the character of a general regulation. Even where only a single respondent is subject to an order, the order seems general in character if it embraces a considerable area of conduct.

LONDONER V. CITY AND COUNTY OF DENVER
Supreme Court of the United States, 1908.
210 U.S. 373, 28 S.Ct. 708, 52 L.Ed. 1103.

MR. JUSTICE MOODY delivered the opinion of the court.

The plaintiffs in error began this proceeding in a state court of Colorado to relieve lands owned by them from an assessment of a tax for the cost of paving a street upon which the lands abutted. The relief sought was granted by the trial court, but its action was reversed by the Supreme Court of the State, which ordered judgment for the defendants. The case is here on writ of error. The Supreme Court held that the tax was assessed in conformity with the constitution and laws of the State, and its decision on that question is conclusive.

* * *

The tax complained of was assessed under the provisions of the charter of the city of Denver, which confers upon the city the power to make local improvements and to assess the cost upon property specially benefited. It does not seem necessary to set forth fully the elaborate provisions of the charter regulating the exercise of this power, except where they call for special examination. The board of public works, upon the petition of a majority of the owners of the frontage to be assessed, may order the paving of a street. The board must, however, first adopt specifications, mark out a district of assessment, cause a map to be made and an estimate of the cost, with the approximate amount to be assessed upon each lot of land. Before action notice by publication and an opportunity to be heard to any person interested must be given by the board.

The board may then order the improvement, but must recommend to the city council a form of ordinance authorizing it, and establishing an assessment district, which is not amendable by the council. The council may then, in its discretion, pass or refuse to pass the ordinance. If the ordinance is passed, the contract for the work is made by the mayor. The charter provides that "the finding of the city council, by ordinance, that any improvements provided for in this article were duly ordered after notice duly given, or that a petition or remonstrance was or was not filed as above provided, or was or was not subscribed by the required number of owners aforesaid shall be conclusive in every court or other tribunal." The charter then provides for the assessment of the cost * * *.

It appears from the charter that, in the execution of the power to make local improvements and assess the cost upon the property specially benefited, the main steps to be taken by the city authorities are plainly marked and separated: 1. The board of public works must transmit to the city council a resolution ordering the work to be done and the form of an ordinance authorizing it and creating an assessment district. This it can do only upon certain conditions, one of which is that there shall first be filed a petition asking the improvement, signed by the owners of the majority of the frontage to be assessed. 2. The passage of that ordinance by the city council, which is given authority to determine conclusively whether the action of the board was duly taken. 3. The assessment of the cost upon the landowners after due notice and opportunity for hearing.

In the case before us the board took the first step by transmitting to the council the resolution to do the work and the form of an ordinance authorizing it. It is contended, however, that there was wanting an essential condition of the jurisdiction of the board, namely, such a petition from the owners as the law requires. The trial court found this contention to be true. But, as has been seen, the charter gave the city council the authority to determine conclusively that the improvements were duly ordered by the board after due notice and a proper petition. In the exercise of this authority the city council, in the ordinance directing the improvement to be made, adjudged, in effect, that a proper petition had been filed. That ordinance, after reciting a compliance by the board with the charter in other respects, and that "certain petitions for said improvements were first presented to the said board, subscribed by the owners of a majority of the frontage to be assessed for said improvements as by the city charter required," enacted "That upon consideration of the premises the city council doth find that in their action and proceedings in relation to said Eighth Avenue Paving District Number One the said board of public works has fully complied with the requirements of the city charter relating thereto." The state Supreme Court held that the determination of the city council was conclusive that a proper petition was filed, and that decision must be accepted by us as the law of the State. The only question for this court is whether the charter provision authorizing such a finding, without notice to the landowners, denies to them due process of law. We think it does not. The proceedings, from the beginning up to and including the passage of the ordinance authorizing the work did not include any assessment or necessitate any assessment, although they laid the foundation for an assessment, which might or might not subsequently be made. Clearly all this might validly be done without hearing to the landowners, provided a hearing upon the assessment itself is afforded. The legislature might have authorized the making of improvements by the city council without any petition. If it chose to exact a petition as a security for wise and just action it could, so far as the Federal Constitution is concerned, accompany that condition with a provision that the council, with or without notice, should determine finally whether it had been performed * * *.

The fifth assignment [of error] * * * fairly raises, we think, the question whether the assessment was made without notice and opportunity for hearing to those affected by it, thereby denying to them due process of law. The trial court found as a fact that no opportunity for hearing was afforded, and the Supreme Court did not disturb this finding. The record discloses what was actually done, and there seems to be no dispute about it. After the improvement was completed the board of public works, in compliance with § 29 of the charter, certified to the city clerk a statement of the cost, and an apportionment of it to the lots of land to be assessed. Thereupon the city clerk, in compliance with § 30, published a notice stating, *inter alia*, that the written complaints or objections of the owners, if filed within thirty days, would be "heard and determined by the city council before the passage of any ordinance assessing the cost." Those interested, therefore, were informed that if they reduced their complaints and objections to writing, and filed them within thirty days, those complaints and objections would be heard, and would be heard before any assessment was made * * *. Resting upon the assurance that they would be heard, the plaintiffs in error filed within the thirty days the following paper:

"Denver, Colorado, January 13, 1900.

"To the Honorable Board of Public Works and the Honorable Mayor and City Council of the City of Denver:

"The undersigned, by Joshua Grozier, their attorney, do hereby most earnestly and strenuously protest and object to the passage of the contemplated or any assessing ordinance against the property in Eighth Avenue Paving District No. 1, so called, for each of the following reasons, to wit:

"1st. That said assessment and all and each of the proceedings leading up to the same were and are illegal, voidable and void, and the attempted assessment if made will be void and uncollectible.

"2nd. That said assessment and the cost of said pretended improvement should be collected, if at all, as a general tax against the city at large and not as a special assessment.

"3d. That property in said city not assessed is benefited by the said pretended improvement and certain property assessed is not benefited by said pretended improvement and other property assessed is not benefited by said pretended improvement to the extent of the assessment; that the individual pieces of property in said district are not benefited to the extent assessed against them and each of them respectively; that the assessment is arbitrary and property assessed in an equal amount is not benefited equally; that the boundaries of said pretended district were arbitrarily created without regard to the benefits or any other method of assessment known to law; that said assessment is outrageously large.

"4th. That each of the laws and each section thereof under which the proceedings in said pretended district were attempted to be had do not confer the authority for such proceedings; that the 1893 city charter was not properly passed and is not a law of the State of Colorado by reason of not properly or at all passing the legislature; that each of the provisions of said charter under which said proceedings were attempted are unconstitutional and violative of fundamental principles of law, the Constitution of the United States and the state constitution, or some one or more of the provisions of one or more of the same.

"5th. Because the pretended notice of assessment is invalid and was not published in accordance with the law, and is in fact no notice at all; because there was and is no valid ordinance creating said district; because each notice required by the 1893 city charter to be given, where it was attempted to give such notice, was insufficient, and was not properly given or properly published.

"6th. Because of non-compliance by the contractor with his contract and failure to complete the work in accordance with the contract; because the contract for said work was let without right or authority; because said pretended district is incomplete and the work under said contract has not been completed in accordance with said contract; because items too numerous to mention, which were not a proper charge in the said assessment, are included therein.

"7th.   Because the work was done under pretended grants of authority contained in pretended laws, which laws were violative of the constitution and fundamental laws of the State and Union.

"8th.   Because the city had <u>no jurisdiction</u> in the premises. <u>No petition</u> subscribed by the owners of a majority of the frontage in the district to be assessed for said improvements was ever obtained or presented.

"9th.   Because of delay by the board of public works in attempting to let the contract and because the said pretended improvement was never properly nor sufficiently petitioned for; because the contracts were not let nor the work done in accordance with the petitions, if any, for the work, and because the city had no jurisdiction in the premises.

"10th. Because before ordering the pretended improvement full <u>details and specifications</u> for the same, permitting and encouraging competition and determining the number of installments and time within which the costs shall be payable, the rate of interest on unpaid installments, and the district of lands to be assessed, together with a map showing the approximate amounts to be assessed, <u>were not adopted</u> by the board of public works before the letting of the contract for the work and furnishing of material; because advertisement for 20 days in two daily newspapers of general circulation, giving notice to the owners of real estate in the district of the kind of improvements proposed, the number of installments and time in which payable, rate of interest and extent of the district, probable cost and time when a resolution ordering the improvement would be considered, was not made either properly or at all, and if ever attempted to be made was not made according to law or as required by the law or charter.

"11th. Because the <u>attempted advertisement for bids</u> on the contract attempted to be let were <u>not properly published</u> and were published and let, and the proceedings had, if at all, in such a way as to be <u>prejudicial to the competition of bidders</u> and to deter bidders; and the completion of the contracts after being attempted to be let was permitted to lag in such a manner as not to comply with the contract, charter or laws, and the power to let the contract attempted to be let was not within the power of the parties attempting to let the same; because the <u>city council is or was by some of the proceedings deprived of legislative discretion</u>, and the board of public works and other pretended bodies <u>given such discretion</u>, which discretion they delegated to others having no right or power to exercise the same; and executive functions were conferred on bodies having no right, power or authority to exercise the same and taken away from others to whom such power was attempted to be granted or given or who should properly exercise the same; that judicial power was attempted to be conferred on the board of public works, so called, and the city council, and other bodies or pretended bodies not judicial or *quasi*-judicial in character, having no right, power or authority to exercise the same, and the courts attempted to be deprived thereof.

"Wherefore, because of the foregoing and numerous other good and sufficient reasons, the undersigned object and protest against the passage of the said proposed assessing ordinance."

This certainly was a complaint against and objection to the proposed assessment. Instead of affording the plaintiffs in error an opportunity to be heard upon its allegations, the city council, without notice to them, met as a board of equalization, not in a stated but in a specially called session, and, without any hearing, adopted the following resolution:

"Whereas, complaints have been filed by the various persons and firms as the owners of real estate included within the Eighth Avenue Paving District No. 1, of the city of Denver against the proposed assessments on said property for the cost of said paving, the names and description of the real estate respectively owned by such persons being more particularly described in the various complaints filed with the city clerk; and

"Whereas, no complaint or objection has been filed or made against the apportionment of said assessment made by the board of public works of the city of Denver, but the complaints and objections filed deny wholly the right of the city to assess any district or portion of the assessable property of the city of Denver; therefore, be it

"Resolved, by the city council of the city of Denver, sitting as a board of equalization, that the apportionments of said assessment made by said board of public works be, and the same are hereby, confirmed and approved."

Subsequently, without further notice or hearing, the city council enacted the ordinance of assessment whose validity is to be determined in this case. The facts out of which the question on this assignment arises may be compressed into small compass. The first step in the assessment proceedings was by the certificate of the board of public works of the cost of the improvement and a preliminary apportionment of it. The last step was the enactment of the assessment ordinance. From beginning to end of the proceedings the landowners, although allowed to formulate and file complaints and objections, were not afforded an opportunity to be heard upon them. Upon these facts was there a denial by the State of the due process of law guaranteed by the Fourteenth Amendment to the Constitution of the United States?

In the assessment, apportionment and collection of taxes upon property within their jurisdiction the Constitution of the United States imposes few restrictions upon the States. In the enforcement of such restrictions as the Constitution does impose this court has regarded substance and not form. But where the legislature of a State, instead of fixing the tax itself, commits to some subordinate body the duty of determining whether, in what amount, and upon whom it shall be levied, and of making its assessment and apportionment, due process of law requires that at some stage of the proceedings before the tax becomes irrevocably fixed, the taxpayer shall have an opportunity to be heard, of which he must have notice, either personal, by publication, or by a law fixing the time and place of the hearing. It must be remembered that the law of Colorado denies the landowner the right to object in the courts to the assessment, upon the ground that the objections are cognizable only by the board of equalization.

If it is enough that, under such circumstances, an opportunity is given to submit in writing all objections to and complaints of the tax to the board, then there was a hearing afforded in the case at bar. But we think that something more than that, even in proceedings for taxation, is required by due process of law. Many requirements essential in strictly judicial proceedings may be dispensed with in proceedings of this nature. But even here a hearing in its very essence demands that he who is entitled to it shall have the right to support his allegations by argument however brief, and, if need by, by proof, however informal. It is apparent that such a hearing was denied to the plaintiffs in error. The denial was by the city council, which, while acting as a board of equalization, represents the State. The assessment was therefore void, and the plaintiffs in error were entitled to a decree discharging their lands from a lien on account of it * * *.

Judgment reversed.

THE CHIEF JUSTICE and MR. JUSTICE HOLMES dissent.

BI-METALLIC INVESTMENT CO. v. STATE BOARD OF EQUALIZATION OF COLORADO

Supreme Court of the United States, 1915.
239 U.S. 441, 36 S.Ct. 141, 60 L.Ed. 372.

MR. JUSTICE HOLMES delivered the opinion of the court.

This is a suit to enjoin the State Board of Equalization and the Colorado Tax Commission from putting in force, and the defendant Pitcher as assessor of Denver from obeying, an order of the boards increasing the valuation of all taxable property in Denver forty per cent. The order was sustained and the suit directed to be dismissed by the Supreme Court of the State. The plaintiff is the owner of real estate in Denver and brings the case here on the ground that it was given no opportunity to be heard and that therefore its property will be taken without due process of law, contrary to the Fourteenth Amendment of the Constitution of the United States * * *.

For the purposes of decision we assume that the constitutional question is presented in the baldest way—that neither the plaintiff nor the assessor of Denver, who presents a brief on the plaintiff's side, nor any representative of the city and county, was given an opportunity to be heard, other than such as they may have had by reason of the fact that the time of meeting of the boards is fixed by law. On this assumption it is obvious that injustice may be suffered if some property in the county already has been valued at its full worth. But if certain property has been valued at a rate different from that generally prevailing in the county the owner has had his opportunity to protest and appeal as usual in our system of taxation, so that it must be assumed that the property owners in the county all stand alike. The question then is whether all individuals have a constitutional right to be heard before a matter can be decided in which all are equally concerned * * *. *[handwritten: ISSUE]*

Where a rule of conduct applies to more than a few people it is impracticable that every one should have a direct voice in its adoption. The Constitution does not require all public acts to be done in town meeting or an assembly of the whole. General statutes within the state power are passed that affect the person or property of individuals, sometimes to the point of ruin, without giving them a chance to be heard. Their rights are protected in the only way that they can be in a complex society, by their power, immediate or remote, over those who make the rule. If the result in this case had been reached as it might have been by the State's doubling the rate of taxation, no one would suggest that the Fourteenth Amendment was violated unless every person affected had been allowed an opportunity to raise his voice against it before the body entrusted by the state constitution with the power. In considering this case in this court we must assume that the proper state machinery has been used, and the question is whether, if the state constitution had declared that Denver had been undervalued as compared with the rest of the State and had decreed that for the current year the valuation should be forty per cent higher, the objection now urged could prevail. It appears to us that to put the question is to answer it. There must be a limit to individual argument in such matters if government is to go on. In *Londoner v. Denver*, 210 U.S. 373, 385, a local board had to determine 'whether, in what amount, and upon whom' a tax for paving a street should be levied for special benefits. A relatively small number of persons was concerned, who were exceptionally affected, in each case upon individual grounds, and it was held that they had a right to a hearing. But that decision is far from reaching a general determination dealing only with the principle upon which all the assessments in a county had been laid. *[handwritten: distinguishes from Londoner v. Denver]*

Judgment affirmed.

5 U.S.C. § 551(4)–(9)
(2012).

For the purpose of * * * [the Administrative Procedure Act]—

(4) "rule" means the whole or a part of an agency statement of general or particular applicability and future effect designed to implement, interpret, or prescribe law or policy or describing the organization, procedure, or practice requirements of an agency and includes the approval or prescription for the future of rates, wages, corporate or financial structures or reorganization thereof, prices, facilities, appliances, services or allowances therefor or of valuations, costs, or accounting, or practices bearing on any of the foregoing;

(5) "rule making" means agency process for formulating, amending, or repealing a rule;

(6) "order" means the whole or a part of a final disposition, whether affirmative, negative, injunctive, or declaratory in form, of an agency in a matter other than rule making but including licensing;

(7) "adjudication" means agency process for the formulation of an order;

(8) "license" includes the whole or a part of an agency permit, certificate, approval, registration, charter, membership, statutory exemption or other form of permission;

(9) "licensing" includes agency process respecting the grant, renewal, denial, revocation, suspension, annulment, withdrawal, limitation, amendment, modification, or conditioning of a license * * *.

SMALL BUSINESS REGULATORY ENFORCEMENT FAIRNESS ACT 5 U.S.C. § 804(3)
(2012).

The term "rule" has the meaning given such term in section 551, except that such term does not include—(A) any rule of particular applicability * * *.

EXECUTIVE ORDER 12866, § 3(D)
5 U.S.C. § 601 note (2012).

"Regulation" or "rule" means an agency statement of general applicability and future effect, which the agency intends to have the force and effect of law, that is designed to implement, interpret, or prescribe law or policy or to describe the procedure or practice requirements of an agency * * *.

LINCOLN V. VIGIL

Supreme Court of the United States, 1993.
508 U.S. 182, 197, 113 S.Ct. 2024, 2034, 124 L.Ed.2d 101.

Determining whether an agency's statement is what the APA calls a "rule" can be a difficult exercise.

NOTES

Sometimes, as under the Due Process Clause at issue in *Londoner* and *Bi-Metallic*, a party will receive more procedures if an agency action is classified as adjudication rather than rulemaking. As Chapter 3 will graphically demonstrate, sometimes the reverse is true. Under the APA, there is a wide range of cases in which a party can be entitled to more procedures if an agency action is classified as rulemaking than if it is classified as adjudication. For the moment, take it on faith that, in the following case, the plaintiff could win on procedural grounds only if the agency action was classified as rulemaking under the APA.

YESLER TERRACE COMMUNITY COUNCIL V. CISNEROS

United States Court of Appeals, Ninth Circuit, 1994.
37 F.3d 442.

Before GOODWIN, CANBY, and KOZINSKI, CIRCUIT JUDGES.

CANBY, CIRCUIT JUDGE.

* * *

Plaintiffs Yesler Terrace Community Council and Eric Bolden (collectively "Yesler") represent a class of tenants in public housing projects in Washington state. Public housing tenants ordinarily may be evicted only after a grievance hearing before the public housing authority (PHA) that administers their residence. In cases of eviction for drug-related or certain other criminal activity, however, PHAs may omit the otherwise mandatory grievance procedures, but only if [the federal Department of Housing and Urban Development ("HUD")] * * * has determined that state court eviction procedures satisfy the elements of due process * * *.

In December 1991, HUD advised the governor of Washington that it had determined that Washington's state court eviction procedures satisfy the elements of due process, and that Washington's PHAs therefore could dispense with grievance hearings for crime-related evictions. Several Washington PHAs subsequently amended their leases and grievance procedures to take advantage of HUD's determination. Then, on March 24, 1992, the Seattle Housing Authority served Marla Davison with an eviction notice stating that she would not be afforded a grievance hearing because her eviction was due to alleged criminal activity.

A few days later, Yesler and Davison brought this action, seeking injunctive and declaratory relief on the ground that HUD violated * * * the Administrative Procedure Act * * * and HUD's own regulations when it issued its due process determination without first providing notice and opportunity to comment * * *.

* * *

* * * HUD maintains that * * * [the legal requirement of procedures for the issuance of rules] does not apply here because the determination that Washington's eviction procedures meet regulatory due process standards is not a rule at all, but instead is an order stemming from an informal adjudication. We find little support for this position, even under the most deferential standard of review.

A rule is:

> [T]he whole or a part of an agency statement of general or particular applicability and future effect designed to implement, interpret, or prescribe law or policy or describing the organization, procedure, or practice requirements of an agency. . .

5 U.S.C. § 551(4). An adjudication (which results in an order) is virtually any agency action that is not rulemaking. 5 U.S.C. § 551(6)(7). Two principal characteristics distinguish rulemaking from adjudication. First, adjudications resolve disputes among specific individuals in specific cases, whereas rulemaking affects the rights of broad classes of unspecified individuals. Second, because adjudications involve concrete disputes, they have an immediate effect on specific individuals (those involved in the dispute). Rulemaking, in contrast, is prospective, and has a definitive effect on individuals only after the rule subsequently is applied. *See Bowen v. Georgetown Univ. Hosp.*, 488 U.S. 204, 216–17, 102 L.Ed.2d 493, 109 S.Ct. 468 (1988) (the "central distinction" between rulemaking and adjudication is that rules have legal consequences "*only* for the future") (Scalia, J., concurring) (emphasis added).

Here, HUD's determination that Washington's state-court eviction procedures met HUD's due process requirements has all the hallmarks of a rule. HUD's determination had no immediate, concrete effect on anyone, but merely permitted PHAs to evict tenants in the future without providing them with informal grievance hearings. At the same time, the determination affected the rights of a broad category of individuals not yet identified. Before the decision was made, all public housing tenants in Washington had a statutory right to a pre-eviction grievance hearing. After the decision, no public housing tenant accused of certain criminal activity had such a right. We conclude that HUD's determination was a rule.

We do not attach great significance to HUD's observation that the manner in which it made its decision shares certain features with adjudications. HUD contends that to make the disputed determination, it merely had to compare the elements of due process * * * with Washington's eviction procedures. This "application of a rule of decision to a particular set of facts," HUD argues, indicates that due process determinations are "adjudicative in nature." HUD's description of the process, however, is incomplete. Nothing in the statute requires HUD to make a due process determination in the first place. Before proceeding to make the determination, HUD had to decide whether to take any action at all. This decision plainly involved more than applying a rule of decision to particular facts. Therefore, even if HUD were correct that the process by which a decision is reached determines whether the decision is a rule or an order, we could not characterize its decision here as an adjudication.

In any event, HUD's premise is flawed. The form of the proceeding is not dispositive; what counts is its effect. *See FTC v. Brigadier Industries Corp.*, 198 U.S.App.D.C. 377, 613 F.2d 1110, 1117 (D.C.Cir.1979) ("The focus is not on whether the particular proceeding involves trial-type devices but instead turns on the nature of the decision to be reached in the proceeding"). HUD's purported "adjudication" had no effect on the State of Washington. The sole effect of HUD's decision was to deprive a broad category of people of the right to an informal grievance hearing prior to eviction, and this effect had legal consequences for yet-to-be-identified individuals only prospectively. These are the effects of a rule, not of an adjudication. An agency cannot avoid the requirement of notice-and-comment rulemaking simply by characterizing its decision as an adjudication.

* * *

[JUDGE KOZINSKI dissented on jurisdictional grounds and did not address the rule/order distinction.]

NOTES

When the court in *Yesler* discusses how to distinguish rulemaking from adjudication, what role does it give to the language in § 551(4) defining a rule as an agency statement of "general or particular applicability"? Consider in this regard the comments about the APA's definition of a rule offered in 1978 by no less a textualist than Justice (then-Professor) Scalia:

> Since every statement is of either general or particular applicability, and since everything an agency does is "designed to implement, interpret, or prescribe law or policy, etc." the only limiting (that is to say, defining) part of the definition [of a rule] is "agency statement of . . . future effect." That is of course absurd * * *. [I]t is generally acknowledged that the only responsible judicial attitude toward this central APA definition is one of benign disregard.

Antonin Scalia, Vermont Yankee: *The APA, the D.C. Circuit, and the Supreme Court,* 1978 Sup. Ct. Rev. 345, 383. A prominent scholar has called § 551(4) the APA's "most blatantly defective provision." Ronald M. Levin, *The Case for (Finally) Fixing the APA's Definition of "Rule,"* 56 Admin.L.Rev. 1077, 1078 (2004).

Consider also how the court in *Yesler* dealt—or failed to deal—with § 551(9). Take a close look at §§ 551(6)–(9), think very hard about exactly what action of the Department of Housing and Urban Development was at issue in *Yesler,* and decide for yourself which section of the APA was most disregarded in this case, benignly or otherwise.

Courts in fact do not often pay much attention to the statutory definition of a "rule" in § 551(4). As was the case in *Yesler,* when the characterization of the agency action is raised by the parties, the focus is normally on the generality or particularity of the agency action in question rather than on the precise language of the APA. *See, e.g., Safari Club Int'l v. Zinke,* 878 F.3d 316, 332–33 (D.C.Cir.2017) (citing, inter alia, the *Londoner* and *Bi-Metallic* cases when discussing the rulemaking/adjudication distinction under the APA). In most administrative law cases, however, the characterization of the agency action is not expressly addressed. It is usually so obvious to all of the parties whether the action at issue is a rulemaking or an adjudication that it simply does not occur to anyone to raise a question about it, even if the broad language of § 551(4) would seem to permit such a question. On the relatively rare occasions when courts do expressly address the rulemaking/adjudication distinction, strange happenings tend to be afoot. In addition to *Yesler,* one must reckon with the likes of *Shell Offshore, Inc. v. Babbitt,* 238 F.3d 622 (5th Cir.2001).

Shell leased some offshore oil-and gas-producing property from the Department of the Interior. Shell was obliged to pay royalties on the value of the production from the land, but was permitted to deduct transportation costs when calculating that value. For many years, the Minerals Management Service of the Interior Department ("MMS") permitted lessees who transported oil through self-owned pipelines to use, as their transportation costs for royalty purposes, the prices reflected in tariffs filed with the Federal Energy Regulatory Commission ("FERC"), which establish the rates that outside parties must pay to use the pipelines. Otherwise, the lessees would have to prove their actual transportation costs—which, if they were using their own pipelines rather than paying a determinate amount to someone else, could be a real burden for the lessees to calculate (and would surely be less than the prices that they charge to third parties for use of their pipelines). At some point in 1993 or 1994, the MMS began concluding that if FERC did not in fact have jurisdiction over a pipeline for which a tariff had been filed, MMS would not allow use of that tariff in calculating transportation costs. Accordingly, when Shell in 1994 asked the MMS to confirm that Shell could use filed tariffs to calculate its transportation costs through its own pipeline, the MMS denied the request "because Shell had failed to petition FERC and receive from FERC a determination affirmatively stating that FERC possessed jurisdiction over the * * * pipeline." *Id.* at 625–26. Shell appealed from the MMS's denial of its request for confirmation on the ground, inter alia, that MMS had changed its practices without using the procedures appropriate for rulemaking. The agency conceded that it had not used rulemaking procedures, but explained that it had not done so because it was engaged in adjudication. Said the court:

> Interior argues that this case merely involves an "adjudication" exempt from the rulemaking requirements of the APA * * *. Shell's response to the first part of Interior's argument is that the decision in the adjudication in this case was wholly predicated upon a new requirement that is, in effect, a new "substantive" rule. We conclude that Shell's argument is the more persuasive. It is clear from Interior's internal memoranda and correspondence with Shell that Interior's denial of Shell's request was the result of a departure from Interior's previous practice of treating as approved all filed FERC tariffs. It is similarly clear that Interior's new policy was the basis for the adjudication rather than the facts of the particular adjudication causing Interior to modify or re-interpret its rule. Interior did not apply a general regulation to the specific facts of Shell's case. Rather, it established a new policy and then applied that new policy to several OCS producers, including Shell. If Shell had submitted its tariff early in 1992 instead of 1994, Interior would have accepted Shell's tariff as "approved by FERC" and Shell would not have been required to petition FERC—there would have been no adjudication prior to 1994. The adjudication resulted because Interior changed its policy, and the district court did not err in reaching the policy change that controlled the adjudicative process.

Id. at 627–28. Exactly what action by the MMS was Shell protesting? And does anything in the APA definitions of rules and orders foreclose an agency from making policy through adjudications? The answer to the last question is obviously no, as courts accustomed to dealing with administrative law matters recognize. *See Neustar, Inc. v. FCC*, 857 F.3d 886, 894 (D.C.Cir.2017). Indeed, in later chapters, you will encounter numerous instances in which agencies make policy and construe statutes through adjudication.

A slightly more involved problem was presented in *City of Arlington, Texas v. FCC*, 668 F.3d 229 (5th Cir.2012), *aff'd*, 569 U.S. 290, 133 S.Ct. 1863, 185 L.Ed.2d 941 (2013), of which you will hear much more in Chapter 4 in connection with another aspect of the case. Federal communications laws limit the ability of local governments to use land use regulation to interfere with the construction and siting of "personal service wireless facilities," 47 U.S.C. § 332(c)(7)(ii) (2012)—essentially meaning cell towers—and specifically requires governmental decisions on construction applications to be made within "a reasonable period of time." *Id.* Wireless companies, concerned about the length of time that local governments were taking to rule on their applications, asked the Federal Communications Commission ("FCC") to clarify the meaning of "reasonable period of time" by establishing maximum time periods within which local governments could act. The FCC responded with a "Declaratory Order" clarifying that either 90 or 150 days would presumptively be "reasonable," depending upon the type of local decision involved. Some local governments challenged the Declaratory Order, which was issued using procedures that were legally adequate if the agency proceeding was an adjudication but plainly inadequate if the proceeding was a rulemaking. So which was it?

On the one hand, the wireless providers requested the agency's clarifying ruling under a Commission procedural regulation providing for declaratory orders, 47 C.F.R. § 1.2, that purports to interpret and apply a provision of the APA authorizing agencies, in the context of adjudications, to "issue a declaratory order to terminate a controversy or remove uncertainty." 5 U.S.C. § 554(e) (2012). On the other hand, the APA's rulemaking section states that agencies must give interested persons "the right to petition for the issuance, amendment, or repeal of a rule." 5 U.S.C. § 553(e) (2012). One might reasonably think that § 554(e)'s provision for declaratory orders in the context of adjudications was designed only to allow agencies to clarify or settle matters within an already existing adjudication rather than to allow the disposition of stand-alone requests for clarification, however general and forward-looking, to be treated as adjudications in themselves. Classification of the agency's action as rulemaking or adjudication would then require a functional assessment of the generality and prospectivity of the action (given that it does not appear to constitute licensing, ratemaking, or anything else that would establish the classification by statutory fiat). On that reasoning, the wireless providers' request for clarification—which was very general, forward-looking, and not in the context of any existing adjudicatory proceeding—surely had to be treated as a petition for rulemaking, and the agency's clarifying order would have to be treated as a rule.

The Fifth Circuit nonetheless, with no analysis and with citation only to cases that involved declaratory orders resolving very specific pre-existing disputes, construed § 554(e), and the accompanying FCC regulation providing for declaratory orders, to authorize all Commission declaratory orders to be treated as adjudicatory orders, whether or not issued in the context of an already-existing adjudication. *See* 668 F.3d at 241. That would seem to settle the matter (however wrongly) in favor of the agency in this case. But the conclusion that an agency could engage in "adjudication" by simply announcing very general time periods applicable to all future cases, outside the context of a specific decision or dispute, was bothersome enough to the court to compel the judges to ponder at great length whether the agency had perhaps abused its discretion by proceeding (as the court assumed it had) through adjudication rather than rulemaking. As we will learn in Chapter 3, agencies almost *never* abuse discretion by choosing to proceed through either adjudication or rulemaking when the governing statutes allow that choice. *See Safari Club*, 878 F.3d at 331 ("When agencies have the statutory authority to engage in rule making and adjudication, they have broad discretion to choose which route to pursue."). A holding that the FCC abused its discretion in the *Arlington* case would have been extraordinary. The court finally buried its doubts by concluding that, even if the agency had engaged in rulemaking (or *had* to have engaged in rulemaking), any error it made by not using the correct procedures to issue its Declaratory Order was harmless. (The APA specifically incorporates the "harmless error" rule into its provisions for judicial review. *See* 5 U.S.C. § 706 (2012).)

The case for treating the agency action in *City of Arlington* as a rulemaking rather than an adjudication is fairly straightforward, but to articulate that case requires a modestly sophisticated understanding of the rulemaking/adjudication distinction and the APA's procedural requirements for rulemaking and adjudication. Your editor's reading of the briefs in this case suggests that the parties, and particularly the cities that were challenging the FCC's decision, did not give the court very much help on this score. And, as the foregoing cases graphically illustrate, courts, especially courts outside the D.C. Circuit Court of Appeals (which deals with administrative law issues on a regular basis), cannot be relied upon to reason these matters out on their own.

A recurring, and difficult, problem concerns how to classify agency action that marks out enforcement policies in broad terms. In general, agency rules are subject to judicial review on procedural and substantive grounds, while particularized agency decisions about how to exercise enforcement discretion are not subject to judicial scrutiny at all. What happens when agencies generally and prospectively define their enforcement plans?

ASSOCIATION OF IRRITATED RESIDENTS V. EPA

United States Court of Appeals for the District of Columbia Circuit, 2007.
494 F.3d 1027.

Before: SENTELLE, ROGERS, and KAVANAUGH, CIRCUIT JUDGES.

SENTELLE, CIRCUIT JUDGE.

Community and environmental groups petition for review of agreements between [the Environmental Protection Agency ("EPA")] * * * and animal feeding operations * * *. Petitioners argue that the agreements are rules disguised as enforcement actions, that EPA did not follow proper procedures for rulemaking, and that EPA exceeded its statutory authority by entering into the agreements. We hold that the agreements do not constitute rules, but rather enforcement actions within EPA's statutory authority. We dismiss the petitions for review because exercises of EPA's enforcement discretion are not reviewable by this court.

I.

Animal feeding operations ("AFOs") are facilities where animals are raised for eggs, dairy, or slaughter * * *. In the course of their operations, AFOs emit a number of pollutants regulated by the Clean Air Act, the Comprehensive Environmental Response, Compensation, and Liability Act, ("CERCLA"), and the Emergency Planning and Community Right-to-Know Act, ("EPCRA") (collectively, the "Acts") * * *. An AFO that releases these pollutants in sufficient quantities may be required to report them under CERCLA and EPCRA, and may be subject to various requirements under the Clean Air Act. *Id.* An AFO emitting these pollutants in quantities below the statutory thresholds, however, has no obligation under the Acts to obtain permits or report its emissions.

Petitioners are a number of community and environmental groups, some of whose members live near AFOs. They assert that the AFOs emit particulate pollution and terrible odors, and that they attract hordes of flies that leave their droppings on everything from cars to outdoor furniture. As a result, petitioners claim that their members suffer effects ranging from reduced enjoyment of the outdoor portion of their property to adverse health effects such as respiratory and heart problems * * *.

Because the Acts apply only to emissions above specified levels, EPA cannot enforce the statutory and regulatory requirements without determining an AFO's emissions * * *. Precise measurements have eluded the government and the AFO industry, which are in agreement that there is no existing methodology to measure reliably an AFO's emissions * * *. EPA's solution to this problem was to invite AFOs to sign a consent agreement under which each AFO will assist in developing an emissions estimating methodology. In exchange, EPA will not pursue administrative actions and lawsuits against the AFOs for a defined period of time. In the agency's judgment, this is the "quickest and most effective way" to achieve compliance.

* * * To date, several thousand AFOs have signed Agreements. Once EPA signs the Agreements, they are forwarded to EPA's Environmental Appeals Board ("EAB") for approval. The Agreements become enforceable against EPA once they are approved by the EAB in a final order. EAB has considered the Agreements in seven sets, and approved a total of 2,568 Agreements.

Although each participating AFO signs an individual Agreement with EPA, all the Agreements have identical terms. The AFO, although not admitting any violation of the Acts, agrees to pay a civil penalty for potential violations based on the size and number of its farms. It agrees to help fund a nationwide study that will monitor, over a two-year period, emissions from animal housing structures and manure storage and treatment areas. The AFO also agrees to permit its facility to be monitored in the study upon request * * *. In consideration for the AFOs' assistance, EPA agrees not to sue participating AFOs for certain potential past and ongoing violations of the Acts for the duration of the study * * *.

* * * [P]etitioners argue * * * that the procedures by which EPA entered into the Agreement did not afford them the meaningful opportunity for comment required [for rulemakings] by the Administrative Procedure Act ("APA") * * *.

In EPA's view, the Agreement is not a rulemaking, but rather a valid exercise of the agency's enforcement discretion * * *.

II.

* * * In this case, subject matter jurisdiction turns on whether the Agreement constitutes a rulemaking subject to APA review, or an enforcement proceeding initiated at the agency's discretion and not reviewable by this court * * *.

Petitioners advance a number of arguments in support of their contention that the Agreement is a rule. They contend that the Agreement meets the definition of "rule" under the APA and that it does not fall within the definition of an enforcement action. They also argue that the Agreement must be a rule because EPA has bound its enforcement discretion, a factor that this court previously found significant in determining whether an agency action is a rule * * *.

EPA's position that the Agreement is an exercise of enforcement discretion rather than a rule is based on case law explaining the substantive difference between the two. In the agency's view, the Agreement's purpose and effect are consistent with enforcement actions and inconsistent with rules. Moreover, EPA believes that the Agreement provides no exemption, but merely defers enforcement of certain statutory requirements in light of the agency's judgment that immediate compliance is impossible or impracticable. We hold that the Agreement represents an enforcement action not subject to our review.

A.

* * * The APA defines a "rule" as "an agency statement of general or particular applicability and future effect designed to implement, interpret, or prescribe law or policy." 5 U.S.C. § 551(4). Petitioners argue that the Agreement is intended to "prescribe law" because it grants an exemption from the Acts for a specified period of time. We disagree. The Agreement merely defers enforcement of the statutory requirements, and makes that deferral subject to enforcement conditions that will ultimately result in compliance. An AFO that fails to fulfill specific obligations loses the protections of the Agreement, leaving EPA free to sue or take other enforcement actions against the AFO. A limited deferral subject to enforcement conditions works no change in the agency's substantive interpretation or implementation of the Acts. As a result, it is not consistent with the concept of a "rule" as that term has been defined.

In *National Association of Home Builders v. U.S. Army Corps of Engineers*, the Corps issued nationwide permits that authorized certain discharges into U.S. waters—something that could not otherwise be done under the governing statute without first obtaining an individual permit. 417 F.3d 1272 (D.C.Cir.2005). This action effectively granted permittees the right to bypass certain requirements of the statute. In holding that the agency had in effect issued a rule, we described the nationwide permit as a "legal prescription . . . which the Corps has issued to implement" the permitting provisions of the applicable statute. *Id*. at 1284. In another case relied on by petitioners, *CropLife America v. EPA,* we held that EPA had promulgated a rule when it announced that the agency would no longer consider certain studies in its regulatory decisionmaking. 329 F.3d 876 (D.C.Cir.2003). These studies had long been submitted by applicants-and accepted by EPA-as evidence of a pesticide's safety. We rejected the agency's argument that the statement was merely one of policy because it was "a firm rule with legal consequences that are binding on both petitioners and the agency." *Id*. at 882. We also noted that petitioners would not have another opportunity to challenge the directive.

Both *Home Builders* and *CropLife* address circumstances not present in the instant case. The AFOs' Agreement with EPA does not express the agency's implementation of any provision of the Clean Air Act, CERCLA or EPCRA. Rather, the Agreement implements a preliminary step— developing a reliable methodology—that the agency deems a prerequisite to enforcement of the Acts. The Agreement makes no determination of an AFO's compliance with the Acts and makes no definitive statement of enforcement or interpretive practices that EPA will apply in its regulatory decisionmaking.

More generally, in the Agreement EPA issues no statement with regard to substantive statutory standards. EPA has not bound itself in a way that reflects "cabining" of its prosecutorial discretion because it imposed no limit on its general enforcement discretion if the substantive statutory standards are violated. It is thus unlike *Community Nutrition Institute v. Young*, 818 F.2d 943, 948 (D.C.Cir.1987) (per curiam), a case in which we held that FDA's announcement of action levels that specified when merchants would be subject to enforcement proceedings under the statute constituted a rule. That was so because "cabining of an agency's prosecutorial discretion can in fact rise to the level of a substantive, legislative rule" when it "is in purpose or likely effect one that *narrowly limits administrative discretion." Id.* (internal quotation marks and citations omitted). In the instant case, EPA's "cabining" of its ability to sue AFOs for a period of time is not based on a substantive interpretation of the statutes, but rather is a way to defer enforcement of those substantive interpretations *until* EPA has determined how their requirements apply in the particular case of AFOs. Moreover, to the extent EPA has limited its enforcement discretion, it has done so only with regard to those AFOs who have signed Agreements * * *.

* * *

III.

The Agreements do not constitute rulemaking, but rather enforcement actions within EPA's statutory authority. EPA's exercises of its enforcement discretion are not reviewable by this court. The petitions for review are dismissed.

So ordered.

ROGERS, CIRCUIT JUDGE, dissenting:

This case involves the intersection of two doctrines. The first involves an agency's unreviewable enforcement discretion, and the second relates to agency rulemaking power. The initial question for the court is whether the scope of enforcement discretion is expansive enough to cover the animal feeding operation ("AFO") protocol formally announced by the Environmental Protection Agency ("EPA") in the Federal Register on January 31, 2005. The court concludes that the enforcement protocol is an exercise of enforcement discretion * * * and that EPA has not promulgated a legislative rule subject to the notice and comment requirements of the Administrative Procedure Act ("APA"). Undoubtedly there is some conceptual overlap between the doctrines to the extent that policies adopted by agencies often reflect discretionary determinations about how to enforce statutes that Congress has entrusted them to implement. However, by imposing a civil penalty on AFOs in the absence of individualized determinations of statutory violations, EPA has attempted to secure the benefits of legislative rulemaking without the burdens of its statutory duties * * *.

* * *

I.

In announcing the new enforcement protocol, EPA advised AFOs in the egg, broiler chicken, turkey, dairy, and swine industries * * * that they could avoid liability for "certain past and ongoing" violations of the Clean Air Act ("CAA"), the Comprehensive Environmental Response Compensation and Liability Act ("CERCLA"), and the Emergency Planning and Community Right to Know Act ("Right to Know Act"). All they had to do was agree to pay a minimal "civil penalty," calibrated by the number of "farms," plus (approximately) $2,500 per farm to fund the collection and study of nationwide emissions data over an (estimated) two-year period, and if selected, to allow EPA to monitor their operations' emissions during that period * * *. AFOs signing the identical form agreements * * * would receive from EPA "a limited release and covenant not to sue" until after the AFO uses the new estimation methodologies * * *. Any AFO would, however, be able to opt out of the agreement at any time without suffering any repercussions beyond the possibility of enforcement actions for past violations * * *.

The [agency's action] * * * has all the earmarks of a legislative rule * * *. Because the proposed enforcement protocol is of "general . . . applicability," will have "future effect," and defines the rights and obligations of members of the regulated community, thereby constraining EPA's enforcement authority, it is a rule. EPA's enforcement protocol is not unlike the enforcement protocol in *Croplife America v. EPA*, 329 F.3d 876, 878 (D.C.Cir.2003), where EPA announced in the Federal Register that it would no longer consider human studies in its regulatory decisionmaking on the safety of pesticides * * *. The court held that the new enforcement policy was a legislative rule because "it create[d] a 'binding norm' that [wa]s 'finally determinative of the issues or rights to which it [wa]s addressed.' " The policy was binding not only on the individuals challenging the rule, but also "on the agency because EPA ha[d] made it clear that it simply 'will not consider' human studies." Similarly here, EPA has announced a new general approach to carrying out its responsibilities under three statutes-provided a "sufficient" number of AFOs sign up and the Environmental Appeals Board ("EAB") approves the individual AFO form agreements. The new protocol is binding on both the AFOs who sign up and the agency, and under its terms, it will bind most of the regulated AFO industry. Under the circumstances, EPA's new enforcement protocol is a legislative rule subject to notice and comment requirements under the APA.

B. THEORIES OF AGENCY BEHAVIOR

How do agencies behave? More importantly, how do the people who can influence the design of the administrative system *believe* that agencies behave? The structure of administrative institutions, and the doctrines of administrative law, cannot help but be shaped by the theories of agency behavior that are dominant at any particular time.

The following materials provide an historical overview of different conceptions of agency behavior. As you read these materials, think about what role in the administrative process the different theories seem to suggest for lawyers and judges.

JAMES MADISON
The Federalist No. 51 (1787).

* * * [W]hat is government itself but the greatest of all reflections on human nature? If men were angels, no government would be necessary. If angels were to govern men, neither external nor internal controls on government would be necessary. In framing a government which is to be administered by men over men, the great difficulty lies in this: you must first enable the government to control the governed; and in the next place oblige it to control itself.

JOSEPH B. EASTMAN, THE PLACE OF THE INDEPENDENT COMMISSION

12 Const. Rev. 95, 100–01 (1928).

* * * [The independent regulatory commissions] * * * are clearly nonpartisan in their makeup, and party policies do not enter into their activities except to the extent that such policies may be definitely registered in the statutes which they are sworn to enforce * * *. Certainly, when once the members are selected their political affiliations cease to be of the slightest consequence * * *.

JAMES M. LANDIS, THE ADMINISTRATIVE PROCESS

(Yale University Press, 1938) pp. 75–76, 154–55.

* * * One of the ablest administrators that it was my good fortune to know, I believe, never read, at least more than casually, the statutes that he translated into reality. He assumed that they gave him power to deal with the broad problems of an industry and, upon that understanding, he sought his own solutions. Limitations upon his powers that counsel brought to his attention, naturally, he respected; but there is an enormous difference between the legalistic form of approach that from the negative vantage of statutory limitations looks to see what it must do, and the approach that considers a problem from the standpoint of finding out what it can do.

* * *

* * * Government today no longer dares to rely for its administration upon the casual office-seeker. Into its service it now seeks to bring men of professional attainment in various fields and to make that service such that they will envisage governance as a career. The desires of these men to share in the mediation of human claims cannot be denied; their contributions dare not casually be tossed aside.

The grandeur that is law loses nothing from such a prospect. Instead, under its banner as a commanding discipline are enlisted armies of men dedicated to the idea of justice. But to use those armies, a sense of the effectiveness of their units is essential and an instillation in those units of morale. "Courts," as Mr. Justice Stone has reminded us, "are not the only agency of government that must be assumed to have capacity to govern"; nor are they, one can add, the only agency moved by the desire for justice. The power of judicial review under our traditions of government lies with the courts because of a deep belief that the heritage they hold makes them experts in the synthesis of design. Such difficulties as have arisen have come because courts cast aside that role to assume to themselves expertness in matters of industrial health, utility engineering, railroad management, even bread baking. The rise of the administrative process represented the hope that policies to shape such fields could most adequately be developed by men bred to the facts. That hope is still dominant, but its possession bears no threat to our ideal of the "supremacy of law." Instead, it lifts it to new heights where the great judge, like a conductor of a many-tongued symphony, from what would otherwise be discord, makes known through the voice of many instruments the vision that has been given him of man's destiny upon this earth.

MARVER H. BERNSTEIN, REGULATING BUSINESS BY INDEPENDENT COMMISSION

(Princeton University Press, 1955) pp. 80, 87. c. 1955 by PUP.
Reprinted by permission of Princeton University Press.

* * * [T]he agency ordinarily begins its administrative career in an aggressive, crusading spirit. It may resolve to meet the opposition of the regulated with firmness in order to promote the public interest. It tends to take a broad view of its responsibilities; and some members of the commission, at least, will develop a fair measure of daring and inventiveness in dealing with their regulatory problems.

* * *

In the period of maturity, * * * [t]he approach and point of view of the regulatory process begins to partake of those of business management. The commission becomes accepted as an essential part of the industrial system * * *. The Commission becomes more concerned with the general health of the industry and tries to prevent changes which adversely affect it. Cut off from the mainstream of political life, the commission's standards of regulation are determined in the light of the desires of the industry affected. It is unlikely that the commission, in this period, will be able to extend regulation beyond the limits acceptable to the regulated groups.

ROGER G. NOLL, REFORMING REGULATION

(Brookings Institution, 1971) pp. 40–43, 46.

In order for a group to decide to carry a battle with a regulatory agency to either the courts or the political arena, the group must expect a substantial gain if the regulatory decision is overturned. Appealing the decision of an agency, either legally or politically, is expensive. To an organized group, costs are incurred through effectively lobbying the politicians or fighting a court case. To an unorganized group, the costs are even higher, for the group must become organized to be effective * * *.

Most regulatory issues are of deep interest to regulated industries, with a very substantial amount of income for these industries riding on the decision. The stake of the general public may in the aggregate be even higher, but it is diffused among a large number of unorganized individuals

* * *. The motivation of a single firm to fight an unfavorable regulatory decision is very high, while a regulatory decision unfavorable to the general public is unlikely to generate enough interest to cause a general public issue to be raised * * *.

An agency that tries to minimize the chance of being overruled by subsequent legal or legislative decisions must, when the interests of a regulated firm and its customers or the public generally are at odds, be overly responsive to the interests of the regulated. First, by giving regulated firms a little more than they deserve, the agencies make certain that the most threatening group has something that could be lost in an appeal. In disputes between well-represented interests, the agency will, for the same reason, seek a compromise that gives something to all disputants, whether economic efficiency or the public interest would favor such a compromise. Second, the regulatory agency will want to be sure that it cannot legitimately be accused of being unfair to the groups that are most likely to challenge the decision. Furthermore, agency determinations of "fact" are bound to be based on evidence supplied by the represented special interests. Most of the information flowing to the agency will come from the regulated, who can afford to use much better resources in regulatory cases than will be employed to represent the interests of the general public.

* * *

The tendency of the legal-political system to reinforce a pro-industry bias in regulatory agencies could well be magnified by the process by which commission members are chosen. Most appointees are politicians with a background in law. Commissioners with this background are likely to place greater weight on legal and political feedback than would, say, economists or academic lawyers, who are more likely to consider efficiency and equity.

In theory, regulatory commissions are composed of neutral, objective experts on the affairs of the regulated industry and on the public interest in the behavior of the regulated. In practice, appointees to commissions must have the tacit approval of the regulated industries. Appointments, almost unnoticed by the general public, are closely watched by regulated firms * * *. While the appointment process does not necessarily produce commissioners who are consciously controlled by the industry they regulate, it nearly always succeeds in excluding persons who are regarded as opposed to the interests of the regulated.

JAMES Q. WILSON, THE POLITICS OF REGULATION, IN THE POLITICS OF REGULATION

(Basic Books, 1980), pp. 372–73, 376–78, 385–87, 394.
Copyright James Q. Wilson.

Anyone who purports to explain the behavior of regulatory agencies must first make clear what behavior is worth explaining. By carefully selecting certain examples and ignoring others, the behavior of many of the regulatory agencies * * * can be made to appear industry-serving in the narrow sense * * *.

But a fuller list suggests that industry-serving behavior is only part of the story. The [Civil Aeronautics Board (CAB)] may have helped the established major air carriers as a group, but * * * by the late-1970s, the CAB was moving toward deregulation in a manner that, at least initially, caused great alarm among the carriers.

The [Food and Drug Administration (FDA)] was energized in the mid-1960s by a series of new appointments and new laws that, by the 1970s, had moved the pharmaceutical industry and many physicians to complain bitterly of costly delays in the introduction of new drugs.

The [Federal Trade Commission (FTC)], after a major reorganization (under a Republican president) began to bring large "structural" cases against such firms as Exxon and the leading cereal manufacturers; at the same time, the Antitrust Division [of the Justice Department] was attempting to expand the reach of the antitrust law by questioning the formation of conglomerates.

* * *

These particular instances might be deemed as exceptions to the normal pattern of industry service by regulatory agencies, but a fair reading * * * suggests that they are a good deal more than that—they are the leading edge of either a broad shift in, or a previously undiscussed dimension of, bureaucratic behavior. To be sure, such examples cannot be found in every agency: the [Federal Maritime Commission (FMC)] continues to approve carrier rate requests without blinking an eye, except when the carrier types its request on the wrong paper or with incorrect margins. But what might be exceptions in these "old" or "traditional" regulatory agencies is clearly the norm in the "new" agencies. [The Environmental Protection Agency (EPA) and the Occupation Safety and Health Administration (OSHA)] have, in general, chosen stricter and more costly standards over more lenient, less expensive ones * * *.

In short, the behavior to be explained is complex and changing; it cannot easily be summarized as serving the interests of either the regulated sector or the public at large * * *.

* * *

Government agencies are more risk averse than imperialistic. They prefer security to rapid growth, autonomy to competition, stability to change * * *.

* * *

That agencies are risk averse does not mean they are timid. Quite the contrary: their desire for autonomy, for a stable environment, and for the freedom [from] blame gives these agencies a strong incentive to make rules and to exercise authority in all aspects of their mission. No agency wishes to be accused of "doing nothing" with respect to a real or imagined problem; hence every agency proliferates rules to cover all possible contingencies. The process is known familiarly in the bureaucracy as "covering your flanks" * * *.

Critics of regulatory agencies notice this proliferation of rules and suppose that it is the result of the "imperialistic" or expansionist instincts of bureaucratic organizations. Though there are such examples, I am struck more by the defensive, threat-avoiding, scandal-minimizing instincts of these agencies.

* * *

* * * [T]he cost of obtaining effective access to the political process has been lowered drastically in the last decade or two. Once national interest groups could exist only if they had corporate sponsors or a mass membership; today, "public interest" lobbies can be sustained by the availability of foundation grants and the use of computerized direct-mail fund drives * * *. Though such groups rarely have the legal staffs or war chests of a well-heeled business lobby, they have at least two offsetting advantages. First, they can enter the federal courts to challenge agency decisions rather easily because the rules governing standing have been liberalized and because in many cases * * * the plaintiffs may be reimbursed for their costs if they win. Second, the public-interest lobbies have many friends in the national media who are happy to cover their activities and publicize their complaints * * *.

The cost of effective political access has also been lowered by the existence within government, especially in Congress, of people who are sympathetic to consumerist and environmental organizations * * *, persons who derive either satisfaction for themselves or political rewards from their superiors from their ability to mount investigations or draft legislation in the regulatory area.

* * *

In short, the political environment of the regulatory agencies changed significantly in a short time. These changes had many sources, but one common characteristic: they reveal the extent to which intellectual descriptions (and criticisms) of institutional arrangements come to have practical consequences. Any generalization about how government works is vulnerable to the behavior of persons who have learned that generalization and wish to repeal it.

* * *

* * * [I]deas as well as interests play a role in shaping policies * * *.
[A] preoccupation with the political role of material interests, while useful
under many circumstances, can detract attention from the greater
challenges to liberty and economic growth raised by the ideas of those
groups in our society—bureaucrats, professionals, academics, the media—
whose political position depends on controlling resources other than wealth
and whose motives are more complex than wealth maximization.

CHAPTER 2

THE CONSTITUTION AND THE
ADMINISTRATIVE STATE

■ ■ ■

A. CONCEPTS OF SEPARATED POWERS

1. THE EIGHTEENTH-CENTURY VISION

JAMES MADISON, THE FEDERALIST
Nos. 48 & 51 (1787).

It is agreed on all sides that the powers properly belonging to one of the departments ought not to be directly and completely administered by either of the other departments. It is equally evident that none of them ought to possess, directly or indirectly, an overruling influence over the other in the administration of their respective powers. It will not be denied that power is of an encroaching nature and that it ought to be effectually restrained from passing the limits assigned to it. After discriminating, therefore, in theory, the several classes of power, as they may in their nature be legislative, executive, or judiciary, the next and most difficult task is to provide some practical security for each, against the invasion of the others. What this security ought to be is the great problem to be solved.

Will it be sufficient to mark, with precision, the boundaries of these departments in the constitution of the government, and to trust to these parchment barriers against the encroaching spirit of power? This is the security which appears to have been principally relied on by the compilers of most of the American constitutions. But experience assures us that the efficacy of the provision has been greatly overstated; and that some more adequate defense is indispensably necessary for the more feeble against the more powerful members of the government.

* * *

To what expedient, then, shall we finally resort, for maintaining in practice the necessary partition of power among the several departments as laid down in the Constitution? The only answer that can be given is that as all these exterior provisions are found to be inadequate the defect must be supplied, by so contriving the interior structure of the government as

83

that its several constituent parts may, by their mutual relations, be the means of keeping each other in their proper places * * *.

In order to lay a due foundation for that separate and distinct exercise of the different powers of government, which to a certain extent is admitted on all hands to be essential to the preservation of liberty, it is evident that each department should have a will of its own; and consequently should be so constituted that the members of each should have as little agency as possible in the appointment of the members of the others * * *.

It is equally evident that the members of each department should be as little dependent as possible on those of the others for the emoluments annexed to their offices. Were the executive magistrate, or the judges, not independent of the legislature in this particular, their independence in every other would be merely nominal.

But the great security against a gradual concentration of the several powers in the same department consists in giving to those who administer each department the necessary constitutional means and personal motives to resist encroachments of the others. The provision for defense must in this, as in all other cases, be made commensurate to the danger of attack. Ambition must be made to counteract ambition. The interest of the man must be connected with the constitutional rights of the place. It may be a reflection on human nature that such devices should be necessary to control the abuses of government. But what is government itself but the greatest of all reflections on human nature? If men were angels, no government would be necessary. If angels were to govern men, neither external nor internal controls on government would be necessary. In framing a government which is to be administered by men over men, the great difficulty lies in this: you must first enable the government to control the governed; and in the next place oblige it to control itself. A dependence on the people is, no doubt, the primary control on the government; but experience has taught mankind the necessity of auxiliary precautions.

THE CONSTITUTION OF THE UNITED STATES

Article I

Section 1. All legislative Powers herein granted shall be vested in a Congress of the United States, which shall consist of a Senate and House of Representatives.

Section 2. [1] The House of Representatives shall be composed of Members chosen every second Year by the People of the several States, and the Electors in each State shall have the Qualifications requisite for Electors of the most numerous Branch of the State Legislature.

[2] No Person shall be a Representative who shall not have attained to the Age of twenty five Years, and been seven Years a Citizen of the

United States, and who shall not, when elected, be an Inhabitant of that State in which he shall be chosen.

[3]   [This clause provides for the apportionment of Representatives among the States on the basis of population.]

[4]   When vacancies happen in the Representation of any State, the Executive Authority thereof shall issue Writs of Election to fill such Vacancies.

[5]   The House of Representatives shall chuse their Speaker and other Officers; and shall have the sole Power of Impeachment.

Section 3. [1] The Senate of the United States shall be composed of two Senators from each State, chosen by the Legislature thereof, for six Years; and each Senator shall have one Vote. [The Seventeenth Amendment, ratified in 1913, replaces this procedure with election by popular vote within each state.]

[2]   [This clause ensures that one-third of the seats in the Senate are up for election each year and it provides for the filling of vacancies. The vacancy provision was amended by the Seventeenth Amendment in 1913.]

[3]   No Person shall be a Senator who shall not have attained to the Age of thirty Years, and been nine Years a Citizen of the United States, and who shall not, when elected, be an Inhabitant of that State for which he shall be chosen.

[4]   The Vice President of the United States shall be President of the Senate, but shall have no Vote, unless they be equally divided.

[5]   The Senate shall chuse their other Officers, and also a President pro tempore, in the Absence of the Vice President, or when he shall exercise the Office of President of the United States.

[6]   The Senate shall have the sole Power to try all Impeachments. When sitting for that Purpose, they shall be on Oath or Affirmation. When the President of the United States is tried, the Chief Justice shall preside: And no Person shall be convicted without the Concurrence of two thirds of the Members present.

[7]   Judgment in Cases of Impeachment shall not extend further than to removal from Office, and disqualification to hold and enjoy any Office of honor, Trust or Profit under the United States: but the Party convicted shall nevertheless be liable and subject to Indictment, Trial, Judgment and Punishment, according to Law.

Section 4. [1] The Times, Places and Manner of holding Elections for Senators and Representatives, shall be prescribed in each State by the Legislature thereof; but the Congress may at any time by Law make or alter such Regulations, except as to the Places of chusing Senators.

[2]   The Congress shall assemble at least once in every Year, and such Meeting shall be on the first Monday in December, unless they shall by Law appoint a different Day.

Section 5. [This section contains a number of provisions dealing with the internal management of Congress.]

Section 6. [1] The Senators and Representatives shall receive a Compensation for their Services, to be ascertained by Law, and paid out of the Treasury of the United States. They shall in all Cases, except Treason, Felony and Breach of the Peace, be privileged from Arrest during their Attendance at the Session of their respective Houses, and in going to and returning from the same; and for any Speech or Debate in either House, they shall not be questioned in any other Place. [The Twenty-Seventh Amendment provides that "No law, varying the compensation for the services of the Senators and Representatives, shall take effect, until an election of Representatives shall have intervened."]

[2]   No Senator or Representative shall, during the Time for which he was elected, be appointed to any civil Office under the Authority of the United States, which shall have been created, or the Emoluments whereof shall have been encreased during such time; and no Person holding any Office under the United States, shall be a Member of either House during his Continuance in Office.

Section 7. [1] All Bills for raising Revenue shall originate in the House of Representatives, but the Senate may propose or concur with Amendments as on other Bills.

[2]   Every Bill which shall have passed the House of Representatives and the Senate, shall, before it becomes a Law, be presented to the President of the United States; If he approve he shall sign it, but if not he shall return it, with his Objections to that House in which it shall have originated, who shall enter the Objections at large on their Journal, and proceed to reconsider it. If after such Reconsideration two thirds of that House shall agree to pass the Bill, it shall be sent, together with the Objections, to the other House, by which it shall likewise be reconsidered, and if approved by two thirds of that House, it shall become a Law. If any Bill shall not be returned by the President within ten Days (Sundays excepted) after it shall have been presented to him, the Same shall be a Law, in like Manner as if he had signed it, unless the Congress by their Adjournment prevent its Return, in which Case it shall not be a Law.

[3]   Every Order, Resolution, or Vote to which the Concurrence of the Senate and House of Representatives may be necessary (except on a question of Adjournment) shall be presented to the President of the United States; and before the Same shall take Effect, shall be approved by him, or being disapproved by him, shall be repassed by two thirds of the Senate

and House of Representatives, according to the Rules and Limitations prescribed in the Case of a Bill.

Section 8. [This Section contains eighteen clauses that specify various powers of Congress. Clauses 1–8 and 10–17 concern such matters as the power to tax and borrow, to regulate interstate and foreign commerce, to establish rules for bankruptcy and naturalization, to coin money and prohibit counterfeiting, to establish a Post Office, to provide for patents and copyrights, to declare war, to establish military forces, and to provide for the governance of the District of Columbia. Clauses 9 and 18 are set forth below.]

The Congress shall have Power * * *

[9]   To constitute Tribunals inferior to the supreme Court;

[18] To make all Laws which shall be necessary and proper for carrying into Execution the foregoing Powers, and all other Powers vested by this Constitution in the Government of the United States, or in any Department or Officer thereof.

Section 9. [This section contains various limitations on Congress. Clauses 1–6 and 8 include limitations on Congress' power to prohibit the slave trade, to suspend the writ of habeas corpus, to enact bills of attainder or ex post facto laws, to impose direct taxes or duties, and to grant titles of nobility. Clause 7 is set forth below.]

[7]   No Money shall be drawn from the Treasury, but in Consequence of Appropriations made by Law.

Section 10. [This section contains a small number of limitations on state governments.]

Article II

Section 1. [1] The executive Power shall be vested in a President of the United States of America.

[Clauses 2–6 of this section set forth the qualifications for and method for electing the President and Vice-President. These provisions have been supplemented or supplanted by the Twelfth, Twentieth, Twenty-Second, Twenty-Third, and Twenty-Fifth Amendments.]

[7]   The President shall, at stated Times, receive for his Services, a Compensation, which shall neither be increased nor diminished during the Period for which he shall have been elected, and he shall not receive within that Period any other Emolument from the United States, or any of them.

[8]   Before he enter on the Execution of his Office, he shall take the following Oath or Affirmation: "I do solemnly swear (or affirm) that I will faithfully execute the Office of President of the United States, and will to

the best of my Ability, preserve, protect and defend the Constitution of the United States."

Section 2. [1] The President shall be Commander in Chief of the Army and Navy of the United States; he may require the Opinion, in writing, of the principal Officer in each of the executive Departments, upon any Subject relating to the Duties of their respective Offices, and he shall have Power to grant Reprieves and Pardons for Offenses against the United States, except in Cases of Impeachment.

[2]   He shall have Power, by and with the Advice and Consent of the Senate, to make Treaties, provided two thirds of the Senators present concur; and he shall nominate, and by and with the Advice and Consent of the Senate, shall appoint Ambassadors, other public Ministers and Consuls, Judges of the supreme Court, and all other Officers of the United States, whose Appointments are not herein otherwise provided for, and which shall be established by Law; but the Congress may by Law vest the Appointment of such inferior Officers, as they think proper, in the President alone, in the Courts of Law, or in the Heads of Departments.

[3]   The President shall have Power to fill up all Vacancies that may happen during the Recess of the Senate, by granting Commissions which shall expire at the End of their next Session.

Section 3. He shall from time to time give to the Congress Information of the State of the Union, and recommend to their Consideration such Measures as he shall judge necessary and expedient; he may, on extraordinary Occasions, convene both Houses, or either of them, and in Case of Disagreement between them, with Respect to the Time of Adjournment, he may adjourn them to such Time as he shall think proper; he shall receive Ambassadors and other public Ministers; he shall take Care that the Laws be faithfully executed, and shall Commission all the Officers of the United States.

Section 4. The President, Vice President and all civil Officers of the United States, shall be removed from Office on Impeachment for, and Conviction of, Treason, Bribery, or other high Crimes and Misdemeanors.

Article III

Section 1. The judicial Power of the United States, shall be vested in one supreme Court, and in such inferior Courts as the Congress may from time to time ordain and establish. The Judges, both of the supreme and inferior Courts, shall hold their Offices during good Behavior, and shall, at stated Times, receive for their Services, a Compensation, which shall not be diminished during their Continuance in Office.

Section 2. [Clauses 1 and 2 of this Section set forth the classes of cases in which the federal courts shall have jurisdiction and in which the Supreme Court will have original jurisdiction.]

[3]   The trial of all Crimes, except in Cases of Impeachment, shall be by jury; and such Trial shall be held in the State where the said Crimes shall have been committed; but when not committed within any State, the Trial shall be at such Place or Places as the Congress may by Law have directed.

Section 3. [This Section defines and limits the power of Congress to prohibit treason.]

Article IV

[The four Sections of this Article contain some provisions dealing with relations among the states, the admission of new states, and the federal government's responsibility to assure each state "a Republican Form of Government * * *." Section 3, clause 2 of this Article is set forth below.]

Section 3. [2] The Congress shall have Power to dispose of and make all needful Rules and Regulations respecting the Territory or other Property belonging to the United States; and nothing in this Constitution shall be so construed as to Prejudice any claims of the United States, or of any particular State.

Article V

[This Article specifies the methods for amending the Constitution.]

Article VI

[1]   All Debts contracted and Engagements entered into, before Adoption of this Constitution, shall be as valid against the United States under this Constitution, as under the Confederation.

[2]   This Constitution, and the Laws of the United States which shall be made in Pursuance thereof; and all Treaties made, or which shall be made, under the Authority of the United States, shall be the supreme Law of the Land; and the Judges in every State shall be bound thereby, any Thing in the Constitution or Laws of any State to the Contrary notwithstanding.

[3]   The Senators and Representatives before mentioned, and the Members of the several State Legislatures, and all executive and judicial Officers, both of the United States and of the several States, shall be bound by Oath or Affirmation, to support this Constitution; but no religious Test shall ever be required as a Qualification to any Office or public Trust under the United States.

Article VII

The Ratification of the Conventions of nine States, shall be sufficient for the Establishment of this Constitution between the States so ratifying the Same.

2. THE TWENTIETH-CENTURY VISION

JAMES LANDIS, THE ADMINISTRATIVE PROCESS
(Yale University Press, 1938) pp. 1–2, 10–12.

The last century has witnessed the rise of a new instrument of government, the administrative tribunal. In its mature form it is difficult to find its parallels in our earlier political history; its development seems indigenous. The rapidity of its growth, the significance of its powers, and the implications of its being, are such as to require notice of the extent to which this new "administrative law" is weaving itself more and more into our governmental fabric.

In terms of political theory, the administrative process springs from the inadequacy of a simple tripartite form of government to deal with modern problems. It represents a striving to adapt governmental technique, that still divides under three rubrics, to modern needs and, at the same time, to preserve those elements of responsibility and those conditions of balance that have distinguished Anglo-American government.

Separation of powers as a political maxim is old; but as a principle of government, sanctified by being elevated to the constitutional level and embroidered by pontifical moral phrases, it has a distinctly American flavor. Our British cousins discover it now and then as they find that its preachment fits some practical or political need. But it was left to us to hallow the tripartite ideal of government, wherein all power delegated by the people was in the purported interests of liberty divided neatly between legislative, executive, and judicial. It was left to us, moreover, not merely to make of this division a convenient way of thinking about government, of considering the desirability of checking and balancing a particular power that might be vested in some official or some body, but also by judicial introspection to distinguish minutely and definitively between these powers. That fineness of logic-chopping that characterizes our courts permits us at will to discern a legislative or a judicial power when we are eager for a determination; at the same time it permits us to avoid decision by the establishment of new categories of quasi-legislative and quasi-judicial powers.

The insistence upon the compartmentalization of power along triadic lines gave way in the nineteenth century to the exigencies of governance. Without too much political theory but with a keen sense of the practicalities of the situation, agencies were created whose functions embraced the three aspects of government. Rule-making, enforcement, and the disposition of competing claims made by contending parties, were all intrusted to them. As the years passed, the process grew. These agencies, tribunals, and rule-making boards were for the sake of convenience distinguished from the existing governmental bureaucracies by terming them "administrative."

The law the courts permitted them to make was named "administrative law," so that now the process in all its component parts can be appropriately termed the "administrative process."

* * *

If in private life we were to organize a unit for the operation of an industry, it would scarcely follow Montesquieu's lines. As yet no organization in private industry either has been conceived along those triadic contours, nor would its normal development, if so conceived, have tended to conform to them. Yet the problems of operating a private industry resemble to a great degree those entailed by its regulation. The direction of any large corporation presents difficulties comparable in character to those faced by an administrative commission. Rates are a concern, likewise wages, hours of employment, safe conditions for labor, and schemes for pensions and gratuities. There must follow the enforcement of pertinent regulations as well as the adjudication of claims of every nature made not only by employees but also by the public * * *.

The significance of this comparison is not that it may point to a need for an expanding concept of the province of governmental regulation, but rather that it points to the form which governmental action tends to take. As the governance of industry, bent upon the shaping of adequate policies and the development of means for their execution, vests powers to this end without regard to the creation of agencies theoretically independent of each other, so when government concerns itself with the stability of an industry it is only intelligent realism for it to follow the industrial rather than the political analogue. It vests the necessary powers with the administrative authority it creates, not too greatly concerned with the extent to which such action does violence to the traditional tripartite theory of governmental organization.

PETER L. STRAUSS, FORMAL AND FUNCTIONAL APPROACHES TO SEPARATION-OF-POWERS QUESTIONS—A FOOLISH INCONSISTENCY?

72 Cornell L. Rev. 488, 492–93 (1987).
Copyright 1987 by Cornell University. All Rights Reserved.

* * * [O]ur formal, three-branch theory of government—at least as traditionally expressed—cannot describe the government we long have had, is not required by the Constitution, and is not necessary to preserve the very real and desirable benefits of "separation of powers" that form so fundamental an element of our constitutional scheme. The Constitution does not define the administrative, as distinct from the political, organs of the federal government; it leaves that entirely to Congress. What the Constitution describes instead are three generalist national institutions (Congress, President, and Supreme Court) which, together with the states, serve as the principal heads of political and legal authority. Each of these three generalist institutions serves as the ultimate authority for a distinctive governmental authority-type (legislative, executive, or judicial). Each may be thought of as having a paradigmatic relationship, characterized by that authority-type, with the working government that Congress creates.

Although these heads of government serve distinct functions, employing distinctive procedures * * *, the same cannot be said of the administrative level of government. Virtually every part of the government Congress has created—the Department of Agriculture as well as the Securities and Exchange Commission—exercises all three of the governmental functions the Constitution so carefully allocates among Congress, President, and Court. These agencies adopt rules having the shape and impact of statutes, mold governmental policy through enforcement decisions and other initiatives, and decide cases in ways that determine the rights of private parties. If in 1787 such a merger of function was unthinkable, in 1987 it is unavoidable given Congress's need to delegate at some level the making of policy for a complex and interdependent economy, and the equal incapacity (and undesirability) of the courts to resolve all matters appropriately characterized as involving "adjudication." A formal theory of separation of powers that says these functions cannot be joined is unworkable; that being so, a theory that locates each agency "in" one or another of the three conventional "branches" of American government, according to its activities, fares no better. Respect for "framers' intent" is only workable in the context of the actual present, and may require some selectivity in just what it is we choose to respect— the open-ended text, the indeterminacy of governmental form, the vision of a changing future, and the general purpose to avoid tyrannical government, rather than a particular three-part model. The problem is finding a way of maintaining the connection between each of the generalist institutions and the paradigmatic function which it alone is empowered to serve, while retaining a grasp on government as a whole that respects our commitments to the control of law.

This object can be achieved conformably to the words of the Constitution * * *, although at some cost to traditional understandings, by observing that the concept of a "branch," as such, is not required by the text. When the Constitution confers power, it confers power on the three generalist political heads of authority, not on branches as such. The constitutional text addresses the powers only of the elected members of Congress, of the President as an individual, and of the Supreme Court and such inferior federal courts as Congress might choose to establish. Its silence about the shape of the inevitable, actual government was a product both of drafting compromises and of the explicit purpose to leave Congress free to make whatever arrangements it deemed "necessary and proper" for the detailed pursuit of government purposes. One can easily and properly infer some relationships that the three named governmental actors must observe as among themselves and, consequently, with whatever subordinate parts of government Congress chooses to create, without having to believe that those parts must be located "here" or "there" in the government structure, or that the governmental functions they may perform are restricted by the accident of that location.

3.   THE EIGHTEENTH CENTURY STRIKES BACK: THE FORMALISM VS. FUNCTIONALISM DEBATE

ARNOLD I. BURNS & STEPHEN J. MARKMAN, UNDERSTANDING SEPARATION OF POWERS
7 Pace L. Rev. 575, 575–83 (1987).

Our Constitution contains explicit directions regarding the organization of the federal government, dividing the responsibilities of government among three separate branches, and enumerating the specific powers each branch is to exercise. This division and enumeration of powers establishes the fundamental terms by which one branch's claim to authority may be deemed valid or invalid, and provides the basis for deciding whether the exercise of power by an agent of government is permitted or prohibited. Too frequently, however, commentators, both inside and outside of government, discuss the separation of powers found in the Constitution as if it were some kind of broad based "constitutional policy" or political philosophy divorced from the specific provisions in the text of the document. This article seeks to refocus that discussion, to move away from abstractions about separation of powers, and to re-anchor the doctrine to its constitutional moorings.

* * *

The concept of separated powers as a political doctrine has, of course, existed at least since the middle of the seventeenth century. Of the various theorists who wrote of the need to divide governmental powers among different institutions, Montesquieu most influenced the Framers. However, it would be a mistake to assume that Montesquieu's view of separation of powers—or any other particular view, for that matter—was specifically incorporated into the Constitution or intended to dictate our understanding of the constitutional structure of our government. Whatever theories may have influenced the Framers, only one specific formulation found expression in the Constitution. Thus, as a jurisprudential matter, there is neither need nor warrant for reliance on abstract conceptual theories about separation of powers divorced from the actual text of the Constitution.

* * * The Constitution distributes the sum total of national governmental power among the three branches * * *. Thus, by its own terms, the Constitution makes clear that the executive and judicial branches have no legislative power; that no part of the judicial power is conferred on the legislature or the executive; and that only the executive branch can exercise executive power. Our system of government, properly viewed, is not, as one scholar has described it, "separated institutions sharing powers." Rather, it consists of three branches assigned different powers and responsibilities that together comprise the full extent of national governmental power.

The Constitution does not permit a branch of government to expand its own authority by encroaching upon the powers conferred on the other branches; nor does an acquiescence in an unconstitutional exercise of power by another branch establish that power in the other branch. Moreover, beyond those powers expressly conferred on the various branches (and such powers as are implicit in their delegation, or incidental to their exercise), there are no "inherent" powers of national government. Thus, neither amorphous concepts of sovereignty, nor the mere possession of legislative or executive power, or of governmental power generally, affords a basis for claiming authority to take action expressly or implicitly authorized by the Constitution.

To insist that the separated powers of the three branches are not shared, however, is not to suggest that these powers may not at times be focused on the same subject or that they must operate with absolute independence. For example, the Constitution confers on the President the power to veto bills "which shall have passed the House of Representatives and the Senate," subject to the power of Congress to override that veto by vote of two-thirds of each House; it grants the Senate the power of consent over treaties and presidential appointments; it gives Congress the power to define the jurisdiction of the judicial branch by virtue of its authority to "ordain and establish . . . inferior [federal] Courts"; and it gives the judiciary, by virtue of its power over cases arising under the Constitution and laws and treaties of the United States, the power to declare legislative and executive acts unconstitutional. Such duties may require different branches to study and act upon the same set of circumstances. However, in each of these instances, the powers of each branch remain discrete: the legislative is exercising legislative power, the President is exercising executive power, and the courts are exercising judicial power; none of them is "sharing" its powers with the other branches. Any "sharing" or "blending" of power relates only to the sharing of the sum of all national governmental power and the concurrent exercise of power by more than one branch.

PETER B. McCUTCHEN, MISTAKES, PRECEDENT, AND THE RISE OF THE ADMINISTRATIVE STATE: TOWARD A CONSTITUTIONAL THEORY OF THE SECOND BEST

80 Cornell L. Rev. 1, 5–11 (1994).

There is general consensus among scholars that the Court has exhibited a "split personality" in separation of powers cases. The Court has alternated between an anything-goes functionalist method * * * and a rigid but principled formalist method that almost always leads to invalidation of the challenged governmental action. There has been little explanation or apparent rationale for the Court's flipping between these two methods of analysis.

Moreover, neither functionalism nor formalism represents a completely satisfactory approach to separation of powers issues. Of the two, functionalism poses the greater threat to the constitutional structures designed to protect individual liberty, check the exercise of power, and assure governmental accountability. Formalism, while faithful to constitutional text, is incomplete—or inadequate—because it fails to bridge the gap between modern administrative government and the formalist paradigm.

Functionalists purport to be concerned with whether a particular exercise of power by one department illegitimately interferes with the "core function" of another department. Central to this inquiry is the issue of whether one department is attempting to "aggrandize" itself at the expense of another. Thus, functionalists are not inclined to worry about the exercise of governmental authority by actors outside of the three named departments. Likewise, functionalists are willing to accommodate substantial innovation below the apex of governmental structure. Ultimately, the functionalist model accepts any distribution of power so long as it does not "undermine the intended distribution of authority" among the President, Congress, and the judiciary.

The "Fourth Branch" therefore does not trouble the functionalists. Because it takes most of the administrative state as a given, functionalism is more "realistic" than formalism—or at least more consistent with the status quo. Despite the Court's wavering, functionalism has been somewhat more prevalent than formalism in the Supreme Court's separation of powers jurisprudence.

Nevertheless, the functionalist approach should be rejected for three reasons. First, functionalism lacks sufficient critical bite: Once a court adopts a functionalist methodology, "no meaningful limitations on interbranch usurpation of power remain." For example, Justice White, who adopted the most consistently functionalist methodology of any member of the Court, consistently refused to hold that separation of powers principles had been violated, except in the most extreme circumstances. The reason for the functionalists' unwillingness to strike down almost any institution on separation of powers grounds is simple. The functionalist notions of "core functions" and "aggrandizement" are so vague and indeterminate that "the judicial reaction will almost always be to defer to the judgments of other branches when separation of powers controversies arise." Thus, functionalism is tantamount to a complete lack of judicial review.

Second, despite its superficial worldliness, functionalism does not appreciate the corrupting effect of power. Functionalism accommodates well-intentioned innovations designed to circumvent the constitutional system of balanced and separated powers in order to overcome a complex, cumbersome, and inefficient method of governance. In the process, however, functionalism has allowed concentrations of virtually unchecked power to pervade a system whose design was largely driven by an almost paranoid distrust of political power * * *. The functionalist insistence that concentrations of power below the apex of governmental authority are not important is, consequently, inconsistent with the Framers' understanding of the tendency of officials to abuse their power. The functionalist notion of aggrandizement and its tendency to accommodate violations of separation of powers principles below the apex of governmental authority therefore fails adequately to protect the constitutional structures that protect individual liberty.

Finally, functionalists only worry when one department tries to take power at the expense of another. They do not worry when a department has some power taken away from it—as long as that power does not go to one of the other coordinate departments. Yet the abdication of power and its corresponding responsibilities is as serious a problem as aggrandizement. The decision of the German Reichstag to relinquish power in 1933 was lamentable not merely because it allowed the Chancellor— Adolph Hitler—to aggrandize his position at the expense of the legislature but also because it involved legislative abdication. If the Congress were to cede all power to an administrative agency in a single legislative act, its decision to do so would be lamentable because it would spell the end of legislative accountability, and therefore of constitutional self-government. The principle remains the same if abdication is accomplished piecemeal. Thus, because it fails to appreciate and counteract the danger inherent in abdication, functionalism should be rejected outright.

The traditional alternative to functionalism is formalism. As in legal discourse generally, formalism in the separation of powers context involves the application of more or less rigid rules, rather than flexible standards, to legal problems. Although the formalist might agree that the separation of powers serves certain goals, the goals are not directly invoked by the formalist in resolving separation of powers cases. Rather, the constitutional text is seen as an "instruction manual" which prescribes particular allocations of power. The three "vesting" clauses "establish[ ] a complete division of otherwise unallocated federal governmental authority among the constitutionally specified legislative, executive, and judicial institutions." Formalism "uses a syllogistic, definitional approach to determining whether a particular exercise of power is legislative, executive, or judicial. It assumes that all exercises of power must fall into one of these categories and takes no ostensible account of the practicalities of administration in arriving at this determination." Thus, under the formalist paradigm, "the constitutional validity of a particular branch action, from the perspective of separation of powers, is to be determined not by resort to functional balancing, but solely by the use of a definitional analysis." No commingling of legislative, executive, or judicial power is permissible, except where specifically provided in the constitutional text.

Any defense of formalism will encounter some resistance. Nonetheless, a formalist approach to separation of powers problems has much to commend it. Most importantly, a formalist approach is the one most consistent with the text of the Constitution. The structural provisions of the Constitution look like an instruction manual. They set forth the role of each department and the modes of interaction among the three departments. There would be no point to these elaborate provisions if Congress were free to prescribe extra-textual modes of governance.

Moreover, the formalist approach furthers the policies behind the separation of powers more than functionalism, which requires the Court to determine on a case-by-case basis if the policies behind the separation of powers are threatened. The constitutional system of balanced and separated powers serves primarily to protect against abuse of governmental authority, or "tyranny." However, it is unclear, in advance, whether a structure that violates the constitutional blueprint is a benign innovation or a malignant threat to liberty. Consequently * * *, the constitutional principle of separation of powers is "inherently prophylactic." "The concept of a prophylactic is that it prevents the creation of a critical situation by proceeding on the assumption that it will be impossible to determine, in the individual instance, the existence of a real threat to the values sought to be fostered." It is therefore unwise to resolve separation of powers cases according to the functionalist model, on a case-by-case basis. Rather, the point of separation of powers jurisprudence is to be rigid and inflexible. The very rigidity of formalism, then, recommends it as the proper mode of interpretation in separation of powers cases.

There is, however, one overriding problem with formalism as a method for evaluating current structures. Under a pure formalist approach, most, if not all, of the administrative state is unconstitutional. Agency rulemaking and adjudication—indeed, the very existence of some agencies—is inconsistent with the formalist model. Formalism, therefore, is "simply incapable of describing the government we have." A useful theory of interpretation must, however, take at least some of our current government as a given. Prudence dictates some accommodation of administrative government. At this point, then, application of undiluted formalism would be unsound and unworkable.

In sum, the problem is that formalism is too principled and rigid while functionalism is not principled or rigid enough.

4.   THE SUPREME COURT SPEAKS

(1)   *Buckley v. Valeo*, 424 U.S. 1, 120–21, 96 S.Ct. 612, 683, 46 L.Ed.2d 659 (1976):

The majority of the Court of Appeals * * * described appellants' argument [concerning the Appointments Clause] as "strikingly syllogistic" * * *. We do not think appellants' arguments * * * can be so easily dismissed * * *.

* * *

The principle of separation of powers was not simply an abstract generalization in the minds of the Framers: it was woven into the document that they drafted in Philadelphia in the summer of 1787 * * *.

It is in the context of these cognate provisions of the document that we must examine the language of [the Appointments Clause] * * *. Because of the importance of its language, we again set out the provision * * *.

(2)   *Nixon v. Administrator of General Services,* 433 U.S. 425, 441, 443, 97 S.Ct. 2777, 2789, 2790, 53 L.Ed.2d 867 (1977):

Appellants' argument is * * * based on an interpretation of the separation-of-powers doctrine inconsistent with the origins of that doctrine, recent decisions of the Court, and the contemporary realities of our political system * * *. [W]e therefore find that appellant's argument rests upon an "archaic view of the separation of powers as requiring three airtight departments of government." Rather, in determining whether the Act disrupts the proper balance between the coordinate branches, the proper inquiry focuses on the extent to which it prevents the Executive Branch from accomplishing its constitutionally assigned functions. Only where the potential for disruption is present must we then determine whether that impact is justified by an overriding need to promote objectives within the constitutional authority of Congress.

(3)   *INS v. Chadha*, 462 U.S. 919, 944, 945, 959, 103 S.Ct. 2764, 2780, 2781, 2789, 77 L.Ed.2d 317 (1983):

[T]he fact that a given law or procedure is efficient, convenient, and useful in facilitating functions of government, standing alone, will not save it if it is contrary to the Constitution. Convenience and efficiency are not the primary objectives—or the hallmarks—of democratic government * * *.

* * *

Explicit and unambiguous provisions of the Constitution prescribe and define the respective functions of the Congress and of the Executive in the legislative process. Since the precise terms of those familiar provisions are critical to the resolution of these cases, we set them out verbatim * * *.

(4) *CFTC v. Schor*, 478 U.S. 833, 847–48, 851, 106 S.Ct. 3245, 3255, 92 L.Ed.2d 675 (1986):

[R]esolution of claims such as Schor's cannot turn on conclusory reference to the language of Article III. Rather, the constitutionality of a given congressional delegation of adjudicative functions to a non-Article III body must be assessed by reference to the purposes underlying the requirements of Article III. This inquiry, in turn, is guided by the principle that "practical attention to substance rather than doctrinaire reliance on formal categories should inform application of Article III."

* * *

In determining the extent to which a given congressional decision to authorize the adjudication of Article III business in a non-Article III tribunal impermissibly threatens the institutional integrity of the Judicial Branch, the Court has declined to adopt formalistic and unbending rules. Although such rules might lend a greater degree of coherence to this area of the law, they might also unduly constrict Congress' ability to take needed and innovative action pursuant to its Article I powers.

(5) *Loving v. United States*, 517 U.S. 748, 757–58, 116 S.Ct. 1737, 1743, 135 L.Ed.2d 36 (1996):

By allocating specific powers and responsibilities to a branch fitted to the task, the Framers created a National Government that is both effective and accountable * * *. The clear assignment of power to a branch, furthermore, allows the citizen to know who may be called to answer for making, or not making, those delicate and necessary decisions essential to government.

(6) *Federal Maritime Comm'n v. South Carolina State Ports Authority*, 535 U.S. 743, 787 122 S.Ct. 1864, 1889, 152 L.Ed.2d 962 (2002)

(Breyer, J., with whom Stevens, J., Souter, J., and Ginsburg, J., join, dissenting):

> An overly restrictive judicial interpretation of the Constitution's structural constraints (unlike its protections of certain basic liberties) will undermine the Constitution's own efforts to achieve its far more basic structural aim, the creation of a representative form of government capable of translating the people's will into effective public action.

> This understanding, underlying constitutional interpretation since the New Deal, reflects the Constitution's demands for structural flexibility sufficient to adapt substantive laws and institutions to rapidly changing social, economic, and technological conditions. It reflects the comparative inability of the Judiciary to understand either those conditions or the need for new laws and new administrative forms they may create. It reflects the Framers' own aspiration to write a document that would "constitute" a democratic, liberty-protecting form of government that would endure through centuries of change. This understanding led the New Deal Court to reject overly restrictive formalistic interpretations of the Constitution's structural provisions, thereby permitting Congress to enact social and economic legislation that circumstances had led the public to demand. And it led that Court to find in the Constitution authorization for new forms of administration, including independent administrative agencies, with the legal authority flexibly to implement, *i.e.*, to "execute," through adjudication, through rulemaking, and in other ways, the legislation that Congress subsequently enacted.

(7) *Wellness Int'l Network, Ltd. v. Sharif*, 575 U.S. ___, ___, 135 S.Ct. 1932, 1944 n.9, 191 L.Ed.2d 911 (2015):

> Here again, the principal dissent's insistence on formalism leads it astray.

(8) *Wellness Int'l Network, Ltd. v. Sharif*, 575 U.S. ___, ___, 135 S.Ct. 1932, 1950, 191 L.Ed.2d 911 (2015) (Roberts, J., with whom Scalia, J., and Thomas, J., join, dissenting):

> The Court justifies its decision largely on pragmatic grounds. I would not yield so fully to functionalism.

B. AGENCIES AND ARTICLE I

The difference between the departments undoubtedly is, that the legislature makes, the executive executes, and the judiciary construes the law; but the maker of the law may commit something to the discretion of the other departments, and the precise boundary of this power is a subject of delicate and difficult inquiry * * *.

Wayman v. Southard, 23 U.S. (10 Wheat.) 1, 42–43, 46, 6 L.Ed. 253 (1825).

Experience has instructed us that no skill in the science of government has yet been able to discriminate and define, with sufficient certainty, its three great provinces—the legislative, executive, and judiciary * * *. Questions daily occur in the course of practice which prove the obscurity which reigns in these subjects, and which puzzle the greatest adepts in political science.

James Madison, The Federalist No. 37 (1787).

Suppose that Congress creates an administrative body, called the Goodness and Niceness Commission, to which Congress gives the authority to promulgate legally binding rules "for the promotion of goodness and niceness on all subjects within Congress' constitutional jurisdiction." Congress then simply ceases to pass laws, leaving the governance of the country to the Goodness and Niceness Commission (subject to the theoretical possibility that Congress could alter or amend the Commission's rules by ordinary legislation).

Does anyone believe that Congress can, under the Constitution, simply empower another entity to perform all of Congress' functions, limited only by the requirement that all of that entity's rules promote goodness and niceness? Surely the Constitution places some limits on the extent to which Congress can entrust authority to other actors; the relevant question is how far those limits extend.

Consider now a statute that was on the books for ninety nine years before its repeal in 1996: the Tea Importation Act. Act of Mar. 2, 1897, ch. 358, 29 Stat. 604 (codified as amended at 21 U.S.C. §§ 41–50 (1994)).[1] As codified just before its repeal, the Act instructed the Secretary of Health and Human Services each year to "appoint a board, to consist of seven members, each of whom shall be an expert in teas, and who shall prepare and submit to him standard samples of tea." 21 U.S.C. § 42. In accordance with the board of experts' recommendations, the Secretary was instructed to "fix and establish uniform standards of purity, quality, and fitness for consumption of all kinds of teas imported into the United States" and to deposit samples of these standards in the customhouses of various ports of entry. *Id.* § 43. Tea importers were required to submit samples of their product for comparison with the standard samples kept at the customhouses. See *id.* § 44. The imported samples were then tested "by a

---

[1]　　The Act was repealed by the Federal Tea Tasters Repeal Act of 1996, Pub. L. No. 104–128, 110 Stat. 1198 (1996).

duly qualified examiner," *id.* § 46, who would test "the purity, quality, and fitness for consumption of the * * * [imported tea samples] according to the usages and customs of the tea trade, including the testing of an infusion of the same in boiling water and, if necessary, chemical analysis." *Id.* The statute declared it unlawful to import into the United States "any merchandise as tea which is inferior in purity, quality, and fitness for consumption to the standards [kept at the customhouses] * * *." *Id.* § 41. In sum, for nearly a century, Congress provided that no imported tea could enter the United States unless federal tea-tasters decided that it measured up to pre-selected standard samples.

If Congress chooses to regulate the importation of tea, does anyone believe that the Constitution requires Congress itself to select the physical samples of tea that serve as the statutory standards for comparison with imported tea, or that it requires each Member of Congress personally to taste each sample of imported tea and then vote on whether it meets standards of purity, quality, and fitness for consumption? Surely the Constitution permits Congress to entrust some measure of authority to other actors; the relevant question is how far that permission extends.

If there is a difference between the Goodness and Niceness Commission and the federal tea-tasting board, what is that difference? Is it the breadth of the agency's authority, the vagueness of the agency's statutory mandate, or both? If one is inclined to focus on the vagueness of the agency's mandate, is a statute authorizing an agency to promulgate standards for the "quality" of tea any more specific than a statute that tells an agency to promote goodness and niceness?[2] Are both statutory schemes unconstitutional in the end?

The following materials explore the way in which legal actors and scholars have, for more than two centuries, wrestled with the "nondelegation doctrine"—that is, the standards for determining when Congress has crossed the constitutional line between delegating legislative authority and simply allowing executive and judicial actors to carry out their constitutionally prescribed functions.

1. BEFORE THE NEW DEAL

a. The First Congress

The state and national governments, under the Articles of Confederation, had provided for pensions to wounded and disabled Revolutionary War veterans. The twenty-fourth statute enacted by the First Congress in 1789 provided that the new United States government would continue paying those previously-granted pensions for one year

---

[2] A tea sample's "purity" and "fitness for consumption" might be more readily determinable by reference to objective criteria than is its "quality."

"under such regulations as the President of the United States may direct." Act of Sept. 29, 1789, ch. XXIV, 1 Stat. 95.

A statute passed in the second session of the First Congress followed up this authority by providing that wounded or disabled military personnel "shall be placed on the list of the invalids of the United States, at such rate of pay, and under such regulations as shall be directed by the President," Act of Apr. 30, 1790, ch. XX, § 11, 1 Stat. 119, 121, subject to some specified maximum pay rates.

Another statute passed that session prohibited unlicensed trade and intercourse with the Indian tribes; instructed the executive department to issue licenses "to any proper person" who posted a specified bond, without providing any definition of a "proper person"; and required all licensees to be "governed in all things touching the said trade and intercourse, by such rules and regulations as the President shall prescribe." Act of July 22, 1790, ch. XXXIII, § 1, 1 Stat. 137.

b.   The Second Congress

The Constitution grants Congress the power to "establish Post Offices and post Roads." U.S. Const. art. I, § 8, cl. 7. A bill introduced in the Second Congress to establish post roads specifically designated, town by town, the routes by which mail was to be carried. An amendment was introduced in the House to authorize the carriage of mail *by such route as the President of the United States shall, from time to time, cause to be established.* 3 Annals of Cong. 229 (1791) (quoting Representative Sedgwick) (emphasis in original). Several representatives objected strenuously that the amendment would unconstitutionally delegate legislative power to the President. Representative Page, for example, declared:

> If the motion before the committee succeeds, I shall make one which will save a deal of time and money, by making a short session of it; for if this House can, with propriety, leave the business of the post office to the President, it may leave to him any other business of legislation; and I may move to adjourn and leave all the objects of legislation to his sole consideration and direction.

Id. at 233 (statement of Rep. Page). *See also id.* at 229 (objecting to the amendment because Congress could not "with propriety delegate that power which they were themselves appointed to exercise") (statement of Rep. Livermore). The amendment was defeated, and the final legislation specifically designated the routes that were established as post roads.[3]

---

[3]   Act of Feb. 20, 1792, ch. VII, § 1, 1 Stat. 232. The first post road established, for example, was described in the statute as follows:

> From Wisscassett in the district of Maine, to Savannah in Georgia, by the following route, to wit: Portland, Portsmouth, Newburyport, Ipswich, Salem, Boston, Worcester,

c.   Cargo of the Brig Aurora v. United States, 11 U.S. (7 Cranch) 382, 3 L.Ed. 378 (1813)

Beginning in 1809, in response to British interference with American shipping, Congress passed a series of statutes restricting trade with Great Britain and subjecting to forfeiture cargo shipped in violation of the statute. The statutes were written to expire within a very short time so that Congress could reassess the state of affairs and provide for the revival of the restrictions if necessary. The 1810 version of the statute provided that the expired 1809 trade prohibition was revived unless the President declared, by proclamation, that Great Britain had ceased to violate the neutral commerce of the United States. Appellant's cargo was seized under the statute at a time when no such presidential proclamation had been made. The appellant's primary arguments against application of the forfeiture statute concerned the date on which Congress intended the statute to take effect and the applicability of a later statute exempting American-owned property from seizure, but counsel for appellant also argued that the forfeiture statute was unconstitutional because "Congress could not transfer the legislative power to the President. To make the revival of a law depend upon the President's proclamation, is to give to that proclamation the force of a law." *Id.* at 386 (argument of Joseph R. Ingersoll). The Supreme Court dismissed the argument in one sentence: "[W]e can see no sufficient reason, why the legislature should not exercise its discretion in reviving the act of March 1st, 1809, either expressly or conditionally, as their judgment should direct." *Id.* at 388.

d.   Wayman v. Southard, 23 U.S. (10 Wheat.) 1, 6 L.Ed. 253 (1825)

A Kentucky statute provided that plaintiffs must accept state bank notes in satisfaction of judicial judgments. The Supreme Court held that this statute did not apply to the execution of federal court judgments in Kentucky, which was instead governed by a federal statute which provided that the "forms of writs, executions, and other processes" would be "subject * * * to such alterations and additions as the * * * [federal] Courts * * * shall, in their discretion, deem expedient, or to such regulations as the Supreme Court of the United States shall think proper, from time to time, by rule, to prescribe to any Circuit or District Court concerning the same." Counsel for defendant, who sought application of the Kentucky state law so his client could pay off the judgment in state bank notes, argued that

---

Springfield, Hartford, Middletown, New Haven, Stratford, Fairfield, Norwalk, Stamford, New York, Newark, Elizabethtown, Woodbridge, Brunswick, Princeton, Trenton, Bristol, Philadelphia, Chester, Wilmington, Elkton, Charlestown, Havre de Grace, Hartford, Baltimore, Bladensburg, Georgetown, Alexandria, Colchester, Dumfries, Fredericksburg, Bowling Green, Hanover Court House, Richmond, Petersburg, Halifax, Tarborough, Smithfield, Fayetteville, Newbridge over Drowning creek, Cheraw Court House, Camden, Statesburg, Columbia, Cambridge and Augusta; and from thence to Savannah * * *.

Id.

this federal statute was inapplicable because it unconstitutionally delegated legislative power to the courts. As Chief Justice Marshall pointed out, the argument was unavailing even if it was right: if the federal statute in question was invalid, that would not establish that state procedural laws rather than other sources of federal law, such as federal common law, would govern the execution of judgments in federal courts. But although it was therefore unnecessary for the Court to decide the delegation issue, Chief Justice Marshall, for a unanimous Court, discussed it at some length in dictum:

> It will not be contended that Congress can delegate to the Courts, or to any other tribunals, powers which are strictly and exclusively legislative. But Congress may certainly delegate to others, powers which the legislature may rightfully exercise itself * * *. [Under the Judiciary Act, which authorizes the federal courts to regulate their practice,] [t]he Courts, for example, may make rules, directing the returning of writs and processes, the filing of declarations and other pleadings, and other things of the same description. It will not be contended, that these things might not be done by the legislature, without the intervention of the Courts; yet it is not alleged that the power may not be conferred on the judicial department.

> The line has not been exactly drawn which separates those important subjects, which must be entirely regulated by the legislature itself, from those of less interest, in which a general provision may be made, and power given to those who are to act under such general provisions to fill up the details * * *.

> * * *

> * * * The power given to the Court to vary the mode of proceeding * * * [concerning such matters as the proper notice to be given a judgment debtor before his or her property is seized for sale and the manner in which the property is held before sale] is a power to vary minor regulations, which are within the great outlines marked out by the legislature in directing the execution. To vary the terms on which a sale is to be made, and declare whether it shall be on credit, or for ready money, is certainly a more important exercise of the power of regulating the conduct of the officer, but is one of the same principle. It is, in all its parts, the regulation of the conduct of the officer of the Court in giving effect to its judgments. A general superintendence over this subject seems to be properly within the judicial province, and has been always so considered. It is, undoubtedly, proper for the legislature to prescribe the manner in which these ministerial offices shall be performed, and this duty will never be devolved on

any other department without urgent reasons. But, in the mode of obeying the mandate of a writ issuing from a Court, so much of that which may be done by the judiciary, under the authority of the legislature, seems to be blended with that for which the legislature must expressly and directly provide, that there is some difficulty in discerning the exact limits within which the legislature may avail itself of the agency of the Courts.

The difference between the departments undoubtedly is, that the legislature makes, the executive executes, and the judiciary construes the law; but the maker of the law may commit something to the discretion of the other departments, and the precise boundary of this power is a subject of delicate and difficult inquiry, into which a Court will not enter unnecessarily.

23 U.S. (10 Wheat.) at 42–43, 45–46.

e.   Marshall Field & Co. v. Clark, 143 U.S. 649, 12 S.Ct. 495, 36 L.Ed. 294 (1892)

Congress by statute provided for duty-free importation of such items as molasses, sugar, coffee, and tea, but specified that the statute's free-trade provisions with respect to any specific country could be suspended by the President if he determined that such country imposed "reciprocally unequal and unreasonable" trade restrictions on American exporters. The plaintiff claimed that this provision unconstitutionally delegated legislative power to the President. The Court rejected the delegation challenge in a lengthy discussion, part of which reads as follows:

That Congress cannot delegate legislative power to the President is a principle universally recognized as vital to the integrity and maintenance of the system of government ordained by the Constitution. The act * * * under consideration is not inconsistent with that principle. It does not, in any real sense, invest the President with the power of legislation * * *. Congress itself determined that the provisions of the act * * * permitting the free introduction of such articles, should be suspended as to any country producing and exporting them that imposed exactions and duties on the agricultural and other products of the United States, which the President deemed, that is, which he found to be, reciprocally unequal and unreasonable. Congress itself prescribed, in advance, the duties to be levied, collected and paid * * * while the suspension lasted. Nothing involving the expediency or the just operation of such legislation was left to the determination of the President * * *. [W]hen he ascertained the fact that duties and exactions, reciprocally unequal and unreasonable, were imposed upon the agricultural products of the

United States * * *, it became his duty to issue a proclamation declaring the suspension, as to that country, which Congress had determined should occur. He had no discretion in the premises except in respect to the duration of the suspension so ordered. But that related only to the enforcement of the policy established by Congress * * *. Legislative power was exercised when Congress declared that the suspension should take effect upon a named contingency. What the President was required to do was simply in execution of the act of Congress. It was not the making of law. He was the mere agent of the law-making department to ascertain and declare the event upon which its expressed will was to take effect.

Id. at 692–93, 12 S.Ct. at 504–505. Two Justices dissented, maintaining that the statute "certainly extends to the executive the exercise of those discretionary powers which the Constitution has vested in the law-making department." *Id.* at 699–700, 12 S.Ct. at 507 (Lamar, J., dissenting).

f.   J.W. Hampton, Jr., & Co. v. United States, 276 U.S. 394, 48 S.Ct. 348, 72 L.Ed. 624 (1928)

A statute authorized the President to alter the amount of a duty on certain imported merchandise in order to "equalize the * * * costs of production" between the United States and the exporting nation. The Court upheld the President's power under the statute against a delegation challenge. In oft-quoted language, the Court stated that the extent to which Congress can vest discretion in the executive or the courts must be determined "according to common sense and the inherent necessities of the governmental co-ordination." *Id.* at 406, 48 S.Ct. at 351. In another oft-quoted passage, the Court observed that "[i]f Congress shall lay down by legislative act an intelligible principle to which the person or body authorized to fix such rates is directed to conform, such legislative action is not a forbidden delegation of legislative power." *Id.* at 409, 48 S.Ct. at 352.

2.   THE NEW DEAL

PANAMA REFINING CO. V. RYAN
Supreme Court of the United States, 1935.
293 U.S. 388, 55 S.Ct. 241, 79 L.Ed. 446.

MR. CHIEF JUSTICE HUGHES delivered the opinion of the Court.

On July 11, 1933, the President, by Executive Order, prohibited "the transportation in interstate and foreign commerce of petroleum and the products thereof produced or withdrawn from storage in excess of the amount permitted to be produced or withdrawn from storage by any State law or valid regulation or order prescribed thereunder, by any board, commission, officer, or other duly authorized agency of a State." This action was based on § 9(c) of Title I of the National Industrial Recovery Act of June 16, 1933. That section provides:

* * *

"(c) The President is authorized to prohibit the transportation in interstate and foreign commerce of petroleum and the products thereof produced or withdrawn from storage in excess of the amount permitted to be produced or withdrawn from storage by any state law or valid regulation or order prescribed thereunder, by any board, commission, officer, or other duly authorized agency of a State. Any violation of any order of the President issued under the provisions of this subsection shall be punishable by fine of not to exceed $1,000, or imprisonment for not to exceed six months, or both."

* * *

* * * Section 9(c) is assailed upon the ground that it is an unconstitutional delegation of legislative power. The section purports to authorize the President to pass a prohibitory law. The subject to which this authority relates is defined. It is the transportation in interstate and foreign commerce of petroleum and petroleum products which are produced or withdrawn from storage in excess of the amount permitted by state authority. Assuming for the present purpose, without deciding, that the Congress has power to interdict the transportation of that excess in interstate and foreign commerce, the question whether that transportation shall be prohibited by law is obviously one of legislative policy. Accordingly, we look to the statute to see whether the Congress has declared a policy with respect to that subject; whether the Congress has set up a standard for the President's action; whether the Congress has required any finding by the President in the exercise of the authority to enact the prohibition.

Section 9(c) is brief and unambiguous. It does not attempt to control the production of petroleum and petroleum products within a State. It does not seek to lay down rules for the guidance of state legislatures or state officers. It leaves to the States and to their constituted authorities the determination of what production shall be permitted. It does not qualify the President's authority by reference to the basis, or extent, of the State's limitation of production. Section 9(c) does not state whether, or in what circumstances or under what conditions, the President is to prohibit the transportation of the amount of petroleum or petroleum products produced in excess of the State's permission. It establishes no criterion to govern the President's course. It does not require any finding by the President as a condition of his action. The Congress in § 9(c) thus declares no policy as to the transportation of the excess production. So far as this section is concerned, it gives to the President an unlimited authority to determine the policy and to lay down the prohibition, or not to lay it down, as he may see fit. And disobedience to his order is made a crime punishable by fine and imprisonment.

We examine the context to ascertain if it furnishes a declaration of policy or a standard of action, which can be deemed to relate to the subject of § 9(c) and thus to imply what is not there expressed * * *. [T]he other provisions of § 9 afford no ground for implying a limitation of the broad grant of authority in § 9(c) * * *.

We turn to the other provisions of Title I of the Act.

The first section is a "declaration of policy." It declares that a national emergency exists "which is productive of widespread unemployment and disorganization of industry, which burdens interstate and foreign commerce, affects public welfare, and undermines the standards of living of the American people." It is declared to be the policy of Congress "to remove obstructions to the free flow of interstate and foreign commerce which tend to diminish the amount thereof"; "to provide for the general welfare by promoting the organization of industry for the purpose of cooperative action among trade groups"; "to induce and maintain united action of labor and management under adequate governmental sanctions and supervision"; "to eliminate unfair competitive practices, to promote the fullest possible utilization of the present productive capacity of industries, to avoid undue restriction of production (except as may be temporarily required), to increase the consumption of industrial and agricultural products by increasing purchasing power, to reduce and relieve unemployment, to improve standards of labor, and otherwise to rehabilitate industry and to conserve natural resources."

This general outline of policy contains nothing as to the circumstances or conditions in which transportation of petroleum or petroleum products should be prohibited,—nothing as to the policy of prohibiting, or not prohibiting, the transportation of production exceeding what the States allow * * *. It is manifest that this broad outline is simply an introduction of the Act, leaving the legislative policy as to particular subjects to be declared and defined, if at all, by the subsequent sections.

* * *

* * * The question whether such a delegation of legislative power is permitted by the Constitution is not answered by the argument that it should be assumed that the President has acted, and will act, for what he believes to be the public good. The point is not one of motives but of constitutional authority, for which the best of motives is not a substitute * * *.

The Constitution provides that "All legislative powers herein granted shall be vested in a Congress of the United States, which shall consist of a

Senate and House of Representatives." Art. I, § 1. And the Congress is empowered "To make all laws which shall be necessary and proper for carrying into execution" its general powers. Art. I, § 8, par. 18. The Congress manifestly is not permitted to abdicate, or to transfer to others, the essential legislative functions with which it is thus vested. Undoubtedly legislation must often be adapted to complex conditions involving a host of details with which the national legislature cannot deal directly. The Constitution has never been regarded as denying to the Congress the necessary resources of flexibility and practicality, which will enable it to perform its function in laying down policies and establishing standards, while leaving to selected instrumentalities the making of subordinate rules within prescribed limits and the determination of facts to which the policy as declared by the legislature is to apply. Without capacity to give authorizations of that sort we should have the anomaly of a legislative power which in many circumstances calling for its exertion would be but a futility. But the constant recognition of the necessity and validity of such provisions, and the wide range of administrative authority which has been developed by means of them, cannot be allowed to obscure the limitations of the authority to delegate, if our constitutional system is to be maintained.

The Court has had frequent occasion to refer to these limitations and to review the course of congressional action * * *.

* * *

* * * [I]n every case in which the question has been raised, the Court has recognized that there are limits of delegation which there is no constitutional authority to transcend. We think that § 9(c) goes beyond those limits. As to the transportation of oil production in excess of state permission, the Congress has declared no policy, has established no standard, has laid down no rule. There is no requirement, no definition of circumstances and conditions in which the transportation is to be allowed or prohibited.

If § 9(c) were held valid, it would be idle to pretend that anything would be left of limitations upon the power of the Congress to delegate its lawmaking function * * *. The question is not of the intrinsic importance of the particular statute before us, but of the constitutional processes of legislation which are an essential part of our system of government.

* * *

MR. JUSTICE CARDOZO, dissenting.

* * *

I am persuaded that a reference, express or implied, to the policy of Congress as declared in § 1 is a sufficient definition of a standard to make the statute valid. Discretion is not unconfined and vagrant. It is canalized within banks that keep it from overflowing * * *. [T]he separation of powers between the Executive and Congress is not a doctrinaire concept to be made use of with pedantic rigor. There must be sensible approximation, there must be elasticity of adjustment, in response to the practical necessities of government, which cannot foresee today the developments of tomorrow in their nearly infinite variety * * *.

A. L. A. SCHECHTER POULTRY CORP. V. UNITED STATES
Supreme Court of the United States, 1935.
295 U.S. 495, 55 S.Ct. 837, 79 L.Ed. 1570.

MR. CHIEF JUSTICE HUGHES delivered the opinion of the Court.

Petitioners in No. 854 were convicted in the District Court of the United States for the Eastern District of New York on eighteen counts of an indictment charging violations of what is known as the "Live Poultry Code," and on an additional count for conspiracy to commit such violations * * *. [T]he defendants contended * * * that the Code had been adopted pursuant to an unconstitutional delegation by Congress of legislative power * * *.

* * *

The "Live Poultry Code" was promulgated under § 3 of the National Industrial Recovery Act. That section * * * authorizes the President to approve "codes of fair competition." Such a code may be approved for a trade or industry, upon application by one or more trade or industrial associations or groups, if the President finds (1) that such associations or groups "impose no inequitable restrictions on admission to membership therein and are truly representative," and (2) that such codes are not designed "to promote monopolies or to eliminate or oppress small enterprises and will not operate to discriminate against them, and will tend to effectuate the policy" of Title I of the Act * * *. Where such a code has not been approved, the President may prescribe one, either on his own motion or on complaint. Violation of any provision of a code (so approved or prescribed) "in any transaction in or affecting interstate or foreign commerce" is made a misdemeanor punishable by a fine of not more than $500 for each offense, and each day the violation continues is to be deemed a separate offense.

The "Live Poultry Code" was approved by the President on April 13, 1934 * * *.

* * *

The Code fixes the number of hours for work-days. It provides that no employee, with certain exceptions, shall be permitted to work in excess of forty (40) hours in any one week, and that no employee, save as stated, "shall be paid in any pay period less than at the rate of fifty (50) cents per hour." The article containing "general labor provisions" prohibits the employment of any person under sixteen years of age, and declares that employees shall have the right of "collective bargaining," and freedom of choice with respect to labor organizations, in the terms of § 7(a) of the Act. The minimum number of employees, who shall be employed by slaughterhouse operators, is fixed, the number being graduated according to the average volume of weekly sales.

* * *

The seventh article, containing "trade practice provisions," prohibits various practices which are said to constitute "unfair methods of competition" * * *.

* * *

* * * The Constitution provides that "All legislative powers herein granted shall be vested in a Congress of the United States, which shall consist of a Senate and House of Representatives." Art I, § 1. And the Congress is authorized "To make all laws which shall be necessary and proper for carrying into execution" its general powers. Art. I, § 8, par. 18. The Congress is not permitted to abdicate or to transfer to others the essential legislative functions with which it is thus vested * * *.

Accordingly, we look to the statute to see whether Congress has overstepped these limitations,—whether Congress in authorizing "codes of fair competition" has itself established the standards of legal obligation, thus performing its essential legislative function, or, by the failure to enact such standards, has attempted to transfer that function to others.

* * *

What is meant by "fair competition" as the term is used in the Act? Does it refer to a category established in the law, and is the authority to make codes limited accordingly? Or is it used as a convenient designation for whatever set of laws the formulators of a code for a particular trade or industry may propose and the President may approve (subject to certain restrictions), or the President may himself prescribe, as being wise and beneficent provisions for the government of the trade or industry in order to accomplish the broad purposes of rehabilitation, correction and expansion which are stated in the first section of Title I?

The Act does not define "fair competition." "Unfair competition," as known to the common law, is a limited concept. Primarily, and strictly, it relates to the palming off of one's goods as those of a rival trader. In recent years, its scope has been extended. It has been held to apply to misappropriation as well as misrepresentation, to the selling of another's goods as one's own,—to misappropriation of what equitably belongs to a competitor. Unfairness in competition has been predicated of acts which lie outside the ordinary course of business and are tainted by fraud, or coercion, or conduct otherwise prohibited by law. But it is evident that in its widest range, "unfair competition," as it has been understood in the law, does not reach the objectives of the codes which are authorized by the National Industrial Recovery Act. The codes may, indeed, cover conduct which existing law condemns, but they are not limited to conduct of that sort. The Government does not contend that the Act contemplates such a limitation. It would be opposed both to the declared purposes of the Act and to its administrative construction.

* * *

For a statement of the authorized objectives and content of the "codes of fair competition" we are referred repeatedly to the "Declaration of Policy" in section one of Title I of the Recovery Act. Thus, the approval of a code by the President is conditioned on his finding that it "will tend to effectuate the policy of this title." § 3(a) * * *. The "policy herein declared" is manifestly that set forth in section one. That declaration embraces a broad range of objectives * * *. It is there declared to be "the policy of Congress"—

> "to remove obstructions to the free flow of interstate and foreign commerce which tend to diminish the amount thereof; and to provide for the general welfare by promotion the organization of industry for the purpose of cooperative action among trade groups, to induce and maintain united action of labor and management under adequate governmental sanctions and supervision, to eliminate unfair competitive practices, to promote the fullest possible utilization of the present productive capacity of industries, to avoid undue restriction of production (except as may be temporarily required), to increase the consumption of industrial and agricultural products by increasing purchasing power, to reduce and relieve unemployment, to improve standards of labor, and otherwise to rehabilitate industry and to conserve natural resources."

Under § 3, whatever "may tend to effectuate" these general purposes may be included in the "codes of fair competition." We think the conclusion is inescapable that the authority sought to be conferred by § 3 was not merely to deal with "unfair competitive practices" which offend against existing law, and could be the subject of judicial condemnation without further legislation, or to create administrative machinery for the application of established principles of law to particular instances of violation. Rather, the purpose is clearly disclosed to authorize new and controlling prohibitions through codes of laws which would embrace what the formulators would propose, and what the President would approve, or prescribe, as wise and beneficent measures for the government of trades and industries in order to bring about their rehabilitation, correction and development, according to the general declaration of policy in section one. Codes of laws of this sort are styled "codes of fair competition."

* * *

* * * [W]ould it be seriously contended that Congress could delegate its legislative authority to trade or industrial associations or groups so as to empower them to enact the laws they deem to be wise and beneficent for the rehabilitation and expansion of their trade or industries? Could trade or industrial associations or groups be constituted legislative bodies for that purpose because such associations or groups are familiar with the problems of their enterprises? And, could an effort of that sort be made valid by such a preface of generalities as to permissible aims as we find in section 1 of title I? The answer is obvious. Such a delegation of legislative power is unknown to our law and is utterly inconsistent with the constitutional prerogatives and duties of Congress.

The question, then, turns upon the authority which § 3 of the Recovery Act vests in the President to approve or prescribe. If the codes have standing as penal statutes, this must be due to the effect of the executive action. But Congress cannot delegate legislative power to the President to exercise an unfettered discretion to make whatever laws he thinks may be needed or advisable for the rehabilitation and expansion of trade or industry.

Accordingly we turn to the Recovery Act to ascertain what limits have been set to the exercise of the President's discretion. *First*, the President, as a condition of approval, is required to find that the trade or industrial associations or groups which propose a code, "impose no inequitable restrictions on admission to membership" and are "truly representative." That condition, however, relates only to the status of the initiators of the new laws and not to the permissible scope of such laws. *Second*, the President is required to find that the code is not "designed to promote monopolies or to eliminate or oppress small enterprises and will not operate to discriminate against them." And, to this is added a proviso that the code "shall not permit monopolies or monopolistic practices." But these restrictions leave virtually untouched the field of policy envisaged by section one, and, in that wide field of legislative possibilities, the proponents of a code, refraining from monopolistic designs, may roam at will and the President may approve or disapprove their proposals as he may see fit * * *.

Nor is the breadth of the President's discretion left to the necessary implications of this limited requirement as to his findings. As already noted, the President in approving a code may impose his own conditions, adding to or taking from what is proposed, as "in his discretion" he thinks necessary "to effectuate the policy" declared by the Act. Of course, he has no less liberty when he prescribes a code on his own motion or on complaint, and he is free to prescribe one if a code has not been approved * * *. And this authority relates to a host of different trades and industries, thus extending the President's discretion to all the varieties of laws which he may deem to be beneficial in dealing with the vast array of commercial and industrial activities throughout the country.

Such a sweeping delegation of legislative power finds no support in the decisions upon which the Government especially relies * * *.

* * *

* * * Section 3 of the Recovery Act is without precedent. It supplies no standards for any trade, industry or activity. It does not undertake to prescribe rules of conduct to be applied to particular states of fact determined by appropriate administrative procedure. Instead of prescribing rules of conduct, it authorizes the making of codes to prescribe them. For that legislative undertaking, § 3 sets up no standards, aside from the statement of the general aims of rehabilitation, correction and expansion described in section one. In view of the scope of that broad declaration, and of the nature of the few restrictions that are imposed, the discretion of the President in approving or prescribing codes, and thus enacting laws for the government of trade and industry throughout the country, is virtually unfettered. We think that the code-making authority thus conferred is an unconstitutional delegation of legislative power.

* * *

MR. JUSTICE CARDOZO, concurring.

The delegated power of legislation which has found expression in this code is not canalized within banks that keep it from overflowing. It is unconfined and vagrant, if I may borrow my own words in an earlier opinion. *Panama Refining Co. v. Ryan*, 293 U.S. 388, 440.

* * *

3.   AFTER THE NEW DEAL

a.   Congressional Directives to Regulatory Agencies

1.   The Federal Communications Commission shall grant broadcast licenses to applicants "if public convenience, interest, or necessity will be served thereby * * *." 47 U.S.C. § 307 (2012) (enacted in 1934). This statute easily survived a nondelegation challenge in *National Broadcasting Co. v. United States*, 319 U.S. 190, 63 S.Ct. 997, 87 L.Ed. 1344 (1943).

2.   "It shall be the duty of the [Securities and Exchange] Commission * * * [t]o require * * * that each registered holding company * * * shall take such steps as the Commission shall find necessary to ensure that the

corporate structure * * * does not unduly or unnecessarily complicate the structure, or unfairly or inequitably distribute voting power among security holders * * *." 15 U.S.C. § 79k (2012) (enacted in 1935). This statute easily survived a nondelegation challenge in *American Power & Light Co. v. SEC*, 329 U.S. 90, 67 S.Ct. 133, 91 L.Ed. 103 (1946).

3.   The Emergency Price Control Act of 1942, 56 Stat. 23, instructed a federal Price Administrator to determine whether commodity prices "have risen or threaten to rise to an extent or in a manner inconsistent with the purposes of this Act," and, if he made such a determination, to fix prices at the level which "in his judgment will be generally fair and equitable and will effectuate the purposes of this Act." The Act's declared purposes were "to stabilize prices and to prevent speculative, unwarranted, and abnormal increases in prices and rents; to eliminate and prevent profiteering, hoarding, manipulation, speculation, and other disruptive practices * * *; to assure that defense appropriations are not dissipated by excessive prices; to protect persons with relatively fixed and limited incomes, consumers, wage earners, investors, and persons dependent on life insurance, annuities, and pensions, from undue impairment of their standard of living; to prevent hardships * * * which would result from abnormal increases in prices; to assist in securing adequate production of commodities and facilities; [and] to prevent a post emergency collapse of values * * *." This statute easily survived a nondelegation challenge in *Yakus v. United States*, 321 U.S. 414, 64 S.Ct. 660, 88 L.Ed. 834 (1944).

b.   The Modern Doctrine

MISTRETTA V. UNITED STATES

Supreme Court of the United States, 1989.
488 U.S. 361, 109 S.Ct. 647, 102 L.Ed.2d 714.

JUSTICE BLACKMUN delivered the opinion of the Court.

In this litigation, we granted certiorari * * * in order to consider the constitutionality of the Sentencing Guidelines promulgated by the United States Sentencing Commission. The Commission is a body created under the Sentencing Reform Act of 1984 (Act), as amended, 18 U.S.C. § 3551 et seq. * * *.

* * *

For almost a century, the Federal Government employed in criminal cases a system of indeterminate sentencing. Statutes specified the penalties for crimes but nearly always gave the sentencing judge wide discretion to decide whether the offender should be incarcerated and for how long, whether restraint, such as probation, should be imposed instead of imprisonment or fine. This indeterminate-sentencing system was supplemented by the utilization of parole, by which an offender was returned to society under the "guidance and control" of a parole officer.

* * *

Historically, federal sentencing—the function of determining the scope and extent of punishment—never has been thought to be assigned by the Constitution to the exclusive jurisdiction of any one of the three Branches of Government. Congress, of course, has the power to fix the sentence for a federal crime, and the scope of judicial discretion with respect to a sentence is subject to congressional control. Congress early abandoned fixed-sentence rigidity, however, and put in place a system of ranges within which the sentencer could choose the precise punishment. Congress delegated almost unfettered discretion to the sentencing judge to determine what the sentence should be within the customarily wide range so selected. This broad discretion was further enhanced by the power later granted the judge to suspend the sentence and by the resulting growth of an elaborate probation system. Also, with the advent of parole, Congress moved toward a "three-way sharing" of sentencing responsibility by granting corrections personnel in the Executive Branch the discretion to release a prisoner before the expiration of the sentence imposed by the judge. Thus, under the indeterminate-sentence system, Congress defined the maximum, the judge imposed a sentence within the statutory range (which he usually could replace with probation), and the Executive Branch's parole official eventually determined the actual duration of imprisonment.

Serious disparities in sentences, however, were common * * *.

* * * Fundamental and widespread dissatisfaction with the uncertainties and the disparities continued to be expressed. Congress had wrestled with the problem for more than a decade when, in 1984, it enacted the sweeping reforms that are at issue here.

* * *

The Act, as adopted, revises the old sentencing process in several ways:

1. It rejects imprisonment as a means of promoting rehabilitation, 28 U.S.C. § 994(k), and it states that punishment should serve retributive, educational, deterrent, and incapacitative goals, 18 U.S.C. § 3553(a)(2).

2. It consolidates the power that had been exercised by the sentencing judge and the Parole Commission to decide what punishment an offender should suffer. This is done by creating the United States Sentencing Commission, directing that Commission to devise guidelines to be used for sentencing, and prospectively abolishing the Parole Commission. 28 U.S.C. §§ 991, 994, and 995(a)(1).

3. It makes all sentences basically determinate. A prisoner is to be released at the completion of his sentence reduced only by any credit earned by good behavior while in custody. 18 U.S.C. §§ 3624(a) and (b).

4. It makes the Sentencing Commission's guidelines binding on the courts, although it preserves for the judge the discretion to depart from the guideline applicable to a particular case if the judge finds an aggravating or mitigating factor present that the Commission did not adequately consider when formulating guidelines. §§ 3553(a) and (b). The Act also requires the court to state its reasons for the sentence imposed and to give "the specific reason" for imposing a sentence different from that described in the guideline. § 3553(c).

5. It authorizes limited appellate review of the sentence. It permits a defendant to appeal a sentence that is above the defined range, and it permits the Government to appeal a sentence that is below that range. It also permits either side to appeal an incorrect application of the guideline. §§ 3742(a) and (b).

Thus, guidelines were meant to establish a range of determinate sentences for categories of offenses and defendants according to various specified factors, "among others." 28 U.S.C. §§ 994(b), (c), and (d). The maximum of the range ordinarily may not exceed the minimum by more than the greater of 25% or six months, and each sentence is to be within the limit provided by existing law. §§ 994(a) and (b)(2).

* * *

On December 10, 1987, John M. Mistretta (petitioner) and another were indicted in the United States District Court for the Western District of Missouri on three counts centering in a cocaine sale. Mistretta moved to have the promulgated Guidelines ruled unconstitutional on the grounds that the Sentencing Commission was constituted in violation of the established doctrine of separation of powers, and that Congress delegated excessive authority to the Commission to structure the Guidelines * * *.

* * *

Petitioner argues that in delegating the power to promulgate sentencing guidelines for every federal criminal offense to an independent Sentencing Commission, Congress has granted the Commission excessive legislative discretion in violation of the constitutionally based nondelegation doctrine. We do not agree.

The nondelegation doctrine is rooted in the principle of separation of powers that underlies our tripartite system of Government. The Constitution provides that "[a]ll legislative Powers herein granted shall be vested in a Congress of the United States," U.S. Const., Art. I, § 1, and we long have insisted that "the integrity and maintenance of the system of government ordained by the Constitution" mandate that Congress generally cannot delegate its legislative power to another Branch. *Field v. Clark*, 143 U.S. 649, 692 (1892). We also have recognized, however, that the separation-of-powers principle, and the nondelegation doctrine in particular, do not prevent Congress from obtaining the assistance of its coordinate Branches. In a passage now enshrined in our jurisprudence, Chief Justice Taft, writing for the Court, explained our approach to such cooperative ventures: "In determining what [Congress] may do in seeking assistance from another branch, the extent and character of that assistance must be fixed according to common sense and the inherent necessities of the government co-ordination." *J.W. Hampton, Jr., & Co. v. United States*, 276 U.S. 394, 406 (1928). So long as Congress "shall lay down by legislative act an intelligible principle to which the person or body authorized to [exercise the delegated authority] is directed to conform, such legislative action is not a forbidden delegation of legislative power." *Id.*, at 409.

Applying this "intelligible principle" test to congressional delegations, our jurisprudence has been driven by a practical understanding that in our increasingly complex society, replete with ever changing and more technical problems, Congress simply cannot do its job absent an ability to delegate power under broad general directives * * *. Accordingly, this Court has deemed it "constitutionally sufficient if Congress clearly delineates the general policy, the public agency which is to apply it, and the boundaries of this delegated authority." *American Power & Light Co. v. SEC*, 329 U.S. 90, 105 (1946).

Until 1935, this Court never struck down a challenged statute on delegation grounds. After invalidating in 1935 two statutes as excessive delegations, see *A. L. A. Schechter Poultry Corp. v. United States* and *Panama Refining Co. v. Ryan*, we have upheld, again without deviation, Congress' ability to delegate power under broad standards.[7] See, *e.g., Lichter v. United States*, 334 U.S. 742, 785–786 (1948) (upholding delegation of authority to determine excessive profits); *American Power & Light Co. v. SEC*, 329 U.S., at 105 (upholding delegation of authority to Securities and Exchange Commission to prevent unfair or inequitable distribution of voting power among security holders); *Yakus v. United States*, 321 U.S. 414, 426 (1944) (upholding delegation to Price Administrator to fix commodity prices that would be fair and equitable, and would effectuate purposes of Emergency Price Control Act of 1942); *FPC v. Hope Natural Gas Co.*, 320 U.S. 591, 600 (1944) (upholding delegation to Federal Power Commission to determine just and reasonable

---

[7]   In *Schechter* and *Panama Refining* the Court concluded that Congress had failed to articulate any policy or standard that would serve to confine the discretion of the authorities to whom Congress had delegated power. No delegation of the kind at issue in those cases is present here * * *. In recent years, our application of the nondelegation doctrine principally has been limited to the interpretation of statutory texts, and, more particularly, to giving narrow constructions to statutory delegations that might otherwise be thought to be unconstitutional. See, *e. g., Industrial Union Dept. v. American Petroleum Institute*, 448 U.S. 607, 646 (1980); *National Cable Television Assn. v. United States*, 415 U.S. 336, 342 (1974).

rates); *National Broadcasting Co. v. United States*, 319 U.S. 190, 225–226 (1943) (upholding delegation to Federal Communications Commission to regulate broadcast licensing "as public interest, convenience, or necessity" require).

In light of our approval of these broad delegations, we harbor no doubt that Congress' delegation of authority to the Sentencing Commission is sufficiently specific and detailed to meet constitutional requirements. Congress charged the Commission with three goals: to "assure the meeting of the purposes of sentencing as set forth" in the Act; to "provide certainty and fairness in meeting the purposes of sentencing, avoiding unwarranted sentencing disparities among defendants with similar records . . . while maintaining sufficient flexibility to permit individualized sentences," where appropriate; and to "reflect, to the extent practicable, advancement in knowledge of human behavior as it relates to the criminal justice process." 28 U.S.C. § 991(b)(1). Congress further specified four "purposes" of sentencing that the Commission must pursue in carrying out its mandate: "to reflect the seriousness of the offense, to promote respect for the law, and to provide just punishment for the offense"; "to afford adequate deterrence to criminal conduct"; "to protect the public from further crimes of the defendant"; and "to provide the defendant with needed . . . correctional treatment." 18 U.S.C. § 3553(a)(2).

In addition, Congress prescribed the specific tool—the guidelines system—for the Commission to use in regulating sentencing. More particularly, Congress directed the Commission to develop a system of "sentencing ranges" applicable "for each category of offense involving each category of defendant." 28 U.S.C. § 994(b). Congress instructed the Commission that these sentencing ranges must be consistent with pertinent provisions of Title 18 of the United States Code and could not include sentences in excess of the statutory maxima. Congress also required that for sentences of imprisonment, "the maximum of the range established for such a term shall not exceed the minimum of that range by more than the greater of 25 percent or 6 months, except that, if the minimum term of the range is 30 years or more, the maximum may be life imprisonment." § 994(b)(2). Moreover, Congress directed the Commission to use current average sentences "as a starting point" for its structuring of the sentencing ranges. § 994(m).

To guide the Commission in its formulation of offense categories, Congress directed it to consider seven factors: the grade of the offense; the aggravating and mitigating circumstances of the crime; the nature and degree of the harm caused by the crime; the community view of the gravity of the offense; the public concern generated by the crime; the deterrent effect that a particular sentence may have on others; and the current incidence of the offense. §§ 994(c)(1)–(7). Congress set forth 11 factors for the Commission to consider in establishing categories of defendants. These include the offender's age, education, vocational skills, mental and emotional condition, physical condition (including drug dependence), previous employment record, family ties and responsibilities, community ties, role in the offense, criminal history, and degree of dependence upon crime for a livelihood. § 994(d)(1)–(11). Congress also prohibited the Commission from considering the "race, sex, national origin, creed, and socioeconomic status of offenders," § 994(d), and instructed that the guidelines should reflect the "general inappropriateness" of considering certain other factors, such as current unemployment, that might serve as proxies for forbidden factors, § 994(e).

In addition to these overarching constraints, Congress provided even more detailed guidance to the Commission about categories of offenses and offender characteristics. Congress directed that guidelines require a term of confinement at or near the statutory maximum for certain crimes of violence and for drug offenses, particularly when committed by recidivists. § 994(h). Congress further directed that the Commission assure a substantial term of imprisonment for an offense constituting a third felony conviction, for a career felon, for one convicted of a managerial role in a racketeering enterprise, for a crime of violence by an offender on release from a prior felony conviction, and for an offense involving a substantial quantity of narcotics. § 994(i). Congress also instructed "that the guidelines reflect . . . the general appropriateness of imposing a term of imprisonment" for a crime of violence that resulted in serious bodily injury. On the other hand, Congress directed that guidelines reflect the general inappropriateness of imposing a sentence of imprisonment "in cases in which the defendant is a first offender who has not been convicted of a crime of violence or an otherwise serious offense." § 994(j). Congress also enumerated various aggravating and mitigating circumstances, such as, respectively, multiple offenses or substantial assistance to the Government, to be reflected in the guidelines. §§ 994(l) and (n). In other words, although Congress granted the Commission substantial discretion in formulating guidelines, in actuality it legislated a full hierarchy of punishment—from near maximum imprisonment, to substantial imprisonment, to some imprisonment, to alternatives—and stipulated the most important offense and offender characteristics to place defendants within these categories.

We cannot dispute petitioner's contention that the Commission enjoys significant discretion in formulating guidelines. The Commission does have discretionary authority to determine the relative severity of federal crimes and to assess the relative weight of the offender characteristics that Congress listed for the Commission to consider. See §§ 994(c) and (d) (Commission instructed to consider enumerated factors as it deems them to be relevant). The Commission also has significant discretion to determine which crimes have been punished too leniently, and which too severely. § 994(m). Congress has called upon the Commission to exercise its judgment about which types of crimes and which types of criminals are to be considered similar for the purposes of sentencing.

But our cases do not at all suggest that delegations of this type may not carry with them the need to exercise judgment on matters of policy. In *Yakus v. United States*, 321 U.S. 414 (1944), the Court upheld a delegation to the Price Administrator to fix commodity prices that "in his judgment will be generally fair and equitable and will effectuate the purposes of this Act" to stabilize prices and avert speculation. See *id.,* at 420. In *National Broadcasting Co. v. United States*, 319 U.S. 190 (1943), we upheld a delegation to the Federal Communications Commission granting it the authority to promulgate regulations in accordance with its view of the "public interest." In *Yakus*, the Court laid down the applicable principle:

> "It is no objection that the determination of facts and the inferences to be drawn from them in the light of the statutory standards and declaration of policy call for the exercise of judgment, and for the formulation of subsidiary administrative policy within the prescribed statutory framework. . .

* * *

> ". . . Only if we could say that there is an absence of standards for the guidance of the Administrator's action, so that it would be impossible in a proper proceeding to ascertain whether the will of Congress has been obeyed, would we be justified in overriding its choice of means for effecting its declared purpose. . ." 321 U.S., at 425–426.

Congress has met that standard here. The Act sets forth more than merely an "intelligible principle" or minimal standards. One court has aptly put it: "The statute outlines the policies which prompted establishment of the Commission, explains what the Commission should do and how it should do it, and sets out specific directives to govern particular situations." *United States v. Chambless*, 680 F. Supp. 793, 796 (ED La.1988).

Developing proportionate penalties for hundreds of different crimes by a virtually limitless array of offenders is precisely the sort of intricate, labor-intensive task for which delegation to an expert body is especially appropriate. Although Congress has delegated significant discretion to the Commission to draw judgments from its analysis of existing sentencing practice and alternative sentencing models, "Congress is not confined to that method of executing its policy which involves the least possible delegation of discretion to administrative officers." *Yakus v. United States*, 321 U.S., at 425–426. We have no doubt that in the hands of the Commission "the criteria which Congress has supplied are wholly adequate for carrying out the general policy and purpose" of the Act. *Sunshine Anthracite Coal Co. v. Adkins*, 310 U.S. 381, 398 (1940).

* * *

JUSTICE SCALIA, dissenting.

While the products of the Sentencing Commission's labors have been given the modest name "Guidelines," see 28 U.S.C. § 994(a)(1), they have the force and effect of laws, prescribing the sentences criminal defendants are to receive. A judge who disregards them will be reversed. I dissent from today's decision because I can find no place within our constitutional system for an agency created by Congress to exercise no governmental power other than the making of laws.

* * *

It should be apparent * * * that the decisions made by the Commission are far from technical, but are heavily laden (or ought to be) with value judgments and policy assessments. This fact is sharply reflected in the Commission's product, as described by the dissenting Commissioner:

> "Under the guidelines, the judge could give the same sentence for abusive sexual contact that puts the child in fear as for unlawfully entering or remaining in the United States. Similarly, the guidelines permit equivalent sentences for the following pairs of offenses: drug trafficking and a violation of the Wild Free-Roaming Horses and Burros Act; arson with a destructive device and failure to surrender a cancelled naturalization certificate; operation of a common carrier under the influence of drugs that causes injury and alteration of one motor vehicle identification number; illegal trafficking in explosives and trespass; interference with a flight attendant and unlawful conduct relating to contraband cigarettes; aggravated assault and smuggling $11,000 worth of fish." Dissenting View of Commissioner Paul H. Robinson on the Promulgation of the Sentencing Guidelines by the United States Sentencing Commission 6–7 (May 1, 1987) (citations omitted).

Petitioner's most fundamental and far-reaching challenge to the Commission is that Congress' commitment of such broad policy responsibility to any institution is an unconstitutional delegation of legislative power. It is difficult to imagine a principle more essential to democratic government than that upon which the doctrine of unconstitutional delegation is founded: Except in a few areas constitutionally committed to the Executive Branch, the basic policy decisions governing society are to be made by the Legislature. Our Members of Congress could not, even if they wished, vote all power to the President and adjourn *sine die*.

But while the doctrine of unconstitutional delegation is unquestionably a fundamental element of our constitutional system, it is not an element readily enforceable by the courts. Once it is conceded, as it must be, that no statute can be entirely precise, and that some judgments, even some judgments involving policy considerations, must be left to the officers executing the law and to the judges applying it, the debate over unconstitutional delegation becomes a debate not over a point of principle but over a question of degree * * *. As the Court points out, we have invoked the doctrine of unconstitutional delegation to invalidate a law only twice in our history, over half a century ago. See *Panama Refining Co. v. Ryan*, 293 U.S. 388 (1935); *A.L.A. Schechter Poultry Corp. v. United States*, 295 U.S. 495 (1935). What legislated standard, one must wonder, can possibly be too vague to survive judicial scrutiny, when we have repeatedly upheld, in various contexts, a "public interest" standard? See, *e. g., National Broadcasting Co. v. United States*, 319 U.S. 190, 216–217 (1943); *New York Central Securities Corp. v. United States*, 287 U.S. 12, 24–25 (1932).

In short, I fully agree with the Court's rejection of petitioner's contention that the doctrine of unconstitutional delegation of legislative authority has been violated because of the lack of intelligible, congressionally prescribed standards to guide the Commission.

* * *

Precisely because the scope of delegation is largely uncontrollable by the courts, we must be particularly rigorous in preserving the Constitution's structural restrictions that deter excessive delegation. The major one, it seems to me, is that the power to make law cannot be exercised by anyone other than Congress, except in conjunction with the lawful exercise of executive or judicial power.

The whole theory of *lawful* congressional "delegation" is not that Congress is sometimes too busy or too divided and can therefore assign its responsibility of making law to someone else; but rather that a certain degree of discretion, and thus of lawmaking, *inheres* in most executive or judicial action, and it is up to Congress, by the relative specificity or generality of its statutory commands, to determine—up to a point—how small or how large that degree shall be. Thus, the courts could be given the power to say precisely what constitutes a "restraint of trade," see *Standard Oil Co. of New Jersey v. United States*, 221 U.S. 1 (1911), or to adopt rules of procedure, see *Sibbach v. Wilson & Co.*, 312 U.S. 1, 18 (1941), or to prescribe by rule the manner in which their officers shall execute their judgments, *Wayman v. Southard*, 10 Wheat. 1, 45 (1825), because that "lawmaking" was ancillary to their exercise of judicial powers. And the Executive could be given the power to adopt policies and rules specifying in detail what radio and television licenses will be in the "public interest, convenience or necessity," because that was ancillary to the exercise of its executive powers in granting and policing licenses and making a "fair and equitable allocation" of the electromagnetic spectrum. See *Federal Radio Comm'n v. Nelson Brothers Bond & Mortgage Co.*, 289 U.S. 266, 285 (1933). Or to take examples closer to the case before us: Trial judges could be given the power to determine what factors justify a greater or lesser sentence within the statutorily prescribed limits because that was ancillary to their exercise of the judicial power of pronouncing sentence upon individual defendants. And the President, through the Parole Commission subject to his appointment and removal, could be given the power to issue Guidelines specifying when parole would be available, because that was ancillary to the President's exercise of the executive power to hold and release federal prisoners.

* * *

The focus of controversy, in the long line of our so-called excessive delegation cases, has been whether the *degree* of generality contained in the authorization for exercise of executive or judicial powers in a particular field is so unacceptably high as to *amount to* a delegation of legislative powers. I say "so-called excessive delegation" because although that convenient terminology is often used, what is really at issue is whether there has been any delegation of legislative power, which occurs (rarely) when Congress authorizes the exercise of executive or judicial power without adequate standards. Strictly speaking, there is *no* acceptable delegation of legislative power * * *. In the present case, however, a pure delegation of legislative power is precisely what we have before us. It is irrelevant whether the standards are adequate, because they are not standards related to the exercise of executive or judicial powers; they are, plainly and simply, standards for further legislation.

The lawmaking function of the Sentencing Commission is completely divorced from any responsibility for execution of the law or adjudication of private rights under the law * * *. The only functions it performs, apart from prescribing the law * * *, are data collection and intragovernmental advice giving and education. These latter activities—similar to functions performed by congressional agencies and even congressional staff—neither determine nor affect private rights, and do not constitute an exercise of governmental power. And the Commission's lawmaking is completely divorced from the exercise of judicial powers since, not being a court, it has no judicial powers itself, nor is it subject to the control of any other body with judicial powers. The power to make law at issue here, in other words, is not ancillary but quite naked. The situation is no different in principle from what would exist if Congress gave the same power of writing sentencing laws to a congressional agency such as the General Accounting Office, or to members of its staff.

The delegation of lawmaking authority to the Commission is, in short, unsupported by any legitimating theory to explain why it is not a delegation of legislative power * * *.

* * *

Today's decision follows the regrettable tendency of our recent separation-of-powers jurisprudence to treat the Constitution as though it were no more than a generalized prescription that the functions of the Branches should not be commingled too much—how much is too much to be determined, case-by-case, by this Court. The Constitution is not that. Rather, as its name suggests, it is a prescribed structure, a framework, for the conduct of government. In designing that structure, the Framers *themselves* considered how much commingling was, in the generality of things, acceptable, and set forth their conclusions in the document * * *. Consideration of the degree of commingling that a particular disposition produces may be appropriate at the margins, where the outline of the framework itself is not clear; but it seems to me far from a marginal question whether our constitutional structure allows for a body which is not the Congress, and yet exercises no governmental powers except the making of rules that have the effect of laws.

I think the Court errs, in other words, not so much because it mistakes the degree of commingling, but because it fails to recognize that this case is not about commingling, but about the creation of a new Branch altogether, a sort of junior varsity Congress. It may well be that in some circumstances such a Branch would be desirable; perhaps the agency before us here will prove to be so. But there are many desirable dispositions that do not accord with the constitutional structure we live under. And in the long run the improvisation of a constitutional structure on the basis of currently perceived utility will be disastrous.

NOTES

The nondelegation doctrine enjoyed one very brief and very modest revival in the decade before *Mistretta*. The following case is important both as a contribution to the law on delegation and as a good introduction to the problems of policymaking in the modern administrative state.

INDUSTRIAL UNION DEP'T, AFL-CIO v. AMERICAN PETROLEUM INST.

Supreme Court of the United States, 1980.
448 U.S. 607, 100 S.Ct. 2844, 65 L.Ed.2d 1010.

MR. JUSTICE STEVENS announced the judgment of the Court and delivered an opinion, in which THE CHIEF JUSTICE and MR. JUSTICE STEWART joined and in Parts I, II, III-A, III-B, III-C, and III-E of which MR. JUSTICE POWELL joined.

The Occupational Safety and Health Act of 1970 (Act), 84 Stat. 1590, 29 U. S. C. § 651 *et seq.*, was enacted for the purpose of ensuring safe and healthful working conditions for every working man and woman in the Nation. This litigation concerns a standard promulgated by the Secretary of Labor to regulate occupational exposure to benzene, a substance which has been shown to cause cancer at high exposure levels. The principal question is whether such a showing is a sufficient basis for a standard that places the most stringent limitation on exposure to benzene that is technologically and economically possible.

The Act delegates broad authority to the Secretary to promulgate different kinds of standards. The basic definition of an "occupational safety and health standard" is found in § 3(8), which provides:

"The term 'occupational safety and health standard' means a standard which requires conditions, or the adoption or use of one or more practices, means, methods, operations, or processes, reasonably necessary or appropriate to provide safe or healthful employment and places of employment." 84 Stat. 1591, 29 U.S.C. § 652(8).

Where toxic materials or harmful physical agents are concerned, a standard must also comply with § 6(b)(5), which provides:

"The Secretary, in promulgating standards dealing with toxic materials or harmful physical agents under this subsection, shall set the standard which most adequately assures, to the extent feasible, on the basis of the best available evidence, that no employee will suffer material impairment of health or functional capacity even if such employee has regular exposure to the hazard dealt with by such standard for the period of his working life. Development of standards under this subsection shall be based upon research, demonstrations, experiments, and such other information as may be appropriate. In addition to the attainment of the highest degree of health and safety protection for the employee, other considerations shall be the latest available scientific data in the field, the feasibility of the standards, and experience gained under this and other health and safety laws." 84 Stat. 1594, 29 U.S.C. § 655(b)(5).

Wherever the toxic material to be regulated is a carcinogen, the Secretary has taken the position that no safe exposure level can be determined and that § 6(b)(5) requires him to set an exposure limit at the lowest technologically feasible level that will not impair the viability of the industries regulated. In this case, after having determined that there is a causal connection between benzene and leukemia (a cancer of the white blood cells), the Secretary set an exposure limit on airborne concentrations of benzene of one part benzene per million parts of air (1 ppm), regulated dermal and eye contact with solutions containing benzene, and imposed complex monitoring and medical testing requirements on employers whose workplaces contain 0.5 ppm or more of benzene.

* * *

* * * [We conclude that] § 3(8) requires the Secretary to find, as a threshold matter, that the toxic substance in question poses a significant health risk in the workplace and that a new, lower standard is therefore "reasonably necessary or appropriate to provide safe or healthful employment and places of employment." Unless and until such a finding is made, it is not necessary to address the further question whether the Court of Appeals correctly held that there must be a reasonable correlation between costs and benefits, or whether, as the federal parties argue, the Secretary is then required by § 6(b)(5) to promulgate a standard that goes as far as technologically and economically possible to eliminate the risk.

* * *

I

Benzene is a familiar and important commodity. It is a colorless, aromatic liquid that evaporates rapidly under ordinary atmospheric conditions. Approximately 11 billion pounds of benzene were produced in the United States in 1976. Ninety-four percent of that total was produced by the petroleum and petrochemical industries, with the remainder produced by the steel industry as a byproduct of coking operations. Benzene is used in manufacturing a variety of products including motor fuels (which may contain as much as 2% benzene), solvents, detergents, pesticides, and other organic chemicals.

The entire population of the United States is exposed to small quantities of benzene, ranging from a few parts per billion to 0.5 ppm, in the ambient air. Over one million workers are subject to additional low-level exposures as a consequence of their employment. The majority of these employees work in gasoline service stations, benzene production (petroleum refineries and coking operations), chemical processing, benzene transportation, rubber manufacturing, and laboratory operations.

Benzene is a toxic substance. Although it could conceivably cause harm to a person who swallowed or touched it, the principal risk of harm comes from inhalation of benzene vapors. When these vapors are inhaled, the benzene diffuses through the lungs and is quickly absorbed into the blood. Exposure to high concentrations produces an almost immediate effect on the central nervous system * * *. Persistent exposures at levels above 25–40 ppm may lead to blood deficiencies and diseases of the blood-forming organs, including aplastic anemia, which is generally fatal.

Industrial health experts have long been aware that exposure to benzene may lead to various types of nonmalignant diseases. By 1948 the evidence connecting high levels of benzene to serious blood disorders had become so strong that the Commonwealth of Massachusetts imposed a 35 ppm limitation on workplaces within its jurisdiction. In 1969 the American National Standards Institute (ANSI) adopted a national consensus standard of 10 ppm averaged over an 8-hour period with a ceiling concentration of 25 ppm for 10-minute periods or a maximum peak concentration of 50 ppm. In 1971, after the Occupational Safety and Health Act was passed, the Secretary adopted this consensus standard as the federal standard, pursuant to 29 U.S.C. § 655(a).

As early as 1928, some health experts theorized that there might also be a connection between benzene in the workplace and leukemia. In the late 1960's and early 1970's a number of epidemiological studies were published indicating that workers exposed to high concentrations of benzene were subject to a significantly increased risk of leukemia. In a 1974 report recommending a permanent standard for benzene, the National Institute for Occupational Safety and Health (NIOSH), OSHA's research arm, noted that these studies raised the "distinct possibility" that benzene caused leukemia. But, in light of the fact that all known cases had occurred at very high exposure levels, NIOSH declined to recommend a change in the 10 ppm standard, which it considered sufficient to protect against nonmalignant diseases. NIOSH suggested that further studies were necessary to determine conclusively whether there was a link between benzene and leukemia and, if so, what exposure levels were dangerous.

Between 1974 and 1976 additional studies were published which tended to confirm the view that benzene can cause leukemia, at least when exposure levels are high. In an August 1976 revision of its earlier recommendation, NIOSH stated that these studies provided "conclusive" proof of a causal connection between benzene and leukemia. Although it acknowledged that none of the intervening studies had provided the dose-response data it had found lacking two years earlier, NIOSH nevertheless recommended that the exposure limit be set as low as possible. As a result of this recommendation, OSHA contracted with a consulting firm to do a study on the costs to industry of complying with the 10 ppm standard then in effect or, alternatively, with whatever standard would be the lowest feasible.

In October 1976, NIOSH sent another memorandum to OSHA, seeking acceleration of the rulemaking process and "strongly" recommending the issuance of an emergency temporary standard pursuant to § 6(c) of the Act, 29 U.S.C. § 655(c), for benzene and two other chemicals believed to be carcinogens. NIOSH recommended that a 1 ppm exposure limit be imposed for benzene. Apparently because of the NIOSH recommendation, OSHA asked its consultant to determine the cost of complying with a 1 ppm standard instead of with the "minimum feasible" standard. It also issued voluntary guidelines for benzene, recommending that exposure levels be limited to 1 ppm on an 8-hour time-weighted average basis wherever possible.

In the spring of 1976, NIOSH had selected two Pliofilm plants in St. Marys and Akron, Ohio, for an epidemiological study of the link between leukemia and benzene exposure. In April 1977, NIOSH forwarded an interim report to OSHA indicating at least a fivefold increase in the expected incidence of leukemia for workers who had been exposed to benzene at the two plants from 1940 to 1949. The report submitted to OSHA erroneously suggested that exposures in the two plants had generally been between zero and 15 ppm during the period in question.[16] As a result of this new evidence and the continued prodding of NIOSH, OSHA did issue an emergency standard, effective May 21, 1977, reducing the benzene exposure limit from 10 ppm to 1 ppm, the ceiling for exposures of up to 10 minutes from 25 ppm to 5 ppm, and eliminating the authority for peak concentrations of 50 ppm. In its explanation accompanying the emergency standard, OSHA stated that benzene had been shown to cause leukemia at exposures below 25 ppm and that, in light of its consultant's report, it was feasible to reduce the exposure limit to 1 ppm.

On May 19, 1977, the Court of Appeals for the Fifth Circuit entered a temporary restraining order preventing the emergency standard from taking effect. Thereafter, OSHA abandoned its efforts to make the

---

[16] The authors' statement with respect to exposure levels was based on a 1946 report by the Ohio Industrial Commission indicating that, after some new ventilation equipment had been installed, exposures at the St. Marys plant had been brought within "safe" limits, in most instances ranging from zero to 10 to 15 ppm. As the authors later admitted, the level considered "safe" in 1946 was 100 ppm. Moreover, only one of the seven workers who died of leukemia had begun working at St. Marys after 1946. Five of the others had worked at the Akron plant, which employed 310 of the 748 workers surveyed. A 1948 report by the Ohio Department of Health indicated exposure levels at the Akron plant of well over 100 ppm, with excursions in some areas up to 1,000 ppm. Surveys taken in the intervening years, as well as testimony by St. Marys employees at the hearing on the proposed standard, indicated that both of the plants may have had relatively high exposures through the 1970's.

Industry representatives argued at the hearing that this evidence indicated that the exposure levels had been very high, as they had been in the other epidemiological studies conducted in the past. NIOSH witnesses, however, simply stated that actual exposure levels for the years in question could not be determined; they did agree, however, that their study should *not* be taken as proof of a fivefold increase in leukemia risk at 10–15 ppm. In its explanation of the permanent standard, OSHA agreed with the NIOSH witnesses that no dose-response relationship could be inferred from the study * * *.

emergency standard effective and instead issued a proposal for a permanent standard patterned almost entirely after the aborted emergency standard.

In its published statement giving notice of the proposed permanent standard, OSHA did not ask for comments as to whether or not benzene presented a significant health risk at exposures of 10 ppm or less. Rather, it asked for comments as to whether 1 ppm was the minimum feasible exposure limit. As OSHA's Deputy Director of Health Standards, Grover Wrenn, testified at the hearing, this formulation of the issue to be considered by the Agency was consistent with OSHA's general policy with respect to carcinogens. Whenever a carcinogen is involved, OSHA will presume that no safe level of exposure exists in the absence of clear proof establishing such a level and will accordingly set the exposure limit at the lowest level feasible. The proposed 1 ppm exposure limit in this case thus was established not on the basis of a proven hazard at 10 ppm, but rather on the basis of "OSHA's best judgment at the time of the proposal of the feasibility of compliance with the proposed standard by the [affected] industries." Given OSHA's cancer policy, it was in fact irrelevant whether there was any evidence at all of a leukemia risk at 10 ppm. The important point was that there was no evidence that there was not some risk, however small, at that level. The fact that OSHA did not ask for comments on whether there was a safe level of exposure for benzene was indicative of its further view that a demonstration of such absolute safety simply could not be made.

Public hearings were held on the proposed standard, commencing on July 19, 1977. The final standard was issued on February 10, 1978. In its final form, the benzene standard is designed to protect workers from whatever hazards are associated with low-level benzene exposures by requiring employers to monitor workplaces to determine the level of exposure, to provide medical examinations when the level rises above 0.5 ppm, and to institute whatever engineering or other controls are necessary to keep exposures at or below 1 ppm.

* * *

The permanent standard is expressly inapplicable to the storage, transportation, distribution, sale, or use of gasoline or other fuels subsequent to discharge from bulk terminals. This exception is particularly significant in light of the fact that over 795,000 gas station employees, who are exposed to an average of 102,700 gallons of gasoline (containing up to 2% benzene) annually, are thus excluded from the protection of the standard.

As presently formulated, the benzene standard is an expensive way of providing some additional protection for a relatively small number of employees. According to OSHA's figures, the standard will require capital investments in engineering controls of approximately $266 million, first-year operating costs (for monitoring, medical testing, employee training, and respirators) of $187 million to $205 million and recurring annual costs of approximately $34 million. The figures outlined in OSHA's explanation of the costs of compliance to various industries indicate that only 35,000 employees would gain any benefit from the regulation in terms of a reduction in their exposure to benzene. Over two-thirds of these workers (24,450) are employed in the rubber-manufacturing industry. Compliance costs in that industry are estimated to be rather low with no capital costs and initial operating expenses estimated at only $34 million ($1,390 per employee); recurring annual costs would also be rather low, totaling less than $1 million. By contrast, the segment of the petroleum refining industry that produces benzene would be required to incur $24 million in capital costs and $600,000 in first-year operating expenses to provide additional protection for 300 workers ($82,000 per employee), while the petrochemical industry would be required to incur $20.9 million in capital costs and $1 million in initial operating expenses for the benefit of 552 employees ($39,675 per employee).

Although OSHA did not quantify the benefits to each category of worker in terms of decreased exposure to benzene, it appears from the economic impact study done at OSHA's direction that those benefits may be relatively small. Thus, although the current exposure limit is 10 ppm, the actual exposures outlined in that study are often considerably lower. For example, for the period 1970–1975 the petrochemical industry reported that, out of a total of 496 employees exposed to benzene, only 53 were exposed to levels between 1 and 5 ppm and only 7 (all at the same plant) were exposed to between 5 and 10 ppm.

II

The critical issue at this point in the litigation is whether the Court of Appeals was correct in refusing to enforce the 1 ppm exposure limit on the ground that it was not supported by appropriate findings.

Any discussion of the 1 ppm exposure limit must, of course, begin with the Agency's rationale for imposing that limit. The written explanation of the standard fills 184 pages of the printed appendix. Much of it is devoted to a discussion of the voluminous evidence of the adverse effects of exposure to benzene at levels of concentration well above 10 ppm. This discussion demonstrates that there is ample justification for regulating occupational exposure to benzene and that the prior limit of 10 ppm, with a ceiling of 25 ppm (or a peak of 50 ppm) was reasonable. It does not, however, provide direct support for the Agency's conclusion that the limit should be reduced from 10 ppm to 1 ppm.

The evidence in the administrative record of adverse effects of benzene exposure at 10 ppm is sketchy at best. OSHA noted that there was "no dispute" that certain nonmalignant blood disorders, evidenced by a reduction in the level of red or white cells or platelets in the blood, could result from exposures of 25–40 ppm. It then stated that several studies had indicated that relatively slight changes in normal blood values could result from exposures below 25 ppm and perhaps below 10 ppm. OSHA did not attempt to make any estimate based on these studies of how significant the risk of nonmalignant disease would be at exposures of 10 ppm or less. Rather, it stated that because of the lack of data concerning the linkage between low-level exposures and blood abnormalities, it was impossible to construct a dose-response curve at this time.[33] OSHA did conclude, however, that the studies demonstrated that the current 10 ppm exposure limit was inadequate to ensure that no single worker would suffer a nonmalignant blood disorder as a result of benzene exposure. Noting that it is "customary" to set a permissible exposure limit by applying a safety factor of 10–100 to the lowest level at which adverse effects had been observed, the Agency stated that the evidence supported the conclusion that the limit should be set at a point "substantially less than 10 ppm" even if benzene's leukemic effects were not considered. OSHA did not state, however, that the nonmalignant effects of benzene exposure justified a reduction in the permissible exposure limit to 1 ppm.

* * *

With respect to leukemia, evidence of an increased risk (i.e., a risk greater than that borne by the general population) due to benzene exposures at or below 10 ppm was even sketchier. Once OSHA acknowledged that the NIOSH study it had relied upon in promulgating the emergency standard did not support its earlier view that benzene had been shown to cause leukemia at concentrations below 25 ppm, there was only one study that provided any evidence of such an increased risk. That study, conducted by the Dow Chemical Co., uncovered three leukemia deaths, versus 0.2 expected deaths, out of a population of 594 workers; it appeared that the three workers had never been exposed to more than 2 to 9 ppm of benzene. The authors of the study, however, concluded that it could not be viewed as proof of a relationship between low-level benzene exposure and leukemia because all three workers had probably been occupationally exposed to a number of other potentially carcinogenic chemicals at other points in their careers and because no leukemia deaths

---

[33] "A dose-response curve shows the relationship between different exposure levels and the risk of cancer [or any other disease] associated with those exposure levels. Generally, exposure to higher levels carries with it a higher risk, and exposure to lower levels is accompanied by a reduced risk." 581 F.2d, at 504, n. 24.

OSHA's comments with respect to the insufficiency of the data were addressed primarily to the lack of data at low exposure levels. OSHA did not discuss whether it was possible to make a rough estimate, based on the more complete epidemiological and animal studies done at higher exposure levels, of the significance of the risks attributable to those levels, nor did it discuss whether it was possible to extrapolate from such estimates to derive a risk estimate for low-level exposures.

had been uncovered among workers who had been exposed to much higher levels of benzene. In its explanation of the permanent standard, OSHA stated that the possibility that these three leukemias had been caused by benzene exposure could not be ruled out and that the study, although not evidence of an increased risk of leukemia at 10 ppm, was therefore "consistent with the findings of many studies that there is an excess leukemia risk among benzene exposed employees." The Agency made no finding that the Dow study, any other empirical evidence, or any opinion testimony demonstrated that exposure to benzene at or below the 10 ppm level had ever in fact caused leukemia * * *.

In the end OSHA's rationale for lowering the permissible exposure limit to 1 ppm was based, not on any finding that leukemia has ever been caused by exposure to 10 ppm of benzene and that it will not be caused by exposure to 1 ppm, but rather on a series of assumptions indicating that some leukemias might result from exposure to 10 ppm and that the number of cases might be reduced by reducing the exposure level to 1 ppm. In reaching that result, the Agency first unequivocally concluded that benzene is a human carcinogen. Second, it concluded that industry had failed to prove that there is a safe threshold level of exposure to benzene below which no excess leukemia cases would occur. In reaching this conclusion OSHA rejected industry contentions that certain epidemiological studies indicating no excess risk of leukemia among workers exposed at levels below 10 ppm were sufficient to establish that the threshold level of safe exposure was at or above 10 ppm.[37] It also rejected an industry witness' testimony that a dose-response curve could be constructed on the basis of the reported epidemiological studies and that this curve indicated that reducing the permissible exposure limit from 10 to 1 ppm would prevent at most one leukemia and one other cancer death every six years.

Third, the Agency applied its standard policy with respect to carcinogens, concluding that, in the absence of definitive proof of a safe level, it must be assumed that *any* level above zero presents *some* increased risk of cancer.[40] As the federal parties point out in their brief, there are a

---

[37] In rejecting these studies, OSHA stated that: "Although the epidemiological method can provide strong evidence of a causal relationship between exposure and disease in the case of positive findings, it is by its very nature relatively crude and an insensitive measure." After noting a number of specific ways in which such studies are often defective, the Agency stated that it is "OSHA's policy when evaluating negative studies, to hold them to higher standards of methodological accuracy." Viewing the industry studies in this light, OSHA concluded that each of them had sufficient methodological defects to make them unreliable indicators of the safety of low-level exposures to benzene.

[40] "As stated above, the positive studies on benzene demonstrate the causal relationship of benzene to the induction of leukemia. Although these studies, for the most part involve high exposure levels, it is OSHA's view that once the carcinogenicity of a substance has been established qualitatively, any exposure must be considered to be attended by risk when considering any given population. OSHA therefore believes that occupational exposure to benzene at low levels poses a carcinogenic risk to workers." 43 Fed. Reg. 5932 (1978).

number of scientists and public health specialists who subscribe to this view, theorizing that a susceptible person may contract cancer from the absorption of even one molecule of a carcinogen like benzene.

Fourth, the Agency reiterated its view of the Act, stating that it was required by § 6(b)(5) to set the standard either at the level that has been demonstrated to be safe or at the lowest level feasible, whichever is higher. If no safe level is established, as in this case, the Secretary's interpretation of the statute automatically leads to the selection of an exposure limit that is the lowest feasible. Because of benzene's importance to the economy, no one has ever suggested that it would be feasible to eliminate its use entirely, or to try to limit exposures to the small amounts that are omnipresent. Rather, the Agency selected 1 ppm as a workable exposure level, and then determined that compliance with that level was technologically feasible and that "the economic impact of . . . [compliance] will not be such as to threaten the financial welfare of the affected firms or the general economy." It therefore held that 1 ppm was the minimum feasible exposure level within the meaning of § 6(b)(5) of the Act.

Finally, although the Agency did not refer in its discussion of the pertinent legal authority to any duty to identify the anticipated benefits of the new standard, it did conclude that some benefits were likely to result from reducing the exposure limit from 10 ppm to 1 ppm. This conclusion was based, again, not on evidence, but rather on the assumption that the risk of leukemia will decrease as exposure levels decrease. Although the Agency had found it impossible to construct a dose-response curve that would predict with any accuracy the number of leukemias that could be expected to result from exposures at 10 ppm, at 1 ppm, or at any intermediate level, it nevertheless "determined that the benefits of the proposed standard are likely to be appreciable." In light of the Agency's disavowal of any ability to determine the numbers of employees likely to be adversely affected by exposures of 10 ppm, the Court of Appeals held this finding to be unsupported by the record.

It is noteworthy that at no point in its lengthy explanation did the Agency quote or even cite §§ 3(8) of the Act. It made no finding that any of the provisions of the new standard were "reasonably necessary or appropriate to provide safe or healthful employment and places of employment." Nor did it allude to the possibility that any such finding might have been appropriate.

III

Our resolution of the issues in these cases turns, to a large extent, on the meaning of and the relationship between § 3(8), which defines a health and safety standard as a standard that is "reasonably necessary and appropriate to provide safe or healthful employment," and § 6(b)(5), which directs the Secretary in promulgating a health and safety standard for toxic materials to "set the standard which most adequately assures, to the extent feasible, on the basis of the best available evidence, that no employee will suffer material impairment of health or functional capacity. . ."

In the Government's view, § 3(8)'s definition of the term "standard" has no legal significance or at best merely requires that a standard not be totally irrational. It takes the position that § 6(b)(5) is controlling and that it requires OSHA to promulgate a standard that either gives an absolute assurance of safety for each and every worker or reduces exposures to the lowest level feasible. The Government interprets "feasible" as meaning technologically achievable at a cost that would not impair the viability of the industries subject to the regulation. The respondent industry representatives, on the other hand, argue that the Court of Appeals was correct in holding that the "reasonably necessary and appropriate" language of § 3(8), along with the feasibility requirement of § 6(b)(5), requires the Agency to quantify both the costs and the benefits of a proposed rule and to conclude that they are roughly commensurate.

In our view, it is not necessary to decide whether either the Government or industry is entirely correct. For we think it is clear that § 3(8) does apply to all permanent standards promulgated under the Act and that it requires the Secretary, before issuing any standard, to determine that it is reasonably necessary and appropriate to remedy a significant risk of material health impairment. Only after the Secretary has made the threshold determination that such a risk exists with respect to a toxic substance, would it be necessary to decide whether § 6(b)(5) requires him to select the most protective standard he can consistent with economic and technological feasibility, or whether, as respondents argue, the benefits of the regulation must be commensurate with the costs of its implementation. Because the Secretary did not make the required threshold finding in these cases, we have no occasion to determine whether costs must be weighed against benefits in an appropriate case.

A

Under the Government's view, § 3(8), if it has any substantive content at all, merely requires OSHA to issue standards that are reasonably calculated to produce a safer or more healthy work environment. Apart from this minimal requirement of rationality, the Government argues that § 3(8) imposes no limits on the Agency's power, and thus would not prevent it from requiring employers to do whatever would be "reasonably necessary" to eliminate all risks of any harm from their workplaces * * *.

If the purpose of the statute were to eliminate completely and with absolute certainty any risk of serious harm, we would agree that it would be proper for the Secretary to interpret §§ 3(8) and 6(b)(5) in this fashion. But we think it is clear that the statute was not designed to require employers to provide absolutely risk-free workplaces whenever it is technologically feasible to do so, so long as the cost is not great enough to destroy an entire industry. Rather, both the language and structure of the Act, as well as its legislative history, indicate that it was intended to require the elimination, as far as feasible, of significant risks of harm.

B

By empowering the Secretary to promulgate standards that are "reasonably necessary or appropriate to provide safe or healthful employment and places of employment," the Act implies that, before promulgating any standard, the Secretary must make a finding that the workplaces in question are not safe. But "safe" is not the equivalent of "risk-free." There are many activities that we engage in every day—such as driving a car or even breathing city air—that entail some risk of accident or material health impairment; nevertheless, few people would consider these activities "unsafe." Similarly, a workplace can hardly be considered "unsafe" unless it threatens the workers with a significant risk of harm.

Therefore, before he can promulgate *any* permanent health or safety standard, the Secretary is required to make a threshold finding that a place of employment is unsafe—in the sense that significant risks are present and can be eliminated or lessened by a change in practices * * *.

* * *

In the absence of a clear mandate in the Act, it is unreasonable to assume that Congress intended to give the Secretary the unprecedented power over American industry that would result from the Government's view of §§ 3(8) and 6(b)(5), coupled with OSHA's cancer policy. Expert testimony that a substance is probably a human carcinogen—either because it has caused cancer in animals or because individuals have contracted cancer following extremely high exposures—would justify the conclusion that the substance poses some risk of serious harm no matter how minute the exposure and no matter how many experts testified that they regarded the risk as insignificant. That conclusion would in turn justify pervasive regulation limited only by the constraint of feasibility. In light of the fact that there are literally thousands of substances used in the workplace that have been identified as carcinogens or suspect carcinogens, the Government's theory would give OSHA power to impose enormous costs that might produce little, if any, discernible benefit.

If the Government were correct in arguing that neither § 3(8) nor § 6(b)(5) requires that the risk from a toxic substance be quantified sufficiently to enable the Secretary to characterize it as significant in an understandable way, the statute would make such a "sweeping delegation of legislative power" that it might be unconstitutional under the Court's reasoning in *A.L.A. Schechter Poultry Corp. v. United States*, 295 U.S. 495, 539, and *Panama Refining Co. v. Ryan*, 293 U.S. 388. A construction of the statute that avoids this kind of open-ended grant should certainly be favored.

C

The legislative history also supports the conclusion that Congress was concerned, not with absolute safety, but with the elimination of significant harm. The examples of industrial hazards referred to in the Committee hearings and debates all involved situations in which the risk was unquestionably significant * * *.

* * *

D

Given the conclusion that the Act empowers the Secretary to promulgate health and safety standards only where a significant risk of harm exists, the critical issue becomes how to define and allocate the burden of proving the significance of the risk in a case such as this, where scientific knowledge is imperfect and the precise quantification of risks is therefore impossible * * *.

* * * As we read the statute, the burden was on the Agency to show, on the basis of substantial evidence, that it is at least more likely than not that long-term exposure to 10 ppm of benzene presents a significant risk of material health impairment * * *.

In this case OSHA did not even attempt to carry its burden of proof * * *.

* * *

E
* * *

In this case the record makes it perfectly clear that the Secretary relied squarely on a special policy for carcinogens that imposed the burden on industry of proving the existence of a safe level of exposure, thereby avoiding the Secretary's threshold responsibility of establishing the need for more stringent standards. In so interpreting his statutory authority, the Secretary exceeded his power.

* * *

MR. CHIEF JUSTICE BURGER, concurring. [omitted]

MR. JUSTICE POWELL, concurring in part and concurring in the judgment.

* * *

OSHA contends that § 6(b)(5) not only permits but actually requires it to promulgate standards that reduce health risks without regard to economic effects, unless those effects would cause widespread dislocation throughout an entire industry. Under the threshold test adopted by the plurality today, this authority will exist only with respect to "significant" risks. But the plurality does not reject OSHA's claim that it must reduce such risks without considering economic consequences less serious than massive dislocation. In my view, that claim is untenable.

* * *

I therefore would not lightly assume that Congress intended OSHA to require reduction of health risks found to be significant *whenever* it also finds that the affected industry can bear the costs. Perhaps more significantly, however, OSHA's interpretation of § 6(b)(5) would force it to regulate in a manner inconsistent with the important health and safety purposes of the legislation we construe today. Thousands of toxic substances present risks that fairly could be characterized as "significant". Even if OSHA succeeded in selecting the gravest risks for earliest regulation, a standard-setting process that ignored economic considerations would result in a serious misallocation of resources and a lower effective level of safety than could be achieved under standards set with reference to the comparative benefits available at a lower cost. I would not attribute such an irrational intention to Congress.

* * *

MR. JUSTICE REHNQUIST, concurring in the judgment.

The statutory provision at the center of the present controversy, § 6(b)(5) of the Occupational Safety and Health Act of 1970, states, in relevant part, that the Secretary of Labor

> ". . . in promulgating standards dealing with toxic materials or harmful physical agents . . . shall set the standard which most adequately assures, *to the extent feasible*, on the basis of the best available evidence, that no employee will suffer material impairment of health or functional capacity even if such employee has regular exposure to the hazard dealt with by such standard for the period of his working life." 84 Stat. 1594, 29 U.S.C. § 655(b)(5) (emphasis added).

According to the Secretary, who is one of the petitioners herein, § 6(b)(5) imposes upon him an absolute duty, in regulating harmful substances like benzene for which no safe level is known, to set the standard for permissible exposure at the lowest level that "can be achieved at bearable cost with available technology." While the Secretary does not attempt to refine the concept of "bearable cost," he apparently believes that a proposed standard is economically feasible so long as its impact "will not be such as to threaten the financial welfare of the affected firms or the general economy."

Respondents reply, and the lower court agreed, that § 6(b)(5) must be read in light of another provision in the same Act, § 3(8), which defines an "occupational health and safety standard" as

> ". . . a standard which requires conditions, or the adoption or use of one or more practices, means, methods, operations, or processes, reasonably necessary or appropriate to provide safe or healthful employment and places of employment." 84 Stat. 1591, 29 U.S.C. § 652(8).

According to respondents, § 6(b)(5), as tempered by § 3(8), requires the Secretary to demonstrate that any particular health standard is justifiable on the basis of a rough balancing of costs and benefits.

In considering these alternative interpretations, my colleagues manifest a good deal of uncertainty, and ultimately divide over whether the Secretary produced sufficient evidence that the proposed standard for benzene will result in any appreciable benefits at all. This uncertainty, I would suggest, is eminently justified, since I believe that this litigation presents the Court with what has to be one of the most difficult issues that could confront a decisionmaker: whether the statistical possibility of future deaths should ever be disregarded in light of the economic costs of preventing those deaths. I would also suggest that the widely varying positions advanced in the briefs of the parties and in the opinions of MR. JUSTICE STEVENS, THE CHIEF JUSTICE, MR. JUSTICE POWELL, and MR. JUSTICE MARSHALL demonstrate, perhaps better than any other fact, that Congress, the governmental body best suited and most obligated to make the choice confronting us in this litigation, has improperly delegated that choice to the Secretary of Labor and, derivatively, to this Court.

I

In his Second Treatise of Civil Government, published in 1690, John Locke wrote that "[the] power of the legislative, being derived from the people by a positive voluntary grant and institution, can be no other than what that positive grant conveyed, which being only to make laws, and not to make legislators, the legislative can have no power to transfer their authority of making laws and place it in other hands." Two hundred years later, this Court expressly recognized the existence of and the necessity for limits on Congress' ability to delegate its authority to representatives of the Executive Branch: "That Congress cannot delegate legislative power to the President is a principle universally recognized as vital to the integrity and maintenance of the system of government ordained by the Constitution." *Field v. Clark*, 143 U.S. 649, 692 (1892).

* * *

During the third and fourth decades of this century, this Court within a relatively short period of time struck down several Acts of Congress on the grounds that they exceeded the authority of Congress under the Commerce Clause or under the nondelegation principle of separation of powers, and at the same time struck down state statutes because they violated "substantive" due process or interfered with interstate commerce. When many of these decisions were later overruled, the principle that Congress could not simply transfer its legislative authority to the Executive fell under a cloud. Yet in my opinion decisions such as *Panama Refining Co. v. Ryan*, 293 U.S. 388 (1935), suffer from none of the excesses of judicial policymaking that plagued some of the other decisions of that era. The many later decisions that have upheld congressional delegations of authority to the Executive Branch have done so largely on the theory that Congress may wish to exercise its authority in a particular field, but because the field is sufficiently technical, the ground to be covered sufficiently large, and the Members of Congress themselves not necessarily expert in the area in which they choose to legislate, the most that may be asked under the separation-of-powers doctrine is that Congress lay down the general policy and standards that animate the law, leaving the agency to refine those standards, "fill in the blanks," or apply the standards to particular cases. These decisions, to my mind, simply illustrate the * * * principle stated more than 50 years ago by Mr. Chief Justice Taft that delegations of legislative authority must be judged "according to common sense and the inherent necessities of the governmental co-ordination."

Viewing the legislation at issue here in light of these principles, I believe that it fails to pass muster. Read literally, the relevant portion of § 6(b)(5) is completely precatory, admonishing the Secretary to adopt the most protective standard if he can, but excusing him from that duty if he cannot. In the case of a hazardous substance for which a "safe" level is either unknown or impractical, the language of § 6(b)(5) gives the Secretary absolutely no indication where on the continuum of relative safety he should draw his line. Especially in light of the importance of the interests at stake, I have no doubt that the provision at issue, standing alone, would violate the doctrine against uncanalized delegations of legislative power. For me the remaining question, then, is whether additional standards are ascertainable from the legislative history or statutory context of § 6(b)(5) or, if not, whether such a standardless delegation was justifiable in light of the "inherent necessities" of the situation.

II

One of the primary sources looked to by this Court in adding gloss to an otherwise broad grant of legislative authority is the legislative history of the statute in question. The opinions of MR. JUSTICE STEVENS and MR. JUSTICE MARSHALL, however, give little more than a tip of the hat to the legislative origins of § 6(b)(5). Such treatment is perhaps understandable, since the legislative history of that section, far from shedding light on what important policy choices Congress was making in the statute, gives one the feeling of viewing the congressional purpose "by the dawn's early light."

The precursor of § 6(b)(5) was placed in the Occupational Safety and Health Act of 1970 while that bill was pending in the House Committee on Education and Labor. At that time, the section read:

> "The Secretary, in promulgating standards under this subsection, shall set the standard which most adequately assures, on the basis of the best available professional evidence, that no employee will suffer any impairment of health, or functional capacity, or diminished life expectancy even if such employee has regular exposure to the hazard dealt with by such standard for the period of his working life." § 7(a)(4), H. R. 16785, 91st Cong., 2d Sess., 49 (1970), Legislative History of the Occupational Safety and Health Act of 1970 (Committee Print compiled for the Senate Committee on Labor and Public Welfare), p. 943 (1971) (hereinafter Leg. Hist.).

Three aspects of this original proposal are particularly significant. First, and perhaps most importantly, as originally introduced the provision contained no feasibility limitation, providing instead that the Secretary "shall set the standard which most adequately assures" that no employee will suffer harm. Second, it would have required the Secretary to protect employees from "any" impairment of health or functional capacity. Third, on its face, although perhaps not in its intent, the provision applied to both health and safety standards promulgated under the Act.

There can be little doubt that, at this point in its journey through Congress, § 6(b)(5) would have required the Secretary, in regulating toxic substances, to set the permissible level of exposure at a safe level or, if no safe level was known, at zero. When the Senate Committee on Labor and Public Welfare considered a provision identical in almost all respects to the House version, however, Senator Javits objected that the provision in question "might be interpreted to require absolute health and safety in all cases, regardless of feasibility. . ." S. Rep. No. 91–1282, p. 58 (1970), Leg. Hist. 197. The Committee therefore amended the bill to provide that the Secretary "shall set the standard which most adequately *and feasibly*" assured that no employee would suffer any impairment of health. The only additional explanation for this change appeared in the Senate Report accompanying the bill to the Senate floor. There, the Committee explained:

> "[Standards] promulgated under section 6(b) shall represent *feasible requirements*, which, where appropriate, shall be based on research, experiments, demonstrations, past experience, and the latest available scientific data. Such standards should be directed at assuring, *so far as possible*, that no employee will suffer impaired health or functional capacity or diminished life

expectancy, by reason of exposure to the hazard involved, even though such exposure may be over the period of his entire working life." S. Rep. No. 91–1282, p. 7 (1970), Leg. Hist. 147 (emphasis added).

Despite Senator Javits' inclusion of the words "and feasibly" in the provision, participants in the floor debate immediately characterized § 6(b)(5) as requiring the Secretary "to establish a utopia free from any hazards" and to "assure that there will not be any risk at all." 116 Cong. Rec. 37614 (1970), Leg. Hist. 480–481 (remarks of Sen. Dominick). Senator Saxbe stated:

> "When we come to saying that an employer must guarantee that such an employee is protected from any possible harm, I think it will be one of the most difficult areas we are going to have to ascertain. . .

> "I believe the terms that we are passing back and forth are going to have to be identified." 116 Cong. Rec., at 26522, Leg. Hist. 345.

In response to these concerns, Senator Dominick introduced a substitute for the proposed provision, deleting the sentence at issue here entirely. He explained that his amendment would delete

> "the requirement in section 6(b)(5) that the Secretary will establish occupational safety and health standards which most adequately and feasibly assure to the extent possible that *no* employee will suffer *any* impairment of health or functional capacity, or diminished life expectancy even if the employee has regular exposure to the hazard dealt with by the standard for the period of his working life.

> "This requirement is inherently confusing and unrealistic. It could be read to require the Secretary to ban all occupations in which there remains *some* risk of injury, impaired health, or life expectancy. In the case of all occupations, it will be impossible to eliminate all risks to safety and health. Thus, the present criteria could, if literally applied, close every business in this nation. In addition, in many cases, the standard which might most 'adequately' and 'feasibly' assure the elimination of the danger would be the prohibition of the occupation itself.

> "If the provision is intended as no more than an admonition to the secretary to do his duty, it seems unnecessary and could, if deemed advisable be included in the legislative history." (Emphasis in original.) 116 Cong. Rec., at 36530, Leg. Hist. 367.

Eventually, Senator Dominick and his supporters settled for the present language of § 6(b)(5). This agreement resulted in three changes from the original version of the provision as amended by Senator Javits. First, the provision was altered to state explicitly that it applied only to standards for "toxic materials or harmful physical agents," in apparent contrast with safety standards. Second, the Secretary was no longer admonished to protect employees from "any" impairment of their health, but rather only from "material" impairments. Third, and most importantly for our purposes, the phrase "most adequately and feasibly assures" was revamped to read "most adequately assures, to the extent feasible."

We have been presented with a number of different interpretations of this shift. According to the Secretary, Senator Dominick recognized that he could not delete the seemingly absolute requirements of § 6(b)(5) entirely, and instead agreed to limit its application to toxic materials or harmful physical agents and to specify that the Secretary was only to protect employees from material impairment of their health. Significantly, the Secretary asserts that his mandate to set such standards at the safest level technologically and economically achievable remained unchanged by the Dominick amendment. According to the Secretary, the change in language from "most adequately and feasibly assures" to "most adequately assures, to the extent feasible," represented only a slight shift in emphasis, perhaps suggesting "a preference for health protection over cost."

MR. JUSTICE MARSHALL reads this history quite differently. In his view, the version of § 6(b)(5) that reached the Senate floor did not "clearly embod[y] the feasibility requirement" and thus was soundly criticized as being unrealistic. It was only as a result of the floor amendments, which replaced "most adequately and feasibly assures" with "most adequately assures, to the extent feasible," that the Secretary clearly was authorized to reject a standard if it proved technologically or economically infeasible.

Respondents cast yet a third light on these events, focusing upon a few places in the legislative history where the words "feasible" and "reasonable" were used more or less interchangeably. It is their contention that, when Congress said "feasible," it meant cost-justified. According to respondents, who agree in this regard with the Secretary, the meaning of the feasibility requirement did not change substantially between the version that left the Senate Committee on Labor and Public Welfare and the version that was ultimately adopted as part of the Act.

To my mind, there are several lessons to be gleaned from this somewhat cryptic legislative history. First, as pointed out by MR. JUSTICE MARSHALL, to the extent that Senator Javits, Senator Dominick, and other Members were worried about imposing upon the Secretary the impossible burden of assuring absolute safety, they did not view § 3(8) of the Act as a limitation on that duty. I therefore find it difficult to accept the conclusion of the lower court, as embellished by respondents, that § 3(8) acts as a general check upon the Secretary's duty under § 6(b)(5) to adopt the most protective standard feasible.

Second, and more importantly, I believe that the legislative history demonstrates that the feasibility requirement, as employed in § 6(b)(5), is a legislative mirage, appearing to some Members but not to others, and assuming any form desired by the beholder. I am unable to accept MR. JUSTICE MARSHALL'S argument that, by changing the phrasing of § 6(b)(5) from "most adequately and feasibly assures" to "most adequately assures, to the extent feasible," the Senate injected into that section something that was not already there. If I am correct in this regard, then the amendment introduced by Senator Javits to relieve the Secretary of the duty to create a risk-free workplace left Senator Dominick free to object to the amended provision on the same grounds. Perhaps Senator Dominick himself offered the aptest description of the feasibility requirement as "no more than an admonition to the Secretary to do his duty. . ." 116 Cong. Rec. 36530 (1970); Leg. Hist. 367.

In sum, the legislative history contains nothing to indicate that the language "to the extent feasible" does anything other than render what had been a clear, if somewhat unrealistic, standard largely, if not entirely, precatory. There is certainly nothing to indicate that these words, as used in § 6(b)(5), are limited to technological and economic feasibility. When Congress has wanted to limit the concept of feasibility in this fashion, it has said so, as is evidenced in a statute enacted the same week as the provision at issue here. I also question whether the Secretary wants to assume the duties such an interpretation would impose upon him. In these cases, for example, the Secretary actually declined to adopt a standard lower than 1 ppm for some industries, not because it was economically or technologically infeasible, but rather because "different levels for different industries would result in serious administrative difficulties." If § 6(b)(5) authorizes the Secretary to reject a more protective standard in the interest of administrative feasibility, I have little doubt that he could reject such standards for any reason whatsoever, including even political feasibility.

* * *

IV

As formulated and enforced by this Court, the nondelegation doctrine serves three important functions. First, and most abstractly, it ensures to the extent consistent with orderly governmental administration that important choices of social policy are made by Congress, the branch of our Government most responsive to the popular will. Second, the doctrine guarantees that, to the extent Congress finds it necessary to delegate authority, it provides the recipient of that authority with an "intelligible principle" to guide the exercise of the delegated discretion. Third, and derivative of the second, the doctrine ensures that courts charged with reviewing the exercise of delegated legislative discretion will be able to test that exercise against ascertainable standards.

I believe the legislation at issue here fails on all three counts. The decision whether the law of diminishing returns should have any place in the regulation of toxic substances is quintessentially one of legislative policy. For Congress to pass that decision on to the Secretary in the manner it did violates, in my mind, John Locke's caveat—reflected in the cases cited earlier in this opinion—that legislatures are to make laws, not legislators. Nor, as I think the prior discussion amply demonstrates, do the provisions at issue or their legislative history provide the Secretary with any guidance that might lead him to his somewhat tentative conclusion that he must eliminate exposure to benzene as far as technologically and economically possible. Finally, I would suggest that the standard of "feasibility" renders meaningful judicial review impossible.

* * *

If we are ever to reshoulder the burden of ensuring that Congress itself make the critical policy decisions, these are surely the cases in which to do it. It is difficult to imagine a more obvious example of Congress simply avoiding a choice which was both fundamental for purposes of the statute and yet politically so divisive that the necessary decision or compromise was difficult, if not impossible, to hammer out in the legislative forge. Far from detracting from the substantive authority of Congress, a declaration that the first sentence of § 6(b)(5) of the Occupational Safety and Health Act constitutes an invalid delegation to the Secretary of Labor would preserve the authority of Congress. If Congress wishes to legislate in an area which it has not previously sought to enter, it will in today's political world undoubtedly run into opposition no matter how the legislation is formulated. But that is the very essence of legislative authority under our system. It is the hard choices, and not the filling in of the blanks, which must be made by the elected representatives of the people. When fundamental policy decisions underlying important legislation about to be enacted are to be made, the buck stops with Congress and the President insofar as he exercises his constitutional role in the legislative process.

I would invalidate the first sentence of § 6(b)(5) of the Occupational Safety and Health Act of 1970 as it applies to any toxic substance or harmful physical agent for which a safe level, that is, a level at which "no employee will suffer material impairment of health or functional capacity even if such employee has regular exposure to [that hazard] for the period of his working life," is, according to the Secretary, unknown or otherwise "infeasible." Absent further congressional action, the Secretary would then have to choose, when acting pursuant to § 6(b)(5), between setting a safe standard or setting no standard at all. Accordingly, for the reasons stated above, I concur in the judgment of the Court affirming the judgment of the Court of Appeals.

MR. JUSTICE MARSHALL, with whom MR. JUSTICE BRENNAN, MR. JUSTICE WHITE, and MR. JUSTICE BLACKMUN join, dissenting.

* * *

In this case the Secretary of Labor found, on the basis of substantial evidence, that (1) exposure to benzene creates a risk of cancer, chromosomal damage, and a variety of nonmalignant but potentially fatal blood disorders, even at the level of 1 ppm; (2) no safe level of exposure has been shown; (3) benefits in the form of saved lives would be derived from the permanent standard; (4) the number of lives that would be saved could turn out to be either substantial or relatively small; (5) under the present state of scientific knowledge, it is impossible to calculate even in a rough way the number of lives that would be saved, at least without making assumptions that would appear absurd to much of the medical community; and (6) the standard would not materially harm the financial condition of the covered industries. The Court does not set aside any of these findings. Thus, it could not be plainer that the Secretary's decision was fully in accord with his statutory mandate "most adequately [to] assur[e] . . . that no employee will suffer material impairment of health or functional capacity . . . ."

The plurality's conclusion to the contrary is based on its interpretation of 29 U.S.C. § 652(8), which defines an occupational safety and health standard as one "which requires conditions . . . reasonably necessary or appropriate to provide safe or healthful employment. . . ." According to the plurality, a standard is not "reasonably necessary or appropriate" unless the Secretary is able to show that it is "at least more likely than not" that the risk he seeks to regulate is a "significant" one. *Ibid.* Nothing in the statute's language or legislative history, however, indicates that the "reasonably necessary or appropriate" language should be given this meaning. Indeed, both demonstrate that the plurality's standard bears no connection with the acts or intentions of Congress and is based only on the plurality's solicitude for the welfare of regulated industries * * *.

Unlike the plurality, I do not purport to know whether the actions taken by Congress and its delegates to ensure occupational safety represent sound or unsound regulatory policy. The critical problem in cases like the ones at bar is scientific uncertainty. While science has determined that exposure to benzene at levels above 1 ppm creates a definite risk of health impairment, the magnitude of the risk cannot be quantified at the present time. The risk at issue has hardly been shown to be insignificant; indeed, future research may reveal that the risk is in fact considerable. But the existing evidence may frequently be inadequate to enable the Secretary to make the threshold finding of "significance" that the Court requires today. If so, the consequence of the plurality's approach would be to subject American workers to a continuing risk of cancer and other fatal diseases, and to render the Federal Government powerless to take protective action on their behalf. Such an approach would place the burden of medical uncertainty squarely on the shoulders of the American worker, the intended beneficiary of the Occupational Safety and Health Act * * *.

* * *

II

The plurality's discussion of the record in this case is both extraordinarily arrogant and extraordinarily unfair. It is arrogant because the plurality presumes to make its own factual findings with respect to a variety of disputed issues relating to carcinogen regulation * * *. And the plurality's discussion is unfair because its characterization of the Secretary's report bears practically no resemblance to what the Secretary actually did in this case. Contrary to the plurality's suggestion, the Secretary did not rely blindly on some Draconian carcinogen "policy." See *ante*, at 2855, 2861. If he had, it would have been sufficient for him to have observed that benzene is a carcinogen, a proposition that respondents do not dispute. Instead, the Secretary gathered over 50 volumes of exhibits and testimony and offered a detailed and evenhanded discussion of the relationship between exposure to benzene at all recorded exposure levels and chromosomal damage, aplastic anemia, and leukemia. In that discussion he evaluated, and took seriously, respondents' evidence of a safe exposure level.

The hearings on the proposed standard were extensive, encompassing 17 days from July 19 through August 10, 1977. The 95 witnesses included epidemiologists, toxicologists, physicians, political economists, industry representatives, and members of the affected work force. Witnesses were subjected to exhaustive questioning by representatives from a variety of interested groups and organizations.

Three basic positions were presented at the hearings. The first position was that the proposed 1 ppm standard was necessary because exposure to benzene would cause material impairment of the health of workers no matter how low the exposure level * * *.

The second position was that a 1 ppm exposure level would itself pose an unwarranted threat to employee health and safety and that the available evidence necessitated a significantly lower level * * *.

The third position was that the 1971 standard should be retained. Proponents of this position suggested that evidence linking low levels of benzene exposure to leukemia was uncertain, that the current exposure limit was sufficiently safe, and that the benefits of the proposed standard would be insufficient to justify the standard's costs * * *.

The regulations announcing the permanent standard for benzene are accompanied by an extensive statement of reasons summarizing and evaluating the results of the hearings. The Secretary found that the evidence showed that exposure to benzene causes chromosomal damage, a variety of nonmalignant blood disorders, and leukemia. 43 Fed. Reg. 5921 (1978). He concluded that low concentrations imposed a hazard that was sufficiently grave to call for regulatory action under the Act.

Evidence of deleterious effects. The Secretary referred to studies which conclusively demonstrated that benzene could damage chromosomes in blood-forming cells. *Id.,* at 5932. There was testimony suggesting a causal relationship between chromosomal damage and leukemia, although it could not be determined whether and to what extent such damage would impair health. *Id.,* at 5933. Some studies had suggested chromosomal damage at exposure levels of 10–25 ppm and lower. No quantitative dose-response curve, showing the relationship between exposure levels and incidence of chromosomal damage could yet be established. *Id.,* at 5933–5934. The evidence of chromosomal damage was, in the Secretary's view, a cause for "serious concern." *Id.,* at 5933.

* * * There was testimony that some of the nonmalignant blood disorders caused by benzene exposure could progress to, or represented, a preleukemic stage which might eventually evolve into a frank leukemia. *Id.,* at 5922.

Considerable evidence showed an association between benzene and nonmalignant blood disorders at low exposure levels. Such an association had been established in one study in which the levels frequently ranged from zero to 25 ppm with some concentrations above 100 ppm, *ibid.*; in another they ranged from 5 to 30 ppm, *id.,* at 5923. Because of the absence of adequate data, a dose-response curve showing the relationship between benzene exposure and blood disorders could not be constructed. There was considerable testimony, however, that such disorders had resulted from exposure to benzene at or near the current level of 10 ppm and lower. The Secretary concluded that the current standard did not provide adequate protection. He observed that a "safety factor" of 10 to 100 was generally used to discount the level at which a causal connection had been found in existing studies. Under this approach, he concluded that, quite apart from any leukemia risk, the permissible exposure limit should be set at a level considerably lower than 10 ppm.

Finally, there was substantial evidence that exposure to benzene caused leukemia * * *.

The Secretary reviewed certain studies suggesting that low exposure levels of 10 ppm and more did not cause any excess incidence of leukemia. Those studies, he suggested, suffered from severe methodological defects, as their authors frankly acknowledged. Finally, the Secretary discussed a study suggesting a statistically significant excess in leukemia at levels of 2 to 9 ppm. *Ibid.* He found that, despite certain deficiencies in the study, it should be considered as consistent with other studies demonstrating an excess leukemia risk among employees exposed to benzene. *Id.*, at 5928.

Areas of uncertainty. The Secretary examined three areas of uncertainty that had particular relevance to his decision. First, he pointed to evidence that the latency period for benzene-induced leukemia could range from 2 to over 20 years. *Id.*, at 5930. Since lower exposure levels lead to an increase in the latency period, it would be extremely difficult to obtain evidence showing the dose-response relationship between leukemia and exposure to low levels of benzene. Because there has been no adequate monitoring in the past, it would be practically impossible to determine what the exposure levels were at a time sufficiently distant so that the latency period would have elapsed. The problem was compounded by the difficulty of conducting a suitable study. Because exposure levels approaching 10 ppm had been required only recently, direct evidence showing the relationship between leukemia and exposure levels between 1 and 10 ppm would be unavailable in the foreseeable future.

Second, the Secretary observed that individuals had differences in their susceptibility to leukemia * * *.

* * *

Finally, the Secretary responded to the argument that the permissible exposure level should be zero or lower than 1 ppm. *Id.*, at 5947. Even though many industries had already achieved the 1 ppm level, he found that a lower level would not be feasible. *Ibid.*

Costs and benefits. The Secretary offered a detailed discussion of the role that economic considerations should play in his determination. He observed that standards must be "feasible," both economically and technologically. In his view the permanent standard for benzene was feasible under both tests. The economic impact would fall primarily on the more stable industries, such as petroleum refining and petrochemical production. *Id.*, at 5934. These industries would be able readily to absorb the costs or to pass them on to consumers. None of the 20 affected industries, involving 157,000 facilities and 629,000 exposed employees, *id.*, at 5935, would be unable to bear the required expenditures, *id.*, at 5934. He concluded that the compliance costs were "well within the financial capability of the covered industries." *Id.*, at 5941. An extensive survey of the national economic impact of the standard, undertaken by a private contractor, found first-year operating costs of between $187 and $205 million, recurring annual costs of $34 million, and investment in engineering controls of about $266 million. Since respondents have not attacked the Secretary's basic conclusions as to cost, the Secretary's extensive discussion need not be summarized here.

Finally, the Secretary discussed the benefits to be derived from the permanent standard * * *. During the hearings an industry witness * * * estimated that the proposed standard would save two lives every six years and suggested that this relatively minor benefit would not justify the regulation's costs.

The Secretary rejected the hypothesis that the standard would save only two lives in six years * * *. He determined that, because of numerous uncertainties in the existing data, it was impossible to construct a dose-response curve by extrapolating from those data to lower exposure levels. More generally, the Secretary observed that it had not been established that there was a safe level of exposure for benzene. Since there was considerable testimony that the risk would decline with the exposure level, *id.*, at 5940, the new standard would save lives. The number of lives saved "may be appreciable," but there was no way to make a more precise determination. The question was "on the frontiers of scientific knowledge." *Ibid.*

The Secretary concluded that, in light of the scientific uncertainty, he was not required to calculate benefits more precisely. *Id.*, at 5941. In any event he gave "careful consideration" to the question of whether the admittedly substantial costs were justified in light of the hazards of benzene exposure. He concluded that those costs were "necessary" in order to promote the purposes of the Act.

III

A

This is not a case in which the Secretary found, or respondents established, that no benefits would be derived from a permanent standard, or that the likelihood of benefits was insignificant. Nor was it shown that a quantitative estimate of benefits could be made on the basis of "the best available evidence." Instead, the Secretary concluded that benefits will result, that those benefits "may" be appreciable, but that the dose-response relationship of low levels of benzene exposure and leukemia, nonmalignant blood disorders, and chromosomal damage was impossible to determine. The question presented is whether, in these circumstances, the Act permits the Secretary to take regulatory action, or whether he must allow continued exposure until more definitive information becomes available.

* * *

The plurality is insensitive to three factors which, in my view, make judicial review of occupational safety and health standards under the substantial evidence test particularly difficult. First, the issues often reach a high level of technical complexity * * *. Second, the factual issues with which the Secretary must deal are frequently not subject to any definitive resolution * * *. Causal connections and theoretical extrapolations may be uncertain. Third, when the question involves determination of the acceptable level of risk, the ultimate decision must necessarily be based on considerations of policy as well as empirically verifiable facts. Factual determinations can at most define the risk in some statistical way; the judgment whether that risk is tolerable cannot be based solely on a resolution of the facts.

* * *

* * * On this record, the Secretary could conclude that regular exposure above the 1 ppm level would pose a definite risk resulting in material impairment to some indeterminate but possibly substantial number of employees * * *. Nothing in the Act purports to prevent the Secretary from acting when definitive information as to the quantity of a standard's benefits is unavailable. Where, as here, the deficiency in knowledge relates to the extent of the benefits rather than their existence, I see no reason to hold that the Secretary has exceeded his statutory authority.

B

The plurality avoids this conclusion through reasoning that may charitably be described as obscure. According to the plurality, the definition of occupational safety and health standards as those "reasonably necessary or appropriate to provide safe or healthful . . . working conditions" requires the Secretary to show that it is "more likely than not" that the risk he seeks to regulate is a "significant" one. *Ante*, at 2869. The plurality does not show how this requirement can be plausibly derived from the "reasonably necessary or appropriate" clause. Indeed, the plurality's reasoning is refuted by the Act's language, structure, and legislative history, and it is foreclosed by every applicable guide to statutory construction. In short, the plurality's standard is a fabrication bearing no connection with the acts or intentions of Congress.

* * * "[R]easonably necessary or appropriate" clauses are routinely inserted in regulatory legislation * * *. The Court has never-until today-interpreted a "reasonably necessary or appropriate" clause as having a substantive content that supersedes a specific congressional directive embodied in a provision that is focused more particularly on an agency's authority * * *.

The plurality suggests that under the "reasonably necessary" clause, a workplace is not "unsafe" unless the Secretary is able to convince a reviewing court that a "significant" risk is at issue. *Ante*, at 2864. That approach is particularly embarrassing in this case, for it is contradicted by the plain language of the Act. The plurality's interpretation renders utterly superfluous the first sentence of § 655(b)(5), which, as noted above, requires the Secretary to set the standard "which most adequately assures

. . . that no employee will suffer material impairment of health." Indeed, the plurality's interpretation reads that sentence out of the Act. By so doing, the plurality makes the test for standards regulating toxic substances and harmful physical agents substantially identical to the test for standards generally-plainly the opposite of what Congress intended. And it is an odd canon of construction that would insert in a vague and general definitional clause a threshold requirement that overcomes the specific language placed in a standard-setting provision * * *.

* * *

* * *[T]he record amply demonstrates that in light of existing scientific knowledge, no purpose would be served by requiring the Secretary to take steps to quantify the risk of exposure to benzene at low levels. Any such quantification would be based not on scientific "knowledge" as that term is normally understood, but on considerations of policy. For carcinogens like benzene, the assumptions on which a dose-response curve must be based are necessarily arbitrary. To require a quantitative showing of a "significant" risk, therefore, would either paralyze the Secretary into inaction or force him to deceive the public by acting on the basis of assumptions that must be considered too speculative to support any realistic assessment of the relevant risk * * *.

* * *

* * * Respondents contend that the term feasible should be read to require consideration of the economic burden of a standard, not merely its technological achievability. I do not understand the Secretary to disagree. But respondents present no argument that the expenditure required by the benzene standard is not feasible in that respect. The Secretary concluded on the basis of substantial evidence that the costs of the standard would be readily absorbed by the 20 affected industries. One need not define the feasibility requirement with precision in order to conclude that the benzene standard is "feasible" in the sense that it will not materially harm the financial condition of the regulated industries.

Respondents suggest that the feasibility requirement should be understood not merely to refer to a standard's expense, but also to mandate a finding that the benefits of an occupational safety and health standard bear a reasonable relation to its costs. I believe that the statute's language, structure, and legislative history foreclose respondents' position. In its ordinary meaning an activity is "feasible" if it is capable of achievement, not if its benefits outweigh its costs * * *.

* * *

IV

In recent years there has been increasing recognition that the products of technological development may have harmful effects whose incidence and severity cannot be predicted with certainty. The responsibility to regulate such products has fallen to administrative agencies. Their task is not an enviable one. Frequently no clear causal link can be established between the regulated substance and the harm to be averted. Risks of harm are often uncertain, but inaction has considerable costs of its own. The agency must decide whether to take regulatory action against possibly substantial risks or to wait until more definitive information becomes available-a judgment which by its very nature cannot be based solely on determinations of fact.

Those delegations, in turn, have been made on the understanding that judicial review would be available to ensure that the agency's determinations are supported by substantial evidence and that its actions do not exceed the limits set by Congress. In the Occupational Safety and Health Act, Congress expressed confidence that the courts would carry out this important responsibility. But in these cases the plurality has far exceeded its authority * * *.

NOTES

Justice Marshall's dissenting opinion dismissed the delegation concerns of the plurality and dissent in a brusque footnote, insisting that "[u]nder the Act, the Secretary is afforded considerably more guidance than are other administrators acting under different regulatory statutes."

In the end, Justice Marshall got the last laugh (or at least the last chortle, if the end result was not quite exactly what he wanted). The next term, the Court addressed the validity of OSHA's standards for cotton dust exposure. *See American Textile Manuf. Inst., Inc. v. Donovan*, 452 U.S. 490, 101 S.Ct. 2478, 69 L.Ed.2d 185 (1981). The cotton dust standard raised no question concerning the significance of the harm under § 3(8) of the OSH Act, as everyone agreed that the health risks easily passed any requirement contained in § 3(8). Accordingly, the only question presented was the appropriate role of cost-benefit analysis in determining feasibility under § 6(b)(5). On that question, Justice Stevens joined the four dissenters in *Industrial Union* in holding that OSHA was not required to use, and indeed was affirmatively forbidden from using, cost-benefit analysis as part of its "to the extent feasibile" determination under § 6(b)(5).

> The plain meaning of the word "feasible" supports respondents' interpretation of the statute. According to Webster's Third New International Dictionary of the English Language 831 (1976), "feasible" means "capable of being done, executed, or effected." Thus, § 6(b)(5) directs the Secretary to issue the standard that "most adequately assures ... that no employee will suffer material

impairment of health," limited only by the extent to which this is "capable of being done." In effect then, as the Court of Appeals held, Congress itself defined the basic relationship between costs and benefits, by placing the "benefit" of worker health above all other considerations save those making attainment of this "benefit" unachievable. Any standard based on a balancing of costs and benefits by the Secretary that strikes a different balance than that struck by Congress would be inconsistent with the command set forth in § 6(b)(5). Thus, cost-benefit analysis by OSHA is not required by the statute because feasibility analysis is.

* * *

Even though the plain language of § 6(b)(5) supports this construction, we must still decide whether § 3(8), the general definition of an occupational safety and health standard, either alone or in tandem with § 6(b)(5), incorporates a cost-benefit requirement for standards dealing with toxic materials or harmful physical agents * * *.

* * * We need not decide whether § 3(8), standing alone, would contemplate some form of cost-benefit analysis. For even if it does, Congress specifically chose in § 6(b)(5) to impose separate and additional requirements for issuance of a subcategory of occupational safety and health standards dealing with toxic materials and harmful physical agents: it required that those standards be issued to prevent material impairment of health *to the extent feasible*. Congress could reasonably have concluded that *health* standards should be subject to different criteria than *safety* standards because of the special problems presented in regulating them.

Agreement with petitioners' argument that § 3(8) imposes an additional and overriding requirement of cost-benefit analysis on the issuance of § 6(b)(5) standards would eviscerate the "to the extent feasible" requirement. Standards would inevitably be set at the level indicated by cost-benefit analysis, and not at the level specified by § 6(b)(5). For example, if cost-benefit analysis indicated a protective standard of 1,000 ug/m ^{3} PEL, while feasibility analysis indicated a 500 ug/m ^{3} PEL, the agency would be forced by the cost-benefit requirement to choose the less stringent point. We cannot believe that Congress intended the general terms of § 3(8) to countermand the specific feasibility requirement of § 6(b)(5). Adoption of petitioners' interpretation would effectively write § 6(b)(5) out of the Act * * *, thereby offending the well-settled rule that all parts of a statute, if possible, are to be given effect * * *.

The legislative history of the Act, while concededly not crystal clear, provides general support for respondents' interpretation of the Act * * *. Perhaps most telling is the absence of any indication whatsoever that Congress intended OSHA to conduct its own cost-benefit analysis before promulgating a toxic material or harmful physical agent standard. The legislative history demonstrates conclusively that Congress was fully aware that the Act would impose real and substantial costs of compliance on industry, and believed that such costs were part of the cost of doing business.

452 U.S. at 508–09, 512–14, 101 S.Ct. at 2490, 2492–93.

Justice Rehnquist renewed his nondelegation attack on the statute, joined this time by Chief Justice Burger. Justice Stewart dissented on substantive grounds not involving the meaning of the statute, and Justice Powell, who had championed a cost-benefit requirement in *Industrial Union*, did not participate in the decision.

4.   LIFE AFTER *MISTRETTA*

a.   What Is Left?

Mistretta was a very strong signal that nondelegation challenges would not be well received by the modern Court. And if the signal was not clear enough, two cases decided shortly after *Mistretta* drove the point home even harder.

Skinner v. Mid-America Pipeline Co., 490 U.S. 212, 109 S.Ct. 1726, 104 L.Ed.2d 250 (1989), concerned a 1986 statute that directed the Secretary of Transportation to "establish a schedule of fees based on the usage, in reasonable relationship to volume-miles, miles, revenues, or an appropriate combination thereof, of natural gas and hazardous liquid pipelines." 49 U.S.C. App. 1682a (2012). The statute placed a number of restrictions on the Secretary's power: "The Secretary may not collect fees from firms not subject to either of the two Pipeline Safety Acts; he may not use the funds for purposes other than administering the two Acts; he may not set fees on a case-by-case basis; in setting fees, he may not apply any criteria other than volume-miles, miles, or revenue; he may not establish a fee schedule that does not bear a 'reasonable relationship' to these criteria." 490 U.S. at 219, 109 S.Ct. at 1731. Mid-America challenged the statute under the nondelegation doctrine. Mid-America conceded that the statute's guidelines to the Secretary "meet the normal requirements of the nondelegation doctrine," *id.*, as applied by the modern Court, but contended that a stricter standard must be applied to delegations of the taxing power. A unanimous Court found "no support * * * for Mid-America's contention that the text of the Constitution or the practices of Congress require the application of a different and stricter nondelegation doctrine in cases where Congress delegates discretionary authority to the Executive under its taxing power." *Id.* at 222–23, 109 S.Ct. at 1733.

Two years later, in *Touby v. United States*, 500 U.S. 160, 111 S.Ct. 1752, 114 L.Ed.2d 219 (1991), the Court again unanimously declined an invitation to find a niche for vigorous application of the nondelegation doctrine. The Controlled Substances Act provides for five categories, or "schedules," of controlled substances, with different penalties for violations of prohibitions on manufacturing, distribution, and possession within the five schedules (violations involving Schedule 1 substances carry the highest penalties). The law allows the Attorney General to add substances to the various schedules and to move substances from one schedule to another, which effectively gives the Attorney General the power to determine the criminal penalties associated with each substance. Touby conceded that the statutory criteria for listing or moving a substance met the lax requirements for an "intelligible principle" under the modern nondelegation doctrine but insisted that "something more than an 'intelligible principle' is required when Congress authorizes another Branch to promulgate regulations that contemplate criminal sanctions." 500 U.S. at 162–63, 165–66, 111 S.Ct. at 1754–55, 1756. The Court found that the statutory listing criteria would satisfy even a more rigorous nondelegation standard and accordingly did not decide whether such a standard was appropriate for criminal penalties. 500 U.S. at 166–67, 111 S,Ct. at 1756–57.

One could reasonably have expected *Mistretta*, *Skinner*, and *Touby*—three effectively unanimous Supreme Court rejections of nondelegation challenges in a three-year span—to put an end to modern litigation under the nondelegation doctrine. But no.

b.   A Spark of Life?

(1). *State of South Dakota v. United States Dep't of the Interior*, 69 F.3d 878 (8th Cir.1995), *vacated and remanded*, 519 U.S. 919, 117 S.Ct. 286, 136 L.Ed.2d 205 (1996).

Section 465 of Title 25 provides that "[t]he Secretary of the Interior is hereby authorized, in his discretion, to acquire * * * any interest in lands * * * within or without existing reservations * * * for the purpose of providing land for Indians." Held by the Eighth Circuit: the statute is an unconstitutional delegation to the Secretary of the Interior.

> By its literal terms, the statute permits the Secretary to purchase a factory, an office building, a residential subdivision, or a golf course in trust for an Indian tribe * * *. Indeed, it would permit the Secretary to purchase the Empire State Building in trust for a tribal chieftain as a wedding present. There are no perceptible "boundaries," no "intelligible principles," within the four corners of the statutory language that constrain this delegated authority—except that the acquisition must be "for Indians." It delegates unrestricted power to acquire land from private citizens for the private use and benefit of Indian tribes or individual Indians.

69 F.3d at 882. A dissenting judge would have found adequate guidance for the Secretary in the statute's legislative history and "historical context." *Id.* at 887. The Supreme Court granted certiorari and, without opinion, vacated the Eighth Circuit's decision and remanded the case for reconsideration in light of updated agency regulations involving judicial review. On the next go-round, the Eighth Circuit, unbound by its vacated prior opinion, rejected the nondelegation challenge and adopted the reasoning of the dissent in the prior case. *South Dakota v. United States Dep't of the Interior,* 423 F.3d 790, 797–98 (8th Cir.2005).

(2). *Loving v. United States,* 517 U.S. 748, 116 S.Ct. 1737, 135 L.Ed.2d 36 (1996).

The President, by executive order, has specified criteria that must be applied by military courts martial when imposing the death penalty. Loving maintained that "Congress, and not the President, must make the fundamental policy determination respecting the factors that warrant the death penalty." 517 U.S. at 754–55, 116 S.Ct. at 1742. Writing for eight Justices, Justice Kennedy stated that "[h]ad the delegations here called for the exercise of judgment or discretion that lies beyond the traditional authority of the President, Loving's * * * argument that Congress failed to provide guiding principles to the President might have more weight." *Id.* at 772, 116 S.Ct. at 1750. The Court concluded, however, that given the President's unique role as commander-in-chief, congressional guidance to the President in this area was unnecessary.

(3). *Clinton v. City of New York,* 524 U.S. 417, 118 S.Ct. 2091, 141 L.Ed.2d 393 (1998).

In 1996, Congress enacted the Line Item Veto Act, 110 Stat. 1200, 2 U.S.C. § 691 *et seq.* (1994 Supp. II). The statute gave the President authority, upon the making of specified determinations, to "cancel in whole," *id.* § 691(a), certain spending and tax-benefit provisions of enacted statutes. The effect of such cancellations was to prevent the relevant provisions "from having legal force or effect." *Id.* § 691e(4)(B)–(C). The parties vigorously disputed whether this statute unconstitutionally delegated legislative authority to the President. The Supreme Court held the statute unconstitutional on other grounds. The Court reasoned that cancellation of a line item in an enacted law was tantamount to an amendment of the statutory text, which can only be achieved through the process for enacting legislation prescribed in Article 1, section 7. The Court said of the nondelegation argument:

> We have been favored with extensive debate about the scope of Congress' power to delegate law-making authority, or its functional equivalent, to the President. The excellent briefs filed by the parties and their *amici curiae* have provided us with valuable historical information that illuminates the delegation

issue but does not really bear on the narrow issue that is dispositive of these cases.

524 U.S. at 447–48, 118 S.Ct. at 2107–08. Justices Breyer, O'Connor, and Scalia thought that the case squarely involved delegation issues and would have upheld the statute as clearly constitutional under a delegation analysis.

(4). *American Trucking Ass'ns v. United States EPA*, 175 F.3d 1027 (D.C.Cir.1999), *modified in part*, 195 F.3d 4 (D.C.Cir.1999), *rev'd*, 531 U.S. 457, 121 S.Ct. 903, 149 L.Ed.2d 1 (2001).

In 1997, the Environmental Protection Agency promulgated air quality standards for particulate matter and ozone. Under the Clean Air Act, primary air quality standards "shall be ambient air quality standards the attainment and maintenance of which in the judgment of the Administrator [of the EPA], based on such criteria and allowing an adequate margin of safety, are requisite to protect the public health." 42 U.S.C. § 7409(b)(1) (2012). Secondary standards "shall specify a level of air quality the attainment and maintenance of which in the judgment of the Administrator, based on such criteria, is requisite to protect the public welfare from any known or anticipated adverse effects associated with the presence of such air pollutant in the ambient air." *Id.* § 7409(b)(2). EPA's stated criteria for evaluating pollution effects are " 'the nature and severity of the health effects involved, the size of the sensitive population(s) at risk, the types of health information available, and the kind and degree of uncertainties that must be addressed.' " 175 F.3d at 1034–35. The EPA has not specified any methodology for measuring or combining the various criteria. A divided D.C. Circuit (which divided further during the court's subsequent denial of en banc rehearing) held that the agency had interpreted the statute with such latitude as to render it unconstitutional:

> Here it is as though Congress commanded EPA to select "big guys," and EPA announced that it would evaluate candidates based on weight and height, but revealed no cut-off point. The announcement, though sensible in what it does say, is fatally incomplete. The reasonable person responds, "How tall? How heavy?"

* * *

> The arguments EPA offers here show only that EPA is applying the stated factors and that larger public health harms (including increased probability of such harms) are, as expected, associated with higher pollutant concentrations. The principle EPA invokes for each increment in stringency * * *—that it is "possible, but not certain" that health effects exist at that level— could, as easily * * * justify a standard of zero. The same

indeterminacy prevails in EPA's decisions *not* to pick a still more stringent level. For example, EPA's reasons for not lowering the ozone standard from 0.08 to 0.07 ppm—that "the more serious effects . . . are less certain" at the lower levels and that the lower levels are "closer to peak background levels"—could also be employed to justify a refusal to reduce levels below those associated with London's "Killer Fog" of 1952 * * *. Thus, the agency rightly recognizes that the question is one of degree, but offers no intelligible principle by which to identify a stopping point.

Id. at 1034, 1036–37. The court remanded to give the agency a chance to interpret the statute in a manner that would pass constitutional muster.

To no one's surprise, the Supreme Court reversed 9–0. *Whitman v. American Trucking Ass'ns*, 531 U.S. 457, 121 S.Ct. 903, 149 L.Ed.2d 1 (2001). The Court, in an opinion authored by Justice Scalia, accepted the government's argument that air quality standards must be "requisite" to meet the public health and that "[r]equisite, in turn, 'mean[s] sufficient but not more than necessary.' " Invoking essentially the same authorities that were cited in *Mistretta*, the Court held that the discretion vested in the EPA by this statute "is in fact well within the outer limits of our nondelegation precedents." The essence of the Court's very brief discussion was as follows:

> It is true enough that the degree of agency discretion that is acceptable varies according to the scope of the power congressionally conferred. While Congress need not provide any direction to the EPA regarding the manner in which it is to define "country elevators," which are to be exempt from new-stationary-source regulations governing grain elevators, it must provide substantial guidance on setting air standards that affect the entire national economy. But even in sweeping regulatory schemes we have never demanded, as the Court of Appeals did here, that statutes provide a "determinate criterion" for saying "how much [of the regulated harm] is too much." 175 F.3d, at 1034. In *Touby*, for example, we did not require the statute to decree how "imminent" was too imminent, or how "necessary" was necessary enough, or even—most relevant here—how "hazardous" was too hazardous. Similarly, the statute at issue in *Lichter* [*v. United States*, 334 U.S. 742 (1948)] authorized agencies to recoup "excess profits" paid under wartime Government contracts, yet we did not insist that Congress specify how much profit was too much. It is therefore not conclusive for delegation purposes that, as respondents argue, ozone and particulate matter are "nonthreshold" pollutants that inflict a continuum of adverse health effects at any airborne concentration greater than zero,

and hence require the EPA to make judgments of degree. "[A] certain degree of discretion, and thus of lawmaking, inheres in most executive or judicial action." *Mistretta v. United States*, at 417, 109 S.Ct. 647 (Scalia, J., dissenting) (emphasis deleted); see 488 U.S., at 378–379, 109 S.Ct. 647 (majority opinion). Section 109(b)(1) of the CAA, which to repeat we interpret as requiring the EPA to set air quality standards at the level that is "requisite"—that is, not lower or higher than is necessary—to protect the public health with an adequate margin of safety, fits comfortably within the scope of discretion permitted by our precedent.

531 U.S. at 475–76, 121 S.Ct. at 913–14. The Court also rejected the D.C. Circuit's suggestion that the EPA could cure any constitutional defects in the statute by adopting regulations that prescribe determinate standards:

> The idea that an agency can cure an unconstitutionally standardless delegation of power by declining to exercise some of that power seems to us internally contradictory. The very choice of which portion of the power to exercise—that is to say, the prescription of the standard that Congress had omitted—would itself be an exercise of the forbidden legislative authority.

Id. at 473, 121 S.Ct. at 912.

Justices Stevens and Souter concurred in the result but thought that the Court should abandon the fiction that agency rulemaking power is executive rather than legislative power under the Constitution. According to the concurrence, the vesting clauses of Articles I and II "do not purport to limit the authority of either recipient of power to delegate authority to others * * *. As long as the delegation provides a sufficiently intelligible principle, there is nothing inherently unconstitutional about it." *Id.* at 489–90, 121 S.Ct. at 921 (Stevens, J., concurring in part and concurring in the judgment).

Justice Thomas joined the majority opinion, but with the following intriguing qualification:

> As it is, none of the parties to this case has examined the text of the Constitution or asked us to reconsider our precedents on cessions of legislative power. On a future day, however, I would be willing to address the question whether our delegation jurisprudence has strayed too far from our Founders' understanding of separation of powers.

Id. at 487, 121 S.Ct. at 920 (Thomas, J., concurring).

(5). *Michigan Gambling Opposition v. Kempthorne*, 525 F.3d 23 (D.C. Cir.2008).

This case involved the same statute at issue in *State of South Dakota v. United States Dep't of the Interior*, *supra*: a statute providing that the "Secretary of the Interior is authorized, in his discretion, to acquire * * * any interest in lands * * * for the purpose of providing land for Indians." 25 U.S.C. § 465 (2012). As had three other circuits, the D.C. Circuit concluded that this statute passed muster under the nondelegation doctrine because it requires the Secretary "to exercise his powers in order to further economic development and self-governance among the Tribes." 525 F.3d at 31. In a lengthy dissent, however, Judge Brown objected because "the statutory language lacks any discernible boundaries. To rely on the purpose of 'providing land for Indians' does nothing to cabin the Secretary's discretion over providing land for Indians because it is tautological. To say the purpose is to provide land for Indians in a broad effort to promote economic development * * * is tautology on steroids." *Id.* at 37. Even in 2008, nondelegation cases sometimes got decided by divided votes in the courts of appeals.

(6). *Reynolds v. United States*, 565 U.S. 432, 132 S.Ct. 975, 181 L.Ed.2d 935 (2012).

In *Mistretta*, Justice Blackmun observed in a footnote that "application of the nondelegation doctrine principally has been limited to the interpretation of statutory texts, and, more particularly, to giving narrow constructions to statutory delegations that might otherwise be thought to be unconstitutional." The plurality opinion in *Industrial Union* is perhaps the prime example of this use of the so-called constitutional avoidance canon. *Reynolds* concerned whether federal registration requirements for sex offenders applied to people convicted before the act was passed. The majority held that it did no so apply until and unless the Attorney General specified by rule that such persons must register. In dissent, Justice Scalia, joined by Justice Ginsburg, maintained that the statute applied to such persons of its own force. He further observed:

> Indeed, it is not entirely clear to me that Congress can constitutionally leave it to the Attorney General to decide—with no statutory standard whatever governing his discretion— whether a criminal statute will or will not apply to certain individuals. That seems to me sailing close to the wind with regard to the principle that legislative powers are nondelegable * * *.

565 U.S. at 450, 132 S.Ct. at 986.

(7). In the slightly more than one decade from *Mistretta* through *American Trucking*, the combined vote in the Supreme Court on the merits of nondelegation challenges was 53–0 against the challenges. Which is more impressive: the unanimous rejection of the challenges or the fact that the Court had to cast 53 votes during that time?

(8). *U.S. Dep't of Transportation v. Ass'n of American Railroads*, 575 U.S. ___, 135 S.Ct. 1225, 191 L.Ed.2d 153 (2015).

The nondelegation doctrine in its classic form deals with Congress vesting power in executive (or judicial) agents. What if Congress vests what appears to be federal legislative power in private actors?

Delegation to private actors has long been treated with great suspicion; the Court once called it "legislative delegation in its most obnoxious form." *Carter v. Carter Coal Co.*, 298 U.S. 238, 311 (1936). In *Ass'n of American Railroads*, the D.C. Circuit Court of Appeals suggested that this principle might still have considerable bite even in the modern era, and the Supreme Court kept that option open.

Amtrak is a government-created (and mostly government-owned) corporation that provides intercity passenger rail service. Amtrak is defined by statute "not [to] be an agency or establishment of the United States Government," 49 U.S.C. § 24301 (2012), and it is statutorily instructed to behave like a private firm. Virtually all of the tracks over which Amtrak's passenger trains travel are owned by private freight-hauling railroads. Amtrak's trains are supposed to be given preference on those tracks in the event of conflict between passenger and freight schedules. The governing statute provides for ongoing measurements of Amtrak's intercity passenger service performance, and if it is determined that any shortfalls in Amtrak service are attributable to a freight railroad's failure to provide the appropriate trackage preference to Amtrak, the federal Surface Transportation Board can award damages or other relief against the offending railroad. *See id.* § 24308(f)(2). The crucial task of devising metrics to measure Amtrak's performance—and thus indirectly to determine potential liabilities of freight carriers for not providing Amtrak with appropriate trackage preferences—is jointly given to the Federal Railroad Administration and Amtrak. *See id.* § 24101 (note). If those entities cannot agree on metrics, the matter can be referred to binding arbitration. Thus, Amtrak, potentially along with an unspecified arbitrator, is given by statute a crucial role in the formulation of norms that can determine the liability of competing private railroads.

The D.C. Circuit found this statutory scheme unconstitutional on the ground that Amtrak was, by both statute and function, a private entity; that Congress had therefore delegated governmental power to a private entity; and that such delegations implicate a far stricter nondelegation principle than applies to grants of power to government agencies. "Even an intelligible principle cannot rescue a statute empowering private parties to wield regulatory authority." 721 F.3d 666, 671 (D.C. Cir. 2013). The court held that while precedent establishes that private parties can be given authority to advise on, and even veto, government regulations, *see, e.g., Currin v. Wallace*, 306 U.S. 1 (1939) (approving a scheme in which growers must consent to regulations before they take effect), they cannot be given authority to promulgate binding regulations. The court further held that Amtrak, given its functions and statutory directives to behave like a business, is a private entity for purposes of the nondelegation doctrine, even though it had previously been held to be a governmental agency for purposes of the First Amendment. *See* page 4, *supra*. On that basis, the court invalidated the provision granting Amtrak authority over metrics.

Again to no one's surprise, the Supreme Court reversed, with eight Justices joining the majority opinion. The Court did not reach the private delegation issue on which the lower court decision turned, because it held that Amtrak is a governmental rather than private entity notwithstanding Congress's statutory assertion to the contrary: "Congressional pronouncements * * * are not dispositive of Amtrak's status as a governmental entity for purposes of separation of powers analysis under the Constitution. And an independent inquiry into Amtrak's status under the Constitution reveals the Court of Appeals' premise was flawed." 135 S.Ct. at 1231. The Court remanded for consideration of other issues in the case, including some issues under the Appointments Clause that were flagged by Justice Alito in a concurring opinion, *see infra* page 229, and a remaining nondelegation issue involving the arbitrator who can determine metrics if Amtrak and the Federal Railroad Administration cannot agree on them. Giving authority to set legally binding metrics to a private arbitrator would presumably raise the same nondelegation issues that the D.C. Circuit thought were raised by a grant of authority to Amtrak. Justice Alito openly telegraphed his views on that question: "If the arbitrator can be a private person, this law is unconstitutional." 135 S.Ct. at 1237 (Alito, J., concurring). Indeed, the government did not really argue otherwise in *Association of American Railroads*, insisting that the statute should be interpreted, using the canon of constitutional avoidance, to refer only to an arbitrator who is a government official. Thus, the scope of any "private party" exception to the demise of the nondelegation principle awaits another day in the Supreme Court.

Do delegations to private parties really raise fundamentally different issues than do delegations to government agencies? Is there any textual basis for this public-private distinction in application of the nondelegation doctrine? On remand in *Ass'n of American Railroads,* the D.C. Circuit found that giving Amtrak power essentially to regulate its competitors violated the Due Process Clause of the Fifth Amendment. *See Ass'n of American Railroads v. United States Dep't of Transportation,* 821 F.3d 19, 27–31 (D.C.Cir.2016). Does the same reasoning apply to delegations to private parties? *See* A. Michael Froomkin, *Wrong Turn in Cyberspace: Using ICANN to Route Around the APA and the Constitution,* 50 Duke L.J. 17, 153 (2000) (suggesting that delegations to private parties raise due process concerns).

Justice Thomas, concurring in the judgment in *Association of American Railroads*, reiterated his long-standing view that the Court should reconsider its entire body of nondelegation jurisprudence and find that even executive officials cannot be given "discretion to formulate generally applicable rules of private conduct." 135 S.Ct. at 1242 (Thomas, J., concurring in the judgment). For many years, Justice Thomas stood alone on the Court in that view. But Justice Thomas may have found reinforcements in Justice Neil Gorsuch, who as a court of appeals judge expressed some sympathy for reviving the nondelegation doctrine. *See Gutierrez-Brizuela v. Lynch*, 834 F.3d 1142, 1154 (10th Cir.2016) (Gorsuch, J., concurring):

> Of course, in relatively recent times the Court has relaxed its approach to claims of unlawful legislative delegation. It has suggested (at least in the civil arena) that Congress may allow the executive to make new rules of general applicability that look a great deal like legislation, so long as the controlling legislation contains an 'intelligible principle' that 'clearly delineates the general policy' the agency is to apply * * *. Some thoughtful judges and scholars have questioned whether standards like these serve as much as a protection against the delegation of legislative authority as a license for it, undermining the separation between the legislative and executive powers that the founders thought essential.

Two is still less than five, so proclaiming the rebirth of the nondelegation doctrine in the Court is a tad premature. But for those who find the prospect intriguing . . . .

(9). A 2006 congressional requirement, and subsequent Department of Justice regulations implementing the requirement, that any convicted sex offender "shall register, and keep the registration current, in each jurisdiction where the offender resides, where the offender is an employee, and where the offender is a student," Sex Offender Registration and Notification Act ["SORNA"], Pub. L No. 109–248, Title I, § 113(a), 120 Stat. 593 (2006) (codified at 34 U.S.C. § 20913(a) (2012)), has been a fertile source of litigation; *see infra* pages 475–482. One very large question is whether the registration requirements should apply to people who were convicted of qualifying offenses *before* the effective date of the act. The statute's answer to that question is: "The Attorney General shall have the authority to specify the applicability of the requirements of this subchapter to sex offenders convicted before the enactment of this chapter or its implementation in a particular jurisdiction, and to prescribe rules for the registration of any such sex offenders * * *." 34 U.S.C. § 20913(d) (2012). There are no criteria identified in the statute for the Attorney General to apply. Does this statute violate the nondelegation doctrine?

Every lower court to consider the matter has said no. In 2017, the Second Circuit, in an unpublished decision, rejected a defendant's nondelegation claim in a dismissive footnote that relied on prior precedent from 2010. *See United States v. Gundy*, 695 Fed. Appx. 639, 641 n.2 (2d Cir.2017). The defendant petitioned for certiorari in the Supreme Court on the delegation issue and on three unrelated matters. The government waived its right to respond to the petition, which the government often does when it thinks that the petition for certiorari is so obviously meritless that it does not require a response and that the Court will surely refuse to take the case. The Supreme Court, however, requested that the government respond to Gundy's petition (as it sometimes does in these situations). The Court then granted certiorari "limited to Question 4 presented by the petition," *Gundy v. United States*, 138 S.Ct. 1260, 200 L.Ed.2d 416 (2018), with Question 4 being: "Whether the federal Sex Offender Registration and Notification Act's delegation of authority to the attorney general to issue regulations under 42 U.S.C. § 16913 violates the nondelegation doctrine."[4] 2017 WL 8132120. There is no split among the circuits on this question. Why would the Court choose to take the case? Perhaps there will be an answer by the time this book sees print.

---

[4] The sex offender registration provisions were originally codified in Title 42 of the United States Code but were moved, without any change in the text of the law, to Title 34 effective September 1, 2017. So when Gundy was convicted, the law had a different label in the United States Code than it does now. For those who find this sort of thing intriguing: The United States Code is just a convenient sorting of laws into a useable, searchable form. The "official" version of the laws is, at least presumptively, the Statutes at Large, which present laws in the chronological order in which they were passed. *See* 1 U.S.C. § 112 (2012) ("The United States Statutes at Large shall be legal evidence of laws, concurrent resolutions, treaties, international agreements other than treaties, proclamations by the President, and proposed or ratified amendments to the Constitution of the United States therein contained, in all the courts of the United States, the several States, and the Territories and insular possessions of the United States.") Congress, however, has formally enacted into law some portions of the United States Code, which converts those portions into official versions that (in the rare event of conflict) trump the earlier versions in the Statutes at Large. *See* 1 U.S.C. § 204(a) (2012) ("The matter set forth in the edition of the Code of Laws of the United States current at any time shall, together with the then current supplement, if any, establish prima facie the laws of the United States, general and permanent in their nature, in force on the day preceding the commencement of the session following the last session the legislation of which is included: *Provided, however*, That whenever titles of such Code shall have been enacted into positive law the text thereof shall be legal evidence of the laws therein contained, in all the courts of the United States, the several States, and the Territories and insular possessions of the United States."). Because "prima facie" evidence can be overcome by more authoritative "legal" evidence, the Statutes at Large prevail in any conflict in which the relevant provisions of the United States Code have not been enacted. Which provisions of the United States Code have been enacted? You can find the list following 1 U.S.C. § 204 in the United States Code Annotated.

5. CONTROLLING DELEGATIONS

a. Legislative Overrides

1. *Statutory Overrides*

The most straightforward way for Congress to control agency discretion is simply to override by statute agency decisions with which Congress disagrees. In extreme cases, Congress can amend the organic statute to eliminate altogether the agency's discretion—or even the agency itself. Less dramatically, Congress can leave in place the agency's basic authority but overrule, on a case-by-case basis, specific exercises of that authority.

A good example of the case-specific technique emerged in the 1970s from efforts by the National Highway Traffic Safety Administration (NHTSA), an agency located within the Department of Transportation, to carry out its statutory mandate to promulgate motor vehicle safety standards. The agency's studies unambiguously showed that one of the easiest, most cost-effective ways to reduce deaths and injuries from motor vehicle accidents was to increase the use of safety belts. For an agency charged with mandating design standards for automobiles, the conclusion was obvious: simply require vehicles to be designed with an "ignition interlock" so that the vehicles will not start (or at least will not start without setting off an irritating buzzer) until the front safety belts are engaged. Accordingly, the agency imposed such a standard on 1974–75 model year vehicles. The agency's conclusions about the relatively low design costs of an ignition interlock and the likely effects of increased belt usage on passenger safety were unchallengeable. The public, however, launched a full-scale revolt against the ignition interlock that is still legendary in administrative law circles. Congress quickly responded to public pressure by passing a statute in 1974 that remains, with some modifications, on the books today:

> A motor vehicle safety standard prescribed under this chapter may not require a manufacturer to comply with the standard by using a safety belt interlock designed to prevent starting or operating a motor vehicle if an occupant is not using a safety belt.

49 U.S.C. § 30124 (2012). Until a 2012 amendment, the statute also prohibited the use of buzzers that lasted for more than eight seconds. End of controversy—at least until NHTSA mandates a breathalyzer ignition interlock, which has been under discussion for some time.

2. *Legislative Vetoes*

Ordinarily, legislative overrides take the form of statutes and thus must clear the constitutional requirements for legislation: passage in both houses of Congress and presentment to the President. This process is deliberately cumbersome and fraught with political obstacles. A more attractive device for Congress is to give the agency discretion that is *conditional* on subsequent approval, or lack of disapproval, by Congress, the House or Senate alone, or even legislative committees. Such a mechanism, popularly known as a legislative veto, allows Congress to reserve to itself, or to some component of itself, the power to override agency decisions without going through the full Article I legislative process. A two-house veto avoids the constitutional presentment requirement for legislation; a one house or committee veto avoids both the presentment and bicameralism requirements. This device became enormously popular in the half-century before 1983, finding its way in some form into nearly 200 federal statutes.[5] In 1983, the Supreme Court dealt the legislative veto a powerful blow.

IMMIGRATION & NATURALIZATION SERVICE V. CHADHA
Supreme Court of the United States, 1983.
462 U.S. 919, 103 S.Ct. 2764, 77 L.Ed.2d 317.

CHIEF JUSTICE BURGER delivered the opinion of the Court.

* * *

Chadha is an East Indian who was born in Kenya and holds a British passport. He was lawfully admitted to the United States in 1966 on a nonimmigrant student visa. His visa expired on June 30, 1972. On October 11, 1973, the District Director of the Immigration and Naturalization Service ordered Chadha to show cause why he should not be deported for having "remained in the United States for a longer time than permitted." Pursuant to § 242(b) of the Immigration and Nationality Act (Act), 8 U.S.C. § 1252(b), a deportation hearing was held before an immigration judge on January 11, 1974. Chadha conceded that he was deportable for overstaying his visa and the hearing was adjourned to enable him to file an application for suspension of deportation under § 244(a)(1) of the Act, 8 U.S.C. § 1254(a)(1). Section 244(a)(1) provides:

> "As hereinafter prescribed in this section, the Attorney General may, in his discretion, suspend deportation and adjust the status to that of an alien lawfully admitted for permanent residence, in the case of an alien who applies to the Attorney General for suspension of deportation and—

---

[5] In 1977, then-Senator James Abourezk, a prominent defender of the legislative veto, explained that "[s]ince 1932, when the first veto provision was enacted into law, 295 congressional veto-type provisions have been inserted in 196 different statutes * * *." James Abourezk, *The Congressional Veto: A Contemporary Response to Executive Encroachment on Legislative Prerogatives*, 52 Ind. L. Rev. 323, 324 (1977). More than half of those provisions were enacted between 1970 and 1975. *See id.*

"(1) is deportable under any law of the United States except the provisions specified in paragraph (2) of this subsection; has been physically present in the United States for a continuous period of not less than seven years immediately preceding the date of such application, and proves that during all of such period he was and is a person of good moral character; and is a person whose deportation would, in the opinion of the Attorney General, result in extreme hardship to the alien or to his spouse, parent, or child, who is a citizen of the United States or an alien lawfully admitted for permanent residence."

* * * The Immigration Judge, on June 25, 1974, ordered that Chadha's deportation be suspended. The immigration judge found that Chadha met the requirements of § 244(a)(1): he had resided continuously in the United States for over seven years, was of good moral character, and would suffer "extreme hardship" if deported.

Pursuant to § 244(c)(1) of the Act, 8 U.S.C. § 1254(c)(1), the immigration judge suspended Chadha's deportation and a report of the suspension was transmitted to Congress. Section 244(c)(1) provides:

"Upon application by any alien who is found by the Attorney General to meet the requirements of subsection (a) of this section the Attorney General may in his discretion suspend deportation of such alien. If the deportation of any alien is suspended under the provisions of this subsection, a complete and detailed statement of the facts and pertinent provisions of law in the case shall be reported to the Congress with the reasons for such suspension. Such reports shall be submitted on the first day of each calendar month in which Congress is in session."

Once the Attorney General's recommendation for suspension of Chadha's deportation was conveyed to Congress, Congress had the power under § 244(c)(2) of the Act, 8 U.S.C. § 1254(c)(2), to veto the Attorney General's determination that Chadha should not be deported. Section 244(c)(2) provides:

"(2) In the case of an alien specified in paragraph (1) of subsection (a) of this subsection—

"if during the session of the Congress at which a case is reported, or prior to the close of the session of the Congress next following the session at which a case is reported, either the Senate or the House of Representatives passes a resolution stating in substance that it does not favor the suspension of such deportation, the Attorney General shall thereupon deport such alien or authorize the alien's voluntary departure at his own expense under the order of deportation in the manner provided by law. If, within the time above specified, neither the Senate nor the House of

Representatives shall pass such a resolution, the Attorney General shall cancel deportation proceedings."

* * *

On December 12, 1975, Representative Eilberg, Chairman of the Judiciary Subcommittee on Immigration, Citizenship, and International Law, introduced a resolution opposing "the granting of permanent residence in the United States to [six] aliens", including Chadha. H. Res. 926, 94th Cong., 1st Sess.; 121 Cong Rec. 40247 (1975). The resolution was referred to the House Committee on the Judiciary. On December 16, 1975, the resolution was discharged from further consideration by the House Committee on the Judiciary and submitted to the House of Representatives for a vote. The resolution had not been printed and was not made available to other Members of the House prior to or at the time it was voted on * * *. The resolution was passed without debate or recorded vote. Since the House action was pursuant to § 244(c)(2), the resolution was not treated as an Article I legislative act; it was not submitted to the Senate or presented to the President for his action.

After the House veto of the Attorney General's decision to allow Chadha to remain in the United States, the immigration judge reopened the deportation proceedings to implement the House order deporting Chadha * * * On November 8, 1976, Chadha was ordered deported pursuant to the House action.

* * *

* * * the [Ninth Circuit] Court of Appeals held that the House was without constitutional authority to order Chadha's deportation; accordingly it directed the Attorney General "to cease and desist from taking any steps to deport this alien based upon the resolution enacted by the House of Representatives." 634 F.2d 408, 436 (1980). The essence of its holding was that § 244(c)(2) violates the constitutional doctrine of separation of powers.

We granted certiorari * * * and we now affirm.

* * *

We turn now to the question whether action of one House of Congress under § 244(c)(2) violates strictures of the Constitution. We begin, of course, with the presumption that the challenged statute is valid. Its wisdom is not the concern of the courts; if a challenged action does not violate the Constitution, it must be sustained * * *.

By the same token, the fact that a given law or procedure is efficient, convenient, and useful in facilitating functions of government, standing alone, will not save it if it is contrary to the Constitution. Convenience and efficiency are not the primary objectives—or the hallmarks—of democratic government and our inquiry is sharpened rather than blunted by the fact that Congressional veto provisions are appearing with increasing frequency in statutes which delegate authority to executive and independent agencies * * *.

* * *

Explicit and unambiguous provisions of the Constitution prescribe and define the respective functions of the Congress and of the Executive in the legislative process. Since the precise terms of those familiar provisions are critical to the resolution of this case, we set them out verbatim. Art. I provides:

> "All legislative Powers herein granted shall be vested in a Congress of the United States, which shall consist of a Senate *and* a House of Representatives." Art. I, § 1. (Emphasis added).

> "Every Bill which shall have passed the House of Representatives *and* the Senate, *shall*, before it becomes a Law, be presented to the President of the United States; . . ." Art. I, § 7, cl. 2. (Emphasis added).

> "*Every* Order, Resolution, or Vote to which the Concurrence of the Senate and House of Representatives may be necessary (except on a question of Adjournment) *shall be* presented to the President of the United States; and before the Same shall take Effect, *shall be* approved by him, or being disapproved by him, *shall be* repassed by two thirds of the Senate and House of Representatives, according to the Rules and Limitations prescribed in the Case of a Bill." Art. I, § 7, cl. 3. (Emphasis added).

These provisions of Art. I are integral parts of the constitutional design for the separation of powers. We have recently noted that "[t]he principle of separation of powers was not simply an abstract generalization in the minds of the Framers: it was woven into the documents that they drafted in Philadelphia in the summer of 1787." *Buckley v. Valeo*, 424 U.S., at 124. Just as we relied on the textual provision of Art. II, § 2, cl. 2, to vindicate the principle of separation of powers in *Buckley*, we find that the purposes underlying the Presentment Clauses and the bicameral requirement * * * guide our resolution of the important question presented in this case. The very structure of the Articles delegating and separating powers under Arts. I, II, and III exemplify the concept of separation of powers, and we now turn to Art. I.

The records of the Constitutional Convention reveal that the requirement that all legislation be presented to the President before becoming law was uniformly accepted by the Framers. Presentment to the President and the Presidential veto were considered so imperative that the draftsmen took special pains to assure that these requirements could not be circumvented. During the final debate on Art. I, § 7, cl. 2, James Madison expressed concern that it might easily be evaded by the simple expedient of calling a proposed law a "resolution" or "vote" rather than a "bill." As a consequence, Art. I, § 7, cl. 3 was added.

The decision to provide the President with a limited and qualified power to nullify proposed legislation by veto was based on the profound conviction of the Framers that the powers conferred on Congress were the powers to be most carefully circumscribed. It is beyond doubt that lawmaking was a power to be shared by both Houses and the President * * * [citing, inter alia, Hamilton and Story].

* * *

The bicameral requirement of Art. I, §§ 1, 7 was of scarcely less concern to the Framers than was the Presidential veto and indeed the two concepts are interdependent. By providing that no law could take effect without the concurrence of the prescribed majority of the Members of both Houses, the Framers reemphasized their belief, already remarked upon in connection with the Presentment Clauses, that legislation should not be enacted unless it has been carefully and fully considered by the Nation's elected officials * * *.

* * *

* * * [T]he Framers were acutely conscious that the bicameral requirement and the Presentment Clauses would serve essential constitutional functions. The President's participation in the legislative process was to protect the Executive Branch from Congress and to protect the whole people from improvident laws. The division of the Congress into two distinctive bodies assures that the legislative power would be exercised only after opportunity for full study and debate in separate settings. The President's unilateral veto power, in turn, was limited by the power of two-thirds of both Houses of Congress to overrule a veto thereby precluding final arbitrary action of one person. It emerges clearly that the prescription for legislative action in Art. I, §§ 1, 7 represents the Framers' decision that the legislative power of the Federal Government be exercised in accord with a single, finely wrought and exhaustively considered, procedure.

The Constitution sought to divide the delegated powers of the new Federal Government into three defined categories, Legislative, Executive and Judicial, to assure, as nearly as possible, that each branch of government would confine itself to its assigned responsibility. The hydraulic pressure inherent within each of the separate Branches to exceed the outer limits of its power, even to accomplish desirable objectives, must be resisted.

Although not "hermetically" sealed from one another, the powers delegated to the three Branches are functionally identifiable. When any Branch acts, it is presumptively exercising the power the Constitution has delegated to it. When the Executive acts, he presumptively acts in an executive or administrative capacity as defined in Art. II. And when, as here, one House of Congress purports to act, it is presumptively acting within its assigned sphere.

Beginning with this presumption, we must nevertheless establish that the challenged action under § 244(c)(2) is of the kind to which the procedural requirements of Art. I, § 7 apply. Not every action taken by either House is subject to the bicameralism and presentment requirements of Art. I. Whether actions taken by either House are, in law and fact, an exercise of legislative power depends not on their form but upon "whether they contain matter which is properly to be regarded as legislative in its character and effect." S. Rep. No. 1335, 54th Cong., 2d Sess., 8 (1897).

Examination of the action taken here by one House pursuant to § 244(c)(2) reveals that it was essentially legislative in purpose and effect. In purporting to exercise power defined in Art. I, § 8, cl. 4 to "establish an uniform Rule of Naturalization," the House took action that had the purpose and effect of altering the legal rights, duties and relations of persons, including the Attorney General, Executive Branch officials and Chadha, all outside the legislative branch * * *.

The legislative character of the one-House veto in this case is confirmed by the character of the Congressional action it supplants. Neither the House of Representatives nor the Senate contends that, absent the veto provision in § 244(c)(2), either of them, or both of them acting together, could effectively require the Attorney General to deport an alien once the Attorney General, in the exercise of legislatively delegated authority,[16] had determined the alien should remain in the United States.

---

[16] Congress protests that affirming the Court of Appeals in these cases will sanction "lawmaking by the Attorney General. . . . Why is the Attorney General exempt from submitting his proposed changes in the law to the full bicameral process?" To be sure, some administrative agency action—rule making, for example, may resemble "lawmaking" * * *. Clearly, however, "[i]n the framework of our Constitution, the President's power to see that the laws are faithfully executed refutes the idea that he is to be a lawmaker." *Youngstown Sheet & Tube Co. v. Sawyer*, 343 U.S. 579, 587 (1952). When the Attorney General performs his duties * * *, he does not exercise "legislative" power * * *. It is clear, therefore, that the Attorney General acts in his presumptively Art. II capacity when he administers the Immigration and Nationality Act. Executive action under legislatively delegated authority that might resemble "legislative" action in some respects is not subject to the approval of both Houses of Congress and the President for the reason that the Constitution does not so require. That kind of Executive action is always subject to check by the terms of the legislation that authorized it; and if that authority is exceeded it is open to judicial review as well as the power of Congress to modify or revoke the authority entirely. A one-House veto is clearly legislative in both character and effect and is not so checked; the need for the the check provided by Art. I, §§ 1, 7 is therefore clear. Congress' authority to delegate portions of its power to administrative agencies provides no support for the argument that Congress can constitutionally control administration of the laws by way of a Congressional veto.

Without the challenged provision in § 244(c)(2), this could have been achieved, if at all, only by legislation requiring deportation * * *.

* * *

Finally, we see that when the Framers intended to authorize either House of Congress to act alone and outside of its prescribed bicameral legislative role, they narrowly and precisely defined the procedure for such action. There are but four provisions in the Constitution, explicit and unambiguous, by which one House may act alone with the unreviewable force of law, not subject to the President's veto:

(a) The House of Representatives alone was given the power to initiate impeachments. Art. I, § 2, cl. 6;

(b) The Senate alone was given the power to conduct trials following impeachment on charges initiated by the House and to convict following trial. Art. I, § 3, cl. 5;

(c) The Senate alone was given final unreviewable power to approve or to disapprove Presidential appointments. Art. II, § 2, cl. 2;

(d) The Senate alone was given unreviewable power to ratify treaties negotiated by the President. Art. II, § 2, cl. 2.

Clearly, when the Draftsmen sought to confer special powers on one House, independent of the other House, or of the President, they did so in explicit, unambiguous terms * * *.

Since it is clear that the action by the House under § 244(c)(2) was not within any of the express constitutional exceptions authorizing one House to act alone, and equally clear that it was an exercise of legislative power, that action was subject to the standards prescribed in Article I * * *. To accomplish what has been attempted by one House of Congress in this case requires action in conformity with the express procedures of the Constitution's prescription for legislative action: passage by a majority of both Houses and presentment to the President.

The veto authorized by § 244(c)(2) doubtless has been in many respects a convenient shortcut; the "sharing" with the Executive by Congress of its authority over aliens in this manner is, on its face, an appealing compromise. In purely practical terms, it is obviously easier for action to be taken by one House without submission to the President; but it is crystal clear from the records of the Convention, contemporaneous writings and debates, that the Framers ranked other values higher than efficiency. The records of the Convention and debates in the states preceding ratification underscore the common desire to define and limit the exercise of the newly created federal powers affecting the states and the people. There is unmistakable expression of a determination that legislation by the national Congress be a step-by-step, deliberate and deliberative process.

The choices we discern as having been made in the Constitutional Convention impose burdens on governmental processes that often seem clumsy, inefficient, even unworkable, but those hard choices were consciously made by men who had lived under a form of government that permitted arbitrary governmental acts to go unchecked. There is no support in the Constitution or decisions of this Court for the proposition that the cumbersomeness and delays often encountered in complying with explicit Constitutional standards may be avoided, either by the Congress or by the President. With all the obvious flaws of delay, untidiness, and potential for abuse, we have not yet found a better way to preserve freedom than by making the exercise of power subject to the carefully crafted restraints spelled out in the Constitution.

We hold that the Congressional veto provision in § 244(c)(2) is severable from the Act and that it is unconstitutional. Accordingly, the judgment of the Court of Appeals is

Affirmed.

POWELL, J., concurring in the judgment.

* * *

[Justice Powell thought that the power to override the Attorney General was judicial power that could not be exercised by a legislative body.]

WHITE, J. dissenting.

* * *

The prominence of the legislative veto mechanism in our contemporary political system and its importance to Congress can hardly be overstated. It has become a central means by which Congress secures the accountability of executive and independent agencies. Without the legislative veto, Congress is faced with a Hobson's choice: either to refrain from delegating the necessary authority, leaving itself with a hopeless task of writing laws with the requisite specificity to cover endless special circumstances across the entire policy landscape, or in the alternative, to abdicate its law-making function to the Executive Branch and independent agencies. To choose the former leaves major national problems unresolved; to opt for the latter risks unaccountable policymaking by those not elected to fill that role * * *.

* * *

* * * We should not find the lack of a specific constitutional authorization for the legislative veto surprising, and I would not infer disapproval of the mechanism from its absence. From the summer of 1787 to the present the Government of the United States has become an endeavor far beyond the contemplation of the Framers. Only within the last half century has the complexity and size of the Federal Government's responsibilities grown so greatly that the Congress must rely on the legislative veto as the most effective if not the only means to insure its role as the Nation's lawmaker. But the wisdom of the Framers was to anticipate that the Nation would grow and new problems of governance would require different solutions. Accordingly, our Federal Government was intentionally chartered with the flexibility to respond to contemporary needs without losing sight of fundamental democratic principles * * *.

* * *

* * * The Court's holding today that all legislative-type action must be enacted through the lawmaking process ignores that legislative authority is routinely delegated to the Executive Branch, to the independent regulatory agencies, and to private individuals and groups * * *.

This Court's decisions sanctioning such delegations make clear that Art. I does not require all action with the effect of legislation to be passed as a law.

Theoretically, agencies and officials were asked only to "fill up the details," and the rule was that "Congress cannot delegate any part of its legislative power except under the limitation of a prescribed standard." *United States v. Chicago, M., St. P. & P.R. Co.*, 282 U.S. 311, 324 (1931) * * *. In practice, however, restrictions on the scope of the power that could be delegated diminished and all but disappeared * * *.

The wisdom and the constitutionality of these broad delegations are matters that still have not been put to rest. But for present purposes, these cases establish that by virtue of congressional delegation, legislative power can be exercised by independent agencies and Executive departments without the passage of new legislation. For some time, the sheer amount of law—the substantive rules that regulate private conduct and direct the operation of government—made by the agencies has far outnumbered the lawmaking engaged in by Congress through the traditional process. There is no question but that agency rulemaking is lawmaking in any functional or realistic sense of the term * * *. When agencies are authorized to prescribe law through substantive rulemaking, the administrator's * * * regulations bind courts and officers of the Federal Government, may pre-empt state law, and grant rights to and impose obligations on the public. In sum, they have the force of law.

If Congress may delegate lawmaking power to independent and Executive agencies, it is most difficult to understand Art. I as prohibiting Congress from also reserving a check on legislative power for itself * * *.

* * *

REHNQUIST, J., dissenting.

[Justice Rehnquist thought that no live case or controversy was presented, so that the Court had no jurisdiction to decide the case one way or the other.]

NOTES

Shortly after the *Chadha* decision, the Court summarily affirmed a lower court invalidation of a two-house legislative veto. *See Consumer Energy Council of America v. FERC*, 673 F.2d 425 (D.C.Cir.1982), *aff'd sub nom. Process Gas Consumers Group v. Consumer Energy Council of America*, 463 U.S. 1216, 103 S.Ct. 3556, 77 L.Ed.2d 1402 (1983). It is therefore clear that the Court regards even a bicameral legislative veto as invalid; violation of the presentment requirement is enough.

3. *Back to the Statutory Drawing Board*

Congress has continued to enact statutes containing legislative veto provisions even after *Chadha* rendered them presently unenforceable in court. Indeed, a substantial number of presidential signing statements that raise constitutional objections to legislation, *see supra* page 43, make specific mention of post-*Chadha* legislative veto provisions. *See* Nelson Lund, *Presidential Signing Statements in Perspective,* 16 Wm. & Mary Bill Rts. J. 95, 104. n.46 (2007). But *Chadha* clearly refocussed attention onto ways of strengthening the ability of Congress to police agency discretion through ordinary legislation rather than through legislative vetoes. In 1996, Congress passed the Small Business Regulatory Enforcement Fairness Act of 1996, part of which provides a systematic mechanism for responding to agency decisions known as the Congressional Review Act. *See* Pub. L. No. 104–121, Title II, 110 Stat. 857 (1996). The mechanism applies only to agency rules,[6] not to orders issued in adjudications, and it contains special provisions for so-called "major rules," which are rules that the Office of Management and Budget "finds has resulted in or is likely to result in an annual effect on the economy of $100,000,000 or more; a major increase in costs or prices for consumers, individual industries, Federal, State, or local government agencies, or geographic regions; or significant adverse effects on competition, employment, investment, productivity, innovation, or on the ability of United States-based enterprises to compete with foreign-based enterprises in domestic and export markets." *Id.* § 804(2).[7]

---

[6] The statute's definitional section incorporates the definition of a rule found in the APA, but excludes, among other things, "any rule of particular applicability," 5 U.S.C. § 804(3)(A) (2012).

[7] Apart from a specific exclusion for rules promulgated under the Telecommunications Act of 1996, *see id.*, this definition of major rules essentially tracks the category of rules that are already subject to internal executive department review by the Office of Management and Budget under a series of executive orders that have been in effect since the mid-1970s. A sample of such orders appears in Appendix D.

Agencies promulgating any covered rules must send an extensive report to Congress detailing the agency's compliance with various procedural requirements. *Id.* § 801(2). Congress may then disapprove (invalidate) the rule through a joint resolution that satisfies the constitutional presentment and bicameralism requirements. The statute, however, prescribes a streamlined legislative process of committee review and floor debate of proposals to disapprove agency rules. *See id.* § 802.[8] If Congress disapproves a rule, the disapproval is retroactive: the rule shall be treated as if it never took effect. *See id.* § 801(f). Moreover, a disapproved rule "may not be reissued in substantially the same form, and a new rule that is substantially the same as such a rule may not be issued, unless the reissued or new rule is specifically authorized by a law enacted after the date of the joint resolution disapproving the original rule." *Id.* § 801(b)(2).

Is this statute an attempt to restore some measure of legislative responsibility to the administrative state, a covert act of sabotage by opponents of regulation, both, or neither? For a thorough treatment of the statute, see Paul Larkin, *Reawakening the Congressional Review Act,* 41 Harv. J.L. & Pub. Pol'y 187 (2018). In its first two decades, the Congressional Review Act was used only once, to overturn agency rules requiring workplaces to be ergonomically sound. In 2017, however, this long-dormant statute came roaring to life; Congress used it fifteen times in the first few months of 2017 to overturn agency regulations. *See id*, at 190. Congress is also considering, as it has considered on other occasions, the so-called REINS Act (for "Regulations from the Executive [I]n Need of Scrutiny"), which would require Congress legislatively to approve all major rules before they take effect. The future of that proposed legislation is uncertain.

b. Appropriations

Article I of the Constitution specifies that "[n]o money shall be drawn from the Treasury, but in Consequence of Appropriations made by Law * * *." U.S. Const. art. I, § 9, cl. 7. On its face, this provision gives Congress exclusive control over federal spending; agencies cannot fix their own budgets, but must rely on congressional appropriations legislation for funding.[9]

A series of statutes confirm and enforce this congressional authority to control federal spending. It is a criminal offense for agency officials to obligate federal funds in excess of appropriations.[10] Agencies may not

---

[8] Either House can change the process simply by changing its internal rules. *See id.* § 802(g).

[9] Is there any circumstance in which government actors, or at least the President, can spend money without congressional authorization? *Compare* J. Gregory Sidak, *The President's Power of the Purse,* 1989 Duke L.J. 1162 (occasionally), *with* Kate Stith, *Congress' Power of the Purse,* 97 Yale L.J. 1343 (1988) (never).

[10] *See* 31 U.S.C. §§ 1341(a), 1350 (2012). Does this mean that agency officials must literally turn out the lights when their budgets run out lest they create an obligation to the local power

augment their statutory budgets with donated funds without specific congressional authorization.[11] And agency officials may not accept volunteer services except in emergencies or with specific congressional authorization.[12]

Congress thus controls the resources that are available to each agency and can use that control to penalize or reward agency behavior through reduced or expanded budgets. If Congress is dissatisfied with an agency's use of its statutory discretion, Congress can simply de-fund the agency until new personnel or policies are in place. In order to get a full sense of an agency's authority, one must therefore look both at its substantive organic statute and its budget. An agency that appears to have very broad statutory powers may have very little real-world power if Congress does not provide the agency with significant funding.

An agency's budget allocation determines the overall level of activity in which the agency can engage. But can Congress use its appropriations power to control the details, as well as the overall level, of agency administration? Could Congress specify, for example, that an appropriation to the Department of Agriculture may be used only to build a water project in the district of Congressman Graft? Or instead of forbidding the Department of Transportation from requiring motor vehicles to have ignition interlocks by amending the agency's organic statute, could Congress leave the agency's statutory authority in place but specify in the agency's appropriation that no portion of the appropriated funds may be used to promulgate or enforce a standard requiring ignition interlocks? The modern answer to all of these questions is "Yes." Congress can, and routinely does, use the appropriations process as a vehicle for making substantive policy and controlling specific agency decisions. Although the use of appropriations legislation to make policy is controversial, Congress is essentially free under modern law to accomplish indirectly through appropriations laws anything that it could accomplish through direct exercise of its legislative authority.

The more difficult question is whether Congress can accomplish indirectly through its appropriations power things that it could *not* accomplish directly. For example, Congress cannot pass a statute forbidding the Supreme Court from overruling its present caselaw concerning abortion—either in favor of or against a greater power on the part of states to legislate concerning abortions. Could Congress, however, specify that no portion of the Supreme Court's appropriated budget may be

---

companies? Yes, that is exactly what it means—as agency officials well recognize whenever a shutdown of the federal government becomes imminent.

[11] *See id.* § 3302(b) (requiring all funds received on behalf of the government to be deposited in the Treasury). Congress has given many agencies such specific "gift authority." *See* Stith, *supra* note 9, at 1368–70.

[12] *See* 31 U.S.C. § 1342 (2012).

used to prepare or issue an opinion that alters the Court's abortion jurisprudence?

c. Legislative History

Chapter 1 introduced the idea of legislative history and its potential, though seemingly waning, impact on judicial interpretation of statutes. *See supra* pages 42–48. Agencies, however, will treat legislative history very seriously whether or not courts use it as an authoritative tool of statutory interpretation. That is because legislative history is a formal way in which members and committees of Congress can communicate their desires to agencies. If a committee report expresses a view on the meaning of a contested term in a statute, a court that is disinclined to use legislative history may regard that document with little interest; after all, it represents at most the views of one committee of one house of Congress, and in all likelihood represents the views only of the staff of a small number of the committee members. To the agency, however, those are precisely the views that are most important—arguably more important than the views of the Supreme Court of the United States. If the agency construes a statute in a way that displeases a court, the agency loses a case. If the agency construes a statute in a way that displeases a congressional committee, or even the staff of a few members of that committee, the agency can lose its funding, its program, and its officials' and employees' futures. The committees that prepare reports on statutes relevant to particular agencies are generally among the committees that oversee those agencies' activities. Such committees are in a strong position to affect further legislation affecting the agencies, including appropriations legislation. They can also make life very unpleasant for the agencies by initiating intrusive oversight hearings or embarrassing media coverage. Moreover, agency officials who offend senators may have to contend with those same senators later on if they are appointed to posts that require Senate confirmation. Even statements by individual legislators who have a particular interest in a specific agency are likely to be looked upon by that agency as significant, if not entirely authoritative.

There is a substantial debate among political scientists about the extent to which congressional committees effectively control agency activity through these informal mechanisms. *See* Mark Seidenfeld, *Why Agencies Act: A Reassessment of the Ossification Critique of Judicial Review,* 70 Ohio St. L.J. 251, 255–56 (2009). Regardless of how that debate comes out, legislative history is and will continue to be an important source of information to agencies about the desires of the members of Congress most directly concerned with the agencies' affairs. For a striking illustration of the extent to which agencies will sometimes treat legislative history (even legislative history only tangentially related to the governing statute) as binding law, see *Northwest Environmental Defense Center v.*

Bonneville Power Administration, 477 F.3d 668, 681–86 (9th Cir.2007) (reversing the agency for treating "committee report language as if the language placed a legal obligation").

6. THE SCHOLARLY DEBATE

The scholarly literature on the delegation problem is voluminous—far too voluminous to summarize here. Certain recurring themes, however, bear a brief mention.

a. Are Delegations Good Policy?

A common-sense case against broad delegations of policymaking authority to agencies argues that such delegations undermine fundamental governmental norms of accountability "by removing basic social policy choices from those who are most representative of and accountable to the electorate," Martin H. Redish, The Constitution As Political Structure 142 (1995), and undermine equally fundamental norms concerning limitations on concentrated powers by circumventing the careful system of checks on policymaking built into the document by the Framers. *See id.* A wide range of scholars, of immensely varying political viewpoints, has elaborated on this commonsense critique.[13] Their general position is aptly summarized by a sequence of chapter and subchapter headings in a leading book on delegation: "Delegation Weakens Democracy," "Delegation Endangers Liberty," "Delegation Makes Law Less Reasonable," "Delegation Shifts the Focus of Lawmakers from Protecting People to Casting Blame," "Delegation Creates Wasteful Fantasies of Cheap, Effective Regulatory Protection," "Delegation Reduces the Public's Sense That Government Is Responsive," and "Delegation Makes Citizens Less Reasonable and More Alienated." David Schoenbrod, Power Without Responsibility: How Congress Abuses the People Through Delegation 99, 107, 119, 126, 128, 129, 130 (1993).

Defenders of modern delegations usually sidestep these concerns, choosing instead to focus on the issue that the Court in *Mistretta* thought decisive: the "practical understanding that in our increasingly complex society, replete with ever changing and more technical problems, Congress simply cannot do its job absent an ability to delegate power under broad general directives." 488 U.S. at 372, 109 S.Ct. at 654. Put crudely, they argue that one cannot have anything resembling the modern activist state if Congress cannot entrust very general authority to administrators.[14] Could Congress avoid that problem by treating agency action under vague

---

[13] Ernest Gellhorn & Glen Robinson, *A Theory of Legislative Delegation*, 68 Cornell L. Rev. 1 (1982).

[14] *See, e.g.,* Louis L. Jaffe, *An Essay on Delegation of Legislative Power*, 47 Colum. L. Rev. 359 (1947); Richard J. Pierce, Jr., *Political Accountability and Delegated Power: A Response to Professor Lowi*, 36 Am. U.L. Rev. 391, 401–02 (1987); Richard B. Stewart, *Beyond Delegation Doctrine*, 36 Am. U.L. Rev. 323, 327–28 (1987).

statutes as legislative proposals and then confirming them through statutes, using a fast-track procedure that minimizes debate and delay? *See* Hon. Stephen Breyer, *Reforming Regulation*, 59 Tul. L. Rev. 4, 11 (1984).

One of the few scholars to tackle head-on the accountability-based critique of delegations is Professor Jerry Mashaw. In addition to criticizing many of the arguments advanced against delegations, Professor Mashaw puts forth a positive argument that accountability concerns often counsel in *favor* of broad delegations.

Strangely enough it may make sense to imagine the delegation of political authority to administrators as a device for improving the responsiveness of government to the desires of the electorate * * *. All we need do is not forget that there are also presidential elections * * *.

* * *

* * * [T]he utilization of vague delegations to administrative agencies takes on significance as a device for facilitating responsiveness to voter preferences expressed in presidential elections * * *. The group of executive officers we commonly call "the Administration" matters only because of the relative malleability of the directives that administrators have in their charge. If congressional statutes were truly specific with respect to the actions that administrators were to take, presidential politics would be a mere beauty contest * * *.

* * * [I]t seems likely that the flexibility that is currently built into the processes of administrative governance by relatively broad delegations of statutory authority permits a more appropriate degree of administrative, or administration, responsiveness to the voter's will than would a strict nondelegation doctrine. For, if we were to be serious about restricting the discretion of administrators, we would have to go much beyond what most nondelegation theorists seem to presume would represent clear congressional choices.

This last point is so neglected in the nondelegation literature that it is worth spelling out in some detail. While most discussions of the nondelegation doctrine focus on the question of substantive criteria for decision, establishing criteria is but one aspect of the exercise of policy discretion. In the formation of regulatory policy, for example, at least the following general types of questions have to be answered: What subjects are to be on the regulatory agenda? What are their priorities? By what criteria are regulations to be formulated? Within what period of time are they to be adopted?

What are the priorities for the utilization of enforcement machinery with respect to adopted policies? What are the rules and procedures by which the relevant facts about the application of legal rules will be found? What are the rules by which facts and law will be combined to yield legal conclusions, that is, "findings" that there have or have not been violations of the regulations? What exceptions or justifications are relevant with respect to noncompliance? If violations are found, what corrective action or remedies will be prescribed?

Each of these questions can, of course, be broken down into a multitude of others and the answer to each question is a policy choice * * *.

Were the Congress to attempt to make statutory meaning uniform over time, it would have to specify the most extraordinarily elaborate criteria for exercising enforcement initiative, for finding facts, for engaging in contextual interpretation, and for determining remedial action * * *. Squeezing discretion out of a statutory-administrative system is indeed so difficult that one is tempted to posit a "Law of Conservation of Administrative Discretion." According to that law the amount of discretion in an administrative system is always constant. Elimination of discretion at one choice point merely causes the discretion that had been exercised there to migrate elsewhere in the system. If Congress were able to adopt specific regulatory criteria in some particular instance, say the OSHA statute, it would only have begun the process of making the real regulatory choices itself.

Nor will it do to suggest that activities beyond the setting of substantive criteria really do not raise the broad policy issues that concern nondelegation theorists. How the facts will be found often determines who wins and who loses. What cases are important enough to pursue entails policy discretion of the broadest sort. When to withhold remedial sanctions or alternatively to make an example of some offender raises issues of basic moral and political values * * *.

* * * [W]ere Congress forced to repeal the Law of Conservation of Administrative Discretion in order to comply with a reinvigorated nondelegation doctrine, it would thereby eliminate executive responsiveness to shifts in voter preferences * * *.

Responsiveness to diversity in voter preferences is not limited to changes through time * * *. [G]overnmental responsiveness also entails situational variance at any one time. If our laws were truly specific, this would also be impossible * * *. [W]e could not have laws that say, "Do something, but be reasonable and take account of local differences." Or at least we could not have them if our idea of democratic responsiveness is that the Congress as a body should make all the decisions necessary to give determinant meaning to the statutes that it passes.

* * * Responsiveness to the will of the people is not a unitary phenomenon that can be embodied in a single institution. Broad delegations recognize that tight accountability linkages at one point in the governmental system may reduce the responsiveness of the system as a whole.

Jerry Mashaw, *Prodelegation: Why Administrators Should Make Political Decisions*, 1 J.L. Econ. & Org. 81, 95–98 (1985).[15] Is Professor Mashaw's argument, even if correct, responsive to the concerns of critics of delegation?

b. Are Delegations Good Law?

The constitutional debate focuses on three questions: (1) does the Constitution in fact place constraints on the degree of generality of congressional statutes, (2) if it does impose constraints, can courts formulate judicially manageable standards for implementing them, and (3) even if they can, do considerations of precedent and reliance counsel against any significant attempt by modern courts to reinvigorate the nondelegation doctrine?

1. Does the Constitution Restrain Delegations?

The Constitution does not contain an express "nondelegation clause." But at least to a formalist, the search for such a clause is misguided. (To a functionalist, the permissibility of delegations is likely to be a postulate of modern government, so that the constitutionality of delegations would not be an interesting or controversial question.) The federal government is a government of limited and enumerated powers. Any institution of the national government can exercise only those powers expressly or impliedly granted to it by the Constitution. This principle applies to the President and the federal courts as much as it does to Congress. Neither the President nor the judiciary is granted "legislative" power. Instead, the President is given the "executive Power" and the federal courts are given the "judicial Power." These powers clearly include the authority to apply and interpret relevant law. Because laws are almost never completely opaque, the ordinary operations of the executive and judicial powers

---

[15] A number of other scholars have also offered an "on the merits" defense of agency policymaking under broad delegations. *See* David B. Spence & Frank Cross, *A Public Choice Case for the Administrative State*, 89 Geo. L.J. 97 (2000); Richard B. Stewart, *The Reformation of American Administrative Law*, 88 Harv. L. Rev. 1669, 1802–13 (1975).

necessarily entail some measure of discretion in application and interpretation. Indeed, this familiar "gap-filling" role is virtually constitutive of the executive and judicial functions. But surely there comes a point where "interpretation" shades into legislation and the executive and judicial powers therefore shade into the legislative power. If Congress enacts a law forbidding transactions in interstate commerce "that fail to promote goodness and niceness," with no further explanation or contextual clarification, the President and the federal courts would arguably exceed their enumerated powers by trying to define the conduct that falls within this statute. They would be legislating rather than executing or judging. As Chief Justice Marshall and James Madison recognized in the passages that begin this section, the line that separates the legislative power from the executive and judicial powers may be difficult to draw, but the line is there nonetheless. Thus, at least for formalists, the nondelegation doctrine is initially grounded in the principle of enumerated powers as it applies to Articles II and III of the Constitution. The President and the courts cannot make law because they have no enumerated power to do so.

Can Congress make these Article II and Article III problems go away? Suppose that Congress adds to the prohibition on interstate transactions "that fail to promote goodness and niceness" an express prescription that the President or some administrative agency "shall promulgate rules to define the conduct proscribed by this statute." In light of this provision, if the executive now defines the conduct prohibited by the statute, it would seem to be "executing" the law in the most obvious sense of the term by following to the letter the congressional command that the executive assume the role of primary lawmaker. How can it violate Article II for executive officers to do precisely what a congressional statute instructs them to do, provided only that the executive officers do not formally cast votes for legislation on the floor of the House or Senate? *See* Eric A. Posner & Adrian Vermeule, *Interring the Nondelegation Doctrine*, 69 U. Chi. L. Rev. 1721 (2002).

In this case, however, the inquiry shifts to whether Congress has the constitutional power to grant that kind of sweeping authority to executive or judicial agents. There are two grounds on which formalists generally think the answer is no.

One ground focuses on the absence of an enumerated congressional power to authorize what amounts to executive or judicial lawmaking. Consider the hypothetical "goodnice and niceness" statute described above. The initial statute prohibiting interstate transactions that fail to promote goodness and niceness is (let us assume) authorized by the Commerce Clause of Article I, which gives Congress power to "regulate Commerce * * * among the several States." The ancillary provision instructing the executive to define the conduct proscribed by the statute, however, is not a regulation of commerce and thus cannot be authorized by the Commerce

Clause. The authorization for such a statute must instead come, if at all, from the Sweeping Clause of Article I, which grants Congress power to "make all Laws which shall be necessary and proper for carrying into Execution" all constitutionally granted powers.[16] A number of modern scholars have invoked this clause as a possible constitutional authorization to Congress to confer broad discretion on administrators.[17] The Sweeping Clause, however, may not be quite as sweeping as is commonly supposed. Your editor and a co-author have argued that the Sweeping Clause only authorizes laws that are consistent with underlying constitutional principles of federalism, separation of powers, and individual rights. *See* Gary Lawson & Patricia B. Granger, *The "Proper" Scope of Federal Power: A Jurisdictional Interpretation of the Sweeping Clause*, 43 Duke L.J. 267 (1993). Thus, according to this argument, far from authorizing broad delegations, the Sweeping Clause is in fact a crucial vehicle through which the specific contours of the nondelegation doctrine are constitutionalized. *See* Gary Lawson, *Delegation and Original Meaning*, 88 Va. L. Rev. 327, 345–52 (2002); Gary Lawson, *Discretion as Delegation: The "Proper" Understanding of the Nondelegation Doctrine*, 73 Geo. Wash. L. Rev. 235 (2005).

A second ground for contesting delegations cuts more broadly than the first. The argument based on the Sweeping Clause only limits congressional power to delegate when the Sweeping Clause is needed as a source of such power. There are some very important contexts, involving the management of government property and the operation of governments in federal territories and the District of Columbia, in which Congress does not need the Sweeping Clause at all, because in those contexts the Constitution contains general grants of power to Congress that are plenary and self-contained. *See* U.S. Const. art. I, § 8, cl. 17; *id.* art. I, § 3, cl. 2. By this reasoning, even a formalist Congress can allow territorial legislatures to make law and can entrust management of federal lands and property to executive agents without worrying about delegation concerns. Your editor, who is something of an arch-formalist, endorsed precisely this set of exceptions to a nondelegation principle through six editions of this book. Your editor now thinks that your editor was wrong.

The federal legislative power does not originate with Congress. It originates with "We the People," who, according to the Constitution's Preamble, delegated some portion of that legislative power to Congress

---

[16] The clause today is generally known as the "Necessary and Proper Clause." The founding generation, however, uniformly called it the "Sweeping Clause."

[17] *See* Harold J. Krent, *Delegation and Its Discontents*, 94 Colum. L. Rev. 710, 736 (1994); Peter M. Shane, *Conventionalism in Constitutional Interpretation and the Place of Administrative Agencies*, 36 Am. U.L. Rev. 573, 597–98 (1987); *cf.* Peter L. Strauss, *Formal and Functional Approaches to Separation-of-Powers Questions—A Foolish Inconsistency?*, 72 Cornell L. Rev. 488, 493 (1987) (suggesting generally that the Constitution left "Congress free to make whatever arrangements it deemed 'necessary and proper' for the detailed pursuit of government purposes," but not specifically discussing the nondelegation doctrine).

when they "ordain[ed] and establish[ed]" the Constitution. U.S. Const., Preamble. Any congressional delegation of authority is therefore a sub-delegation of previously delegated power, *see* Philip Hamburger, Is Administrative Law Unlawful? 377–80 (2014), and therein lies the problem. The Constitution, in both form and substance, is a kind of fiduciary instrument in which a principal—"We the People"—authorizes agents—various governmental institutions—to manage some portion of the principal's affairs. This not only imposes fiduciary duties on the governmental actors but also brings into play various background rules of interpretation from the law of agency (which is *not* to be confused with the law of *agencies,* or administrative law; the "law of agency" is a huge field of law which involves both private and public actors and concerns what happens when some people are authorized, often through contracts, to act on behalf of others). *See* Gary Lawson, Guy I. Seidman & Robert G. Natelson, *The Fiduciary Foundations of Federal Equal Protection,* 94 B.U. L. Rev. 415 (2014). One of the most basic of those interpretative norms, which was well established in the late eighteenth century, is that agents exercising delegated power must personally exercise that power. They cannot sub-delegate away delegated power unless the authorizing instrument specifically permits it. *See* Robert G. Natelson, *The Legal Origins of the Necessary and Proper Clause, in* Gary Lawson, Geoffrey P. Miller, Robert G. Natelson & Guy Seidman, The Origins of the Necessary and Proper Clause 52, 58–59 (2010). Because there is no specific pro-delegation provision in the Constitution—the Sweeping Clause, as noted above, is much more plausibly read as an anti-delegation provision—there can be no delegation of congressional authority, regardless of the context or subject matter. This argument about the characterization of the Constitution as a fiduciary instrument, including the implication of that characterization for subdelegation of legislative (and, for that matter, executive and judicial) authority, is developed at length in Gary Lawson & Guy Seidman, "A Great Power of Attorney": Understanding the Fiduciary Constitution (2017).

Your editor, of course, might be all wet, either in his choice of interpretative methodology, his application of that methodology to the problem of delegation, or both. But that is the argument.

Even if the Constitution does contain a nondelegation principle of some sort, however, there remains the problem of determining when grants of discretion to administrators constitute delegations of legislative authority. Administrators, after all, are constitutionally capable of exercising Article II "executive Power," and that power surely includes some ability to exercise discretion. What is the point at which administrative discretion crosses the line from executive to legislative authority?

2.   Is the Nondelegation Doctrine Justiciable?

Mistretta holds essentially that the nondelegation doctrine is effectively nonjusticiable: except perhaps in very extreme circumstances, the Court will not involve itself in decisions concerning the required specificity of congressional statutes. That holding was based partly on concerns about the necessity of delegations, but also partly on concerns about whether any judicially manageable standard can be determined for separating permissible from impermissible grants of authority. That was certainly Justice Scalia's concern in his dissenting opinion, and many scholars agree that no judicially manageable standards for identifying improper delegations can be (or, at a minimum, have yet been) devised.[18]

Proponents of a judicially enforceable nondelegation doctrine have put forth four different formulations for such a doctrine. The first is Chief Justice Marshall's 1825 formulation in *Wayman v. Southard*:

> The line has not been exactly drawn which separates *those important subjects*, which must be entirely regulated by the legislature itself, from *those of less interest*, in which a general provision may be made, and power given to those who are to act under such general provisions to fill up the details.

23 U.S. (10 Wheat.) at 43 (emphasis added). In other words, under Chief Justice Marshall's formulation, the Constitution requires Congress to make whatever decisions are important enough to the statutory scheme at issue so that the Constitution requires Congress to make them. That seems flagrantly circular and unhelpful. Can we do better?

A second formulation of the nondelegation principle comes from Professor David Schoenbrod. For Professor Schoenbrod, the crucial distinction is between statutes that establish rules and statutes that set *goals*. A valid statute must set forth a *rule of conduct* and not merely a *goal* or *set of goals* to which executive or judicial actors must strive. The act of legislation is not completed simply by announcing an ambition; the Constitution requires the legislature to specify *how* and *to what extent* that ambition should be realized. "[T]he statute itself must speak to what people cannot do; the statute may not merely recite regulatory goals and leave it to an agency to promulgate the rules to achieve those goals." David Schoenbrod, *The Delegation Doctrine: Could the Court Give It Substance?*, 83 Mich. L. Rev. 1223, 1227 (1985). Goals statutes are per se unconstitutional, according to Professor Schoenbrod. A rules statute, by contrast, "demarcates permissible from impermissible conduct," David Schoenbrod, *Goals Statutes or Rules Statutes: The Case of the Clean Air Act*, 30 U.C.L.A. L. Rev. 740, 783 (1983), and therefore constitutes valid

---

[18]   *See, e.g.,* Pierce, *supra* note 14, at 393–403; Stewart, *supra* note 14, at 324–28.

legislation.[19] The problem, of course, is to distinguish permissible rules statutes from impermissible goals statutes. Most rules leave some room for interpretation and discretion in application. This feature of rules does not necessarily raise nondelegation problems because interpretation of rules is an appropriate executive and judicial function. A statute that appears to state a rule, however, may nonetheless be a "goals" statute in Professor Schoenbrod's parlance if the stated "rule" has so little meaning independent of the act of interpretation that articulation of the rule essentially constitutes an act of legislation. How does one tell in any given case whether a seeming "rules" statute defines enough permissible and impermissible conduct to qualify as a valid act of legislation? Presumably, one must pay close attention to the particular terms, context, and character of the statute to determine both the kind and quantity of conduct that it regulates. In other words, one might fairly say that a rules statute must regulate the "important subjects" in any given statutory scheme, but that the act of interpretation can involve determination of ancillary matters of "less interest"—all of which brings us back to Chief Justice Marshall's seemingly circular formulation in *Wayman v. Southard.*

A third formulation for a nondelegation principle has been advanced by Professor Martin Redish. Drawing on conceptions of political legitimacy and accountability, Professor Redish proposes what he calls the "political commitment" principle:

> * * * [A]ccountability for lawmakers constitutes the sine qua non of a representative democracy. It therefore seems reasonable to demand as the prerequisite for legislative action some meaningful level of normative political commitment by the enacting legislators, thus enabling the electorate to judge its representatives * * *. Statutes that fail to make such a commitment, instead effectively amounting to nothing more than a mandate to an executive agency to create policy, should be deemed unconstitutional delegations of legislative power. A reviewing court will be able to determine whether the necessary political commitment has been made by deciding whether the voters would be better informed about their representatives' positions by learning how their representatives voted on the statute.

Martin H. Redish, The Constitution As Political Structure 136–37 (1995). Unlike Professor Schoenbrod's (functionally similar) formulation, Professor Redish's "political commitment" principle draws attention to the

---

[19] Professor Schoenbrod would impose a lesser standard of specificity on Congress when it is legislating concerning the management of government property. Your editor once defended that seemingly odd qualification, *see* Gary Lawson, *Who Legislates?*, 1995 Pub. Int. L. Rev. 147, 154–55, but now thinks it inconsistent with the delegated nature of federal legislative power, which permits no subdelegation.

importance of the issues involved to the electorate. Legislators need not make every conceivable choice embodied in a statute, but they must make those choices that are necessary for the political responsibility contemplated by the Constitution's scheme of representation. How does one tell, however, whether a particular statute provides enough information to the electorate about their representatives to satisfy the political commitment principle? Surely the test must involve examining whether the issues left unresolved by the statute concern "important subjects" or matters "of lesser interest"—which brings us back once again to reconsider Chief Justice Marshall's circular formulation in *Wayman v. Southard.*

Your editor has suggested a fourth formulation for a constitutional nondelegation principle: "Congress must make whatever policy decisions are sufficiently important to the statutory scheme at issue so that Congress must make them." Gary Lawson, *The Rise and Rise of the Administrative State*, 107 Harv. L. Rev. 1231, 1239 (1994). In short:

> Chief Justice Marshall's circular formulation was right all along, and rather than wind our way back to it indirectly, we might as well take the freeway. The line between legislative and executive power (or between legislative and judicial power) must be drawn in the context of each particular statutory scheme. In every case, Congress must make the central, fundamental decisions, but Congress can leave ancillary matters to the President or the courts. One can try to find alternative ways to express the distinction between fundamental and ancillary matters, such as focusing on case-resolving power or demonstrations of political commitment or choices among salient alternatives, but in the end, one cannot really get behind or beneath the fact that law execution and application involve discretion in matters of "less interest" but turn into legislation when that discretion extends to "important subjects." That is the line that the Constitution draws, and there is no escape from it.

Gary Lawson, *Delegation and Original Meaning*, 88 Va. L. Rev. 327, 376–77 (2002). One might express this point with a bit more legal precision by saying that subdelegation of delegated discretionary authority, such as Congress's legislative powers, is permissible if, but only if, the capacity to delegate is *incidental* to the granted authority. The term "incidental" in this context is a term of art from fiduciary theory: "[T]he power to sub-delegate can be incidental only with respect to ministerial tasks, or where delegation is necessary in a strict sense, or where there was in the eighteenth century an established custom or usage of subdelegation." Gary Lawson & Guy Seidman, "A Great Power of Attorney": Understanding the Fiduciary Constitution 117 (2017).

Are any of these tests judicially manageable? Perhaps more to the point, as Professor Redish has forcefully asked, *see Redish, supra,* at 137, are they any *less* manageable than many other tests that courts routinely apply—and that critics of a more restrictive nondelegation doctrine generally do not question?

3.   *What About Precedent?*

Even if a judicially-manageable nondelegation doctrine can be devised, should courts apply it in the modern world, when doing so would require overruling a substantial body of case law, call into question the validity of many long-established institutions, and unravel settled expectations about the political process? This question probably cannot be answered without engaging, at a very fundamental level, the larger issue of the role of precedent in judicial (and, for that matter, legislative and executive) decisionmaking. And that, alas, would take us too far afield from the current mission. For an especially thoughtful attempt to wrestle with these issues, see Peter B. McCutchen, *Mistakes, Precedent, and the Rise of the Administrative State: Toward a Constitutional Theory of the Second Best,* 80 Cornell L. Rev. 1 (1994).

C. AGENCIES AND ARTICLE II

1. APPOINTMENT OF AGENCY OFFICIALS

Much of the Constitution is devoted to establishing who will staff the federal government. There are elaborate provisions, both in the original document and in subsequent amendments, for the selection and qualifications of the President and Vice President,[20] members of the House of Representatives[21] and the Senate,[22] and the federal electorate.[23] This set of provisions is clearly among the centerpieces of the Constitution.

What about the rest of the federal government? In modern times, the twin demises of the enumerated powers and nondelegation doctrines have made administrative agencies perhaps the most important power centers in American life. The federal government now has virtually (not totally, but virtually) unlimited legislative jurisdiction over national affairs, and Congress has virtually unlimited power to delegate that expansive legislative jurisdiction to administrative agencies. It is therefore very important to know how the administrators of those agencies, who in fact exercise most of the federal government's near-plenary power, are selected

---

[20] *See* U.S. Const. art. I, § 2, cl. 2–6; *id.* amend. XII, XX, XXII-XXIII & XXV.

[21] *See id.* art. I, § 2, cl. 2–4; *id.* art. I, § 4, cl. 1; *id.* art. I, § 5, cl. 1; *id.* art. I, § 6, cl. 2.

[22] *See id.* art. I, § 3, cl. 1–3; *id.* art. I, § 4, cl. 1; *id.* art. I, § 5, cl. 1; *id.* art. I, § 6, cl. 2; *id.* amend. XVII.

[23] *See id.* art. I, § 2, cl. 1; *id.* art. I, § 3, cl. 1; *id.* art. II, § 1, cl. 2 & 4; *id.* amend. XV, XVII, XIX, XXIV & XXVI.

for office. It is also important to know what legal and political controls exist on the administrators' decisionmaking once they are appointed; that topic will occupy much of the rest of this course.

All significant federal positions other than the few specifically created by the Constitution—the President, the Vice President, the Supreme Court, and Congress—are created by Congress under its power "[t]o make all Laws which shall be necessary and proper for carrying into Execution" all powers vested in the institutions of the national government. There are no Cabinet Secretaries, Cabinet Undersecretaries or Deputies, agency heads, or agency general counsels unless and until Congress creates those offices.[24] *See, e.g.,* 31 U.S.C. § 301 (2012) (creating twenty six key positions in the Department of the Treasury, including the Secretary of the Treasury). Once the agencies, and the key officers who head them, come into existence, those agencies can then create the enormous volume of staff and support positions within the government, pursuant to statutory authorizations to hire personnel[25] and/or general authorizations to perform agency functions, and subject to the overall budgetary strictures and hiring procedures imposed by Congress. If it so desired, Congress could micromanage the number and duties of even low-level positions within each agency, but there is no reason to think that Congress would wish to do so.

Congress by statute can determine the titles, duties, salaries, and perquisites of virtually all federal officials (with some modest limitations on its ability to control the salaries and duties of federal judges). Can it also determine the methods of selection of those officials?

Not necessarily. The Constitution contains an Appointments Clause that specifies a method of selection for at least some of the government positions that Congress creates. This clause provides:

> [the President] shall nominate, and by and with the Advice and Consent of the Senate, shall appoint Ambassadors, other public Ministers and Consuls, Judges of the supreme Court, and all other Officers of the United States, whose Appointments are not herein otherwise provided for, and which shall be established by Law; but the Congress may by Law vest the Appointment of such

---

[24] One must carve out a modest exception to this statement for certain positions created by the President pursuant to governmental reorganization plans. These plans, in which pre-existing duties and functions are moved around within the executive department by presidential order, are themselves authorized by statute. *See* 5 U.S.C. § 903 (2012). The Environmental Protection Agency, for example, was created by President Nixon as part of a reorganization plan in which existing governmental functions in other agencies were transferred to the new unit. The position of Administrator of the EPA was created by that reorganization as well. *See* Reorganization Plan No. 3 of 1970, § 1(a), 35 Fed. Reg. 15623 (1970).

[25] *See, e.g.,* 26 U.S.C. § 7804(a) (2012) ("[u][n]less otherwise prescribed by the Secretary [of the Treasury], the Commissioner of Internal Revenue is authorized to employ such number of persons as the Commissioner deems proper for the administration and enforcement of the internal revenue laws").

inferior Officers, as they think proper, in the President alone, in the Courts of Law, or in the Heads of Departments.

U.S. Const. art. II, § 2, cl. 2. The Appointments Clause thus sets forth a specific method—actually, two specific methods—by which the personnel described in it may constitutionally be appointed to office. Despite the clause's seeming detail, however, it raises as many questions as it answers.

First, which government workers must be selected in accordance with the Appointments Clause? All of them? Or is there a constitutional distinction between, on the one hand, the named officials and "other Officers of the United States" and, on the other hand, people who work for the government in positions that do not involve a substantial degree of decisionmaking responsibility (secretaries, technical support personnel, staff attorneys and other professionals, janitors, guards, etc.)? If some government employees are not "Officers of the United States" within the meaning of the Appointments Clause, the mode of appointment of such employees is not dictated by the Constitution, and Congress can presumably set whatever terms of appointment are "necessary and proper" for carrying into effect government functions, including selection by competitive examination through a civil service process. It seems clear that the term "Officers" refers only to a subset, and indeed a rather small subset, of government employees. The section of Article II following the Appointments Clause provides that the President "shall Commission all the Officers of the United States." *Id.* art. II, § 3. It has never been thought that the President must personally sign papers certifying the employment of each and every government worker. Instead, it has always been understood that "Officers" refers to some class of especially important government workers—such as high-level agency officials, federal judges, and other figures such as (at least in earlier days) justices of the peace for the District of Columbia. So the first question posed by the Appointments Clause is: precisely who are these "Officers of the United States" for whom the clause prescribes a constitutional rule of appointment?[26]

Second, the Appointments Clause prescribes two distinct modes of appointment: (1) presidential appointment subject to advice and consent by the Senate and (2) appointment, without Senate participation, by the

---

[26] To be precise, the clause refers to "Officers of the United States, whose Appointments are not herein otherwise provided for * * *." Other than the President, Vice President, and members of Congress, whose appointment does the Constitution provide for? The list is small, but important: the two houses of Congress get to choose their own officers, *see id.* art. I, § 2, cl. 5 ("[t]he House of Representatives shall chuse their Speaker and other Officers"); *id.* art. I, § 3, cl. 5 ("[t]he Senate shall chuse their other Officers, and also a President pro tempore, in the Absence of the Vice President, or when he shall exercise the Office of President of the United States"), and the states get to appoint officers of the militia. *See id.* art. I, § 8, cl. 16. It is very possible that such officials would not in any event be "Officers of the United States" for purposes of the Appointments Clause, but there are many things that the Framers of the Constitution did not leave to chance. The possibility that the President would claim the authority to appoint legislative or militia officers was one of them.

President, the courts, or department heads. The second mode is available only for "inferior Officers" and only when Congress chooses to utilize that mode. The first mode is thus the *default* mode for all officers and the *exclusive* mode for all officers who are not constitutionally "inferior." So which subset of "Officers of the United States" are "inferior," and thus capable of being appointed under the second mode?

Third, if the second mode of appointment is available and Congress makes use of it, who other than the President is capable of exercising the appointment power? Who are the "Courts of Law" and the "Heads of Departments" in whom Congress may choose to vest power to appoint inferior officers? And are there any limitations on the kinds of appointments these people can make?

Fourth, once an officer is properly appointed, can Congress expand that officer's duties without requiring a separate appointment? It is clear that Congress cannot simply designate by name the person who will fill a particular position that is subject to the Appointments Clause.[27] But can Congress circumvent this limitation by expanding the authority of already-appointed officers? Could Congress, for example, give the existing Secretary of Defense statutory responsibility for administering national pollution regulations without requiring a separate appointment for that task?

The last few decades have produced, by historical standards, a veritable torrent of litigation on the Appointments Clause. The following cases, which represent only a small fraction of the modern case law, explore (but do not necessarily answer) many of the questions raised by the clause's text.

BUCKLEY V. VALEO
Supreme Court of the United States, 1976.
424 U.S. 1, 96 S.Ct. 612, 46 L.Ed.2d 659.

PER CURIAM:

These appeals present constitutional challenges to the key provisions of the Federal Election Campaign Act of 1971 * * *.

* * *

The 1974 amendments to the Act create an eight-member Federal Election Commission (Commission), and vest in it primary and substantial responsibility for administering and enforcing the Act. The question that

---

[27] That doesn't mean that Congress won't try. *See* Olympic Federal Savings & Loan Ass'n v. Director, Office of Thrift Supervision, 732 F.Supp. 1183 (D.D.C.) (holding unconstitutional an attempt by Congress to name by statute the director of the OTS, who was responsible for administering bankrupt savings and loan institutions), *vacated as moot*, 903 F.2d 837 (D.C.Cir.1990).

we address in this portion of the opinion is whether, in view of the manner in which a majority of its members are appointed, the Commission may under the Constitution exercise the powers conferred upon it * * *.

Chapter 14 of Title 2 makes the Commission the principal repository of the numerous reports and statements which are required by that chapter to be filed by those engaging in the regulated political activities * * *.

Beyond these recordkeeping, disclosure, and investigative functions, however, the Commission is given extensive rulemaking and adjudicative powers. Its duty under § 438(a)(10) is "to prescribe suitable rules and regulations to carry out the provisions of . . . chapter (14)." Under § 437d(a)(8) the Commission is empowered to make such rules "as are necessary to carry out the provisions of this Act." Section 437d(a)(9) authorizes it to "formulate general policy with respect to the administration of this Act" and enumerated sections of Title 18's Criminal Code, as to all of which provisions the Commission "has primary jurisdiction with respect to (their) civil enforcement." § 437c(b). The Commission is authorized under § 437f(a) to render advisory opinions with respect to activities possibly violating the Act, the Title 18 sections, or the campaign funding provisions of Title 26, the effect of which is that "(n)otwithstanding any other provision of law, any person with respect to whom an advisory opinion is rendered . . . who acts in good faith in accordance with the provisions and findings (thereof) shall be presumed to be in compliance with the (statutory provision) with respect to which such advisory opinion is rendered." § 437f(b). In the course of administering the provisions for Presidential campaign financing, the Commission may authorize convention expenditures which exceed the statutory limits.

The Commission's enforcement power is both direct and wide ranging. It may institute a civil action for (i) injunctive or other relief against "any acts or practices which constitute or will constitute a violation of this Act," § 437g(a)(5); (ii) declaratory or injunctive relief "as may be appropriate to implement or con[s]true any provisions" of Chapter 95 of Title 26, governing administration of funds for Presidential election campaigns and national party conventions; and (iii) "such injunctive relief as is appropriate to implement any provision" of Chapter 96 of Title 26, governing the payment of matching funds for Presidential primary campaigns. If after the Commission's post-disbursement audit of candidates receiving payments under Chapter 95 or 96 it finds an overpayment, it is empowered to seek repayment of all funds due the Secretary of the Treasury. In no respect do the foregoing civil actions require the concurrence of or participation by the Attorney General; conversely, the decision not to seek judicial relief in the above respects would appear to rest solely with the Commission. With respect to the referenced Title 18 sections, § 437g(a)(7) provides that if, after notice and opportunity for a hearing before it, the Commission finds an actual or threatened criminal violation, the Attorney General "upon request by the Commission . . . shall institute a civil action for relief." Finally, as "(a)dditional enforcement authority," § 456(a) authorizes the Commission, after notice and opportunity for hearing, to make "a finding that a person . . . while a candidate for Federal office, failed to file" a required report of contributions or expenditures. If that finding is made within the applicable limitations period for prosecutions, the candidate is thereby "disqualified from becoming a candidate in any future election for Federal office for a period of time beginning on the date of such finding and ending one year after the expiration of the term of the Federal office for which such person was a candidate."

The body in which this authority is reposed consists of eight members. The Secretary of the Senate and the Clerk of the House of Representatives are *ex officio* members of the Commission without the right to vote. Two members are appointed by the President *pro tempore* of the Senate "upon the recommendations of the majority leader of the Senate and the minority leader of the Senate." Two more are to be appointed by the Speaker of the House of Representatives, likewise upon the recommendations of its respective majority and minority leaders. The remaining two members are appointed by the President. Each of the six voting members of the Commission must be confirmed by the majority of both Houses of Congress, and each of the three appointing authorities is forbidden to choose both of their appointees from the same political party.

* * *

Appellants urge that since Congress has given the Commission wide-ranging rulemaking and enforcement powers with respect to the substantive provisions of the Act, Congress is precluded under the principle of separation of powers from vesting in itself the authority to appoint those who will exercise such authority. Their argument is based on the language of Art. II, § 2, cl. 2, of the Constitution, which provides in pertinent part as follows:

> "[The President] shall nominate, and by and with the Advice and Consent of the Senate, shall appoint . . . all other Officers of the United States, whose Appointments are not herein otherwise provided for, and which shall be established by Law: but the Congress may by Law vest the Appointment of such inferior Officers, as they think proper, in the President alone, in the Courts of Law, or in the Heads of Departments."

Appellants' argument is that this provision is the exclusive method by which those charged with executing the laws of the United States may be chosen. Congress, they assert, cannot have it both ways. If the Legislature wishes the Commission to exercise all of the conferred powers, then its members are in fact "Officers of the United States" and must be appointed under the Appointments Clause. But if Congress insists upon retaining the power to appoint, then the members of the Commission may not discharge those many functions of the Commission which can be performed only by "Officers of the United States," as that term must be construed within the doctrine of separation of powers.

* * *

The majority of the Court of Appeals * * * described appellants' argument based upon Art. II, § 2, cl. 2, as "strikingly syllogistic," and concluded that Congress had sufficient authority under the Necessary and Proper Clause of Art. I of the Constitution not only to establish the Commission but to appoint the Commission's members * * *.

We do not think appellants' arguments * * * may be so easily dismissed * * *.

* * *

* * * Because of the importance of [the Appointment Clause's] language, we again set out the provision:

> "[The President] shall nominate, and by and with the Advice and Consent of the Senate, shall appoint Ambassadors, other public Ministers and Consuls, Judges of the supreme Court, and all other Officers of the United States, whose Appointments are not herein otherwise provided for, and which shall be established by Law: but the Congress may by Law vest the Appointment of such inferior Officers, as they think proper, in the President alone, in the Courts of Law, or in the Heads of Departments."

The Appointments Clause could, of course, be read as merely dealing with etiquette or protocol in describing "Officers of the United States," but the drafters had a less frivolous purpose in mind * * *.

We think that the term "Officers of the United States" as used in Art. II * * * is a term intended to have substantive meaning. We think its fair import is that any appointee exercising significant authority pursuant to the laws of the United States is an "Officer of the United States," and must, therefore, be appointed in the manner prescribed by § 2, cl. 2, of that Article.

* * * If a postmaster first class, *Myers v. United States*, 272 U.S. 52, 47 S.Ct. 21, 71 L.Ed. 160 (1926), and the clerk of a district court, *Ex parte Hennen*, 38 U.S. 225, 13 Pet. 225, 10 L.Ed. 136 (1839), are inferior officers of the United States within the meaning of the Appointments Clause, as they are, surely the Commissioners before us are at the very least such "inferior Officers" within the meaning of that Clause.[162]

---

[162] "*Officers of the United States*" does not include all employees of the United States, but there is no claim made that the Commissioners are employees of the United States rather than officers.

Although two members of the Commission are initially selected by the President, his nominations are subject to confirmation not merely by the Senate, but by the House of Representatives as well. The remaining four voting members of the Commission are appointed by the President *pro tempore* of the Senate and by the Speaker of the House. While the second part of the Clause authorizes Congress to vest the appointment of the officers described in that part in "the Courts of Law, or in the Heads of Departments," neither the Speaker of the House nor the President *pro tempore* of the Senate comes within this language.

The phrase "Heads of Departments," used as it is in conjunction with the phrase "Courts of Law," suggests that the Departments referred to are themselves in the Executive Branch or at least have some connection with that branch. While the Clause expressly authorizes Congress to vest the appointment of certain officers in the "Courts of Law," the absence of similar language to include Congress must mean that neither Congress nor its officers were included within the language "Heads of Departments" in this part of cl. 2.

Thus with respect to four of the six voting members of the Commission, neither the President, the head of any department, nor the Judiciary has any voice in their selection.

* * *

Appellee Commission and *amici* urge that because of what they conceive to be the extraordinary authority reposed in Congress to regulate elections, this case stands on a different footing than if Congress had exercised its legislative authority in another field. There is, of course, no doubt that Congress has express authority to regulate congressional elections * * *. But Congress has plenary authority in all areas in which it has substantive legislative jurisdiction, so long as the exercise of that authority does not offend some other constitutional restriction. We see no reason to believe that the authority of Congress over federal election practices is of such a wholly different nature from the other grants of authority to Congress that it may be employed in such a manner as to offend well-established constitutional restrictions stemming from the separation of powers.

The position that because Congress has been given explicit and plenary authority to regulate a field of activity, it must therefore have the power to appoint those who are to administer the regulatory statute is both novel and contrary to the language of the Appointments Clause. Unless their selection is elsewhere provided for, *all* Officers of the United States are to be appointed in accordance with the Clause. Principal officers are

---

Employees are lesser functionaries subordinate to officers of the United States, whereas the Commissioners, appointed for a statutory term, are not subject to the control or direction of any other executive, judicial, or legislative authority.

selected by the President with the advice and consent of the Senate. Inferior officers Congress may allow to be appointed by the President alone, by the heads of departments, or by the Judiciary. No class or type of officer is excluded because of its special functions * * *.

* * *

We are also told by appellees and *amici* that Congress had good reason for not vesting in a Commission composed wholly of Presidential appointees the authority to administer the Act, since the administration of the Act would undoubtedly have a bearing on any incumbent President's campaign for re-election. While one cannot dispute the basis for this sentiment as a practical matter, it would seem that those who sought to challenge incumbent Congressmen might have equally good reason to fear a Commission which was unduly responsive to members of Congress whom they were seeking to unseat. But such fears, however rational, do not by themselves warrant a distortion of the Framers' work.

Appellee Commission and *amici* finally contend, and the majority of the Court of Appeals agreed with them, that whatever shortcomings the provisions for the appointment of members of the Commission might have under Art. II, Congress had ample authority under the Necessary and Proper Clause of Art. I to effectuate this result. We do not agree. The proper inquiry when considering the Necessary and Proper Clause is not the authority of Congress to create an office or a commission, which is broad indeed, but rather its authority to provide that its own officers may make appointments to such office or commission.

So framed, the claim that Congress may provide for this manner of appointment under the Necessary and Proper Clause of Art. I stands on no better footing than the claim that it may provide for such manner of appointment because of its substantive authority to regulate federal elections. Congress could not, merely because it concluded that such a measure was "necessary and proper" to the discharge of its substantive legislative authority, pass a bill of attainder or *ex post facto* law contrary to the prohibitions contained in § 9 of Art. I. No more may it vest in itself, or in its officers, the authority to appoint officers of the United States when the Appointments Clause by clear implication prohibits it from doing so.

* * *

Insofar as the powers confided in the Commission are essentially of an investigative nature, falling in the same general category as those powers which Congress might delegate to one of its own committees, there can be no question that the Commission as presently constituted may exercise them * * *.

But when we go beyond this type of authority to the more substantial powers exercised by the Commission, we reach a different result. The

Commission's enforcement power, exemplified by its discretionary power to seek judicial relief, is authority that cannot possibly be regarded as merely in aid of the legislative function of Congress * * *.

Congress may undoubtedly under the Necessary and Proper Clause create "offices" in the generic sense and provide such method of appointment to those "offices" as it chooses. But Congress' power under that Clause is inevitably bounded by the express language of Art. II, § 2, cl. 2, and unless the method it provides comports with the latter, the holders of those offices will not be "Officers of the United States." They may, therefore, properly perform duties only in aid of those functions that Congress may carry out by itself, or in an area sufficiently removed from the administration and enforcement of the public law as to permit their being performed by persons not "Officers of the United States."

* * *

We hold that these provisions of the Act, vesting in the Commission primary responsibility for conducting civil litigation in the courts of the United States for vindicating public rights, violate Art. II, § 2, cl. 2, of the Constitution. Such functions may be discharged only by persons who are "Officers of the United States" within the language of that section.

All aspects of the Act are brought within the Commission's broad administrative powers: rulemaking, advisory opinions, and determinations of eligibility for funds and even for federal elective office itself. These functions, exercised free from day-to-day supervision of either Congress or the Executive Branch, are more legislative and judicial in nature than are the Commission's enforcement powers, and are of kinds usually performed by independent regulatory agencies or by some department in the Executive Branch under the direction of an Act of Congress. Congress viewed these broad powers as essential to effective and impartial administration of the entire substantive framework of the Act. Yet each of these functions also represents the performance of a significant governmental duty exercised pursuant to a public law * * *. These administrative functions may therefore be exercised only by persons who are "Officers of the United States."

* * *

NOTES

Does *Buckley*, in effect, define an officer of the United States for purposes of the Appointments Clause as any federal official who is important enough to be considered an officer of the United States for purposes of the Appointments Clause? Is a better definition available?

The Office of Legal Counsel ("OLC") in the United States Department of Justice took up that challenge in 2007 in a memorandum to agency general counsels. *See* Office of Legal Counsel, U.S. Department of Justice, *Officers of the United States Within the Meaning of the Appointments Clause* (April 16, 2007). The OLC memo noted that "the Supreme Court has not articulated the precise scope and application of the [Appointments] Clause's requirements; the Executive Branch * * * has adopted differing interpretations since *Buckley*; and questions about the Clause continue to arise regularly, both in the operation of the Executive branch and in proposed legislation." *Id.* at 3. The OLC analysis concluded that "a position, however labeled, is in fact a federal office if (1) it is invested by legal authority with a portion of the sovereign power of the federal Government, and (2) it is 'continuing.'" *Id.* at 1. Delegated sovereign power is "power lawfully conferred by the Government to bind third parties, or the Government itself," *id.* at 11, which entails the authority to administer, execute, or interpret the law," *id.* at 11, or to perform certain other functions traditionally associated with the executive arm of the national government such as military affairs and diplomacy, *id.* at 13–14. The proviso that power be "conferred by the Government" explains why state officials enforcing federal law are not subject to the Appointments Clause: state officials get their enforcement power from their own state governments rather than from the federal government (though Congress can always forbid state enforcement when it is "necessary and proper" to do so). *See id.* at 20–21; Gary Lawson, *Territorial Governments and the Limits of Formalism*, 78 Cal. L. Rev. 853, 866–67 (1990). The requirement that a position be "continuing" in order to constitute an office explains away cases such as *Auffmordt v. Hedden*, 137 U.S. 310, 11 S.Ct. 103, 34 L.Ed. 674 (1890), in which a merchant engaged by the Customs Service to appraise the value of imported goods was not considered an officer; the many historical situations in which special agents or envoys have been used in diplomatic missions without going through the constitutional appointments process; and the long tradition of *qui tam* litigation, in which private citizens can, in a limited fashion, sue on behalf of the United States and collect bounties, *see United States ex rel. Stone v. Rockwell Int'l Corp.*, 282 F.3d 787, 804–05 (10th Cir.2002). But the OLC memorandum makes very clear that "continuing" does not mean "permanent": "a temporary position may also be 'continuing,' if it is not personal, 'transient,' or 'incidental.'" *OLC Memorandum* at 21. "For example, the position of Attorney General presumably still would be an office if Congress provided for it to expire each year * * *." *Id.* at 29. When all is said and done, does OLC's forty-page definition of an officer differ markedly from the definition of an officer as someone important enough to be an officer?

A recent scholarly survey of eighteenth-century usage suggests that the term "Officer" might have a broader original meaning than *Buckley* and ensuing authorities suggest, referring to anyone "whom the government entrusts with ongoing responsibility to perform a statutory duty of any level of importance." Jennifer Mascott, *Who Are "Officers of the United States"?*, 70 Stan. L. Rev.443 (2018). In other words, an officer is anyone exercising non-trivial—rather than, as *Buckley* puts it, "significant"—authority. According to this analysis, the primary limit on who is an officer under the Constitution comes from the requirement that the official's responsibility be "ongoing."

Under this test, many officials now chosen through competitive processes rather than appointments, or appointed by officials below the level of department head, would likely be constitutional officers subject to the Appointments Clause and therefore unconstitutional in their current guises. An even broader study of linguistic practices in the eighteenth century reaches similar but not identical conclusions, finding that "the original meaning of 'officers of the United States' is messy, but arguably closer to Professor Mascott's views than the Supreme Court's." *See* James Cleith Phillips, Jacob Crump & Benjamin Lee, *Investigating the Original Meaning of "Officers of the United States" with the Corpus of Founding-Era American English*, https://papers.ssrn.com/sol3/papers.cfm?abstract_id=3126975.

The Supreme Court again considered the boundaries of the term "Officers of the United States" in *Freytag v. Commissioner of Internal Revenue*, 501 U.S. 868, 111 S.Ct. 2631, 115 L.Ed.2d 764 (1991), which concerned whether the Chief Judge of the United States Tax Court could constitutionally appoint special trial judges to hear cases and, in some instances, to render decisions. The Tax Court is one of many so-called "legislative courts," which are specialized tribunals that resolve disputes much as do regular courts, but whose judges do not have the guarantees of salary and tenure provided in Article III of the Constitution. The Tax Court, for example, consists of judges "appointed to 15-year terms by the President, by and with the advice and consent of the Senate." *Id.* at 871, 111 S.Ct. at 2635. Special trial judges are additional personnel who assist the regular Tax Court judges in their duties, much the way that magistrates assist District Court judges.

If special trial judges are employees rather than officers, the Appointments Clause has no bearing on their selection. The Supreme Court, however, had no trouble holding that special trial judges are "Officers of the United States" rather than mere employees for purposes of the Appointments Clause. Although special trial judges do not always render final decisions, they "perform more than ministerial tasks. They take testimony, conduct trials, rule on the admissibility of evidence, and have the power to enforce compliance with discovery orders." *Id.* at 881–82, 111 S.Ct. at 2640–41. Moreover, in a limited class of cases the special trial judges can actually render, with finality, the Tax Court's decisions. *Id.* at 882, 111 S.Ct. at 2640. They must therefore be appointed in accordance with the Appointments Clause—raising the question, discussed *infra* pages 230–232, whether the Chief Judge of the Tax Court is a permissible appointing authority.

Legislative courts are not the only judge-like entities in the administrative world. Administrative law judges, or ALJs, are a special breed of agency personnel who preside over many important agency adjudications (and a small handful of rulemakings). ALJs have most of the powers normally associated with trial judges, and their decisions become the final decisions of the agency if they are not appealed. *See* 5 U.S.C. § 557(b) (2012). For a more detailed look at the peculiar role of ALJs in the administrative state, *see infra* pages 313–318. Oddly enough given their importance, the constitutional status of ALJs was unresolved for a very long time.

ALJs traditionally have not been appointed in the fashion prescribed in the Appointments Clause. In the case of the Securities and Exchange Commission until 2018, for example, "the SEC's Office of Administrative Law Judges, with input from the Chief Administrative Law Judge, human resources, and OPM, identifies and selects SEC ALJs. The SEC Commissioners are not involved in the appointment process in any way." Linda D. Jellum & Moses M. Tincher, *The Shadow of* Free Enterprise: *The Unconstitutionality of the Securities & Exchange Commission Administrative Law Judges*, 70 S.M.U. L. Rev. 3, 15–16 (2017). The lower-level staff members who chose the ALJs under this scheme are clearly not among the "Heads of Departments" capable of appointing inferior officers.

The D.C. Circuit first considered the constitutional status of ALJs in 2000, holding, in a 2–1 decision, that ALJs generally were not officers under the reasoning of *Freytag. See Landry v. FDIC*, 204 F.3d 1125 (D.C.Cir.2000). A decade later, the constitutional status of ALJs rose to the legal forefront when multiple parties challenged adjudications conducted by ALJs of the SEC. The Dodd-Frank Wall Street Reform and Consumer Protection Act, Pub. L. No. 111–203, 124 Stat. 1376 (2010), allowed the SEC for the first time to pursue monetary penalty claims in administrative adjudications rather than in court. Those adjudications were conducted by ALJs. Challenges to those adjudications based on the Appointments Clause yielded a circuit split, with the D.C. Circuit finding, largely on the strength of *Landry*, that the ALJs were not constitutional officers and thus could be appointed by SEC staff, *see Raymond J. Lucia Companies, Inc. v. SEC*, 832 F.3d 277 (D.C.Cir.2016), *review denied by an equally divided court*, 868 F.3d 1021 (D.C.Cir.2017), and the Tenth Circuit holding the SEC's adjudicative structure unconstitutional. *See Bandimere v. SEC*, 844 F.3d 1168 (10th Cir.2016). The Supreme Court resolved the matter in 2018, in a decision whose full implications may take some time to process.

LUCIA V. SEC
Supreme Court of the United States, 2018.
138 S.Ct. 2044.

JUSTICE KAGAN delivered the opinion of the Court.

The Appointments Clause of the Constitution lays out the permissible methods of appointing "Officers of the United States," a class of government officials distinct from mere employees. This case requires us to decide whether administrative law judges (ALJs) of the Securities and Exchange Commission (SEC or Commission) qualify as such "Officers." In keeping with *Freytag v. Commissioner*, 501 U.S. 868, 111 S.Ct. 2631, 115 L.Ed.2d 764 (1991), we hold that they do.

I

The SEC has statutory authority to enforce the nation's securities laws. One way it can do so is by instituting an administrative proceeding against an alleged wrongdoer. By law, the Commission may itself preside over such a proceeding. *See* 17 CFR § 201.110 (2017). But the Commission also may, and typically does, delegate that task to an ALJ. *See ibid.*; 15 U.S.C. § 78d–1(a). The SEC currently has five ALJs. Other staff members, rather than the Commission proper, selected them all.

An ALJ assigned to hear an SEC enforcement action has extensive powers—the "authority to do all things necessary and appropriate to discharge his or her duties" and ensure a "fair and orderly" adversarial proceeding. §§ 201.111, 200.14(a). Those powers "include, but are not limited to," supervising discovery; issuing, revoking, or modifying subpoenas; deciding motions; ruling on the admissibility of evidence; administering oaths; hearing and examining witnesses; generally "[r]egulating the course of" the proceeding and the "conduct of the parties and their counsel"; and imposing sanctions for "[c]ontemptuous conduct" or violations of procedural requirements. §§ 201.111, 201.180. As that list suggests, an SEC ALJ exercises authority "comparable to" that of a federal district judge conducting a bench trial. *Butz v. Economou*, 438 U.S. 478, 513, 98 S.Ct. 2894, 57 L.Ed.2d 895 (1978).

After a hearing ends, the ALJ issues an "initial decision." § 201.360(a)(1). That decision must set out "findings and conclusions" about all "material issues of fact [and] law"; it also must include the "appropriate order, sanction, relief, or denial thereof." § 201.360(b). The Commission can then review the ALJ's decision, either upon request or sua sponte. *See* § 201.360(d)(1). But if it opts against review, the Commission "issue[s] an order that the [ALJ's] decision has become final." § 201.360(d)(2). At that point, the initial decision is "deemed the action of the Commission." § 78d–1(c).

This case began when the SEC instituted an administrative proceeding against petitioner Raymond Lucia and his investment company. Lucia marketed a retirement savings strategy called "Buckets of Money." In the SEC's view, Lucia used misleading slideshow presentations to deceive prospective clients. The SEC charged Lucia under the Investment Advisers Act, § 80b–1 et seq., and assigned ALJ Cameron Elliot to adjudicate the case. After nine days of testimony and argument, Judge Elliot issued an initial decision concluding that Lucia had violated the Act and imposing sanctions, including civil penalties of $300,000 and a lifetime bar from the investment industry. In his decision, Judge Elliot made factual findings about only one of the four ways the SEC thought Lucia's slideshow misled investors. The Commission thus remanded for factfinding on the other three claims, explaining that an ALJ's "personal experience with the witnesses" places him "in the best position to make findings of fact" and "resolve any conflicts in the evidence." App. to Pet. for Cert. 241a. Judge Elliot then made additional findings of deception and issued a revised initial decision, with the same sanctions.

On appeal to the SEC, Lucia argued that the administrative proceeding was invalid because Judge Elliot had not been constitutionally appointed. According to Lucia, the Commission's ALJs are "Officers of the United States" and thus subject to the Appointments Clause. Under that Clause, Lucia noted, only the President, "Courts of Law," or "Heads of Departments" can appoint "Officers." And none of those actors had made Judge Elliot an ALJ. To be sure, the Commission itself counts as a "Head[ ] of Department[ ]." *Ibid.; see Free Enterprise Fund v. Public Company Accounting Oversight Bd.,* 561 U.S. 477, 511–513, 130 S.Ct. 3138, 177 L.Ed.2d 706 (2010). But the Commission had left the task of appointing ALJs, including Judge Elliot, to SEC staff members. As a result, Lucia contended, Judge Elliot lacked constitutional authority to do his job.

The Commission rejected Lucia's argument. It held that the SEC's ALJs are not "Officers of the United States." Instead, they are "mere employees"—officials with lesser responsibilities who fall outside the Appointments Clause's ambit. App. to Pet. for Cert. 87a. The Commission reasoned that its ALJs do not "exercise significant authority independent of [its own] supervision." *Id.*, at 88a. Because that is so (said the SEC), they need no special, high-level appointment.

Lucia's claim fared no better in the Court of Appeals for the D.C. Circuit. A panel of that court seconded the Commission's view that SEC ALJs are employees rather than officers, and so are not subject to the Appointments Clause. *See* 832 F.3d 277, 283–289 (2016). Lucia then petitioned for rehearing en banc. The Court of Appeals granted that request and heard argument in the case. But the ten members of the en banc court divided evenly, resulting in a per curiam order denying Lucia's claim. *See* 868 F.3d 1021 (2017). That decision conflicted with one from the Court of Appeals for the Tenth Circuit. *See Bandimere v. SEC,* 844 F.3d 1168, 1179 (2016).

Lucia asked us to resolve the split by deciding whether the Commission's ALJs are "Officers of the United States within the meaning of the Appointments Clause." Pet. for Cert. i. Up to that point, the Federal Government (as represented by the Department of Justice) had defended the Commission's position that SEC ALJs are employees, not officers. But in responding to Lucia's petition, the Government switched sides.[1] So when we granted the petition, 583 U.S. ___ (2018), we also appointed an amicus curiae to defend the judgment below. We now reverse.

---

[1] In the same certiorari-stage brief, the Government asked us to add a second question presented: whether the statutory restrictions on removing the Commission's ALJs are constitutional. See Brief in Response 21. When we granted certiorari, we chose not to take that step. See 583 U.S. ___ (2018). The Government's merits brief now asks us again to address the removal issue. *See* Brief for United States 39–55. We once more decline. No court has addressed that question, and we ordinarily await "thorough lower court opinions to guide our analysis of the merits." *Zivotofsky v. Clinton,* 566 U.S. 189, 201, 132 S.Ct. 1421, 182 L.Ed.2d 423 (2012).

II

The sole question here is whether the Commission's ALJs are "Officers of the United States" or simply employees of the Federal Government. The Appointments Clause prescribes the exclusive means of appointing "Officers." Only the President, a court of law, or a head of department can do so. And as all parties agree, none of those actors appointed Judge Elliot before he heard Lucia's case; instead, SEC staff members gave him an ALJ slot. So if the Commission's ALJs are constitutional officers, Lucia raises a valid Appointments Clause claim. The only way to defeat his position is to show that those ALJs are not officers at all, but instead non-officer employees—part of the broad swath of "lesser functionaries" in the Government's workforce. *Buckley v. Valeo*, 424 U.S. 1, 126, n. 162, 96 S.Ct. 612, 46 L.Ed.2d 659 (1976) (per curiam). For if that is true, the Appointments Clause cares not a whit about who named them. *See United States v. Germaine*, 99 U.S. 508, 510, 25 L.Ed. 482 (1879).

Two decisions set out this Court's basic framework for distinguishing between officers and employees. *Germaine* held that "civil surgeons" (doctors hired to perform various physical exams) were mere employees because their duties were "occasional or temporary" rather than "continuing and permanent." *Id.*, at 511–512. Stressing "ideas of tenure [and] duration," the Court there made clear that an individual must occupy a "continuing" position established by law to qualify as an officer. *Id.*, at 511. *Buckley* then set out another requirement, central to this case. It determined that members of a federal commission were officers only after finding that they "exercis[ed] significant authority pursuant to the laws of the United States." 424 U.S., at 126. The inquiry thus focused on the extent of power an individual wields in carrying out his assigned functions.

Both the amicus and the Government urge us to elaborate on *Buckley's* "significant authority" test * * *. And maybe one day we will see a need to refine or enhance the test *Buckley* set out so concisely. But that day is not this one, because in *Freytag v. Commissioner*, 501 U.S. 868, 111 S.Ct. 2631, 115 L.Ed.2d 764 (1991), we applied the unadorned "significant authority" test to adjudicative officials who are near-carbon copies of the Commission's ALJs. As we now explain, our analysis there (sans any more detailed legal criteria) necessarily decides this case.

The officials at issue in *Freytag* were the "special trial judges" (STJs) of the United States Tax Court. The authority of those judges depended on the significance of the tax dispute before them. In "comparatively narrow and minor matters," they could both hear and definitively resolve a case for the Tax Court. *Id.*, at 873. In more major matters, they could preside over the hearing, but could not issue the final decision; instead, they were to "prepare proposed findings and an opinion" for a regular Tax Court judge to consider. *Ibid.* The proceeding challenged in *Freytag* was a major one, involving $1.5 billion in alleged tax deficiencies. After conducting a 14-week trial, the STJ drafted a proposed decision in favor of the Government. A regular judge then adopted the STJ's work as the opinion of the Tax Court. The losing parties argued on appeal that the STJ was not constitutionally appointed.

This Court held that the Tax Court's STJs are officers, not mere employees. Citing *Germaine,* the Court first found that STJs hold a continuing office established by law. *See* 501 U.S., at 881. They serve on an ongoing, rather than a "temporary [or] episodic[,] basis"; and their "duties, salary, and means of appointment" are all specified in the Tax Code. *Ibid.* The Court then considered, as *Buckley* demands, the "significance" of the "authority" STJs wield. 501 U.S., at 881. In addressing that issue, the Government had argued that STJs are employees, rather than officers, in all cases (like the one at issue) in which they could not "enter a final decision." *Ibid.* But the Court thought the Government's focus on finality "ignore[d] the significance of the duties and discretion that [STJs] possess." *Ibid.* Describing the responsibilities involved in presiding over adversarial hearings, the Court said: STJs "take testimony, conduct trials, rule on the admissibility of evidence, and have the power to enforce compliance with discovery orders." *Id.,* at 881–882. And the Court observed that "[i]n the course of carrying out these important functions, the [STJs] exercise significant discretion." *Id.,* at 882. That fact meant they were officers, even when their decisions were not final.[4]

Freytag says everything necessary to decide this case. To begin, the Commission's ALJs, like the Tax Court's STJs, hold a continuing office established by law. Indeed, everyone here—Lucia, the Government, and the amicus—agrees on that point. Far from serving temporarily or episodically, SEC ALJs "receive[ ] a career appointment." 5 CFR § 930.204(a) (2018). And that appointment is to a position created by statute, down to its "duties, salary, and means of appointment." *Freytag,* 501 U.S., at 881; see 5 U.S.C. §§ 556–557, 5372, 3105.

Still more, the Commission's ALJs exercise the same "significant discretion" when carrying out the same "important functions" as STJs do. Both sets of officials have all the authority needed to ensure fair and

---

[4]   The Court also provided an alternative basis for viewing the STJs as officers. "Even if the duties of [STJs in major cases] were not as significant as we . . . have found them," we stated, "our conclusion would be unchanged." *Freytag,* 501 U.S., at 882. That was because the Government had conceded that in minor matters, where STJs could enter final decisions, they had enough "independent authority" to count as officers. *See ibid.* And we thought it made no sense to classify the STJs as officers for some cases and employees for others. *See ibid.* Justice SOTOMAYOR relies on that back-up rationale in trying to reconcile *Freytag* with her view that "a prerequisite to officer status is the authority" to issue at least some "final decisions." But *Freytag* has two parts, and its primary analysis explicitly rejects Justice SOTOMAYOR's theory that final decisionmaking authority is a sine qua non of officer status. *See* 501 U.S., at 881–882. As she acknowledges, she must expunge that reasoning to make her reading work. See post, at 5 ("That part of the opinion[ ] was unnecessary to the result").

orderly adversarial hearings—indeed, nearly all the tools of federal trial judges * * *. [T]he Commission's ALJs have equivalent duties and powers as STJs in conducting adversarial inquiries.

And at the close of those proceedings, ALJs issue decisions much like that in *Freytag*—except with <u>potentially more independent effect</u>. As the *Freytag* Court recounted, STJs "prepare proposed findings and an opinion" adjudicating charges and assessing tax liabilities. 501 U.S., at 873. Similarly, the Commission's ALJs issue decisions containing factual findings, legal conclusions, and appropriate remedies. *See* § 201.360(b). And what happens next reveals that the ALJ can play the more autonomous role. In a major case like *Freytag*, a regular Tax Court judge must always review an STJ's opinion. And that opinion counts for nothing unless the regular judge adopts it as his own. *See* 501 U.S., at 873. By contrast, the SEC can decide against reviewing an ALJ decision at all. And when the SEC declines review (and issues an order saying so), the ALJ's decision itself "becomes final" and is "deemed the action of the Commission." § 201.360(d)(2); 15 U.S.C. § 78d–1(c). That last-word capacity makes this an a fortiori case: If the Tax Court's STJs are officers, as *Freytag* held, then the Commission's ALJs must be too.

The amicus offers up two distinctions to support the opposite conclusion. His main argument relates to "the power to enforce compliance with discovery orders" * * *. 501 U.S., at 882. The Tax Court's STJs, he states, had that power "because they had authority to punish contempt" (including discovery violations) through fines or imprisonment. Brief for Amicus Curiae 37; see id., at 37, n. 10 (citing 26 U.S.C. § 7456(c)). By contrast, he observes, the Commission's ALJs have less capacious power to sanction misconduct. The amicus's secondary distinction involves how the Tax Court and Commission, respectively, review the factfinding of STJs and ALJs. The Tax Court's rules state that an STJ's findings of fact "shall be presumed" correct. Tax Court Rule 183(d). In comparison, the amicus notes, the SEC's regulations include no such deferential standard. *See* Brief for Amicus Curiae 10, 38, n. 11.

But those distinctions make no difference for officer status. To start with the amicus's primary point, *Freytag* referenced only the general "power to enforce compliance with discovery orders," not any particular method of doing so. 501 U.S., at 882. True enough, the power to toss malefactors in jail is an especially muscular means of enforcement—the nuclear option of compliance tools. But just as armies can often enforce their will through conventional weapons, so too can administrative judges. As noted earlier, the Commission's ALJs can respond to discovery violations and other contemptuous conduct by excluding the wrongdoer (whether party or lawyer) from the proceedings—a powerful disincentive to resist a court order. *See* § 201.180(a)(1)(i). Similarly, if the offender is an attorney, the ALJ can "[s]ummarily suspend" him from representing his client—not something the typical lawyer wants to invite. § 201.180(a)(1)(ii). And finally, a judge who will, in the end, issue an opinion complete with factual findings, legal conclusions, and sanctions has substantial informal power to ensure the parties stay in line * * *.

And the amicus's standard-of-review distinction fares just as badly. The *Freytag* Court never suggested that the deference given to STJs' factual findings mattered to its Appointments Clause analysis. Indeed, the relevant part of *Freytag* did not so much as mention the subject (even though it came up at oral argument, *see* Tr. of Oral Arg. 33–41). And anyway, the Commission often accords a similar deference to its ALJs, even if not by regulation. The Commission has repeatedly stated, as it did below, that its ALJs are in the "best position to make findings of fact" and "resolve any conflicts in the evidence." App. to Pet. for Cert. 241a (quoting *In re Nasdaq Stock Market, LLC*, SEC Release No. 57741 (Apr. 30, 2008)). (That was why the SEC insisted that Judge Elliot make factual findings on all four allegations of Lucia's deception.) And when factfinding derives from credibility judgments, as it frequently does, acceptance is near-automatic. Recognizing ALJs' "personal experience with the witnesses," the Commission adopts their "credibility finding[s] absent overwhelming evidence to the contrary." App. to Pet. for Cert. 241a; *In re Clawson*, SEC Release No. 48143 (July 9, 2003). That practice erases the constitutional line the amicus proposes to draw.

[The Court then held that Lucia was entitled to a new hearing before a different adjudicator than Judge Eliott, even if Eliott was subsequently given a proper appointment.]

　　* * *

JUSTICE THOMAS, with whom JUSTICE GORSUCH joins, concurring.

I agree with the Court that this case is indistinguishable from *Freytag v. Commissioner*, 501 U.S. 868, 111 S.Ct. 2631, 115 L.Ed.2d 764 (1991). If the special trial judges in *Freytag* were "Officers of the United States," Art. II, § 2, cl. 2, then so are the administrative law judges of the Securities and Exchange Commission. Moving forward, however, this Court will not be able to decide every Appointments Clause case by comparing it to *Freytag*. And, as the Court acknowledges, our precedents in this area do not provide much guidance. While precedents like *Freytag* discuss what is sufficient to make someone an officer of the United States, our precedents have never clearly defined what is necessary. I would resolve that question based on the original public meaning of "Officers of the United States." To the Founders, this term encompassed all federal civil officials " 'with responsibility for an ongoing statutory duty.' " *NLRB v. SW General, Inc.*, 580 U.S. ___, ___ (2017) (THOMAS, J., concurring) (slip op., at 4); Mascott, *Who Are "Officers of the United States"?* 70 Stan. L.Rev. 443, 564 (2018) (Mascott).

* * *

The Founders likely understood the term "Officers of the United States" to encompass all federal civil officials who perform an ongoing, statutory duty—no matter how important or significant the duty. *See* Mascott 454 * * *. The ordinary meaning of "officer" was anyone who performed a continuous public duty. *See id.,* at 484–507; e.g., *United States v. Maurice*, 26 F. Cas. 1211, 1214 (No. 15,747) (CC Va. 1823) (defining officer as someone in " 'a public charge or employment' " who performed a "continuing" duty); 8 Annals of Cong. 2304–2305 (1799) (statement of Rep. Harper) (explaining that the word officer "is derived from the Latin word *officium*" and "includes all persons holding posts which require the performance of some public duty"). For federal officers, that duty is "established by Law"—that is, by statute. Art. II, § 2, cl. 2. The Founders considered individuals to be officers even if they performed only ministerial statutory duties—including recordkeepers, clerks, and tidewaiters (individuals who watched goods land at a customhouse). *See* Mascott 484–507 * * *.

Applying the original meaning here, the administrative law judges of the Securities and Exchange Commission easily qualify as "Officers of the United States." These judges exercise many of the agency's statutory duties, including issuing initial decisions in adversarial proceedings. *See* 15 U.S.C. § 78d–1(a); 17 CFR §§ 200.14, 200.30–9 (2017). As explained, the importance or significance of these statutory duties is irrelevant. All that matters is that the judges are continuously responsible for performing them.

* * * Because the Court reaches the same conclusion by correctly applying *Freytag*, I join its opinion.

JUSTICE BREYER, with whom JUSTICE GINSBURG and JUSTICE SOTOMAYOR join as to Part III, concurring in the judgment in part and dissenting in part.

I agree with the Court that the Securities and Exchange Commission did not properly appoint the Administrative Law Judge who presided over petitioner Lucia's hearing. But I * * * would rest our conclusion upon statutory, not constitutional, grounds. I believe it important to do so because I cannot answer the constitutional question that the majority answers without knowing the answer to a different, embedded constitutional question, which the Solicitor General urged us to answer in this case: the constitutionality of the statutory "for cause" removal protections that Congress provided for administrative law judges. *Cf. Free Enterprise Fund v. Public Company Accounting Oversight Bd.*, 561 U.S. 477, 130 S.Ct. 3138, 177 L.Ed.2d 706 (2010) * * *.

I

The relevant statute here is the Administrative Procedure Act. That Act governs the appointment of administrative law judges. It provides (as it has, in substance, since its enactment in 1946) that "[e]ach agency shall appoint as many administrative law judges as are necessary for" hearings governed by the Administrative Procedure Act. 5 U.S.C. § 3105. In the case of the Securities and Exchange Commission, the relevant "agency" is the Commission itself. But the Commission did not appoint the Administrative Law Judge who presided over Lucia's hearing. Rather, the Commission's staff appointed that Administrative Law Judge, without the approval of the Commissioners themselves.

I do not believe that the Administrative Procedure Act permits the Commission to delegate its power to appoint its administrative law judges to its staff * * *.

I have found no other statutory provision that would permit the Commission to delegate the power to appoint its administrative law judges to its staff * * *.

The analysis may differ for other agencies that employ administrative law judges. Each agency's governing statute is different, and some, unlike the Commission's, may allow the delegation of duties without a published order or rule. *See*, e.g., 42 U.S.C. § 902(a)(7) (applicable to the Social Security Administration). Similarly, other agencies' administrative law judges perform distinct functions, and their means of appointment may therefore not raise the constitutional questions that inform my reading of the relevant statutes here.

The upshot, in my view, is that for statutory, not constitutional, reasons, the Commission did not lawfully appoint the Administrative Law Judge here at issue. And this Court should decide no more than that.

II

A

The reason why it is important to go no further arises from the holding in a case this Court decided eight years ago, *Free Enterprise Fund, supra.* The case concerned statutory provisions protecting members of the Public Company Accounting Oversight Board from removal without cause. The Court held in that case that the Executive Vesting Clause of the Constitution, Art. II, § 1 ("[t]he executive Power shall be vested in a President of the United States of America"), forbade Congress from providing members of the Board with "multilevel protection from removal" by the President. *Free Enterprise Fund*, 561 U.S., at 484; *see id.*, at 514 ("Congress cannot limit the President's authority" by providing "two levels of protection from removal for those who . . . exercise significant executive power"). *But see id.*, at 514–549 (BREYER, J., dissenting). Because, in the

Court's view, the relevant statutes (1) granted the Securities and Exchange Commissioners protection from removal without cause, (2) gave the Commissioners sole authority to remove Board members, and (3) protected Board members from removal without cause, the statutes provided Board members with two levels of protection from removal and consequently violated the Constitution. *Id.*, at 495–498.

* * *

If the *Free Enterprise Fund* Court's holding applies equally to the administrative law judges—and I stress the "if"—then to hold that the administrative law judges are "Officers of the United States" is, perhaps, to hold that their removal protections are unconstitutional. This would risk transforming administrative law judges from independent adjudicators into dependent decisionmakers, serving at the pleasure of the Commission * * *.

* * *

* * * [I]f a holding that administrative law judges are "inferior Officers" brings with it application of *Free Enterprise Fund's* limitation on "for cause" protections from removal, then a determination that administrative law judges are, constitutionally speaking, "inferior Officers" would directly conflict with Congress' intent, as revealed in the statute. In that case, it would be clear to me that Congress did not intend that consequence, and that it therefore did not intend to make administrative law judges "inferior Officers" at all.

B

Congress' intent on the question matters, in my view, because the Appointments Clause is properly understood to grant Congress a degree of leeway as to whether particular Government workers are officers or instead mere employees not subject to the Appointments Clause * * *.

The use of the words "by Law" to describe the establishment and means of appointment of "Officers of the United States," together with the fact that Article I of the Constitution vests the legislative power in Congress, suggests that (other than the officers the Constitution specifically lists) Congress, not the Judicial Branch alone, must play a major role in determining who is an "Office[r] of the United States." And Congress' intent in this specific respect is often highly relevant. Congress' leeway is not, of course, absolute—it may not, for example, say that positions the Constitution itself describes as "Officers" are not "Officers." But given the constitutional language, the Court, when deciding whether other positions are "Officers of the United States" under the Appointments Clause, should give substantial weight to Congress' decision.

How is the Court to decide whether Congress intended that the holder of a particular Government position count as an "Office[r] of the United

States"? Congress might, of course, write explicitly into the statute that the employee "is an officer of the United States under the Appointments Clause," but an explicit phrase of this kind is unlikely to appear. If it does not, then I would approach the question like any other difficult question of statutory interpretation * * *.

* * *

* * * I would not answer the question whether the Securities and Exchange Commission's administrative law judges are constitutional "Officers" without first deciding * * * what effect that holding would have on the statutory "for cause" removal protections that Congress provided for administrative law judges. If, for example, *Free Enterprise Fund* means that saying administrative law judges are "inferior Officers" will cause them to lose their "for cause" removal protections, then I would likely hold that the administrative law judges are not "Officers," for to say otherwise would be to contradict Congress' enactment of those protections in the Administrative Procedure Act. In contrast, if *Free Enterprise Fund* does not mean that an administrative law judge (if an "Office[r] of the United States") would lose "for cause" protections, then it is more likely that interpreting the Administrative Procedure Act as conferring such status would not run contrary to Congress' intent. In such a case, I would more likely hold that, given the other features of the Administrative Procedure Act, Congress did intend to make administrative law judges inferior "Officers of the United States."

* * *

The Court's decision to address the Appointments Clause question separately from the constitutional removal question is problematic. By considering each question in isolation, the Court risks (should the Court later extend *Free Enterprise Fund*) unraveling, step-by-step, the foundations of the Federal Government's administrative adjudication system as it has existed for decades, and perhaps of the merit-based civil-service system in general. And the Court risks doing so without considering that potential consequence. For these reasons, I concur in the judgment in part and, with respect, I dissent in part.

[Part III of Justice Breyer's opinion, joined by Justices Ginsburg and Sotomayor, dissented from the majority's remedial holding that Judge Elliot could not hear Lucia's case on remand.]

JUSTICE SOTOMAYOR, with whom JUSTICE GINSBURG joins, dissenting.

* * *

As the majority notes, this Court's decisions currently set forth at least two prerequisites to officer status: (1) an individual must hold a "continuing" office established by law, *United States v. Germaine*, 99 U.S. 508, 511–512, 25 L.Ed. 482 (1879), and (2) an individual must wield "significant authority," *Buckley v. Valeo*, 424 U.S. 1, 126, 96 S.Ct. 612, 46 L.Ed.2d 659 (1976) (per curiam). The first requirement is relatively easy to grasp; the second, less so. To be sure, to exercise "significant authority," the person must wield considerable powers in comparison to the average person who works for the Federal Government * * *. But this Court's decisions have yet to articulate the types of powers that will be deemed significant enough to constitute "significant authority."

To provide guidance to Congress and the Executive Branch, I would hold that one requisite component of "significant authority" is the ability to make final, binding decisions on behalf of the Government. Accordingly, a person who merely advises and provides recommendations to an officer would not herself qualify as an officer.

* * *

Confirming that final decisionmaking authority is a prerequisite to officer status would go a long way to aiding Congress and the Executive Branch in sorting out who is an officer and who is a mere employee. At the threshold, Congress and the Executive Branch could rule out as an officer any person who investigates, advises, or recommends, but who has no power to issue binding policies, execute the laws, or finally resolve adjudicatory questions.

Turning to the question presented here, it is true that the administrative law judges (ALJs) of the Securities and Exchange Commission wield "extensive powers." They preside over adversarial proceedings that can lead to the imposition of significant penalties on private parties. In the hearings over which they preside, Commission ALJs also exercise discretion with respect to important matters.

Nevertheless, I would hold that Commission ALJs are not officers because they lack final decisionmaking authority. As the Commission explained below, the Commission retains " 'plenary authority over the course of [its] administrative proceedings and the rulings of [its] law judges.' " *In re Raymond J. Lucia Companies, Inc. & Raymond J. Lucia, Sr.*, SEC Release No. 75837 (Sept. 3, 2015). Commission ALJs can issue only "initial" decisions. 5 U.S.C. § 557(b). The Commission can review any initial decision upon petition or on its own initiative. 15 U.S.C. § 78d–1(b). The Commission's review of an ALJ's initial decision is de novo. 5 U.S.C. § 557(c). It can "make any findings or conclusions that in its judgment are proper and on the basis of the record." 17 CFR § 201.411(a) (2017). The Commission is also in no way confined by the record initially developed by an ALJ. The Commission can accept evidence itself or refer a matter to an ALJ to take additional evidence that the Commission deems relevant or necessary. *See ibid.*; § 201.452. In recent years, the Commission has accepted review in every case in which it was sought. Even where the Commission does not review an ALJ's initial decision, as in cases in which no party petitions for review and the Commission does not act sua sponte, the initial decision still only becomes final when the Commission enters a finality order. 17 CFR. § 201.360(d)(2). And by operation of law, every action taken by an ALJ "shall, for all purposes, . . . be deemed the action of the Commission." 15 U.S.C. § 78d–1(c) (emphasis added). In other words, Commission ALJs do not exercise significant authority because they do not, and cannot, enter final, binding decisions against the Government or third parties.

The majority concludes that this case is controlled by *Freytag v. Commissioner*, 501 U.S. 868, 111 S.Ct. 2631, 115 L.Ed.2d 764 (1991). In *Freytag,* the Court suggested that the Tax Court's special trial judges (STJs) acted as constitutional officers even in cases where they could not enter final, binding decisions. In such cases, the Court noted, the STJs presided over adversarial proceedings in which they exercised "significant discretion" with respect to "important functions," such as ruling on the admissibility of evidence and hearing and examining witnesses. 501 U.S., at 881–882. That part of the opinion, however, was unnecessary to the result. The Court went on to conclude that even if the STJs' duties in such cases were "not as significant as [the Court] found them to be," its conclusion "would be unchanged." *Id.*, at 882. The Court noted that STJs could enter final decisions in certain types of cases, and that the Government had conceded that the STJs acted as officers with respect to those proceedings. *Ibid.* Because STJs could not be "officers for purposes of some of their duties . . . , but mere employees with respect to other[s]," the Court held they were officers in all respects. *Ibid. Freytag* is, therefore, consistent with a rule that a prerequisite to officer status is the authority, in at least some instances, to issue final decisions that bind the Government or third parties.

* * *

NOTES

Justice Breyer's concurring opinion focuses heavily on the proposition that if ALJs are constitutional "Officers," they likely must, pursuant to the Court's decision (to which Justice Breyer vigorously dissented) in *Free Enterprise Fund v. Public Company Accounting Oversight Bd.*, 561 U.S. 477, 130 S.Ct. 3138, 177 L.Ed.2d 706 (2010), be removable at will by the agency that employs them, which would undo the scheme of (semi-)independent adjudication established by the APA. We will take up *Free Enterprise Fund* at some length later, *see infra* pages 262–276; be prepared to reconsider then some of the issues raised by *Lucia.*

The federal government is filled with persons who are not appointed as constitutional "Officers" but who share at least some of the characteristics of officers found relevant in *Buckley, Freytag,* and *Lucia.* Before the government issues a lien on, or attempts to levy upon, a taxpayer's property for alleged unpaid tax liabilities, the taxpayer is entitled to a hearing within the Internal Revenue Service, conducted in accordance with specified statutory procedures, *see* 26 U.S.C. §§ 6320, 6330 (2012), at which liability is determined and settlement or compromise offers are entertained. Those hearings must be conducted within the IRS Office of Appeals (which the statute assumes to exist but does not create), either by settlement officers, appeals officers, appeals account resolution specialists, or appeals team managers, Internal Revenue Manual 8.22.4.5, the latter of whom have supervisory responsibility over the other appeals personnel. None of these officials, including the team managers, is appointed in conformance with the Appointments Clause. *Freytag* seems to say that determination of tax liability is a significant governmental function. The statute provides that taxpayers can challenge Office of Appeals decisions in the Tax Court, 26 U.S.C. §§ 6320(c), 6330(d)(1) (2012), which seems to give those decisions the kind of administrative finality deemed relevant (even if not dispositive) in *Freytag* and *Lucia*. So are these officials—or at least the supervisory team managers—"Officers of the United States"?

The D.C. Circuit said "no" in *Tucker v. Commissioner of Internal Revenue*, 676 F.3d 1129 (D.C.Cir.2012):

> Although the cases are not altogether clear, the main criteria for drawing the line between inferior Officers and employees * * * are (1) the significance of the matters resolved by the officials, (2) the discretion they exercise in reaching their decisions, and (3) the finality of those decisions. In light of *Freytag* we can assume here that the issue of a person's tax liability is substantively significant enough to meet factor (1), in which case degrees of discretion and finality will ultimately be determinative * * *.

> * * *[I]n this case * * *, we conclude that the lack of discretion is determinative, offsetting the effective finality of Appeals employees' decisions within the executive branch.

> Appeals employees' discretion is highly constrained * * *. The office is authorized to compromise disputed tax liability on the basis of its probabilistic estimates of the hazards of litigation * * *.

> But in reaching such decisions (and indeed in all its decisions), Appeals is subject to consultation requirements, to guidelines, and to supervision. First, the office is instructed in the Internal Revenue Manual to "[r]equest legal advice from an Associate Chief Counsel office on novel or significant issues. Second, the Manual tells Appeals to seek a "Technical Advice Memorandum" from the Chief Counsel's Office "when a lack of uniformity exists on the disposition of the issue or the issue is unusual or complex enough to warrant consideration by the Office of Chief Counsel." (The Chief Counsel is appointed by the President with the advice and consent of the Senate.) Third, Appeals is required to follow any established technical or legal IRS position that is favorable to the taxpayer. Fourth, various regulations and the Internal Revenue Manual impose detailed guidelines for

what settlements Appeals may accept. Fifth, Appeals must obtain a favorable opinion from the General Counsel for the Treasury for any compromise in which the unpaid amount of tax is $50,000 or more, and its compromises of smaller amounts are subject to "continuing quality review by the Secretary." * * * Sixth, any "closing agreement" relieving a taxpayer of liability must be approved by the Secretary * * *.

* * *

Accordingly, we find even Appeals employees' authority over tax liability insufficient to rank them as inferior Officers.

This being so, it is plain that the authority they exercise in the pure collection aspects of * * * [the] hearings is not enough. As to those functions, the government is simply a creditor, and accordingly Appeals employees must make decisions based largely on the same mundane and practical concerns that any creditor faces * * *. [T]he significance and discretion involved in the decisions seem well below the level necessary to require an "Officer."

Id. at 1133–35. Would the court have been better off just to say that these employees are not important enough to be officers for purposes of the Appointments Clause? Did the court actually say something different? Does this decision survive *Lucia*?

The Appointments Clause only applies to "Officers of the United States, whose Appointments are not herein otherwise provided for." Because the appointments of the President and Vice President are "otherwise provided for," this phrasing could lead one to conclude that the President and Vice President are "Officers of the United States." The same phrase, however, also describes the officials who must receive presidential commissions. U.S. Const. art. II, § 3. It is not impossible that the President must commission himself or herself, but the idea has an odd ring. More substantively, the Impeachment Clause extends to "[t]he President, Vice President and all civil Officers of the United States." *Id.* § 4. The absence of the word "other" between "all" and "civil Officers" is strong textual evidence that the President and Vice President are not themselves "Officers of the United States." 2 Joseph Story, Commentaries on the Constitution § 791 (1833). So, if the President and Vice President are not "Officers of the United States," then what are they?

The Constitution at various times refers to "the Office of the President of the United States," "Office of honor, Trust or Profit under the United States," "civil Office under the Authority of the United States," "Office under the United States," "Office of Profit or Trust under [the United States]," "executive and judicial Officers, both of the United States and of the several States," and also to "Officer[s]" generically, without any modifiers. The scope of these phrases in their particular constitutional contexts determines, among other things, which officials are subject to Congress' impeachment powers; the scope of the removal flowing from a Senate conviction following impeachment; the extent of various disqualifications from holding federal positions; and who is precluded from receiving gifts from foreign governments. These kinds of questions seldom reach the courts, but they are among the many questions of governmental structure with which executive and legislative department lawyers must often struggle. For an intriguing account of the significance of, and the vigorous debates concerning, the Constitution's varying usages of the word "officer," see Seth Barrett Tillman, *Interpreting Precise Constitutional Text: The Argument for a "New" Interpretation of the Incompatibility Clause, the Removal & Disqualification Clause, and the Religious Test Clause—A Response to Professor Josh Chafetz's* Impeachment and Assassination, 61 Cleveland St. L. Rev. 285 (2013).

Once one determines that a federal official is an "Officer of the United States," one may further need to determine whether that officer is an "inferior Officer" whose appointment can be vested by statute in the President, department heads, or courts of law without Senate consent. (If no statute prescribes such a mode of appointment, then the officer must be appointed by the President with the advice and consent of the Senate, which is the constitutional default rule for all officers and the exclusive rule for non-inferior officers.) How does one distinguish an inferior officer from a non-inferior officer?

One terminological point might lead to confusion. At least since *Buckley v. Valeo*, it has been conventional to describe officers who must, regardless of Congress's wishes, constitutionally be appointed by the President with the advice and consent of the Senate as "principal" officers. That is a mistake. The term "principal Officer" does not appear in the Appointments Clause; it appears in the Opinions Clause, which says that the President "may require the Opinion, in writing, of the principal Officer in each of the executive Departments, upon any Subject relating to the Duties of their respective Offices." U.S. Const. art. II, § 2, cl. 1. The phrasing of the Opinions Clause indicates that there is one and only one "principal" officer in each department, meaning that the "principal" officers are really the "Heads of Departments" who are capable of appointing inferior officers (or the chair of a multi-member commission if such a commission can be a constitutional "Department" with a collegial "Head[ ]" as an appointing authority). That does not mean that all non-principal officers are inferior. The opposite of an inferior officer is a *superior* officer, and many superior officers are not principal officers. This was very clear at the Constitutional Convention. When the inferior officers provision of the Appointments Clause was introduced by Gouverneur Morris on September 15, 1787, James Madison claimed: "It does not go far enough if it be necessary at all—Superior Officers below Heads of Departments ought in some cases to have the appointment of lesser offices." 2 The Records of the Federal Convention of 1787, at 627 (Max Farrand ed. 1911). Madison clearly had the understanding that the class of "Superior Officers" was broader than the class of department heads (or "principal Officers"). Nonetheless, the uniform modern practice has been to refer to non-inferior officers as "principal," though without drawing (thus far) the implication of exactly-one-principal-officer-per-department that might be gleaned from cross-referencing that term with the Opinions Clause. Your editor, with much heavy sighing, defers to this practice of describing superior officers as "principal" in the rest of these materials.

MORRISON V. OLSON

Supreme Court of the United States, 1988.
487 U.S. 654, 108 S.Ct. 2597, 101 L.Ed.2d 569.

CHIEF JUSTICE REHNQUIST delivered the opinion of the Court.

This case presents us with a challenge to the independent counsel provisions of the Ethics in Government Act of 1978, 28 U.S.C. §§ 49, 591 *et seq.* (1982 ed., Supp. V) * * *.

* * *

Briefly stated, Title VI of the Ethics in Government Act (Title VI or the Act), 28 U.S.C. §§ 591–599, allows for the appointment of an "independent counsel" to investigate and, if appropriate, prosecute certain high-ranking Government officials for violations of federal criminal laws. The Act requires the Attorney General, upon receipt of information that he determines is "sufficient to constitute grounds to investigate whether any person [covered by the Act] may have violated any Federal criminal law," to conduct a preliminary investigation of the matter. When the Attorney General has completed this investigation, or 90 days has elapsed, he is required to report to a special court (the Special Division) created by the Act "for the purpose of appointing independent counsels." 28 U.S.C. § 49. If the Attorney General determines that "there are no reasonable grounds to believe that further investigation is warranted," then he must notify the Special Division of this result. In such a case, "the division of the court shall have no power to appoint an independent counsel." § 592(b)(1). If, however, the Attorney General has determined that there are "reasonable grounds to believe that further investigation or prosecution is warranted," then he "shall apply to the division of the court for the appointment of an independent counsel." The Attorney General's application to the court "shall contain sufficient information to assist the [court] in selecting an independent counsel and in defining that independent counsel's prosecutorial jurisdiction." § 592(d). Upon receiving this application, the Special Division "shall appoint an appropriate independent counsel and shall define that independent counsel's prosecutorial jurisdiction." § 593(b).

With respect to all matters within the independent counsel's jurisdiction, the Act grants the counsel "full power and independent authority to exercise all investigative and prosecutorial functions and powers of the Department of Justice, the Attorney General, and any other officer or employee of the Department of Justice." § 594(a) * * *. Under

§ 594(a)(9), the counsel's powers include "initiating and conducting prosecutions in any court of competent jurisdiction, framing and signing indictments, filing informations, and handling all aspects of any case, in the name of the United States." The counsel may appoint employees, may request and obtain assistance from the Department of Justice, and may accept referral of matters from the Attorney General if the matter falls within the counsel's jurisdiction as defined by the Special Division. The Act also states that an independent counsel "shall, except where not possible, comply with the written or other established policies of the Department of Justice respecting enforcement of the criminal laws." § 594(f) * * *.

Two statutory provisions govern the length of an independent counsel's tenure in office * * *. Section 596(a)(1) provides:

> "An independent counsel appointed under this chapter may be removed from office, other than by impeachment and conviction, only by the personal action of the Attorney General and only for good cause, physical disability, mental incapacity, or any other condition that substantially impairs the performance of such independent counsel's duties." * * *

Under the current version of the Act, an independent counsel can obtain judicial review of the Attorney General's action * * *.

* * * Under § 596(b)(1), the office of an independent counsel terminates when he or she notifies the Attorney General that he or she has completed or substantially completed any investigations or prosecutions undertaken pursuant to the Act. In addition, the Special Division, acting either on its own or on the suggestion of the Attorney General, may terminate the office of an independent counsel at any time if it finds that "the investigation of all matters within the prosecutorial jurisdiction of such independent counsel . . . have been completed or so substantially completed that it would be appropriate for the Department of Justice to complete such investigations and prosecutions." § 596(b)(2).

Finally, the Act provides for congressional oversight of the activities of independent counsel * * *.

* * *

* * * The initial question is * * * whether appellant is an "inferior" or a "principal" officer.[12] If she is the latter, as the Court of Appeals concluded, then the Act is in violation of the Appointments Clause.

The line between "inferior" and "principal" officers is one that is far from clear, and the Framers provided little guidance into where it should be drawn. See, *e.g.*, 2 J. Story, Commentaries on the Constitution § 1536, pp. 397–398 (3d ed. 1858) ("In the practical course of the government there

---

[12] It is clear that appellant is an "officer" of the United States, not an "employee."

does not seem to have been any exact line drawn, who are and who are not to be deemed *inferior* officers, in the sense of the constitution, whose appointment does not necessarily require the concurrence of the senate"). We need not attempt here to decide exactly where the line falls between the two types of officers, because in our view appellant clearly falls on the "inferior officer" side of that line. Several factors lead to this conclusion.

First, appellant is subject to removal by a higher Executive Branch official. Although appellant may not be "subordinate" to the Attorney General (and the President) insofar as she possesses a degree of independent discretion to exercise the powers delegated to her under the Act, the fact that she can be removed by the Attorney General indicates that she is to some degree "inferior" in rank and authority. Second, appellant is empowered by the Act to perform only certain, limited duties. An independent counsel's role is restricted primarily to investigation and, if appropriate, prosecution for certain federal crimes. Admittedly, the Act delegates to appellant "full power and independent authority to exercise all investigative and prosecutorial functions and powers of the Department of Justice," but this grant of authority does not include any authority to formulate policy for the Government or the Executive Branch, nor does it give appellant any administrative duties outside of those necessary to operate her office. The Act specifically provides that in policy matters appellant is to comply to the extent possible with the policies of the Department.

Third, appellant's office is limited in jurisdiction. Not only is the Act itself restricted in applicability to certain federal officials suspected of certain serious federal crimes, but an independent counsel can only act within the scope of the jurisdiction that has been granted by the Special Division pursuant to a request by the Attorney General. Finally, appellant's office is limited in tenure. There is concededly no time limit on the appointment of a particular counsel. Nonetheless, the office of independent counsel is "temporary" in the sense that an independent counsel is appointed essentially to accomplish a single task, and when that task is over the office is terminated, either by the counsel herself or by action of the Special Division. Unlike other prosecutors, appellant has no ongoing responsibilities that extend beyond the accomplishment of the mission that she was appointed for and authorized by the Special Division to undertake * * *.

* * *

This does not, however, end our inquiry under the Appointments Clause. Appellees argue that even if appellant is an "inferior" officer, the Clause does not empower Congress to place the power to appoint such an officer outside the Executive Branch. They contend that the Clause does not contemplate congressional authorization of "interbranch appointments," in which an officer of one branch is appointed by officers of another branch. The relevant language of the Appointments Clause is worth repeating. It reads: ". . . but the Congress may by Law vest the Appointment of such inferior Officers, as they think proper, in the President alone, in the courts of Law, or in the Heads of Departments." On its face, the language of this "excepting clause" admits of no limitation on interbranch appointments. Indeed, the inclusion of "as they think proper" seems clearly to give Congress significant discretion to determine whether it is "proper" to vest the appointment of, for example, executive officials in the "courts of Law" * * *.

* * *

We do not mean to say that Congress' power to provide for interbranch appointments of "inferior officers" is unlimited. In addition to separation-of-powers concerns, which would arise if such provisions for appointment had the potential to impair the constitutional functions assigned to one of the branches, *[Ex parte] Siebold* * * * suggested that Congress' decision to vest the appointment power in the courts would be improper if there was some "incongruity" between the functions normally performed by the courts and the performance of their duty to appoint. 100 U.S. [10 Otto], at 398 ("[T]he duty to appoint inferior officers, when required thereto by law, is a constitutional duty of the courts; and in the present case there is no such incongruity in the duty required as to excuse the courts from its performance, or to render their acts void"). In this case, however, we do not think it impermissible for Congress to vest the power to appoint independent counsel in a specially created federal court * * *.

* * *

SCALIA, J., dissenting:

* * *

* * * [T]he Court does not attempt to "decide exactly" what establishes the line between principal and "inferior" officers, but is confident that, whatever the line may be, appellant "clearly falls on the 'inferior officer' side" of it. The Court gives three reasons: *First*, she "is subject to removal by a higher Executive Branch official," namely, the Attorney General. *Second*, she is "empowered by the Act to perform only certain, limited duties." *Third*, her office is "limited in jurisdiction" and "limited in tenure."

The first of these lends no support to the view that appellant is an inferior officer. Appellant is removable only for "good cause" or physical or mental incapacity. By contrast, most (if not all) *principal* officers in the Executive Branch may be removed by the President *at will*. I fail to see how the fact that appellant is more difficult to remove than most principal officers helps to establish that she is an inferior officer * * *.

The second reason offered by the Court—that appellant performs only certain, limited duties—may be relevant to whether she is an inferior officer, but it mischaracterizes the extent of her powers. As the Court states: "Admittedly, the Act delegates to appellant [the] *'full power and independent authority to exercise all investigative and prosecutorial functions and powers of the Department of Justice.'* " ([E]mphasis added) * * *. Once all of this is "admitted," it seems to me impossible to maintain that appellant's authority is so "limited" as to render her an inferior officer * * *.

The final set of reasons given by the Court for why the independent counsel clearly is an inferior officer emphasizes the limited nature of her jurisdiction and tenure. Taking the latter first, I find nothing unusually limited about the independent counsel's tenure. To the contrary, unlike most high-ranking Executive Branch officials, she continues to serve until she (or the Special Division) decides that her work is substantially completed. This particular independent prosecutor has already served more than two years, which is at least as long as many Cabinet officials. As to the scope of her jurisdiction, there can be no doubt that is small (though far from unimportant). But within it she exercises more than the full power of the Attorney General. The Ambassador to Luxembourg is not anything less than a principal officer, simply because Luxembourg is small. And the federal judge who sits in a small district is not for that reason "inferior in rank and authority" * * *.

More fundamentally, however, it is not clear from the Court's opinion why the factors it discusses—even if applied correctly to the facts of this case—are determinative of the question of inferior officer status * * *. [T]he independent counsel is not an inferior officer because she is not *subordinate* to any officer in the Executive Branch (indeed, not even to the President) * * *. At the only other point in the Constitution at which the word "inferior" appears, it plainly connotes a relationship of subordination. Article III vests the judicial power of the United States in "one supreme Court, and in such *inferior* Courts as the Congress may from time to time ordain and establish." U.S. Const., Art. III, § 1 (emphasis added). In Federalist No. 81, Hamilton pauses to describe the "inferior" courts authorized by Article III as inferior in the sense that they are "subordinate" to the Supreme Court.

* * *

To be sure, it is not a *sufficient* condition for "inferior" officer status that one be subordinate to a principal officer. Even an officer who is subordinate to a department head can be a principal officer * * *. But it is surely a *necessary* condition for inferior officer status that the officer be subordinate to another officer * * *.

* * *

NOTES

1.   Who Is "Inferior"?

Does the majority in *Morrison* define a principal officer for purposes of the Appointments Clause as any officer who is important enough to be considered a principal officer for purposes of the Appointments Clause? Is a better definition available?

A few years after *Morrison*, Justice Scalia found himself in the majority— and, intriguingly enough, assigned by the author of *Morrison v. Olson* to write the opinion—in *Edmond v. United States*, 520 U.S. 651, 117 S.Ct. 1573, 137 L.Ed.2d 917 (1997), which concerned the appointment process for members of the Coast Guard Court of Criminal Appeals. As with the Tax Court judges in *Freytag,* these officials perform adjudicatory functions but do not conform to the requirements of Article III. The Coast Guard Court of Criminal Appeals judges are appointed by the Secretary of Transportation. The secretary is clearly a department head under the Appointments Clause and thus capable of appointing inferior officers. The issue in *Edmond* was whether the judges were in fact principal officers who had to be appointed by the President with Senate confirmation. Justice Scalia wrote for an eight-Justice majority that the judges in question were inferior officers, using the following reasoning:

> Our cases have not set forth an exclusive criterion for distinguishing between principal and inferior officers for Appointment Clause purposes. Among the offices that we have found to be inferior are that of a district court clerk, an election supervisor, a vice-consul charged temporarily with the duties of the consul, and a "United States commissioner" in district court proceedings. Most recently, in *Morrison v. Olson*, 487 U.S. 654, 108 S.Ct. 2597, 101 L.Ed.2d 569 (1988), we held that the independent counsel created by provisions of the Ethics in Government Act of 1978 was an inferior officer. In reaching that conclusion, we relied on several factors: that the independent counsel was subject to removal by a higher officer (the Attorney General), that she performed only limited duties, that her jurisdiction was narrow, and that her tenure was limited.

> Petitioners are quite correct that the last two of these conclusions do not hold with regard to the office of military judge at issue here. It is not "limited in tenure," as that phrase was used in *Morrison* to describe "appoint[ment] essentially to accomplish a single task [at the end of which] the office is terminated." Nor are military judges "limited in jurisdiction," as used in *Morrison* to refer to the fact that an independent counsel may investigate and prosecute only those individuals, and for only those crimes, that are within the scope of jurisdiction granted by the special three judge appointing panel. However, *Morrison* did not purport to set forth a definitive test for whether an office is "inferior" under the Appointments Clause. To the contrary, it explicitly stated: "We need not attempt here to decide exactly where the line falls between the

two types of officers, because in our view [the independent counsel] clearly falls on the 'inferior officer' side of the line." 487 U.S., at 671, 108 S.Ct., at 2608.

To support principal-officer status, petitioners emphasize the importance of the responsibilities that Court of Criminal Appeals judges bear. They review those court-martial proceedings that result in the most serious sentences, including those "in which the sentence, as approved, extends to death, dismissal . . . , dishonorable or bad-conduct discharge, or confinement for one year or more." Art. 66(b)(1), UCMJ, 10 U.S.C. § 866(b)(1). They must ensure that the court-martial's finding of guilt and its sentence are "correct in law and fact," *id.* Art. 66(c), § 866(c), which includes resolution of constitutional challenges. And finally, unlike most appellate judges, Court of Criminal Appeals judges are not required to defer to the trial court's factual findings, but may independently "weigh the evidence, judge the credibility of witnesses, and determine controverted questions of fact, recognizing that the trial court saw and heard the witnesses." *Ibid.* We do not dispute that military appellate judges are charged with exercising significant authority on behalf of the United States. This, however, is also true of offices that we have held were "inferior" within the meaning of the Appointments Clause. The exercise of "significant authority pursuant to the laws of the United States" marks, not the line between principal and inferior officer for Appointments Clause purposes, but rather, as we said in *Buckley*, the line between officer and non-officer. 424 U.S., at 126, 96 S.Ct., at 685–686.

Generally speaking, the term "inferior officer" connotes a relationship with some higher ranking officer or officers below the President: Whether one is an "inferior" officer depends on whether he has a superior. It is not enough that other officers may be identified who formally maintain a higher rank, or possess responsibilities of a greater magnitude. If that were the intention, the Constitution might have used the phrase "lesser officer." Rather, in the context of a Clause designed to preserve political accountability relative to important Government assignments, we think it evident that "inferior officers" are officers whose work is directed and supervised at some level by others who were appointed by Presidential nomination with the advice and consent of the Senate.

* * *

Supervision of the work of Court of Criminal Appeals judges is divided between the Judge Advocate General (who in the Coast Guard is subordinate to the Secretary of Transportation) and the Court of Appeals for the Armed Forces. The Judge Advocate General exercises administrative oversight over the Court of Criminal Appeals * * *. It is conceded by the parties that the Judge Advocate

General may also remove a Court of Criminal Appeals judge from his judicial assignment without cause. The power to remove officers, we have recognized, is a powerful tool for control.

The Judge Advocate General's control over Court of Criminal Appeals judges is, to be sure, not complete. He may not attempt to influence (by threat of removal or otherwise) the outcome of individual proceedings, Art. 37, UCMJ, 10 U.S.C. § 837, and has no power to reverse decisions of the court. This latter power does reside, however, in another Executive Branch entity, the Court of Appeals for the Armed Forces. That court reviews every decision of the Courts of Criminal Appeals in which: (a) the sentence extends to death; (b) the Judge Advocate General orders such review; or (c) the court itself grants review upon petition of the accused. *id.*, Art. 67(a), § 867(a). The scope of review is narrower than that exercised by the Court of Criminal Appeals: so long as there is some competent evidence in the record to establish each element of the offense beyond a reasonable doubt, the Court of Appeals for the Armed Forces will not reevaluate the facts. This limitation upon review does not in our opinion render the judges of the Court of Criminal Appeals principal officers. What is significant is that the judges of the Court of Criminal Appeals have no power to render a final decision on behalf of the United States unless permitted to do so by other Executive officers.

Finally, petitioners argue that *Freytag v. Commissioner*, 501 U.S. 868, 111 S.Ct. 2631, 115 L.Ed.2d 764 (1991), which held that special trial judges charged with assisting Tax Court judges were inferior officers and could be appointed by the Chief Judge of the Tax Court, suggests that Court of Criminal Appeals judges are principal officers. Petitioners contend that Court of Criminal Appeals judges more closely resemble Tax Court judges—who we implied (according to petitioners) were principal officers—than they do special trial judges. We note initially that *Freytag* does not hold that Tax Court judges are principal officers; only the appointment of special trial judges was at issue in that case. Moreover, there are two significant distinctions between Tax Court judges and Court of Criminal Appeals judges. First, there is no Executive Branch tribunal comparable to the Court of Appeals for the Armed Forces that reviews the work of the Tax Court; its decisions are appealable only to courts of the Third Branch. And second, there is no officer comparable to a Judge Advocate General who supervises the work of the Tax Court, with power to determine its procedural rules, to remove any judge without cause, and to order any decision submitted for review.

Id. at 661–66, 117 S.Ct. at 1580–82. Justice Souter concurred separately, insisting that the Court's (new?) understanding of the line between inferior and principal officers was too narrow.

Because the term "inferior officer" implies an official superior, one who has no superior is not an inferior officer. This unexceptionable maxim will in some instances be dispositive of status; it might, for example, lead to the conclusion that United States district judges cannot be inferior officers, since the power of appellate review does not extend to them personally, but is limited to their judgments.

It does not follow, however, that if one is subject to some supervision and control, one is an inferior officer. Having a superior officer is necessary for inferior officer status, but not sufficient to establish it. *See, e.g., Morrison v. Olson, supra,* at 654, 722, 108 S.Ct., at 2599, 2635 (1988) ("To be sure, it is not a sufficient condition for 'inferior' officer status that one be subordinate to a principal officer. Even an officer who is subordinate to a department head can be a principal officer") (SCALIA, J., dissenting). Accordingly, in *Morrison,* the Court's determination that the independent counsel was "to some degree 'inferior' " to the Attorney General, see *id.,* at 671, 108 S.Ct., at 2608–2609, did not end the enquiry. The Court went on to weigh the duties, jurisdiction, and tenure associated with the office before concluding that the independent counsel was an inferior officer. Thus, under *Morrison,* the Solicitor General of the United States, for example, may well be a principal officer, despite his statutory "inferiority" to the Attorney General * * *.

In this case, as the Court persuasively shows, the Judge Advocate General has substantial supervisory authority over the judges of the Coast Guard Court of Criminal Appeals * * *. While these facts establish that the condition of supervision and control necessary for inferior officer status has been met, I am wary of treating them as sufficient to demonstrate that the judges of the Court of Criminal Appeals are actually inferior officers under the Constitution.

In having to go beyond the Court's opinion to decide that the criminal appeals judges are inferior officers, I do not claim the convenience of a single sufficient condition, and, indeed, at this stage of the Court's thinking on the matter, I would not try to derive a single rule of sufficiency. What is needed, instead, is a detailed look at the powers and duties of these judges to see whether reasons favoring their inferior officer status within the constitutional scheme weigh more heavily than those to the contrary.

Id. at 667–68, 117 S.Ct. at 1582–83. Would Justice Scalia, who (as Justice Souter noted) said in *Morrison v. Olson* that "[e]ven an officer who is subordinate to a department head can be a principal officer," disagree with Justice Souter?

In *Free Enterprise Fund v. Public Company Accounting Oversight Board,* 561 U.S. 477, 130 S.Ct. 3138, 177 L.Ed.2d 706 (2010), discussed in more detail *infra* pages 232–233, 262–275, the Supreme Court, without acknowledging any possible conflict between the methodologies of *Morrison* and *Edmond*, brusquely held that members of the Public Company Accounting Oversight Board ("PCAOB"), who exercise broad powers over financial accounting for publicly-traded companies, are inferior officers as long as they are removable at will by the Securities and Exchange Commission; and Congress could therefore allow the Commission rather than the President and Senate to appoint the PCAOB members: "Given that the Commission is properly viewed, under the Constitution, as possessing the power to remove Board members at will, and given the Commission's other oversight authority, we have no hesitation in concluding that under *Edmond* the Board members are inferior officers whose appointment Congress may permissibly vest in a 'Hea[d] of Departmen[t].' " 561 U.S. at 510, 130 S.Ct. at 3162. Does this terse statement— and it is all that the Supreme Court had to say on the subject of inferior officer status in *Free Enterprise Fund*—mean inferior officer status is now solely a function of the officer's place in the chain of command? Are the Solicitor General (who supervises all federal appellate litigation) and the Deputy Attorney General (who runs much of the day-to-day activity of the Department of Justice) inferior officers because they are below the Attorney General in the chain of command within the Department of Justice? Interestingly, the vigorous, four-Justice dissent in *Free Enterprise Fund*, discussed *infra*, appeared to agree completely with the majority's resolution of all Appointments Clause issues regarding the PCAOB members, including their status as inferior officers.

The Copyright Royalty Board sets rates for transmissions of copyrighted musical works through various media, including webcasts, when the parties cannot agree upon a licensing fee. 17 U.S.C. § 114(d)–(f) (2012). The Board thus has rate-setting authority over "musical works not only on traditional media such as CDs, cassettes and vinyl, but also on digital music downloaded through iTunes and Amazon.com, digital streaming via the web, rates paid by satellite carriers, non-commercial broadcasting, and certain cable transmissions." *Intercollegiate Broadcasting System, Inc. v. Copyright Royalty Board*, 684 F.3d 1332, 1338 (D.C.Cir.2012). The Board consists of three Copyright Royalty Judges, who are appointed (to six-year terms) by the Librarian of Congress. "When a ratemaking proceeding is initiated, the Judges are tasked with 'mak[ing] determinations and adjustments of reasonable terms and rates of royalty payments,' 17 U.S.C. § 801(b)(1), where 'reasonable' means payments that 'most clearly represent the rates and terms that would have been negotiated in the marketplace between a willing buyer and a willing seller,' *id.* § 114(f)(2)(B)." *Id.* at 1335. The statute provides for removal of the judges by the Librarian of Congress only for misconduct or neglect of duty. 17 U.S.C. § 801(i) (2012). Are the Board members principal officers who must be appointed by the President with the advice and consent of the Senate?

The D.C. Circuit has said yes—*if* the restrictive removal provision is valid. Following *Free Enterprise Fund*, however, the court found the removal restriction invalid and held that the Librarian of Congress can remove the

Board members at will. On that understanding, the Board members are inferior officers who can be appointed by the Librarian as a department head. *Intercollegiate Broadcasting System, Inc. v. Copyright Royalty Board*, 684 F.3d at 1340–41. The court noted that *Morrison* and *Edmond* seem to disagree about whether the importance of the officer's duties, and not simply the officer's place in the chain of command, can affect the officer's status as principal or inferior. For an argument that an officer with important enough duties (such as the Solicitor General and the Deputy Attorney General) can be principal officers even if they are answerable to other officers, see Gary Lawson, *The "Principal" Reason Why the PCAOB Is Unconstitutional,* 62 Vand. L. Rev. En Banc 73 (2009).

Some issues involving the meaning of "inferior officers" in the Appointments Clause lurk as well in the structure of Amtrak, discussed on pages 163–164, *supra.* The Board of Amtrak consists of the Secretary of Transportation, seven other members appointed by the President with the advice and consent of the Senate, 49 U.S.C. § 24302(a)(1) (2012), and a ninth member, the president of Amtrak, who is selected by the other eight Board members. *Id.* § 24302(a)(1)(B). If all of the Board members must be principal officers, the appointment of Amtrak's president by the other Board members is obviously unconstitutional, as principal officers must be appointed by the President with the advice and consent of the Senate. Is the president of Amtrak an inferior officer because the other Board members can replace him or her at will? Or is everyone on the Board, with equal voting power, necessarily a principal officer since there is no other entity, other than perhaps the President of the United States, to whom the Amtrak Board must answer? *See Dep't of Transportation v. Ass'n of American Railroads*, 135 S.Ct. 1225, 1239 (2015) (Alito, J., concurring).

On remand from the Court's decision in *Ass'n of American Railroads*, the D.C. Circuit concluded that an arbitrator who decides with finality upon the metrics for determining railroad performance was a principal officer, and thus could not validly be appointed by a department head, because no one supervised or reviewed the arbitrator's decision:

> And while it may seem peculiar to demand "primary class" treatment for a position as banal as the PRIIA [Passenger Rail Investment and Improvement Act of 2008] arbitrator, it also seems inescapable. Nowhere does PRIIA suggest the arbitrator "is directed and supervised at some level by others who were appointed by Presidential nomination with the advice and consent of the Senate." [*Edmond,* 520 U.S. at 663, 117 S.Ct. at 1581.] PRIIA doesn't provide any procedure by which the arbitrator's decision is reviewable by the STB [Surface Transportation Board]. Instead, it empowers the arbitrator to determine the metrics and standards "through binding arbitration." *See Dep't of Transp.,* 135 S.Ct. at 1239 (Alito, J., concurring) ("As to that 'binding' decision, who is the supervisor?"). The result? A final agency action, the promulgation of metrics and standards as though developed jointly by Amtrak and the FRA.

Without providing for the arbitrator's direction or supervision by principal officers, PRIIA impermissibly vests power to appoint an arbitrator in the STB.

821 F.3d 19, 39 (D.C.Cir.2016). The same problem might infect the Patent Trial and Appeal Board, which has final executive authority to cancel or modify already-issued patents. Only one member of the PTAB is appointed by the President with the advice and consent of the Senate, and the agency must act through panels of three or more members, so at least two members of every panel will have been appointed only as inferior officers. There is no further executive review of PTAB decisions; they are appealed directly to federal court. Does *Edmond* make this an easy case for unconstitutionality? *See* Gary Lawson, *Appointments and Illegal Adjudication: The AIA Through a Constitutional Lens,* 41 Geo. Mason U.L. Rev. ___ (2018).

2. *Who May Appoint "Inferior" Officers?*

Inferior officers may be appointed by the President, "Courts of Law," or "Heads of Departments" if Congress chooses to give them appointment authority. Who are the "Courts of Law" and "Heads of Departments" contemplated by the Appointments Clause?

In *Freytag*, the Supreme Court unanimously held that the Chief Judge of the Tax Court could constitutionally appoint "special trial judges." The Justices split 5–4, however, on the rationale for the decision. As inferior officers, special trial judges can only be appointed by the President, the courts of law, or the heads of departments. Does the Chief Judge of the Tax Court fall into either of the two latter categories? A majority of the Court held that the Chief Judge of the Tax Court is not a head of a department under the Appointments Clause, but that the Tax Court is a "Court[ ] of Law" and therefore capable of appointing inferior officers. With respect to the former point, the Court said:

> This court for more than a century has held that the term "Departmen[t]" refers only to " 'a part or division of the executive government, as the Department of State, or of the Treasury,' " expressly "creat[ed]" and "giv[en] . . . the name of a department" by congress. *Germaine*, 99 U.S., at 510–511. Accordingly, the term "heads of departments" does not embrace "inferior commissioners and bureau officers." *Germaine*, 99 U.S., at 511 * * *. Confining the term "heads of Departments" in the appointments Clause to executive divisions like the Cabinet-level departments constrains the distribution of the appointment power just as the Commissioner's interpretation, in contrast, would diffuse it.

Id. at 886, 111 S.Ct. at 2643. With respect to the latter point, the petitioners argued, with considerable force, that the phrase "the Courts of Law" in the Appointments Clause obviously refers to the courts described in Article III of the Constitution—that is, courts whose judges have salary protection and tenure during good behavior. The Court answered:

The text of the [Appointments] Clause does not limit the "Courts of Law" to those courts established under Article III of the Constitution. The Appointments Clause does not provide that Congress can vest appointment power only in "one Supreme Court" and other courts established under Article III, or only in tribunals that exercise broad common-law jurisdiction * * *. Petitioners * * * underestimate the importance of this Court's time-honored reading of the Constitution as giving Congress wide discretion to assign the task of adjudication in cases arising under federal law to legislative tribunals. *See, e.g., American Insurance Co. v. Canter*, 1 Pet. 511, 546, 7 L.Ed. 242 (1828) (the judicial power of the United States is not limited to the judicial power defined under Article III and may be exercised by legislative courts); *Williams v. United States*, 289 U.S. 553, 565–567, 53 S.Ct. 751, 754–755, 77 L.Ed. 1372 (1933) (same).

* * *

* * * The Tax Court exercises judicial, rather than executive, legislative, or administrative, power. It was established by Congress to interpret and apply the Internal Revenue Code in disputes between taxpayers and the Government. By resolving these disputes, the court exercises a portion of the judicial power of the United States.

Id. at 888–91, 111 S.Ct. at 2644, 2645.

Four Justices, led by Justice Scalia, strongly resisted the characterization of the Tax Court as a constitutional "Court[ ] of Law," insisting instead that it performs executive rather than judicial functions:

The [Appointments] Clause does not refer generally to "Bodies exercising judicial Functions," or even to "Courts" generally, or even to "Courts of Law" generally. It refers to *the* Courts of Law." Certainly this does not mean *any* "Cour[t] of Law" (the Supreme Court of Rhode Island would not do). The definite article "the" obviously narrows the class of eligible "Courts of Law" to those courts of law envisioned by the Constitution. Those are Article III courts, and the Tax Court is not one of them.

* * *

I agree with the unremarkable proposition that "Congress [has] wide discretion to assign the task of adjudication in cases arising under federal law to legislative tribunals" * * *. Such tribunals, like any other administrative board, exercise the executive power, not the judicial power of the United States * * *.

* * * [T]here is nothing "inherently judicial" about "adjudication." To be a federal officer and to adjudicate are necessary

but not sufficient conditions for the exercise of federal judicial power
* * *.

* * *

In short, given the performance of adjudicatory functions by a federal officer, it is the identity of the officer—not something intrinsic about the mode of decisionmaking or type of decision—that tells us whether the judicial power is being exercised * * *.

Id. at 902, 909, 911, 111 S.Ct. at 2651, 2655, 2656. The four Justices joined the Court's judgment, however, because they believed that the Chief Judge is among the "Heads of Departments" referenced in the Appointments Clause:

* * * [T]he Tax Court is a freestanding, self-contained entity in the Executive Branch, whose Chief Judge is removable by the President (and, save impeachment, no one else). Nevertheless, the Court holds that the Chief Judge is not the head of a department.

It is not at all clear what the Court's reason for this conclusion is. I had originally thought that the Court was adopting petitioners' theory—wrong, but at least coherent—that "Heads of Departments" means Cabinet officers * * *. Elsewhere, however, the Court seemingly disclaims Cabinet status as the criterion * * *. Unfortunately, it never specifies what characteristic it is that causes an agency to *be* "like a Cabinet-level department," or even provides any intelligible clues as to what it might have in mind * * *.

* * * [The position that "Heads of Departments" means "Cabinet officers" has] no basis in text or precedent * * *. The term "Cabinet" does not appear in the Constitution * * *.

* * *

* * * I would give the term ["Departments"] its ordinary meaning * * *. As an American dictionary roughly contemporaneous with adoption of the Appointments Clause provided, and as remains the case, a department is "[a] separate allotment or part of business; a distinct province, in which a class of duties are allotted to a particular person. . ." 1 N. Webster, American Dictionary 58 (1828) * * *. [T]he Founders * * * chose the word "Departmen[t]," * * * not to connote size or function (much less Cabinet status), but separate organization—a connotation that still endures even in colloquial usage today ("that is not my department") * * *.

Id. at 915–16, 920, 111 S.Ct. at 2658–59, 2660.

Once again, as with the methodology for determining inferior officer status, the Court's 2010 decision in *Free Enterprise Fund* appears to have vindicated Justice Scalia's position. The Court, citing the same nineteenth-century dictionary as did Justice Scalia in *Freytag*, held that the Securities and

Exchange Commission, an independent regulatory agency, qualifies as a "Department[ ]" under the Appointments Clause:

> Respondents' reading of the Appointments Clause is consistent with the common, near-contemporary definition of a "department" as a "separate allotment or part of business; a distinct province, in which a class of duties are allotted to a particular person." 1 N. Webster, American Dictionary of the English Language (1828) (def.2) (1995 facsimile ed.). It is also consistent with the early practice of Congress, which in 1792 authorized the Postmaster General to appoint "an assistant, and deputy postmasters, at all places where such shall be found necessary," § 3, 1 Stat. 234—thus treating him as the "Hea[d] of [a] Departmen[t]" without the title of Secretary or any role in the President's Cabinet. And it is consistent with our prior cases, which have never invalidated an appointment made by the head of such an establishment. Because the Commission is a freestanding component of the Executive Branch, not subordinate to or contained within any other such component, it constitutes a "Departmen[t]" for the purposes of the Appointments Clause.

561 U.S. at 511, 130 S.Ct. at 3162–63. The Court also brushed aside the Free Enterprise Fund's suggestion that only a single person could be a constitutional department head and that the members of the SEC, as a collective body, therefore could not be proper appointing authorities as "Heads of Departments":

> As a constitutional matter, we see no reason why a multimember body may not be the "Hea[d]" of a "Departmen[t]" that it governs. The Appointments Clause necessarily contemplates collective appointments by the "Courts of Law," and each House of Congress, too, appoints its officers collectively. Petitioners argue that the Framers vested the nomination of principal officers in the President to avoid the perceived evils of collective appointments, but they reveal no similar concern with respect to inferior officers, whose appointments may be vested elsewhere, including in multimember bodies. Practice has also sanctioned the appointment of inferior officers by multimember agencies. Classification Act of 1923, ch. 265, § 2, 42 Stat. 1488 (defining "the head of the department" to mean "the officer *or group of officers* . . . who are not subordinate or responsible to any other officer of the department" (emphasis added)); 37 Op. Atty. Gen. 227, 231 (1933) (endorsing collective appointment by the Civil Service Commission). We conclude that the Board members have been validly appointed by the full Commission.

561 U.S. at 512–13, 130 S.Ct. at 3163–64.

As for where all of this leaves the majority opinion in *Freytag* and its seemingly far more limited view of what counts as "Departments," consider the following colloquy at oral argument in *Free Enterprise Fund* between Justice Scalia, Chief Justice Roberts, and Mike Carvin, counsel for Free Enterprise

Fund who was arguing that SEC commissioners could not properly appoint Board members because the SEC was not a constitutional "Department[ ]":

> MR. CARVIN: * * * The SEC cannot be a department under *Freytag*, because it is an independent agency indistinguishable from the Tax Court. And—and what the *Freytag* majority opinion said was, if you are unlike a [C]abinet department because you are not subject to political oversight, then—
>
> JUSTICE SCALIA: I hope your case doesn't rest on *Freytag*.
>
> [Laughter.]
>
> MR. CARVIN: So do I. I want to take an opportunity to focus on the real point of *Freytag*, which was made very eloquently in the *Freytag* dissenting opinion, which was—
>
> [Laughter.]
>
> CHIEF JUSTICE ROBERTS: And the brief.
>
> [Laughter.]

https://www.supremecourt.gov/oral_arguments/argument_transcripts/2009/08 -861.pdf, at 23–24. Deputy Solicitor General John Roberts argued *Freytag* on behalf of the United States in 1991 (and presumably wrote the brief to which Chief Justice John Roberts referred in 2010), urging the broad view of "Departments" embraced by Justice Scalia in his concurrence in *Freytag*. Has this aspect of *Freytag* now been overruled by laughter at an oral argument?

If the SEC is a constitutional "Department[ ]" under the Appointments Clause, what other entities might qualify as "Departments"? The majority in *Free Enterprise Fund* suggested that the SEC is a department because it "is a freestanding component of the Executive Branch, not subordinate to or contained within any other such component." But is it really a department because it is "freestanding," or is it a department because it has sufficient power and distinctive identity to be a department, in which case it could conceivably be a department even if it was somehow situated within or subject to some measure of control by another department? Recall from Chapter 1 that an entity can be an agency under the APA "whether or not it is within or subject to review by another agency." 5 U.S.C. 551(1) (2012). Does the same hold true for constitutional "Departments"? If so, might the PCAOB itself be a "Department[ ]"—in which case its members would be "Heads of Departments" and therefore principal officers for that reason? *See* Gary Lawson, *The "Principal" Reason Why the PCAOB Is Unconstitutional,* 62 Vand. L. Rev. En Banc 73 (2009). Is the FBI a "Department[ ]" even though it is situated within the Department of Justice? Is each United States Attorney's office its own "Department[ ]"?

Is Amtrak a constitutional "Department[ ]"? If it is not, then members of the Amtrak Board are not "Heads of Departments" and presumably cannot appoint the president of Amtrak, who also serves on the Board. *See Dep't of Transportation v. Ass'n of American Railroads,* 575 U.S. ___, ___, 135 S.Ct.

1225, 1239–40 (2015) (Alito, J., concurring). And if Amtrak is in fact a constitutional "Department[ ]," does that mean that all of its board members must be principal officers? Can an inferior officer be the head of a federal department? Did the Association of American Railroads focus on the wrong constitutional challenge by emphasizing the nondelegation doctrine rather than the Appointments Clause?

3. *New Duties, New Officers?*

The Coast Guard Court of Criminal Appeals, which was the subject of *Edmond*, is just one example of a military court. The structure of the military justice system is quite complex. *See Ortiz v. United States,* 138 S.Ct. 2165 (2018). The decision in *Weiss v. United States,* 510 U.S. 163, 114 S.Ct. 752, 127 L.Ed.2d 1 (1994), concerned the appointments process for military judges, who comprise one component of that structure. As the Court explained:

> The military judge, a position that has officially existed only since passage of the Military Justice Act of 1968, acts as presiding officer at a special or general court-martial. The judge rules on all legal questions, and instructs court-martial members regarding the law and procedures to be followed * * *.

> Military trial judges must be commissioned officers of the armed forces[2] and members of the bar of a federal court or a State's highest court. The judges are selected and certified as qualified by the Judge Advocate General of their branch of the armed forces.[3] They do not serve for fixed terms and may perform judicial duties only when assigned to do so by the appropriate Judge Advocate General. While serving as judges, officers may also, with the approval of the Judge Advocate General, perform other tasks unrelated to their judicial duties.

Id. at 167–68, 114 S.Ct. at 756. Thus, military judges are appointed in conformance with the Appointments Clause to their positions as commissioned military officers, but they do not receive a separate appointment under the Appointments Clause to their positions as military judges (the Judge Advocates General are clearly not proper recipients of the appointment power, even assuming that military judges are inferior rather than principal officers). The question in *Weiss* was whether an additional appointment was necessary before military officers could carry out the duties of military judges. The Court unanimously held that no additional appointment was necessary:

> * * * [O]ur decisions in *Buckley*, *Freytag*, and *Morrison* * * * undoubtedly establish * * * that a military judge is an "officer of the United States"—a proposition to which both parties agree. But the decisions simply do not speak to the issue of whether, and when, the Appointments Clause may require a second appointment.

---

[2]   All commissioned officers are appointed by the President, with the advice and consent of the Senate.

[3]   The Judge Advocate General for each service is the principal legal officer for that service.

The lead and dissenting opinions in the Court of Military Appeals devoted considerable attention to, and the parties before us have extensively briefed, the significance of our opinion in *Shoemaker v. United States*, 147 U.S. 282, 13 S.Ct. 361, 37 L.Ed. 170 (1893). There Congress had enacted a statute establishing a commission to supervise the development of Rock Creek Park in the District of Columbia. Three of the members were appointed by the President with the advice and consent of the Senate, but the remaining two members were the Chief of Engineers of the Army and the Engineer Commissioner of the District of Columbia. Both of the latter were already commissioned as military officers, but it was contended that the Appointments Clause required that they again be appointed to their new positions. The Court rejected the argument, saying:

> "[T]he argument is, that while Congress may create an office, it cannot appoint the officer; that the officer can only be appointed by the President with the approval of the Senate. . . As, however, the two persons whose eligibility is questioned were at the time of the passage of the act . . . officers of the United States who had been theretofore appointed by the President and confirmed by the Senate, we do not think that, because additional duties, germane to the offices already held by them, were devolved upon them by the act, it was necessary that they should be again appointed by the President and confirmed by the Senate. It cannot be doubted, and it has frequently been the case, that Congress may increase the power and duties of an existing office without thereby rendering it necessary that the incumbent should be again nominated and appointed." *Id.*, at 300–301, 13 S.Ct., at 391.

The present case before us differs from *Shoemaker* in several respects, at least one of which is significant for purposes of Appointments Clause analysis. In *Shoemaker*, Congress assigned new duties to two existing offices, each of which was held by a single officer. This no doubt prompted the Court's description of the argument as being that "while Congress may create an office, it cannot appoint the officer." By looking to whether the additional duties assigned to the offices were "germane," the Court sought to ensure that Congress was not circumventing the Appointments Clause by unilaterally appointing an incumbent to a new and distinct office. But here the statute authorized an indefinite number of military judges, who could be designated from among hundreds or perhaps thousands of qualified commissioned officers. In short, there is no ground for suspicion here that Congress was trying to both create an office and also select a particular individual to fill the office * * *.

Even if we assume, *arguendo*, that the principle of "germaneness" applies to the present situation, we think that principle is satisfied here * * *. Although military judges obviously perform certain unique and important functions, all military officers, consistent with a long tradition, play a role in the operation of the military justice system.

Commissioned officers, for example, have the power and duty to "quell quarrels, frays, and disorders among persons subject to [the Uniform Code of Military Justice (UCMJ)] and to apprehend persons subject to [the UCMJ] who take part therein." Art. 7(c), UCMJ. Commanding officers can impose nonjudicial disciplinary punishment for minor offenses, without the intervention of a court martial, which includes correctional custody, forfeiture of pay, reduction in grade, extra duties, restriction to certain limits, and detention of pay. A commissioned officer may serve as a summary court-martial or a member of a special or general court-martial. When acting as a summary court-martial or as the president of a special court-martial without a military judge, this officer conducts the proceedings and resolves all issues that would be handled by the military judge, except for challenges for cause against the president of a special court-martial without a military judge. Convening authorities, finally, have the authority to review and modify the sentence imposed by courts-martial. Art. 60, UCMJ. Thus, by contrast to civilian society, nonjudicial military officers play a significant part in the administration of military justice.

By the same token, the position of military judge is less distinct from other military positions than the office of full-time civilian judge is from other offices in civilian society * * *. Neither military trial nor appellate judges * * * have a fixed term of office. Commissioned officers are assigned or detailed to the position of military judge by a Judge Advocate General for a period of time he deems necessary or appropriate, and then they may be reassigned to perform other duties. Even while serving as military trial judges, officers may perform, with the permission of the Judge Advocate General, duties unrelated to their judicial responsibilities. Whatever might be the case in civilian society, we think that the role of military judge is "germane" to that of military officer.

Id. at 173–76, 114 S.Ct. at 759–760. The majority assumed, without deciding, that military judges were inferior rather than principal officers—a proposition that Justice Souter sought to establish at length in a concurring opinion. *See id.* at 191–94, 114 S.Ct. at 768–69 (Souter, J., concurring).

Justice Scalia and Justice Thomas agreed with the Court's conclusion that no new appointment was necessary in this case, but they focussed more heavily on whether the additional duties that a military officer assumes by becoming a military judge are "germane" to the position to which the officer was initially appointed.

Germaneness analysis must be conducted, it seems to me, whenever that is necessary to assure that the conferring of new duties does not violate the Appointments Clause. Violation of the Appointments Clause occurs not only when (as in *Shoemaker*) Congress may be aggrandizing *itself* (by effectively appropriating the appointment power over the officer exercising the new duties), but also when Congress, *without* aggrandizing itself, effectively lodges appointment power in any person other than those whom the Constitution specifies. Thus, "germaneness" is relevant whenever Congress gives power to confer new duties to anyone other than the few potential recipients of the appointment power specified in the Appointments Clause—*i.e.*, the President, the Courts of Law, and Heads of Departments.

The Judges Advocate General are none of these. Therefore, if acting as a military judge under the Military Justice Act is nongermane to serving as a military officer, giving Judges Advocate General the power to appoint military officers to serve as military judges would violate the Appointments Clause, even if there were "hundreds or perhaps thousands" of individuals from whom the selections could be made. For taking on the nongermane duties of military judge would amount to assuming a new "Offic[e]" within the meaning of Article II, and the appointment to that office would have to comply with the strictures of Article II. I find the Appointments Clause not to have been violated in the present case, only because I agree with the Court's dictum that the new duties are germane.*

Id. at 196, 114 S.Ct. at 770.

Are Justices Scalia and Thomas saying that Congress cannot vest new duties in an officer without providing for a new appointment if the new duties are sufficiently important to require a new appointment? Is the majority saying something different? Is a better test available? *See* Matthew Hunter, *Legislating Around the Appointments Clause*, 91 B.U.L. Rev. 753 (2011).

4. *Recess Appointments*

Recent events have brought to the fore another oft-neglected feature of the constitutional appointments process. The Constitution actually contains two separate appointments clauses: The Appointments Clause that is the main subject of these materials and the Recess Appointments Clause, which provides that the "President shall have Power to fill up all Vacancies that may happen during the Recess of the Senate, by granting Commissions which shall expire at the End of their next Session." U.S. Const. art. II, § 2, cl. 3. In the

---

* The further issues perceptively discussed in JUSTICE SOUTER's concurrence—namely, whether the Appointments Clause permits conferring principal-officer responsibilities upon an inferior officer in a manner other than that required for the appointment of a principal officer (and, if not, whether the responsibilities of a military judge are those of a principal officer)—were in my view wisely avoided by the Court, since they were inadequately presented and not at all argued * * *. As JUSTICE SOUTER's opinion demonstrates, the issues are complex; they should be resolved only after full briefing and argument.

founding era, in which the Senate typically would meet for less than half the year and transportation was time-consuming, the need for such a provision was obvious: If a vacancy in a crucial position—say, Secretary of State or Secretary of War during wartime—arose during the six- to nine-month annual break in the Senate's business, it would likely be impossible to summon a quorum of the Senate into session in a timely fashion to provide advice and consent for key presidential appointments. Some mechanism for permitting appointments without Senate participation was essential.

The text of the Recess Appointments Clause suggests a very limited role for these appointments made without Senate participation. First, the clause refers to vacancies that "happen" during the Senate recess; the facial meaning is thus that vacancies that arise while the Senate is in session rather than in recess are not eligible for recess appointments. Second, because the clause refers to "the" recess of the Senate rather than to "recesses" or "any recess," the facial meaning is that vacancies must arise during "the" main recess between sessions of the Senate rather than during any intrasession breaks or recesses. A further structural implication, though one not commanded by the text, would likely be that appointments for any vacancies can avoid Senate confirmation only if the appointments themselves are made during an intersession recess when the Senate is not available to advise and consent. For extended discussions of this view of the clause's meaning, see Robert G. Natelson, *The Origins and Meaning of "Vacancies that May Happen During the Recess" in the Constitution's Recess Appointments Clause,* 37 Harv. J.L. & Pub. Pol'y 199 (2014); Michael B. Rappaport, *The Original Meaning of the Recess Appointments Clause,* 52 U.C.L.A. L. Rev. 1487 (2005).

Modern practice—by presidents of both parties—has treated the clause more broadly, permitting recess appointments for any vacancies that *exist* during a Senate recess even if the vacancies *arose* while the Senate was in session. *See* Office of Legal Counsel, U.S. Department of Justice, *Lawfulness of Recess Appointments During a Recess of the Senate Notwithstanding Periodic Pro Forma Sessions,* at 1 (Jan. 6, 2012). Moreover, modern presidential practice—again under presidents of both parties—has extended the meaning of "the Recess of the Senate" to include intrasession recesses, provided that such intrasession breaks are of "substantial length." *See id.* at 5 (citing numerous prior Department of Justice opinions). For a scholarly view defending these positions, see Edward A. Hartnett, *Recess Appointments of Article III Judges: Three Constitutional Questions,* 26 Cardozo L. Rev. 377 (2005).

The issue garnered wide attention when President Obama in 2012 made recess appointments to three vacancies on the National Labor Relations Board. Without those recess appointments, the NLRB had only two members and thus lacked a quorum for taking any legally binding action. *See New Process Steel, L.P., v. NLRB,* 560 U.S. 674, 130 S.Ct. 2635 (2010). The vacancies did not arise, and the appointments were not made, during an intersession recess. Instead, they were made during a period in which the Senate was operating under a unanimous consent agreement which provided for ongoing pro forma sessions with the stipulation (which could be, and on some occasions was, overridden) that no business be conducted during those "sessions." Thus, the Senate was either in session or, if one treats the pro forma sessions as functional nullities, in an intrasession recess.

In *Noel Canning v. NLRB*, 705 F.3d 490 (D.C.Cir.2013), the D.C. Circuit held that the recess appointments were invalid and the NLRB was therefore disabled from acting for lack of a quorum. The court unanimously reasoned that recess appointments could only be made during an intersession Senate recess, *see id.* at 499–507, specifically rejecting a contrary holding by the Eleventh Circuit a decade earlier. *See Evans v. Stephens*, 387 F.3d 1220 (11th Cir.2004). Two judges (with one judge not reaching the issue) also determined that the Recess Appointments Clause only applies to vacancies that arise during the Senate's intersession recess. *See id.* at 507–14.

A unanimous Supreme Court affirmed the judgment of the D.C. Circuit finding the appointments invalid, *NLRB v. Noel Canning*, 573 U.S. ___, 134 S.Ct. 2550, 189 L.Ed.2d 538 (2014), but the Court sharply split 5–4 on the reasoning. The majority, relying largely on historical practice, concluded that a "recess" for purposes of the Recess Appointments Clause can include an intrasession break provided that it is not too short (with a period shorter than ten days being presumptively too short). *See* 134 S.Ct. at 2567. Similarly relying on considerations of practice and purpose, it also concluded that recess appointments can occur for vacancies that did not arise during a recess. *See id.* at 2573. But it held that, on the facts of the case before it, the Senate was not in recess when it conducted pro forma sessions, leaving as the only relevant "recess" a three-day break between pro forma sessions, which the Court considered too short to trigger the Recess Appointments Clause. The key for the Court was the Senate's own characterization of its actions: "We hold that, for purposes of the Recess Appointments Clause, the Senate is in session when it says it is, provided that, under its own rules, it retains the capacity to transact Senate business. The Senate met that standard here." *Id.* at 2574.

Justice Scalia, writing for himself and three other Justices, concurred only in the result. Relying primarily on original meaning, he would have found both that recesses can only occur between sessions and that any vacancies for purposes of the Recess Appointments Clause must occur during that recess. He found the majority's reliance on practice and purpose both unsound and unconvincing: "What the majority needs to sustain its judgment is an ambiguous text and a clear historical practice. What it has is a clear text and an at-best-ambiguous historical practice." *Id.* at 2617 (Scalia, J., concurring in the judgment).

Given that the majority determined that the recess appointments in this particular case were invalid under any plausible theory, does that make its rejection of the broader arguments embraced by Justice Scalia dictum? If not, is the upshot of this decision, in the wake of cases like *Buckley v. Valeo,* that the Appointments Clause is generally to be construed formalistically while the Recess Appointments Clause is generally to be construed functionally? Or is the search for generalizations in the Court's separation of powers jurisprudence something of a fool's errand?

2. REMOVAL OF AGENCY OFFICIALS

Some of the provisions dealing with the selection of government officials also address removal from office. The President, Vice President, and members of Congress are automatically "removed" whenever their terms of office expire. The Constitution also gives Congress some explicit removal authority. Each house of Congress can expel—remove—its members by a two-thirds vote. *See* U.S. Const. art. I, § 5, cl. 2 ("Each House may * * *, with the concurrence of two thirds, expel a Member"). Congress may also remove the President, Vice President, and all other civil officers through impeachment. Six provisions of the Constitution deal with removal of officials through impeachment. All civil officers of the United States, including the President and Vice President, are subject to removal upon impeachment for and conviction of "Treason, Bribery, or other high Crimes and Misdemeanors." *Id.* art. II, § 4.[28] The House is given the power of impeachment, *see id.* art. I, § 2, cl. 5, and the Senate is given the power to try all impeachments and to convict with a two-thirds majority. *See id.* art. I, § 3, cl. 6.[29] The sole consequence of a conviction is removal from office and disqualification from holding further offices, though conviction does not preclude prosecution under applicable criminal laws. *Id.* art. I, § 3, cl. 7. The President's pardon power does not extend to impeachments, *see id.* art. II, § 2, cl. 1, and impeached officers are not entitled to trial by jury in the Senate proceedings, *see id.* art. III, § 2, cl. 3.

Apart from the elaborate impeachment provisions, the Constitution says nothing explicit about the removal of non-elected executive officials. There is no "Removal Clause" analogous to the Appointments Clause.

One could plausibly draw at least four different inferences about executive removal from the Constitution's text. First, one could say that because impeachment is the only mode of removal for executive officers specifically mentioned in the Constitution, it is the only permissible mode. Second, one could say that removal is an executive function and that Article II therefore gives the President the power of removal when it vests "[t]he executive Power * * * in a President of the United States of America." *Id.* art. II, § 1, cl. 1. The impeachment clauses, on this understanding, give Congress an additional, strictly limited and defined, removal power. Third,

---

[28] The phrase "high Crimes and Misdemeanors" describes a class of conduct that goes beyond ordinary indictable crimes. It does not include mere policy disagreements with Congress, but it most likely includes things like corruption, abuse of power, and neglect of duty. See Gary Lawson & Christopher D. Moore, *The Executive Power of Constitutional Interpretation*, 81 Iowa L. Rev. 1267, 1307–10 (1996).

[29] Ordinarily, the Vice President presides over the Senate. The Chief Justice, however, presides over impeachment trials when the President is being tried. See U.S. Const. art. I, § 3, cl. 6.

one could say that the mode of removal ordinarily follows the mode of appointment, so that officials appointed, for example, by the President with the advice and consent of the Senate can be removed only by the same procedure. And finally, one could say that Congress can set whatever terms of removal are "necessary and proper" whenever it uses its Sweeping Clause power to create offices.

All of these positions are textually and structurally plausible, and all of them were advanced with considerable vigor in the First Congress. That Congress had to face squarely the Constitution's relative silence on executive removal when it began creating executive departments and offices in 1789. The issue came to a head in connection with the Secretary of the Department of Foreign Affairs. In discussing the appropriate legislative specification, if any, for the Secretary's removal, the House of Representatives engaged in one of the most spirited and sophisticated constitutional debates in American history.[30] Substantial arguments were made for the exclusivity of impeachment as a mode of removal,[31] for a presidential removal power,[32] for a removal power that follows the mode of appointment,[33] and for a congressional power to specify the mode of removal.[34] In the end, the House endorsed a provision that implied an inherent presidential removal power. The Senate divided evenly on the same provision, and the Vice President broke the tie in favor of the House's position. This implicit legislative endorsement of a presidential power to remove executive officials is so important that it is known simply as "the decision of 1789." Reflect on all of the decisions that the First Congress made in 1789 and you will realize the magnitude of this label. For a thorough treatment of this historic event, see Saikrishna Prakash, *New Light on the Decision of 1789*, 91 Cornell L. Rev. 1021 (2006).

Perhaps surprisingly, given the importance of the issue, the Supreme Court did not issue a major opinion[35] on the removal question until 1926.

---

[30] The Senate did not begin keeping records of its debates until 1795, so we do not have any information about the course of the debate in the Senate.

[31] *See* 1 Annals of Cong. 389 (1789) (statement of Rep. Jackson); *id.* at 477 (statement of Rep. Huntington).

[32] *See, e.g., id.* at 387, 479–82, 514–19 (statement of Rep. Madison); *id.* at 387–88, 525–27 (statement of Rep. Benson); *id.* at 388, 482–84, 531–32 (statement of Rep. Vining); *id.* at 393 (statement of Rep. Goodhue); *id.* at 397–98, 508–09 (statement of Rep. Clymer); *id.* at 478–79 (statement of Rep. Sedgwick); *id.* at 486–88, 548–50 (statement of Rep. Boudinot); *id.* at 492–96, 561–64 (statement of Rep. Ames); *id.* at 498–500 (statement of Rep. Hartley).

[33] *See, e.g., id.* at 389–90 (statement of Rep. Bland); *id.* at 391, 473–74 (statement of Rep. White); *id.* at 393 (statement of Rep. Sylvester); *id.* at 395–96, 490–92 (statement of Rep. Gerry); *id.* at 509–10 (statement of Rep. Page); *id.* at 585–91 (statement of Rep. Stone).

[34] *See, e.g., id.* at 391 (statement of Rep. Thatcher); *id.* at 391–92 (statement of Rep. Jackson); *id.* at 393–92, 500–05 (statement of Rep. Lawrence); *id.* at 496–98 (statement of Rep. Livermore).

[35] A relatively minor 1886 decision held that Congress could limit the President's power to remove inferior officers who are appointed without Senate confirmation. *See United States v. Perkins*, 116 U.S. 483, 21 Ct.Cl. 499, 6 S.Ct. 449, 29 L.Ed. 700 (1886).

See Myers v. United States, 272 U.S. 52, 47 S.Ct. 21, 71 L.Ed. 160 (1926).[36] An 1876 statute provided that "Postmasters of the first, second and third classes shall be appointed and may be removed by the President by and with the advice and consent of the Senate and shall hold their offices for four years unless sooner removed or suspended according to law." Act of July 12, 1876, 19 Stat. 80, 81, c. 179. Myers, a first class postmaster, was removed before the end of his four-year term by the President (acting through the Postmaster General) without action by the Senate. Myers' estate sued for back pay for the remainder of the term. The Court held in favor of a constitutionally-based presidential removal power over executive officers. The majority and three dissenting opinions consume 240 pages of the United States Reports, many of which are devoted to differing interpretations of the extensive legal and political history of the removal controversy. The gist of the majority opinion, however, is its discussion— and endorsement—of the reasoning put forward during the decision of 1789 by proponents of a presidential removal power, most notably James Madison:

> First. Mr. Madison insisted that Article II by vesting the executive power in the President was intended to grant to him the power of appointment and removal of executive officers except as thereafter expressly provided in that Article * * *.

> * * *

> The vesting of the executive power in the President was essentially a grant of the power to execute the laws * * *. It was urged that the natural meaning of the term "executive power" granted the President included the appointment and removal of executive subordinates. If such appointments and removals were not an exercise of the executive power, what were they? They certainly were not the exercise of legislative or judicial power in government as usually understood.

> It is quite true that, in state and colonial governments at the time of the Constitutional Convention, power to make appointments and removals had sometimes been lodged in the legislatures or in the courts, but such a disposition of it was really vesting part of the executive power in another branch of the Government. In the British system, the Crown, which was the executive, had the power of appointment and removal of executive officers, and it was

---

[36] This does not mean that the removal issue was dormant for the intervening 150 years. Quite to the contrary, the issue of removal of executive officials was at the heart of some of the most important events in American legal history, including *Marbury v. Madison* and the impeachment and near-conviction of President Andrew Johnson. *See* Myers, 272 U.S. at 139–42, 164–67, 47 S.Ct. at 32–34, 41–43.

natural, therefore, for those who framed our Constitution to regard the words "executive power" as including both * * *.

* * *

Second. The view of Mr. Madison and his associates was that * * * the power of removal of executive officers was incident to the power of appointment * * *.

Under section 2 of Article II, however, the power of appointment by the Executive is restricted in its exercise by the provision that the Senate * * * may check the action of the Executive by rejecting the officers he selects * * *.

The history of the [Appointments] [C]lause * * * makes it clear that it was not prompted by any desire to limit removals * * *. [T]he important purpose of those who brought about the restriction was to lodge in the Senate, where the small States had equal representation with the larger States, power to prevent the President from making too many appointments from the larger States * * *.

* * *

* * * The rejection of a nominee of the President for a particular office does not greatly embarrass him in the conscientious discharge of his high duties in the selection of those who are to aid him, because the President usually has an ample field from which to select * * *.

The power to prevent the removal of an officer who has served under the President is different * * *. [T]he defects in ability or intelligence or loyalty in the administration of the laws of one who has served as an officer under the President, are facts as to which the President, or his trusted subordinates, must be better informed than the Senate * * *.

* * *

Third. Another argument * * * is that, in the absence of an express power of removal granted to the President, power to make provision for removal of all such officers is vested in the Congress by section 8 of Article I.

* * *

A reference of the whole power of removal to general legislation by Congress is quite out of keeping with the plan of government devised by the framers of the Constitution. It could never have been intended to leave to Congress unlimited discretion to vary fundamentally the operation of the great independent executive branch of government and thus most seriously to weaken it * * *.

* * *

Fourth. Mr. Madison and his associates pointed out with great force the unreasonable character of the view that the Convention intended, with express provision, to give to Congress or the Senate, in case of political or other differences, the means of thwarting the Executive in the exercise of his great powers and in the bearing of his great responsibility, by fastening upon him, as subordinate executive officers, men who by their inefficient service under him, by their lack of loyalty to the service, or by their different views of policy, might make his taking care that the laws be faithfully executed most difficult or impossible.

As Mr. Madison said in the debate in the First Congress:

"Vest this power in the Senate jointly with the President, and you abolish at once that great principle of unity and responsibility in the Executive department, which was intended for the security and liberty and the public good * * *."

* * *

We have devoted much space to this discussion and decision of the question of the Presidential power of removal in the First Congress, not because a Congressional conclusion on a constitutional issue is conclusive, but, first, because of our agreement with the reasons upon which it was avowedly based; second, because this was the decision of the First Congress, on a question of primary importance in the organization of the Government, made within two years after the Constitutional Convention and within a much shorter time after its ratification; and, third, because that Congress numbered among its leaders those who had been members of the Convention. It must necessarily constitute a precedent upon which many future laws supplying the machinery of the new Government would be based.

Id. at 115–36, 47 S.Ct. at 25–31.

Chief Justice Taft then devoted 38 pages to the judicial, political, and scholarly history of the removal question since the decision of 1789, considering the views of, inter alia, Marshall, Story, Hamilton, Webster, Calhoun, and virtually every President and attorney general through the first half of the nineteenth century. He concluded that "from 1789 until 1863, a period of 74 years, there was no act of Congress, no executive act, and no decision of this Court at variance with the declaration of the First Congress, but there was * * * clear, affirmative recognition of it by each branch of the Government." *Id.* at 163, 47 S.Ct. at 41.

The first major rejection of the decision of 1789 by Congress was the Tenure of Office Act of 1867, *see* Act of March 2, 1867, 14 Stat. 430, ch. 154, in which Congress provided, in Taft's words, "that all officers appointed by and with the consent of the Senate should hold their offices until their successors should have in like manner been appointed and qualified, and that certain heads of departments, including the Secretary of War, should hold their offices during the term of the President by whom appointed and one month thereafter subject to removal by consent of the Senate." 272 U.S. at 166, 47 S.Ct. at 42. The object of the statute was to prevent President Andrew Johnson from packing the executive department with persons hostile to the post-Civil War Reconstruction program and thereby blocking implementation of Reconstruction. President Johnson's refusal to obey the statute, which was enacted over his veto, was the principal grounds for his impeachment and near-conviction (the Senate failed by a single vote to muster the necessary two-thirds majority for conviction). Taft declined to give this episode much significance.[37]

Myers appeared to be a sweeping decision that rendered all of the most important executive officials—at a minimum, all "heads of departments and bureaus," *id.* at 134, 47 S.Ct. at 31—subject to unlimited presidential removal. Remember, the case involved a first class postmaster, not the Secretary of State or an agency commissioner. This outcome is entirely agreeable to persons who believe that executive unity, and its resulting accountability, is a vital political value. It is less agreeable to Progressives who believe that governance is primarily a subject for apolitical expertise. Such persons would urge us to insulate government officials from the play of political forces, including (and perhaps especially) presidential influence.

An exemplary Progressive-era statute is the Federal Trade Commission Act, passed in 1914 and largely unchanged today. The Commission is given potentially sweeping authority "to prevent * * * unfair methods of competition in or affecting commerce and unfair or deceptive acts or practices in or affecting commerce." 15 U.S.C. § 45(a)(2) (2012). Commissioners are appointed to seven-year terms, and the statute specifies that they "may be removed by the President for inefficiency, neglect of duty, or malfeasance in office." *Id.* § 41. Does this statute purport to limit the President's removal power to the named circumstances, and is such a limitation constitutional?

The Court addressed both questions in 1935 in the landmark case *Humphrey's Executor v. United States*, 295 U.S. 602, 55 S.Ct. 869, 79 L.Ed.

---

[37] "The extremes to which the majority in both Houses carried legislative measures in that matter are now recognized by all who calmly review the history of that episode * * *. [W]e are certainly justified in saying that they should not be given the weight affecting proper constitutional construction to be accorded to that reached by the First Congress during a political calm and acquiesced in by the whole Government for three-quarters of a century, especially when the new construction contended for has never been acquiesced in by either the executive or the judicial departments." *Id.* at 175–76, 47 S.Ct. at 45–46.

1611 (1935). Only nine years had passed since *Myers*, but they were nine eventful years. The nation was in the midst of the Great Depression. President Roosevelt was pressing a revolutionary legislative agenda that included an enormous expansion of agency power, most notably through the National Industrial Recovery Act that was invalidated in *Schechter Poultry*. Indeed, *Humphrey's Executor* was argued the day before *Schechter*, and both decisions were handed down on May 27, 1935.

Humphrey's Executor resulted from President Roosevelt's attempt to remove William E. Humphrey, who had been appointed to the Federal Trade Commission by President Hoover in 1931. In 1933, five years before Humphrey's term of office expired, President Roosevelt asked Humphrey to resign on the ground " 'that the aims and purposes of the Administration * * * can be carried out most effectively with personnel of my own selection.' " 295 U.S. at 618, 55 S.Ct. at 870. Humphrey refused to resign, and President Roosevelt declared him removed. Humphrey, and his estate after he died, sought his salary for the remainder of his statutory term of office.

The Court in *Humphrey's Executor* first held that the Federal Trade Commission Act was intended to limit the President's power to remove FTC commissioners.

> * * * [I]f the intention of Congress that no removal should be made during the specified term except for one or more of the enumerated causes were not clear upon the face of the statute, as we think it is, it would be made clear by a consideration of the character of the commission and the legislative history which accompanied and preceded the passage of the act.
>
> The commission is to be non-partisan; and it must, from the very nature of its duties, act with entire impartiality. It is charged with the enforcement of no policy except the policy of the law. Its duties are neither political nor executive, but predominantly quasi-judicial and quasi-legislative * * *. [I]ts members are called upon to exercise the trained judgment of a body of experts * * *.

* * *

> The debates in both houses demonstrate that the prevailing view was that the commission was not to be "subject to anybody in the government but . . . only to the people of the United States"; free from "political domination or control" or the "probability or possibility of such a thing"; to be "separate and apart from any existing department of the government—not subject to the orders of the President."

* * *

Thus, the language of the act, the legislative reports, and the general purposes of the legislation as reflected by the debates, all combine to demonstrate the Congressional intent to create a body of experts who shall gain experience by length of service; a body which shall be independent of executive authority, *except in its selection*, and free to exercise its judgment without the leave or hindrance of any other official or any department of the government.

Id. at 623–26, 55 S.Ct. at 872–73. Could this classically Progressive vision of administration be squared with the constitutional holding of *Myers*? Here, with nothing of substance omitted, was the Court's answer:

* * * [T]he government's chief reliance is *Myers v. United States*. That case has been so recently decided, and the prevailing and dissenting opinions so fully review the general subject of the power of executive removal, that further discussion would add little of value to the wealth of material there collected. These opinions * * * occupy 243 pages of the volume in which they are printed. Nevertheless, the narrow point actually decided was only that the President had power to remove a postmaster of the first class, without the advice and consent of the Senate as required by act of Congress. In the course of the opinion of the court, expressions occur which tend to sustain the government's contention, but these are beyond the point involved and, therefore, do not come within the rule of *stare decisis*. In so far as they are out of harmony with the views here set forth, these expressions are disapproved * * *.

* * *

The office of a postmaster is so essentially unlike the office now involved that the decision in the *Myers* case cannot be accepted as controlling our decision here. A postmaster is an executive officer restricted to the performance of executive functions. He is charged with no duty at all related to either the legislative or judicial power. The actual decision in the *Myers* case finds support in the theory that such an officer is merely one of the units in the executive department and, hence, inherently subject to the exclusive and illimitable power of removal by the Chief Executive, whose subordinate and aid he is. Putting aside *dicta*, which may be followed if sufficiently persuasive but which are not controlling, the necessary reach of the decision goes far enough to include all purely executive officers. It goes no farther;—much less does it include an officer who occupies no place in the executive department and who exercises no part of the executive power vested by the Constitution in the President.

The Federal Trade Commission is an administrative body created by Congress to carry into effect legislative policies embodied in the statute in accordance with the legislative standard therein prescribed, and to perform other specified duties as a legislative or as a judicial aid. Such a body cannot in any proper sense be characterized as an arm or an eye of the executive. Its duties are performed without executive leave and, in the contemplation of the statute, must be free from executive control. In administering the provisions of the statute in respect of "unfair methods of competition"—that is to say, in filling in and administering the details embodied by that general standard—the commission acts in part quasi-legislatively and in part quasi-judicially. In making investigations and reports thereon for the information of Congress under § 6, in aid of the legislative power, it acts as a legislative agency. Under § 7, which authorizes the commission to act as a master in chancery under rules prescribed by the court, it acts as an agency of the judiciary. To the extent that it exercises any executive function—as distinguished from executive power in the constitutional sense—it does so in the discharge and effectuation of its quasi-legislative or quasi-judicial powers, or as an agency of the legislative or judicial departments of the government.

If Congress is without authority to prescribe causes for removal of members of the trade commission and limit executive power of removal accordingly, that power at once becomes practically all-inclusive in respect of civil officers with the exception of the judiciary provided for by the Constitution. The Solicitor General, at the bar, apparently recognizing this to be true, with commendable candor, agreed that his view in respect of the removability of members of the Federal Trade Commission necessitated a like view in respect of the Interstate Commerce Commission and the Court of Claims * * *.

We think it plain under the Constitution that illimitable power of removal is not possessed by the President in respect of officers of the character of those just named. The authority of Congress, in creating quasi-legislative or quasi-judicial agencies, to require them to act in discharge of their duties independently of executive control cannot well be doubted; and that authority includes, as an appropriate incident, power to fix the period during which they shall continue in office, and to forbid their removal except for cause in the meantime. For it is quite evident that one who holds his office only during the pleasure of another cannot be depended upon to maintain an attitude of independence against the latter's will.

The fundamental necessity of maintaining each of the three general departments of government entirely free from the control or coercive influence, direct or indirect, of either of the others, has often been stressed and is hardly open to serious question. So much is implied in the very fact of the separation of the powers of these departments by the Constitution; and in the rule which recognizes their essential co-equality. The sound application of a principle that makes one master in his own house precludes him from imposing his control in the house of another who is master there * * *.

The power of removal here claimed for the President falls within this principle, since its coercive influence threatens the independence of a commission, which is not only wholly disconnected from the executive department, but which, as already fully appears, was created by Congress as a means of carrying into operation legislative and judicial powers, and as an agency of the legislative and judicial departments.

In the light of the question now under consideration, we have reexamined the precedents referred to in the *Myers* case, and find nothing in them to justify a conclusion contrary to that which we have reached. The so-called 'decision of 1789' had relation to a bill proposed by Mr. Madison to establish an executive Department of Foreign Affairs * * *. [T]he office under consideration by Congress was not only purely executive, but the officer one who was responsible to the President, and to him alone, in a very definite sense. A reading of the debates shows that the President's illimitable power of removal was not considered in respect of other than executive officers * * *.

* * *

The result of what we now have said is this: Whether the power of the President to remove an officer shall prevail over the authority of Congress to condition the power by fixing a definite term and precluding a removal except for cause, will depend upon the character of the office; the *Myers* decision, affirming the power of the President alone to make the removal, is confined to purely executive officers; and as to officers of the kind here under consideration, we hold that no removal can be made during the prescribed term for which the officer is appointed, except for one or more of the causes named in the applicable statute.

Id. at 626–32, 55 S.Ct. at 873–75.

For half a century, *Humphrey's Executor* was taken as an unchallenged, and unchallengeable, validation of the structure of independent agencies. More importantly, because of its refusal neatly to categorize FTC commissioners as legislative, executive, or judicial officers, *Humphrey's Executor* came to stand for a definitive judicial rejection of formalist methodology in separation of powers cases. The rebirth of formalism in the wake of *Buckley* and *Chadha*, and the increased attention those cases paid to presidential prerogatives, gave rise to questions about the continued validity of *Humphrey's Executor*. Indeed, the Reagan administration, through Attorney General Edwin Meese III, openly declared its hostility to *Humphrey's Executor* and its limited view of presidential removal power.

A slightly different wrinkle on the removal problem arose in 1986 in *Bowsher v. Synar*, 478 U.S. 714, 106 S.Ct. 3181, 92 L.Ed.2d 583 (1986). The Gramm-Rudman-Hollings Act, enacted in 1985, called for across-the-board spending cuts in certain federal programs if specified deficit-reduction targets were not met. The final determination of whether the spending cuts were triggered was assigned to the Comptroller General, a presidential appointee (with Senate confirmation) who is removable either by impeachment or by joint resolution of Congress for any of five specified causes: "(i) permanent disability; (ii) inefficiency; (iii) neglect of duty; (iv) malfeasance; or (v) a felony or conduct involving moral turpitude." 31 U.S.C. § 703(e)(1)(B) (2012). The Court, through a five-Justice majority, determined that the task of estimating deficit figures and applying them to the statute at hand was an executive task, *see* 478 U.S. at 732–34, 106 S.Ct. at 3191–92, and that "Congress cannot reserve for itself the power of removal of an officer charged with the execution of the laws except by impeachment." *Id.* at 726, 106 S.Ct. at 3188. Because Congress could remove the Comptroller General by joint resolution, even if only for specified causes, the Comptroller General's authority under the statute was invalid. Two Justices concurred on the very different ground that the Comptroller General was an agent of Congress and that Congress could act "to make policy that will bind the Nation," 478 U.S. at 737, 106 S.Ct. at 3193 (Stevens, J., concurring), only through the bicameral procedures for legislation set forth in Article I of the Constitution. Two Justices dissented. Justice White in particular decried the majority's "willingness to interpose its distressingly formalistic view of separation of powers as a bar to the attainment of governmental objectives through the means chosen by the Congress and the President * * *." *Id.* at 759, 106 S.Ct. at 3204 (White, J., dissenting). The majority, for its part, clearly stated that it was not saying anything about the power of Congress to restrict presidential removal power, but was only discussing attempts by Congress to reserve to itself some degree of removal power over executive officials beyond its constitutional impeachment power. *See id.* at 725 n.4, 106 S.Ct. at 3187 n.4.

The larger question about the power of Congress to restrict presidential removal, however, could not be avoided in *Morrison v. Olson*. The statute at issue in *Morrison* provided that the independent counsel "may be removed from office, other than by impeachment and conviction, only by the personal action of the Attorney General and only for good cause, physical disability, mental incapacity, or any other condition that substantially impairs the performance of such independent counsel's duties * * *." The independent counsel, who conducts criminal investigations and prosecutions, is very clearly an executive official, as *Myers* and *Humphrey's Executor* understood that term, and unless "good cause" is read much more broadly than is plausible, the statute quite clearly and sharply restricts the President's removal power (and that of the President's agent, the Attorney General).

MORRISON V. OLSON

Supreme Court of the United States, 1988.
487 U.S. 654, 108 S.Ct. 2597, 101 L.Ed.2d 569.

[Other portions of this case are reprinted at pages 219–223.]

We now turn to consider whether the [Ethics in Government] Act is invalid under the constitutional principle of separation of powers. Two related issues must be addressed: The first is whether the provision of the Act restricting the Attorney General's power to remove the independent counsel to only those instances in which he can show "good cause," taken by itself, impermissibly interferes with the President's exercise of his constitutionally appointed functions. The second is whether, taken as a whole, the Act violates the separation of powers by reducing the President's ability to control the prosecutorial powers wielded by the independent counsel.

* * *

Unlike both *Bowsher* and *Myers*, this case does not involve an attempt by Congress itself to gain a role in the removal of executive officials other than its established powers of impeachment and conviction. The Act instead puts the removal power squarely in the hands of the Executive Branch * * *. There is no requirement of congressional approval of the Attorney General's removal decision * * *. In our view, the removal provisions of the Act make this case more analogous to *Humphrey's Executor v. United States*, 295 U.S. 602, 55 S.Ct. 869, 79 L.Ed. 1611 (1935), and *Wiener v. United States*, 357 U.S. 349, 78 S.Ct. 1275, 2 L.Ed.2d 1377 (1958), than to *Myers* or *Bowsher*.

In *Humphrey's Executor* * * *, we found it "plain" that the Constitution did not give the President "illimitable power of removal" over the officers of independent agencies. Were the President to have the power to remove

FTC Commissioners at will, the "coercive influence" of the removal power would "threate[n] the independence of [the] commission."

Similarly, in *Wiener* we considered whether the President had unfettered discretion to remove a member of the War Claims Commission * * *. The Commission's function was to receive and adjudicate certain claims for compensation from those who had suffered personal injury or property damage at the hands of the enemy during World War II. Commissioners were appointed by the President, with the advice and consent of the Senate, but the statute made no provision for the removal of officers, perhaps because the Commission itself was to have a limited existence. As in *Humphrey's Executor*, however, the Commissioners were entrusted by Congress with adjudicatory powers that were to be exercised free from executive control. In this context, "Congress did not wish to have hang over the Commission the Damocles' sword of removal by the President for no reason other than that he preferred to have on that Commission men of his own choosing." 357 U.S., at 356, 78 S.Ct., at 1279. Accordingly, we rejected the President's attempt to remove a Commissioner "merely because he wanted his own appointees on [the] Commission," stating that "no such power is given to the President directly by the Constitution, and none is impliedly conferred upon him by statute." *Ibid.*

Appellees contend that *Humphrey's Executor* and *Wiener* are distinguishable from this case because they did not involve officials who performed a "core executive function." They argue that our decision in *Humphrey's Executor* rests on a distinction between "purely executive" officials and officials who exercise "quasi-legislative" and "quasi-judicial" powers * * *.

We undoubtedly did rely on the terms "quasi-legislative" and "quasi-judicial" to distinguish the officials involved in *Humphrey's Executor* and *Wiener* from those in *Myers*, but our present considered view is that the determination of whether the Constitution allows Congress to impose a "good cause"-type restriction on the President's power to remove an official cannot be made to turn on whether or not that official is classified as "purely executive." The analysis contained in our removal cases is designed not to define rigid categories of those officials who may or may not be removed at will by the President, but to ensure that Congress does not interfere with the President's exercise of the "executive power" and his constitutionally appointed duty to "take care that the laws be faithfully executed" under Article II. *Myers* was undoubtedly correct in its holding, and in its broader suggestion that there are some "purely executive" officials who must be removable by the President at will if he is to be able to accomplish his constitutional role.[29] But as the Court noted in *Wiener*:

---

[29] The dissent says that the language of Article II vesting the executive power of the United States in the President requires that every officer of the United States exercising any part of that power must serve at the pleasure of the President and be removable by him at will. This rigid

"The assumption was short-lived that the *Myers* case recognized the President's inherent constitutional power to remove officials no matter what the relation of the executive to the discharge of their duties and no matter what restrictions Congress may have imposed regarding the nature of their tenure." 357 U.S., at 352, 78 S.Ct., at 1277.

* * * We do not mean to suggest that an analysis of the functions served by the officials at issue is irrelevant. But the real question is whether the removal restrictions are of such a nature that they impede the President's ability to perform his constitutional duty, and the functions of the officials in question must be analyzed in that light.

Considering for the moment the "good cause" removal provision in isolation from the other parts of the Act at issue in this case, we cannot say that the imposition of a "good cause" standard for removal by itself unduly trammels on executive authority. There is no real dispute that the functions performed by the independent counsel are "executive" in the sense that they are law enforcement functions that typically have been undertaken by officials within the Executive Branch. As we noted above, however, the independent counsel is an inferior officer under the Appointments Clause, with limited jurisdiction and tenure and lacking policymaking or significant administrative authority. Although the counsel exercises no small amount of discretion and judgment in deciding how to carry out his or her duties under the Act, we simply do not see how the President's need to control the exercise of that discretion is so central to the functioning of the Executive Branch as to require as a matter of constitutional law that the counsel be terminable at will by the President.

Nor do we think that the "good cause" removal provision at issue here impermissibly burdens the President's power to control or supervise the independent counsel, as an executive official, in the execution of his or her duties under the Act. This is not a case in which the power to remove an executive official has been completely stripped from the President, thus providing no means for the President to ensure the "faithful execution" of the laws. Rather, because the independent counsel may be terminated for "good cause," the Executive, through the Attorney General, retains ample authority to assure that the counsel is competently performing his or her statutory responsibilities in a manner that comports with the provisions of the Act. Although we need not decide in this case exactly what is encompassed within the term "good cause" under the Act, the legislative history of the removal provision also makes clear that the Attorney General

---

demarcation—a demarcation incapable of being altered by law in the slightest degree, and applicable to tens of thousands of holders of offices neither known nor foreseen by the Framers— depends upon an extrapolation from general constitutional language which we think is more than the text will bear. It is also contrary to our holding in *United States v. Perkins*, decided more than a century ago.

may remove an independent counsel for "misconduct." *See* H.R. Conf. Rep. No. 100–452, p. 37 (1987) * * *. We do not think that this limitation as it presently stands sufficiently deprives the President of control over the independent counsel to interfere impermissibly with his constitutional obligation to ensure the faithful execution of the laws.

The final question to be addressed is whether the Act, taken as a whole, violates the principle of separation of powers by unduly interfering with the role of the Executive Branch. Time and again we have reaffirmed the importance in our constitutional scheme of the separation of governmental powers into the three coordinate branches * * *. On the other hand, we have never held that the Constitution requires that the three branches of Government "operate with absolute independence." *United States v. Nixon*, 418 U.S., at 707, 94 S.Ct., at 3107. In the often-quoted words of Justice Jackson:

> "While the Constitution diffuses power the better to secure liberty, it also contemplates that practice will integrate the dispersed powers into a workable government. It enjoins upon its branches separateness but interdependence, autonomy but reciprocity." *Youngstown Sheet & Tube Co. v. Sawyer*, 343 U.S. 579, 635, 72 S.Ct. 863, 870, 96 L.Ed. 1153 (1952) (concurring opinion).

* * * [T]his case does not involve an attempt by Congress to increase its own powers at the expense of the Executive Branch. Unlike some of our previous cases, most recently *Bowsher v. Synar*, this case simply does not pose a "dange[r] of congressional usurpation of Executive Branch functions" * * *.

* * *

* * * It is undeniable that the Act reduces the amount of control or supervision that the Attorney General and, through him, the President exercises over the investigation and prosecution of a certain class of alleged criminal activity. The Attorney General is not allowed to appoint the individual of his choice; he does not determine the counsel's jurisdiction; and his power to remove a counsel is limited. Nonetheless, the Act does give the Attorney General several means of supervising or controlling the prosecutorial powers that may be wielded by an independent counsel. Most importantly, the Attorney General retains the power to remove the counsel for "good cause," a power that we have already concluded provides the Executive with substantial ability to ensure that the laws are "faithfully executed" by an independent counsel. No independent counsel may be appointed without a specific request by the Attorney General, and the Attorney General's decision not to request appointment if he finds "no reasonable grounds to believe that further investigation is warranted" is committed to his unreviewable discretion. The Act thus gives the Executive

a degree of control over the power to initiate an investigation by the independent counsel. In addition, the jurisdiction of the independent counsel is defined with reference to the facts submitted by the Attorney General, and once a counsel is appointed, the Act requires that the counsel abide by Justice Department policy unless it is not "possible" to do so. Notwithstanding the fact that the counsel is to some degree "independent" and free from executive supervision to a greater extent than other federal prosecutors, in our view these features of the Act give the Executive Branch sufficient control over the independent counsel to ensure that the President is able to perform his constitutionally assigned duties.

* * *

JUSTICE SCALIA, dissenting.

It is the proud boast of our democracy that we have "a government of laws and not of men." Many Americans are familiar with that phrase; not many know its derivation. It comes from Part the First, Article XXX, of the Massachusetts Constitution of 1780, which reads in full as follows:

> "In the government of this Commonwealth, the legislative department shall never exercise the executive and judicial powers, or either of them: The executive shall never exercise the legislative and judicial powers, or either of them: The judicial shall never exercise the legislative and executive powers, or either of them: to the end it may be a government of laws and not of men."

The Framers of the Federal Constitution similarly viewed the principle of separation of powers as the absolutely central guarantee of a just Government * * *. Without a secure structure of separated powers, our Bill of Rights would be worthless, as are the bills of rights of many nations of the world that have adopted, or even improved upon, the mere words of ours.

* * *

* * * [J]ust as the mere words of a Bill of Rights are not self-effectuating, the Framers recognized "[t]he insufficiency of a mere parchment delineation of the boundaries" to achieve the separation of powers. Federalist No. 73, p. 442 (A. Hamilton). "[T]he great security," wrote Madison, "against a gradual concentration of the several powers in the same department consists in giving to those who administer each department the necessary constitutional means and personal motives to resist encroachments of the others. The provision for defense must in this, as in all other cases, be made commensurate to the danger of attack." Federalist No. 51, pp. 321–322. Madison continued:

> "But it is not possible to give to each department an equal power of self-defense. In republican government, the legislative

authority necessarily predominates. The remedy for this inconveniency is to divide the legislature into different branches; and to render them, by different modes of election and different principles of action, as little connected with each other as the nature of their common functions and their common dependence on the society will admit. . . . As the weight of the legislative authority requires that it should be thus divided, the weakness of the executive may require, on the other hand, that it should be fortified." *Id.*, at 322–323.

The major "fortification" provided, of course, was the veto power. But in addition to providing fortification, the Founders conspicuously and very consciously declined to sap the Executive's strength in the same way they had weakened the Legislature: by dividing the executive power. Proposals to have multiple executives, or a council of advisers with separate authority were rejected. See 1 M. Farrand, Records of the Federal Convention of 1787, pp. 66, 71–74, 88, 91–92 (rev. ed. 1966); 2 *id.*, at 335–337, 533, 537, 542. Thus, while "[a]ll legislative Powers herein granted shall be vested in a Congress of the United States, which shall consist of a Senate *and* House of Representatives," U.S. Const., Art. I, § 1 (emphasis added), "[t]he executive Power shall be vested in *a President of the United States,*" Art. II, § 1, cl. 1 (emphasis added).

That is what this suit is about. Power. The allocation of power among Congress, the President, and the courts in such fashion as to preserve the equilibrium the Constitution sought to establish—so that "a gradual concentration of the several powers in the same department," Federalist No. 51, p. 321 (J. Madison), can effectively be resisted. Frequently an issue of this sort will come before the Court clad, so to speak, in sheep's clothing: the potential of the asserted principle to effect important change in the equilibrium of power is not immediately evident, and must be discerned by a careful and perceptive analysis. But this wolf comes as a wolf.

* * *

If to describe this case is not to decide it, the concept of a government of separate and coordinate powers no longer has meaning. The Court devotes most of its attention to such relatively technical details as the Appointments Clause and the removal power, addressing briefly and only at the end of its opinion the separation of powers * * *. I think that has it backwards. Our opinions are full of the recognition that it is the principle of separation of powers * * * which gives comprehensible content to the Appointments Clause, and determines the appropriate scope of the removal power. Thus, while I will subsequently discuss why our appointments and removal jurisprudence does not support today's holding, I begin with a consideration of the fountainhead of that jurisprudence, the separation and equilibration of powers.

* * *

* * * Article II, § 1, cl. 1, of the Constitution provides:

"The executive Power shall be vested in a President of the United States".

* * * [T]his does not mean *some of* the executive power, but *all of* the executive power. It seems to me, therefore, that the decision of the Court of Appeals invalidating the present statute must be upheld on fundamental separation-of-powers principles if the following two questions are answered affirmatively: (1) Is the conduct of a criminal prosecution (and of an investigation to decide whether to prosecute) the exercise of purely executive power? (2) Does the statute deprive the President of the United States of exclusive control over the exercise of that power? Surprising to say, the Court appears to concede an affirmative answer to both questions, but seeks to avoid the inevitable conclusion that since the statute vests some purely executive power in a person who is not the President of the United States it is void.

The Court concedes that "[t]here is no real dispute that the functions performed by the independent counsel are 'executive'" * * *. There is no possible doubt that the independent counsel's functions fit this description. She is vested with the "full power and independent authority to exercise all *investigative and prosecutorial* functions and powers of the Department of Justice [and] the Attorney General." 28 U.S.C. § 594(a) (emphasis added). Governmental investigation and prosecution of crimes is a quintessentially executive function.

As for the second question, whether the statute before us deprives the President of exclusive control over that quintessentially executive activity: The Court does not, and could not possibly, assert that it does not. That is indeed the whole object of the statute. Instead, the Court points out that the President, through his Attorney General, has at least some control. That concession is alone enough to invalidate the statute, but I cannot refrain from pointing out that the Court greatly exaggerates the extent of that "some" Presidential control. "Most importan[t]" among these controls, the Court asserts, is the Attorney General's "power to remove the counsel for 'good cause.'" This is somewhat like referring to shackles as an effective means of locomotion. As we recognized in *Humphrey's Executor v. United States*, 295 U.S. 602, 55 S.Ct. 869, 79 L.Ed. 1611 (1935)—indeed, what *Humphrey's Executor* was all about—limiting removal power to "good cause" is an impediment to, not an effective grant of, Presidential control * * *.

Moving on to the presumably "less important" controls that the President retains * * *, * * * the Court points out that the Act directs the independent counsel to abide by general Justice Department policy, except when not "possible." The exception alone shows this to be an empty promise. Even without that, however, one would be hard put to come up with many investigative or prosecutorial "policies" (other than those imposed by the Constitution or by Congress through law) that are absolute. Almost all investigative and prosecutorial decisions—including the ultimate decision whether, after a technical violation of the law has been found, prosecution is warranted—involve the balancing of innumerable legal and practical considerations. Indeed, even political considerations (in the nonpartisan sense) must be considered, as exemplified by the recent decision of an independent counsel to subpoena the former Ambassador of Canada, producing considerable tension in our relations with that country. See N.Y. Times, May 29, 1987, p. A12, col. 1. Another pre-eminently political decision is whether getting a conviction in a particular case is worth the disclosure of national security information that would be necessary. The Justice Department and our intelligence agencies are often in disagreement on this point, and the Justice Department does not always win. The present Act even goes so far as specifically to take the resolution of that dispute away from the President and give it to the independent counsel. 28 U.S.C. § 594(a)(6). In sum, the balancing of various legal, practical, and political considerations, none of which is absolute, is the very essence of prosecutorial discretion. To take this away is to remove the core of the prosecutorial function, and not merely "some" Presidential control.

As I have said, however, it is ultimately irrelevant *how much* the statute reduces Presidential control. The case is over when the Court acknowledges, as it must, that "[i]t is undeniable that the Act reduces the amount of control or supervision that the Attorney General and, through him, the President exercises over the investigation and prosecution of a certain class of alleged criminal activity" * * *. It is not for us to determine, and we have never presumed to determine, how much of the purely executive powers of government must be within the full control of the President. The Constitution prescribes that they *all* are.

* * *

* * * I will not discuss at any length why the restrictions upon the removal of the independent counsel also violate our established precedent dealing with that specific subject * * *. I cannot avoid commenting, however, about the essence of what the Court has done to our removal jurisprudence today.

* * *

Since our 1935 decision in *Humphrey's Executor v. United States*, 295 U.S. 602, 55 S.Ct. 869, 79 L.Ed. 1611—which was considered by many at the time the product of an activist, anti-New Deal Court bent on reducing the power of President Franklin Roosevelt—it has been established that the line of permissible restriction upon removal of principal officers lies at the point at which the powers exercised by those officers are no longer purely executive. Thus, removal restrictions have been generally regarded as lawful for so-called "independent regulatory agencies" * * *, which engage substantially in what has been called the "quasi-legislative activity" of rulemaking, and for members of Article I courts, such as the Court of Military Appeals, who engage in the "quasi-judicial" function of adjudication. It has often been observed, correctly in my view, that the line between "purely executive" functions and "quasi-legislative" or "quasi-judicial" functions is not a clear one or even a rational one. But at least it permitted the identification of certain officers, and certain agencies, whose functions were entirely within the control of the President. Congress had to be aware of that restriction in its legislation. Today, however, *Humphrey's Executor* is swept into the dustbin of repudiated constitutional principles * * *.

One can hardly grieve for the shoddy treatment given today to *Humphrey's Executor*, which, after all, accorded the same indignity (with much less justification) to Chief Justice Taft's opinion 10 years earlier in *Myers v. United States*, 272 U.S. 52, 47 S.Ct. 21, 71 L.Ed. 160 (1926)—gutting, in six quick pages devoid of textual or historical precedent for the novel principle it set forth, a carefully researched and reasoned 70-page opinion. It is in fact comforting to witness the reality that he who lives by the *ipse dixit* dies by the *ipse dixit*. But one must grieve for the Constitution. *Humphrey's Executor* at least had the decency formally to observe the constitutional principle that the President had to be the repository of *all* executive power, which, as *Myers* carefully explained, necessarily means that he must be able to discharge those who do not perform executive functions according to his liking * * *. By contrast, "our present considered view" is simply that *any* executive officer's removal can be restricted, so long as the President remains "able to accomplish his constitutional role." There are now no lines. If the removal of a prosecutor, the virtual embodiment of the power to "take care that the laws be faithfully executed," can be restricted, what officer's removal cannot? This is an open invitation for Congress to experiment. What about a special Assistant Secretary of State, with responsibility for one very narrow area of foreign policy, who would not only have to be confirmed by the Senate but could also be removed only pursuant to certain carefully designed restrictions? Could this possibly render the President "[un]able to accomplish his constitutional role"? Or a special Assistant Secretary of Defense for Procurement? The possibilities are endless, and the Court does not understand what the separation of powers, what "[a]mbition . . . counteract[ing] ambition," Federalist No. 51, p. 322 (Madison), is all about, if it does not expect Congress to try them. As far as I can discern from the Court's opinion, it is now open season upon the President's removal power for all executive officers, with not even the superficially principled restriction of *Humphrey's Executor* as cover. The Court essentially says to the President: "Trust us. We will make sure that you are able to accomplish your constitutional role." I think the Constitution gives the President—and the people—more protection than that.

NOTES

The independent counsel statute at issue in *Morrison* lapsed by its own terms in 1999 and was not renewed by Congress. Appointments of independent counsels since that time have resulted from internal Justice Department regulations rather than statutes.

For the most part, Justice Scalia's dire predictions about a rash of novel congressional attempts to immunize executive officers from presidential removal have not been realized. One major exception was the Public Company Accounting Oversight Board ("PCAOB") created by Title I of the Sarbanes-Oxley Act of 2002, 15 U.S.C. §§ 7211–19 (2012). In the wake of a series of accounting scandals that rocked the financial world in the 1990s, the PCAOB was vested with broad authority to regulate and oversee the audit practices of accounting firms, including the authority to register, inspect, investigate, and sanction such firms. *See id.* § 7211(c), (f). The members of the PCAOB are chosen by the Securities and Exchange Commission ("SEC"), *id.* § 7211(e)(4), and "may be removed by the Commission, in accordance with section 7217(d)(3) * * *, for good cause shown." *Id.* § 7211(e)(6). Section 7217(d)(3) provides that the SEC may censure or remove PCAOB officials upon a finding by the Commission (after a formal hearing) that a member of the PCAOB "(**A**) has willfully violated any provision of this Act, the rules of the Board, or the securities laws; (**B**) has willfully abused the authority of that member; or (**C**) without reasonable justification or excuse, has failed to enforce compliance with any such provision or rule, or any professional standard by any registered public accounting firm or any associated person thereof." *Id.* § 7217(d)(3). The SEC, in turn, is an independent agency whose members are removable by the President only for cause.

In 2005, the constitutionality of the PCAOB was challenged on two grounds: that its members are principal officers[38] who can only be appointed by the President with Senate confirmation and that the statute's double for-cause removal arrangement (the President can only remove SEC commissioners for cause and SEC commissioners can only remove PCAOB members for cause) improperly insulates PCAOB members from presidential control. Three years later, in a split decision, the D.C. Circuit rejected both challenges. *Free Enterprise Fund v. PCAOB*, 537 F.3d 667 (D.C.Cir.2008). Two years later, the Supreme Court issued its first opinion on removal since *Morrison v. Olson.*

---

[38] The statute creating the PCAOB declares that the Board is not a government agency and that its members are not federal officers at all. *See* 15 U.S.C. § 7211(b) (2012). Congress cannot define who is and is not an officer for constitutional purposes, *see supra* page 4, and no one defending the constitutionality of the PCAOB relied on this provision.

FREE ENTERPRISE FUND V. PUBLIC COMPANY ACCOUNTING OVERSIGHT BOARD

Supreme Court of the United States, 2010.
561 U.S. 477, 130 S.Ct. 3138, 177 L.Ed.2d 706.

CHIEF JUSTICE ROBERTS delivered the opinion of the Court.

Our Constitution divided the "powers of the new Federal Government into three defined categories, Legislative, Executive, and Judicial." *INS v. Chadha*, 462 U.S. 919, 951, 103 S.Ct. 2764 (1983). Article II vests "[t]he executive Power * * * in a President of the United States of America," who must "take Care that the Laws be faithfully executed." In light of "[t]he impossibility that one man should be able to perform all the great business of the State," the Constitution provides for executive officers to "assist the supreme Magistrate in discharging the duties of his trust." 30 Writings of George Washington 334 (J. Fitzpatrick ed.1939).

Since 1789, the Constitution has been understood to empower the President to keep these officers accountable—by removing them from office, if necessary. See generally *Myers v. United States*, 272 U.S. 52, 47 S.Ct. 21 (1926). This Court has determined, however, that this authority is not without limit. In *Humphrey's Executor v. United States*, 295 U.S. 602, 55 S.Ct. 869 (1935), we held that Congress can, under certain circumstances, create independent agencies run by principal officers appointed by the President, whom the President may not remove at will but only for good cause. Likewise, in *United States v. Perkins*, 116 U.S. 483, 6 S.Ct. 449 (1886), and *Morrison v. Olson*, 487 U.S. 654, 108 S.Ct. 2597 (1988), the Court sustained similar restrictions on the power of principal executive officers—themselves responsible to the President—to remove their own inferiors. The parties do not ask us to reexamine any of these precedents, and we do not do so.

We are asked, however, to consider a new situation not yet encountered by the Court. The question is whether these separate layers of protection may be combined. May the President be restricted in his ability to remove a principal officer, who is in turn restricted in his ability to remove an inferior officer, even though that inferior officer determines the policy and enforces the laws of the United States?

We hold that such multilevel protection from removal is contrary to Article II's vesting of the executive power in the President * * *.

* * *

The Constitution provides that "[t]he executive Power shall be vested in a President of the United States of America." As Madison stated on the floor of the First Congress, "if any power whatsoever is in its nature Executive, it is the power of appointing, overseeing, and controlling those who execute the laws." 1 Annals of Cong. 463 (1789).

The removal of executive officers was discussed extensively in Congress when the first executive departments were created. The view that "prevailed, as most consonant to the text of the Constitution" and "to the requisite responsibility and harmony in the Executive Department," was that the executive power included a power to oversee executive officers through removal; because that traditional executive power was not "expressly taken away, it remained with the President." Letter from James Madison to Thomas Jefferson (June 30, 1789), 16 Documentary History of the First Federal Congress 893 (2004). "This Decision of 1789 provides contemporaneous and weighty evidence of the Constitution's meaning since many of the Members of the First Congress had taken part in framing that instrument." *Bowsher v. Synar*, 478 U.S. 714, 723–24, 106 S.Ct. 3181 (1986) (internal quotation marks omitted). And it soon became the "settled and well understood construction of the Constitution." *Ex parte Hennen*, 38 U.S. 230, 13 Pet. 230, 259.

The landmark case of *Myers v. United States* reaffirmed the principle that Article II confers on the President "the general administrative control of those executing the laws." 272 U.S. at 164, 47 S.Ct. 21 * * *. As we explained in *Myers* the President therefore must have some "power of removing those for whom he can not continue to be responsible." *Id.* at 117, 47 S.Ct. 21.

Nearly a decade later in *Humphrey's Executor*, this Court held that *Myers* did not prevent Congress from conferring good-cause tenure on the principal officers of certain independent agencies * * *.

Humphrey's Executor did not address the removal of inferior officers, whose appointment Congress may vest in heads of departments. If Congress does so, it is ordinarily the department head, rather than the President, who enjoys the power of removal. This Court has upheld for-cause limitations on that power as well.

* * *

We again considered the status of inferior officers in *Morrison* * * *. We recognized that the independent counsel was undoubtedly an executive officer, rather than " 'quasi-legislative' " or " 'quasi-judicial,' " but we stated as "our present considered view" that Congress had power to impose good-cause restrictions on her removal. 487 U.S., at 689–91, 108 S.Ct. 2597 * * *. *Morrison* did not, however, address the consequences of more than one level of good-cause tenure * * *.

B

As explained, we have previously upheld limited restrictions on the President's removal power. In those cases, however, only one level of protected tenure separated the President from an officer exercising executive power. It was the President—or a subordinate he could remove at will—who decided whether the officer's conduct merited removal under the good-cause standard.

The Act before us does something quite different. It not only protects Board members from removal except for good cause, but withdraws from the President any decision on whether that good cause exists. That decision is vested instead in other tenured officers—the [Securities and Exchange] Commissioners—none of whom is subject to the President's direct control. The result is a Board that is not accountable to the President, and a President who is not responsible for the Board.

The added layer of tenure protection makes a difference. Without a layer of insulation between the Commission and the Board, the Commission could remove a Board member at any time, and therefore would be fully responsible for what the Board does. The President could then hold the Commission to account for its supervision of the Board, to the same extent that he may hold the Commission to account for everything else it does.

A second level of tenure protection changes the nature of the President's review. Now the Commission cannot remove a Board member at will. The President therefore cannot hold the Commission fully accountable for the Board's conduct, to the same extent that he may hold the Commission accountable for everything else that it does. The Commissioners are not responsible for the Board's actions. They are only responsible for their own determination of whether the Act's rigorous good-cause standard is met. And even if the President disagrees with their determination, he is powerless to intervene—unless that determination is so unreasonable as to constitute "inefficiency, neglect of duty, or malfeasance in office." *Humphrey's Executor*, 295 U.S., at 620, 55 S.Ct. 869 (internal quotation marks omitted).

This novel structure does not merely add to the Board's independence, but transforms it. Neither the President, nor anyone directly responsible to him, nor even an officer whose conduct he may review only for good cause, has full control over the Board. The President is stripped of the power our precedents have preserved, and his ability to execute the laws— by holding his subordinates accountable for their conduct—is impaired.

That arrangement is contrary to Article II's vesting of the executive power in the President * * *.

Indeed, if allowed to stand, this dispersion of responsibility could be multiplied. If Congress can shelter the bureaucracy behind two layers of good-cause tenure, why not a third? At oral argument, the Government was unwilling to concede that even *five* layers between the President and the Board would be too many. Tr. of Oral Arg. 47–48. The officers of such an agency—safely encased within a Matryoshka doll of tenure protections—

would be immune from Presidential oversight, even as they exercised power in the people's name.

* * *

The diffusion of power carries with it a diffusion of accountability. The people do not vote for the "Officers of the United States." They instead look to the President to guide the "assistants or deputies * * * subject to his superintendence." The Federalist No. 72, p. 487 (J. Cooke ed.1961) (A. Hamilton). Without a clear and effective chain of command, the public cannot "determine on whom the blame or the punishment of a pernicious measure, or series of pernicious measures ought really to fall." *Id., No. 70,* at 476 (same). That is why the Framers sought to ensure that "those who are employed in the execution of the law will be in their proper situation, and the chain of dependence be preserved; the lowest officers, the middle grade, and the highest, will depend, as they ought, on the President, and the President on the community." 1 Annals of Cong., at 499 (J. Madison).

By granting the Board executive power without the Executive's oversight, this Act subverts the President's ability to ensure that the laws are faithfully executed—as well as the public's ability to pass judgment on his efforts. The Act's restrictions are incompatible with the Constitution's separation of powers.

C

* * *

No one doubts Congress's power to create a vast and varied federal bureaucracy. But where, in all this, is the role for oversight by an elected President? The Constitution requires that a President chosen by the entire Nation oversee the execution of the laws. And the " 'fact that a given law or procedure is efficient, convenient, and useful in facilitating functions of government, standing alone, will not save it if it is contrary to the Constitution,' " for " '[c]onvenience and efficiency are not the primary objectives-or the hallmarks-of democratic government.' " *Bowsher,* 478 U.S., at 736, 106 S.Ct. 3181 (quoting *Chadha,* 462 U.S., at 944, 103 S.Ct. 2764).

One can have a government that functions without being ruled by functionaries, and a government that benefits from expertise without being ruled by experts. Our Constitution was adopted to enable the people to govern themselves, through their elected leaders. The growth of the Executive Branch, which now wields vast power and touches almost every aspect of daily life, heightens the concern that it may slip from the Executive's control, and thus from that of the people. This concern is largely absent from the dissent's paean to the administrative state.

For example, the dissent dismisses the importance of removal as a tool of supervision, concluding that the President's "power to get something done" more often depends on "who controls the agency's budget requests and funding, the relationships between one agency or department and another, . . . purely political factors (including Congress' ability to assert influence)," and indeed whether particular *unelected* officials support or "resist" the President's policies. *Post,* at 11, 13 (emphasis deleted). The Framers did not rest our liberties on such bureaucratic minutiae. As we said in *Bowsher, supra,* at 730, 106 S.Ct. 3181, "[t]he separated powers of our Government cannot be permitted to turn on judicial assessment of whether an officer exercising executive power is on good terms with Congress."

* * *

The President has been given the power to oversee executive officers; he is not limited, as in Harry Truman's lament, to "persuad[ing]" his unelected subordinates "to do what they ought to do without persuasion." *Post,* at 11 (internal quotation marks omitted). In its pursuit of a "workable government," Congress cannot reduce the Chief Magistrate to a cajoler-in-chief.

D

The United States concedes that some constraints on the removal of inferior executive officers might violate the Constitution. See Brief for United States 47. It contends, however, that the removal restrictions at issue here do not.

To begin with, the Government argues that the Commission's removal power over the Board is "broad," and could be construed as broader still, if necessary to avoid invalidation. See, *e.g., id.,* at 51, and n. 19; cf. PCAOB Brief 22–23. But the Government does not contend that simple disagreement with the Board's policies or priorities could constitute "good cause" for its removal. See Tr. of Oral Arg. 41–43, 45–46. Nor do our precedents suggest as much * * *.

Indeed, this case presents an even more serious threat to executive control than an "ordinary" dual for-cause standard. Congress enacted an unusually high standard that must be met before Board members may be removed. A Board member cannot be removed except for willful violations of the Act, Board rules, or the securities laws; willful abuse of authority; or unreasonable failure to enforce compliance-as determined in a formal Commission order, rendered on the record and after notice and an opportunity for a hearing. The Act does not even give the Commission power to fire Board members for violations of *other* laws that do not relate to the Act, the securities laws, or the Board's authority. The President might have less than full confidence in, say, a Board member who cheats on his taxes; but that discovery is not listed among the grounds for removal * * *.

* * *

Alternatively, respondents portray the Act's limitations on removal as irrelevant, because—as the Court of Appeals held—the Commission wields "at-will removal power over Board *functions* if not Board members." 537 F.3d, at 683 (emphasis added); accord, Brief for United States 27–28; PCAOB Brief 48 * * *.

Broad power over Board functions is not equivalent to the power to remove Board members * * *. [A]ltering the budget or powers of an agency as a whole is a problematic way to control an inferior officer. The Commission cannot wield a free hand to supervise individual members if it must destroy the Board in order to fix it.

* * *

Finally, respondents suggest that our conclusion is contradicted by the past practice of Congress. But the Sarbanes-Oxley Act is highly unusual in committing substantial executive authority to officers protected by two layers of for-cause removal—including at one level a sharply circumscribed definition of what constitutes "good cause," and rigorous procedures that must be followed prior to removal.

* * *

The dissent here suggests that other such positions might exist, and complains that we do not resolve their status in this opinion. *Post,* at 23–31. The dissent itself, however, stresses the very size and variety of the Federal Government, see *post,* at 7–8, and those features discourage general pronouncements on matters neither briefed nor argued here. In any event, the dissent fails to support its premonitions of doom; none of the positions it identifies are similarly situated to the Board. See *post,* at 28–31.

For example, many civil servants within independent agencies would not qualify as "Officers of the United States," who "exercis[e] significant authority pursuant to the laws of the United States," *Buckley,* 424 U.S., at 126, 96 S.Ct. 612. The parties here concede that Board members are executive "Officers," as that term is used in the Constitution * * *.

Nor do the employees referenced by the dissent enjoy the same significant and unusual protections from Presidential oversight as members of the Board. Senior or policymaking positions in government may be excepted from the competitive service to ensure Presidential control, see §§ 2302(a)(2)(B), 3302, 7511(b)(2), and members of the Senior Executive Service may be reassigned or reviewed by agency heads (and entire agencies may be excluded from that Service by the President), see, *e.g.,* §§ 3132(c), 3395(a), 4312(d), 4314(b)(3), (c)(3). While the full extent of that authority is not before us, any such authority is of course wholly absent with respect to the Board. Nothing in our opinion, therefore, should be read to cast doubt on the use of what is colloquially known as the civil service system within independent agencies.[10]

* * *

There is no reason for us to address whether these positions identified by the dissent, or any others not at issue in this case, are so structured as to infringe the President's constitutional authority * * *. The only issue in this case is whether Congress may deprive the President of adequate control over the Board, which is the regulator of first resort and the primary law enforcement authority for a vital sector of our economy. We hold that it cannot.

* * *

BREYER, J., with whom JUSTICE STEVENS, JUSTICE GINSBURG, and JUSTICE SOTOMAYOR join, dissenting.

The Court holds unconstitutional a statute providing that the Securities and Exchange Commission can remove members of the Public Company Accounting Oversight Board from office only for cause. It argues that granting the "inferior officer[s]" on the Accounting Board "more than one level of good-cause protection . . . contravenes the President's 'constitutional obligation to ensure the faithful execution of the laws.'" I agree that the Accounting Board members are inferior officers. But in my view the statute does not significantly interfere with the President's "executive Power." It violates no separation-of-powers principle. And the Court's contrary holding threatens to disrupt severely the fair and efficient administration of the laws. I consequently dissent.

I

A

The legal question before us arises at the intersection of two general constitutional principles. On the one hand, Congress has broad power to enact statutes "necessary and proper" to the exercise of its specifically enumerated constitutional authority. As Chief Justice Marshall wrote for the Court nearly 200 years ago, the Necessary and Proper Clause reflects the Framers' efforts to create a Constitution that would "endure for ages to come." *McCulloch v. Maryland*, 17 U.S. 316, 4 Wheat. 316, 415 (1819). It

---

[10] For similar reasons, our holding also does not address that subset of independent agency employees who serve as administrative law judges. Whether administrative law judges are necessarily "Officers of the United States" is disputed. See, *e.g. Landry v. FDIC,* 204 F.3d 1125 (C.A.D.C.2000). And unlike members of the Board, many administrative law judges of course perform adjudicative rather than enforcement or policymaking functions or possess purely recommendatory powers. The Government below refused to identify either "civil service tenure-protected employees in independent agencies" or administrative law judges as "precedent for the PCAOB." 537 F.3d 667, 699, n. 8 (C.A.D.C.2008) (Kavanaugh, J., dissenting); see Tr. of Oral Arg. in No. 07–5127 (CADC), pp. 32, 37–38, 42.

embodies their recognition that it would be "unwise" to prescribe "the means by which government should, in all future time, execute its powers." *Ibid.* Such "immutable rules" would deprive the Government of the needed flexibility to respond to future "exigencies which, if foreseen at all, must have been seen dimly." *Ibid.* * * *.

On the other hand, the opening sections of Articles I, II, and III of the Constitution separately and respectively vest "all legislative Powers" in Congress, the "executive Power" in the President, and the "judicial Power" in the Supreme Court (and such "inferior Courts as Congress may from time to time ordain and establish"). In doing so, these provisions imply a structural separation-of-powers principle. And that principle, along with the instruction in Article II, § 3 that the President "shall take Care that the Laws be faithfully executed," limits Congress' power to structure the Federal Government.

But neither of these two principles is absolute in its application to removal cases. The Necessary and Proper Clause does not grant Congress power to free *all* Executive Branch officials from dismissal at the will of the President. Nor does the separation-of-powers principle grant the President an absolute authority to remove *any and all* Executive Branch officials at will. Rather, depending on, say, the nature of the office, its function, or its subject matter, Congress sometimes may, consistent with the Constitution, limit the President's authority to remove an officer from his post. And we must here decide whether the circumstances surrounding the statute at issue justify such a limitation.

In answering the question presented, we cannot look to more specific constitutional text, such as the text of the Appointments Clause or the Presentment Clause, upon which the Court has relied in other separation-of-powers cases. That is because, with the exception of the general "vesting" and "take care" language, the Constitution is completely "silent with respect to the power of removal from office." *Ex parte Henne,* 13 Pet. 230, 258 (1839).

Nor does history offer significant help. The President's power to remove Executive Branch officers "was not discussed in the Constitutional Convention." *Myers, supra*, at 109–110, 47 S.Ct. 21 * * *. Scholars, like Members of this Court, have continued to disagree, not only about the inferences that should be drawn from the inconclusive historical record, but also about the nature of the original disagreement.

Nor does this Court's precedent fully answer the question presented. At least it does not clearly invalidate the provision in dispute * * *.

* * *

B

When previously deciding this kind of nontextual question, the Court has emphasized the importance of examining how a particular provision, taken in context, is likely to function * * *. The Court has thereby written into law Justice Jackson's wise perception that "the Constitution . . . contemplates that practice will integrate the dispersed powers into *a workable government.*" *Youngstown Sheet & Tube Co. v. Sawyer*, 343 U.S. 579, 635, 72 S.Ct. 863 (1952) (opinion concurring in judgment) (emphasis added).

It is not surprising that the Court in these circumstances has looked to function and context, and not to bright-line rules. For one thing, that approach embodies the intent of the Framers. As Chief Justice Marshall long ago observed, our Constitution is fashioned so as to allow the three coordinate branches, including this Court, to exercise practical judgment in response to changing conditions and "exigencies," which at the time of the founding could be seen only "dimly," and perhaps not at all. *McCulloch,* 4 Wheat. at 415.

For another, a functional approach permits Congress and the President the flexibility needed to adapt statutory law to changing circumstances * * *. [T]he Federal Government at the time of the founding consisted of about 2,000 employees and served a population of about 4 million. Today, however, the Federal Government employs about *4.4 million workers* who serve a Nation of more than 310 million people living in a society characterized by rapid technological, economic, and social change.

* * *

The upshot is that today vast numbers of statutes governing vast numbers of subjects, concerned with vast numbers of different problems, provide for, or foresee, their execution or administration through the work of administrators organized within many different kinds of administrative structures, exercising different kinds of administrative authority, to achieve their legislatively mandated objectives. And, given the nature of the Government's work, it is not surprising that administrative units come in many different shapes and sizes.

The functional approach required by our precedents recognizes this administrative complexity and, more importantly, recognizes the various ways presidential power operates within this context—and the various ways in which a removal provision might affect that power. As human beings have known ever since Ulysses tied himself to the mast so as safely to hear the Sirens' song, sometimes it is necessary to disable oneself in order to achieve a broader objective. Thus, legally enforceable commitments—such as contracts, statutes that cannot instantly be changed, and, as in the case before us, the establishment of independent administrative institutions—hold the potential to empower precisely because of their ability to constrain. If the President seeks to regulate through impartial adjudication, then insulation of the adjudicator from removal at will can help him achieve that goal. And to free a technical decisionmaker from the fear of removal without cause can similarly help create legitimacy with respect to that official's regulatory actions by helping to insulate his technical decisions from nontechnical political pressure.

* * *

Thus, here, as in similar cases, we should decide the constitutional question in light of the provision's practical functioning in context. And our decision should take account of the Judiciary's comparative lack of institutional expertise.

II

A

To what extent then is the Act's "for cause" provision likely, as a practical matter, to limit the President's exercise of executive authority? In practical terms no "for cause" provision can, in isolation, define the full measure of executive power. This is because a legislative decision to place ultimate administrative authority in, say, the Secretary of Agriculture rather than the President, the way in which the statute defines the scope of the power the relevant administrator can exercise, the decision as to who controls the agency's budget requests and funding, the relationships between one agency or department and another, as well as more purely political factors (including Congress' ability to assert influence) are more likely to affect the President's power to get something done. That is why President Truman complained that " 'the powers of the President amount to' " bringing " 'people in and try[ing] to persuade them to do what they ought to do without persuasion.' " C. Rossiter, The American Presidency 154 (2d rev. ed.1960). And that is why scholars have written that the President "is neither dominant nor powerless" in his relationships with many Government entities, "whether denominated executive or independent." Strauss, The Place of Agencies in Government: Separation of Powers and the Fourth Branch, 84 Colum. L. Rev. 573, 583 (1984). Those entities "are *all* subject to presidential direction in significant aspects of their functioning, and [are each] able to resist presidential direction in others." *Ibid.* (emphasis added).

Indeed, notwithstanding the majority's assertion that the removal authority is "*the* key" mechanism by which the President oversees inferior officers in the independent agencies, it appears that no President has ever actually sought to exercise that power by testing the scope of a "for cause" provision.

But even if we put all these other matters to the side, we should still conclude that the "for cause" restriction before us will not restrict presidential power significantly. For one thing, the restriction directly limits, not the President's power, but the power of an already independent agency. The Court seems to have forgotten that fact when it identifies its central constitutional problem: According to the Court, the President "is powerless to intervene" if he has determined that the Board members' "conduct merit[s] removal" because "[t]hat decision is vested instead in other tenured officers—the Commissioners—none of whom is subject to the President's direct control." But so long as the President is *legitimately* foreclosed from removing the *Commissioners* except for cause (as the majority assumes), nullifying the Commission's power to remove Board members only for cause will not resolve the problem the Court has identified: The President will *still* be "powerless to intervene" by removing the Board members if the Commission reasonably decides not to do so.

In other words, the Court fails to show why *two* layers of "for cause" protection—Layer One insulating the Commissioners from the President, and Layer Two insulating the Board from the Commissioners—impose any more serious limitation upon the *President's* powers than *one* layer * * *.

* * *

* * * [O]nce we leave the realm of hypothetical logic and view the removal provision at issue in the context of the entire Act, its lack of practical effect becomes readily apparent. That is because the statute provides the Commission with full authority and virtually comprehensive control over all of the Board's functions * * *.

* * *

C

Where a "for cause" provision is so unlikely to restrict presidential power and so likely to further a legitimate institutional need, precedent strongly supports its constitutionality. First, in considering a related issue in *Nixon v. Administrator of General Services*, 433 U.S. 425, 97 S.Ct. 2777 (1977), the Court made clear that when "determining whether the Act disrupts the proper balance between the coordinate branches, the proper inquiry focuses on the extent to which it prevents the Executive Branch from accomplishing its constitutionally assigned functions." *Id.*, at 443, 97 S.Ct. 2777 * * *. Here, the removal restriction may somewhat diminish the *Commission's* ability to control the Board, but it will have little, if any, negative effect in respect to the President's ability to control the Board, let alone to coordinate the Executive Branch. Indeed, given *Morrison*, where the Court upheld a restriction that significantly interfered with the

President's important historic power to control criminal prosecutions, a " 'purely executive' " function, the constitutionality of the present restriction would seem to follow *a fortiori*.

Second * * *, this Court has repeatedly upheld "for cause" provisions where they restrict the President's power to remove an officer with adjudicatory responsibilities. And we have also upheld such restrictions when they relate to officials with technical responsibilities that warrant a degree of special independence. The Accounting Board's functions involve both kinds of responsibility * * *.

* * *

Fourth, the Court has said that "[o]ur separation-of-powers jurisprudence generally focuses on the danger of one branch's *aggrandizing its power* at the expense of another branch." *Freytag, supra,* at 878, 111 S.Ct. 2631 (emphasis added) * * *. Congress here has "drawn" no power to itself to remove the Board members. It has instead sought to *limit* its own power, by, for example, providing the Accounting Board with a revenue stream independent of the congressional appropriations process * * *.

In sum, the Court's prior cases impose functional criteria that are readily met here. Once one goes beyond the Court's elementary arithmetical logic (*i.e.,* "one plus one is greater than one") our precedent virtually dictates a holding that the challenged "for cause" provision is constitutional.

D

We should ask one further question. Even if the "for cause" provision before us does not itself significantly interfere with the President's authority or aggrandize Congress' power, is it nonetheless necessary to adopt a bright-line rule forbidding the provision lest, through a series of such provisions, each itself upheld as reasonable, Congress might undercut the President's central constitutional role? The answer to this question is that no such need has been shown. Moreover, insofar as the Court seeks to create such a rule, it fails. And in failing it threatens a harm that is far more serious than any imaginable harm this "for cause" provision might bring about.

The Court fails to create a bright-line rule because of considerable uncertainty about the scope of its holding—an uncertainty that the Court's opinion both reflects and generates. The Court suggests, for example, that its rule may not apply where an inferior officer "perform[s] adjudicative . . . functions." But the Accounting Board performs adjudicative functions. What, then, are we to make of the Court's potential exception? And would such an exception apply to an administrative law judge who also has important administrative duties beyond pure adjudication * * * ?

The Court further seems to suggest that its holding may not apply to inferior officers who have a different relationship to their appointing agents than the relationship between the Commission and the Board. But the only characteristic of the "relationship" between the Commission and the Board that the Court apparently deems relevant is that the relationship includes two layers of for-cause removal. Why then would any different relationship that also includes two layers of for-cause removal survive where this one has not? * * *

The Court begins to reveal the practical problems inherent in its double for-cause rule when it suggests that its rule may not apply to "the civil service." The "civil service" is defined by statute to include "all appointive positions in . . . the Government of the United States," excluding the military, but including *all* civil "officer[s]" up to and including those who are subject to Senate confirmation. The civil service thus includes many officers indistinguishable from the members of both the Commission and the Accounting Board * * *.

* * *

The potential list of those whom today's decision affects is yet larger. As JUSTICE SCALIA has observed, administrative law judges (ALJs) "are all executive officers." And ALJs are each removable "only for good cause established and determined by the Merit Systems Protection Board," 5 U.S.C. §§ 7512(a)–(b). But the members of the Merit Systems Protection Board are themselves protected from removal by the President absent good cause. § 1202(d).

* * *

And what about the military? * * * There are over 210,000 active-duty commissioned officers currently serving in the armed forces. And such officers can generally be so removed only by *other* commissioned officers, who themselves enjoy the same career protections.

* * *

The majority sees "no reason . . . to address whether" any of "these positions," "or any others," might be deemed unconstitutional under its new rule, preferring instead to leave these matters for a future case. But what is to happen in the meantime? Is the work of all these various officials to be put on hold while the courts of appeals determine whether today's ruling applies to them? Will Congress have to act to remove the "for cause" provisions? Can the President then restore them via executive order? And, still, what about the military? A clearer line would help avoid these practical difficulties.

* * *

In my view the Court's decision is wrong—very wrong * * *. Its rule of decision is both imprecise and overly broad. In light of the present imprecision, it must either narrow its rule arbitrarily, leaving it to apply virtually alone to the Accounting Board, or it will have to leave in place a broader rule of decision applicable to many other "inferior officers" as well. In doing the latter, it will undermine the President's authority. And it will create an obstacle, indeed pose a serious threat, to the proper functioning of that workable Government that the Constitution seeks to create-in provisions this Court is sworn to uphold.

With respect I dissent.

NOTES

Administrative law judges in independent agencies such as the SEC are statutorily subject to "double-cause" removal. In *Lucia v. SEC, supra* pages 203–215, Justice Breyer's concurring opinion worried that the majority's holding that ALJs are constitutional "Officers," combined with the majority's holding in *Free Enterprise Fund,* might invalidate that removal arrangement. The majority in both *Lucia* and *Free Enterprise Fund* claimed not to have decided that question. Is that claim tenable? Is the result feared by Justice Breyer now inevitable? Will subjecting ALJs to at-will removal be a bad thing? Is it constitutionally relevant whether it would be a bad thing? If ALJ independence is a paramount value, would a simple solution be to convert all ALJs—or at the least the 200 or so ALJs who adjudicate enforcement actions (the vast majority of ALJs decide only benefits claims)—into Article III judges?

Virtually all independent agencies—that is, agencies whose heads are not removable at the will of the President—are multi-member bodies. *See supra* page 6. The few exceptions are all of relatively modern vintage: the independent counsel discussed in *Morrison v. Olson*; the Federal Housing Finance Agency, created in 2008; the Social Security Administration, which was converted (over the constitutional doubts of President Clinton) to an independent agency in 1994 after six decades as an executive agency; and the Consumer Financial Protection Bureau (CFPB), which was created in 2010 as part of the Dodd-Frank Act. Does an agency's internal organizational structure make any constitutional difference when it comes to congressional restrictions on removal of agency officials? In 2016, a panel of the D.C. Circuit, in an opinion by Judge Brett Kavanaugh, said yes, holding that the CFPB was unconstitutional because the CFPB is headed by a single director and limitations on presidential removal of agency heads are permissible only when the agency is multi-membered. *See PHH Corp. v. CFPB,* 839 F.3d 1 (D.C.Cir.2016). The other single-headed independent agencies listed above were dismissed as anomalies or distinguished as not having direct regulatory authority over private parties. *See id.* at 18–21. The panel majority (one judge would have decided the case on narrower grounds without reaching the constitutional removal issues) essentially started with unlimited presidential removal as the baseline and then asked whether Supreme Court precedent approving certain removal restrictions mandated a different result in the case of the CFPB. *See, e.g., id.* at 5 ("In 1935, however, the Supreme Court carved out an exception to * * * Article II by permitting Congress to create *independent* agencies that exercise executive power"). Is that consistent with the methodology of *Free Enterprise Fund?* With the methodology of *Morrison v. Olson?* With how one normally expects lower courts to deal with Supreme Court precedents? In any event, the *en banc* D.C. Circuit overturned the panel decision and upheld the structure of the CFPB. *See PHH Corp. v. CFPB,* 881 F.3d 75 (D.C.Cir.2018). The plaintiff chose not to seek Supreme Court review of that decision. Shortly thereafter, however, a district judge in New York adopted the reasoning of the panel majority (which had been repeated in dissenting opinions in the D.C. Circuit's *en banc* proceeding) and held that the CFPB could not constitutionally pursue lawsuits. *See CFPB v. RD Legal Funding, LLC,* 2018 WL 3094916, *35 (S.D.N.Y).

On the heels of that decision, in July 2018, the Federal Housing Finance Agency, one of the few other independent agencies headed by a single director, was found (by a 2–1 vote) unconstitutional by the Fifth Circuit. *See Collins v. Mnuchin,* 896 F.3d 640 (5th Cir.2018). The court relied in part on the absence of a multi-member board at the top of the agency, reasoning (as had the D.C. Circuit panel that found the CFPB unconstitutional) that presidents are likely to be able to appoint at least some members of such a board and thus exert a degree of control over its actions, whereas "the FHFA's single-Director leadership structure insulates the agency from presidential oversight." *Id.* at 667. *Cf. PHH Corp.,* 881 F.3d at 167 (Kavanaugh, J., dissenting) ("a President may be stuck for years with a Director who was appointed by the prior President and who vehemently opposes the current President's agenda"). The court also invoked a multiplicity of other factors, such as the agency's self-funding provisions which exempt it from the usual appropriations process (and thus exempt it from the risk of a presidential veto of its funding), as evidence that the agency's structure removed it too far from presidential control and direction to be constitutional. *See Collins,* 896 F.3d at 666 (grounding a finding of unconstitutionality on "(1) for-cause removal restriction; (2) single-Director leadership structure; (3) lack of a bipartisan leadership composition requirement; (4) funding stream outside the normal appropriations process; and (5) Federal Housing Finance Oversight Board's purely advisory oversight role").

Does it seem at all odd that, after 230 years, there is no consensus about something as basic to governance as the President's constitutional relationship to administrative agencies?

3. THE UNITARY EXECUTIVE

Justice Roberts' opinion in *Free Enterprise Fund* and Justice Scalia's dissent in *Morrison* both emphasize the connection between the removal controversy and what is often called "the unitary executive": the Constitution's vesting of executive power in the person of the President rather than in the executive department as a whole. Advocates of the unitary executive typically reason that the President must, by constitutional command, have supervisory authority over all discretionary decisions vested by statute in executive officials; otherwise, Congress could effectively vest executive power in subordinate officials. Recent decades have seen a steady stream of highly sophisticated, and often highly contentious, scholarship debating presidential power to control the operations of the executive department.[39] Those debates are more than occasionally misdirected by confusion about what is meant by a "unitary executive." Literally, the term means only that the "executive Power," whatever its scope may be, is entirely vested in the person of the President. So understood, the "unitary executive" idea says nothing about *how much power* is encompassed by the term "executive Power." It just says that whatever that power may be, the President has it. At times, however, debates seemingly framed in terms of the "unitary executive" are really debates about the scope and extent of the "executive Power," so that advocates of the unitary executive are often (mis)cast as advocates of broad presidential power. But the questions of scope and location are quite distinct. One might believe in a very modest conception of "executive Power" but think that that (very limited) power must be under the control and direction of the President. Alternatively, one might believe that there is a very broad scope to the "executive Power" but that Congress may, if it wishes, divide that power up among the President and subordinates. Or one might believe in neither or both a unitary executive and a broad presidential power. Arguments for one are not necessarily arguments for the other.

With some reluctance, this book leaves questions about the scope of presidential power primarily to courses in constitutional law or to advanced seminars, though warm and happy thoughts go out to any instructor who wants to supplement this book with materials on the constitutional extent of presidential power. The focus here is on the debate concerning the unitary or non-unitary status of the "executive Power," whatever the scope of that power may be. At the heart of that debate is the question whether the President's constitutional power comes, at least in part, from the vesting of the "executive Power" in the first sentence of Article II or solely from the more specific (and quite limited) enumerations of power in sections 2 and 3 of Article II. There is no express "Control and

---

[39] For a sampling of some of the scholarship, see Steven G. Calabresi, *Some Normative Arguments for the Unitary Executive*, 48 Ark. L. Rev. 23 (1995); Steven G. Calabresi, *The Vesting Clauses as Power Grants*, 88 Nw. U.L. Rev. 1377 (1994); Steven G. Calabresi & Saikrishna B. Prakash, *The President's Power to Execute the Laws*, 104 Yale L.J. 541 (1994); Steven G. Calabresi & Kevin H. Rhodes, *The Structural Constitution: Unitary Executive, Plural Judiciary*, 105 Harv. L. Rev. 1153 (1992); Martin Flaherty, *The Most Dangerous Branch*, 105 Yale L.J. 1725 (1996); Lawrence Lessig & Cass R. Sunstein, *The President and the Administration*, 94 Colum. L. Rev. 1 (1994); Robert G. Natelson, *The Original Meaning of the Constitution's "Executive Vesting Clause"—Evidence from Eighteenth-Century Drafting Practice,* 31 Whittier L. Rev. 1 (2009).

Direction Clause" in sections 2 and 3 of Article II, so if the "Vesting Clause" that opens Article II does not actually grant to the President "[t]he executive Power," the case for a constitutionally unitary executive becomes harder (though not impossible) to make. For a partisan but hopefully informative look at this question, see Gary Lawson & Guy Seidman, *The Jeffersonian Treaty Clause*, 2006 Ill. L. Rev. 1, 22–43.

Does it strike you as at all odd that, after 230 years, there is no consensus on something as basic to governance as the constitutional source of presidential power? Does it strike you as odder still that there has never been a definitive Supreme Court pronouncement on that question? Indeed, the Supreme Court pointedly ducked the question in 2015 in *Zivotofsky v. Kerry*, 576 U.S. ___, 135 S.Ct. 2076, 192 L.Ed.2d 83 (2015). In holding that the President has the exclusive power to recognize foreign governments, so that Congress could not require the State Department (which did not recognize any country as having sovereignty over Jerusalem) to list "Israel" as the country of birth on a passport at the request of an American citizen born in Jerusalem, the Court identified a range of enumerated presidential functions—to initiate treaties, receive foreign ambassadors, and nominate American ambassadors—that "give the President control over recognition decisions." 135 S.Ct. at 2085. "Because these specific Clauses confer the recognition power on the President, the Court need not consider whether or to what extent the Vesting Clause, which provides that the 'executive Power' shall be vested in the President, provides further support for the President's action here." *Id.* at 2086. Justice Thomas specifically endorsed the so-called Vesting Clause Thesis in a separate opinion. *See id.* at 2097–98 (Thomas, J., concurring in the judgment in part and dissenting in part).

The debate over the unitary executive has focused largely on the issue of removal, with unitarians urging an essentially unlimited power of presidential removal and nonunitarians (of various stripes) urging differing degrees of congressional power to restrict presidential removal of subordinate officials. Removal is not, however, the only context in which the unitary executive concept can play a role. In the nineteenth century, there was a major debate within the executive department over whether presidents had the power, not merely to remove subordinates, but personally to make discretionary decisions vested in those subordinates by statute. That debate has largely disappeared from the contemporary scene, though it may be an even more fruitful context than the removal issue for considering the constitutional scope of presidential (and congressional) power to control the administration of the laws. If the President has the power to make all executive decisions, or at least to nullify any executive decisions contrary to his or her instructions, does the President really need a removal power in order to effectuate the "executive Power"? *See* Gary Lawson, *The Rise and Rise of the Administrative State*, 107 Harv. L. Rev. 1231, 1241–45 (1994). And if the answer to that question is "no," on what basis could one infer a presidential removal power not expressly granted by the Constitution? Or does the vesting of the "executive Power" in the President by itself amount to an express grant of removal power?

D. AGENCIES AND ARTICLE III

When agencies make substantive rules with the force and effect of law, their activity looks enough like legislation to raise questions about whether the agencies are improperly exercising the "legislative Power" vested in Congress by Article I. When agencies adjudicate—resolve disputes by applying the law to particular facts—does their activity look enough like judging to raise questions about whether the agencies are improperly exercising the "judicial Power" vested in life-tenured and salary-guaranteed federal courts by Article III?

It certainly raises the questions, but finding the answers proves to be one of the most difficult tasks in American jurisprudence. The case law—more than 200 years of it—is among the most confused and confusing bodies of judicial thinking that one will ever encounter. Mercifully, unless your professor is considerably bolder than your editor, you will not have to deal much with the issue in this course. You should, however, be familiar at least with the broad outlines of the problem. To make a long story irresponsibly short:

Consider William Marbury's appointment as a Justice of the Peace of the District of Columbia circa 1803. Officials such as Marbury had both civil and criminal jurisdiction and had the same powers as their counterparts in the states of Virginia or Maryland. If Marbury and his fellow Justices of the Peace exercised the "judicial Power of the United States," they would need to have life tenure and salary guarantees in accordance with the terms of Article III. Congress behaved as though they had or needed neither. As Chief Justice Marshall pointed out five different times in *Marbury v. Madison*, Marbury was appointed under a statute providing for a five-year term of office rather than for tenure during good behavior. And Congress several times changed the terms of compensation of these officers. Were these tenure and compensation statutes unconstitutional? Or did Marbury exercise something other than federal "judicial Power"?

In 1803—the same year that *Marbury v. Madison* was decided—a federal circuit court held, by a 2–1 vote, that the District of Columbia Justices of the Peace exercised federal "judicial Power" and that the statutes changing their forms of compensation were unconstitutional diminishments of the salaries of federal judges. *See United States v. More*, 7 U.S. (3 Cranch) 159, 160 n[*] (1805) (reporting the 1803 circuit court opinion). Presumably, that meant that the Justices of the Peace also constitutionally held office during good behavior, though the court (in a perhaps extravagant bit of judicial restraint) declined to comment on that issue. The decision was appealed to the Supreme Court, which dismissed the case on jurisdictional grounds without reaching the merits.

A quarter-century later, however, the Supreme Court said, in powerful and influential language, that adjudicatory officials in federal territories (Florida before statehood, in that particular case) exercising admiralty jurisdiction do not possess Article III judicial power but are instead "legislative Courts" exercising power granted by Congress under its Article IV power to govern federal territory. *See American Insurance Co. v. 356 Bales of Cotton*, 26 U.S. (1 Pet.) 511 (1828). The same reasoning would apply to judges in the District of Columbia, which is governed by Congress under the Article I District Clause. The upshot of this decision was to validate a class of federal officials who look like federal judges, act like federal judges, and rule like federal judges (including handing out death sentences in appropriate cases) but who do not constitutionally count as Article III federal judges.

Another quarter-century later, the Court further held that military courts martial involved the exercise of Article I congressional power and Article II presidential power to regulate and govern the military rather than Article III "judicial Power." *Dynes v. Hoover*, 61 U.S. (20 How.) 65 (1857). And shortly thereafter, Congress created a federal tribunal, without life tenure or salary guarantees, to rule on money claims against the federal government. This form of non-Article III adjudication was validated on the ground of sovereign immunity: The federal government does not have to provide *any* forum for claims against it, so no one has a right to complain about the forums that Congress does choose to provide. *See United States v. Sherwood*, 312 U.S. 584, 61 S.Ct. 767, 85 L.Ed. 1058 (1941).

None of these forms of non-Article III adjudication—territorial tribunals, military courts martial, or suits against the United States—encompasses administrative agencies resolving claims by one person against another, such as a claim by a shipper that a railroad has charged an unlawful rate or a claim by a maritime worker that he is owed compensation from his employer under a federal workers' compensation statute. The latter issue came up in 1932 in *Crowell v. Benson*, 285 U.S. 22, 52 S.Ct. 285, 76 L.Ed. 598 (1932). The Longshoremen's and Harbor Workers' Compensation Act of 1927 ("LHWCA"), of which we will hear more in Chapter 4, required (and still requires) employers to compensate employees for certain injuries "occurring upon the navigable waters of the United States." 33 U.S.C. § 903 (2012). Claims under the act were to be adjudicated by Deputy Commissioners of the United States Employees' Compensation Commission, subject to judicial review. The decision in *Crowell* turned on the effects of the findings of the Deputy Commissioners.

The Deputy Commissioner in *Crowell* awarded compensation to the claimant. The trial court held a trial *de novo*, effectively giving no legal effect to the findings of the agency, and overturned the award. The court of appeals affirmed, as did the Supreme Court by a 5–3 vote.

There are two facets to the Supreme Court's decision in *Crowell*. By affirming the trial court's decision to hold a trial *de novo*, the strict holding of the Court seems to cut strongly *against* the propriety of allowing executive agents to adjudicate the monetary liability of one private citizen to another. The Court, however, limited its holding in this respect to facts that go to the very *jurisdiction* of the agency to decide the claim, "in the sense that their existence is a condition precedent to the operation of the statutory scheme." *Id.* at 54, 52 S.Ct. at 294. The Court explained that, in the context of *Crowell*, "[t]hese fundamental requirements are that the injury occurs upon the navigable waters of the United States, and that the relation of master and servant exists. These conditions are indispensable to the application of the statute * * * because the power of the Congress to enact the legislation turns upon the existence of these conditions." *Id.* at 54–55, 52 S.Ct. at 294.

By contrast, the determination of non-jurisdictional facts such as "the facts relating to the circumstances of the injuries received, as well as their nature and consequences, may appropriately be subjected to the scheme of administration for which the act provides." *Id.* at 65, 52 S.Ct. at 298. The Court explained:

> As to determinations of fact, the distinction is at once apparent between cases of private right and those which arise between the government and persons subject to its authority in connection with the performance of the constitutional functions of the executive or legislative departments * * *. Thus the Congress, in exercising the powers confided to it, may establish 'legislative' courts (as distinguished from 'constitutional courts in which the judicial power conferred by the Constitution can be deposited') which are to form part of the government of territories or of the District of Columbia, or to serve as special tribunals 'to examine and determine various matters, arising between the government and others, which from their nature do not require judicial determination and yet are susceptible of it.' * * * Familiar illustrations of administrative agencies created for the determination of such matters are found in connection with the exercise of the congressional power as to interstate and foreign commerce, taxation, immigration, the public lands, public health, the facilities of the post office, pensions, and payments to veterans.

The present case does not fall within the categories just described, but is one of private right, that is, of the liability of one individual to another under the law as defined. But, in cases of that sort, there is no requirement that, in order to maintain the essential attributes of the judicial power, all determinations of fact in constitutional courts shall be made by judges. On the common-law side of the federal courts, the aid of juries is not only deemed appropriate but is required by the Constitution itself. In cases of equity and admiralty, it is historic practice to call to the assistance of the courts, without the consent of the parties, masters, and commissioners or assessors, to pass upon certain classes of questions, as, for example, to take and state an account or to find the amount of damages. While the reports of masters and commissioners in such cases are essentially of an advisory nature, it has not been the practice to disturb their findings when they are properly based upon evidence, in the absence of errors of law, and the parties have no right to demand that the court shall redetermine the facts thus found * * *.

* * *

In deciding whether the Congress, in enacting the statute under review, has exceeded the limits of its authority to prescribe procedure in cases of injury upon navigable waters, regard must be had, as in other cases where constitutional limits are invoked, not to mere matters of form, but to the substance of what is required. The statute has a limited application, being confined to the relation of master and servant, and the method of determining the questions of fact, which arise in the routine of making compensation awards to employees under the act, is necessary to its effective enforcement. The act itself, where it applies, establishes the measure of the employer's liability, thus leaving open for determination the questions of fact as to the circumstances, nature, extent, and consequences of the injuries sustained by the employee for which compensation is to be made in accordance with the prescribed standards. Findings of fact by the deputy commissioner upon such questions are closely analogous to the findings of the amount of damages that are made according to familiar practice by commissioners or assessors, and the reservation of full authority to the court to deal with matters of law provides for the appropriate exercise of the judicial function in this class of cases. For the purposes stated, we are unable to find any constitutional obstacle to the action of the Congress in availing itself of a method shown by experience to be essential in order to apply its standards to the thousands of cases involved, thus relieving the courts of a most serious burden while preserving their complete authority to insure the proper application of the law.

Id. at 50–54, 52 S.Ct. at 292–94. Three Justices would have reversed the trial court, leaving the initial determination of even "jurisdictional" facts to the agency.

It is fair to say that the dictum of *Crowell* approving the general permissibility of agency adjudication has had far more lasting impact than its narrow holding regarding "jurisdictional" facts, which has fallen into desuetude. That is because the facts considered "jurisdictional" by *Crowell* are the facts necessary to *Congress's constitutional power to enact the statute* rather than the facts statutorily necessary for agency action under constitutionally valid laws. Fewer facts affect the scope of Congress's constitutional powers today than was the case in 1932. "After the New Deal constitutional revolution it would be rare that facts determined by administrative agencies were fundamental in *Crowell's* sense. As a result, *Crowell's* holding on de novo review * * * has for all practical purposes almost vanished." Mark Tushnet, *The Story of* Crowell: *Grounding the Administrative State, in* Federal Courts Stories 354, 387 (Vicki C. Jackson & Judith Resnick eds., 2010).

Consider what the following two cases say about the ability of Congress to charge politically accountable administrators rather than tenured federal judges with the adjudication of claims against private citizens.

COMMODITY FUTURES TRADING COMM'N V. SCHOR

Supreme Court of the United States, 1986.
478 U.S. 833, 106 S.Ct. 3245, 92 L.Ed.2d 675.

JUSTICE O'CONNOR delivered the opinion of the Court.

[The Commodity Futures Trading Commission (CFTC) is an independent agency that enforces the Commodity Exchange Act (CEA), which regulates commodity futures transactions. The CFTC is authorized by statute to adjudicate claims for damages, or reparations, brought by customers of commodity brokers for the brokers' violations of the CEA or CFTC regulations. The CFTC additionally promulgated a regulation permitting itself to adjudicate counterclaims brought by brokers in reparations proceedings when the counterclaim arises out of the transaction(s) giving rise to the customer's complaint.

Schor sought reparations for numerous alleged violations of the CEA by his broker, ContiCommodity Services of America, Inc. (Conti), which Schor maintained was responsible for the debit (negative) balance in his trading account with Conti. Conti counterclaimed for the debit balance in the CFTC reparations proceeding. The agency ruled in favor of Conti on all counts, and Schor then questioned the statutory authority for the agency's regulation permitting it to adjudicate Conti's counterclaim. The agency rejected the challenge to its authority, and Schor appealed. The Court of Appeals reversed, on the ground that construing the CEA to deny the agency power to adjudicate ordinary contract-law counterclaims "avoids significant constitutional questions" that would be raised by such agency authority.]

* * *

* * * Our examination of the CEA and its legislative history and purpose reveals that Congress plainly intended the CFTC to decide counterclaims asserted by respondents in reparations proceedings, and just as plainly delegated to the CFTC the authority to fashion its counterclaim jurisdiction in the manner the CFTC determined necessary to further the purposes of the reparations program.

* * *

* * * We therefore are squarely faced with the question whether the CFTC's assumption of jurisdiction over common law counterclaims violates Article III of the Constitution.

* * *

Article III, § 1, directs that the "judicial Power of the United States shall be vested in one supreme Court and in such inferior Courts as the Congress may from time to time ordain and establish," and provides that these federal courts shall be staffed by judges who hold office during good behavior, and whose compensation shall not be diminished during tenure in office. Schor claims that these provisions prohibit Congress from authorizing the initial adjudication of common law counterclaims by the CFTC, an administrative agency whose adjudicatory officers do not enjoy the tenure and salary protections embodied in Article III.

Although our precedents in this area do not admit of easy synthesis, they do establish that the resolution of claims such as Schor's cannot turn on conclusory reference to the language of Article III. Rather, the constitutionality of a given congressional delegation of adjudicative functions to a non-Article III body must be assessed by reference to the purposes underlying the requirements of Article III. This inquiry, in turn, is guided by the principle that "practical attention to substance rather than doctrinaire reliance on formal categories should inform application of Article III." *Thomas* [*v. Union Carbide Agricultural Products Co.*, 473 U.S. 568, 587 (1985)] * * *.

* * *

In determining the extent to which a given congressional decision to authorize the adjudication of Article III business in a non-Article III tribunal impermissibly threatens the institutional integrity of the Judicial Branch, the Court has declined to adopt formalistic and unbending rules. Although such rules might lend a greater degree of coherence to this area of the law, they might also unduly constrict Congress' ability to take needed and innovative action pursuant to its Article I powers. Thus, in reviewing Article III challenges, we have weighed a number of factors, none of which has been deemed determinative, with an eye to the practical effect that the congressional action will have on the constitutionally assigned role of the federal judiciary. Among the factors upon which we have focused are the extent to which the "essential attributes of judicial power" are reserved to Article III courts, and, conversely, the extent to which the non-Article III forum exercises the range of jurisdiction and powers normally vested only in Article III courts, the origins and importance of the right to be adjudicated, and the concerns that drove Congress to depart from the requirements of Article III.

An examination of the relative allocation of powers between the CFTC and Article III courts in light of the considerations given prominence in our precedents demonstrates that the congressional scheme does not impermissibly intrude on the province of the judiciary. The CFTC's adjudicatory powers depart from the traditional agency model in just one respect: the CFTC's jurisdiction over common law counterclaims. While wholesale importation of concepts of pendent or ancillary jurisdiction into the agency context may create greater constitutional difficulties, we decline to endorse an absolute prohibition on such jurisdiction out of fear of where some hypothetical "slippery slope" may deposit us. Indeed, the CFTC's exercise of this type of jurisdiction is not without precedent. Thus, in *RFC v. Bankers Trust Co.*, 318 U.S. 163, 168–171 (1943), we saw no constitutional difficulty in the initial adjudication of a state law claim by a federal agency, subject to judicial review, when that claim was ancillary to a federal law dispute. Similarly, in *Katchen v. Landy*, 382 U.S. 323 (1966), this Court upheld a bankruptcy referee's power to hear and decide state law counterclaims against a creditor who filed a claim in bankruptcy when those counterclaims arose out of the same transaction. We reasoned that, as a practical matter, requiring the trustee to commence a plenary action to recover on its counterclaim would be a "meaningless gesture." *Id.*, at 334.

In the instant cases, we are likewise persuaded that there is little practical reason to find that this single deviation from the agency model is fatal to the congressional scheme * * *.

* * * The CFTC, like the agency in *Crowell*, deals only with a "particularized area of law," *Northern Pipeline, supra,* 458 U.S., at 85, 102 S.Ct., at 2878, whereas the jurisdiction of the bankruptcy courts found unconstitutional in *Northern Pipeline* extended to broadly "all civil proceedings arising under title 11 or arising in or *related to* cases under title 11." 28 U.S.C. § 1471(b) (quoted in *Northern Pipeline,* 458 U.S., at 85,

102 S.Ct., at 2878) (emphasis added). CFTC orders, like those of the agency in *Crowell,* but unlike those of the bankruptcy courts under the 1978 Act, are enforceable only by order of the district court. CFTC orders are also reviewed under the same "weight of the evidence" standard sustained in *Crowell,* rather than the more deferential standard found lacking in *Northern Pipeline.* See 7 U.S.C. § 9; *Northern Pipeline, supra,* at 85, 102 S.Ct., at 2879. The legal rulings of the CFTC, like the legal determinations of the agency in *Crowell,* are subject to *de novo* review. Finally, the CFTC, unlike the bankruptcy courts under the 1978 Act, does not exercise "all ordinary powers of district courts," and thus may not, for instance, preside over jury trials or issue writs of habeas corpus. 458 U.S., at 85, 102 S.Ct., at 2878

Of course, the nature of the claim has significance in our Article III analysis quite apart from the method prescribed for its adjudication. The counterclaim asserted in this litigation is a "private" right for which state law provides the rule of decision. It is therefore a claim of the kind assumed to be at the "core" of matters normally reserved to Article III courts. Yet this conclusion does not end our inquiry; just as this Court has rejected any attempt to make determinative for Article III purposes the distinction between public rights and private rights, *Thomas, supra,* at 585–586, there is no reason inherent in separation of powers principles to accord the state law character of a claim talismanic power in Article III inquiries.

* * * The risk that Congress may improperly have encroached on the federal judiciary is obviously magnified when Congress "[withdraws] from judicial cognizance any matter which, from its nature, is the subject of a suit at the common law, or in equity, or admiralty" and which therefore has traditionally been tried in Article III courts, and allocates the decision of those matters to a non-Article III forum of its own creation. *Murray's Lessee v. Hoboken Land & Improvement Co.,* 18 How. 272, 284 (1856). Accordingly, where private, common law rights are at stake, our examination of the congressional attempt to control the manner in which those rights are adjudicated has been searching. In this litigation, however, "[looking] beyond form to the substance of what" Congress has done, we are persuaded that the congressional authorization of limited CFTC jurisdiction over a narrow class of common law claims as an incident to the CFTC's primary, and unchallenged, adjudicative function does not create a substantial threat to the separation of powers.

It is clear that Congress has not attempted to "withdraw from judicial cognizance" the determination of Conti's right to the sum represented by the debit balance in Schor's account. Congress gave the CFTC the authority to adjudicate such matters, but the decision to invoke this forum is left entirely to the parties and the power of the federal judiciary to take jurisdiction of these matters is unaffected. In such circumstances, separation of powers concerns are diminished, for it seems self-evident that just as Congress may encourage parties to settle a dispute out of court or resort to arbitration without impermissible incursions on the separation of powers, Congress may make available a quasi-judicial mechanism through which willing parties may, at their option, elect to resolve their differences. This is not to say, of course, that if Congress created a phalanx of non-Article III tribunals equipped to handle the entire business of the Article III courts without any Article III supervision or control and without evidence of valid and specific legislative necessities, the fact that the parties had the election to proceed in their forum of choice would necessarily save the scheme from constitutional attack. But this case obviously bears no resemblance to such a scenario, given the degree of judicial control saved to the federal courts, as well as the congressional purpose behind the jurisdictional delegation, the demonstrated need for the delegation, and the limited nature of the delegation.

* * *

It also bears emphasis that the CFTC's assertion of counterclaim jurisdiction is limited to that which is necessary to make the reparations procedure workable. The CFTC adjudication of common law counterclaims is incidental to, and completely dependent upon, adjudication of reparations claims created by federal law, and in actual fact is limited to claims arising out of the same transaction or occurrence as the reparations claim.

In such circumstances, the magnitude of any intrusion on the Judicial Branch can only be termed *de minimis*. Conversely, were we to hold that the Legislative Branch may not permit such limited cognizance of common law counterclaims at the election of the parties, it is clear that we would "defeat the obvious purpose of the legislation to furnish a prompt, continuous, expert and inexpensive method for dealing with a class of questions of fact which are peculiarly suited to examination and determination by an administrative agency specially assigned to that task." *Crowell v. Benson*, [285 U.S. 22 (1932)] at 46. See also *Thomas, supra*, at 583–584. We do not think Article III compels this degree of prophylaxis.

Nor does our decision in *Bowsher v. Synar* require a contrary result. Unlike *Bowsher*, this case raises no question of the aggrandizement of congressional power at the expense of a coordinate branch. Instead, the separation of powers question presented in this litigation is whether Congress impermissibly undermined, without appreciable expansion of its own power, the role of the Judicial Branch. In any case, we have, consistent with *Bowsher*, looked to a number of factors in evaluating the extent to which the congressional scheme endangers separation of powers principles under the circumstances presented, but have found no genuine threat to those principles to be present in this litigation.

In so doing, we have also been faithful to our Article III precedents, which counsel that bright-line rules cannot effectively be employed to yield broad principles applicable in all Article III inquiries. Rather, due regard must be given in each case to the unique aspects of the congressional plan at issue and its practical consequences in light of the larger concerns that underlie Article III. We conclude that the limited jurisdiction that the CFTC asserts over state law claims as a necessary incident to the adjudication of federal claims willingly submitted by the parties for initial agency adjudication does not contravene separation of powers principles or Article III.

* * *

JUSTICE BRENNAN, with whom JUSTICE MARSHALL joins, dissenting.

Article III, § 1, of the Constitution provides that "[the] judicial Power of the United States, shall be vested in one supreme Court, and in such inferior Courts as the Congress may from time to time ordain and establish." It further specifies that the federal judicial power must be exercised by judges who "shall hold their Offices during good Behaviour, and [who] shall, at stated Times, receive for their Services a Compensation, which shall not be diminished during their Continuance in Office."

On its face, Article III, § 1, seems to prohibit the vesting of any judicial functions in either the Legislative or the Executive Branch. The Court has, however, recognized three narrow exceptions to the otherwise absolute mandate of Article III: territorial courts, see, *e.g.*, *American Ins. Co. v. Canter*, 1 Pet. 511 (1828); courts-martial, see, *e.g.*, *Dynes v. Hoover*, 20 How. 65 (1857); and courts that adjudicate certain disputes concerning public rights, see, *e. g.*, *Murray's Lessee v. Hoboken Land & Improvement Co.*, 18 How. 272 (1856); *Ex parte Bakelite Corp.*, 279 U.S. 438 (1929); *Crowell v. Benson*, 285 U.S. 22 (1932); *Thomas v. Union Carbide Agricultural Products Co.*, 473 U.S. 568 (1985). See generally *Northern Pipeline Construction Co. v. Marathon Pipe Line Co.*, 458 U.S. 50 (1982) (opinion of BRENNAN, J.). Unlike the Court, I would limit the judicial authority of non-Article III federal tribunals to these few, long-established exceptions and would countenance no further erosion of Article III's mandate.

* * *

The Framers knew that "[the] accumulation of all powers, Legislative, Executive, and Judiciary, in the same hands, whether of one, a few, or many, and whether hereditary, self-appointed, or elective, may justly be pronounced the very definition of tyranny." The Federalist No. 46, p. 334 (H. Dawson ed. 1876) (J. Madison) * * *. The federal judicial power, then, must be exercised by judges who are independent of the Executive and the Legislature in order to maintain the checks and balances that are crucial to our constitutional structure.

The Framers also understood that a principal benefit of the separation of the judicial power from the legislative and executive powers would be the protection of individual litigants from decisionmakers susceptible to majoritarian pressures. Article III's salary and tenure provisions promote impartial adjudication by placing the judicial power of the United States "in a body of judges insulated from majoritarian pressures and thus able to enforce [federal law] without fear of reprisal or public rebuke." *United States v. Raddatz*, 447 U.S. 667, 704 (1980) (MARSHALL, J., dissenting) * * *.

These important functions of Article III are too central to our constitutional scheme to risk their incremental erosion. The exceptions we have recognized for territorial courts, courts-martial, and administrative courts were each based on "certain exceptional powers bestowed upon Congress by the Constitution or by historical consensus." *Northern Pipeline, supra,* at 70 (opinion of BRENNAN, J.). Here, however, there is no equally forceful reason to extend further these exceptions to situations that are distinguishable from existing precedents. The Court, however, engages in just such an extension. By sanctioning the adjudication of state-law counterclaims by a federal administrative agency, the Court far exceeds the analytic framework of our precedents.

* * *

* * * The Court requires that the legislative interest in convenience and efficiency be weighed against the competing interest in judicial independence. In doing so, the Court pits an interest the benefits of which are immediate, concrete, and easily understood against one, the benefits of which are almost entirely prophylactic, and thus often seem remote and not worth the cost in any single case. Thus, while this balancing creates the illusion of objectivity and ineluctability, in fact the result was foreordained, because the balance is weighted against judicial independence. The danger of the Court's balancing approach is, of course, that as individual cases accumulate in which the Court finds that the short-term benefits of efficiency outweigh the long-term benefits of judicial independence, the protections of Article III will be eviscerated.

Perhaps the resolution of reparations claims such as respondents' may be accomplished more conveniently under the Court's decision than under my approach, but the Framers foreswore this sort of convenience in order to preserve freedom * * *.

STERN V. MARSHALL
Supreme Court of the United States, 2011.
564 U.S. 462, 131 S.Ct. 2594, 180 L.Ed.2d 475.

CHIEF JUSTICE ROBERTS delivered the opinion of the Court.

* * *

* * * This is the second time we have had occasion to weigh in on this long-running dispute between Vickie Lynn Marshall and E. Pierce Marshall over the fortune of J. Howard Marshall II, a man believed to have been one of the richest people in Texas. The Marshalls' litigation has worked its way through state and federal courts in Louisiana, Texas, and California, and two of those courts—a Texas state probate court and the Bankruptcy Court for the Central District of California—have reached contrary decisions on its merits. The Court of Appeals below held that the Texas state decision controlled, after concluding that the Bankruptcy Court lacked the authority to enter final judgment on a counterclaim that Vickie brought against Pierce in her bankruptcy proceeding. To determine whether the Court of Appeals was correct in that regard, we must resolve two issues: (1) whether the Bankruptcy Court had the statutory authority * * * to issue a final judgment on Vickie's counterclaim; and (2) if so, whether conferring that authority on the Bankruptcy Court is constitutional.

Although the history of this litigation is complicated, its resolution ultimately turns on very basic principles. Article III, § 1, of the Constitution commands that "[t]he judicial Power of the United States, shall be vested in one supreme Court, and in such inferior Courts as the Congress may from time to time ordain and establish." That Article further provides that the judges of those courts shall hold their offices during good behavior, without diminution of salary. *Ibid.* Those requirements of Article III were not honored here. The Bankruptcy Court in this case exercised the judicial power of the United States by entering final judgment on a common law tort claim, even though the judges of such courts enjoy neither tenure during good behavior nor salary protection. We conclude that, although the Bankruptcy Court had the statutory authority to enter judgment on Vickie's counterclaim, it lacked the constitutional authority to do so.

I

* * * Known to the public as Anna Nicole Smith, Vickie was J. Howard's third wife and married him about a year before his death. Although J. Howard bestowed on Vickie many monetary and other gifts during their courtship and marriage, he did not include her in his will. Before J. Howard passed away, Vickie filed suit in Texas state probate court, asserting that Pierce—J. Howard's younger son—fraudulently induced J. Howard to sign a living trust that did not include her, even though J. Howard meant to give her half his property. Pierce denied any fraudulent activity and defended the validity of J. Howard's trust and, eventually, his will.

After J. Howard's death, Vickie filed a petition for bankruptcy in the Central District of California. Pierce filed a complaint in that bankruptcy proceeding, contending that Vickie had defamed him by inducing her lawyers to tell members of the press that he had engaged in fraud to gain control of his father's assets * * *. Vickie responded to Pierce's initial complaint by asserting truth as a defense to the alleged defamation and by filing a counterclaim for tortious interference with the gift she expected from J. Howard * * * *.

On November 5, 1999, the Bankruptcy Court issued an order granting Vickie summary judgment on Pierce's claim for defamation. On September 27, 2000, after a bench trial, the Bankruptcy Court issued a judgment on Vickie's counterclaim in her favor. The court later awarded Vickie over $400 million in compensatory damages and $25 million in punitive damages.

In post-trial proceedings, Pierce argued that the Bankruptcy Court lacked jurisdiction over Vickie's counterclaim * * * because Vickie's counterclaim was not a "core proceeding" under 28 U.S.C. § 157(b)(2)(C) * * *. [B]ankruptcy courts may hear and enter final judgments in "core proceedings" in a bankruptcy case. In non-core proceedings, the bankruptcy courts instead submit proposed findings of fact and conclusions of law to the district court, for that court's review and issuance of final judgment. The Bankruptcy Court in this case concluded that Vickie's counterclaim was "a core proceeding" under § 157(b)(2)(C), and the court therefore had the "power to enter judgment" on the counterclaim * * *.

* * *

[The Supreme Court held, as a matter of statutory interpretation, that the (late) Vickie's counterclaim "is a 'core proceeding' under the plain text of § 157(b)(2)(C)" and that bankruptcy courts have statutory power to enter final judgments on all core proceedings and not merely, as (the equally late) Pierce argued, on a limited set of core proceedings.]

III

Although we conclude that § 157(b)(2)(C) permits the Bankruptcy Court to enter final judgment on Vickie's counterclaim, Article III of the Constitution does not.

A

Article III, § 1, of the Constitution mandates that "[t]he judicial Power of the United States, shall be vested in one supreme Court, and in such inferior Courts as the Congress may from time to time ordain and establish." The same section provides that the judges of those constitutional courts "shall hold their Offices during good Behaviour" and "receive for their Services[ ] a Compensation[ ] [that] shall not be diminished" during their tenure.

* * *

Article III protects liberty not only through its role in implementing the separation of powers, but also by specifying the defining characteristics of Article III judges. The colonists had been subjected to judicial abuses at the hand of the Crown, and the Framers knew the main reasons why: because the King of Great Britain "made Judges dependent on his Will alone, for the tenure of their offices, and the amount and payment of their salaries." The Declaration of Independence ¶ 11. The Framers undertook in Article III to protect citizens subject to the judicial power of the new Federal Government from a repeat of those abuses. By appointing judges to serve without term limits, and restricting the ability of the other branches to remove judges or diminish their salaries, the Framers sought to ensure that each judicial decision would be rendered, not with an eye toward currying favor with Congress or the Executive, but rather with the "[c]lear heads . . . and honest hearts" deemed "essential to good judges." 1 Works of James Wilson 363 (J. Andrews ed. 1896).

Article III could neither serve its purpose in the system of checks and balances nor preserve the integrity of judicial decisionmaking if the other branches of the Federal Government could confer the Government's "judicial Power" on entities Article III. That is why we have long recognized that, in general, Congress may not "withdraw from judicial cognizance any matter which, from its nature, is the subject of a suit at the common law, or in equity, or admiralty." *Murray's Lessee v. Hoboken Land & Improvement Co.*, 59 U.S. 272, 18 How. 272, 284, 15 L.Ed. 372 (1856) * * *.

B

This is not the first time we have faced an Article III challenge to a bankruptcy court's resolution of a debtor's suit. In [*Northern Pipeline Constr. Co. v. Marathon Pipe Line Co.*, 458 U.S. 50, 102 S.Ct. 2858, 73 L.Ed.2d 598 (1982)], we considered whether bankruptcy judges serving under the Bankruptcy Act of 1978—appointed by the President and confirmed by the Senate, but lacking the tenure and salary guarantees of Article III—could "constitutionally be vested with jurisdiction to decide [a] state-law contract claim" against an entity that was not otherwise part of the bankruptcy proceedings. The Court concluded that assignment of such state law claims for resolution by those judges "violates Art. III of the Constitution." *Id.*, at 52, 87, 102 S.Ct. 2858 (plurality opinion); *id.*, at 91, 102 S.Ct. 2858 (Rehnquist, J., concurring in judgment).

The [four-Justice] plurality in *Northern Pipeline* recognized that there was a category of cases involving "public rights" that Congress could constitutionally assign to "legislative" courts for resolution. That opinion concluded that this "public rights" exception extended "only to matters arising between" individuals and the Government "in connection with the performance of the constitutional functions of the executive or legislative departments . . . that historically could have been determined exclusively by those" branches. *Id,.* at 67–68, 102 S.Ct. 2858 (internal quotation marks omitted). A full majority of the Court, while not agreeing on the scope of the exception, concluded that the doctrine did not encompass adjudication of the state law claim at issue in that case.

A full majority of Justices in *Northern Pipeline* also rejected the debtor's argument that the bankruptcy court's exercise of jurisdiction was constitutional because the bankruptcy judge was acting merely as an adjunct of the district court or court of appeals.

After our decision in *Northern Pipeline*, Congress revised the statutes governing bankruptcy jurisdiction and bankruptcy judges * * *. Congress permitted the newly constituted bankruptcy courts to enter final judgments only in "core" proceedings.

With respect to such "core" matters, however, the bankruptcy courts under the 1984 Act exercise the same powers they wielded under the Bankruptcy Act of 1978 * * *. As in *Northern Pipeline*, the new courts in core proceedings "issue final judgments, which are binding and enforceable even in the absence of an appeal." And, as in *Northern Pipeline*, the district courts review the judgments of the bankruptcy courts in core proceedings only under the usual limited appellate standards. That requires marked deference to, among other things, the bankruptcy judges' findings of fact. See § 158(a); Fed. Rule Bkrcy Proc. 8013 (findings of fact "shall not be set aside unless clearly erroneous").

C

* * * It is clear that the Bankruptcy Court in this case exercised the "judicial Power of the United States" in purporting to resolve and enter final judgment on a state common law claim * * *.

* * *

1

Vickie's counterclaim cannot be deemed a matter of "public right" that can be decided outside the Judicial Branch. As explained above, in *Northern Pipeline* we rejected the argument that the public rights doctrine permitted a bankruptcy court to adjudicate a state law suit brought by a debtor against a company that had not filed a claim against the estate. Although our discussion of the public rights exception since that time has not been entirely consistent, and the exception has been the subject of some debate, this case does not fall within any of the various formulations of the concept that appear in this Court's opinions.

We first recognized the category of public rights in *Murray's Lessee v. Hoboken Land & Improvement Co.*, 59 U.S. 272, 18 How. 272, 15 L.Ed. 372 (1856). That case involved the Treasury Department's sale of property belonging to a customs collector who had failed to transfer payments to the Federal Government that he had collected on its behalf. The plaintiff, who claimed title to the same land through a different transfer, objected that the Treasury Department's calculation of the deficiency and sale of the property was void, because it was a judicial act that could not be assigned to the Executive under Article III.

"To avoid misconstruction upon so grave a subject," the Court laid out the principles guiding its analysis. *Id.,* at 284. It confirmed that Congress cannot "withdraw from judicial cognizance any matter which, from its nature, is the subject of a suit at the common law, or in equity, or admiralty." *Ibid.* The Court also recognized that "[a]t the same time there are matters, involving public rights, which may be presented in such form that the judicial power is capable of acting on them, and which are susceptible of judicial determination, but which congress may or may not bring within the cognizance of the courts of the United States, as it may deem proper." *Ibid.*

As an example of such matters, the Court referred to "[e]quitable claims to land by the inhabitants of ceded territories" and cited cases in which land issues were conclusively resolved by Executive Branch officials. *Ibid.* In those cases "it depends upon the will of congress whether a remedy in the courts shall be allowed at all," so Congress could limit the extent to which a judicial forum was available. [*Ibid.*] * * *. The point of *Murray's Lessee* was simply that Congress may set the terms of adjudicating a suit when the suit could not otherwise proceed at all [because of sovereign immunity].

Subsequent decisions from this Court contrasted cases within the reach of the public rights exception—those arising "between the Government and persons subject to its authority in connection with the performance of the constitutional functions of the executive or legislative departments"—and those that were instead matters "of private right, that is, of the liability of one individual to another under the law as defined." *Crowell v. Benson*, 285 U.S. 22, 50, 51, 52 S.Ct. 285, 76 L.Ed. 598 (1932).[6]

---

[6]   Although the Court in *Crowell* went on to decide that the facts of the private dispute before it could be determined by a non-Article III tribunal in the first instance, subject to judicial review, the Court did so only after observing that the administrative adjudicator had only limited authority to make specialized, narrowly confined factual determinations regarding a particularized area of law and to issue orders that could be enforced only by action of the District Court. In other words, the agency in *Crowell* functioned as a true "adjunct" of the District Court. That is not the case here.

Shortly after *Northern Pipeline*, the Court rejected the limitation of the public rights exception to actions involving the Government as a party. The Court has continued, however, to limit the exception to cases in which the claim at issue derives from a federal regulatory scheme, or in which resolution of the claim by an expert government agency is deemed essential to a limited regulatory objective within the agency's authority. In other words, it is still the case that what makes a right "public" rather than private is that the right is integrally related to particular federal government action.

Our decision in *Thomas v. Union Carbide Agricultural Products Co.*, for example, involved a data-sharing arrangement between companies under a federal statute providing that disputes about compensation between the companies would be decided by binding arbitration. 473 U.S. 568, 571–575, 105 S.Ct. 3325, 87 L.Ed.2d 409 (1985). This Court held that the scheme did not violate Article III, explaining that "[a]ny right to compensation . . . results from [the statute] and does not depend on or replace a right to such compensation under state law." *Id.* at 584, 105 S.Ct. 3325.

Commodity Futures Trading Commission v. Schor concerned a statutory scheme that created a procedure for customers injured by a broker's violation of the federal commodities law to seek reparations from the broker before the Commodity Futures Trading Commission (CFTC). A customer filed such a claim to recover a debit balance in his account, while the broker filed a lawsuit in Federal District Court to recover the same amount as lawfully due from the customer. The broker later submitted its claim to the CFTC, but after that agency ruled against the customer, the customer argued that agency jurisdiction over the broker's counterclaim violated Article III. This Court disagreed, but only after observing that (1) the claim and the counterclaim concerned a "single dispute"—the same account balance; (2) the CFTC's assertion of authority involved only "a narrow class of common law claims" in a " 'particularized area of law' "; (3) the area of law in question was governed by "a specific and limited federal regulatory scheme" as to which the agency had "obvious expertise"; (4) the parties had freely elected to resolve their differences before the CFTC; and (5) CFTC orders were "enforceable only by order of the district court. Most significantly, given that the customer's reparations claim before the agency and the broker's counterclaim were competing claims to the same amount, the Court repeatedly emphasized that it was "necessary" to allow the agency to exercise jurisdiction over the broker's claim, or else "the reparations procedure would have been confounded."

---

* * * *Crowell* may well have additional significance in the context of expert administrative agencies that oversee particular substantive federal regimes, but we have no occasion to and do not address those issues today * * *.

The most recent case in which we considered application of the public rights exception—and the only case in which we have considered that doctrine in the bankruptcy context since *Northern Pipeline*—is *Granfinanciera, S.A. v. Nordberg*, 492 U.S. 33, 109 S.Ct. 2782, 106 L.Ed.2d 26 (1989). In *Granfinanciera*, we rejected a bankruptcy trustee's argument that a fraudulent conveyance action filed on behalf of a bankruptcy estate against a noncreditor in a bankruptcy proceeding fell within the "public rights" exception. We explained that, "[i]f a statutory right is not closely intertwined with a federal regulatory program Congress has power to enact, and if that right neither belongs to nor exists against the Federal Government, then it must be adjudicated by an Article III court." *Id*. at 54–55, 109 S.Ct. 2782 * * *. [W]e concluded that fraudulent conveyance actions were "more accurately characterized as a private rather than a public right as we have used those terms in our Article III decisions." *Id*. at 55, 109 S.Ct. 2782.

Vickie's counterclaim—like the fraudulent conveyance claim at issue in Granfinancier—does not fall within any of the varied formulations of the public rights exception in this Court's cases. * * *. The claim is instead one under state common law between two private parties * * *. Congress has nothing to do with it.

In addition, Vickie's claimed right to relief does not flow from a federal statutory scheme, as in *Thomas* * * *.

Furthermore, the asserted authority to decide Vickie's claim is not limited to a "particularized area of the law," as in *Crowell, Thomas*, and *Schor*. We deal here not with an agency but with a court, with substantive jurisdiction reaching any area of the *corpus juris*. This is not a situation in which Congress devised an "expert and inexpensive method for dealing with a class of questions of fact which are particularly suited to examination and determination by an administrative agency specially assigned to that task." *Crowell*, 285 U.S., at 46, 52 S.Ct. 285 * * *.

* * *

We recognize that there may be instances in which the distinction between public and private rights—at least as framed by some of our recent cases—fails to provide concrete guidance as to whether, for example, a particular agency can adjudicate legal issues under a substantive regulatory scheme. Given the extent to which this case is so markedly distinct from the agency cases discussing the public rights exception in the context of such a regime, however, we do not in this opinion express any view on how the doctrine might apply in that different context.

* * *

JUSTICE SCALIA, concurring.

I agree with the Court's interpretation of our Article III precedents, and I accordingly join its opinion. I adhere to my view, however, that—our contrary precedents notwithstanding—"a matter of public rights . . . must at a minimum arise between the government and others," *Granfinanciera, S.A., v. Nordberg*, 492 U.S. 33, 65, 109 S.Ct. 2782, 106 L.Ed.2d 26 (1989) (SCALIA, J., concurring in part and concurring in judgment) internal quotation marks omitted).

The sheer surfeit of factors that the Court was required to consider in this case should arouse the suspicion that something is seriously amiss with our jurisprudence in this area. I count at least seven different reasons given in the Court's opinion for concluding that an Article III judge was required to adjudicate this lawsuit: that it was one "under state common law" which was "not a matter that can be pursued only by grace of the other branches," that it was "not 'completely dependent upon' adjudication of a claim created by federal law," that "Pierce did not truly consent to resolution of Vickie's claim in the bankruptcy court proceedings," that "the asserted authority to decide Vickie's claim is not limited to a 'particularized area of the law,'" that "there was never any reason to believe that the process of adjudicating Pierce's proof of claim would necessarily resolve Vickie's counterclaim," that the trustee was not "asserting a right of recovery created by federal bankruptcy law," and that the Bankruptcy Judge "ha[d] the power to enter 'appropriate orders and judgments'—including final judgments—subject to review only if a party chooses to appeal."

Apart from their sheer numerosity, the more fundamental flaw in the many tests suggested by our jurisprudence is that they have nothing to do with the text or tradition of Article III. For example, Article III gives no indication that state-law claims have preferential entitlement to an Article III judge; nor does it make pertinent the extent to which the area of the law is "particularized." The multifactors relied upon today seem to have entered our jurisprudence almost randomly.

Leaving aside certain adjudications by federal administrative agencies, which are governed (for better or worse) by our landmark decision in *Crowell v. Benson*, in my view an Article III judge is required in *all* federal adjudications, unless there is a firmly established historical practice to the contrary. For that reason—and not because of some intuitive balancing of benefits and harms—I agree that Article III judges are not required in the context of territorial courts, courts-martial, or true "public rights" cases * * *. But Vickie points to no historical practice that authorizes a non-Article III judge to adjudicate a counterclaim of the sort at issue here.

JUSTICE BREYER, with whom JUSTICE GINSBURG, JUSTICE SOTOMAYOR, and JUSTICE KAGAN, join, dissenting.

* * *

I

My disagreement with the majority's conclusion stems in part from my disagreement about the way in which it interprets, or at least emphasizes, certain precedents. In my view, the majority overstates the current relevance of statements this Court made in an 1856 case, *Murray's Lessee v. Hoboken Land & Improvement Co.*, and it overstates the importance of an analysis that did not command a Court majority in *Northern Pipeline Constr. Co. v. Marathon Pipe Line Co.*, and that was subsequently disavowed. At the same time, I fear the Court understates the importance of a watershed opinion widely thought to demonstrate the constitutional basis for the current authority of administrative agencies to adjudicate private disputes, namely, *Crowell v. Benson.* And it fails to follow the analysis that this Court more recently has held applicable to the evaluation of claims of a kind before us here, namely, claims that a congressional delegation of adjudicatory authority violates separation-of-powers principles derived from Article III.

* * *

* * * I believe the majority places insufficient weight on *Crowell*, a seminal case that clarified the scope of the dictum in *Murray's Lessee.* In that case, the Court considered whether Congress could grant to an Article I administrative agency the power to adjudicate an employee's workers' compensation claim against his employer. The Court assumed that an Article III court would review the agency's decision *de novo* in respect to questions of law but it would conduct a less searching review (looking to see only if the agency's award was "supported by evidence in the record") in respect to questions of fact. The Court pointed out that the case involved a dispute between private persons (a matter of "private rights") and (with one exception not relevant here) it upheld Congress' delegation of primary factfinding authority to the agency.

* * *

Crowell has been hailed as "the greatest of the cases validating administrative adjudication." Bator, The Constitution as Architecture: Legislative and Administrative Courts Under Article III, 65 Ind. L.J. 233, 251 (1990). Yet, in a footnote, the majority distinguishes *Crowell* as a case in which the Court upheld the delegation of adjudicatory authority to an administrative agency simply because the agency's power to make the "specialized, narrowly confined factual determinations" at issue arising in a "particularized area of law," made the agency a "true 'adjunct' of the District Court." Were *Crowell*'s holding as narrow as the majority suggests, one could question the validity of Congress' delegation of authority to adjudicate disputes among private parties to other agencies such as the National Labor Relations Board, the Commodity Futures Trading Commission, the Surface Transportation Board, and the Department of Housing and Urban Development, thereby resurrecting important legal questions previously thought to have been decided.

* * *

Rather than leaning so heavily on the approach taken by the plurality in *Northern Pipeline*, I would look to this Court's more recent Article III cases *Thomas* and *Schor*—cases that commanded a clear majority. In both cases the Court took a more pragmatic approach to the constitutional question. It sought to determine whether, in the particular instance, the challenged delegation of adjudicatory authority posed a genuine and serious threat that one branch of Government sought to aggrandize its own constitutionally delegated authority by encroaching upon a field of authority that the Constitution assigns exclusively to another branch.

* * *

This case law * * * requires us to determine pragmatically whether a congressional delegation of adjudicatory authority to a non-Article III judge violates the separation-of-powers principles inherent in Article III. That is to say, we must determine through an examination of certain relevant factors whether that delegation constitutes a significant encroachment by the Legislative or Executive Branches of Government upon the realm of authority that Article III reserves for exercise by the Judicial Branch of Government. Those factors include (1) the nature of the claim to be adjudicated; (2) the nature of the non-Article III tribunal; (3) the extent to which Article III courts exercise control over the proceeding; (4) the presence or absence of the parties' consent; and (5) the nature and importance of the legislative purpose served by the grant of adjudicatory authority to a tribunal with judges who lack Article III's tenure and compensation protections. The presence of "private rights" does not automatically determine the outcome of the question but requires a more "searching" examination of the relevant factors.

Insofar as the majority would apply more formal standards, it simply disregards recent, controlling precedent. *Thomas, supra,* at 587, 105 S.Ct. 3325 ("[P]ractical attention to substance rather than doctrinaire reliance on formal categories should inform application of Article III"); *Schor, supra,* at 851, 106 S.Ct. 3425 ("[T]he Court has declined to adopt formalistic and unbending rules" for deciding Article III cases).

* * * Applying *Schor*'s approach here, I conclude that the delegation of adjudicatory authority before us is constitutional * * *.

First, I concede that *the nature of the claim to be adjudicated* argues against my conclusion * * *.

At the same time the significance of this factor is mitigated here by the fact that bankruptcy courts often decide claims that similarly resemble various common-law actions. Suppose, for example, that ownership of 40 acres of land in the bankruptcy debtor's possession is disputed by a creditor. If that creditor brings a claim in the bankruptcy court, resolution of that dispute requires the bankruptcy court to apply the same state property law that would govern in a state court proceeding. This kind of dispute arises with regularity in bankruptcy proceedings.

* * *

Second, *the nature of the non-Article III tribunal* argues in favor of constitutionality. That is because the tribunal is made up of judges who enjoy considerable protection from improper political influence * * *.

Third, *the control exercised by Article III judges over bankruptcy proceedings* argues in favor of constitutionality. Article III judges control and supervise the bankruptcy court's determinations—at least to the same degree that Article III judges supervised the agency's determinations in *Crowell,* if not more so * * *.

Moreover, in one important respect Article III judges maintain greater control over the bankruptcy court proceedings at issue here than they did over the relevant proceedings in any of the previous cases in which this Court has upheld a delegation of adjudicatory power. The District Court here may "withdraw, in whole or in part, any case or proceeding referred [to the Bankruptcy Court] . . . on its own motion or on timely motion of any party, for cause shown." 28 U.S.C. § 157(d).

Fourth, the fact that *the parties have consented* to Bankruptcy Court jurisdiction argues in favor of constitutionality, and strongly so * * *.

* * *

Fifth, *the nature and importance of the legislative purpose served* by the grant of adjudicatory authority to bankruptcy tribunals argues strongly in favor of constitutionality. Congress' delegation of adjudicatory powers over counterclaims asserted against bankruptcy claimants constitutes an important means of securing a constitutionally authorized end * * *.

* * *

* * * [A] bankruptcy court's determination * * * plays a critical role in Congress' constitutionally based effort to create an efficient, effective federal bankruptcy system. At the least, that is what Congress concluded. We owe deference to that determination, which shows the absence of any legislative or executive motive, intent, purpose, or desire to encroach upon

areas that Article III reserves to judges to whom it grants tenure and compensation protections.

Considering these factors together, I conclude that, as in *Schor*, "the magnitude of any intrusion on the Judicial Branch can only be termed *de minimis.*" 478 U.S., at 856, 106 S.Ct. 3425. I would similarly find the statute before us constitutional.

NOTES

In a sequel to *Stern* that is likely of more interest to constitutional than administrative lawyers, a divided Court—with the majority and dissent hurling accusations of "formalism" and "functionalism" at each other, *see supra* page 100—held that litigant consent could obviate any Article III problem with having Article I bankruptcy judges enter final orders in the kind of "non-core" claims at issue in *Stern. See Wellness Int'l Network, Ltd. v. Sharif*, 575 U.S. ___, 135 S.Ct. 1932, 191 L.Ed.2d 911 (2015). And patents have been held to be "public rights" that can be cancelled by a non-Article-III administrative tribunal. *See Oil States Energy Services, LLC v. Greene's Energy Group, LLC*, 138 S.Ct. 1365, 200 L.Ed.2d 671 (2018).

1. FORMALISM AND ARTICLE III

How would a formalist handle the problem of agency adjudication? Formalists are unanimous in their dislike of *Schor* (and *Crowell*), but they have had a very hard time coming up with a convincing demarcation of the line between permissible agency administration and impermissible agency judging. Functionalists, by the same token, face the problem of explaining why Congress cannot simply transfer all adjudicative functions to politically controllable officials. And everyone faces the problem of construing the Supreme Court's case law on the subject, which has aptly been characterized as "notoriously obscure." Harold Bruff, *Specialized Courts in Administrative Law*, 43 Ad. L. Rev. 329, 352 (1991).

Consider one formalist's (extremely tentative) proposed solution.

Administrative adjudication is problematic only if it must be considered an exercise of judicial power. But an activity is not exclusively judicial merely because it is adjudicative—that is, because it involves the application of legal standards to particular facts. Much adjudicative activity by executive officials—such as granting or denying benefits under entitlement statutes—is *execution* of the laws by any rational standard, though it also fits comfortably within the concept of the judicial power if conducted by judicial officers. This overlap between the executive and judicial functions is not surprising; under many pre-American conceptions of separation of powers, the judicial power was treated as an aspect of the executive power.

Agency adjudication is therefore constitutionally permissible under Article III as long as the activity in question can fairly fit the definition of executive power, even if it also fairly fits the definition of judicial power. Some forms of adjudication, however, are quintessentially judicial. The conviction of a defendant under the criminal laws, for example, is surely something that requires the exercise of judicial rather than executive power. Although it is difficult to identify those activities that are strictly judicial in the constitutional sense, perhaps Justice Curtis had the right answer in *Murray's Lessee v. Hoboken Land & Improvement Co.* when he suggested that the Article III inquiry merges with questions of due process: if the government is depriving a citizen of "life, liberty, or property," it generally must do so by *judicial* process, which in the federal system requires an Article III court; but if it is denying a citizen (to use discredited but still useful language) a mere privilege, it can do so by purely executive action.

Gary Lawson, *The Rise and Rise of the Administrative State*, 107 Harv. L. Rev. 1231, 1246–47 (1994).

At this point, with a substantial body of case law under one's belt, it might be fruitful to reexamine what labels such as "formalism" and "functionalism" might mean. *See supra* pages 91–98. With the caveat that the following excerpt was authored by a partisan in the formalism/functionalism debate, consider whether it helps make sense out of at least some of the Supreme Court's (and the legal academy's) work product.

GARY LAWSON, PROLEGOMENON TO ANY FUTURE ADMINISTRATIVE LAW COURSE: SEPARATION OF POWERS AND THE TRANSCENDENTAL DEDUCTION

49 St. Louis U.L. Rev. 885 (2005).
Reprinted with permission of the Saint Louis University Law Journal © 2005 St. Louis University School of Law, St. Louis, Missouri.

The Constitution of 1788, as amended, is a set of instructions about how to set up and operate a government. The people who drafted and ratified the document no doubt had expectations (possibly conflicting, possibly overlapping) regarding the likely consequences of following those instructions. But there is a conceptual difference between the instructions on the one hand and the consequences, or expectations of consequences, of following those instructions on the other * * *.

Formalism chooses the instructions rather than the consequences or expectations as the starting point for reasoning about federal governmental structure. Formalism takes the provisions of the Constitution of 1788 as the major premises of reasoning about separation of powers and tries to deduce from those premises subsidiary propositions about the constitutionality of various institutions and practices * * *. The Constitution of 1788 is the starting point in this reasoning. It is the baseline against which modern institutions and practices must be judged * * *.

Functionalism reverses the order of the argument. Functionalism starts with the constitutionality of some important subset of modern institutions as the major premise of constitutional argument about governmental structure. Propositions about these institutions serve functionalism as postulates—that is, as propositions that must be accepted as true by any viable constitutional theory. There are three, and perhaps four, such propositions that together constitute the basic contours of functionalism:

    1.   The federal government has near-plenary regulatory power, or at least enough regulatory power to reach manufacturing, contracting, and most economic activity.

    2.   Congress has near-plenary power to delegate its near-plenary legislative power to other actors.

    3.   Congress may combine legislative, executive, and judicial functions in a single administrative entity.

    4.   It is permissible to insulate administrative decision makers from political influence.

Together, these propositions define the modern administrative state. If one rejects any of these propositions, one will inflict major damage on modern institutions of governance * * *.

For functionalists, these propositions, and the modern institutions that they validate, are the baseline against which the Constitution, or at least constitutional theory, must be judged. Any theory of constitutional interpretation, either in general or of a particular clause, that challenges these basic postulates and thus leads to the invalidation of a substantial portion of the modern administrative state is by definition wrong under functionalism. The whole point of functionalism, in other words, is to provide a constitutional justification for the modern administrative state * * *.

* * *

Does that mean that, for functionalists, every institution of the modern administrative state is by definition constitutional? Not at all. It means only that certain core institutions of the modern administrative state such as a national government of near-plenary powers, the permissibility of broad delegations to agencies, and the combination of legislative, executive, and judicial functions in administrative agencies are off the table. These institutions are constitutional by definition, literally by definition, as they define the practical meaning of the Constitution. But other, less fundamental institutions can be unconstitutional under functionalism if they are inconsistent with either the logical implications of the core institutions, the text of the Constitution, or whatever is regarded as relevant for constitutional meaning when the integrity of modern governance is not at stake. For instance, functionalists can agree wholeheartedly with formalists that Congress cannot directly appoint executive officials. This conclusion in no way threatens the basic integrity of modern administrative governance, and it does not call into question the legitimacy of the core institutions of the modern state. Functionalists might even be able to agree with formalists that the legislative veto is unconstitutional. Invalidating the legislative veto certainly sent shockwaves through the government, but it did not seriously threaten the integrity of the basic institutions of modern governance. The administrative state trundles along with or without legislative vetoes. Indeed, legislative vetoes might even be inconsistent with the core premises of modern governance if one regards them as an undue extension of political influence into the agency process. Functionalists, it seems to me, can go either way on the legislative veto and still be good functionalists. Finally, functionalists need not object to the Supreme Court's recent modest revival of the doctrine of enumerated powers. Rulings that Congress cannot enact the Violence Against Women Act or the Gun-Free School Zones Act simply do not affect the missions of mainstream federal agencies as long as the holdings are confined to the periphery of non-economic activity, as they seem to be thus far. If the Court were once again to hold that manufacturing is not commerce within the meaning of Article I, section 8, that would be inconsistent with functionalism, but no one expects any such thing to happen.

The mystery of the Supreme Court's apparent vacillation between formalism and functionalism can now be solved. There is no vacillation. The Court is solidly, consistently, unshakably functionalist. When the basic institutions of modern administrative governance are at stake, the Court closes ranks and hurls the constitutional text into the Potomac River. When subsidiary institutions are at stake, the various Justices are free to indulge their own interpretative preferences, which for some involve deductive application of textual instructions and for others involve reasoning from consequences * * *.

Thus, formalism and functionalism are distinguished more by their starting points than by the methods of reasoning that are employed once those starting points are established.

2. ADMINISTRATIVE ADJUDICATION AND JURY TRIAL

In federal court, in addition to a judge with the salary and tenure guarantees of Article III, you often get a jury as well. The jury as decisionmaker is not beholden to any established governmental body, which is why it was so important to the founding generation. The Seventh Amendment provides that "In Suits at common law, where the value in controversy shall exceed twenty dollars, the right of trial by jury shall be preserved * * *." U.S. Const. amend. VII. When politically accountable agencies adjudicate, and perhaps impose fines on defendants totaling hundreds of thousands or millions of dollars, does the Seventh Amendment require the use of a jury?

In *Atlas Roofing Co., Inc. v. OSHRC*, 430 U.S. 442, 97 S.Ct. 1261, 51 L.Ed.2d 464 (1977), a unanimous Supreme Court resoundingly answered "No." Atlas Roofing faced substantial fines imposed by the Occupational Safety and Health Review Commission, an independent agency that adjudicates violations of federal workplace safety standards alleged by the Occupational Safety and Health Administration. It argued that the imposition of a fine was a classic "Suit[ ] at common law" within the meaning of the Seventh Amendment. The Court answered:

> At least in cases in which "public rights" are being litigated—*e.g.*, cases in which the Government sues in its sovereign capacity to enforce public rights created by statutes within the power of Congress to enact—the Seventh Amendment does not prohibit Congress from assigning the factfinding function and initial adjudication to an administrative forum with which the jury would be incompatible.
>
> Congress has often created new statutory obligations, provided for civil penalties for their violation, and committed exclusively to an administrative agency the function of deciding whether a violation has in fact occurred. These statutory schemes have been sustained by this Court, albeit often without express reference to the Seventh Amendment * * *.

* * *

> * * * Congress is not required by the Seventh Amendment to choke the already crowded federal courts with new types of litigation or prevented from committing some new types of litigation to administrative agencies with special competence in the relevant field. This is the case even if the Seventh Amendment would have required a jury where the adjudication of those rights is assigned instead to a federal court of law instead of an administrative agency.

430 U.S. at 450, 454, 97 S.Ct. at 1269. Under this doctrine, patents can be cancelled by an administrative agency without need for a jury. *See Oil States Energy Services, LLC v. Greene's Energy Group, LLC,* 138 S.Ct. 1365, 200 L.Ed.2d 671 (2018).

E. AGENCIES AND THE SEPARATION OF POWERS

The concept of the "separation of powers," by its name alone, describes a specific mechanism for securing liberty: conferring different governmental functions on different actors. The combination of the various functions of government in the same hands, wrote Madison, "may justly be pronounced the very definition of tyranny." The Federalist No. 46. The whole point of a scheme of separated powers is to insure that the power to make rules of conduct, the power to apply and enforce those rules, and the power to adjudicate claimed violations are in different, independent hands.

Modern administrative agencies are Madison's worst nightmare come true. Agencies routinely combine in one body the executive power of enforcement and administration, the legislative-like power of rulemaking, and the judicial-like power of adjudication. To grasp just how profound this combination of functions has become in modern times, consider the enforcement activities of a typical federal agency, such as the Federal Trade Commission:

> The Commission promulgates substantive rules of conduct. The Commission then considers whether to authorize investigations into whether the Commission's rules have been violated. If the Commission authorizes an investigation, the investigation is conducted by the Commission, which reports its findings to the Commission. If the Commission thinks that the Commission's findings warrant an enforcement action, the Commission issues a complaint. The Commission's complaint that a Commission rule has been violated is then prosecuted by the Commission and adjudicated by the Commission. This Commission adjudication can either take place before the full Commission or before a semi-autonomous Commission administrative law judge. If the Commission chooses to adjudicate before an administrative law judge rather than before the Commission and the decision is adverse to the Commission, the Commission can appeal to the Commission. If the Commission ultimately finds a violation, then, and only then, the affected private party can appeal to an Article III court. But the agency decision, even before the bona fide Article III tribunal, possesses a very strong presumption of correctness on matters both of fact and of law.

Gary Lawson, *The Rise and Rise of the Administrative State,* 107 Harv. L. Rev. 1231, 1243 (1994).

The modern Supreme Court has never questioned the compatibility of this combination of functions in agencies with traditional (or, for that matter, untraditional) understandings of separation of powers. It has, however, ruled on whether allowing an enforcer of rules to adjudicate his or her own enforcement action is compatible with the Constitution's requirement (for both state and federal governments) of due process.

WITHROW V. LARKIN

Supreme Court of the United States, 1975.
421 U.S. 35, 95 S.Ct. 1456, 43 L.Ed.2d 712.

MR. JUSTICE WHITE delivered the opinion of the Court.

The statutes of the State of Wisconsin forbid the practice of medicine without a license from an Examining Board composed of practicing physicians. The statutes also define and forbid various acts of professional misconduct * * *. To enforce these provisions, the Examining Board is empowered under Wis. Stat. Ann. §§ 448.17 and 448.18 (1974) to warn and reprimand, temporarily to suspend the license, and "to institute criminal action or action to revoke license when it finds probable cause therefor under criminal or revocation statutes. . ." When an investigative proceeding before the Examining Board was commenced against him, appellee brought this suit against appellants, the individual members of the Board, seeking an injunction against the enforcement of the statutes. The District Court issued a preliminary injunction, the appellants appealed, and we noted probable jurisdiction.

* * *

Appellee, a resident of Michigan and licensed to practice medicine there, obtained a Wisconsin license in August 1971 under a reciprocity agreement between Michigan and Wisconsin governing medical licensing. His practice in Wisconsin consisted of performing abortions at an office in Milwaukee. On June 20, 1973, the Board sent to appellee a notice that it would hold an investigative hearing on July 12, 1973, under Wis. Stat. Ann. § 448.17 to determine whether he had engaged in certain proscribed acts. The hearing would be closed to the public, although appellee and his attorney could attend. They would not, however, be permitted to cross-examine witnesses. Based upon the evidence presented at the hearing, the Board would decide "whether to warn or reprimand if it finds such practice and whether to institute criminal action or action to revoke license if probable cause therefor exists under criminal or revocation statutes."

* * *

On September 18, 1973, the Board sent to appellee a notice that a "contested hearing" would be held on October 4, 1973, to determine whether appellee had engaged in certain prohibited acts and that based upon the evidence adduced at the hearing the Board would determine whether his license would be suspended temporarily under Wis. Stat. Ann. § 448.18 (7). Appellee moved for a restraining order against the contested hearing. The District Court granted the motion on October 1, 1973. Because the Board had moved from purely investigative proceedings to a hearing aimed at deciding whether suspension of appellee's license was appropriate, the District Court concluded that a substantial federal question had arisen, namely, whether the authority given to appellants both "to investigate physicians and present charges [and] to rule on those charges and impose punishment, at least to the extent of reprimanding or temporarily suspending" violated appellee's due process rights. Appellee's motion to request the convening of a three-judge court was also granted, and appellants' motion to dismiss was denied.

The Board complied and did not go forward with the contested hearing. Instead, it noticed and held a final investigative session on October 4, 1973, at which appellee's attorney, but not appellee, appeared. The Board thereupon issued "Findings of Fact," "Conclusions of Law," and a "Decision" in which the Board found that appellee had engaged in specified conduct proscribed by the statute * * *.

* * *

* * * On the present record, it is quite unlikely that appellee would ultimately prevail on the merits of the due process issue presented to the District Court * * *.

Concededly, a "fair trial in a fair tribunal is a basic requirement of due process." *In re Murchison*, 349 U.S. 133, 136 (1955). This applies to administrative agencies which adjudicate as well as to courts. *Gibson v. Berryhill*, 411 U.S. 564, 579 (1973). Not only is a biased decisionmaker constitutionally unacceptable but "our system of law has always endeavored to prevent even the probability of unfairness." *In re Murchison*, *supra*, at 136; *cf. Tumey v. Ohio*, 273 U.S. 510, 532 (1927). In pursuit of this end, various situations have been identified in which experience teaches that the probability of actual bias on the part of the judge or decisionmaker is too high to be constitutionally tolerable. Among these cases are those in which the adjudicator has a pecuniary interest in the outcome and in which he has been the target of personal abuse or criticism from the party before him.

The contention that the combination of investigative and adjudicative functions necessarily creates an unconstitutional risk of bias in administrative adjudication has a much more difficult burden of persuasion to carry. It must overcome a presumption of honesty and integrity in those serving as adjudicators; and it must convince that, under a realistic appraisal of psychological tendencies and human weakness, conferring investigative and adjudicative powers on the same individuals poses such a risk of actual bias or prejudgment that the practice must be forbidden if the guarantee of due process is to be adequately implemented.

Very similar claims have been squarely rejected in prior decisions of this Court. In *FTC v. Cement Institute*, 333 U.S. 683 (1948), the Federal Trade Commission had instituted proceedings concerning the respondents' multiple basing-point delivered-price system. It was demanded that the Commission members disqualify themselves because long before the Commission had filed its complaint it had investigated the parties and reported to Congress and to the President, and its members had testified before congressional committees concerning the legality of such a pricing system. At least some of the members had disclosed their opinion that the system was illegal. The issue of bias was brought here and confronted "on the assumption that such an opinion had been formed by the entire membership of the Commission as a result of its prior official investigations." *Id.*, at 700.

The Court rejected the claim, saying:

"[T]he fact that the Commission had entertained such views as the result of its prior *ex parte* investigations did not necessarily mean that the minds of its members were irrevocably closed on the subject of the respondents' basing point practices. Here, in contrast to the commission's investigations, members of the cement industry were legally authorized participants in the hearings. They produced evidence—volumes of it. They were free to point out to the Commission by testimony, by cross-examination of witnesses, and by arguments, conditions of the trade practices under attack which they thought kept these practices within the range of legally permissible business activities." *Id.*, at 701.

In specific response to a due process argument, the Court asserted:

"No decision of this Court would require us to hold that it would be a violation of procedural due process for a judge to sit in a case after he had expressed an opinion as to whether certain types of conduct were prohibited by law. In fact, judges frequently try the same case more than once and decide identical issues each time, although these issues involve questions both of law and fact. Certainly, the Federal Trade Commission cannot possibly be under stronger constitutional compulsions in this respect than a court." *Id.*, at 702–703 (footnote omitted).

This Court has also ruled that a hearing examiner who has recommended findings of fact after rejecting certain evidence as not being probative was not disqualified to preside at further hearings that were required when reviewing courts held that the evidence had been erroneously excluded. *NLRB v. Donnelly Garment Co.*, 330 U.S. 219, 236–

237 (1947). The Court of Appeals had decided that the examiner should not again sit because it would be unfair to require the parties to try "issues of fact to those who may have prejudged them. . ." 151 F.2d 854, 870 (C.A.8 1945). But this Court unanimously reversed, saying:

> "Certainly it is not the rule of judicial administration that, statutory requirements apart . . . a judge is disqualified from sitting in a retrial because he was reversed on earlier rulings. We find no warrant for imposing upon administrative agencies a stiffer rule, whereby examiners would be disentitled to sit because they ruled strongly against a party in the first hearing." 330 U.S. at 236–237.

More recently we have sustained against due process objection a system in which a Social Security examiner has responsibility for developing the facts and making a decision as to disability claims, and observed that the challenge to this combination of functions "assumes too much and would bring down too many procedures designed, and working well, for a governmental structure of great and growing complexity." *Richardson v. Perales*, 402 U.S. 389, 410 (1971).

That is not to say that there is nothing to the argument that those who have investigated should not then adjudicate. The issue is substantial, it is not new, and legislators and others concerned with the operations of administrative agencies have given much attention to whether and to what extent distinctive administrative functions should be performed by the same persons. No single answer has been reached. Indeed, the growth, variety, and complexity of the administrative processes have made any one solution highly unlikely. Within the Federal Government itself, Congress has addressed the issue in several different ways, providing for varying degrees of separation from complete separation of functions to virtually none at all. For the generality of agencies, Congress has been content with § 5 of the Administrative Procedure Act, 5 U.S.C. § 554(d), which provides that no employee engaged in investigating or prosecuting may also participate or advise in the adjudicating function, but which also expressly exempts from this prohibition "the agency or a member or members of the body comprising the agency."

It is not surprising, therefore, to find that "[t]he case law, both federal and state, generally rejects the idea that the combination [of] judging [and] investigating functions is a denial of due process. . ." 2 K. Davis, Administrative Law Treatise § 13.02, p. 175 (1958). Similarly, our cases, although they reflect the substance of the problem, offer no support for the bald proposition applied in this case by the District Court that agency members who participate in an investigation are disqualified from adjudicating. The incredible variety of administrative mechanisms in this country will not yield to any single organizing principle.

Appellee relies heavily on *In re Murchison, supra,* in which a state judge, empowered under state law to sit as a "one-man grand jury" and to compel witnesses to testify before him in secret about possible crimes, charged two such witnesses with criminal contempt, one for perjury and the other for refusing to answer certain questions, and then himself tried and convicted them. This Court found the procedure to be a denial of due process of law not only because the judge in effect became part of the prosecution and assumed an adversary position, but also because as a judge, passing on guilt or innocence, he very likely relied on "his own personal knowledge and impression of what had occurred in the grand jury room," an impression that "could not be tested by adequate cross-examination." 349 U.S., at 138.

Plainly enough, *Murchison* has not been understood to stand for the broad rule that the members of an administrative agency may not investigate the facts, institute proceedings, and then make the necessary adjudications. The Court did not purport to question the *Cement Institute* case, *supra,* or the Administrative Procedure Act and did not lay down any general principle that a judge before whom an alleged contempt is committed may not bring and preside over the ensuing contempt proceedings. The accepted rule is to the contrary.

Nor is there anything in this case that comes within the strictures of *Murchison.* When the Board instituted its investigative procedures, it stated only that it would investigate whether proscribed conduct had occurred. Later in noticing the adversary hearing, it asserted only that it would determine if violations had been committed which would warrant suspension of appellee's license. Without doubt, the Board then anticipated that the proceeding would eventuate in an adjudication of the issue; but there was no more evidence of bias or the risk of bias or prejudgment than inhered in the very fact that the Board had investigated and would now adjudicate. Of course, we should be alert to the possibilities of bias that may lurk in the way particular procedures actually work in practice. The processes utilized by the Board, however, do not in themselves contain an unacceptable risk of bias. The investigative proceeding had been closed to the public, but appellee and his counsel were permitted to be present throughout; counsel actually attended the hearings and knew the facts presented to the Board. No specific foundation has been presented for suspecting that the Board had been prejudiced by its investigation or would be disabled from hearing and deciding on the basis of the evidence to be presented at the contested hearing. The mere exposure to evidence presented in nonadversary investigative procedures is insufficient in itself to impugn the fairness of the Board members at a later adversary hearing. Without a showing to the contrary, state administrators "are assumed to be men of conscience and intellectual discipline, capable of judging a particular controversy fairly on the basis of its own circumstances." *United States v. Morgan*, 313 U.S. 409, 421 (1941).

* * *

Nor do we think the situation substantially different because the Board, when it was prevented from going forward with the contested hearing, proceeded to make and issue formal findings of fact and conclusions of law asserting that there was probable cause to believe that appellee had engaged in various acts prohibited by the Wisconsin statutes. These findings and conclusions were verified and filed with the district attorney for the purpose of initiating revocation and criminal proceedings. Although the District Court did not emphasize this aspect of the case before it, appellee stresses it in attempting to show prejudice and prejudgment. We are not persuaded.

Judges repeatedly issue arrest warrants on the basis that there is probable cause to believe that a crime has been committed and that the person named in the warrant has committed it. Judges also preside at preliminary hearings where they must decide whether the evidence is sufficient to hold a defendant for trial. Neither of these pretrial involvements has been thought to raise any constitutional barrier against the judge's presiding over the criminal trial and, if the trial is without a jury, against making the necessary determination of guilt or innocence. Nor has it been thought that a judge is disqualified from presiding over injunction proceedings because he has initially assessed the facts in issuing or denying a temporary restraining order or a preliminary injunction. It is also very typical for the members of administrative agencies to receive the results of investigations, to approve the filing of charges or formal complaints instituting enforcement proceedings, and then to participate in the ensuing hearings. This mode of procedure does not violate the Administrative Procedure Act, and it does not violate due process of law. We should also remember that it is not contrary to due process to allow judges and administrators who have had their initial decisions reversed on appeal to confront and decide the same questions a second time around.

Here, the Board stayed within the accepted bounds of due process. Having investigated, it issued findings and conclusions asserting the commission of certain acts and ultimately concluding that there was probable cause to believe that appellee had violated the statutes.

The risk of bias or prejudgment in this sequence of functions has not been considered to be intolerably high or to raise a sufficiently great possibility that the adjudicators would be so psychologically wedded to their complaints that they would consciously or unconsciously avoid the appearance of having erred or changed position. Indeed, just as there is no logical inconsistency between a finding of probable cause and an acquittal in a criminal proceeding, there is no incompatibility between the agency filing a complaint based on probable cause and a subsequent decision, when all the evidence is in, that there has been no violation of the statute. Here, if the Board now proceeded after an adversary hearing to determine that appellee's license to practice should not be temporarily suspended, it would not implicitly be admitting error in its prior finding of probable cause. Its position most probably would merely reflect the benefit of a more complete view of the evidence afforded by an adversary hearing.

The initial charge or determination of probable cause and the ultimate adjudication have different bases and purposes. The fact that the same agency makes them in tandem and that they relate to the same issues does not result in a procedural due process violation. Clearly, if the initial view of the facts based on the evidence derived from nonadversarial processes as a practical or legal matter foreclosed fair and effective consideration at a subsequent adversary hearing leading to ultimate decision, a substantial due process question would be raised. But in our view, that is not this case.

That the combination of investigative and adjudicative functions does not, without more, constitute a due process violation, does not, of course, preclude a court from determining from the special facts and circumstances present in the case before it that the risk of unfairness is intolerably high. Findings of that kind made by judges with special insights into local realities are entitled to respect, but injunctions resting on such factors should be accompanied by at least the minimum findings required by Rules 52(a) and 65(d).

The judgment of the District Court is reversed and the case is remanded to that court for further proceedings consistent with this opinion.

1.   SEPARATION OF POWERS AND SEPARATION OF FUNCTIONS

Withrow dealt only with the question whether the combination of investigation, prosecution, and adjudication in a single agency necessarily violates due process of law. It did not address any questions of the separation of powers, for the simple reason that state agencies, such as the Wisconsin agency at issue in *Withrow*, are not subject to the separation-of-powers limitations of the federal Constitution (though they are subject to whatever limitations are contained in their own state constitutions). No one doubts, however, that a broad-based separation-of-powers challenge to the modern combination of functions in federal agencies would meet the same fate as the broad-based due process challenge in *Withrow*.

One need not be a strict devotee of the Constitution of 1789 in order to feel some unease at the consequences of the demise of the separation of powers. One could, in principle, applaud the Court's unwillingness to find the whole enterprise of modern administrative government unconstitutional while still recognizing that Madison and his ilk had a valid point about the dangers of concentrated power. Modern constitutional doctrine permits a near-limitless combination of functions in agencies, but Congress can draw a nonconstitutional line at an earlier point.

The Administrative Procedure Act draws several such lines. The most important line is that in many agency proceedings—known as *formal proceedings*—that use procedures resembling those of a judicial trial, the proceeding is conducted, and an initial (and sometimes final) decision is made, by an agency official called an *administrative law judge*. Such officials, who were encountered several times already in this chapter, were originally known as *hearing officers* or *hearing examiners*; their titles, though not their duties or powers, were changed by statute in 1978. Keep in mind that pre-1978 judicial opinions, and even a few post-1978 opinions, use the old titles. Administrative law judges—or *ALJs*, as they are generally known—perform many of the adjudicative, judge-like functions carried out by agencies.[40]

They can:

(1)   administer oaths and affirmations;

(2)   issue subpoenas authorized by law;

(3)   rule on offers of proof and receive relevant evidence;

(4)   take depositions or have depositions taken when the ends of justice would be served;

(5)   regulate the course of the hearing;

(6)   hold conferences for the settlement or simplification of the issues by consent of the parties * * * ;

(7)   inform the parties as to the availability of one or more alternative means of dispute resolution, and encourage use of such methods;

(8)   require the attendance at any conference held pursuant to paragraph (6) of at least one representative of each party who has authority to negotiate concerning resolution of issues in controversy;

(9)   dispose of procedural requests or similar matters;

(10) make or recommend decisions * * * ; and

(11) take other action authorized by agency rule * * * .

---

[40] Do not confuse ALJs with the similarly-named administrative judges (AJs). AJs preside over many agency proceedings (largely involving immigration, veterans benefits, and government personnel matters), but they do not have the statutory protections afforded ALJs that are discussed below. And AJs are not authorized to preside over formal agency proceedings. For a detailed, and critical, look at the important and often-overlooked role of AJs, see Kent Barnett, *Against Administrative Judges*, 49 U.C. Davis L. Rev. 1643 (2016); Kent Barnett, *Why Bias Challenges to Administrative Adjudication Should Succeed,* 81 Mo. L. Rev. 1023 (2016).

5 U.S.C. § 556(c) (2012). This looks—and is—very much like the list of powers of a trial judge in an Article III federal court. But ALJs are not judges in the constitutional sense. They do not benefit from constitutional guarantees of salary and tenure. They are executive agency officials, though agency officials of a special kind. Each agency hires its own ALJs, *see* 5 U.S.C. § 3105 (2012),[41] but the salaries of ALJs are set on a government-wide basis, in accordance with regulations set forth by an agency called the Office of Personnel Management ("OPM"). *See* 5 U.S.C. § 5372 (2012). Thus, the hiring agency does not control the salaries of its ALJs. ALJs may be removed or disciplined by the agency for which they work, but only for "good cause established and determined by the Merit System Protection Board * * *." 5 U.S.C. § 7521(a) (2012). Thus, as with salary, an agency other than the hiring agency is ultimately responsible for the ALJs' tenure.[42] The agency, however, is permitted to set standards for acceptable quantity and quality of decisionmaking; failure to meet those standards would presumably be "good cause" for removal or discipline. *See Nash v. Bowen*, 869 F.2d 675 (2d Cir.1989) (upholding the Social Security Administration's use of peer review and production quotas to supervise its corps of ALJs). Thus, ALJs have some measure of statutory independence from the agencies that employ them, though considerably less independence than the Constitution grants to Article III judges.[43] Of course, after *Lucia v. SEC*, pages 203–215, *supra*, at least some of these features of ALJs may require some modification if they are legally challenged, as they surely will be in the coming years. That modification process has already begun in the Trump Administration as a matter of policy. Until July 2018, agencies would select ALJs from a list of candidates provided by the OPM, which oversees the government's civil service system. Candidates were identified by OPM based on an evaluation process that included competitive examinations (essentially the government's version of the LSAT or GRE), which is standard practice for civil service positions. Following the *Lucia* decision, President Trump issued an executive order exempting ALJs from some of the civil service selection processes:

> By the authority vested in me as President by the Constitution and the laws of the United States of America,

---

[41] Under some circumstances, agencies may also "borrow" ALJs from other agencies. *See* 5 U.S.C. § 3344 (2012).

[42] And decisions of the Merit Systems Protection Board are subject to Article III judicial review.

[43] Even that measure of independence is fairly recent. Prior to enactment of the APA in 1946, hearing examiners were "on a par with other agency employees, their compensation and promotion dependent upon agency ratings. The expanding scope of agency activity during the 1930s and early 1940s led to increasingly heavy criticism, however, because the hearing examiners came to be perceived as 'mere tools of the agency concerned.' *Ramspeck v. Federal Trial Examiners Conference*, 345 U.S. 128, 131, 73 S.Ct. 570, 572, 97 L.Ed. 872 (1953). In response, Congress * * * [in the APA removed] control over the hearing examiners' tenure and compensation from the agencies * * *." Nash v. Califano, 613 F.2d 10, 16 (2d Cir.1980).

including sections 3301 and 3302 of title 5, United States Code, it is hereby ordered as follows:

Section 1. Policy. The Federal Government benefits from a professional cadre of administrative law judges (ALJs) appointed under section 3105 of title 5, United States Code, who are impartial and committed to the rule of law. As illustrated by the Supreme Court's recent decision in *Lucia v. Securities and Exchange Commission*, No. 17–130 (June 21, 2018), ALJs are often called upon to discharge significant duties and exercise significant discretion in conducting proceedings under the laws of the United States. As part of their adjudications, ALJs interact with the public on issues of significance. Especially given the importance of the functions they discharge—which may range from taking testimony and conducting trials to ruling on the admissibility of evidence and enforcing compliance with their orders—ALJs must display appropriate temperament, legal acumen, impartiality, and sound judgment. They must also clearly communicate their decisions to the parties who appear before them, the agencies that oversee them, and the public that entrusts them with authority.

Previously, appointments to the position of ALJ have been made through competitive examination and competitive service selection procedures. The role of ALJs, however, has increased over time and ALJ decisions have, with increasing frequency, become the final word of the agencies they serve. Given this expanding responsibility for important agency adjudications, and as recognized by the Supreme Court in *Lucia*, at least some—and perhaps al—ALJs are "Officers of the United States" and thus subject to the Constitution's Appointments Clause, which governs who may appoint such officials.

As evident from recent litigation, *Lucia* may also raise questions about the method of appointing ALJs, including whether competitive examination and competitive service selection procedures are compatible with the discretion an agency head must possess under the Appointments Clause in selecting ALJs. Regardless of whether those procedures would violate the Appointments Clause as applied to certain ALJs, there are sound policy reasons to take steps to eliminate doubt regarding the constitutionality of the method of appointing officials who discharge such significant duties and exercise such significant discretion.

Pursuant to my authority under section 3302(1) of title 5, United States Code, I find that conditions of good administration make necessary an exception to the competitive hiring rules and examinations for the position of ALJ. These conditions include the need to provide agency heads with additional flexibility to assess prospective appointees without the limitations imposed by competitive examination and competitive service selection procedures. Placing the position of ALJ in the excepted service will mitigate concerns about undue limitations on the selection of ALJs, reduce the likelihood of successful Appointments Clause challenges, and forestall litigation in which such concerns have been or might be raised. This action will also give agencies greater ability and discretion to assess critical qualities in ALJ candidates, such as work ethic, judgment, and ability to meet the particular needs of the agency. These are all qualities individuals should have before wielding the significant authority conferred on ALJs, and each agency should be able to assess them without proceeding through complicated and elaborate examination processes or rating procedures that do not necessarily reflect the agency's particular needs. This change will also promote confidence in, and the durability of, agency adjudications.

Executive Order Excepting Administrative Law Judges from the Competitive Service, July 10, 2018. The Order goes on to provide:

To the extent permitted by law and the provisions of this part, and subject to the suitability and fitness requirements of the applicable Civil Service Rules and Regulations, appointments and position changes in the excepted service shall be made in accordance with such regulations and practices as the head of the agency concerned finds necessary. These shall include, for the position of administrative law judge appointed under 5 U.S.C. 3105, the requirement that, at the time of application and any new appointment, the individual, other than an incumbent administrative law judge, must possess a professional license to practice law * * *. This requirement shall constitute a minimum standard for appointment to the position of administrative law judge, and such appointments may be subject to additional agency requirements where appropriate

Id. § 3(ii) (amending 5 C.F.R. 6.3(b)). The effect of this order is to give the agencies more flexibility in who they choose as ALJs. Is this likely to make ALJs more attuned to their agency's policy priorities? Given the function of ALJs, is that good, bad, or indifferent? Would you want to participate in an adjudication in which the presiding judge was hand-picked by the opposing party?

Another important line drawn by the Administrative Procedure Act provides some insulation between agency prosecutors and agency adjudicators. When an ALJ presides over a hearing, the ALJ may not "be responsible to or subject to the supervision or direction of an employee or agent engaged in the performance of investigative or prosecuting functions for an agency." 5 U.S.C. § 554(d) (2012). Furthermore, "An employee or agent engaged in the performance of investigative or prosecuting functions for an agency in a case may not, in that or a factually related case, participate or advise in the decision * * * except as witness or counsel in public proceedings." *Id.* Thus, the agency as an entity is permitted to combine prosecutorial and adjudicative functions, but different personnel in the agency generally must perform those functions. This is known as the *separation of functions*. It is a statutory effort to build into the administrative process some of the safeguards that are automatically provided by the largely-defunct traditional separation of powers doctrine.

There is a gaping hole in the separation provided by the separation of functions doctrine. Formal, trial-like agency proceedings must be conducted either by an ALJ or by "the agency * * * [or] one or more members of the body which comprises the agency." *Id.* § 556(b). Thus, a formal adjudication—to determine, for example, whether conduct constitutes an unfair trade practice in violation of a Federal Trade Commission rule—can be conducted *either* by a semi-autonomous ALJ *or* by some or all of the Commissioners. If one or more of the Commissioners presides over the hearing, the separation of functions provisions of the APA do not apply. *See id.* § 554(d). Agency heads thus may personally investigate, prosecute, and adjudicate the same case.

2. THE PROBLEM OF BIAS

In addition to their prosecutorial and adjudicatory powers, agency heads also promulgate rules and formulate policy. *Withrow* makes it clear that the combination of functions does not by itself constitute grounds for finding impermissible bias in agency adjudication. Other cases make clear that improper bias will only be found in adjudicatory settings when there is very strong evidence that an agency adjudicator has prejudged both the facts and the law of a particular case. As a modern case put it,

> We review an agency member's decision not to recuse himself from a proceeding under a deferential, abuse of discretion standard. In an adjudicatory proceeding, recusal is required only where "a disinterested observer may conclude that [the decisionmaker] has in some measure adjudged the facts as well as the law of a particular case in advance of hearing it." *Cinderella Career and Finishing Schools, Inc.*, 425 F.2d [583, 591 (D.C.Cir.1970)]. In other words, we will set aside a commission member's decision not to recuse himself from his duties only where he has "demonstrably made up [his] mind about important and specific factual questions and [is] impervious to contrary

evidence." *United Steelworkers of America v. Marshall*, 647 F.2d 1189, 1209 (D.C.Cir.1980).

Metropolitan Council of NAACP Branches v. FCC, 46 F.3d 1154, 1164–65 (D.C.Cir.1995). The standard is difficult, but not impossible, to meet. On several occasions, the public statements of a member of the Federal Trade Commission convinced a federal court that he had prejudged the guilt of specific defendants. *See Cinderella Career and Finishing Schools v. FTC*, 425 F.2d 583 (D.C.Cir.1970) (concluding that public statements by Commissioner Paul Rand Dixon concerning a specific case required his recusal); *Texaco, Inc. v. FTC*, 336 F.2d 754 (D.C.Cir.1964), *vac. on other grounds*, 381 U.S. 739, 85 S.Ct. 1798, 14 L.Ed.2d 714 (1965) (same). A commissioner of the Consumer Products Safety Commission was found to have unalterably prejudged whether notices and limitations on marketing could adequately reduce risks from swallowing small magnets when he said, prior to any adjudication: "the conclusion that I reach is that if these magnet sets remain on the market irrespective of how strong the warnings on the boxes in which they're sold or how narrowly they are marketed to adults, children will continue to be at risk of debilitating harm or death from this product." *See Zen Magnets, LLC v. CPSC*, 2018 WL 2938326, at *13 (D.Colo.2018) ("I find that Commissioner Adler's statement during the Meeting on the Final Rule demonstrated an irrevocably closed mind, or at the very least a reasonable appearance that he had prejudged the key questions of fact and law at issue in the adjudication."). On the other hand, a court refused to hold that a member of the Nuclear Regulatory Commission should have been disqualified for bias even though he had described the petitioner Nuclear Information and Resource Service as the "Nuclear Disinformation Resource Service," had accused the group of using "factoids or made-up facts or irrelevant facts," and described one of the group's witnesses as a "person who doesn't know anything about radiation." *Nuclear Information and Resource Service v. NRC*, 509 F.3d 562, 571 (D.C.Cir.2007). The court explained:

> Given the roles that agency officials must play in the give-and-take of sometimes rough-and-tumble policy debates, courts must tread lightly when presented with this kind of challenge. Administrative officers are presumed objective * * *. A party cannot overcome this presumption with a mere showing that an official "has taken a public position, or had expressed strong views, or holds an underlying philosophy with respect to an issue in dispute." *United Steelworkers of Am. v. Marshall*, 647 F.2d 1189, 1208 (D.C.Cir.1980) * * *.

> Here, as the Commissioner noted, his "personal style" was to "speak vigorously, sometimes colorfully," to "spark debate." Decision on Motion at 3, J.A. ["Joint Appendix"] 1311. Such comments, particularly when made in an entirely separate

proceeding, do not support the conclusion that Commissioner McGaffigan had "adjudged the facts as well as the law" regarding the particular license application at issue here. Commissioner McGaffigan did not abuse his discretion in denying petitioners' motion [for disqualification].

509 F.3d at 571.

What about an agency engaged in rulemaking? We do not require elected legislators to maintain open minds about policy matters; indeed, closed-mindedness, sometimes called consistency and adherence to principle, is often seen as a virtue in a lawmaker. Nonetheless, courts hold agencies to a minimal level of open-mindedness in rulemaking, though a level considerably lower than is required in adjudication. *See Association of Nat'l Advertisers, Inc. v. FTC,* 627 F.2d 1151, 1170 (D.C.Cir.1979) (holding that recusal is required in a rulemaking "only when there has been a clear and convincing showing that the Department member has an unalterably closed mind on matters critical to the disposition of the proceeding," and finding, by a 2–1 vote, that the recusal standard was not met in a case involving the regulation of cereal advertising on children's television programs by a letter from FTC Commissioner Michael Pertschuk to the head of the Food and Drug Administration declaring that "one of the evils flowing from the unfairness of children's advertising is the resulting distortion of children's perception of nutritional values" and concluding that "[c]hildren's advertising is inherently unfair").

CHAPTER 3

STATUTORY CONSTRAINTS ON AGENCY PROCEDURE

■ ■ ■

A. INTRODUCTION: THE ADMINISTRATIVE PROCEDURE ACT

Modern constitutional law places few substantive constraints on the scope of power that can be exercised by federal administrative agencies. Today's Congress has a very broad (if not quite unlimited) legislative jurisdiction and a very broad (if not quite unlimited) power to transfer that jurisdiction to agencies.

This does not mean that agencies operate free of legal constraints. Far from it; agency action is constrained to some extent by a wide range of legal forces that regulates both the substance of the agencies' decisions and the procedures employed in reaching those decisions. Chapter 4 explores legal constraints on the substantive decisions that agencies can reach; this chapter and Chapter 5 concentrate on the procedures that agencies must follow in order to generate binding rules or orders. You will quickly find that this distinction between substance and procedure is hard to maintain: the procedural constraints on agencies cannot fully be understood without reference to the substantive constraints and vice versa. Modern administrative law, however, largely speaks the language of procedure, so that is where we begin.

One might guess that a statute called the Administrative Procedure Act[1] would be a good place to start a search for legal limits on administrative agency procedures. And the APA is indeed one source of procedural (and, for that matter, substantive) constraints on agencies. But it is only one source. The federal Constitution, organic statutes, agency regulations, agency practice, court decisions, and, at least from an agency's perspective, presidential directives[2] are all potential sources of procedural law. Indeed, as we shall see, the APA's procedural requirements generally

---

[1] The text of the statute is found in Appendix B.

[2] Most presidential directives to agencies are, by presidential design, unenforceable in court against agencies by private parties. They are "enforced" by the President and his or her staff through political pressure and, where necessary and possible, removal of recalcitrant agency officials.

cannot be understood without reference to some of these other sources of law.

The APA is nonetheless a good starting point and focus for an inquiry into the procedural law of the modern administrative state. To conduct that inquiry, one must have some sense of the history and structure of the statute.[3]

1. ORIGINS OF THE APA

The APA was enacted in 1946. Obviously, there was a considerable body of administrative law, including procedural law, for the century and a half prior to the APA's enactment. *See* Jerry L. Mashaw, Creating the Administrative Constitution: The Lost One Hundred Years of American Administrative Law (2012); Joseph Postell, Bureaucracy in America: The Administrative's State Challenge to Constitutional Government 73–206 (2017). Indeed, much of the APA was a codification of pre-existing law that was embedded in organic statutes and court decisions. But the APA was the first statute to systematize administrative law on a government-wide basis. The timing of its enactment was not accidental; only after the enormous proliferation of administrative governance under the New Deal was there a strongly felt need for systematic controls on agency behavior. For most of the nation's history up to that point, constitutional law and political reality combined to limit the scope of federal agency activity. The New Deal, however, heralded an expanded conception of federal agency involvement in people's lives, coupled with an across-the-board retreat from constitutional doctrines of federalism and separation of powers that had foreclosed the emergence of an activist administrative state. Hence, administrative law gained significantly in importance during the mid-1930s.

The APA was the culmination of more than a decade of strong, often partisan, debate over the emerging administrative state.[4] For a time, opponents of the New Deal could rely on the Supreme Court to place constitutional limits on the scope of agency authority. When that avenue was closed off in 1937 by the Supreme Court's large-scale retreat from policing the structural boundaries of congressional power, *see, e.g.*, *NLRB v. Jones & Laughlin Steel Corp.*, 301 U.S. 1, 57 S.Ct. 615, 81 L.Ed. 893 (1937) (upholding the National Labor Relations Act against challenges that it exceeds Congress' enumerated powers and violates the right to jury trial). the debate was channeled wholly into the legislative arena. New Deal opponents did not have the political strength to abolish or amend the

---

[3]   For a comprehensive history of the APA, which the following discussion draws upon, see George B. Shepherd, *Fierce Compromise: The Administrative Procedure Act Emerges from New Deal Politics*, 90 Nw. U.L. Rev. 1557 (1996).

[4]   *See* Joanna L. Grisinger, The Unwieldy American State: Administrative Politics Since the New Deal 59–82 (2012).

organic statutes of their disfavored agencies. Accordingly, they concentrated on procedural reform, which could draw on a broader constituency that included persons who supported the New Deal's substantive goals but harbored doubts about the methods by which at least some administrative agencies effected those goals.[5] Many proposals for statutory reform of agency practices were offered during the 1930s; these ranged from mild proposals for special administrative courts to substantial proposals to provide for heightened judicial scrutiny of agency action and to require agencies to use elaborate adjudicative procedures. The hope of New Deal opponents (and the fear of the New Deal supporters who opposed these reforms) was that elaborate procedural requirements would at least slow down agency activity, if not halt it altogether.

In 1940, Congress passed the Walter-Logan bill, which would have imposed substantial procedural requirements on many of the most important federal agencies. President Roosevelt vetoed the bill, on the stated ground that extensive reforms should await completion of a study of the federal administrative process being conducted by the Attorney General (the study was completed in 1941). Congress failed to override the veto.

Administrative reform then took a back seat to World War II until 1946, when the APA passed by a unanimous voice-vote of both houses of Congress and was signed by President Truman. This unanimity, however, probably reflected less a widespread sense of satisfaction about the legislation than a sense on the part of strong, partisan factions that the relevant political forces had come to equilibrium. The statute was, as Professor George Shepherd terms it, a "fierce compromise."

That "fierce compromise" has survived to this day with very few substantive amendments: the text of the APA today is largely the text of the APA as it was enacted in 1946. As you will see, however, the APA's text sometimes does and sometimes does not play much of a role in the modern world. In many important respects, agency and judicial application of the APA bears no real relationship to the statute that was enacted in 1946. Nonetheless, one must have a good grasp of the 1946 statute in order to understand the nature of, and reasons for, modern departures from it as well as to understand the respects in which the original statute still governs administrative behavior.

2. THE STRUCTURE OF THE APA

The APA's provisions cover four main subjects. One set of provisions, which has been amended substantially over the past half-century, concerns

---

[5] The National Labor Relations Board was especially notorious for its blatant bias in the administration of New Deal labor legislation. *See* Grisinger, *supra* note 4, at 23–26. The Securities and Exchange Commission was also a favorite target. *See* Shepherd, *supra* note 3, at 1606–08.

[Handwritten margin notes, left side:]

APA covers 4 main subjects:

① agency disclosure of info

② availability, timing, + form of judicial review

③ scope of judicial review

④ procedural reqmts for making decisions

APA's 2 fundamtl distinctions:
① rulemaking v. adjudication
② formal v. informal procedural modes

---

①agency disclosure of information. *See* 5 U.S.C. §§ 552–552b (2012). This is an enormously important topic that is omitted from this book, with great reluctance, for lack of space. ②Another set of provisions governs the availability, timing, and form of judicial review of agency action. *See id.* §§ 701–05. Those provisions are studied in Chapter 6, *infra* ③Another provision concerns the scope of judicial review of agency decisions, *see id.* § 706; that provision is covered in Chapter 4, *infra* ④Finally, a large set of provisions regulates the procedures that agencies must employ when making decisions. Those provisions are among the subjects of this chapter.

The APA's procedural framework relies on two fundamental distinctions concerning agency action. First, it distinguishes rulemaking from adjudication. That distinction was presented in Chapter 1, *see supra* pages 52–76, and you should at this point review those materials, especially the APA's definitions of rulemaking and adjudication. Second, the APA distinguishes between what have come to be called *formal* and *informal* procedural modes, though the APA itself does not use the words "formal" or "informal." Sections 556 and 557 of the APA[6] spell out a set of highly formal procedures for rulemaking and adjudication that bear a strong resemblance to a full-dress judicial trial. (Section 554 specifies some additional procedures that apply only to adjudications.) These provisions prescribe in considerable detail a process of settlement negotiations, formal presentation of evidence, and agency decision, presided over by an administrative law judge (or, in rare cases, an agency head) who directs the proceedings and issues an initial decision. Agency proceedings conducted in accordance with these elaborate hearing procedures are called *formal rulemakings*[7] or *formal adjudications*. Such proceedings are also sometimes called *trial-type proceedings* to reflect their court-like character or *on-the-record proceedings* to reflect § 556(e)'s requirement that agency decisions in such proceedings be based solely (subject to limited exceptions for facts subject to official notice) on the material actually presented during the stylized, trial-type hearing.

Formal agency proceedings under the APA differ from judicial trials in a number of ways. Most obviously, there is no jury or Article III judge in the agency proceeding. In addition, the rules of evidence that play such an important role in court proceedings do not necessarily apply in agency

[Handwritten margin notes, bottom left:]

Formal agency proceedings

· no jury
· no Art III judge
· rules of evid. don't necess. apply
· more freedom to restrict to written materials

---

[6] It is conventional to refer to the APA's provisions by their codification in Title 5 of the United States Code (as in "section 556 of the APA" or "section 702 of the APA") rather than by the section numbers in the enacted bill. Technically, of course, this is wrong: one should refer to "section 553 of Title 5, which is section 4 of the APA". On rare occasions, you will see cases refer to the section numbers in the original legislation. But most sources today, including this casebook, use the U.S. Code section numbers.

[7] Be aware that courts are not always careful in their use of this terminology. Oftentimes, courts will use the term "formal rulemaking" to describe any agency rulemaking that results in legally binding norms, without regard to the procedures required for those rulemakings. *See, e.g.,* Gray v. Sec. of Veterans Affairs, 875 F.3d 1102, 1109 (Fed.Cir.2017); CFTC v. McDonnell, 387 F.Supp.3d 213, 224 (E.D.N.Y.2018).

hearings. The APA declares simply that "[a]ny oral or documentary evidence may be received, but the agency as a matter of policy shall provide for the exclusion of irrelevant, immaterial, or unduly repetitious evidence." § 556(d). This is a very generous rule of admissibility. Hearsay evidence, for example, is freely admissible in agency proceedings under this standard, though agencies may choose to adopt rules of evidence that more closely track the familiar judicial models,[8] and Congress may on occasion prescribe more rigid rules of evidence for specific agencies.[9] Moreover, although oral presentations and cross-examination are ordinarily a part of formal agency proceedings, *see id.* ("A party is entitled to present his case or defense by oral or documentary evidence, to submit rebuttal evidence, and to conduct such cross-examination as may be required for a full and true disclosure of the facts"), agencies have more freedom than do courts to restrict the record to written materials, at least in limited circumstances. *See id.* ("In rule making or determining claims for money or benefits or applications for initial licenses an agency may, when a party will not be prejudiced thereby, adopt procedures for the submission of all or part of the evidence in written form.").

Despite these differences between formal agency hearings and judicial trials, the APA's package of formal procedures is quite impressive. It looks even more impressive when placed alongside the APA's informal procedural prescriptions for rulemaking and adjudication.

When agencies seek to adopt legislative rules through informal rulemaking,[10] § 553 of the APA prescribes a fairly minimal set of procedures. First, the agency must give notice of its intention to consider adopting a rule. According to the statute, the notice can contain "*either* the terms or substance of the proposed rule *or* a description of the subjects and issues involved." § 553(b) (emphasis added).[11] Under the text of the second clause, it is sufficient notice for the agency merely to describe a problem that it is investigating. The text of the APA does not require the agency to enter a rulemaking proceeding with a specific rule in mind. Second, after providing the required notice, the agency "shall give interested persons an

---

[8] *See* Michael H. Graham, *Application of the Rules of Evidence in Administrative Agency Formal Adversarial Adjudications: A New Approach*, 1991 U. Ill. L. Rev. 353, 368–69, 372.

[9] The leading example is Congress's requirement that unfair labor proceedings adjudicated by the National Labor Relations Board "shall, so far as practicable, be conducted in accordance with the rules of evidence applicable in the district courts * * *." 29 U.S.C. § 160(b) (2012).

[10] In general, the APA's procedural requirements for rulemaking apply only to legislative rules—that is, rules that govern the rights and responsibilities of persons subject to the agency's jurisdiction. Agencies adopt many rules that are not legislative. The variety of such rules, and how to distinguish them from legislative rules, are discussed *infra*, pages 434–484.

[11] The notice must also contain "a statement of the time, place, and nature of public rule making proceedings." *Id.* This is not a requirement that public proceedings, in the sense of actual hearings open to the public, in fact be held, but merely a requirement that any hearings actually held be disclosed. As we shall see, informal rulemakings do not require, and generally do not employ, such public proceedings. The notice must also contain "a reference to the legal authority under which the rule is proposed * * *." *Id.*

opportunity to participate in the rule making through submission of written data, views, or arguments *with or without opportunity for oral presentation.*" *Id.* § 553(c) (emphasis added). The public, in other words, has a right to comment on the agency's proposal, but the agency determines the form in which those comments are presented. Nothing in the text of § 553 requires those comments to be made available to the public during the rulemaking proceeding.[12] Third, "[a]fter consideration of the relevant matter presented, the agency shall incorporate in the rules adopted a concise general statement of their basis and purpose." *Id.* That is the full measure of the procedures required by the text of the APA for informal rulemaking. Importantly, because § 556(e)'s "on the record" requirement does not apply to informal rulemakings, rules that emerge from informal rulemakings do not need to be based solely on material presented during the rulemaking proceeding.

Because informal rulemaking procedures require the agency only to provide the public with notice and a right to comment (and to offer a brief explanation of any rule that is finally adopted), such proceedings are often called *notice-and-comment rulemakings.* Obviously, the procedural difference between formal and informal rulemaking under the text of the APA is substantial.[13]

The difference between formal and informal adjudication is even more substantial. The APA provides no specific procedures that must be employed in informal adjudication—not even the minimal notice-and-comment requirements applicable to informal rulemaking. Section 555 contains some general requirements governing party participation and agency collection of information that might be relevant to adjudication, and § 555(e) requires prompt notice of any denial of a written application made to an agency in connection with an agency proceeding, but those are literally the only procedural requirements that the text of the APA imposes on informal agency adjudications.

The APA of 1946 thus sets up a feast-or-famine procedural dichotomy. In formal rulemakings or adjudications, agencies must provide elaborate, trial-type hearings before adopting legally binding rules or orders and must justify those rules or orders solely on the basis of the material presented in the formal proceedings. In informal rulemakings, agencies need only provide minimal notice and a right to file written comments on the agency's proposals. In informal adjudications, the APA requires virtually no procedures at all.

---

[12] Section 552 of the APA—the so-called Freedom of Information Act—does provide a vehicle for compelling agency disclosure of such comments, but given the reality of litigation under the Freedom of Information Act, there is no assurance that disclosure will take place before the rulemaking process is completed.

[13] As we shall see later in this chapter, modern developments have made the difference far less substantial than the text of the APA suggests.

This look at the text of the APA provides a radically incomplete story. Modern developments have rendered the APA's provisions for informal procedures unrecognizable to their 1946 drafters. Much of this chapter—and subsequent chapters—traces those developments and their profound effect on informal agency proceedings. Moreover, the APA is not the only relevant source of procedural law. As this chapter will demonstrate, organic statutes and agency regulations, for example, can require procedures in informal proceedings even when the APA does not. And as Chapter 5 will illustrate, the Constitution often requires procedures in informal adjudications.

developments to informal procedures

— pay attn to additional sources of procedural law!

Nonetheless, the distinction between formal and informal agency proceedings remains one of the most important distinctions in administrative law. Very large consequences, for the agencies and for the parties appearing before them, can turn on whether an agency is required to use formal or informal procedures under the APA. So how does one determine which procedural mode an agency must employ in any given case?

For rulemaking, agencies must employ the formal procedures of §§ 556–57, rather than the informal notice-and-comment procedures of § 553, "[w]hen rules are required by statute to be made on the record after opportunity for an agency hearing * * *." *Id.* § 553(c). For adjudication, agencies must employ the formal procedures of §§ 556–57, along with a few other procedures required by § 554, "in every case of adjudication required by statute to be determined on the record after opportunity for an agency hearing." *Id.* § 554(a). Thus, the APA uses essentially the same language in both rulemakings and adjudications to trigger the use of formal procedures: whether proceedings are "required by statute to be [made/determined] on the record after opportunity for an agency hearing." Two questions immediately suggest themselves about that language.

When must formal v. informal proceedings be used?

First, where does one look to see if there is a "statute" that requires a particular agency proceeding to be made "on the record after opportunity for an agency hearing"? This question, at least, has a clear answer: one looks at the organic statutes that empower and limit the agency in question. The APA specifies the package of procedures that apply to formal proceedings, but it leaves matters up to Congress on a case-by-case basis to trigger application of that procedural package by appropriate language in the organic statutes of each agency. Thus, one cannot determine whether the APA's formal procedures apply in a given case by consulting the APA alone. One must read the APA in conjunction with the relevant agency's organic statutes to see whether any of those organic statutes, in the case at hand, require a determination to be made "on the record after opportunity for an agency hearing."

look to reQmt of "organic statute"

What statutory lang. triggers formal APA procedures?

Second, what does an organic statute have to say in order to trigger formal APA procedures? This question, alas, does not have such an easy answer, as the following materials demonstrate. In particular, one might assume that because the APA's rulemaking and adjudication provisions use exactly the same language to describe the applicability of formal procedures, the same legal standard always governs the triggering of such procedures. Be prepared to test that assumption.

B. FORMAL RULEMAKING

1. THE ORIGINAL UNDERSTANDING

Shortly after enactment of the APA in 1946, the Department of Justice prepared a manual instructing its attorneys on the implementation and interpretation of the new statute. The Supreme Court has often used this manual as a guide to interpreting the APA.[14] The manual had the following to say about the circumstances under which organic statutes trigger formal rulemaking:

> Statutes rarely require hearings prior to the issuance of rules of general applicability * * *. The Federal Food, Drug and Cosmetic Act 21 U.S.C. § 801) is almost unique in that it specifically provides that agency action issuing, amending, or repealing specified classes of substantive rules may be taken only after notice and hearing, and that "The Administrator shall base his order only on substantial evidence of record at the hearing and shall set forth as part of his order detailed findings of fact on which the order is based." Upon review in a circuit court of appeals, a transcript of the record is filed * * *. It is clear that such rules are "required by statute to be made on the record after opportunity for an agency hearing" * * *.
>
> Statutes authorizing agencies to prescribe future rates (i.e., rules of either general or particular applicability) for public utilities and common carriers typically require that such rates be established only after an opportunity for a hearing before the agency. Such statutes rarely specify in terms that the agency action must be taken on the basis of the "record" developed in the hearing. However, where rates or prices are established by an agency after a hearing required by statute, the agencies

---

[14] *See, e.g.,* Shinseki v. Sanders, 556 U.S. 396, 406, 129 S.Ct. 1696, 1704, 173 L.Ed.2d 532 (2009); Norton v. Southern Utah Wilderness Alliance, 542 U.S. 55, 63–64, 124 S.Ct. 2373, 2379, 159 L.Ed.2d 137 (2004); Director, Office of Workers' Compensation Programs, Dep't of Labor v. Newport News Shipbuilding & Dry Dock Co., 514 U.S. 122, 126–27, 115 S.Ct. 1278, 1283, 131 L.Ed.2d 160 (1995); Steadman v. SEC, 450 U.S. 91, 103 n.22, 101 S.Ct. 999, 1009 n.22, 67 L.Ed.2d 69 (1981); Chrysler Corp. v. Brown, 441 U.S. 281, 302 n.31, 99 S.Ct. 1705, 1718 n.31, 60 L.Ed.2d 208 (1979); Vermont Yankee Nuclear Power Corp. v. NRDC, Inc., 435 U.S. 519, 546, 98 S.Ct. 1197, 1213, 55 L.Ed.2d 460 (1978).

themselves and the courts have long assumed that the agency's action must be based upon the evidence adduced at the hearing * * *.

The Interstate Commerce Commission and the Secretary of Agriculture may, after hearing, prescribe rates for carriers and stockyard agencies, respectively * * *. Nothing in the Interstate Commerce Act * * * requires in terms that such rate orders be "made on the record" * * *. However, * * * the courts have long assumed that such rate orders must be based upon the record made in the hearing * * *.

With respect to the types of rule making discussed above, the statutes not only specifically require the agencies to hold hearings but also, specifically, or by clear implication, or by established administrative and judicial construction, require such rules to be formulated upon the basis of the evidentiary record made in the hearing. In these situations, the public rule making procedures required by section 4(b) [§ 553(b)] will consist of a hearing conducted in accordance with sections 7 and 8 [§§ 556–57].

There are other statutes which require agencies to hold hearings before issuing rules, but contain no language from which the further requirement of decision "on the record" can be inferred * * *. In this type of statute, there is no requirement, express or implied, that rules be formulated "on the record."

United States Department of Justice, Attorney General's Manual on the Administrative Procedure Act 32–34 (1947).

2. THE FLORIDA EAST COAST RAILWAY SAGA

Every administrative law case involves, at least indirectly, an organic statute that confers power on the agency in question and directs and limits the exercise of that power. An understanding of the organic statute is often essential to an understanding of the case. You should therefore get into the habit of identifying the relevant organic statute in each case and reading it *carefully*.

For the present story, the relevant statute was § 1(14)(a) of the Interstate Commerce Act, 24 Stat. 379, popularly known as the Esch Car Service Act of 1917. The statute was administered by the now-defunct Interstate Commerce Commission ("ICC" or "Commission"), which was abolished in 1995, 109 Stat. 932, though many of the ICC's functions continue under the administration of other agencies. At all times relevant to our story, the Esch Car Service Act read:

The Commission may, after hearing, on a complaint or upon its own initiative without complaint, establish reasonable rules, regulations, and practices with respect to car service by common carriers by railroad subject to this chapter, including the compensation to be paid and other terms of any contract, agreement, or arrangement for the use of any locomotive, car, or other vehicle not owned by the carrier using it (and whether or not owned by another carrier), and the penalties or other sanctions for nonobservance of such rules, regulations, or practices. In fixing such compensation to be paid for the use of any type of freight car, the Commission shall give consideration to the national level of ownership of such type of freight car and to other factors affecting the adequacy of the national freight car supply, and shall, on the basis of such consideration, determine whether compensation should be computed solely on the basis of elements of ownership expense involved in owning and maintaining such type of freight car, including a fair return on value, or whether such compensation should be increased by such incentive element or elements of compensation as in the Commission's judgment will provide just and reasonable compensation to freight car owners, contribute to sound car service practices (including efficient utilization and distribution of cars) and encourage the acquisition and maintenance of a car supply adequate to meet the needs of commerce and the national defense. The Commission shall not make any incentive element applicable to any type of freight car the supply of which the Commission finds to be adequate and may exempt from the compensation to be paid by any group of carriers such incentive element or elements if the Commission finds it to be in the national interest.

49 U.S.C. § 1(14)(a) (1976). (The statute has evolved into 49 U.S.C. § 11122 (2012), which is substantively similar to the version quoted above and is now administered by the Surface Transportation Board.) The statute consists of three sentences. The first sentence—which from 1917 to 1966 was the only sentence—authorizes the ICC to "establish reasonable rules, regulations, and practices with respect to car service by common carriers by railroad," including specifically the power to regulate the terms by which railroads borrow rail cars from each other and "the compensation to be paid" under car-hire rental contracts. It is a common practice in the railroad industry to rent cars from competing railroads when that is the quickest way of getting a shipment delivered. In the absence of such a practice, each railroad would have to maintain a much larger fleet of cars and thus incur much larger capital and maintenance expenses. When the ICC set car-hire rates under this statute, it was obviously engaged in *ratemaking*, which the APA specifically defines in §§ 551(4)–(5) to be rulemaking. Accordingly, any rate-setting activity by the ICC that occurred after enactment of the APA in 1946 was necessarily classified as rulemaking for purposes of the APA.

The first sentence of the statute also sets forth some procedural requirements for the Commission's rulemaking activity: the Commission is empowered to promulgate rules "after hearing." There is no further explanation in the organic statute about the form that such a hearing must take, nor is there any explicit reference to a hearing taking place "on the record."

The second sentence of the statute was added in 1966. When the statute was originally enacted in 1917, it was understood to constrain quite severely the ICC's power to set car hire rates. Specifically, the ICC was permitted to consider *only* whether the rates that it set or approved gave the renting carrier a fair return on its investment in the rented rail cars. No, the statute does not say that expressly; it speaks only of "reasonable" rules, regulations, and practices. The statute, however, was enacted against a long history of rate regulation, which made clear that rate-setting agencies were supposed to ensure a fair return on investment and nothing more (or less). In 1917, when the Esch Car Service Act was enacted, everyone, including Congress, knew that "reasonable" compensation for car rentals was fair-return compensation. Thus, prior to 1966, the Commission did not have the statutory power to require rail carriers to pay more than a "fair return on investment" price for car rentals.

Members of Congress in some of the farming states, however, frequently heard complaints from their constituents about regional and seasonal shortages of rail cars. These shortages were often blamed on the widespread car-rental practice, which encouraged railroads to skimp on new car purchases by hoping to meet enhanced seasonal needs through renting cars from other carriers. Congress thus amended the statute in 1966 to *compel* the ICC to consider ("the Commission shall give consideration to") criteria other than fair return when setting car-hire rates, including "whether such compensation should be increased by such incentive element or elements of compensation as in the Commission's judgment will provide just and reasonable compensation to freight car owners * * *." In other words, the ICC was ordered in 1966 to think long and hard about setting car hire rates high enough to encourage railroads to buy more cars, or at least to return borrowed cars more quickly so that they could carry more traffic.

The third sentence of the statute, which was also added in 1966, simply lets the Commission exempt certain classes of cars (for example, specialized refrigerated cars that not every railroad would sensibly own in abundance) from any increased rental rates that it comes up with. The 1966 amendments did not alter the first sentence of the Esch Car Service Act in any manner.

After the 1966 amendment ordered the Commission to think about incentive elements in car hire rates, the ICC on July 6, 1966 announced an investigation into car hire practices. Here is the document announcing that investigation:

INTERSTATE COMMERCE COMMISSION EX PARTE NO. 252
USE OF FREIGHT CARS: INCENTIVE PER DIEM CHARGES
31 Fed. Reg. 9240 (1966).

* * *

Section 1(14)(a) of the Interstate Commerce Act, as amended by Public Law 89–430, effective May 26, 1966, requires the Commission, after consideration of the national level of ownership of each type of freight car and other factors affecting the adequacy of the national freight car supply, to determine whether the compensation for the use of such cars should be increased by incentive elements which will provide just and reasonable compensation to car owners, contribute to sound car service practices (including efficient utilization and distribution of cars), and encourage the acquisition and maintenance of a car supply adequate to meet the needs of commerce and national defense.

The legislative history of this public law, as well as the Commission's experience with the existing car shortage problem indicates that the need for expedition is imperative. Therefore, the Commission proposes to consider, under the schedule shown below, whether an incentive per diem charge of either $2.50 or some other amount should be prescribed on an interim experimental basis. Thereafter, the Commission will conduct a further investigation for the purpose of prescribing an incentive per diem rate or rates on a continuing basis as needed * * *.

It is ordered, That an investigation be, and it is hereby, instituted by the Commission, upon its own motion, for the purpose of determining whether the establishment, on an interim basis, of an incentive per diem rate of either $2.50 per day or some other amount, to be added to the regular rate of per diem and to be paid to the car owner for the use of certain types of cars during periods of car shortages, will promote greater efficiency in the use of and increase the national freight car supply.

It is further ordered, That all common carriers by railroad subject to the Interstate Commerce Act be, and they are hereby, made respondents to this proceeding.

It is further ordered, That all respondents shall, on or before October 1, 1966, file and serve verified representations (original and 20 copies should be filed), including their recommendations on the tentative proposal indicated above, any additional facts or formula that the Commission should consider in rendering its decision herein, or in any later proceeding, and the most effective and appropriate method by which incentive elements may be employed to accomplish the stated purposes of section 1(14)(a), as amended, with the reasons therefor.

The representations should include, but not be limited to, the following subjects:

* * *

* * * [The order asked for views on twelve specific questions concerning the implementation of an incentive per diem charge for the use by rail carriers of the railroad cars of other carriers.]

It is further ordered, That this proceeding be, and it is hereby, assigned for prehearing conference and hearing on November 1, 1966, at 10 a.m., U.S. standard time, at the offices of the Interstate Commerce Commission, Washington, D.C. Should any party desire to cross-examine on any matter contained in any of the above specified representations, he must so notify the Commission and the witness or his counsel not later than October 20, 1966.

It is further ordered, That this proceeding be, and it is hereby, referred to Hearing Examiner R.C. Bamford for the prehearing conference and hearing. Due and timely execution of our functions imperatively and unavoidably require the omission of a recommended report. The initial decision shall be by the entire Commission.

NOTES

The foregoing document is a Notice of Proposed Rulemaking ("NPR") under § 553 of the APA. In its Notice, the Commission did not propose a specific rate (rule) for car hires. Rather, it simply indicated that it was commencing a proceeding in order to consider whether to adopt a per diem incentive charge "of either $2.50 or some other amount." Observe that at the very end of the NPR, the matter is assigned for hearing before a hearing examiner (who today would be called an administrative law judge), and the parties are instructed to notify the ICC about their intentions to "cross-examine on any matter contained in any of the above specified representations." The Commission itself was to make the initial decision. These procedures are all features of *formal rulemaking* under §§ 556–57. In 1966, the ICC clearly thought that it was engaging in a formal rulemaking proceeding.

The proceeding eventually concluded in October 1967, with the ICC complaining of insufficient data and doing nothing. This was not unusual; agencies often commence rulemaking proceedings and then determine not to adopt any rules as a result of those proceedings. In this case, however, the agency did not drop the matter altogether but instead soon commenced another rulemaking proceeding. On December 29, 1967, the ICC published another NPR:

INTERSTATE COMMERCE COMMISSION EX PARTE NO. 252 SUB 1 INCENTIVE PER DIEM CHARGES FOR 1968 NOTICE OF PROPOSED RULE MAKING

32 Fed. Reg. 20987 (1967).

* * *

Public Law 89–430, effective May 26, 1966, amended section 1(14)(a) of the Interstate Commerce Act, so as to require this Commission to determine the adequacy and requirements of the national freight car supply and to impose incentive elements of per diem charges upon the users of such cars if found to be necessary, subject to specified limitations. The investigation in Docket Ex Parte No. 252, Incentive Per Diem Charges, 332 I.C.C. 11, demonstrated the inadequacy of information now available to make the determinations required by the aforesaid statute, as amended. Whether a need exists for enforcement of the incentive element authority, and the manner and amount thereof, require further proceedings and the accumulation of reliable current data on a continuing basis. Therefore:

It is ordered, That under authority of Part I of the Interstate Commerce Act 49 U.S.C. 1, et seq.) more particularly section 1(14)(a) and the Administrative Procedure Act (5 U.S.C. 553, 556, and 557), a proceeding be, and it is hereby, instituted for the purpose of implementing those provisions of the law relating to our authority to encourage the acquisition and maintenance of an adequate car supply as specified in Public Law 89–430.

It is further ordered, That all common carriers by railroad subject to the Interstate Commerce Act be, and they are hereby, made respondents to this proceeding.

* * *

It is further ordered, That this proceeding be, and it is hereby, assigned for hearing at the offices of the Interstate Commerce Commission, Washington, D.C., on a date hereafter to be fixed. Prehearing conference may be held upon notice by the Hearing Examiner. Upon timely requests, by shippers, associations, or other interested parties, consideration will be given to the setting of hearings at other places. Requests for leave to intervene may be made orally at the time of the hearing and should not be made prior thereto.

It is further ordered, That each carrier listed in the Appendix hereto, shall complete and file, in accordance with the accompanying instructions, the Data Sheet for Railroad Freight Car Study (both attached) and, until further ordered, shall maintain the underlying records. (A list of study dates, not necessarily the same dates, is being furnished each carrier named in the appendix. A list of stations at which the study is to be made is also furnished each Class I carrier shown in the appendix. Selected Class II carriers are required to make the study at all stations).

NOTES

Unlike the initial notice, this second NPR did not propose any specific rule—not even of the indefinite "$2.50 or something else" variety. The notice simply called for input into a study of car hire rates. As the agency explained: "Whether a need exists for enforcement of the incentive element authority, and the manner and amount thereof, require further proceedings and the accumulation of reliable current data on a continuing basis." The agency did not believe that it could formulate a proper proposed rule without first undertaking a rulemaking process to gather necessary information. Once again, the notice was couched in the language of *formal rulemaking*, complete with references to hearing examiners and public proceedings. Observe in particular that the NPR lists §§ 556–57 of the APA—the APA's formal procedural sections—among the legal authorities for the proceeding. The ICC clearly thought in late 1967, as it had in 1966, that the car hire proceedings had to take place with the full panoply of procedures specified by APA §§ 556–57.

During this second rulemaking, data was presented to the agency, a few informal information-gathering meetings were held, and matters generally proceeded apace. The railroads from the start expressed serious doubts about the Commission's methods of gathering and processing data. The ICC eventually prepared a study and sent it to Congress, but no specific incentive element was proposed. The rulemaking process yielded information but no rule.

On May 13, 1969, the ICC's chairperson and general counsel were hauled before the Senate Subcommittee on Surface Transportation of the Committee on Commerce, where they got roasted alive by farm state senators for having failed quickly to raise car hire rates:

Senator Hartke [of Indiana]: All right * * *. It is my understanding that the Commission and its legal authorities have taken the position that before any kind of basic action can be taken * * *, it must be shown that there is an actual shortage [of boxcars] which is determined in accordance with a hearing.

* * *

Mr. Ginnane [the ICC general counsel]: Yes; there must be a hearing. That is in the beginning of section 1(14)(4)[a] the Commission may, after hearing, on a complaint or upon its own initiative.

Senator Hartke: That is the Commission may, after hearing on a complaint, or upon its own initiative without complaint.

Mr. Ginnane: But in either event only after a hearing.

Senator Hartke: Why?

Mr. Ginnane: Because the Congress has so reported it in the opening clause of section 1(14). The Commission may after a hearing.

* * *

Senator Hartke: Do you have trouble having a hearing, I mean since 1966?

* * *

Mrs. Brown [the ICC chairperson]: Well, I can simply say, as you know, the study has been presented to you in the form that it is now and—

Senator Hartke: And it has one of those little hookers on the end of it that the railroads are now going to claim that they want an advisory commission that you are going to come in and recommend an advisory commission and we are going to have this S of S syndrome right back in our face again.

If you raise the basic per diem to $4.50 or $5, would not these cars find their way home very fast? Wagging their tail behind them?

Mrs. Brown: Well, that precisely, I don't know about the amount, but that precisely is the position that the Commission is trying to get itself in which our lawyers have told us there must be a hearing * * *.

The Chairman [Senator Magnuson of Washington]: Why do you say there must be a hearing? You have authority, unless I am wrong when I wrote the act, to act on your own initiative without a hearing. I mean it is advisable if you can have a hearing, I understand that, or am I wrong?

Mrs. Brown: Well, I am going to defer to my general counsel again because I am told that you have to have a hearing.

The Chairman: You can issue an emergency order at any time without a hearing. If the act doesn't allow that we are going to change it, I will tell you that. What is the use of having a hearing on these things? I just don't understand. I don't understand what you are doing here. What is this exhibit appendix D? Can anybody understand that?

If C is greater than 1.96, the chances are 95 out of 100 that the difference is significant. If C is greater than 2.58, the chances are 99 out of 100 that the difference is significant. The difference is ratio 1 minus ratio 2. Compute the standard area of the difference and when 2 over 1 is squared with the sampling error, the square of the sampling error is the second ratio and you compute the difference between C and D.

Now, what has that to do with boxcar service?

Mrs. Brown: I am doing to defer this question to Mr. Bybee, who heads the staff.

The Chairman: I don't think anybody can understand this thing. I thought the income tax form was bad enough, but this is something else. In other words, let's get down to some basic facts here.

We have been going at this thing how many years? Long before any of you were even down at the ICC. I hate to repeat this but I am sure that your Chairman will allow me to, the very first meeting of the Commerce Committee I went to 25 years ago, we were discussing boxcar shortages. Twenty-five years ago.

Here we are again with studies C over D and X over C. Now, we know we are going to have a boxcar shortage in the fall.

Isn't there someone of us that can do something about it and if you haven't got enough authority under the law, we will change it for you. You can hold these hearings until doomsday on these things. I suspect that we have a storeroom full of hearings on boxcar shortages. We have to move them out to Virginia, to a fieldhouse out there because we can't handle them here, the building isn't big enough.

Now the Department of Transportation is going to study it. In other words, why study boxcar shortages, you have a shortage. You are going to have one with this year's crop. A big one.

What can we do about it, have another study? This, I don't understand.

I will ask a simple question, you can act without a hearing, am I wrong?

Mr. Ginnane: In my opinion the Commission cannot fix compensation without an opportunity for a hearing.

Florida East Coast Ry. Co. v. United States, 322 F.Supp. 725, 729–31 (M.D.Fla.1971). Once again, it was clear that the Commission thought that it could only set car-hire rates under the Esch Car Service Act through formal rulemaking, replete with statutorily required public hearings.

Six months after being harangued by the Senate committee, the Commission issued a report declaring that incentive rates were obviously a wonderful idea, and it published a rule for public comment proposing a detailed schedule of rates:

INTERSTATE COMMERCE COMMISSION EX PARTE NO. 252
(SUB-NO. 1) INCENTIVE PER DIEM CHARGES—1968
34 Fed. Reg. 20438 (1969).

* * *

It appearing, that by order of the Commission, dated December 15, 1967, this rulemaking proceeding was instituted for the purpose of implementing those provisions of the law relating to the Commission's authority to encourage the acquisition and maintenance of an adequate car supply as specified in * * * section 1(14)(a) of the Interstate Commerce Act:

And it further appearing, that investigation of the matters and things involved in this proceedings has been made and that the Commission has made and filed an interim report herein containing its tentative findings of fact and provisional conclusions thereon, including the proposed rules and regulations set forth below * * *:

It is ordered, That verified statements of facts, briefs, and statements of position respecting the tentative conclusions reached in the said interim report, the rules and regulations set forth below, and any other pertinent matter, are hereby invited to be submitted pursuant to the filing schedule set forth below * * *.

* * *

It is further ordered, That initial verified statements of facts, briefs, and statements of position in response to the said interim report may be filed on or before February 24, 1970; and that replies thereto may be filed on or before March 24, 1970.

It is further ordered, That any party requesting oral hearing shall set forth with specificity the need therefor and the evidence to be adduced.

* * *

[The notice provided a detailed schedule of proposed rates based on the dollar value of the freight and the age of the boxcar.]

NOTES

Again, this NPR speaks the language of formal rulemaking by discussing responsive filings and requests for oral argument. A number of railroads requested oral hearings and an opportunity to cross-examine the Commission staff members who prepared the studies on which the proposed rules were based.

In April 1970, the ICC adopted the proposed rules, denying all requests for oral hearings and cross-examination. Significantly, the Commission did not deny the requests on the ground that the Commission was conducting notice-and-comment rulemaking under § 553, which by its terms does not require oral participation. The ICC still thought at this point that it was conducting a formal rulemaking subject to §§ 556–57. Rather, the Commission sought to invoke the "escape clause" in § 556(d), which allows an agency in a formal rulemaking to dispense with oral presentations and cross-examination (though not with the other procedures required in formal proceedings) "when a party will not be prejudiced thereby." The Commission simply insisted that denial of these procedures did not prejudice the railroads.

Two separate challenges to the Commission's car-hire rates were filed based on the Commission's denial of various railroads' requests for cross-examination. In one case, the agency survived the procedural challenge on the ground that the affected railroad had not shown by sufficient evidence that it had been prejudiced by its inability to cross-examine Commission staffers. *See Long Island R.R. Co. v. United States*, 318 F.Supp. 490 (E.D.N.Y.1970). In the other case, the railroad won on the ground that it *had* sufficiently shown prejudice. *See Florida East Coast Ry. Co. v. United States*, 322 F.Supp. 725 (M.D.Fla.1971) (*"FECR"*). Both decisions expressly held that the "after hearing" language in the Esch Act triggered the APA's requirements for formal rulemaking.

The United States appealed from the lower court decision in *FECR* that had ruled in favor of the railroad. Its jurisdictional statement to the Supreme Court raised one and only one issue: Florida East Coast Railway had failed to demonstrate that it was prejudiced by the absence of cross-examination, and that under § 556(d) the agency could therefore properly conduct its formal rulemaking without oral proceedings. Accordingly, right up to the point when the United States filed its appeal in the Supreme Court, everyone thought that this proceeding involved formal rulemaking and that the only question before the Supreme Court was the applicability of the § 556(d) exemption from oral proceedings in certain circumstances.

UNITED STATES V. FLORIDA EAST COAST RY.

Supreme Court of the United States, 1973.
410 U.S. 224, 93 S.Ct. 810, 35 L.Ed.2d 223.

MR. JUSTICE REHNQUIST delivered the opinion of the Court.

Appellees, two railroad companies, brought this action in the District Court for the Middle District of Florida to set aside the incentive per diem rates established by appellant Interstate Commerce Commission in a rulemaking proceeding. *Incentive Per Diem Charges—1968, Ex parte* No. 252 (Sub-No. 1), 337 I.C.C. 217 (1970). They challenged the order of the Commission on both substantive and procedural grounds. The District Court sustained appellees' position that the Commission had failed to comply with the applicable provisions of the Administrative Procedure Act and therefore set aside the order without dealing with the railroads' other contentions. The District Court held that the language of § 1(14)(a) of the Interstate Commerce Act, 24 Stat. 379, as amended, 49 U.S.C. § 1(14)(a), required the Commission in a proceeding such as this to act in accordance with the Administrative Procedure Act, 5 U.S.C. § 556(d), and that the Commission's determination to receive submissions from the appellees only in written form was a violation of that section because the appellees were "prejudiced" by that determination within the meaning of that section.

Following our decision last Term in *United States v. Allegheny-Ludlum Steel Corp.*, 406 U.S. 742 (1972), we noted probable jurisdiction and requested the parties to brief the question of whether the Commission's proceeding was governed by 5 U.S.C. § 553 or by §§ 556 and 557 of the Administrative Procedure Act. We here decide that the Commission's proceeding was governed only by § 553 of that Act, and that appellees received the "hearing" required by § 1(14)(a) of the Interstate Commerce Act. We, therefore, reverse the judgment of the District Court and remand the case to that court for further consideration of appellees' other contentions that were raised there, but which we do not decide.

I.   BACKGROUND OF CHRONIC FREIGHT CAR SHORTAGES

This case arises from the factual background of a chronic freight-car shortage on the Nation's railroads * * *. Judge Simpson, writing for the District Court in this case, noted that "[f]or a number of years portions of the nation have been plagued with seasonal shortages of freight cars in which to ship goods." 322 F.Supp. 725, 726 (M.D.Fla.1971). Judge Friendly, writing for a three-judge District Court in the Eastern District of New York in the related case of *Long Island R.R Co. v. United States*, 318 F.Supp. 490, 491 (E.D.N.Y.1970), described the Commission's order as "the latest chapter in a long history of freight-car shortages in certain regions and seasons and of attempts to ease them." Congressional concern for the problem was manifested in the enactment in 1966 of an amendment to § 1(14)(a) of the Interstate Commerce Act, enlarging the Commission's authority to prescribe per diem charges for the use by one railroad of freight cars owned by another * * *.

The Commission in 1966 commenced an investigation, *Ex parte* No. 252, Incentive Per Diem Charges, "to determine whether information presently available warranted the establishment of an incentive element increase, on an interim basis, to apply pending further study and investigation." Statements of position were received from the Commission staff and a number of railroads. Hearings were conducted at which witnesses were examined. In October 1967, the Commission rendered a decision discontinuing the earlier proceeding, but announcing a program of further investigation into the general subject.

In December 1967, the Commission initiated the rulemaking procedure giving rise to the order that appellees here challenge. It directed Class I and Class II line-haul railroads to compile and report detailed information with respect to freight-car demand and supply at numerous sample stations for selected days of the week during 12 four-week periods, beginning January 29, 1968.

Some of the affected railroads voiced questions about the proposed study or requested modification in the study procedures outlined by the Commission in its notice of proposed rulemaking. In response to petitions setting forth these carriers' views, the Commission staff held an informal conference in April 1968, at which the objections and proposed modifications were discussed. Twenty railroads, including appellee Seaboard, were represented at this conference, at which the Commission's staff sought to answer questions about reporting methods to accommodate individual circumstances of particular railroads. The conference adjourned on a note that undoubtedly left the impression that hearings would be held at some future date. A detailed report of the conference was sent to all parties to the proceeding before the Commission.

The results of the information thus collected were analyzed and presented to Congress by the Commission during a hearing before the Subcommittee on Surface Transportation of the Senate Committee on Commerce in May 1969. Members of the Subcommittee expressed dissatisfaction with the Commission's slow pace in exercising the authority that had been conferred upon it by the 1966 Amendments to the Interstate Commerce Act * * *.

* * *

The Commission, now apparently imbued with a new sense of mission, issued in December 1969 an interim report announcing its tentative decision to adopt incentive per diem charges on standard boxcars based on the information compiled by the railroads. The substantive decision reached by the Commission was that so-called "incentive" per diem charges should be paid by any railroad using on its lines a standard boxcar owned by another railroad * * *. It did so by means of a proposed schedule that established such charges on an across-the-board basis for all common carriers by railroads subject to the Interstate Commerce Act. Embodied in the report was a proposed rule adopting the Commission's tentative conclusions and a notice to the railroads to file statements of position within 60 days * * *.

Both appellee railroads filed statements objecting to the Commission's proposal and requesting an oral hearing, as did numerous other railroads. In April 1970, the Commission, without having held further "hearings," issued a supplemental report making some modifications in the tentative conclusions earlier reached, but overruling *in toto* the requests of appellees.

The District Court held that in so doing the Commission violated § 556(d) of the Administrative Procedure Act, and it was on this basis that it set aside the order of the Commission.

II. APPLICABILITY OF ADMINISTRATIVE PROCEDURE ACT

In *United States v. Allegheny-Ludlum Steel Corp., supra*, we held that the language of § 1(14)(a) of the Interstate Commerce Act authorizing the Commission to act "after hearing" was not the equivalent of a requirement that a rule be made "on the record after opportunity for an agency hearing" as the latter term is used in § 553(c) of the Administrative Procedure Act.[15] Since the 1966 amendment to § 1(14)(a), under which the Commission was here proceeding, does not by its terms add to the hearing requirement contained in the earlier language, the same result should obtain here unless that amendment contains language that is tantamount to such a requirement. Appellees contend that such language is found in the provisions of that Act requiring that:

> "[T]he Commission shall give consideration to the national level of ownership of such type of freight car and to other factors affecting the adequacy of the national freight car supply, and shall, on the basis of such consideration, determine whether compensation should be computed. . ."

While this language is undoubtedly a mandate to the Commission to consider the factors there set forth in reaching any conclusion as to imposition of per diem incentive charges, it adds to the hearing requirements of the section neither expressly nor by implication. We know of no reason to think that an administrative agency in reaching a decision cannot accord consideration to factors such as those set forth in the 1966

---

15 [Ed. note: The *Allegheny-Ludlum* decision involved a challenge to the evidentiary basis for Commission rules governing a different aspect of the car-hire practice. At the very end of its opinion, the Court said the following about the procedural requirements for Commission rulemaking activities under the Esch Act:

> Appellees claim that the Commission's procedure here departed from the provisions of 5 U.S.C. §§ 556 and 557 * * *. Those sections, however, govern a rulemaking proceeding only when 5 U.S.C. § 553 so requires. The latter section, dealing generally with rulemaking, makes applicable the provisions of §§ 556 and 557 only "when rules are required by statute to be made on the record after opportunity for an agency hearing. . . ." The Esch Act, authorizing the Commission "after hearing, on a complaint or upon its own initiative without complaint, [to] establish reasonable rules, regulations, and practices with respect to car service . . . ," 49 U.S.C. § 1(14)(a), does not require that such rules "be made on the record." 5 U.S.C. § 553. That distinction is determinative for this case. "A good deal of significance lies in the fact that some statutes do expressly require determinations on the record." 2 K. Davis, *Administrative Law Treatise* § 13.08, p. 225 (1958). Sections 556 and 557 need be applied "only where the agency statute, in addition to providing a hearing, prescribes explicitly that it be 'on the record.'" *Siegel v. Atomic Energy Comm'n*, 130 U.S. App. D.C. 307, 314, 400 F.2d 778, 785 (1968); *Joseph E. Seagram & Sons Inc. v. Dillon*, 120 U.S. App. D.C. 112, 115 n. 9, 344 F.2d 497, 500 n. 9 (1965). We do not suggest that only the precise words "on the record" in the applicable statute will suffice to make §§ 556 and 557 applicable to rulemaking proceedings, but we do hold that the language of the Esch Car Service Act is insufficient to invoke these sections.]

amendment by means other than a trial-type hearing or the presentation of oral argument by the affected parties. Congress by that amendment specified necessary components of the ultimate decision, but it did not specify the method by which the Commission should acquire information about those components.

Both of the district courts that reviewed this order of the Commission concluded that its proceedings were governed by the stricter requirements of §§ 556 and 557 of the Administrative Procedure Act, rather than by the provisions of § 553 alone.[6] The conclusion of the District Court for the Middle District of Florida, which we here review, was based on the assumption that the language in § 1(14)(a) of the Interstate Commerce Act requiring rulemaking under that section to be done "after hearing" was the equivalent of a statutory requirement that the rule "be made on the record after opportunity for an agency hearing." Such an assumption is inconsistent with our decision in *Allegheny-Ludlum, supra.*

The District Court for the Eastern District of New York reached the same conclusion by a somewhat different line of reasoning. That court felt that because § 1(14)(a) of the Interstate Commerce Act had required a "hearing," and because that section was originally enacted in 1917, Congress was probably thinking in terms of a "hearing" such as that described in the opinion of this Court in the roughly contemporaneous case of *ICC v. Louisville & Nashville R. Co.,* 227 U.S. 88, 93 (1913). The ingredients of the "hearing" were there said to be that "[a]ll parties must be fully apprised of the evidence submitted or to be considered, and must be given opportunity to cross-examine witnesses, to inspect documents and to offer evidence in explanation or rebuttal." Combining this view of congressional understanding of the term "hearing" with comments by the Chairman of the Commission at the time of the adoption of the 1966 legislation regarding the necessity for "hearings," that court concluded that Congress had, in effect, required that these proceedings be "on the record after opportunity for an agency hearing" within the meaning of § 553(c) of the Administrative Procedure Act.

---

[6]   Both district court opinions were handed down before our decision in *United States v. Allegheny-Ludlum Steel Corp.,* 406 U.S. 742 (1972), and it appears from the record before us that the Government in those courts did not really contest the proposition that the Commission's proceedings were governed by the stricter standards of §§ 556 and 557.

The dissenting opinion of MR. JUSTICE DOUGLAS relies in part on indications by the Commission that it proposed to apply the more stringent standards of §§ 556 and 557 of the Administrative Procedure Act to these proceedings. This Act is not legislation that the Interstate Commerce Commission, or any other single agency, has primary responsibility for administering. An agency interpretation involving, at least in part, the provisions of that Act does not carry the weight, in ascertaining the intent of Congress, that an interpretation by an agency "charged with the responsibility" of administering a particular statute does. Moreover, since any agency is free under the Act to accord litigants appearing before it more procedural rights than the Act requires, the fact that an agency may choose to proceed under §§ 556 and 557 does not carry the necessary implication that the agency felt it was required to do so.

Insofar as this conclusion is grounded on the belief that the language "after hearing" of § 1(14)(a), without more, would trigger the applicability of §§ 556 and 557, it, too, is contrary to our decision in *Allegheny-Ludlum*, *supra*. The District Court observed that it was "rather hard to believe that the last sentence of § 553(c) was directed only to the few legislative sports where the words 'on the record' or their equivalent had found their way into the statute book." 318 F.Supp., at 496. This is, however, the language which Congress used, and since there are statutes on the books that do use these very words, see, *e. g.*, the Fulbright Amendment to the Walsh-Healey Act, 41 U.S.C. § 43a, and 21 U.S.C. § 371(e)(3), the regulations provision of the Food and Drug Act, adherence to that language cannot be said to render the provision nugatory or ineffectual. We recognized in *Allegheny-Ludlum* that the actual words "on the record" and "after . . . hearing" used in § 553 were not words of art, and that other statutory language having the same meaning could trigger the provisions of §§ 556 and 557 in rulemaking proceedings. But we adhere to our conclusion, expressed in that case, that the phrase "after hearing" in § 1(14)(a) of the Interstate Commerce Act does not have such an effect.

III. "HEARING" REQUIREMENT OF § 1(14)(a) OF THE INTERSTATE COMMERCE ACT

Inextricably intertwined with the hearing requirement of the Administrative Procedure Act in this case is the meaning to be given to the language "after hearing" in § 1(14)(a) of the Interstate Commerce Act. Appellees, both here and in the court below, contend that the Commission procedure here fell short of that mandated by the "hearing" requirement of § 1(14)(a), even though it may have satisfied § 553 of the Administrative Procedure Act. The Administrative Procedure Act states that none of its provisions "limit or repeal additional requirements imposed by statute or otherwise recognized by law." 5 U.S.C. § 559. Thus, even though the Commission was not required to comply with §§ 556 and 557 of that Act, it was required to accord the "hearing" specified in § 1(14)(a) of the Interstate Commerce Act. Though the District Court did not pass on this contention, it is so closely related to the claim based on the Administrative Procedure Act that we proceed to decide it now.

If we were to agree with the reasoning of the District Court for the Eastern District of New York with respect to the type of hearing required by the Interstate Commerce Act, the Commission's action might well violate those requirements, even though it was consistent with the requirements of the Administrative Procedure Act.

The term "hearing" in its legal context undoubtedly has a host of meanings. Its meaning undoubtedly will vary, depending on whether it is used in the context of a rulemaking-type proceeding or in the context of a proceeding devoted to the adjudication of particular disputed facts. It is by no means apparent what the drafters of the Esch Car Service Act of 1917, 40 Stat. 101, which became the first part of § 1(14)(a) of the Interstate Commerce Act, meant by the term. Such an intent would surely be an ephemeral one if, indeed, Congress in 1917 had in mind anything more specific than the language it actually used, for none of the parties refer to any legislative history that would shed light on the intended meaning of the words "after hearing." What is apparent, though, is that the term was used in granting authority to the Commission to make rules and regulations of a prospective nature.

* * *

Under these circumstances, confronted with a grant of substantive authority made after the Administrative Procedure Act was enacted,[8] we think that reference to that Act, in which Congress devoted itself exclusively to questions such as the nature and scope of hearings, is a satisfactory basis for determining what is meant by the term "hearing" used in another statute. Turning to that Act, we are convinced that the term "hearing" as used therein does not necessarily embrace either the right to present evidence orally and to cross-examine opposing witnesses, or the right to present oral argument to the agency's decisionmaker.

Section 553 excepts from its requirements rulemaking devoted to "interpretative rules, general statements of policy, or rules of agency organization, procedure, or practice," and rulemaking "when the agency for good cause finds . . . that notice and public procedure thereon are impracticable, unnecessary, or contrary to the public interest." This exception does not apply, however, "when notice or hearing is required by statute"; in those cases, even though interpretative rulemaking be involved, the requirements of § 553 apply. But since these requirements themselves do not mandate any oral presentation, see *Allegheny-Ludlum*, *supra*, it cannot be doubted that a statute that requires a "hearing" prior to rulemaking may in some circumstances be satisfied by procedures that meet only the standards of § 553 * * *.

Similarly, even where the statute requires that the rulemaking procedure take place "on the record after opportunity for an agency hearing," thus triggering the applicability of § 556, subsection (d) provides that the agency may proceed by the submission of all or part of the evidence in written form if a party will not be "prejudiced thereby." Again, the Act makes it plain that a specific statutory mandate that the proceedings take place on the record after hearing may be satisfied in some circumstances by evidentiary submission in written form only.

We think this treatment of the term "hearing" in the Administrative Procedure Act affords a sufficient basis for concluding that the requirement

---

[8]   The Interstate Commerce Act was amended in May 1966 * * *.

of a "hearing" contained in § 1(14)(a), in a situation where the Commission was acting under the 1966 statutory rulemaking authority that Congress had conferred upon it, did not by its own force require the Commission either to hear oral testimony, to permit cross-examination of Commission witnesses, or to hear oral argument * * *.

Appellee railroads cite a number of our previous decisions dealing in some manner with the right to a hearing in an administrative proceeding. Although appellees have asserted no claim of constitutional deprivation in this proceeding, some of the cases they rely upon expressly speak in constitutional terms, while others are less than clear as to whether they depend upon the Due Process Clause of the Fifth and Fourteenth Amendments to the Constitution, or upon generalized principles of administrative law formulated prior to the adoption of the Administrative Procedure Act.

* * *

ICC v. Louisville & Nashville R. Co., 227 U.S. 88 (1913), involved what the Court there described as a "quasi-judicial" proceeding of a quite different nature from the one we review here * * *. The type of proceeding there, in which the Commission adjudicated a complaint by a shipper that specified rates set by a carrier were unreasonable, was sufficiently different from the nationwide incentive payments ordered to be made by all railroads in this proceeding so as to make the *Louisville & Nashville* opinion inapplicable in the case presently before us.

The basic distinction between rulemaking and adjudication is illustrated by this Court's treatment of two related cases under the Due Process Clause of the Fourteenth Amendment [citing and describing *Londoner v. Denver*, 210 U.S. 373 (1908), and *Bi-Metallic Investment Co. v. State Board of Equalization*, 239 U.S. 441 (1915)] * * *.

Later decisions have continued to observe the distinction adverted to in *Bi-Metallic Investment Co., supra* * * *. While the line dividing them may not always be a bright one, these decisions represent a recognized distinction in administrative law between proceedings for the purpose of promulgating policy-type rules or standards, on the one hand, and proceedings designed to adjudicate disputed facts in particular cases on the other.

Here, the incentive payments proposed by the Commission * * * were applicable across the board to all of the common carriers by railroad subject to the Interstate Commerce Act. No effort was made to single out any particular railroad for special consideration based on its own peculiar circumstances. Indeed, one of the objections of appellee Florida East Coast was that it and other terminating carriers should have been treated differently from the generality of the railroads. But the fact that the order may in its effects have been thought more disadvantageous by some railroads than by others does not change its generalized nature. Though the Commission obviously relied on factual inferences as a basis for its order, the source of these factual inferences was apparent to anyone who read the order of December 1969. The factual inferences were used in the formulation of a basically legislative-type judgment, for prospective application only, rather than in adjudicating a particular set of disputed facts.

The Commission's procedure satisfied both the provisions of § 1(14)(a) of the Interstate Commerce Act and of the Administrative Procedure Act, and were not inconsistent with prior decisions of this Court. We, therefore, reverse the judgment of the District Court, and remand the case so that it may consider those contentions of the parties that are not disposed of by this opinion.

It is so ordered.

MR. JUSTICE POWELL took no part in the consideration or decision of this case.

MR. JUSTICE DOUGLAS, with whom MR. JUSTICE STEWART concurs, dissenting.

The present decision makes a sharp break with traditional concepts of procedural due process. The Commission order under attack is tantamount to a rate order. Charges are fixed that nonowning railroads must pay owning railroads for boxcars of the latter that are on the tracks of the former * * *. This is the imposition on carriers by administrative fiat of a new financial liability. I do not believe it is within our traditional concepts of due process to allow an administrative agency to saddle anyone with a new rate, charge, or fee without a full hearing that includes the right to present oral testimony, cross-examine witnesses, and present oral argument. That is required by the Administrative Procedure Act, 5 U.S.C. § 556(d); § 556(a) states that § 556 applies to hearings required by § 553. Section 553(c) provides that § 556 applies "when rules are required by statute to be made on the record after opportunity for an agency hearing." A hearing under § 1(14)(a) of the Interstate Commerce Act fixing rates, charges, or fees is certainly adjudicatory, not legislative in the customary sense.

* * *

* * * I believe that "prejudice" was shown when it was claimed that the very basis on which the Commission rested its finding was vulnerable because it lacked statistical validity or other reasoned basis. At least in that narrow group of cases, prejudice for lack of a proper hearing has been shown.

* * *

The more exacting hearing provisions of the Administrative Procedure Act, 5 U.S.C. §§ 556–557, are only applicable, of course, if the "rules are required by statute to be made on the record after opportunity for an agency hearing." *Id.*, § 553(c).

United States v. Allegheny-Ludlum Steel Corp., 406 U.S. 742, was concerned strictly with a rulemaking proceeding of the Commission for the promulgation of "car service rules" that in general required freight cars, after being unloaded, to be returned "in the direction of the lines of the road owning the cars." *Id.*, at 743. We sustained the Commission's power with respect to these two rules on the narrow ground that they were wholly legislative * * *.

The rules in question here established "incentive" per diem charges to spur the prompt return of existing cars and to make the acquisition of new cars financially attractive to the railroads. Unlike those we considered in *Allegheny-Ludlum*, these rules involve the creation of a new financial liability. Although quasi-legislative, they are also adjudicatory in the sense that they determine the measure of the financial responsibility of one road for its use of the rolling stock of another road * * *.

* * *

Accordingly, I would hold that appellees were not afforded the hearing guaranteed by § 1(14)(a) of the Interstate Commerce Act and 5 U.S.C. §§ 553, 556, and 557, and would affirm the decision of the District Court.

NOTES

1.   *The Story Behind the Story*

United States v. Florida East Coast Ry. Co., 410 U.S. 224, 93 S.Ct. 810, 35 L.Ed.2d 223 (1973) ("*FECR*"), is, in its own peculiar fashion, one of the most important milestones in American administrative law.[16] The case also illustrates a general point about the reading of court opinions: in order to understand a case, it is often necessary to look beyond the opinion itself.

In 1972, while the appeal in *FECR* was pending, the Supreme Court decided *United States v. Allegheny-Ludlum Steel Corp.*, 406 U.S. 742, 92 S.Ct. 1941, 32 L.Ed.2d 453 (1972). This decision profoundly affected the proceedings in *FECR* in two ways. First, the parties, you should recall, had all proceeded up to the time of appeal in *FECR* on the assumption that the ICC had been obliged to engage in formal rulemaking to set rates under the Esch Car Service Act. After the *Allegheny-Ludlum* decision, the Supreme Court, on its own motion, ordered the parties in *FECR* to brief the question whether formal hearings were required by law. Second, the decision on this issue in *FECR* was ultimately resolved in favor of the ICC solely on the authority of

---

[16] It is also the answer to a trivia question: What case appears in the United States Reports immediately after the companion cases of *Roe v. Wade* and *Doe v. Bolton*?

Allegheny-Ludlum, with no additional analysis. That is not surprising: *Allegheny-Ludlum* unambiguously construed the very statute at issue in *FECR* not to require formal rulemaking proceedings.

And thereby hangs a tale. *Allegheny-Ludlum* concerned a different set of car-hire rules which, in essence, required rented cars to be returned in the general direction of the borrowing railroad. Thus, under the new rules, if you borrowed cars from a Maine railroad in order to ship goods to Florida, you could not return the cars to Maine via Houston via Denver via San Francisco via Minneapolis. The cars had to be sent back more or less in the direction from whence they came. These rules, as with the rules at issue in *FECR*, were challenged in lawsuits brought in different districts. The rules were upheld in one case (which again involved Florida East Coast Railway), *see Florida East Coast Ry. Co. v. United States*, 327 F.Supp. 1076 (M.D.Fla.1971), and were invalidated in another, *see Allegheny-Ludlum Steel Corp. v. United States*, 325 F.Supp. 352 (W.D.Pa.1971). In both cases, the rules were challenged on *substantive* rather than *procedural* grounds. That is, the challenging parties insisted that the Commission had insufficient evidence to support its conclusion that there was a serious enough boxcar shortage to warrant the new rules. No one complained that they did not get enough, or the right kind of, hearings. The *Allegheny Ludlum* lower court opinion did not even cite the Administrative Procedure Act, much less invoke it to challenge the Commission's decision. Florida East Coast Railway, in the other case, did argue very briefly that the Commission violated § 556(d) of the APA by failing to identify certain documents of which it took official notice during its rulemaking, but this was a minor, throwaway point in an argument directed primarily to the Commission's evidentiary basis for its rules.

The United States' brief to the Supreme Court in *Allegheny-Ludlum* made no reference whatsoever to the APA. Allegheny-Ludlum's brief made passing reference to the official notice problem and questioned whether the agency had made adequate findings of fact under § 557(c)(A), but the latter challenge was obviously intended as a substantive rather than procedural challenge—*i.e.,* the complaint was that the agency did a lousy job of finding facts, not that it failed to lay out those (according to the railroads lousy) factual finding with sufficient procedural formality. The United States' reply brief made no reference to these very minor arguments and did not so much as cite the APA. The transcript of oral argument before the Supreme Court shows that no procedural challenge was ever raised at oral argument.

Nonetheless, at the very end of a lengthy opinion holding that the ICC had adequate factual support for its rules, the Supreme Court in *Allegheny-Ludlum* added the discussion found at note 15 in the *FECR* opinion. The only authorities relied upon by the Court in that discussion were a treatise by Professor Kenneth Culp Davis and two lower court opinions. The statement from Professor Davis' treatise was part of his discussion of the procedural requirements for agency *adjudication* and had nothing to do with rulemaking. *See* 2 Kenneth Culp Davis, Administrative Law Treatise § 13.08, at 223 (1958). One of the lower court opinions involved an organic statute that did not even require a hearing. *See Joseph E. Seagram & Sons, Inc. v. Dillon*, 344 F.2d 497, 499 (D.C.Cir.1965). The other opinion did state that formal rulemaking procedures were required only when the organic statute *explicitly* called for "on the record" proceedings, *see Siegel v. AEC*, 400 F.2d 778, 785 n.9 (D.C.Cir.1968), but its only authority for that claim was the *Attorney General's Manual on the Administrative Procedure Act*, which says no such thing. *See supra* pages 328–329.

In other words, the decision in *FECR*, holding that the ICC did not have to employ formal rulemaking when setting car-hire rates under the Esch Car Service Act, relied solely on a prior decision which resolved that question, on the basis of highly dubious authorities, without briefing or argument by the parties. For a detailed, fascinating (at least to administrative law junkies), and meticulously researched account of how the decision in *FECR* came about, see Kent Barnett, *How the Supreme Court Derailed Formal Rulemaking*, 85 Geo. Wash. L. Rev. Arguendo 1 (2017).

2.   *The Aftermath*

The Court in *FECR* specifically said that it was not requiring organic statutes to contain the magic words "on the record" in order to trigger formal rulemaking. Nonetheless, the decision, and the prior decision in *Allegheny-Ludlum*, very clearly made such language the focus of analysis. Lower courts were quick to seize on the presence or absence of explicit "on the record" language as dispositive, reasoning that *FECR* "virtually established it as a touchstone test of when §§ 556–57 procedures are required." *Mobil Oil Corp. v. FPC*, 483 F.2d 1238, 1250 (D.C.Cir.1973). Statutory rulemaking provisions calling for a "full hearing," *Farmers Union Central Exchange v. FERC*, 734 F.2d 1486, 1498–99 (D.C.Cir.1984), and "full opportunity for hearing," *American Telephone & Telegraph Co. v. FCC*, 572 F.2d 17, 22 (2d Cir.1978), for example, have been found to require only informal rulemaking procedures under the APA. Indeed, since *FECR* was decided, no statute that does not contain the magic words "on the record" has been found to require formal rulemaking. Apart from the few rulemaking statutes that contain an express "on the record" requirement, *see, e.g.,* 21 U.S.C. 811(a) (2012) (requiring classifications of controlled substances by the Attorney General to be made on the record), formal rulemaking has virtually disappeared as a procedural category.

The modern legal academy has almost unanimously celebrated the effective demise of formal rulemaking, on the grounds that procedural formality is generally unsuited to the policy decisions that often dominate rulemakings and that the extensive machinery of formal proceedings would unduly slow down the regulatory process. For modest dissenting views, suggesting that at least on some occasions the transparency and accountability generated through formal rulemaking might outweigh the associated costs, see Gary Lawson, *Reviving Formal Rulemaking: Openness and Accountability for Obamacare,* Backgrounder No. 2585, July 25, 2011 (available at http:// report.heritage.org/bg2585); Aaron L. Nielson, *In Defense of Formal*

Rulemaking, 75 Ohio St. L.J. 237 (2014). The ever-iconoclastic Justice Thomas has also raised a glass to formal rulemaking:

> Although almost all rulemaking is today accomplished through informal notice and comment, the APA actually contemplated a much more formal process for most rulemaking * * *.

> Today, however, formal rulemaking is the Yeti of administrative law. There are isolated sightings of it in the ratemaking context, but elsewhere it proves elusive. It is somewhat ironic for the Court so adamantly to insist that agencies be subject to no greater procedures than those required by the APA when we have not been adamant in requiring agencies to comply with even those baseline procedures. See *United States v. Florida East Coast R. Co.*, 410 U.S. 224, 237–38, 93 S.Ct. 810, 35 L.Ed.2d 223 (1973).

Perez v. Mortgage Bankers Ass'n, 575 U.S. ___, ___ n.5, 135 S.Ct. 1199, 1222 n.5, 191 L.Ed.2d 186 (2015).

3. *The Stakes*

FECR made it more difficult for organic statutes to trigger formal rulemaking—including statutes that had for decades been understood to require formal rulemaking—at precisely the time that rulemaking was dramatically gaining importance as a procedural mode. Until the 1960s, adjudication was by far the most important form of agency action. Prior to that time, the major activity of agencies such as the Federal Communications Commission, the Interstate Commerce Commission (which no longer exists), the Federal Power Commission (which has become the Federal Energy Regulatory Commission), the Atomic Energy Commission (which has become the Nuclear Regulatory Commission), and the Food and Drug Administration was licensing, which by definition is adjudication under the APA. Agencies engaged in dispensing benefits, such as the Social Security Administration and the Veterans Administration (which has become the Department of Veterans Affairs), also engaged—and today still engage—primarily in adjudication. The National Labor Relations Board, one of the most important of the New Deal agencies, chose as a matter of policy to proceed exclusively by adjudication.[17] The Federal Trade Commission did not even have the statutory power to engage in substantive rulemaking until the mid-1970s.[18] The primary avenue for rulemaking was the ratemaking activity of the various agencies charged with rate authority, such as the ICC in the *FECR* matter. Although ratemaking is defined as rulemaking by the APA, it does not neatly fit the

---

[17] Only in very recent years has the NLRB engaged in any substantive rulemaking, and it continues to make policy almost exclusively through adjudication.

[18] In 1973, the D.C. Circuit held for the first time—and almost surely incorrectly—that the FTC had the power to make policy through rulemaking. *See* National Petroleum Refiners Ass'n v. FTC, 482 F.2d 672 (D.C.Cir.1973) . The agency explicitly received rulemaking power two years later in the Federal Trade Commission Improvement Act of 1975. *See* 15 U.S.C. § 57a (2012). That rulemaking authority requires something that is not technically formal rulemaking under the APA but which includes, by specific statutory command, most of the procedures associated with formal rulemaking. *See id.* at § 57a(c).

classic model of rulemaking as legislative-like policymaking. Rulemaking of that variety was largely the province of the Securities and Exchange Commission.

This focus on adjudication changed in a major way in the 1960s and 1970s. During that period, agencies en masse engaged in a "constant and accelerating flight away from individualized, adjudicatory proceedings to generalized disposition through rulemaking." Antonin Scalia, Vermont Yankee: *The APA, The D.C. Circuit, and the Supreme Court*, 1978 Sup. Ct. Rev. 345, 376. Rulemaking thus became the center of attention in the administrative state. This flight to rulemaking had a number of sources. First, and most importantly, Congress empowered a new breed of agencies to deal with health, safety, and environmental problems (the National Highway Traffic Safety Administration in 1966, the Environmental Protection Agency and the Occupational Safety and Health Administration in 1970, and the Consumer Product Safety Commission in 1972). These agencies' statutes explicitly authorized, and in many instances affirmatively *required*, the use of rulemaking. Second, as federal intervention in the economy continued to grow, the new and old agencies alike increasingly realized that they simply could not carry out their missions effectively through case-by-case adjudication. They needed the more sweeping coverage that results from rulemaking. The pressures of the growing regulatory state led inexorably to an increase in rulemaking.[19]

Thus, rulemaking activity was dramatically increasing just as *FECR* substantially reduced the procedural requirements in many rulemakings. At the same time, confidence in agency decisionmaking was on the decline; by the 1970s, agencies were widely viewed as tools of the regulated industries ripe for capture rather than apolitical technocrats disinterestedly seeking a well-defined public good. The combination of increased rulemaking activity under sharply decreased procedural constraints and a gloomy view of agency behavior proved highly volatile. Indeed, much of this course charts the consequences of this combination.

C. FORMAL ADJUDICATION

The shadow of *FECR* dominates the modern law of formal rulemaking. The Supreme Court, however, has never decided a case involving the language that organic statutes must contain in order to trigger formal *adjudication*. Thus, the lower courts have been left to fend for themselves. A lower court judge who is attempting to determine when organic statutes mandate formal adjudication has many questions to consider: Does *FECR* apply to adjudication as well as rulemaking, given that the triggering language of § 553 and § 554 is identical? Are there differences between

---

[19] *See* Reuel Schiller, *Rulemaking's Promise: Administrative Law and Legal Culture in the 1960s and 1970s,* 53 Admin. L. Rev. 1139 (2001). For an alternative account of the flight to rulemaking that emphasizes the persistent efforts of scholars to promote rulemaking, see Richard J. Pierce, *Rulemaking and the Administrative Procedure Act*, 32 Tulsa L.J. 185, 188–90 (1996).

rulemaking and adjudication as forms of action that justify giving identical language a different meaning in the two contexts? Are there other administrative law doctrines at work that bear on this question?

Perhaps the most obvious answer is to say that *FECR* governs both rulemaking and adjudication. The D.C. Circuit endorsed this position in 1978 (though we will soon see that it has since changed its mind). In *United States Lines, Inc. v. FMC*, 584 F.2d 519 (D.C.Cir.1978), the Federal Maritime Commission had approved a joint service agreement between two water carriers. The approval proceeding was clearly an adjudication under the APA. The organic statute required a hearing, but did not specify that the hearing had to be on the record. Relying on *FECR* and *Allegheny-Ludlum*, the court held that §§ 556–57 of the APA did not apply: "While the exact phrase 'on the record' is not an absolute prerequisite to application of the formal hearing requirements [of the APA], the Supreme Court has made clear that these provisions do not apply unless Congress has clearly indicated that the 'hearing' required by statute must be a trial-type hearing on the record." 584 F.2d at 536. A similar answer is at least implicit in the following case.

CITY OF WEST CHICAGO, ILLINOIS V. NRC

United States Court of Appeals, Seventh Circuit, 1983.
701 F.2d 632.

Before CUMMINGS, CHIEF JUDGE, BAUER, CIRCUIT JUDGE, and GRANT, SENIOR DISTRICT JUDGE.

CUMMINGS, CHIEF JUDGE.

This appeal by the City of West Chicago (City) * * * challenges a Nuclear Regulatory Commission (NRC) order of February 11, 1982, granting to Kerr-McGee Corporation (KM) a license amendment (Amendment No. 3) authorizing demolition of certain buildings at KM's West Chicago facility, and acceptance for on site storage of contaminated soil from offsite locations * * *. We uphold the NRC order * * *.

I. FACTS

KM operated a milling facility in West Chicago for the production of thorium and thorium compounds from 1967 to 1973. Although the plant closed in 1973, there is presently on site approximately 5 million cubic feet of contaminated waste material consisting of building rubble, contaminated soil, and tailings from the milling of thorium ore. The NRC has been studying KM's proposed plan to decommission the site—ultimately dispose of the tailings and other contaminated materials—since submission of the plan in August 1979 * * *.

The current NRC license for the West Chicago site is a "source material" license issued pursuant to NRC regulations and authorizing KM to possess and store thorium ores.[1] In March 1980 and March 1981 KM submitted emergency requests to demolish Buildings Nos. 1 and 3 at the West Chicago site. On April 24, 1981, the NRC staff granted these requests as Amendment No. 1 to KM's existing license. Amendment No. 3, which is the focus of the City's suit challenging the NRC order, was issued in September 1981 and allowed demolition of six additional buildings on site in a non-emergency situation. Amendment No. 3 also authorized receipt and storage on site of contaminated material that was formerly taken from the site for use as landfill.

* * * [T]he City brought suit challenging the issuance of Amendment No. 3 as well as the NRC's delay in adopting a final decommissioning plan for the site and issuing an EIS [Environmental Impact Statement] for the plan. The City requested the district court to set aside Amendment No. 3, claiming, *inter alia*, that the amendment violated the National Environmental Policy Act (NEPA) because no EIS was issued before approval, and that the City had no notice of KM's request for the amendment and consequently had no opportunity to request a hearing. The City also sought an order compelling NRC to issue an EIS for, and to take final action on, KM's proposed plan for decommissioning and stabilization of the site. Judge McGarr temporarily enjoined KM's activities under the amendment and ordered the NRC to give notice to the City and consider any request for hearing that the City might make. NRC did so, and on February 11, 1982, issued its order denying the City's request for a formal, trial-type hearing, addressing the contentions raised by the City in the written materials it submitted, and issuing Amendment No. 3 * * *.

II. REVIEW OF THE NRC ORDER

The City challenges the NRC order on both procedural and substantive grounds, contending first, that the NRC violated its own regulations, the Atomic Energy Act, due process, and the National Environmental Policy Act (NEPA) in issuing Amendment No. 3, and second, that the order must be set aside because it is both unsupported by substantial evidence in the record and arbitrary and capricious. We address the procedural issues first.

A. *The NRC order cannot be set aside on procedural grounds*

The Atomic Energy Act of 1954 (AEA), § 189(a), 42 U.S.C. § 2239(a), clearly requires NRC to grant a "hearing" if requested "in any proceeding under this chapter, for the granting, suspending, revoking, or amending of any license or construction permit * * *."[2] The parties in this case are

---

[1] "Source material" is defined in Section 11 of the Atomic Energy Act, 42 U.S.C. § 2014(z), as "(1) uranium, thorium, or any other material which is determined by the Commission pursuant to the provisions of section 2091 of this title to be source material; or (2) ores containing one or more of the foregoing materials, in such concentration as the Commission may by regulation determine from time to time." * * *

[2] § 189(a). Hearings and judicial review.

arguing about the kind of "hearing" the NRC is required to conduct when issuing an amendment to a source materials license. The City argues that NRC must hold a formal, adversarial, trial-type hearing as provided by NRC regulations, 10 C.F.R. §§ 2.104 and 2.105. We shall refer to the hearing process outlined in those Sections as a "formal hearing." NRC and intervenor KM argue that the NRC may hold an informal hearing in which it requests and considers written materials without providing for traditional trial-type procedures such as oral testimony and cross-examination. We shall refer to this kind of hearing as an "informal hearing." In the circumstances of this case, we find that an informal hearing suffices.

1.   NRC did not violate its own regulations.

Under Commission regulations, a formal hearing is triggered by * * * a notice of hearing under 10 C.F.R. § 2.104 * * *.

Section 2.104 provides that a notice of hearing will issue when "a hearing is required by the Act or this chapter [10 C.F.R. ch. 1] or [when] the Commission finds that a hearing is required in the public interest."[4] The City argues that NRC must issue a notice of hearing because the first sentence of Section 189(a) of the AEA requires a hearing upon the request of an interested party. NRC however offers a narrower interpretation of the phrase "required by the Act" in Section 2.104. It contends that a formal hearing is "required by the Act" within the meaning of Section 2.104 when

---

(a)   In any proceeding under this chapter, for the granting, suspending, revoking, or amending of any license or construction permit, or application to transfer control * * *, the Commission shall grant a hearing upon the request of any person whose interest may be affected by the proceeding, and shall admit any such person as a party to such proceeding. The Commission shall hold a hearing after thirty days' notice and publication once in the Federal Register, on each application under section 2133 or 2134(b) of this title for a construction permit for a facility, and on any application under section 2134(c) of this title for a construction permit for a testing facility. In cases where such a construction permit has been issued following the holding of such a hearing, the Commission may, in the absence of a request therefor by any person whose interest may be affected, issue an operating license or an amendment to a construction permit or an amendment to an operating license without a hearing, but upon thirty days' notice and publication once in the Federal Register of its intent to do so. The Commission may dispense with such thirty days' notice and publication with respect to any application for an amendment to a construction permit or an amendment to an operating license upon a determination by the Commission that the amendment involves no significant hazards consideration.

* * *

4   § 2.104 Notice of hearing.

(a)   In the case of an application on which a hearing is required by the Act or this chapter, or in which the Commission finds that a hearing is required in the public interest, the Secretary will issue a notice of hearing to be published in the Federal Register as required by law at least fifteen (15) days, and in the case of an application concerning a construction permit for a facility of the type described in § 50.21(b) or § 50.22 of this chapter or a testing facility, at least thirty (30) days, prior to the date set for hearing in the notice * * *. The notice will state:

(1)   The time, place, and nature of the hearing and/or prehearing conference, if any;

(2)   The authority under which the hearing is to be held;

(3)   The matters of fact and law to be considered; and

(4)   The time within which answers to the notice shall be filed.

* * *

the AEA mandates a hearing even absent a request for one; in other words, even when a proceeding under Section 189(a) will be uncontested. The second sentence of Section 189(a) provides that NRC shall automatically hold a hearing on certain applications for a construction permit even absent a request for a hearing. The first sentence of Section 189(a) on the other hand requires NRC to grant a hearing only upon the request of an interested person. By distinguishing the two sentences in this manner, NRC interprets Section 2.104 to "require" a hearing only in cases falling under the second, rather than the first sentence. Because a materials license amendment clearly falls within the first sentence of Section 189(a), it does not, we hold, trigger the Section 2.104 notice of hearing, or the formal procedures provided therein.

* * *

* * * When a court is called upon to construe administrative regulations, "the ultimate criterion is the administrative interpretation, which becomes of controlling weight unless it is plainly erroneous or inconsistent with the regulation." *Bowles v. Seminole Rock & Sand Co.*, 325 U.S. 410, 414, 89 L.Ed. 1700, 65 S.Ct. 1215, quoted in *First Bank v. Avenue Bank and Trust Co.*, 605 F.2d 372, 376 (7th Cir.1979). Although NRC's interpretation of its regulations is at times somewhat convoluted, it is not plainly erroneous or inconsistent with the text of the regulations. We therefore hold that NRC acted in conformance with its regulations in denying the City a formal hearing.

2.   NRC did not violate the Atomic Energy Act.

Our inquiry cannot end with a finding that the NRC acted in conformance with its own regulations, for we must determine whether those regulations as interpreted violate the governing statute. If the AEA requires a formal hearing in the case of a materials license amendment, then the NRC must provide one, despite its interpretation of the regulations.

The City claims that a materials licensing hearing under Section 189(a) of the AEA must be in accordance with Section 5 of the Administrative Procedure Act (APA), 5 U.S.C. § 554. Section 554 does not by its terms dictate the type of hearing to which a party is entitled; rather it triggers the formal hearing provisions of Section 556 and 557 of the APA if the adjudication in question is required by the agency's governing statute to be "determined on the record after opportunity for an agency hearing * * *."[7] *United States v. Allegheny-Ludlum Steel Corp.*, 406 U.S. 742, 757, 32 L.Ed.2d 453, 92 S.Ct. 1941. The City argues that Section 189(a) of the AEA triggers the formal hearing provisions of the APA because it provides that the "Commission shall grant a hearing upon the request of any person

---

[7]   The parties agree that under the APA, all licensing proceedings are adjudications. 5 U.S.C. §§ 551(6)–(7), (9).

whose interest may be affected by the proceeding, and shall admit any such person as a party to such proceeding."

Although Section 554 specifies that the governing statute must satisfy the "on the record" requirement, those three magic words need not appear for a court to determine that formal hearings are required. See, e.g., *Seacoast Anti-Pollution League v. Costle*, 572 F.2d 872, 876 (1st Cir.), certiorari denied *sub nom. Public Serv. Co. v. Seacoast Anti Pollution League*, 439 U.S. 824, 58 L.Ed.2d 117, 99 S.Ct. 94 (1978); *Marathon Oil Co. v. EPA*, 564 F.2d 1253, 1263 (9th Cir.1977). However, even the City agrees that in the absence of these magic words, Congress must clearly indicate its intent to trigger the formal, on-the-record hearing provisions of the APA. We find no such clear intention in the legislative history of the AEA, and therefore conclude that formal hearings are not statutorily required for amendments to materials licenses.

The parties agree that the legislative history of the 1954 AEA sheds little light on the hearing requirement of the first sentence of Section 189(a). While Section 181 of the AEA made the provisions of the APA applicable to all agency actions, it did not specify the "on the record" requirement necessary to trigger Section 554 of the APA. Thus despite the fact that the statute required the Commission to grant a hearing to any materially interested party, there is no indication that Congress meant the hearing to be a formal one. Similarly, the legislative history of the 1957 and 1962 amendments to the AEA shows little concern with the procedures required by the hearing provision in the first sentence of Section 189(a). Rather, Congress was concerned mainly with facilities or reactor licenses as opposed to the source, special nuclear, or byproduct materials licenses covered under the first sentence of Section 189(a).

In adopting rules to carry out the AEA, however, the Atomic Energy Commission (AEC) did provide by regulation for formal hearings on request in all licensing cases. 10 C.F.R. §§ 2.102, 2.708, 21 Fed. Reg. 804 (Feb. 4, 1956). The agency did not indicate whether the formal hearings were a matter of discretion or statutory mandate * * *.

The AEC continued to hold formal hearings in all contested reactor cases, as well as in materials licensing cases. However, based on the threadbare legislative history concerning materials licenses, we are unable to conclude that the AEC's procedures were mandated by statute. Even if the legislative history indicates that formal procedures are required by statute in reactor licensing cases under the second, third, and fourth sentences of Section 189(a), we do not accept the City's argument that this by necessity indicates that all hearings under the first sentence must be formal as well. While the first sentence of Section 189(a) speaks in terms of "any license or construction permit," it does so in the context of a statute that distinguishes between the licensing of nuclear materials and reactor facilities. In this case, we have no difficulty ascribing different meanings to the word "hearing" even though it appears in succeeding sentences of the same statutory section.

* * *

Despite the fact that licensing is adjudication under the APA, there is no evidence that Congress intended to require formal hearings for all Section 189(a) activities. In light of the above analysis, we conclude that NRC did not violate the AEA when it denied the City's request for a formal hearing.

3.   NRC hearing procedures satisfy the requirements of due process.

The City argues that the NRC proceedings deprived it of liberty or property interests without due process of law. Yet generalized health, safety and environmental concerns do not constitute liberty or property subject to due process protection. Although the City claims that it has presented "specific documented concerns" to the NRC in its petitions, such "concerns" do not, without more, require due process protection.

Even if we were to find a protected liberty or property interest in this case, we would hold that Commission procedures constituted sufficient process * * *.

* * *

NRC concluded, and we concur, that in this particular case, the Commission procedures afforded the City all the process that was constitutionally necessary.

* * *

The orders under review * * * are affirmed.

NOTES

It is certainly plausible to say that, because § 553 and § 554 use essentially the same language to trigger the application of formal proceedings, essentially the same legal rules should govern the necessity for formal rulemaking and formal adjudication. It is therefore plausible to say that the Supreme Court has "implied that formal adjudication procedures are only necessary when a statute uses the magic words 'on the record.'" *Crestview Parke Care Center v. Thompson*, 373 F.3d 743, 748 (6th Cir.2004). *See also Arwady Hand Trucks Sales, Inc. v. Vander Werf*, 507 F.Supp.2d 754, 759 (S.D. Tex.2007) (no formal adjudication where the organic statute provides for a "hearing" but not a "hearing on the record"). But is it necessary to say it? Can one just as plausibly distinguish rulemaking from adjudication in some respect that is potentially relevant to the procedures that might be triggered by a facially ambiguous statutory reference to a "hearing"?

In 1977, the Ninth Circuit came up with what it thought was a plausible distinction: rulemakings often (not always, but often) focus on broad policy questions that do not lend themselves well to treatment in adversarial proceedings, while adjudications often (not always, but often) focus on specific factual disputes that seem better suited to formal procedural mechanisms. The court thought this sufficient to treat "hearing" requirements in adjudicatory statutes as more likely to trigger formal APA proceedings than similar or identical language in rulemaking statutes. See *Marathon Oil Co. v. EPA*, 564 F.2d 1253, 1261–64 (9th Cir.1977). The following year, a panel of the First Circuit articulated the same distinction.

SEACOAST ANTI-POLLUTION LEAGUE V. COSTLE

United States Court of Appeals, First Circuit, 1978.
572 F.2d 872.

Before COFFIN, CHIEF JUDGE, CAMPBELL and BOWNES, CIRCUIT JUDGES.

COFFIN, CHIEF JUDGE.

This case is before us on a petition by the Seacoast Anti-Pollution League and the Audubon Society of New Hampshire (petitioners) to review a decision by the Administrator of the Environmental Protection Agency (EPA) * * *.

The Public Service Company of New Hampshire (PSCO) filed an application with the EPA for permission to discharge heated water into the Hampton-Seabrook Estuary which runs into the Gulf of Maine. The water would be taken from the Gulf of Maine, be run through the condenser of PSCO's proposed nuclear steam electric generating station at Seabrook, and then be directly discharged back into the Gulf at a temperature 39 degrees F higher than at intake. The water is needed to remove waste heat, some 16 billion BTU per hour, generated by the nuclear reactor but not converted into electrical energy by the turbine. Occasionally, in a process called backflushing, the water will be recirculated through the condenser, and discharged through the intake tunnel at a temperature of 120 degrees F in order to kill whatever organisms may be living in the intake system.

Section 301(a) of the [Federal Water Pollution Control Act of 1972 (FWPCA)], 33 U.S.C. § 1311(a), prohibits the discharge of any pollutant unless the discharger, the point source operator, has obtained an EPA permit. Heat is a pollutant. 33 U.S.C. § 1362(6). Section 301(b) directs the EPA to promulgate effluent limitations. The parties agree that the cooling system PSCO has proposed does not meet the EPA standards because PSCO would utilize a once-through open cycle system—the water would not undergo any cooling process before being returned to the sea. Therefore, in August, 1974, PSCO applied not only for a discharge permit under § 402 of the FWPCA, 33 U.S.C. § 1342, but also an exemption from the EPA standards pursuant to § 316 of the FWPCA, 33 U.S.C. § 1326. Under § 316(a) a point source operator who "after opportunity for public hearing, can demonstrate to the satisfaction of the Administrator" that the EPA's standards are "more stringent than necessary to assure the projection [sic] and propagation of a balanced, indigenous population of shellfish, fish, and wildlife in and on the body of water" may be allowed to meet a lower standard. Moreover, under § 316(b) the cooling water intake structure must "reflect the best technology available for minimizing adverse environmental impact."

In January, 1975, the Regional Administrator of the EPA held a non-adjudicatory hearing at Seabrook. He then authorized the once-through system in June, 1975. Later, in October, 1975, he specified the location of the intake structure. The Regional Administrator granted a request by petitioners that public adjudicative hearings on PSCO's application be held. These hearings were held in March and April, 1976, pursuant to the EPA's regulations establishing procedures for deciding applications for permits under § 402 of the FWPCA. The hearings were before an administrative law judge who certified a record to the Regional Administrator for decision. The Regional Administrator decided in November, 1976, to reverse his original determinations and deny PSCO's application.

PSCO * * * appealed the decision to the Administrator who agreed to review it. Thereafter, a new Administrator was appointed, and he assembled a panel of six in-house advisors to assist in his technical review. This panel met between February 28 and March 3, 1977, and submitted a report finding that with one exception PSCO had met its burden of proof. With respect to that exception, the effect of backflushing, the Administrator asked PSCO to submit further information, offered other parties the opportunity to comment upon PSCO's submission, and stated that he would hold a hearing on the new information if any party so requested and could satisfy certain threshold conditions * * *. Petitioners did request a hearing, but the Administrator denied the request.

The Administrator's final decision followed the technical panel's recommendations and, with the additional information submitted, reversed the Regional Administrator's decision, finding that PSCO had met its burden under § 316. It is this decision that petitioners have brought before us for review.

Petitioners assert that the proceedings by which the EPA decided this case contravened certain provisions of the APA governing adjudicatory hearings, 5 U.S.C. §§ 554, 556, and 557. Respondents answer that the APA does not apply to proceedings held pursuant to § 316 or § 402 of the FWPCA, 33 U.S.C. §§ 1326, 1342.

The dispute centers on the meaning of the introductory phrases of § 554(a) of the APA:[4]

"This section applies . . . in every case of adjudication required by statute to be determined on the record after opportunity for an agency hearing. . ."

Both § 316(a) and § 402(a)(1) of the FWPCA provide for public hearings, but neither states that the hearing must be "on the record". We are now the third court of appeals to face this issue. The Ninth Circuit and the Seventh Circuit have each found that the APA does apply to proceedings pursuant to § 402. *Marathon Oil Co. v. EPA*, 564 F.2d 1253 (9th Cir.1977); *United States Steel Corp. v. Train*, 556 F.2d 822 (7th Cir.1977). We agree.

At the outset we reject the position of intervenor PSCO that the precise words "on the record" must be used to trigger the APA. The Supreme Court has clearly rejected such an extreme reading even in the context of rule making under § 553 of the APA. See *United States v. Florida East Coast Ry. Co.*, 410 U.S. 224, 245, 35 L.Ed.2d 223, 93 S.Ct. 810 (1973); *United States v. Allegheny-Ludlum Steel Corp.*, 406 U.S. 742, 757, 32 L.Ed.2d 453, 92 S.Ct. 1941 (1972). Rather, we think that the resolution of this issue turns on the substantive nature of the hearing Congress intended to provide.

We begin with the nature of the decision at issue. The EPA Administrator must make specific factual findings about the effects of discharges from a specific point source. On the basis of these findings the Administrator must determine whether to grant a discharge permit to a specific applicant. Though general policy considerations may influence the decision, the decision will not make general policy. Only the rights of the specific applicant will be affected. "As the instant proceeding well demonstrates, the factual questions involved in the issuance of section 402 permits will frequently be sharply disputed. Adversarial hearings will be helpful, therefore, in guaranteeing both reasoned decisionmaking and meaningful judicial review. In summary, the proceedings below were conducted in order 'to adjudicate disputed facts in particular cases,' not 'for the purposes of promulgating policy-type rules or standards.' " *Marathon Oil Co., supra*, at 1262.

---

[4] The determination that the EPA must make under § 316 of the FWPCA is not a rule because it is not "designed to implement, interpret, or prescribe law or policy". 5 U.S.C. § 551(4). Rather the EPA must decide a specific factual question already prescribed by statute. Since the determination is not a rule, it is an order. 5 U.S.C. § 551(6). The agency process for formulating an order is an adjudication. 5 U.S.C. § 551(7). Therefore, § 554 rather than § 553 of the APA is the relevant section. The same result is dictated because § 316(a) of the FWPCA is a licensing, 5 U.S.C. § 551(9), since it results in the granting or denial of a form of permission. See 5 U.S.C. § 551(8). A license is an order. 5 U.S.C. § 551(6).

This is exactly the kind of quasi-judicial proceeding for which the adjudicatory procedures of the APA were intended * * *. If determinations such as the one at issue here are not made on the record, then the fate of the Hampton-Seabrook Estuary could be decided on the basis of evidence that a court would never see or, what is worse, that a court could not be sure existed. We cannot believe that Congress would intend such a result.

* * * [W]e view the crucial part of the limiting language [in section 554] to be the requirement of a statutorily imposed hearing. We are willing to presume that, unless a statute otherwise specifies, an adjudicatory hearing subject to judicial review must be on the record * * *.

This rationale and conclusion also are supported by our holding in *South Terminal Corp. v. EPA*, 504 F.2d 646, 660 (1st Cir.1974) ("public hearing" not tantamount to "on the record"), and the other rule making cases cited to us for similar propositions.[9] The presumption in rule making cases is that formal, adjudicatory procedures are not necessary. A hearing serves a very different function in the rule making context. Witnesses may bring in new information or different points of view, but the agency's final decision need not reflect the public input. The witnesses are not the only source of the evidence on which the Administrator may base his factual findings. For these reasons, we place less importance on the absence of the words "on the record" in the adjudicatory context.

* * *

Here the statute certainly does not indicate that the determination need not be on the record, and we find no indication of a contrary congressional intent. Therefore, we will judge the proceedings below according to the standards set forth in §§ 554, 556, and 557 of the APA.

* * *

[The court then held that the agency violated § 556(e) of the APA by basing its decision on the report of the six-person technical review panel established by the Administrator to help evaluate the evidence provided by PSCO. That report, which was produced *after* the initial hearing on PSCO's application, was never subjected to adversarial investigation in subsequent proceedings, and the court determined that it was therefore not properly part of the record for decision. The court also remanded for an initial determination by the Administrator whether, with respect to PSCO's evidence concerning the effects of backflushing, cross-examination was "required for a full and true disclosure of the facts" under § 556(d).]

---

9   *United States v. Florida East Coast Ry.*, *supra*; *United States v. Allegheny-Ludlum Steel Corp.*, *supra*. The Supreme Court explicitly confined its holding to rule making cases. *Id.*, 406 U.S. at 757, 92 S.Ct. at 1941.

NOTES

Seacoast and *West Chicago* offer dueling presumptions: the *Seacoast* court was willing to presume (subject to rebuttal by evidence of contrary congressional intent) that any language in an organic statute calling for a "hearing" triggers formal adjudication, while the *West Chicago* court appeared to presume (subject to rebuttal by evidence of contrary congressional intent) that the restrictive rule of *FECR* applies to adjudications as well as rulemakings.[20] As we saw earlier, in 1978 one panel of the D.C. Circuit expressly endorsed the *West Chicago* position. At other times, however, the D.C. Circuit seemed instead to endorse the opposite presumption that "hearing" language ordinarily triggered formal adjudication. *See Union of Concerned Scientists v. NRC*, 735 F.2d 1437, 1444 n.12 (D.C.Cir.1984) ("when a statute calls for a hearing in an adjudication the hearing is presumptively governed by 'on the record' procedures").

In 1989, the D.C. Circuit resolved its intra-circuit conflict between presumptions by selecting "none of the above."

In order to understand the D.C. Circuit's choice, however, we need to get a bit ahead of ourselves. Chapter 4 will cover the standards by which courts review the substance of agency decisionmaking—that is, the factual, legal and policy determinations that agencies make in the course of rulemakings or adjudications. In a wide range of circumstances, courts give a considerable amount of deference to an agency's substantive determinations; the precise contours and scope of that deference are the chief topic of Chapter 4. Oftentimes, that deference extends to agency legal determinations. For example, the NRC's interpretation of its regulations in *City of West Chicago* was a legal determination: the agency was construing a legal text. The court gave—correctly under then-governing doctrine—a great deal of deference to the agency's view of the law. In other words, for the City of West Chicago to win on its claim that agency regulations required the formal procedures that it requested, the City had to show not only that it had the better of the legal argument but that the agency's legal position was seriously wrong. The agency went into that dispute with a big thumb (and several fingers) on its side of the scale. A similar doctrine often applies to agency interpretations of statutes. When you are litigating against an agency, you will often have to show more than that the agency is probably wrong about the law; you may well have to show that the agency's interpretation of the law is downright unreasonable. This doctrine is most often associated with *Chevron U.S.A. v. Natural Resources Defense Council*, 467 U.S. 837, 104 S.Ct. 2778, 81 L.Ed.2d 694 (1984). You will study *Chevron*, its predecessors, and its aftermath in gruesome detail later in this course. For now, it is enough to recognize that *Chevron* often effectively functions as a presumption in favor of the agency's interpretation of a statute. In light of that doctrine, consider. . .

---

[20] One must say "appears to" because, if the court is to be believed, the city's lawyers conceded that this was the appropriate standard.

CHEMICAL WASTE MGM'T, INC. V. UNITED STATES EPA

United States Court of Appeals, District of Columbia Circuit, 1989.
873 F.2d 1477.

Before WALD, CHIEF JUDGE, and STARR and D.H. GINSBURG, CIRCUIT JUDGES.

D.H. GINSBURG, CIRCUIT JUDGE:

Petitioners Chemical Waste Management, Inc. and Waste Management of North America seek review of Environmental Protection Agency regulations that establish informal procedures for administrative hearings concerning the issuance of corrective action orders under § 3008(h) of the Resource Conservation and Recovery Act (RCRA), as modified by the Hazardous and Solid Waste Amendments of 1984. 42 U.S.C. § 6928(h). We conclude that the regulations represent a reasonable interpretation of an ambiguous statutory provision and are not, on their face, inconsistent with the requirement of due process. Accordingly, we deny the petition for review.

I.   BACKGROUND

Congress enacted RCRA in 1976 to establish a comprehensive program for regulation of hazardous waste management and disposal. The statute requires generally that the operator of any hazardous waste treatment, storage, or disposal facility obtain a permit, but facilities in existence as of 1980 may continue to operate as "interim facilities" pending agency action on their permit applications.

A.   *Formal Adjudication under Part 22*

Subsection (a) of RCRA § 3008 authorizes EPA to enter orders assessing civil penalties, including suspension or revocation of permits, for violation of RCRA regulations. 42 U.S.C. § 6928(a). Subsection (b) provides that, upon request made within thirty days of the issuance of a subsection (a) order, EPA "shall promptly conduct a public hearing." Accordingly, the agency is authorized to "issue subpoenas for the attendance and testimony of witnesses and the production of relevant papers, books, and documents, and may promulgate rules for discovery procedures." RCRA § 3008(b), 42 U.S.C. § 6928(b).

In 1978, EPA promulgated procedural regulations to implement the "public hearing" provision of subsection (a). 40 C.F.R. Part 22. These procedures conform to the provisions of the Administrative Procedure Act for formal adjudication. 5 U.S.C. §§ 556 & 557. For example, an Administrative Law Judge presides at the hearing, 40 C.F.R. § 22.03(a), and each party has the right to call and to cross-examine witnesses, 40 C.F.R. § 22.22(b).

In the preamble accompanying these regulations, EPA explained its selection of formal adjudicatory procedures. Although, in EPA's view, there are "many cases" in which the term "public hearing" should not be read to require formal adjudicatory procedures, EPA concluded that "the nature of the decision at issue in [subsection (a)] cases indicates . . . that such formal procedures were probably intended." 43 Fed. Reg. 34738 (1978). In such cases, the agency "will be accusing someone of violating established legal standards through their past conduct, and will be seeking to impose a sanction for it. . . In addition, the facts at issue will be specific ones involving the past conduct of regulated persons." *Id.*

B. *Informal Adjudication Under Part 24*

In the Hazardous and Solid Waste Amendments of 1984, Congress added to § 3008 a new subsection (h), authorizing the Administrator of EPA to issue "an order requiring corrective action" whenever he "determines that there is or has been a release of hazardous waste into the environment" from an interim facility. RCRA § 3008(h)(1), 42 U.S.C. § 6928(h)(1). Such orders must indicate "the nature of the required corrective action or other response measure, and . . . specify a time for compliance," and may include suspension or revocation of the facility's authorization to operate as an interim facility. RCRA § 3008(h)(2), 42 U.S.C. § 6928(h)(2). The Administrator may assess a civil penalty of up to $25,000 per day for noncompliance with a corrective action order. *Id.* The 1984 Amendments also modified subsection (b) to make it clear that those subject to corrective action orders under the new subsection (h) have the right to a "public hearing."

To govern subsection (h) hearings, EPA promulgated the procedural regulations here under review, 40 C.F.R. Part 24. Those rules specifically provide that the formal adjudicatory procedures of Part 22 shall be applicable only to challenges to subsection (h) corrective action orders that include a suspension or revocation of interim status or an assessment of civil penalties for noncompliance. 40 C.F.R. § 24.01. If the order calls upon the interim facility operator merely to undertake an investigation or to do so in combination with interim corrective measures, then, depending upon the burden entailed by such measures, the agency will use either the informal adjudicatory procedures provided in Subpart B of Part 24 (for interim corrective measures that are "neither costly nor technically complex," 40 C.F.R. § 24.80) or those in Subpart C of Part 24.

The procedures in Subparts B and C are substantially similar insofar as is relevant to this case. The crucial point is that both subparts set forth informal rather than formal adjudicatory procedures. Under either subpart, the operator of a hazardous waste facility may submit written information and argument for inclusion in the record, 40 C.F.R. §§ 24.10(b) & 24.14(a)(1); make an oral presentation at the hearing itself, 40 C.F.R.

§§ 24.11 & 24.15(a); and be assisted at hearing by legal and technical advisors, *id*. Direct examination and cross-examination of witnesses is not permitted, but the Presiding Officer may direct questions to either party. *Id*. The Presiding Officer is to be either "the Regional Judicial Officer . . . or another attorney employed by the Agency, who has had no prior connection with the case, including performance of any investigative or prosecuting functions." 40 C.F.R. §§ 24.09 & 24.13(a). With respect to both Subpart B and Subpart C proceedings, EPA, when issuing a corrective action order, shall deliver to the operator "all relevant documents and oral information (which has been reduced to writing), which the Agency considered in the process of developing and issuing the order, exclusive of privileged internal communications." 40 C.F.R. § 24.03(b).

The Presiding Officer is to review the record and to file a recommended decision with the EPA Regional Administrator, 40 C.F.R. §§ 12 & 24.17. The Regional Administrator, in turn, is to receive comments from the parties and to render a final decision, 40 C.F.R. § 24.18, from which an aggrieved party may seek judicial review under the APA.

II.   *CHEVRON* ANALYSIS

Petitioners argue initially that the informal procedures of Part 24 are inconsistent with the intent of Congress in enacting and amending § 3008 * * *.

* * *

We approach petitioners' arguments within the framework that the Supreme Court decreed in *Chevron U.S.A. v. Natural Resources Defense Council*, 467 U.S. 837, 81 L.Ed.2d 694, 104 S.Ct. 2778 (1984), for judicial review of an agency's interpretation of a statute under its administration. At the outset, we ask whether "Congress has directly spoken to the precise question at issue," *id*. at 842; if so, then we "must give effect to the unambiguously expressed intent of Congress" and may not defer to a contrary agency interpretation, *id*. at 842–43. If the statute is "silent or ambiguous with respect to the specific issue," however, we proceed to ask "whether the agency's answer is based on a permissible construction of the statute," *id*. at 843; if so, then we must defer to the agency's construction.

* * *

* * * [T]he statutory language, taken alone, does not show that Congress "has directly spoken to the precise question at issue." Subsection (b) requires a "public hearing" but does not, by its terms, indicate whether Congress intended that formal or informal hearing procedures be used * * *.

* * *

3. *Circuit Precedent.* Petitioners point to our statement in a footnote in *Union of Concerned Scientists v. U.S. NRC*, 237 U.S.App.D.C. 1, 735 F.2d 1437, 1444 n. 12 (D.C.Cir.1984) (*UCS*), that "when a statute calls for a hearing in an adjudication the hearing is presumptively governed by 'on the record' procedures," notwithstanding omission of the phrase "on the record" in the statute. See also *Seacoast Anti-Pollution League v. Costle*, 572 F.2d 872, 877 (1st Cir.1978); *Marathon Oil v. EPA*, 564 F.2d 1253, 1264 (9th Cir.1977). For the reasons set out below, however, we decline to adhere any longer to the presumption raised in *UCS*.

* * *

* * * *UCS* and its kin, *Seacoast* and *Marathon*, all predate the Supreme Court's decision in *Chevron*. Under that decision, it is not our office to presume that a statutory reference to a "hearing," without more specific guidance from Congress, evinces an intention to require formal adjudicatory procedures, since such a presumption would arrogate to the court what is now clearly the prerogative of the agency, *viz.*, to bring its own expertise to bear upon the resolution of ambiguities in the statute that Congress has charged it to administer. In effect, the presumption in *UCS* truncates the *Chevron* inquiry at the first step by treating a facially ambiguous statutory reference to a "hearing" as though it were an unambiguous constraint upon the agency. We will henceforth make no presumption that a statutory "hearing" requirement does or does not compel the agency to undertake a formal "hearing on the record," thereby leaving it to the agency, as an initial matter, to resolve the ambiguity.*

While an agency might not be able reasonably to read a requirement that it conduct a "hearing on the record" to permit informal procedures in the converse situation to that presented here, an agency that *reasonably* reads a simple requirement that it hold a "hearing" to allow for informal hearing procedures must prevail under the second step of *Chevron*. As usual in cases involving *Chevron*'s second step, the court will evaluate the reasonableness of the agency's interpretation using the normal tools of statutory interpretation—such as legislative history, structural inferences, or exceptional circumstances of the type presented in *UCS*.

* * *

[The court concluded that the agency's interpretation of the statute was reasonable and reasonably explained, and it rejected as well a constitutional due process challenge to the regulations.]

* * *

---

* Our discussion rejecting the presumption set forth in the *UCS* dictum has been separately circulated to and approved by the entire court, and thus constitutes the law of this circuit. *See Irons v. Diamond*, 216 U.S. App. D.C. 107, 670 F.2d 265, 268 n. 11 (D.C.Cir.1981).

* * * [T]he petition for review is

Denied.

NOTES

With *Chemical Waste* in the mix, there are at least three options for a court trying to decide (in the absence of binding circuit precedent) when ambiguous "hearing" language in an organic statute triggers formal agency adjudication. Is a fourth option to abandon altogether the search for presumptions and simply figure out the best answer in each case? For a spirited and thoughtful defense of precisely this position, see Melissa M. Berry, *Beyond* Chevron's *Domain: Agency Interpretations of Statutory Procedural Provisions*, 30 Seattle U.L. Rev. 541 (2007).

In 2006, the First Circuit abandoned *Seacoast* and joined the D.C. Circuit in holding that *Chevron* governs when agencies construe organic statutes that are ambiguous about the need for an "on the record" formal proceeding. *See Dominion Energy Brayton Point, LLC v. Johnson*, 443 F.3d 12 (1st Cir. 2006). The court determined, as had the D.C. Circuit in *Chemical Waste*, that post-1984 Supreme Court cases required reappraisal of its past doctrine and mandated deference to agency interpretations of ambiguous organic statutes. (Of course, if an organic statute unambiguously calls for formal adjudication, an agency cannot escape that conclusion by interpreting the statute otherwise. How does one know when a statute is unambiguous? Hold that question until Chapter 4.) Thus, *Seacoast* is no longer good law in the First Circuit. In the absence of controlling Supreme Court precedent, it could, of course, still be "good law" in some other court that has not yet ruled on the standard for triggering formal adjudication and finds *Seacoast* persuasive.

D. INFORMAL RULEMAKING

1. THE ORIGINAL UNDERSTANDING

The Department of Justice's 1947 *Manual on the Administrative Procedure Act* had the following to say about the procedures in informal rulemaking:

> * * * Under section 4(b) [section 553(b)] each agency * * * may conduct its rule making by affording interested persons opportunity to submit written data only, or by receiving a combination of written and oral evidence, or by adopting any other method it finds most appropriate for public participation in the rule making process * * *.

> * * *

> * * * [A]n agency may state the proposed rule itself or the substance of the rule in the notice required by section 4(a). On the other hand, the agency, if it desires, may issue a more general

"description of the subjects and issues involved" * * *. When there is a "description of the subjects and issues involved," the notice should be sufficiently informative to assure interested persons an opportunity to participate intelligently in the rule making process.

* * * [S]ection 4(a) * * * confers discretion upon the agency, except where statutes require "formal rule making subject to sections 7 and 8, to designate in each case the procedure for public participation in rule making. Such informal rule making procedure may take a variety of forms: informal hearings (with or without a stenographic transcript), conferences, consultation with industry committees, submission of written views, or any combination of these * * * ".

Each agency is affirmatively required to consider "all relevant matter presented" in the proceeding * * *. It is entirely clear, however, that section 4(b) does not require the formulation of rules upon the exclusive basis of any "record" made in informal rule making proceedings. Accordingly, except in formal rule making governed by sections 7 and 8, an agency is free to formulate rules upon the basis of materials in its files and the knowledge and experience of the agency, in addition to the materials adduced in public rule making proceedings.

Section 4(b) provides that upon the completion of public rule making proceedings "after consideration of all relevant matter presented, the agency shall incorporate in any rules adopted a concise general statement of their basis and purpose." The required statement will be important in that the courts and the public may be expected to use such statements in the interpretation of the agency's rules. The statement is to be "concise" and "general". Except as required by statutes providing for "formal" rule making procedure, findings of fact and conclusions of law are not necessary. Nor is there required an elaborate analysis of the rules or of the considerations upon which the rules were issued. Rather, the statement is intended to advise the public of the general basis and purpose of the rules.

United States Dep't of Justice, Attorney General's Manual on the Administrative Procedure Act 29–32 (1947). This suggests a minimal set of procedures that it would be almost impossible for an agency to fail to provide (or to fail to provide in a fashion that would not be harmless error). Indeed, your editor is unaware of any significant case in the first two decades after enactment of the APA that turned on the inadequacy of agency procedures in an informal rulemaking. Until the late 1960s, it is fair to say that there was effectively no substantial body of doctrine concerning the procedural law of informal rulemaking. Under the text of section 553 of the APA, it is difficult even to imagine what such a body of doctrine would look like.

As it happens, this is one of the those areas of administrative law in which the text of the APA has played a relatively modest role in modern legal development, though the statute does make doctrinal appearances in seemingly odd places. As you examine the following materials, see if you can detect any rhyme or reason in the ways in which the text of section 553 affects judicial decisions regarding the procedural requirements for informal rulemaking. (Spoiler alert: Your editor has no grand theory as to either rhyme or reason, so do not spend excessive energy on this search.)

2. THE *VERMONT YANKEE* SAGA

The law governing *formal* rulemaking is best understood through the story of a railroad and its car-hire rates: the *Florida East Coast Railway* saga. Similarly, the law governing *informal* rulemaking is best understood through the story of a power company and its nuclear plant: the *Vermont Yankee* saga. It is perhaps the most important saga in modern administrative law.

a. The Agency Speaks

In 1954, Congress enacted the Atomic Energy Act in order to promote and channel the commercial use of nuclear power. Under the statute, nuclear power plants must have federal licenses in order to be built or operated.[21] These licensing proceedings are adjudications under the APA and, under the same statute at issue in *City of West Chicago,* require a "hearing." 42 U.S.C. § 2239(a) (2012). In addition, the Nuclear Regulatory Commission (which assumed the functions of the Atomic Energy Commission in 1974) has general authority to "make, promulgate, issue, rescind and amend such rules and regulations as may be necessary to carry out the purposes of this Chapter." 42 U.S.C. § 2201(p) (2012). This grant of general rulemaking authority does not require rules to be made "on the record," does not require any kind of hearing, and indeed does not specify any procedures whatsoever for such rulemakings. Even if the *FECR* decision did not exist, or had come out the other way, it would be indisputable that this statute authorizes informal, notice-and-comment rulemaking under the APA.

On December 2, 1966, Vermont Yankee Nuclear Power Corporation applied for a license to construct and operate a nuclear power plant in

---

[21] For the first 35 years of the statute, separate licensing proceedings had to be held for construction and operation of nuclear reactors. In 1989, the Nuclear Regulatory Commission by rule created a streamlined procedure for obtaining a "combined" construction/operation license (and also for obtaining approval of site locations and generic reactor designs). *See Early Site Permits; Standard Design Certifications; and Combined Licenses for Nuclear Power Reactors*, 54 Fed. Reg. 15,372 (1989) (codified at 10 C.F.R. pts. 2, 50–52 & 170).

Vernon, Vermont. Roughly a year later, the construction license was granted. The request for an operating license was the subject of an adjudicatory hearing by a three-person Atomic Safety and Licensing Board on August 10, 1971. One of the main issues that opponents of the plant tried to raise throughout the proceedings was the potential problem of dealing with the waste products from nuclear fission, which remain radioactive for a very long time. One must either dispose of these wastes by burying them in stable underground facilities or reprocess them into usable fuel. At the 1971 hearing, the Licensing Board ruled that it would not consider the environmental effects of the reprocessing or disposal of nuclear wastes generated by the plant in its decision whether to grant an operating license, though it *would* consider the environmental effects of transporting the spent fuel to storage or disposal sites.[22] This decision was affirmed by the agency's Atomic Safety and Licensing Appeal Board, which (as the name suggests) was constituted to hear internal agency appeals from adjudicatory decisions of licensing boards.

The agency had to deal with similar questions about waste disposal and reprocessing every time that someone sought to build or operate a nuclear reactor. One sensible way to deal with recurring issues is to promulgate a *rule* that will resolve those issues for all future adjudications, so that they do not have to be considered on a case-by-case basis. Accordingly, shortly after the decision of the agency's Appeal Board, the agency issued a notice of proposed rulemaking to consider a rule "that would specifically deal with the question of consideration of environmental effects associated with the uranium fuel cycle in the individual cost-benefit analyses for light water cooled nuclear power reactors." *Notice of Proposed Rulemaking: Environmental Effects of the Uranium Fuel Cycle*, 37 Fed. Reg. 24,191, 24,191 (Nov. 15, 1972). As part of the rulemaking, the Commission's staff prepared an "Environmental Survey of the Nuclear Fuel Cycle," dated November 6, 1972, which foresaw few, if any, environmental problems from nuclear waste reprocessing or disposal. Based on that study, the Commission proposed a rule that specified very small values for the environmental effects of fuel reprocessing or disposal to be used in all reactor licensing proceedings. The Commission expressly stated that the proceeding to consider that rule would be "informal" and "legislative-type," *id.* at 24,193, with no cross-examination or discovery allowed. It nonetheless invited interested persons to "attend the hearing and present *oral or written* statements," *id.* (emphasis added), and it made available for inspection the staff-generated Environmental Survey of the Nuclear Fuel Cycle. *See id.* ("Copies of . . . [the survey] may be examined at

---

[22] This was not as weird as it might sound. The Board reasoned that the highly speculative effects of the reprocessing or disposal of nuclear wastes were better considered in decisions to license the reprocessing or disposal facilities themselves than in proceedings to license individual reactors. Transportation issues, on the other hand, were more plausibly site-specific and therefore appropriately handled on a reactor-by-reactor basis.

the Commission's Public Document Room . . . [or] may be obtained upon request"). The text of § 553 of the APA expressly does not require oral proceedings in informal rulemakings, and it says nothing about public availability of agency documents in rulemakings.[23] Nor did any agency regulation or organic statute require those kinds of procedures in informal rulemakings under 42 U.S.C. § 2201(p).

The Commission ultimately adopted the proposed rule with minor variations. *See Environmental Effects of the Uranium Fuel Cycle*, 39 Fed. Reg. 14,188 (1974). The rule was challenged in the D.C. Circuit by the National Resources Defense Council (NRDC) and other environmental lobbying groups.

b.   The D.C. Circuit Speaks

The D.C. Circuit sided with the NRDC and invalidated the proposed rule. *See NRDC v. NRC*, 547 F.2d 633 (D.C.Cir.1976). The vast bulk of the opinion, and of the challengers' arguments, focused on the scanty *substantive* support for the agency's action. And, indeed, the Environmental Survey that formed the basis for the agency's rule was long on conclusions but remarkably short on detail given the large role that it played in the agency's ultimate decision. The petitioning environmental groups, however, also strongly objected to the absence of cross-examination and discovery, which they argued was necessary in order to reveal the basis for the agency's Environmental Survey. The D.C. Circuit agreed that the agency's procedures were legally inadequate:

> Many procedural devices for creating a genuine dialogue on these issues [of waste reprocessing and disposal] were available to the agency—including informal conferences between intervenors and staff, document discovery, interrogatories, technical advisory committees comprised of outside experts with differing perspectives, limited cross-examination, funding independent research by intervenors, detailed annotation of technical reports, surveys of existing literature, memoranda explaining methodology. We do not presume to intrude on the agency's province by dictating to it which, if any, of these devices it must adopt to flesh out the record. It may be that no combination of the procedures mentioned above will prove adequate, and the agency will be required to develop new procedures. . . On the other hand, the procedures the agency adopted in this case, if administered in a more sensitive, deliberate manner, might suffice. Whatever

---

[23] The Freedom of Information Act, which is technically part of the APA, requires agencies to make any documents, including rulemaking documents, publicly available upon request unless the requested information comes within one of nine stated exceptions. But the agency in this case was making the documents available without requiring parties to go through the machinery of the FOIA, and there is nothing in the text of § 553 that required the agency to extend that courtesy.

techniques the Commission adopts, before it promulgates a rule limiting further consideration of waste disposal and reprocessing issues, it must in one way or another generate a record in which the factual issues are fully developed.

547 F.2d at 653–54.

The text of the APA seems to provide no support for any such procedural claims in an informal notice-and-comment rulemaking. Indeed, the petitioners got *more* procedures than the APA contemplates: the agency gave them access to the Environmental Survey and allowed them to participate in oral proceedings, neither of which is strictly mandated by the text of § 553. Nonetheless, in 1976, the argument that the agency also had to provide opportunities for discovery and cross-examination during the informal rulemaking was a slam-dunk winner in any lower court in the country, and the D.C. Circuit's discussion of this point was a straightforward application of then-governing circuit-court precedent.

The story of how a textually frivolous claim in 1946 became an easy winner in 1976 comprises the next chapter in the unfolding saga of American administrative law. The materials following *Florida East Coast Railway* briefly described the flight to rulemaking, and in particular to informal rulemaking, that resulted from the large-scale expansion of agencies and agency jurisdictions.[24] The next series of events, which forms the critical backdrop to *Vermont Yankee*, arose out of two other major developments in the 1960s and early 1970s.

The first development concerned theories of agency behavior. At the same time that agencies were exercising ever-increasing authority under ever-decreasing procedural restraints, confidence in agency decisionmaking among scholars, judges, and participants in the administrative process was reaching a new low. The New Deal and the informal rulemaking provisions of the APA were driven by James Landis' vision of disinterested, apolitical management of economic activity by technically expert government officials. By the 1960s and early 1970s, that model of agency decisionmaking had fallen into disrepute. The dominant model of agency behavior, as reflected in the excerpt in Chapter 1 from Roger Noll's 1971 book *Reforming Regulation*,[25] instead viewed agencies as pawns of special industry interests who would use the agency process to shield themselves from economic competition and public scrutiny. Indeed, "dominant" does not quite describe the power exercised by the "agency capture" model during this time period; it was treated by virtually everyone, regardless of ideological orientation, as an established fact of

---

[24] *See supra* pages 351–352.
[25] *See supra* pages 78–79.

regulatory life.[26] Opponents of regulation could, of course, try to argue that the threat of agency capture counseled against granting broad powers to administrators. But there is no necessary logical link between endorsement of capture theory and opposition to regulation. If one is substantively committed to the regulatory agenda of the activist state, one could instead view capture theory as an invitation to (as the title of Professor Noll's book suggests) *reform* rather than *limit* the administrative process. Certainly, many proponents of capture theory did not view it as in any way antagonistic to regulation in general. Indeed, the people who arguably gave capture theory its widest public airing were Ralph Nader and his supporters, who certainly did not view capture theory as a clarion call for deregulation. It is impossible in one paragraph to communicate the extent to which the capture theory of agency behavior dominated and influenced administrative law in the 1960s and 1970s. For a longer discussion that elaborates on many of the themes in this chapter, see Thomas W. Merrill, *Capture Theory and the Courts, 1967–1983*, 72 Chi.Kent L. Rev. 1039 (1997).

The second important development in the 1960s was the emergence on the D.C. Circuit of a solid majority of "activist liberal" judges, who all wore that label openly and proudly as a badge of honor. To appreciate the significance of this development, however, one first needs to understand the D.C. Circuit's role in the formulation of administrative law.

From the perspective of administrative law, the D.C. Circuit has for decades been by far the most important court in the country—*much* more important than the Supreme Court. The Supreme Court decides perhaps half a dozen administrative law cases (broadly construed) each year. By contrast, the D.C. Circuit hears approximately 1/3 of all major federal administrative law appeals. In part, this concentration of authority is a natural result of geography: because all agencies have offices in Washington, D.C., judicial review statutes almost always provide that venue for challenges to agency action is at least *proper* in the D.C. Circuit. And in part, it is the result of deliberate statutory design, which in many important cases makes the D.C. Circuit the *exclusive* venue for challenging agency action.[27] In any event, the effect of this concentration of review is that participants in the administrative process often care a lot more about the views of the D.C. Circuit than about the views of the Supreme Court. An agency that is unhappy with some aspect of the D.C. Circuit's

---

[26] Even James Landis succumbed to some degree; in 1960, he wrote a report to President-elect Kennedy that was witheringly critical of much agency practice since the onset of the New Deal.

[27] *See, e.g.* 42 U.S.C. 7607(b)(1) (2012) (providing for exclusive review in the D.C. Circuit of air quality standards or rules promulgated by the Administrator of the Environmental Protection Agency); 42 U.S.C. § 9613(a) (2012) (providing for exclusive review in the D.C. Circuit of regulations promulgated under the Comprehensive Environmental Response, Compensation, and Liability Act).

administrative law jurisprudence will recognize that its chances of getting Supreme Court review are very slim,[28] and even if it obtains review, the appellate process can take years, with its accompanying disruption of the agency's program. It is generally easier and cheaper simply to do whatever the D.C. Circuit wants. As then-Professor (later Justice) Scalia put it in his classic article on *Vermont Yankee*: "As a practical matter, the D.C. Circuit is something of a resident manager, and the Supreme Court an absentee landlord." Antonin Scalia, Vermont Yankee: *The APA, the D.C. Circuit, and the Supreme Court*, 1978 Sup. Ct. Rev. 345, 371. On the whole, it is not too much to say that the D.C. Circuit's *dicta* often has more influence on the actual practice of administrative law than do the Supreme Court's *holdings*.

In the 1960s, this critical power center of administrative law came to be dominated by a powerful bloc of judges, spearheaded by a quartet with whom every student of administrative law should be familiar: David Bazelon (the author of the D.C. Circuit's opinion in *Vermont Yankee*), J. Skelly Wright, Carl McGowan, and Harold Leventhal. For a detailed look at these judges and their jurisprudential philosophies, see Matthew Warren, *Active Judging: Judicial Philosophy and the Development of the Hard Look Doctrine in the D.C. Circuit*, 90 Geo. L.J. 2599 (2002). All of these men were very savvy, *very* smart,[29] and *VERY* liberal, and along with fellow-travellers Spottswood Robinson and Edward Tamm, they formed an unbreakable majority on the D.C. Circuit in the decade before *Vermont Yankee* (1968–78).[30] All four were self-conscious judicial activists,[31] though,

---

[28] The lower court judges recognize this as well. A possibly apocryphal story is told of a former D.C. Circuit judge who, when asked how he could justify an opinion in which he had flagrantly flouted governing Supreme Court precedent, responded, "Well, they can't reverse 'em all."

[29] Even while serving on the bench, all four judges were frequent contributors to law reviews on a wide variety of subjects, and McGowan was a former professor of Administrative Law.

[30] For most of this period, the court also had three conservative judges: Malcolm Wilkey, Roger Robb, and George MacKinnon. Wilkey often voted with the liberals on administrative law issues, and neither Robb nor MacKinnon had a consistent administrative law philosophy to offer in opposition to their colleagues.

[31] This is not a normative judgment—it is a simple statement of fact which the judges themselves would have happily endorsed. McGowan was the quiet one of the group, but here are some selected self-descriptions of Bazelon, Leventhal, and Wright:

Wright on Wright and Bazelon (from J. Skelly Wright, *A Colleague's Tribute to Judge David L. Bazelon, on the Twenty-Fifth Anniversary of His Appointment*, 123 U. Pa. L. Rev. 250, 250 (1974)):

I am probably the only judge on any federal court of appeals who can call Judge David L. Bazelon conservative. We have been members of the same court for twelve years. In that time, we have often agreed on the answer to questions of law, and our agreement has generally put us both on the liberal side of the court.

Bazelon on Bazelon and Wright (from David L. Bazelon, *A Colleague's Tribute to Chief Judge J. Skelly Wright*, 7 Hastings Const. L.Q. 864, 865 (1980)):

Judge Wright and I are members of an inferior federal court * * *. [I]t is fair to say that we are both examples of a species sometimes called "liberal, activist federal judges" * * *.

Wright on Wright and Leventhal (from J. Skelly Wright, *Harold Leventhal*, 80 Colum. L. Rev. 882, 882 (1980)):

as we shall see, they sometimes disagreed among themselves about exactly what kinds of activism were appropriate. They were especially concerned about environmental issues, which were becoming major subjects of regulatory concern in the 1960s and early 1970s, and they were well schooled in the theory of agency capture. As a result, they were deeply worried that agencies—particularly the new breed of single-headed executive agencies such as the National Highway Traffic Safety Administration and the Environmental Protection Agency—would sell out their lofty mandates under industry pressure and political influence. Even worse from their perspective, they had to watch dourly as Richard Nixon was elected President in 1968, and in the following years they had to watch dourly as President Nixon appointed the administrators to run the various health, safety, and environmental agencies.

Their views on agency behavior showed through transparently in their opinions. Recall James Landis' exalted vision of agency competence and compare it to Wright's view, expressed in a 1971 opinion (joined by Robinson and Tamm):

> These cases are only the beginning of what promises to become a flood of new litigation—litigation seeking judicial assistance in protecting our natural environment. Several recently enacted statutes attest to the commitment of the Government to control, at long last, the destructive engine of material "progress." But it remains to be seen whether the promise of this legislation will become a reality. Therein lies the judicial role. In these cases, we must for the first time interpret the broadest and perhaps most important of the recent statutes: the National Environmental Policy Act of 1969 (NEPA). We must assess claims that one of the agencies charged with its administration has failed to live up to the congressional mandate. Our duty, in short, is to see that important legislative purposes, heralded in the halls of Congress, are not lost or misdirected in the vast hallways of the federal bureaucracy.

Calvert Cliffs' Coordinating Committee, Inc. v. United States AEC, 449 F.2d 1109, 1111 (D.C.Cir.1971) (footnotes omitted). Leventhal (joined by McGowan) was even more explicit about agency capture concerns: "The essential point is that a procedure not requiring an opportunity for oral

---

Judge Leventhal * * * did not blink at the need for bold initiatives when traditional approaches would not work * * *. [H]e was never reluctant to turn "outside" the law for solutions to hard problems.

And here is Geoff Stone, former Dean of the University of Chicago Law School and a former clerk to Judge Wright, on Wright (from Geoffrey R. Stone, *A Passion for Justice*, 98 Yale L.J. 213, 218 (1988)):

We live in an era in which the terms "judicial activism" and "liberalism" are often hurled as insults. This is a tragedy of our times. Judge Wright was both a "judicial activist" and a "liberal." He wore both labels proudly.

presentation to the Department [of Agriculture] on crucial matters, and not requiring evidence in the record, is a seed bed for the weed of industry domination." *Walter Holm & Co. v. Hardin*, 449 F.2d 1009 (D.C.Cir.1971). Not to be outdone, Wright added in 1977:

> Although it is impossible to draw any firm conclusions about the effect of ex parte presentations upon the ultimate shape of the pay cable rules, the evidence is certainly consistent with the oft-voiced claims of undue industry influence over Commission proceedings, and we are particularly concerned that the final shaping of the rules we are reviewing here may have been by compromise among contending industry forces, rather than by exercise of the independent discretion in the public interest the Communications Act vests in individual commissioners.

Home Box Office, Inc. v. FCC, 567 F.2d 9, 53 (D.C.Cir.1977). Bazelon, in a separate concurring statement in *Vermont Yankee*, emphasized the judges' deep concern about environmental matters: "Decisions in areas touching the environment or medicine affect the lives and health of all. These interests, like the First Amendment, have 'always had a special claim to judicial protection.'" *NRDC v. NRC*, 547 F.2d 633, 657 (D.C.Cir.1976) (footnote omitted).[32]

So, imagine that you are a liberal activist judge in the early 1970s with a strong environmental consciousness. You fully expect agencies—especially Nixonite agencies—to lay a "seed bed for the weed of industry domination" and thereby unleash "the destructive engine of material 'progress.'" At the same time, however, you are strongly in favor of the agencies' substantive missions and believe in an extensive post-New Deal regulatory state. What do you do?

One solution is to second-guess the *substantive* decisions of the agencies. That is, you simply decide directly whether you think an agency's decision constitutes desirable social policy. This substantive approach, however, involves a rather bald assertion of judicial authority, which may or may not give you pause. More importantly, it assumes that you can recognize a desirable social policy when you see one. That assumption of judicial competence may be unwarranted with respect to many of the complicated, cutting-edge scientific issues involved in much environmental policymaking. It also assumes that you, as a judge, will have access to sufficient information to be able to determine whether agencies are pursuing your vision of the public good.

---

[32] The quotation in this passage supporting the claim of a special judicial role in environmental protection was from a prior opinion by Bazelon. *See* EDF v. Ruckelshaus , 598 (D.C.Cir.1971). The passage's only other authority was a "see also" citation to a law review article by Leventhal. *See* Harold Leventhal, *Environmental Decisionmaking and the Role of the Courts*, 122 U. Pa. L. Rev. 509 (1974).

Given all of these concerns, you might instead decide to concentrate on regulating the agencies' decisionmaking *procedures*, on the assumptions that (1) judges are generally competent to identify good decisionmaking procedures, (2) procedures are a good in themselves because they promote participatory values and expose agency decisionmaking to public scrutiny, and (3) good decisionmaking procedures might at least marginally improve the chances of reaching good results when courts cannot identify or command good results directly.

Throughout the early 1970s, Bazelon, McGowan, Leventhal, and Wright openly and forcefully debated the merits of these two approaches in a series of important judicial opinions and law review articles. (One of the most famous of those debates, in *Ethyl Corp. v. EPA,* 541 F.2d 1 (D.C.Cir.1976) (en banc), is partially reproduced at pages 752–756, *infra.*) The end result of that debate was intensive judicial review of both procedure *and* substance.

If the issue in an administrative law case was substantive (did the law or regulation really apply? were the environmental consequences adequately considered? did the agency give undue consideration to economic feasibility? were consumer interests appropriately addressed?), there is no question that industries on the wrong end of a regulation or a rate order were at something of a disadvantage when arguing to the D.C. Circuit in the 1970s. While it is possible to overstate the extent of the court's raw result orientation, it was significant enough to make forum shopping a critical element in any administrative law litigation strategy. In some cases, forum shopping was impossible because the venue provisions in the relevant judicial review statutes concentrated all appeals from agency action in the D.C. Circuit. However, where venue was appropriate in more than one jurisdiction, the race to the courthouse was on.[33]

We will take up the details of substantive review of agency decisionmaking in Chapter 4. For now, the focus is on the D.C. Circuit's pre-*Vermont Yankee procedural* activism. All of the D.C. Circuit's liberals, and on frequent occasion one of its conservatives (Malcolm Wilkey), were in favor of procedural activism.[34] The result was that in the decade preceding *Vermont Yankee,* the D.C. Circuit invented something that has come to be called "hybrid APA rulemaking," which involved judicially

---

[33] For more on forum shopping, and the modern solution to it, *see infra* pages 1020–1021.

[34] It is worth noting that the liberal bloc did not display any significant party bias when reviewing agency decisions for procedural rather than substantive errors. Their doctrines were "articulated at a level of generality that permitted a wide variety of groups, including not just public interest intervenors but also regulated businesses and their competitors, to enlist the court in their struggles with agency regulators." Thomas W. Merrill, *Capture Theory and the Courts: 1967–1983,* 72 Chi.Kent L. Rev. 1039, 1040 (1997). Industries as well as environmental groups seeking to challenge agency decisions on *procedural* grounds were delighted to litigate in the D.C. Circuit.

grafting onto the basic § 553 notice-and-comment requirements a series of procedural additions that varied from case to case, though almost always stopping well short of the full range of procedures required in formal rulemaking. Oral hearings and cross-examination were among the most common judicially imposed procedures.

There were three dimensions to this procedural revolution, corresponding to the three legally relevant[35] features of the informal rulemaking process: the issuance of a notice of proposed rulemaking, the actual conduct of the rulemaking proceeding, and (in the event that a rule is adopted) the publication of a statement of basis and purpose for the rule. The text of § 553 of the APA requires only that agencies engaged in informal rulemaking give notice of proposed rulemakings, offer an opportunity for interested persons to comment, and then provide a "concise general statement of the[ ] basis and purpose" of any adopted rules. Herein follows the fate of those provisions in the D.C. Circuit in the period from 1968–78.

Consider first the requirement of a "concise general statement of * * * basis and purpose." For twenty years after enactment of the APA, it was perfectly obvious what that meant: an agency adopting a rule had to provide, for want of a better phrase, a concise general statement of its basis and purpose. The *Attorney General's Manual* devoted only one paragraph to this requirement, which merely said: "[t]he statement is to be 'concise' and 'general'. Except as required by statutes providing for 'formal' rule making procedure, findings of fact and conclusions of law are not necessary. Nor is there required an elaborate analysis of the rules or of the considerations upon which the rules were issued. Rather, the statement is intended to advise the public of the general basis and purpose of the rules." United States Dep't of Justice, Attorney General's Manual on the Administrative Procedure Act 32 (1947). According to the Manual, the primary purpose of the statement was not to facilitate judicial review of the agency's decision but to aid the courts and the public "in the interpretation of the agency's rules." An ordinary reader would probably suppose that a few paragraphs would be more than adequate in most situations.

The first hint that matters might be otherwise came in a 1968 opinion by McGowan (joined by Bazelon and Robinson) reviewing the very first rulemaking proceeding conducted by the National Highway Traffic Safety Administration under the National Traffic and Motor Vehicle Safety Act of

---

[35] One should never forget that "legally relevant" does not mean "practically relevant." The most important events in a rulemaking proceeding usually happen *before* the agency issues a notice of proposed rulemaking—that is, before the rulemaking proceeding legally exists. At that preliminary stage, the agency is formulating its policy views and marshalling information. By the time the notice of proposed rulemaking is published, the agency has often already decided on its course of action, and the actual rulemaking proceeding is just a technical formality. If you want to influence agency outcomes, you are well advised to make your input known to the agency through nonlegal channels at a very early, pre-rulemaking stage.

1966. *See Automotive Parts & Accessories Ass'n v. Boyd*, 407 F.2d 330 (D.C.Cir.1968). The court held (correctly) that the agency was permitted to use informal rather than formal rulemaking, and it also held that the agency's explanation of its rule (which included a lengthy analysis issued as part of a denial of rehearing) satisfied the "concise general statement" requirement of § 553. The court then added in dicta:

> However, on the occasion of this first challenge to the implementation of the new statute it is appropriate for us to remind the Administrator of the ever present possibility of judicial review, and to caution against an overly literal reading of the statutory terms "concise" and "general." These adjectives must be accommodated to the realities of judicial scrutiny, which do not contemplate that the court itself will, by a laborious examination of the record, formulate in the first instance the significant issues faced by the agency and articulate the rationale of their resolution. We do not expect the agency to discuss every item of fact or opinion included in the submissions made to it in informal rule making. We do expect that, if the judicial review which Congress has thought it important to provide is to be meaningful, the "concise general statement of . . . basis and purpose" mandated by Section [553] will enable us to see what major issues of policy were ventilated by the informal proceedings and why the agency reacted to them as it did.

Id. at 338. And with that they were off to the races. In a very short time, it became clear that in order for a "concise general statement of * * * basis and purpose" to pass muster in the D.C. Circuit (and soon thereafter in other circuits, which often look to the D.C. Circuit for guidance on administrative law questions), it had to respond in some detail to every significant comment made by private parties participating in the rulemaking. In an even moderately complicated rulemaking, such a statement must be voluminous, consuming tens, or even hundreds, of tiny-typed pages in the *Federal Register* and hundreds, or even thousands, of pages of supporting documents.

Section 553's requirement that an agency give "[g]eneral notice of proposed rule making," including "either the terms or substance of the proposed rule or a description of the subjects and issues involved," underwent a similar transformation in the 1970s. A good illustration is a famous Leventhal opinion from 1973 involving Environmental Protection Agency (EPA) pollution standards for cement plants. *See Portland Cement Ass'n v. Ruckelshaus*, 486 F.2d 375 (D.C.Cir.1973). The EPA's notice of proposed rulemaking had published the actual text of the proposed emissions standards, which itself is more than the text of § 553 requires, and went on to explain that the proposed rules were "based on stationary source testing conducted by the Environmental Protection Agency and/or contractors." 36 Fed. Reg. 24,876 (1971). Along with the notice, the EPA issued an extensive background document which disclosed much of the underlying data then in its possession, but which did not disclose the methodology of certain tests that ultimately proved relevant to the adoption of the final rules. Leventhal's opinion discussed at some length the importance of these methodologies to the decisionmaking process and to the ability of interested parties to make informed and critical comments to the agency, *see* 486 F.2d at 392–93, and then announced, "It is not consonant with the purpose of a rule-making proceeding to promulgate rules on the basis of * * * data that, [to a] critical degree, is known only to the agency." *Id.* at 393. The case did not formally *hold* that notices of proposed rulemakings must reveal all relevant underlying studies and data in the agency's possession, but it was taken to *mean* that by just about everyone. It was clear, in other words, that the D.C. Circuit was firing a shot across the bow of the regulatory establishment, and that if agencies did not want their rules tied up in court for years to come, they had better start putting a lot more information into their rulemaking notices than had been previously expected.

The product of ten years of D.C. Circuit interpretations of the procedural requirements for the "front end" (notice of proposed rulemaking) and "back end" (statement of basis and purpose) of the rulemaking process was nicely summarized in an opinion by Wright issued in 1977:

> The APA sets out three procedural requirements: notice of the proposed rulemaking, an opportunity for interested persons to comment, and "a concise general statement of [the] basis and purpose" of the rules ultimately adopted. As interpreted by recent decisions of this court, these procedural requirements are intended to assist judicial review as well as to provide fair treatment for persons affected by a rule. To this end there must be an *exchange* of views, information, and criticism between interested persons and the agency. Consequently, the notice required by the APA, or information subsequently supplied to the public, must disclose in detail the thinking that has animated the form of a proposed rule and the data upon which that rule is based. Moreover, a dialogue is a two-way street: the opportunity to comment is meaningless unless the agency responds to significant points raised by the public * * *.

From this survey of the case law emerge two dominant principles. First, an agency proposing informal rulemaking has an obligation to make its views known to the public in a concrete and focused form so as to make criticism or formulation of alternatives possible. Second, the "concise and general" statement that must accompany the rules finally promulgated must be accommodated to the realities of judicial scrutiny, which do not contemplate that the court itself will, by a laborious examination of the record, formulate in the first instance the significant issues faced by the agency and articulate the rationale of their resolution. . . [The record must] enable us to see what major issues of policy were ventilated by the informal proceedings and why the agency reacted to them as it did.

HBO, Inc. v. FCC, 567 F.2d 9, 35–36 (D.C.Cir.) (footnote and copious citations omitted) (quoting *Boyd*, 407 F.2d at 338).

The procedural issues in *Vermont Yankee*, of course, did not involve the adequacy of the Commission's notice of proposed rulemaking or statement of basis and purpose. Rather, it concerned the *conduct* of the agency's rulemaking proceeding, for which the text of § 553 provides almost no structure, other than a requirement that interested parties be allowed to submit comments. As with the front and back ends of the informal rulemaking process, however, the D.C. Circuit *circa* 1976 was not deeply concerned with the text of § 553. Its opinion in *Vermont Yankee* was merely the latest in a line of decisions imposing a wide range of procedural requirements, beyond the opportunity for comment specified in § 553, on the conduct of agency rulemakings. As Bazelon (joined, *inter alia*, by Wilkey) wrote in 1974:

> The fact that an agency action falls into the traditional category of "rulemaking" does not, of course, mean that traditional procedures are automatically adequate. This Court has long recognized that basic considerations of fairness may dictate procedural requirements not specified by Congress. Oral submissions may be required even in legislative-type proceedings, and cross-examination may be necessary if critical issues cannot be otherwise resolved. Broad issues of public health and safety may, for example, require an expanded right of confrontation * * *.

O'Donnell v. Shaffer, 491 F.2d 59, 62 (D.C.Cir.1974) (footnotes omitted). Given this case law, the outcome in the D.C. Circuit in *Vermont Yankee* was hardly shocking. It was considerably more shocking that the Supreme Court granted certiorari to review the D.C. Circuit's decision. And that shock was nothing compared to what followed.

c. The Supreme Court Speaks

VERMONT YANKEE NUCLEAR POWER CORP. v. NATURAL RESOURCES DEFENSE COUNCIL, INC.

Supreme Court of the United States, 1978.
435 U.S. 519, 98 S.Ct. 1197, 55 L.Ed.2d 460.

MR. JUSTICE REHNQUIST delivered the opinion of the Court.

In 1946, Congress enacted the Administrative Procedure Act, which as we have noted elsewhere was not only "a new, basic and comprehensive regulation of procedures in many agencies," *Wong Yang Sung v. McGrath*, 339 U.S. 33 (1950), but was also a legislative enactment which settled "long-continued and hard-fought contentions, and enacts a formula upon which opposing social and political forces have come to rest." *Id.*, at 40. Section 4 of the Act, 5 U.S.C. § 553, dealing with rulemaking, requires in subsection (b) that "notice of proposed rule making shall be published in the Federal Register . . . ," describes the contents of that notice, and goes on to require in subsection (c) that after the notice the agency "shall give interested persons an opportunity to participate in the rule making through submission of written data, views, or arguments with or without opportunity for oral presentation. After consideration of the relevant matter presented, the agency shall incorporate in the rules adopted a concise general statement of their basis and purpose." Interpreting this provision of the Act in *United States v. Allegheny-Ludlum Steel Corp.*, 406 U.S. 742 (1972), and *United States v. Florida East Coast R. Co.*, 410 U.S. 224 (1973), we held that generally speaking this section of the Act established the maximum procedural requirements which Congress was willing to have the courts impose upon agencies in conducting rulemaking procedures. Agencies are free to grant additional procedural rights in the exercise of their discretion, but reviewing courts are generally not free to impose them if the agencies have not chosen to grant them. This is not to say necessarily that there are no circumstances which would ever justify a court in overturning agency action because of a failure to employ procedures beyond those required by the statute. But such circumstances, if they exist, are extremely rare.

Even apart from the Administrative Procedure Act this Court has for more than four decades emphasized that the formulation of procedures was basically to be left within the discretion of the agencies to which Congress had confided the responsibility for substantive judgments * * *.

It is in the light of this background of statutory and decisional law that we granted certiorari to review two judgments of the Court of Appeals for the District of Columbia Circuit because of our concern that they had seriously misread or misapplied this statutory and decisional law cautioning reviewing courts against engrafting their own notions of proper procedures upon agencies entrusted with substantive functions by Congress. We conclude that the Court of Appeals has done just that in these cases, and we therefore remand them to it for further proceedings. We also find it necessary to examine the Court of Appeals' decision with respect to agency action taken after full adjudicatory hearings. We again conclude that the court improperly intruded into the agency's decisionmaking process, making it necessary for us to reverse and remand with respect to this part of the cases also.

I

A

Under the Atomic Energy Act of 1954, the Atomic Energy Commission[2] was given broad regulatory authority over the development of nuclear energy. Under the terms of the Act, a utility seeking to construct and operate a nuclear power plant must obtain a separate permit or license at both the construction and the operation stage of the project. In order to obtain the construction permit, the utility must file a preliminary safety analysis report, an environmental report, and certain information regarding the antitrust implications of the proposed project. This application then undergoes exhaustive review by the Commission's staff and by the Advisory Committee on Reactor Safeguards (ACRS), a group of distinguished experts in the field of atomic energy. Both groups submit to the Commission their own evaluations, which then become part of the record of the utility's application. The Commission staff also undertakes the review required by the National Environmental Policy Act of 1969 (NEPA), and prepares a draft environmental impact statement, which, after being circulated for comment, is revised and becomes a final environmental impact statement. Thereupon a three-member Atomic Safety and Licensing Board conducts a public adjudicatory hearing, and reaches a decision[4] which can be appealed to the Atomic Safety and Licensing Appeal Board, and currently, in the Commission's discretion, to the Commission itself. The final agency decision may be appealed to the courts of appeals. The same sort of process occurs when the utility applies for a license to operate the plant, except that a hearing need only be held in contested cases and may be limited to the matters in controversy.[5]

---

[2]   The licensing and regulatory functions of the Atomic Energy Commission (AEC) were transferred to the Nuclear Regulatory Commission (NRC) by the Energy Reorganization Act of 1974. Hereinafter both the AEC and NRC will be referred to as the Commission.

[4]   The Licensing Board issues a permit if it concludes that there is reasonable assurance that the proposed plant can be constructed and operated without undue risk and that the environmental cost-benefit balance favors the issuance of a permit.

[5]   When a license application is contested, the Licensing Board must find reasonable assurance that the plant can be operated without undue risk and will not be inimical to the common defense and security or to the health and safety of the public. The Licensing Board's decision is subject to review similar to that afforded the Board's decision with respect to a construction permit.

These cases arise from two separate decisions of the Court of Appeals for the District of Columbia Circuit. In the first, the court remanded a decision of the Commission to grant a license to petitioner Vermont Yankee Nuclear Power Corp. to operate a nuclear power plant. In the second, the court remanded a decision of that same agency to grant a permit to petitioner Consumers Power Co. to construct two pressurized water nuclear reactors to generate electricity and steam.

B

In December 1967, after the mandatory adjudicatory hearing and necessary review, the Commission granted petitioner Vermont Yankee a permit to build a nuclear power plant in Vernon, Vt. Thereafter, Vermont Yankee applied for an operating license. Respondent Natural Resources Defense Council (NRDC) objected to the granting of a license, however, and therefore a hearing on the application commenced on August 10, 1971. Excluded from consideration at the hearings, over NRDC's objection, was the issue of the environmental effects of operations to reprocess fuel or dispose of wastes resulting from the reprocessing operations.[6] This ruling was affirmed by the Appeal Board in June 1972.

comm. granted permit

In November 1972, however, the Commission, making specific reference to the Appeal Board's decision with respect to the Vermont Yankee license, instituted rulemaking proceedings "that would specifically deal with the question of consideration of environmental effects associated with the uranium fuel cycle in the individual cost-benefit analyses for light water cooled nuclear power reactors." The notice of proposed rulemaking offered two alternatives, both predicated on a report prepared by the Commission's staff entitled Environmental Survey of the Nuclear Fuel Cycle. The first would have required no quantitative evaluation of the environmental hazards of fuel reprocessing or disposal because the Environmental Survey had found them to be slight. The second would have specified numerical values for the environmental impact of this part of the fuel cycle, which values would then be incorporated into a table, along with the other relevant factors, to determine the overall cost-benefit balance for each operating license.

Much of the controversy in this case revolves around the procedures used in the rulemaking hearing which commenced in February 1973. In a supplemental notice of hearing the Commission indicated that while discovery or cross-examination would not be utilized, the Environmental

controversy: procedures used in rulemaking hearing

---

[6] The nuclear fission which takes place in light-water nuclear reactors apparently converts its principal fuel, uranium, into plutonium, which is itself highly radioactive but can be used as reactor fuel if separated from the remaining uranium and radioactive waste products. Fuel reprocessing refers to the process necessary to recapture usable plutonium. Waste disposal, at the present stage of technological development, refers to the storage of the very long lived and highly radioactive waste products until they detoxify sufficiently that they no longer present an environmental hazard. There are presently no physical or chemical steps which render this waste less toxic, other than simply the passage of time.

Survey would be available to the public before the hearing along with the extensive background documents cited therein. All participants would be given a reasonable opportunity to present their position and could be represented by counsel if they so desired. Written and, time permitting, oral statements would be received and incorporated into the record. All persons giving oral statements would be subject to questioning by the Commission. At the conclusion of the hearing, a transcript would be made available to the public and the record would remain open for 30 days to allow the filing of supplemental written statements. More than 40 individuals and organizations representing a wide variety of interests submitted written comments. On January 17, 1973, the Licensing Board held a planning session to schedule the appearance of witnesses and to discuss methods for compiling a record. The hearing was held on February 1 and 2, with participation by a number of groups, including the Commission's staff, the United States Environmental Protection Agency, a manufacturer of reactor equipment, a trade association from the nuclear industry, a group of electric utility companies, and a group called Consolidated National Intervenors which represented 79 groups and individuals including respondent NRDC.

After the hearing, the Commission's staff filed a supplemental document for the purpose of clarifying and revising the Environmental Survey. Then the Licensing Board forwarded its report to the Commission without rendering any decision. The Licensing Board identified as the principal procedural question the propriety of declining to use full formal adjudicatory procedures. The major substantive issue was the technical adequacy of the Environmental Survey.

In April 1974, the Commission issued a rule which adopted the second of the two proposed alternatives described above. The Commission also approved the procedures used at the hearing, and indicated that the record, including the Environmental Survey, provided an "adequate data base for the regulation adopted." Finally, the Commission ruled that to the extent the rule differed from the Appeal Board decisions in Vermont Yankee "those decisions have no further precedential significance," but that since "the environmental effects of the uranium fuel cycle have been shown to be relatively insignificant, . . . it is unnecessary to apply the amendment to applicant's environmental reports submitted prior to its effective date or to Final Environmental Statements for which Draft Environmental Statements have been circulated for comment prior to the effective date."

[handwritten margin note: Commission approved procedures used]

Respondents appealed from both the Commission's adoption of the rule and its decision to grant Vermont Yankee's license to the Court of Appeals for the District of Columbia Circuit.

* * *

D

With respect to the challenge of Vermont Yankee's license, the [appeals] court first ruled that in the absence of effective rulemaking proceedings,[13] the Commission must deal with the environmental impact of fuel reprocessing and disposal in individual licensing proceedings. The court then examined the rulemaking proceedings and, despite the fact that it appeared that the agency employed all the procedures required by 5 U.S.C. § 553 and more, the court determined the proceedings to be inadequate and overturned the rule. Accordingly, the Commission's determination with respect to Vermont Yankee's license was also remanded for further proceedings.[14]

* * *

II

* * *

* * * [B]efore determining whether the Court of Appeals reached a permissible result, we must determine exactly what result it did reach, and in this case that is no mean feat. Vermont Yankee argues that the court invalidated the rule because of the inadequacy of the procedures employed in the proceedings. Respondents, on the other hand, labeling petitioner's view of the decision a "straw man," argue to this Court that the court merely held that the record was inadequate to enable the reviewing court to determine whether the agency had fulfilled its statutory obligation. But we unfortunately have not found the parties' characterization of the opinion to be entirely reliable; it appears here, as in *Orloff v. Willoughby*,

---

[13] In the Court of Appeals no one questioned the Commission's authority to deal with fuel cycle issues by informal rulemaking as opposed to adjudication. Neither does anyone seriously question before this Court the Commission's authority in this respect.

[14] After the decision of the Court of Appeals the Commission promulgated a new interim rule pending issuance of a final rule * * *. The Commission has also indicated in its brief that it intends to complete the proceedings currently in progress looking toward the adoption of a final rule regardless of the outcome of this case. Following oral argument, respondent NRDC, relying on the above facts, filed a suggestion of mootness and a motion to dismiss the writ of certiorari as improvidently granted. We hold that the case is not moot, and deny the motion to dismiss the writ of certiorari as improvidently granted.

* * *

As we read the opinion of the Court of Appeals, its view that reviewing courts may in the absence of special circumstances justifying such a course of action impose additional procedural requirements on agency action raises questions of such significance in this area of the law as to warrant our granting certiorari and deciding the case. Since the vast majority of challenges to administrative agency action are brought to the Court of Appeals for the District of Columbia Circuit, the decision of that court in this case will serve as precedent for many more proceedings for judicial review of agency actions than would the decision of another Court of Appeals. Finally, this decision will continue to play a major role in the instant litigation regardless of the Commission's decision to press ahead with further rulemaking proceedings * * *. [N]ot only is the NRDC relying on the decision of the Court of Appeals as a device to force the agency to provide more procedures, but it is also challenging the interim rules promulgated by the agency in the Court of Appeals, alleging again the inadequacy of the procedures and citing the opinion of the Court of Appeals as binding precedent to that effect.

345 U.S. 83, 87 (1953), that "in this Court the parties changed positions as nimbly as if dancing a quadrille."[15]

After a thorough examination of the opinion itself, we conclude that while the matter is not entirely free from doubt, the majority of the Court of Appeals struck down the rule because of the perceived inadequacies of the procedures employed in the rulemaking proceedings. The court first determined the intervenors' primary argument to be "that the decision to preclude 'discovery or cross-examination' denied them a meaningful opportunity to participate in the proceedings as guaranteed by due process." The court then went on to frame the issue for decision thus:

> "Thus, we are called upon to decide whether the procedures provided by the agency were sufficient to ventilate the issues."

The court conceded that absent extraordinary circumstances it is improper for a reviewing court to prescribe the procedural format an agency must follow, but it likewise clearly thought it entirely appropriate to "scrutinize the record as a whole to insure that genuine opportunities to participate in a meaningful way were provided. . ." The court also refrained from actually ordering the agency to follow any specific procedures, but

---

[15] Vermont Yankee's interpretation has been consistent throughout the litigation. That cannot be said of the other parties, however. The Government, Janus-like, initially took both positions. While the petition for certiorari was pending, a brief was filed on behalf of the United States and the Commission, with the former indicating that it believed the court had unanimously held the record to be inadequate, while the latter took Vermont Yankee's view of the matter. When announcing its intention to undertake licensing of reactors pending the promulgation of an "interim" fuel cycle rule, however, the Commission said:

"[The] court found that the rule was inadequately supported by the record insofar as it treated two particular aspects of the fuel cycle—the impacts from reprocessing of spent fuel and the impacts from radioactive waste management." 41 Fed. Reg. 45850 (1976).

And even more recently, in opening another rulemaking proceeding to replace the rule overturned by the Court of Appeals, the Commission stated:

"The original procedures proved adequate for the development and illumination of a wide range of fuel cycle impact issues. . . .

". . . The court here indicated that the procedures previously employed could suffice, and indeed did for other issues.

* * *

"Accordingly, notice is hereby given that the rules for the conduct of the reopened hearing and the authorities and responsibilities of the Hearing Board will be the same as originally applied in this matter except that specific provision is hereby made for the Hearing Board to entertain suggestions from participants as to questions which the Board should ask of witnesses for other participants." 42 Fed. Reg. 26988–26989 (1977).

Respondent NRDC likewise happily switches sides depending on the forum. As indicated above, it argues here that the Court of Appeals held only that the record was inadequate. Almost immediately after the Court of Appeals rendered its decision, however, NRDC filed a petition for rulemaking with the Commission which listed over 13 pages of procedural suggestions it thought "necessary to comply with the Court's order and with the mandate of [NEPA]." These proposals include cross-examination, discovery, and subpoena power. NRDC likewise challenged the interim fuel cycle rule and suggested to the Court of Appeals that it hold the case pending our decision in this case because the interim rules were "defective due to the inadequacy of the procedures used in developing the rule. . . ." NRDC has likewise challenged the procedures being used in the final rulemaking proceeding as being "no more than a re-run of hearing procedures which were found inadequate [by the Court of Appeals]."

there is little doubt in our minds that the ineluctable mandate of the court's decision is that the procedures afforded during the hearings were inadequate. This conclusion is particularly buttressed by the fact that after the court examined the record, particularly the testimony of Dr. Pittman, and declared it insufficient, the court proceeded to discuss at some length the necessity for further procedural devices or a more "sensitive" application of those devices employed during the proceedings. The exploration of the record and the statement regarding its insufficiency might initially lead one to conclude that the court was only examining the sufficiency of the evidence, but the remaining portions of the opinion dispel any doubt that this was certainly not the sole or even the principal basis of the decision. Accordingly, we feel compelled to address the opinion on its own terms, and we conclude that it was wrong.

In prior opinions we have intimated that even in a rule-making proceeding when an agency is making a " 'quasi-judicial' " determination by which a very small number of persons are " 'exceptionally affected, in each case upon individual grounds,' " in some circumstances additional procedures may be required in order to afford the aggrieved individuals due process.[16] It might also be true, although we do not think the issue is presented in this case and accordingly do not decide it, that a totally unjustified departure from well-settled agency procedures of long standing might require judicial correction.

But this much is absolutely clear. Absent constitutional constraints or extremely compelling circumstances the "administrative agencies 'should be free to fashion their own rules of procedure and to pursue methods of inquiry capable of permitting them to discharge their multitudinous duties.' " *FCC v. Schreiber*, 381 U.S., at 290, quoting from *FCC v. Pottsville Broadcasting Co.*, 309 U.S., at 143. Indeed, our cases could hardly be more explicit in this regard. The Court has * * * upheld this principle in a variety of applications * * *.

* * *

Respondent NRDC argues that § 4 of the Administrative Procedure Act, 5 U.S.C. § 553, merely establishes lower procedural bounds and that a court may routinely require more than the minimum when an agency's proposed rule addresses complex or technical factual issues or "Issues of Great Public Import." We have, however, previously shown that our decisions reject this view. We also think the legislative history, even the part which it cites, does not bear out its contention * * *. And the Attorney General's Manual on the Administrative Procedure Act 31, 35 (1947), a contemporaneous interpretation previously given some deference by this

---

[16] Respondent NRDC does not now argue that additional procedural devices were required under the Constitution. Since this was clearly a rulemaking proceeding in its purest form, we see nothing to support such a view.

Court because of the role played by the Department of Justice in drafting the legislation, further confirms that view. In short, all of this leaves little doubt that Congress intended that the discretion of the *agencies* and not that of the courts be exercised in determining when extra procedural devices should be employed.

Reasoning

There are compelling reasons for construing § 4 in this manner. In the first place, if courts continually review agency proceedings to determine whether the agency employed procedures which were, in the court's opinion, perfectly tailored to reach what the court perceives to be the "best" or "correct" result, judicial review would be totally unpredictable. And the agencies, operating under this vague injunction to employ the "best" procedures and facing the threat of reversal if they did not, would undoubtedly adopt full adjudicatory procedures in every instance. Not only would this totally disrupt the statutory scheme * * *, but all the inherent advantages of informal rulemaking would be totally lost.

Secondly, it is obvious that the court in these cases reviewed the agency's choice of procedures on the basis of the record actually produced at the hearing, and not on the basis of the information available to the agency when it made the decision to structure the proceedings in a certain way. This sort of Monday morning quarterbacking not only encourages but almost compels the agency to conduct all rulemaking proceedings with the full panoply of procedural devices normally associated only with adjudicatory hearings.

Finally, and perhaps most importantly, this sort of review fundamentally misconceives the nature of the standard for judicial review of an agency rule. The court below uncritically assumed that additional procedures will automatically result in a more adequate record because it will give interested parties more of an opportunity to participate in and contribute to the proceedings. But informal rulemaking need not be based solely on the transcript of a hearing held before an agency. Indeed, the agency need not even hold a formal hearing. See 5 U.S.C. § 553(c). Thus, the adequacy of the "record" in this type of proceeding is not correlated directly to the type of procedural devices employed, but rather turns on whether the agency has followed the statutory mandate of the Administrative Procedure Act or other relevant statutes. If the agency is compelled to support the rule which it ultimately adopts with the type of record produced only after a full adjudicatory hearing, it simply will have no choice but to conduct a full adjudicatory hearing prior to promulgating every rule. In sum, this sort of unwarranted judicial examination of perceived procedural shortcomings of a rulemaking proceeding can do nothing but seriously interfere with that process prescribed by Congress.

Respondent NRDC also argues that the fact that the Commission's inquiry was undertaken in the context of NEPA somehow permits a court to require procedures beyond those specified in § 4 of the APA when investigating factual issues through rulemaking. The Court of Appeals was apparently also of this view, indicating that agencies may be required to "develop new procedures to accomplish the innovative task of implementing NEPA through rulemaking." But we search in vain for something in NEPA which would mandate such a result * * *. [J]ust two Terms ago, we emphasized that the only procedural requirements imposed by NEPA are those stated in the plain language of the Act. *Kleppe v. Sierra Club*, 427 U.S. 390, 405–406 (1976). Thus, it is clear NEPA cannot serve as the basis for a substantial revision of the carefully constructed procedural specifications of the APA.

In short, nothing in the APA, NEPA, the circumstances of this case, the nature of the issues being considered, past agency practice, or the statutory mandate under which the Commission operates permitted the court to review and overturn the rulemaking proceeding on the basis of the procedural devices employed (or not employed) by the Commission so long as the Commission employed at least the statutory *minima*, a matter about which there is no doubt in this case.

There remains, of course, the question of whether the challenged rule finds sufficient justification in the administrative proceedings that it should be upheld by the reviewing court. Judge Tamm, concurring in the result reached by the majority of the Court of Appeals, thought that it did not. There are also intimations in the majority opinion which suggest that the judges who joined it likewise may have thought the administrative proceedings an insufficient basis upon which to predicate the rule in question. We accordingly remand so that the Court of Appeals may review the rule as the Administrative Procedure Act provides. We have made it abundantly clear before that when there is a contemporaneous explanation of the agency decision, the validity of that action must "stand or fall on the propriety of that finding, judged, of course, by the appropriate standard of review. If that finding is not sustainable on the administrative record made, then the Comptroller's decision must be vacated and the matter remanded to him for further consideration." *Camp v. Pitts*, 411 U.S. 138, 143, 93 S.Ct. 1241, 1244, 36 L.Ed.2d 106 (1973). See also *SEC v. Chenery Corp.*, 318 U.S. 80, 63 S.Ct. 454, 87 L.Ed. 626 (1943). The court should engage in this kind of review and not stray beyond the judicial province to explore the procedural format or to impose upon the agency its own notion of which procedures are "best" or most likely to further some vague, undefined public good.

* * *

Reversed and remanded.

MR. JUSTICE BLACKMUN and MR. JUSTICE POWELL took no part in the consideration or decision of these cases.

NOTES

The Supreme Court's unanimous opinion in *Vermont Yankee*, holding that the D.C. Circuit improperly required the agency to employ rulemaking procedures in excess of those required by the text of the APA, has a harshness of tone that is unmistakable. It seems obvious that more is involved here than the fate of one rulemaking proceeding.

Nor is the tone the opinion's only odd feature. The Supreme Court did not *have* to hear this case; it was before the Court on a discretionary grant of certiorari, not a mandatory appeal. In light of that fact, consider the following:

(1) As the opinion notes in footnote 14, shortly after certiorari was granted, the Nuclear Regulatory Commission (NRC or Commission) adopted a new interim rule for assessing the environmental effects of the nuclear fuel cycle. Then, in its principal brief in *Vermont Yankee*, the Commission affirmed its intention to adopt a new permanent rule shortly thereafter, regardless of the Supreme Court's disposition of the case. So why was the Court wasting its time and precious docket space deciding a case involving the now-and-forevermore-defunct old rule? The NRDC asked this question in a post-argument motion to dismiss, suggesting that, in light of the Commission's actions and representations, the Court should dismiss the writ of certiorari as improvidently granted.[36] Of course, the NRDC sought dismissal only because its position on the merits was clearly headed for the legal equivalent of a meltdown in the Court, but its motion was nonetheless eminently reasonable. Note that the Court's reasons for proceeding with the case included both the importance of the issue presented *and the importance of the lower court involved*. The implication is that the Court would not have decided the case if it had come up from, for example, the First Circuit or Fourth Circuit rather than the D.C. Circuit.

(2) More importantly, the Court expends a considerable amount of energy simply trying to decipher the precise holding of the D.C. Circuit: did the lower court reverse the agency for not using appropriate rulemaking procedures or for not having a sufficient evidentiary basis for its rule? The question is important, because if the real reason for the D.C. Circuit's decision was an insufficient evidentiary basis, the case would contain no issue of general legal significance warranting the Supreme Court's attention. The fact that a case is wrongly decided, or even idiotically decided, is typically not a sufficient reason for Supreme Court review. The Court is ordinarily quite reluctant to involve itself in cases that turn on questions of fact rather than questions of law, and an issue like whether one particular agency in one particular proceeding had sufficient evidentiary support for one particular rule is a classic example of a fact-bound question. It is also noteworthy that the D.C.

---

[36] In the Court's lingo, this is called DIG-ging a case, and it generally occurs several times each term. The Court will agree to hear a case in order to address a particular issue, only to discover after briefing or oral argument that the issue is not actually presented or is not presented squarely and cleanly enough for the Court's taste. Rather than waste time deciding a case that it never should have agreed to hear in the first place, the Court will simply dismiss the case from its docket, which has the effect of allowing the lower court judgment to stand.

Circuit was far from clearly wrong about the shoddy evidentiary basis for the agency's decision.

The Court ultimately concluded that the D.C. Circuit's decision was based on procedural rather than evidentiary deficiencies in the agency proceeding, but only after observing that "the matter is not entirely free from doubt." That is putting it mildly. Not even the various federal agencies involved in the litigation could agree on the meaning of the lower court's opinion: the Solicitor General's Office, which has responsibility for representing the United States before the Supreme Court, concluded that the D.C. Circuit had determined that there was inadequate record evidence, while the Nuclear Regulatory Commission insisted that the opinion was a major legal precedent that broadly required more and better rulemaking procedures.[37] Meanwhile, the NRDC was earnestly telling the Supreme Court that of course the case involved only narrow factual disputes concerning one particular rulemaking record. That is noteworthy because, as note 15 of the opinion observes, the NRDC took a very different view in other Commission proceedings, and the Commission also switched positions as convenience dictated.

This widespread (and entirely justifiable) confusion over the meaning of the D.C. Circuit's opinion is significant in view of the fact that the Supreme Court generally prefers to hear cases that neatly and cleanly present discrete legal issues. Uncertainty about the scope or meaning of a lower court opinion is almost always sufficient reason to deny certiorari. Judged by the Court's usual standards, the grant of certiorari in this case was very surprising.

By reaching out to take this case (and to hold onto it notwithstanding the agency's issuance of a new rule), the Supreme Court obviously thought that it had something important to say about administrative procedure.

d. So They Spoke. Did Anyone Listen?

DC circ. decision

CONNECTICUT LIGHT AND POWER CO. v. NRC

United States Court of Appeals, District of Columbia Circuit, 1982.
673 F.2d 525.

Before WALD, MIKVA and GINSBURG, CIRCUIT JUDGES.

fire protection for nuclear power plants

MIKVA, CIRCUIT JUDGE.

Connecticut Light and Power Company ("Connecticut Light" or "Company") challenges a decision by the Nuclear Regulatory Commission ("NRC" or "Commission") to adopt a stringent fire protection program for nuclear power plants in service before January 1, 1979. In the wake of a

---

[37] Indeed, at the certiorari stage, the Solicitor General filed a brief on behalf of the United States opposing Vermont Yankee's petition for certiorari, on the ground that the case involved only factual issues unfit for Supreme Court review. However, in a *very* unusual maneuver, the brief noted the conflicting position of the Commission. Ordinarily, the Solicitor General will simply present his or her own views as "the" views of the United States; any prior disagreement among agencies is either settled or squelched by the time the briefs are filed.

damaging fire at the Browns Ferry Nuclear Power Plant, a 1976 Commission report recommended improved fire protection standards for operating nuclear power plants. Based on the *Browns Ferry Report*, the Commission developed technical guidelines for evaluating the fire safety of both new and operating nuclear plants. Because of the extensive problems involved in redesigning a nuclear plant already built and in service, the guidelines for operating plants differed from those for plants not completed. For several years after the promulgation of the guidelines, Commission staff pursued the approach of evaluating the safety of operating plants by applying the guidelines on a plant by plant basis. In a number of cases, the evaluation process resulted in fire protection programs acceptable to both Commission staff and the plants in question. Disagreements persisted, however, on some issues that were common to a number of plants. As a result, some five years after the Browns Ferry fire the Commission decided to embark on the rule-making challenged here.

Connecticut Light and Power Company, licensed by the Commission to operate nuclear generating plants, objects to a number of features of the Commission's adoption of the fire protection program. First, Connecticut Light contends that the notice of proposed rule-making was inadequate because it gave no indication of the technical basis on which the Commission had relied in formulating the proposed rules and because the rules as adopted differed in major respects from the rules proposed in the notice * * *. Second, Connecticut Light argues that the Commission failed to offer an adequate technical justification for the fire protection rules in the form in which they were ultimately adopted. Finally, Connecticut Light claims that the Commission failed to comply with its own regulations governing the imposition of new requirements for nuclear plants already in service.

We affirm the fire protection regulations as adopted by the Commission. The administrative record contains adequate support for the Commission's determination that adoption of the rules was urgently needed to protect the public safety. We cannot conceal, however, our concerns about some of the procedures followed by the Commission in the rule-making process by which the program was adopted. The Commission complied but barely with the procedures mandated by the Administrative Procedure Act for notice and comment rule-making.

The process of notice and comment rule-making is not to be an empty charade. It is to be a process of reasoned decision-making. One particularly important component of the reasoning process is the opportunity for interested parties to participate in a meaningful way in the discussion and final formulation of rules. *Ethyl Corp. v. Environmental Protection Agency*, 176 U.S. App. D.C. 373, 541 F.2d 1, 48 (D.C.Cir.) (en banc). The procedures followed by the NRC here came perilously close to foreclosing any useful participation whatsoever during the rule-making process itself.

An equally important component of the process of reasoned decision-making is the agency's own explanation for the rules it adopts. While an agency need not justify the rules it selects in every detail, it should explain the general bases for the rules chosen. Such explanations help assure public confidence in the rule-making process. Disclosure of the agency's rationale is particularly important in order that a reviewing court may fulfill its statutory obligation to determine whether the agency's choice of rules was arbitrary or capricious. The NRC has not made our task on review easy. If the Commission had provided any less in the way of reasoned explanation for the fire protection program selected, we would be compelled to remand the program to the NRC.

I.   THE FIRE PROTECTION PROGRAM

The NRC proposed and adopted a comprehensive program to prevent, detect, control, and extinguish fires in operating nuclear power plants. Although the program includes a number of specific requirements debated in the plant evaluations that followed the Browns Ferry fire, three specific parts of the program are challenged in this appeal. They are the methodology mandated for protecting duplicate systems to shut down reactor units safely in case of fire, the requirements for the design of alternative shutdown mechanisms when needed as a substitute for duplicate systems, and the method stipulated for protecting the lubrication system for the reactor's coolant pump.

In most cases in a nuclear power plant, it is possible to design duplicate systems for shutting down reactor units in case of an emergency such as a fire. The duplicate system is provided as a back-up, in case the primary shutdown system should be damaged or destroyed. It is thus especially important to ensure that the duplicate shutdown system cannot be damaged by whatever emergency disables the primary shutdown system.

protecting duplicate system

In the plant by plant evaluations after the Browns Ferry fire, and in the notice of proposed rule-making, the Commission followed a "postulated hazards" approach to the protection of duplicate safe shutdown capacity. On this approach, a plant's protection of such redundant shutdown capacity is tested by reference to a number of factors. In the fire protection program as proposed, these factors included the likely area within which a fire might spread, the fire extinguishing system used in the area, the accessibility of the area to fire fighters and equipment, the relative fire danger in the area, the availability of alternative methods for shutting down the reactor unit safely, and the fire retardant capacity of protective devices such as fire retardant coatings. 45 Fed.Reg. 36,087 (1980). Pursuant to these guidelines, NRC staff had approved the methods used to protect duplicate shutdown capacity in a number of nuclear plants in service before January 1979. The final rule adopted by the Commission, however, abandoned the postulated hazards approach. In its stead, the

[margin note: In new rule, only 3 approved methods]

Commission stipulated three approved methods for protecting duplicate shutdown capacity. These are: separation of the redundant system by a barrier able to withstand fire for at least three hours; separation of the redundant system by a distance of twenty feet containing no intervening combustible material, together with fire detectors and an automatic fire suppression system; and enclosure of the redundant system in a fire barrier able to withstand fire for one hour, coupled with fire detectors and an automatic fire suppression system. 10 C.F.R. § 50, App. R, III.G.2 (1980). These methods give no credit for fire retardant coatings and do not consider the relative fire danger of the area in which the redundant shutdown system is located.

[margin note: alternative shutdown capacity]

In some cases, it is also necessary to provide alternative shutdown capacity in order to protect the reactor unit in case of fire. For example, it may be impossible to redesign an operating plant in order to protect a duplicate shutdown system adequately. To protect the public safety, alternative shutdown systems must be protected against damage, just as redundant shutdown systems must be. The Commission proposed a postulated hazards approach to the evaluation of alternative shutdown capacity, under which a plant was to be required to show it could protect at least one means for shutting down the plant from damage for at least seventy-two hours following a fire. *Notice of Proposed Rule-Making*, 45 Fed.Reg. 36,089 (May 29, 1980).

The final rules adopted by the Commission, however, abandoned the postulated hazards approach to the protection of alternative shutdown capacity. Instead, the final rules stipulated that alternative shutdown capacity must be protected by one of the methods acceptable for the protection of redundant shutdown capacity. 10 C.F.R. § 50, App. R, III.G.2 (1980). In addition, the Commission continued to require that one back up method for ensuring safe shutdown in case of fire should be able to remain operable for at least seventy-two hours following a fire. *Id.* § 50, App. R. III.L.1. One important aspect of this requirement is that the back up method should be sufficiently isolated from associated electrical circuitry to prevent damaged circuits from spreading a continuing fire into the back up system. *Id.* § 50, App. R. III.L.7. It may be especially difficult and expensive to redesign operating nuclear power plants to meet this last provision.

[margin note: protection of lubricant for cooling system]

The third aspect of the fire protection program challenged here concerns the protection of lubricant for the reactor's coolant system. The lubrication oil in the reactor's coolant system must be protected in order to protect the coolant system, and ultimately the reactor itself. Because the oil is flammable, however, it poses a significant fire hazard. The NRC originally proposed two acceptable methods for protecting the lubricant: an oil collection system, which drains the pump lubricant away from the reach of the fire; and an automatic fire suppression system, which attempts to put out the fire before it can reach the lubricant. *Notice of Proposed Rule-Making*, 45 Fed.Reg. 36,090 (May 29, 1980). During the process of plant by plant evaluation that preceded the rule-making, NRC staff had approved fire suppression systems for protecting the lubricant in a number of plants. The Commission, however, concluded that only an oil collection system could sufficiently protect the coolant pump lubricant from fire. The final rule, therefore, stipulates only one method for protecting the lubrication oil: an oil collection system. 10 C.F.R. § 50, App.R, III.O (1980).

This rule-making followed an extensive process of plant by plant evaluations that had culminated in NRC staff approval of entire fire protection programs at many nuclear power plants and of important portions of such programs at others. Even so, the original notice of proposed rule-making contained no indication of whether plants would be required to alter approved features to comply with the new regulations. The final rule specified that most of the particular requirements would not be imposed upon plants that had received staff approval of features before the effective date of the new rule. 10 C.F.R. § 50.48(b) (1980). Three particular requirements, however, were to be applied to all nuclear plants operating before January 1, 1979, regardless of whether they had received staff approval of these aspects of their fire protection program. *Id.* These include the portions of the fire protection program challenged here: the standards for protecting duplicate and alternative safe shutdown capacity and the method for protecting the reactor coolant pump lubricant.

The final rules, however, contain an additional, critical element of flexibility. Within thirty days of the rules' effective date, licensees were allowed to apply for exemptions from any aspect of the fire protection program, including those requirements applied to plants in spite of prior staff approval of protection systems that did not conform to the new rules. *Id.* § 50.48(c)(6). Implementation of the new rules is tolled pending final Commission action on the exemption request. *Id.* Exemptions are to be granted by the Commission upon a showing by the licensee that the required plant modification "would not enhance fire protection safety in the facility or that such modifications may be detrimental to overall facility safety." *Id.* Apparently a number of such exemption requests were filed within the time provided and are now under consideration by the NRC. Final decisions by the NRC on the exemption requests will themselves be subject to judicial review, 5 U.S.C. § 702 (1976).

[margin note: w/in 30 days, licensees could apply for exemptions]

II.　THE ADEQUACY OF THE NOTICE OF PROPOSED RULE-MAKING

[margin note: Adequacy of Notice]

A. *Disclosure of the Technical Basis* for the Proposed Rules. The Administrative Procedure Act requires an agency engaged in informal rule-making to publish a notice of proposed rule-making in the Federal Register that includes "either the terms or substance of the proposed rule or a description of the subjects and issues involved." 5 U.S.C. § 553(b)(3).

Connecticut Light's most serious complaint about the notice of proposed rule-making here is that it failed to indicate or explain the technical basis on which the Commission had relied in selecting the proposed rules.

The purpose of the comment period is to allow interested members of the public to communicate information, concerns, and criticisms to the agency during the rule-making process. If the notice of proposed rule-making fails to provide an accurate picture of the reasoning that has led the agency to the proposed rule, interested parties will not be able to comment meaningfully upon the agency's proposals. As a result, the agency may operate with a one-sided or mistaken picture of the issues at stake in a rule-making. In order to allow for useful criticism, it is especially important for the agency to identify and make available technical studies and data that it has employed in reaching the decisions to propose particular rules. To allow an agency to play hunt the peanut with technical information, hiding or disguising the information that it employs, is to condone a practice in which the agency treats what should be a genuine interchange as mere bureaucratic sport. An agency commits serious procedural error when it fails to reveal portions of the technical basis for a proposed rule in time to allow for meaningful commentary.

The notice proposing the fire protection program made little reference to technical material. It referred only to the *Browns Ferry Report* and to the guidelines laid down in *Branch Technical Position* 9.5–1 and employed in the plant by plant safety evaluations. 45 Fed.Reg. 36,082 (May 29, 1980). Otherwise the Commission asserted that "(t)he position of the staff and the licensees regarding the provisions of this rule is documented and well known." *Id.*

Connecticut Light contends to the contrary that the Commission's position was not well-known at all. Some technical papers relied upon by the Commission, Connecticut Light asserts, were either not public or were not identified as relevant by the Commission until long after the comment period had closed. Utilities wishing to comment on these technical studies, the Company argues, would thus have either been unable to review some relevant documents, or would have faced the situation of having to guess which of a myriad of entries in the Commission's public documents room has played an important role in the development of the fire protection program.

The Commission's belief that its position was well-known was not entirely unreasonable. It was based in the first instance on the wide circulation of the *Browns Ferry Report* and *Branch Technical Position* 9.5–1. Indeed, Connecticut Light does not contest the availability or importance of these documents in this appeal. The Commission also contends that it relied heavily on the safety evaluations that had been prepared by NRC staff during the plant by plant evaluation process. These safety reports were on file in the NRC public documents room during the comment period. Of course, it would be unfair to charge one utility with knowledge of the details of what went on during a safety review of another utility's nuclear power plants. The NRC, however, did not assume that the utility companies had or should have shared information developed in individualized safety reviews. Instead, it relied on the utilities' common knowledge of problems that had recurred in plant after plant and of reports that had been publicly filed. There was in fact a common store of experience on which the NRC drew, that had been developed and accumulated in interaction with the utilities during the five-year period that followed the Browns Ferry fire.

Finally, the Commission did rely on some technical studies that were not mentioned in the notice of proposed rule-making. Two sets of studies made by Sandia Laboratories, both important to the development of the proposals for protecting duplicate and alternative shutdown capacity, are paramount examples of this. These studies concerning the effectiveness of separation distances in preventing fire from spreading from one set of cables to another and the usefulness of fire retardant coatings, however, had already been subject to widespread public comment. The separation distance studies were part of the basis of a petition by the Union of Concerned Scientists (UCS) to require the NRC to alter its fire protection standards. They were subject to public comment during the review of the UCS petition and a public memorandum by the NRC staff responded specifically to criticisms of the separations tests submitted during that review. The fire retardant coatings studies, also public, formed part of the basis for a petition for reconsideration by the UCS.

During the comment period, the utilities repeatedly asked the NRC to identify the technical studies upon which the proposed rules were based. The NRC was unhelpful and the comments submitted are noticeably general. Certainly, it would have been better practice for the NRC to have identified these technical materials specifically in the notice of proposed rule-making. Nonetheless, this rule-making process took place against a background of five years during which the Commission explored safety proposals in a public forum and exposed the important technical studies to adversarial comment. Given this context, we conclude that the technical background of the rules was sufficiently identified to allow for meaningful comment during the rule-making process.

B. *Differences Between the Fire Protection Program as Proposed and as Adopted.* Connecticut Light's second major challenge to the NRC procedures here is that the Commission adopted final rules that differed significantly from the rules announced in the notice of proposed rule-making. Connecticut Light contends that because of the differences the NRC should have renoticed the changed rules and set a new comment period. Connecticut Light regards three particular changes as crucial: the

① change from the postulated hazards approach to a list of three acceptable methods for protecting duplicate and alternative shutdown capacity, the ② decision to give no credit for fire retardant coatings, and the ③ determination that a collection system is the only acceptable means for protecting the coolant pump lubrication oil. We find that the rules as adopted were sufficiently similar to the rules as proposed that renoticing was not required. An important factor in our decision, however, is that with the exemption provision the practical impact of the final rules is very similar to what it would have been if the proposed rules had gone into effect.

An agency adopting final rules that differ from its proposed rules is required to renotice when the changes are so major that the original notice did not adequately frame the subjects for discussion. The purpose of the new notice is to allow interested parties a fair opportunity to comment upon the final rules in their altered form. The agency need not renotice changes that follow logically from or that reasonably develop the rules it proposed originally. Otherwise, the comment period would be a perpetual exercise rather than a genuine interchange resulting in improved rules.

Here, the final rules were a "logical outgrowth" of the rules as proposed. The NRC had proposed two methods for protecting coolant pump lubrication oil; the final rule mandated one of these methods, a collection system, because of concern about the flammability of the lubrication oil. The NRC had proposed a method for protecting alternate and duplicate shutdown capacity that included consideration of the effects of fire retardant coatings; the final rule ignored the coatings because of concern about their reliability. With respect to both of these changes, the notice of proposed rule-making clearly revealed both the precise "subject matter" and the "issues" involved as required by the APA, 5 U.S.C. § 553(b)(3) (1976). The final rules were simply more stringent versions of the proposed rules.

The question is somewhat closer with respect to the change in methods of protecting duplicate shutdown capacity from the postulated hazards approach to the stipulation of the three acceptable alternatives. Connecticut Light contends that it did not have a fair opportunity to comment on the latter approach, because the approach was entirely novel. The NRC replies that it adopted the stipulated alternatives approach because of criticism about the complexity of the postulated hazards approach. It also points out that with the exemption procedure the stipulated alternatives approach is not a major shift in NRC policy.

In explaining the interplay between the adoption of the stipulated alternatives approach and the exemption procedure, the Commission stated:

> Requirements that account for all of the parameters that are important to fire protection and consistent with safety

requirements for all plant-unique configurations have not yet been developed. In light of the experience gained in fire protection evaluations over the past four years, the Commission believes that the licensees should reexamine those previously approved configurations of fire protection that do not meet the requirements as specified in Section III.G. to Appendix R. Based on this reexamination the licensee must either meet the requirements of Section III.G. of Appendix R or apply for an exemption that justifies alternatives by a fire hazard analysis.

45 Fed.Reg. 76,603 (Nov. 19, 1980). The practical effect of the exemption procedure is thus to give utilities a fourth alternative: if the company can prove that another method works as well as one of the three stipulated by the NRC, in light of the identified fire hazards at its plant, it may continue to employ that method. The NRC at oral argument characterized the final rule as adopted with the exemption provision as "functionally . . . the same" as the postulated hazards approach * * *.

* * *

Certainly, a rule that continues to allow a proposed approach as an alternative to other stipulated methods may be regarded as the logical successor to the proposed approach. On this basis, we conclude that the NRC was not obligated to renotice the fire protection program when it shifted from reliance on the postulated hazards approach to the stipulated alternatives approach in conjunction with the exemption procedure.

* * *

III. The NRC's Justification for the Final Rules

Under the Administrative Procedure Act, an agency adopting rules by notice and comment rule-making must provide "a concise general statement of (the rules') basis and purpose." 5 U.S.C. § 553(c) (1976). This statement need not be comprehensive, but it must indicate sufficiently the agency's reasons for the rules selected, so that the reviewing court is not faced with the task of "rummaging" through the record to elicit a rationale on its own. In this case, the Commission has come close indeed to requiring this court to search dusty attic corners of the record to bring to light an adequate rationale for the Commission's action. [The court then upholds the agency decision on the merits after a lengthy, detailed, and often critical analysis.]

* * *

V. Conclusion

Our decision to uphold the NRC's adoption of the fire protection program is reluctant. At almost every step of the way, the NRC's procedures were less than exemplary. The notice of proposed rule-making was cursory and gave the industry the minimum acceptable opportunity to respond. The agency's statement of the basis for the program in its final form provided limited technical guidance indeed. Surely, the NRC is entitled to use its discretion to err on the side of protecting the public safety when it regulates nuclear power plants. If the NRC treats the safeguards of the administrative process in too cavalier a fashion, however, it may be impossible for the reviewing court to discern that its action has indeed furthered the public safety.

Nonetheless, this is a case in which the rule as tempered by the exemption procedure must be upheld. The fire protection program with the exemption procedure is not a radical departure from the program as it was developed after the Browns Ferry fire and as it was originally proposed. With the exemption procedure, power plants will be able to show that alternative fire protection systems protect the public safety at the same high level as the system chosen by the Commission. Their failure to make such showings will only be further proof that the Commission was indeed correct that the public safety urgently required a stringent fire protection program for nuclear power plants.

NOTES

Modern court decisions sound many of the same themes concerning the purposes and requirements of informal rulemaking as did Connecticut Light. For example, in 1995, the D.C. Circuit explained:

> The APA requires an agency to provide notice of a proposed rule, an opportunity for comment, and a statement of the basis and purpose of the final rule adopted. These requirements, which serve important purposes of agency accountability and reasoned decision-making, impose a significant duty on the agency. Notice of a proposed rule must include sufficient detail on its content and basis in law and evidence to allow for meaningful and informed comment: "the Administrative Procedure Act requires the agency to make available to the public, in a form that allows for meaningful comment, the data the agency used to develop the proposed rule." *Engine Mfrs. Ass'n v. EPA*, 20 F.3d 1177, 1181 (D.C.Cir.1994); *see also Connecticut Light & Power Co. v. NRC*, 673 F.2d 525, 530–31 (D.C.Cir.1982) ("An agency commits serious procedural error when it fails to reveal portions of the technical basis for a proposed rule in time to allow for meaningful commentary.") *Home Box Office, Inc. v. FCC*, 567 F.2d 9, 55 (D.C.Cir.1977) (proposed rule must provide sufficient information to permit informed "adversarial critique"). Likewise, in adopting the final rule, the agency must "articulate with reasonable clarity its reasons for decision, and identify the significance of the crucial facts." *Greater Boston Television Corp. v. FCC*, 444 F.2d 841, 851 (D.C.Cir.1970).

American Medical Ass'n v. Reno, 57 F.3d 1129, 1132–33 (D.C.Cir.1995). Ten years later, the same court was sounding precisely the same themes, explaining that notice requirements in informal rulemakings "are designed (1) to ensure that agency regulations are tested via exposure to diverse public comment, (2) to ensure fairness to affected parties, and (3) to give affected parties an opportunity to develop evidence in the record to support their objections to the rule and thereby enhance the quality of judicial review." *International Union, United Mine Workers of America v. Mine Safety & Health Admin.*, 407 F.3d 1250, 1259 (D.C.Cir.2005). To the same effect, see *Prometheus Radio Project v. FCC*, 652 F.3d 433, 449 (3d Cir.2011).

Connecticut Light, American Medical Ass'n, United Mine Workers, and *Prometheus Radio Project* all read—and cite cases—as though they could have been written in 1977. Did *Vermont Yankee*'s fierce language about adherence to the text of the APA change nothing?

Quite to the contrary, *Vermont Yankee* has had a major influence on administrative law. But the scope of that influence must be clearly understood. Recall that an informal rulemaking has three major components: (1) the issuance of a notice of proposed rulemaking, (2) the conduct of the rulemaking itself, during which the agency receives comments and formulates its views, and (3) the issuance (or not) of a final rule, along with a statement of basis and purpose for any rule adopted. The holding of *Vermont Yankee*—that federal courts cannot require agencies to use specific procedures during a rulemaking proceeding simply because the courts consider them a good idea—concerns only phase (2) of the informal rulemaking process and is solidly a part of American administrative law. *Vermont Yankee*'s language was certainly broad enough to suggest that courts should stick to the original understanding of the APA with respect to phases (1) and (3) as well. Courts, however, including the Supreme Court, have not read *Vermont Yankee* as broadly as its language permits. In important respects, that outcome is not surprising. The forces that led the D.C. Circuit to transform the informal rulemaking process did not disappear because of the *Vermont Yankee* decision. The full range of those forces will not become clear until more of this course unfolds, but a brief (and incomplete) assessment of those forces may be helpful.

The late 1960s saw the convergence of many important events: the rise of capture theory (and the decline in confidence in agency decisionmaking), the increasing importance of rulemaking, especially informal rulemaking, the rise of environmentalism and environmental regulation, and the emergence of the Bazelon-Leventhal-McGowan-Wright bloc on the D.C. Circuit. In this atmosphere, the APA's informal rulemaking philosophy, which was designed to facilitate agency discretion, was entirely out of place. The new conception of rulemaking viewed the rulemaking process more as a means of checking agency abuses than of facilitating agency expertise (though the hope was that agencies, once adequately checked, would then use their expertise in the service of the public interest). More procedures obviously serve this purpose, both by exposing agency decisionmaking to more public scrutiny and by promoting the involvement of interested members of the public who, unlike the courts, have the expertise to identify flaws in agency decisionmaking even at the highest levels of technical sophistication.

The D.C. Circuit's procedural innovations, however, also served another, more functional purpose. In addition to reviewing the adequacy of agency procedures, courts also review the substance of agency decisionmaking to ensure that agency rules and orders conform to statutory directives, are supported by adequate factual evidence, and represent defensible exercises of discretion. The details of this review are taken up in Chapter 4. For the moment, however, place yourself in the position of a reviewing court in 1967. An agency adopts a rule involving a highly technical health or safety issue. A party (and perhaps more than one party) seeks judicial review of the rule on the ground that it does not represent state-of-the-art scientific reasoning in the field. What materials will you, as a reviewing court, examine in order to determine whether the agency's decision is substantively valid?

The informal rulemaking process, *circa* 1967, will produce virtually nothing that can be used as a basis for judicial review. It generates a notice of proposed rulemaking that need only indicate that the agency is studying a problem, a set of comments by interested parties that the agency need not consider in any formal way, and a statement of basis and purpose that will likely say nothing that is not evident on the face of the rule. When, as often happens, judicial review of agency action takes place directly in a court of appeals, bypassing the district court level, there has been no trial at which facts and evidence were developed. There has been no adversary proceeding, in the traditional sense, in which the agency's reasoning and assumptions were tested by parties with comparable levels of understanding and expertise. And because of a long-standing administrative law doctrine that we will examine shortly,[38] judicial review must take place solely on the basis of the reasoning adopted by the agency; one cannot supplement the agency's justifications for its rule in briefs or arguments on appeal. In short, the "record" generated by an informal rulemaking is wholly unsuited to any form of substantive judicial review other than an examination of the face of the rule itself.

And indeed, the procedural and substantive provisions of the 1946 APA nicely dovetail. The APA originally contemplated that judges would overturn agency rules only when those rules were unreasonable, or perhaps even only when they were patently absurd—a determination that could be made simply by examining the rules. No elaborate "record" for review was needed, because judges were not expected to look very closely at the agencies' work product. This highly deferential judicial review may have been well suited to an era that placed great confidence in agency expertise and impartiality, but it hardly commends itself to judges worried about industry capture and agency neglect of the public interest. Such judges will want to engage in some form of substantial scrutiny of agency decisions. Any kind of energetic substantive review, however, requires a set of agency *procedures* that generates an

---

[38] *See infra* pages 516–518.

adequate record for review. The procedures prescribed by § 553 won't do the trick; something more is needed.

The D.C. Circuit's procedural innovations are tailored precisely to provide the requisite record for vigorous substantive review. An elaborate notice of proposed rulemaking exposes the agency's reasoning to public scrutiny and criticism, an enhanced set of rulemaking procedures ensures that the agency's arguments are put through an adversarial testing process, and an extensive statement of basis and purpose that responds to all serious criticisms and suggestions of commenters provides the court with an opportunity (or at least a fighting chance) to identify whether the agency is really pursuing its statutory mission or is instead using its power for private ends. To do away with all of these procedural innovations is to do away with serious substantive review of agency decisions. No one in 1978 was prepared to do this—or believed that the Supreme Court was prepared to do this. As it turned out, the Court was no more willing than was the D.C. Circuit to abandon substantive review of agency decisions, which means that much of the D.C. Circuit's pre-1978 revolution had to survive *Vermont Yankee*.

If this short discussion is unclear or confusing, it will become clearer when you study the law of substantive review, and clearer still when you study the law governing the timing of judicial review. For now, it is enough simply to accept on faith the bottom line concerning the scope of *Vermont Yankee*: as far as the notice of proposed rulemaking and the statement of basis and purpose are concerned, the D.C. Circuit's pre-*Vermont Yankee* innovations are all still good law, but once a valid notice of proposed rulemaking has been issued, courts may not require an agency to use specific procedures during the rulemaking unless there is some source of statutory, regulatory, or constitutional law that imposes those specific procedural requirements.

[margin note: impact of Vermont Yankee]

Informal rulemaking is thus a much more procedurally elaborate enterprise than was contemplated in 1946. It is not nearly as elaborate as formal rulemaking—there is no requirement of an ALJ, formal presentation of evidence, oral presentations and cross-examination, etc.—but it is far more elaborate than the simple notice-and-comment process described in the text of § 553. Hybrid rulemaking may not be as vibrant as it was in 1977, but it is still very much alive.

3. THE NOTICE OF PROPOSED RULEMAKING

Prior to the rise of hybrid rulemaking, it was very difficult for a notice of proposed rulemaking to be procedurally inadequate. The notice merely had to contain a statement of the agency's legal authority for its rulemaking, an announcement of the time and location of any public proceedings, and either the text or substance of any proposed rule *or a description of the subject matter of the rulemaking*. If the agency was considering, for example, adding an incentive element to railroad car hire rates, it was sufficient to issue a notice of proposed rulemaking that said, in essence, "We are thinking about incentive elements for car hire rates."

The level of detail contained in the notice was primarily left up to the agency. That was entirely consonant with the original understanding of the informal rulemaking process, which was designed for the benefit of the regulators, not the regulated. The purpose of the informal rulemaking process, as envisioned in the 1946 APA, was to allow the agency to educate itself about the subject matter of its rulemaking so that it could formulate intelligent rules. Under that conception of rulemaking, it would be almost bizarre for a party outside the agency to protest that a notice of proposed rulemaking did not sufficiently alert the public to the agency's plans.

The modern understanding of the rulemaking process, however, is quite different. In the post-1968 era, the rulemaking process is viewed more as a *check* on agencies than as a facilitative device. The participation of interested parties in rulemakings is seen both as an end in itself and as a means by which flaws in the agencies' thinking can be brought to the attention of the agencies—and, eventually, to the reviewing court. Under this model of rulemaking, it is essential that agencies give detailed notice of their plans to the public so that comments can be directed at the agencies' actual proposals. Challenges to the adequacy of an agency's notice of proposed rulemaking are now commonplace.[39]

Such challenges typically take one of three forms. First, a party might object that an agency's notice of proposed rulemaking failed to disclose all of the relevant data that animated the agency's thinking and therefore did not give the public an adequate opportunity to address the agency's proposals. Second, a party might claim that the agency failed adequately to disclose the nature of its proposals and ended up adopting a rule that no one could have seen coming (and therefore no one could have intelligently commented upon). Third, parties might contend that the rule finally adopted by the agency differs so dramatically from its initial proposal that a new round of comments is required in order to provide an adequate vetting of the agency action.

Start with the first kind of challenge, which focuses on the extent to which the agency disclosed its reasoning process when it first gave notice that it was considering a rule. There are actually two sub-species of this kind of challenge. One focuses on the information that was in the agency's possession at the moment that it issued its notice of proposed rulemaking: the claim in such cases is that the agency failed to disclose important information that motivated its notice of proposed rulemaking. This was the basis for the challenges to the procedural adequacy of the notices of proposed rulemaking in *Portland Cement* and *Connecticut Light & Power*:

---

[39] For reasons that are explained in Chapter 6 (review is only available for "final" agency action), a challenge to a notice of proposed rulemaking can take place only if a rule is issued. Parties will then seek to invalidate the rule on the ground that the notice was procedurally defective.

the agency allegedly failed to disclose all of the technical data upon which its rule was ultimately based. Cases raising claims of this sort are legion.

AMERICAN RADIO RELAY LEAGUE, INC. v. FCC

United States Court of Appeals, District of Columbia Circuit, 2008.
524 F.3d 227.

Before: ROGERS, TATEL and KAVANAUGH, CIRCUIT JUDGES.

ROGERS, CIRCUIT JUDGE.

[Certain broadband operators, known as Access Broadband over Power Line ("Access BPL") operators, use electrical power lines to transmit their data. The process poses risks of interference with radio communications. In 2004, the Federal Communications Commission ("FCC") adopted rules regulating the use of the radio spectrum by Access BPL operators. The American Radio Relay League, an organization representing licensed amateur radio operators, objected that the rules did not provide adequate protection against spectrum interference by Access BPL providers. The court rejected all but one of the League's substantive challenges to the FCC's rules—and JUDGE KAVANAUGH, partially dissenting on this ground, would have rejected all of them.]

* * *

More persuasive is the League's contention that the Commission has failed to comply with the APA by not disclosing in full certain studies by its staff upon which the Commission relied in promulgating the rule.

* * *

Under APA notice and comment requirements, "[a]mong the information that must be revealed for public evaluation are the 'technical studies and data' upon which the agency relies [in its rulemaking]." *Chamber of Commerce v. SEC (Chamber of Commerce II)*, 443 F.3d 890, 899 (D.C.Cir.2006) (citation omitted). Construing section 553 of the APA, the court explained long ago that "[i]n order to allow for useful criticism, it is especially important for the agency to identify and make available *technical studies and data* that it has employed in reaching the decisions to propose particular rules." *Conn. Light & Power Co. v. Nuclear Regulatory Comm'n*, 673 F.2d 525, 530 (D.C.Cir.1982) (emphasis added). More particularly, "[d]isclosure of *staff reports* allows the parties to focus on the information relied on by the agency and to point out where that information is erroneous or where the agency may be drawing improper conclusions from it." *Nat'l Ass'n of Regulatory Util. Comm'rs ("NARUC") v. FCC*, 737 F.2d 1095, 1121 (D.C.Cir.1984) (emphasis added).

Public notice and comment regarding relied-upon technical analysis, then, are "[t]he safety valves in the use of . . . sophisticated methodology." *Sierra Club v. Costle*, 657 F.2d 298, 334, 397–98 & n. 484 (D.C.Cir.1981).

> By requiring the "most critical factual material" used by the agency be subjected to informed comment, the APA provides a procedural device to ensure that agency regulations are tested through exposure to public comment, to afford affected parties an opportunity to present comment and evidence to support their positions, and thereby to enhance the quality of judicial review.

Chamber of Commerce II, 443 F.3d at 900 * * *. The failure to disclose for public comment is subject, however, to "the rule of prejudicial error," 5 U.S.C. § 706, and the court will not set aside a rule absent a showing by the petitioners "that they suffered prejudice from the agency's failure to provide an opportunity for public comment," *Gerber v. Norton*, 294 F.3d 173, 182 (D.C.Cir.2002), in sufficient time so that the agency's "decisions . . . [may be] framed with . . . comment in full view," *NARUC*, 737 F.2d at 1121.

[handwritten in margin: petitioners must show "prejudicial error"]

At issue are five scientific studies consisting of empirical data gathered from field tests performed by the Office of Engineering and Technology. Two studies measured specific Access BPL companies' emissions, and three others measured location-specific emissions in pilot Access BPL areas in New York, North Carolina, and Pennsylvania. In placing the studies in the rulemaking record, the Commission has redacted parts of individual pages, otherwise relying on those pages * * *. [T]he Commission reaffirmed that "the redacted portions . . . referred to internal communications that were not relied upon in the decision making process," while reiterating that Commission statements in the [rulemaking] *Order* "point" to the partially redacted studies—including the Commission's "own field investigations of [Access] BPL experimental sites"—and "clarify[ing] that in this proceeding, the Commission relied . . . on its own internally conducted studies." The court, pursuant to the Commission's offer, Resp.'s Br. at 44 n. 35, has reviewed *in camera* the partially redacted pages in unredacted form; they show staff summaries of test data, scientific recommendations, and test analysis and conclusions regarding the methodology used in the studies. All pages in the studies are stamped "for internal use only."

It would appear to be a fairly obvious proposition that studies upon which an agency relies in promulgating a rule must be made available during the rulemaking in order to afford interested persons meaningful notice and an opportunity for comment * * *. Where, as here, an agency's determination "is based upon 'a complex mix of controversial and uncommented upon data and calculations,'" there is no APA precedent allowing an agency to cherry-pick a study on which it has chosen to rely in part.

The League has met its burden to demonstrate prejudice by showing that it "ha[s] something useful to say" regarding the unredacted studies, *Chamber of Commerce II*, 443 F.3d at 905, that may allow it to "mount a credible challenge" if given the opportunity to comment. As suggested by the League, the partially redacted pages indicate that a study's core scientific recommendations may reveal the limitations of its own data and that its conclusions may reveal methodology or illuminate strengths and weaknesses of certain data or the study as a whole. For example, the League points to the unredacted headings of otherwise redacted pages referring to "New Information Arguing for Caution on HF BPL" and "BPL Spectrum Tradeoffs," subjects on which it seeks the opportunity to comment. The unredacted pages thus appear to "contain information in tension with the [Commission's] conclusion" that "[Access] BPL's acknowledged interference risks are 'manageable.'" Pet.'s Br. at 18. Allowing such "omissions in data and methodology" may "ma[ke] it impossible to reproduce" an agency's results or assess its reliance upon them. *City of Brookings Mun. Tel. Co. v. FCC*, 822 F.2d 1153, 1168 (D.C.Cir.1987).

The Commission nonetheless maintains that it need not publish for notice and comment the five studies in full, including portions which it styles as "its staff's internal analysis of data in a rulemaking proceeding," Resp.'s Br. at 44, "regardless of whether the agency accepts or rejects or ignores" this material, *id.* at 22. It relies on *EchoStar Satellite L.L.C. v. FCC*, 457 F.3d 31 (D.C.Cir.2006), but that case is inapposite. In *EchoStar*, the court held that neither late disclosure of data submitted by a commenter nor non-disclosure of certain staff analysis, in the absence of a timely objection to the completeness of the rulemaking record, violated the notice and comment requirements. The study in that case on which the Commission had relied was made part of the rulemaking record two months before the Commission issued its order upon reconsideration and the non-disclosed staff analysis represented "merely . . . cogitations upon the evidence" that was part of the rulemaking record. *Id.* at 40. By contrast, the challenged orders indicate that the five staff studies were never fully disclosed for comment even though they were, according to the Commission, a central source of data for its critical determinations.

* * *

* * * The Commission has chosen to rely on the data in those studies and to place the redacted studies in the rulemaking record. Individual pages relied upon by the Commission reveal that the unredacted portions are likely to contain evidence that could call into question the Commission's decision to promulgate the rule. Under the circumstances, the Commission can point to no authority allowing it to rely on the studies in a rulemaking but hide from the public parts of the studies that may contain contrary evidence, inconvenient qualifications, or relevant explanations of the

methodology employed. The Commission has not suggested that any other confidentiality considerations would be implicated were the unredacted studies made public for notice and comment. The Commission also has not suggested that the redacted portions of the studies contain only "supplementary information" merely "clarify[ing], expand[ing], or amend[ing] other data that has been offered for comment." *See Chamber of Commerce II*, 443 F.3d at 903. Of course, it is within the Commission's prerogative to credit only certain parts of the studies. But what it did here was redact parts of those studies that are inextricably bound to the studies as a whole and thus to the data upon which the Commission has stated it relied, parts that explain the otherwise unidentified methodology underlying data cited by the Commission for its conclusions, and parts that signal caution about that data. This is a critical distinction and no precedent sanctions such a "hide and seek" application of the APA's notice and comment requirements.

* * *

NOTES

Then-Judge Kavanaugh joined the opinion in *American Radio Relay League* because he thought it was "the best interpretation of our *Portland Cement* line of cases," *id.* at 246, but he wrote separately to

> underscore that *Portland Cement* stands on a shaky legal foundation (even though it may make sense as a policy matter in some cases). Put bluntly, the *Portland Cement* doctrine cannot be squared with the text of § 553 of the APA. And *Portland Cement's* lack of roots in the statutory text creates a serious jurisprudential problem because the Supreme Court later [in *Vermont Yankee*] rejected this kind of freeform interpretation of the APA.

Id. Your editor agrees. *See* Jack M. Beermann & Gary Lawson, *Reprocessing* Vermont Yankee, 75 Geo. Wash. L. Rev. 856, 894 (2007). The majority responded to Judge Kavanaugh by maintaining that "the procedures invalidated in *Vermont Yankee* were not anchored to any statutory provision." 524 F.3d at 239. Is the *Portland Cement* doctrine anchored, in any meaningful sense of that word, to any statutory provision in the APA? The American Bar Association's Section on Administrative Law and Regulatory Practice has recommended that Congress amend the APA expressly to codify the *Portland Cement* doctrine. *See* Christopher J. Walker, *Modernizing the Administrative Procedure Act*, 69 Admin. L. Rev. 629, 639–40 (2017).

A second sub-species of complaint about agency non-disclosure of information in a notice of proposed rulemaking focuses, not on what the agency knew when it issued its notice, but on what the agency learned during the rulemaking and accordingly knew when it issued its final rule. Assume that a notice of proposed rulemaking adequately discloses the information that animates the agency's decision to propose a certain rule. Assume further that during the comment period, the agency comes across new information that is directly relevant to its ultimate decision. If the agency bases its decision to adopt a rule in part on this newly-acquired information, does it have to begin a whole new notice-and-comment period so that interested parties can address the adequacy of this new information? A "yes" answer would create strong incentives for agencies to refuse to learn anything from the comment period— a conclusion that seems utterly perverse. A "no" answer threatens to undermine the theory behind hybrid rulemaking by allowing agencies to base rules on data that were not made available for public criticism during the comment period.

A typical illustration of this problem is *Building Industry Ass'n of Superior California v. Norton*, 247 F.3d 1241 (D.C.Cir.2001):

> In those regions of California with Mediterranean climates, one finds shallow depressions called "vernal pools" that fill with rainwater in fall and winter only to evaporate in spring. In these pools reside numerous indigenous aquatic invertebrates that have evolved to survive in the pools' variable environmental conditions. In 1992 the Fish and Wildlife Service proposed to list as endangered species five tiny crustaceans resident in California's vernal pools: the vernal pool fairy shrimp, Conservancy fairy shrimp, longhorn fairy shrimp, California linderiella, and vernal pool tadpole shrimp (collectively, "fairy shrimp") * * *.

> After a comment period, the Service withdrew the proposal to list the California linderiella. It listed vernal pool fairy shrimp as threatened and the three remaining species as endangered * * *.

* * *

> * * * [T]he rule relies heavily on the Simovich study, which was released after the proposal and which the agency received only during the comment period. The study was therefore not among the materials published for public comment. Appellants argue that the Service's failure to seek comment on the study violated the APA.

> It is not disputed that the Service placed great weight on the Simovich study. It is cited frequently in the rule, which touted it as "[s]cientifically credible." 59 Fed. Reg. at 48,141. The Service concedes that the study is "the first long-term multidisciplinary study" and "the most scientifically based and well-documented professional study" of California vernal pools ever attempted, that it is "more comprehensive than any previous study," and that "the final rule relied substantially on the findings in the Simovich study."

> The Service nonetheless contends that it was not required to publish the Simovich study for public comment, and we agree. The APA generally obliges an agency to publish for comment the technical studies and data on which it relies. But to avoid "perpetual cycles of new notice and comment periods," *Ass'n of Battery Recyclers v. EPA*,

208 F.3d 1047, 1058 (D.C.Cir. 2000), a final rule that is a logical outgrowth of the proposal does not require an additional round of notice and comment even if the final rule relies on data submitted during the comment period. Such is the case here. The Simovich study, while the best available, only confirmed the findings delineated in the proposal * * *. Essentially, the proposal advanced for comment a hypothesis and some supporting data. The Simovich study provided additional support for that hypothesis—indeed, better support than was previously available—but it did not reject or modify the hypothesis such that additional comment was necessary.

247 F.3d at 1243, 1245–46. *Accord: Competitive Enterprise Inst. v. United States Dep't of Transportation*, 863 F.3d 911, 920 (D.C.Cir.2017) ("An agency cannot include material 'critical' to its decision for the first time in the final rule, but it may include new 'supplementary' information that 'expands upon and confirms' data in the rulemaking record") (citations omitted); *Kern County Farm Bureau v. Allen*, 450 F.3d 1072, 1076–80 (9th Cir.2006) (agency can use materials obtained subsequent to the notice of proposed rulemaking and never submitted for public comment when the agency uses the new material "merely to refine and expand on its pre-existing data").

A similar problem—with a different result—was presented in *Chamber of Commerce of U.S. v. SEC*, 443 F.3d 890 (D.C.Cir 2006). The Securities and Exchange Commission promulgated a rule exempting mutual funds from certain regulatory burdens if they had corporate boards with at least 75 percent outside directors and an outside director as the board's chairperson. The rule was initially remanded to the agency because the SEC had failed to determine (and therefore adequately to consider) the costs to the companies of meeting those conditions. *See Chamber of Commerce v. SEC*, 412 F.3d 133 (D.C.Cir.2005). On remand, the SEC reaffirmed its original decision based on materials concerning likely compliance costs that it gathered after remand but had not submitted for public comment. The D.C. Circuit ruled that it was error to rely on such material:

> [F]urther notice and comment are not required when additional fact gathering merely supplements information in the rulemaking record by checking or confirming prior assessments without changing methodology, by confirming or corroborating data in the rulemaking record, or by internally generating information using a methodology disclosed in the rulemaking record * * *.

> * * *

> The Commission's extensive reliance upon extra-record materials in arriving at its cost estimates, and thus in determining not to modify the two conditions, however, required further opportunity for comment under section 553(c) * * *. To the extent that the Commission suggests that the "publicly available" extra-record materials merely supplemented the rulemaking record * * *, it ignores what is obvious * * *.

To develop cost estimates for the Rule's two conditions, the Commission relied on privately produced "Management Practice Inc. Bulletin[s] and a nonpublic survey of compensation and governance practices in the mutual fund industry that is summarized in one of these bulletins." Neither the bulletins nor the survey were part of the rulemaking record * * *. Yet these extra-record materials supply the basic assumptions used by the Commission to establish the range of costs that mutual funds are likely to bear in complying with the two conditions * * *.

* * *

Other aspects of the Commission's decision illustrate that it treated extra-record data as primary, rather than supplementary, evidence * * *. [F]or extra-record data to be "supplementary," it must clarify, expand, or amend other data that has been offered for comment * * *.

[handwritten margin note: primary v. supplementary evidence — clarify, expand, or amend]

* * *

In sum, the combination of circumstances—inadequate notice that the Commission would base its cost estimates for the two conditions on "publicly available" extra-record materials on which it did not typically rely in rulemakings [and] the Commission's acknowledgment that the rulemaking record contained gaps and did not include reliable cost data * * *—suffices to show * * * the Commission's reliance on materials not in, nor merely "supplementary" to, the rulemaking record.

443 F.3d at 901–06.

A second form of challenge to the adequacy of a notice of proposed rulemaking argues that the agency's final rule concerns a subject that was not adequately "flagged" by the notice. Agencies cannot give notice that they are considering A, B, and C, and then adopt a rule concerning D. The public must be made aware of the agency's proposals. Problems of this sort are relatively rare, but on occasion, agencies will go to what seem like considerable lengths to obscure their true ambitions in a rulemaking. *See MCI Telecommunications Corp. v. FCC*, 57 F.3d 1136 (D.C. Cir. 1995) (holding invalid a rule that was foreshadowed in the notice of proposed rulemaking only in an obscure, misplaced footnote that knowledgeable participants in the rulemaking almost surely would have skipped).

A third form of challenge to the adequacy of a notice of proposed rulemaking is one of the challenges presented in *Connecticut Light & Power*. Suppose that an agency adequately provides notice to the public that it is considering rules A and B. After conducting the rulemaking proceeding and receiving comments, the agency adopts rules that cover the same essential subject matter as A and B but differ to some degree from the initially proposed rules in substance and details. Under the rulemaking philosophy prevalent in 1946, it would be very strange for a party to argue that a notice was inadequate because the agency adopted a rule that was different from its original proposal. The whole point of a rulemaking proceeding, *circa* 1946, was to allow the agency to educate itself and make an informed judgment. The expectation was that agencies would often change their minds as a result of the comments they received and the information acquired during the rulemaking; if the final product differed, even significantly, from the original proposal, that was a normal part of the process. The APA provides for rule *making* procedures, not rule *adoption* procedures. Under the post-1968 conception of rulemaking, however, if the final rule differs from the proposals put forward in the notice, it is open to parties to argue that they never got the chance to comment effectively on the agency's actual work product. It would be foolish, however, to hold agencies strictly to the terms of the proposals in their notices; agencies should be encouraged to correct their initial proposals and adopt better rules if that is what the rulemaking proceeding suggests is the wisest course. Indeed, the agency's rule would be substantively invalid if the agency stubbornly clung to its original proposal in the face of persuasive arguments for change.

As *Connecticut Light & Power* suggests, courts have tried to tread a middle ground between allowing agencies flexibility to adapt rules to new information and arguments and requiring that agency proposals be subjected to public scrutiny. If a final rule is a "logical outgrowth" of the proposals in the notice of proposed rulemaking, no new notice is required even if the adopted rules differ from the proposals. But if the final rule departs too drastically from the original proposals, then a new notice, and a new comment period, is required. How much of a departure is too much? There is no formula that will give an answer, and the case law applying the vague "logical outgrowth" concept to particular facts is voluminous and growing. *See, e.g., Environmental Integrity Project v. EPA,* 425 F.3d 992 (D.C. Cir. 2005); *Louisiana Federal Land Bank Ass'n, FLCA v. Farm Credit Administration,* 336 F.3d 1075, 1081–82 (D.C.Cir.2003); *Alto Dairy v. Veneman,* 336 F.3d 560, 569–70 (7th Cir.2003). For a good introduction, see Phillip M. Kannan, *The Logical Outgrowth Doctrine in Rulemaking,* 48 Admin. L. Rev. 213 (1996).

In *Int'l Union, United Mine Workers v. Mine Safety & Health Administration,* 626 F.3d 84 (D.C. Cir. 2010), the D.C. Circuit considered a rule adopted by the Mine Safety and Health Administration (MSHA) addressing, inter alia, the design of refuge chambers in mines to be used in the event of an accident. Pursuant to statutory directive, the rule was based on a report prepared by the National Institute of Occupational Safety and Health (NIOSH) and was challenged by the United Mine Workers of America (UMWA).

Refuge Volume. The NIOSH Report recommended providing at least 15 square feet of unrestricted floor space and at least 85 cubic feet of unrestricted volume per miner in the refuge alternatives to enable miners to perform basic functions. However, the Report advised that "[t]he values listed . . . should not be considered as absolute, but rather as reasonable starting points for specifications." Beyond noting that "it may be impractical to implement viable refuge alternatives in the few mines that operate in very low coal, e.g. less than 36 inches," the NIOSH Report did not include specific recommendations on how to tailor volume in these low-height mines.

MSHA proposed that a refuge chamber provide 60 cubic feet per miner, including 15 square feet of floor space. *See* NPRM ["Notice of Proposed Rulemaking"], 73 Fed. Reg. at 34,146. It also noted the problem of low-height mines, explaining that "[f]or mines with lower heights, the 60 cubic feet of space may need to be attained by increasing the length or floor area." *Id.* The NPRM noted the NIOSH recommendation of 85/15. MSHA generally "solicit[ed] comments on these minimum space and volume requirements," instructing that "[c]omments should be specific, including alternatives, rationale, safety benefits to miners, technological and economic feasibility, and supporting data." *Id.* MSHA also specifically "solicit[ed] comment on these proposed values for floor space and volume, particularly in low mining heights," *id.* at 34,157, with the same instructions about comments.

The UMWA commented that 60 cubic feet was inadequate, explaining that it was "always the intent [of Congress] to provide not only the necessary protections for miners to sustain life while they are inside a chamber/shelter, but to also allow miners to be comfortable while awaiting rescue." Such adequate volume was important, the UMWA emphasized, to protect miners' mental stability while trapped for up to 96 hours; it pointed to testimony at congressional hearings recounting experiences of trapped miners and how they survived physically and mentally in confined quarters while awaiting rescue. The UMWA also noted that the reduced space would subject miners to greater risk of CO_2 exposure and/or excessive heat within the chamber. In UMWA's view, the nearly 30% reduction from the NIOSH recommendation was without justification and "does not make sense." *Id.* at 10. In "urg[ing] MSHA to adopt the 85 cubic foot recommendation of NIOSH to all refuges," *id.,* UMWA stated that it would support using more than one chamber to accommodate the space needed.

* * *

The Final Rule adopted the proposed 60 cubic feet per miner for refuge chambers and also included a sliding scale based on the height of each mine allowing as little as 30 cubic feet for refuge chambers in mines with heights ranging from 36 inches or less to 54 inches.

* * *

The UMWA * * * contends the requirement is not a logical outgrowth of the proposed rule, specifically maintaining that it was not afforded an opportunity to submit comments regarding the mental well-being of miners in "coffin-sized spaces," or about "larger persons," i.e., "a mildly obese miner," or the ability to perform basic survival tasks.

A final rule is a logical outgrowth of the proposed rule "only if interested parties should have anticipated that the change was possible, and thus reasonably should have filed their comments on the subject during the notice-and-comment period." *Int'l Union, United Mine Workers of Am. v. MSHA*, 407 F.3d 1250, 1259 (D.C.Cir.2005) (internal quotations omitted). However, "a final rule will be deemed to be the logical outgrowth of a proposed rule if a new round of notice and comment would not provide commentators with their first occasion to offer new and different criticisms which the agency might find convincing." *Fertilizer Inst. v. EPA*, 935 F.2d 1303, 1311 (D.C.Cir.1991) (citation and internal quotation marks omitted). Notice of the agency's intention is crucial to "ensure that agency regulations are tested via exposure to diverse public comment, . . . to ensure fairness to affected parties, and . . . to give affected parties an opportunity to develop evidence in the record to support their objections to the rule and thereby enhance the quality of judicial review." *Int'l Union*, 40 F.3d at 1259.

Thus, in *Int'l Union*, 407 F.3d at 1259, the court held that a proposed rule providing for a minimum air velocity did not put parties on notice that the maximum air velocity might be regulated. In *Shell Oil Co. v. EPA*, 950 F.2d 741, 751–52 (D.C.Cir.1991), the court held that there was no logical outgrowth where there was "a marked shift in emphasis between the proposed regulations and the final rules" because the listing of hazardous waste went from a "largely supplementary function" to having a "heavy emphasis" in the regulatory scheme. By contrast, in *Nat'l-Mining Ass'n v. MSHA*, 512 F.3d 696, 699 (D.C.Cir.2008), where the proposed rule requiring that "rescue devices be provided for each miner in both the primary and the alternative escapeways" left open the questions of where the devices would be stored, how they would be available to miners, and whether one common cache of devices would be sufficient where escapeways were proximate, the court held that the rule providing for a hardened room cache between the escapeways was a "logical outgrowth" of the proposal.

The proposed [refuge alternative] rule identified the potential problem with attaining 60 cubic feet of space per miner, explaining that "for mines with lower heights, the 60 cubic feet of space may need to be attained by increasing the length or floor area," 73 Fed. REg. at 34,416. The Final Rule dealt with the problem by reducing the volume to as little as 30 cubic feet per miner where mine heights are 36 inches or less. The UMWA contends that the proposed rule contained "[t]he explicit assurance . . . that any problem presented by lower mine heights would be addressed by increasing the length or floor area of the refuge chamber . . . *not* . . . through further reduction in the volume requirement." Pet'r Br. 34. However, this overlooks MSHA's statement that "achieving the volume per mine in refute alternatives for low coal mines could be problematic, 73 Fed. Reg. at 34,157, and its specific call for comments on the proposed floor space and volume requirements in low mining heights, *see id.* MSHA was free to adopt a different solution in the Final Rule, as long as it gave interested parties fair notice and an opportunity to respond.

The UMWA "does not suggest that it lacked adequate notice that the Secretary in her [Final] Rule may have further reduced the proposed rule's 60 cubic feet volume requirement," but rather emphasizes that MSHA's reduction of ceiling heights in low mining areas without increasing the floor space presents a logical outgrowth problem. Reply Br. 30. The UMWA views the change as of the more extreme kind in *Int'l Union*, 407 F.3d at 1259, maintaining that MSHA, in "slash[ing] in half" the volume requirement, Reply Br. 30, flipped the potential solution entirely. But the court has held "a final rule represents a logical outgrowth where the NPRM expressly asked for comments on a particular issue or otherwise made clear that the agency was contemplating a particular change." *CSX Transp., Inc. v. STB*, 584 F.3d 1076, 10871 (D.C.Cir.2009) * * *. Here MSHA's proposed rule identified the problem of low height mines and specifically solicited detailed comments on it.

626 F.3d at 89–90, 94–96.

The Second Circuit reached a different result on a similar issue in *Time Warner Cable, Inc. v. FCC*, 729 F.3d 137 (2d.Cir. 2013). The Cable Television Consumer Protection and Competition Act of 1992, 106 Stat. 1460 (codified at 47 U.S.C. § 536(a)(3), (5)) forbids multichannel video programming distributors ("MVPDs"), such as major cable networks, from discriminating against content produced by non-affiliated networks. The statute provides for complaint procedures if non-affiliated networks think themselves aggrieved, and an FCC regulation promulgated in 2011—known as the "standstill rule"— requires the MVPDs to continue carrying the non-affiliated programming until the complaint is resolved. *See Revision of the Commission's Program Carriage Rules*, 26 FCC Rcd. 11494 (2011), 47 C.F.R. § 76.1302(k)(1). The 2007 notice of proposed rulemaking that led to the standstill rule had sought comments on "the need to clarify the elements" of a discrimination charge, on whether the Commission needed to " 'adopt rules to address the complaint process itself,' " and " 'on any other issues that would properly inform [its] program carriage inquiry.' " 729 F.3d, at 148. The court found this notice insufficient to sustain the standstill rule.

Here, the *2007 NPRM* did not specifically indicate that the FCC was considering adopting a standstill rule. Nor can that rule be considered the logical outgrowth of the issues described in the *2007 NPRM*. While the 2007 NPRM did seek comment on whether the FCC should "adopt rules to address the complaint process itself" and, specifically, whether it "should adopt additional rules to protect [programming networks] from potential retaliation if they file a complaint," those solicitations are too general to provide adequate notice that a standstill rule was under consideration as a means to provide such protection. Thus, interested parties had no reason to comment on such a measure. . . .

Indeed, the record shows that the public did not, in fact, anticipate that the FCC would adopt a standstill rule based on the 2007 NPRM. None of the commenters addressed such a rule during the official comment period—a fact that strongly suggests that the 2007 NPRM provided insufficient notice.

That conclusion is reinforced by the fact that, in a similar context, under the program access provision of the Cable Act, the FCC expressly sought comment on whether it should adopt a standstill rule. That the FCC, with release of the *2011 FCC Order,* solicited comment on several key aspects of the standstill rule's implementation, including whether its authority to issue standstill orders in the program carriage context is statutorily or otherwise limited, further indicates that the agency did not adequately solicit comments on the standstill rule in the first instance.

729 F.3d at 170–71. *See also Allina Health Services v. Sebelius,* 746 F.3d 1102 (D.C.Cir. 2014) (notice proposing to "clarify" existing practices did not provide adequate notice for a rule significantly changing those practices).

If your mind is now spinning about when a final rule is a "logical outgrowth" of a notice of proposed rulemaking, see if the following case slows down or speeds up the rotation.

MID CONTINENT NAIL CORP. v. UNITED STATES

United States Court of Appeals for the Federal Circuit, 2017.
846 F.3d 1364.

Before: NEWMAN, LOURIE, and DYK, CIRCUIT JUDGES.

DYK, CIRCUIT JUDGE.

[The Department of Commerce has responsibility for enforcing "antidumping" laws that determine whether foreign competitors of American firms are selling products in the United States at discriminatorily low prices. There are statutorily prescribed methodologies that the Commerce Department must use for calculating whether imported products are subject to import duties (which effectively raise their prices) because of the anti-dumping laws. Normally, one compares either average or specific transactional prices of imported merchandise to the average or specific transactional prices of comparable merchandise. *See* 19 U.S.C. § 1677f–1(d)(1)(A)(i)–(ii) (2012). But in exceptional cases, in which the agency suspects "targeted" dumping aimed at relatively narrow markets, the agency is allowed to compare average prices to specific transactional prices, instead of comparing average-to-average or transactional-to-transactional prices, if the agency detects a suspicious pattern of pricing that cannot be explained using the normal methodologies. *See id.* § 1677f–1(d)(1)(B). Because this methodology to some extent compares apples to oranges, the Commerce Department, by a rule adopted through notice-and-comment procedures, limited its use of that methodology even more strictly than the methodology's use is limited by statute by confining its application "to those sales that constitute targeted dumping," 19 C.F.R. § 351.414(f)(2) (2008), rather than to all sales by the supposedly offending importer. Under that rule, which the court in this case calls the "Limiting Regulation," the American sales of steel nails in 2011 by Precision Fasteners, LLC, a United Arab Emirates company, would *not* violate the anti-dumping rules. If, however, one applied that exceptional average-to-transactional methodology to all of Precision's sales and not just to those sales which the agency could identify as targeted dumping, one would calculate a violation of the anti-dumping laws, and a duty on Precision's nails would be imposed—to the benefit of Mid Continent Nail Corp., which brought the anti-dumping challenge.

[In 2008, the Commerce Department withdrew its rule confining application of the average-to-transactional methodology to identified targeted dumping sales. *See* Withdrawal of the Regulatory Provisions Governing Targeted Dumping in Antidumping Duty Investigations, Interim Final Rule, 73 Fed. Reg. 74,930, 74,931 (Dec. 10, 2008) ("*Withdrawal Notice*"). The agency did *not* use notice-and-comment procedures to repeal the rule. Initially, the agency claimed that it could repeal the rule using the "good cause" exception to notice-and-comment procedures in § 553, which you will hear about shortly. *See infra* pages 472–484. In a portion of the opinion not reproduced here, the Federal Circuit rejected that argument. The agency's next line of defense was that repeal of the rule had actually been foreshadowed in certain notices of proposed rulemaking, so that the repeal, while not the subject of its own dedicated rulemaking proceedings, was a "logical outgrowth" of various other rulemaking proceedings in which notice-and-comment procedures had been provided. The Commerce Department then applied the average-to-transactional methodology to Precision and imposed a duty. Precision appealed, arguing that the limiting rule had never been properly repealed and was thus still in force. Everyone agreed that Precision should win if the withdrawal of the limiting rule was invalid.]

*   *   *

I

We first address Mid Continent's contention that Commerce provided adequate notice for the repeal of the Limiting Regulation through two

Federal Register notices issued in 2007 and 2008: (1) Targeted Dumping in Antidumping Investigations; Request for Comment, 72 Fed. Reg. 60,651 (Oct. 25, 2007) [hereinafter *Request for Comment*]; and (2) Proposed Methodology for Identifying and Analyzing Targeted Dumping in Antidumping Investigations; Request for Comment, 73 Fed. Reg. 26,371 (May 9, 2008) [hereinafter *Proposed Methodology*].

A

The requirement that an agency provide adequate notice before altering its regulations is rooted in the APA's provisions governing the administrative rulemaking process. Under the APA, whenever an agency decides to "formulat[e], amend[ ], or repeal[ ] a rule," it must first publish an NPRM [notice of proposed rulemaking] setting forth "either the terms or substance of the proposed rule[,] or a description of the subjects and issues involved." 5 U.S.C. §§ 553(b), 551(5). For the purposes of notice and comment, withdrawal or repeal of an existing regulation is treated the same as promulgation of a new regulation. *See Tunik v. MSPB*, 407 F.3d 1326, 1342 (Fed. Cir. 2005). Although the notice "need not specify every precise proposal which [the agency] may ultimately adopt," it "must be sufficient to fairly apprise interested parties of the issues involved." *Nuvio Corp. v. FCC*, 473 F.3d 302, 310 (D.C. Cir. 2006) (quoting *Action for Children's Television v. FCC*, 564 F.2d 458, 470 (D.C. Cir. 1977)). Adequate notice "is crucial to 'ensure that agency regulations are tested via exposure to diverse public comment, . . . to ensure fairness to affected parties, and . . . to give affected parties an opportunity to develop evidence in the record to support their objections to the rule and thereby enhance the quality of judicial review.'" *Int'l Union, United Mine Workers of Am. v. Mine Safety & Health Admin.*, 626 F.3d 84, 95 (D.C. Cir. 2010) (quoting *Int'l Union, United Mine Workers of Am. v. Mine Safety & Health Admin.*, 407 F.3d 1250, 1259 (D.C. Cir. 2005)).

The dispositive question in assessing the adequacy of notice under the APA is whether an agency's final rule is a "logical outgrowth" of an earlier request for comment.

The logical outgrowth doctrine recognizes that a certain degree of change between an NPRM and a final rule is inherent to the APA's scheme of rulemaking through notice and comment. Accordingly, judicial formulations of the doctrine have sought to "balance" the values served by adequate notice, *see Int'l Union*, 626 F.3d at 94–95, with "the public interest in expedition and finality." *Small Refiner Lead Phase-Down Task Force v. EPA*, 705 F.2d 506, 547 (D.C. Cir. 1983) * * *.

* * *

Nonetheless, there are limits to how far a notice of proposed rulemaking may be stretched under the logical outgrowth doctrine. In some cases, these limits may be difficult to discern, *Kooritzky v. Reich*, 17 F.3d 1509, 1513 (D.C. Cir. 1994), but certain clear lines have been drawn. "The logical outgrowth doctrine does not extend to a final rule that finds no roots in the agency's proposal because something is not a logical outgrowth of nothing, . . . [or] where interested parties would have had to divine the agency's unspoken thoughts, because the final rule was surprisingly distant from the [a]gency's proposal." *Envtl. Integrity Project v. EPA*, 425 F.3d 992, 996 (D.C. Cir. 2005) (internal quotation marks and citations omitted).

B

Having summarized the principles animating the logical outgrowth doctrine, we turn to whether Commerce's repeal of the Limiting Regulation in *Withdrawal Notice* was a logical outgrowth of *Request for Comment* and *Proposed Methodology* * * *.

* * *

Ten years after promulgating the Limiting Regulation, Commerce published *Request for Comment,* in which the agency sought guidance regarding an appropriate test to determine the existence of targeted dumping. In this notice, Commerce admitted that it had accrued only "limited experience with targeted dumping" despite the intervening years; that it had yet to develop a standard targeted dumping test; and that its "experience with regard to the use of the [average-to-transaction] method ha[d] been very limited." 72 Fed. Reg. at 60,651. By publishing *Request for Comment*, Commerce hoped to solicit the public's views on "its development of a methodology for determining whether targeted dumping is occurring in antidumping investigations," and "input on standards and tests that may be appropriate in a targeted dumping analysis." *Id.* Specifically, the agency sought guidance on: (1) how to determine the existence of a "pattern of export prices . . . among purchasers, regions, or periods of time"; (2) how to determine if such a pattern "differ[s] significantly"; and (3) the "appropriate statistical techniques" to assess targeted dumping. *Id.*

Despite raising these concerns, *Request for Comment* was not published in the Federal Register as an NPRM, meaning that the notice on its face did not indicate that Commerce was considering a rulemaking. More problematically, *Request for Comment* did not propose any kind of rule or raise any question about the scope of the average-to-transaction methodology, much less the conditions under which the agency should depart from its "normal" practice of not applying the methodology to all sales. *Request for Comment* did not even include a citation to the Limiting Regulation. Instead, in *Request for Comment*, Commerce simply sought information on the broad issue of how the agency should determine the existence of targeted dumping—a distinct, predicate issue to the problem addressed by the Limiting Regulation (i.e., the scope of the average-to-transaction methodology).

The consequence of these deficiencies is that *Request for Comment* falls short of satisfying the APA's requirements for notice and opportunity for comment * * *. *Request for Comment* gave no indication that Commerce was contemplating a potential change in the Limiting Regulation. Nor did commentators responding to *Request for Comment* perceive the agency to be raising the issue of the regulation's repeal or revision, or suggest such repeal or revision themselves. We therefore have no doubt that Commerce's repeal of the Limiting Regulation was not a logical outgrowth of *Request for Comment* because, as in *Kooritzky,* "[s]omething is not a logical outgrowth of nothing." 17 F.3d at 1513.

C

Six months after *Request for Comment*, Commerce—still concerned with the appropriate test for determining the existence of targeted dumping—proposed a new two-part test addressing the problem in *Proposed Methodology* * * *. In particular, the agency "request[ed] comment on the application of the [average-to-transaction methodology] and the conditions, if any, under which the [average-to-transaction] methodology should apply to *all* sales to the target, even if some sales of a control number do not pass the targeted dumping test." *Id.* at 26,372 (emphasis added).

Proposed Methodology thus presents a closer question under the logical outgrowth doctrine than *Request for Comment*. The Limiting Regulation had provided that Commerce would "normally" apply the average-to-transaction methodology only to "those sales" found to "constitute targeted dumping." 19 C.F.R. § 351.414(f)(2) (2008). Therefore, by seeking public comment on "the conditions, if any," under which the average-to-transaction methodology should be applied to all sales made by a respondent—instead of just the respondent's targeted sales—Commerce effectively raised the general subject of the Limiting Regulation, perhaps suggesting wholesale elimination of the agency's discretion to apply the average-to-transaction methodology to all sales.

Although courts have found logical outgrowths when an NPRM "expressly asked for comments on a particular issue or otherwise made clear that the agency was contemplating a particular change," *CSX*, 584 F.3d at 1081, we do not think that this principle supports holding *Proposed Methodology* to have provided the "necessary predicate" for *Withdrawal Notice. Kooritzky,* 17 F.3d at 1513. For starters, like *Request for Comment, Proposed Methodology* on its face did not indicate that further action to withdraw the Limiting Regulation was being considered. Instead, *Proposed Methodology* merely sought public views on how to interpret the regulation itself—which provided that the agency would "normally" not apply the average-to-transaction methodology to all sales—that is, how exactly Commerce should apply the "normally" limitation. Because the agency had left the circumstances in which it would have applied the average-to-transaction methodology to all sales largely undefined, "interested persons" would have perceived the question regarding the Limiting Regulation posed in *Proposed Methodology* as simply Commerce's first step in clarifying the scope of its own regulation. Indeed, comments that the agency received in response to *Proposed Methodology* did not understand Commerce to be raising a broader question, *i.e.*, whether to repeal the Limiting Regulation.

Posing such a general "scope" question does not suffice to provide the requisite "fair notice" for an agency rule to be upheld as a logical outgrowth. In *CSX*, the D.C. Circuit confronted a similar problem in addressing a rule promulgated by the Surface Transportation Board ("STB") to resolve railroad rate disputes. The STB had originally proposed a rule allowing such disputes to be resolved using "comparison groups drawn from the most recent year of waybill sampling." 584 F.3d at 1078. In the rule finally adopted, however, the agency "switch[ed] from one year to four years' worth of data." *Id*. The STB argued that the final rule was a logical outgrowth because "mention[ing] . . . the release of one-year data . . . gave notice that the amount of data available . . . might change." *Id*. at 1082.

The D.C. Circuit rejected this argument for two reasons. First, the court observed that although the STB's notice had proposed a number of related regulatory changes, "it nowhere even hinted that [the agency] might consider expanding the number of years from which comparison groups could be derived." *Id*. Second, permitting the "mere mention" of the one-year timeframe for drawing comparison groups to provide adequate notice would allow the agency "to justify any final rule it might be able to devise by whimsically picking and choosing within the four corners of a lengthy 'notice.'" *Id*. (quoting *Envtl. Integrity Project*, 425 F.3d at 998). "Such a rule would hardly promote the purposes of the APA's notice requirement." *Id*.

The same reasoning applies to *Proposed Methodology*. Despite mentioning the subject matter of the Limiting Regulation, Commerce's primary purpose in the *Proposed Methodology* was to propose a new test for determining whether a respondent was engaged in targeted dumping and to seek public comment on this proposal. As a "related issue" the agency posed a general question of when to apply the average-to-transaction methodology to all sales, not just targeted sales. But this question did not raise the "particular issue" of withdrawing the Limiting Regulation; it sought only to clarify the meaning of the Limiting Regulation's recitation of the word "normally." And, as in *CSX*, allowing Commerce's question in *Proposed Methodology* to provide adequate notice for *Withdrawal Notice* would permit the agency to adopt a final rule from a limitless continuum of regulatory actions * * *.

D

Mid Continent argues that even if Commerce did not itself provide the required notice, comments made in response to *Request for Comment* and *Proposed Methodology* urged Commerce to apply the average-to-transaction methodology to "all sales" and thereby effectively raised the issue of repealing the Limiting Regulation.

Although responses by commentators may be relevant to the court's inquiry under the logical outgrowth doctrine, as a general matter, an agency "cannot bootstrap notice from a comment." *Fertilizer Inst. v. EPA*, 935 F.2d 1303, 1312 (D.C. Cir. 1991). Here, the comments relied on by Mid Continent never urged Commerce to repeal the Limiting Regulation; commentators simply asked the agency to construe the regulation more or less broadly * * *. [T]he fact that comments * * * were entirely silent on the issue of repealing the Limiting Regulation supports the conclusion that these notices were insufficient to render the agency's actions in *Withdrawal Notice* a "logical outgrowth." *See, e.g., Council Tree Commc'ns, Inc. v. FCC*, 619 F.3d 235, 256 (3d Cir. 2010).

Finally, our conclusion that *Withdrawal Notice* is not a logical outgrowth of either *Request for Comment* or *Proposed Methodology* is further bolstered by * * * other considerations. First, Commerce never referred to *Request for Comment* or *Proposed Methodology* in *Withdrawal Notice*, nor responded to the comments it had received in response to the two earlier notices * * *. Last but not least, Commerce did not suggest in *Withdrawal Notice* that it had in fact complied with the APA by issuing the earlier notices. To the contrary, Commerce thought it necessary to invoke the APA's good cause exception, which implies that the agency did not consider its prior notices to have satisfied the statute's procedural requirements. Although the inconsistency of simultaneously invoking good cause and arguing post hoc compliance with the APA is not dispositive, the tension between these conflicting positions strongly supports our view that Commerce's (and now, Mid Continent's) assertion that the agency had complied with notice-and-comment rulemaking is not supportable.

In summary, we hold that Commerce's repeal of the Limiting Regulation in *Withdrawal Notice* was not a logical outgrowth of *Request for Comment* and *Proposed Methodology*, and that [the] agency failed to provide adequate notice under the APA.

NOTES

The text of the APA states that notices of proposed rulemaking can contain "*either* the terms or substance of the proposed rule *or a description of the subjects and issues involved*." § 553(b)(3) (emphasis added). The tacit assumption in modern law, however, reflected most clearly in the "logical outgrowth" doctrine, is that notices of proposed rulemaking will generally propose rules for adoption. Indeed, one frequent agency response by agencies to the rise of the "logical outgrowth" doctrine is to offer a wide range of alternative proposed rules in the notice of proposed rulemaking to ensure that any final rule will be able to trace its lineage to something in the initial document.

This modern emphasis on rule-proposal is so strong that, in 2006, an agency's failure to offer a concrete proposal in a notice of proposed rulemaking prompted a serious, though unsuccessful, legal challenge. *See Nuvio Corp. v. FCC*, 473 F.3d 302, 309–10 (D.C.Cir.2006) ("Petitioners' final argument faults the Commission because . . . [the notice] lacked proposed rules or even tentative conclusions . . . The Commission fairly apprised the parties and the public of the issues covered").

In 2011, it prompted another serious challenge—this time with a markedly different outcome. Over the years, the Federal Communications Commission ("FCC") has conducted extensive rulemakings concerning cross-ownership of different media outlets (television stations, radio stations, and newspapers). Those rulemakings typically address a variety of topics concerning such ownership, ranging from the permissible degrees of concentration in various markets to the promotion of race and gender diversity. Prior to 2008, those rules forbade the same entity from owning a broadcast television station and a daily newspaper in the same market. In a rule issued on December 18, 2007 (but generally known as the "2008 Order"), the FCC replaced that flat ban on such cross-ownership with a case-by-case, multi-factor review process. *See 2006 Quadrennial Regulatory Review—Review of the Commission's Broadcast Ownership Rules and Other Rules Adopted Pursuant to Section 202 of the Telecommunications Act of 1996, Report and Order on Reconsideration*, 23 F.C.C.R. 2010, 2055–56 (2007). The relevant portion of the FCC's notice of proposed rulemaking on this topic—described by the reviewing court as "paragraph 32"—read as follows:

> * * * [W]e seek comment on how we should approach cross-ownership limits. Should limits vary depending upon the characteristic of local markets? If so, what characteristics should be considered, and how should they be factored into any limits? We seek comment on the newspaper/broadcast rule and the radio/television cross-ownership rule. Are there aspects of television and radio broadcast operations that make cross-ownership with a newspaper different for each of these media? If so, should limits on newspaper/radio combinations be different from limits on newspaper/television combinations? Lastly, are the newspaper/broadcast cross-ownership rule and the radio/television cross-ownership rule necessary in the public interest as a result of competition?

2006 Quadrennial Regulatory Review; 2002 Biennial Regulatory Review—Review of the Commission's Broadcast Ownership Rules, 71 Fed. Reg. 45511,

45514 (2006) ("*FNPR*"). The Third Circuit found this "description of the subjects and issues involved," § 553(b)(3), to be <u>inadequate notice</u> under the APA to support a rule changing the cross-ownership regime:

> * * * [T]he Commission relies on paragraph 32 of the *FNPR* to satisfy its notice obligations under the APA. It argues that "[a] notice that contains no rule proposals complies with the APA so long as it is 'sufficient to fairly apprise interested parties of all significant subjects and issues involved.' " [FCC Br. at 37] (quoting *NVE, Inc. v. Dep't of Health and Human Servs.*, 436 F.3d 182, 191 (3d Cir.2006)). However, an agency also <u>"must 'describe the range of alternatives being considered with reasonable specificity</u>. Otherwise, interested parties will not know what to comment on, and notice will not lead to better-informed agency decision-making.' " *Horsehead Res. Dev. Co., Inc. v. Browner*, 16 F.3d 1246, 1268 (D.C.Cir.1994).

On these facts, we <u>cannot conclude that the Commission met this obligation</u>, as we fail to see how the *FNPR*, with its two general questions related to the NBCO [newspaper/broadcasting cross-ownership] rule, and the irregular comment period that followed, satisfy the APA. The *FNPR* <u>makes plain that the FCC was planning significant revision to the NBCO rule</u> and looking for an alternative to the Diversity Index for measuring diversity. Paragraph 32 of the *FNPR* asks only <u>whether cross-ownership limits should vary</u> "depending upon the characteristics of local markets," and, "if so, what characteristics should be considered . . . ?"

While the new rule varies limits depending on characteristics of markets—specifically, market size and the number of media voices— it was <u>not clear from the *FNPR* which characteristics the Commission was considering or why</u>. The phrase "characteristics of markets" was <u>too open-ended</u> to allow for meaningful comment on the Commission's approach. In addition, many central elements of the rule are not based on "characteristics of markets" at all. For example, key aspects of the rule rely on: the amount of "local news" produced by an individual station involved in a potential merger and how that term is defined; the definition of "major media voices," including what counts as a major newspaper; how "market concentration" is measured; whether a station is "failing"; whether a station exercises "independent news judgment" and how that term is defined; and whether a case-by-case approach or a categorical approach to proposed mergers would better serve the public interest. The *FNPR* also did not solicit comment on the overall framework under consideration, how potential factors might operate together, or how the new approach might affect the FCC's other ownership rules. These were significant omissions.

* * *

* * * [I]nterested parties were prejudiced by the inadequacy of the *FNPR*. During the official comment period, some commenters noted that their submission would be limited because the *FNPR* "makes no proposals and suggests no options." *Comments of UCC et al*, MB Docket No. 06–121 at 60 (Oct. 23, 2006) ("*10/23/06 UCC Comments*"). Indeed, in an 87-page submission, there was only *one paragraph* on how a relaxed approach to cross-ownership "might work" if the FCC eliminated the existing ban, but over 11 pages discussing data on the benefits of retaining a ban and several more pages regarding closing "loopholes" in the ban. *10/23/06 UCC Comments* at 61–74. These comments, like many others, were largely limited to discussing whether the ban should be retained or eliminated. *See, e.g., Comments of Bonneville International Corp.,* MB Docket No. 06–121 at 15 (Oct. 23, 2006) (arguing that the ban should be eliminated); *Comments of Belo Corp.,* MB Docket No. 06–121 at 9–10 (Oct. 23, 2006) (same); *Comments of AFL-CIO,* MB Docket No. 06–121 at 57 (Oct. 23, 2006) (urging retention of the ban); *Comments of American Federation of Radio and Television Artists,* MB Docket No. 06–121 at 20–22 (Oct. 23, 2006) (same). This occurred, we suspect, in large measure because a discussion of the actual issues involved—including the factors, presumptions, and exceptions the FCC was considering—was impossible based on the sparse *FNPR*.

* * *

In this context, we have little choice but to conclude that the FCC did not, through the *FNPR*, fulfill its "obligation to make its views known to the public in a concrete and focused form so as to make criticism or formulation of alternatives possible." *Home Box Office,* 567 F.2d at 36. The two sentences in paragraph 32 of the *FNPR* are simply too general and open-ended to have fairly apprised the public of the Commission's new approach to cross-ownership.

Prometheus Radio Project v. FCC, 652 F.3d 431 (3d Cir.2011).

Can you challenge a rulemaking proceeding because the agency did not provide enough time for interested parties to file comments? Interestingly, the APA does not specify a time period for comments after issuance of a notice of proposed rulemaking. Recommendations have been made to codify a presumptive sixty-day period for comments, at least for matters of great significance. *See* Christopher J. Walker, *Modernizing the Administrative Procedure Act,* 69 Admin. L. Rev. 629, 641–42 (2017). Absent such a statute, any challenge to the length of the comment period would have to be based on "arbitrary or capricious" review, discussed at length in Chapter 4.

4. THE STATEMENT OF BASIS AND PURPOSE

The statement of basis and purpose for a rule contains the agency's justification for its rule—much as a judicial opinion contains the court's justification for its decision. For reasons that will become clear a bit later in this chapter, when courts evaluate the substantive adequacy of a rule, they generally will not look beyond the arguments advanced by the agency in its statement of basis and purpose. As a result, the modern statement of basis and purpose is often a monstrously long and complex document that contains a detailed exposition of the agency's reasoning and the agency's response to the views expressed by commenters during the rulemaking.

Because the statement of basis and purpose is the vehicle by which an agency justifies the product of its informal rulemakings, to say that a statement of basis and purpose is "procedurally inadequate" often is really to say that the agency failed adequately to explain its decision on the merits. Accordingly, arguments about the adequacy of the statement of basis and purpose are best viewed—and are generally viewed by courts—as arguments about the *substance* of the agency's decision and decisionmaking process, and that is a topic for Chapter 4.

Several questions about the statement of basis and purpose, however, seem more "procedural" than "substantive." First, does a statement of basis and purpose have to address every argument that is put forward by commenters during a rulemaking proceeding? Although agencies sometimes might feel as though the answer is "yes," courts have not gone that far. Rather, "[a]n agency need not address every comment, but it must respond in a reasoned manner to those that raise significant problems." *Reytblatt v. United States NRC*, 105 F.3d 715, 722 (D.C.Cir.1997). The level of detail required in a response "depends on the subject of the regulation and the nature of the comments received." *Action on Smoking and Health v. CAB*, 699 F.2d 1209, 1216 (D.C.Cir.1983). A good example of the problem is *Louisiana Federal Land Bank Ass'n, FLCA v. Farm Credit Administration*, 336 F.3d 1075 (D.C.Cir.2003):

> The Congress established the Farm Credit System in order to "improv[e] the income and well-being of American farmers and ranchers by furnishing sound, adequate, and constructive credit . . . to them." 12 U.S.C. § 2001(a) * * *. The System * * * currently comprises six Farm Credit Banks (FCBs) * * * and over 100 local "associations," such as the Louisiana Federal Land Bank Association. The FCBs finance the local associations, which in turn provide eligible borrowers with credit * * *.

> The Act authorizes * * * direct loans and loan participations. In a loan participation, an institution such as an FCB buys an interest in a direct loan * * *.

> The Act itself contains no geographic restriction upon lending * * *. Nevertheless, the F[arm] C[redit] A[dministration] historically has imposed such restrictions by chartering only one lender of each type to serve any given geographic territory * * *.

In November 1998 the FCA proposed * * * removing the geographic restrictions * * *.

The FCA received more than 270 comments on the proposal, including one submitted by the plaintiffs, which argued that the FCA lacked statutory authority to promulgate the Proposed Rule, geographic limitations were integral to the statutory scheme, and permitting out-of-territory lending would hurt the System and its customers, especially small farmers * * *.

On April 25, 2000 the FCA published the Final Rule * * * [which] removed geographic restrictions from loan participations but not from direct loans, allowing an FCB to participate in a loan outside its territory without the consent of any other System institution * * *.

* * *

As noted above, the Proposed Rule prompted over 270 comments, including the one submitted by the plaintiffs. The preamble to the Final Rule said almost nothing about the comments, noting merely:

> [No commenter cited any statutory provision that restricts the authority of System banks and associations to participate in loans outside of their chartered territory.] Only one comment letter mentioned the statutory authorities of System institutions to participate in loans.

65 Fed. Reg. at 24,101/2. The plaintiffs claim this statement did not adequately address their comment protesting the introduction of competition by the lifting of the geographic restrictions. In response, the FCA points out that in the preamble to the Proposed Rule it had discussed out-of-territory participations separately, whereas the plaintiffs' comment did not make such a distinction and was not specifically directed to the part of the Proposed Rule dealing with participations. Therefore, it argues, none of the comments it received was relevant to the Final Rule authorizing only out-of-territory participations and none required a response.

The FCA should have responded to the plaintiffs' comment. Although the FCA is not required "to discuss every item of fact or opinion included in the submissions" it receives in response to a Notice of Proposed Rulemaking, *Pub. Citizen, Inc. v. Fed. Aviation Admin.*, 988 F.2d 186, 197 (D.C.Cir.1993), it must respond to those "comments which, if true, . . . would require a change in [the] proposed rule." *Am. Mining Cong. v. United States EPA*, 907 F.2d 1179, 1188 (D.C.Cir.1990). In this case the plaintiffs' comment was applicable equally to a rule limited to participations and to one that also removed the geographic restriction upon direct lending: it argued against the introduction into the System of competition generally, without regard to form * * *. The plaintiffs complained that the Proposed Rule would, by authorizing "out-of-territory lending," effectively "abolish Congress's carefully wrought statutory scheme of geographic boundaries and limitations." That would be undesirable, the plaintiffs argued, because "cooperation and interdependence are essential characteristics of the Farm Credit System."

We find unpersuasive the FCA's response that the plaintiffs' comment lacked adequate specificity to out-of-territory participations * * *. The FCA asserts that the term "out-of-territory lending" as used in the *Plaintiffs' Comment* denotes only direct loans and not loan participations, but it offers no reason, and we see none, to believe that. We interpret the plaintiffs' comment, in keeping with the rationale that underlies it, to relate to all forms of out-of-territory lending, including but not limited to participations in loans originated by others. As such, their comment deserves an answer.

336 F.3d, at 1078–81. *See also PPL Wallingford Energy LLC v. FERC*, 419 F.3d 1194 (D.C. Cir. 2005) (agency entirely failed to respond to a seemingly important argument).

Second, if the statement of basis and purpose responds to comments by making reference to materials that were not specifically disclosed in the notice of proposed rulemaking, is that a problem? As with concerns about agency reliance on data that comes to light during the comment period, a "yes" answer would have very large consequences for agency incentives to take the comment period seriously. Accordingly, courts are generally reluctant to order new rounds of notice and comment simply because material that shows up in the statement of basis and purpose as a response to commenters was not mentioned in the notice of proposed rulemaking:

The Rybacheks allege that the EPA's addition of over 6,000 pages to the administrative record, after the public review-and-comment period had ended, violated their right to comment on the record.

We disagree. The EPA has not violated the Rybacheks' right to meaningful public participation. The additional material was the EPA's response to comments made during a public-comment period. Nothing prohibits the Agency from adding supporting documentation for a final rule in response to public comments. In fact, adherence to the Rybacheks' view might result in the EPA's never being able to issue a final rule capable of standing up to review: every time the Agency responded to public comments, such as those in this rulemaking, it would trigger a new comment period. Thus, either the comment period would continue in a never-ending circle, or, if the EPA chose not to respond to the last set of public comments, any final rule could be struck down for lack of support in the record. *Cf.* BASF Wyandotte Corp. v. Costle, 598 F.2d 637, 644–45 (1st Cir.1979) (noting that it is "perfectly predictable" that an administrative agency will collect new data during the comment period "in a continuing effort to give the regulations a more accurate foundation" and stating that "[t]he agency should be encouraged to use such information in its final calculations without thereby risking the requirement of a new comment period"). The Rybacheks' unviolated right was to comment on the proposed regulations, not to comment in a never-ending way on the EPA's responses to their comments.

Rybachek v. United States EPA, 904 F.2d 1276, 1286 (9th Cir.1990).

5. STATUTORY HYBRID RULEMAKING

Congress as well as the courts often adds procedures to the informal rulemaking process. Congress can, of course, provide for formal rulemaking by specifying an "on the record" requirement in the agency's organic statute, but Congress may prefer a degree of procedural formality somewhere between the extremes of formal and informal rulemaking. By adding statutory procedures to the basic informal rulemaking package, Congress can produce any level of procedural formality that it desires on a case-by-case basis.[40]

The Clean Air Act Amendments of 1977 are a good example. The judicial review provisions of that statute, 42 U.S.C. § 7607 (2012), impose an elaborate set of procedural requirements on certain rulemakings by the Environmental Protection Agency and define a record for purposes of judicial review, but do not trigger formal rulemaking under the APA. Indeed, the statute expressly provides that the APA's procedural provisions are inapplicable to a wide range of agency actions except to the extent that they are specifically made applicable by the statute. Consider how, if at all, the prescribed procedures in this context differ from formal rulemaking under the APA.

   (d) Rulemaking

   (1) This subsection applies to * * * [21 specific kinds of air quality regulations and "such other actions as the Administrator may determine"].

---

[40] For a sample of such statutes, see Kenneth Culp Davis & Richard J. Pierce, Jr., I Administrative Law Treatise § 7.7, pp. 340–46 (3d ed. 1994).

The provisions of section 553 through 557 and section 706 of title 5 shall not, except as expressly provided in this subsection, apply to actions to which this subsection applies. This subsection shall not apply in the case of any rule or circumstance referred to in subparagraphs (A) or (B) of subsection 553(b) of title 5.

(2) Not later than the date of proposal of any action to which this subsection applies, the Administrator shall establish a rulemaking docket for such action (hereinafter in this subsection referred to as a "rule"). Whenever a rule applies only within a particular State, a second (identical) docket shall be simultaneously established in the appropriate regional office of the Environmental Protection Agency.

(3) In the case of any rule to which this subsection applies, notice of proposed rulemaking shall be published in the Federal Register, as provided under section 553(b) of Title 5, shall be accompanied by a statement of its basis and purpose and shall specify the period available for public comment (hereinafter referred to as the "comment period"). The notice of proposed rulemaking shall also state the docket number, the location or locations of the docket, and the times it will be open to public inspection. The statement of basis and purpose shall include a summary of—

(A) the factual data on which the proposed rule is based;

(B) the methodology used in obtaining the data and in analyzing the data; and

(C) the major legal interpretations and policy considerations underlying the proposed rule.

The statement shall also set forth or summarize and provide a reference to any pertinent findings, recommendations, and comments by the Scientific Review Committee established under section 7409(d) of this title and the National Academy of Sciences, and, if the proposal differs in any important respect from any of these recommendations, an explanation of the reasons for such differences. All data, information, and documents referred to in this paragraph on which the proposed rule relies shall be included in the docket on the date of publication of the proposed rule.

(4)(A) The rulemaking docket required under paragraph (2) shall be open for inspection by the public at reasonable times specified in the notice of proposed rulemaking. Any person may copy documents contained in the docket. The Administrator shall provide copying facilities which may be used at the expense of the person seeking copies, but the Administrator may waive or reduce such expenses in such instances as the public interest requires. Any person may request copies by mail if the person pays the expenses, including personnel costs to do the copying.

(B)(i) Promptly upon receipt by the agency, all written comments and documentary information on the proposed rule received from any person for inclusion in the docket during the comment period shall be placed in the docket. The transcript of public hearings, if any, on the proposed rule shall also be included in the docket promptly upon receipt from the person who transcribed such hearings. All documents which become available after the proposed rule has been published and which the Administrator determines are of central relevance to the rulemaking shall be placed in the docket as soon as possible after their availability.

(ii) The drafts of proposed rules submitted by the Administrator to the Office of Management and Budget for any interagency review process prior to proposal of any such rule, all documents accompanying such drafts, and all written comments thereon by other agencies and all written responses to such written comments by the Administrator shall be placed in the docket no later than the date of proposal of the rule. The drafts of the final rule submitted for such review process prior to promulgation and all such written comments thereon, all documents accompanying such drafts, and written responses thereto shall be placed in the docket no later than the date of promulgation.

(5) In promulgating a rule to which this subsection applies (i) the Administrator shall allow any person to submit written comments, data, or documentary information; (ii) the Administrator shall give interested persons an opportunity for the oral presentation of data, views, or arguments, in addition to an opportunity to make written submissions; (iii) a transcript shall be kept of any oral presentation; and (iv) the Administrator shall keep the record of such proceeding open for thirty days after completion of the proceeding to provide an opportunity for submission of rebuttal and supplementary information.

(6)(A) The promulgated rule shall be accompanied by (i) a statement of basis and purpose like that referred to in paragraph (3) with respect to a proposed rule and (ii) an explanation of the reasons for any major changes in the promulgated rule from the proposed rule.

(B) The promulgated rule shall also be accompanied by a response to each of the significant comments, criticisms, and new data submitted in written or oral presentations during the comment period.

(C) The promulgated rule may not be based (in part or whole) on any information or data which has not been placed in the docket as of the date of such promulgation.

(7)(A) The record for judicial review shall consist exclusively of the material referred to in paragraph (3), clause (i) of paragraph (4)(B), and subparagraphs (A) and (B) of paragraph (6).

Id. at § 7607(d).

A number of government-wide statutes also impose procedural requirements on agency rulemaking. The Regulatory Flexibility Act, 5 U.S.C. §§ 601–612 (2012), and the Small Business Regulatory Enforcement Fairness Act of 1996, 5 U.S.C. §§ 801–808 (2012), both require all covered agencies to produce various reports and analyses as part of their rulemakings.

Presidents can also affect the procedures employed in the rulemaking process. Every president since the mid-1970s has issued instructions to executive agencies to guide their rulemaking efforts; those instructions require agencies to prepare reports on proposed rules, to be submitted to an important arm of the White House called the Office of Management and Budget, to facilitate internal executive department oversight of agency action. Several of those executive orders dealing with rulemakings are reproduced in Appendix D. A detailed study of executive orders is probably beyond the scope of this course (though you will be well served if your professor disagrees with this judgment). Two points, however, are worth noting. First, these presidential orders, by their terms, do not create rights in private parties that can be enforced in court. They are internal management devices enforced, if at all, by political pressure and the risk of termination of agency officials who do not comply. Second, perhaps the most remarkable feature of modern executive orders in this area is their consistency. President Clinton's Executive Order 12866, dating back to 1993, has remained the cornerstone of executive review of agency rulemaking, with only relatively minor amendments, through the presidencies of George W. Bush, Barack Obama, and Donald Trump. The problem of how to manage the sprawling bureaucracy of the modern American executive department crosses party and ideological lines. Because those problems partake more of political science and management theory than of formal legal doctrine, we will, with more than modest regret, pass them over for now.

6. EXEMPTIONS FROM RULEMAKING PROCEDURES

Not all rulemakings are subject to the APA's procedures. Section 553 specifically states that its provisions do not apply to rules concerning (1) a military or foreign affairs function of the United States; or (2) a matter relating to agency management or personnel or to public property, loans, grants, benefits, or contracts." This subject-matter exclusion covers a good percentage of the federal budget, though it leaves most agency regulation of private conduct subject to § 553's requirements.[41] There is, however, another set of exemptions from § 553 that is based on the *character* rather than the *subject matter* of the rules. Unless an organic statute requires otherwise, the notice and comment provisions of § 553 do not apply "(A) to interpretative rules, general statements of policy, or rules of agency organization, procedure, or practice; or (B) when the agency for good cause finds (and incorporates the finding and a brief statement of reasons therefor in the rules issued) that notice and public procedure thereon are impracticable, unnecessary, or contrary to the public interest." *Id.* § 553(b).

The scope of these exemptions is much more important today than was the case prior to the 1970s, for two simple reasons. First, informal rulemaking was not a significant agency activity until fairly recently. Second, when agencies did employ informal rulemaking, it did not much matter either to agencies or to private parties whether the agency used § 553's notice-and-comment procedures or invoked an exemption. Parties gained very little, and agencies lost very little, when agencies used the rulemaking procedures prescribed by the actual text of § 553 as originally conceived and interpreted, and parties accordingly lost very little if those procedures were not employed. The stakes are much higher, however, when compliance with § 553 entails modern hybrid procedures. Accordingly, agencies seeking to avoid the procedural burdens of hybrid rulemaking have good reason to invoke § 553's exemptions, and parties have many reasons to challenge agency use of exemptions (for example, to invalidate rules, to discourage further rulemaking, or just to get more input into the rulemaking process).

You should always keep in mind, however, that an exemption from the APA's rulemaking procedures is not an exemption from all procedural requirements. Sources of law other than the APA may require procedures even for rules that fall squarely within one of the APA's exemptions.

a. Procedural Rules

Ever since the Supreme Court decided *Erie R.R. v. Tompkins*, 304 U.S. 64, 58 S.Ct. 817, 82 L.Ed. 1188 (1938), federal courts have had to wrestle with the problem of distinguishing substantive rules from procedural rules in determining whether state or federal law governs issues arising in

---

[41] There are long-standing proposals to eliminate or modify this exclusion. *See* Christopher J. Walker, *Modernizing the Administrative Procedure Act,* 69 Admin.L. Rev. 629, 646 (2017). In practice, agencies whose activities are (in whole or in part) covered by this exclusion can, and often do, choose by regulation to be bound by the APA's rulemaking provisions. *See, e.g., Public Participation in Rule Making,* 36 Fed. Reg. 2532 (Feb. 5, 1971) (waiving the § 553(2) exemption for rules promulgated by the Department of Health and Human Services).

diversity cases. The result is not a pretty sight. It is therefore not surprising that courts have had difficulty distinguishing exempt rules of "agency organization, procedure, or practice" (which are generally known collectively as "procedural rules") from non-exempt substantive rules. Rules prescribing the conduct of adjudicatory hearings, such as rules establishing the permissible scope of discovery, look like rules of "procedure," but they can influence the outcome of adjudications as much or more than can pure rules of law. Are such rules therefore substantive rather than procedural? What about rules defining what evidence is admissible in agency proceedings? Or rules setting forth evidentiary presumptions? There are, alas, no clear answers to these questions. In 1990, however, a panel of the D.C. Circuit took an interesting stab at the issue in the following case. The case was ultimately dismissed as moot and the decision was vacated, which means that the case has no formal legal status. Both the majority and dissenting opinions, however, can be (and are more than occasionally) offered as persuasive authorities, and they are worthy of consideration. Keep in mind that because the decision was vacated, the dissent now stands on the same legal footing as the majority.

Note: decision was vacated, so no legal authority (but can be used persuasively)

AIR TRANSPORT ASSOCIATION OF AMERICA V. DEPARTMENT OF TRANSPORTATION

United States Court of Appeals, District of Columbia Circuit, 1990.
900 F.2d 369, remanded, 498 U.S. 1023, 111 S.Ct. 669, 112 L.Ed.2d 662 (1991),
vacated as moot, 933 F.2d 1043 (D.C.Cir.1991).

Before MIKVA, EDWARDS, and SILBERMAN, CIRCUIT JUDGES.

EDWARDS, CIRCUIT JUDGE:

The issue in this case is whether respondent governmental agencies (collectively "Federal Aviation Administration" or "FAA") were obliged to engage in notice and comment procedures before promulgating a body of regulations governing the adjudication of administrative civil penalty actions. See 53 Fed. Reg. 34,646 (1988) (codified at 14 C.F.R. pt. 13) ("Penalty Rules" or "Rules") * * *. Petitioner Air Transport Association of America ("Air Transport") contends that the FAA's failure to comply with the notice and comment requirements of the Administrative Procedure Act ("APA") renders the Penalty Rules invalid. The FAA maintains that it was justified in dispensing with notice and comment under the "rules of agency organization, procedure, or practice" * * * exception[ ] to section 553.

* * *

In December of 1987, Congress enacted a series of amendments to the Federal Aviation Act relating to civil penalties. Among other things, these amendments * * * established a "demonstration program" authorizing the FAA to prosecute and adjudicate administrative penalty actions involving less than $50,000 * * *.

* * *

* * * Congress provided that the FAA could assess a civil penalty "only" after notice and opportunity for a hearing on the record in accordance with section 554 of [the APA]." 49 U.S.C. app. § 1475(d)(1) * * *.

Approximately nine months after enactment of section 1475, the FAA promulgated the Penalty Rules. Effective immediately upon their issuance, the Penalty Rules established a schedule of civil penalties * * *. *See* 14 C.F.R. § 13.16(a)(3) (1989). The Penalty Rules also established a comprehensive adjudicatory scheme providing for formal notice, settlement procedures, discovery, an adversary hearing before an ALJ and an administrative appeal. *See id.* §§ 13.201–13.235. In explaining why it dispensed with prepromulgation notice and comment, the FAA emphasized the procedural character of the Penalty Rules and the time constraints of section 1475 * * *.

[handwritten margin note: Penalty Rules · schedule of civ. penalties · comprehensive adj. scheme]

* * *

Section 553 of the APA obliges an agency to provide notice and an opportunity to comment before promulgating a final rule. No question exists that the Penalty Rules fall within the scope of the APA's rulemaking provisions. Nonetheless, the FAA maintains that the Penalty Rules were exempt from the notice and comment requirements * * * because they are "rules of agency organization, procedure, or practice," *id.* § 553(b)(A) * * *.

Section 553's notice and comment requirements are essential to the scheme of administrative governance established by the APA * * *. [B]y mandating "openness, explanation, and participatory democracy" in the rulemaking process, these procedures assure the legitimacy of administrative norms. *Weyerhaeuser Co. v. Costle,* 590 F.2d 1011, 1027 (D.C. Cir. 1978). For these reasons, we have consistently afforded a narrow cast to the exceptions to section 553, permitting an agency to forgo notice and comment only when the subject matter or the circumstances of the rulemaking divest the public of any legitimate stake influencing the outcome. In the instant case, because the Penalty Rules substantially affected civil penalty defendants' right to avail themselves of an administrative adjudication, we cannot accept the FAA's contention that the Rules could be promulgated without notice and comment.

[handwritten margin note: majority finds against FAA]

* * *

Our cases construing section 553(b)(A) have long emphasized that a rule does not fall within the scope of the exception merely because it is capable of bearing the label "procedural." *See, e.g., Reeder v. FCC,* 865 F.2d 1298 (D.C. Cir. 1989) (*per curiam*). In *Reeder,* we examined a body of rules governing the submission of "counterproposals" to the allotment of FM radio frequencies by the Federal Communications Commission. Although the rules purported merely to define the procedures for the submission of counterproposals, we recognized that these procedures in fact foreclosed agency consideration of counterproposals based on the upgrading of existing FM stations. *See id.* at 1305. Because the agency previously *did* permit applicants to submit counterproposals based on upgrading plans, we held that the agency should have engaged in notice and comment before depriving applicants' of this right.

Rather than focus on whether a particular rule is "procedural" or "substantive," these decisions employ a functional analysis * * *. Where nominally "procedural" rules "encode[ ] a substantive value judgment" or "substantially alter the rights or interests of regulated" parties * * *, the rules must be preceded by notice and comment. [*American Hosp. Ass'n v. Bowen,* 834 F.2d 1037, 1047, 1041 (D.C.Cir.1987)].

[margin note: majority takes functionalist approach]

The Penalty Rules fall outside the scope of section 553(b)(A) because they substantially affect a civil penalty defendant's *right to an administrative adjudication.* Under both the due process clause and the APA, a party has a right to notice and a hearing before being forced to pay a monetary penalty. Congress expressly directed the FAA to incorporate these rights into its civil penalty program. In implementing this mandate, the FAA made discretionary—indeed, in many cases, highly contentious— choices concerning what process civil penalty defendants are due. Each one of these choices "encode[d] a substantive value judgment," *American Hosp. Ass'n,* 834 F.2d at 1047, on the appropriate balance between a defendant's *rights* to adjudicatory procedures and the agency's interest in efficient prosecution.[8] The FAA was no less obliged to engage in notice and comment before taking action affecting these adjudicatory rights than it would have been had it taken action affecting aviators' "substantive" obligations under the Federal Aviation Act. *See, e.g., National Ass'n v. Schweiker,* 690 F.2d 932, 949 (D.C. Cir. 1982) (notice and comment required for rules "eliminating the qualified right" to present reimbursement claims to agency secretary rather than intermediary); *Brown Express, Inc. v. United States,* 607 F.2d 695, 702–03 (5th Cir. 1979) (notice and comment required for rules eliminating notice of award of temporary carrier licenses).

Indeed, this is the teaching of the seminal decision in *National Motor Freight Traffic Ass'n v. United States,* 268 F.Supp. 90 (D.D.C.1967) (three-judge panel), *aff'd mem.,* 393 U.S. 18, 89 S.Ct. 49, 21 L.Ed.2d 19 (1968). In *National Motor Freight,* the court reviewed a body of Interstate Commerce Commission rules establishing a scheme for the administrative adjudication of carrier overcharge claims. Rejecting the claim that the rules merely established procedures for implementing substantive statutory rights, the court held that the agency's decision to establish "[a] right to

---

[8] In noting that the FAA made discretionary choices determining the *specific form* of civil penalty defendants' adjudicatory rights, we do not, of course, suggest that the choices made *violated* those rights. Section 553 stands for the proposition that interested parties have a right to influence agency decisionmaking even when the decisions made are substantively lawful.

avail oneself of an administrative adjudication" was itself one that the APA required to be open to public participation. *National Motor Freight* was summarily affirmed by the Supreme Court, and remains binding precedent. In our view, it is controlling in the case before us.

The cases cited by the FAA do not suggest a contrary conclusion. The FAA puts its primary emphasis on *American Hospital Association*. At issue in that case were a series of agency directives and manuals defining the "enforcement strategy" of review boards assigned to investigate Medicare reimbursement claims by hospitals. We held that these materials were covered by section 553(b)(A) because we recognized that the public has no legitimate interest in influencing an agency's "discretionary deployment of enforcement resources," *id.* at 1057 n. 4—a classic "internal" matter, essential to how an agency constitutes itself. Nothing in *American Hospital Association* detracts from the principle that the public *does* have a legitimate interest in participating in agency decisions affecting statutory and constitutional rights "to avail oneself of an administrative adjudication."

Also inapposite are various decisions in which we have applied section 553(b)(A) to rules that regulate such matters as the timing of applications for benefits or the timing of the agency's processing of such applications. The rules at issue in these cases did affect "the manner in which the parties present themselves or their viewpoints to the agency," *Batterton v. Marshall*, 648 F.2d [694] at 707 [D.C. Cir. 1980] but they did *not* affect any component of a party's statutory or constitutional right to avail himself of an administrative adjudication. They were all cases, in short, in which "the need for public participation" in the rulemaking process was "too small to warrant it." *Id.* at 704. The Penalty Rules, in contrast, affect the entire range of adjudicatory rights guaranteed by the due process clause, the APA and section 1475(d)(1)—matters far too important to be withdrawn from public deliberation.

In criticizing our reliance on *National Motor Freight,* the dissent argues that agency action that is expressly exempt under the APA is not subject to notice and comment rulemaking simply because it has a "substantial impact" on regulated parties. We agree with this assertion, but it is irrelevant because it begs the question whether the Penalty Rules are included within the exemption of section 553(b)(A). We rely on *National Motor Freight* not to show that the Penalty Rules have a "substantial impact" on aviators, but to show that rules affecting *the right to avail oneself of an administrative adjudication* are *not* within the express terms of section 553(b)(A). *No* case in this circuit has ever suggested otherwise.

The dissent also contends that we have "obliterated" the distinction between substance and procedure. But, as the case law clearly illustrates, there is no such "distinction" to obliterate for purposes of section 553(b)(A).

The dissent refuses to come to terms with the precedent characterizing this exception to notice and comment rulemaking as * * * applicable to rules " 'organizing [agencies'] *internal* operations.' " *American Hosp. Ass'n,* 834 F.2d at 1047 (quoting *Batterton,* 648 F.2d at 707 (emphasis added)). The dissent's infusion of a rigid "procedure"—"substance" distinction is * * * also inconsistent with the statutory text. Section 553(b)(A) does not exempt "rules of procedure" *per se,* but rather "rules of *agency organization, procedure, or practice*" * * *.

* * * In using the terms "rules of agency organization, procedure, or practice," Congress intended to distinguish not between rules affecting different *classes of rights*—"substantive" and "procedural"—but rather to distinguish between rules affecting different *subject matters*—"the rights or interests of regulated" parties, *American Hosp. Ass'n,* 834 F.2d at 1041, and agencies' " 'internal operations,' " *id.* at 1047 (quoting *Batterton,* 648 F.2d at 707). Because the Penalty Rules substantially affect civil penalty defendants' " right to avail [themselves] of an administrative adjudication," members of the aviation community had a legitimate interest in participating in the rulemaking process.

* * *

SILBERMAN, CIRCUIT JUDGE, dissenting.

* * * I think the rules fall, by ample measure, within the "procedural" exemption of section 553(b)(A), which exempts from notice and comment "rules of agency organization, procedure, or practice." To be sure, the rules in this case could as well be described as rules of "practice" (covering the practice of the parties and attorneys before the FAA) and also in some respects rules of "agency organization" (dealing with the interrelationship between the administrative law judges and the Administrator). I use the term "procedure" here to cover all three concepts.

Lines between substance and procedure in various areas of the law are difficult to draw and therefore often perplex scholars and judges. But Congress, when it passed the Administrative Procedure Act, made that difference critical, and we are therefore obliged to implement a viable distinction between "procedural" rules and those that are substantive. The majority opinion, in effect, abandons the effort * * *.

If we assume a spectrum of rules running from the most substantive to the most procedural, I would describe the former as those that regulate "primary conduct" * * * and the latter are those furthest away from primary conduct. In other words, if a given regulation purports to direct, control, or condition the behavior of those institutions or individuals subject to regulation by the authorizing statute it is not procedural, it is substantive. At the other end of the spectrum are those rules, such as the ones before us in this case, which deal with enforcement or adjudication of claims of violations of the substantive norm but which do not *purport* to affect the substantive norm. These kinds of rules are, in my view, clearly procedural.

Rules are no less procedural because they are thought to be important or affect outcomes. Congress did not state, when it passed the APA, that all but insignificant rules must be put out for notice and comment. And to say, as does the majority, that the rules are covered by section 553's notice and comment requirement because they "substantially affect a civil defendant's *right to an administrative adjudication*" is, I respectfully submit, circular reasoning. It assumes the conclusion by describing petitioner's interest in the agency's adjudicatory procedures as if it were a substantive right. It also implicitly suggests that petitioner is correct on the merits in claiming the agency's adjudicatory procedures are illegal * * *.

Admittedly, not all our cases fit precisely along the continuum I described above. When an agency, rather than publishing rules which define a substantive norm to which regulated groups must conform or which flesh out enforcement procedures to effectuate such compliance, instead adopts rules dealing with the award of *benefits,* a slightly different but similar analysis is used to distinguish substantive from procedural rules. Sometimes the Government's prospective award of benefits is actually designed, in part, to affect primary conduct—such as the standards used to determine whether to renew a broadcast license or the criteria employed to determine eligibility for unemployment insurance. But typically, benefits are bestowed in accordance with preexisting qualifications or status. In those circumstances, it cannot be said that the rules seek to condition primary conduct. We still think of such rules as substantive because defining eligibility for a benefit program is the very essence of the program. It is in this context that in *Batterton v. Marshall*, 648 F.2d 694 (D.C. Cir. 1980), we said that substantive rules are those that affect the "rights and interests of parties." *See id.* at 707. In *Batterton,* Maryland challenged the Department of Labor's adoption of a new method of calculating local unemployment rates, which in turn determined the amount of CETA job training funds each state and locality would receive. We categorized those new rules as substantive because they altered the criteria by which Government benefits would be distributed rather than simply change the manner in which claimants for benefits communicated to the agency the nature of their substantive claim. Similarly, in *Reeder v. FCC*, 865 F.2d 1298 (D.C.Cir. 1989), a radio station objected to the FCC's adoption of rules governing counterproposals to the agency's allotment of new FM channels throughout the United States. We decided that the procedural exemption was inapplicable because the FCC had altered its decisionmaking criteria for new station allotments. *See id.* at 1304–05.

In contrast, in *Neighborhood TV Co., Inc. v. FCC*, 742 F.2d 629 (D.C.Cir. 1984), we concluded that FCC rules that froze contested applications for "translators" (devices which amplify and rebroadcast television signals) and then processed rural applications before urban ones were procedural because the rules did not alter the standards by which those applications would be judged. *See id.* at 637–38. We also pointed out that * * * earlier decisions * * * found the challenged rules exempted from the notice and comment requirements precisely because the FCC rules did not regulate the radio stations' right to broadcast its signals at a particular station.

Of course, procedure impacts on outcomes and thus can virtually always be described as affecting substance, but to pursue that line of analysis results in the obliteration of the distinction that Congress demanded. We avoided that snare only recently in *American Hosp. Ass'n v. Bowen*, 834 F.2d 1037, 1047 (D.C.Cir. 1987), where we held, over a strong dissent in many respects redolent of the majority opinion here, that HHS rules that set forth the enforcement priorities for peer review organizations (acting as agents to ensure medically reasonable and necessary hospital health care), as well as some adjudicatory procedures similar to those contained in the rules before us, did not have to be published for comment. Although it was argued that the procedures would affect hospital behavior by discouraging activity in the zone of an enforcement priority, we nevertheless held that the rules did not "encode [ ] a substantive value judgment or put[ ] a stamp of approval or disapproval on a given type of behavior." *Id.* at 1047. We recognized that hospital costs would be affected by the enforcement scheme, but that was not enough to bring the rules out of the procedural safe harbor. *See id.* at 1051. The case at bar involves rules that are, *a fortiori,* procedural because, unlike in *American Hospital Ass'n,* it is not even argued here that primary behavior—the safety efforts of the airlines—is even affected by the adjudicatory rules.

Deviating from our previous and recent emphasis on primary conduct, the majority asserts that a proposed rule that *allegedly* infringes on "the right to avail oneself of an administrative adjudication" is "substantive." But the quoted language comes from an old and now discredited district court case, *National Motor Freight Traffic Ass'n v. United States*, 268 F.Supp. 90 (D.D.C. 1967), *aff'd mem.,* 393 U.S. 18, 89 S.Ct. 49, 21 L.Ed. 2d 19 (1968). The Supreme Court summarily affirmed the judgment of the district court in *National Motor Freight* and therefore we are not bound by the district court's reasoning. We have specifically disapproved of *National Motor Freight's* "substantial impact" analysis, moreover, because of the Supreme Court's command in *Vermont Yankee* to avoid engrafting additional procedures on agency action beyond those required by the APA.[3]

---

[3]   Even if *National Motor Freight* were still good law and binding on us, our case is arguably distinguishable because the only issue before us is the specific content of FAA adjudicative

It might be thought that there is something vaguely underhanded about an agency publishing important rules without an opportunity for those affected to comment. And lawyers and judges tend to prefer, on the margin, added procedure. But * * * we have been admonished somewhat dramatically by *Vermont Yankee* to not add more procedure to the APA than Congress required. I am afraid the majority opinion by obliterating the distinction between substance and procedure in section 553 does just that.

NOTES

In *JEM Broadcasting Co., Inc. v. FCC*, 22 F.3d 320 (D.C.Cir.1994), the court suggested that Judge Silberman's dissenting opinion, with its insistence upon a categorical distinction between substance and procedure, is likely to prevail. The FCC adopted rules, known as the "hard look" rules, that called for rejection without opportunity for amendment of any broadcast license application that did not unambiguously contain all required information. JEM submitted an application that contained some incorrect coordinates; the application was summarily rejected pursuant to the "hard look" rules. JEM, which sought an opportunity to correct the error in its application, challenged the rules on the ground that they had been promulgated without notice-and-comment procedures. The court held that the rules "fall comfortably within the realm of the 'procedural' as we have defined it in other cases." *Id.* at 327. With respect to *Air Transport*, the court explained:

> * * * JEM argues that we cannot find the instant rule to be procedural because it encodes the substantive value judgment that applications containing minor errors should be sacrificed to promote efficient application processing * * *. JEM's reasoning threatens to swallow the procedural exception to notice and comment, for agency housekeeping rules often embody a judgment about what mechanics and processes are most efficient. In *Air Transport*, a divided panel of this court held that the Department of Transportation's adoption of a comprehensive scheme for adjudicating civil penalty actions required notice and comment, in part because the rules encoded a substantive value judgment "on the appropriate balance between a defendant's *rights* to adjudicatory procedures and the agency's interest in efficient prosecution." Although *Air Transport* is no longer binding precedent, we recognize that our opinion there extended the "value judgment" rationale further than any other case of this circuit of

procedures and not whether such a remedial avenue exists at all. In *National Motor Freight* freight carriers challenged an ICC plan of administrative adjudication of alleged carrier overcharges. Congress had explicitly authorized only judicial remedies to recover excessive rates. In the absence of such authority, the district court concluded that the right to an administrative route to reparations itself was a significant determination by the Commission that granted shippers an easier path to recover excess payments. *See National Motor Freight*, 268 F.Supp. at 95–96. Thus, the court decided that the provision of a *new remedy* was a new right or interest afforded to shippers. In contrast, Congress specifically empowered the FAA to adopt rules to adjudicate civil penalties * * *.

> which we are aware; and to the extent that it suggests a different result here, we disavow its reasoning.

Id. at 328. Subsequent cases in the D.C. Circuit have applied but have not materially clarified the analysis in *JEM Broadcasting. See, e.g., James V. Hurson Associates, Inc. v. Glickman*, 229 F.3d 277, 281 (D.C.Cir.2000) (a rule eliminating routine face-to-face meetings between food producers and regulators in the review of commercial food labels is "procedural" because the agency "did not alter the substantive criteria by which it would approve or deny proposed labels; it simply changed the procedures it would follow in applying those substantive standards"); *Chamber of Commerce of the United States v. United States Dep't of Labor*, 174 F.3d 206, 212 (D.C.Cir.1999) (a rule providing that worksites can avoid an otherwise mandatory inspection by participating in a compliance program is substantive, not procedural, because the rule "will affect employers' interests in the same way that a plainly substantive rule mandating a comprehensive safety program would affect their rights"). Cases in other courts do not fare much better. *See Time Warner Cable, Inc. v. FCC*, 729 F.3d 137, 168–69 (2d. Cir.2013) (FCC rule requiring a cable operator to continue to carry unaffiliated network programming until the parties' rights were definitively resolved is substantive rather than procedural because it " 'substantively affects the public to a degree sufficient to implicate the policy interests animating notice-and-comment rulemaking.' " (quoting *Electronic Privacy Info. Ctr. v. U.S. Dep't of Homeland Sec.*, 653 F.3d 1, 5 (D.C.Cir.2011)).

b. Interpretative Rules and Policy Statements

The terms "legislative rules" or "substantive rules" have long been used as synonyms to describe rules that create rights or obligations for regulated parties.[42] Typically, such rules are based on interpretations of organic statutes and/or reflect general policies adopted by the agency. So how do such rules differ from "interpretative rules" or "general statements of policy"? That question has proven to be one of the most troublesome in all of administrative law—not because the answer is difficult, but because the easy answer is, at least to modern sensibilities, unacceptable. The result has been four different tests for distinguishing legislative rules from interpretative rules or policy statements, at least three of which continue to have some relevance to modern doctrine.

A lawyer in 1946 would have had a ready answer to the problem of distinguishing interpretative from legislative rules: a legislative rule operates just like a statute, and violation of such a rule is itself grounds for liability without anything further, while an interpretative rule (or policy

---

[42] Technically, the commonplace equation of "substantive rules" and "legislative rules" is sloppy nomenclature. Legislative rules establish rights and obligations and are therefore distinguishable from interpretative rules. Substantive rules are distinguishable from procedural rules, but can include non-legislative interpretative rules. *See* Robert A. Anthony, *Interpretive Rules, Policy Statements, Guidances, Manuals, and the Like—Should Federal Agencies Use Them to Bind the Public?*, 41 Duke L.J. 1311, 1321 n.37 (1992). You may now safely ignore this footnote, because virtually everyone else in the administrative law world does as well.

statement) merely offers the agency's opinion on matters of law or policy. Violation of an interpretative rule, on this understanding, is not sufficient grounds for liability: the agency must further prove that the conduct in question violates a legislative rule or an underlying statute. This test for distinguishing interpretative from legislative rules is known as the *legal effects test,* as it focuses on the legal effect of the rule. If the rule creates a binding norm on regulated parties, it is legislative; otherwise, it is interpretative.

The leading case applying the legal effects test is *Pacific Gas & Electric Co. v. FPC*, 506 F.2d 33 (D.C.Cir.1974). The Federal Power Commission, without using notice-and-comment rulemaking procedures, issued an order specifying which natural gas customers should be given priority by pipelines if shortages prevented all customers from getting their full amount of ordered gas. The agency described its order as a "statement of policy," and the language of the order suggested (albeit ambiguously) that the agency would make its actual priority determinations through case-by-case adjudications, though presumably the policy statement would guide those determinations. The court held that notice-and-comment procedures were not required. In influential language, the court described the difference between a legislative rule and a policy statement:

> An administrative agency has available two methods for formulating policy that will have the force of law. An agency may establish binding policy through rulemaking procedures by which it promulgates substantive rules, or through adjudications which constitute binding precedents. A general statement of policy is the outcome of neither a rulemaking nor an adjudication; it is neither a rule nor a precedent but is merely an announcement to the public of the policy which the agency hopes to implement in future rulemakings or adjudications. A general statement of policy, like a press release, presages an upcoming rulemaking or announces the course which the agency intends to follow in future adjudications.

* * *

The critical distinction between a substantive rule and a general statement of policy is the different practical effect that these two types of pronouncements have in subsequent administrative proceedings. A properly adopted substantive rule establishes a standard of conduct which has the force of law. In subsequent administrative proceedings involving a substantive rule, the issues are whether the adjudicated facts conform to the rule and whether the rule should be waived or applied in that particular instance. The underlying policy embodied in the rule is not generally subject to challenge before the agency.

A general statement of policy, on the other hand, does not establish a "binding norm." It is not finally determinative of the issues or rights to which it is addressed. The agency cannot apply or rely upon a general statement of policy as law because a general statement of policy only announces what the agency seeks to establish as policy. A policy statement announces the agency's tentative intentions for the future. When the agency applies the policy in a particular situation, it must be prepared to support the policy just as if the policy statement had never been issued. An agency cannot escape its responsibility to present evidence and reasoning supporting its substantive rules by announcing binding precedent in the form of a general statement of policy.

506 F.2d at 38–39.

The legal effects test is easy to administer: if the agency wants to characterize a rule as interpretative, and thus exempt from notice-and-comment procedures, it cannot use the rule as binding law in subsequent adjudications. The problem with the legal effects test is that it is readily subject to agency gamesmanship. Policy statements or interpretative rules that are not "law," in the strict sense required by the legal effects test, can nonetheless serve many of the same functions as legislative rules. If you are a regulated party, and the agency issues an interpretative rule or policy statement indicating its present view of the law, you will probably make serious efforts to comply with that rule even if it is not formally binding. At a minimum, the rule alerts you to the kind of conduct that the agency regards as worthy of prosecution; at a maximum, the rule may effectively dictate how the agency will conduct its prosecutorial adjudications. The *practical effect* of such rules on regulated parties may be hard to distinguish from the practical effect of legislative rules. Thus, an agency can often get a great deal of mileage, in terms of compliance by regulated parties, from the issuance of interpretative rules or policy statements, without undergoing the extensive procedures associated with modern hybrid rulemaking.

Courts that are willing to rewrite § 553 of the APA to require extensive procedures in informal rulemaking are not likely to look favorably on devices that allow agencies to circumvent those procedural requirements by issuing rules that govern conduct practically but not formally. And indeed, some courts in the late 1960s and early 1970s suggested that notice-and-comment procedures were required for rules that had a substantial impact on regulated parties, even if those rules did not satisfy the formal legal effects test. *See Lewis-Mota v. Secretary of Labor*, 469 F.2d 478 (2d Cir.1972); *Texaco, Inc. v. FPC*, 412 F.2d 740 (3d Cir.1969); *National Motor Freight Traffic Ass'n v. United States*, 268 F.Supp. 90 (D.D.C.1967), *aff'd per curiam*, 393 U.S. 18, 89 S.Ct. 49, 21 L.Ed.2d 19 (1968). This doctrine came to be called the substantial impact test.

The substantial impact test has <u>no plausible grounding in the text or</u> history of § 553 of the APA. And although *Vermont Yankee*'s call for adherence to the text of the APA has had decidedly mixed results, it has generally been taken <u>to invalidate the substantial impact test</u>. As the D.C. Circuit explained in 1982,

> [The district] court <u>erred</u> in using the substantial impact test. At one time, the test was used to determine the applicability of APA procedures by asking essentially whether the agency action had an impact on the rights and interests of private parties. Since *Vermont Yankee Nuclear Power Corp. v. Natural Resources Defense Council, Inc.*, 435 U.S. 519, 98 S.Ct. 1197, 55 L.Ed.2d 460, it is clear that a court cannot engraft <u>additional procedures</u> on agency action beyond those contemplated by the APA (or another specific Act). Simply because agency action has <u>substantial impact</u> <u>does not mean</u> it is subject to notice and comment if it is otherwise expressly exempt under the APA.

Cabais v. Egger, 690 F.2d 234, 237 (D.C.Cir.1982).

Rejection of the substantial impact test, however, <u>did not mean a</u> <u>simple return to the legal effects test</u> as the exclusive basis for determining when agency rules were legislative.[43] The problem of agency gamesmanship that prompted courts to invent the substantial impact test still remained. Courts accordingly changed their focus from the impact of rules on regulated parties to the <u>impact of rules on *agencies*</u>. Suppose, for instance, that an agency issues (without notice-and-comment procedures) a rule that it declares is an interpretative rule or policy statement. The agency announces that, in subsequent adjudications, it will not treat the rule as binding law and will gladly entertain all arguments that parties are willing to offer as to why conduct covered by the "interpretative" rule is nonetheless not unlawful. But lo and behold, when the agency <u>actually</u> conducts adjudications, <u>virtually everyone who violates the "nonbinding"</u> "<u>interpretative</u>" <u>rule ends up being punished</u>. The rule fails the legal effects test, but is its practical impact on the agency enough to make it legislative?

---

[43] The legal effects test has always been, and continues to be, at least one of the applicable standards for determining when notice-and-comment procedures are required. A rule that is substantive according to the legal effects test will be regarded as substantive by all courts. The question is whether a rule that is not substantive according to the legal effects test is nonetheless substantive because of some other test.

[handwritten margin note:] Vermont Yankee generally seen as invalidating substantial impact test

UNITED STATES TELEPHONE ASS'N v. FCC

United States Court of Appeals, District of Columbia Circuit, 1994.
28 F.3d 1232.

Before WALD, SILBERMAN and HENDERSON, CIRCUIT JUDGES.

SILBERMAN, CIRCUIT JUDGE:

penalties for violations of Communications Act

The Commission issued, without notice and comment, a schedule of base penalties and adjustments to determine the appropriate fines for violations of the Communications Act. We conclude that the penalty schedule is not a policy statement and, therefore, should have been put out for comment under the Administrative Procedure Act.

Holding

Section 503(b) of the Communications Act authorizes the FCC to impose "monetary forfeitures" (fines) on licensees for violations of the Act or of regulations promulgated thereunder * * *. The statute provides a maximum fine schedule in accordance with classification of licensee: $25,000 for broadcasters and cable television operators, $100,000 for common carriers (such as telephone companies), and $10,000 for other service providers. For each day of a continuing violation, the Commission may assess up to $250,000 for broadcasters, $1,000,000 for common carriers, and $75,000 for others.

The FCC decided in 1991 to abandon its traditional case-by-case approach to implementing section 503(b) and issued an order to "adopt more specific standards for assessing forfeitures." *Standards for Assessing Forfeitures*, 6 F.C.C.R. 4695 (1991), *recon. denied* 7 F.C.C.R. 5339 (1992), *revised*, 8 F.C.C.R. 6215 (1993). The forfeiture standards, set forth in a schedule appended to its order, contemplate a base forfeiture amount for each type of violation, which amount is calculated as a percentage (varying on the violation) of the statutory maxima for the different services. Thus, the base forfeiture amount for false distress communications is 80% of the statutory maxima: *i.e.*, $20,000 per violation for broadcasters, $80,000 for common carriers, and $8,000 for others * * *. The fines schedule also provides for adjustments to the base amount depending on various aggravating or mitigating factors. The base amount, for instance, is increased 20–50% for "substantial economic gain" and reduced 30–60% for "good faith or voluntary disclosure."

Petitioner, a trade group of telephone companies that unsuccessfully sought reconsideration before the agency, * * * claims that the Commission violated the Administrative Procedure Act by issuing the standards without notice and an opportunity to comment * * *.

* * *

FCC claims penalty sched. = policy statmt

The Commission claims that the standards are only general statements of policy exempt from the notice and comment obligation that the APA imposes on the adoption of substantive rules. The distinction between the two types of agency pronouncements has not proved an easy one to draw, but we have said repeatedly that it turns on an agency's intention to bind itself to a particular legal policy position. The Commission, mindful of this precedent, labeled the standards as a policy statement and reiterated 12 times that it retained discretion to depart from the standards in specific applications.

The difficulty we see in the Commission's position is that the appendix affixed to the short "policy statement" sets forth a detailed schedule of penalties applicable to specific infractions as well as the appropriate adjustments for particular situations. It is rather hard to imagine an agency wishing to publish such an exhaustive framework for sanctions if it did not intend to use that framework to cabin its discretion. Indeed, no agency to our knowledge has ever claimed that such a schedule of fines was a policy statement. It simply does not fit the paradigm of a policy statement, namely, an indication of an agency's current position on a particular regulatory issue.

Although sometimes we face the difficulty of reviewing a statement before it has been applied and therefore are unsure whether the agency intends to be bound, that is not so in this case. The schedule of fines has been employed in over 300 cases and only in 8 does the Commission even claim that it departed from the schedule. In three cases, the Commission maintains that it did not apply the guidelines at all to certain violations of a new tariff-filing requirement. That, however, is a mischaracterization * * *. The most that could be said about these cases is that the Commission exercised enforcement discretion *not to prosecute*—but adhered to the standards when it calculated the penalties that would have applied had it prosecuted.

FCC only departed from schedule in 8/300+ cases

In *Cargo Vessel Kodiak Enterprise*, 7 F.C.C.R. 1847 (1992), the Commission ordered a forfeiture of $50,000 where strict application of the standards would have amounted to $155,000. The reason given, however, was that "[w]hen an inspection certificate expires while a vessel is at sea, our policy is not to assess a forfeiture for the period between the expiration of the certificate and the vessel's arrival in port." 7 F.C.C.R. at 1848. The deviation thus resulted not from relaxation of the standards but again from a non-prosecution policy independent of the standards—that under certain conditions no fines at all, however they are calculated, will attach. In three other cases, the Commission applied the base amounts under the forfeiture standards but did not insist on upward adjustments. *See Dial-A-Page, Inc.*, 8 F.C.C.R. 2767, 2768 (1993) (potential increase for "repeated violations"); *TVX Broadcast Group*, 6 F.C.C.R. 7494, 7496 (1991) (same); *David Price*, 7 F.C.C.R. 6550, 6551 n. 4 (1992) ("lengthy continuous violation"). That the Commission deviated from a minor portion of the standards, while probative, does not vitiate its adherence to the schedule of base amounts.

The Commission is left to rely on a single opinion, *James Scott Martin*, 7 F.C.C.R. 3524 (1992), in which it noted that under the standards, the base forfeiture amount would have been $8000. "Under the circumstances of this case," however, the Commission imposed a fine of $1000. *Id.* The decision admittedly is ambiguous as to whether the Commission applied downward adjustment criteria under the standards (which, petitioner contends, could yield a $1000 bottom line) or exercised independent discretion in reaching that amount. But even if we resolved the ambiguity in the Commission's favor, that would mean that the Commission exercised discretion in only one out of over 300 cases, which is little support for the Commission's assertion that it intended not to be bound by the forfeiture standards.

* * *

Accordingly, we grant the petition for review and set aside the forfeiture standards.

PROFESSIONALS AND PATIENTS FOR CUSTOMIZED CARE v. SHALALA

United States Court of Appeals, Fifth Circuit, 1995.
56 F.3d 592.

Before WISDOM, WIENER, and PARKER, CIRCUIT JUDGES.

WIENER, CIRCUIT JUDGE:

In this challenge brought pursuant to the Administrative Procedure Act (APA), Plaintiff-Appellant Professionals and Patients for Customized Care (P2C2) contends that the district court erred in concluding that Food & Drug Administration (FDA) Compliance Policy Guide 7132.16 (CPG 7132.16) is not a substantive rule and thus is not subject to the APA's notice-and-comment requirement. Finding no reversible error, we affirm.

I

FACTS AND PROCEEDINGS

In 1992, the FDA promulgated CPG 7132.16 to address what the agency perceived to be a burgeoning problem in the pharmaceutical industry—the manufacture of drugs by establishments with retail pharmacy licenses. Pharmacies have long engaged in the practice of traditional compounding, the process whereby a pharmacist combines ingredients pursuant to a physician's prescription to create a medication for an individual patient. This type of compounding is commonly used to prepare medications that are not commercially available, such as diluted doses for children and altered forms of medications for easier consumption.

Pharmacies that practice traditional compounding are regulated primarily by state law, and the drugs that they blend are exempt from many federal misbranding provisions. Drug manufacturers and their products, however, are subject to rigorous federal oversight.

By the 1990s, the FDA had become aware that many establishments with retail pharmacy licenses were purchasing large quantities of bulk drug substances; combining those substances into specific drug products before ever receiving any valid prescriptions; and then marketing those drug products to practitioners and patients. The FDA suspected that establishments engaged in this large-scale speculative "compounding" were doing so to circumvent those new drug, adulteration, and misbranding provisions of the Food, Drug, and Cosmetic Act (Act) that regulate the manufacture of drugs.

To combat this perceived problem, the FDA issued CPG 7132.16, in an effort to establish the following "policy":

POLICY

FDA recognizes that a licensed pharmacist may compound drugs extemporaneously after receipt of a valid prescription for an individual patient. . .

Pharmacies that do not otherwise engage in practices that extend beyond the limits set forth in this CPG may prepare drugs in very limited quantities before receiving a valid prescription, provided they can document a history of receiving valid prescriptions that have been generated solely within an established professional practitioner-patient-pharmacy relationship and provided further that they maintain the prescription on file for all such products dispensed at the pharmacy as required by state law.

If a pharmacy compounds finished drugs from bulk active ingredient materials considered to be unapproved new drug substances, as defined in 21 CFR 310.3(g), such activity must be covered by an FDA-sanctioned investigational new drug application (IND) that is in effect in accordance with 21 U.S.C. Section 355(i) and 21 CFR 312.

. . .

Pharmacies may not, without losing their status as retail entities, compound, provide, and dispense drugs to third parties for resale to individual patients.

FDA will generally continue to defer to state and local officials (sic) regulation of the day-to-day practice of retail pharmacy and related activities. . .

FDA may, in the exercise of its enforcement discretion, initiate federal enforcement actions against entities and responsible persons when the scope and nature of a pharmacy's activity raises the kind of concerns normally associated with a manufacturer and that results in significant violations of the new drug, adulteration, or misbranding provisions of the Act.

This CPG goes on to identify nine factors that the FDA "will consider" in determining whether to initiate an enforcement action, but explains that the "list of factors is not intended to be exhaustive and other factors may be appropriate for consideration in a particular case."

[Editor's note: The opinion does not specifically identify those nine factors, but they are—

1.   Compounding of drugs in anticipation of receiving prescriptions, except in very limited quantities in relation to the amount of drugs compounded after receiving valid prescriptions.

2.   Compounding drugs that were withdrawn or removed from the market for safety reasons * * *.

3.   Compounding finished drugs from bulk active ingredients that are not components of FDA approved drugs without an FDA sanctioned investigational new drug application * * *.

4.   Receiving, storing, or using drug substances without first obtaining written assurance from the supplier that each lot of the drug substance has been made in an FDA-registered facility.

5.   Receiving, storing, or using drug components not guaranteed or otherwise determined to meet official compendia requirements.

6.   Using commercial scale manufacturing or testing equipment for compounding drug products.

7.   Compounding drugs for third parties who resell to individual patients or offering compounded drug products at wholesale to other state licensed persons or commercial entities for resale.

8.   Compounding drug products that are commercially available in the marketplace or that are essentially copies of commercially available FDA-approved drug products. In certain circumstances, it may be appropriate for a pharmacist to compound a small quantity of a drug that is only slightly different than an FDA-approved drug that is commercially available. In these circumstances, FDA will consider whether there is documentation of the medical need for the particular variation of the compound for the particular patient.

9.   Failing to operate in conformance with applicable state law regulating the practice of pharmacy.]

The FDA issued CPG 7132.16 without complying with APA notice-and-comment procedures, as the agency considered CPG 7132.16 to be for internal guidance. The FDA explains that CPG 7132.16 was intended to be used within the agency, primarily by FDA district offices, as an aid in identifying those pharmacies that manufacture drugs under the guise of traditional compounding.

P2C2, an organization comprising individuals and entities engaged in the practice of pharmacy, interprets CPG 7132.16 differently. Soon after CPG 7132.16 issued, the FDA notified some of the organization's members that their activities were more consistent with drug manufacturing than with traditional compounding, and that they and their products were thus subject to the regulations applicable to drug manufacturers. On behalf of those and other members, P2C2 filed suit in federal district court, claiming that CPG 7132.16 is invalid because it is a substantive rule issued in violation of the APA's notice-and-comment requirement * * *. Following a two-day bench trial, the district court made extensive findings of fact and conclusions of law, and ruled that CPG 7132.16 is either an "interpretative rule" or "policy statement," but it is not a "substantive rule." Consequently, held the district court, the FDA was exempt from complying with the APA's notice-and-comment requirements, and CPG 7132.16 was validly promulgated.

DC found it to be either interp. rule or policy statmt

* * *

II

ANALYSIS

* * *

If CPG 7132.16 were a substantive rule it would be unlawful, for it was promulgated without the requisite notice-and-comment. The pivotal issue in this case, therefore, is whether CPG 7132.16 is a substantive rule. *ISSUE* Although the APA itself does not define "substantive rules," "interpretive rules," or "statements of policy," courts over the years have developed a body of jurisprudence that is helpful in drawing the necessary—but often illusory—distinctions among the three types of rules * * *.

In *Community Nutrition Institute v. Young*, the D.C. Circuit reiterated two "criteria" to which courts have looked to distinguish substantive rules from nonsubstantive rules:

> First, courts have said that, unless a pronouncement acts prospectively, it is a binding norm. Thus . . . a statement of policy may not have a present effect: "a 'general statement of policy' is one that does not impose any rights and obligations". . .

> The second criterion is whether a purported policy statement genuinely leaves the agency and its decisionmakers free to exercise discretion.

free to exercise discretion

The court further explained that "binding effect, not the timing, . . . is the essence of criterion one." In analyzing these criteria, we are to give some deference, "albeit 'not overwhelming,' " to the agency's characterization of its own rule. While mindful but suspicious of the agency's own characterization, we follow the D.C. Circuit's analysis in determining whether CPG 7132.16 is a substantive rule under the APA, focusing primarily on whether the rule has binding effect on agency discretion or severely restricts it * * *.

1. Agency Deference: FDA's Characterization

* * * It is undisputed that the FDA has consistently classified the instant rule as a statement of policy. The rule is self-described as "Policy," and it was promulgated as a "compliance *policy* guide." In addition, the FDA has steadfastly insisted, both before us and before the district court, that CPG 7132.16 was intended to propound policy.

* * *

2. Binding Effect of CPG 7132.16

* * * P2C2 argues that CPG 7132.16 establishes a binding norm, as it imposes on compounding pharmacists significant new obligations. Most of these new obligations are manifested in the nine "factors," which, according to P2C2, are tantamount to binding norms. The district court found that the nine factors merely provide guidance to help FDA agents distinguish traditional compounding from drug manufacturing, and that the factors are not finally determinative of whether a particular pharmacy is violating the Act. According to the court, enforcement actions are brought only for violations of the Act, and CPG 7132.16 merely restates a long-standing FDA position regarding the traditional practice of pharmacy; it does not represent a change in FDA policy and does not have a significant effect on pharmacy practice or traditional compounding. To ascertain whether CPG 7132.16 creates binding norms, we first consider its plain language and then address the manner in which it had been implemented by the FDA.

a. Plain Language of CPG 7132.16

* * *

We observe initially the statement in CPG 7132.16 that the FDA "will consider" the nine factors in determining whether to initiate an enforcement action against a pharmacy. We also note that, even though the mandatory tone of the factors is undoubtedly calculated to encourage compliance, CPG 7132.16 affords an opportunity for individualized determinations. It expressly provides that "[t]he foregoing list of factors is not intended to be exhaustive," recognizes that "other factors may be appropriate for consideration in a particular case," and states that, even if the factors are present, the FDA retains discretion whether to bring an enforcement action * * *.

* * *

b. *FDA's Enforcement of CPG 7132.16*

P2C2 urges that, even if the plain language of the rule does not create a binding norm, the agency has *treated* CPG 7132.16 as though it establishes binding norms, and thus we should hold that it does. P2C2 reminds us that the pertinent inquiry is not only what CPG 7132.16 states that the agency will do, but also " 'what the agency does in fact.' "

P2C2 relies on numerous informal agency communications as evidence that the FDA has treated CPG 7132.16 as establishing a binding norm. P2C2 cites in particular to evidence that, since CPG 7132.16's promulgation: (1) the FDA has used the nine factors listed in CPG 7132.16 when inspecting pharmacies, and has relied on those factors to determine whether federal enforcement actions were warranted; (2) in numerous letters the FDA has warned pharmacists that they were engaged in drug manufacturing, rather than traditional compounding, because they were conducting some, or all, of the activities listed in CPG 7132.16, and (3) the FDA has furnished copies of CPG 7132.16 to pharmacists who inquired about the legal restrictions on drug compounding. P2C2's reliance is misplaced.

The fact that FDA inspectors refer to CPG 7132.16 to help determine whether a pharmacy is engaged in traditional compounding or drug manufacturing is not particularly probative whether the rule is substantive. We would expect agency employees to consider all sources of pertinent information in performing that task, whether the information be contained in a substantive rule, an interpretive rule, or a statement of policy. Indeed, what purpose would an agency's statement of policy serve if agency employees could not refer to it for guidance?

More probative of the nature of CPG 7132.16, however, is the language used by the FDA in warning letters to pharmacies. In one such letter, the FDA wrote that firms engaged in activities that "exceed the limits of CPG 7132.16 are considered manufacturers and are subject to all the provisions of the Act." We would not dispute that if this statement were viewed in a vacuum, one could be led to conclude that the FDA was in fact treating CPG 7132.16 as a binding norm. But statements are not to be considered out of context or in isolation, and in that very same letter the FDA clearly stated that CPG 7132.16 was only used by the agency as "internal guidance." Moreover, informal communications often exhibit a lack of "precision of draftsmanship" and such internal inconsistencies are not unexpected, which is why such documents are generally entitled to limited weight. We cannot conclude, in light of all of the other circumstances, that these warning letters are sufficient to transform CPG 7132.16 into a substantive rule.

As with that use of CPG 7132.16, we do not find particularly probative the fact that the FDA enclosed copies of CPG 7132.16 in letters responding to some pharmacists' questions regarding the legality of compounding activities. In that correspondence, the agency pointed out that CPG 7132.16 is "policy" and explained further that "[t]his document includes a list of factors which the FDA feels differentiates [sic]" traditional compounding from drug manufacturing. The FDA noted in particular that "[t]his list is not intended to be exhaustive, and other situations or factors may be considered in particular cases." By so doing, the letters made clear that CPG 7132.16 was used for guidance, but that the FDA retained discretion to conduct an individualized inquiry and to consider other factors outside the list. CPG 7132.16, for example, provides that pharmacies engaged in nontraditional compounding are subject to certain provisions of *the Act*, and the FDA explains in warning letters that a pharmacy's compounding may be subject to regulation *under the Act*.

We cannot conclude that the FDA has treated the factors in CPG 7132.16 as binding norms. Rather, the agency has used CPG 7132.16 for guidance to help identify those pharmacies that might be engaged in drug manufacturing activities under the guise of compounding.

3.   Degree of Enforcement Discretion Accorded FDA

Even if CPG 7132.16 does not create binding norms, argues P2C2, the rule so narrowly constricts FDA enforcement discretion that the CPG should be deemed to be a substantive rule.[43] P2C2 contends that CPG 7132.16 acts essentially to identify those pharmacies against which the FDA will bring enforcement actions, thereby denying the agency any semblance of discretion. We disagree.

True, the FDA had even greater discretion in bringing enforcement actions before CPG 7132.16 issued; prior to that time inspectors were apparently provided with no official guidance whatsoever. In that sense, therefore, CPG 7132.16 has "channeled" the FDA's enforcement discretion, providing direction—where once there was none—by helping to determine whether a pharmacy is engaged in traditional compounding or drug manufacturing. But all statements of policy channel discretion to some degree—indeed, that is their purpose. The more cogent question therefore is whether CPG 7132.16 is so restrictive in defining which pharmacies are engaged in drug manufacturing that it effectively removes most, if not all, of the FDA's discretion in deciding against which pharmacies it will bring an enforcement action. We cannot read CPG 7132.16 that restrictively.

CPG 7132.16 makes clear that it was not intended to foreclose the agency's exercise of its discretion in bringing an enforcement action. In fact,

---

[43]   The concept of constricted enforcement discretion is closely related to that of "binding norms," as both reduce the leeway with which the agency can perform its tasks.

the rule expressly refers to the discretionary nature of bringing such actions * * *.

* * *

We further observe that the language of CPG 7132.16 that purports to distinguish traditional compounding from drug manufacturing is imprecise and discretionary—not exact and certain. The rule, for example, states what action the FDA "may" take in its "discretion" to address "significant violations"; it does not mandate a particular agency response once precisely fixed thresholds are exceeded. CPG 7132.16 also expresses that the list of nine factors is neither dispositive nor exhaustive. Although CPG 7132.16 may assist the FDA in identifying pharmacies engaged in the manufacture of drugs, it clearly leaves to the sound discretion of the agency in each case the ultimate decision whether to bring an enforcement action.

* * *

In sum, nowhere does CPG 7132.16 draw a "line in the sand" that, once crossed, removes all discretion from the agency. We cannot agree with P2C2, therefore, that CPG 7132.16 so significantly restricts the discretionary role of the FDA in determining whether to bring an enforcement action against a pharmacy as to transform it into a substantive rule. In our view, CPG 7132.16 merely identifies some indicia of drug manufacturing; it neither compels the conclusion that a pharmacy is engaged in drug manufacturing nor provokes an automatic or nondiscretionary response from the agency. Rather, FDA inspectors are free to consider in toto those nine factors, as well as others, and then, based on that guidance and their own judgment, decide whether the pharmacy in question is engaged in drug manufacturing. Such is the nature of a discretionary rule, not of a substantive one.

4. Statement of Policy or Interpretative Rule?

The district court held that CPG 7132.16 is not a substantive rule, finding it to be either a statement of policy or an interpretative rule. Although our plenary determination that the rule is not substantive is sufficient to affirm the district court's judgment, we continue, albeit briefly, to explain how CPG 7132.16 fits into the narrow exemptions from the APA notice-and-comment requirements.

a. Statement of Policy

As we recently explained, "[a] general statement of policy is a statement by an administrative agency announcing motivating factors the agency will consider, or tentative goals toward which it will aim, in determining the resolution of a substantive question of regulation." This definition fits CPG 7132.16 to a tee, as in it the FDA announced some of the factors that it will consider in resolving "a substantive question of regulation," *i.e.*, whether a pharmacy is engaged in traditional compounding or drug manufacturing.

b. Interpretative Rule

CPG 7132.16 could arguably be considered an interpretative rule as well * * *.

It reminds parties of the existing regulations that pertain to drug manufacturing and explains the FDA's view of what distinguishes drug manufacturing from traditional compounding. It clarifies, rather than creates, law.

* * *

* * * As we agree, then, that CPG 7132.16 is not a substantive rule, and thus is not subject to APA notice-and-comment requirements, the district court's judgment is, in all respects,

AFFIRMED.

NOTES

The legal effects test and the (now-discarded) substantial impact test have in common that they both allow a determination of the status of an agency rule at the moment the rule is promulgated. The rule as issued either operates as a binding norm or it does not; the rule as issued would either foster substantial compliance by a reasonable regulated party or it would not. The "impact on agencies" test represented by *United States Telephone Ass'n* and *P2C2*, however, requires considerable experience with an agency's application of a rule (300 adjudications in the case of *United States Telephone Ass'n*) before one can determinatively say whether a seemingly "interpretative" rule is in fact legislative. At the time that the rule is promulgated, neither the agency nor outside parties can tell for certain whether the rule requires notice-and-comment procedures. But that, of course, is precisely the point in time when one most wants to know what procedures, if any, are needed.

Is there some other test, either in addition to or instead of the "impact on agencies" test, that can be used to separate legislative from interpretative rules *at the moment that the rules are promulgated*? Consider whether the test put forth in the following case by Judge (and former administrative law professor) Stephen Williams adequately solves the problems encountered by previous tests.

AMERICAN MINING CONGRESS v. MINE SAFETY & HEALTH ADMIN.

[handwritten: ← DC Circuit decision]

United States Court of Appeals, District of Columbia Circuit, 1993.
995 F.2d 1106.

[handwritten left margin: x-ray readings re. lung disease]

Before WILLIAMS, SENTELLE and RANDOLPH, CIRCUIT JUDGES.

STEPHEN F. WILLIAMS, CIRCUIT JUDGE:

This case presents a single issue: whether Program Policy Letters of the Mine Safety and Health Administration, stating the agency's position that certain x-ray readings qualify as "diagnose[s]" of lung disease within the meaning of agency reporting regulations, are interpretive rules under the Administrative Procedure Act. We hold that they are.

[handwritten right margin: ← ISSUE]

The Federal Mine Safety and Health Act, 30 U.S.C. § 801 *et seq.*, extensively regulates health and safety conditions in the nation's mines and empowers the Secretary of Labor to enforce the statute and relevant regulations * * *. The Act makes a general grant of authority to the Secretary to issue "such regulations as . . . [he] deems appropriate to carry out" any of its provisions. *Id.* at § 957.

Pursuant to its statutory authority, the Mine Safety and Health Administration (acting on behalf of the Secretary of Labor) maintains regulations known as "Part 50" regulations, which cover the "Notification, Investigation, Reports and Records of Accidents, Injuries, Illnesses, Employment, and Coal Production in Mines." See 30 CFR Part 50. These were adopted via notice-and-comment rulemaking. Subpart C deals with the "Reporting of Accidents, Injuries, and Illnesses" and requires mine operators to report to the MSHA within ten days "each accident, occupational injury, or occupational illness" that occurs at a mine. See 30 CFR § 50.20(a). Of central importance here, the regulation also says that whenever any of certain occupational illnesses are "*diagnosed*," the operator must similarly report the diagnosis within ten days. *Id.* (emphasis added) * * *.

As the statute and formal regulations contain ambiguities, the MSHA from time to time issues Program Policy Letters ("PPLs") intended to coordinate and convey agency policies, guidelines, and interpretations to agency employees and interested members of the public. One subject on which it has done so—apparently in response to inquiries from mine operators about whether certain x-ray results needed to be reported as "diagnos[es]"—has been the meaning of the term diagnosis for purposes of Part 50.

The first of the PPLs at issue here, PPL No. 91–III–2 (effective September 6, 1991), stated that any chest x-ray of a miner who had a history of exposure to pneumonoconiosis-causing dust that rated 1/0 or higher on the International Labor Office (ILO) classification system would be considered a "diagnosis that the x-rayed miner has silicosis or one of the other pneumoconioses" for the purposes of the Part 50 reporting requirements * * *. The 1991 PPL also set up a procedure whereby, if a mine operator had a chest x-ray initially evaluated by a relatively unskilled reader, the operator could seek a reading by a more skilled one; if the latter rated the x-ray below 1/0, the MSHA would delete the "diagnosis" from its files * * *.

The second letter, PPL No. P92–III–2 (effective May 6, 1992), superseded the 1991 PPL but largely repeated its view about a Part 50 diagnosis * * *.

The final PPL under dispute, PPL No. P92–III–2 (effective August 1, 1992), replaced the May 1992 PPL and again restated the MSHA's basic view that a chest x-ray rating above 1/0 on the ILO scale constituted a "diagnosis" of silicosis or some other pneumoconiosis. The August 1992 PPL also modified the MSHA's position on additional readings. Specifically, when the first reader is not a "B" reader (*i.e.*, one certified by the National Institute of Occupational Safety and Health to perform ILO ratings), and the operator seeks a reading from a "B" reader, the MSHA will stay enforcement for failure to report the first reading. If the "B" reader concurs with the initial determination that the x-ray should be scored a 1/0 or higher, the mine operator must report the "diagnosis". If the "B" reader scores the x-ray below 1/0, the MSHA will continue to stay enforcement if the operator gets a third reading, again from a "B" reader; the MSHA then will accept the majority opinion of the three readers.

The MSHA did not follow the notice and comment requirements of 5 U.S.C. § 553 in issuing any of the three PPLs. In defending its omission of notice and comment, the agency relies solely on the interpretive rule exemption of § 553(b)(3)(A).

* * *

The distinction between those agency pronouncements subject to APA notice-and-comment requirements and those that are exempt has been aptly described as "enshrouded in considerable smog," *General Motors Corporation v. Ruckelshaus*, 742 F.2d 1561, 1565 (D.C.Cir.1984) (en banc) (quoting *Noel v. Chapman*, 508 F.2d 1023, 1030 (2d Cir.1975)); *see also American Hospital Association v. Bowen*, 834 F.2d 1037, 1046 (D.C.Cir.1987) (calling the line between interpretive and legislative rules "fuzzy"); *Community Nutrition Institute v. Young*, 818 F.2d 943, 946 (D.C.Cir.1987) (quoting authorities describing the present distinction between legislative rules and policy statements as "tenuous," "blurred" and "baffling").

Given the confusion, it makes some sense to go back to the origins of the distinction in the legislative history of the Administrative Procedure

Act. Here the key document is the *Attorney General's Manual on the Administrative Procedure Act* (1947), which offers "the following working definitions":

> *Substantive rules*—rules, other than organizational or procedural under section 3(a)(1) and (2), issued by an agency pursuant to statutory authority and which implement the statute, as, for example, the proxy rules issued by the Securities and Exchange Commission pursuant to section 14 of the Securities Exchange Act of 1934 (15 U.S.C. 78n). Such rules have the force and effect of law.

> *Interpretative rules*—rules or statements issued by an agency to advise the public of the agency's construction of the statutes and rules which it administers. . .

> *General statements of policy*—statements issued by an agency to advise the public prospectively of the manner in which the agency proposes to exercise a discretionary power.

Id. at 30 n. 3. *See also* Michael Asimow, *Public Participation in the Adoption of Interpretive Rules and Policy Statements*, 75 Mich.L.Rev. 520, 542 & n. 95 (1977) (reading legislative history of Administrative Procedure Act as "suggest[ing] an intent to adopt the legal effect test" as marking the line between substantive and interpretive rules).

Our own decisions have often used similar language, inquiring whether the disputed rule has "the force of law". We have said that a rule has such force only if Congress has delegated legislative power to the agency and if the agency intended to exercise that power in promulgating the rule.

On its face, the "intent to exercise" language may seem to lead only to more smog, but in fact there are a substantial number of instances where such "intent" can be found with some confidence. The first and clearest case is where, in the absence of a legislative rule by the agency, the legislative basis for agency enforcement would be inadequate. The example used by the Attorney General's Manual fits exactly—the SEC's proxy authority under § 14 of the Securities Exchange Act of 1934. Section 14(b), for example, forbids certain persons, "to give, or to refrain from giving a proxy" "in contravention of such rules and regulations as the Commission may prescribe". The statute itself forbids *nothing* except acts or omissions to be spelled out by the Commission in "rules or regulations". The present case is similar, as to Part 50 itself, in that § 813(h) merely requires an operator to maintain "such records . . . as the Secretary . . . may reasonably require from time to time". 30 U.S.C. § 813(h). Although the Secretary might conceivably create some "require[ments]" ad hoc, clearly some agency creation of a duty is a necessary predicate to any enforcement against an operator for failure to keep records. Analogous cases may exist in which an agency may offer a government benefit only after it formalizes the prerequisites.

Second, an agency seems likely to have intended a rule to be legislative if it has the rule published in the Code of Federal Regulations; 44 U.S.C. § 1510 limits publication in that code to rules "having general applicability and legal effect". *See Brock v. Cathedral Bluffs Shale Oil Co.*, 796 F.2d 533, 539 (D.C.Cir.1986) (Scalia, J.).

Third, " '[i]f a second rule repudiates or is irreconcilable with [a prior legislative rule], the second rule must be an amendment of the first; and, of course, an amendment to a legislative rule must itself be legislative.' " *National Family Planning & Reproductive Health Ass'n v. Sullivan*, 979 F.2d 227, 235 (D.C.Cir.1992) (quoting Michael Asimow, *Nonlegislative Rulemaking and Regulatory Reform*, 1985 Duke L.J. 381, 396).

There are variations on these themes. For example, in *Chamber of Commerce v. OSHA*, 636 F.2d 464 (D.C.Cir.1980), the agency had on a prior occasion claimed that a certain statutory term, correctly understood, itself imposed a specific requirement on affected businesses. We found that interpretation substantively invalid, but noted the agency's power to promulgate such a requirement on the basis of more general authority. *Leone v. Mobil Oil Corp.*, 523 F.2d 1153 (D.C.Cir.1975). The agency then issued a purported interpretive rule to fill the gap (without notice and comment), and we struck it down as an invalid exercise of the agency's legislative powers. *Chamber of Commerce*, 636 F.2d at 469.

We reviewed a similar juxtaposition of different agency modes in *Fertilizer Institute v. EPA*, 935 F.2d 1303, 1308 (D.C.Cir.1991). There a statute created a duty to report any "release" of a "reportable quantity" or "RQ" of certain hazardous materials, specifying the RQs but authorizing the EPA to change them by regulation. In the preamble to a legislative rule exercising its authority to amend the RQs, the EPA also expatiated on the meaning of the statutory term "release"—improperly broadening it, as petitioners claimed and as we ultimately found. 935 F.2d at 1309–10. But we rejected a claim that the agency's attempted exposition of the term "release" was not an interpretation and therefore required notice and comment. *Id*. at 1307–09.

* * *

This focus on whether the agency needs to exercise legislative power (to provide a basis for enforcement actions or agency decisions conferring benefits) helps explain some distinctions that may, out of context, appear rather metaphysical. For example, in *Fertilizer Institute* we drew a distinction between instances where an agency merely "declare[s] its understanding of what a statute requires" (interpretive), and ones where an agency "go[es] beyond the text of a statute" (legislative). *Id*. at 1308. *See* *also Chamber of Commerce*, 636 F.2d at 469 (distinguishing between "constru[ing]" a statutory provision and "supplement[ing]" it). The difficulty with the distinction is that almost every rule may seem to do both. But if the dividing line is the necessity for agency legislative action, then a rule supplying that action will be legislative no matter how grounded in the agency's "understanding of what the statute requires", and an interpretation that spells out the scope of an agency's or regulated entity's pre-existing duty (such as EPA's interpretation of "release" in *Fertilizer Institute*), will be interpretive * * *.

* * *

In an occasional case we have appeared to stress whether the disputed rule is one with "binding effect"—"binding" in the sense that the rule does not " 'genuinely leave[ ] the agency . . . free to exercise discretion.' " *State of Alaska v. DOT*, 868 F.2d at 445 (quoting *Community Nutrition Institute v. Young*, 818 F.2d 943, 945–46 (D.C.Cir.1987)). That inquiry arose in a quite different context, that of distinguishing policy statements, rather than interpretive rules, from legislative norms. The classic application is *Pacific Gas & Electric Co. v. FPC*, 506 F.2d 33, 38 (D.C.Cir.1974) * * *.

But while a good rule of thumb is that a norm is less likely to be a general policy statement when it purports (or, even better, has proven) to restrict agency discretion, restricting discretion tells one little about whether a rule is interpretive. Nor is there much explanatory power in any distinction that looks to the use of mandatory as opposed to permissive language. While an agency's decision to use "will" instead of "may" may be of use when drawing a line between *policy statements* and legislative rules, the endeavor miscarries in the interpretive/legislative rule context. Interpretation is a chameleon that takes its color from its context; therefore, an interpretation will use imperative language—or at least have imperative meaning—if the interpreted term is part of a command; it will use permissive language—or at least have a permissive meaning—if the interpreted term is in a permissive provision.

A non-legislative rule's capacity to have a binding effect is limited in practice by the fact that agency personnel at every level act under the shadow of judicial review. If they believe that courts may fault them for brushing aside the arguments of persons who contest the rule or statement, they are obviously far more likely to entertain those arguments * * *. Because the threat of judicial review provides a spur to the agency to pay attention to facts and arguments submitted in derogation of any rule not supported by notice and comment, even as late as the enforcement stage, *any* agency statement not subjected to notice-and-comment rulemaking will be more vulnerable to attack not only in court but also within the agency itself.

Not only does an agency have an incentive to entertain objections to an interpretive rule, but the ability to promulgate such rules, without notice and comment, does not appear more hazardous to affected parties than the likely alternative. Where a statute or legislative rule has created a legal basis for enforcement, an agency can simply let its interpretation evolve ad hoc in the process of enforcement or other applications (*e.g.*, grants). The protection that Congress sought to secure by requiring notice and comment for legislative rules is not advanced by reading the exemption for "interpretive rule" so narrowly as to drive agencies into pure ad hocery—an ad hocery, moreover, that affords less notice, or less convenient notice, to affected parties.

Accordingly, insofar as our cases can be reconciled at all, we think it almost exclusively on the basis of whether the purported interpretive rule has "legal effect", which in turn is best ascertained by asking (1) whether in the absence of the rule there would not be an adequate legislative basis for enforcement action or other agency action to confer benefits or ensure the performance of duties, (2) whether the agency has published the rule in the Code of Federal Regulations, (3) whether the agency has explicitly invoked its general legislative authority, or (4) whether the rule effectively amends a prior legislative rule. If the answer to any of these questions is affirmative, we have a legislative, not an interpretive rule.

Here we conclude that the August 1992 PPL is an interpretive rule. The Part 50 regulations themselves require the reporting of diagnoses of the specified diseases, so there is no legislative gap that required the PPL as a predicate to enforcement action. Nor did the agency purport to act legislatively, either by including the letter in the Code of Federal Regulations, or by invoking its general legislative authority under 30 U.S.C. § 811(a). The remaining possibility therefore is that the August 1992 PPL is a de facto amendment of prior legislative rules, namely the Part 50 regulations.

A rule does not, in this inquiry, become an amendment merely because it supplies crisper and more detailed lines than the authority being interpreted. If that were so, no rule could pass as an interpretation of a legislative rule unless it were confined to parroting the rule or replacing the original vagueness with another.

Although petitioners cite some definitions of "diagnosis" suggesting that with pneumoconiosis and silicosis, a diagnosis requires more than a chest x-ray—specifically, additional diagnostic tools as tissue examination or at least an occupational history, MSHA points to some administrative rules that make x-rays at the level specified here the basis for a finding of pneumoconiosis. A finding of a disease is surely equivalent, in normal terminology, to a diagnosis, and thus the PPLs certainly offer no interpretation that repudiates or is irreconcilable with an existing legislative rule.

We stress that deciding whether an interpretation is an amendment of a legislative rule is different from deciding the substantive validity of that interpretation. An interpretive rule may be sufficiently within the language of a legislative rule to be a genuine interpretation and not an amendment, while at the same time being an incorrect interpretation of the agency's statutory authority. Here, petitioners have made no attack on the PPLs' substantive validity. Nothing that we say upholding the agency's decision to act without notice and comment bars any such substantive claims.

Accordingly, the petitions for review are

Dismissed.

NOTES

To no one's great surprise, *American Mining* did not resolve all (or even much) of the uncertainty surrounding legislative rules, interpretative rules, and policy statements. In particular, *American Mining's* attempt to give substance to the distinction between interpretative rules and policy statements—and to prescribe different tests for identifying each kind of entity—has not attracted a large following. In 1997, the D.C. Circuit took up the task once again.

DC Circuit

SYNCOR INTERNATIONAL CORP. V. SHALALA

United States Court of Appeals, District of Columbia Circuit, 1997.
127 F.3d 90.

Before SILBERMAN, ROGERS and TATEL, CIRCUIT JUDGES.

SILBERMAN, CIRCUIT JUDGE:

Appellant[ ] Syncor * * * appeals the district court's decision that FDA's 1995 "Notice," entitled "Regulation of Positron Emission Tomography Radiopharmaceutical Drug Products; Guidance; Public Workshop," was a "non-substantive" rule not subject to notice and comment rulemaking. We reverse.

I.

Positron emission tomography (PET) is a diagnostic imaging method that uses a subset of radioactive pharmaceuticals, called PET drugs, to determine biochemistry, physiology, anatomy, and pathology within various body organs and tissues by measuring the concentration of radioactivity in a targeted area of the body. The active component of PET drugs is a positron-emitting isotope. This component has a short half-life, so the drug remains effective for only brief periods of time. As a consequence, PET drugs are not manufactured by pharmaceutical companies; instead, they are prepared by physicians and pharmacists operating accelerators in facilities known as nuclear pharmacies, which most often are part of major teaching hospitals or their adjacent universities, and always are located very near to the place where the PET drug will be administered to patients. These nuclear pharmacists compound the isotope with a chemical solution called a substrate. The substrate is used to carry the isotope to the targeted organ or tissue, and the precise solution used depends on the targeted area. For example, a nuclear pharmacist might combine an isotope with a glucose substrate if the brain was being targeted, since the brain is an area of high glucose uptake. In part for this reason, PET drugs are compounded pursuant to a prescription.

On February 25, 1995, FDA announced that PET radiopharmaceuticals "should be regulated" under the drug provisions of the Federal Food, Drug, and Cosmetic Act. In this publication, labeled a "Notice," and referred to alternatively in its text as "guidance" and a "policy statement," FDA indicated that it would require PET "radiopharmaceutical manufacturers" to comply with the [adulteration, misbranding, approval, and registration provisions] * * * of the Act * * *.

FDA indicated that its 1995 publication was to supersede its prior 1984 publication—directed at all nuclear pharmacies, not just those compounding PET radiopharmaceuticals—entitled "Nuclear Pharmacy Guideline; Criteria for Determining When to Register as a Drug Establishment." The 1984 Guideline had unequivocally stated that nuclear pharmacists who operated an accelerator to produce radioactive drugs to be dispensed under a prescription—which precisely describes the process by which nuclear pharmacies compound PET radiopharmaceuticals—were not [subject to the Act] * * *.

Syncor [claimed that] * * * FDA violated the Administrative Procedure Act's [notice and comment requirements] * * *. The district judge granted summary judgment in FDA's favor * * *.

II.

The APA exempts from notice and comment interpretative rules or general statements of policy. 5 U.S.C. § 553(b)(3)(A) (1994). Before the district court the FDA characterized its 1995 publication as merely "guidance" (a general statement of policy). The district judge disagreed, concluding that it was a rule, but an interpretative one. Here, FDA concedes that the publication is a "rule," and adopts the district court's conclusion. Syncor still contends that the publication is a substantive regulation.

We have long recognized that it is quite difficult to distinguish between substantive and interpretative rules. *See Paralyzed Veterans of Am. v. D.C.*

Arena L.P., 117 F.3d 579, 587 (D.C.Cir.1997); *American Mining Congress v. Mine Safety & Health Admin.*, 995 F.2d 1106, 1108–09 (D.C.Cir.1993). Further confusing the matter is the tendency of courts and litigants to lump interpretative rules and policy statements together in contrast to substantive rules, a tendency to which we have ourselves succumbed on occasion. That causes added confusion because interpretative rules and policy statements are quite different agency instruments. An agency policy statement does not seek to impose or elaborate or interpret a legal norm. It merely represents an agency position with respect to how it will treat—typically enforce—the governing legal norm. By issuing a policy statement, an agency simply lets the public know its current enforcement or adjudicatory approach. The agency retains the discretion and the authority to change its position—even abruptly—in any specific case because a change in its policy does not affect the legal norm. We thus have said that policy statements are binding on neither the public nor the agency * * *.

An interpretative rule, on the other hand, typically reflects an agency's construction of a statute that has been entrusted to the agency to administer. The legal norm is one that Congress has devised; the agency does not purport to modify that norm, in other words, to engage in lawmaking. To be sure, since an agency's interpretation of an ambiguous statute is entitled to judicial deference * * *, it might be thought that the interpretative rule—particularly if it changes a prior statutory interpretation as an agency may do without notice and comment—is, in reality, a change in the legal norm. Still, in such a situation the agency does not claim to be exercising authority to itself make positive law. Instead, it is construing the product of congressional lawmaking "based on specific statutory provisions." *See United Technologies Corp. v. U.S. EPA*, 821 F.2d 714, 719 (D.C.Cir.1987). That is why we have said that "[t]he distinction between an interpretative rule and substantive rule . . . likely turns on how tightly the agency's interpretation is drawn linguistically from the actual language of the statute." *Paralyzed Veterans*, 117 F.3d at 588.

We should note, in order to be complete (although this variation is not implicated in the case before us), that an interpretative rule can construe an agency's substantive regulation as well as a statute. In that event, the interpretative rule is, in a sense, even more binding on the agency because its modification, unlike a modification of an interpretative rule construing a statute, will likely require a notice and comment procedure. Otherwise, the agency could evade its notice and comment obligation by "modifying" a substantive rule that was promulgated by notice and comment rulemaking.

A substantive rule has characteristics of both the policy statement and the interpretative rule; it is certainly in part an exercise of policy, and it is a rule. But the crucial distinction between it and the other two techniques is that a substantive rule *modifies* or *adds* to a legal norm based on the agency's *own authority*. That authority flows from a congressional delegation to promulgate substantive rules, to engage in supplementary lawmaking. And, it is because the agency is engaged in lawmaking that the APA requires it to comply with notice and comment.

It is apparent to us, in light of the foregoing discussion, that FDA's 1995 publication is not an interpretative rule. It does not purport to construe any language in a relevant statute or regulation; it does not interpret anything. Instead, FDA's rule uses wording consistent only with the invocation of its general rulemaking authority to extend its regulatory reach. *See American Mining Congress*, 995 F.2d at 1112. The publication is entitled *Regulation* of Positron Emission Topography Radiopharmaceutical Drug Products. In the text, FDA explained that "as [PET] technology has advanced, questions have been raised about the most appropriate approach to *regulation* of PET radiopharmaceuticals." And then FDA stated, "[h]aving considered the available information * * *, FDA has *concluded* that radiopharmaceuticals *should be regulated* under the drug provisions of the Federal Food, Drug, and Cosmetic Act."

* * *

* * * This is not a change in interpretation or in enforcement policy, but rather, is fundamentally new regulation. The reasons FDA has advanced for its rule—advancement in PET technology, the expansion of procedures in which PET is used, and the unique nature of PET radiopharmaceuticals—are exactly the sorts of changes in fact and circumstance which notice and comment rulemaking is meant to inform.

The FDA nevertheless focuses on *American Mining Congress*, in which, recognizing that an agency often has an option to proceed through *adjudication*, we warned against construing the interpretative rule exception to the APA's notice and comment provisions "so narrowly as to drive agencies into pure [adjudicatory] ad hocery—an ad hocery, moreover, that affords less notice, or less convenient notice, to affected parties." *American Mining Congress*, 995 F.2d at 1112. Accordingly, we identified four factors, any one of which, if present, would identify a supposed interpretative rule as really legislative. The first of those factors, on which FDA concentrates, is whether in the absence of the rule there would not have been "an adequate legislative basis for enforcement action or other agency action to confer benefits or ensure the performance of duties," which is another way of asking whether the disputed rule really adds content to the governing legal norms.

The government contends that the rule in question qualifies as an interpretative rule, under that factor, because in the absence of its issuance the government could have proceeded to enforce regulatory requirements against manufacturers of PET drugs. In the past, pursuant to FDA's 1984 Guideline, those requirements were merely "deferred." The government does not clearly explain what it means by "deferred," but seems to suggest that it exercised enforcement discretion in not asserting regulatory authority over appellants until 1995, and therefore simply is reversing that discretionary decision. The obvious difficulty with the government's argument is that it is supportive of a claim that the rule was really a policy statement—a claim which the government abandoned on appeal. As we have said, enforcement discretion is relevant in determining whether an agency intended to bind itself, and therefore, in determining whether a pronouncement is a legislative rule or a general statement of policy, but "tells one little about whether a rule is interpretive." *American Mining Congress*, 995 F.2d at 1111.

In any event, we think the government misreads *American Mining Congress*. We never suggested in that case that a rule that does not purport to interpret any language in a statute or regulation could be thought an interpretative rule. We do not have to decide, therefore, whether FDA could have succeeded in an enforcement proceeding against a nuclear pharmacy that was operating pursuant to the 1984 Guideline, under the secure impression that their activities were totally unregulated (although we find it hard to imagine the government facing a hospitable reception in any federal district court). We think it a kindness also to say that we doubt that the government would have done any better in this case to have relied on the policy statement exception on appeal. The 1995 publication is as far removed from the typical policy statement as it is from an interpretative rule; it drew a boundary to the agency's regulatory reach.

Accordingly, we reverse and remand to the district court with instructions to enter summary judgment in Syncor's favor, and to vacate FDA's rule as not in accordance with law * * *.

NOTES

Does *Syncor* clarify at all the relevant difference (if indeed there is one) between policy statements and interpretative rules? Is it decisive to this inquiry that policy statements "are binding on neither the public nor the agency"? *See Hudson v. FAA*, 192 F.3d 1031, 1034–35 (D.C.Cir.1999) (emphasizing the non-binding character of policy statements). After all, if a purportedly interpretative rule binds either the public or the agency, doesn't that ipso facto make it a legislative rather than interpretative rule? And if the only remaining difference between interpretative rules and policy statements is the difference between articulating and applying a legal norm, is that enough to warrant different treatment under § 553? Courts frequently do not distinguish between interpretative rules and policy statements but instead treat them as a single category of exempt rules. *See, e.g., American Tort Reform Ass'n v. OSHA*, 738 F.3d 387, 394 (D.C.Cir.2013). Whatever the answers to these questions may be, the *American Mining* approach, after finding relatively little favor in its early years, seems to be making a comeback, *see*, *e.g., Hemp Industries Ass'n v. Drug Enforcement Administration*, 333 F.3d 1082 (9th Cir.2003), and must be viewed as part of the legal landscape.

The requirement, highlighted in the penultimate paragraph of *Syncor*, that an interpretative rule actually interpret something has bite in many settings. For example, the Secretary of Health and Human Services produces a Provider Reimbursement Manual to instruct Medicare intermediaries—private firms that review Medicare claims—how to determine the "reasonable costs" of, and therefore the validity and amount of claims for payment from, medical providers. The Manual is not promulgated through notice-and-comment rulemaking. Medical malpractice and other insurance premiums paid by medical providers are generally recoverable costs, even when those premiums are paid to insurance companies owned or controlled by the providers. When such "captive" insurance companies are based outside the United States, however, a provision of the Manual provides very detailed rules restricting the investments that can be made by those insurance companies and denies reimbursement for premiums paid to companies that do not comply with those rules. Section 2152.2.A.4 of the Manual specifies, for instance, that no more than ten percent of the assets of the insurer can be invested in equity securities and no more than ten percent of the total equity investment can be in any one specific equity issue. In *Catholic Health Initiatives v. Sebelius,* 617 F.3d 490 (D.C.Cir.2010), the court held that this requirement could not be sustained as an interpretative rule and required notice and comment procedures:

> To fall within the category of interpretive, the rule must "derive a proposition from an existing document whose meaning compels or logically justifies the proposition. The substance of the derived proposition must flow fairly from the substance of the existing document." Robert A. Anthony, *"Interpretive" Rules, "Legislative" Rules, and "Spurious" Rules: Lifting the Smog,* 8 Admin. L.J. Am. U. 1, 6 n.21 (1994). If the rule cannot fairly be seen as interpreting a statute or a regulation, and if (as here) it is enforced, "the rule is not an interpretive rule exempt from notice-and-comment rulemaking." *Central Tex. Tel. Coop v. FCC,* 402 F.3d 205, 212 (D.C.Cir.2005).

> Although § 2152.2.A.4 of the Manual does not identify what it is purporting to interpret, the Manual's Foreword claims that every Manual provision rests on the "reasonable cost" language in the statute and the regulations. But as Professor Anthony has written, if the relevant statute or regulation "consists of vague or vacuous terms—such as 'fair and equitable,' 'just and reasonable,' 'in the public interest,' and the like—the process of announcing propositions that specify applications of those terms is not ordinarily one of interpretation, because those terms in themselves do not supply substance from which the propositions can be derived." *Lifting the Smog,* at 6 n.21 * * *.

The short of the matter is that there is no way an interpretation of "reasonable costs" can produce the sort of detailed—and rigid—investment code set forth in § 2162.2.A.4. This is essentially the point of the dissenting Board members. The statute gives the Secretary authority to promulgate regulations defining "the method or methods to be used, and the items to be included, in determining" what constitutes a provider's "reasonable costs." 42 U.S.C. § 1395x(v)(1)(A). We may assume, without deciding, that the Manual's investment limitations are an "extension" of the reasonable cost provisions in this section and the corresponding regulation, as the Board majority thought, and we may assume that the limitations are "consistent" with those provisions, as the Secretary has argued. But neither assumption leads to the conclusion that the Manual's limitations represent an interpretation of the Medicare Act or of the regulations. Consistency with the statute may be enough to sustain a rule duly promulgated after notice and comment, just as consistency with the Commerce Clause, Art. I, § 8, cl. 3, may be enough to sustain the constitutionality of a statute. But no one would say, for instance, that the detailed provisions of the Clean Air Act were interpretations of the language of the Constitution. The same is true here. The connection between § 2162.2.A.4 of the Manual and "reasonable costs" is simply too attenuated to represent an interpretation of those terms as used in the statute and the regulations.

617 F.3d at 494–96. Of course, for a provision in an agency manual to constitute a legislative rule, the manual's instructions must in some sense be binding on the agency or some other party, such as the private intermediaries in *Catholic Health Initiatives*. Manual provisions, including HHS Medicare manual provisions, often fail that threshold test for being a legislative rule. *See, e.g., Clarian Health West, LLC v. Hargan*, 878 F.3d 346, 356–58 (D.C.Cir.2018) (manual instruction to Medicare intermediaries on how to calculate hospital eligibility for extra payments held not binding and therefore a statement of policy rather than a legislative rule).

If, after all of this, you are having trouble distinguishing legislative rules from procedural rules from interpretative rules from general statements of policy, take heart that you are far from alone:

The APA divides agency [rulemaking] action * * * into three boxes: legislative rules, interpretive rules, and general statements of policy. A lot can turn on which box an agency action falls into. In terms of reviewability, legislative rules and sometimes even interpretive rules may be subject to pre-enforcement judicial review, but general statements of policy are not. Legislative rules generally require notice and comment, but interpretive rules and general statements of policy do not. Legislative rules generally receive *Chevron* deference, but interpretive rules and general statements of policy often do not.

So, given all of that, we need to know how to classify an agency action as a legislative rule, interpretive rule, or general statement of policy. That inquiry turns out to be quite difficult and confused. It should not be that way. Rather, given all of the consequences that flow, all relevant parties should instantly be able to tell whether an agency action is a legislative rule, an interpretive rule, or a general statement of policy—and thus immediately know the procedural and substantive requirements and consequences. An important continuing project for the Executive Branch, the courts, the administrative bar, and the legal academy—and perhaps for Congress—will be to get the law into such a place of clarity and predictability.

National Mining Ass'n v. McCarthy, 758 F.3d 243, 251 (D.C.Cir.2014). So just think of this section of the course as part of a "continuing project."

The *Syncor* decision notes in passing that modification of an interpretative rule that interprets a regulation, "unlike a modification of an interpretative rule construing a statute, will likely require a notice and comment procedure." That innovation was known as the *"Paralyzed Veterans"* doctrine, after *Paralyzed Veterans of America v. D.C. Arena L.P.*, 117 F.3d 579 (D.C.Cir. 1997). On its face, the idea that a change in agency interpretation of a regulation (even though not the initial interpretation itself) requires notice and comment is quite peculiar: Aren't agency interpretations of regulations the classic example of interpretative rules that are exempt from the APA's notice and comment requirements? The Supreme Court put this doctrine to rest in 2015 in *Perez v. Mortgage Bankers Ass'n*, 575 U.S. ___, 135 S.Ct. 1199, 191 L.Ed.2d 186 (2015). In deciding whether mortgage loan officers are covered by certain exemptions to the overtime rules of the Fair Labor Standards Act, the Department of Labor issued a series of flip-flopping interpretations of a regulation defining the exemptions, and its 2010 flip (not exempted) from its 2006 flop (exempted) was challenged on the ground that the agency did not employ notice and comment procedures before issuing its 2010 "Administrator's Interpretation" of the relevant regulation. The Supreme Court unanimously, albeit in four separate opinions discussing a wide range of issues not directly pertinent to the basic holding, concluded that requiring notice and comment in this circumstance was inconsistent with the APA (and *Vermont Yankee)*, as it would effectively require notice and comment procedures for agency pronouncements that everyone agreed were interpretative rules. In an important sidebar discussion, three Justices expressed views on the extent of the judicial deference that is appropriate to these agency interpretations of regulations; we will hear much more of that topic in Chapter 4.

c.   Good Cause

By far the most common § 553 exemption invoked by agencies concerns circumstances "when the agency for good cause finds (and incorporates the finding and a brief statement of reasons therefor in the rules issued) that notice and public procedures thereon are impracticable, unnecessary, or contrary to the public interest." § 553(b). A study of rules promulgated during the first half of 1987 showed that almost one-third of all such rules invoked the "good cause" exemption from notice-and-comment procedures; an additional nine percent invoked the other exemptions. *See* Juan J. Lavilla, *The Good Cause Exemption to Notice and Comment Rulemaking Requirements under the Administrative Procedure Act*, 3 Admin. L.J. 317, 338–39 & n.86 (1989). More recent studies confirm that a remarkable number of rules continue to be put forward by agencies without notice and comment procedures, primarily on the basis of the "good cause" exemption. *See infra* pages 483–484. The scope of the "good cause" exemption is therefore very important.

Unfortunately, determinations of whether rulemaking procedures are "impracticable, unnecessary, or contrary to the public interest" are inherently fact-specific; useful generalizations are hard to draw. The starting point, however, is that

> the good cause exception is to be "narrowly construed and only reluctantly countenanced." *State of New Jersey v. EPA*, 626 F.2d 1038, 1045 (D.C.Cir.1980). It is "not [an] escape clause[ ] that may be arbitrarily utilized at the agency's whim." *American Fed'n of Gov't Employees v. Block*, 655 F.2d 1153, 1156 (D.C.Cir.1981). "Rather, use of the[ ] exception[ ] by administrative agencies should be limited to emergency situations * * *." *Id.*

Tennessee Gas Pipeline Co. v. FERC, 969 F.2d 1141, 1144 (D.C.Cir.1992). *See also Mid Continent Nail Corp. v. United States*, 846 F.3d 1364, 1380 (Fed.Cir.2017) (laying out a similarly strict test for "good cause").

Oftentimes, that strong language has bite. In *Tennessee Gas*, for example, the Federal Energy Regulatory Commission promulgated a rule requiring pipelines to give the agency advance notification of the construction or replacement of pipeline facilities.

> The Commission explained that it was issuing the interim rule without notice and comment or prepublication but was instead invoking the good cause exception of the APA, which permits an agency to dispense with those requirements under certain circumstances. In support of this decision, the Commission emphasized the interim nature of the rule, the fact that the notification requirements were not unduly burdensome, and the public interest in oversight during the period before a final rule could be issued. The agency was particularly

> > concerned that construction activities may take place during the period of time between issuance of the NOPR and adoption of a final rule without the opportunity for Commission intervention. Once the NOPR is issued, pipelines

may respond to the proposed changes in the regulations by commencing construction in order to avoid either the inherent uncertainty associated with proposed changes to existing regulations or application of the proposed changes, if adopted, to a particular project.

To ensure that the establishment of a procedure to review construction and replacement activities for potential environmental damage would not itself be the source of such damage, the Commission concluded that "it is imperative that the opportunity for some form of oversight on an interim basis be provided immediately."

* * *

Here, the Commission has provided little factual basis for its belief that pipelines will seek to avoid its future rule by rushing new construction and replacements with attendant damage to the environment. Section 2.55(b) has been in effect for some forty years; section 284.3(c) for about thirteen. Yet the agency has cited only one case in which a pipeline company operating under either of those sections has been found to have harmed the environment. In that case, which involved new construction pursuant to section 284.3(c), the Commission imposed a $37 million civil penalty against the company for damage to archaeological sites in violation of the National Historic Preservation Act. It goes without saying that evidence of harm resulting from the past construction of a new pipeline provides no support for the rule's requirement of advance notification of replacement work performed pursuant to section 2.55(b). Moreover, evidence of a single violation in the case of new construction, while not insubstantial, is a thin reed on which to base a waiver of the APA's important notice and comment requirements.

The Commission's counsel maintained, at oral argument, that the agency has had ample practical experience on which to support its claim that the absence of oversight over section 284.3(c) and 2.55(b) projects had resulted in avoidable damage to the environment and thus would predictably do so in the future. That may well be the case, but that does not excuse the Commission's failure to cite such examples in support of its claim of a good cause exception from the APA's notice and comment requirements.

* * *

FERC has claimed good cause without offering any evidence, beyond its asserted expertise, as to why the public interest is served by the immediate implementation of the interim rule. Accordingly, the petition is granted and the interim rule vacated.

969 F.2d at 1143, 1145–46.

Does the following case, which involves an invocation of the good cause exemption that split the circuits as well as the judges in this case, represent a materially different understanding of the agency's burden of explanation for dispensing with notice-and-comment procedures?

retroactivity of sex offender reg. requirements

UNITED STATES V. DEAN

← 11th circuit

United States Court of Appeals for the Eleventh Circuit, 2010.
604 F.3d 1275.

Before HULL, WILSON and FARRIS, CIRCUIT JUDGES.

FARRIS, SENIOR CIRCUIT JUDGE:

Christopher Dean appeals his guilty plea to the charge of having traveled in interstate commerce and knowingly failing to register as a sex offender under the Sex Offender Registration and Notification Act, in violation of 18 U.S.C. § 2250(a) (2006). Dean asserts that the Attorney General did not have good cause to promulgate a rule making SORNA retroactive without notice and comment as required by the Administrative Procedure Act * * *.

I.

On January 18, 1994, Dean was convicted of criminal sexual conduct in the third degree in Minnesota. As a result of the conviction, Dean was required to register as a sex offender. Dean relocated to Montana in 2003 and registered as a sex offender there. Dean then subsequently relocated to Georgia and registered in 2005 as a sex offender and provided notice to Montana. Dean traveled to Alabama sometime between July 2007 and August 2007 and failed to register as a sex offender there. Dean was arrested in Alabama for failing to register. On March 14, 2008, Dean was charged in federal district court with one count of having traveled in interstate commerce and knowingly failing to register as a sex offender as required by SORNA * * *.

* * *

II.

Congress enacted the Sex Offender Registration and Notification Act, which became effective on July 27, 2006 * * *. SORNA sets out an initial registration requirement for sex offenders in 42 U.S.C. § 16913(b). Subsection (b) provides that:

The sex offender shall initially register—

(1) before completing a sentence of imprisonment with respect to the offense giving rise to the registration requirement; or

(2) not later than 3 business days after being sentenced for that offense, if the sex offender is not sentenced to a term of imprisonment.

Id. SORNA also provides specifically * * * that:

The Attorney General shall have the authority to specify the applicability of the requirements of this subchapter to sex offenders convicted before July 27, 2006 or its implementation in a particular jurisdiction, and to prescribe rules for the registration of any such sex offenders and for other categories of sex offenders who are unable to comply with subsection (b) of this section.

42 U.S.C. §§ 16913(b), (d).

On February 28, 2007, the Attorney General promulgated an interim rule pursuant to § 16913(d) making SORNA retroactive to all sex offenders convicted prior to SORNA's enactment. 28 C.F.R. § 72.3 (2007). In promulgating the rule, the Attorney General invoked the "good cause" exceptions of the Administrative Procedure Act at 5 U.S.C. §§ 553(b)(3)(B) and (d)(3) and did not have a pre-promulgation notice and comment period. 72 Fed.Reg. 8894, 8896–7 (2007).

AG claimed "good cause" exemption

The Attorney General issued a statement of good cause with the rule, noting the practical dangers of additional sexual assaults and child sexual abuse or exploitation offenses if SORNA were not made immediately retroactive:

The immediate effectiveness of this rule is necessary to eliminate any possible uncertainty about the applicability of the Act's requirements * * * to sex offenders whose predicate convictions predate the enactment of SORNA. Delay in the implementation of this rule would impede the effective registration of such sex offenders and would impair immediate efforts to protect the public from sex offenders who fail to register through prosecution and the imposition of criminal sanctions. The resulting practical dangers include the commission of additional sexual assaults and child sexual abuse or exploitation offenses by sex offenders that could have been prevented had local authorities and the community been aware of their presence, in addition to greater difficulty in apprehending perpetrators who have not been registered and tracked as provided by SORNA. This would thwart the legislative objective of "protect[ing] the public from sex offenders and offenders against children" by establishing "a comprehensive national system for the registration of those offenders," SORNA § 102, because a substantial class of sex offenders could evade the Act's registration requirements and enforcement mechanisms during the pendency of a proposed rule and delay in the effectiveness of a final rule.

It would accordingly be <u>contrary to the public interest</u> to adopt this rule with the prior notice and comment period normally required * * *.

Id. at 8896–97. The rule took effect immediately * * *.

* * *

IV.

* * * Dean does not dispute that SORNA would apply to him if the rule making it retroactive is valid. Whether the Attorney General had good cause to bypass the notice and comment requirements of the APA is an <u>issue of first impression</u> in this Court and <u>one that has split our sister circuits</u>. *See United States v. Gould*, 568 F.3d 459 (4th Cir.2009), *cert. denied*, 559 U.S. 974, 130 S.Ct. 1686 (2010); *United States v. Cain*, 583 F.3d 408 (6th Cir.2009).

* * *

The Attorney General concedes that he <u>did not follow the standard notice and comment procedures</u> required by the APA. Instead, the Attorney General invoked the "good cause" exceptions * * *. The good cause exceptions allow the agency to skip notice and comment "when the agency for good cause finds (and incorporates the finding and a brief statement of reasons therefor in the rules issued) that notice and public procedure thereon are impracticable, unnecessary, or contrary to the public interest." 5 U.S.C. § 553(b)(3)(B).

We have indicated previously that the good cause exception "should be read narrowly." *United States Steel Corp. v. United States Environmental Protection Agency*, 595 F.2d 207, 214 (5th Cir.1979); *see also Jifry v. F.A.A.*, 370 F.3d 1174, 1179 (D.C.Cir.2004) (indicating that the exception should be "narrowly construed and only reluctantly countenanced"). The exception is, however, "an important safety valve to be used where delay would do real harm." *United States Steel Corp.*, 595 F.2d at 214 * * *.

The Attorney General's two reasons for good cause both relate to the public interest. He asserts that the rule (1) provides guidance to <u>eliminate uncertainty</u>; and (2) <u>prevents the delay in registration</u> of sex offenders who would evade the registration requirements during the notice and comment period, commit additional sexual assaults, and be harder to apprehend.

Only two other circuits have addressed this issue, and they reached different conclusions. *United States v. Gould*, 568 F.3d 459, 470 (4th Cir.2009), upheld the Attorney General's invocation of good cause to bypass the notice and comment requirements for the rule making SORNA

4th Cir upheld AG's actions

retroactive. The Gould court held that "[t]here was a need for legal certainty about SORNA's 'retroactive' application to sex offenders convicted before SORNA and a concern for public safety that these offenders be registered in accordance with SORNA as quickly as possible." *Id.* In particular the court found that "[d]elaying implementation of the regulation to accommodate notice and comment could reasonably be found to put the public safety at greater risk." *Id.* The court also noted that the Attorney General allowed post-promulgation comments, which were addressed in the proposed National Guidelines issued in May 2007 and in the final National Guidelines issued in May 2008. *Id.*

6th Cir. rejected AG's actions

The Sixth Circuit disagreed in *United States v. Cain*, 583 F.3d 408 (6th Cir.2009) * * *. The Sixth Circuit concluded that uncertainty was not good cause because every regulation is designed to provide some type of guidance. *Id.* at 421. It also concluded that Congress had already built in some amount of uncertainty and delay into the design of the statute. The court highlighted the Attorney General's own seven-month delay in issuing the regulation. The court concluded that Congress had already balanced the costs and benefits of delay in not exempting SORNA from APA procedures. The court contrasted this situation with a situation where an agency is facing a statutory deadline.

The *Cain* court then turned to the Attorney General's safety justification. *Id.* at 422. The court noted several cases where safety concerns justified bypassing the notice and comment period. However, the court indicated that the safety concern had previously been used when the "emergency situation arose *after* the statutory enactment at issue." It also noted that agencies have previously given specific reasons "to conclude that [their] regulations insufficiently protected public safety, and those reasons arose after the existing regulations went into effect." The court concluded that the "Attorney General gave no specific evidence of actual harm to the public in his conclusory statement of reasons, and gave no explanation for why he could act in an emergency fashion when Congress had not deemed the situation so critical seven months earlier."

* * *

We address the Attorney General's guidance argument first. We have addressed a somewhat similar guidance argument previously. In *United States Steel Corp.*, the EPA alleged that an immediate rule without notice and comment was necessary to provide guidance to the states. 595 F.2d at 214. We found the need to provide guidance rationale faltered because States already had most of the information the EPA rule provided, the designations at issue were actually based on submissions by the States, and the EPA's role "is limited to reviewing the state designations and modifying them where necessary." *Id.*

In stark contrast, the agency here was granted sole discretion to determine whether SORNA applies retroactively, and there was no guidance at all in place in that matter. The guidance rationale is particularly important here as the persons who were affected by the rule were already convicted of their prior crimes and need to know whether to register. As the Fourth Circuit said, "[t]here was a need for legal certainty about SORNA's 'retroactive' application." *Gould*, 568 F.3d at 471. While this reason alone may not have established the good cause exception, it does count to some extent.

* * *

We now turn to the Attorney General's public safety justification. We conclude that the public safety argument advanced by the Attorney General is good cause for bypassing the notice and comment period. Retroactive application of the rule allowed the federal government to immediately start prosecuting sex offenders who failed to register in state registries. In practical terms, the retroactive rule reduced the risk of additional sexual assaults and sexual abuse by sex offenders by allowing federal authorities to apprehend and prosecute them. The retroactive application of SORNA also removes a barrier to timely apprehension of sex offenders.

The majority in *Cain* reads two cases, one from the D.C. Circuit and one from the Ninth Circuit, to hold that the safety prong of the good cause exception can only be invoked in emergency situations. However, the D.C. Circuit has noted that "the exception excuses notice and comment in emergency situations, or where delay could result in serious harm." *Jifry*, 370 F.3d at 1179. Similarly, the Ninth Circuit has noted that "notice and comment procedures should be waived only when delay would do real harm. Emergencies, though not the only situations constituting good cause, are the most common." *Natural Resources Defense Council, Inc. v. Evans*, 316 F.3d 904, 910 (9th Cir.2003). Both of these decisions are consistent with our precedent in *United States Steel Corp.*, where we indicated that the good cause exceptions were "to be used where delay would do real harm." 595 F.2d at 214. We hold that there does not need to be an emergency situation and the Attorney General only has to show that there is good cause to believe that delay would do real harm.

The dissent in *Gould* argues the retroactive application of SORNA does not improve public safety because it does not compel additional registration and "merely allowed the federal government to prosecute under SORNA sex offenders who were currently violating state registration laws." *Gould*, 568 F.3d at 478 (Michael, J., dissenting). This argument is premised on the notion that those who failed to register are subject to state prosecution already, and that is sufficient for public safety. We are not persuaded. Public safety is improved by federal law that allows the federal

[handwritten margin note: Ct finds public safety argmt to be "good cause"]

government to pursue sex offenders regardless of existing state laws providing for state prosecution. SORNA brings to bear the power of federal law enforcement, including the United States Marshals Service, to assist in locating and apprehending sex offenders who fail to register. The additional criminal sanction also increases the likelihood of registration. Furthermore, Congress has already made the judgment that a federal law for tracking sex offenders, in addition to existing state law, would improve public safety.

* * *

The majority in *Cain* also reasoned that Congress built in a period of delay and the Attorney General delayed seven-months; therefore delay cannot constitute good cause. *Cain*, 583 F.3d at 421. We disagree. All Congressional directives to an agency to implement rules are subject to delay as the agency considers the rule and then promulgates it. If Congress were required to create the substantive administrative rules by itself to avoid notice and comment, then the good cause exception would be meaningless. An agency could never demonstrate good cause since delay is inevitably built in as the agency brings its expertise to bear on the issue. The question is whether further delay will cause harm, and here it was reasonably determined that waiting thirty additional days for the notice and comment period to pass would do real harm.

* * *

The Attorney General had good cause to bypass the Administrative Procedure Act's notice and comment requirement.

AFFIRMED.

Concurrence

WILSON, CIRCUIT JUDGE, concurring in the result:

The Attorney General failed to show good cause to avoid the notice and comment requirements of the Administrative Procedure Act. At oral argument, the government conceded that at the time of his arrest Dean could have been charged with failing to register under either of two existing laws * * *. The government's concession highlights the lack of an emergency or threat of real harm attending the promulgation of the regulation. There was little if any support for the Attorney General's public safety justification that notice and comment "would impair immediate efforts to protect the public from sex offenders who fail to register *through prosecution and the imposition of criminal sanctions.*" The issue is not whether sex offenders should register, but rather whether the addition of one more layer of federal protection atop a substantial quilt of existing state and federal laws merited emergency treatment. Administrative law imposes the doctrine of harmless error, however, and because I conclude Dean suffered no prejudice, I concur with the majority's decision to uphold his conviction.

I.   The Attorney General's Claims of Emergency Fell Short

While I take seriously Congress's mandate that sex offenders register their whereabouts, I accord equal respect to Congress's requirement that executive agencies provide notice and accept comment before binding this nation with their rules. The majority opinion quotes but does not give due weight to our circuit's law requiring us to construe narrowly the good cause exceptions to notice and comment. As I stated above, the existence of stringent state and federal criminal sanctions on the books at the time the regulation was promulgated obviated the case for an emergency. Indeed, every state already had its own registration law * * *.

The majority opinion cites "the power of federal law enforcement, including the United States Marshals Service," as a reason to augment the federal prosecutorial arsenal without notice and comment. But in this case the Prattville Police Department received the initial tip about Dean and arrested him. That local and not federal law enforcement made the case is hardly anomalous. Local and state law enforcement shoulder much of the burden of registering and tracking sex offenders * * *.

* * *

II.   In Passing SORNA, Congress Factored in Delay

The bottom line is that Congress factored delay into SORNA when it wrote the law. To this point the majority opinion has no good reply. In drafting SORNA Congress clearly took the larger view on the problem of unregistered sex offenders. Congress unquestionably had the power to release the Attorney General from the requirements of the APA. Indeed, Congress could have decided on its own to make SORNA apply to pre-enactment convictions, instead of delegating that decision to the Attorney General. Congress however unambiguously declined to adopt either option. Congress balanced the costs and benefits of allowing the Attorney General to determine SORNA's pre-enactment reach, and in doing so it countenanced the inevitable delays of administrative rulemaking. Notably, the Attorney General took seven months from the passage of SORNA to publish its interim rule. Yet that time-span is absent from the Attorney General's claims of emergency timing. What's more, Congress's allocation of three years, plus extensions, to the states to comply with SORNA means Congress did not perceive an emergency. In short, the intent of Congress as captured in the plain words of SORNA was *not* to relieve the Attorney General of the requirement for notice and comment.

III.   Harmless Error Analysis Dooms Dean's Appeal

Here, however, Dean's argument falters. I concur in the result upholding his conviction because another, equally potent requirement of the APA compels it: harmless error review. The passage of five months between promulgation of the regulation and Dean's arrest rendered harmless the lack of pre-enactment notice and comment.

* * *

IV. Conclusion

* * *

I am troubled by the precedent the majority opinion sets today. It is now easier for an administrative agency to avoid notice and comment in our circuit by claiming an emergency or threat of serious harm, whether or not the facts support one. As Dean's counsel pointed out at oral argument, today's holding will apply to APA appeals unrelated to SORNA.

For these reasons, I concur in the result.

NOTES

A number of other circuits have rejected the Justice Department's claim of good cause. *See United States v. Ross,* 848 F.3d 1129 (D.C.Cir.2017); *United States v. Brewer, e.g.,* 766 F.3d 884 8th Cir.2014); *United States v. Valverde,* 628 F.3d 1159 (9th Cir.2010). Supreme Court review of the issue seems unlikely, however, as the Attorney General has subsequently promulgated new rules.

The Third Circuit has also rejected the Justice Department's claims of good cause in this context. *See United States v. Reynolds,* 710 F.3d 498 (3d Cir.2013). The *Reynolds* decision noted and discussed (without resolving) an apparent ambiguity about the standard of review for agency claims of good cause: should the court give weight or deference to the agency's position when passing on the applicability of the good cause exception or simply decide for itself whether the statutory criteria are met? *See id.* at 507–09. The purposes of the good cause exception would suggest the latter, though more general standards of court review of agency decisions provide some modest grounds for arguing the former. The D.C. Circuit weighed in on that question in 2014, holding squarely that no deference is due to the agency's claims when deciding whether good cause exists for issuing a rule without notice and comment. *See Sorenson Communications Inc. v. FCC,* 755 F.3d 702, 706 (D.C.Cir.2014) ("our review of the agency's legal conclusion of good cause is *de novo*"). Does that include *de novo* review of the agency's predictions of likely consequences of delaying issuance of a rule? *Sorenson* rather plainly says yes—in the course of rejecting the FCC's prediction that a fund for providing telecommunications services for the hearing-impaired would run out unless rules were immediately promulgated restricting certain marketing practices:

> Though we do not exclude the possibility that a fiscal calamity could conceivably justify bypassing the notice-and-comment requirement, this case does not provide evidence of such an exigency. The Commission's record is simply too scant to establish a fiscal emergency. It does not reveal when the Fund was expected to run out

of money, whether the Fund would have run out of money before a notice-and-comment period could elapse, or whether there were reasonable alternatives available to the Commission, such as temporarily raising Fund contribution amounts or borrowing in anticipation of future collections. Though no particular catechism is necessary to establish good cause, <u>something more than an unsupported assertion is required</u>.

755 F.3d at 707.

Suppose that an agency publishes a rule without going through notice-and-comment procedures, perhaps because it <u>thinks that it can</u> successfully invoke the "good cause" exception. The rule is an "interim rule," meaning that the agency intends to revisit the issues addressed <u>by the rule in the near future</u> but wants some kind of rule in place immediately. <u>After</u> the interim rule takes effect, the agency <u>asks for public comments</u>, with the expectation that the comments will help shape a new, or final, rule.

interim rule

This is a remarkably <u>common</u> pattern. A 2012 study by the Government Accountability Office examined agency rulemaking from 2003–2010 in order "to provide information on the frequency, reasons, and potential effects of issuing final rules without an NPRM." Government Accountability Office, Federal Rulemaking: Agencies Could Take Additional Steps to Respond to Public Comments 3 (2012), https://www.gao.gov/assets/660/651052.pdf. The report determined that "[d]uring calendar years 2003 through 2010, agencies published 568 major rules and about 30,000 nonmajor rules * * *. [A]gencies published about 35 percent of major rules and about 44 percent of nonmajor rules without an NPRM during those years." *Id.* at 8. (A "major" rule, for this purpose, is a rule which "has resulted in or is likely to result in an annual effect on the economy of $100 million or more." *Id.* at 7.) The vast majority of these rules issued without notices of proposed rulemaking were issued under the "good cause" exception. *See id.* at 15–21. About two-thirds of the time, agencies followed up these rules by asking for comments, which often resulted in new rules that differed in some fashion from the original, or interim, rules. *See id.* at 24–27.

It is virtually certain that at least some of these invocations of the good cause exemption are unwarranted under current doctrine. *See* Kristin E. Hickman, *Coloring Outside the Lines: Examining Treasury's (Lack of) Compliance with Administrative Procedure Act Rulemaking Requirements,* 82 Notre Dame L. Rev. 1727 (2007). But if the agency has provided opportunity for comment by the time a challenge to an interim rule reaches a court, <u>has the post-promulgation notice-and-comment opportunity cured the original defect</u> (or at least rendered it harmless error)? If the answer is yes, agencies have incentives to promulgate first and give notice later, which is exactly the opposite sequence contemplated by the APA's notice-and-comment procedures. Some courts accordingly take a hard line against the practice, holding that if there was no valid exemption from notice-and-comment procedures, <u>then even a procedurally proper final rule following an interim rule is invalid</u>. *See U.S.*

Steel Corp. v. U.S. EPA, 595 F.2d 207, 214–15 (5th Cir.1979). The rationale for invaliding the final rule as well as the interim rule is that the opportunity to comment once an interim rule is in place is qualitatively different from an opportunity to comment when there is no rule yet in place. The D.C. Circuit, while generally accepting that rationale, is willing to allow subsequent notice-and-comment to cure prior procedural defects when the agency has an "open mind" throughout the integrated rulemaking process. *See Advocates for Highway and Auto Safety v. Federal Highway Admin.,* 28 F.3d 1288, 1291–92 (D.C.Cir.1994). On the other hand, if the final rule comes after notice and comment, then, as a formal matter, there is nothing to complain about regarding that rule whether or not the agency has an "open mind." *Cf. Salman Ranch, Ltd. v. Comm'r,* 647 F.3d 929, 940 (10th Cir.2011) (finding, in context of agency's claim for deference, procedural challenge to interim rule was moot once a final rule was properly promulgated). But the interim rule would still seemingly be invalid with respect to parties against whom it was applied if no applicable exception from notice-and-comment procedures excused the failure to provide pre-promulgation procedures for the interim rule. Is the right answer thus categorically to invalidate procedurally improper interim rules and categorically to validate procedurally proper (as a formal matter) final rules, or do functional concerns call for some kind of compromise position? For a thoughtful exploration of these important but oft-ignored questions, see Kristin E. Hickman & Mark Thomson, *Open Minds and Harmless Errors: Judicial Review of Postpromulgation Notice and Comment,* 101 Cornell L. Rev. 261 (2016).

E. INFORMAL ADJUDICATION

The text of the APA imposes essentially no procedural constraints on informal agency adjudication—that is, adjudication that is not required by statute to be held "on the record after opportunity for an agency hearing." In creating hybrid rulemaking requirements, courts at least had § 553's requirement of a notice of proposed rulemaking and a statement of basis and purpose to work with. In informal adjudication, the APA does not even provide those minimal materials to serve as a basis for more elaborate procedures. And surely, one might think, *Vermont Yankee* prohibits courts from requiring more procedures in informal adjudications simply because they regard them as wise checks on agency discretion.

The materials thus far have sharply differentiated judicial review of agency *procedures* from judicial review of the *substance* of agency decisions—that is, whether agencies properly found facts, construed the law, and applied their discretion. That distinction is pedagogically necessary but unrealistic; procedural review and substantive review in the modern administrative state are inextricably interconnected. Procedural law dictates the possible scope of substantive review and vice versa. Nowhere is that clearer than in the cases that develop the modern procedural law for informal adjudication.

Nonetheless, a full discussion of substantive review is postponed to Chapter 4. The following materials, however, at least give a sense of the bottom-line APA requirements imposed on agencies in informal adjudications, even if those materials cannot fully be understood outside the context of a detailed study of substantive review.

CITIZENS TO PRESERVE OVERTON PARK V. VOLPE

Supreme Court of the United States, 1971.
401 U.S. 402, 91 S.Ct. 814, 28 L.Ed.2d 136.

constructing highways through public parks

Opinion of the Court by MR. JUSTICE MARSHALL, announced by MR. JUSTICE STEWART.

The growing public concern about the quality of our natural environment has prompted Congress in recent years to enact legislation designed to curb the accelerating destruction of our country's natural beauty. We are concerned in this case with § 4(f) of the Department of Transportation Act of 1966, as amended,[2] and § 18(a) of the Federal-Aid Highway Act of 1968.[44] These statutes prohibit the Secretary of Transportation from authorizing the use of federal funds to finance the construction of highways through public parks if a "feasible and prudent" alternative route exists. If no such route is available, the statutes allow him to approve construction through parks only if there has been "all possible planning to minimize harm" to the park.

Petitioners, private citizens as well as local and national conservation organizations, contend that the Secretary has violated these statutes by authorizing the expenditure of federal funds for the construction of a six-lane interstate highway through a public park in Memphis, Tennessee. Their claim was rejected by the District Court, which granted the Secretary's motion for summary judgment, and the Court of Appeals for the Sixth Circuit affirmed. After oral argument, this Court granted a stay that halted construction and, treating the application for the stay as a

DC granted SJ
↓
COA affirmed
↓
SCOTUS stay
↓
reverses lower ct

---

[2] "It is hereby declared to be the national policy that special effort should be made to preserve the natural beauty of the countryside and public park and recreation lands, wildlife and waterfowl refuges, and historic sites. The Secretary of Transportation shall cooperate and consult with the Secretaries of the Interior, Housing and Urban Development, and Agriculture, and with the States in developing transportation plans and programs that include measures to maintain or enhance the natural beauty of the lands traversed. After August 23, 1968, the Secretary shall not approve any program or project which requires the use of any publicly owned land from a public park, recreation area, or wildlife and waterfowl refuge of national, State, or local significance as determined by the Federal, State, or local officials having jurisdiction thereof, or any land from an historic site of national, State, or local significance as so determined by such officials unless (1) there is no feasible and prudent alternative to the use of such land, and (2) such program includes all possible planning to minimize harm to such park, recreational area, wildlife and waterfowl refuge, or historic site resulting from such use." 82 Stat. 824, 49 U.S.C. § 1653(f).

[44] [Editor's note: This statute is substantively identical to section 4(f) of the Department of Transportation Act of 1966.]

petition for certiorari, granted review. We now reverse the judgment below and remand for further proceedings in the District Court.

Overton Park is a 342-acre city park located near the center of Memphis. The park contains a zoo, a nine-hole municipal golf course, an outdoor theater, nature trails, a bridle path, an art academy, picnic areas, and 170 acres of forest. The proposed highway, which is to be a six-lane, high-speed expressway, will sever the zoo from the rest of the park. Although the roadway will be depressed below ground level except where it crosses a small creek, 26 acres of the park will be destroyed * * *.

Although the route through the park was approved by the Bureau of Public Roads in 1956 and by the Federal Highway Administrator in 1966, the enactment of § 4(f) of the Department of Transportation Act prevented distribution of federal funds for the section of the highway designated to go through Overton Park until the Secretary of Transportation determined whether the requirements of § 4(f) had been met. Federal funding for the rest of the project was, however, available; and the state acquired a right-of-way on both sides of the park. In April 1968, the Secretary announced that he concurred in the judgment of local officials that I-40 should be built through the park. And in September 1969 the State acquired the right-of-way inside Overton Park from the city.[15] Final approval for the project—the route as well as the design—was not announced until November 1969, after Congress had reiterated in § 138 of the Federal-Aid Highway Act that highway construction through public parks was to be restricted. Neither announcement approving the route and design of I-40 was accompanied by a statement of the Secretary's factual findings. He did not indicate why he believed there were no feasible and prudent alternative routes or why design changes could not be made to reduce the harm to the park.

Petitioners contend that the Secretary's action is invalid without such formal findings and that the Secretary did not make an independent determination but merely relied on the judgment of the Memphis City Council. They also contend that it would be "feasible and prudent" to route I-40 around Overton Park either to the north or to the south. And they argue that if these alternative routes are not "feasible and prudent," the present plan does not include "all possible" methods for reducing harm to the park. Petitioners claim that I-40 could be built under the park by using either of two possible tunneling methods,[18] and they claim that, at a

---

[15] The State paid the City $2,000,000 for the 26-acre right-of-way and $206,000 to the Memphis Park Commission to replace park facilities that were to be destroyed by the highway. The city of Memphis has used $1,000,000 of these funds to pay for a new 160-acre park and it is anticipated that additional parkland will be acquired with the remaining money.

[18] Petitioners argue that either a bored tunnel or a cut-and-cover tunnel, which is a fully depressed route covered after construction, could be built. Respondents contend that the construction of a tunnel by either method would greatly increase the cost of the project, would create safety hazards, and because of increases in air pollution would not reduce harm to the park.

minimum, by using advanced drainage techniques[19] the expressway could be depressed below ground level along the entire route through the park including the section that crosses the small creek.

Respondents argue that it was <u>unnecessary</u> for the Secretary to make formal findings, and that he did, in fact, exercise his own independent judgment which was supported by the facts. In the District Court, respondents introduced affidavits, prepared specifically for this litigation, which indicated that the Secretary had made the decision and that the decision was supportable. These affidavits were contradicted by affidavits introduced by petitioners, who also sought to take the deposition of a former Federal Highway Administrator who had participated in the decision to route I-40 through Overton Park.

[Respondents' arguments:]

The <u>District Court and the Court of Appeals found that formal findings by the Secretary were not necessary</u> and refused to order the deposition of the former Federal Highway Administrator because those courts believed that probing of the mental processes of an administrative decisionmaker was prohibited. And, believing that the Secretary's authority was wide and reviewing courts' authority narrow in the approval of highway routes, the lower courts held that the affidavits contained no basis for a determination that the Secretary had exceeded his authority.

We agree that <u>formal findings were not required</u> But we do <u>not</u> believe that in this case <u>judicial review based solely on litigation affidavits</u> was adequate.

[SCOTUS conclusion]

* * *

* * * [T]he existence of judicial review is only the start: the <u>standard for review</u> must also be determined. For that we must look to § 706 of the Administrative Procedure Act, which provides that a "reviewing court shall . . . hold unlawful and set aside agency action, findings, and conclusions found" not to meet six separate standards. In all cases agency action must be set aside if the action was "<u>arbitrary, capricious, an abuse of discretion, or otherwise not in accordance with law</u>" or if the action <u>failed to meet statutory, procedural, or constitutional requirements</u>. 5 U.S.C. §§ 706(2)(A), (B), (C), (D). In certain narrow, specifically limited situations, the agency action is to be set aside if the action was not supported by "<u>substantial evidence</u>." And in other equally narrow circumstances the reviewing court is to engage in a *de novo* review of the action and set it aside if it was "<u>unwarranted by the facts</u>." 5 U.S.C. §§ 706(2)(E), (F).

[standard of review]
[• arbitrary, capricious, abuse of discr.]
[• substantial evidence]
[• unwarranted by the facts]

Petitioners argue that the Secretary's approval of the construction of I-40 through Overton Park is subject to one or the other of these latter two

---

[19] Petitioners contend that adequate drainage could be provided by using mechanical pumps or some form of inverted siphon. They claim that such devices are often used in expressway construction.

standards of limited applicability. First, they contend that the "substantial evidence" standard of § 706(2)(E) must be applied. In the alternative, they claim that § 706(2)(F) applies and that there must be a *de novo* review to determine if the Secretary's action was "unwarranted by the facts." Neither of these standards is, however, applicable.

Review under the substantial-evidence test is authorized only when the agency action is taken pursuant to a rulemaking provision of the Administrative Procedure Act itself, 5 U.S.C. § 553, or when the agency action is based on a public adjudicatory hearing. See 5 U.S.C. §§ 556, 557. The Secretary's decision to allow the expenditure of federal funds to build I-40 through Overton Park was plainly not an exercise of a rulemaking function. And the only hearing that is required by either the Administrative Procedure Act or the statutes regulating the distribution of federal funds for highway construction is a public hearing conducted by local officials for the purpose of informing the community about the proposed project and eliciting community views on the design and route. The hearing is nonadjudicatory, quasi-legislative in nature. It is not designed to produce a record that is to be the basis of agency action—the basic requirement for substantial-evidence review.

Petitioners' alternative argument also fails. *De novo* review of whether the Secretary's decision was "unwarranted by the facts" is authorized by § 706(2)(F) in only two circumstances. First, such *de novo* review is authorized when the action is adjudicatory in nature and the agency factfinding procedures are inadequate. And, there may be independent judicial factfinding when issues that were not before the agency are raised in a proceeding to enforce nonadjudicatory agency action. Neither situation exists here.

Even though there is no *de novo* review in this case and the Secretary's approval of the route of I-40 does not have ultimately to meet the substantial-evidence test, the generally applicable standards of § 706 require the reviewing court to engage in a substantial inquiry. Certainly, *presumption of regularity* the Secretary's decision is entitled to a presumption of regularity. But that presumption is not to shield his action from a thorough, probing, in-depth review.

Q #1: whether Secr. acted w/in scope of authority The court is first required to decide whether the Secretary acted within the scope of his authority. This determination naturally begins with a delineation of the scope of the Secretary's authority and discretion. As has been shown, Congress has specified only a small range of choices that the Secretary can make. Also involved in this initial inquiry is a determination of whether on the facts the Secretary's decision can reasonably be said to be within that range. The reviewing court must consider whether the Secretary properly construed his authority to approve the use of parkland as limited to situations where there are no feasible alternative routes or where feasible alternative routes involve uniquely difficult problems. And the reviewing court must be able to find that the Secretary could have reasonably believed that in this case there are no feasible alternatives or that alternatives do involve unique problems.

Scrutiny of the facts does not end, however, with the determination that the Secretary has acted within the scope of his statutory authority. Section 706(2)(A) requires a finding that the actual choice made was not ["arbitrary, capricious, an abuse of discretion, or otherwise not in accordance with law."] 5 U.S.C. § 706(2)(A). To make this finding the court must consider whether the decision was based on a consideration of the relevant factors and whether there has been a clear error of judgment. Although this inquiry into the facts is to be searching and careful, the ultimate standard of review is a narrow one. The court is not empowered to substitute its judgment for that of the agency.

The final inquiry is whether the Secretary's action followed the necessary procedural requirements. Here the only procedural error alleged is the failure of the Secretary to make formal findings and state his reason for allowing the highway to be built through the park.

Undoubtedly, review of the Secretary's action is hampered by his failure to make such findings, but the absence of formal findings does not necessarily require that the case be remanded to the Secretary. Neither the Department of Transportation Act nor the Federal-Aid Highway Act requires such formal findings. Moreover, the Administrative Procedure Act requirements that there be formal findings in certain rulemaking and adjudicatory proceedings do not apply to the Secretary's action here. See 5 U.S.C. §§ 553(a)(2), 554(a). And, although formal findings may be required in some cases in the absence of statutory directives when the nature of the agency action is ambiguous, those situations are rare. Plainly, there is no ambiguity here; the Secretary has approved the construction of I-40 through Overton Park and has approved a specific design for the project.

* * *

* * * [T]here is an administrative record that allows the full, prompt review of the Secretary's action that is sought without additional delay which would result from having a remand to the Secretary.

That administrative record is not, however, before us. The lower courts based their review on the litigation affidavits that were presented. These affidavits were merely *"post hoc"* rationalizations, which have traditionally been found to be an inadequate basis for review. And they clearly do not constitute the "whole record" compiled by the agency: the basis for review required by § 706 of the Administrative Procedure Act.

Thus it is necessary to remand this case to the District Court for plenary review of the Secretary's decision. That review is to be based on the full administrative record that was before the Secretary at the time he made his decision. But since the bare record may not disclose the factors that were considered or the Secretary's construction of the evidence it may be necessary for the District Court to require some explanation in order to determine if the Secretary acted within the scope of his authority and if the Secretary's action was justifiable under the applicable standard.

The court may require the administrative officials who participated in the decision to give testimony explaining their action. Of course, such inquiry into the mental processes of administrative decisionmakers is usually to be avoided. *United States v. Morgan*, 313 U.S. 409, 422 (1941). And where there are administrative findings that were made at the same time as the decision, as was the case in *Morgan*, there must be a strong showing of bad faith or improper behavior before such inquiry may be made. But here there are no such formal findings and it may be that the only way there can be effective judicial review is by examining the decisionmakers themselves.

The District Court is not, however, required to make such an inquiry. It may be that the Secretary can prepare formal findings * * * that will provide an adequate explanation for his action. Such an explanation will, to some extent, be a "*post hoc* rationalization" and thus must be viewed critically. If the District Court decides that additional explanation is necessary, that court should consider which method will prove the most expeditious so that full review may be had as soon as possible.

Reversed and remanded.

MR. JUSTICE DOUGLAS took no part in the consideration or decision of this case.

Separate opinion of MR. JUSTICE BLACK, with whom MR. JUSTICE BRENNAN joins.

I agree with the Court that the judgment of the Court of Appeals is wrong and that its action should be reversed. I do not agree that the whole matter should be remanded to the District Court. I think the case should be sent back to the Secretary of Transportation * * *. The Act of Congress in connection with other federal highway aid legislation, it seems to me, calls for hearings—hearings that a court can review, hearings that demonstrate more than mere arbitrary defiance by the Secretary. Whether the findings growing out of such hearings are labeled "formal" or "informal" appears to me to be no more than an exercise in semantics. Whatever the hearing requirements might be, the Department of Transportation failed to meet them in this case * * *. I dissent from the Court's failure to send the case back to the Secretary, whose duty has not yet been performed.

NOTES

Overton Park, decided in 1971, pointed towards procedural requirements in informal adjudication that are not specified in the APA. A D.C. Circuit decision from 1982 even more explicitly declared: "The distinct and steady trend of the courts has been to demand in informal adjudications procedures similar to those already required in informal rulemaking. Courts have required *some explanation* for agency action and, to ensure the adequacy of that explanation, some opportunity for interested parties to be informed of and comment upon the relevant evidence before the agency." *Independent U.S. Tanker Owners Committee v. Lewis,* 690 F.2d 908, 922–23 (D.C.Cir.1982). *Vermont Yankee*, decided in 1978, at least strongly suggested that no such requirements should be imposed. Are *Vermont Yankee* and *Overton Park* truly in conflict, and if so, can they be reconciled?

PENSION BENEFIT GUARANTY CORP. v. LTV

Supreme Court of the United States, 1990.
496 U.S. 633, 110 S.Ct. 2668, 110 L.Ed.2d 579.

Pension Benefit Guaranty Corp.

BLACKMUN, J.

In this case we must determine whether the decision of the Pension Benefit Guaranty Corporation (PBGC) to restore certain pension plans under § 4047 of the Employee Retirement Income Security Act of 1974 (ERISA), was, as the Court of Appeals concluded, arbitrary and capricious or contrary to law, within the meaning of § 706 of the Administrative Procedure Act (APA).

ERISA

I

Petitioner PBGC is a wholly owned United States Government corporation, modeled after the Federal Deposit Insurance Corporation. The Board of Directors of the PBGC consists of the Secretaries of the Treasury, Labor, and Commerce. The PBGC administers and enforces Title IV of ERISA. Title IV includes a mandatory Government insurance program that protects the pension benefits of over 30 million private-sector American workers who participate in plans covered by the Title * * *.

When a plan covered under Title IV terminates with insufficient assets to satisfy its pension obligations to the employees, the PBGC becomes trustee of the plan, taking over the plan's assets and liabilities. The PBGC then uses the plan's assets to cover what it can of the benefit obligations. The PBGC then must add its own funds to ensure payment of the most of the remaining "nonforfeitable" benefits, *i.e.,* those benefits to which participants have earned entitlement under the plan terms as of the date of termination * * *.

The cost of the PBGC insurance is borne primarily by employers that maintain ongoing pension plans. Sections 4006 and 4007 of ERISA require these employers to pay annual premiums. The insurance program is also financed by statutory liability imposed on employers who terminate underfunded pension plans. Upon termination, the employer becomes liable to the PBGC for the benefits that the PBGC will pay out. Because the PBGC historically has recovered only a small portion of that liability, Congress repeatedly has been forced to increase the annual premiums. Even with these increases, the PBGC in its most recent Annual Report noted liabilities of $4 billion and assets of only $2.4 billion, leaving a deficit of over $1.5 billion.

PBGC deficit

As noted above, plan termination is the insurable event under Title IV. Plans may be terminated "voluntarily" by an employer or "involuntarily" by the PBGC. An employer may terminate a plan voluntarily in one of two ways. It may proceed with a "standard termination" only if it has sufficient assets to pay all benefit commitments. A standard termination thus does not implicate PBGC insurance responsibilities. If an employer wishes to terminate a plan whose assets are insufficient to pay all benefits, the employer must demonstrate that it is in financial "distress" as defined in 29 U.S.C. § 1341(c) (1982 ed., Supp. IV). Neither a standard nor a distress termination by the employer, however, is permitted if termination would violate the terms of an existing collective-bargaining agreement.

The PBGC, though, may terminate a plan "involuntarily," notwithstanding the existence of a collective-bargaining agreement. Section 4042 of ERISA provides that the PBGC may terminate a plan whenever it determines that:

> "(1) the plan has not met the minimum funding standard required under section 412 of title 26, or has been notified by the Secretary of the Treasury that a notice of deficiency under section 6212 of title 26 has been mailed with respect to the tax imposed under section 4971(a) of title 26,

> "(2) the plan will be unable to pay benefits when due,

> "(3) the reportable event described in section 1343(b)(7) of this title has occurred, or

> "(4) the possible long-run loss of the [PBGC] with respect to the plan may reasonably be expected to increase unreasonably if the plan is not terminated." 29 U.S.C. § 1342(a).

Termination can be undone by PBGC. Section 4047 of ERISA, 29 U.S.C. § 1347, provides:

> "In the case of a plan which has been terminated under section 1341 or 1342 of this title the [PBGC] is authorized in any such case in which [it] determines such action to be appropriate and consistent with its duties under this subchapter, to take such

action as may be necessary to restore the plan to its pretermination status, including, but not limited to, the transfer to the employer or a plan administrator of control of part or all of the remaining assets and liabilities of the plan."

When a plan is restored, full benefits are reinstated, and the employer, rather than the PBGC, again is responsible for the plan's unfunded liabilities.

II

This case arose after respondent The LTV Corporation (LTV Corp.) and many of its subsidiaries, including LTV Steel Company Inc., (LTV Steel) (collectively LTV), in July 1986 filed petitions for reorganization under Chapter 11 of the Bankruptcy Code. At that time, LTV Steel was the sponsor of three defined benefit pension plans (the Plans) covered by Title IV of ERISA * * *. Chronically underfunded, the Plans, by late 1986, had unfunded liabilities for promised benefits of almost $2.3 billion. Approximately $2.1 billion of this amount was covered by PBGC insurance.

It is undisputed that one of LTV Corp's principal goals in filing the Chapter 11 petitions was the restructuring of LTV Steel's pension obligations, a goal which could be accomplished if the Plans were terminated and responsibility for the unfunded liabilities was placed on the PBGC * * *. LTV therefore sought to have the PBGC terminate the Plans.

To that end, LTV advised the PBGC in 1986 that it could not continue to provide complete funding for the Plans. PBGC estimated that, without continued funding, the Plans' $2.1 billion underfunding could increase by as much as $65 million by December 1987 and by another $63 million by December 1988, unless the Plans were terminated. Moreover, extensive plant shutdowns were anticipated. These shutdowns, if they occurred before the Plans were terminated, would have required the payment of significant "shutdown benefits." The PBGC estimated that such benefits could increase the Plans' liabilities by as much as $300 million to $700 million, of which up to $500 million was covered by PBGC insurance. Confronted with this information, the PBGC * * * determined that the Plans should be terminated in order to protect the insurance program from the unreasonable risk of large losses, and commenced termination proceedings in the District Court. With LTV's consent, the Plans were terminated effective January 13, 1987.

* * *

In early August 1987, the PBGC determined that the financial factors on which it had relied in terminating the Plans had changed significantly. Of particular significance to the PBGC was its belief that the steel industry, including LTV Steel, was experiencing a dramatic turnaround. As a result, the PBGC concluded it no longer faced the imminent risk, central to its original termination decision, of large unfunded liabilities stemming from plant shutdowns * * *.

The Director issued a Notice of Restoration on September 22, 1987, indicating the PBGC's intent to restore the terminated Plans * * *. Restoration meant that the Plans were ongoing, and that LTV again would be responsible for administering and funding them.

LTV refused to comply with the restoration decision. This prompted the PBGC to initiate an enforcement action in the District Court. The court vacated the PBGC's restoration decision * * *.

The Court of Appeals for the Second Circuit affirmed, holding * * * that the agency's restoration decision was arbitrary and capricious because the PBGC's decision-making process of informal adjudication lacked adequate procedural safeguards.

Because of the significant administrative law questions raised by this case, and the importance of the PBGC's insurance program, we granted certiorari.

III

[The Court determined that PBGC's actions were legally justified on the merits.]

* * *

Finally, we consider the Court of Appeals' ruling that the agency procedures were inadequate in this particular case. Relying upon a passage in *Bowman Transportation, Inc. v. Arkansas-Best Freight System, Inc.*, 419 U.S. 281, 288, n. 4 (1974), the court held that the PBGC's decision was arbitrary and capricious because the "PBGC neither apprised LTV of the material on which it was to base its decision, gave LTV an adequate opportunity to offer contrary evidence, proceeded in accordance with ascertainable standards . . . , nor provided [LTV] a statement showing its reasoning in applying those standards." 875 F.2d, at 1021. The court suggested that on remand the agency was required to do each of these things.

The PBGC argues that this holding conflicts with *Vermont Yankee Nuclear Power Corp. v. Natural Resources Defense Council, Inc.*, 435 U.S. 519 (1978), where, the PBGC contends, this Court made clear that when the Due Process Clause is not implicated and an agency's governing statute contains no specific procedural mandates, the Administrative Procedure Act establishes the maximum procedural requirements a reviewing court may impose on agencies. Although *Vermont Yankee* concerned additional procedures imposed by the Court of Appeals for the District of Columbia Circuit on the Atomic Energy Commission when the agency was engaging in informal rulemaking, the PBGC argues that the informal adjudication process by which the restoration decision was made should be governed by the same principles.

Respondents counter by arguing that courts, under some circumstances, do require agencies to undertake additional procedures. As support for this proposition, they rely on *Citizens to Preserve Overton Park, Inc. v. Volpe*, 401 U.S. 402 (1971). In *Overton Park*, the Court concluded that the Secretary of Transportation's "*post hoc* rationalizations" regarding a decision to authorize the construction of a highway did not provide "an adequate basis for [judicial] review" for purposes of § 706 of the APA. *Id.*, at 419. Accordingly, the Court directed the District Court on remand to consider evidence that shed light on the Secretary's reasoning at the time he made the decision. Of particular relevance for present purposes, the Court in *Overton Park* intimated that one recourse for the District Court might be a remand to the agency for a fuller explanation of the agency's reasoning at the time of the agency action. Subsequent cases have made clear that remanding to the agency in fact is the preferred course. See *Florida Power & Light Co. v. Lorion*, 470 U.S. 729, 744 (1985) ("If the reviewing court simply cannot evaluate the challenged agency action on the basis of the record before it, the proper course, except in rare circumstances, is to remand to the agency for additional investigation or explanation"). Respondents contend that the instant case is controlled by *Overton Park* rather than *Vermont Yankee*, and that the Court of Appeals' ruling was thus correct.

[margin note: Respondents' argmt]

We believe that respondents' argument is wide of the mark. We begin by noting that although one initially might feel that there is some tension between *Vermont Yankee* and *Overton Park*, the two cases are not necessarily inconsistent. *Vermont Yankee* stands for the general proposition that courts are not free to impose upon agencies specific procedural requirements that have no basis in the APA. At most, *Overton Park* suggests that § 706(2)(A) of the APA, which directs a court to ensure that an agency action is not arbitrary and capricious or otherwise contrary to law, imposes a general "procedural" requirement of sorts by mandating that an agency take whatever steps it needs to provide an explanation that will enable the court to evaluate the agency's rationale at the time of decision.

[margin note: SCOTUS disagrees w/respondents]

Here, unlike in *Overton Park*, the Court of Appeals did not suggest that the administrative record was inadequate to enable the court to fulfill its duties under § 706. Rather, to support its ruling, the court focused on "fundamental fairness" to LTV. 875 F.2d, at 1020–1021. With the possible exception of the absence of "ascertainable standards"—by which we are not exactly sure what the Court of Appeals meant—the procedural inadequacies cited by the court all relate to LTV's role in the PBGC's decisionmaking process. But the court did not point to any provision in ERISA or the APA which gives LTV the procedural rights the court identified. Thus, the court's holding runs afoul of *Vermont Yankee* and finds no support in *Overton Park*.

Nor is *Arkansas-Best*, the case on which the Court of Appeals relied, to the contrary. The statement relied upon (which was dictum) said: "A party is entitled, of course, to know the issues on which decision will turn and to be apprised of the factual material on which the agency relies for decision so that he may rebut it." 419 U.S., at 288, n.4. That statement was entirely correct in the context of *Arkansas-Best*, which involved a formal adjudication by the Interstate Commerce Commission pursuant to the trial-type procedures set forth in §§ 5, 7 and 8 of the APA, 5 U.S.C. §§ 554, 556–557, which include requirements that parties be given notice of "the matters of fact and law asserted," § 554(b)(3), an opportunity for "the submission and consideration of facts [and] arguments," § 554(c)(1), and an opportunity to submit "proposed findings and conclusions" or "exceptions," § 557(c)(1), (2). The determination in this case, however, was lawfully made by informal adjudication, the minimal requirements for which are set forth in § 555 of the APA, and do not include such elements. A failure to provide them where the Due Process Clause itself does not require them (which has not been asserted here) is therefore not unlawful.

determination here was lawfully made via inf. adjud.

* * *

[JUSTICES WHITE, O'CONNOR, and STEVENS dissented on grounds unrelated to the APA argument.]

NOTES

In theory, some structure for informal adjudication could be provided by § 555(e) of the APA, which states that "[p]rompt notice shall be given of the denial in whole or in part of a written application, petition, or other request of an interested person made in connection with any agency proceeding. Except in affirming a prior denial or when the denial is self-explanatory, the notice shall be accompanied by a brief statement of the grounds for denial." One can imagine this provision producing procedural requirements for an agency to explain its decisions not unlike those generated through application of substantive review principles as in *Overton Park* and *LTV*. For reasons that remain somewhat mysterious, however, § 555(e) has not played much of a role in administrative law. For a relatively rare decision that characterizes an agency's inadequate response as a violation of § 555(e) in addition to (as is typical) a violation of § 706(2)(A), see *Butte County, California v. Hogen*, 613 F.3d 190, 194–95 (D.C.Cir.2010).

F. THE CHOICE BETWEEN RULEMAKING AND ADJUDICATION

1. THE STRANGE SAGA OF C.T. CHENERY

SEC v. CHENERY CORP.

Supreme Court of the United States, 1943.
318 U.S. 80, 63 S.Ct. 454, 87 L.Ed. 626.

public utility holding company

MR. JUSTICE FRANKFURTER delivered the opinion of the Court.

The respondents, who were officers, directors, and controlling stockholders of the Federal Water Service Corporation (hereafter called Federal),[45] a holding company registered under the Public Utility Holding Company Act of 1935, c. 687, 49 Stat. 803, 15 U.S.C. § 79 et seq., brought this proceeding under § 24(a) of the Act to review an order made by the Securities and Exchange Commission on September 24, 1941, approving a plan of reorganization for the company. Under the Commission's order, preferred stock acquired by the respondents during the period in which successive reorganization plans proposed by the management of the company were before the Commission, was not permitted to participate in the reorganization on an equal footing with all other preferred stock * * *.

The relevant facts are as follows. In 1937 Federal was a typical public utility holding company. Incorporated in Delaware, its assets consisted of securities of subsidiary water, gas, electric, and other companies in thirteen states and one foreign country. The respondents controlled Federal through their control of its parent, Utility Operators Company, which owned all of the outstanding shares of Federal's Class B common stock, representing the controlling voting power in the company. On November 8, 1937, when Federal registered as a holding company under the Public Utility Holding Company Act of 1935, its management filed a plan for reorganization under §§ 7 and 11 of the Act, the relevant portions of which are copied in the margin.[1] This plan, as well as two other plans

plan for reorganization

---

45 [Editor's note: The principal respondents were C.T. Chenery, the president of Federal, and Chenery Corp., Mr. Chenery's personal company.]

1 "SEC. 7. (a) A registered holding company or subsidiary company thereof may file a declaration with the Commission, regarding any of the acts enumerated in subsection (a) of section 6, in such form as the Commission may by rules and regulations prescribe as necessary or appropriate in the public interest or for the protection of investors or consumers * * *.

"(d)   If the requirements of subsections (c) and (g) are satisfied, the Commission shall permit a declaration regarding the issue or sale of a security to become effective unless the Commission finds that—

* * *

"(6)   the terms and conditions of the issue or sale of the security are detrimental to the public interest or the interest of investors or consumers.

"(e)   If the requirements of subsection (g) are satisfied, the Commission shall permit a declaration to become effective regarding the exercise of a privilege or right to alter the priorities, preferences, voting power, or other rights of the holders of an outstanding security unless the later submitted by Federal, provided for participation by Class B stockholders in the equity of the proposed reorganized company. This feature of the plans was unacceptable to the Commission, and all were ultimately withdrawn. On March 30, 1940, a fourth plan was filed by Federal. This plan, proposing a merger of Federal, Utility Operators Company, and Federal Water and Gas Corporation, a wholly-owned inactive subsidiary of Federal, contained no provision for participation by the Class B stock. Instead, that class of stock was to be surrendered for cancellation, and the preferred and Class A common stock of Federal were to be converted into common stock of the new corporation. As the Commission pointed out in its analysis of the proposed plan, "except for the 5.3% of new common allocated to the present holders of Class A stock, substantially all of the equity of the reorganized company will be given to the present preferred stockholders."

During the period from November 8, 1937, to June 30, 1940, while the successive reorganization plans were before the Commission, the respondents purchased a total of 12,407 shares of Federal's preferred stock. (The total number of outstanding shares of Federal's preferred stock was 159,269.) These purchases were made on the over-the-counter market through brokers at prices lower than the book value of the common stock of the new corporation into which the preferred stock would have been converted under the proposed plan. If this feature of the plan had been approved by the Commission, the respondents through their holdings of Federal's preferred stock would have acquired more than 10 per cent of the common stock of the new corporation. The respondents frankly admitted

Commission finds that such exercise of such privilege or right will result in an unfair or inequitable distribution of voting power among holders of the securities of the declarant or is otherwise detrimental to the public interest or the interest of investors or consumers.

"(f)   Any order permitting a declaration to become effective may contain such terms and conditions as the Commission finds necessary to assure compliance with the conditions specified in this section * * *.

"SEC. 11. (a) It shall be the duty of the Commission to examine the corporate structure of every registered holding company and subsidiary company thereof, the relationships among the companies in the holding-company system of every such company and the character of the interests thereof and the properties owned or controlled thereby to determine the extent to which the corporate structure of such holding-company system and the companies therein may be simplified, unnecessary complexities therein eliminated, voting power fairly and equitably distributed among the holders of securities thereof, and the properties and business thereof confined to those necessary or appropriate to the operations of an integrated public-utility system * * *.

"(e)   In accordance with such rules and regulations or order as the Commission may deem necessary or appropriate in the public interest or for the protection of investors or consumers, any registered holding company or any subsidiary company of a registered holding company may, at any time after January 1, 1936, submit a plan to the Commission for the divestment of control, securities, or other assets, or for other action by such company or any subsidiary company thereof for the purpose of enabling such company or any subsidiary company thereof to comply with the provisions of subsection (b). If, after notice and opportunity for hearing, the Commission shall find such plan, as submitted or as modified, necessary to effectuate the provisions of subsection (b) and fair and equitable to the persons affected by such plan, the Commission shall make an order approving such plan; and the Commission, at the request of the company, may apply to a court, in accordance with the provisions of subsection (f) of section 18, to enforce and carry out the terms and provisions of such plan * * *."

that their purpose in buying the preferred stock was to protect their interests in the company.

In ascertaining whether the terms of issuance of the new common stock were "fair and equitable" or "detrimental to the interests of investors" within § 7 of the Act, the Commission found that it could not approve the proposed plan so long as the preferred stock acquired by the respondents would be permitted to share on a parity with other preferred stock. The Commission did not find fraud or lack of disclosure, but it concluded that the respondents, as Federal's managers, were fiduciaries and hence under a "duty of fair dealing" not to trade in the securities of the corporation while plans for its reorganization were before the Commission. It recommended that a formula be devised under which the respondents' preferred stock would participate only to the extent of the purchase prices paid plus accumulated dividends since the dates of such purchases. Accordingly, the plan was thereafter amended to provide that the preferred stock acquired by the respondents, unlike the preferred stock held by others, would not be converted into stock of the reorganized company, but could only be surrendered at cost plus 4 per cent interest. The Commission, over the respondents' objections, approved the plan as thus amended, and it is this order which is now under review.

* * *

The Commission did not find that the respondents as managers of Federal acted covertly or traded on inside knowledge, or that their position as reorganization managers enabled them to purchase the preferred stock at prices lower than they would otherwise have had to pay, or that their acquisition of the stock in any way prejudiced the interests of the corporation or its stockholders.[46] To be sure, the new stock into which the

---

46 [Editor's note: The Court of Appeals, in the decision under review, described the purchases by the Chenery group:

When the first plan was proposed, members of the Commission's staff objected to the retention of voting power in Federal by its Class B common stock, substantially all of which belonged to Utility Operators Company, which in turn was controlled by officers and directors of Federal. This opposition held in suspense for two and a half years the proposed plan and various subsequently suggested amendments. Notice of the Commission's position in this regard was made public both by the Commission and Federal, and it is agreed was known and understood by stockholders or investors. Realizing that if the Commission persisted in this stand the officers and employees of Federal who had invested in this class of stock would find themselves without either a stake or influence in the company they had helped create and by which they were employed, Chenery, president of Federal, suggested to many of them that they use what money they could spare to buy preferred stock, stating that he would follow the same course. This resulted in purchases over a period of two and a half to three years on the part of various officers and directors of the corporation. The average purchase of each of the 16 officers and directors, other than Chenery, and one Vandenberg was around 130 shares. Chenery, for the account of a family corporation controlled by him, purchased approximately 8,000 shares, of which a lot of 2,700 shares was not a purchase but an exchange for $100,000 of Federal's prior debenture gold bonds, and as to which the other party to the transaction testified that he preferred to have the bonds to the stock "and today I am very much delighted we made the trade". The remaining director, Vandenberg,

respondents' preferred stock would be converted under the plan of reorganization would have a book value—which may or may not represent market value—considerably greater than the prices paid for the preferred stock. But that would equally be true of purchases of preferred stock made by other investors. The respondents, the Commission tells us, acquired their stock as the outside world did, and [upon no better terms.] The Commission dealt with this as a specific case, and not as the application of a general rule formulating rules of conduct for reorganization managers. Consequently, it is a vital consideration that the Commission conceded that the respondents did not acquire their stock through any favoring circumstances. In its own words, "honesty, full disclosure, and purchase at a fair price" characterized the transactions. The Commission did not suggest that, as a result of their purchases of preferred stock, the respondents would be unjustly enriched. On the contrary, the question before the Commission was [whether the respondents, simply because they were reorganization managers, should be denied the benefits to be received by the 6,000 other preferred stockholders.] Some technical rule of law must have moved the Commission to single out the respondents and deny their preferred stock the right to participate equally in the reorganization. To ascertain the precise basis of its determination, we must look to the Commission's opinion.

The Commission stated that "in the process of formulation of a 'voluntary' reorganization plan, the management of a corporation occupies a fiduciary position toward all of the security holders to be affected, and that it is subjected to the same standards as other fiduciaries with respect to dealing with the property which is the subject matter of the trust." Applying by analogy the restrictions imposed on trustees in trafficking in property held by them in trust for others, the Commission ruled that even though the management does not hold the stock of the corporation in trust for the stockholders, nevertheless the "duty of fair dealing" which the management owes to the stockholders is violated if those in control of the corporation purchase its stock, even at a fair price, openly and without fraud. The Commission concluded that "honesty, full disclosure, and purchase at a fair price do not take the case outside the rule."

In reaching this result the Commission stated that it was merely applying "the broad equitable principles enunciated in the cases heretofore cited", namely, *Pepper v. Litton*, 308 U.S. 295, 60 S.Ct. 238, 84 L.Ed. 281; *Michoud v. Girod*, 4 How. 503, 557, 11 L.Ed. 1076; *Magruder v. Drury*, 235 U.S. 106, 119, 120, 35 S.Ct. 77, 81, 82, 59 L.Ed. 151; and *Meinhard v. Salmon*, 249 N.Y. 458, 164 N.E. 545, 62 A.L.R. 1. Its opinion plainly shows

---

who at the time of the merger—we gather from the record—had ceased to be an officer and director of the corporation, purchased in the open market approximately 1,700 shares.

Chenery Corp. v. SEC, 128 F.2d 303, 306 (D.C.Cir.1942).]

that the Commission purported to be acting only as it assumed a court of equity would have acted in a similar case. Since the decision of the Commission was explicitly based upon the applicability of principles of equity announced by courts, its validity must likewise be judged on that basis. The grounds upon which an administrative order must be judged are those upon which the record discloses that its action was based.

principles of equity

In confining our review to a judgment upon the validity of the grounds upon which the Commission itself based its action, we do not disturb the settled rule that, in reviewing the decision of a lower court, it must be affirmed if the result is correct "although the lower court relied upon a wrong ground or gave a wrong reason." *Helvering v. Gowran*, 302 U.S. 238, 245, 58 S.Ct. 154, 158, 82 L.Ed. 224. The reason for this rule is obvious. It would be wasteful to send a case back to a lower court to reinstate a decision which it had already made but which the appellate court concluded should properly be based on another ground within the power of the appellate court to formulate. But it is also familiar appellate procedure that where the correctness of the lower court's decision depends upon a determination of fact which only a jury could make but which has not been made, the appellate court cannot take the place of the jury. Like considerations govern review of administrative orders. If an order is valid only as a determination of policy or judgment which the agency alone is authorized to make and which it has not made, a judicial judgment cannot be made to do service for an administrative judgment. For purposes of affirming no less than reversing its orders, an appellate court cannot intrude upon the domain which Congress has exclusively entrusted to an administrative agency.

✳

If, therefore, the rule applied by the Commission is to be judged solely on the basis of its adherence to principles of equity derived from judicial decisions, its order plainly cannot stand. As the Commission concedes here, the courts do not impose upon officers and directors of a corporation any fiduciary duty to its stockholders which precludes them, merely because they are officers and directors, from buying and selling the corporation's stock. The cases upon which the Commission relied do not establish principles of law and equity which in themselves are sufficient to sustain its order. The only question in *Pepper v. Litton*, 308 U.S. 295, 60 S.Ct. 238, 84 L.Ed. 281, was whether claims obtained by the controlling stockholders of a bankrupt corporation were to be treated equally with the claims of other creditors where the evidence revealed "a scheme to defraud creditors * * *." Another case relied upon, *Woods v. City National Bank Co.*, 312 U.S. 262, 61 S.Ct. 493, 85 L.Ed. 820, held only that a bankruptcy court * * * could deny compensation to protective committees representing conflicting interests. *Michoud v. Girod*, 4 How. 503, 11 L.Ed. 1076, and *Magruder v. Drury*, 235 U.S. 106, 35 S.Ct. 77, 59 L.Ed. 151, dealt with the specific obligations of express trustees and not with those of persons in control of a corporate enterprise toward its stockholders.

Determination of what is "fair and equitable" calls for the application of ethical standards to particular sets of facts. But these standards are not static. In evolving standards of fairness and equity, the Commission is not bound by settled judicial precedents. Congress certainly did not mean to preclude the formulation by the Commission of standards expressing a more sensitive regard for what is right and what is wrong than those prevalent at the time the Public Utility Holding Company Act of 1935 became law. But the Commission did not in this case proffer new standards reflecting the experience gained by it in effectuating the legislative policy. On the contrary, it explicitly disavowed any purpose of going beyond those which the courts had theretofore recognized. Since the Commission professed to decide the case before it according to settled judicial doctrines, its action must be judged by the standards which the Commission itself invoked. And judged by those standards, *i.e.*, those which would be enforced by a court of equity, we must conclude that the Commission was in error in deeming its action controlled by established judicial principles.

But the Commission urges here that the order should nevertheless be sustained because "the effect of trading by management is not measured by the fairness of individual transactions between buyer and seller, but by its relation to the timing and dynamics of the reorganization which the management itself initiates and so largely controls." Its argument lays stress upon the "strategic position enjoyed by the management in this type of reorganization proceeding and the vesting in it of statutory powers available to no other representative of security holders". It contends that these considerations warrant the stern rule applied in this case since the Commission "has dealt extensively with corporate reorganizations, both under the Act, and other statutes entrusted to it", and "has, in addition, exhaustively studied protective and reorganization committees", and that the situation was therefore "peculiarly within the Commission's special administrative competence".

In determining whether to approve the plan of reorganization proposed by Federal's management, the Commission could inquire, under § 7(d)(6) and (e) of the Act, whether the proposal was "detrimental to the public interest or the interest of investors or consumers", and, under § 11(e), whether it was "fair and equitable". That these provisions were meant to confer upon the Commission broad powers for the protection of the public plainly appears from the reports of the Congressional committees in charge of the legislation * * *.

* * *

* * * [T]herefore, the Commission could take appropriate action for the correction of reorganization abuses found to be "detrimental to the public

interest or the interest of investors or consumers." It was entitled to take into account those more subtle factors in the marketing of utility company securities that gave rise to the very grave evils which the Public Utility Holding Act of 1935 was designed to correct * * *.

But the difficulty remains that the considerations urged here in support of the Commission's order were not those upon which its action was based. The Commission did not rely upon "its special administrative competence"; it formulated no judgment upon the requirements of the "public interest or the interest of investors or consumers" in the situation before it. Through its preoccupation with the special problems of utility reorganizations the Commission accumulates an experience and insight denied to others. Had the Commission, acting upon its experience and peculiar competence, promulgated a general rule of which its order here was a particular application, the problem for our consideration would be very different. Whether and to what extent directors or officers should be prohibited from buying or selling stock of the corporation during its reorganization, presents problems of policy for the judgment of Congress or of the body to which it has delegated power to deal with the matter. Abuse of corporate position, influence, and access to information may raise questions so subtle that the law can deal with them effectively only by prohibitions not concerned with the fairness of a particular transaction. But before transactions otherwise legal can be outlawed or denied their usual business consequences, they must fall under the ban of some standards of conduct prescribed by an agency of government authorized to prescribe such standards—either the courts or Congress or an agency to which Congress has delegated its authority. Congress itself did not proscribe the respondents' purchases of preferred stock in Federal. Established judicial doctrines do not condemn these transactions. Nor has the Commission, acting under the rule-making powers delegated to it by § 11(e), promulgated new general standards of conduct. It purported merely to be applying an existing judge-made rule of equity. The Commission's determination can stand, therefore, only if it found that the specific transactions under scrutiny showed misuse by the respondents of their position as reorganization managers, in that as such managers they took advantage of the corporation or the other stockholders or the investing public. The record is utterly barren of any such showing. Indeed, such a claim against the respondents was explicitly disavowed by the Commission.

* * *

Judged, therefore, as a determination based upon judge-made rules of equity, the Commission's order cannot be upheld. Its action must be measured by what the Commission did, not by what it might have done * * *. The Commission's action cannot be upheld merely because findings might have been made and considerations disclosed which would justify its order as an appropriate safeguard for the interests protected by the Act. There must be such a responsible finding. There is no such finding here.

* * * In finding that the Commission's order cannot be sustained, we are not imposing any trammels on its powers. We are not enforcing formal requirements. We are not suggesting that the Commission must justify its exercise of administrative discretion in any particular manner or with artistic refinement. We are not sticking in the bark of words. We merely hold that an administrative order cannot be upheld unless the grounds upon which the agency acted in exercising its powers were those upon which its action can be sustained.

Holding

The cause should therefore be remanded to the Court to Appeals with directions to remand to the Commission for such further proceedings, not inconsistent with this opinion, as may be appropriate.

So ordered.

MR. JUSTICE DOUGLAS took no part in the consideration and decision of this case.

MR. JUSTICE BLACK, with whom MR. JUSTICE REED and MR. JUSTICE MURPHY concur, dissenting.

* * *

I can see nothing improper in the Commission's findings and determinations. On the contrary, the rule they evolved appears to me to be a salutary one, adequately supported by cogent reasons and thoroughly consistent with the high standards of conduct which should be required of fiduciaries * * *.

* * *

That the Commission has chosen to proceed case by case rather than by a general pronouncement does not appear to me to merit criticism. The intimation is that the Commission can act only through general formulae rigidly adhered to. In the first place, the rule of the single case is obviously a general advertisement to the trade, and in the second place the briefs before us indicate that this is but one of a number of cases in which the Commission is moving to an identical result on a broad front. But aside from these considerations the Act gives the Commission wide powers to evolve policy standards, and this may well be done case by case, as under the Federal Trade Commission Act.

* * *

IN RE FEDERAL WATER SERVICE CORP.
Securities and Exchange Commission, 1945.
18 S.E.C. 231.

[On remand, the Chenery group proposed precisely the same plan that the Commission had rejected in the decision under review in *Chenery I*. The Commission again rejected the plan and reaffirmed its original order in a 30-page opinion. The following excerpt does not omit from those thirty pages any reference by the Commission to any legal authority in support of its decision.]

* * *

For the reasons stated hereafter, we are unable to find that the plan if amended as proposed would be "fair and equitable to the persons affected thereby" * * *.

We are led to this result not by proof that the interveners committed acts of conscious wrongdoing but by the character of the conflicting interests created by the intervenors' program of stock purchases carried out while plans for reorganization were under consideration * * *.

* * *

It is our view that no management of a holding company can engage in a program of buying its company's stock during the course of a reorganization under the Act, without raising the probability that in one way or another the personal interests it seeks to further through its program will be opposed to its duties to exercise disinterested judgment in matters pertaining to subsidiaries' accounting, budgetary and dividend policies, to present publicly an unprejudiced financial picture of the enterprise, and to effectuate a fair and feasible plan expeditiously. The natural inclination of any person to buy cheaply, coupled with the normal and extraordinary powers of a holding company management to further that objective by creating the conditions which make cheap buying possible during the course of a reorganization before us, are bound to create a risk— perhaps in some cases merely potential but in all cases very real—of harm to all of the company's public security holders whether or not they elect to sell. In such a case the managers are not buying merely against future market risks. They are buying against a reorganization which they themselves are planning, during a period in which they exercise, as far as the corporation is concerned, a dominant influence over most of the factors that affect the progress and outcome of the reorganization * * *.

* * *

* * * [W]e do not believe the statute limits our power and duty to withhold approval solely to cases in which someone is able to establish by affirmative evidence that actual misconduct accompanied such a conflict of interests * * *.

* * *

Turning now to the case before us the salient fact is, as the interveners have stated, that their primary object in buying the preferred stock of Federal was to <u>obtain the voting power</u> that was accruing to that stock through the reorganization, and to profit from their investment therein. This stock they had purchased in the market at prices that were depressed in relation to what they anticipated would be, and what in fact was, the earning and asset value of its reorganization equivalent. We think we need look no further than this.

* * *

The interveners urge that we have no alternative but to act first by general rule or published statement of policy if we are to act at all in a matter of this kind. The Supreme Court indicated the advisability of promulgating a general rule, though <u>we do not understand its opinion to hold that the absence of a preexisting rule is fatal to the decision we have reached</u>. Now that we have had the question sharply focused in this and other cases before us, and have had an extensive period in which to consider the problems involved, we may well decide that a general rule, with adequately flexible provisions, would be both practicable and desirable; but <u>we do not see how the promulgation of such a rule now or later would affect our duty to act by order in this case</u> in deciding whether this plan is fair and equitable and meets the other standards of the Act. We therefore <u>reserve</u> for further consideration the question whether or not a rule should be adopted.

CHENERY CORP. v. SEC
United States Court of Appeals, District of Columbia Circuit, 1946.
154 F.2d 6.

Before GRONER, CHIEF JUSTICE, and CLARK and WILBUR K. MILLER, ASSOCIATE JUSTICES.

GRONER, C.J.

* * *

* * * [T]he immediate question is whether the Commission's action in again outlawing petitioners' purchases of stocks, considered in the light of the Supreme Court's opinion, is a permissible exercise of administrative discretion * * *. <u>We are of opinion that its action cannot be sustained on that ground</u> * * *.

* * *

The Commission's position actually amounts to neither more nor less than a definite holding that purchases of stock of a corporation in process or reorganization are unlawful, when made by officers or employees of the corporation,—and this without regard to any factor of good or bad faith, or any other factor which might impute special knowledge, secret information, or indeed anything tending to show a lack of bona fides in the transaction * * *. In practical effect, therefore, the Commission now insists upon doing precisely what the Supreme Court said it could not do; that is to say, in applying to this specific case a standard which has never been promulgated, either by the Commission in its regulations or by legislative act, and which the Commission says can not fairly be generally applied.

* * *

In nothing we have said do we wish to be understood as expressing any opinion as to the right of the Commission under its broad powers to promulgate a rule of general application forbidding officers and directors of a corporation in process of reorganization from buying—and perhaps also from selling—securities of the corporation during the pendency of proceedings before the Commission. That question is not present in this case. What we do say is that, without such a rule, of which notice is given so that all may know of its existence, transactions in themselves fair and just and honest and in accord with traditional business practices, and which "Congress itself did not proscribe," and which "judicial doctrines do not condemn," may not properly be "outlawed or denied" their ordinary effect.

But here the Commission's position goes beyond the mere question of the necessity of a rule. It insists upon an absolute right to approve in one case and to refuse to approve in another. In says, quite frankly, that it would be inappropriate to condemn a transaction such as we have here in a case in which the cost of the security purchased was in excess of its reorganization value; and again that it might be inconvenient to apply it if to do so would embarrass the corporation's finances. These are but instances which demonstrate its claim to unfettered discretion, irrespective of adequate findings based upon a fair appraisal of the evidence. Nothing that we find in the opinion of the Supreme Court warrants such a conclusion and nothing could be more directly in conflict with the terms and spirit of the law.

SEC v. CHENERY CORP.

Supreme Court of the United States, 1947.
332 U.S. 194, 67 S.Ct. 1575, 91 L.Ed. 1995.

MR. JUSTICE MURPHY delivered the opinion of the Court.

This case is here for the second time. *In S.E.C. v. Chenery Corporation*, 318 U.S. 80, 63 S.Ct. 454, 87 L.Ed. 626, we held that an order of the *original holding*

Securities and Exchange Commission could not be sustained on the grounds upon which that agency acted. We therefore directed that the case be remanded to the Commission for such further proceedings as might be appropriate. On remand, the Commission reexamined the problem, recast its rationale and reached the same result. The issue now is whether the Commission's action is proper in light of the principles established in our prior decision.

ISSUE

When the case was first here, we emphasized a simple but fundamental rule of administrative law. That rule is to the effect that a reviewing court, in dealing with a determination or judgment which an administrative agency alone is authorized to make, must judge the propriety of such action solely by the grounds invoked by the agency. If those grounds are inadequate or improper, the court is powerless to affirm the administrative action by substituting what it considers to be a more adequate or proper basis. To do so would propel the court into the domain which Congress has set aside exclusively for the administrative agency.

We also emphasized in our prior decision an important corollary of the foregoing rule. If the administrative action is to be tested by the basis upon which it purports to rest, that basis must be set forth with such clarity as to be understandable. It will not do for a court to be compelled to guess at the theory underlying the agency's action; nor can a court be expected to chisel that which must be precise from what the agency has left vague and indecisive. In other words, 'We must know what a decision means before the duty becomes ours to say whether it is right or wrong.' *United States v. Chicago, M., St. P. & P.R. Co.*, 294 U.S. 499, 511, 55 S.Ct. 462, 467, 79 L.Ed. 1023.

Applying this rule and its corollary, the Court was unable to sustain the Commission's original action * * *.

* * *

The Court interpreted the Commission's order approving this amended plan as grounded solely upon judicial authority * * *.

* * *

The latest order of the Commission definitely avoids the fatal error of relying on judicial precedents which do not sustain it. This time, after a thorough reexamination of the problem in light of the purposes and standards of the Holding Company Act, the Commission has concluded that the proposed transaction is inconsistent with the standards of §§ 7 and 11 of the Act. It has drawn heavily upon its accumulated experience in dealing with utility reorganizations. And it has expressed its reasons with a clarity and thoroughness that admit of no doubt as to the underlying basis of its order.

The argument is pressed upon us, however, that the Commission was foreclosed from taking such a step following our prior decision. It is said that, in the absence of findings of conscious wrongdoing on the part of Federal's management, the Commission could not determine by an order in this particular case that it was inconsistent with the statutory standards to permit Federal's management to realize a profit through the reorganization purchases. All that it could do was to enter an order allowing an amendment to the plan so that the proposed transaction could be consummated. Under this view, the Commission would be free only to promulgate a general rule outlawing such profits in future utility reorganizations; but such a rule would have to be prospective in nature and have no retroactive effect upon the instant situation.

We reject this contention, for it grows out of a misapprehension of our prior decision and of the Commission's statutory duties. We held no more and no less than that the Commission's first order was unsupportable for the reasons supplied by that agency. But when the case left this Court, the problem whether Federal's management should be treated equally with other preferred stockholders still lacked a final and complete answer. It was clear that the Commission could not give a negative answer by resort to prior judicial declarations. And it was also clear that the Commission was not bound by settled judicial precedents in a situation of this nature. Still unsettled, however, was the answer the Commission might give were it to bring to bear on the facts the proper administrative and statutory considerations, a function which belongs exclusively to the Commission in the first instance * * *.

* * *

The absence of a general rule or regulation governing management trading during reorganization did not affect the Commission's duties in relation to the particular proposal before it. The Commission was asked to grant or deny effectiveness to a proposed amendment to Federal's reorganization plan whereby the management would be accorded parity treatment on its holdings. It could do that only in the form of an order, entered after a due consideration of the particular facts in light of the relevant and proper standards. That was true regardless of whether those standards previously had been spelled out in a general rule or regulation. Indeed, if the Commission rightly felt that the proposed amendment was inconsistent with those standards, an order giving effect to the amendment merely because there was no general rule or regulation covering the matter would be unjustified.

It is true that our prior decision explicitly recognized the possibility that the Commission might have promulgated a general rule dealing with this problem under its statutory rule-making powers, in which case the issue for our consideration would have been entirely different from that which did confront us. But we did not mean to imply thereby that the failure of the Commission to anticipate this problem and to promulgate a general rule withdrew all power from that agency to perform its statutory duty in this case. To hold that the Commission had no alternative in this proceeding but to approve the proposed transaction, while formulating any general rules it might desire for use in future cases of this nature, would be to stultify the administrative process. That we refuse to do.

Since the Commission, unlike a court, does have the ability to make new law prospectively through the exercise of its rule-making powers, it has less reason to rely upon *ad hoc* adjudication to formulate new standards of conduct within the framework of the Holding Company Act. The function of filling in the interstices of the Act should be performed, as much as possible, through this quasi-legislative promulgation of rules to be applied in the future. But any rigid requirement to that effect would make the administrative process inflexible and incapable of dealing with many of the specialized problems which arise. Not every principle essential to the effective administration of a statute can or should be cast immediately into the mold of a general rule. Some principles must await their own development, while others must be adjusted to meet particular, unforeseeable situations. In performing its important functions in these respects, therefore, an administrative agency must be equipped to act either by general rule or by individual order. To insist upon one form of action to the exclusion of the other is to exalt form over necessity.

In other words, problems may arise in a case which the administrative agency could not reasonably foresee, problems which must be solved despite the absence of a relevant general rule. Or the agency may not have had sufficient experience with a particular problem to warrant rigidifying its tentative judgment into a hard and fast rule. Or the problem may be so specialized and varying in nature as to be impossible of capture within the boundaries of a general rule. In those situations, the agency must retain power to deal with the problems on a case-to-case basis if the administrative process is to be effective. There is thus a very definite place for the case-by-case evolution of statutory standards. And the choice made between proceeding by general rule or by individual, *ad hoc* litigation is one that lies primarily in the informed discretion of the administrative agency.

Hence we refuse to say that the Commission, which had not previously been confronted with the problem of management trading during reorganization, was forbidden from utilizing this particular proceeding for announcing and applying a new standard of conduct. That such action might have a retroactive effect was not necessarily fatal to its validity. Every case of first impression has a retroactive effect, whether the new principle is announced by a court or by an administrative agency. But such retroactivity must be balanced against the mischief of producing a result which is contrary to a statutory design or to legal and equitable principles. If that mischief is greater than the ill effect of the retroactive application of a new standard, it is not the type of retroactivity which is condemned by law.

And so in this case, the fact that the Commission's order might retroactively prevent Federal's management from securing the profits and control which were the objects of the preferred stock purchases may well be outweighed by the dangers inherent in such purchases from the statutory standpoint. If that is true, the argument of retroactivity becomes nothing more than a claim that the Commission lacks power to enforce the standards of the Act in this proceeding. Such a claim deserves rejection.

The problem in this case thus resolves itself into a determination of whether the Commission's action in denying effectiveness to the proposed amendment to the Federal reorganization plan can be justified on the basis upon which it clearly rests. As we have noted, the Commission avoided placing its sole reliance on inapplicable judicial precedents. Rather it has derived its conclusions from the particular facts in the case, its general experience in reorganization matters and its informed view of statutory requirements * * *.

* * *

The purchase by a holding company management of that company's securities during the course of a reorganization may well be thought to be so fraught with danger as to warrant a denial of the benefits and profits accruing to the management. The possibility that such a stock purchase program will result in detriment to the public investors is not a fanciful one. The influence that program may have upon the important decisions to be made by the management during reorganization is not inconsequential. Since the officers and directors occupy fiduciary positions during this period, their actions are to be held to a higher standard than that imposed upon the general investing public. There is thus a reasonable basis for a value judgment that the benefits and profits accruing to the management from the stock purchases should be prohibited, regardless of the good faith involved. And it is a judgment that can justifiably be reached in terms of fairness and equitableness, to the end that the interests of the public, the investors and the consumers might be protected. But it is a judgment based upon public policy, a judgment which Congress has indicated is of the type for the Commission to make.

The Commission's conclusion here rests squarely in that area where administrative judgments are entitled to the greatest amount of weight by appellate courts. It is the product of administrative experience, appreciation of the complexities of the problem, realization of the statutory policies, and responsible treatment of the uncontested facts. It is the type of judgment which administrative agencies are best equipped to make and which justifies the use of the administrative process. Whether we agree or disagree with the result reached, it is an allowable judgment which we cannot disturb.

Reversed.

MR. JUSTICE BURTON concurs in the result.

THE CHIEF JUSTICE and MR. JUSTICE DOUGLAS took no part in the consideration or decision of this case.

MR. JUSTICE JACKSON [with whom MR. JUSTICE FRANKFURTER joins], dissenting.

The Court by this present decision sustains the identical administrative order which only recently it held invalid * * *. There being no change in the order, no additional evidence in the record and no amendment of relevant legislation, it is clear that there has been a shift in attitude between that of the controlling membership of the Court when the case was first here and that of those who have the power of decision on this second review.

I feel constrained to disagree with the reasoning offered to rationalize this shift. It makes judicial review of administrative orders a hopeless formality for the litigant, even where granted to him by Congress. It reduces the judicial process in such cases to a mere feint. While the opinion does not have the adherence of a majority of the full Court, if its pronouncements should become governing principles they would, in practice, put most administrative orders over and above the law.

I.

The essential facts are few and are not in dispute. This corporation filed with the Securities and Exchange Commission a voluntary plan of reorganization. While the reorganization proceedings were pending sixteen officers and directors bought on the open market about 7 ½% of the corporation's preferred stock. Both the Commission and the Court admit that these purchases were not forbidden by any law, judicial precedent, regulation or rule of the Commission. Nevertheless, the Commission has ordered these individuals to surrender their shares to the corporation at cost, plus 4% interest, and the Court now approves that order.

It is helpful, before considering whether this order is authorized by law, to reflect on what it is and what it is not. It is not conceivably a discharge of the Commission's duty to determine whether a proposed plan of reorganization would be "fair and equitable." It has nothing to do with the corporate structure, or the classes and amounts of stock, or voting rights or dividend preferences. It does not remotely affect the impersonal financial or legal factors of the plan. It is a personal deprivation denying particular persons the right to continue to own their stock and to exercise its privileges. Other persons who bought at the same time and price in the open market would be allowed to keep and convert their stock. Thus, the order is in no sense an exercise of the function of control over the terms and relations of the corporate securities.

Neither is the order one merely to regulate the future use of property. It literally takes valuable property away from its lawful owners for the benefit of other private parties without full compensation and the Court expressly approves the taking. It says that the stock owned by these persons is denied conversion along with similar stock owned by others * * *.

It should also be noted that neither the Court nor the Commission purports to adjudge a forfeiture of this property as a consequence of sharp dealing or breach of trust * * *.

II.

The reversal of the position of this Court is due to a fundamental change in prevailing philosophy. The basic assumption of the earlier opinion as therein stated was, *"But before transactions otherwise legal can be outlawed or denied their usual business consequences, they must fall under the ban of some standards of conduct prescribed by an agency of government authorized to prescribe such standards. . ."* Securities and Exchange Commission v. Chenery Corp., 318 U.S. 80, 92, 93, 63 S.Ct. 454, 461, 87 L.Ed. 626. The basic assumption of the present opinion is stated thus: *"The absence of a general rule or regulation governing management trading during reorganization did not affect the Commission's duties in relation to the particular proposal before it."* This puts in juxtaposition the two conflicting philosophies which produce opposite results in the same case and on the same facts. The difference between the first and the latest decision of the Court is thus simply the difference between holding that administrative orders must have a basis in law and a holding that absence of a legal basis is no ground on which courts may annul them.

As there admittedly is no law or regulation to support this order we peruse the Court's opinion diligently to find on what grounds it is now held that the Court of Appeals, on pain of being reversed for error, was required to stamp this order with its approval. We find but one. That is the principle of judicial deference to administrative experience. That argument is five times stressed in as many different contexts * * *.

What are we to make of this reiterated deference to "administrative experience" when in another context the Court says, "Hence we refuse to say that the Commission, *which had not previously been confronted with the problem of management trading during reorganization,* was forbidden from utilizing this particular proceeding for announcing and applying *a new standard of conduct.*"? (Emphasis supplied.)

The Court's reasoning adds up to this: The Commission must be sustained because of its accumulated experience in solving a problem with which it had never before been confronted!

Of course, thus to uphold the Commission by professing to find that it has enunciated a "new standard of conduct," brings the Court squarely against the invalidity of retroactive law-making. But the Court does not falter. "That such action might have a retroactive effect was not necessarily fatal to its validity." "But such retroactivity must be balanced against the mischief of producing a result which is contrary to a statutory design or to legal and equitable principles." Of course, if what these parties did really was condemned by "statutory design" or "legal and equitable principles," it could be stopped without resort to a new rule and there would be no retroactivity to condone. But if it had been the Court's view that some law already prohibited the purchases, it would hardly have been necessary three sentences earlier to hold that the Commission was not prohibited "from utilizing this particular proceeding for announcing and applying a *new standard of conduct*." (Emphasis supplied.)

I give up. Now I realize fully what Mark Twain meant when he said, "The more you explain it, the more I don't understand it."

III.

* * *

Even if the Commission had, as the Court says, utilized this case to announce a new legal standard of conduct, there would be hurdles to be cleared, but we need not dwell on them now. Because to promulgate a general rule of law, either by regulation or by case law, is something the Commission expressly declined to do. It did not previously promulgate, and it does not by this order profess to promulgate, any rule or regulation to prohibit such purchases absolutely or under stated conditions. On the other hand, its position is that no such rule or standard would be fair and equitable in all cases.

IV.

Whether, as matter of policy, corporate managers during reorganization should be prohibited from buying or selling its stock, is not a question for us to decide. But it is for us to decide whether, so long as no law or regulation prohibits them from buying, their purchases may be forfeited, or not, in the discretion of the Commission. If such a power exists in words of the statute or in their implication, it would be possible to point it out and thus end the case. Instead, the Court admits that there was no law prohibiting these purchases when they were made, or at any time thereafter. And, except for this decision, there is none now.

The truth is that in this decision the Court approves the Commission's assertion of power to govern the matter *without* law, power to force surrender of stock so purchased whenever it will, <u>and power also to overlook such acquisitions if it so chooses</u>. The reasons which will lead it to take one course as against the other remain locked in its own breast, and it has not and apparently does not intend to commit them to any rule or regulation. This administrative authoritarianism, this power to decide without law, is what the Court seems to approve in so many words * * *.

V.

The Court's averment concerning this order that "It is the type of judgment which administrative agencies are best equipped to make and which justifies the use of the administrative process," is the first instance in which the administrative process is sustained by reliance on that disregard of law which enemies of the process have always alleged to be its principal evil. <u>It is the first encouragement this Court has given to conscious lawlessness as a permissible rule of administrative action</u>. This decision is an ominous one to those who believe that men should be governed by laws that they may ascertain and abide by, and which will guide the action of those in authority as well as of those who are subject to authority.

I have long urged, and still believe, that the administrative process deserves fostering in our system as an expeditious and nontechnical method of *applying law* in specialized fields. I can not agree that it be used, and I think its continued effectiveness is endangered when it is used, as a method of *dispensing with law* in those fields.

NOTES

Epilogue. After the events of *Chenery II*, Federal Water & Gas Corp. dissolved and its assets were distributed to shareholders and creditors. The Chenery group sought to participate in the dissolution as shareholders, but the SEC ruled that they could participate only as creditors. The Chenery group once again appealed. The court of appeals held that the Chenery group's status had been finally determined in the prior proceeding and that reconsideration was barred by res judicata. One argument advanced by the Chenery group, however, bears mention.

> The Chenery group strongly urges that the rule which the Commission drew from the Act and which it held denied them the right to participate in the merger as stockholders, has subsequently been rejected by the Commission and *has never been applied by it in any later reorganization*. Accordingly, they urge, it should not be applied here. This argument, however, while it has its appeal, is not available to defeat the operation of the rule of res judicata since the effect of a final judgment may not be avoided on any such ground as this. On the contrary it is settled that a judgment of a court of competent jurisdiction, once final, is binding under the rules of res judicata even though it was based upon a patently erroneous view of

the law. A fortiori, if all that appears is that there has been a subsequent change in the law.

In re Federal Water & Gas Corp., 188 F.2d 100, 105 (3d Cir.) (emphasis added), *cert. denied*, 341 U.S. 953, 71 S.Ct. 1018, 95 L.Ed. 1375 (1951).

2. THE LAW OF *CHENERY I*

The Supreme Court in the first *Chenery* decision ("*Chenery I*") emphasized that judicial review of agency decisions differs from review of lower court decisions in one important respect. Parties seeking to defend a lower court judgment are not bound to defend the reasoning of the lower court. Lower court judgments can be sustained on any grounds properly supported by the record, even if the lower court expressly rejected those grounds. Agency decisions, however, can be sustained only on the grounds specifically relied upon by the agencies. The agency decisionmakers at the time of their decision, not the agency's lawyers on appeal, determine the basis on which agency action must be judged. As the Supreme Court stated in oft-quoted language, courts "may not accept appellate counsel's post-hoc rationalizations for agency action." *Burlington Truck Lines, Inc. v. United States*, 371 U.S. 156, 168, 83 S.Ct. 239, 9 L.Ed.2d 207 (1962). This principle is sometimes known as "the *Chenery I* principle." It remains a bedrock principle of federal administrative law, applicable both to adjudications (the setting of *Chenery I*) and to rulemakings.

Despite the clarity of *Chenery I*'s warning against defending agency decisions on grounds not relied on by the agency, parties seeking affirmance of agency decisions violate the *Chenery I* principle with considerable abandon. In a survey done before the first edition of this book, at least eleven reported court of appeals decisions from the period January 1996 through July 1997 invoked the *Chenery I* principle against often blatant efforts by parties to advance reasons for affirmance of agency decisions that were not relied upon by the agency. *See, e.g., Graceba Total Communications v. FCC*, 115 F.3d 1038, 1041 (D.C.Cir.1997) ("Whatever the force of this reasoning, like so many of the Commission's arguments in its brief, it appears nowhere in the Commission's order. As the Supreme Court has made clear, we 'may not accept appellate counsel's post hoc rationalizations for agency action,' *Burlington Truck Lines*, 371 U.S. at 168, 83 S.Ct. at 246, and are 'powerless to affirm' agency action on 'grounds [that] are inadequate or improper.' *SEC v. Chenery Corp.*, 332 U.S. 194, 196, 67 S.Ct. 1575, 1577, 91 L.Ed. 1995 (1947).") A quick-and-dirty check on June 18, 2009, consisting of nothing more sophisticated than a WESTLAW search for "Chenery," disclosed half a dozen flagrant *Chenery I* violations in the first half of 2009 alone. The actual number is surely much higher, as many cases applying the *Chenery I* principle cite subsequent cases rather than *Chenery*. *See, e.g., LePage's 2000, Inc. v. Postal Regulatory Commission*, 642 F.3d 225, 231 (D.C.Cir.2011); *NRDC v.*

U.S. EPA, 658 F.3d 200, 217 (2d Cir.2011). The pace of "*Chenery I*" violations does not seem to have abated since then. *See, e.g., Fibertower Spectrum Holdings, LLC v. FCC*, 782 F.3d 692, 700 (D.C.Cir.2015); *NRDC v. EPA*, 755 F.3d 1010, 1020–21 (D.C.Cir.2014).

On some occasions, these efforts to avoid the *Chenery I* principle are successful. Courts will sometimes refuse to send the case back to the agency when the outcome on remand seems clear and further proceedings would be futile. *See, e.g., Envirocare of Utah, Inc. v. NRC*, 194 F.3d 72 (D.C.Cir.1999); *Yang v. INS*, 109 F.3d 1185 (7th Cir.1997); *NLRB v. American Geri-Care, Inc.*, 697 F.2d 56 (2d Cir.1982). More specifically, affirmance on newly raised grounds is warranted where the agency's result was mandated by law, because in such a case the agency has no discretion to do anything other than reach the legally mandated result. *See Morgan Stanley Capital Group, Inc. v. Public Utility District No. 1 of Snohomish County*, 554 U.S. 527, 544–45, 128 S.Ct. 2733, 2745, 171 L.Ed.2d 607 (2008) (the Federal Energy Regulatory Commission ("FERC") changed its rationale on appeal in apparent violation of *Chenery I*, "but FERC has lucked out: The *Chenery* doctrine has no application to these cases, because we conclude that the Commission was *required* * * * to apply the *Mobile-Sierra* presumption in its evaluation of the contracts here. That it provided a different rationale for the necessary result is no cause for upsetting its ruling"). The Federal Circuit, especially in patent cases, has long held *Chenery* inapplicable whenever the case turns on issues of law rather than on factual issues. *See In re Aoyama*, 656 F.3d 1293, 1299 (Fed.Cir.2011); *In re Comiskey*, 554 F.3d 967, 974–75 (Fed. Cir.2009). On other occasions, courts sometimes engage in creative interpretation of agency decisions in order to find that agencies in fact adopted the reasoning advanced in court by appellate counsel. *See, e.g., RNS Services, Inc. v. Secretary of Labor*, 115 F.3d 182 (3d Cir.1997). For the most part, however, the *Chenery* principle effectively, and powerfully, limits the defense of agency decisions to the grounds actually relied upon by the agencies.

There are two important corollaries of the *Chenery* principle. The first concerns the appropriate remedy when an agency decision cannot be supported on the grounds advanced by the agency. The usual remedy is to remand the case back to the agency for further consideration rather than to reverse the agency outright. *See I.N.S. v. Ventura*, 537 U.S. 12, 123 S.Ct. 353, 154 L.Ed.2d 272 (2002). If there are grounds that could support the agency's decision but were not in fact relied on by the agency, courts ordinarily give the agency the option to rely on those grounds. The second corollary is that the rationale for the agency's decision must be clear: courts must understand the agency's reasons for action before they can decide whether those reasons are adequate. Courts, however, generally do not enforce this requirement with much rigor. As the Supreme Court has said in oft-quoted language, "[w]hile we may not supply a reasoned basis for the

[handwritten margin note: note: Chenery I does not apply where agency's result was mandated by law] agency's action that the agency itself has not given, we will uphold a decision of less than ideal clarity if the agency's path may reasonably be discerned." *Bowman Transportation, Inc. v. Arkansas-Best Freight System, Inc.*, 419 U.S. 281, 285–86, 95 S.Ct. 438, 42 L.Ed.2d 447 (1974). *See Press Communications, LLC v. FCC,* 875 F.3d 1117, 1122 (D.C.Cir.2017) ("The FCC's discussion * * * is admittedly sparse, but * * * [w]e can reasonably discern the Bureau's path"). Even a rationale that the agency never articulated can be a basis for affirmance if it is clear that the rationale actually underlaid the agency's decision. *See National R.R. Passenger Corp. v. Boston & Maine Corp.*, 503 U.S. 407, 420, 112 S.Ct. 1394, 1403, 118 L.Ed.2d 52 (1992) (affirming, by a 6–3 vote, an agency interpretation of a statute that was never expressly advanced by the agency in its decision because "the only reasonable reading of the agency's opinion, and the only plausible explanation of the issues that the agency addressed after considering the factual submissions by all of the parties, is that the ICC's decision was based on the proffered interpretation.").

3.   THE LAW OF *CHENERY II*

a.   Too Much Adjudication?

The *Chenery I* decision, and the lower court decisions throughout the *Chenery* proceedings, strongly suggested that the SEC could create a new principle of law only through rulemaking. The Supreme Court's second *Chenery* decision (*Chenery II*) flatly rejected that suggestion, holding that "the choice made between proceeding by general rule or by individual, ad hoc litigation is one that lies primarily in the informed discretion of the administrative agency." This, too, remains a bedrock principle of federal administrative law—though, as with the *Chenery I* principle, it displays a few fault lines.

"Over the years, commentators, judges, and Justices have shown near unanimity in extolling the virtues of the rulemaking process over the process of making 'rules' through case-by-case adjudication."[47] Kenneth Culp Davis & Richard J. Pierce, Jr., I Administrative Law Treatise § 6.7, at 261 (3d ed. 1994). Rulemaking is generally viewed as a fairer, more efficient process than adjudication for the formulation of new legal standards. One might expect this consensus to generate considerable pressure for courts to require agencies to proceed by rulemaking in many instances in which they have that option.[48] *Chenery II*'s statement that the choice between rulemaking and adjudication "lies primarily in the informed discretion of the administrative agency" left two openings for

---

[47] One can add "legislators" to this list, as Congress sometimes *requires* agencies to proceed by rulemaking.

[48] Obviously, agencies only have the choice to engage in rulemaking if their organic statutes confer rulemaking authority upon them.

courts that might wish to impose such a requirement. First, the choice between rulemaking and adjudication is "primarily", not "exclusively," left to agency discretion; *Chenery II* clearly contemplates some judicial role in policing the agencies' choices. Second, as we will later see in detail, if a court characterizes an agency's exercise of discretion, such as a choice between adjudication and rulemaking, as an *abuse* of that discretion, courts are generally empowered to overturn such choices. Thus, *Chenery II* left ample legal materials from which courts could have fashioned a fairly wide-ranging requirement that agencies employ rulemaking.

Courts, however, have not generally utilized the openings left by *Chenery II*. Apart from some dictum in one Supreme Court decision, *see Morton v. Ruiz*, 415 U.S. 199, 236, 94 S.Ct. 1055, 1075, 39 L.Ed.2d 270 (1974), and one rogue holding by a court of appeals panel that has not been followed by any other federal court, *see Ford Motor Co. v. FTC*, 673 F.2d 1008 (9th Cir.1981), caselaw clearly supports a very wide agency power to choose its mode of proceeding. In 1974, the Supreme Court soundly reaffirmed *Chenery II*'s strong language. *See NLRB v. Bell Aerospace Co.*, 416 U.S. 267, 294, 94 S.Ct. 1757, 1771, 40 L.Ed.2d 134 (1974) ("the Board is not precluded from announcing new principles in an adjudicative proceeding and * * * the choice between rulemaking and adjudication lies in the first instance within the Board's discretion."). Any claim that an agency has abused its discretion by choosing to make policy through adjudication rather than rulemaking is unlikely to succeed.[49]

b. Too Much Rulemaking?

Chenery II makes it difficult to complain about an agency's choice to make policy through adjudication rather than rulemaking. Can one ever complain about an agency's choice to proceed through rulemaking rather than adjudication? Suppose that an organic statute guarantees you a right to a formal adjudicatory hearing on an application for a broadcast license. The Federal Communications Commission then adopts a rule declaring that no one who already owns more than five broadcasting stations will receive any further licenses. You own more than five stations, and your application is summarily dismissed on that basis. No hearing is held, because there are no facts to find or issues to resolve. Can the Commission do this?

The answer is obviously yes. *See United States v. Storer Broadcasting Co.*, 351 U.S. 192, 205, 76 S.Ct. 763, 771, 100 L.Ed. 1081 (1956). An important purpose of rules is to resolve classes of cases on the basis of

---

[49] Other arguments for a rulemaking requirement are possible but also unlikely to succeed. Some courts have suggested that constitutional due process may require agencies to use rulemaking to cabin their discretion. *See, e.g.*, Holmes v. New York City Housing Authority, 398 F.2d 262, 265 (2d Cir.1968). Modern due process law probably renders this kind of claim near-frivolous. A few other courts have creatively (mis)construed organic statutes to require rulemaking. *See, e.g.*, Curry v. Block, 738 F.2d 1556 (11th Cir.1984).

certain identifiable considerations, such as the number of broadcast stations owned by license applicants. If the rule is within the agency's substantive power, that would seem to be the end of the matter. The Supreme Court appears to have said as much: "even if a statutory scheme requires individualized determinations, the decisionmaker has the authority to rely on rulemaking to resolve certain issues of general applicability unless Congress clearly expresses an intent to withhold that authority." *American Hosp. Ass'n v. NLRB*, 499 U.S. 606, 612, 111 S.Ct. 1539, 1543, 113 L.Ed.2d 675 (1991). But are there any limits to an agency's ability to resolve issues by rule rather than by consideration of individualized facts?

In 1978, the Social Security Administration adopted guidelines for determining eligibility for social security disability benefits. The guidelines

> consist of a matrix of the four factors identified by Congress—physical ability, age, education, and work experience—and set forth rules that identify whether jobs requiring specific combinations of these factors exist in significant numbers in the national economy. Where a claimant's qualifications correspond to the job requirements identified by a rule,[5] the guidelines direct a conclusion as to whether work exists that the claimant could perform. If such work exists, the claimant is not considered disabled.

Heckler v. Campbell, 461 U.S. 458, 461–62, 103 S.Ct. 1952, 1954–55, 76 L.Ed.2d 66 (1983). A disappointed claimant objected that the statute required consideration of each applicant's individual circumstances. The Supreme Court did not disagree, but found use of the guidelines consistent with that statutory command.

> We do not think that the Secretary's reliance on medical-vocational guidelines is inconsistent with the Social Security Act. It is true that the statutory scheme contemplates that disability hearings will be individualized determinations based on evidence adduced at a hearing. See 42 U.S.C. § 423(d)(2)(A) (specifying consideration of each individual's condition); 42 U.S.C. § 405(b) (1976 ed., Supp. V) (disability determination to be based on evidence adduced at hearing). But this does not bar the Secretary from relying on rulemaking to resolve certain classes of issues. The Court has recognized that even where an agency's enabling statute expressly requires it to hold a hearing, the agency may

---

[5]   The regulations recognize that the rules only describe "major functional and vocational patterns." If an individual's capabilities are not described accurately by a rule, the regulations make clear that the individual's particular limitations must be considered. Additionally, the regulations declare that the Administrative Law Judge will not apply the age categories "mechanically in a borderline situation," and recognize that some claimants may possess limitations that are not factored into the guidelines. Thus, the regulations provide that the rules will be applied only when they describe a claimant's abilities and limitations accurately.

rely on its rulemaking authority to determine issues that do not require case-by-case consideration. *See FPC v. Texaco, Inc.*, 377 U.S. 33, 41–44, 84 S.Ct. 1105, 1110–1112, 12 L.Ed.2d 112 (1964); *United States v. Storer Broadcasting Co.*, 351 U.S. 192, 205, 76 S.Ct. 763, 771, 100 L.Ed. 1081 (1956). A contrary holding would require the agency continually to relitigate issues that may be established fairly and efficiently in a single rulemaking proceeding.

The Secretary's decision to rely on medical-vocational guidelines is consistent with *Texaco* and *Storer*. As noted above, in determining whether a claimant can perform less strenuous work, the Secretary must make two determinations. She must assess each claimant's individual abilities and then determine whether jobs exist that a person having the claimant's qualifications could perform. The first inquiry involves a determination of historic facts, and the regulations properly require the Secretary to make these findings on the basis of evidence adduced at a hearing. We note that the regulations afford claimants ample opportunity both to present evidence relating to their own abilities and to offer evidence that the guidelines do not apply to them.[11] The second inquiry requires the Secretary to determine an issue that is not unique to each claimant—the types and numbers of jobs that exist in the national economy. This type of general factual issue may be resolved as fairly through rulemaking as by introducing the testimony of vocational experts at each disability hearing.

As the Secretary has argued, the use of published guidelines brings with it a uniformity that previously had been perceived as lacking. To require the Secretary to relitigate the existence of jobs in the national economy at each hearing would hinder needlessly an already overburdened agency. We conclude that the Secretary's use of medical-vocational guidelines does not conflict with the statute, nor can we say on the record before us that they are arbitrary and capricious.

Campbell, 461 U.S. at 467–68, 103 S.Ct. at 1957–58.

Campbell emphasizes, as did the Court's prior cases, that the rules in question were not applied inflexibly. Rather, applicants were allowed to demonstrate that the rules should not be applied to them if the rules did

---

[11] Both *FPC v. Texaco, Inc.*, 377 U.S. 33, 40, 84 S.Ct. 1105, 1109, 12 L.Ed.2d 112 (1964), 40, 84 S.Ct. 1105, 1109, 12 L.Ed.2d 112 (1964), and *United States v. Storer Broadcasting Co.*, 351 U.S. 192, 205, 76 S.Ct. 763, 771, 100 L.Ed. 1081 (1956), were careful to note that the statutory scheme at issue allowed an individual applicant to show that the rule promulgated should not be applied to him. The regulations here provide a claimant with equal or greater protection since they state that an Administrative Law Judge will not apply the rules contained in the guidelines when they fail to describe a claimant's particular limitations.

not fairly reflect the applicants' situations. But what if the rules contain no such escape clause? Rules by definition focus on certain abstract features of fact situations and will therefore almost always be over-or under-inclusive. Many of the benefits of rules are lost if rules must precisely mirror the results that would be reached in case-by-case adjudications. How accurate do rules have to be, and are agencies obliged to provide mechanisms for waiving application of rules if they deviate too far from reality?

We do not have good answers to either question. With regard to the latter, the Supreme Court has noted in passing that none of its decisions squarely holds that an agency "may never adopt a rule that lacks a waiver provision," *FCC v. WNCN Listeners Guild*, 450 U.S. 582, 601 n.44, 101 S.Ct. 1266, 1277 n.44, 67 L.Ed.2d 521 (1981). The statement is a thin reed on which to rest any strong claims about the law. *Compare Macon County Samaritan Memorial Hosp. v. Shalala*, 7 F.3d 762, 768 (8th Cir.1993) ("bright-line tests are a fact of regulatory life, and the Supreme Court has declined to hold that an agency may never adopt a rule that lacks a waiver provision") *with Thomas Radio Co. v. FCC*, 716 F.2d 921, 925 (D.C.Cir.1983) ("Because the FCC did not adopt an absolute no-waiver policy in the context of dual city coverage requirements, we need not decide whether such a policy, if adopted, would be so inflexible as to constitute an abuse of agency discretion.").

Any discussion of the degree of precision required of rules must await consideration in Chapter 4 of the standards governing substantive review of agency decisions. For now, it suffices to say that rules must generally be reasonable, and their degree of over-and under-inclusiveness is an important aspect of reasonableness. With one very notable exception, *see* Colin Diver, *The Optimal Precision of Administrative Rules*, 93 Yale L.J. 65 (1983), scholars have had little to say on the subject.

4.   A NOTE ON RETROACTIVITY

The new principle of law devised by the Commission in the *Chenery* proceedings was applied to the Chenery group retroactively, in the sense that no enunciated principle of law prohibited or penalized their stock purchases at the time they were made. Adjudications, whether by courts or agencies, generally operate retroactively in this fashion. For many centuries, the justification for this practice was that adjudicators found rather than made law. When they applied their announced rules to the parties, there was therefore no retroactivity; the governing law already existed and was merely being articulated by the adjudicator. That justification is transparently false in many modern settings. Agencies, in particular, often make new policy through adjudications and then apply those new principles to the parties before them. *Chenery II* suggested that such retroactivity is generally permitted whenever viewed by the agency as appropriate. Modern courts are less accommodating to agencies, though it is unclear how much less:

> * * * [T]here is a robust doctrinal mechanism for alleviating the hardships that may befall regulated parties who rely on "quasi-judicial" determinations that are altered by subsequent agency action * * *.

In the ensuing years [after *Chenery II*], in considering whether to give retroactive application to a new rule, the courts have held that

> [t]he governing principle is that when there is a "substitution of new law for old law that was reasonably clear," the new rule may justifiably be given prospectively-only effect in order to "protect the settled expectations of those who had relied on the preexisting rule." *Williams Natural Gas Co. v. FERC*, 3 F.3d 1544, 1554 (D.C.Cir.1993). By contrast, retroactive effect is appropriate for "new applications of [existing] law, clarifications, and additions." *Id.*

Pub. Serv. Co. of Colo. v. FERC, 91 F.3d 1478, 1488 (D.C.Cir.1996). In a case in which there is a "substitution of new law for old law that was reasonably clear," a decision to deny retroactive effect is uncontroversial. In cases in which there are "new applications of existing law, clarifications, and additions," the courts start with a presumption in favor of retroactivity. However, retroactivity will be denied "when to apply the new rule to past conduct or to prior events would work a 'manifest injustice.'" *Clark-Cowlitz Joint Operating Agency v. FERC*, 826 F.2d 1074, 1081 (D.C.Cir.1987) (en banc).

This court has not been entirely consistent in enunciating a standard to determine when to deny retroactive effect in cases involving "new applications of existing law, clarifications, and additions" resulting from adjudicatory actions. In *Clark-Cowlitz*, the *en banc* court adopted a non-exhaustive five-factor balancing test, *see* 826 F.2d at 1081–86 (citing *Retail, Wholesale & Dep't Store Union, AFL-CIO v. NLRB*, 466 F.2d 380, 390 (D.C.Cir.1972)).[50] In a subsequent case, however, we substituted a similar three-factor test. *See Dist. Lodge 64 v. NLRB*, 949 F.2d 441, 447–49 (D.C.Cir.1991). And in other cases, the court has jettisoned multi-pronged balancing approaches altogether. *See*

---

[50] [Editor's note: the five non-exhaustive factors were "(1) whether the particular case is one of first impression, (2) whether the new rule represents an abrupt departure from well established practice or merely attempts to fill a void in an unsettled area of law, (3) the extent to which the party against whom the new rule is applied relied on the former rule, (4) the degree of the burden which a retroactive order imposes on a party, and (5) the statutory interest in applying a new rule despite the reliance of a party on the old standard." 466 F.2d at 390.]

Cassell v. FCC, 154 F.3d 478, 486 (D.C.Cir.1998) (declining to "plow laboriously" through the *Clark-Cowlitz* factors, which "boil down to a question of concerns grounded in notions of equity and fairness").

Verizon Telephone Companies v. FCC, 269 F.3d 1098, 1109–10 (D.C.Cir.2001).

What about retroactive rulemaking? The Constitution flatly prohibits either Congress or the states from enacting ex post facto laws, *see* U.S. Const. art. I, § 9, cl. 3 (Congress); *id.* art. I, § 10, cl. 1 (states), but those prohibitions have long been understood to apply only to criminal laws. *See Calder v. Bull*, 3 U.S. (3 Dall.) 386, 1 L.Ed. 648 (1798). In the civil context, retroactive imposition of liability is generally permitted, *see Pension Benefit Guaranty Corp. v. R.A. Gray & Co.*, 467 U.S. 717, 104 S.Ct. 2709, 81 L.Ed.2d 601 (1984), but is strongly disfavored by rules of construction that require clear statements of legislative intent to alter preexisting rights. *See Landgraf v. USI Film Products*, 511 U.S. 244, 114 S.Ct. 1483, 128 L.Ed.2d 229 (1994). Do—and should—the same principles apply to agency rulemaking?

In *Bowen v. Georgetown University Hospital*, 488 U.S. 204, 109 S.Ct. 468, 102 L.Ed.2d 493 (1988), the Supreme Court answered directly:

> Retroactivity is not favored in the law. Thus, congressional enactments and administrative rules will not be construed to have retroactive effect unless their language requires this result. By the same principle, a statutory grant of legislative rulemaking authority will not, as a general matter, be understood to encompass the power to promulgate retroactive rules unless that power is conveyed by Congress in express terms. See *Brimstone R. Co. v. United States*, 276 U.S. 104, 122 (1928) ("The power to require readjustments for the past is drastic. It . . . ought not to be extended so as to permit unreasonably harsh action without very plain words"). Even where some substantial justification for retroactive rulemaking is presented, courts should be reluctant to find such authority absent an express statutory grant.

488 U.S. at 208–09, 109 S.Ct. at 471. Justice Scalia, in a concurring opinion, found additional support for this position in the APA's definition of a rule as a statement of "future effect." *Id.* at 216–20, 109 S.Ct. at 475–477 (Scalia, J., concurring).

Notwithstanding this seemingly strong presumption against finding grants of retroactive rulemaking authority, it has been held (over vigorous protest) that implicit authority to issue retroactive rules can be found in the structure of statutes, without need for a clear congressional grant of such authority. *See Nat'l Petrochemical & Refiners Ass'n v. EPA*, 630 F.3d 145, 162–66 (D.C.Cir.2010) (finding such authority); *Nat'l Petrochemical &*

Refiners Ass'n v. EPA, 643 F.3d 958 (D.C.Cir.2011) (Brown, J., joined by Sentelle, C.J., dissenting from denial of rehearing en banc) (vigorously protesting). It is also sometimes far from obvious whether a rule operates retroactively. Certainly if a rule attaches legal consequences to past conduct, it is retroactive. But many rules change the *economic* consequences of past conduct without formally changing their *legal* consequences, and formally forward-looking rules can wreak havoc with settled expectations. For a careful discussion, see *Nat'l Petrochemical*, 630 F.3d at 159–62.

CHAPTER 4

SCOPE OF REVIEW OF AGENCY ACTION

▪ ▪ ▪

A. INTRODUCTION

1. DEGREES OF DEFERENCE

Quite often, the most important question for legal decisionmakers is how much weight, if any, they should give to the views of prior decisionmakers when reaching their own conclusions. Appellate courts do not always ask whether lower court judges got the right answers. On many occasions, appellate courts instead decide whether lower court determinations satisfy some minimal standard of reasonableness. For example, Federal Rule of Civil Procedure 52(a) states that findings of fact made by federal district courts in civil cases "shall not be set aside unless clearly erroneous, and due regard shall be given to the opportunity of the trial court to judge of the credibility of the witnesses." The Supreme Court has made clear that this standard can require appellate courts to accept findings of fact even when the appellate court, all things considered, would have reached a different result:

> Although the meaning of the phrase "clearly erroneous" is not immediately apparent, certain general principles governing the exercise of the appellate court's power to overturn findings of a district court may be derived from our cases. The foremost of these principles * * * is that "[a] finding is 'clearly erroneous' when although there is evidence to support it, the reviewing court on the entire evidence is left with the definite and firm conviction that a mistake has been committed." *United States v. United States Gypsum Co.*, 333 U.S. 364, 395, 68 S.Ct. 525, 542, 92 L.Ed. 746 (1948). This standard plainly does not entitle a reviewing court to reverse the finding of the trier of fact simply because it is convinced that it would have decided the case differently. The reviewing court oversteps the bounds of its duty under Rule 52(a) if it undertakes to duplicate the role of the lower court. "In applying the clearly erroneous standard to the findings of a district court sitting without a jury, appellate courts must constantly have in mind that their function is not to decide factual issues *de novo*." *Zenith Radio Corp. v. Hazeltine Research, Inc.*, 395 U.S. 100, 123, 89 S.Ct. 1562, 1576, 23 L.Ed.2d 129 (1969). If

[handwritten margin note: clearly erroneous standard]

the district court's account of the evidence is plausible in light of the record viewed in its entirety, the court of appeals may not reverse it even though convinced that had it been sitting as the trier of fact, it would have weighed the evidence differently. Where there are two permissible views of the evidence, the factfinder's choice between them cannot be clearly erroneous.

This is so even when the district court's findings do not rest on credibility determinations, but are based instead on physical or documentary evidence or inferences from other facts * * *.

The rationale for deference to the original finder of fact is not limited to the superiority of the trial judge's position to make determinations of credibility. The trial judge's major role is the determination of fact, and with experience in fulfilling that role comes expertise. Duplication of the trial judge's efforts in the court of appeals would very likely contribute only negligibly to the accuracy of fact determination at a huge cost in diversion of judicial resources. In addition, the parties to a case on appeal have already been forced to concentrate their energies and resources on persuading the trial judge that their account of the facts is the correct one; requiring them to persuade three more judges at the appellate level is requiring too much * * *. For these reasons, review of factual findings under the clearly-erroneous standard—with its deference to the trier of fact—is the rule, not the exception.

Anderson v. City of Bessemer City, N.C., 470 U.S. 564, 573–75, 105 S.Ct. 1504, 1511–1512, 84 L.Ed.2d 518 (1985). As the Supreme Court suggests, there are many reasons—reasons of expertise, economy, and fairness—why appellate courts will often give a degree of deference to the prior determinations of other tribunals. The mere fact that a decisionmaker has already decided a question often counts for a great deal in the law.

The "clearly erroneous" standard is only one manifestation of this principle of deference. When juries rather than trial courts have found facts, appellate courts are obliged to be even more deferential to those determinations: an appellate court may overturn a jury's factual conclusion only when no reasonable person could possibly have reached such a conclusion. The law does not have a catchy name for this standard of review, so we will simply call it "the jury standard."

On some occasions, appellate courts do directly substitute their judgment for that of the lower court. Most notably, appellate courts ordinarily review the legal determinations of lower courts *de novo*—that is, with no weight given to the fact that a prior determination has been made. *See Salve Regina College v. Russell*, 499 U.S. 225, 231, 111 S.Ct. 1217, 1221, 113 L.Ed.2d 190 (1991). But some legal determinations by trial courts receive substantial deference on appeal. Trial courts make numerous legal decisions concerning the propriety of preliminary injunctions, the admissibility of evidence, and the permissible structure of proof at trial that are reviewed by appellate courts only for *abuse of discretion*—a highly deferential standard that is more similar to the jury standard than to the clearly erroneous standard.

abuse of discretion [handwritten]

These standards of review can be placed on a scale running from the least deferential (de novo) to the most deferential (jury standard), with the "clearly erroneous" and "abuse of discretion" standards each falling somewhere between those two points. There is obviously no way to give numerical values to these standards, but they can be ranked ordinally: the clearly erroneous standard is more deferential than de novo review but less deferential than the abuse of discretion standard, which in turn is less deferential than the standard for review of jury factfinding. One might even be able to make comparative judgments—for example, that the abuse of discretion standard is "closer" to the jury standard than to the clearly erroneous standard.

Of course, these standards of review do not exhaust the universe of possible standards: one can imagine countless levels of deference ranging from no deference at all to absolute deference in which there is no possibility of reversal. But these four standards—de novo, clearly erroneous, abuse of discretion, and the jury standard—are the benchmarks that are most familiar in appellate review of court decisions.

One can readily imagine applying these familiar standards to appellate court review of *agency* decisionmaking. After all, many of the same considerations of expertise and economy that justify deferential review of some (but not other) lower court determinations seem to apply with just as much force to agency determinations. Thus, a perfectly sensible scheme of judicial review of administrative action could rely entirely on the existing benchmarks: agency legal conclusions could ordinarily be reviewed de novo, agency factual conclusions could be reviewed deferentially (whether on the clearly erroneous standard or the jury standard would be a matter of political choice), and agency exercises of discretion, including the formulation of policy under broad delegations from Congress, could be reviewed for abuse of discretion much as are discretionary decisions by trial courts.

For the most part, the contemporary system of judicial review of federal administrative agency action employs *none* of the benchmarks familiar from appellate review of lower court decisionmaking. The statement is remarkable enough to bear repetition: For the most part, the contemporary system of judicial review of federal administrative agency action employs *none* of the benchmarks familiar from appellate review of lower court decisionmaking. Instead, federal administrative law has developed its own unique set of standards for review. As you will see as this chapter unfolds, agency legal conclusions are generally reviewed deferentially rather than de novo, though the precise scope of that deference is ill-defined; agency factual conclusions have generally been reviewed deferentially, though under a standard that corresponds neither to the clearly erroneous standard nor to the jury standard; and agency exercises of discretion are reviewed deferentially, though the level and kind of deference varies enormously with the context and often has little in common with the abuse of discretion standard applicable to lower courts.

In each case, there are reasons why the system of administrative review has developed its own set of standards instead of co-opting the standards already available elsewhere in the legal system, though you will have to judge for yourself whether those reasons are persuasive. This chapter aims both to identify those reasons and to provide an overview of contemporary law. Accordingly, we will spend much of our time tracing the evolution of modern scope-of-review doctrine; we will examine the standards that have been rejected as well as the standards that the law has ultimately—at least for now—adopted. One cannot truly learn scope-of-review doctrine by memorizing verbal formulas; a decent grasp of the law in this area requires some understanding of the forces at work that have shaped, and continue to shape, the formulas.

2.   IS THIS FOR REAL?

The discussion thus far has tacitly assumed that scope of review doctrine—in administrative law and elsewhere—consists of a highly formalistic, categorical approach in which issues on review are classified as matters of fact, law, or discretion and an appropriate standard of review is then attached to each issue to establish the weight that the reviewing court should give to the views of a prior decisionmaker. This description raises both conceptual and empirical questions.

At the conceptual level, there are serious questions about whether either the scheme of classification or the array of standards makes any sense. Scholars have long argued that the distinction between issues of law and fact—much less the more complex distinction among issues of law, fact, and discretion—breaks down very quickly. Issues do not sort themselves neatly into prefabricated boxes of law, fact, or discretion. One does not have to look far for examples of difficult and pervasive problems: is the question whether a defendant in a tort suit was negligent a question of law, fact, or discretion? It would seem to be a legal question, in the sense that it requires application of abstract legal standards of care to particular facts, but for scope of review purposes the legal system generally assigns the determination of negligence to juries and then gives great weight to the jury determinations, effectively treating the conclusion of negligence as a species of factfinding.

Once one has successfully classified an issue, it is often unclear what to make of the law's prescribed standard of review. What does it mean to say that a conclusion is "clearly erroneous" or "an abuse of discretion"? How does one distinguish an erroneous conclusion from a clearly erroneous conclusion from a conclusion that represents an abuse of discretion from a conclusion that no reasonable person could reach? It is one thing to state a verbal formula representing a standard of review; it is another thing altogether to find something in reality to which that formula corresponds.

These conceptual questions spawn an empirical one: do courts actually perform appellate review, of either lower court or agency decisions, by categorizing issues and applying formulas? A substantial segment of the academic community thinks not. This skeptical view was well captured in 1975 by Professors Ernest Gellhorn and Glen Robinson in their oft-quoted suggestion "that the rules governing judicial review have no more substance at the core than a seedless grape." Ernest Gellhorn & Glen O. Robinson, *Perspectives in Administrative Law*, 75 Colum. L. Rev. 771, 780–81 (1975). According to different proponents of this skeptical view, when courts review agency decisions, they might simply substitute their views of good policy for the agency's, or they might decide based on the identity of the parties, or they might make judgments of the relative institutional competence of courts and agencies, or they might make even more complex judgments about the appropriate judicial role. But the skeptics all agree that the one thing that courts are not doing—and probably could not be doing even if they wanted to—is categorizing issues as law, fact, or discretion, applying a specified standard of review, and giving a degree of deference to the decision under review that corresponds to the standard.

Interestingly, one seldom hears *judges* express this kind of extreme skepticism about the doctrinal approach (as we will henceforth call it) to scope of review. On the contrary, judges generally profess to take the various deference formulas and classification schemes very seriously. For instance, in *Texas World Service Co., Inc. v. NLRB*, 928 F.2d 1426 (5th Cir.1991), an ALJ determined, as a matter of fact, that certain firms were not acting as joint employers. The National Labor Relations Board disagreed. The court of appeals affirmed the Board:

> Having read the ALJ's comprehensive opinion, we are not convinced that we would have found World, Whitewood, and Lucky to be joint employers had we been charged with determining that issue afresh. Certainly, had the clearly erroneous standard been the appropriate standard of review, the ALJ could not have been reversed. Nevertheless, we acknowledge that substantial evidence exists on the record considered as a whole to support the Board's findings.

928 F.2d at 1431. And in *Dickinson v. Zurko*, 527 U.S. 150, 119 S.Ct. 1816, 144 L.Ed.2d 143 (1999), the parties, the patent bar, the Federal Circuit Court of Appeals, and the Supreme Court devoted a great deal of energy—including, in the Supreme Court, a review of 89 pre-APA cases reviewing patent office decisions—to resolving the same seemingly metaphysical question whether the "clearly erroneous" standard or the "substantial evidence" standard applies to court review of factual findings by the Patent and Trademark Office. Everybody behaved as though this decision mattered in some important, even if small and unspecifiable, way.

It is possible, of course, that the judges and lawyers who profess to take scope of review categories and formulas seriously either misunderstand or misrepresent what they are doing. Indeed, there is some empirical support for a modest skepticism about scope-of-review standards, as at least one study shows that federal court affirmance rates of agencies are remarkably invariant across scope-of-review provisions, suggesting that perhaps a unitary standard of reasonableness rather than a mélange of differing standards is operative. *See* David Zaring, *Reasonable Agencies*, 96 Va. L. Rev. 135 (2010). One must, however, be very wary in this context of the fallacy of the hard case. There are certainly some instances in which application of the doctrinal approach to scope of review is very difficult, and there are certainly other instances in which such application is easy but judges choose to ignore (or at least willfully to misconstrue) the doctrine. No one contends that partisan politics, for example, never determines the outcomes in administrative law cases. But as you examine a large number of administrative law decisions—a far larger number than you will encounter in this course—you will (so your editor firmly believes) discover that in the vast run of routine cases that dominate the courts' and agencies' dockets, the doctrinal approach strongly influences the administrative process. And it is the routine rather than the exceptional cases that ought to be the basis for descriptions of the legal system.[1]

These materials take the doctrinal approach very seriously. So should you—even if you ultimately decide (as you might) that your editor is simply wrong about the way in which the legal system actually works. For whether they apply it conscientiously or simply invoke it as a pretense, agencies, lawyers, legislators, and judges clearly speak the doctrinal language of classification and standards. Indeed, the basic distinction between law and fact, which sophisticated academics will often tell you is a naive misconception, happens to be embodied in the United States Constitution[2]

---

[1] Exceptional cases, of course, tend to show up disproportionately in law school casebooks. That is true of this book as well, though it makes a conscious, determined effort to present at least some cases that are selected precisely for their routineness rather than their novelty.

[2] *See* U.S. Const. amend. VII ("In Suits at common law, where the value in controversy shall exceed twenty dollars, the right of trial by jury shall be preserved, and no *fact* tried by a jury, shall be otherwise re-examined in any Court of the United States, than according to the rules of the common law.") (emphasis added).

as well as in numerous statutes.[3] Many of the operative standards of review in administrative law are prescribed by statute; the APA, for example, instructs courts to ask whether certain agency decisions are "arbitrary, capricious, an abuse of discretion, or otherwise not in accordance with law," 5 U.S.C. § 706(2)(A) (2012), or "unsupported by substantial evidence," *id.* § 706(2)(E), and numerous other statutes contain similar instructions. Judicial opinions and lawyers' briefs are filled with discussions of the proper classification of questions and the appropriate standard of review for those questions. The language of judicial review of agency decisions is the language of classification and standards. You need to know that language in order to function effectively within the modern system of administrative law.

3. IS THERE A BETTER WAY?

The law may in fact speak the language of classification and standards, but does it have to do so? Are there other, and perhaps better, ways of structuring a scheme of appellate review of agency decisions?

There is a powerful alternative to the doctrinal approach that is known generally as the "legal process" approach.[4] This approach reasons that the purpose and function of appellate review, in administrative law and elsewhere, is to allocate decisionmaking responsibility between the initial and reviewing tribunals. Any system of review, including a system of classification and standards, will generate such an allocation, and the system is justifiable if and only if its allocation is a good one. But if the object of the enterprise is to reach a sensible allocation of responsibility between agencies and reviewing courts, why not ask *directly* which body is best suited to making the decision under review? A well-crafted system of classification and standards can and will reflect such judgments about relative institutional competence, and possibly reflect them quite effectively, but why not employ those judgments directly rather than filter them through a complicated scheme of classifications and standards? Accordingly, on this view, scope of review doctrine should self-consciously seek to determine whether, and to what degree, courts or agencies are best suited to decide the specific issue under review. The nature of the issue— whether it is one of law, fact, or discretion—may well be relevant to that determination, but it is not dispositive. Courts should consider the particular features, and not simply the general categorization, of the issue

---

[3] *See, e.g.*, 29 U.S.C. § 660(a) (2012) ("The findings of the Commission with respect to *questions of fact*, if supported by substantial evidence on the record considered as a whole, shall be conclusive.") (emphasis added); Fed. R. Civ. P. 52(a) ("In all actions tried upon the facts without a jury or with an advisory jury, the court shall find the facts specially and state separately its conclusions of law thereon.").

[4] This approach was perhaps most prominent at the Harvard Law School in the 1950s and 1960s, though its influence extended, and still extends, far beyond Cambridge, Massachusetts.

under review, as well as the particular features of the agency, court, and statute involved.

This is a very powerful theory (to which this discussion does not do justice), and it has had a significant measure of influence on modern law. A substantial number of scholars endorse it, and a substantial number of judges, agency officials, and practitioners were trained in it. You will see this "legal process," or "institutional competence," approach reflected in some of the cases in this chapter. Indeed, to a large extent, the doctrinal approach and legal process approach can and do peacefully coexist, as they prescribe precisely the same results in a vast range of cases. Nonetheless, there are some important instances in which the legal process and doctrinal approaches lead in different directions. For the most part, the doctrinal approach has prevailed in such cases,[5] though it would be unwise to conclude that the battle is over. The story of federal administrative law has been the story of change—and much of that change has centered on scope-of-review doctrine.

B. REVIEW OF FINDINGS OF FACT IN FORMAL PROCEEDINGS

5 U.S.C. § 706
(2012).

* * * The reviewing court shall * * * (2) hold unlawful and set aside agency action, findings, and conclusions found to be * * * (E) unsupported by substantial evidence in a case subject to sections 556 and 557 of this title or otherwise reviewed on the record of an agency hearing provided by statute * * *. In making the foregoing determinations, the court shall review the whole record or those parts of it cited by a party, and due account shall be taken of the rule of prejudicial error.

UNITED STATES DEP'T OF JUSTICE, ATTORNEY GENERAL'S MANUAL ON THE ADMINISTRATIVE PROCEDURE ACT
109 (1947).

* * * [Section 706(2)(E)] is a general codification of the substantial evidence rule which, either by statute or judicial rule, has long been applied

---

[5] It is difficult to say definitively why the doctrinal approach has prevailed. The doctrinal approach gives more of an appearance of objectivity and constraint, though in reality application of the various standards of review is probably no more objective and constraining than would be application of an "institutional competence" principle. The doctrinal approach is reflected in many scope-of-review statutes, but fidelity to statutory command has not always been a hallmark of federal administrative law. Perhaps, in the end, the doctrinal approach is simply easier for lawyers and judges to apply. You may find that proposition hard to swallow by the time you are finished with these materials, but consider the awful possibility that the alternatives to existing law are even worse.

to the review of Federal administrative action. *Consolidated Edison Co. v. National Labor Relations Board*, 305 U.S. 197 (1938); *National Labor Relations Board v. Remington Rand*, 94 F.2d 862 (C.C.A.2, 1938).

UNIVERSAL CAMERA CORP. V. NLRB
Supreme Court of the United States, 1951.
340 U.S. 474, 71 S.Ct. 456, 95 L.Ed. 456.

MR. JUSTICE FRANKFURTER delivered the opinion of the Court.

The essential issue raised by this case * * * is the effect of the Administrative Procedure Act and the legislation colloquially known as the Taft-Hartley Act on the duty of Courts of Appeals when called upon to review orders of the National Labor Relations Board.

The Court of Appeals for the Second Circuit granted enforcement of an order directing, in the main, that petitioner reinstate with back pay an employee found to have been discharged because he gave testimony under the Wagner Act[6] and cease and desist from discriminating against any employee who files charges or gives testimony under that Act.[7] The court below, Judge Swan dissenting, decreed full enforcement of the order * * *. [T]he views of that court regarding the effect of the new legislation on the relation between the Board and the courts of appeals in the enforcement of the Board's orders conflicted with those of the Court of Appeals for the Sixth Circuit * * *. The clash of opinion obviously required settlement by this Court.

I.

Want of certainty in judicial review of Labor Board decisions partly reflects the intractability of any formula to furnish definiteness of content for all the impalpable factors involved in judicial review. But in part doubts as to the nature of the reviewing power and uncertainties in its application derive from history, and to that extent an elucidation of this history may clear them away.

The Wagner Act provided: "The findings of the Board as to the facts, if supported by evidence, shall be conclusive." Act of July 5, 1935, § 10(e), 49 Stat. 449, 454, 29 U.S.C. § 160(e), 29 U.S.C.A. § 160(e). This Court read

---

6 [Ed. note: The Wagner Act was one of the principal New Deal statutes. It heavily regulates the process of collective bargaining, and in many situations requires employers to deal with unions. The Taft-Hartley Act was enacted in 1947 to amend some features of the Wagner Act that were deemed to tilt the balance too far against employers.]

7 [Ed. note: The employee, named Chairman, claimed that he was fired because of testimony that he gave at an NLRB hearing concerning union representation of the company's maintenance employees. The company maintained that Chairman was fired because he accused the firm's personnel manager of drunkenness during a heated argument about employee discipline. The hearing examiner (who today would be called an administrative law judge) "was not satisfied that the respondent's motive in discharging Chairman was reprisal for his testimony; but on review of the record a majority of the Board found the opposite * * *." NLRB v. Universal Camera Corp., 179 F.2d 749, 750 (2d. Cir.1950).]

"evidence" to mean "substantial evidence," *Washington, V. & M. Coach Co. v. Labor Board*, 301 U.S. 142, 57 S.Ct. 648, 81 L.Ed. 965, and we said that "[s]ubstantial evidence is more than a mere scintilla. It means such relevant evidence as a reasonable mind might accept as adequate to support a conclusion." *Consolidated Edison Co. v. National Labor Relations Board*, 305 U.S. 197, 229, 59 S.Ct. 206, 217, 83 L.Ed. 126. Accordingly, it "must do more than create a suspicion of the existence of the fact to be established. . . it must be enough to justify, if the trial were to a jury, a refusal to direct a verdict when the conclusion sought to be drawn from it is one of fact for the jury." *National Labor Relations Board v. Columbian Enameling & Stamping Co.*, 306 U.S. 292, 300, 59 S.Ct. 501, 505, 83 L.Ed. 660.

The very smoothness of the "substantial evidence" formula as the standard for reviewing the evidentiary validity of the Board's findings established its currency. But the inevitably variant applications of the standard to conflicting evidence soon brought contrariety of views and in due course bred criticism. Even though the whole record may have been canvassed in order to determine whether the evidentiary foundation of a determination by the Board was "substantial," the phrasing of this Court's process of review readily lent itself to the notion that it was enough that the evidence supporting the Board's result was "substantial" when considered by itself. It is fair to say that by imperceptible steps regard for the fact-finding function of the Board led to the assumption that the requirements of the Wagner Act were met when the reviewing court could find in the record evidence which, when viewed in isolation, substantiated the Board's findings. This is not to say that every member of this Court was consciously guided by this view or that the Court ever explicitly avowed this practice as doctrine. What matters is that the belief justifiably arose that the Court had so construed the obligation to review.

Criticism of so contracted a reviewing power reinforced dissatisfaction felt in various quarters with the Board's administration of the Wagner Act in the years preceding the war. The scheme of the Act was attacked as an inherently unfair fusion of the functions of prosecutor and judge. Accusations of partisan bias were not wanting. The "irresponsible admission and weighing of hearsay, opinion, and emotional speculation in place of factual evidence" was said to be a "serious menace."[5] No doubt some, perhaps even much, of the criticism was baseless and some surely was reckless. What is here relevant, however, is the climate of opinion thereby generated and its effect on Congress. Protests against "shocking injustices" and intimations of judicial "abdication" with which some courts

---

[5]   This charge was made by the majority of the Special Committee of the House appointed in 1939 to investigate the National Labor Relations Board. H.R. Rep. No. 1902, 76th Cong., 3d Sess. 76.

granted enforcement of the Board's order stimulated pressures for legislative relief from alleged administrative excesses.

The strength of these pressures was reflected in the passage in 1940 of the Walter-Logan Bill. It was vetoed by President Roosevelt, partly because it imposed unduly rigid limitations on the administrative process, and partly because of the investigation into the actual operation of the administrative process then being conducted by an experienced committee appointed by the Attorney General. It is worth noting that despite its aim to tighten control over administrative determinations of fact, the Walter-Logan Bill contented itself with the conventional formula that an agency's decision could be set aside if "the findings of fact are not supported by substantial evidence."

The final report of the Attorney General's Committee was submitted in January, 1941. The majority concluded that "[d]issatisfaction with the existing standards as to the scope of judicial review derives largely from dissatisfaction with the fact-finding procedures now employed by the administrative bodies." Departure from the "substantial evidence" test, it thought, would either create unnecessary uncertainty or transfer to courts the responsibility for ascertaining and assaying matters the significance of which lies outside judicial competence. Accordingly, it recommended against legislation embodying a general scheme of judicial review.

Three members of the Committee registered a dissent * * *. They reported that under a "prevalent" interpretation of the "substantial evidence" rule "if what is called 'substantial evidence' is found anywhere in the record to support conclusions of fact, the courts are said to be obliged to sustain the decision without reference to how heavily the countervailing evidence may preponderate—unless indeed the stage of arbitrary decision is reached. Under this interpretation, the courts need to read only one side of the case and, if they find any evidence there, the administrative action is to be sustained and the record to the contrary is to be ignored." Their view led them to recommend that Congress enact principles of review applicable to all agencies not excepted by unique characteristics. One of these principles was expressed by the formula that judicial review could extend to "findings, inferences, or conclusions of fact unsupported, upon the whole record, by substantial evidence." So far as the history of this movement for enlarged review reveals, the phrase "upon the whole record" makes its first appearance in this recommendation of the minority of the Attorney General's Committee. This evidence of the close relationship between the phrase and the criticism out of which it arose is important, for the substance of this formula for judicial review found its way into the statute books when Congress with unquestioning—we might even say uncritical—unanimity enacted the Administrative Procedure Act.

One is tempted to say "uncritical" because the legislative history of that Act hardly speaks with that clarity of purpose which Congress supposedly furnishes courts in order to enable them to enforce its true will. On the one hand, the sponsors of the legislation indicated that they were reaffirming the prevailing "substantial evidence" test. But with equal clarity they expressed disapproval of the manner in which the courts were applying their own standard. The committee reports of both houses refer to the practice of agencies to rely upon "suspicion, surmise, implications, or plainly incredible evidence," and indicate that courts are to exact higher standards "in the exercise of their independent judgment 'and on consideration of' the whole record."

Similar dissatisfaction with too restricted application of the "substantial evidence" test is reflected in the legislative history of the Taft-Hartley Act. The bill as reported to the House provided that the "findings of the Board as to the facts shall be conclusive unless it is made to appear to the satisfaction of the court either (1) that the findings of fact are against the manifest weight of the evidence, or (2) that the findings of fact are not supported by substantial evidence." The bill left the House with this provision. Early committee prints in the Senate provided for review by "weight of the evidence" or "clearly erroneous" standards. But, as the Senate Committee Report relates, "it was finally decided to conform the statute to the corresponding section of the Administrative Procedure Act where the substantial evidence test prevails. In order to clarify any ambiguity in that statute, however, the committee inserted the words 'questions of fact, if supported by substantial evidence *on the record considered as a whole. . .'*"

This phraseology was adopted by the Senate. The House conferees agreed * * *.

It is fair to say that in all this Congress expressed a mood. And it expressed its mood not merely by oratory but by legislation. As legislation that mood must be respected, even though it can only serve as a standard for judgment and not as a body of rigid rules assuring sameness of applications. Enforcement of such broad standards implies subtlety of mind and solidity of judgment. But it is not for us to question that Congress may assume such qualities in the federal judiciary.

From the legislative story we have summarized, two concrete conclusions do emerge. One is the identity of aim of the Administrative Procedure Act and the Taft-Hartley Act regarding the proof with which the Labor Board must support a decision. The other is that now Congress has left no room for doubt as to the kind of scrutiny which a court of appeals must give the record before the Board to satisfy itself that the Board's order rests on adequate proof.

It would be mischievous word-playing to find that the scope of review under the Taft-Hartley Act is any different from that under the Administrative Procedure Act. The Senate Committee which reported the review clause of the Taft-Hartley Act expressly indicated that the two standards were to conform in this regard, and the wording of the two Acts is for purposes of judicial administration identical. And so we hold that the standard of proof specifically required of the Labor Board by the Taft-Hartley Act is the same as that to be exacted by courts reviewing every administrative action subject to the Administrative Procedure Act.

Whether or not it was ever permissible for courts to determine the substantiality of evidence supporting a Labor Board decision merely on the basis of evidence which in and of itself justified it, without taking into account contradictory evidence or evidence from which conflicting inferences could be drawn, the new legislation definitively precludes such a theory of review and bars its practice. The substantiality of evidence must take into account whatever in the record fairly detracts from its weight. This is clearly the significance of the requirement in both statutes that courts consider the whole record * * *.

* * *

There remains, then, the question whether enactment of these two statutes has altered the scope of review other than to require that substantiality be determined in the light of all that the record relevantly presents. A formula for judicial review of administrative action may afford grounds for certitude but cannot assure certainty of application. Some scope for judicial discretion in applying the formula can be avoided only by falsifying the actual process of judging or by using the formula as an instrument of futile casuistry. It cannot be too often repeated that judges are not automata. The ultimate reliance for the fair operation of any standard is a judiciary of high competence and character and the constant play of an informed professional critique upon its work.

Since the precise way in which courts interfere with agency findings cannot be imprisoned within any form of words, new formulas attempting to rephrase the old are not likely to be more helpful than the old. There are no talismanic words that can avoid the process of judgment. The difficulty is that we cannot escape, in relation to this problem, the use of undefined defining terms.

Whatever changes were made by the Administrative Procedure and Taft-Hartley Acts are clearly within this area where precise definition is impossible. Retention of the familiar "substantial evidence" terminology indicates that no drastic reversal of attitude was intended.

But a standard leaving an unavoidable margin for individual judgment does not leave the judicial judgment at large even though the phrasing of the standard does not wholly fence it in. The legislative history of these Acts demonstrates a purpose to impose on courts a responsibility which has not always been recognized. Of course it is a statute and not a committee report which we are interpreting. But the fair interpretation of a statute is often "the art of proliferating a purpose", *Brooklyn National Corp. v. Commissioner*, 2 Cir., 157 F.2d 450, 451, revealed more by the demonstrable forces that produced it than by its precise phrasing. The adoption in these statutes of the judicially-constructed "substantial evidence" test was a response to pressures for stricter and more uniform practice, not a reflection of approval of all existing practices. To find the change so elusive that it cannot be precisely defined does not mean it may be ignored. We should fail in our duty to effectuate the will of Congress if we denied recognition to expressed Congressional disapproval of the finality accorded to Labor Board findings by some decisions of this and lower courts, or even of the atmosphere which may have favored those decisions.

We conclude, therefore, that the Administrative Procedure Act and the Taft-Hartley Act direct that courts must now assume more responsibility for the reasonableness and fairness of Labor Board decisions than some courts have shown in the past. Reviewing courts must be influenced by a feeling that they are not to abdicate the conventional judicial function. Congress has imposed on them responsibility for assuring that the Board keeps within reasonable grounds. That responsibility is not less real because it is limited to enforcing the requirement that evidence appear substantial when viewed, on the record as a whole, by courts invested with the authority and enjoying the prestige of the Courts of Appeals. The Board's findings are entitled to respect; but they must nonetheless be set aside when the record before a Court of Appeals clearly precludes the Board's decision from being justified by a fair estimate of the worth of the testimony of witnesses or its informed judgment on matters within its special competence or both.

* * *

II.

Our disagreement with the view of the court below that the scope of review of Labor Board decisions is unaltered by recent legislation does not of itself, as we have noted, require reversal of its decision. The court may have applied a standard of review which satisfies the present Congressional requirement.

The decision of the Court of Appeals is assailed on two grounds. It is said (1) that the court erred in holding that it was barred from taking into account the report of the examiner on questions of fact insofar as that report was rejected by the Board, and (2) that the Board's order was not supported by substantial evidence on the record considered as a whole, even apart from the validity of the court's refusal to consider the rejected portions of the examiner's report.

The latter contention is easily met * * *. [I]t is clear from the court's opinion in this case that it in fact did consider the "record as a whole," and did not deem itself merely the judicial echo of the Board's conclusion. The testimony of the company's witnesses was inconsistent, and there was clear evidence that the complaining employee had been discharged by an officer who was at one time influenced against him because of his appearance at the Board hearing. On such a record we could not say that it would be error to grant enforcement.

The first contention, however, raises serious questions to which we now turn.

III.

The Court of Appeals deemed itself bound by the Board's rejection of the examiner's findings because the court considered these findings not "as unassailable as a master's." They are not. Section 10(c) of the Labor Management Relations Act provides that "If upon the preponderance of the testimony taken the Board shall be of the opinion that any person named in the complaint has engaged in or is engaging in any such unfair labor practice, then the Board shall state its findings of fact * * *." 61 Stat. 147, 29 U.S.C.(Supp. III) § 160(c), 29 U.S.C.A. § 160(c). The responsibility for decision thus placed on the Board is wholly inconsistent with the notion that it has power to reverse an examiner's findings only when they are "clearly erroneous." Such a limitation would make so drastic a departure from prior administrative practice that explicitness would be required.

The Court of Appeals concluded from this premise "that, although the Board would be wrong in totally disregarding his findings, it is practically impossible for a court, upon review of those findings which the Board itself substitutes, to consider the Board's reversal as a factor in the court's own decision. This we say, because we cannot find any middle ground between doing that and treating such a reversal as error, whenever it would be such, if done by a judge to a master in equity." 179 F.2d at 753. Much as we respect the logical acumen of the Chief Judge of the Court of Appeals, we do not find ourselves pinioned between the horns of his dilemma.

We are aware that to give the examiner's findings less finality than a master's and yet entitle them to consideration in striking the account, is to introduce another and an unruly factor into the judgmatical process of review. But we ought not to fashion an exclusionary rule merely to reduce the number of imponderables to be considered by reviewing courts.

The Taft-Hartley Act provides that "The findings of the Board with respect to questions of fact if supported by substantial evidence on the record considered as a whole shall be conclusive." Surely an examiner's report is as much a part of the record as the complaint or the testimony. According to the Administrative Procedure Act, "All decisions (including initial, recommended, or tentative decisions) shall become a part of the record. . ."[8] We found that this Act's provision for judicial review has the same meaning as that in the Taft-Hartley Act. The similarity of the two statutes in language and purpose also requires that the definition of "record" found in the Administrative Procedure Act be construed to be applicable as well to the term "record" as used in the Taft-Hartley Act.

It is therefore difficult to escape the conclusion that the plain language of the statutes directs a reviewing court to determine the substantiality of evidence on the record including the examiner's report. The conclusion is confirmed by the indications in the legislative history that enhancement of the status and function of the trial examiner was one of the important purposes of the movement for administrative reform.

* * *

* * * Nothing in the statutes suggests that the Labor Board should not be influenced by the examiner's opportunity to observe the witnesses he hears and sees and the Board does not. Nothing suggests that reviewing courts should not give to the examiner's report such probative force as it intrinsically commands * * *.

* * *

We do not require that the examiner's findings be given more weight than in reason and in the light of judicial experience they deserve. The "substantial evidence" standard is not modified in any way when the Board and its examiner disagree. We intend only to recognize that evidence supporting a conclusion may be less substantial when an impartial, experienced examiner who has observed the witnesses and lived with the case has drawn conclusions different from the Board's than when he has reached the same conclusion. The findings of the examiner are to be considered along with the consistency and inherent probability of testimony. The significance of his report, of course, depends largely on the importance of credibility in the particular case. To give it this significance does not seem to us materially more difficult than to heed the other factors which in sum determine whether evidence is "substantial."

* * *

We therefore remand the cause to the Court of Appeals. On reconsideration of the record it should accord the findings of the trial examiner the relevance that they reasonably command in answering the comprehensive question whether the evidence supporting the Board's order

---

8   [Ed. note: The precise language of the APA, as presently codified, is, "All decisions, including initial, recommended, and tentative decisions, are a part of the record * * *." 5 U.S.C. § 557(c) (2012)].

is substantial. But the court need not limit its reexamination of the case to the effect of that report on its decision. We leave it free to grant or deny enforcement as it thinks the principles expressed in this opinion dictate.

Judgment vacated and cause remanded.

MR. JUSTICE BLACK and MR. JUSTICE DOUGLAS concur with parts I and II of this opinion but as to part III agree with the opinion of the court below.

NOTES

For more than two-thirds of a century, *Universal Camera* has been the leading case on the meaning of the APA's "substantial evidence" test for review of agency factual conclusions in formal proceedings; it has (as of 2018) been cited almost 9,000 times by other federal court decisions. The Court addressed three distinct questions: (1) what is the overall level of deference required by the substantial evidence test, (2) what materials should the reviewing court consult in assessing the agency's decision, and (3) what weight should be given to the findings of initial agency adjudicators (such as ALJs) when the agency rejects their findings?

The answer to the first question is not entirely clear, is it? The weight of authority in 1946 (or 1947) would clearly have supported the view that a "substantial evidence" standard is equivalent to the jury standard: evidence that would be sufficient to sustain a jury verdict on appeal would also be "substantial evidence" for purposes of appellate review of agency decisions. Justice Frankfurter, however, found the APA and the Taft-Hartley Act to reflect a congressional "mood" of stricter judicial scrutiny of agency decisions than had characterized pre-APA law. No verbal formula adequately expresses the quantum of evidence needed to satisfy this new test, but one can fairly say that the substantial evidence standard, as articulated by the Court in *Universal Camera* and as applied day-to-day by the lower courts that have followed it, is less deferential than the jury standard but more deferential than the clearly erroneous standard of Fed. R. Civ. Proc. 52(a). *See Chen v. Mukasey*, 510 F.3d 797, 801 (8th Cir.2007).

The Court, however, has muddied the waters a bit. In *Allentown Mack Sales & Service, Inc. v. NLRB*, 522 U.S. 359, 118 S.Ct. 818, 139 L.Ed.2d 797 (1998), the Court, per Justice Scalia, held that an agency cannot evaluate evidence on the basis of unarticulated presumptions and practices, even if those presumptions and practices could survive judicial scrutiny if they were explicitly adopted. This is not really a holding about the accuracy of the agency's findings of fact but rather concerns the agency's reasoning process and methodology, which we shall later see is governed by a standard of review different from the substantial evidence test. *See Changzhou Wujin Fine Chemical Factory Co, Ltd. v. United States*, 701 F.3d 1367, 1377 (Fed.Cir.2012) (explaining that an agency decision can be supported by substantial evidence but still be invalid because of flaws in the agency's reasoning process). In the course of its decision, however, the Court observed in passing: "We must decide whether * * * [the agency's] conclusion is supported by substantial evidence on the record as a whole [citing, inter alia, *Universal Camera*]. Put differently, we must decide whether on this record it would have been possible for a reasonable jury to reach the Board's conclusion. See, *e.g.*, *NLRB v. Columbian Enameling & Stamping Co.*, 306 U.S. 292, 300, 59 S.Ct. 501, 83 L.Ed. 660 (1939); *Consolidated Edison Co. v. NLRB*, 305 U.S. 197, 229, 59 S.Ct. 206, 83 L.Ed. 126 (1938)." 522 U.S. at 366–67. If taken seriously, this formulation of the substantial evidence test would undo the intermediate standard introduced by Justice Frankfurter in *Universal Camera* and replace it with the pre-APA jury standard. It is unclear how seriously to take the Court's remarks. *Compare W & M Properties of Connecticut, Inc. v. NLRB*, 514 F.3d 1341, 1348–49 (D.C.Cir.2008) (applying the jury standard while citing *Allentown Mack*) *with Int'l Union, UAW, AFL-CIO v. NLRB*, 514 F.3d 574, 580–81 (6th Cir.2008) (citing *Universal Camera*, with no mention of the jury standard or *Allentown Mack*). Despite its articulation of the jury standard, the Court in *Allentown Mack* scrutinized the agency's findings with a rigor that it would never have applied to a jury verdict. Other courts that have cited *Allentown Mack's* language have behaved similarly. *See, e.g, Podewils v. NLRB*, 274 F.3d 536 (D.C.Cir.2001); *NLRB v. Beverly Enterprises-Massachusetts, Inc.*, 174 F.3d 13 (1st Cir.1999). The courts that purport to apply *Allentown Mack* may thus be doing precisely what *Allentown Mack* said that an agency cannot do: declaring one standard for evaluating evidence and applying another.

The answer to the question what material reviewing courts should consult is much more straightforward: under the APA, reviewing courts must consult the "whole record," not merely those parts of it that tend to support the agency's decision. This is a small matter that can make a large difference. Suppose, for example, that the agency concludes that an employer fired an employee because of the employee's union activities. The agency relies on a document prepared by the employer setting forth a policy of punishing or firing all employees who are union activists. Standing alone, the document would seem to provide "substantial evidence" to support the Board's conclusion concerning the employer's motive. But suppose that there is extensive, uncontradicted testimony elsewhere in the record stating that the document was an April Fool's prank written by a known jokester in the company's management. Considered in light of the "whole record," the document may not constitute "substantial evidence" after all. This requirement that courts consult the "whole record" has not been a subject of controversy since *Universal Camera*—nor could it be, given the express language of the APA. In practice, of course, courts generally consult only "those parts of [the record] cited by a party." Courts will not often scour the entire record of the agency proceeding looking for evidence that the parties' lawyers have not chosen to emphasize in their briefs—though the APA clearly permits such judicial diligence, as hapless law clerks discover from time to time.

As for the weight to be given to findings of initial decisionmakers such as ALJs, most of the time decisions of initial agency adjudicators simply become the final decisions of agencies—occasionally through explicit agency adoption, but more often through the operation of § 557(b) of the APA, which provides that an initial decision "becomes the decision of the agency without further proceedings unless there is an appeal to, or review on motion of, the agency within time provided by rule." When, however, there is an appeal and the agency disagrees with the findings of the initial adjudicator, the rule of *Universal Camera* governs: the findings of initial adjudicators are part of the record, and agencies and reviewing courts must give them due consideration.

In practice, such initial findings often carry great weight with reviewing courts, especially when the findings turn on determinations of witness credibility. When agencies review the decisions of initial adjudicators, they generally do not hold new hearings and take testimony from witnesses (though they have the power to do so). Rather, they review the paper record from the initial adjudication. There is a long tradition in our legal system—whether wise or foolish—of treating the appearance and demeanor of witnesses as relevant to their credibility.[9] Accordingly, agencies generally need to have very good reasons for rejecting credibility determinations made by adjudicators who actually saw the witnesses.

KIMM V. DEPARTMENT OF THE TREASURY

United States Court of Appeals, Federal Circuit, 1995.
61 F.3d 888.

Before RICH, LOURIE, and RADER, CIRCUIT JUDGES.

LOURIE, CIRCUIT JUDGE.

Kevin R. Kimm petitions for review of the August 18, 1994 final decision of the Merit Systems Protection Board, reversing the March 25, 1994 initial decision of the Administrative Judge ("AJ") and sustaining Kimm's thirty-day suspension from his position with the Department of the Treasury ("agency"). Kimm was suspended for willfully using a government-owned vehicle for other than official purposes in violation of 31 U.S.C. § 1349(b). Because the board's determination that Kimm's use was willful was not supported by substantial evidence, we reverse.

BACKGROUND

Kimm is a highly decorated criminal investigator who has served for more than ten years at the agency's Bureau of Alcohol, Tobacco and Firearms ("AT"). By letter dated April 1, 1993, Kimm was notified that the agency proposed to suspend him from duty and pay status for thirty calendar days based on a charge that he willfully used a government-owned vehicle ("GOV") for other than official purposes in violation of 31 U.S.C. § 1349(b).

---

[9] For an unusually explicit judicial discussion and assessment of this tradition, see *Penasquitos Village, Inc. v. NLRB*, 565 F.2d 1074, 1079–80 (9th Cir.1977); *id.* at 1084–86 (Duniway, J., concurring in part and dissenting in part).

As support for the suspension, the agency cited Kimm's alleged admission to an agency investigator that Kimm had driven his son to day care in his GOV one time during November 1992 and on two or three other occasions during the preceding year. In a written reply, Kimm denied informing the investigator that he had transported his son in the GOV in November 1992, but stated instead that he had transported his son to and from day care in his GOV on a few occasions during August 1992 when his wife was placed on bed rest due to complications arising from her pregnancy.[1] Kimm was accordingly suspended.

In an initial decision issued March 25, 1994, the AJ reversed the agency's action, holding that the agency failed to prove by preponderant evidence that Kimm willfully used his GOV for other than official reasons. The AJ summarized Kimm's testimony at his hearing regarding his belief that his GOV use would not constitute a nonofficial use under the circumstances as follows:

> [Kimm] testified that ordinarily his wife drove their son to and from day care. However, in August, 1992, his wife was going through a difficult pregnancy. She had suffered previous miscarriages, and because she had begun to again experience early contractions (the due date was in October), she was ordered by her doctor to remain in bed. [Kimm] testified that on the Friday before the first work week in August, his wife's doctor had ordered her to avoid stressful activity, but that on Tuesday of the following week, he called and ordered her to remain in bed at all times.

> [Kimm] testified that it was during the remainder of this week in August that he transported his son to and from day care three or four times. During the second work week of August, he was home on sick leave, and transported his son to and from day care in one of his [personal vehicles]. Following that week, [Kimm's] wife's parents stayed with them, and provided the necessary transportation.

> [Kimm] testified that his position required him to be "on call" around the clock, seven days-a-week, that he was often called out in the middle of the night, and occasionally had to sleep in his GOV. He testified that his GOV was equipped with weapons and an encrypted radio, so that he could be in constant contact with his office. [He] testified that during August, 1992, he was working a great deal of overtime, was often the Acting Resident Agent in Charge, and that he had been heavily involved in an extremely dangerous conspiracy investigation.

---

[1]   The board found that the agency did not prove the alleged November 1992 use. Only the August 1992 use remains at issue.

[Kimm] testified that he deviated from the most direct route to and from work by 2.6 miles each way in order to take his son to or from day care. [If Kimm] had taken his son to day care in a [personal vehicle], then returned home to obtain his GOV, and then proceeded to work, the round trip would have been 21.2 miles, and would have taken a total of approximately 40 minutes, due to heavy commuter traffic. [Kimm] testified that due to his extremely heavy work load and long hours, he believed that he was making the most efficient use of his and the agency's time by providing transportation to his son in the GOV during his wife's "medical emergency." [Kimm] testified that he believed the agency's regulations allowed him discretion to make a "minor deviation." He testified that it was standard practice, for example, to make minor deviations to find a place to eat dinner while on a mission, or to alter one's route to and from the office, if a death threat had been received. He also testified that the agency was lax in the enforcement of its GOV regulations, and cited a number of incidents that he believed had occurred to support this belief.

* * * [T]he AJ found that Kimm did not act with the requisite knowledge or reckless disregard that his GOV use constituted a nonofficial use. Instead, because Kimm was continuously on call and authorized to use his GOV for commuting, the AJ found that "his belief that he had discretion to rectify a family emergency and simultaneously maximize the time he was available to perform his agency functions, was a good faith belief, and not in reckless disregard of the agency's regulations." Thus, the AJ found that the agency did not prove willful misuse within the meaning of § 1349(b). The agency petitioned the full board for review of the initial decision.

On August 18, 1994, the board reversed the initial decision and sustained the suspension. The board stated that

a reasonable person in [Kimm's] position could not have determined that the presence of his 3-year old son in the GOV was essential to the completion of an official mission * * *. Further, there is no indication in the record that, on the occasions when [Kimm] transported his son in his GOV, the presence of his son was necessary for [Kimm's] protection while engaged in foreseeable arrests and seizures. We therefore find that the appellant did not reasonably exercise the discretion afforded him under the agency's Orders, which did not permit the transportation of unauthorized persons in a GOV in order to maximize an employee's availability for work during a "medical emergency" involving a family member. We find that the purpose of the presence of the appellant's son in the GOV was to further the appellant's personal convenience in transporting his son to day care during his wife's illness.

The board concluded that "more likely than not, [Kimm's] use of his GOV constitutes willful misuse." Kimm petitioned for review of the board's final decision * * *.

DISCUSSION

Our standard of review for board decisions is governed by statute, which directs us to set aside board actions, findings, or conclusions found to be—

(1) arbitrary, capricious, an abuse of discretion, or otherwise not in accordance with law;

(2) obtained without procedures required by law, rule, or regulation having been followed; or

(3) unsupported by substantial evidence. . .

5 U.S.C. § 7703(c) (1988). Under this standard, we will reverse the board's decision if it is not supported by "such relevant evidence as a reasonable mind might accept as adequate to support a conclusion." *Brewer v. United States Postal Serv.*, 647 F.2d 1093, 1096, 227 Ct.Cl. 276 (1981) (quoting *Consolidated Edison Co. v. National Labor Relations Bd.*, 305 U.S. 197, 229, 59 S.Ct. 206, 217, 83 L.Ed. 126 (1938)). The question before us is not how the court would rule upon a *de novo* appraisal of the facts of the case, but whether the administrative determination is supported by substantial evidence in the record as a whole.

* * *

Section 1349(b) of Title 31, United States Code, provides in pertinent part that

[a]n officer or employee who *willfully uses* or authorizes the use of *a passenger motor vehicle . . . owned . . . by the United States Government (except for an official purpose authorized by section 1344 of this title) . . . shall be suspended without pay by the head of the agency.* The officer or employee shall be suspended for at least one month, and when circumstances warrant, for a longer period or summarily removed from office.

31 U.S.C. § 1349(b) (1988) (emphasis added). In *Felton v. Equal Employment Opportunity Commission*, 820 F.2d 391 (Fed.Cir.1987), we held that a violation of § 1349(b) required more than a showing that the employee intended to take the action that provided the foundation for the charge. *Id.* at 393. Rather, in order for the action to constitute a willful use for a nonofficial purpose within the meaning of the act, the employee must have had actual knowledge that the use would be characterized as

"nonofficial" or have acted in reckless disregard as to whether the use was for nonofficial purposes. *Id.* at 394. The board in this case did not specify whether, in its view, the agency had proved that Kimm actually knew or had acted with reckless disregard of the nonofficial nature of his GOV use; however, the record supports neither view.

After hearing Kimm's testimony and considering all the evidence, the AJ specifically found that Kimm did not have actual knowledge that the use would constitute a nonofficial use. The AJ characterized Kimm's demeanor during his testimony as "straightforward and unwavering . . . and consistent with his written and oral replies." In contrast, the AJ found the agency's evidence "inherently improbable." The AJ considered the fact that Kimm is a highly decorated AT agent with more than ten years of service, a flawless record, and an excellent reputation, making it unlikely that Kimm would knowingly violate a rule or, if he did so, would then lie about his motives. When, as with a determination concerning a witness's state of mind, the AJ's finding is explicitly or implicitly based on the demeanor of a witness, the board may not simply disagree with the AJ's assessment of credibility. If the board reverses such a finding, we will not sustain its decision on appeal unless the board has articulated sound reasons, based on the record, for its contrary evaluation of the testimonial evidence. Here, the board did not articulate any reason for a contrary evaluation of the testimony and we therefore will not sustain its decision to the extent that it was based on Kimm's knowledge that the use of the GOV was nonofficial.

The AJ also specifically determined that the agency did not prove that Kimm acted with "reckless disregard" concerning whether the use was for other than official purposes. Rather, the AJ held that, under the circumstances, Kimm could reasonably have determined that his GOV use would promote the successful operation of the agency by saving considerable time and by maintaining contact with his agency during a time when Kimm was on call around the clock. In reversing the AJ, the board stated that "the agency's Orders . . . did not permit the transportation of unauthorized persons in a GOV in order to maximize an employee's availability for work during a 'medical emergency' involving a family member."

The agency's policy with regard to GOV use provides that employees are responsible for using GOVs for official purposes only, including transporting only those persons whose presence is essential to the successful completion of an official mission * * *. The orders also call for the employee's exercise of judgment in determining whether the transportation of a particular person is essential to the success of the mission.

* * *

* * * Kimm was involved in an around-the-clock, dangerous investigation, which required him to be on call at all times. He was authorized to commute to work in his GOV, which contained specialized equipment necessary to remain in contact with the agency. Kimm was under considerable stress, not only from long hours of overtime, but from the possibility of his wife miscarrying. Kimm was also aware of the culture of the agency, which allowed minor deviations in the use of GOVs. Given the circumstances, Kimm could reasonably have concluded that bringing his son to and from day care on his way to and from work during a limited medical emergency, saving time and maintaining contact with his agency, was essential to successful completion of his mission. Even if Kimm could have first secured permission to transport his son, his failure to do so given the circumstances does not amount to "reckless disregard" for the regulations.

The board also concluded that "a reasonable person in [Kimm's] position could not have determined that the presence of his 3-year old son in the GOV was essential to the completion of an official mission." To support this conclusion, the board explained that on the occasions in question, the presence of Kimm's son was not actually necessary for Kimm's protection * * *.

It is of course absurd to consider the presence of a three-year-old child as being necessary for Kimm's protection. The point is whether, under the circumstances, Kimm's use of the GOV was in reckless disregard as to whether the use was nonofficial. Clearly, Kimm was not acting in reckless disregard. Kimm thought he was conscientiously fulfilling his duties to the best of his ability.

Thus, there is no evidence of record to support a finding that Kimm knew or should have known that the use of the vehicle in the circumstances of this case would be held to constitute use for a nonofficial purpose or that he acted in reckless disregard for whether the use was or was not for an official purpose. Official use was left to good judgment and we think it clear that Kimm could reasonably have determined that the use would promote the success of his mission by saving time and maintaining contact with the agency when he was authorized to commute and was on call at all times.

CONCLUSION

The finding of the board that Kimm willfully used a GOV for other than an official purpose is not supported by substantial evidence. Therefore, we reverse.

* * *

NOTES

Kimm illustrates how the credibility findings of initial adjudicators can count for a great deal. One can find cases in which appellate courts openly reject such credibility findings, *see, e.g., Sasol North America Inc. v. NLRB,* 275 F.3d 1106, 1112 (D.C.Cir.2002) ("[w]hile an agency's credibility decision normally enjoys almost overwhelming deference, it does not do so when it rests explicitly on a mistaken notion"); *Be-Lo Stores v. NLRB,* 126 F.3d 268 (4th Cir.1997) (rejecting an ALJ's credibility determinations when the ALJ systematically credited all of the literally dozens of witnesses for one side and discredited all of the literally dozens of witnesses on the other side), but they are few and far between.

Kimm does not involve § 706(2)(E) of the APA. Instead, the case involves an organic statute that prescribes a "substantial evidence" standard for review of facts. The Court in *Universal Camera* also dealt with a scope-of-review provision in an organic statute—the Taft-Hartley Act—but held that the "substantial evidence" provisions in the 1947 Taft-Hartley Act and in the 1946 APA were designed to codify the same level of judicial scrutiny of agency decisions. *Kimm*'s discussion of the meaning of 5 U.S.C. § 7703(c), however, suggests a standard more like the pre—*Universal Camera*, and perhaps post—*Allentown Mack*, jury standard. But, as in *Allentown Mack*, it is hard to imagine an appellate court treating a jury verdict the way that the Federal Circuit treated the decision of the Merit Systems Protection Board in *Kimm*. The decision reflects a judicial "mood" that is entirely compatible with the approach articulated in *Universal Camera* and incompatible with the highly deferential jury standard.

In another respect, *Kimm* is consistent with the general practice of reviewing courts under the APA. The court emphasized that the agency *failed to offer any explanation* for its rejection of the AJ's findings. As you shall later see, this demand for reasoned agency explanation is a hallmark of modern administrative law in many contexts. In this context, it means that agencies must explicitly *account for* the findings of initial adjudicators. They can choose to reject those findings, but they must provide reasons for that rejection, *see David Saxe Productions, LLC v. NLRB,* 888 F.3d 1305, 1311–12 (D.C.Cir.2018); *ARC Bridges, Inc. v. NLRB,* 861 F.3d 193, 200 (D.C.Cir.2017), especially when the agency is overturning a credibility determination solely on the basis of a written record. *See Local 702, Int'l Brotherhood of Electrical Workers v. NLRB,* 215 F.3d 11, 15 (D.C.Cir.2000).

Factual disputes often turn less on what the evidence directly says than on what inferences can properly be drawn from that evidence. The following case is typical.

LARO MAINTENANCE CORP. v. NLRB

United States Court of Appeals, District of Columbia Circuit, 1995.
56 F.3d 224.

Before WALD, RANDOLPH, and ROGERS, CIRCUIT JUDGE.

ROGERS, CIRCUIT JUDGE.

Laro Maintenance Corporation petitions for review of the decision and order of the National Labor Relations Board finding that Laro had violated §§ (8)(a)(1) and (3) of the National Labor Relations Act, 29 U.S.C. §§ 158(a)(1) and (3), by discriminating against certain applicants for employment based on their union membership. Specifically, Laro contends that the Board impermissibly presumed anti-union animus and lacked substantial evidence to support its finding of discriminatory intent. Because the Board applied the appropriate legal standard and substantial evidence in the record considered as a whole supports its determination that Laro's failure to hire any of the thirteen applicants was based on their union membership, we deny the petition for review and grant the Board's cross-petition for enforcement.

I.

For about six years ending on September 30, 1990, Prompt Maintenance Services, Inc. cleaned and maintained the federal government building at 225 Cadman Plaza in Brooklyn, New York under a contract with the General Services Administration ("GSA"). Prompt employees performed this work under a collective bargaining agreement between Prompt and Local 32B-32J, Service Employees International Union, AFL-CIO ("Local 32B"). In April 1990, the GSA solicited bids for a new cleaning contract at Cadman Plaza. The bid solicitation required the new contractor to pay the same wages as Prompt and to have an initial work force of which at least fifty percent comprised experienced cleaners. Laro was awarded the contract to begin October 1, 1990.

On or about September 17, 1990, Local 32B requested that Laro hire Prompt's Cadman Plaza employees. On September 18, Laro's President, Robert Bertuglia, toured the Cadman Plaza building. A GSA official mentioned the names of various employees as being "good workers," and Bertuglia observed two Prompt employees sleeping. Bertuglia did not take note of the names of either the good workers or the sleeping workers. After the inspection, the building manager (another GSA employee) informed Bertuglia that the GSA had taken deductions from Prompt's fee, presumably for deficient performance. Bertuglia told the building manager that he did not intend to hire any of Prompt's employees because of the deductions and the two employees he had seen sleeping on the job. The building manager informed Bertuglia that certain judges whose chambers were in the Cadman Plaza building wanted Laro to retain the Prompt employees who cleaned their chambers. The building manager also advised

Bertuglia to interview all Prompt employees and stated that it would be advantageous for Laro to hire as many of them as possible. Several days later, the GSA official who conducted the inspection gave Bertuglia a list of ten "better cleaners from Prompt Maintenance," and urged Laro to hire them.

Despite Bertuglia's stated desire not to hire any Prompt employees, Laro agreed to hire the ten Prompt employees on the GSA's list. Laro accepted applications from other Prompt employees but had already decided that it would not hire any of them; consequently Laro asked the Prompt employees who were not on the GSA's list virtually no questions about their background or experience and did not seek information about individual Prompt employees who had good work records and had worked at Cadman Plaza for a number of years for Prompt and its predecessor. Instead, to complete its Cadman Plaza work force, Laro hired eight workers who had not previously worked for Prompt. Laro had previously employed four of these workers. Two had good work records and requested transfers to Cadman Plaza. Laro transferred the other two to Cadman Plaza at least in part because of their poor performance at Laro's Jamaica, New York site: Laro had discharged one for poor attendance and insubordination three weeks before it hired her to work at Cadman Plaza, and transferred the other because he required constant supervision, did not get his work done, made frivolous excuses for his failure to complete tasks, and constantly complained. Laro also hired four workers who had not previously been employed by either Prompt or Laro. Laro admitted that three of them had no relevant work experience, and although the fourth worker listed factory and office cleaning as relevant experience on his application, he did not list any positions at which he would have gained such experience. On September 28, 1990, just before commencing work at Cadman Plaza under its contract with GSA, Laro entered into a supplemental agreement with Amalgamated Local Union 355 ("Local 355")—with which Laro had a collective bargaining agreement (August 1, 1990, through July 1, 1993) for its employees in Jamaica, New York—covering its employees at Cadman Plaza.

Thereafter, Local 32B filed an unfair labor practice charge against Laro * * * on the ground that Laro had bargained with Local 355 knowing that it represented a minority of the workers at Cadman Plaza and that it had refused to consider employing Prompt employees, other than those on the GSA's list, because of their union membership. When these charges came before an Administrative Law Judge ("ALJ") for a hearing, Laro admitted that it had recognized Local 355 although Local 32B represented a majority of the employees at Cadman Plaza * * *. Following a hearing on the remaining complaint allegations, the ALJ concluded that Laro violated §§ 8(a)(1) and (3) upon finding that Laro had declined to consider any Prompt employees who were not on the "better cleaners" list in order to recognize and bargain with Local 355 rather than Local 32B. The Board adopted the ALJ's findings and conclusions with minor modifications and ordered Laro to offer employment and back pay to the Prompt employees it had refused to consider.[2] Laro petitioned for review * * *, and the Board cross-petitioned for enforcement * * *.

II.

Section 8(a)(3) of the Act makes it an unfair labor practice for an employer "to encourage or discourage membership in any labor organization," "by discrimination in regard to hire or tenure of employment or any term or condition of employment. . ." 29 U.S.C. § 158(a)(3).[3] Under this section, a successor employer not the alter ego of its predecessor is not obligated to hire its predecessor's employees. *Howard Johnson Co. v. Detroit Local Joint Executive Bd., Hotel & Restaurant Employees Int'l Union*, 417 U.S. 249, 259 n. 5, 261, 94 S.Ct. 2236, 2242 n. 5, 2243, 41 L.Ed.2d 46 (1974). However, "a new owner [can]not refuse to hire the employees of [its] predecessor solely because they were union members or to avoid having to recognize the union." *Id.* at 262 n. 8, 94 S.Ct. at 2243 n. 8.

When a violation of § 8(a)(3) is alleged, the Board applies the two-stage causation test established in *Wright Line*, 251 N.L.R.B. 1083, 1980 WL 12312 (1980), *enf'd*, 662 F.2d 899 (1st Cir.1981), and approved by the Supreme Court in *NLRB v. Transportation Mgt. Corp.*, 462 U.S. 393, 103 S.Ct. 2469, 76 L.Ed.2d 667 (1983). Under *Wright Line*, the Board's General Counsel bears the initial burden to "make a prima facie showing sufficient to support the inference that protected [i.e., legitimate, union-related] conduct was a 'motivating factor' in the employer's decision" to take adverse employment action. *Wright Line*, 251 N.L.R.B. at 1089. The employer may then rebut the inference by showing by a preponderance of the evidence that "the same action would have taken place even in the absence of the protected conduct." *Id.*

* * *

III.

* * * Laro contends that the Board's finding of a *prima facie* case, that Laro's failure to hire any of the thirteen Prompt employees was motivated by its desire to avoid bargaining with Local 32B, is unsupported by substantial evidence. Similarly Laro contends that substantial evidence does not support the Board's rejection of Laro's claim under the second prong of *Wright Line* that it would have hired the same employees regardless of the Prompt employees' union membership. The court's review

---

[2]   The ALJ found that Laro failed to hire thirteen Prompt employees because of their union affiliation * * *.

[3]   Such conduct also violates § 8(a)(1) of the Act because it "interfere [s] with, restrain[s], or coerce[s] employees in the exercise of" their labor rights. 29 U.S.C. § 158(a)(1).

of the Board's factual conclusions is highly deferential, upholding a decision if it is supported by substantial evidence considering the record as a whole. *Universal Camera Corp. v. NLRB*, 340 U.S. 474, 488, 71 S.Ct. 456, 465, 95 L.Ed. 456 (1951). "So long as the Board's findings are *reasonable*, they may not be displaced on review even if the court might have reached a different result had the matter been before it *de novo*." *Clark & Wilkins Indus., Inc. v. NLRB*, 887 F.2d 308, 312 (D.C.Cir.1989).

The court's review of the Board's determination with respect to motive is even more deferential. Motive is a question of fact that may be inferred from direct or circumstantial evidence. In most cases only circumstantial evidence of motive is likely to be available. Drawing such inferences from the evidence to assess an employer's hiring motive invokes the expertise of the Board, and consequently, the court gives "substantial deference to inferences the Board has drawn from the facts," including inferences of impermissible motive. *Gold Coast Restaurant Corp. v. NLRB*, 995 F.2d 257, 263 (D.C.Cir.1993).

The Board relied principally on three factual findings for its determination that Laro's motive for failing to hire any of the thirteen Prompt employees was its desire to avoid bargaining with Local 32B: (1) Laro's admitted unfair labor practice of recognizing Local 355 as the representative of employees at Cadman Plaza when a majority of those employees were members of Local 32B; (2) Laro's hiring practices at other sites that reveal anti-union bias; and (3) the pretextual nature of Laro's explanations for its actions. Because there is substantial evidence of record to support these findings and the Board's inference is reasonable, the court has no basis to conclude that the Board erred.

From the time Laro took over the Cadman Plaza site until the hearing before the ALJ—a period of nineteen months—Laro engaged in an unfair labor practice by recognizing Local 355 as the collective bargaining representative of the Cadman Plaza workers even though Laro knew that a majority of Laro's Cadman Plaza employees (ten of eighteen) were members of Local 32B. In addition, the Board adopted the ALJ's finding that Laro knowingly engaged in this unfair labor practice and actively attempted to conceal it. The Board found that a Laro supervisor told one of Laro's employees at the Jamaica site, Sebatine Acosta, that Laro was being sued by another union and needed two Jamaica employees to tell the Board that they also worked at Cadman Plaza. Laro instructed Acosta to inform the Board that he had worked at Cadman Plaza for an entire month when, in fact, he had only worked there one night. Laro's bad faith recognition of Local 355 rather than Local 32B, followed by Laro's attempt to conceal its unfair labor practice, presented the Board with substantial evidence that Laro's motive in failing to hire any of the Prompt employees was to avoid bargaining with Local 32B. The Board could properly consider this unfair labor practice in determining Laro's motive for its contemporaneous failure to hire the Prompt employees.

Laro's contention that once it hired former Prompt employees as a majority of its Cadman Plaza work force, it had no further incentive to discriminate against Local 32B members, is undermined by its own action. Because the majority of Local 32B members at Cadman Plaza was so small (ten of eighteen), the addition of two individuals to the unit would destroy Local 32B's majority status, and Laro attempted, through Acosta and his supervisor, to accomplish this goal. Had Laro hired additional former Prompt employees, it could not as easily conceal the Local 32B majority * * *.

As further evidence of impermissible motive, the Board relied on Laro's employment decisions at other cleaning contract sites. Of the three sites where Laro acquired the cleaning contract, including Cadman Plaza, two were unionized under the previous employer and one was not. Laro attempted to avoid hiring any of the incumbent employees at both unionized locations but willingly hired one-third of the incumbent employees at the non-union location. These actions undermine Laro's claim that its reasons for limiting its hires of Prompt employees were related to performance; there is no performance-based rationale for the disparate treatment of incumbent employees at unionized and non-unionized sites in the absence of record evidence regarding employee quality. The Board's inference that this disparate treatment was based on union membership is thus based on substantial evidence and provides further evidence of unlawful motive for Laro's refusal to hire any of the thirteen Prompt employees.

Finally, the Board determined that Laro's explanation for its refusal to consider the applications of the thirteen Prompt employees was pretextual. Although Laro was not obliged to offer any explanation for its actions, the Board has held that a "case of discriminatory motivation may be supported by consideration of the lack of any legitimate basis for a respondent's actions." *Weco Cleaning Specialists, Inc.*, 308 N.L.R.B. 310, 310 n. 4, 1992 WL 206968 (1992); *Wright Line*, 251 N.L.R.B. at 1088 n. 12. This is especially true when the employer presents a legitimate basis for its actions which the factfinder concludes is pretextual. In such cases, the factfinder may not only properly infer that there is some other motive, but "that the motive is one that the employer desires to conceal—an unlawful motive—at least where . . . the surrounding facts tend to reinforce that inference." *Shattuck Denn Mining Corp. v. NLRB*, 362 F.2d 466, 470 (9th Cir.1966).

Laro maintains that it refused to consider employing any Prompt employees who were not on the GSA's recommended list for two related legitimate reasons. First, Laro claims that it wanted to start work with "fresh" employees, untainted by different methods that may have been used by Prompt or bad habits acquired during previous employment at Cadman Plaza. Second, Laro points out that it knew that Prompt employees had performed inadequately based on the deductions from Prompt's fees and Bertuglia's observation of two Prompt employees sleeping on the job. Laro correctly maintains that the Board, albeit on distinguishable records where the factfinder credited the proffered explanation, has previously found similar reasons sufficient defenses to allegations of discriminatory actions. However, assertions of a legitimate business reason for preferring inexperienced workers can be overcome by evidence that an anti-union motive influenced the decision to exclude experienced employees.

The Board's rejection of Laro's proffered business reasons for refusing to consider any of the thirteen Prompt employees is supported by substantial evidence. Both proffered reasons stem from Laro's alleged desire to hire workers who would perform best. Yet the record and Laro's actions belie such an intent on Laro's part. Laro transferred one worker from Jamaica to Cadman Plaza because of his poor work and need for constant supervision, and it hired another worker who had recently been fired from the Jamaica site for absenteeism and insubordination. Laro also hired at least three workers for Cadman Plaza with no relevant experience, rather than attempting to determine who among Prompt's experienced employees were sleeping on the job or responsible for the deductions (whose nature, extent and causes were unknown to Laro). None of these actions comports with a desire to employ only the most productive workers.

Most telling is Laro's treatment of two individuals who sought employment during the week before Laro took over the Cadman Plaza contract. One former Prompt employee, Luis Quebrada, requested his old job back at Cadman Plaza, while a former Laro employee, Yonette Mathurin, who had been fired by Laro, requested her old job back at the Jamaica site. Laro hired both, but instead of giving them their requested assignments, it told Quebrada that no positions were left at Cadman Plaza and he would have to work at the Jamaica site, while informing Mathurin precisely the opposite, that no job was available at the Jamaica site but she could work at Cadman Plaza.

Based on this evidence, the Board drew the reasonable inference that Laro's explanations for not hiring any of the thirteen Prompt employees were pretextual. A desire for better quality employees does not explain Laro's hiring of demonstrably poor employees, rather than making any attempt to determine the quality of Prompt's experienced employees. Nor does Laro's explanation elucidate why Laro would allow the former Prompt employee, Quebrada, to work only at the Jamaica site, while permitting the former Laro employee, Mathurin, to take a job only at Cadman Plaza.

Laro's desire to exclude Prompt employees from the Cadman Plaza site because of their union membership explains all of these actions.

Laro has offered the ALJ, the Board, and the court innocent explanations for virtually all of the evidence from which the Board inferred impermissible motive. For example, Laro explained that it assigned its two previous employees with poor records to Cadman Plaza because one would do better work for the supervisor at Cadman Plaza than he did for the supervisor at Jamaica and the other, who had been fired, repeatedly entreated her supervisor for reinstatement until he agreed to give her a second chance. However, the Board was not required to credit these explanations, and specifically declined to overturn the ALJ's evaluations because it was not convinced by "the clear preponderance of all the relevant evidence . . . that they [were] incorrect." One component of the Board's determination that Laro's explanation for its actions was pretextual is the Board's view of Bertuglia's credibility. "[T]he ALJ's credibility determinations, as adopted by the Board, will be upheld unless they are patently insupportable." *Gold Coast*, 995 F.2d at 265; *Williams Enterprises, Inc. v. NLRB*, 956 F.2d 1226, 1232 (D.C.Cir.1992). Consistent with the applicable standard of review, even if the court concluded that Laro's explanations were reasonable, the court would nevertheless uphold the Board's inferences as supported by substantial, if not overwhelming, evidence. We therefore conclude that the first prong of *Wright Line* was satisfied; substantial evidence supports a *prima facie* case that Laro failed to consider or hire any of the thirteen Prompt employees because of its desire to avoid recognizing and bargaining with Local 32B in violation of §§ 8(a)(1) and (3).

Laro fares no better under the *Wright Line* test's second prong. Laro asserted the affirmative defense that even in the absence of impermissible motivation, it would have made the same hiring decisions and declined to hire any of the thirteen Prompt employees. Specifically, Laro maintains that it would have hired the eight non-incumbent employees whom it did hire because of its legitimate desire for workers who had experience working for Laro or who were recommended by a person with such experience. The ALJ concluded that Laro failed to prove that any of the thirteen Prompt employees would not have been hired absent Laro's impermissible motivation. The Board agreed, noting that Laro had failed to offer any legitimate reason for refusing to interview or consider the pool of experienced employees. The Board's rejection of Laro's argument is based on substantial evidence. As noted, the Board rejected Laro's claim that it legitimately preferred workers previously employed by Laro because two of those workers had demonstrated their inability to work under Laro's system. Similarly, the Board rejected Laro's claim that it legitimately preferred inexperienced workers recommended by Laro employees because the Board found that this preference was applied disparately to union members and was therefore a pretext for discrimination based on union membership.

Thus, the Board's determination that Laro refused to hire any of the thirteen former Prompt employees because of their union membership is supported by substantial evidence in the record considered as a whole, including Laro's predetermination not to hire any more Prompt employees than GSA required, its disparate treatment of union-represented employees, its admitted contemporaneous unfair labor practice, and the absence of a legitimate reason for refusing to consider or make inquiries about the thirteen Prompt employees while hiring inexperienced employees and employees with poor work records. Accordingly, we deny the petition for review and grant the Board's petition for enforcement.

RANDOLPH, CIRCUIT JUDGE, dissenting:

The Board's decision in this case makes no sense. Prompt's 23 employees had been doing a lousy job cleaning Cadman Plaza and Laro knew it, not only from GSA's report but also from observing two of Prompt's employees sleeping on the job. When Laro took over, it decided to streamline operations, thinking it could do a better job with 5 fewer workers. Yet according to the Board, Laro had a legal obligation to fill its 18 slots with the former Prompt employees. Why? Because, according to the Board, the only reason Laro did not hire all its employees from the Prompt pool was Laro's anti-Local 32B animus. There is no substantial evidence, indeed there is no evidence whatever, to support the Board's conclusion—a conclusion that entails the utterly ridiculous proposition that but for the Prompt employees' membership in Local 32B, Laro would have hired them.

Too bad for Laro that it did not stick to its initial plan of not hiring any of Prompt's 23 employees. Had Laro done so in light of what it learned from GSA, no unfair labor practice charge could possibly have stuck. The labor laws do not require new employers to keep any of their predecessor's workers on board, so long as the new employer does not refuse to hire them "solely" because they belong to a union. But at GSA's urging, Laro caved in and retained 10 Prompt employees, designated by GSA as the best of the bunch. The remaining 13 Prompt employees were thus necessarily the worst of the lot, or at least Laro was entitled to so believe. Laro harbored no anti-union animus in filling 10 of its 18 positions—a majority—with Prompt workers, all of whom were members of Local 32B. How then can it be that Laro violated § 8(a)(3), 29 U.S.C. § 158(a)(3), by not hiring more? (Actually, Laro did hire one more former Prompt employee and set him to work at another site. When he quit two days later, complaining that he had been "overworked," he fell back into the pool of the unhired 13.)

The ALJ's answer to this question, adopted by the Board, is irrational: Laro "did not want to hire any more of Prompt's incumbent employees than it believed it was required to by GSA, in an effort to avoid a bargaining obligation with Local 32B." It is tempting to place a couple of exclamation points and a few question marks at the end of the ALJ's statement, a statement upon which the entire case turns. Why in the world would Laro think it could "avoid a bargaining obligation" by not hiring more Prompt employees? A "bargaining obligation" arises from a union's majority status. Local 32B was already over the top at Cadman Plaza. Ten of 18 is a majority. A bigger majority is still a majority. Are we supposed to believe that Laro could not do simple arithmetic?

The truth is that Laro's refusal to recognize Local 32B was not on the basis that the union lacked a majority at Cadman Plaza. Laro refused to bargain with Local 32B because Laro considered—incorrectly it turned out—the Cadman Plaza operation an accretion to the bargaining unit in Jamaica, Queens, where Laro cleaned another federal office building pursuant to a GSA contract. A different union, Local 355, represented Laro's Jamaica employees. The number of employees represented by Local 355 exceeded 18. Hence, no matter how many more former Prompt employees Laro hired at Cadman Plaza, the unit as Laro viewed it would still have had a majority of Local 355 members.

The fact that Laro hired a majority of its Cadman Plaza work force from the pool of Prompt employees gives the lie to the ALJ's—and the Board's—notion that Laro's alleged intent to avoid bargaining with Local 32B was a "motivating factor" behind the company's hiring decisions. Had Laro been thinking the thoughts the ALJ placed in its head it would have pared down GSA's list to 8 or less.

The rest of the ALJ's reasoning is makeweight, and just as nonsensical. Two examples should suffice. Consider first what the ALJ deduced from Laro's take-over of two other cleaning operations. When the company succeeded to the cleaning contract at the federal facility in Jamaica, Laro hired one-third of the incumbent employees, who were not then unionized. Upon taking over operations at Dowling College, Laro initially decided not to hire any incumbent employees, but wound up hiring all of them at the college's insistence; the incumbent employees were unionized. According to the ALJ, what happened at Jamaica and Dowling College shows that Laro did not really "like[ ] to 'start fresh' with a new complement of employees" unless a union represented the incumbent workers. Nonsense again. There is no evidence whatever that Laro's initial desire at Dowling stemmed from anti-union sentiments. If Laro is so anti-union, how can one account for the fact that the Jamaica employees became organized without Laro's committing any unfair labor practices? All we know, all the Board and the ALJ knew, is that on one occasion Laro hired some incumbents and on another occasion it did not want to, but did. About the only thing to be gleaned from this bit of history is a common fact of business life having nothing to do with anti-union animus: sometimes there are good workers in the group of incumbents; sometimes there are not; and sometimes it is not worth trying to sort out the good from the bad.

Consider last the ALJ's "reasoning" that because Laro hired some inexperienced workers, anti-union bias must have moved it not to hire any of the 13 experienced Prompt employees. This too crosses the boggle threshold. In the ALJ's mind, experience must equal competence. Nonsense again. If you were in the cleaning business would you prefer an experienced Prompt employee, experienced that is in sleeping on the job, over a fresh face willing to work and eager to learn how to run a vacuum cleaner and empty a trash can?

My colleagues deeply bow in deference to the Board when they should be furrowing their brows at what the Board offered. More can be said, but this is enough to indicate why I respectfully dissent.

NOTES

How does one tell whether evidence is "substantial" enough to sustain an agency decision? Was the NLRB's evidence in *Laro Maintenance* really more "substantial" than the MSPB's evidence in *Kimm*? These questions do not have simple answers. Most of the time, lawyers know substantial evidence when they see it.[10] When the evidence gets close to the margins, judgments become difficult, which is why we have appellate decisions—and occasionally split appellate decisions—determining whether agencies have satisfied the substantial evidence test. For other good examples of decisions involving the reasonableness of agency inferences from circumstantial evidence, see *Jackson Hospital Corp. v. NLRB*, 647 F.3d 1137 (D.C.Cir.2011) (rejecting an agency inference not unlike the inference in *Laro Maintenance*); *Federated Logistics & Operations v. NLRB,* 400 F.3d 920 (D.C.Cir.2005) (upholding an agency inference by a 2–1 vote); *Elliott v. CFTC*, 202 F.3d 926 (7th Cir.2000) (upholding an agency inference by a 2–1 vote).

C. REVIEW OF FINDINGS OF FACT IN INFORMAL PROCEEDINGS

Section 706(2)(E) by its terms applies only to formal agency proceedings—that is, cases "subject to sections 556 and 557 of this title or otherwise reviewed on the record of an agency hearing provided by statute." What happens when agencies find facts in informal proceedings to which the APA's substantial evidence test does not apply? Sometimes the agency's organic statute will prescribe a standard of review—most likely a "substantial evidence" standard, as with the organic statutes in *Universal Camera* and *Kimm*. What is the relationship between those

---

[10] They know it, of course, from experience: if you see enough agency proceedings, you can get a "feel" for the kind of evidence that will support or undermine an agency position. To make matters worse, the kind and quantum of evidence that will be deemed "substantial" may vary a bit with the agency and court involved.

extra-APA standards and § 706(2)(E)? And what if the organic statute does not provide a standard of review? The APA states that reviewing courts should overturn agency action that is "arbitrary, capricious, an abuse of discretion, or otherwise not in accordance with law." § 706(2)(A). Is there anything in this cryptic provision that can apply to judicial review of agency factfinding in informal proceedings?

Consider the answers provided by then-Judge, later-Justice, and (most importantly) former-Administrative-Law-professor Scalia (joined by then-Judge, now-Justice, former-Civil-Procedure-professor Ginsburg) in this difficult but now-classic opinion:

ASSOCIATION OF DATA PROCESSING SERVICE ORGANIZATIONS, INC. v. BOARD OF GOVERNORS OF THE FEDERAL RESERVE SYSTEM

United States Court of Appeals, District of Columbia Circuit, 1984.
745 F.2d 677.

Before GINSBURG and SCALIA, CIRCUIT JUDGES, and VAN PELT, SENIOR DISTRICT JUDGE.

SCALIA, CIRCUIT JUDGE:

The Association of Data Processing Service Organizations, Inc. ("ADAPSO"), a national trade association representing the data processing industry, and two of its members petition this court for review of two orders of the Board of Governors of the Federal Reserve System, pursuant to 12 U.S.C. § 1848 (1982). In No. 82–1910, they seek review of the Board's July 9, 1982 order approving Citicorp's application to establish a subsidiary, Citishare, to engage in certain data processing and transmission services. *Order Approving Engaging in Data Processing and Data Transmission Activities*, 68 Fed.Res.Bull. 505 (1982) ("Citicorp Order"). In No. 82–2108, they seek review of the Board's August 23, 1982 order, entered after notice and comment rulemaking, amending those portions of Regulation Y which dealt with the performance of data processing activities by bank holding companies. *Data Processing and Electronic Funds Transfer Activities*, 47 Fed.Reg. 37,368 (1982) ("Regulation Y Order"). We consolidated the two appeals.

The Bank Holding Company Act of 1956, ch. 240, 70 Stat. 133 (codified as amended at 12 U.S.C. §§ 1841–50 (1982)) (the "Act"), requires all bank holding companies to seek prior regulatory approval before engaging in nonbanking activities. The restrictions do not apply to:

> activities . . . which the Board after due notice and opportunity for hearing has determined (by order or regulation) to be so closely related to banking or managing or controlling banks as to be a proper incident thereto. . . In determining whether a particular

> activity is a proper incident to banking or managing or controlling banks the Board shall consider whether its performance by an affiliate of a holding company can reasonably be expected to produce benefits to the public, such as greater convenience, increased competition, or gains in efficiency, that outweigh possible adverse effects, such as undue concentration of resources, decreased or unfair competition, conflicts of interests, or unsound banking practices.

12 U.S.C. § 1843(c)(8). Section 1848, the source of our review authority, provides that "[t]he findings of the Board as to the facts, if supported by substantial evidence, shall be conclusive." *Id.* at § 1848.

On February 23, 1979, Citicorp applied for authority to engage, through its subsidiary Citishare, in the processing and transmission of banking, financial, and economic related data through timesharing, electronic funds transfer, home banking and other techniques. It also sought permission to sell its excess computing capacity and some computer hardware. The Board published notice of Citicorp's application, which was protested by ADAPSO, and set it for formal hearing. Before the hearing was held, Citicorp amended its application to add certain activities and to request amendment of Regulation Y to permit the activities it had specified. The Board published an Amended Order for Hearing and invited public comments and participation. A formal hearing was held before an Administrative Law Judge in which the merits of both the application and the proposed rule were considered. In addition, more than sixty companies and individuals submitted written comments on the proposed rule. On March 29, 1982, the ALJ decided that the activities proposed by Citicorp were closely related to banking and would produce benefits to the public which would outweigh their costs. The ALJ also recommended amendments to Regulation Y that would permit those activities contained in the Citicorp application. On July 9, 1982, the Board adopted the ALJ's recommendation to approve the Citicorp application, with certain restrictions. On August 23, 1982, the Board adopted the ALJ's recommended amendments to Regulation Y, again with certain restrictions. ADAPSO, and two of its members, participants in the actions below, filed these petitions for review.

I.   STANDARD OF REVIEW

We are faced at the outset with a dispute regarding the proper standard of review. These consolidated appeals call for us to review both an on-the-record adjudication and an informal notice and comment rulemaking. Petitioners contend that the substantial evidence standard, which presumably authorizes more rigorous judicial review, should govern our review of both orders. The Board agrees, noting that § 1848 applies a substantial evidence standard to factual determinations. Intervenor

Citicorp contends that while the substantial evidence standard should govern review of the Citicorp order, Regulation Y should be upset only if arbitrary or capricious. Intervenor California Bankers Clearing House Association, addressing only Regulation Y, also advocates review under the arbitrary or capricious review standard. The parties' submissions on this point reflect considerable confusion, which is understandable when one examines decisions defining the standard of review under this statute.

Both of the Supreme Court's opinions reviewing action of the Board in amending Regulation Y noted that the Board's determination "is entitled to the greatest deference," *Board of Governors of the Federal Reserve System v. Investment Company Institute*, 450 U.S. 46, 56, 101 S.Ct. 973, 981–82, 67 L.Ed.2d 36 (1981) ("*ICI*"); *Securities Industry Association v. Board of Governors of the Federal Reserve System*, [468] U.S. [207], 104 S.Ct. 3003, 3009, 82 L.Ed.2d 158 (1984) ("*SIA*"), but neither of them discussed the applicable standard of review, or even referred to § 1848. The courts of appeals, however, have applied the substantial evidence standard of § 1848 to Board adjudications such as the authorization in the first order here under review, *Securities Industry Association v. Board of Governors of the Federal Reserve System*, 716 F.2d 92, 101–02 (2d Cir.1983), aff'd, [468] U.S. [207], 104 S.Ct. 3003, 82 L.Ed.2d 158 (1984), while applying the arbitrary or capricious standard, despite § 1848, to Board rules, including specifically amendments of Regulation Y, *National Courier Association v. Board of Governors of the Federal Reserve System*, 516 F.2d 1229 (D.C.Cir.1975); *Association of Bank Travel Bureaus v. Board of Governors of the Federal Reserve System*, 568 F.2d 549 (7th Cir.1978); *see Investment Company Institute v. Board of Governors of the Federal Reserve System*, 551 F.2d 1270, 1281 (D.C.Cir.1977) (dicta). In fact one appellate opinion has, like this one, addressed precisely the situation in which *both* an adjudicatory authorization *and* an amendment of Regulation Y were at issue in the same case—and applied the § 1848 substantial evidence standard to the former but the arbitrary or capricious standard to the latter. *Compare Alabama Association of Insurance Agents v. Board of Governors of the Federal Reserve System*, 533 F.2d 224, 246 (5th Cir.1976), with *id.* at 240. This would make a lot of sense if, as the Board has argued in some cases, § 1848 in its totality applies only to adjudication rather than rulemaking, since it is limited to "orders" of the Board, a word which the Administrative Procedure Act ("APA") defines to mean the product of an adjudication. *See* 5 U.S.C. § 551(4), (6) (1982). Such a technical interpretation of the provision, however, has been uniformly and quite correctly rejected. *See Investment Company Institute, supra*, 551 F.2d at 1276–78; *Alabama Association of Insurance Agents, supra*, 533 F.2d at 234–35. That leaves the courts with the difficult task of explaining why the last sentence of § 1848, unlike all the rest of it, should be deemed to apply only to adjudication and not to rulemaking. Difficult, because there is nothing in either the text or the legislative history of the section to suggest such a result. The courts applying the arbitrary or capricious standard to Board rulemaking (which, as stated above, include all the courts that have confronted the issue) dispose of this problem either by totally ignoring it, *see Alabama Association of Insurance Agents, supra,* 533 F.2d at 240, 246, or by noting that the parties "do not appear to contest" the point, *National Courier, supra,* 516 F.2d at 1235 n. 8, or by the *ipse dixit* that "[w]e interpret [the last sentence of § 1848] to apply to findings of fact 'on the record' in an adjudicatory hearing as contrasted with a rulemaking proceeding," *Association of Bank Travel Bureaus, supra,* 568 F.2d at 552 n. 5.

We think that there is no basis for giving the last sentence of § 1848 anything less than the general application given to the rest of the section. The Supreme Court's pronouncement that the "greatest deference" is to be given to the determinations of the Board, and the court of appeals decisions applying the arbitrary or capricious test to Board rulemaking, seem to us explicable on quite different grounds—namely, that in their application to the requirement of factual support the substantial evidence test and the arbitrary or capricious test are one and the same. The former is only a specific application of the latter, separately recited in the APA not to establish a more rigorous standard of factual support but to emphasize that in the case of formal proceedings the factual support must be found in the closed record as opposed to elsewhere. We shall elaborate upon this point because it is not uncommon for parties to expend great effort in appeals before us to establish which of the two standards is applicable where in fact their operation is precisely the same.

The "scope of review" provisions of the APA are cumulative. Thus, an agency action which is supported by the required substantial evidence may in another regard be "arbitrary, capricious, an abuse of discretion, or otherwise not in accordance with law"—for example, because it is an abrupt and unexplained departure from agency precedent. Paragraph (A) of subsection 706(2)—the "arbitrary or capricious" provision—is a catchall, picking up administrative misconduct not covered by the other more specific paragraphs. Thus, in those situations where paragraph (E) has no application (informal rulemaking, for example, which is not governed by §§ 556 and 557 to which paragraph (E) refers), paragraph (A) takes up the slack, so to speak, enabling the courts to strike down, as arbitrary, agency action that is devoid of needed factual support. When the arbitrary or capricious standard is performing that function of assuring factual support, there is no *substantive* difference between what it requires and what would be required by the substantial evidence test, since it is impossible to conceive of a "nonarbitrary" factual judgment supported only by evidence that is not substantial in the APA sense—*i.e.*, not " 'enough to justify, if the trial were to a jury, a refusal to direct a verdict when the conclusion sought to be drawn . . . is one of fact for the jury,' " *Illinois Central R.R. v. Norfolk*

& Western Ry., 385 U.S. 57, 66, 87 S.Ct. 255, 260, 17 L.Ed.2d 162 (1966) (quoting *NLRB v. Columbian Enameling & Stamping Co.*, 306 U.S. 292, 300, 59 S.Ct. 501, 505, 83 L.Ed. 660 (1939)).

We have noted on several occasions that the distinction between the substantial evidence test and the arbitrary or capricious test is "largely semantic," *Aircraft Owners and Pilots Association v. FAA*, 600 F.2d 965, 971 n. 28 (D.C.Cir.1979); *Pacific Legal Foundation v. Department of Transportation*, 593 F.2d 1338, 1343 n. 35 (D.C.Cir.1979); *American Public Gas Association v. FPC*, 567 F.2d 1016, 1028–29 (D.C.Cir.1977), and have indeed described that view as "the emerging consensus of the Courts of Appeals," *Pacific Legal Foundation, supra*, 593 F.2d at 1343 n. 35. Leading commentators agree:

> Does the extent of required factual support for rules depend in part on whether the standard for review is "substantial evidence" or "arbitrary and capricious"? Although from 1946 until some time during the 1970s the dominant answer probably was yes, a change to a no answer has probably occurred during the 1970s. . .

1 K. DAVIS, ADMINISTRATIVE LAW TREATISE § 6:13 at 512 (2d ed. 1978).

> In review of rules of general applicability made after "notice and comment" rule-making, [substantial evidence and arbitrary or capricious] criteria converge into a test of reasonableness.
>
> . . .
>
> Review without an agency record thus comes down to review of reasonableness. [T]he question of reasonableness is also the one which the court must now ask itself in reviewing findings of fact under the post-APA substantial evidence rule.

B. SCHWARTZ, ADMINISTRATIVE LAW 604, 606 (1976).

As noted earlier, this does not consign paragraph (E) of the APA's judicial review section to pointlessness. The distinctive function of paragraph (E)—what it achieves that paragraph (A) does not—is to require substantial evidence to be found *within the record of closed-record proceedings* to which it exclusively applies. The importance of that requirement should not be underestimated. It is true that, as the Supreme Court said in *Camp v. Pitts*, 411 U.S. 138, 142, 93 S.Ct. 1241, 1244, 36 L.Ed.2d 106 (1973), even informal agency action (not governed by paragraph (E)) must be reviewed only on the basis of "the administrative record already in existence." But that is quite a different and less onerous requirement, meaning only that whether the administrator was arbitrary must be determined on the basis of what he had before him when he acted, and not on the basis of "some new record made initially in the reviewing court," *id*. That "administrative record" might well include crucial material that was neither shown to nor known by the private parties in the proceeding—as indeed appears to have been the situation in *Camp v. Pitts* itself. It is true that, in informal rulemaking, at least the most critical factual material that is used to support the agency's position on review must have been made public in the proceeding and exposed to refutation. That requirement, however, does not extend to all data, and it only applies in rulemaking and not in other informal agency action, since it derives not from the arbitrary or capricious test but from the command of 5 U.S.C. § 553(c) that "the agency . . . give interested persons an opportunity to participate in the rule making." *See Portland Cement Association v. Ruckelshaus*, 486 F.2d 375, 393 n. 67 (D.C.Cir.1973).

Consolidated cases such as those before us here—involving simultaneous review of a rule (whose factual basis is governed only by paragraph (A)'s catch-all control against "arbitrary or capricious" action) and of a formal adjudication dealing with the same subject (whose factual basis is governed by paragraph (E)'s requirement of substantial evidence)—demonstrate why the foregoing interpretation of the two standards is the only interpretation that makes sense. If the standards were substantively different (and leaving aside for the moment consideration of any special effect of § 1848), the Citicorp order, authorizing one bank holding company's data processing services, would be subject to more rigorous judicial review of factual support than the Regulation Y order which, due to its general applicability, would affect the operations of every bank holding company in the nation. Or, to put the point another way: If the Board had never issued any Regulation Y, and simply determined in the context of a particular application that the provision of timesharing services is "closely related" to banking, that determination, which could be reconsidered and revised in the context of the next adjudication, would require more factual support than the same determination in a rulemaking, which would have immediate nationwide application and, until amended by further rulemaking, would have to be applied to all subsequent applications.

This seemingly upside-down application of varying standards is not an issue in the present case since, as we have observed, § 1848 makes it clear that only *one* standard—the substantial evidence test—applies to review of all Board actions. The relevance of the foregoing discussion here is to determine what that standard *means*. What we have said suggests that the normal (APA) meaning of the "substantial evidence" terminology connotes a substantive standard no different from the arbitrary or capricious test. One cannot dismiss out of hand, however, the possibility that, in this particular statute, a different meaning was intended—in which case that different standard would govern review of both rulemaking and adjudication. A number of "substantial evidence" review provisions have been attached to rulemaking authority, particularly in recent years. *See, e.g.,* 29 U.S.C. § 655(f) (1982) (Occupational Safety and Health Act); 30 U.S.C. § 816(a) (1982) (Federal Coal Mine Health and Safety Act); 15 U.S.C. § 1193(e)(3) (1982) (Flammable Fabrics Act); 15 U.S.C. § 57a(e)(3)(A) (1982) (FTC Improvement Act of 1975). It is conceivable that some of these were intended, as the Fifth Circuit found with regard to such a provision in the Consumer Product Safety Act, 15 U.S.C. § 2060 (1982), to require the courts "to scrutinize [agency] actions more closely than an 'arbitrary and capricious' standard would allow." *Aqua Slide 'N' Dive Corp. v. CPSC,* 569 F.2d 831, 837 (5th Cir.1978). Congress's unpropitious use of the "substantial evidence" APA language for such a purpose is plausible, since the standard has acquired a reputation for being more stringent.[6] One should not be too quick, however, to impute such a congressional intent. There is surely little appeal to an ineffable review standard that lies somewhere in-between the quantum of factual support required to go to a jury (the traditional "substantial evidence" test) and the "preponderance of the evidence" standard that would apply in *de novo* review. Moreover, 5 U.S.C. § 559 provides that a subsequent statute shall not be held to supersede or modify the APA provisions "except to the extent that it does so expressly." While the provision for "substantial evidence" review where the APA would otherwise require only "arbitrary or capricious" review is unquestionably an "express" alteration, surely the import of the § 559 instruction is that Congress's *intent to make a substantive change* be clear. This can lead to some fairly convoluted inquiries. Suppose, for example, that Congress clearly intended to switch to a stricter test, but was also clearly operating on the mistaken belief that the existing test ("arbitrary or capricious") was more lenient than the "substantial evidence" standard. Should one give effect to the congressional intent to adopt a stricter standard, or rather to the congressional intent to adopt the "substantial evidence" standard (which is in fact, as we have discussed, no stricter)? Several decisions of this court stand for the proposition that a "substantial evidence" provision in the substantive statute under consideration did not have the effect of requiring increased factual support beyond that demanded by the normal "arbitrary or capricious" rulemaking standard of review. *Public Systems v. FERC,* 606 F.2d 973, 980 n. 34 (D.C.Cir.1979) (interpreting the predecessors of § 19(b) of the Natural Gas Act, 15 U.S.C. § 717r(b) (1982), and the corresponding provision of the Federal Power Act, 16 U.S.C. § 825l(b) (1982)); *American Public Gas Association v. FPC, supra,* 567 F.2d at 1028–29 (interpreting the predecessor of § 19(b) of the Natural Gas Act).

---

[6]   *See, e.g.,* the quotation from K. DAVIS, *supra.* The reason for this reputation, one may surmise, is that under the APA the substantial evidence test applies almost exclusively to formal adjudication (formal rulemaking is rare), which is, by contrast to rulemaking, characteristically long on facts and short on policy—so that the inadequacy of factual support is typically the central issue in the judicial appeal and is the most common reason for reversal.

Fortunately, it is not necessary to engage in these speculations with regard to the "substantial evidence" provision of § 1848. The Supreme Court has evidently rejected the notion that it alters normal APA review requirements, since the Court's opinions reviewing Board action deem the provision unworthy of mention, and specifically accord the Board "the greatest deference." We hold, therefore, that the § 1848 "substantial evidence" requirement applicable to our review here demands a quantum of factual support no different from that demanded by the substantial evidence provision of the APA, which is in turn no different from that demanded by the arbitrary or capricious standard.

* * *

[In a lengthy discussion, the court upholds the agency on the merits.]

NOTES

The dictum of *Data Processing* "that in their application to the requirement of factual support the substantial evidence test and the arbitrary or capricious test are one and the same" has become settled law in the D.C. Circuit, *see Center for Auto Safety v. FHA*, 956 F.2d 309, 313 (D.C.Cir.1992), though its influence on other circuits is less clear. *Compare Zen Magnets, LLC v. CPSC*, 841 F.3d 1141, 1148 n.8 (10th Cir.2016) (endorsing the *Data Processing* approach); *GTE South v. Morrison*, 199 F.3d 733, 745 n.5 (4th Cir.1999) (same); *Wileman Brothers & Elliott, Inc. v. Espy*, 58 F.3d 1367, 1374–75 (9th Cir.1995) (same) *with Browning-Ferris Industries of South Jersey, Inc. v. Muszynski*, 899 F.2d 151, 164 (2d Cir.1990) (describing *Data Processing* as "conflating" the arbitrary or capricious and substantial evidence tests for review of factual judgments).

Judge/Justice/Professor Scalia's analysis of the relationship between § 706(2)(A) and § 706(2)(E) is characteristically intricate and elegant. But is it *correct* to equate the quanta of evidence required by § 706(2)(A) and § 706(2)(E) to support agency factual findings? It is too early in this course to make that judgment, as we have not yet studied § 706(2)(A) in depth. Suffice it to say that Justice Scalia may be wrong with respect to the original meaning of the APA, which arguably supports the view that § 706(2)(E) calls for stricter judicial scrutiny than does § 706(2)(A), but right about which interpretation of § 706(2)(A) best fits into the overall modern scheme of judicial review.

Data Processing's discussion of the APA was all dictum, as the case clearly held that the organic statute prescribed the standard of review—"substantial evidence"—for factual findings in both formal and informal proceedings. Judge Scalia held that the "substantial evidence" test specified in the Bank Holding Company Act of 1956 requires the same standard of judicial review as does the APA—just as Justice (and former Administrative Law professor) Frankfurter held in *Universal Camera* with respect to the 1947 Taft-Hartley Act's substantial evidence provision. Judge Scalia acknowledged, however, the possibility that "substantial evidence" provisions in some organic statutes may call for a different—either more or less deferential—standard of review than is found in the APA. In *Corrosion Proof Fittings v. EPA*, 947 F.2d 1201 (5th Cir.1991), the Fifth Circuit expressly held that a "substantial evidence" provision in the Toxic Substances Control Act (TSCA) prescribes a different, more rigorous standard of review for factual findings in informal rulemaking than do either of the potentially applicable APA provisions:

> Contrary to the EPA's assertions, the arbitrary and capricious standard found in the APA and the substantial evidence standard found in TSCA are different standards, even in the context of an informal rulemaking. Congress specifically went out of its way to provide that "the standard of review prescribed by paragraph (2)(E) of section 706 [of the APA] shall not apply and the court shall hold unlawful and set aside such rule if the court finds that the rule is not supported by substantial evidence in the rulemaking record . . . taken as a whole." 15 U.S.C. § 2618(c)(1)(B)(i). "The substantial evidence standard mandated by [TSCA] is generally considered to be more rigorous than the arbitrary and capricious standard normally applied to informal rulemaking," Environmental Defense Fund v. EPA, 636 F.2d 1267, 1277 (D.C.Cir.1980), and "afford[s] a considerably more generous judicial review" than the arbitrary and capricious test.

947 F.2d at 1213–14. The Fifth Circuit did not cite *Data Processing*.

In the course of his discussion of how organic statutes might prescribe standards of review that are different from the APA standards, Judge Scalia cautioned against casually reading such statutes to call for varying levels of review, because "[t]here is surely little appeal to an ineffable review standard that lies somewhere in-between the quantum of factual support required to go to a jury (the traditional 'substantial evidence' test) and the 'preponderance of the evidence' standard that would apply in *de novo* review." Is it true, and was it true in 1984, that the "traditional 'substantial evidence' test" was the jury standard? Does that square at all with *Universal Camera*? Didn't *Universal Camera* already create just such "an ineffable review standard"? Was Justice Scalia in *Allentown Mack* trying to make his decision as Judge Scalia in *Data Processing* correct nunc pro tunc?

D. REVIEW OF AGENCY LEGAL CONCLUSIONS

1. THEORY AND HISTORY

The primary function of appellate courts is to decide questions of law. One might therefore expect reviewing courts to engage in de novo review of agency legal conclusions. This instinct finds support in the language of the APA, which instructs courts to overturn agency action that is "in excess of statutory jurisdiction, authority, or limitations, or short of statutory right," § 706(2)(C), without specifying a deferential standard of review.

Nonetheless, agencies have long received a substantial measure of deference for many of their legal conclusions. The precise domain and scope of that deference, however, has been—and continues to be—one of the major battlegrounds in administrative law. In order to understand the present law (and the likely direction of future law) in this area, one must understand the past. Accordingly, we begin with discussion of some cases that in many respects are no longer good law,[11] but without which the present law is incomprehensible.

Consider three noteworthy cases that were decided between 1941 and 1951 involving judicial review of agency interpretations of statutes: *Gray v. Powell*, 314 U.S. 402, 62 S.Ct. 326, 86 L.Ed. 301 (1941); *NLRB v. Hearst*, 322 U.S. 111, 64 S.Ct. 851, 88 L.Ed.1170 (1944); and *O'Leary v. Brown-Pacific-Maxon, Inc.*, 340 U.S. 504, 71 S.Ct. 470, 95 L.Ed. 483 (1951). These cases, alone and collectively, reflect a pattern of judicial review that serves as a framework for the law leading up to modern developments.[12]

Gray v. Powell concerned an interpretation of the Bituminous Coal Act of 1937 by the Director of the Bituminous Coal Division of the Department of the Interior. The Act authorized the agency to prescribe a detailed code for the regulation, or more precisely the cartelization, of the bituminous coal industry, as part of the general New Deal antipathy towards what was regarded as wasteful and destructive competition. In order to coerce coal producers to submit to the regulatory codes, the Act imposed a punitive 19 ½ percent tax "upon the sale or other disposal of bituminous coal produced within the United States, when sold or otherwise disposed of by the producer thereof," § 3(b), 50 Stat. 75, with a blanket exception from the tax for any producer who was a "code member" under the statute and whose transaction complied with the code. (There was also an exception from the tax for any coal sold exclusively to a governmental entity. *See* § 3(e), 50 Stat. 75–76.) For purposes of the tax provision, the Act defined "disposal" of coal to "include[ ] consumption or use * * * by a producer, and any transfer of title by the producer other than by sale," § 3(a), 50 Stat. 75, but then carved out an exception from the terms of the coal code for "coal consumed by the producer or * * * coal transported by the producer to himself for consumption by him." § 4(*l*), 50 Stat. 83. The net effect of these provisions was to exempt from the punitive tax for non-compliance with the code any "sale or other disposal" of coal that was consumed by its producer. Of course, if there was never any "sale or other disposal" of coal

[handwritten margin note: Gray v. Powell]

---

[11] Any case involving judicial review of agency legal conclusions that was decided before 1984 is immediately suspect. Some such cases may still be good law, but you must be very careful with them.

[12] The ensuing discussion is adapted, largely verbatim, from Gary Lawson & Stephen Kam, *Making Law Out of Nothing At All: The Origins of the* Chevron *Doctrine*, 65 Admin. L. Rev. 1, 13–23 (2013).

in the first place, the tax would not apply regardless of who consumed or produced it.

Seaboard Air Line Railway Company was a large coal consumer. If it had bought coal for its locomotives on the open market from a coal mine, there is no doubt that such transactions would have come within the statute and thus would have needed to comply with the code provisions in order to avoid the tax penalty. If it had owned its own mine, hired its own employees to mine coal, and then consumed the coal from its own mines, there is no doubt that it would have fallen within the statute's producer/consumer exception to the tax. Seaboard did neither of these things. Instead, it leased coal lands and then hired an independent contractor to mine the coal and deliver it to Seaboard. Seaboard owned the coal, for all common-law purposes, from ground to locomotive, but at some point the coal had to be transferred from the possession of the independent mining company that dug it up to Seaboard. Seaboard asked the Director of the Bituminous Coal Division to declare these transfers of possession exempt from the coal code, and the Director refused.

seaboard asked for exemption, Director refused

On appeal, Seaboard advanced two arguments. First, it argued that it was actually the producer of the coal, just as much as if it had hired its own employees rather than independent contractors to dig it up. If that argument had been correct, Seaboard would clearly be exempt from the code as a producer/consumer. Second, it argued that even if its independent contractor was actually the producer of the coal for purposes of the statute, the transfer of possession of the coal from the contractor to Seaboard was not a "sale or other disposal," subject to tax for non-compliance, because title to the coal never changed hands. The independent contractor, in essence, was handing Seaboard's own coal to Seaboard.

The Supreme Court (by a 5–3 vote) ruled in favor of the agency on both counts—but it did so for very different reasons on each count and with very different assumptions about the deference owed to agencies.

With respect to whether Seaboard was actually the producer of the coal, the Court majority declared, after examining in some detail the contractual arrangements between Seaboard and one of its contractors:

> The separation of production and consumption is complete when a buyer obtains supplies from a seller totally free from buyer connection. Their identity is undoubted when the consumer extracts coal from its own land with its own employees. Between the two extremes are the innumerable variations that bring the arrangements closer to one pole or the other of the range between exemption and inclusion. To determine upon which side of the median line the particular instance falls calls for the expert, experienced judgment of those familiar with the industry. Unless we can say that a set of circumstances deemed by the Commission

to bring them within the concept "producer" is so unrelated to the tasks entrusted by Congress to the Commission as in effect to deny a sensible exercise of judgment, it is the Court's duty to leave the Commission's judgment undisturbed.

314 U.S. at 413, 62 S.Ct. at 333. This is very strong deference indeed for the agency's understanding of the statutory term "producer" in this context. The Court reviewed the agency decision for reasonableness rather than correctness.

strong deference for agency's interp. of statutory term

With respect to whether transactions between a producer (assuming, as the agency and Court found, that the independent contractor was the producer) and Seaboard were outside the scope of the Act because there was no transfer of title to the coal, and therefore no "sale or other disposal" within the statute, the Court affirmed the agency in a lengthy discussion that made no reference at all to deference:

> The core of the Act is the requirement that coal be put under the code or pay the 19 1/2 per cent exercise. We said in *Sunshine Anthracite Coal Co. v. Adkins*, 310 U.S. 381, 392, 50 S.Ct. 907, 912, 84 L.Ed. 1263, that the sanction tax applied to non-code members. Since they were not members, it was there contended that their coal would not be subject to the code, but it was explained in the *Adkins* case that the code was intended to apply to sales "in or directly affecting interstate commerce in bituminous coal," Section 4, 3rd paragraph, and that non-code coal "would be" subject to the code when it was interstate coal or coal affecting interstate commerce and therefore subject to the regulatory power of Congress. So here, the purpose of Congress which was to stabilize the industry through price regulation, would be hampered by an interpretation that required a transfer of title, in the technical sense, to bring a producer's coal, consumed by another party, within the ambit of the coal code. We find no necessity to so interpret the act. This conclusion seems to us in accord with the plain language of Section 3(a) and (b) providing for a tax on "other disposal" as well as sale. The definition of disposal as including "consumption or use by a producer, and any transfer of title by the producer other than by sale" cannot be said to put a meaning on disposal limited to the inclusion. It is true that Section 4, part II(e) speaks of a violation of the price provisions by "sale or delivery or offer for sale of coal at a price below" the minimum without reference to "other disposition," the phrase generally used, but the failure to include those words at that point does not, we think, justify an interpretation that coal covered by the code may be disposed of otherwise than by a transfer of title without penalty * * *.

314 U.S. at 415–16, 62 S.Ct. at 334–35. The Court simply determined, after what appears to be strict de novo review, that the agency had correctly construed the statute. The shift in both analysis and tone from one issue to the other within the opinion is striking.

There is an obvious difference between those issues that possibly explains the Court's differential treatment of them. The question whether a "sale or other disposal" of coal within the meaning of § 3(a) of the Bituminous Coal Act of 1937 requires a transfer of title to the coal is a question that requires no special knowledge of the coal industry to answer. A law professor in an ivory tower who has never seen a lump of coal could apply ordinary tools of statutory interpretation (language, structure, legislative history, purpose, etc.) to figure out the best construction of the statute. The legal question involved is abstract, or *pure*, in the sense that it can be addressed in principle using nothing more than conventional tools of legal analysis. By contrast, or so the Court could reasonably have thought, the question whether Seaboard was a "producer" of coal when it leased the mines but hired contractors to mine them is not necessarily something that can be answered abstractly from an ivory tower. To be sure, one *could* conclude that any arrangement in which the consumer owns the mine makes that consumer the "producer," in which case one needs only the same legal skills necessary to determine whether a transfer of title is a statutory prerequisite for a "sale or other disposal" of coal. But one could also believe that the Act's failure to provide a definition of "producer" suggests a more calibrated inquiry, in which case "producer" status other than at the obvious poles (open-market purchases and own-employee mining) may turn on subtleties in the particular arrangements between the mine-owning consumer and the workers who mine the coal. In that circumstance, detailed knowledge of and expertise in the coal industry may well be essential to a reasoned determination of whether any particular entity is a "producer." More precisely, figuring out whether an entity such as Seaboard is a producer may require an *inductive* rather than *deductive* form of inquiry. Instead of fixing the meaning of the statute and then asking whether Seaboard maps onto that meaning, one might instead define the statute by a common-law-like process of inclusion and exclusion, based on detailed study of the specific facts governing transactions such as Seaboard's. This kind of inquiry is best described as *law application*—the application of legal terms to specific factual settings—rather than *law determination*—the abstract ascertainment of statutory meaning—to reflect its inductive character. And in that context it makes a measure of sense to give deference regarding the nature and structure of the coal-production process to the supposedly expert agency charged with the task of applying the Bituminous Coal Act.[13]

---

[13] Of course, to say that it makes a measure of sense does not mean that it is inevitable, much less a good idea. Three Justices dissented in *Gray v. Powell*, and that was on the second hearing

So understood, *Gray v. Powell* describes a framework in which the deference afforded agencies in their legal interpretations depends to a great degree upon the *kind* of legal interpretation involved. Pure, abstract, "ivory tower" legal questions call for de novo review, while fact-bound, inductive, law application questions call for a good measure of deference.

This pattern was at work in many pre-*Chevron* cases after 1941. In *NLRB v. Hearst*, one of the most famous of the New Deal-era administrative law cases, the National Labor Relations Board determined that newsboys—who were generally adult vendors with fixed sales locations—were "employees" for purposes of the mandatory-bargaining provisions of the Wagner Act, with the result that Hearst Publications had a statutory duty to bargain with a union representing the newsboys. The statute unhelpfully defined (and still defines) an "employee" as "any employee." 29 U.S.C. § 152(3) (2012). The newspaper company refused to bargain with the newsboys' union on the ground that the Wagner Act's definition of an "employee" incorporated the common-law distinction between employees and independent contractors and that the newsboys were independent contractors rather than employees under generally accepted common-law principles. The Court, with only one dissenting vote, affirmed the agency decision, but as in *Gray* did so in two distinct steps.

[handwritten: NLRB v. Hearst]

[handwritten: Ct. affirmed agency]

First, the Court rejected the newspaper's claim that the Wagner Act's definition of "employee" incorporated common-law standards for determining employee status. The Court's discussion of that point of statutory interpretation was lengthy, *see* 322 U.S. at 120–29, 64 S.Ct. at 855–59, employing a range of considerations including the need for national uniformity, the uncertainty of the common-law standard(s), and the purposes of the policies of the Wagner Act. At no point did the Court indicate that it was at all relevant that the NLRB had already construed the statute in that fashion. Rather, the Court engaged in de novo review—as one would expect from the framework set forth in *Gray v. Powell*. After all, the question whether the word "employee" in the Wagner Act is meant to incorporate pre-existing common-law standards for determining employee status is a classic pure, abstract, "ivory tower" legal question. One can ask and answer it without knowing anything about the newspaper industry—and indeed without even knowing that there is a controversy involving the newspaper industry. One only needs traditional tools of statutory interpretation.

Once one has decided that the common law does not determine the statute's meaning, however, there still remains the problem of interpreting

---

of the case after an initial 4–4 split. It might also make a measure of sense to review all questions of law, pure or mixed, de novo. For an argument that universal de novo review, subject to application of a number of canons that would give weight to consistent and contemporaneous constructions by agencies, was the practice before *Gray v. Powell*, see Aditya Bamzai, *The Origins of Judicial Deference to Executive Interpretation*, 126 Yale L.J. 908 (2017).

and applying the statute in the case at hand. The newspaper likely would have won (as it did in the lower court) if the common law controlled the case, but that does not mean that the newspaper necessarily must lose if the common law does not control the case. One must still determine whether the newsboys at issue were "employees" under whatever non-common-law meaning of the term applies in the Wagner Act. On that question, the Court said that "where the question is one of specific application of a broad statutory term in a proceeding in which the agency administering the statute must determine it initially, the reviewing court's function is limited * * *. [T]he Board's determination that specified persons are 'employees' under this Act is to be accepted if it has 'warrant in the record' and a reasonable basis in law." *Id.* at 131, 64 S.Ct. at 860–61.

As with determining who is a "producer" under the Bituminous Coal Act, determining who is an "employee" under the Wagner Act seems like an inductive process of inclusion and exclusion based on detailed understanding of factual settings, at least once one has rejected the common law as controlling. The process of filling out the meaning of "employee," after abstractly concluding that its meaning cannot be deduced from the common law, is a process of law application rather than strict law determination, and that process plausibly warrants deference to the agency charged with administering the statute.

This bifurcated framework also appeared in 1951 in *O'Leary v. Brown-Pacific-Maxon, Inc.* John Valak was an employee of the defendant company in Guam. The company provided a recreation center that was near a channel "so dangerous for swimmers that its use was forbidden and signs to that effect erected." 340 U.S. at 505, 71 S.Ct. at 471. While at the recreation center one day, Valak braved the channel in an attempt to rescue some men trapped on a reef, and he drowned in the process. His mother brought a claim under the Longshoremen's and Harbor Workers' Compensation Act of 1927 ("LHWCA"), which requires the company to provide benefits for "accidental injury or death arising out of and in the course of employment." 33 U.S.C. § 902(2) (2012). The agency awarded a death benefit under the statute. The company objected that the statutory term "in the course of employment" was meant (shades of *Hearst*) to incorporate pre-existing common-law standards, and that however heroic Valak's actions may have been, they were surely, as the Court of Appeals had concluded, a frolic and detour at common law and hence not subject to the statutory compensation provisions.

The Court agreed with the agency that the statute extended beyond the common-law meaning of "course of employment," but as in *Gray* and *Hearst* did so with no mention of deference to the agency. The question whether the LHWCA meant to define "course of employment" by strict reference to the common law is clearly a pure, abstract, "ivory tower" kind of legal question that requires no special expertise in employment relations to resolve. One could ask and answer it without even knowing whether any specific dispute turns on the answer.

Once one extends the statute beyond the common law, however, there remains the problem, as there was in *Hearst*, of determining whether this particular action by this particular employee fell within the extended boundaries of the statute. The resolution of that problem, as with establishing the statutory meanings of "producer" and "employee," is the kind of inductive, fact-specific, law application question for which deference is appropriate under the *Gray* framework. As the Court explained, such questions are not "so severable from the experience of industry nor of such a nature as to be peculiarly appropriate for independent judicial ascertainment as 'questions of law.'" Accordingly, the appropriate standard of review was "that discussed in *Universal Camera Corp. v. National Labor Relations Board*," meaning that the agency got plenty of deference. *See* 340 U.S. at 507–09, 71 S.Ct. at 472.[14]

The Gray/Hearst/O'Leary framework provides a workable and plausible, even if not inevitable or incontestable, mechanism for reviewing agency legal determinations. It is not always easy to determine whether a legal question is a "pure" question of law determination or a "mixed" question of law application, but much of the time it is a pretty straightforward inquiry. And once that classification is made, the appropriate deference rule seems to follow automatically.

Of course, the framework was never that simple. Understanding the foundations of modern law requires attention to several important modifications to the framework.

The need for some kind of modification became very clear in 1947 when the Court decided *Packard Motor Car Co. v. NLRB*, 330 U.S. 485, 67 S.Ct. 789, 91 L.Ed. 1040. As in *Hearst*, the question concerned whether a particular class of persons were "employees" under the Wagner Act. This time, the class of persons was a group of foremen at an auto plant, who the NLRB determined were an appropriate bargaining unit under the statute. The company countered that the foremen, with responsibility for managing, disciplining, and making recommendations concerning line employees, were part of the "employer" under the statute rather than employees. The Court, by a 5–4 vote, agreed with the NLRB—and Congress

---

[14] The Court's discussion of this point was a bit muddled by its willingness to indulge the agency Deputy Commissioner's labeling of the question of "course of employment" as a question of *fact*. Of course it is not a question of fact, and of course Justice (and former Administrative Law professor) Frankfurter, who authored the majority opinion, knew that it was not a question of fact. The best reading of the opinion, given that it was issued on the same day as *Universal Camera Corp. v. NLRB*, 340 U.S. 474 (1951), is that Justice Frankfurter meant that the *degree* of deference afforded agency applications of law is comparable in scope to the *degree* of deference afforded agency findings of fact under the "substantial evidence" standard of review. This conflation of factual and legal categories supports Aditya Bamzai's thesis that the rise of deference to executive legal interpretation during and after the New Deal was driven in part by rising skepticism about the meaningfulness of lines between fact and law. *See* Bamzai, *supra* note 13.

[handwritten margin note: Congress amended law to override Ct's decision]

agreed with the company by promptly passing the Taft-Hartley Act and overruling the decision in *Packard*.

For our purposes, it does not matter whether the Court in *Packard* correctly or incorrectly interpreted the Wagner Act. All that matters is that the Court affirmed the agency without resorting to any deference. Indeed, the only mention of the agency's prior interpretations was a recitation offered by *the company* of the agency's checkered history of "inaction, vacillation and division * * * in applying this Act to foremen." 330 U.S. at 492, 67 S.Ct. at 793. The Court's response was that "[i]f we were obliged to depend upon administrative interpretation for light in finding the meaning of the statute, the inconsistency of the Board's decisions would leave us in the dark," but that it was unnecessary to make such reference to the agency's actions in this case "in deciding the naked question of law whether the Board is now * * * acting within the terms of the statute." *Id.* at 492–93, 67 S.Ct. at 793–94.

Of course, if the relevant issue of statutory meaning really was a "naked question of law," the conclusion of "no deference" followed logically from the *Gray* framework. That characterization of the issue would only be accurate, however, if the relevant legal issue was whether all people who bore the label "foreman" at all times and under all circumstances were outside the coverage of the Act. That was not the issue. No one believed or argued that a company could simply apply the label "foreman" to someone and thereby remove that person from the statute. The real question was whether persons with the specific responsibilities, duties, and status of the people labeled "foremen" *in this particular case* were "employees" within the statute. One could perhaps resolve even that issue as a "naked question of law" by saying, as the majority opinion at some points seemed to say, that anyone who draws a salary from the company is an "employee." But that would have the intriguing consequence, as the dissenting opinion pointed out, of making corporate executives, including the president of the company, employees subject to the Wagner Act. Charity demands that one not attribute such a position to the Court. Accordingly, the best interpretation of the opinion is that it really was treating the relevant issue as more akin to the inductive, fact-specific, law-applying process involved in deciding whether newsboys are "employees." The Court did in fact go into considerable detail describing the specific functions of the foremen who were at issue. On that understanding, one would expect the agency decision to receive a great deal of deference, amounting essentially to reasonableness review, rather than the strict de novo review that was actually provided.

If that is the correct characterization of the case, so that *Packard* represents a break, and a fairly sharp one at that, with the *Gray/Hearst/O'Leary* framework, one must ask why the Court might have deferred to the agency's inductive construction of the term "employee" in *Hearst* but not in *Packard*.

There are many possible reasons, and scholars were quick to point them out in the wake of *Packard*. First, and most obviously, the issue in *Packard* was much more important than the issue in *Hearst*.[15] The question whether, and to what extent, supervisory personnel could be the subjects of mandatory collective bargaining went to the very heart of the system of labor regulation. Very few people other than newsboys and newspaper owners cared who won in *Hearst*, but the entire nation would be affected by the outcome in *Packard* (and whatever subsequent cases it would spawn). Second, and relatedly, the NLRB of that era had a (well-deserved) reputation for being blatantly pro-labor. The Court may well have been reluctant to extend quite as much deference to the legal interpretations of the NLRB as it would extend, for example, to the Director of the Bituminous Coal Division of the Department of the Interior, especially on a matter of major importance. Third, the Court acknowledged that the agency had been inconsistent in its application of the statute to foremen. While the Court did not regard this as a reason to construe the statute not to cover foremen, it did suggest that it might be a reason not to pay too much attention to the Board's present actions.

All of these considerations—the importance of the issue, the reputation of the agency, and the agency's consistency—are plausible explanations for the Court's actions *and plausible normative justifications for declining to give deference to an agency's applications of legal terms to particular facts*.[16] Once one acknowledges, however, that there can be good reasons for declining to defer to particular instances of agency law application, the list of plausible reasons grows very quickly. Is the issue one for which the agency's expertise is likely to be valuable? How carefully has the agency considered the question and explained its reasoning? What procedures did the agency use to reach its conclusion? How strongly has Congress indicated an intention to commit administration of the statute to the agency? Was the agency involved in the drafting of the statute? Did the agency issue its interpretation soon after enactment of the statute or did it "sandbag" for many years? A creative reader can easily add another half-

[handwritten margin notes: · importance of issue · reputation of agency · agency's consistency]

---

[15] See Louis B. Jaffe, Judicial Control of Administrative Action 561 (1965) ("[I]n Hearst the Justices * * * did not regard the classification as raising a significant legal issue. In Packard they did.").

[16] Could they also provide sound normative reasons for declining to give deference to agency factfinding? As an abstract matter, quite possibly yes. But deference to agency factfinding is ordinarily mandated by statute. Congress has presumably considered and balanced all of the relevant normative considerations before requiring judicial deference to agency factfinding. Deference to agency legal conclusions, however, is almost never mandated (or forbidden) by statute. The principles of judicial review of agency legal conclusions are primarily court-created. To be sure, the APA instructs reviewing courts to "decide all relevant questions of law," § 706, which certainly could be read as a command to engage in de novo review of all legal questions. It must suffice for now to say that, rightly or wrongly, that view of § 706 has never had any serious traction in the courts.

dozen reasons to this list. And as the list grows, so does the complexity of the scheme for judicial review. Instead of a simple two-part scheme (pure question equals no deference, law applying question equals deference equivalent in degree to the substantial evidence test), one now has an ill-structured, multi-faceted inquiry. Once one has identified a question as one of law application, one must now determine whether any or all of a long list of factors justify departing from the *Gray-Hearst-O'Leary* rule of deference. Nor can this reasoning be limited to questions of law application. If these factors can justify *declining* to give deference to agencies on questions of law application, can they also justify *granting* agencies deference on pure questions of law that would normally be reviewed de novo? There is no reason why not. *See, e.g., FEC v. Democratic Senatorial Campaign Committee,* 454 U.S. 27, 102 S.Ct. 38, 70 L.Ed.2d 23 (1981) (deferring to the agency's view that a statute forbidding political committees from making expenditures on behalf of candidates did not prevent those committees from acting as spending agents for other organizations). Accordingly, *every* case involving judicial review of an agency legal interpretation becomes an invitation for a many-factored inquiry into the appropriateness of deference.

Another important modification to the *Gray* framework stems from the language of certain kinds of statutes. On occasion, Congress will specifically and expressly indicate that an ambiguous term is to be defined by the agency, even where the process of definition could involve abstract law determination rather than inductive law application. For example, in *Batterton v. Francis,* 432 U.S. 416, 97 S.Ct. 2399, 53 L.Ed.2d 448 (1977), the relevant statute expressly gave the Secretary of HEW the power to determine, through rulemaking, the standards for "unemployment" by referring to "unemployment (as determined in accordance with standards prescribed by the Secretary)." 42 U.S.C. § 607(a) (1976). While defining such a term through a rulemaking would ordinarily involve abstract law determination, the Court noted that Congress

> expressly delegated to the Secretary the power to prescribe standards for determining what constitutes 'unemployment' for purposes of AFDC-UF eligibility. In a situation of this kind, Congress entrusts to the Secretary, rather than to the courts, the primary responsibility for interpreting the statutory term. In exercising that responsibility, the Secretary adopts regulations with legislative effect. A reviewing court is not free to set aside those regulations simply because it would have interpreted the statute in a different manner.

432 U.S. at 425, 97 S.Ct. at 2405.

Once it is settled that assigning this law-determining power to agencies does not violate the nondelegation doctrine, express congressional grants of this kind amount to a command to courts to afford legal deference to agency decisions pursuant to such statutes. Conceivably, one might be able to infer such a command from language that is less than express, but presumably that would require some kind of unusual, statute-specific evidence indicating that Congress intends for agencies rather than courts to provide statutory meaning.

And all of the foregoing is only part of the picture. *Gray, Hearst, Packard,* and *O'Leary* involved statutes which the relevant agency was clearly charged with implementing, and the agencies' actions in those cases were all intended to have formal legal effect. What if either or both of those assumptions are relaxed? What if an agency interprets a statute in an advisory capacity? The Court's answer was provided in a case that has, as we shall soon see, risen to the fore of administrative law in recent years after a period of relative neglect.

SKIDMORE V. SWIFT & CO.

Supreme Court of the United States, 1944.
323 U.S. 134, 65 S.Ct. 161, 89 L.Ed. 124.

MR. JUSTICE JACKSON delivered the opinion of the Court.

Seven employees of the Swift and Company packing plant at Fort Worth, Texas, brought an action under the Fair Labor Standards Act, 29 U.S.C. § 201 et seq., to recover overtime, liquidated damages, and attorneys' fees, totalling approximately $77,000. The District Court rendered judgment denying this claim wholly, and the Circuit Court of Appeals for the Fifth Circuit affirmed.

It is not denied that the daytime employment of these persons was working time within the Act. Two were engaged in general fire hall duties and maintenance of fire-fighting equipment of the Swift plant. The others operated elevators or acted as relief men in fire duties. They worked from 7:00 a.m. to 3:30 p.m., with a half-hour lunch period, five days a week. They were paid weekly salaries.

Under their oral agreement of employment, however, petitioners undertook to stay in the fire hall on the Company premises, or within hailing distance, three and a half to four nights a week. This involved no task except to answer alarms, either because of fire or because the sprinkler was set off for some other reason. No fires occurred during the period in issue, the alarms were rare, and the time required for their answer rarely exceeded an hour. For each alarm answered the employees were paid in addition to their fixed compensation an agreed amount, fifty cents at first, and later sixty-four cents. The Company provided a brick fire hall equipped with steam heat and air-conditioned rooms. It provided sleeping quarters, a pool table, a domino table, and a radio. The men used their time in sleep or amusement as they saw fit, except that they were required to stay in or close by the fire hall and be ready to respond to alarms. It is stipulated that "they agreed to remain in the fire hall and stay in it or within hailing distance, subject to call, in event of fire or other casualty, but were not required to perform any specific tasks during these periods of time, except in answering alarms." The trial court found the evidentiary facts as stipulated; it made no findings of fact as such as to whether under the arrangement of the parties and the circumstances of this case * * * the fire hall duty or any part thereof constituted working time. It said, however, as a "conclusion of law" that "the time plaintiffs spent in the fire hall subject to call to answer fire alarms does not constitute hours worked, for which overtime compensation is due them under the Fair Labor Standards Act, as interpreted by the Administrator and the Courts," and in its opinion observed, "of course we know pursuing such pleasurable occupations or performing such personal chores does not constitute work." The Circuit Court of Appeals affirmed.

Margin note: DC made no finding of fact ↓ just concl. of law

* * * [W]e hold that no principle of law found either in the statute or in Court decisions precludes waiting time from also being working time. We have not attempted to, and we cannot, lay down a legal formula to resolve cases so varied in their facts as are the many situations in which employment involves waiting time. Whether in a concrete case such time falls within or without the Act is a question of fact to be resolved by appropriate findings of the trial court. This involves scrutiny and construction of the agreements between the particular parties, appraisal of their practical construction of the working agreement by conduct, consideration of the nature of the service, and its relation to the waiting time, and all of the surrounding circumstances. Facts may show that the employee was engaged to wait, or they way show that he waited to be engaged. His compensation may cover both waiting and task, or only performance of the task itself. Living quarters may in some situations be furnished as a facility of the task and in another as a part of its compensation. The law does not impose an arrangement upon the parties. It imposes upon the courts the task of finding what the arrangement was.

We do not minimize the difficulty of such an inquiry where the arrangements of the parties have not contemplated the problem posed by the statute. But it does not differ in nature or in the standards to guide judgment from that which frequently confronts courts where they must find retrospectively the effect of contracts as to matters which the parties failed to anticipate or explicitly to provide for.

Congress did not utilize the services of an administrative agency to find facts and to determine in the first instance whether particular cases fall within or without the Act. Instead, it put this responsibility on the courts. But it did create the office of Administrator, impose upon him a variety of duties, endow him with powers to inform himself of conditions in industries and employments subject to the Act, and put on him the duties of bringing injunction actions to restrain violations. Pursuit of his duties has accumulated a considerable experience in the problems of ascertaining working time in employments involving periods of inactivity and a knowledge of the customs prevailing in reference to their solution. From these he is obliged to reach conclusions as to conduct without the law, so that he should seek injunctions to stop it, and that within the law, so that he has no call to interfere. He has set forth his views of the application of the Act under different circumstances in an interpretative bulletin and in informal rulings. They provide a practical guide to employers and employees as to how the office representing the public interest in its enforcement will seek to apply it. Wage and Hour Division, Interpretative Bulletin No. 13.

The Administrator thinks the problems presented by inactive duty require a flexible solution, rather than the all-in or all-out rules respectively urged by the parties in this case, and his Bulletin endeavors to suggest standards and examples to guide in particular situations. In some occupations, it says, periods of inactivity are not properly counted as working time even though the employee is subject to call. Examples are an operator of a small telephone exchange where the switchboard is in her home and she ordinarily gets several hours of uninterrupted sleep each night; or a pumper of a stripper well or watchman of a lumber camp during the off season, who may be on duty twenty-four hours a day but ordinarily "has a normal night's sleep, has ample time in which to eat his meals, and has a certain amount of time for relaxation and entirely private pursuits." Exclusion of all such hours the Administrator thinks may be justified. In general, the answer depends "upon the degree to which the employee is free to engage in personal activities during periods of idleness when he is subject to call and the number of consecutive hours that the employee is subject to call without being required to perform active work." "Hours worked are not limited to the time spent in active labor but include time given by the employee to the employer. * * * "

The facts of this case do not fall within any of the specific examples given, but the conclusion of the Administrator, as expressed in the brief amicus curiae, is that the general tests which he has suggested point to the exclusion of sleeping and eating time of these employees from the work-week and the inclusion of all other on-call time: although the employees were required to remain on the premises during the entire time, the evidence shows that they were very rarely interrupted in their normal sleeping and eating time, and these are pursuits of a purely private nature which would presumably occupy the employees' time whether they were on duty or not and which apparently could be pursued adequately and comfortably in the required circumstances; the rest of the time is different because there is nothing in the record to suggest that, even though

[handwritten margin note: Admin's approach]

pleasurably spent, it was spent in the ways the men would have chosen had they been free to do so.

There is no statutory provision as to what, if any, deference courts should pay to the Administrator's conclusions. And, while we have given them notice, we have had no occasion to try to prescribe their influence. The rulings of this Administrator are not reached as a result of hearing adversary proceedings in which he finds facts from evidence and reaches conclusions of law from findings of fact. They are not, of course, conclusive, even in the cases with which they directly deal, much less in those to which they apply only by analogy. They do not constitute an interpretation of the Act or a standard for judging factual situations which binds a district court's processes, as an authoritative pronouncement of a higher court might do. But the Administrator's policies are made in pursuance of official duty, based upon more specialized experience and broader investigations and information than is likely to come to a judge in a particular case. They do determine the policy which will guide applications for enforcement by injunction on behalf of the Government. Good administration of the Act and good judicial administration alike require that the standards of public enforcement and those for determining private rights shall be at variance only where justified by very good reasons. The fact that the Administrator's policies and standards are not reached by trial in adversary form does not mean that they are not entitled to respect. This Court has long given considerable and in some cases decisive weight to Treasury Decisions and to interpretative regulations of the Treasury and of other bodies that were not of adversary origin.

Skidmore factors —

We consider that the rulings, interpretations and opinions of the Administrator under this Act, while not controlling upon the courts by reason of their authority, do constitute a body of experience and informed judgment to which courts and litigants may properly resort for guidance. The weight of such a judgment in a particular case will depend upon the thoroughness evident in its consideration, the validity of its reasoning, its consistency with earlier and later pronouncements, and all those factors which give it power to persuade, if lacking power to control.

* * * [A]lthough the District Court referred to the Administrator's Bulletin, its evaluation and inquiry were apparently restricted by its notion that waiting time may not be work, an understanding of the law which we hold to be erroneous. Accordingly, the judgment is reversed and the cause remanded for further proceedings consistent herewith.

NOTES

Skidmore is important for two independent reasons. First, it demonstrates that deference can be appropriate even when an agency does not have formal responsibility for administering a statute. That is an insight that will be crucial later in this chapter. Second, it suggests that the *amount* of deference to which an agency might be entitled is as open to argument as the threshold question *whether* an agency is entitled to any deference in the first place. Thus, not only are we faced with an indeterminate list of factors that can affect *whether* we defer to agency legal conclusions, but the same factors can affect, in an indeterminate way, the *level* of deference that is appropriate in any given case. The seemingly simple pattern laid out in *Gray, Hearst,* and *O'Leary* has thus become an administrative nightmare.

Accordingly, the best description of pre-1984 law (or so at least one casebook editor thinks) is that it required reviewing courts to conduct roughly the following inquiry:

[handwritten margin note: description of pre-1984 law]

(1) Does the agency administer the statutory provision at issue? If not, then the agency gets, at most, some measure of deference pursuant to *Skidmore v. Swift* if warranted by all of the facts and circumstances. If yes, then . . .

(2) Is the agency's legal interpretation a pure, abstract, "ivory tower" legal question that can be asked and answered without knowing anything about the particular dispute before the agency? If no, then the agency presumptively gets a strong measure of deference, tantamount to reasonableness review, unless a constellation of factors counsels otherwise. If yes, then the court presumptively reviews the matter de novo, against subject to a constellation of factors that might counsel otherwise.

(3) Also, if Congress has *expressly* entrusted the law-determination function to the agency, then courts must honor the congressional allocation of authority and give the agency's decision great deference regardless of the classification of the legal question involved.

Judges and scholars widely criticized the indeterminacy, inconsistency, and unpredictability that this scope-of-review regime generated. A famous law review article published in 1985 noted that "[t]he decision whether to grant deference [to an agency's legal interpretation] depends on various attributes of the agency's legal authority and functions and of the administrative interpretation at issue," Colin S. Diver, *Statutory Interpretation in the Administrative State,* 133 U. Pa. L. Rev. 549, 562 (1985), and then identified ten different factors (contemporaneousness, long-standing duration, consistency, reliance, importance of the issue, complexity, presence of rulemaking authority, the need for agency action to implement the statute, congressional ratification, and quality of agency explanation) that had been applied by Supreme Court decisions. *Id.* at 562 n.95. No judge really wants to apply a ten-factor test to a foundational inquiry in administrative law cases. It would not be surprising if judges in the trenches of administrative law actively looked for an alternative to this potentially messy legal world. Did the following case offer them one?

2. THEORY AND CURRENT PRACTICE

a. The Quiet Revolution

**CHEVRON U.S.A. v. NATURAL RESOURCES
DEFENSE COUNCIL, INC.**

Supreme Court of the United States, 1984.
467 U.S. 837, 104 S.Ct. 2778, 81 L.Ed.2d 694.

JUSTICE STEVENS delivered the opinion of the Court.

In the Clean Air Act Amendments of 1977, Pub. L. 95–95, 91 Stat. 685, Congress enacted certain requirements applicable to States that had not achieved the national air quality standards established by the Environmental Protection Agency (EPA) pursuant to earlier legislation. The amended Clean Air Act required these "nonattainment" States to establish a permit program regulating "new or modified major stationary sources" of air pollution. Generally, a permit may not be issued for a new or modified major stationary source unless several stringent conditions are met. The EPA regulation promulgated to implement this permit requirement allows a State to adopt a plantwide definition of the term "stationary source." Under this definition, an existing plant that contains several pollution-emitting devices may install or modify one piece of equipment without meeting the permit conditions if the alteration will not increase the total emissions from the plant. The question presented by these cases is whether EPA's decision to allow States to treat all of the pollution-emitting devices within the same industrial grouping as though they were encased within a single "bubble" is based on a reasonable construction of the statutory term "stationary source."

I

The EPA regulations containing the plantwide definition of the term stationary source were promulgated on October 14, 1981. Respondents filed a timely petition for review in the United States Court of Appeals for the District of Columbia Circuit pursuant to 42 U.S.C. § 7607(b)(1). The Court of Appeals set aside the regulations.

The court observed that the relevant part of the amended Clean Air Act "does not explicitly define what Congress envisioned as a 'stationary source', to which the permit program . . . should apply," and further stated that the precise issue was not "squarely addressed in the legislative history." In light of its conclusion that the legislative history bearing on the question was "at best contradictory," it reasoned that "the purposes of the non-attainment program should guide our decision here." Based on two of its precedents concerning the applicability of the bubble concept to certain Clean Air Act programs, the court stated that the bubble concept was "mandatory" in programs designed merely to maintain existing air quality, but held that it was "inappropriate" in programs enacted to improve air quality. Since the purpose of the permit program—its "*raison d'etre*," in the court's view—was to improve air quality, the court held that the bubble concept was inapplicable in these cases under its prior precedents. It therefore set aside the regulations embodying the bubble concept as contrary to law. We granted certiorari to review that judgment, and we now reverse.

SCOTUS sides w/ EPA

The basic legal error of the Court of Appeals was to adopt a static judicial definition of the term "stationary source" when it had decided that Congress itself had not commanded that definition * * *.

II

When a court reviews an agency's construction of the statute which it administers, it is confronted with two questions. First, always, is the question whether Congress has directly spoken to the precise question at issue. If the intent of Congress is clear, that is the end of the matter; for the court, as well as the agency, must give effect to the unambiguously expressed intent of Congress.[9] If, however, the court determines Congress has not directly addressed the precise question at issue, the court does not simply impose its own construction on the statute, as would be necessary in the absence of an administrative interpretation. Rather, if the statute is silent or ambiguous with respect to the specific issue, the question for the court is whether the agency's answer is based on a permissible construction of the statute.[11]

Questions
① whether Cong has directly spoken to a

② whether agency's interp = based on permissible construction

"The power of an administrative agency to administer a congressionally created . . . program necessarily requires the formulation of policy and the making of rules to fill any gap left, implicitly or explicitly, by Congress." *Morton v. Ruiz*, 415 U.S. 199, 231 (1974). If Congress has explicitly left a gap for the agency to fill, there is an express delegation of authority to the agency to elucidate a specific provision of the statute by regulation. Such legislative regulations are given controlling weight unless they are arbitrary, capricious, or manifestly contrary to the statute. Sometimes the legislative delegation to an agency on a particular question is implicit rather than explicit. In such a case, a court may not substitute its own construction of a statutory provision for a reasonable interpretation made by the administrator of an agency.

EXPRESS: arbitrary + capricious

IMPLICIT: reasonableness

* * *

---

[9]   The judiciary is the final authority on issues of statutory construction and must reject administrative constructions which are contrary to clear congressional intent. If a court, employing traditional tools of statutory construction, ascertains that Congress had an intention on the precise question at issue, that intention is the law and must be given effect.

[11]   The court need not conclude that the agency construction was the only one it permissibly could have adopted to uphold the construction, or even the reading the court would have reached if the question initially had arisen in a judicial proceeding.

In light of these well-settled principles it is clear that the Court of Appeals misconceived the nature of its role in reviewing the regulations at issue. Once it determined, after its own examination of the legislation, that Congress did not actually have an intent regarding the applicability of the bubble concept to the permit program, the question before it was not whether in its view the concept is "inappropriate" in the general context of a program designed to improve air quality, but whether the Administrator's view that it is appropriate in the context of this particular program is a reasonable one. Based on the examination of the legislation and its history which follows, we agree with the Court of Appeals that Congress did not have a specific intention on the applicability of the bubble concept in these cases, and conclude that the EPA's use of that concept here is a reasonable policy choice for the agency to make.

EPA's interp = reasonable policy choice

* * *

IV

The Clean Air Act Amendments of 1977 are a lengthy, detailed, technical, complex, and comprehensive response to a major social issue. A small portion of the statute expressly deals with nonattainment areas. The focal point of this controversy is one phrase in that portion of the Amendments.[22]

* * *

The 1977 Amendments contain no specific reference to the "bubble concept." Nor do they contain a specific definition of the term "stationary source," though they did not disturb the definition of "stationary source" contained in § 111(a)(3) [of the 1970 Clean Air Act amendments], applicable by the terms of the Act to the NSPS [(new source performance standard)] program. Section 302(j), however, defines the term "major stationary source" as follows:

"major stationary source"

> "(j) Except as otherwise expressly provided, the terms 'major stationary source' and 'major emitting facility' mean any stationary facility or source of air pollutants which directly emits, or has the potential to emit, one hundred tons per year or more of any air pollutant (including any major emitting facility or source of fugitive emissions of any such pollutant, as determined by rule by the Administrator)."

V

The legislative history of the portion of the 1977 Amendments dealing with nonattainment areas does not contain any specific comment on the

---

[22] Specifically, the controversy in these cases involves the meaning of the term "major stationary sources" in § 172(b)(6) of the Act * * *.

"bubble concept" or the question whether a plantwide definition of a stationary source is permissible under the permit program * * *.

* * *

VI

As previously noted, prior to the 1977 Amendments, the EPA had adhered to a plantwide definition of the term "source" under a NSPS program. After adoption of the 1977 Amendments, proposals for a plantwide definition were considered in at least three formal proceedings.

In January 1979 * * *, [i]n those areas that did not have a revised SIP [(state implementation plan)] in effect by July 1979, the EPA rejected the plantwide definition; on the other hand, it expressly concluded that the plantwide approach would be permissible in certain circumstances if authorized by an approved SIP * * *.

In April, and again in September 1979, the EPA published additional comments in which it indicated that revised SIP's could adopt the plantwide definition of source in nonattainment areas in certain circumstances * * *.

In August 1980, however, the EPA adopted a regulation that, in essence, applied the basic reasoning of the Court of Appeals in these cases. The EPA took particular note of the two then-recent Court of Appeals decisions, which had created the bright-line rule that the "bubble concept" should be employed in a program designed to maintain air quality but not in one designed to enhance air quality. Relying heavily on those cases, EPA adopted a dual definition of "source" for nonattainment areas that required a permit whenever a change in either the entire plant, or one of its components, would result in a significant increase in emissions even if the increase was completely offset by reductions elsewhere in the plant. The EPA expressed the opinion that this interpretation was "more consistent with congressional intent" than the plantwide definition because it "would bring in more sources or modifications for review," 45 Fed. Reg. 52697 (1980), but its primary legal analysis was predicated on the two Court of Appeals decisions.

In 1981 a new administration took office and initiated a "Government-wide reexamination of regulatory burdens and complexities." 46 Fed. Reg. 16281. In the context of that review, the EPA reevaluated the various arguments that had been advanced in connection with the proper definition of the term "source" and concluded that the term should be given the same definition in both nonattainment areas and PSD areas.

In explaining its conclusion, the EPA first noted that the definitional issue was not squarely addressed in either the statute or its legislative history and therefore that the issue involved an agency "judgment as how to best carry out the Act." *Ibid.* It then set forth several reasons for concluding that the plantwide definition was more appropriate. It pointed out that the dual definition "can act as a disincentive to new investment and modernization by discouraging modifications to existing facilities" and "can actually retard progress in air pollution control by discouraging replacement of older, dirtier processes or pieces of equipment with new, cleaner ones." *Ibid.* Moreover, the new definition "would simplify EPA's rules by using the same definition of 'source' for PSD, nonattainment new source review and the construction moratorium. This reduces confusion and inconsistency." *Ibid.* Finally, the agency explained that additional requirements that remained in place would accomplish the fundamental purposes of achieving attainment with NAAQS's as expeditiously as possible. These conclusions were expressed in a proposed rulemaking in August 1981 that was formally promulgated in October.

conclusions led to new rule

VII

In this Court respondents expressly reject the basic rationale of the Court of Appeals' decision. That court viewed the statutory definition of the term "source" as sufficiently flexible to cover either a plantwide definition, a narrower definition covering each unit within a plant, or a dual definition that could apply to both the entire "bubble" and its components. It interpreted the policies of the statute, however, to mandate the plantwide definition in programs designed to maintain clean air and to forbid it in programs designed to improve air quality. Respondents place a fundamentally different construction on the statute. They contend that the text of the Act requires the EPA to use a dual definition—if either a component of a plant, or the plant as a whole, emits over 100 tons of pollutant, it is a major stationary source. They thus contend that the EPA rules adopted in 1980, insofar as they apply to the maintenance of the quality of clean air, as well as the 1981 rules which apply to nonattainment areas, violate the statute.

Respondents' argument.

Statutory Language

The definition of the term "stationary source" in § 111(a)(3) refers to "any building, structure, facility, or installation" which emits air pollution. This definition is applicable only to the NSPS program by the express terms of the statute; the text of the statute does not make this definition applicable to the permit program. Petitioners therefore maintain that there is no statutory language even relevant to ascertaining the meaning of stationary source in the permit program aside from § 302(j), which defines the term "major stationary source." We disagree with petitioners on this point.

The definition in § 302(j) tells us what the word "major" means—a source must emit at least 100 tons of pollution to qualify—but it sheds virtually no light on the meaning of the term "stationary source."

* * * Basically * * *, the language of § 302(j) simply does not compel any given interpretation of the term "source."

Respondents recognize that, and hence point to § 111(a)(3). Although the definition in that section is not literally applicable to the permit program, it sheds as much light on the meaning of the word "source" as anything in the statute * * *.

We are not persuaded that parsing of general terms in the text of the statute will reveal an actual intent of Congress. We know full well that this language is not dispositive; the terms are overlapping and the language is not precisely directed to the question of the applicability of a given term in the context of a larger operation. To the extent any congressional "intent" can be discerned from this language, it would appear that the listing of overlapping, illustrative terms was intended to enlarge, rather than to confine, the scope of the agency's power to regulate particular sources in order to effectuate the policies of the Act.

parsing terms here will not reveal Cong's intent

Legislative History

In addition, respondents argue that the legislative history and policies of the Act foreclose the plantwide definition, and that the EPA's interpretation is not entitled to deference because it represents a sharp break with prior interpretations of the Act.

← R's arg.

Based on our examination of the legislative history, we agree with the Court of Appeals that it is unilluminating. The general remarks pointed to by respondents "were obviously not made with this narrow issue in mind and they cannot be said to demonstrate a Congressional desire. . ." *Jewell Ridge Coal Corp. v. Mine Workers*, 325 U.S. 161, 168–169 (1945) * * *.

* * *

Our review of the EPA's varying interpretations of the word "source"— both before and after the 1977 Amendments—convinces us that the agency primarily responsible for administering this important legislation has consistently interpreted it flexibly—not in a sterile textual vacuum, but in the context of implementing policy decisions in a technical and complex arena. The fact that the agency has from time to time changed its interpretation of the term "source" does not, as respondents argue, lead us to conclude that no deference should be accorded the agency's interpretation of the statute. An initial agency interpretation is not instantly carved in stone. On the contrary, the agency, to engage in informed rulemaking, must consider varying interpretations and the wisdom of its policy on a continuing basis. Moreover, the fact that the agency has adopted different definitions in different contexts adds force to the argument that the definition itself is flexible, particularly since Congress has never indicated any disapproval of a flexible reading of the statute.

EPA's varying interps.

↑ flexible interp.

*Note: EPA's change in interp does NOT mean no deference should be given

Significantly, it was not the agency in 1980, but rather the Court of Appeals that read the statute inflexibly to command a plantwide definition for programs designed to maintain clean air and to forbid such a definition for programs designed to improve air quality. The distinction the court drew may well be a sensible one, but our labored review of the problem has surely disclosed that it is not a distinction that Congress ever articulated itself, or one that the EPA found in the statute before the courts began to review the legislative work product. We conclude that it was the Court of Appeals, rather than Congress or any of the decisionmakers who are authorized by Congress to administer this legislation, that was primarily responsible for the 1980 position taken by the agency.

Policy

The arguments over policy that are advanced in the parties' briefs create the impression that respondents are now waging in a judicial forum a specific policy battle which they ultimately lost in the agency and in the 32 jurisdictions opting for the "bubble concept," but one which was never waged in the Congress. Such policy arguments are more properly addressed to legislators or administrators, not to judges.

In these cases the Administrator's interpretation represents a reasonable accommodation of manifestly competing interests and is entitled to deference: the regulatory scheme is technical and complex, the agency considered the matter in a detailed and reasoned fashion, and the decision involves reconciling conflicting policies. Congress intended to accommodate both interests, but did not do so itself on the level of specificity presented by these cases. Perhaps that body consciously desired the Administrator to strike the balance at this level, thinking that those with great expertise and charged with responsibility for administering the provision would be in a better position to do so; perhaps it simply did not consider the question at this level; and perhaps Congress was unable to forge a coalition on either side of the question, and those on each side decided to take their chances with the scheme devised by the agency. For judicial purposes, it matters not which of these things occurred.

Judges are not experts in the field, and are not part of either political branch of the Government. Courts must, in some cases, reconcile competing political interests, but not on the basis of the judges' personal policy preferences. In contrast, an agency to which Congress has delegated policymaking responsibilities may, within the limits of that delegation, properly rely upon the incumbent administration's views of wise policy to inform its judgments. While agencies are not directly accountable to the people, the Chief Executive is, and it is entirely appropriate for this political branch of the Government to make such policy choices—resolving the competing interests which Congress itself either inadvertently did not resolve, or intentionally left to be resolved by the agency charged with the administration of the statute in light of everyday realities.

When a challenge to an agency construction of a statutory provision, fairly conceptualized, really centers on the wisdom of the agency's policy, rather than whether it is a reasonable choice within a gap left open by Congress, the challenge must fail. In such a case, federal judges—who have no constituency—have a duty to respect legitimate policy choices made by those who do. The responsibilities for assessing the wisdom of such policy choices and resolving the struggle between competing views of the public interest are not judicial ones: "Our Constitution vests such responsibilities in the political branches." *TVA v. Hill*, 437 U.S. 153, 195 (1978).

[handwritten: duty to respect legitimate policy choices]

We hold that the EPA's definition of the term "source" is a permissible construction of the statute which seeks to accommodate progress in reducing air pollution with economic growth. "The Regulations which the Administrator has adopted provide what the agency could allowably view as . . . [an] effective reconciliation of these twofold ends. . ." *United States v. Shimer*, 367 U.S., at 383.

[handwritten: Holding]

The judgment of the Court of Appeals is reversed.

It is so ordered.

JUSTICE MARSHALL and JUSTICE REHNQUIST took no part in the consideration or decision of these cases.

JUSTICE O'CONNOR took no part in the decision of these cases.

NOTES

Occasionally, as in *Vermont Yankee* or *Universal Camera*, there are cases in which the Supreme Court writes an opinion that is self-consciously designed to settle important issues and either restate or alter the law in a definitive fashion. *Chevron*, which has become among the most cited Supreme Court decisions in history and the subject of a scholarly literature that would fill libraries, was *not* such a case.

The opinion in *Chevron* does not have the magisterial tone and sweep of decisions like *Vermont Yankee* or *Universal Camera*. The opinion does, of course, contain some very broad, general language concerning deference to agency legal interpretations. Because the issue in *Chevron* was a pure question of law, it is therefore barely possible to conclude from *Chevron*'s broad language that the Court was instructing lower courts to replace the long-standing distinction between pure legal questions (generally reviewed de novo) and questions of law application (generally reviewed deferentially) with a single, uniform principle of deference applicable to all legal questions, whether pure or otherwise. But this reading—sometimes called the broad reading of *Chevron*—is hardly the only, or even the most natural, reading of the case. Near the end of its opinion, the Court in *Chevron* emphasized that "the regulatory scheme is technical and complex, the agency considered the matter in a detailed and reasoned fashion, and the decision involves reconciling conflicting policies." These are all among the factors that, under the traditional approach, could strongly affect the degree of deference afforded agency legal interpretations. It is therefore <u>possible, and even natural, to read *Chevron* simply as a straightforward application of settled principles</u> of judicial review of agency legal conclusions, with the case presenting one of the unusual but not unheard-of situations in which the traditional panoply of factors warranted granting an agency deference on a pure question of law.

There is little doubt that the Court in 1984 intended this second, or weak, reading of *Chevron*. Publicly available papers of the Court's deliberations reveal no evidence that the Court in 1984 regarded *Chevron* as a major administrative law case, much less as a case that could fundamentally alter scope-of-review doctrine. *See* Robert V. Percival, *Environmental Law in the Supreme Court: Highlights from the Marshall Papers*, 23 Envtl. L. Rep. 10606, 10613 (1993). The briefs and argument in the case did not at all engage broad issues of methodology or scope of review. Instead, all of the parties and the Justices understood the case to be an important but relatively narrow dispute about the scope of the Clean Air Act, with no broader implications for administrative law doctrine. *See* Thomas W. Merrill, *The Story of* Chevron USA Inc. v. Natural Resources Defense Council, Inc.: *Sometimes Great Cases Are Made Not Born, in* Statutory Interpretation Stories 164 (William N. Eskridge, Jr. et al eds., 2011).

The strong reading, however, quickly gained substantial momentum. Within months, some lower courts, most notably some panels of the D.C. Circuit, <u>took *Chevron* to prescribe a major change in scope-of-review law</u>, substituting a seemingly simple two-step test for the elaborate, multi-factor scheme prescribed by traditional law. *See, e.g., Rettig v. Pension Benefit Guaranty Corp.,* 744 F.2d 133 (D.C.Cir.1984); *Railway Labor Executives' Ass'n v. United States Railroad Retirement Bd.,* 749 F.2d 856 (D.C.Cir.1984). These decisions applying a broad reading of *Chevron* did so with little fanfare or discussion, and many other contemporaneous decisions continued, either implicitly or explicitly, to employ the traditional pre-*Chevron* analysis. By imperceptible but gradual steps, however, *Chevron* took hold, until by the end of 1986 the broad reading of *Chevron* was clearly settled law, at least in the D.C. Circuit. For a detailed account of the case-by-case process through which the *Chevron* doctrine was constructed by lower court judges, see Gary Lawson & Stephen Kam, *Making Law Out of Nothing At All: The Origins of the* Chevron *Doctrine,* 65 Admin. L. Rev. 1 (2013). By 1986, *Chevron* was also emerging as a major—and arguably *the* major—subject of academic commentary on administrative law.

Much of the early commentary was hostile, as the broad rule of deference prescribed by the strong reading of *Chevron* seemed hard to square either with traditional understandings of the role of appellate courts or with modern skepticism about agency performance. Many lower court judges also had grave doubts about the new regime. Many judges were trained at law schools (such as Harvard) steeped in the "legal process" tradition. From the perspective of that tradition, a broad rule of deference to agencies on questions of pure law makes no sense: courts, not politically appointed agencies, are the institutions best situated to define the abstract meaning of statutes, even if agencies are often better at applying statutes to particular facts. An advocate of the legal process approach would surely prefer the traditional scheme of judicial review, with its emphasis on the details of the particular agency and issue under review, to *Chevron*'s blunderbuss attitude of deference to agencies even on pure or abstract legal questions.

The Supreme Court had very little to say about *Chevron* until 1987. Certainly, there was no indication during that time that the Court believed that it had made any significant change to scope of review doctrine.

There were two major events involving the Court between 1984 and 1987 that are important to the *Chevron* saga. First, in 1986 Justice Scalia was elevated to the Court (replacing Chief Justice Burger) from the D.C. Circuit, where he had witnessed the establishment of the broad reading of *Chevron* as controlling circuit law (though, perhaps counterintuitively, he personally played relatively little role in its establishment). Second, the Court in 1987 was heavily staffed with law clerks who had previously worked on the D.C. Circuit and were thus well versed in the battles taking place in the lower courts. That year, those battles were renewed in a higher forum, as the following excerpt explains.

GARY LAWSON & STEPHEN KAM, MAKING LAW OUT OF NOTHING AT ALL: THE ORIGINS OF THE *CHEVRON* DOCTRINE

65 Admin. L. Rev. 1 (2013).

The initial battle [over *Chevron*] was fought in an unlikely context. Section 243(h) of the Immigration and Nationality Act provided, as of 1987, that "[t]he Attorney General shall not deport any alien . . . [with some exceptions not relevant here] to a country if the Attorney General determines that such alien's life or freedom *would be threatened* in such country on account of race, religion, nationality, membership in a particular social group, or political opinion."[1] If the otherwise-deportable alien could show he or she "would be threatened" in their country of return, which the Supreme Court construed to mean that it was "more likely than not that the alien would be subject to persecution"[2] upon return, then the Attorney General—typically acting through the Immigration and Naturalization Service ("INS")—was *required* to withhold deportation ("shall not deport"). Alternatively, the Refugee Act allowed the Attorney General, in his or her discretion, to grant asylum to a refugee,[3] defined as

---

[1]   8 U.S.C. § 1253(h) (1982) (emphasis added).

[2]   *INS v. Stevic*, 467 U.S. 407, 429–30 (1984).

[3]   *See* 8 U.S.C. § 1158(a) (1982) ("The Attorney General shall establish a procedure for an alien . . . and the alien may be granted asylum in the discretion of the Attorney General.").

a person "who is unable or unwilling to return to, and is unable or unwilling to avail himself or herself of the protection of, that [person's home] country because of persecution or *a well-founded fear of persecution* on account of race, religion, nationality, membership in a particular social group, or political opinion."[4]

In *INS v. Cardoza-Fonseca*,[5] the government argued the standard of proof for establishing refugee status, via a showing of a "well-founded fear of persecution," was the same "more likely than not" standard governing proof of entitlement to a withholding of deportation under the Immigration and Nationality Act. The respondent argued that one could have a "well-founded fear of persecution" even if it was not "more likely than not" to occur—meaning a forty-nine percent chance of imprisonment or execution upon return to one's home country, in other words, is enough to ground a "well-founded fear." The case thus revolved around a pure question of law: whether the legislatively prescribed standards of proof under two different statutes were the same.

The Ninth Circuit had agreed with respondent that the standard for proving a "well-founded fear" was different, and more generous to the alien, than was the standard for showing that life or freedom "would be threatened"[6] upon return. The court made no reference to *Chevron* or any kind of deference to the INS, as prior circuit precedent controlled the case instead.[7]

In its brief to the Supreme Court, the government briefly but forcefully urged deference to the INS's views, though *Chevron* was only one of many cases cited and received no special attention.[8] The brief concentrated on statutory analysis and administrative policy. The respondent's brief argued, citing *Chevron* in a footnote, that deference to the INS was appropriate only when Congress specifically delegates interpretative authority, as had arguably occurred in some prior immigration cases,[9] and that section 208(a) of the Refugee Act delegates no such authority. The discussion of deference was brief, and *Chevron* was decidedly in the background. The government's reply brief did not cite *Chevron*.

The oral argument, held on October 7, 1986, raised the stakes. The government (through long-time Deputy Solicitor General Larry Wallace) opened its argument with a call for deference to the INS, but intriguingly

---

4   *Id.* § 1101(a)(42)(A) (emphasis added).

5   480 U.S. 421 (1987).

6   *Cardoza-Fonseca v. U.S. INS*, 767 F.2d 1448 (9th Cir. 1985).

7   *See id.* at 1451–52 (citing cases from the Sixth, Seventh, and Ninth Circuits, but not *Chevron*).

8   *See* Brief for the Petitioner at 18–19, *Cardoza-Fonseca,* 480 U.S. 421 (1987) (No. 85–782), 1986 U.S. S. Ct. Briefs LEXIS 367. The string citation on page 18 was the brief's only mention of *Chevron*.

9   *See, e.g., INS v. Wang*, 450 U.S. 139, 145 (1981).

did not cite, invoke, or otherwise mention *Chevron*. The deference argument instead focused on the INS's expertise as "an active participant in the legislation as it developed," and its opportunity to "study the legislative background against the experience that it has had in applying the standards." This was consistent with the position in the government's brief, which easily could have been written without any mention of *Chevron*.

Chevron was introduced into the oral argument in a question addressed to Dana Marks Keener, counsel for the respondent * * *. The first words out of Ms. Keener's mouth after "may it please the Court" were:

> Understandably, the Government is putting considerable emphasis on their deference argument. That's because it's the only argument that it has. Unfortunately, there are some—or fortunately for our side—there are some considerable problems with deference to the agency in this particular context.
>
> By reviewing the statutory canons that apply to deference, the first place you start is with the fact that a court is the expert in terms of statutory construction. The meaning of the "well-founded fear" standard is an issue of law. It's clearly within the traditional function of this Court to interpret. It is not an area * * *.

At that point, Ms. Keener was interrupted by a question from Chief Justice Rehnquist: "Are you suggesting that the INS in this case should be given no deference simply because it is construing a term of the statute?" Her response included the argument's first mention of *Chevron*: "No. Of course the Court also looks at other factors, and deference cases talk about the fact, *Chevron* for example, that first always is Congress' intent." That narrow view of *Chevron* [which treated *Chevron* as an argument *against* deference] incited an exchange that, for the first time in the *Cardoza-Fonseca* litigation, and indeed for the first time in quite a while in the federal courts, brought to the fore the traditional, pre-*Chevron* distinction between pure and mixed questions of law:

> QUESTION (from Chief Justice Rehnquist): Well, my question to you was, which I don't think you've yet answered, is [ ] the agency entitled to no deference because what it is construing is a term of the statute?
>
> MS. KEENER: I think that answer is probably correct. But in arriving at whether deference is considered or not, the courts usually look at several factors, which include the legislative history, the plain language of the statute.
>
> QUESTION (from Chief Justice Rehnquist): Well, is deference one of those factors or not?

MS. KEENER: Well, it can be if a standard is not a question of pure law, if it is an application of the law to a specific set of facts. And courts often look to the agency's expertise to decide whether or not that's the kind of situation presented. However, that's not the case here.

QUESTION (from Justice Scalia): What was *Chevron*? Wasn't that a question of pure law? And didn't we say there that we, and in other cases, that we will accept the expert agency's interpretation of its governing statute where it's a reasonable one?

MS. KEENER: There was a technical gap in *Chevron*, and it was involved in the implementation. So it was construing a term involved in implementing a standard.

And with that the game was on.

By a vote of 6–3 (with Justices Powell, Rehnquist, and White dissenting), the Court agreed with respondent and the Ninth Circuit that the agency could not permissibly read the "well-founded fear" criterion in the discretionary withholding-of-deportation provision of the Refugee Act to require the same "more likely than not" standard of proof required by the "would be threatened" criterion in the mandatory withholding-of-deportation provision of the Immigration and Nationality Act. So framed, the decision's holding is an unexceptional and perhaps obviously correct bit of statutory interpretation. The fireworks were in the dicta.

As Justice Scalia pointed out in his concurring opinion, once one concluded—as had the Court—that the statute's plain meaning foreclosed the government's interpretation, there was no occasion to discuss deference, *Chevron*, or anything else. No amount of deference can justify an agency position contrary to the clear meaning of a statute. Nonetheless, in an opinion authored by Justice Stevens—who not at all coincidentally authored *Chevron*—a clean majority of five Justices took the occasion to explicitly and pointedly comment about the *Chevron* framework:

> The INS's second principal argument in support of the proposition that the "well founded fear" and "clear probability" standard are equivalent is that the BIA so construes the two standards. The INS argues that the BIA's construction of the Refugee Act of 1980 is entitled to substantial deference, even if we conclude that the Court of Appeals' reading of the statutes is more in keeping with Congress' intent. This argument is unpersuasive.

> The question whether Congress intended the two standards to be identical is a pure question of statutory construction for the courts to decide. Employing traditional tools of statutory construction, we have concluded that Congress did not intend the two standards to be identical. In *Chevron U.S.A., Inc. v. Natural*

Resources Defense Council, Inc., 467 U.S. 837, 104 S.Ct. 2778, 81 L.Ed.2d 694 (1984), we explained:

> "The judiciary is the final authority on issues of statutory construction and must reject administrative constructions which are contrary to clear congressional intent. If a court, employing traditional tools of statutory construction, ascertains that Congress had an intention on the precise question at issue, that intention is the law and must be given effect." *Id.*, at 843, n. 9.

> The narrow legal question whether the two standards are the same is, of course, quite different from the question of interpretation that arises in each case in which the agency is required to apply either or both standards to a particular set of facts. There is obviously some ambiguity in a term like "well-founded fear" which can only be given concrete meaning through a process of case-by-case adjudication. In that process of filling " 'any gap left, implicitly or explicitly, by Congress,' " the courts must respect the interpretation of the agency to which Congress has delegated the responsibility for administering the statutory program. See *Chevron, supra*, at 843. But our task today is much narrower, and is well within the province of the judiciary. We do not attempt to set forth a detailed description of how the "well-founded fear" test should be applied. Instead, we merely hold that the Immigration Judge and the BIA were incorrect in holding that the two standards are identical.[10]

The implications of this passage in 1987 were potentially enormous. Justice Stevens, writing for five Justices all of whom were part of the *Chevron* majority, effectively announced that the pre-*Chevron* distinction between pure and mixed questions of law still governed, which essentially adopted the position of Cardoza-Fonseca's counsel that the interpretation in *Chevron* partook more of law application than of law interpretation. The issue in *Cardoza-Fonseca* itself was characterized as "a pure question of statutory construction *for the courts to decide*." Any doubt Justice Stevens was taking specific aim at the emergent *Chevron* doctrine evaporates with a long footnote * * * omitted from the quoted passage. Justice Stevens pointedly introduced the footnote by observing, "In view of the INS's heavy reliance on the principle of deference as described in *Chevron* . . . , we set forth the relevant text in its entirety"—followed by four full paragraphs from the *Chevron* decision. The wording of this sentence was not accidental. The INS did not rely on *Chevron* itself, as we have seen and as Justice Stevens surely knew. The footnote refers to the "principle of deference *as described* in *Chevron*," meaning Justice Stevens was clarifying the

---

[10]   480 U.S. at 445–48 (footnotes omitted) (brackets in original).

"principle of deference" that he, speaking for a unanimous Court, intended to prescribe in 1984. The fourth of the full paragraphs quoted from the *Chevron* opinion begins with the words, "[i]n light of these well-settled principles," indicating *Chevron* was applying settled law rather than setting forth any new conception of deference. The message to the lower courts that had fashioned—however sketchily—their own distinctive "*Chevron* doctrine" was clear: there is no "*Chevron* doctrine" beyond the principles that were "well-settled" in the summer 1984, which required distinguishing between pure questions of law and mixed questions of law application.

The message was not lost on Justice Scalia. He agreed with the majority that the government's interpretation of the statute was unsustainable, and therefore concurred in the result, but he emphatically objected to the majority's characterization of *Chevron*:

> This Court has consistently interpreted *Chevron*—which has been an extremely important and frequently cited opinion, not only in this Court but in the Courts of Appeals—as holding that courts must give effect to a reasonable agency interpretation of a statute unless that interpretation is inconsistent with a clearly expressed congressional intent. The Court's discussion is flatly inconsistent with this well-established interpretation . . . .

> The Court . . . implies that courts may substitute their interpretation of a statute for that of an agency whenever they face "a pure question of statutory construction for the courts to decide," rather than a "question of interpretation [in which] the agency is required to apply [a legal standard] to a particular set of facts." No support is adduced for this proposition, which is contradicted by the case the Court purports to be interpreting, since in *Chevron* the Court deferred to the Environmental Protection Agency's abstract interpretation of the phrase "stationary source."

> In my view, the Court badly misinterprets *Chevron*. More fundamentally, however, I neither share nor understand the Court's eagerness to refashion important principles of administrative law in a case in which such questions are completely unnecessary to the decision and have not been fully briefed by the parties.[11]

Presumably, Justice Scalia was not telling Justice Stevens the latter misunderstood his own opinion. As the reference to *Chevron*'s prevalence in the lower courts illustrates, Justice Scalia instead was no doubt identifying that *Chevron* had taken on a life of its own, whether Justice

---

[11]   480 U.S. at 454–55 (Scalia, J., concurring) (internal quotations omitted).

Stevens so intended it in 1984; and to seek casually to alter or undo that structure—especially in a case in which no party was calling for a reconsideration or clarification of *Chevron*—could have serious doctrinal consequences.

No Justice joined Justice Scalia's concurring opinion. The three dissenting Justices found the agency's interpretation of the statute reasonable, but they did not engage in debate over the proper meaning of *Chevron*.

Was the *Chevron* revolution over before it actually began?

A substantial number of lower courts thought so, quite reasonably given the strong dictum of *Cardoza-Fonseca*. There was a surge of decisions in the courts of appeals announcing that deference * * * would no longer be given to agency decisions involving pure questions of law but only to agency applications of law to particular facts.[12] Not every case understood *Cardoza-Fonseca* to cut short the *Chevron* revolution,[13] and because the discussion in *Cardoza-Fonseca* was plainly dictum, there was no requirement that it be so understood, but there were enough decisions cutting down on *Chevron* to question *Chevron*'s future.

The stage was set for what promised to be one of the most profound battles over administrative law doctrine in American legal history. The lower courts, on their own accord, had constructed a method for reviewing agency legal conclusions that, however uncertain at the margins and in the mechanics, was materially different from what preceded it. That method flew in the face of strongly and widely held precepts about sound allocation of institutional authority, but it offered some promise of a cleaner, simpler, and less intrusive judicial role in administrative review. There was ample room, and strong ammunition, on both sides of that divide. Once the issues raised by *Chevron* had migrated to the Supreme Court—which had happened by the time *Cardoza-Fonseca* was decided—it seemed inevitable that those issues would come to a head in something other than an exchange of dictum.

* * *

In 1987, Justice Scalia was the only vote on the Supreme Court for the proposition that courts should routinely give some measure of legal deference to agencies even on pure questions of law interpretation. By 1988, the number had risen to four, with no change in the Court's

---

[12] *See, e.g., NLRB Union v. FLRA*, 834 F.2d 191, 198 (D.C. Cir. 1987); *FEC v. Sailors' Union of the Pac. Political Fund*, 828 F.2d 502, 505–06 (9th Cir. 1987); *Union of Concerned Scientists v. NRC*, 824 F.2d 108, 113 (D.C. Cir. 1987); *Regular Common Carrier Conference v. United States*, 820 F.2d 1323, 1330 (D.C. Cir. 1987); *Adams House Health Care v. Heckler*, 817 F.2d 587 (9th Cir. 1987); *Int'l Union, United Automobile, Aerospace and Agricultural Implement Workers of America v. Brock*, 816 F.2d 761, 764–65 (D.C. Cir. 1987).

[13] *See, e.g., Grinspoon v. DEA*, 828 F.2d 881, 884–85 (1st Cir. 1987) (holding that *Cardoza-Fonseca* in fact reaffirmed *Chevron*).

membership other than the retirement of Justice Powell, who had not taken sides in the *Cardoza-Fonseca* controversy. *NLRB v. United Food & Commercial Workers Union, Local 23, AFL-CIO*[14] concerned "whether a federal court has authority to review a decision of the National Labor Relations Board's General Counsel dismissing an unfair labor practice complaint pursuant to an informal settlement in which the charging party refused to join."[15] A unanimous Court of eight Justices—this was during the interregnum before Justice Kennedy became an active member—found the courts had no such authority. The case came down to whether the proceeding at issue was prosecutorial (not reviewable) or adjudicatory (reviewable). The Court's discussion of the scope of review for this question intriguingly invoked *Cardoza-Fonseca* but made no specific mention of distinguishing between pure and mixed questions of law. The Court's disposition on the merits observed:

> [T]he general congressional framework, dividing the final authority of the General Counsel and the Board along a prosecutorial and adjudicatory line, is easy to discern. Some agency decisions can be said with certainty to fall on one side or the other of this line. For example, as already discussed, decisions whether to file a complaint are prosecutorial. In contrast, the resolution of contested unfair labor practice cases is adjudicatory. But between these extremes are cases that might fairly be said to fall on either side of the division. Our task, under *Cardoza-Fonseca* and *Chevron,* is not judicially to categorize each agency determination, but rather to decide whether the agency's regulatory placement is permissible.[16]

Justice Scalia highlighted the Court's deferential posture in a concurring opinion, this time joined by Justices Rehnquist, White, and O'Connor:

> I join the Court's opinion, and write separately only to note that our decision demonstrates the continuing and unchanged vitality of the test for judicial review of agency determinations of law set forth in *Chevron* . . . . Some courts have mistakenly concluded otherwise, on the basis of dicta in *INS v. Cardoza-Fonseca* . . . . If the dicta of *Cardoza-Fonseca*, as opposed to its expressed adherence to *Chevron*, were to be applied here, surely the question whether dismissal of complaints requires board approval and thus qualifies for judicial review . . . would be "a pure question of statutory construction" rather than the application of a "standar[d] to a particular set of facts," as to which "the courts

---

[14] 484 U.S. 112 (1988).

[15] *Id.* at 114.

[16] *Id.* at 125.

must respect the interpretation of the agency[.]" Were we to follow those dicta, therefore, we would be deciding this issue conclusively and authoritatively, rather than merely "decid[ing] whether the agency's regulatory placement is permissible[.]" The same would be true, moreover, of the many other decisions alluded to by the court in which "we have traditionally accorded the board deference with regard to its interpretation of the NLRA." Those cases, and this, are decided correctly only because "the statute is silent or ambiguous" with respect to an issue relevant to the agency's administration of the law committed to its charge— which is the test for deference set forth in *Chevron*.[17]

The Court's opinion made no response to this concurrence. A response was certainly available: by describing the decision in terms of line drawing, the Court left open an ability to challenge Justice Scalia's characterization of the case as involving a pure question of law. Line drawing smacks of law application, so it would be possible to slot *United Foods* into the circumstances in which deference was permitted by *Cardoza-Fonseca*. The Court made no such effort.

If one enjoyed reading tea leaves, by 1988 it looked as though there might be a 4–4 split on the Court concerning applying deference to pure questions of law, awaiting resolution by Justice Kennedy when he joined the Court. One needed only reasonably assume that Justices Stevens, Brennan (who authored the opinion in *United Foods*), Marshall, and Blackmun continued to adhere to the strong dictum of *Cardoza-Fonseca*. It remained only for the fully staffed Court to decide a case that squarely, neatly, and cleanly settled the status of Justice Stevens' dictum in *Cardoza-Fonseca*.

It never happened. No such decision came—or has come since. Through a process that we can observe but do not purport to explain, the 4–4 split in *United Foods* was almost universally taken by the lower courts as a vindication of Justice Scalia's position in his concurrence, that *Chevron* would extend deference to agency determinations involving pure legal questions.[18] To be sure, litigants were still pushing, albeit unsuccessfully, the distinction between pure and mixed legal questions as late as 1991[19] * * *. But at least some form of the *Chevron* revolution has dominated the

---

[17]   484 U.S. at 133–34 (Scalia, J., concurring).

[18]   *See*, e.g., *City of Boston v. U.S. Dep't of Hous. & Urban Dev.*, 898 F.2d 828, 831 (1st Cir. 1990); *CSX Transp. v. United States*, 867 F.2d 1439, 1444–45 (D.C. Cir. 1989) (Edwards, J., dissenting) (expressing dislike for *Chevron* but conceding it governs); *Theodus v. McLaughlin*, 852 F.2d 1380, 1382–84 (D.C. Cir. 1988); *Ry. Labor Execs' Ass'n v. U.S. R.R. Bd.*, 842 F.2d 466, 471–72 (D.C. Cir. 1988); *Fernandez v. Brock*, 840 F.2d 622, 631–32 (9th Cir. 1988); *Mead Johnson Pharm. Grp. v. Bowen*, 838 F.2d 1332, 1335–36 (D.C. Cir. 1988); *Cablevision Syss. Dev. Co. v. Motion Picture Ass'n of Am.*, 836 F.2d 599, 607 n.12 (D.C. Cir. 1988).

[19]   *See Wagner Seed Co., Inc. v. Bush*, 946 F.2d 918, 922 (D.C. Cir. 1991); *Central States Motor Freight Bureau, Inc. v. ICC*, 924 F.2d 1099, 1102 (D.C. Cir 1991).

lower courts for more than two decades now * * *. The great debate over the soul of *Chevron* thus ended with nary a whimper, much less a bang.

NOTES

But that does not mean that the battle is over. In *Negusie v. Holder*, 555 U.S. 511, 129 S.Ct. 1159, 173 L.Ed.2d 20 (2009), the majority declined to apply *Chevron* to an interpretation of the immigration laws by the Board of Immigration Appeals because the agency had not independently interpreted the statute but had (wrongly) considered a prior Supreme Court decision controlling in the case. The majority remanded the case back to the agency so that the agency could interpret the statute free of its mistaken view of the Court's precedents. Justices Stevens and Breyer concurred with the refusal to apply *Chevron* but would have decided the statutory issue without reference to any subsequent agency interpretation:

> In cases involving agency adjudication, we have sometimes described the court's role as deciding pure questions of statutory construction and the agency's role as applying law to fact [citing *Cardozo-Fonseca* and *United Foods*]. While this phrasing is peculiar to the adjudicatory context, the principle applies to *Chevron*'s domain more broadly. In the context of agency rulemaking, for instance, we might distinguish between pure questions of statutory interpretation and policymaking, or between central legal issues and interstitial questions. The label is immaterial. What matters is the principle: Certain aspects of statutory interpretation remain within the purview of the courts, even when the statute is not entirely clear * * *.

> * * *

> The threshold question the Court addresses today is the kind of "pure question of statutory construction for the courts to decide" that we answered in *Cardozo-Fonseca* rather than a fact-intensive question * * *.

> * * *

> Because I remain convinced that the narrower interpretation of *Chevron* endorsed by the Court in *Cardozo-Fonseca* was more faithful to the rationale of that case than the broader view the Court adopts today, I am unable to join its opinion.

Id. at 531, 534, 538. Opposition on the bench to a broad application, or in some cases *any* application, of *Chevron* has become more open in recent years. When he was a court of appeals judge, Justice Gorsuch authored a lengthy diatribe against *Chevron* (in a concurrence to one of his own majority opinions). *See Gutierrez-Brizuela v. Lynch,* 834 F.3d 1142, 1151–58 (10th Cir.2016) (Gorsuch, J., concurring). Other judges have launched subtler but forceful attacks on *Chevron. See Zurich American Ins. Group v. Duncan,* 889 F.3d 293, 307–08 (6th Cir.2018) (Kethledge, J., concurring in the judgment) ("For the narrow purpose of deciding this case * * *, it makes little difference whether we agree with the agency's interpretation (as I do) or defer to it (as the majority does). For purposes of our constitutional separation of powers, however, it matters a great deal whether we exercise our Article III power to " 'say what the law is,' " or instead hand over that power to an executive agency."); *Waterkeeper Alliance v. EPA*, 853 F.3d 527, 539 (D.C.Cir.2017) (Brown, J., concurring) ("An Article III renaissance is emerging against the judicial abdication performed in *Chevron's* name"); *Egan v. Delaware River Port. Auth.*, 851 F.3d 263, 278 (3d Cir.2017) (Jordan, J., concurring in the judgment) ("*Chevron* and *Auer* and their like are, with all respect, contrary to the roles assigned to the separate branches of government; they embed perverse incentives in the operations of government; they spread the spores of the ever-expanding administrative state; they require us at times to lay aside fairness and our own best judgment and instead bow to the nation's most powerful litigant, the government, for no reason other than that it is the government. The problems they create are serious and ought to be fixed."). *See also* Brett M. Kavanaugh, *Book Review*, 129 Harv. L. Rev. 2118, 2150 (2016) ("*Chevron* * * * has no basis in the Administrative Procedure Act. So *Chevron* itself is an atextual invention by courts. In many ways, *Chevron* is nothing more than a judicially orchestrated shift of power from Congress to the Executive Branch"). And in 2018 the Supreme Court was asked by a party formally to overrule *Chevron* but (in an opinion by Justice Gorsuch) declined the invitation and ruled for that party on other grounds. *See SAS Inst., Inc. v. Iancu*, 138 S.Ct. 1348, 1358 (2018) ("SAS replies that we might use this case as an opportunity to abandon *Chevron* * * *. But whether *Chevron* should remain is a question we may leave for another day."). Until "another day" comes, every administrative lawyer needs to have a solid understanding of the ins and outs of *Chevron*.

b.   Dancing the *Chevron* Two-Step

When compared to pre-1984 law, *Chevron* appears to offer the virtue of simplicity: instead of an indeterminate, multi-factor test for deference, one merely asks whether the statute or regulation in question is clear and, if not, whether the agency's interpretation is reasonable. Indeed, this seeming simplicity may have been an important factor in the emergence and ultimate triumph (for now) of the strong reading of *Chevron*. But how deceptive is this seeming simplicity? The implementation of "the *Chevron* two-step," as it is widely called,[17] has generated an enormous range of

(handwritten margin note: (1) Is the statute/reg clear? If not... (2) Is the agency's interp reasonable?)

---

[17] *Chevron* inquiries typically get structured in this "two step" manner because of the language used by Justice Stevens in the *Chevron* decision. But if Justice Stevens had no intention of creating a new regime for appellate review of agency decisionmaking—and there is no doubt whatsoever that he had no such intention—does it make sense to parse the language of the decision so carefully to flesh out the contours of the doctrine? Once one has decided to adopt a strong reading of *Chevron*, doesn't it make more sense to frame the inquiry as a "one step" analysis that asks whether the agency's interpretation is, all things considered, reasonable—keeping in mind that an interpretation contrary to the clear meaning of the statute is per se unreasonable? A number of administrative law scholars have argued over the years for this "one-step" formulation. *See* Matthew C. Stephenson & Adrian Vermeule, Chevron *Has Only One Step*, 95 Va.L.Rev. 597 (2009); Gary Lawson, *Proving the Law*, 86 Nw.U.L.Rev. 859, 884 n.78 (1992). *But see* Kenneth A.

problems—and, of course, an enormous body of case law and academic commentary. A full study of the *Chevron* doctrine would be a course in itself; these materials can only touch on the highlights.

3.   WHEN DOES *CHEVRON* APPLY?

Despite its breadth, the broad reading of *Chevron* does not require judicial deference to *all* agency legal interpretations. *Chevron* discussed the principles for judicial review of "an agency's construction of the *statute* which it administers" (emphasis added). But agencies can interpret many legal documents other than statutes, and in those contexts the *Chevron* doctrine may not apply.

Most notably, agencies frequently construe their own regulations. As a formal matter, the extent to which agencies receive deference in regulatory construction is governed by a line of cases separate from both the pre-and post-*Chevron* cases concerning statutory interpretation. The leading decision concerning deference to agency regulatory construction is *Bowles v. Seminole Rock & Sand Co.,* 325 U.S. 410, 65 S.Ct. 1215, 89 L.Ed. 1700 (1945), which declared that an agency's construction of its own regulation "becomes of controlling weight unless it is plainly erroneous or inconsistent with the regulation." *Id.* at 414. This doctrine was restated and reaffirmed in *Auer v. Robbins,* 519 U.S. 452, 461–63, 117 S.Ct. 905, 137 L.Ed.2d 79 (1997). Accordingly, deference to agency regulatory construction is often called "*Seminole Rock* deference" or "*Auer* deference." Courts sometimes describe this deference "as even greater than our deference to an agency's interpretation of ambiguous statutory terms," *C.F. Communications Corp. v. FCC*, 128 F.3d 735, 738 (D.C.Cir.1997). *See also Paradissiotis v. Rubin*, 171 F.3d 983, 987 (5th Cir.1999) (stating that agency interpretations of their own regulations are entitled to a higher level of deference than the *Chevron* standard). Other courts are more doubtful whether the *Seminole Rock/Auer* formulation differs meaningfully from the rule of *Chevron*. "After all, *Chevron* requires a reviewing court to affirm a permissible (or reasonable) interpretation of an ambiguous statute, and we very much doubt that we would defer to an *unreasonable* agency interpretation of an ambiguous regulation." *Paralyzed Veterans of America v. D.C. Arena L.P.*, 117 F.3d 579, 584

Bamberger & Peter L. Strauss, Essay, Chevron's *Two Steps*, 95 Va. L. Rev. 611 (2009) (defending the two-step formulation)., In 2009, a former administrative law scholar made the same point writing for a majority of the Court. *See* Entergy Corp. v. Riverkeeper, Inc., 556 U.S. 208, 218 n.4 129 S.Ct. 1498, 173 L.Ed.2d 369 (2009) ("The dissent finds it 'puzzling' that we invoke this proposition (that a reasonable agency interpretation prevails) at the 'outset,' omitting the supposedly prior inquiry of ' "whether congress has directly spoken to the precise question at issue." ' But surely if Congress has directly spoken to an issue then any agency interpretation contradicting what Congress has said would be unreasonable") (opinion by Scalia, J.). It is too soon to tell whether this language will have any impact on the way in which the administrative law community formulates the *Chevron* inquiry. For now, at least, *Chevron* is generally understood to require two distinct steps: determine whether the meaning of the statute is clear and, if not, affirm the agency's interpretation as long as it is reasonable.

(D.C.Cir.1997). Indeed, many courts simply declare directly that *Chevron* governs review of agency regulatory construction. *See, e.g., Smith v. Scott*, 223 F.3d 1191, 1195 (10th Cir.2000); *Transitional Learning Community of Galveston, Inc. v. United States OPM*, 220 F.3d 427, 430 (5th Cir.2000). Given the different origins of the *Chevron* and *Seminole Rock/Auer* doctrines, however, the correct approach is to keep them separate—as did the Supreme Court in *Gonzales v. Oregon*, 546 U.S. 243, 126 S.Ct. 904, 163 L.Ed.2d 748 (2006). In any event, deference to the agency does not necessarily mean victory for the agency: it is quite possible for agencies unreasonably to interpret their own regulations. *See, e.g., Kaiser Foundation Hospitals v. Sebelius*, 708 F.3d 226 (D.C.Cir.2013) (finding unreasonable an agency's "narrow, arbitrarily applied" interpretation of its regulation).

Seminole Rock/Auer deference, which allows agencies to get great deference in the interpretation of their own work product, is not universally admired. For a critical analysis of the doctrine, see John F. Manning, *Constitutional Structure and Judicial Deference to Agency Interpretations of Agency Rules*, 96 Colum. L. Rev. 612 (1996). Professor Manning's critique eventually won over an important convert: the author of the opinion in *Auer v. Robbins. See Talk America, Inc. v. Michigan Bell Telephone Co.*, 564 U.S. 50, 131 S.Ct. 2254 (2011) (Scalia, J., concurring):

> It is comforting to know that I would reach the Court's result even without *Auer*. For while I have in the past uncritically accepted that rule, I have become increasingly doubtful of its validity. On the surface, it seems to be a natural corollary—indeed, an *a fortiori* application—of the rule that we will defer to an agency's interpretation of the statute it is charged with implementing. But it is not. When Congress enacts an imprecise statute that it commits to the implementation of an executive agency, it has no control over that implementation (except, of course, through further, more precise, legislation). The legislative and executive functions are not combined. But when an agency promulgates an imprecise rule, it leaves *to itself* the implementation of that rule, and thus the initial determination of the rule's meaning. And though the adoption of a rule is an exercise of the executive rather than the legislative power, a properly adopted rule has fully the effect of law. It seems contrary to fundamental principles of separation of powers to permit the person who promulgates a law to interpret it as well. "When the legislative and executive powers are united in the same person, or in the same body of magistrates, there can be no liberty; because apprehensions may arise, lest the same monarch or senate should enact tyrannical laws, to execute them in a tyrannical manner."

[Handwritten margin note: sep. of powers issue and letting the one who promulgates the rule also interpret it]

Montesquieu, Spirit of the Laws bk. XI, ch. 6, pp. 151–152 (O. Piest ed., T. Nugent transl.1949).

Deferring to an agency's interpretation of a statute does not encourage Congress, out of a desire to expand its power, to enact vague statutes; the vagueness effectively cedes power to the Executive. By contrast, deferring to an agency's interpretation of its own rule encourages the agency to enact vague rules which give it the power, in future adjudications, to do what it pleases. This frustrates the notice and predictability purposes of rulemaking, and promotes arbitrary government. The seeming inappropriateness of *Auer* deference is especially evident in cases such as these, involving an agency that has repeatedly been rebuked in its attempts to expand the statute beyond its text, and has repeatedly sought new means to the same ends.

There are undoubted advantages to *Auer* deference. It makes the job of a reviewing court much easier, and since it usually produces affirmance of the agency's view without conflict in the Circuits, it imparts (once the agency has spoken to clarify the regulation) certainty and predict-ability to the administrative process. The defects of *Auer* deference, and the alternatives to it, are fully explored in Manning, *Constitutional Structure and Judicial Deference to Agency Interpretations of Agency Rules*, 96 Colum. L. Rev. 612 (1996). We have not been asked to reconsider *Auer* in the present case. When we are, I will be receptive to doing so.

564 U.S. at 68–69, 131 S.Ct. at 2266.

Does the following case suggest that Justice Scalia was not alone in his doubts?

CHRISTOPHER V. SMITHKLINE BEECHAM CORP.

Supreme Court of the United States, 2012.
567 U.S. 142, 132 S.Ct. 2156, 183 L.Ed.2d 153.

JUSTICE ALITO delivered the opinion of the Court.

The Fair Labor Standards Act (FLSA) imposes minimum wage and maximum hours requirements on employers, see 29 U.S.C. §§ 206–207 (2006 ed. and Supp. IV), but those requirements do not apply to workers employed "in the capacity of outside salesman," § 213(a)(1). This case requires us to decide whether the term "outside salesman," as defined by Department of Labor (DOL or Department) regulations, encompasses pharmaceutical sales representatives whose primary duty is to obtain nonbinding commitments from physicians to prescribe their employer's prescription drugs in appropriate cases. We conclude that these employees qualify as "outside salesm[e]n."

I

A

*　*　* [T]he FLSA obligates employers to compensate employees for hours in excess of 40 per week at a rate of 1 1/2 times the employees' regular wages. See § 207(a). The overtime compensation requirement, however, does not apply with respect to all employees. As relevant here, the statute exempts workers "employed . . . in the capacity of outside salesman." § 213(a)(1).

Congress did not define the term "outside salesman," but it delegated authority to the DOL to issue regulations "from time to time" to "defin[e] and delimi[t]" the term. Ibid. The DOL promulgated such regulations in 1938, 1940, and 1949. In 2004, following notice-and-comment procedures, the DOL reissued the regulations with minor amendments. The current regulations are nearly identical in substance to the regulations issued in the years immediately following the FLSA's enactment. See 29 C.F.R. §§ 541.500–541.504 (2011).

Three of the DOL's regulations are directly relevant to this case: §§ 541.500, 541.501, and 541.503. We refer to these three regulations as the "general regulation," the "sales regulation," and the "promotion-work regulation," respectively.

The general regulation sets out the definition of the statutory term "employee employed in the capacity of outside salesman." It defines the term to mean "any employee . . . [w]hose primary duty is . . . making sales within the meaning of [29 U.S.C. § 203(k)]" and "[w]ho is customarily and regularly engaged away from the employer's place or places of business in performing such primary duty." §§ 541.500(a)(1)–(2). The referenced statutory provision, 29 U.S.C. § 203(k), states that " '[s]ale' or 'sell' includes any sale, exchange, contract to sell, consignment for sale, shipment for sale, or other disposition." Thus, under the general regulation, an outside salesman is any employee whose primary duty is making any sale, exchange, contract to sell, consignment for sale, shipment for sale, or other disposition.

The sales regulation restates the statutory definition of sale discussed above and clarifies that "[s]ales within the meaning of [29 U.S.C. § 203(k)] include the transfer of title to tangible property, and in certain cases, of tangible and valuable evidences of intangible property." 29 C.F.R. § 541.501(b).

Finally, the promotion-work regulation identifies "[p]romotion work" as "one type of activity often performed by persons who make sales, which may or may not be exempt outside sales work, depending upon the circumstances under which it is performed." § 541.503(a). Promotion work that is "performed incidental to and in conjunction with an employee's own outside sales or solicitations is exempt work," whereas promotion work that is "incidental to sales made, or to be made, by someone else is not exempt outside sales work." *Ibid.*

Additional guidance concerning the scope of the outside salesman exemption can be gleaned from reports issued in connection with the DOL's promulgation of regulations in 1940 and 1949, and from the preamble to the 2004 regulations. See Dept. of Labor, Wage and Hour Division, Report and Recommendations of the Presiding Officer at Hearings Preliminary to Redefinition (1940) (hereinafter 1940 Report); Dept. of Labor, Wage and Hour Division, Report and Recommendations on Proposed Revisions of Regulations, Part 541 (1949) (hereinafter 1949 Report); 69 Fed.Reg. 22160–22163 (hereinafter Preamble). Although the DOL has rejected proposals to eliminate or dilute the requirement that outside salesmen make their own sales, the Department has stressed that this requirement is met whenever an employee "in some sense make [s] a sale." 1940 Report 46; see also Preamble 22162 (reiterating that the exemption applies only to an employee who "in some sense, has made sales"). And the DOL has made it clear that "[e]xempt status should not depend" on technicalities, such as "whether it is the sales employee or the customer who types the order into a computer system and hits the return button," Preamble 22163, or whether "the order is filled by [a] jobber rather than directly by [the employee's] own employer," 1949 Report 83.

B

Respondent SmithKline Beecham Corporation is in the business of developing, manufacturing, and selling prescription drugs. The prescription drug industry is subject to extensive federal regulation, including the now-familiar requirement that prescription drugs be dispensed only upon a physician's prescription. In light of this requirement, pharmaceutical companies have long focused their direct marketing efforts, not on the retail pharmacies that dispense prescription drugs, but rather on the medical practitioners who possess the authority to prescribe the drugs in the first place. Pharmaceutical companies promote their prescription drugs to physicians through a process called "detailing," whereby employees known as "detailers" or "pharmaceutical sales representatives" provide information to physicians about the company's products in hopes of persuading them to write prescriptions for the products in appropriate cases. The position of "detailer" has existed in the pharmaceutical industry in substantially its current form since at least the 1950's, and in recent years the industry has employed more than 90,000 detailers nationwide.

Respondent hired petitioners Michael Christopher and Frank Buchanan as pharmaceutical sales representatives in 2003. During the roughly four years when petitioners were employed in that capacity, they were responsible for calling on physicians in an assigned sales territory to discuss the features, benefits, and risks of an assigned portfolio of respondent's prescription drugs. Petitioners' primary objective was to obtain a nonbinding commitment from the physician to prescribe those drugs in appropriate cases, and the training that petitioners received underscored the importance of that objective.

Petitioners spent about 40 hours each week in the field calling on physicians. These visits occurred during normal business hours, from about 8:30 a.m. to 5 p.m. Outside of normal business hours, petitioners spent an additional 10 to 20 hours each week attending events, reviewing product information, returning phone calls, responding to e-mails, and performing other miscellaneous tasks * * *.

* * * It is undisputed that respondent did not pay petitioners time-and-a-half wages when they worked in excess of 40 hours per week.

* * *

II

We must determine whether pharmaceutical detailers are outside salesmen as the DOL has defined that term in its regulations. The parties agree that the regulations themselves were validly promulgated and are therefore entitled to deference under *Chevron U.S.A. Inc. v. Natural Resources Defense Council, Inc.*, 467 U.S. 837, 104 S.Ct. 2778, 81 L.Ed.2d 694 (1984). But the parties disagree sharply about whether the DOL's interpretation of the regulations is owed deference under *Auer v. Robbins*, 519 U.S. 452, 117 S.Ct. 905, 137 L.Ed.2d 79 (1997). It is to that question that we now turn.

A

The DOL first announced its view that pharmaceutical detailers are not exempt outside salesmen in an *amicus* brief filed in the Second Circuit in 2009, and the Department has subsequently filed similar *amicus* briefs in other cases, including the case now before us. While the DOL's ultimate conclusion that detailers are not exempt has remained unchanged since 2009, the same cannot be said of its reasoning. In both the Second Circuit and the Ninth Circuit, the DOL took the view that "a 'sale' for the purposes of the outside sales exemption requires a consummated transaction directly involving the employee for whom the exemption is sought." Secretary's *Novartis* Brief 11; see also Brief for Secretary of Labor as *Amicus Curiae* in No. 10–15257 (CA9), p. 12. Perhaps because of the nebulous nature of this "consummated transaction" test, the Department changed course after we granted certiorari in this case. The Department now takes the position that "[a]n employee does not make a 'sale' for purposes of the 'outside salesman' exemption unless he actually transfers title to the property at issue." Brief for United States as *Amicus Curiae* 12–13 (hereinafter U.S. Brief). Petitioners and the DOL assert that this new interpretation of the regulations is entitled to controlling deference. See Brief for Petitioners 31–42; U.S. Brief 30–34.

Although *Auer* ordinarily calls for deference to an agency's interpretation of its own ambiguous regulation, even when that interpretation is advanced in a legal brief, this general rule does not apply in all cases. Deference is undoubtedly inappropriate, for example, when the agency's interpretation is " 'plainly erroneous or inconsistent with the regulation.' " *Id.* at 461, 117 S.Ct. 905 (quoting *Robertson v. Methow Valley Citizens Council*, 490 U.S. 332, 359, 109 S.Ct. 1835, 104 L.Ed.2d 351 (1989)). And deference is likewise unwarranted when there is reason to suspect that the agency's interpretation "does not reflect the agency's fair and considered judgment on the matter in question." *Auer, supra*, at 462, 117 S.Ct. 905. This might occur when the agency's interpretation conflicts with a prior interpretation, see, *e.g., Thomas Jefferson Univ. v. Shalala*, 512 U.S. 504, 515, 114 S.Ct. 2381, 129 L.Ed.2d 405 (1994), or when it appears that the interpretation is nothing more than a "convenient litigating position," *Bowen v. Georgetown Univ. Hospital*, 488 U.S. 204, 213, 109 S.Ct. 468, 102 L.Ed.2d 493 (1988), or a " ' *post hoc* rationalizatio[n]' advanced by an agency seeking to defend past agency action against attack," *Auer, supra*, at 462, 117 S.Ct. 905 (quoting *Bowen, supra*, at 212, 109 S.Ct. 468 (alteration in original)).

In this case, there are strong reasons for withholding the deference that *Auer* generally requires. Petitioners invoke the DOL's interpretation of ambiguous regulations to impose potentially massive liability on respondent for conduct that occurred well before that interpretation was announced. To defer to the agency's interpretation in this circumstance would seriously undermine the principle that agencies should provide regulated parties "fair warning of the conduct [a regulation] prohibits or requires." *Gates & Fox Co. v. Occupational Safety and Health Review Comm'n*, 790 F.2d 154, 156 (C.A.D.C.1986) (Scalia, J.). Indeed, it would result in precisely the kind of "unfair surprise" against which our cases have long warned. See *Long Island Care at Home, Ltd. v. Coke*, 551 U.S. 158, 170–171, 127 S.Ct. 2339, 168 L.Ed.2d 54 (2007) (deferring to new interpretation that "create[d] no unfair surprise" because agency had proceeded through notice-and-comment rulemaking); *Martin v. Occupational Safety and Health Review Comm'n*, 499 U.S. 144, 158, 111 S.Ct. 1171, 113 L.Ed.2d 117 (1991) (identifying "adequacy of notice to regulated parties" as one factor relevant to the reasonableness of the agency's interpretation).

This case well illustrates the point. Until 2009, the pharmaceutical industry had little reason to suspect that its longstanding practice of treating detailers as exempt outside salesmen transgressed the FLSA. The statute and regulations certainly do not provide clear notice of this. The general regulation adopts the broad statutory definition of "sale," and that definition, in turn, employs the broad catchall phrase "other disposition." This catchall phrase could reasonably be construed to encompass a nonbinding commitment from a physician to prescribe a particular drug, and nothing in the statutory or regulatory text or the DOL's prior guidance plainly requires a contrary reading.

Even more important, despite the industry's decades-long practice of classifying pharmaceutical detailers as exempt employees, the DOL never initiated any enforcement actions with respect to detailers or otherwise suggested that it thought the industry was acting unlawfully. We acknowledge that an agency's enforcement decisions are informed by a host of factors, some bearing no relation to the agency's views regarding whether a violation has occurred. But where, as here, an agency's announcement of its interpretation is preceded by a very lengthy period of conspicuous inaction, the potential for unfair surprise is acute * * *.

[handwritten margin note: concern re: unfair surprise]

Our practice of deferring to an agency's interpretation of its own ambiguous regulations undoubtedly has important advantages, but this practice also creates a risk that agencies will promulgate vague and open-ended regulations that they can later interpret as they see fit, thereby "frustrat[ing] the notice and predictability purposes of rulemaking." Talk America, Inc. v. Michigan Bell Telephone Co., 564 U.S. ___, ___, 131 S.Ct. 2254, 2266, 180 L.Ed.2d 96 (2011) (SCALIA, J., concurring); see also Stephenson & Pogoriler, *Seminole Rock's* Domain, 79 Geo. Wash. L. Rev. 1449, 1461–1462 (2011); Manning, Constitutional Structure and Judicial Deference to Agency Interpretations of Agency Rules, 96 Colum. L. Rev. 612, 655–668 (1996). It is one thing to expect regulated parties to conform their conduct to an agency's interpretations once the agency announces them; it is quite another to require regulated parties to divine the agency's interpretations in advance or else be held liable when the agency announces its interpretations for the first time in an enforcement proceeding and demands deference.

Accordingly, whatever the general merits of *Auer* deference, it is unwarranted here. We instead accord the Department's interpretation a measure of deference proportional to the " 'thoroughness evident in its consideration, the validity of its reasoning, its consistency with earlier and later pronouncements, and all those factors which give it power to persuade.' " *United States v. Mead Corp.,* 533 U.S. 218, 228, 121 S.Ct. 2164, 150 L.Ed.2d 292 (2001) (quoting *Skidmore v. Swift & Co.,* 323 U.S. 134, 140, 65 S.Ct. 161, 89 L.Ed. 124 (1944)).

[handwritten margin note: Auer deference = "unwarranted" here]

NOTES

The Court in *Christopher* found the agency's interpretation of its regulations unpersuasive on the merits, and it further held that the employees were outside salesmen and therefore exempt from the statute. Four Justices (Justices Breyer, Ginsburg, Sotomayor, and Kagan) dissented from the majority's application of the statute, but they agreed that no deference should be given to the government's interpretation of the regulations, albeit for seemingly narrower reasons than the majority. *See* 132 S.Ct. at 2175 (Breyer, J., dissenting) ("[i]n light of important, near-contemporaneous differences in the Justice Department's views as to the meaning of relevant Labor Department regulations, I also agree that we should not give the Solicitor General's current interpretive view any especially favorable weight").

The looming battle over the continuing vitality of *Seminole Rock* or *Auer* deference heated up considerably in 2015 in *Perez v. Mortgage Bankers Ass'n,* 575 U.S. ___, 135 S.Ct. 1199 (2015), discussed on page 472, *supra*. In *Mortgage Bankers Ass'n,* the Court unanimously rejected the D.C. Circuit's *Paralyzed Veterans* doctrine that agencies must use notice and comment procedures when substantially changing their interpretations of their own regulations. That is clearly right if the agency's interpretation is an interpretative rule. But might an agency's especially creative "interpretation" or "reinterpretation" of a regulation be tantamount to the issuance of a new regulation, and thus tantamount to a legislative rule, if it fundamentally changes the operative meaning of the regulation? As long as the agency's interpretation has no real legal effect or binding quality, the answer is no; the agency will simply be offering its opinion as to the meaning of the regulation, and parties are free to challenge that opinion in court. The regulation has legal force; the agency's interpretation does not. If, however, the courts will defer to the agency's interpretation, that simple answer starts to dissolve, because the agency's interpretation now moves the legal needle to some degree. Mortgage Bankers Association, in defending the *Paralyzed Veterans* doctrine, made precisely that argument, to which the Court responded as follows:

> MBA alternatively suggests that interpretive rules have the force of law because an agency's interpretation of its own regulations may be entitled to deference under *Auer v. Robbins*. Even in cases where an agency's interpretation receives *Auer* deference, however, it is the court that ultimately decides whether a given regulation means what the agency says. Moreover, *Auer* deference is not an inexorable command in all cases. See *Christopher v. SmithKline Beecham Corp.*

135 S.Ct. at 1208 n.4.

Three Justices were not convinced that MBA's argument could be so easily dismissed. Justice Scalia extended and expanded his criticism of *Seminole Rock* and *Auer*, in comments that might have broader implications for *Chevron* as well:

I agree with the Court's decision, and all of its reasoning demonstrating the incompatibility of the D.C. Circuit's *Paralyzed Veterans* holding with the Administrative Procedure Act * * *. Considered alongside our law of deference to administrative determinations, however, today's decision produces a balance between power and procedure quite different from the one Congress chose when it enacted the APA.

* * * The Act guards against excesses in rulemaking by requiring notice and comment.

The APA exempts interpretive rules from these requirements. But this concession to agencies was meant to be more modest in its effects than it is today. For * * * the Act provides that "the *reviewing court* shall * * * interpret constitutional and statutory provisions, and determine the meaning or applicability of the terms of an agency action." § 706 (emphasis added). The Act thus contemplates that courts, not agencies, will authoritatively resolve ambiguities in statutes and regulations. In such a regime, the exemption for interpretive rules does not add much to agency power. An agency may use interpretive rules to *advise* the public by explaining its interpretation of the law. But an agency may not use interpretive rules to *bind* the public by making law, because it remains the responsibility of the court to decide whether the law means what the agency says it means.

Heedless of the original design of the APA, we have developed an elaborate law of deference to agencies' interpretations of statutes and regulations. Never mentioning § 706's directive that the "reviewing court * * * interpret * * * statutory provisions," we have held [in *Chevron*] that *agencies* may authoritatively resolve ambiguities in statutes * * * [and] we have—relying on a case decided before the APA, *Bowles v. Seminole Rock & Sand Co.*, 325 U.S. 410, 65 S.Ct. 1215, 89 L.Ed. 1700 (1945)—held [in *Auer*] that *agencies* may authoritatively resolve ambiguities in regulations.

By supplementing the APA with judge-made doctrines of deference, we have revolutionized the import of interpretive rules' exemption from notice-and-comment rulemaking. Agencies may now use these rules not just to advise the public, but also to bind them. After all, if an interpretive rule gets deference, the people are bound to obey it on pain of sanction, no less surely than they are bound to obey substantive rules, which are accorded similar deference. Interpretive rules that command deference *do* have the force of law.

The Court's reasons for resisting this obvious point would not withstand a gentle breeze * * *. Of course an interpretive rule must meet certain conditions before it gets deference—the interpretation must, for instance, be reasonable—but once it does so it is every bit as binding as a substantive rule. So the point stands: By deferring to interpretive rules, we have allowed agencies to make binding rules unhampered by notice-and-comment procedures.

The problem is bad enough, and perhaps insoluble if *Chevron* is not to be uprooted, with respect to interpretive rules setting forth agency interpretation of statutes. But an agency's interpretation of its own regulations is another matter. By giving that category of interpretive rules *Auer* deference, we do more than allow the agency to make binding regulations without notice and comment. Because the agency (not Congress) drafts the substantive rules that are the object of those interpretations, giving them deference allows the agency to control the extent of its notice-and-comment-free domain. To expand this domain, the agency need only write substantive rules more broadly and vaguely, leaving plenty of gaps to be filled in later, using interpretive rules unchecked by notice and comment. The APA does not remotely contemplate this regime.

Still and all, what are we to do about the problem? The *Paralyzed Veterans* doctrine is a courageous (indeed, brazen) attempt to limit the mischief by requiring an interpretive rule to go through notice and comment if it revises an earlier definitive interpretation of a regulation. That solution is unlawful for the reasons set forth in the Court's opinion: It contradicts the APA's unqualified exemption of interpretive rules from notice-and-comment rulemaking.

But I think there is another solution—one unavailable to the D.C. Circuit since it involves the overruling of one [of] this Court's decisions (that being even a greater fault than merely ignoring the APA). As I have described elsewhere, the rule of *Chevron,* if it did not comport with the APA, at least was in conformity with the long history of judicial review of executive action, where "[s]tatutory ambiguities * * * were left to reasonable resolution by the Executive." *United States v. Mead Corp.,* 533 U.S. 218, 243, 121 S.Ct. 2164, 150 L.Ed.2d 292 (2001) (SCALIA, J, dissenting). I am unaware of any such history justifying deference to agency interpretations of its own regulations * * *. I would therefore restore the balance originally struck by the APA with respect to an agency's interpretation of its own regulations, not by rewriting the Act in order to make up for *Auer,* but by abandoning *Auer* and applying the Act as written. The agency is free to interpret its own regulations with or without notice and comment; but courts will decide—with no deference to the agency—whether that interpretation is correct.

135 S.Ct. at 1211–13 (Scalia, J., concurring in the judgment). As we will shortly see, Justice Scalia's comments on *Chevron* reflected his own view of the scope of *Chevron* deference, which does not necessarily reflect the view of the Court. After 2001, interpretative rules do not receive *Chevron* deference, *see infra* page 646, though Justice Scalia bitterly dissented from the decision setting out the framework from which that doctrine sprang.

Justice Thomas, in a lengthy concurrence in *Mortgage Bankers*, suggested that *Seminole Rock/Auer* deference (and, by implication, *Chevron* deference, *see infra* pages 746–748) is actually unconstitutional because "[i]t represents a transfer of judicial power to the Executive Branch, and it amounts to an erosion of the judicial obligation to serve as a 'check' on the political branches." *Id.* at 1217 (Thomas, J., concurring in the judgment). And Justice Alito separately noted that he "await[s] a case in which the validity of *Seminole Rock* may be explored through full briefing and argument." *Id.* at 1210–11 (Alito, J., concurring in part and concurring in the judgment). Justices Thomas and Gorsuch have expressly called for reconsideration of *Seminole Rock/Auer* deference. *See Garco Construction, Inc. v. Speer*, 138 S.Ct. 1052, 1052–53 (2018) (Thomas, J., with whom Gorsuch, J. joins, dissenting from the denial of certiorari). Justice Thomas has said of *Seminole Rock/Auer* that "[a]ny reader of this Court's opinions should think that the doctrine is on its last gasp." That may represent the triumph of hope over experience. In any event, until there is formal reconsideration of the doctrine by the Supreme Court, deference to agency interpretation of regulations is likely to be the norm in the lower courts. *See, e.g., Via Christi Hospitals Wichita, Inc. v. Burwell*, 820 F.3d 451, 456–57 (D.C.Cir.2016).

If *Seminole Rock* and *Auer* are, for some reason, overruled in the future, would that discourage agencies from engaging in rulemaking? Would that be a good or bad thing on balance? *See* Aaron L. Nielson, *Beyond* Seminole Rock, 105 Geo. L. Rev. 943 (2017) (suggesting that if *Seminole Rock* and *Auer* are overruled, then agencies, utilizing the broad discretion conferred by the *Chenery II* doctrine, *see supra* pages 518–519, will choose to engage in adjudication, to the detriment of parties who would prefer the predictability of even vague rules). Is it relevant for administrative law doctrine whether it would be a good or bad thing on balance?

Agency legal interpretation arises in many other contexts where it is—or at least ought to be—clear that *Chevron* does not apply. Agencies must often interpret the Constitution to determine whether their actions violate substantive or procedural rights guaranteed by that document. Agencies receive no deference from courts on constitutional matters. *See Gulf Power Co. v. FCC*, 208 F.3d 1263, 1271 (11th Cir.2000). Similarly, agencies must often interpret and apply court decisions that construe statutes and regulations. *Chevron* deference does not extend to agency interpretations of court opinions, even when the agency is entitled to deference in the interpretation of the statutes or regulations that were the subject of the court opinions. *See Negusie v. Holder*, 555 U.S. 511, 129 S.Ct. 1159, 173 L.Ed.2d 20 (2009); *Reno v. Bossier Parish School Board*, 528 U.S. 320, 120 S.Ct. 866, 876 n.5, 145 L.Ed.2d 845 (2000). One court has even extended *Chevron* deference to a *state* agency's interpretations of *state* statutes and regulations, *see Smith v. Scott, supra*, which is clearly off the wall. State agencies do not receive *Chevron* deference even in the interpretation of federal law. *See GTE South, Inc. v. Morrison*, 199 F.3d 733, 745 (4th Cir.1999) (collecting cases). *But cf. AT & T Corp. v. Iowa Utilities Board*, 525 U.S. 366, 386 n.10, 119 S.Ct. 721, 142 L.Ed.2d 835 (1999) (describing as "novel" the question "whether federal courts must defer to state agency interpretations of federal law"). Furthermore, agencies must often interpret contracts, deeds, and other legal instruments. In principle, *Chevron* deference does not extend to these instruments; in practice, the results are mixed. *Compare National Fuel Gas Supply Corp. v. FERC*, 811 F.2d 1563 (D.C.Cir.1987) (holding that *Chevron* counsels in favor of deference to the Federal Energy Regulatory Commission's interpretation of gas supply contracts) *with Meadow Green-Wildcat Corp. v. Hathaway*, 936 F.2d 601 (1st Cir.1991) (holding that Forest Service permits should be treated like contracts, and that the Forest Service accordingly should get no deference in their interpretation). *See also Markwest Michigan Pipeline Co., LLC v. FERC*, 646 F.3d 30 (D.C.Cir.2011) (giving *Chevron* deference to an agency's interpretation of a settlement agreement approved by the agency); *Transitional Learning Community, supra*, 220 F.3d at 430–31 (reserving judgment on whether *Chevron* applies to contract interpretation). *Cf. Southeast Power Pool v. FERC*, 736 F.3d 995, 997 (D.C.Cir.2013) (describing deference to agency contract interpretation as " '*Chevron*-like' "). Three Justices have indicated that the application of *Chevron* to interpretation of at least some kinds of contracts is a question warranting Supreme Court review in an appropriate case. *See Scenic America, Inc. v. Dep't of Transportation*, 138 S.Ct. 2, 2–3 (2017) (Gorsuch, with whom the Chief Justice and Justice Alito join, respecting the denial of certiorari).

Nor does *Chevron* even apply to all federal agency interpretations of statutes. *Chevron* calls for deference to "an agency's construction of the statute which it *administers*" (emphasis added).[18] What does it mean to "administer" a statute? The term "administer" in this context is a term of art that has no explicit definition. In general, however, agencies are said to "administer" statutes for which they have some special responsibility. Agencies will often *interpret* and *apply* statutes that they do not *administer* in this limited, specialized sense. All agencies, for example, must apply and interpret general statutes such as the APA, the Federal Tort Claims Act, the Regulatory Flexibility Act, and the like, but no agency bears any *special* responsibility with respect to such statutes and thus no agency gets *Chevron* deference for its interpretations of these statutes. *See, e.g., Epic Systems Corp. v. Lewis,* 138 S.Ct. 1612 (2018) (NLRB does not administer the Federal Arbitration Act and thus gets no *Chevron* deference in its interpretation); *Aeronautical Repair Station Ass'n, Inc. v. FAA*, 494 F.3d 161, 176 (D.C.Cir.2007) (FAA does not administer the Regulatory Flexibility Act and thus gets no deference in its interpretation); *SSA, Baltimore, Maryland v. FLRA*, 201 F.3d 465, 471 (D.C.Cir.2000) ("We do not defer to the FLRA's interpretation of the Back Pay Act, a general statute not committed to the Authority's administration."). Rate-setting agencies may often have to interpret and apply the internal revenue code in order to assess the tax consequences of certain transactions, but these

---

[18] Similar language is found in pre-*Chevron* cases granting deference to agency legal judgments. *See, e.g.,* Hearst, 322 U.S. at 131 ("where the question is one of specific application of a broad statutory term in a proceeding in which the agency administering the statute must determine it initially, the reviewing court's function is limited").

agencies do not have a *special responsibility* with respect to the tax laws. The Internal Revenue Service has such a responsibility, and accordingly "administers" those statutes for *Chevron* purposes, *see Mayo Foundation for Medical Education and Research v. United States*, 562 U.S. 44, 131 S.Ct. 704, 178 L.Ed.2d 588 (2011), but other agencies do not, even if they must occasionally deal with and interpret the tax code.

Ordinarily, agencies "administer," and thus receive *Chevron* deference concerning, the substantive provisions of the organic statutes that they enforce. Most of the time, it is fairly obvious whether an agency "administers" a particular statute within the meaning of *Chevron*. But what happens when the statutory provision at issue does not directly implicate the agency's regulatory mission? Few cases present this question, and even fewer address it. *Wagner Seed Co., Inc. v. Bush,* 946 F.2d 918 (D.C.Cir.1991), involved a clean-up order issued by the Environmental Protection Agency pursuant to section 106(a) of the Comprehensive Environmental Response, Compensation, and Liability Act of 1980 (CERCLA), 42 U.S.C. § 9606(a) (2012), which authorizes the EPA to compel the removal of toxic wastes from various sites. Wagner Seed's warehouse had been hit by lightning, which resulted in the release of some toxic substances. The EPA ordered removal of those substances.

By October 17, 1986, Wagner had substantially completed the clean-up. (The Government asserts, and Wagner does not dispute, that it had by then expended 98% of its ultimate clean-up costs.) On that date, the Congress passed the Superfund Amendments and Reauthorization Act of 1986 (SARA), which amended CERCLA by adding, *inter alia*, the following provision:

> Any person who *receives and complies* with the terms of any order issued under subsection (a) of this section may, within 60 days after completion of the required action, petition the President for reimbursement from the [Superfund] for the reasonable costs of such action, plus interest.

§ 106(b)(2)(A), 42 U.S.C. § 9606(b)(2)(A) (emphasis added).

In January 1988, the EPA certified that Wagner had complied with the clean-up order, and within 60 days Wagner petitioned for reimbursement under § 106(b)(2)(A), on the ground that the release of hazardous materials was caused by an act of God. In June 1988, the agency rejected Wagner's claim in a letter holding that the reimbursement provision of SARA applies only to clean-up orders received after the Congress adopted that provision. Wagner then instituted this suit, as authorized by § 106(b)(2)(B).

Wagner asserts that the EPA erred in interpreting the phrase "receives and complies" in § 106(b)(2). As Wagner reads the statute, it requires only that an order have been received and complied with by the time reimbursement is sought. The crux of its dispute with the EPA, therefore, is whether the Congress intended the term "receives" to apply retrospectively or only prospectively from the date the statute was adopted.

946 F.2d at 919–20. The majority in the D.C. Circuit held that the agency was entitled to *Chevron* deference. On the merits, the court determined that the statute was ambiguous on whether reimbursement applied only to clean-up orders issued before the effective date of SARA and concluded that the agency's interpretation was reasonable. The court did not expressly discuss whether the EPA "administered" the reimbursement provisions of SARA. Judge (and former Administrative Law professor) Stephen Williams, however, addressed that issue in dissent:

> * * * If we owed the EPA deference on this interpretive issue, I would agree with the majority's decision to reject Wagner's suit; the statute does not clearly resolve the question and the EPA's reading is not unreasonable. But *Chevron* calls for deference only when a court reviews an agency's construction of a statute "which it administers." While Congress put the President in charge of many aspects of CERCLA, it gave the administration of § 106(b)(2) to the courts, *not* to him or his delegee. EPA has occasion to interpret the "receives and complies" language of § 106(b)(2) only because of its authority (as the President's delegee) to pay the petitioner off and thus avert a suit. This involvement seems to me too peripheral to make *Chevron* applicable.

> *Adams Fruit Co. v. Barrett*, 494 U.S. 638, 110 S.Ct. 1384, 108 L.Ed.2d 585 (1990), represents the opposite pole from *Chevron*. There the Court unanimously refused to defer to the Department of Labor on the question of whether exclusivity provisions in state workers' compensation law "reverse pre-empted" a federal private right of action created by § 1854 of the Migrant and Seasonal Agricultural Worker Protection Act, 29 U.S.C. §§ 1801–72. Despite the Secretary's power to administer the act generally, including her power to set safety standards (and the concomitant judicial deference to those judgments, *see* 494 U.S. at [650], 110 S.Ct. at 1391), and her general rulemaking authority * * *, the Court refused to defer to the Secretary's views on the scope of § 1854: "Congress has expressly established the Judiciary and not the Department of Labor as the adjudicator of private rights of action arising under the statute." *Adams Fruit*, 494 U.S. at [649], 110 S.Ct. at 1390. The agency could not "bootstrap" its § 1841 authority over standards into an area in which it had "no jurisdiction". *Id.* 494 U.S. at [650], 110 S.Ct. at 1391.

> This case is not quite so strongly against deference as *Adams Fruit*. There Congress had not charged the Secretary of Agriculture with any administrative task that called on her to interpret § 1854, so her construction was quite gratuitous. Here, as a result of the President's delegation, the EPA had to construe § 106(b)(2) as a predicate to its own action. But government agencies often construe

a statute as a prelude to litigation. Prosecutors must interpret criminal statutes in order to bring indictments and faithfully enforce the law, yet no court defers to their view of the statute. A more "specific responsibility for administering the law" is needed to trigger *Chevron. Crandon v. United States*, 494 U.S. 152, 110 S.Ct. 997, 1011, 108 L.Ed.2d 132 (1990) (Scalia, J., concurring in the judgment).

* * *

As EPA does not administer § 106(b), I would not apply *Chevron* deference to its view that § 106(b)(2)(A) contains a timing requirement in addition to the one that section adopts explicitly. Construing the provision independently, I would not adopt any such view myself. Accordingly I would reverse the judgment below.

946 F.2d at 925–26, 930 (Williams, J., dissenting).

Recall from the materials on formal adjudication that the D.C. Circuit and the First Circuit give *Chevron* deference to agencies' interpretations of procedural provisions providing for hearings in organic statutes. *See Chemical Waste Mgmt., Inc. v. United States EPA*, 873 F.2d 1477 (D.C.Cir.1989); *Dominion Energy Brayton Point, LLC v. Johnson*, 443 F.3d 12 (1st Cir. 2006). Does it really make sense to give deference to agencies' interpretations of the procedural provisions of their statutes? Does anyone think for a moment that the courts would give *Chevron* deference to agency interpretations of scope-of-review provisions in their organic statutes or to provisions providing for judicial review? *See Murphy Exploration & Production Co. v. United States Dep't of the Interior,* 252 F.3d 473, 478–80 (D.C.Cir.2001) (explaining at some length that *Chevron* does not apply to the provisions of a statute establishing rights of judicial review); *see also Shweika v. Department of Homeland Security,* 723 F.3d 710, 717–19 (6th Cir.2013) (holding that *Chevron* does not apply to statutes establishing federal court jurisdiction over agency action). Are procedural provisions materially different? For arguments against *Chevron* deference to procedural provisions (and hence against *Chemical Waste* and *Dominion Energy*), see Melissa M. Berry, *Beyond* Chevron's *Domain: Agency Interpretations of Statutory Procedural Provisions,* 30 Seattle U.L. Rev. 541 (2007); William S. Jordan, III, Chevron *and Hearing Rights: An Unintended Combination,* 61 Admin. L. Rev. 249 (2009); William Funk, *Slip Slidin' Away: The Erosion of APA Adjudication,* 122 Penn. St. L. Rev. 141 (2017).

It is also unclear whether agencies will receive *Chevron* deference for interpretations of statutes of limitations that are specific to that agency. (If a statute of limitations is broadly applicable, then it is like the APA or the Federal Tort Claims Act and clearly no deference is due. *See DLS Precision Fab, LLC. v. United States Immigration & Customs Enforcement,* 867 F.3d 1079, 1087 n.1 (9th Cir.2017).) In theory, the answer should be "no," for the same reason that agencies do not (and should not) get deference for interpretations of judicial review provisions. In practice, the answer is muddy. *See AKM LLC v. Secretary of Labor,* 675 F.3d 752, 754–55 (D.C.Cir.2012) (leaving the question open); *id.* at 764–69 (Brown, J., concurring) (forcefully arguing against such deference); *Romanyuk v. Lynch,* 151 F.Supp.3d 559, 563 (E.D.Pa.2015) ("A statute of limitations is not a matter requiring 'particular expertise' that only an implementing agency possesses. It follows that a statute of limitations challenge does not require any deference").

What about a statute that splits regulatory jurisdiction over the sale of electrical energy between federal and state regulatory agencies? Does the federal agency "administer" that statute for *Chevron* purposes? The Supreme Court avoided that question by finding the statute clear so that deference was unnecessary. *See FERC v. Electric Power Supply Ass'n*, 136 S.Ct. 760, 773 n.5 (2016).

As Judge Williams' dissent in *Wagner Seed* makes clear, courts do not give deference to the Justice Department's interpretation of federal criminal statutes, even though that agency clearly has a special responsibility for the enforcement of the criminal laws. Indeed, under the traditional rule of lenity, one might even say that courts give deference to the interpretations of criminal defendants rather than to the agency's interpretations. Apart from a very limited holding that the Sentencing Commission's commentary on its sentencing guidelines is entitled to a large measure of deference, *see Stinson v. United States*, 508 U.S. 36, 113 S.Ct. 1913, 123 L.Ed.2d 598 (1993), there is no evident movement in the courts to extend *Chevron* to the criminal context. *But see* Dan M. Kahan, *Is* Chevron *Relevant to Federal Criminal Law?*, 110 Harv. L. Rev. 469 (1996) (arguing for such deference). Matters get more complicated when, as is often the case, regulatory statutes have both civil and criminal application, so that *Chevron* and the rule of lenity, which urges courts to construe ambiguous criminal statutes against the government, directly collide. Does *Chevron* apply to the civil application but not to the criminal? To both? To neither? The D.C. Circuit applies *Chevron* at least to civil cases in these circumstances. *See Competitive Enterprise Inst. v. Dep't of Transportation,* 863 F.3d 911, 915 n.4 (D.C.Cir.2017). For thoughtful explorations of this enduring, important, and as-yet unresolved problem, see *Whitman v. United States,* 135 S.Ct. 352 (Statement of Justice Scalia, with whom Justice Thomas joins, respecting the denial of certiorari); *Carter v. Welles-Bowen Realty, Inc.,* 736 F.3d 722, 729 (6th Cir.2013) (Sutton, J., concurring); Sanford N. Greenberg, *Who Says It's a Crime?* Chevron *Deference to Agency Interpretations of Regulatory Statutes That Create Criminal Liability*, 58 U. Pitt. L. Rev. 1 (1996).

Normally, when we think of an agency "administering" a statute, we think of a statute that is the special responsibility of a particular agency, such as the National Labor Relations Board's responsibility for executing the substantive provisions of the National Labor Relations Act or the Environmental Protection Agency's authority with respect to the substantive provisions of the Clean Air Act. Everyone agrees that the relevant agencies "administer" such statutes for *Chevron* purposes. At the other pole are statutes, such as the APA, that are applied by all agencies but specially enforced by none; everyone agrees that *Chevron* does not apply in such cases. But what happens when, as is often the case, more than one agency, but fewer than all agencies, has enforcement responsibility with respect to a statute. Do they all get deference? Do none get deference?

RAPAPORT V. UNITED STATES DEP'T OF THE TREASURY, OFFICE OF THRIFT SUPERVISION

United States Court of Appeals, District of Columbia Circuit, 1995.
59 F.3d 212.

Before GINSBURG, RANDOLPH, and ROGERS, CIRCUIT JUDGES.

GINSBURG, CIRCUIT JUDGE:

Robert D. Rapaport was the majority shareholder of a savings and loan association that failed. Thereafter the Office of Thrift Supervision, as successor to the Federal Savings and Loan Insurance Corporation, ordered him to pay approximately $1.5 million pursuant to his agreement personally to maintain the capital in the institution at no less than the minimum required by regulation. We hold that because the OTS has not shown that Rapaport was "unjustly enriched," it may not enforce the agreement against him in an administrative (as opposed to judicial) proceeding. Accordingly, we grant Rapaport's petition for review and set aside the agency's order.

* * *

In order for the OTS to order a party to undertake any "affirmative action to correct conditions resulting from violations or practices," it must show either that the party has been "unjustly enriched" or that his conduct "involved a reckless disregard for the law or any applicable regulations or prior order of [a] Federal banking agency." 12 U.S.C. § 1818(b)(6)(A). The OTS's only theory throughout this case has been that Rapaport was "unjustly enriched," and therefore it must show as much before it can require him to pay a pro rata share of Great Life's capital deficiency.

The Acting Director's sole basis for concluding that Rapaport had, in fact, been unjustly enriched was simply that Rapaport "retain[ed] funds . . . belong [ing] to [Great Life]"—*i.e.*, the contested capital contribution— "while [Great Life] received the benefits of deposit insurance." Rapaport claims that this is insufficient to make out a case of unjust enrichment within the meaning of § 1818(b)(6)(A), and we agree.

As a preliminary matter, the OTS argues that we should defer to its construction of § 1818 under *Chevron, U.S.A., Inc. v. Natural Resources Defense Council*, 467 U.S. 837, 104 S.Ct. 2778, 81 L.Ed.2d 694 (1984). We have already held in *Wachtel* [*v. OTS*, 982 F.2d 581 (D.C.Cir.1993)] that we owe no such deference to the OTS's interpretation of § 1818 because that agency shares responsibility for the administration of the statute with at least three other agencies. 982 F.2d at 585. The alternative would lay the groundwork for a regulatory regime in which either the same statute is interpreted differently by the several agencies or the one agency that happens to reach the courthouse first is allowed to fix the meaning of the text for all. Neither outcome is unthinkable, of course, but neither has the OTS suggested any reason to believe that the congressional delegation of administrative authority contemplates such peculiar corollaries. Hence, we proceed de novo.

* * *

[On the merits, the court rejected the agency's interpretation of "unjust enrichment."]

ROGERS, CIRCUIT JUDGE, concurring in part and concurring in the judgment:

In rejecting OTS's contention that the court should defer to its construction of 12 U.S.C. § 1818(b)(6)(A)(i) under *Chevron U.S.A. Inc. v. Natural Resources Defense Council, Inc.*, 467 U.S. 837, 104 S.Ct. 2778, 81 L.Ed.2d 694 (1984), the majority concludes that "[w]e have already held in *Wachtel* [*v. OTS*, 982 F.2d 581, 585 (D.C.Cir.1993),] that we owe no such deference to the OTS's interpretation of § 1818 because that agency shares responsibility for administration of the statute with at least three other agencies." However, *Wachtel*'s suggestion that deference is inappropriate when more than one agency administers a statute was dictum that relied on distinguishable caselaw * * *.

In *Wachtel*, a bank holding company sought review of OTS's order, pursuant to § 1818(b)(1), to make payments based on an alleged agreement to maintain the bank's net worth. 982 F.2d at 582–83. Although finding neither unjust enrichment nor reckless disregard of banking laws, OTS maintained that it could order the holding company to make the payments under § 1818(b)(1) without making these findings. *Id.* at 585. The court rejected OTS's position as "almost frivolous," and proceeded to observe that even if *Chevron* deference were applicable, OTS's interpretation would fail because the statute was not ambiguous and OTS's interpretation was arbitrary. *Id.* While the court suggested that *Chevron* was inapplicable because OTS administered § 1818 jointly with other agencies, this was unnecessary to the court's holding that, under any standard of review, OTS's order was invalid. As dictum, the court's suggestion in *Wachtel* is not binding circuit law.

Although the court has stated that it does not defer to an agency's construction of a statute interpreted by more than one agency, *e.g.*, *Association of Am. Physicians & Surgeons, Inc. v. Clinton*, 997 F.2d 898, 913 (D.C.Cir.1993), the cases other than *Wachtel* itself appear readily distinguishable. For example, in *Clinton*, 997 F.2d at 913, which involved the Federal Advisory Committee Act, the court cited two cases involving statutes that apply to all agencies. *See FLRA v. United States Dep't of*

Treasury, 884 F.2d 1446, 1451 (D.C.Cir.1989) (no deference to FLRA's interpretation of the Freedom of Information Act ("FOIA") and the Privacy Act because "the FLRA is not charged with a special duty to interpret" these statutes); *Reporters Comm. for Freedom of the Press v. United States Dep't of Justice*, 816 F.2d 730, 734 (D.C.Cir.1987) (no deference to any agency interpretation of FOIA because "it applies to all government agencies, and thus no one executive branch entity is entrusted with its primary interpretation"), *rev'd on other grounds*, 489 U.S. 749, 109 S.Ct. 1468, 103 L.Ed.2d 774 (1989). Similarly, in *Wachtel*, the court relied on *Professional Reactor Operator Soc'y v. United States Nuclear Regulatory Comm'n*, 939 F.2d 1047, 1051 (D.C.Cir.1991), in which the court declined to defer to [the] Commission's interpretation of the Administrative Procedure Act because the statute applies to all agencies and is not within the Commission's area of expertise. Even more readily distinguished are cases in which the court has declined to defer to an agency's interpretation of a statute whose administration is entrusted to another agency. *E.g., Illinois Nat'l Guard v. FLRA*, 854 F.2d 1396, 1400 (D.C.Cir.1988); *Department of Treasury v. FLRA*, 837 F.2d 1163, 1167 (D.C.Cir.1988). At the same time, the court has acknowledged that where two agencies were charged with administering a statute, there "might well be a compelling case to afford deference if it were necessary for decision [where] both agencies agree as to which of them has exclusive jurisdiction." *CF Indus., Inc. v. FERC*, 925 F.2d 476, 478 n. 1 (D.C.Cir.1991) (dictum).

Consequently, it appears too facile to conclude that deference is inappropriate simply because more than one agency is involved in administering a statute. The question of whether deference is due more likely depends on the nature of the statute and how Congress has decided it shall be administered. Under FIRREA, Congress provided for joint decisions among the several administering banking agencies on the allocation of transferred functions. The statute instructs how to determine the "appropriate" entity for administering provisions of the statute. *See* 12 U.S.C. § 1813(q)(4) (the Director of OTS is the "appropriate Federal banking agency" "in the case of any savings association or any savings and loan holding company"). As is evident, Congress intended the several agencies that administer FIRREA to agree regarding their respective roles and exercise their expertise accordingly.

Thus, while *Wachtel* correctly reminds that consideration be given to the fact that more than one agency administers the statute, 982 F.2d at 585 n. 4, deference may nonetheless be appropriate where only expert banking agencies administer the statute and there is no disagreement among them about their respective responsibilities or the agency position under review. Two circuits considering OTS's administration of the provision at issue here appear, at least implicitly, to agree. *Simpson v. OTS*, 29 F.3d 1418, 1425 (9th Cir.1994) (applying *Chevron* deference to

OTS's definition of "reckless disregard for the law" under § 1818(b)(6)(A)(ii)); *Akin v. OTS*, 950 F.2d 1180, 1184 (5th Cir.1992) (same, for interpretation of cease and desist power under § 1818(b), and applying "arbitrary and capricious"/abuse of discretion standard to OTS's determination that an individual had been "unjustly enriched" under § 1818(b)(6)(A)(i)). Another circuit has staked out a middle ground. *1185 Ave. of Ams. Assocs. v. RTC*, 22 F.3d 494, 497 (2d Cir.1994) (declining to give "full *Chevron* deference to the RTC's interpretation" of 12 U.S.C. § 1821(e) because several other agencies administer FIRREA).

The instant case does not require the court to decide whether *Chevron* deference should apply to OTS's interpretation of § 1818(b)(6)(A) because, as in *Wachtel*, the same result follows whether the court applies *de novo* review or *Chevron* deference. Even without reference to the common law definition of unjust enrichment, the legislative history indicates that Congress did not intend the phrase used in § 1818(b)(6)(A)(i) to encompass the retention of funds owed under a net worth maintenance agreement. Hence, OTS failed to prove that Rapaport was unjustly enriched.

Accordingly, notwithstanding the majority's interpretation of *Wachtel* and its observations regarding conditions for deference, I concur in granting the petition for review.

NOTES

Do either Judge Ginsburg or Judge Rogers respond at all to the other's concerns? The Seventh Circuit has suggested that it does not agree with *Rapaport*, at least in cases involving only two agencies. *See Board of Trade of the City of Chicago v. SEC*, 187 F.3d 713, 718–19 (7th Cir.1999). And the D.C. Circuit has (sensibly) said that *Chevron* applies when multiple agencies administer a statute but the agencies can only act jointly and thus must speak with a single voice. *See Loan Syndication and Trading Ass'n v. SEC*, 882 F.3d 220, 222 (D.C.Cir.2018). For an enlightening analysis of the doctrinal, practical, and normative problems raised by interpretative authority spread across multiple agencies, see Daniel A. Farber & Anne Joseph O'Connell, *Agencies as Adversaries*, 105 Cal. L. Rev. 1375, 1450–56 (2017).

One point may seem obvious but occasionally causes some problems: <u>For *Chevron* to apply, there must actually be an agency interpretation of a statute for a court to consider</u>. If the agency could have interpreted the statute but <u>did not</u>, there is nothing to which a court can defer, and *Chevron* drops out of the picture. A subtler problem arises when the agency offers an interpretation of a statute but there is no indication of how that interpretation was reached. (Is an interpretation that does not reflect a genuine effort to uncover the meaning of a statute really an "interpretation"?) We will later explore in some detail the extent to which courts will scrutinize the process by which agencies reach decisions. *See infra* pages 748–851. For now, it is enough to observe there is some authority for the proposition that agencies <u>cannot get *Chevron*</u> deference for interpretations that do not actually exhibit the process of interpretation that yielded them. *See Montgomery County, Maryland v. FCC*, 863 F.3d 485 (6th Cir.2017) ("if an agency wants the federal courts to adopt (much less defer to) its interpretation of a statute, the agency must do the work of actually interpreting it. The FCC's orders reflect none of that work as to the question whether 'in-kind' cable-related exactions are 'franchise fees' "). In other words, agencies, like students writing exams, may need to "show their work" in order to get *Chevron* credit for their interpretations.

What if the agency initially interpreted the statute, but by the time the case reaches court, the agency's composition has changed and the agency no longer defends its prior interpretation (but has not yet formally revoked the rule or order on review)? The D.C. Circuit at one point said that *Chevron*, and even *Skidmore,* does not apply in that circumstance, *see Global Tel*Link v. FCC*, 866 F.3d 397, 407–08 (D.C.Cir.2017); *id.* at 418 (Silberman, J., concurring), *but see id.* at 425 (Pillard, J., concurring in part and dissenting in part), but then oddly seemed to back off from that position in a clarification issued in response to a rehearing petition. *See id.* at 417 ("We need not and do not decide whether we were required to follow *Chevron* Step Two even though the agency declined to defend its position before the court.").

Perhaps the most perplexing problem concerning the scope of *Chevron* in the decade and a half following the decision was whether agency legal decisions have to take a certain *form* in order to receive *Chevron* deference. Agency legal interpretations can emerge from formal or informal proceedings and from rulemakings or adjudications. Rules that embody legal interpretations can be legislative or interpretative. And legal interpretations can result from opinion letters, staff manuals, amicus brief, or countless other documents. Does the existence or extent of *Chevron* deference vary with the form in which the agency's legal interpretation is expressed?

For *Chevron's* first fifteen years, the Supreme Court had little to say on such questions. The lower courts, left to their own devices, splintered along several lines. For instance, the D.C. Circuit consistently gave *Chevron* deference to interpretations embodied in interpretative rules. *See Health Ins. Ass'n of Am. v. Shalala*, 23 F.3d 412, 424 n.8 (D.C.Cir.1994) (collecting cases in which the D.C. Circuit gave *Chevron* deference to interpretative rules). The Third Circuit agreed, *see Elizabeth Blackwell Health Center for Women v. Knoll*, 61 F.3d 170, 182 (3d Cir.1995), but most other circuits did not. *See Southern Ute Indian Tribe v. Amoco Production Co.*, 119 F.3d 816 (10th Cir.1997) (collecting cases). In addition, several courts suggested that *Chevron* deference should only apply to agencies that have been granted legislative rulemaking authority, *see Atchison, Topeka & Santa Fe Ry. Co. v. Pena*, 44 F.3d 437 (7th Cir.1994) (en banc), *aff'd on other grounds*, 516 U.S. 152, 116 S.Ct. 595, 133 L.Ed.2d 535 (1996); *Merck & Co., Inc. v. Kessler*, 80 F.3d 1543 (Fed.Cir.1996), though the basis for that doctrine was difficult to discern: It has long been clear that agencies can receive *Chevron* deference for interpretations issued during legally binding adjudications, *see National R.R. Passenger Corp. v. Boston & Maine Corp.*, 503 U.S. 407, 112 S.Ct. 1394, 118

L.Ed.2d 52 (1992), and it is hard to fathom why deference to adjudicating agencies should turn on whether such agencies also have rulemaking power that they chose not to employ.

In 2000 and 2001, the Supreme Court issued two important decisions that address (but do not necessarily fully answer) some of these questions.

CHRISTENSEN V. HARRIS COUNTY

Supreme Court of the United States, 2000.
529 U.S. 576, 120 S.Ct. 1655, 146 L.Ed.2d 621.

JUSTICE THOMAS delivered the opinion of the Court.

Under the Fair Labor Standards Act of 1938 (FLSA), 29 U.S.C. § 201 *et seq.*, States and their political subdivisions may compensate their employees for overtime by granting them compensatory time or "comp time," which entitles them to take time off work with full pay. If the employees do not use their accumulated compensatory time, the employer is obligated to pay cash compensation under certain circumstances. Fearing the fiscal consequences of having to pay for accrued compensatory time, Harris County adopted a policy requiring its employees to schedule time off in order to reduce the amount of accrued compensatory time. Employees of the Harris County Sheriff's Department sued, claiming that the FLSA prohibits such a policy. The Court of Appeals rejected their claim. Finding that nothing in the FLSA or its implementing regulations prohibits an employer from compelling the use of compensatory time, we affirm.

I

A

The FLSA generally provides that hourly employees who work in excess of 40 hours per week must be compensated for the excess hours at a rate not less than 1 1/2 times their regular hourly wage * * *.

* * * States and their political subdivisions * * * [may] compensate employees for overtime by granting them compensatory time at a rate of 1 1/2 hours for every hour worked. To provide this form of compensation, the employer must arrive at an agreement or understanding with employees that compensatory time will be granted instead of cash compensation.

The FLSA expressly regulates some aspects of accrual and preservation of compensatory time. For example, the FLSA provides that an employer must honor an employee's request to use compensatory time within a "reasonable period" of time following the request, so long as the use of the compensatory time would not "unduly disrupt" the employer's operations. § 207(*o*)(5); 29 CFR § 553.25 (1999). The FLSA also caps the number of compensatory time hours that an employee may accrue. After an employee reaches that maximum, the employer must pay cash compensation for additional overtime hours worked. § 207(*o*)(3)(A). In addition, the FLSA permits the employer at any time to cancel or "cash out" accrued compensatory time hours by paying the employee cash compensation for unused compensatory time. § 207(*o*)(3)(B); 29 CFR § 553.26(a) (1999). And the FLSA entitles the employee to cash payment for any accrued compensatory time remaining upon the termination of employment. § 207(*o*)(4).

B

Petitioners are 127 deputy sheriffs employed by respondents Harris County, Texas, and its sheriff, Tommy B. Thomas (collectively, Harris County). It is undisputed that each of the petitioners individually agreed to accept compensatory time, in lieu of cash, as compensation for overtime. As petitioners accumulated compensatory time, Harris County became concerned that it lacked the resources to pay monetary compensation to employees who worked overtime after reaching the statutory cap on compensatory time accrual and to employees who left their jobs with sizable reserves of accrued time. As a result, the county began looking for a way to reduce accumulated compensatory time. It wrote to the United States Department of Labor's Wage and Hour Division, asking "whether the Sheriff may schedule non-exempt employees to use or take compensatory time." Brief for Petitioners 18–19. The Acting Administrator of the Division replied:

DOL

> "[I]t is our position that a public employer may schedule its nonexempt employees to use their accrued FLSA compensatory time as directed if the prior agreement specifically provides such a provision * * *.

> "Absent such an agreement, it is our position that neither the statute nor the regulations permit an employer to require an employee to use accrued compensatory time." Opinion Letter from Dept. of Labor, Wage and Hour Div. (Sept. 14, 1992), 1992 WL 845100 (Opinion Letter).

After receiving the letter, Harris County implemented a policy under which the employees' supervisor sets a maximum number of compensatory hours that may be accumulated. When an employee's stock of hours approaches that maximum, the employee is advised of the maximum and is asked to take steps to reduce accumulated compensatory time. If the employee does not do so voluntarily, a supervisor may order the employee to use his compensatory time at specified times.

Petitioners sued, claiming that the county's policy violates the FLSA because § 207(*o*)(5)—which requires that an employer reasonably accommodate employee requests to use compensatory time—provides the exclusive means of utilizing accrued time in the absence of an agreement or understanding permitting some other method. The District Court

Petitioners' legal claim

agreed, granting summary judgment for petitioners and entering a declaratory judgment that the county's policy violated the FLSA. The Court of Appeals for the Fifth Circuit reversed, holding that the FLSA did not speak to the issue and thus did not prohibit the county from implementing its compensatory time policy * * *. We granted certiorari * * *.

II

* * *

[The Court held that the statute permitted Harris County to compel the employees to use their excess compensatory time.]

III

In an attempt to avoid the conclusion that the FLSA does not prohibit compelled use of compensatory time, petitioners and the United States contend that we should defer to the Department of Labor's opinion letter, which takes the position that an employer may compel the use of compensatory time only if the employee has agreed in advance to such a practice. Specifically, they argue that the agency opinion letter is entitled to deference under our decision in *Chevron U.S.A., Inc. v. Natural Resources Defense Council, Inc.*, 467 U.S. 837, 104 S.Ct. 2778, 81 L.Ed.2d 694 (1984). In *Chevron*, we held that a court must give effect to an agency's regulation containing a reasonable interpretation of an ambiguous statute. *Id.*, at 842–844, 104 S.Ct. 2778.

Here, however, we confront an interpretation contained in an opinion letter, not one arrived at after, for example, a formal adjudication or notice-and-comment rulemaking. Interpretations such as those in opinion letters—like interpretations contained in policy statements, agency manuals, and enforcement guidelines, all of which lack the force of law—do not warrant *Chevron*-style deference. Instead, interpretations contained in formats such as opinion letters are "entitled to respect" under our decision in *Skidmore v. Swift & Co.*, 323 U.S. 134, 140, 65 S.Ct. 161, 89 L.Ed. 124 (1944), but only to the extent that those interpretations have the "power to persuade," *ibid.* As explained above, we find unpersuasive the agency's interpretation of the statute at issue in this case.

Of course, the framework of deference set forth in *Chevron* does apply to an agency interpretation contained in a regulation. But in this case the Department of Labor's regulation does not address the issue of compelled compensatory time. The regulation provides only that "[t]he agreement or understanding [between the employer and employee] *may* include other provisions governing the preservation, use, or cashing out of compensatory time so long as these provisions are consistent with [§ 207(*o*)]." 29 CFR § 553.23(a)(2) (1999) (emphasis added). Nothing in the regulation even arguably requires that an employer's compelled use policy must be included in an agreement. The text of the regulation itself indicates that its command is permissive, not mandatory.

Seeking to overcome the regulation's obvious meaning, the United States asserts that the agency's opinion letter interpreting the regulation should be given deference under our decision in *Auer v. Robbins*, 519 U.S. 452, 117 S.Ct. 905, 137 L.Ed.2d 79 (1997). In *Auer*, we held that an agency's interpretation of its own regulation is entitled to deference. *Id.*, at 461, 117 S.Ct. 905. See also *Bowles v. Seminole Rock & Sand Co.*, 325 U.S. 410, 65 S.Ct. 1215, 89 L.Ed. 1700 (1945). But *Auer* deference is warranted only when the language of the regulation is ambiguous * * *. Because the regulation is not ambiguous on the issue of compelled compensatory time, *Auer* deference is unwarranted.

US argues for Auer deference

reg ≠ ambiguous, so no Auer def.

* * *

* * * The judgment of the Court of Appeals is affirmed.

JUSTICE SOUTER, concurring.

Concurrence

I join the opinion of the Court on the assumption that it does not foreclose a reading of the Fair Labor Standards Act of 1938 that allows the Secretary of Labor to issue regulations limiting forced use.

JUSTICE SCALIA, concurring in part and concurring in the judgment.

Concurrence

I join the judgment of the Court and all of its opinion except Part III, which declines to give effect to the position of the Department of Labor in this case because its opinion letter is entitled only to so-called "*Skidmore* deference." *Skidmore* deference to authoritative agency views is an anachronism, dating from an era in which we declined to give agency interpretations (including interpretive regulations, as opposed to "legislative rules") authoritative effect. This former judicial attitude accounts for that provision of the 1946 Administrative Procedure Act which exempted "interpretative rules" (since they would not be authoritative) from the notice-and-comment requirements applicable to rulemaking.

That era came to an end with our watershed decision in *Chevron U.S.A., Inc. v. Natural Resources Defense Council, Inc.*, 467 U.S. 837, 844, 104 S.Ct. 2778, 81 L.Ed.2d 694 (1984), which established the principle that "a court may not substitute its own construction of a statutory provision for a reasonable interpretation made by the administrator of an agency." While *Chevron* in fact involved an interpretive regulation, the rationale of the case was not limited to that context * * *. Quite appropriately, therefore, we have accorded *Chevron* deference not only to agency regulations, but to authoritative agency positions set forth in a variety of other formats. See, *e.g., INS v. Aguirre-Aguirre*, 526 U.S. 415, 425, 119 S.Ct. 1439, 143 L.Ed.2d 590 (1999) (adjudication); *NationsBank of N.C., N.A. v. Variable Annuity Life Ins. Co.*, 513 U.S. 251, 256–257, 115 S.Ct. 810, 130 L.Ed.2d 740 (1995) (letter of Comptroller of the Currency); *Pension*

Benefit Guaranty Corporation v. LTV Corp., 496 U.S. 633, 647–648, 110 S.Ct. 2668, 110 L.Ed.2d 579 (1990) (decision by Pension Benefit Guaranty Corp. to restore pension benefit plan); *Young v. Community Nutrition Institute*, 476 U.S. 974, 978–979, 106 S.Ct. 2360, 90 L.Ed.2d 959 (1986) (Food and Drug Administration's "longstanding interpretation of the statute," reflected in no-action notice published in the Federal Register).

In my view, therefore, the position that the county's action in this case was unlawful unless permitted by the terms of an agreement with the sheriff's department employees warrants *Chevron* deference if it represents the authoritative view of the Department of Labor. The fact that it appears in a single opinion letter signed by the Acting Administrator of the Wage and Hour Division might not alone persuade me that it occupies that status. But the Solicitor General of the United States, appearing as an *amicus* in this action, has filed a brief, cosigned by the Solicitor of Labor, which represents the position set forth in the opinion letter to be the position of the Secretary of Labor. That alone, even without existence of the opinion letter, would in my view entitle the position to *Chevron* deference. What we said in a case involving an agency's interpretation of its own regulations applies equally, in my view, to an agency's interpretation of its governing statute:

> "Petitioners complain that the Secretary's interpretation comes to us in the form of a legal brief; but that does not, in the circumstances of this case, make it unworthy of deference. The Secretary's position is in no sense a 'post hoc rationalizatio[n]' advanced by an agency seeking to defend past agency action against attack. There is simply no reason to suspect that the interpretation does not reflect the agency's fair and considered judgment on the matter in question." *Auer v. Robbins*, 519 U.S. 452, 462, 117 S.Ct. 905, 137 L.Ed.2d 79 (1997).

I nonetheless join the judgment of the Court because, for the reasons set forth in Part II of its opinion, the Secretary's position does not seem to me a reasonable interpretation of the statute.

JUSTICE STEVENS, with whom JUSTICE GINSBURG and JUSTICE BREYER join, dissenting.

* * *

DISSENT

[The dissenters disagreed with the majority's construction of the statute.]

JUSTICE BREYER, with whom JUSTICE GINSBURG joins, dissenting.

JUSTICE SCALIA may well be right that the position of the Department of Labor, set forth in both brief and letter, is an "authoritative" agency view that warrants deference under *Chevron*. But I do not object to the majority's citing *Skidmore v. Swift & Co.*, 323 U.S. 134, 65 S.Ct. 161, 89

L.Ed. 124 (1944), instead. And I do disagree with JUSTICE SCALIA'S statement that what he calls "*Skidmore* deference" is "an anachronism."

Skidmore made clear that courts may pay particular attention to the views of an expert agency where they represent "specialized experience," 323 U.S., at 139, 65 S.Ct. 161, even if they do not constitute an exercise of delegated lawmaking authority. The Court held that the "rulings, interpretations and opinions of" an agency, "while not controlling upon the courts by reason of their authority, do constitute a body of experience and informed judgment to which courts and litigants may properly resort for guidance." *Id.*, at 140, 65 S.Ct. 161. As Justice Jackson wrote for the Court, those views may possess the "power to persuade," even where they lack the "power to control." *Skidmore*, *supra*, at 140, 65 S.Ct. 161.

Chevron made no relevant change. It simply focused upon an additional, separate legal reason for deferring to certain agency determinations, namely, that Congress had delegated to the agency the legal authority to make those determinations. And, to the extent there may be circumstances in which *Chevron*-type deference is inapplicable—*e.g.*, where one has doubt that Congress actually intended to delegate interpretive authority to the agency (an "ambiguity" that *Chevron* does not presumptively leave to agency resolution)—I believe that *Skidmore* nonetheless retains legal vitality. If statutes are to serve the human purposes that called them into being, courts will have to continue to pay particular attention in appropriate cases to the experienced-based views of expert agencies.

I agree with JUSTICE STEVENS that * * *, for the reasons he sets forth, the Labor Department's position in this matter is eminently reasonable, hence persuasive, whether one views that decision through *Chevron's* lens, through *Skidmore's*, or through both.

[margin note: DOL's position is reasonable]

UNITED STATES v. MEAD

Supreme Court of the United States, 2001.
533 U.S. 218, 121 S.Ct. 2164, 150 L.Ed.2d 292.

[margin note: tariff classification]

JUSTICE SOUTER delivered the opinion of the Court.

The question is whether a tariff classification ruling by the United States Customs Service deserves judicial deference. The Federal Circuit rejected Customs's invocation of *Chevron, U.S.A., Inc. v. Natural Resources Defense Council, Inc.*, 467 U.S. 837, 104 S.Ct. 2778, 81 L.Ed.2d 694 (1984), in support of such a ruling, to which it gave no deference. We agree that a tariff classification has no claim to judicial deference under *Chevron*, there being no indication that Congress intended such a ruling to carry the force of law, but we hold that under *Skidmore v. Swift & Co.*, 323 U.S. 134, 65 S.Ct. 161, 89 L.Ed. 124 (1944), the ruling is eligible to claim respect according to its persuasiveness.

[margin note: no Chevron deference, but possible Skidmore def.]

I

Imports are taxed under the Harmonized Tariff Schedule of the United States (HTSUS). Title 19 U.S.C. § 1500(b) provides that Customs "shall, under rules and regulations prescribed by the Secretary [of the Treasury] . . . fix the final classification and rate of duty applicable to . . . merchandise" under the HTSUS. Section 1502(a) provides that

> "[t]he Secretary of the Treasury shall establish and promulgate such rules and regulations not inconsistent with the law (including regulations establishing procedures for the issuance of binding rulings prior to the entry of the merchandise concerned), and may disseminate such information as may be necessary to secure a just, impartial, and uniform appraisement of imported merchandise and the classification and assessment of duties thereon at the various ports of entry."

* * *

The Secretary provides for tariff rulings before the entry of goods by regulations authorizing "ruling letters" setting tariff classifications for particular imports. 19 C.F.R. § 177.8 (2000). A ruling letter

> "represents the official position of the Customs Service with respect to the particular transaction or issue described therein and is binding on all Customs Service personnel in accordance with the provisions of this section until modified or revoked. In the absence of a change of practice or other modification or revocation which affects the principle of the ruling set forth in the ruling letter, that principle may be cited as authority in the disposition of transactions involving the same circumstances." § 177.9(a).

After the transaction that gives it birth, a ruling letter is to "be applied only with respect to transactions involving articles identical to the sample submitted with the ruling request or to articles whose description is identical to the description set forth in the ruling letter." § 177.9(b)(2). As a general matter, such a letter is "subject to modification or revocation without notice to any person, except the person to whom the letter was addressed," § 177.9(c), and the regulations consequently provide that "no other person should rely on the ruling letter or assume that the principles of that ruling will be applied in connection with any transaction other than the one described in the letter," *ibid.* Since ruling letters respond to transactions of the moment, they are not subject to notice and comment before being issued, may be published but need only be made "available for public inspection," 19 U.S.C. § 1625(a), and, at the time this action arose, could be modified without notice and comment under most circumstances, 19 C.F.R. § 177.10(c) (2000). A broader notice-and-comment requirement for modification of prior rulings was added by statute in 1993 and took effect after this case arose.

Any of the 46 port-of-entry Customs offices may issue ruling letters, and so may the Customs Headquarters Office * * *. Most ruling letters contain little or no reasoning, but simply describe goods and state the appropriate category and tariff. A few letters, like the Headquarters ruling at issue here, set out a rationale in some detail.

Respondent, the Mead Corporation, imports "day planners," three-ring binders with pages having room for notes of daily schedules and phone numbers and addresses, together with a calendar and suchlike. The tariff schedule on point falls under the HTSUS heading for "[r]egisters, account books, notebooks, order books, receipt books, letter pads, memorandum pads, diaries and similar articles," HTSUS subheading 4820.10, which comprises two subcategories. Items in the first, "[d]iaries, notebooks and address books, bound; memorandum pads, letter pads and similar articles," were subject to a tariff of 4.0% at the time in controversy. Objects in the second, covering "[o]ther" items, were free of duty.

Between 1989 and 1993, Customs repeatedly treated day planners under the "other" HTSUS subheading. In January 1993, however, Customs changed position, and issued a Headquarters ruling letter classifying Mead's day planners as "Diaries . . . , bound" subject to tariff under subheading 4820.10.20. That letter was short on explanation, but after Mead's protest, Customs Headquarters issued a new letter, carefully reasoned but never published, reaching the same conclusion. This letter considered two definitions of "diary" from the Oxford English Dictionary, the first covering a daily journal of the past day's events, the second a book including " 'printed dates for daily memoranda and jottings; also . . . calendars . . .' " Customs concluded that "diary" was not confined to the first, in part because the broader definition reflects commercial usage and hence the "commercial identity of these items in the marketplace." As for the definition of "bound," Customs concluded that HTSUS was not referring to "bookbinding," but to a less exact sort of fastening described in the Harmonized Commodity Description and Coding System Explanatory Notes to Heading 4820, which spoke of binding by " 'reinforcements or fittings of metal, plastics, etc.' "

Customs rejected Mead's further protest of the second Headquarters ruling letter, and Mead filed suit in the Court of International Trade (CIT). The CIT granted the Government's motion for summary judgment, adopting Customs's reasoning without saying anything about deference.

Mead then went to the United States Court of Appeals for the Federal Circuit. While the case was pending there this Court decided *United States v. Haggar Apparel Co.*, 526 U.S. 380, 119 S.Ct. 1392, 143 L.Ed.2d 480 (1999), holding that Customs regulations receive the deference described in *Chevron*. The appeals court requested briefing on the impact of *Haggar*, and the Government argued that classification rulings, like Customs regulations, deserve *Chevron* deference.

The Federal Circuit, however, reversed the CIT and held that Customs classification rulings should not get *Chevron* deference, owing to differences from the regulations at issue in *Haggar*. Rulings are not preceded by notice and comment as under the Administrative Procedure Act (APA), they "do not carry the force of law and are not, like regulations, intended to clarify the rights and obligations of importers beyond the specific case under review." 185 F.3d, at 1307. The appeals court thought classification rulings had a weaker *Chevron* claim even than Internal Revenue Service interpretive rulings, to which that court gives no deference; unlike rulings by the IRS, Customs rulings issue from many locations and need not be published.

The Court of Appeals accordingly gave no deference at all to the ruling classifying the Mead day planners and rejected the agency's reasoning as to both "diary" and "bound" * * *.

We granted certiorari in order to consider the limits of *Chevron* deference owed to administrative practice in applying a statute. We hold that administrative implementation of a particular statutory provision qualifies for *Chevron* deference when it appears that Congress delegated authority to the agency generally to make rules carrying the force of law, and that the agency interpretation claiming deference was promulgated in the exercise of that authority. Delegation of such authority may be shown in a variety of ways, as by an agency's power to engage in adjudication or notice-and-comment rulemaking, or by some other indication of a comparable congressional intent. The Customs ruling at issue here fails to qualify, although the possibility that it deserves some deference under *Skidmore* leads us to vacate and remand.

II

When Congress has "explicitly left a gap for an agency to fill, there is an express delegation of authority to the agency to elucidate a specific provision of the statute by regulation," *Chevron*, 467 U.S., at 843–44, 104 S.Ct. 2778, and any ensuing regulation is binding in the courts unless procedurally defective, arbitrary or capricious in substance, or manifestly contrary to the statute. But whether or not they enjoy any express delegation of authority on a particular question, agencies charged with applying a statute necessarily make all sorts of interpretive choices, and while not all of those choices bind judges to follow them, they certainly may influence courts facing questions the agencies have already answered. "[T]he well-reasoned views of the agencies implementing a statute 'constitute a body of experience and informed judgment to which courts and litigants may properly resort for guidance,' " *Bragdon v. Abbott,* 524 U.S.

624, 642, 118 S.Ct. 2196, 141 L.Ed.2d 540 (1998) (quoting *Skidmore*, 323 U.S. at 139–40, 65 S.Ct. 161), and "[w]e have long recognized that considerable weight should be accorded to an executive department's construction of a statutory scheme it is entrusted to administer. . ." *Chevron, supra*, at 844, 104 S.Ct. 2778 (footnote omitted). The fair measure of deference to an agency administering its own statute has been understood to vary with circumstances, and courts have looked to the degree of the agency's care, its consistency, formality, and relative expertness, and to the persuasiveness of the agency's position. The approach has produced a spectrum of judicial responses, from great respect at one end, see, *e.g., Aluminum Co. of America v. Central Lincoln Peoples' Util. Dist.*, 467 U.S. 380, 389–90, 104 S.Ct. 2472, 81 L.Ed.2d 301 (1984) ("'substantial deference'" to administrative construction), to near indifference at the other, see, *e.g., Bowen v. Georgetown Univ. Hospital,* 488 U.S. 204, 212–13, 109 S.Ct. 468, 102 L.Ed.2d 493 (1988) (interpretation advanced for the first time in a litigation brief). Justice Jackson summed things up in *Skidmore v. Swift & Co.*:

> "The weight [accorded to an administrative] judgment in a particular case will depend upon the thoroughness evident in its consideration, the validity of its reasoning, its consistency with earlier and later pronouncements, and all those factors which give it power to persuade, if lacking power to control." 323 U.S., at 140, 65 S.Ct. 161.

Since 1984, we have identified a category of interpretive choices distinguished by an additional reason for judicial deference. This Court in *Chevron* recognized that Congress not only engages in express delegation of specific interpretive authority, but that "[s]ometimes the legislative delegation to an agency on a particular question is implicit." 467 U.S., at 844, 104 S.Ct. 2778. Congress, that is, may not have expressly delegated authority or responsibility to implement a particular provision or fill a particular gap. Yet it can still be apparent from the agency's generally conferred authority and other statutory circumstances that Congress would expect the agency to be able to speak with the force of law when it addresses ambiguity in the statute or fills a space in the enacted law, even one about which "Congress did not actually have an intent" as to a particular result. *Id.,* at 845, 104 S.Ct. 2778. When circumstances implying such an expectation exist, a reviewing court has no business rejecting an agency's exercise of its generally conferred authority to resolve a particular statutory ambiguity simply because the agency's chosen resolution seems unwise, but is obliged to accept the agency's position if Congress has not previously spoken to the point at issue and the agency's interpretation is reasonable.

We have recognized a very good indicator of delegation meriting *Chevron* treatment in express congressional authorizations to engage in the process of rulemaking or adjudication that produces regulations or rulings for which deference is claimed. It is fair to assume generally that Congress contemplates administrative action with the effect of law when it provides for a relatively formal administrative procedure tending to foster the fairness and deliberation that should underlie a pronouncement of such force [citing Merrill & Hickman, *Chevron's Domain*, 89 Geo. L.J. 833, 872 (2001)]. Thus, the overwhelming number of our cases applying *Chevron* deference have reviewed the fruits of notice-and-comment rulemaking or formal adjudication. That said, and as significant as notice-and-comment is in pointing to *Chevron* authority, the want of that procedure here does not decide the case, for we have sometimes found reasons for *Chevron* deference even when no such administrative formality was required and none was afforded, see, *e.g., NationsBank of N.C., N.A. v. Variable Annuity Life Ins. Co.*, 513 U.S. 251, 256–57, 115 S.Ct. 810, 130 L.Ed.2d 740 (1995). The fact that the tariff classification here was not a product of such formal process does not alone, therefore, bar the application of *Chevron*.

[margin handwritten note: lack of rulemaking/adjud. does not necessarily preclude chevron]

There are, nonetheless, ample reasons to deny *Chevron* deference here. The authorization for classification rulings, and Customs's practice in making them, present a case far removed not only from notice-and-comment process, but from any other circumstances reasonably suggesting that Congress ever thought of classification rulings as deserving the deference claimed for them here.

No matter which angle we choose for viewing the Customs ruling letter in this case, it fails to qualify under *Chevron*. On the face of the statute, to begin with, the terms of the congressional delegation give no indication that Congress meant to delegate authority to Customs to issue classification rulings with the force of law. We are not, of course, here making any global statement about Customs's authority, for it is true that the general rulemaking power conferred on Customs, see 19 U.S.C. § 1624, authorizes some regulation with the force of law, or "legal norms," as we put it in *Haggar*, 526 U.S., at 391, 119 S.Ct. 1392. It is true as well that Congress had classification rulings in mind when it explicitly authorized, in a parenthetical, the issuance of "regulations establishing procedures for the issuance of binding rulings prior to the entry of the merchandise concerned," 19 U.S.C. § 1502(a).[15] The reference to binding classifications does not, however, bespeak the legislative type of activity that would naturally bind more than the parties to the ruling, once the goods classified are admitted into this country. And though the statute's direction to disseminate "information" necessary to "secure" uniformity, 19 U.S.C. § 1502(a), seems to assume that a ruling may be precedent in later transactions, precedential value alone does not add up to *Chevron* entitlement; interpretive rules may sometimes function as precedents, see Strauss, *The Rulemaking Continuum*, 41 Duke L.J. 1463, 1472–73 (1992),

[margin handwritten note: precedential value alone does not add up to chevron entitlement]

---

[15] The ruling in question here, however, does not fall within that category.

and they enjoy no *Chevron* status as a class. In any event, any precedential claim of a classification ruling is counterbalanced by the provision for independent review of Customs classifications by the CIT, see 28 U.S.C. §§ 2638–40; the scheme for CIT review includes a provision that treats classification rulings on par with the Secretary's rulings on "valuation, rate of duty, marking, restricted merchandise, entry requirements, drawbacks, vessel repairs, or similar matters," § 1581(h). It is hard to imagine a congressional understanding more at odds with the *Chevron* regime.[16]

It is difficult, in fact, to see in the agency practice itself any indication that Customs ever set out with a lawmaking pretense in mind when it undertook to make classifications like these. Customs does not generally engage in notice-and-comment practice when issuing them, and their treatment by the agency makes it clear that a letter's binding character as a ruling stops short of third parties; Customs has regarded a classification as conclusive only as between itself and the importer to whom it was issued, and even then only until Customs has given advance notice of intended change. Other importers are in fact warned against assuming any right of detrimental reliance.

Indeed, to claim that classifications have legal force is to ignore the reality that 46 different Customs offices issue 10,000 to 15,000 of them each year. Any suggestion that rulings intended to have the force of law are being churned out at a rate of 10,000 a year at an agency's 46 scattered offices is simply self-refuting. Although the circumstances are less startling here, with a Headquarters letter in issue, none of the relevant statutes recognizes this category of rulings as separate or different from others; there is thus no indication that a more potent delegation might have been understood as going to Headquarters even when Headquarters provides developed reasoning, as it did in this instance.

* * *

In sum, classification rulings are best treated like "interpretations contained in policy statements, agency manuals, and enforcement guidelines." *Christensen.* 529 U.S., at 587, 120 S.Ct. 1655. They are beyond the *Chevron* pale.

To agree with the Court of Appeals that Customs ruling letters do not fall within *Chevron* is not, however, to place them outside the pale of any deference whatever. *Chevron* did nothing to eliminate *Skidmore's* holding that an agency's interpretation may merit some deference whatever its form, given the "specialized experience and broader investigations and information" available to the agency, 323 U.S., at 139, 65 S.Ct. 161, and

---

[16] Although Customs's decision "is presumed to be correct" on review, 28 U.S.C. § 2639(a)(1), the CIT "may consider any new ground" even if not raised below, § 2638, and "shall make its determinations upon the basis of the record made before the court," rather than that developed by Customs, § 2640(a).

given the value of uniformity in its administrative and judicial understandings of what a national law requires, *id.*, at 140, 65 S.Ct. 161.

There is room at least to raise a *Skidmore* claim here, where the regulatory scheme is highly detailed, and Customs can bring the benefit of specialized experience to bear on the subtle questions in this case * * *. Such a ruling may surely claim the merit of its writer's thoroughness, logic and expertness, its fit with prior interpretations, and any other sources of weight.

Underlying the position we take here, like the position expressed by JUSTICE SCALIA in dissent, is a choice about the best way to deal with an inescapable feature of the body of congressional legislation authorizing administrative action. That feature is the great variety of ways in which the laws invest the Government's administrative arms with discretion, and with procedures for exercising it, in giving meaning to Acts of Congress. Implementation of a statute may occur in formal adjudication or the choice to defend against judicial challenge; it may occur in a central board or office or in dozens of enforcement agencies dotted across the country; its institutional lawmaking may be confined to the resolution of minute detail or extend to legislative rulemaking on matters intentionally left by Congress to be worked out at the agency level.

Although we all accept the position that the Judiciary should defer to at least some of this multifarious administrative action, we have to decide how to take account of the great range of its variety. If the primary objective is to simplify the judicial process of giving or withholding deference, then the diversity of statutes authorizing discretionary administrative action must be declared irrelevant or minimized. If, on the other hand, it is simply implausible that Congress intended such a broad range of statutory authority to produce only two varieties of administrative action, demanding either *Chevron* deference or none at all, then the breadth of the spectrum of possible agency action must be taken into account. JUSTICE SCALIA'S first priority over the years has been to limit and simplify. The Court's choice has been to tailor deference to variety. This acceptance of the range of statutory variation has led the Court to recognize more than one variety of judicial deference, just as the Court has recognized a variety of indicators that Congress would expect *Chevron* deference.[18]

Our respective choices are repeated today. JUSTICE SCALIA would pose the question of deference as an either-or choice * * *.

* * *

---

[18] It is, of course, true that the limit of *Chevron* deference is not marked by a hard-edged rule. But *Chevron* itself is a good example showing when *Chevron* deference is warranted, while this is a good case showing when it is not. Judges in other, perhaps harder, cases will make reasoned choices between the two examples, the way courts have always done.

We think, in sum, that JUSTICE SCALIA'S efforts to simplify ultimately run afoul of Congress's indications that different statutes present different reasons for considering respect for the exercise of administrative authority or deference to it. Without being at odds with congressional intent much of the time, we believe that judicial responses to administrative action must continue to differentiate between *Chevron* and *Skidmore,* and that continued recognition of *Skidmore* is necessary for just the reasons Justice Jackson gave when that case was decided.[19]

* * *

Since the *Skidmore* assessment called for here ought to be made in the first instance by the Court of Appeals for the Federal Circuit or the Court of International Trade, we go no further than to vacate the judgment and remand the case for further proceedings consistent with this opinion.

It is so ordered.

JUSTICE SCALIA, dissenting.

Today's opinion makes an avulsive change in judicial review of federal administrative action. Whereas previously a reasonable agency application of an ambiguous statutory provision had to be sustained so long as it represented the agency's authoritative interpretation, henceforth such an application can be set aside unless "it appears that Congress delegated authority to the agency generally to make rules carrying the force of law," as by giving an agency "power to engage in adjudication or notice-and-comment rulemaking, or . . . some other [procedure] indicati[ng] comparable congressional intent," and "the agency interpretation claiming deference was promulgated in the exercise of that authority." What was previously a general presumption of authority in agencies to resolve ambiguity in the statutes they have been authorized to enforce has been changed to a presumption of no such authority, which must be overcome by affirmative legislative intent to the contrary. And whereas previously, when agency authority to resolve ambiguity did not exist the court was free

---

[19] Surely Justice Jackson's practical criteria, along with *Chevron's* concern with congressional understanding, provide more reliable guideposts than conclusory references to the "authoritative" or "official." Even if those terms provided a true criterion, there would have to be something wrong with a standard that accorded the status of substantive law to every one of 10,000 "official" customs classifications rulings turned out each year from over 46 offices placed around the country at the Nation's entryways. JUSTICE SCALIA tries to avoid that result by limiting what is "authoritative" or "official" to a pronouncement that expresses the "judgment of central agency management, approved at the highest level," as distinct from the pronouncements of "underlings." But that analysis would not entitle a Headquarters ruling to *Chevron* deference; the "highest level" at Customs is the source of the regulation at issue in *Haggar,* the Commissioner of Customs with the approval of the Secretary of the Treasury. The Commissioner did not issue the Headquarters ruling. What JUSTICE SCALIA has in mind here is that because the Secretary approved the Government's position in its brief to this Court, *Chevron* deference is due. But if that is so, *Chevron* deference was not called for until sometime after the litigation began, when central management at the highest level decided to defend the ruling, and the deference is not to the classification ruling as such but to the brief. This explains why the Court has not accepted JUSTICE SCALIA'S position.

to give the statute what it considered the best interpretation, henceforth the court must supposedly give the agency view some indeterminate amount of so-called *Skidmore* deference. We will be sorting out the consequences of the *Mead* doctrine, which has today replaced the *Chevron* doctrine, for years to come. I would adhere to our established jurisprudence, defer to the reasonable interpretation the Customs Service has given to the statute it is charged with enforcing, and reverse the judgment of the Court of Appeals.

I

* * *

The Court's new doctrine is neither sound in principle nor sustainable in practice.

As to principle: The doctrine of *Chevron*—that all *authoritative* agency interpretations of statutes they are charged with administering deserve deference—was rooted in a legal presumption of congressional intent, important to the division of powers between the Second and Third Branches. When, *Chevron* said, Congress leaves an ambiguity in a statute that is to be administered by an executive agency, it is presumed that Congress meant to give the agency discretion, within the limits of reasonable interpretation, as to how the ambiguity is to be resolved. By committing enforcement of the statute to an agency rather than the courts, Congress committed its initial and primary interpretation to that branch as well.

* * *

The basis in principle for today's new doctrine can be described as follows: The background rule is that ambiguity in legislative instructions to agencies is to be resolved not by the agencies but by the judges. Specific congressional intent to depart from this rule must be found—and while there is no single touchstone for such intent it can generally be found when Congress has authorized the agency to act through (what the Court says is) relatively formal procedures such as informal rulemaking and formal (and informal?) adjudication, and when the agency in fact employs such procedures * * *. There is no necessary connection between the formality of procedure and the power of the entity administering the procedure to resolve authoritatively questions of law. The most formal of the procedures the Court refers to—formal adjudication—is modeled after the process used in trial courts, which of course are not generally accorded deference on questions of law. The purpose of such a procedure is to produce a closed record for determination and review of the facts—which implies nothing about the power of the agency subjected to the procedure to resolve authoritatively questions of law.

As for informal rulemaking: While formal adjudication procedures are *prescribed* (either by statute or by the Constitution), informal rulemaking is more typically *authorized* but not required. Agencies with such authority are free to give guidance through rulemaking, but they may proceed to administer their statute case-by-case, "making law" as they implement their program (not necessarily through formal adjudication). Is it likely— or indeed even plausible—that Congress meant, when such an agency chooses rulemaking, to accord the administrators of that agency, *and their successors,* the flexibility of interpreting the ambiguous statute now one way, and later another; but, when such an agency chooses case-by-case administration, to eliminate all future agency discretion by having that same ambiguity resolved authoritatively (and forever) by the courts? Surely that makes no sense. It is also the case that certain significant categories of rules—those involving grant and benefit programs, for example, are exempt from the requirements of informal rulemaking. See 5 U.S.C. § 553(a)(2). Under the Court's novel theory, when an agency takes advantage of that exemption its rules will be deprived of *Chevron* deference, *i.e.,* authoritative effect. Was this either the plausible intent of the APA rulemaking exemption, or the plausible intent of the Congress that established the grant or benefit program?

[handwritten margin note: when agency uses rulemaking exception, should it be deprived of Chevron?]

Some decisions that are neither informal rulemaking nor formal adjudication are required to be made personally by a Cabinet Secretary, without any prescribed procedures. Is it conceivable that decisions specifically committed to these high-level officers are meant to be accorded no deference, while decisions by an administrative law judge left in place without further discretionary agency review, see 5 U.S.C. § 557(b), are authoritative? This seems to me quite absurd, and not at all in accord with any plausible actual intent of Congress.

As for the practical effects of the new rule:

The principal effect will be protracted confusion. As noted above, the one test for *Chevron* deference that the Court enunciates is wonderfully imprecise: whether "Congress delegated authority to the agency generally to make rules carrying the force of law, . . . as by . . . adjudication[,] notice-and-comment rulemaking, or . . . some other [procedure] indicati[ng] comparable congressional intent." But even this description does not do justice to the utter flabbiness of the Court's criterion, since, in order to maintain the fiction that the new test is really just the old one, applied consistently throughout our case law, the Court must make a virtually open-ended exception to its already imprecise guidance: In the present case, it tells us, the absence of notice-and-comment rulemaking (and "[who knows?] [of] some other [procedure] indicati[ng] comparable congressional intent") is not enough to decide the question of *Chevron* deference, "for we have sometimes found reasons for *Chevron* deference even when no such administrative formality was required and none was afforded." The opinion then goes on to consider a grab bag of other factors—including the factor that used to be the sole criterion for *Chevron* deference: whether the interpretation represented the *authoritative* position of the agency. It is hard to know what the lower courts are to make of today's guidance.

Another practical effect of today's opinion will be an artificially induced increase in informal rulemaking. Buy stock in the G[overnment] P[rinting] O[ffice]. Since informal rulemaking and formal adjudication are the only more-or-less safe harbors from the storm that the Court has unleashed; and since formal adjudication is not an option but must be mandated by statute or constitutional command; informal rulemaking— which the Court was once careful to make voluntary unless required by statute—will now become a virtual necessity. As I have described, the Court's safe harbor requires not merely that the agency have been given rulemaking authority, but also that the agency have *employed* rulemaking as the means of resolving the statutory ambiguity. (It is hard to understand why that should be so. Surely the mere *conferral* of rulemaking authority demonstrates—if one accepts the Court's logic—a congressional intent to allow the agency to resolve ambiguities. And given that intent, what difference does it make that the agency chooses instead to use another perfectly permissible means for that purpose?) Moreover, the majority's approach will have a perverse effect on the rules that do emerge, given the principle (which the Court leaves untouched today) that judges must defer to reasonable agency interpretations of their own regulations. Agencies will now have high incentive to rush out barebones, ambiguous rules construing statutory ambiguities, which they can then in turn further clarify through informal rulings entitled to judicial respect.

* * *

And finally, the majority's approach compounds the confusion it creates by breathing new life into the anachronism of *Skidmore,* which sets forth a sliding scale of deference owed an agency's interpretation of a statute * * *.

It was possible to live with the indeterminacy of *Skidmore* deference in earlier times. But in an era when federal statutory law administered by federal agencies is pervasive, and when the ambiguities (intended or unintended) that those statutes contain are innumerable, totality-of-the-circumstances *Skidmore* deference is a recipe for uncertainty, unpredictability, and endless litigation. To condemn a vast body of agency action to that regime (all except rulemaking, formal (and informal?)) adjudication, and whatever else might now and then be included within today's intentionally vague formulation of affirmative congressional intent to "delegate" is irresponsible.

* * *

[handwritten margin note: informal rulemaking will now become a virtual necess.]

To decide the present case, I would adhere to the original formulation of *Chevron* * * *. *Chevron* sets forth an across-the-board presumption, which operates as a background rule of law against which Congress legislates: [Ambiguity means Congress intended agency discretion.] Any resolution of the ambiguity by the administering agency that is authoritative—that represents the official position of the agency—must be accepted by the courts if it is reasonable.

Nothing in the statute at issue here displays an intent to modify the background presumption on which *Chevron* deference is based * * *.

There is no doubt that the Customs Service's interpretation represents the authoritative view of the agency. Although the actual ruling letter was signed by only the Director of the Commercial Rulings Branch of Customs Headquarters' Office of Regulations and Rulings, the Solicitor General of the United States has filed a brief, cosigned by the General Counsel of the Department of the Treasury, that represents the position set forth in the ruling letter to be the official position of the Customs Service.[6]

There is also no doubt that the Customs Service's interpretation is a reasonable one, whether or not judges would consider it the best. I will not belabor this point, since the Court evidently agrees: An interpretation that was unreasonable would not merit the remand that the Court decrees for consideration of *Skidmore* deference.

* * *

For the reasons stated, I respectfully dissent from the Court's judgment * * *. I dissent even more vigorously from the reasoning that produces the Court's judgment, and that makes today's decision one of the most significant opinions ever rendered by the Court dealing with the

---

[6] * * * The "authoritativeness" of an agency interpretation does not turn upon whether it has been enunciated by someone who is actually employed by the agency. It must represent the judgment of central agency management, approved at the highest levels. I would find that condition to have been satisfied when, a ruling having been attacked in court, the general counsel of the agency has determined that it should be defended. If one thinks that that does not impart sufficient authoritativeness, then surely the line has been crossed when, as here, the General Counsel of the agency and the Solicitor General of the United States have assured this Court that the position represents the agency's authoritative view. (Contrary to the Court's suggestion), there would be nothing bizarre about the fact that this latter approach would entitle the ruling to deference here, though it would not have been entitled to deference in the lower courts. Affirmation of the official agency position before this court—if that is thought necessary—is no different from the agency's issuing a new rule after the Court of Appeals determination. It establishes a new legal basis for the decision, which this Court must take into account (or remand for that purpose), even though the Court of Appeals could not. The *authoritativeness* of the agency ruling may not be a bright-line standard—but it is infinitely brighter than the line the Court asks us to draw today * * *. And, most important of all, it is a line that focuses attention on the right question: not whether Congress "affirmatively intended" to delegate interpretive authority (if it entrusted administration of the statute to an agency, it did, because that is how our system works); but whether it is truly the agency's considered view, or just the opinions of some underlings, that are at issue.

judicial review of administrative action. Its consequences will be enormous, and almost uniformly bad.

NOTES

Christensen and *Mead* clearly answer some questions that had plagued courts for most of *Chevron's* first two decades. It is now clear (as it should have been from the start) that rulemaking authority is not a *sine qua non* for *Chevron* deference; Congress can give agencies power to render decisions "with the force and effect of law" by granting power to make legislative rules, power to adjudicate, or both. It is also clear that interpretative rules are not entitled to *Chevron* deference. True, the Court did not expressly say in *Mead* that interpretative rules can *never* be entitled to *Chevron* deference; it said only that such rules "enjoy no *Chevron* status as a class." But *Mead* and *Christensen* both emphasize that the touchstone for *Chevron* deference is evidence that "Congress delegated authority to the agency generally to make rules [or adjudicatory orders] carrying the force of law, and that the agency interpretation claiming deference was promulgated in the exercise of that authority." Interpretative rules, by definition, are not "promulgated in the exercise of th[e] authority" to make law, and accordingly they seem to be outside the scope of *Chevron* as the Court has now defined it. This will be true even if the agency employs notice and comment procedures for its interpretative rules (as agencies are always free to do even when the APA exempts the rules from any mandatory procedural requirement). *See Coke v. Long Island Care at Home, Ltd.*, 376 F.3d 118, 131–32 (2d Cir. 2004) (declining to give *Chevron* deference to an interpretative rule promulgated with notice and comment procedures). On the other hand, the occasional interpretative rule or policy statement may still slip through the net with lower courts that continue to puzzle over the meaning of *Mead*. *See, e.g., Kruse v. Wells Fargo Home Mortgage, Inc.*, 383 F.3d 49 (2d Cir. 2004) (granting *Chevron* deference to a policy statement that the court conclusorily found—somehow—to have been promulgated pursuant to lawmaking authority).

The (re-)emergence of *Skidmore v. Swift* as a major part of the legal landscape is also a significant development, though perhaps less significant than Justice Scalia's opinions in *Christensen* and *Mead* suggest. After all, many agency legal interpretations do not get *Chevron* deference under any approach to *Chevron*—because, for example, the agency does not administer the statute in question. Courts in such cases are not *obliged* to defer to the agency's views, but they are surely *permitted* to do so if they are persuaded that the agency's views were well-considered, so *Skidmore* deference will always exist in some settings. It is clear, however, that more agency decisions would receive *Chevron* rather than *Skidmore* deference under Justice Scalia's view of *Chevron* than under the Court's view in *Mead*, and *Skidmore* accordingly now has a broader role to play than was acknowledged in the past.

Other matters about the application of *Chevron*, however, remain somewhat unclear after *Mead*. Most fundamentally, there is the problem of determining when Congress has signaled its intention to delegate to the agency authority to make pronouncements "carrying the force of law." If such a delegation exists, then one can argue about whether the agency has acted pursuant to that authority, but if no such delegation exists, *Mead* seems to foreclose *Chevron* deference. Is it enough for Congress to grant the agency a general rulemaking power (as it usually does), or does there need to be some stronger signal that such rules are meant to give the agencies lawmaking power? For an enlightening and exhaustive study of this problem, *see* Thomas W. Merrill & Kathryn Tongue Watts, *Agency Rules with the Force of Law: The Original Convention*, 116 Harv. L. Rev. 467 (2002). And what is the relevance, if any, of the procedures employed by the agency to promulgate the rule or order at issue? *Mead* establishes that an agency interpretation that is promulgated as law and has an adequate procedural pedigree (informal notice-and-comment rulemaking qualifies for this purpose) will definitely get *Chevron* deference, but it does not establish that interpretations promulgated as law that lack such a pedigree will *not* get *Chevron* deference. If an agency, for example, issues a legislative rule and properly invokes § 553(b)'s "good cause" exception from notice and comment procedures, *Mead* neither forecloses nor mandates *Chevron* deference (the emphasis on the agency's exercise of lawmaking power suggests deference, while the emphasis on the use of adequate procedures suggests otherwise). In footnote 18 of *Mead,* the Court expressly leaves resolution of such issues to future case-by-case adjudication. In principle, one would think that the procedures actually employed by an agency should be irrelevant, though the procedures required by Congress might be one indication of whether Congress intended for the agency action in question to be the kind of action for which *Chevron* deference is appropriate. In practice, courts often continue to give significant weight to procedures employed by the agency—perhaps because footnote 18 leaves them with so little guidance about what else to weigh in the balance. *See, e.g., Sinclair Wyoming Refining Co. v. U.S. EPA,* 867 F.3d 1211, 1217 (10th Cir.2017); *Knox Creek Coal Corp. v. Secretary of Labor,* 811 F.3d 148, 159–60 (4th Cir.2016); *Fogo de Chao (Holdings), Inc. v. U.S. Dep't of Homeland Security,* 769 F.3d 1127, 1136–37 (D.C.Cir.2014); *Village of Barrington, Ill. v. Surface Transportation Board,* 636 F.3d 650, 658–59 (D.C.Cir.2011). On the other hand, courts considering whether to defer to highly informal, unpublished decisions of single members of the Board of Immigration Appeals have split. *See De Leon-Ochoa v. Attorney General of the United States,* 622 F.3d 341, 349–51 (3d Cir.2010) ("No consensus exists among our sister Courts of Appeals as to what quantum of deference, if any, should be accorded to those opinions * * *. Because it was not briefed, barely argued, and is not dispositive for the issues before us, we decline to resolve the question."). Of course, if a rule or order is procedurally (or substantively) *defective,* it is not a valid rule or order at all. In that case, the rule or order has no force of law and therefore cannot receive *Chevron* deference. *See Encino Motorcars, LLC v. Navarro,* 136 S.Ct. 2117, 2125 (2016).

A great many regulations promulgated by agencies literally repeat the language of the underlying statute. Can the agency then claim *Seminole*

Rock/Auer deference for interpretation of the regulation in a circumstance in which *Mead* might foreclose deference in the interpretation of the underlying statute? The Supreme Court said "no" in 2006:

> In *Auer*, the underlying regulations gave specificity to a statutory scheme the Secretary was charged with enforcing and reflected the considerable experience and expertise the Department of Labor had acquired over time with respect to the complexities of the Fair Labor Standards Act. Here, on the other hand, the underlying regulation does little more than restate the terms of the statute itself * * *, and the near-equivalence of the statute and regulation belies the Government's argument for *Auer* deference.

Gonzales v. Oregon, 546 U.S. 243, 256–57, 126 S.Ct. 904, 915, 163 L.Ed.2d 748 (2006).

Gonzalez could plausibly be read as a general instruction to deny deference to agency interpretations of all "parroting" regulations that repeat statutory language, or it could plausibly be construed narrowly in light of the unique facts (and politically charged context) of the case, which involved efforts by the United States Attorney General to outlaw prescriptions for drugs to be used in assisted suicide. The early returns suggest that *Gonzalez's* "anti-parroting" doctrine will be construed narrowly, *see Plateau Mining Corp. v. Federal Mine Safety & Health Review Comm'n*, 519 F.3d 1176, 1192–93 (10th Cir.2008) (giving deference to agency interpretation of regulations that closely tracked, but did not precisely echo, the underlying statute), though there have been cases in which the anti-parroting rule has had serious bite. *See, e.g., Fogo de Chao (Holdings), Inc. v. U.S. Dep't of Homeland Security*, 769 F.3d 1127, 1135–36 (D.C.Cir.2014) (denying *Auer* deference where the regulation "largely parrots, rather than interprets, the key statutory language"). The issue is only important if agencies get more deference for interpretations of regulations than for interpretations of statutes. That could happen in either of two ways. First, the degree of deference under *Auer* might be considered broader than the degree of deference under *Chevron*. As was previously noted, *see supra* page 606, an agency in 2001 had good reason to think this the case. In view of the unsettled future of *Auer* deference, that may be a less plausible position in 2018. Second, there may be certain preconditions for *Chevron* deference that are not satisfied for interpretation of the underlying statute, and the agency may hope to do an end run around those preconditions by essentially converting the statute into a regulation, to which *Mead* and other "step zero" cases do not apply. Until quite recently, that was a plausible line of argument, because there were no recognized analogues to "step zero" for *Auer* deference. *See Talk America, Inc. v. Michigan Bell Telephone Co.*, 564 U.S. 50, 131 S.Ct. 2254, 180 L.Ed.2d 96 (2011) (giving *Auer* deference to agency interpretations of regulations offered in an amicus brief); *see also Chase Bank USA, N.A. v. McCoy*, 562 U.S. 195, 131 S.Ct. 871, 178 L.Ed.2d 716 (2011) (same). That line of argument may be less plausible in light of *Christopher v. Smithkline Beecham Corp.*, *supra* pages 608–613, which seems to indicate that there are (unspecified) preconditions for deference to agency interpretations of regulations. *See, e.g., Vietnam Veterans of America v. CIA*, 811 F.3d 1068, 1078 (9th Cir.2016) ("*Auer* deference is not warranted in all circumstances * * *. The government's proposed interpretation is a 'convenient litigating position' that does not warrant *Auer* deference.") The future of the anti-parroting rule likely depends on the broader future of *Auer* deference.

The "parroting" problem involves the interplay between *Chevron* deference to agency interpretations of ambiguous statutes and *Auer* deference to agency interpretations of ambiguous regulations. The boundaries between those doctrines, however, are not always kept as crisp as one might like. Consider in this regard *Coeur Alaska, Inc. v. Southeast Alaska Conservation Council*, 557 U.S. 261, 129 S.Ct. 2458 (2009).

[handwritten margin note: Coeur Alaska v. SE Alaska Conservation]

The Clean Water Act forbids "the discharge of any pollutant by any person" into the navigable waters of the United States. 33 U.S.C. § 1311(a) (2012). The Environmental Protection Agency can authorize such discharges by issuing a "permit for the discharge of any pollutant," *id.* § 1342(a), in accordance with the statute's substantive and procedural guidelines. Section 1316(e) adds that "new sources" of pollution may only discharge pollutants if the activity complies with an "applicable performance standard" promulgated by the EPA. *Id.* § 1316(e). One such performance standard effectively forbids mine operators from discharging "process wastewater" into the waters of the United States. 40 C.F.R. § 440.104(b)(1).

That would seem to be bad news for companies like Coeur Alaska, which wanted to reopen a gold mine that had been closed since 1928. The company planned to use a method called "froth flotation" that processes rock from the mine in churning water and uses chemicals to isolate the gold-bearing minerals. Once the gold has been removed, one is left with a large mass of crushed rock and water, called slurry, that must be deposited somewhere. Coeur Alaska proposed to deposit its slurry into a nearby lake that everyone agreed was navigable waters and thus subject to the requirements of the Clean Water Act. Under the Clean Water Act regime just described, this plan would seem to be flagrantly and obviously illegal, as the slurry fits nicely within the category of "process wastewater."

The EPA, however, is not the only federal agency that grants permits under the Clean Water Act. Yet another provision of the statute authorizes the Army Corps of Engineers to grant permits for the discharge of "dredged or fill material," 33 U.S.C. § 1344(a) (2012), under EPA guidelines and subject to an EPA veto if the latter agency finds a Corps-permitted plan to have an "unacceptable adverse effect * * *." *Id.* § 1344(c). Coeur Alaska's slurry fits nicely within the definition of "dredged or fill material." The EPA's general permitting authority under § 1342(a) specifically declares that it does not apply to matters governed by the Corps' permitting authority under § 1344, and Coeur Alaska accordingly sought and received a permit from the Corps (which the EPA did not veto). But what about § 1316—the "new source" permitting provision? That section says nothing expressly about its relationship to 1344. "On the one hand, [§ 1316] provides that a discharge that violates an EPA new source performance standard is 'unlawful'—without any exception for fill material. On the other hand, [§ 1344] grants the Corps blanket authority to permit the discharge of fill material—without any mention of [§ 1316]." 557 U.S. at 281, 129 S.Ct. at 2471–72. Is § 1316 inapplicable to matters within the jurisdiction of the Corps under § 1344, or does any new source discharge, even a discharge of "dredged or fill material" subject to Corps rather than EPA approval, have to comply with § 1316 performance standards?

Six Justices said the former and three said the latter. The majority, citing *Chevron*, noted that "[b]ecause Congress has not 'directly spoken' to the 'precise question' of whether an EPA performance standard applies to discharges of fill material, the statute alone does not resolve the case." 557 U.S. at 277, 129 S.Ct. at 2469. Nor do any agency regulations directly attempt to address the evident conflict between the statutory provisions: "Rather than address the tension between §§ [1316 and 1344], the regulations instead implement the statutory framework without elaboration on this point." 557 U.S. at 282, 129 S.Ct. at 2472. The Court, however, found indirect resolution of the conflict in other agency pronouncements:

> The question is addressed and resolved in a reasonable and coherent way by the practice and policy of the two agencies, all as recited in a memorandum written in May 2004 by Diane Regas, then the Director of the EPA's Office of Wetlands, Oceans and Watersheds, to Randy Smith, the Director of the EPA's regional Office of Water with responsibility over the mine. The Memorandum, though not subject to sufficiently formal procedures to merit *Chevron* deference, see *Mead*, is entitled to a measure of deference because it interprets the agencies' own regulatory scheme. See *Auer*.

The Regas Memorandum explains:

> As a result [of the fact that the discharge is regulated under § [1344]], the regulatory regime applicable to discharges under section 1342, including effluent limitations guidelines and standards, such as those applicable to gold ore mining * * * do not apply to the placement of tailings into the proposed impoundment [of Lower Slate Lake]. See 40 CFR § 122.3(b).

The regulation that the Memorandum cites—40 CFR § 122.3—is one we considered above and found ambiguous. That regulation provides: "[d]ischarges of dredged or fill material into waters of the United States which are regulated under section [1344] of CWA" "do not require [§ 1342] permits." The Regas Memorandum takes an instructive interpretive step when it explains that because the discharge "do[es] not require" an EPA permit, the EPA's performance standard "do[es] not apply" to the discharge. The Memorandum presents a reasonable interpretation of the regulatory regime. We defer to the interpretation because it is not "plainly erroneous or inconsistent with the regulation[s]." *Auer*.

557 U.S. at 283–84, 129 S.Ct. at 2473. Justice Scalia concurred with the following commentary:

> I join the opinion of the Court, except for its protestation that it is not according *Chevron* deference to the reasonable interpretation set forth in the [Regas] memorandum * * *. The opinion purports to give this agency interpretation "a measure of deference" because it involves an interpretation of "the agencies' own regulatory scheme," and "the regulatory regime" (citing *Auer v. Robbins*). *Auer, however* stands only for the principle that we defer to an agency's interpretation *of its own ambiguous regulation*. But it becomes obvious from the ensuing discussion that the referenced "regulatory scheme" and "regulatory regime" for which the Court accepts the agency interpretation includes not just the agencies' own regulations but also (and indeed primarily) the conformity of those regulations with the ambiguous governing statute, which is the primary dispute here.

> Surely the Court is not adding to our already inscrutable opinion in *United States v. Mead Corp.* the irrational fillip that an agency position which otherwise does not qualify for *Chevron* deference *does* receive *Chevron* deference if it clarifies not just an ambiguous statute but *also* an ambiguous regulation. One must conclude, then, that if today's opinion is *not* according the agencies' reasonable and authoritative interpretation of the Clean Water Act *Chevron* deference, it is according some *new* type of deference—perhaps to be called in the future *Coeur Alaska* deference—which is identical to *Chevron* deference except for the name.

> * * * Of course the only reason a new name is required is our misguided opinion in *Mead*, whose incomprehensible criteria for *Chevron* deference have produced so much confusion in the lower courts that there has now appeared the phenomenon of *Chevron* avoidance—the practice of declining to opine whether *Chevron* applies or not. *See* Bressman, How *Mead* Has Muddled Judicial Review of Agency Action, 58 Vand. L. Rev. 1443, 1464 (2005).

> I favor overruling *Mead*. Failing that, I am pleased to join an opinion that effectively ignores it.

557 U.S. at 295–96, 129 S.Ct. at 2479–80 (Scalia, J., concurring in part and concurring in the judgment). Since Justice Scalia is obviously right about the irrelevance of *Auer* in this circumstance (no one was really arguing about the meaning of 40 C.F.R. § 122.3, were they?), why did the majority not simply cite *Skidmore* and declare victory? Is it because the Regas Memorandum was conclusory rather than carefully reasoned and was therefore a poor candidate for *Skidmore* deference? If so, and if no other deference doctrines seemed applicable, was it unthinkable to decide the case without mentioning deference at all?

In 2013, the Supreme Court appeared to resolve another of the many issues that have divided courts and commentators about the reach of the *Chevron* doctrine. From the early days of *Chevron* onward, some courts refused to give deference to agency interpretations that otherwise seemed to meet the criteria for *Chevron* but which defined the scope of the agency's own statutory jurisdiction, *see, e.g., Northern Illinois Steel Supply Co. v. Secretary of Labor*, 294 F.3d 844 (7th Cir. 2002)—a refusal that had considerable academic support. *See, e.g.,* Nathan Alexander Sales & Jonathan H. Adler, *The Rest Is Silence:* Chevron *Deference, Agency Jurisdiction, and Statutory Silences*, 2009 U. Ill. L. Rev. 1497. In *City of Arlington, Texas v. FCC*, 133 S.Ct. 1863 (2013), the facts of which are discussed in another context at pages 69–71, *supra*, the Federal Communications Commission construed its statutory power to place limits on the land-use decisions of state and local governments. A five-Justice majority—consisting of the intriguing combination of Justices Scalia, Thomas, Ginsburg, Sotomayor, and Kagan—held that *Chevron* applied to the Commission's interpretation of the statute and rejected any purported distinction between "jurisdictional" and "nonjurisdictional" agency interpretations:

> The question here is whether a court must defer under *Chevron* to an agency's interpretation of a statutory ambiguity that concerns the scope of the agency's statutory authority (that is, its jurisdiction). The argument against deference rests on the premise that there exist two distinct classes of agency interpretations: Some interpretations—the big, important ones, presumably—define the agency's "jurisdiction." Others—humdrum, run-of-the-mill stuff—are simply applications of jurisdiction the agency plainly has. That premise is false, because the distinction between "jurisdictional" and "nonjurisdictional" interpretations is a mirage. No matter how it is framed, the question a court faces when confronted with an agency's interpretation of a statute it administers is always, simply, *whether the agency has stayed within the bounds of its statutory authority*.

> The misconception that there are, for *Chevron* purposes, separate "jurisdictional" questions on which no deference is due derives, perhaps, from a reflexive extension to agencies of the very real division between the jurisdictional and nonjurisdictional that is applicable to courts. In the judicial context, there *is* a meaningful line: Whether the court decided *correctly* is a question that has different consequences from the question whether it had the power to decide at *all* * * *. A court's power to decide a case is independent of whether its decision is correct, which is why even an erroneous judgment is entitled to res judicata effect. Put differently, a jurisdictionally proper but substantively incorrect judicial decision is not ultra vires.

> That is not so for agencies charged with administering congressional statutes. Both their power to act and how they are to act is authoritatively prescribed by Congress, so that when they act

improperly, no less than when they act beyond their jurisdiction, what they do is ultra vires. Because the question—whether framed as an incorrect application of agency authority or an assertion of authority not conferred—is always whether the agency has gone beyond what Congress has permitted it to do, there is no principled basis for carving out some arbitrary subset of such claims as "jurisdictional."

* * *

Those who assert that applying *Chevron* to "jurisdictional" interpretations "leaves the fox in charge of the henhouse" overlook the reality that a separate category of "jurisdictional" interpretations does not exist. The fox-in-the-henhouse syndrome is to be avoided not by establishing an arbitrary and undefinable category of agency decisionmaking that is accorded no deference, but by taking seriously, and applying rigorously, in all cases, statutory limits on agencies' authority. Where Congress has established a clear line, the agency cannot go beyond it; and where Congress has established an ambiguous line, the agency can go no further than the ambiguity will fairly allow. But in rigorously applying the latter rule, a court need not pause to puzzle over whether the interpretive question presented is "jurisdictional." If "the agency's answer is based on a permissible construction of the statute," that is the end of the matter.

Id. at 1868–69, 1874–75.

Justice Breyer agreed with the majority that there is no meaningful line between jurisdictional and nonjurisdictional agency interpretations and that the relevant question is always whether the agency acted within the boundaries of its statutory authority. He wrote separately to emphasize that determining those boundaries, and specifically determining whether "Congress has left a deference-warranting gap for the agency to fill," *id.* at 1875, requires a case-specific, multi-faceted inquiry, as was emphasized in *Mead.* On the facts of *City of Arlington*, he found that

> many factors favor the agency's view: (1) the language of the Telecommunications Act grants the FCC broad authority (including rulemaking authority) to administer the Act; (2) the words are open-ended—*i.e.* "ambiguous"; (3) the provision concerns an interstitial administrative matter, in respect to which the agency's expertise could have an important role to play; and (4) the matter, in context, is complex, likely making the agency's expertise useful in helping to answer the "reasonableness" question that the statute poses.

Id. at 1876 (Breyer, J., concurring in part and concurring in the judgment).

Chief Justice Roberts, joined by Justices Kennedy and Alito, vigorously *dissent* dissented:

> My disagreement with the Court is fundamental. It is also easily expressed: A court should not defer to an agency until the court

decides, on its own, that the agency is entitled to deference. Courts defer to an agency's interpretation of law when and because Congress has conferred on the agency interpretive authority over the question at issue. An agency cannot exercise interpretive authority until it has it; the question whether an agency enjoys that authority must be decided by a court, without deference to the agency.

* * * Although modern administrative agencies fit most comfortably within the Executive Branch, as a practical matter they exercise legislative power, by promulgating regulations with the force of law; executive power, by policing compliance with those regulations; and judicial power, by adjudicating enforcement actions and imposing sanctions on those found to have violated their rules. The accumulation of these powers in the same hands is not an occasional or isolated exception to the constitutional plan; it is a central feature of modern American government.

The administrative state "wields vast power and touches almost every aspect of daily life." *Free Enterprise Fund v. Public Company Accounting Oversight Bd.*, 561 U.S. ___, ___, 130 S.Ct. 3138, 3156, 177 L.Ed.2d 706 (2010). The Framers could hardly have envisioned today's "vast and varied federal bureaucracy" and the authority administrative agencies now hold over our economic, social, and political activities. *Ibid.* * * *. And the federal bureaucracy continues to grow; in the last 15 years, Congress has launched more than 50 new agencies.

* * *

[T]he danger posed by the growing power of the administrative state cannot be dismissed.

* * *

It is against this background that we consider whether the authority of administrative agencies should be augmented even further, to include not only broad power to give definitive answers to questions left to them by Congress, but also the same power to decide when Congress has given them that power.

Before proceeding to answer that question, however, it is necessary to sort through some confusion over what this litigation is about. The source of the confusion is a familiar culprit: the concept of "jurisdiction," which we have repeatedly described as a word with " 'many, too many, meanings.' " *Union Pacific R. Co. v. Locomotive Engineers*, 558 U.S. 67, 81, 130 S.Ct. 584, 175 L.Ed.2d 428 (2009).

The Court states that the question "is whether a court must defer under Chevron to an agency's interpretation of a statutory ambiguity that concerns the scope of the agency's statutory authority (that is, its jurisdiction)." That is fine—until the parenthetical. The parties, *amici*, and court below too often use the term "jurisdiction" imprecisely, which leads the Court to misunderstand the argument it must confront. That argument is not that "there exist two distinct classes of agency interpretations," some "big, important ones" that "define the agency's 'jurisdiction,'" and other "humdrum, run-of-the-mill" ones that "are simply applications of jurisdiction the agency plainly has." The argument is instead that a court should not defer to an agency on whether Congress has granted the agency interpretive authority over the statutory ambiguity at issue.

* * * [B]efore a court may grant * * * deference, it must on its own decide whether Congress—the branch vested with lawmaking authority under the Constitution—has in fact delegated to the agency lawmaking power over the ambiguity at issue.

* * *

In *Mead*, we * * * made clear that the "category of interpretative choices" to which *Chevron* deference applies is defined by congressional intent. *Chevron* deference, we said, rests on a recognition that Congress has delegated to an agency the interpretive authority to implement "a particular provision" or answer "'a particular question.'"

* * *

* * * *Chevron* deference is based on, and finds legitimacy as, a congressional delegation of interpretive authority. An agency interpretation warrants such deference only if Congress has delegated authority to definitively interpret a particular ambiguity in a particular manner. Whether Congress has done so must be determined by the court on its own before *Chevron* can apply.

* * *

Despite these precedents, the FCC argues that a court need only locate an agency and a grant of general rulemaking authority over a statute. *Chevron* deference then applies, it contends, to the agency's interpretation of any ambiguity in the Act, including ambiguity in a provision said to carve out specific provisions from the agency's general rulemaking authority. If Congress intends to exempt part of the statute from the agency's interpretive authority, the FCC says, Congress "can ordinarily be expected to state that intent explicitly." Brief for Federal Respondents 30.

If a congressional delegation of interpretive authority is to support *Chevron* deference, however, that delegation must extend to the specific statutory ambiguity at issue. The appropriate question is whether the delegation covers the "specific provision" and "particular question" before the court. *Chevron*, 467 U.S., at 844, 104 S.Ct. 2778. A congressional grant of authority over some portion of a statute does not necessarily mean that Congress granted the agency interpretive authority over all its provisions.

* * *

* * * [W]hen Congress provides interpretive authority to a[n] * * * agency, a court must decide if the ambiguity the agency has purported to interpret with the force of law is one to which the congressional delegation extends. A general delegation to the agency to administer the statute will often suffice to satisfy the court that Congress has delegated interpretive authority over the ambiguity at issue. But if Congress has exempted particular provisions from that authority, that exemption must be respected, and the determination whether Congress has done so is for the courts alone.

The FCC's argument that Congress "can ordinarily be expected to state that intent explicitly," Brief for Federal Respondents 30, goes to the merits of that determination, not to whether a court should decide the question *de novo* or defer to the agency * * *.

* * *

In these cases, the FCC issued a declaratory ruling interpreting the term "reasonable period of time" in 47 U.S.C. § 332(c)(7)(B)(ii). The Fifth Circuit correctly recognized that it could not apply *Chevron* deference to the FCC's interpretation unless the agency "possessed statutory authority to administer § 332(c)(7)(B)(ii)," but it erred by granting *Chevron* deference to the FCC's view on that antecedent question. Because the court should have determined on its own whether Congress delegated interpretive authority over § 332(c)(7)(B)(ii) to the FCC before affording *Chevron* deference, I would vacate the decision below and remand the cases to the Fifth Circuit to perform the proper inquiry in the first instance.

Id. at 1874–84, 1886 (Roberts. J., dissenting). The majority directly responded to the dissent:

The question on which we granted certiorari was whether "a court should apply *Chevron* to review an agency's determination of its own jurisdiction." Pet. for Cert. i. Perhaps sensing the incoherence of the "jurisdictional-nonjurisdictional" line, the dissent does not even attempt to defend it, but proposes a much broader scope for *de novo* judicial review: Jurisdictional or not, and even where a rule is at issue and the statute contains a broad grant of rulemaking authority, the dissent would have a court search provision-by-provision to determine "whether [that] delegation covers the 'specific provision' and 'particular question' before the court."

The dissent is correct that *United States v. Mead Corp.*, 533 U.S. 218, 121 S.Ct. 2164, 150 L.Ed.2d 292 (2001), requires that, for *Chevron* deference to apply, the agency must have received congressional authority to determine the particular matter at issue in the particular manner adopted. No one disputes that. But *Mead* denied *Chevron* deference to action, by an agency with rulemaking authority, that was not rulemaking. What the dissent needs, and fails to produce, is a single case in which a general conferral of rulemaking or adjudicative authority has been held insufficient to support *Chevron* deference for an exercise of that authority within the agency's substantive field. There is no such case, and what the dissent proposes is a massive revision of our *Chevron* jurisprudence.

Where we differ from the dissent is in its apparent rejection of the theorem that the whole includes all of its parts—its view that a general conferral of rulemaking authority does not validate rules for *all* the matters the agency is charged with administering. Rather, the dissent proposes that even when general rulemaking authority is clear, *every* agency rule must be subjected to a *de novo* judicial determination of whether *the particular issue* was committed to agency discretion. It offers no standards at all to guide this open-ended hunt for congressional intent (that is to say, for evidence of congressional intent more specific than the conferral of general rulemaking authority). It would simply punt that question back to the Court of Appeals, presumably for application of some sort of totality-of-the-circumstances test—which is really, of course, not a test at all but an invitation to make an ad hoc judgment regarding congressional intent. Thirteen Courts of Appeals applying a totality-of-the-circumstances test would render the binding effect of agency rules unpredictable and destroy the whole stabilizing purpose of *Chevron*. The excessive agency power that the dissent fears would be replaced by chaos. There is no need to wade into these murky waters. It suffices to decide this case that the preconditions to deference under *Chevron* are satisfied because Congress has unambiguously vested the FCC with general authority to administer the Communications Act through rulemaking and adjudication, and the agency interpretation at issue was promulgated in the exercise of that authority.

Id. at 1873–74.

Three (at the very least) points to ponder about this decision: First, although the Court clearly took the case in order to resolve a deep, long-standing circuit split about whether "jurisdictional" agency interpretations receive *Chevron* deference, isn't the majority correct that the dissent is not defending that line? Instead, isn't the argument really about how to apply *Mead*? The dissenters—joined in this respect by Justice Breyer—appear to want a case-by-case, statute-by-statute, provision-by-provision assessment of whether Congress intended to grant interpretative deference to the agency on the particular question involved, with courts conducting de novo review of that issue. The majority is content to allow a general grant of authority, such as the provision empowering the FCC to implement its statutory mandates by prescribing "such rules and regulations as may be necessary in the public interest," 47 U.S.C. § 201(b) (2012), to serve as a blanket source of authority for *Chevron* deference. Presumably, the majority is fine with de novo review within that sphere; under any standard of review, no one doubts that general rulemaking authorizations mean what they say. If those general authorizations are sufficient to constitute the evidence of congressional intent to delegate demanded by *Mead,* agencies with such general authority will almost always find their interpretations falling within *Chevron* (assuming that the more particularized preconditions for *Chevron*, such as administering the statute, or perhaps solely administering the statute, are satisfied). Has Justice Scalia thus avulsively changed what in 2001 he termed *Mead's* "avulsive change in judicial review of federal administrative action"? Or has that always been the law even after *Mead,* and does the dissent essentially agree with the majority on this point by declaring that "[a] general delegation to the agency to administer the statute will often suffice to satisfy the court that Congress has delegated interpretive authority over the ambiguity at issue"? If the dissent believes that last statement, what exactly did it want the Fifth Circuit to determine on remand?

Second, recall from Chapter 1 that the Fifth Circuit held that the agency action in this case was *not* an exercise of rulemaking authority but was instead adjudication—a holding that was necessary to sustain the agency action because of the absence of notice-and-comment procedures accompanying the agency's Clarifying Ruling. *See supra* pages 69–71. (The parties did not seek certiorari on that aspect of the Fifth Circuit's decision.) Observe that former Administrative Law professor Scalia, along with former Administrative Law professors Breyer and Kagan, assumed without discussion that the agency *must* have exercised rulemaking authority in this case—because of course to a person well-versed in administrative law doctrine the Clarifying Ruling cannot sensibly be understood as anything other than a rule. The majority distinguished this case from *Mead* because "*Mead* denied *Chevron* deference to action, by an agency with rulemaking authority, that was not rulemaking." But isn't that exactly this case, given that the parties did not challenge the Fifth Circuit's characterization of the agency action as adjudication? Was the majority opinion therefore wrong, because even if the FCC's general rulemaking authority is enough to bring *Chevron* into play, the agency interpretation in this instance was not "promulgated in the exercise of that authority"? Did the petitioning cities ask for certiorari on the wrong question?

Third, has there ever been in a modern Supreme Court opinion anything like the attack on the administrative state seen in Chief Justice Roberts' dissent? Is Chief Justice Roberts right that the considerations that he raises are an important part of the "background" against which issues like the one in this case should be addressed?

For a thorough and perceptive (and, as it happened, prescient) treatment of many of the issues surrounding the scope of *Chevron*, see Thomas W. Merrill & Kristin E. Hickman, *Chevron's Domain*, 89 Geo. L.J. 833 (2001).

4. HOW CLEAR IS "CLEAR"?

Under the two-step formulation of *Chevron*, if Congress "has directly spoken to the precise question at issue * * *, that is the end of the matter; for the court, as well as the agency, must give effect to the unambiguously expressed intent of Congress." 467 U.S. at 842–43. If the statute is ambiguous, however, the court must determine "whether the agency's answer is based on a permissible construction of the statute." *Id.* at 843. This infelicitous formulation[19] is often restated in some variation of the following: if the meaning of the statute is not *clear*, then courts must accept any *reasonable* agency interpretation.

This formulation immediately suggests a very large problem. We saw in Chapter 1 that there is no consensus in the legal system about how to determine the meaning of statutes. *See supra* pages 10–11. If there is no consensus about what it takes to determine a statute's meaning, can there possibly be a consensus about what it takes to determine whether a statute's meaning is *clear*? This is perhaps the most important question in the implementation of *Chevron*, and as yet no case has self-consciously attempted to provide an answer. The foregoing is one of many statements about administrative law remarkable enough to bear repetition: This is perhaps the most important question in the implementation of *Chevron*, and as yet no case has self-consciously attempted to provide an answer. But, as a logical matter, courts *must* be providing at least implicit answers to that question every time that they decide a *Chevron* case. That necessity was evident from the early days of *Chevron*.

DOLE v. UNITED STEELWORKERS OF AMERICA

Supreme Court of the United States, 1990.
494 U.S. 26, 110 S.Ct. 929, 108 L.Ed.2d 23.

JUSTICE BRENNAN delivered the opinion of the Court.

Among the regulatory tools available to Government agencies charged with protecting public health and safety are rules which require regulated entities to disclose information directly to employees, consumers, or others. Disclosure rules protect by providing access to information about what dangers exist and how these dangers can be avoided. Today we decide whether the Office of Management and Budget (OMB) has the authority under the Paperwork Reduction Act of 1980, 44 U.S.C. § 3501 *et seq.*, to review such regulations.

I

In 1983, pursuant to the Occupational Safety and Health Act of 1970 (OSH Act), which authorizes the Department of Labor (DOL) to set health

---

[19] It is not helpful to tell courts to ask whether an agency's construction of a statute is "permissible" unless courts know what agencies are permitted to do.

and safety standards for workplaces, DOL promulgated a hazard communication standard. The standard imposed various requirements on manufacturers aimed at ensuring that their employees were informed of the potential hazards posed by chemicals found at their workplace. Specifically, the standard required chemical manufacturers to label containers of hazardous chemicals with appropriate warnings. "Downstream" manufacturers—commercial purchasers who used the chemicals in their manufacturing plants—were obliged to keep the original labels intact or else transfer the information onto any substitute containers. The standard also required chemical manufacturers to provide "material safety data sheets" to downstream manufacturers. The data sheets were to list the physical characteristics and hazards of each chemical, the symptoms caused by overexposure and any pre-existing medical conditions aggravated by exposure. In addition, the data sheets were to recommend safety precautions and first aid and emergency procedures in case of overexposure, and provide a source for additional information. Both chemical manufacturers and downstream manufacturers were required to make the data sheets available to their employees and to provide training on the dangers of the particular hazardous chemicals found at each workplace.

* * *

* * * [DOL subsequently issued] a revised hazard communication standard that applied to work sites in all sectors of the economy [rather than just the manufacturing sector]. At the same time, DOL submitted the standard to OMB for review of any paperwork requirements. After holding a public hearing, OMB approved all but three of its provisions. OMB rejected a requirement that employees who work at multiemployer sites (such as construction sites) be provided with data sheets describing the hazardous substances to which they were likely to be exposed, through the activities of any of the companies working at the same site. The provision permitted employers either to exchange data sheets and make them available at their home offices or to maintain all relevant data sheets at a central location on the work site. OMB also disapproved a provision exempting consumer products used in the workplace in the same manner, and resulting in the same frequency and duration of exposure, as in normal consumer use. Finally, OMB vetoed an exemption for drugs sold in solid, final form for direct administration to patients.

OMB disapproved these provisions based on its determination that the requirements were not necessary to protect employees. OMB's objection to the exemptions was that they were too narrow, and that the standard, therefore, applied to situations in which disclosure did not benefit employees. DOL disagreed with OMB's assessment, but it published notice that the three provisions were withdrawn. DOL added its reasons for believing that the provisions were necessary, proposed that they be retained, and invited public comment.

* * * [In response to a suit by the respondent union,] the Third Circuit * * * ordered DOL to reinstate the OMB-disapproved provisions. The court reasoned that the provisions represented good-faith compliance by DOL with the court's prior orders, that OMB lacked authority under the Paperwork Reduction Act to disapprove the provisions, and that, therefore, DOL had no legitimate basis for withdrawing them.

Petitioners sought review in this Court. We granted certiorari to answer the important question whether the Paperwork Reduction Act authorizes OMB to review and countermand agency regulations mandating disclosure by regulated entities directly to third parties. We hold that the Paperwork Reduction Act does not give OMB that authority, and therefore affirm.

II

The Paperwork Reduction Act * * * charges OMB with developing uniform policies for efficient information processing, storage, and transmittal systems, both within and among agencies * * *.

The Act prohibits any federal agency from adopting regulations which impose paperwork requirements on the public unless the information is not available to the agency from another source within the Federal Government, and the agency must formulate a plan for tabulating the information in a useful manner. Agencies are also required to minimize the burden on the public to the extent practicable. In addition, the Act institutes a second layer of review by OMB for new paperwork requirements. After an agency has satisfied itself that an instrument for collecting information—termed an "information collection request"—is needed, the agency must submit the request to OMB for approval. If OMB disapproves the request, the agency may not collect the information.

Typical information collection requests include tax forms, Medicare forms, financial loan applications, job applications, questionnaires, compliance reports, and tax or business records. These information requests share at least one characteristic: The information requested is provided to a federal agency, either directly or indirectly. Agencies impose the requirements on private parties in order to generate information to be used by the agency in pursuing some other purpose. For instance, agencies use these information requests in gathering background on a particular subject to develop the expertise with which to devise or fine-tune appropriate regulations, amassing diffuse data for processing into useful statistical form, and monitoring business records and compliance reports for signs or proof of nonfeasance to determine when to initiate enforcement measures.

By contrast, disclosure rules do not result in information being made available for agency personnel to use. The promulgation of a disclosure rule is a final agency action that represents a substantive regulatory choice. An agency charged with protecting employees from hazardous chemicals has a variety of regulatory weapons from which to choose: It can ban the chemical altogether; it can mandate specified safety measures, such as gloves or goggles; or it can require labels or other warnings alerting users to dangers and recommended precautions. An agency chooses to impose a warning requirement because it believes that such a requirement is the least intrusive measure that will sufficiently protect the public, not because the measure is a means of acquiring information useful in performing some other agency function.

No provision of the Act expressly declares whether Congress intended the Paperwork Reduction Act to apply to disclosure rules as well as information-gathering rules. The Act applies to "information collection requests" by a federal agency which are defined as

> "a written report form, application form, schedule, questionnaire, reporting or recordkeeping requirement, collection of information requirement, or other similar method calling for the collection of information." 44 U.S.C. § 3502(11).

"Collection of information," in turn, is defined as

> "the obtaining or soliciting of facts or opinions by an agency through the use of written report forms, application forms, schedules, questionnaires, reporting or recordkeeping requirements, or other similar methods calling for either—

> "(A) answers to identical questions posed to, or identical reporting or recordkeeping requirements imposed on, ten or more persons, other than agencies, instrumentalities, or employees of the United States; or

> "(B) answers to questions posed to agencies, instrumentalities, or employees of the United States which are to be used for general statistical purposes." 44 U.S.C. § 3502(4).

Petitioners urge us to read the words "obtaining or soliciting of facts by an agency through . . . reporting or recordkeeping requirements" as encompassing disclosure rules * * *. We believe, however, that the language, structure, and purpose of the Paperwork Reduction Act reveal that petitioners' position is untenable because Congress did not intend the Act to encompass these or any other third-party disclosure rules.

"On a pure question of statutory construction, our first job is to try to determine congressional intent, using traditional tools of statutory construction." *NLRB v. Food and Commercial Workers*, 484 U.S. 112, 123, 108 S.Ct. 413, 421, 98 L.Ed.2d 429 (1987). Our "starting point is the language of the statute," *Schreiber v. Burlington Northern, Inc.*, 472 U.S. 1, 5, 105 S.Ct. 2458, 2461, 86 L.Ed.2d 1 (1985), but " 'in expounding a statute, we are not guided by a single sentence or member of a sentence, but look to the provisions of the whole law, and to its object and policy.' " *Massachusetts v. Morash*, 490 U.S. 107, 115, 109 S.Ct. 1668, 1673, 104 L.Ed.2d 98 (1989), quoting *Pilot Life Ins. Co. v. Dedeaux*, 481 U.S. 41, 51, 107 S.Ct. 1549, 1555, 95 L.Ed.2d 39 (1987).

Petitioners' interpretation of "obtaining or soliciting facts by an agency through . . . reporting or recordkeeping requirements" is not the most natural reading of this language. The commonsense view of "obtaining or soliciting facts *by an agency*" is that the phrase refers to an agency's efforts to gather facts for its own use and that Congress used the word "solicit" in addition to the word "obtain" in order to cover information requests that rely on the voluntary cooperation of information suppliers as well as rules which make compliance mandatory. Similarly, data sheets consisting of advisory material on health and safety do not fall within the normal meaning of "records," and a Government-imposed reporting requirement customarily requires reports to be made to the Government, not training and labels to be given to someone else altogether.

That a more limited reading of the phrase "reporting and recordkeeping requirements" was intended derives some further support from the words surrounding it. The traditional canon of construction, *noscitur a sociis*, dictates that " 'words grouped in a list should be given related meaning.' "*Massachusetts v. Morash, supra*, 490 U.S., at 114–115, 109 S.Ct., at 1673, quoting *Schreiber, supra*, 472 U.S., at 8, 105 S.Ct., at 2462. The other examples listed in the definitions of "information collection request" and "collection of information" are forms for communicating information to the party requesting that information. If "reporting and recordkeeping requirements" is understood to be analogous to the examples surrounding it, the phrase would comprise only rules requiring information to be sent or made available to a federal agency, not disclosure rules.

The same conclusion is produced by a consideration of the object and structure of the Act as a whole. Particularly useful is the provision detailing Congress' purposes in enacting the statute. The Act declares that its purposes are:

> "(1) to minimize the Federal paperwork burden for individuals, small businesses, State and local governments, and other persons;

> "(2) to minimize the cost *to the Federal Government* of collecting, maintaining, using, and disseminating information;

> "(3) to maximize the usefulness of information collected, maintained, and disseminated *by the Federal Government*;

"(4)   to coordinate, integrate and, to the extent practicable and appropriate, make uniform Federal information policies and practices;

"(5)   to ensure that automatic data processing, telecommunications, and other information technologies are acquired and used by the Federal Government in a manner which improves service delivery and program management, increases productivity, improves the quality of decisionmaking, reduces waste and fraud, and wherever practicable and appropriate, reduces the information processing burden for the Federal Government and *for persons who provide information to and for the Federal Government*; and

"(6)   to ensure that the collection, maintenance, use and dissemination of information *by the Federal Government* is consistent with applicable laws relating to confidentiality, including . . . the Privacy Act." 44 U.S.C. § 3501 (emphasis added).

Disclosure rules present none of the problems Congress sought to solve through the Paperwork Reduction Act, and none of Congress' enumerated purposes would be served by subjecting disclosure rules to the provisions of the Act. The statute makes clear that the first purpose—avoiding a burden on private parties and state and local governments—refers to avoiding "the time, effort, or financial resources expended by persons to provide information *to a Federal agency*." 44 U.S.C. § 3502(3) (defining "burden") (emphasis added). Because Congress expressed concern only for the burden imposed by requirements to provide information to a federal agency, and not for any burden imposed by requirements to provide information to a third party, OMB review of disclosure rules would not further this congressional aim.

Congress' second purpose—minimizing the Federal Government's cost of handling information—also would not be advanced by review of disclosure rules because such rules do not impose any information processing costs on the Federal Government. Because the Federal Government is not the consumer of information "requested" by a disclosure rule nor an intermediary in its dissemination, OMB review of disclosure rules would not serve Congress' third, fourth, fifth, or sixth purposes. Thus, nothing in Congress' itemized and exhaustive textual description of its reasons for enacting this particular Act indicates any legislative purpose to have OMB screen proposed disclosure rules. We find this to be strong evidence that Congress did not intend the Act to authorize OMB review of such regulations.

This conclusion is buttressed by the language and import of other provisions of the Act * * *. [The Court examines, at considerable length, three other provisions of the statute that suggest that only information provided to the government is covered.]

* * *

III

* * *

Petitioners rely on statements from various stages of the Act's legislative history as evidence that Congress intended "collection of information" to include disclosure rules. However, the statements show merely that the Act was intended to reach not only statistical compilations but also information collected for law enforcement purposes and information filed with an agency for possible dissemination to the public (*i.e.*, when the agency is an intermediary in the process of data dissemination). This sheds no light on the issue before this Court: Whether the Act reaches rules mandating disclosure by one party directly to a third party. Moreover, other statements in the committee reports reinforce respondents' position.

Because we find that the statute, as a whole, clearly expresses Congress' intention, we decline to defer to OMB's interpretation. See *Board of Governors of the Federal Reserve System v. Dimension Financial Corp.*, 474 U.S. 361, 368, 106 S.Ct. 681, 686, 88 L.Ed.2d 691 (1986) ("The traditional deference courts pay to agency interpretation is not to be applied to alter the clearly expressed intent of Congress"); *Chevron U.S.A., Inc. v. Natural Resources Defense Council, Inc.*, 467 U.S. 837, 842–843, 104 S.Ct. 2778, 2781–2782, 81 L.Ed.2d 694 (1984) ("If the intent of Congress is clear, that is the end of the matter"). We affirm the judgment of the Third Circuit insofar as it held that the Paperwork Reduction Act does not give OMB the authority to review agency rules mandating disclosure by regulated entities to third parties.

It is so ordered.

JUSTICE WHITE, with whom the CHIEF JUSTICE joins, dissenting.

The Court's opinion today requires more than 10 pages, including a review of numerous statutory provisions and legislative history, to conclude that the Paperwork Reduction Act of 1980 (PRA or Act) is clear and unambiguous on the question whether it applies to agency directives to private parties to collect specified information and disseminate or make it available to third parties. On the basis of that questionable conclusion, the Court refuses to give *any* deference to the Office of Management and Budget's (OMB's) longstanding and consistently applied interpretation that such requirements fall within the Act's scope. Because in my view the Act is not clear in that regard and deference is due OMB under *Chevron U.S.A., Inc. v. Natural Resources Defense Council, Inc.*, 467 U.S. 837, 104 S.Ct. 2778, 81 L.Ed.2d 694 (1984), I respectfully dissent.

* * *

As the Court acknowledges, there is no question in this case that OMB is the agency charged with administering the PRA. Unless Congress has directly spoken to the issue whether an agency request that private parties disclose to, or maintain for, third parties information such as material safety data sheets (MSDS's) is an "information collection request" or a "recordkeeping requirement" within the Act's scope, OMB's interpretation of the Act is entitled to deference, provided of course that it is based on a permissible construction of the statute.

The Court concedes that the Act does not expressly address "whether Congress intended the Paperwork Reduction Act to apply to disclosure rules as well as information-gathering rules." Curiously, the Court then almost immediately asserts that interpreting the Act to provide coverage for disclosure requests is untenable. The plain language of the Act, however, suggests the contrary. Indeed, the Court appears to acknowledge that petitioners' interpretation of the Act, although not the one the Court prefers, is nonetheless reasonable: "Petitioners' interpretation . . . is not the *most* natural reading of this language." (emphasis added). The Court goes on to arrive at what it believes is the *most* reasonable of plausible interpretations; it cannot rationally conclude that its interpretation is the *only* one that Congress could possibly have intended. The Court neglects to even mention that the only other Court of Appeals besides the Third Circuit in this case to address a similar question rejected the interpretation that the Court now adopts. In addition, there is evidence that for years OMB has been reviewing proposals similar to the standard at issue in this case routinely and without objection from other agencies. As I see it, by independently construing the statute rather than asking if the agency's interpretation is a permissible one and deferring to it if that is the case, the Court's approach is clearly contrary to *Chevron*.

PAULEY v. BETHENERGY MINES, INC.

Supreme Court of the United States, 1991.
501 U.S. 680, 111 S.Ct. 2524, 115 L.Ed.2d 604.

JUSTICE BLACKMUN delivered the opinion of the Court.

The black lung benefits program, created by Congress, was to be administered first by the Social Security Administration (SSA) under the auspices of the then-existent Department of Health, Education, and Welfare (HEW), and later by the Department of Labor (DOL). Congress authorized these Departments, during their respective tenures, to adopt interim regulations governing the adjudication of claims for black lung benefits, but constrained the Secretary of Labor by providing that the DOL regulations "shall not be more restrictive than" HEW's. This litigation calls upon us to determine whether the Secretary of Labor has complied with that constraint.

* * *

[The Federal Coal Mine Health and Safety Act of 1969 (FCMHSA) provides benefits to coal miners and their dependents for disabilities resulting from pneumoconiosis, or so-called "black lung disease." The statute, and the numerous regulations that have been promulgated under it, establish the means by which miners prove that their disabilities can be attributed, wholly or partially, to pneumoconiosis. The usual mode of proof is through one or more statutory or regulatory presumptions that give rise to an inference of pneumoconiosis upon a showing, for example, of an x-ray indicating pneumoconiosis or of the presence of certain respiratory illnesses after more than fifteen years of coal mining. Once a presumption of disability from pneumoconiosis was established, regulations from HEW which were applicable to claims filed before June 30, 1973 ("Part B claims") permitted rebuttal of that presumption "upon a showing that the miner is doing his usual coal mine work or comparable and gainful work, or is capable of doing such work."

The Black Lung Benefits Reform Act of 1977 (BLBRA) expanded in some ways the methods by which miners could establish eligibility for benefits. The statute also authorized the DOL to promulgate regulations for processing claims filed after June 30, 1973 but before March 31, 1980 ("Part C claims"), with the proviso that the "[c]riteria applied by the Secretary of Labor . . . shall not be more restrictive than the criteria applicable to a claim filed on June 30, 1973."

Under the DOL regulations, it was easier for miners to invoke a presumption of pneumoconiosis than it was under the HEW regulations. But it was also, at least arguably, easier for the Social Security Administration, the agency administering the benefits program, to rebut the presumption once it is established.]

* * * [T]he DOL interim regulations provide four methods for rebutting the presumptions * * *. Two of the rebuttal provisions mimic those in the HEW regulations, permitting rebuttal upon a showing that the miner is performing, or is able to perform, his coal mining or comparable work. The other two rebuttal provisions are at issue in these cases. Under these provisions, a presumption of total disability due to pneumoconiosis can be rebutted if "[t]he evidence establishes that the total disability or death of the miner did not arise in whole or in part out of coal mine employment," or if "[t]he evidence establishes that the miner does not, or did not, have pneumoconiosis."

* * *

* * * [W]e must determine whether the third and fourth rebuttal provisions in the DOL regulations render the DOL regulations more restrictive than were the HEW regulations. These provisions permit rebuttal of the presumption of eligibility upon a showing that the miner's disability did not arise in whole or in part out of coal mine employment or that the miner does not have pneumoconiosis.

* * *

In the BLBRA, Congress specifically constrained the Secretary of Labor's discretion through the directive that the criteria applied to part C claims could "not be more restrictive than" that applied to part B claims. 30 U.S.C. § 902(f)(2). The claimants and the dissent urge that this restriction is unambiguous, and that no deference is due the Secretary's determination that her interim regulations are not more restrictive than HEW's * * *.

Judicial deference to an agency's interpretation of ambiguous provisions of the statutes it is authorized to implement reflects a sensitivity to the proper roles of the political and judicial branches. *See Chevron U.S.A., Inc. v. Natural Resources Defense Council, Inc.*, 467 U.S. 837, 866, 104 S.Ct. 2778, 2793, 81 L.Ed.2d 694 (1984) * * *. When Congress, through express delegation or the introduction of an interpretive gap in the statutory structure, has delegated policy-making authority to an administrative agency, the extent of judicial review of the agency's policy determinations is limited.

It is precisely this recognition that informs our determination that deference to the Secretary is appropriate here. The Benefits Act has produced a complex and highly technical regulatory program. The identification and classification of medical eligibility criteria necessarily require significant expertise and entail the exercise of judgment grounded in policy concerns. In those circumstances, courts appropriately defer to the agency entrusted by Congress to make such policy determinations.

* * *

Having determined that the Secretary's position is entitled to deference, we must decide whether this position is reasonable. *See Chevron*, 467 U.S., at 845, 104 S.Ct., at 2783. The claimants and the dissent argue that this issue can be resolved simply by comparing the two interim regulations. This argument is straightforward; it reasons that the mere existence of regulatory provisions permitting rebuttal of statutory elements not rebuttable under the HEW interim regulations renders the DOL interim regulations more restrictive than HEW's and, as a consequence, renders the Secretary's interpretation unreasonable. Specifically, the claimants and the dissent assert that the HEW interim regulations plainly contain no provision, either in the invocation subsection or in the rebuttal subsection, that directs factual inquiry into the issue of disability causation or the existence of pneumoconiosis. Accordingly, under the claimants' reading of the regulations, there is no manner in which the DOL interim regulations can be seen to be "not . . . more restrictive than" the HEW regulations.

The regulatory scheme, however, is not so straightforward as the claimants would make it out to be. We have noted before the Byzantine character of these regulations. In our view, the Secretary presents the more reasoned interpretation of this complex regulatory structure, an interpretation that has the additional benefit of providing coherence among the statute and the two interim regulations.

The premise underlying the Secretary's interpretation of the HEW interim regulations is that the regulations were adopted to ensure that miners who were disabled due to pneumoconiosis arising out of coal mine employment would receive benefits from the black lung program. Under the Secretary's view, it disserves congressional intent to interpret HEW's interim regulations to allow recovery by miners who do not have pneumoconiosis or whose total disability did not arise, at least in part, from their coal mine employment. We agree.

[In a lengthy analysis—much of which is simply a description of the competing arguments—the Court upholds the DOL's interpretation as reasonable. In the course of that discussion, the Court observed: "While it is possible that the claimants' parsing of these impenetrable regulations would be consistent with accepted canons of construction, it is axiomatic that the Secretary's interpretation need not be the best or most natural one by grammatical or other standards."]

* * *

JUSTICE KENNEDY took no part in the consideration or decision of this litigation.

JUSTICE SCALIA, dissenting.

I respectfully dissent. The disputed regulatory language is complex, but it is not ambiguous, and I do not think *Chevron* deference requires us to accept the strained and implausible construction advanced by the Department of Labor (DOL) * * *.

* * *

As an initial matter, the Court misconstrues our *Chevron* jurisprudence. *Chevron* requires that we defer to an agency's interpretation of its organic statute once we determine that that statute is ambiguous. No one contends that the relevant *statutory* language ("shall not be more restrictive than") is ambiguous. The only serious question surrounds the regulations of the then-extant Department of Health, Education, and

Welfare (HEW) to which the statute refers. I agree that those regulations are complex, perhaps even "Byzantine," but that alone is insufficient to invoke *Chevron* deference. Deference is appropriate where the relevant language, carefully considered, can yield more than one reasonable interpretation, not where discerning the only possible interpretation requires a taxing inquiry. *Chevron* is a recognition that the ambiguities in statutes are to be resolved by the agencies charged with implementing them, not a declaration that, when statutory construction becomes difficult, we will throw up our hands and let regulatory agencies do it for us. In my view the HEW regulations referred to by the present statute are susceptible of only one meaning, although they are so intricate that that meaning is not immediately accessible.

* * *

The relationship between the * * * [HEW and DOL] regulations is apparent because they use a similar structure and, in large part, similar language. Both allow claimants to invoke a presumption of disability due to pneumoconiosis upon the presentation of certain medical evidence (the HEW regulations provide for two types of medical evidence while the DOL regulations provide for four). Both specify certain ways in which that presumption may be rebutted. The HEW regulations, however, specify only two methods of rebuttal (both relating to the extent of the disability), while the DOL regulations authorize four methods (the two expressed in the HEW regulations plus two more: (1) that pneumoconiosis did not cause the disability, and (2) that the miner does not have pneumoconiosis).

Obviously, if the DOL regulations provide more opportunities for rebuttal, they are less favorable to claimants. I think it quite apparent that they do. The present case is illustrative. Claimant Pauley invoked the presumption by submitting X-ray evidence of pneumoconiosis * * *. BethEnergy, the employer, rebutted the presumption by arguing * * * that although Pauley had pneumoconiosis it did not cause his disability. Had the case proceeded under the HEW regulations, Pauley's presentation would have been the same * * *. For BethEnergy, however, things would have been different * * *. The only rebuttal expressly contemplated by the HEW regulations is that the claimant is not in fact disabled—but Pauley concededly was. It appears, therefore, that BethEnergy could not have challenged the causal link between the pneumoconiosis and the disability under the HEW regulations and thus would have had no defense.

In my view this argument is self-evidently correct and is obscured only by the technical complexity of the regulatory provisions. But the statutory *structure*, as opposed to the actual language, is simple. Under the HEW regulations, we assume "x," but "x" may be rebutted by a showing of "a" or "b." Under the DOL regulations, we likewise assume "x," but "x" may be rebutted by a showing of "a" or "b" *or* "c" *or* "d." It defies common sense to argue that, given this structure, the two regulations are in fact identical, and that Pauley, whose claim could be defeated by a showing of "c" but not by a showing of "a" or "b," was no worse off under the latter regime. Yet that is precisely the argument the Court accepts.

* * *

NOTES

Dole and Pauley reflect quite different understandings of what it means for a statute to be "clear." At a minimum, Pauley (and Justice White's dissent in Dole) suggest that clarity has something to do with the degree of effort required to find meaning, while Dole (and Justice Scalia's dissent in Pauley) suggest that clarity is a function, not of the effort required to find a meaning, but of the confidence that one has in the meaning that one ultimately finds. Put another way, Dole seems to understand clarity in terms of the *degree of certainty* that one can have in an answer to a question of statutory meaning, while Pauley seems to define clarity in terms of the *obviousness* of the answer. Consider whether the next case, which was one of the most high-profile administrative law case of recent times, resolves—or even recognizes—that underlying clash.

FDA v. BROWN & WILLIAMSON TOBACCO CORP.

Supreme Court of the United States, 2000.
529 U.S. 120, 120 S.Ct. 1291, 146 L.Ed.2d 121.

JUSTICE O'CONNOR delivered the opinion of the Court.

This case involves one of the most troubling public health problems facing our Nation today: the thousands of premature deaths that occur each year because of tobacco use. In 1996, the Food and Drug Administration (FDA), after having expressly disavowed any such authority since its inception, asserted jurisdiction to regulate tobacco products. The FDA concluded that nicotine is a "drug" within the meaning of the Food, Drug, and Cosmetic Act (FDCA or Act) and that cigarettes and smokeless tobacco are "combination products" that deliver nicotine to the body. 61 Fed.Reg. 44397 (1996). Pursuant to this authority, it promulgated regulations intended to reduce tobacco consumption among children and adolescents. The agency believed that, because most tobacco consumers begin their use before reaching the age of 18, curbing tobacco use by minors could substantially reduce the prevalence of addiction in future generations and thus the incidence of tobacco-related death and disease.

Regardless of how serious the problem an administrative agency seeks to address, however, it may not exercise its authority "in a manner that is inconsistent with the administrative structure that Congress enacted into law." *ETSI Pipeline Project v. Missouri*, 484 U.S. 495, 517, 108 S.Ct. 805, 98 L.Ed.2d 898 (1988). And although agencies are generally entitled to deference in the interpretation of statutes that they administer, a reviewing "court, as well as the agency, must give effect to the unambiguously expressed intent of Congress." *Chevron U.S.A., Inc. v. Natural Resources Defense Council, Inc.*, 467 U.S. 837, 842–843, 104 S.Ct. 2778, 81 L.Ed.2d 694 (1984). In this case, we believe that Congress has clearly precluded the FDA from asserting jurisdiction to regulate tobacco products. Such authority is inconsistent with the intent that Congress has expressed in the FDCA's overall regulatory scheme and in the tobacco-specific legislation that it has enacted subsequent to the FDCA. In light of this clear intent, the FDA's assertion of jurisdiction is impermissible.

I

The FDCA grants the FDA, as the designee of the Secretary of Health and Human Services, the authority to regulate, among other items, "drugs" and "devices." See 21 U.S.C. §§ 321(g)–(h), 393 (1994 ed. and Supp. III). The Act defines "drug" to include "articles (other than food) intended to affect the structure or any function of the body." 21 U.S.C. § 321(g)(1)(C). It defines "device," in part, as "an instrument, apparatus, implement, machine, contrivance, . . . or other similar or related article, including any component, part, or accessory, which is . . . intended to affect the structure or any function of the body." § 321(h). The Act also grants the FDA the authority to regulate so-called "combination products," which "constitute a combination of a drug, device, or biologic product." § 353(g)(1). The FDA has construed this provision as giving it the discretion to regulate combination products as drugs, as devices, or as both.

On August 11, 1995, the FDA published a proposed rule concerning the sale of cigarettes and smokeless tobacco to children and adolescents * * *. A public comment period followed, during which the FDA received over 700,000 submissions, more than "at any other time in its history on any other subject." 61 Fed.Reg. 44418 (1996).

On August 28, 1996, the FDA issued a final rule * * *. The FDA determined that nicotine is a "drug" and that cigarettes and smokeless tobacco are "drug delivery devices," and therefore it had jurisdiction under the FDCA to regulate tobacco products as customarily marketed—that is, without manufacturer claims of therapeutic benefit. First, the FDA found that tobacco products " 'affect the structure or any function of the body' " because nicotine "has significant pharmacological effects." *Id.*, at 44631. Specifically, nicotine "exerts psychoactive, or mood-altering, effects on the brain" that cause and sustain addiction, have both tranquilizing and stimulating effects, and control weight. *Id.*, at 44631–44632. Second, the FDA determined that these effects were "intended" under the FDCA because they "are so widely known and foreseeable that [they] may be deemed to have been intended by the manufacturers," *id.*, at 44687 * * *. Finally, the agency concluded that cigarettes and smokeless tobacco are "combination products" because, in addition to containing nicotine, they include device components that deliver a controlled amount of nicotine to the body.

Having resolved the jurisdictional question, the FDA next explained the policy justifications for its regulations, detailing the deleterious health effects associated with tobacco use. It found that tobacco consumption was "the single leading cause of preventable death in the United States." *Id.*, at 44398. According to the FDA, "[m]ore than 400,000 people die each year from tobacco-related illnesses, such as cancer, respiratory illnesses, and heart disease." *Ibid.* The agency also determined that the only way to reduce the amount of tobacco-related illness and mortality was to reduce the level of addiction, a goal that could be accomplished only by preventing children and adolescents from starting to use tobacco * * *.

Based on these findings, the FDA promulgated regulations concerning tobacco products' promotion, labeling, and accessibility to children and adolescents. The access regulations prohibit the sale of cigarettes or smokeless tobacco to persons younger than 18; require retailers to verify through photo identification the age of all purchasers younger than 27; prohibit the sale of cigarettes in quantities smaller than 20; prohibit the distribution of free samples; and prohibit sales through self-service displays and vending machines except in adult-only locations. The promotion regulations require that any print advertising appear in a black-and-white, text-only format unless the publication in which it appears is read almost exclusively by adults; prohibit outdoor advertising within 1,000 feet of any public playground or school; prohibit the distribution of any promotional items, such as T-shirts or hats, bearing the manufacturer's brand name; and prohibit a manufacturer from sponsoring any athletic, musical, artistic, or other social or cultural event using its brand name. The labeling regulation requires that the statement, "A Nicotine-Delivery Device for Persons 18 or Older," appear on all tobacco product packages.

The FDA promulgated these regulations pursuant to its authority to regulate "restricted devices." See 21 U.S.C. § 360j(e). The FDA construed § 353(g)(1) as giving it the discretion to regulate "combination products" using the Act's drug authorities, device authorities, or both, depending on "how the public health goals of the act can be best accomplished." 61 Fed.Reg. 44403 (1996). Given the greater flexibility in the FDCA for the regulation of devices, the FDA determined that "the device authorities provide the most appropriate basis for regulating cigarettes and smokeless tobacco." *Id.*, at 44404. Under 21 U.S.C. § 360j(e), the agency may "require that a device be restricted to sale, distribution, or use . . . upon such other conditions as [the FDA] may prescribe in such regulation, if, because of its potentiality for harmful effect or the collateral measures necessary to its use, [the FDA] determines that there cannot otherwise be reasonable assurance of its safety and effectiveness." The FDA reasoned that its regulations fell within the authority granted by § 360j(e) because they related to the sale or distribution of tobacco products and were necessary for providing a reasonable assurance of safety.

Respondents, a group of tobacco manufacturers, retailers, and advertisers, filed suit in United States District Court for the Middle District of North Carolina challenging the regulations * * *. The [district] court held that the FDCA authorizes the FDA to regulate tobacco products as customarily marketed and that the FDA's access and labeling regulations are permissible, but it also found that the agency's advertising and promotion restrictions exceed its authority under § 360j(e) * * *.

The Court of Appeals for the Fourth Circuit reversed, holding that Congress has not granted the FDA jurisdiction to regulate tobacco products * * *.

We granted the Government's petition for certiorari to determine whether the FDA has authority under the FDCA to regulate tobacco products as customarily marketed.

II

The FDA's assertion of jurisdiction to regulate tobacco products * * * contravenes the clear intent of Congress.

A threshold issue is the appropriate framework for analyzing the FDA's assertion of authority to regulate tobacco products. Because this case involves an administrative agency's construction of a statute that it administers, our analysis is governed by *Chevron U.S.A., Inc. v. Natural Resources Defense Council, Inc.*, 467 U.S. 837, 104 S.Ct. 2778, 81 L.Ed.2d 694 (1984). Under *Chevron*, a reviewing court must first ask "whether Congress has directly spoken to the precise question at issue." *Id.*, at 842, 104 S.Ct. 2778. If Congress has done so, the inquiry is at an end; the court "must give effect to the unambiguously expressed intent of Congress." *Id.*, at 843, 104 S.Ct. 2778. But if Congress has not specifically addressed the question, a reviewing court must respect the agency's construction of the statute so long as it is permissible. Such deference is justified because "[t]he responsibilities for assessing the wisdom of such policy choices and resolving the struggle between competing views of the public interest are not judicial ones," *Chevron, supra*, at 866, 104 S.Ct. 2778, and because of the agency's greater familiarity with the ever-changing facts and circumstances surrounding the subjects regulated.

In determining whether Congress has specifically addressed the question at issue, a reviewing court should not confine itself to examining a particular statutory provision in isolation. The meaning—or ambiguity—of certain words or phrases may only become evident when placed in context * * *. A court must therefore interpret the statute "as a symmetrical and coherent regulatory scheme," *Gustafson v. Alloyd Co.*, 513 U.S. 561, 569, 115 S.Ct. 1061, 131 L.Ed.2d 1 (1995), and "fit, if possible, all parts into an harmonious whole," *FTC v. Mandel Brothers, Inc.*, 359 U.S. 385, 389, 79 S.Ct. 818, 3 L.Ed.2d 893 (1959). Similarly, the meaning of one statute may be affected by other Acts, particularly where Congress has spoken subsequently and more specifically to the topic at hand. In addition, we must be guided to a degree by common sense as to the manner in which Congress is likely to delegate a policy decision of such economic and political magnitude to an administrative agency.

With these principles in mind, we find that Congress has directly spoken to the issue here and precluded the FDA's jurisdiction to regulate tobacco products.

A

Viewing the FDCA as a whole, it is evident that one of the Act's core objectives is to ensure that any product regulated by the FDA is "safe" and "effective" for its intended use * * *. Thus, the Act generally requires the FDA to prevent the marketing of any drug or device where the "potential for inflicting death or physical injury is not offset by the possibility of therapeutic benefit." *United States v. Rutherford*, 442 U.S. 544, 556, 99 S.Ct. 2470, 61 L.Ed.2d 68 (1979).

In its rulemaking proceeding, the FDA quite exhaustively documented that "tobacco products are unsafe," "dangerous," and "cause great pain and suffering from illness." 61 Fed.Reg. 44412 (1996). It found that the consumption of tobacco products "presents extraordinary health risks," and that "tobacco use is the single leading cause of preventable death in the United States." *Id.*, at 44398. It stated that "[m]ore than 400,000 people die each year from tobacco-related illnesses, such as cancer, respiratory illnesses, and heart disease, often suffering long and painful deaths," and that "[t]obacco alone kills more people each year in the United States than acquired immunodeficiency syndrome (AIDS), car accidents, alcohol, homicides, illegal drugs, suicides, and fires, combined." *Ibid.* * * *.

These findings logically imply that, if tobacco products were "devices" under the FDCA, the FDA would be required to remove them from the market. Consider, first, the FDCA's provisions concerning the misbranding of drugs or devices. The Act prohibits "[t]he introduction or delivery for introduction into interstate commerce of any food, drug, device, or cosmetic that is adultered or misbranded." 21 U.S.C. § 331(a). In light of the FDA's findings, two distinct FDCA provisions would render cigarettes and smokeless tobacco misbranded devices. First, § 352(j) deems a drug or device misbranded "[i]f it is dangerous to health when used in the dosage or manner, or with the frequency or duration prescribed, recommended, or suggested in the labeling thereof." The FDA's findings make clear that tobacco products are "dangerous to health" when used in the manner prescribed. Second, a drug or device is misbranded under the Act "[u]nless its labeling bears . . . adequate directions for use . . . in such manner and form, as are necessary for the protection of users," except where such directions are "not necessary for the protection of the public health." § 352(f)(1). Given the FDA's conclusions concerning the health consequences of tobacco use, there are no directions that could adequately protect consumers. That is, there are no directions that could make tobacco products safe for obtaining their intended effects. Thus, were tobacco products within the FDA's jurisdiction, the Act would deem them misbranded devices that could not be introduced into interstate commerce. Contrary to the dissent's contention, the Act admits no remedial discretion once it is evident that the device is misbranded.

Second, the FDCA requires the FDA to place all devices that it regulates into one of three classifications. See § 360c(b)(1). The agency relies on a device's classification in determining the degree of control and regulation necessary to ensure that there is "a reasonable assurance of safety and effectiveness." 61 Fed.Reg. 44412 (1996). The FDA has yet to classify tobacco products. Instead, the regulations at issue here represent so-called "general controls," which the Act entitles the agency to impose in advance of classification. Although the FDCA prescribes no deadline for device classification, the FDA has stated that it will classify tobacco products "in a future rulemaking" as required by the Act. *Id.*, at 44412. Given the FDA's findings regarding the health consequences of tobacco use, the agency would have to place cigarettes and smokeless tobacco in Class III because, even after the application of the Act's available controls, they would "presen[t] a potential unreasonable risk of illness or injury." 21 U.S.C. § 360c(a)(1)(C). As Class III devices, tobacco products would be subject to the FDCA's premarket approval process. Under these provisions, the FDA would be prohibited from approving an application for premarket approval without "a showing of reasonable assurance that such device is safe under the conditions of use prescribed, recommended, or suggested on the labeling thereof." 21 U.S.C. § 360e(d)(2)(A). In view of the FDA's conclusions regarding the health effects of tobacco use, the agency would have no basis for finding any such reasonable assurance of safety. Thus, once the FDA fulfilled its statutory obligation to classify tobacco products, it could not allow them to be marketed.

The FDCA's misbranding and device classification provisions therefore make evident that were the FDA to regulate cigarettes and smokeless tobacco, the Act would require the agency to ban them. In fact, based on these provisions, the FDA itself has previously taken the position that if tobacco products were within its jurisdiction, "they would have to be removed from the market because it would be impossible to prove they were safe for their intended us[e]." Public Health Cigarette Amendments of

1971: Hearings before the Commerce Subcommittee on S. 1454, 92d Cong., 2d Sess., 239 (1972) (statement of FDA Commissioner Charles Edwards).

Congress, however, has foreclosed the removal of tobacco products from the market. A provision of the United States Code currently in force states that "[t]he marketing of tobacco constitutes one of the greatest basic industries of the United States with ramifying activities which directly affect interstate and foreign commerce at every point, and stable conditions therein are necessary to the general welfare." 7 U.S.C. § 1311(a). More importantly, Congress has directly addressed the problem of tobacco and health through legislation on six occasions since 1965. When Congress enacted these statutes, the adverse health consequences of tobacco use were well known, as were nicotine's pharmacological effects. Nonetheless, Congress stopped well short of ordering a ban. Instead, it has generally regulated the labeling and advertisement of tobacco products, expressly providing that it is the policy of Congress that "commerce and the national economy may be . . . protected to the maximum extent consistent with" consumers "be[ing] adequately informed about any adverse health effects." 15 U.S.C. § 1331. Congress' decisions * * * reveal its intent that tobacco products remain on the market. Indeed, the collective premise of these statutes is that cigarettes and smokeless tobacco will continue to be sold in the United States. A ban of tobacco products by the FDA would therefore plainly contradict congressional policy.

The FDA apparently recognized this dilemma and concluded, somewhat ironically, that tobacco products are actually "safe" within the meaning of the FDCA. In promulgating its regulations, the agency conceded that "tobacco products are unsafe, as that term is conventionally understood." 61 Fed.Reg. 44412 (1996). Nonetheless, the FDA reasoned that, in determining whether a device is safe under the Act, it must consider "not only the risks presented by a product but also any of the countervailing effects of use of that product, including the consequences of not permitting the product to be marketed." *Id.*, at 44412–44413. Applying this standard, the FDA found that, because of the high level of addiction among tobacco users, a ban would likely be "dangerous." *Id.*, at 44413. In particular, current tobacco users could suffer from extreme withdrawal, the health care system and available pharmaceuticals might not be able to meet the treatment demands of those suffering from withdrawal, and a black market offering cigarettes even more dangerous than those currently sold legally would likely develop. *Ibid.* The FDA therefore concluded that, "while taking cigarettes and smokeless tobacco off the market could prevent some people from becoming addicted and reduce death and disease for others, the record does not establish that such a ban is the appropriate public health response under the act." *Id.*, at 44398.

It may well be, as the FDA asserts, that "these factors must be considered when developing a regulatory scheme that achieves the best public health result for these products." *Id.*, at 44413. But the FDA's judgment that leaving tobacco products on the market "is more effective in achieving public health goals than a ban," *ibid.*, is no substitute for the specific safety determinations required by the FDCA's various operative provisions. Several provisions in the Act require the FDA to determine that the product itself is safe as used by consumers. That is, the product's probable therapeutic benefits must outweigh its risk of harm. In contrast, the FDA's conception of safety would allow the agency, with respect to each provision of the FDCA that requires the agency to determine a product's "safety" or "dangerousness," to compare the aggregate health effects of alternative administrative actions. This is a qualitatively different inquiry. Thus, although the FDA has concluded that a ban would be "dangerous," it has not concluded that tobacco products are "safe" as that term is used throughout the Act.

* * *

Consequently, the analogy made by the FDA and the dissent to highly toxic drugs used in the treatment of various cancers is unpersuasive. Although "dangerous" in some sense, these drugs are safe within the meaning of the Act because, for certain patients, the therapeutic benefits outweigh the risk of harm * * *. The same is not true for tobacco products. As the FDA has documented in great detail, cigarettes and smokeless tobacco are an unsafe means to obtaining any pharmacological effect.

* * * The FDA, consistent with the FDCA, may clearly regulate many "dangerous" products without banning them. Indeed, virtually every drug or device poses dangers under certain conditions. What the FDA may not do is conclude that a drug or device cannot be used safely for any therapeutic purpose and yet, at the same time, allow that product to remain on the market. Such regulation is incompatible with the FDCA's core objective of ensuring that every drug or device is safe and effective.

Considering the FDCA as a whole, it is clear that Congress intended to exclude tobacco products from the FDA's jurisdiction * * *. [I]f tobacco products were within the FDA's jurisdiction, the Act would require the FDA to remove them from the market entirely. But a ban would contradict Congress' clear intent as expressed in its more recent, tobacco-specific legislation. The inescapable conclusion is that there is no room for tobacco products within the FDCA's regulatory scheme. If they cannot be used safely for any therapeutic purpose, and yet they cannot be banned, they simply do not fit.

B

In determining whether Congress has spoken directly to the FDA's authority to regulate tobacco, we must also consider in greater detail the tobacco-specific legislation that Congress has enacted over the past 35 years. At the time a statute is enacted, it may have a range of plausible meanings. Over time, however, subsequent acts can shape or focus those meanings * * *. This is particularly so where the scope of the earlier statute is broad but the subsequent statutes more specifically address the topic at hand * * *.

Congress has enacted six separate pieces of legislation since 1965 addressing the problem of tobacco use and human health * * *. In adopting each statute, Congress has acted against the backdrop of the FDA's consistent and repeated statements that it lacked authority under the FDCA to regulate tobacco absent claims of therapeutic benefit by the manufacturer. In fact, on several occasions over this period, and after the health consequences of tobacco use and nicotine's pharmacological effects had become well known, Congress considered and rejected bills that would have granted the FDA such jurisdiction. Under these circumstances, it is evident that Congress' tobacco-specific statutes have effectively ratified the FDA's long-held position that it lacks jurisdiction under the FDCA to regulate tobacco products. Congress has created a distinct regulatory scheme to address the problem of tobacco and health, and that scheme, as presently constructed, precludes any role for the FDA.

* * *

* * * [O]ur conclusion does not rely on the fact that the FDA's assertion of jurisdiction represents a sharp break with its prior interpretation of the FDCA. Certainly, an agency's initial interpretation of a statute that it is charged with administering is not "carved in stone." *Chevron*, 467 U.S., at 863, 104 S.Ct. 2778. As we recognized in *Motor Vehicle Mfrs. Assn. of United States, Inc. v. State Farm Mut. Automobile Ins. Co.*, 463 U.S. 29, 103 S.Ct. 2856, 77 L.Ed.2d 443 (1983), agencies "must be given ample latitude to 'adapt their rules and policies to the demands of changing circumstances.'" *Id.*, at 42, 103 S.Ct. 2856 (quoting *Permian Basin Area Rate Cases*, 390 U.S. 747, 784, 88 S.Ct. 1344, 20 L.Ed.2d 312 (1968)). The consistency of the FDA's prior position is significant in this case for a different reason: it provides important context to Congress' enactment of its tobacco-specific legislation. When the FDA repeatedly informed Congress that the FDCA does not grant it the authority to regulate tobacco products, its statements were consistent with the agency's unwavering position since its inception, and with the position that its predecessor agency had first taken in 1914. Although not crucial, the consistency of the FDA's prior position bolsters the conclusion that when Congress created a distinct regulatory scheme addressing the subject of tobacco and health, it understood that the FDA is without jurisdiction to regulate tobacco products and ratified that position.

The dissent also argues that the proper inference to be drawn from Congress' tobacco-specific legislation is "critically ambivalent." We disagree. In that series of statutes, Congress crafted a specific legislative response to the problem of tobacco and health, and it did so with the understanding, based on repeated assertions by the FDA, that the agency has no authority under the FDCA to regulate tobacco products. Moreover, Congress expressly preempted any other regulation of the labeling of tobacco products concerning their health consequences, even though the oversight of labeling is central to the FDCA's regulatory scheme. And in addressing the subject, Congress consistently evidenced its intent to preclude any federal agency from exercising significant policymaking authority in the area. Under these circumstances, we believe the appropriate inference—that Congress intended to ratify the FDA's prior position that it lacks jurisdiction—is unmistakable.

* * *

C

Finally, our inquiry into whether Congress has directly spoken to the precise question at issue is shaped, at least in some measure, by the nature of the question presented. Deference under *Chevron* to an agency's construction of a statute that it administers is premised on the theory that a statute's ambiguity constitutes an implicit delegation from Congress to the agency to fill in the statutory gaps. In extraordinary cases, however, there may be reason to hesitate before concluding that Congress has intended such an implicit delegation. This is hardly an ordinary case. Contrary to its representations to Congress since 1914, the FDA has now asserted jurisdiction to regulate an industry constituting a significant portion of the American economy. In fact, the FDA contends that, were it to determine that tobacco products provide no "reasonable assurance of safety," it would have the authority to ban cigarettes and smokeless tobacco entirely. See Brief for Petitioners 35–36; Reply Brief for Petitioners 14. Owing to its unique place in American history and society, tobacco has its own unique political history. Congress, for better or for worse, has created a distinct regulatory scheme for tobacco products, squarely rejected proposals to give the FDA jurisdiction over tobacco, and repeatedly acted to preclude any agency from exercising significant policymaking authority in the area. Given this history and the breadth of the authority that the FDA has asserted, we are obliged to defer not to the agency's expansive construction of the statute, but to Congress' consistent judgment to deny the FDA this power * * *.

* * *

By no means do we question the seriousness of the problem that the FDA has sought to address. The agency has amply demonstrated that tobacco use, particularly among children and adolescents, poses perhaps the single most significant threat to public health in the United States. Nonetheless, no matter how "important, conspicuous, and controversial" the issue, and regardless of how likely the public is to hold the Executive Branch politically accountable, an administrative agency's power to regulate in the public interest must always be grounded in a valid grant of authority from Congress * * *. Reading the FDCA as a whole, as well as in conjunction with Congress' subsequent tobacco-specific legislation, it is plain that Congress has not given the FDA the authority that it seeks to exercise here * * *.

JUSTICE BREYER, with whom JUSTICE STEVENS, JUSTICE SOUTER, and JUSTICE GINSBURG join, dissenting.

The Food and Drug Administration (FDA) has the authority to regulate "articles (other than food) intended to affect the structure or any function of the body. . ." Federal Food, Drug and Cosmetic Act (FDCA), 21 U.S.C. § 321(g)(1)(C). Unlike the majority, I believe that tobacco products fit within this statutory language.

In its own interpretation, the majority nowhere denies the following two salient points. First, tobacco products (including cigarettes) fall within the scope of this statutory definition, read literally * * *.

Second, the statute's basic purpose—the protection of public health— supports the inclusion of cigarettes within its scope * * *.

Despite the FDCA's literal language and general purpose (both of which support the FDA's finding that cigarettes come within its statutory authority), the majority nonetheless reads the statute as excluding tobacco products for two basic reasons:

(1) the FDCA does not "fit" the case of tobacco because the statute requires the FDA to prohibit dangerous drugs or devices (like cigarettes) outright, and the agency concedes that simply banning the sale of cigarettes is not a proper remedy; and

(2) Congress has enacted other statutes, which, when viewed in light of the FDA's long history of denying tobacco-related jurisdiction and considered together with Congress' failure explicitly to grant the agency tobacco-specific authority, demonstrate that Congress did not intend for the FDA to exercise jurisdiction over tobacco.

In my view, neither of these propositions is valid. Rather, the FDCA does not significantly limit the FDA's remedial alternatives. And the later statutes do not tell the FDA it cannot exercise jurisdiction, but simply leave FDA jurisdictional law where Congress found it.

* * * In short, I believe that the most important indicia of statutory meaning—language and purpose—along with the FDCA's legislative history * * * are sufficient to establish that the FDA has authority to regulate tobacco. The statute-specific arguments against jurisdiction that

the tobacco companies and the majority rely upon * * * are based on erroneous assumptions and, thus, do not defeat the jurisdiction-supporting thrust of the FDCA's language and purpose. The inferences that the majority draws from later legislative history are not persuasive, since * * * one can just as easily infer from the later laws that Congress did not intend to affect the FDA's tobacco-related authority at all. And the fact that the FDA changed its mind about the scope of its own jurisdiction is legally insignificant because * * * the agency's reasons for changing course are fully justified. Finally, * * * the degree of accountability that likely will attach to the FDA's action in this case should alleviate any concern that Congress, rather than an administrative agency, ought to make this important regulatory decision.

* * *

The majority nonetheless reaches the "inescapable conclusion" that the language and structure of the FDCA as a whole "simply do not fit" the kind of public health problem that tobacco creates. That is because, in the majority's view, the FDCA requires the FDA to ban outright "dangerous" drugs or devices (such as cigarettes); yet, the FDA concedes that an immediate and total cigarette-sale ban is inappropriate. This argument is curious because it leads with similarly "inescapable" force to precisely the opposite conclusion, namely, that the FDA does have jurisdiction but that it must ban cigarettes. More importantly, the argument fails to take into account the fact that a statute interpreted as requiring the FDA to pick a more dangerous over a less dangerous remedy would be a perverse statute, causing, rather than preventing, unnecessary harm whenever a total ban is likely the more dangerous response. And one can at least imagine such circumstances. Suppose, for example, that a commonly used, mildly addictive sleeping pill (or, say, a kind of popular contact lens), plainly within the FDA's jurisdiction, turned out to pose serious health risks for certain consumers. Suppose further that many of those addicted consumers would ignore an immediate total ban, turning to a potentially more dangerous black-market substitute, while a less draconian remedy (say, adequate notice) would wean them gradually away to a safer product. Would the FDCA still force the FDA to impose the more dangerous remedy? For the following reasons, I think not.

First, the statute's language does not restrict the FDA's remedial powers in this way. The FDCA permits the FDA to regulate a "combination product"—i.e., a "device" (such as a cigarette) that contains a "drug" (such as nicotine)—under its "device" provisions. 21 U.S.C. § 353(g)(1). And the FDCA's "device" provisions explicitly grant the FDA wide remedial discretion * * *.

The Court points to other statutory subsections which it believes require the FDA to ban a drug or device entirely, even where an outright ban risks more harm than other regulatory responses. But the cited provisions do no such thing. It is true, as the majority contends, that "the FDCA requires the FDA to place all devices" in "one of three classifications" and that Class III devices require "premarket approval." But it is not the case that the FDA must place cigarettes in Class III because tobacco itself "present[s] a potential unreasonable risk of illness or injury." 21 U.S.C. § 360c(a)(1)(C). In fact, Class III applies only where regulation cannot otherwise "provide reasonable assurance of . . . safety." §§ 360c(a)(1)(A), 360c(a)(1)(B) (placing a device in Class I or Class II when regulation can provide that assurance). Thus, the statute plainly allows the FDA to consider the relative, overall "safety" of a device in light of its regulatory alternatives, and where the FDA has chosen the least dangerous path, *i.e.*, the safest path, then it can—and does—provide a "reasonable assurance" of "safety" within the meaning of the statute. A good football helmet provides a reasonable assurance of safety for the player even if the sport itself is still dangerous. And the safest regulatory choice by definition offers a "reasonable" assurance of safety in a world where the other alternatives are yet more dangerous.

* * *

Noting that the FDCA requires banning a "misbranded" drug, the majority also points to 21 U.S.C. § 352(j), which deems a drug or device "misbranded" if "it is dangerous to health when used" as "prescribed, recommended, or suggested in the labeling." In addition, the majority mentions § 352(f)(1), which calls a drug or device "misbranded" unless "its labeling bears . . . adequate directions for use" as "are necessary for the protection of users." But this "misbranding" language is not determinative, for it permits the FDA to conclude that a drug or device is not "dangerous to health" and that it does have "adequate" directions when regulated so as to render it as harmless as possible. And surely the agency can determine that a substance is comparatively "safe" (not "dangerous") whenever it would be less dangerous to make the product available (subject to regulatory requirements) than suddenly to withdraw it from the market. Any other interpretation risks substantial harm of the sort that my sleeping pill example illustrates. And nothing in the statute prevents the agency from adopting a view of "safety" that would avoid such harm. Indeed, the FDA already seems to have taken this position when permitting distribution of toxic drugs, such as poisons used for chemotherapy, that are dangerous for the user but are not deemed "dangerous to health" in the relevant sense.

* * *

The statute's language, then, permits the agency to choose remedies consistent with its basic purpose—the overall protection of public health.

The second reason the FDCA does not require the FDA to select the more dangerous remedy is that, despite the majority's assertions to the contrary, the statute does not distinguish among the kinds of health effects that the agency may take into account when assessing safety. The Court insists that the statute only permits the agency to take into account the health risks and benefits of the "product itself" as used by individual consumers, and, thus, that the FDA is prohibited from considering that a ban on smoking would lead many smokers to suffer severe withdrawal symptoms or to buy possibly stronger, more dangerous, black market cigarettes * * *. But the FDCA expressly permits the FDA to take account of comparative safety in precisely this manner. See, *e.g.*, 21 U.S.C. § 360h(e)(2)(B)(i)(II) (no device recall if "risk of recal[l]" presents "a greater health risk than" no recall); § 360h(a) (notification "unless" notification "would present a greater danger" than "no such notification").

* * *

I concede that, as a matter of logic, one could consider the FDA's "safety" evaluation to be different from its choice of remedies. But to read the statute to forbid the agency from taking account of the realities of consumer behavior either in assessing safety or in choosing a remedy could increase the risks of harm * * *. Why would Congress insist that the FDA ignore such realities, even if the consequent harm would occur only unusually, say, where the FDA evaluates a product (a sleeping pill; a cigarette; a contact lens) that is already on the market, potentially habit forming, or popular? I can find no satisfactory answer to this question. And that, I imagine, is why the statute itself says nothing about any of the distinctions that the Court has tried to draw.

* * *

In my view, where linguistically permissible, we should interpret the FDCA in light of Congress' overall desire to protect health. That purpose requires a flexible interpretation that both permits the FDA to take into account the realities of human behavior and allows it, in appropriate cases, to choose from its arsenal of statutory remedies. A statute so interpreted easily "fit[s]" this, and other, drug-and device-related health problems.

In the majority's view, laws enacted since 1965 require us to deny jurisdiction, whatever the FDCA might mean in their absence. But why? Do those laws contain language barring FDA jurisdiction? The majority must concede that they do not * * *.

* * * [W]hatever individual Members of Congress after 1964 may have assumed about the FDA's jurisdiction, the laws they enacted did not embody any such "no jurisdiction" assumption. And one cannot automatically infer an antijurisdiction intent, as the majority does, for the later statutes are both (and similarly) consistent with quite a different

congressional desire, namely, the intent to proceed without interfering with whatever authority the FDA otherwise may have possessed * * *.

* * *

I now turn to the final historical fact that the majority views as a factor in its interpretation of the subsequent legislative history: the FDA's former denials of its tobacco-related authority. Until the early 1990's, the FDA expressly maintained that the 1938 statute did not give it the power that it now seeks to assert. It then changed its mind. The majority agrees with me that the FDA's change of positions does not make a significant legal difference. Nevertheless, it labels those denials "important context" for drawing an inference about Congress' intent. In my view, the FDA's change of policy, like the subsequent statutes themselves, does nothing to advance the majority's position.

* * *

What changed? For one thing, the FDA obtained evidence sufficient to prove the necessary "intent" despite the absence of specific "claims." This evidence, which first became available in the early 1990's, permitted the agency to demonstrate that the tobacco companies knew nicotine achieved appetite-suppressing, mood-stabilizing, and habituating effects through chemical (not psychological) means, even at a time when the companies were publicly denying such knowledge.

Moreover, scientific evidence of adverse health effects mounted, until, in the late 1980's, a consensus on the seriousness of the matter became firm * * *.

Finally, administration policy changed. Earlier administrations may have hesitated to assert jurisdiction * * *. Commissioners of the current administration simply took a different regulatory attitude.

Nothing in the law prevents the FDA from changing its policy for such reasons. By the mid-1990's, the evidence needed to prove objective intent— even without an express claim—had been found. The emerging scientific consensus about tobacco's adverse, chemically induced, health effects may have convinced the agency that it should spend its resources on this important regulatory effort. As for the change of administrations, I agree with then-JUSTICE REHNQUIST'S statement in a different case, where he wrote:

> "The agency's changed view * * * seems to be related to the election of a new President of a different political party. It is readily apparent that the responsible members of one administration may consider public resistance and uncertainties to be more important than do their counterparts in a previous administration. A change in administration brought about by the people casting their votes is a perfectly reasonable basis for an

executive agency's reappraisal of the costs and benefits of its programs and regulations. As long as the agency remains within the bounds established by Congress, it is entitled to assess administrative records and evaluate priorities in light of the philosophy of the administration." *Motor Vehicle Mfrs. Assn. of United States, Inc. v. State Farm Mut. Automobile Ins. Co.*, 463 U.S. 29, 59, 103 S.Ct. 2856, 77 L.Ed.2d 443 (1983) (concurring in part and dissenting in part).

* * *

* * * [O]ne might claim that courts, when interpreting statutes, should assume in close cases that a decision with "enormous social consequences" should be made by democratically elected Members of Congress rather than by unelected agency administrators. If there is such a background canon of interpretation, however, I do not believe it controls the outcome here.

Insofar as the decision to regulate tobacco reflects the policy of an administration, it is a decision for which that administration, and those politically elected officials who support it, must (and will) take responsibility. And the very importance of the decision taken here, as well as its attendant publicity, means that the public is likely to be aware of it and to hold those officials politically accountable. Presidents, just like Members of Congress, are elected by the public. Indeed, the President and Vice President are the only public officials whom the entire Nation elects. I do not believe that an administrative agency decision of this magnitude— one that is important, conspicuous, and controversial—can escape the kind of public scrutiny that is essential in any democracy. And such a review will take place whether it is the Congress or the Executive Branch that makes the relevant decision.

The upshot is that the Court today holds that a regulatory statute aimed at unsafe drugs and devices does not authorize regulation of a drug (nicotine) and a device (a cigarette) that the Court itself finds unsafe. Far more than most, this particular drug and device risks the life-threatening harms that administrative regulation seeks to rectify. The majority's conclusion is counter-intuitive. And, for the reasons set forth, I believe that the law does not require it.

Consequently, I dissent.

NOTES

If one counts pages in the Federal Reporter system, it is evident that courts implicitly use the "clarity as degree of certainty" approach of *Dole* substantially more often than they use the "clarity as obviousness" approach of *Pauley, see, e.g., Ragsdale v. Wolverine World Wide, Inc.*, 535 U.S. 81, 122 S.Ct. 1155, 152 L.Ed.2d 167 (2002); *Sierra Club. v. EPA*; 551 F.3d 1019, 1027–

28 (D.C.Cir.2008), though the latter continues to make appearances. *See, e.g., Secretary of Labor, Mine Safety & Health Admin. v. Excel Mining, LLC,* 334 F.3d 1, 13 (D.C.Cir.2003) (finding a statute ambiguous essentially "because of the complicated syntax of the statutory and regulatory language"). Beyond that, it is difficult to make useful generalizations about lower courts' treatment of step one of *Chevron.* Sometimes, courts are relatively quick to find statutes ambiguous, *see Verizon California, Inc. v. FCC,* 555 F.3d 270, 273 (D.C.Cir.2009) (finding the statute ambiguous even when the petitioner's proposed interpretation is "the first reading that comes to mind"), while on other occasions courts seem to work very hard to find clarity. *See Sierra Club,* 551 F.3d at 1024–26. It does not help that courts seem blissfully unaware that there are different conceptions of the nature of step one from which they logically must be choosing. *See, e.g., Esquivel-Quintana v. Sessions,* 137 S.Ct. 1562, 1572, 198 L.Ed.2d 22 (2017) (declaring that a statute "unambiguously forecloses" the agency interpretation without any discussion of what it means for a statute to be unambiguous); *Wisconsin Central Ltd v. United States,* 138 S.Ct. 2067 (2018) (splitting 5–4 on whether the meaning of "money remuneration" in a statute was clear, with neither the majority nor the dissent explicitly identifying what it means for a statute to be clear).

At least one prominent jurist, however, is acutely aware of the importance, and difficulty, of defining what it means for a statute to be "clear": "That simple threshold determination of clarity versus ambiguity may affect billions of dollars, the individual rights of millions of citizens, and the fate of clean air rules, securities regulations, labor laws, or the like. And yet there is no particularly principled guide for making that clarity versus ambiguity decision, and no good way for judges to find neutral principles on which to debate and decide that question." Brett M. Kavanaugh, *Book Review,* 129 Harv. L. Rev. 2118, 2153 (2016). *See also id.* at 2137–42 (exploring at some length what it might mean for a statute to be clear or ambiguous). Only time will tell whether Justice Kavanaugh can bring this issue to wider judicial attention.

The canonical formulation of *Chevron's* step one asks whether Congress has directly spoken to the "precise" question at issue. How precisely must Congress speak in order clearly to resolve an issue? There is no crisp answer, though the best rough approximation is "pretty precisely." *See, e.g., Mayo Foundation for Medical Education and Research v. United States,* 562 U.S. 44, 131 S.Ct. 704, 711 (2011) ("The statute does not define the term 'student,' and does not otherwise attend to the precise question whether medical residents are subject to FICA").

The majority in *Brown & Williamson* rather plainly thought that it was performing a straightforward, even if controverted, application of step one of *Chevron,* in which the overall structure and context of the statute yielded a clear meaning. Some judges and scholars, however, see cases such as *Brown & Williamson* as representing what is sometimes called a "major issues" or "major questions" exception to *Chevron,* in which the Court denies *Chevron* deference to agencies when the issue involved is highly sensitive. *See, e.g., U.S.*

Telecom Ass'n v. FCC, 855 F.3d 381, 419–22 (D.C.Cir.2017) (Kavanaugh, J., dissenting from denial of rehearing en banc); Abigail Moncrieff, *Reincarnating the "Major Questions" Exception to* Chevron *Deference As a Doctrine of Non-Interference (or Why* Massachusetts v. EPA *Got It Wrong)*, 60 Admin. L. Rev. 593 (2008). Your editor has always been skeptical of this vision, on the theory that all of the relevant cases can better be explained on more mundane grounds without positing a free-floating but unstated "major issues" inquiry. Your editor's position is a bit harder to maintain in light of *King v. Burwell*, ___ U.S. ___, 135 S.Ct. 2480, 192 L.Ed.2d 483 (2015), in which the Court held that a statute providing health insurance subsidies to participants in "an Exchange established by the State," 26 U.S.C. §§ 36B(b)–(c) (2012), allowed subsidies to be paid to participants in exchanges established by the federal government. The administering agency for the provision, the Internal Revenue Service, had construed the statute to allow such subsidies. The Court, while affirming the agency decision, specifically declined to grant the agency *Chevron* deference:

> When analyzing an agency's interpretation of a statute, we often apply the two-step framework announced in *Chevron*, 467 U.S. 837, 104 S.Ct. 2778, 81 L.Ed.2d 694. Under that framework, we ask whether the statute is ambiguous and, if so, whether the agency's interpretation is reasonable. This approach "is premised on the theory that a statute's ambiguity constitutes an implicit delegation from Congress to the agency to fill in the statutory gaps." *FDA v. Brown & Williamson Tobacco Corp.*, 529 U.S. 120, 159, 120 S.Ct. 1291, 146 L.Ed.2d 121 (2000). "In extraordinary cases, however, there may be reason to hesitate before concluding that Congress has intended such an implicit delegation." *Ibid.*
>
> This is one of those cases. The tax credits are among the Act's key reforms, involving billions of dollars in spending each year and affecting the price of health insurance for millions of people. Whether those credits are available on Federal Exchanges is thus a question of deep "economic and political significance" that is central to this statutory scheme; had Congress wished to assign that question to an agency, it surely would have done so expressly. *Utility Air Regulatory Group v. EPA*, 573 U.S. ___, ___, 134 S.Ct. 2427, 2444, 189 L.Ed.2d 372 (2014) (quoting *Brown & Williamson,* 529 U.S., at 160, 120 S.Ct. 1291). It is especially unlikely that Congress would have delegated this decision to the *IRS,* which has no expertise in crafting health insurance policy of this sort. See *Gonzales v. Oregon,* 546 U.S. 243, 266–267, 126 S.Ct. 904, 163 L.Ed.2d 748 (2006). This is not a case for the IRS.

135 S.Ct. at 2488–89. Is that a "major questions" exception to *Chevron* or just ordinary statutory interpretation?

Every so often judges agree that the meaning of a statute is clear (however they understand that conclusion) but disagree about the content of that clear meaning. Oftentimes, the disagreement concerns which words in the statute need interpreting. For example, in *Scialabba v. Cuellar de Osorio*, 573 U.S. 41, 134 S.Ct. 2191, 189 L.Ed.2d 98 (2014), the majority and dissent disagreed primarily on which words in the relevant statute were the key words to interpret. *See also Sierra Club v. EPA*, 536 F.3d 673 (D.C.Cir.2008) (the majority and dissent both thought that there was clear statutory meaning for relevant provisions of a statute, but each thought that a different provision of the statute was relevant). Always keep in mind that "statutory interpretation," whether under *Chevron* or otherwise, always involves specific statutes, and indeed specific parts of statutes. One may need to look beyond those specific statutes or parts in order to engage in proper interpretation, but one is always interpreting some particular provision.

And sometimes everyone agrees on the terms to be interpreted, everyone agrees that the meaning of the relevant statutory provision is clear, but judges disagree about which way that clear meaning cuts. *Compare, e.g., FERC v. Electric Power Supply Ass'n*, 136 S.Ct. 760, 773 n.5, 193 L.Ed.2d 661 (2016) (no need for *Chevron* deference because the statute clearly supports the agency's position) *with id.* at 785 (Scalia, J., dissenting) (no need for *Chevron* deference because the statute clearly defeats the agency's position).

5.   HOW REASONABLE IS "REASONABLE"?

If the court cannot resolve the case at *Chevron*'s first step, the second step tells courts to accept any agency interpretation that is reasonable. How does one know a "reasonable" agency interpretation when one sees it? Where does *Chevron*'s reasonableness requirement fit along the spectrum of deference? Is it analogous to *Hearst*'s and *O'Leary*'s reasonableness requirement? Or is reasonableness something that depends heavily on context? And what should courts look for in an agency interpretation when assessing reasonableness: fit with the statute, careful reasoning, good policy sense, all of the above? Perhaps surprisingly, the cases contain as little explicit theoretical discussion of the meaning of *Chevron*'s second step as they do of its first.

At least one thing, however, is evident: although courts have not articulated very well the standard(s) that they are applying at step two of *Chevron*, agencies very seldom lose at that stage of the analysis. One comprehensive study finds that when courts of appeals reach *Chevron* step two, the agency wins 93.8 percent of the time. *See* Kent Barnett & Christopher J. Walker, Chevron *in the Circuit Courts*, 116 Mich. L. Rev. 1, 6 (2017). (When the case is resolved at step one, by contrast, agencies win about 40 percent of the time. *See id.* at 34.) Courts generally affirm agencies at step two in cursory fashion, *see, e.g., Air Transport Ass'n of America v. FAA*, 169 F.3d 1 (D.C.Cir.1999), and often with no more than a single conclusory sentence. *See, e.g., Automated Power Exchange, Inc. v. FERC*, 204 F.3d 1144 (D.C.Cir.2000); *Natural Resources Defense Council v. EPA*, 749 F.3d 1055, 1060 (D.C.Cir.2014). For a particularly dramatic example, see *Adirondack Medical Center v. Sebelius*, 740 F.3d 692 (D.C.Cir.2014) (spending seven pages on step one of *Chevron* and one sentence on step two). Frequently, the court will simply apply its step-one analysis: The same reasons why the agency does not lose at step one generally establish that its interpretation is at least reasonable. *See, e.g., Competitive Enterprise Inst. v. United States Dep't of Transportation*, 863 F.3d 911, 917 (D.C.Cir.2017) ("Petitioners present no arguments under *Chevron's* second step beyond those already discussed as part of step one. The *Chevron*-one analysis supports a reasonableness finding."). Cases that affirm agencies after more than a cursory discussion of step two typically do so by concluding that the agency's interpretation is *better* than competing interpretations, *see, e.g., County of Los Angeles v. Shalala*, 192 F.3d 1005, 1017–20 (D.C.Cir.1999), which sheds little light on what constitutes a "reasonable" interpretation.

In the infrequent cases in which agencies lose at step two, the agency interpretations typically either fail completely to advance the goals of the underlying statute, *see Chemical Manufacturers Ass'n v. EPA*, 217 F.3d 861 (D.C.Cir.2000), or are so bizarre that close analysis is unnecessary. *See NRDC v. Daley*, 209 F.3d 747 (D.C.Cir.2000); *Whitecliff, Inc. v. Shalala*, 20 F.3d 488 (D.C.Cir.1994). For example, in the first case in the Supreme Court in which an agency lost at step two, *AT & T Corp. v. Iowa Utilities Board*, 525 U.S. 366, 119 S.Ct. 721, 142 L.Ed.2d 835 (1999), the agency effectively construed an important statutory requirement out of existence. A statute required local phone companies to make elements of their facilities available to competitors when such access was "necessary" and lack of access would "impair" the ability of a competitor to provide service. 47 U.S.C. § 251(d)(2). The FCC, charged with applying this statute, required access essentially to anything that competitors requested. While agreeing with the agency that the statute was ambiguous, the Court (with Justice Souter dissenting and three other Justices dissenting on unrelated grounds) concluded that the agency's interpretation was beyond the bounds of reasonableness:

> [T]he Act requires the FCC to apply *some* limiting standard, rationally related to the goals of the Act, which it has simply failed to do * * *. [T]he Commission announced that it would regard the "necessary" standard as having been met regardless of whether "requesting carriers can obtain the requested proprietary element from a source other than the incumbent," since "[r]equiring new entrants to duplicate unnecessarily even a part of the incumbent's network could generate delay and higher costs for new entrants, and thereby impede entry by competing local providers and delay competition, contrary to the goals of the 1996 Act." First Report & Order ¶ 283. And it announced that it would regard the "impairment" standard as having been met if "the failure of an incumbent to provide access to a network element would decrease

the quality, or increase the financial or administrative cost of the service a requesting carrier seeks to offer, compared with providing that service *over other unbundled elements in the incumbent LEC's network,*" *id.* 285 (emphasis added)—which means that comparison with self-provision, or with purchasing from another provider, is excluded. Since any entrant will request the most efficient network element that the incumbent has to offer, it is hard to imagine when the incumbent's failure to give access to the element would not constitute an "impairment" under this standard. The Commission asserts that it deliberately limited its inquiry to the incumbent's own network because no rational entrant would seek access to network elements from an incumbent if it could get better service or prices elsewhere. That may be. But that judgment allows entrants, rather than the Commission, to determine whether access to proprietary elements is necessary, and whether the failure to obtain access to nonproprietary elements would impair the ability to provide services. The Commission cannot, consistent with the statute, blind itself to the availability of elements outside the incumbent's network. That failing alone would require the Commission's rule to be set aside. In addition, however, the Commission's assumption that *any* increase in cost (or decrease in quality) imposed by denial of a network element renders access to that element "necessary," and causes the failure to provide that element to "impair" the entrant's ability to furnish its desired services is simply not in accord with the ordinary and fair meaning of those terms. An entrant whose anticipated annual profits from the proposed service are reduced from 100% of investment to 99% of investment has perhaps been "impaired" in its ability to amass earnings, but has not *ipso facto* been "impair[ed] . . . in its ability to provide the services it seeks to offer"; and it cannot realistically be said that the network element enabling it to raise its profits to 100% is "necessary" In a world of perfect competition, in which all carriers are providing their service at marginal cost, the Commission's total equating of increased cost (or decreased quality) with "necessity" and "impairment" might be reasonable; but it has not established the existence of such an ideal world. We cannot avoid the conclusion that, if Congress had wanted to give blanket access to incumbents' networks on a basis as unrestricted as the scheme the Commission has come up with, it would not have included § 251(d)(2) in the statute at all. It would simply have said (as the Commission in effect has) that whatever requested element can be provided must be provided.

* * * The Commission began with the premise that an incumbent was obliged to turn over as much of its network as was "technically feasible," and viewed (d)(2) as merely permitting it to soften that obligation by regulatory grace * * *. The Commission's premise was wrong. Section 251(d)(2) does not authorize the Commission to create isolated exemptions from some underlying duty to make all network elements available. It requires the Commission to determine on a rational basis *which* network elements must be made available, taking into account the objectives of the Act and giving some substance to the "necessary" and "impair" requirements. The latter is not achieved by disregarding entirely the availability of elements outside the network, and by regarding *any* "increased cost or decreased service quality" as establishing a "necessity" and an "impair[ment]" of the ability to "provide . . . services."

* * * Because the Commission has not interpreted the terms of the statute in a reasonable fashion, we must vacate 47 CFR § 51.319 (1997).

525 U.S. at 388–92.

The pace of agency step two losses has noticeably picked up in the years since *AT & T, see, e.g., Natural Resources Defense Council v. EPA,* 777 F.3d 456 (D.C.Cir.2014); *Echostar Satellite L.L.C. v. FCC,* 704 F.3d 992 (D.C.Cir.2013), though, as noted above, it is still extremely small. (A 6.2 percent agency loss rate represents a "picked up" pace? Yes, actually, it does. In 1999, it was possible to list, in a very modest footnote, literally every reported case in which an agency had lost at step two of *Chevron.*) If an agency makes it to step two, which happens about 70 percent of the time in *Chevron* cases, *see* Barnett & Walker, *supra,* at 6, the agency is in pretty good shape.

What exactly was the agency's step two error in the following case? Some background is necessary: In 2007, in a sharply divided 5–4 decision (with Justice Scalia writing the dissent), the Supreme Court held that the definition of an "air pollutant" in the Clean Air Act, 42 U.S.C. § 7521(a)(1) (2012), included carbon dioxide and other "greenhouse gases." *See Massachusetts v. EPA,* 549 U.S. 497, 127 S.Ct. 1438, 167 L.Ed.2d 248 (2007). The Court thus rejected the EPA's then-position that it had no statutory authority to regulate "greenhouse gases" under the existing terms of the Clean Air Act. By 2014, the EPA (under a different presidential administration) had embraced regulation of "greenhouse gases" as a central part of its mission. There are far more sources of "greenhouse gases" than of more conventional pollutants. The question in the following case was how to adapt application of the Clean Air Act, which was designed to deal with a limited set of large polluting sources, to the newly expanded set of pollutants.

UTILITY AIR REGULATORY GROUP V. EPA

Supreme Court of the United States, 2014.
573 U.S. 302, 134 S.Ct. 2427, 189 L.Ed.2d 372.

JUSTICE SCALIA announced the judgment of the Court and delivered the opinion of the Court with respect to Parts I and II.

Acting pursuant to the Clean Air Act, 69 Stat. 322, as amended, 42 U.S.C. §§ 7401–7671q, the Environmental Protection Agency recently set standards for emissions of "greenhouse gases" (substances it believes contribute to "global climate change") from new motor vehicles. We must decide whether it was permissible for EPA to determine that its motor-vehicle greenhouse-gas regulations automatically triggered permitting requirements under the Act for stationary sources that emit greenhouse gases.

I.   Background

A.   Stationary-Source Permitting

The Clean Air Act regulates pollution-generating emissions from both stationary sources, such as factories and powerplants, and moving sources, such as cars, trucks, and aircraft. This litigation concerns permitting obligations imposed on stationary sources under Titles I and V of the Act.

Title I charges EPA with formulating national ambient air quality standards (NAAQS) for air pollutants. §§ 7408–7409. To date, EPA has issued NAAQS for six pollutants: sulfur dioxide, particulate matter, nitrogen dioxide, carbon monoxide, ozone, and lead. States have primary responsibility for implementing the NAAQS by developing "State implementation plans." A State must designate every area within its borders as "attainment," "nonattainment," or "unclassifiable" with respect to each NAAQS, and the State's implementation plan must include permitting programs for stationary sources that vary according to the classification of the area where the source is or is proposed to be located.

Stationary sources in areas designated attainment or unclassifiable are subject to the Act's provisions relating to "Prevention of Significant Deterioration" (PSD). §§ 7470–7492. EPA interprets the PSD provisions to apply to sources located in areas that are designated attainment or unclassifiable for any NAAQS pollutant, regardless of whether the source emits that specific pollutant. Since the inception of the PSD program, every area of the country has been designated attainment or unclassifiable for at least one NAAQS pollutant; thus, on EPA's view, all stationary sources are potentially subject to PSD review.

It is unlawful to construct or modify a "major emitting facility" in "any area to which [the PSD program] applies" without first obtaining a permit. To qualify for a permit, the facility must not cause or contribute to the violation of any applicable air-quality standard, and it must comply with emissions limitations that reflect the "best available control technology" (or BACT) for "each pollutant subject to regulation under" the Act. The Act defines a "major emitting facility" as any stationary source with the potential to emit 250 tons per year of "any air pollutant" (or 100 tons per year for certain types of sources). § 7479(1). It defines "modification" as a physical or operational change that causes the facility to emit more of "any air pollutant." § 7411(a)(4).

In addition to the PSD permitting requirements for construction and modification, Title V of the Act makes it unlawful to *operate* any "major source," wherever located, without a comprehensive operating permit. Unlike the PSD program, Title V generally does not impose any substantive pollution-control requirements. Instead, it is designed to facilitate compliance and enforcement by consolidating into a single document all of a facility's obligations under the Act. The permit must include all "emissions limitations and standards" that apply to the source, as well as associated inspection, monitoring, and reporting requirements. Title V defines a "major source" by reference to the Act-wide definition of "major stationary source," which in turn means any stationary source with the potential to emit 100 tons per year of "any air pollutant." §§ 7661(2)(B), 7602(j).

B.   EPA's Greenhouse-Gas Regulations

In 2007, the Court held that Title II of the Act "authorize[d] EPA to regulate greenhouse gas emissions from new motor vehicles" if the Agency "form[ed] a 'judgment' that such emissions contribute to climate change." *Massachusetts v. EPA*, 549 U. S. 497, 528 (quoting § 7521(a)(1)) * * *.

* * *

In 2009 * * * EPA found that greenhouse-gas emissions from new motor vehicles contribute to elevated atmospheric concentrations of greenhouse gases, which endanger public health and welfare by fostering global "climate change." 74 Fed. Reg. 66523, 66537 (hereinafter Endangerment Finding). It denominated a "single air pollutant" the "combined mix" of six greenhouse gases that it identified as "the root cause of human-induced climate change": carbon dioxide, methane, nitrous oxide, hydrofluorocarbons, perfluorocarbons, and sulfur hexafluoride. *Id.*, at 66516, 66537 * * *.

Next, EPA issued its "final decision" regarding the prospect that motor-vehicle greenhouse-gas standards would trigger stationary-source permitting requirements. 75 Fed. Reg. 17004 (2010) (hereinafter Triggering Rule). EPA announced that beginning on the effective date of its greenhouse-gas standards for motor vehicles, stationary sources would be subject to the PSD program and Title V on the basis of their potential to emit greenhouse gases. As expected, EPA in short order promulgated greenhouse-gas emission standards for passenger cars, light-duty trucks, and medium-duty passenger vehicles to take effect on January 2, 2011. 75 Fed. Reg. 25324 (hereinafter Tailpipe Rule).

EPA then announced steps it was taking to "tailor" the PSD program and Title V to greenhouse gases. 75 Fed. Reg. 31514 (hereinafter Tailoring Rule). Those steps were necessary, it said, because the PSD program and Title V were designed to regulate "a relatively small number of large industrial sources," and requiring permits for all sources with greenhouse-gas emissions above the statutory thresholds would radically expand those programs, making them both unadministrable and "unrecognizable to the Congress that designed" them. *Id.*, at 31555, 31562. EPA nonetheless rejected calls to exclude greenhouse gases entirely from those programs, asserting that the Act is not "ambiguous with respect to the need to cover [greenhouse-gas] sources under either the PSD or title V program." *Id.*, at 31548, n. 31. Instead, EPA adopted a "phase-in approach" that it said would "appl[y] PSD and title V at threshold levels that are as close to the statutory levels as possible, and do so as quickly as possible, at least to a certain point." *Id.*, at 31523.

* * *

C.   Decision Below

Numerous parties, including several States, filed petitions for review in the D. C. Circuit * * * challenging EPA's greenhouse-gas-related actions. The Court of Appeals * * * found it "crystal clear that PSD permittees must install BACT for greenhouse gases." [684 F.3d 102, 137 (D.C.Cir.2012)] * * *.

We granted * * * certiorari * * * to decide * * *: " 'Whether EPA permissibly determined that its regulation of greenhouse gas emissions from new motor vehicles triggered permitting requirements under the Clean Air Act for stationary sources that emit greenhouse gases.' " 571 U.S. ___ (2013).

II.   Analysis

This litigation presents two distinct challenges to EPA's stance on greenhouse-gas permitting for stationary sources. First, we must decide whether EPA permissibly determined that a source may be subject to the PSD and Title V permitting requirements on the sole basis of the source's potential to emit greenhouse gases. Second, we must decide whether EPA permissibly determined that a source already subject to the PSD program because of its emission of conventional pollutants (an "anyway" source) may be required to limit its greenhouse-gas emissions by employing the "best available control technology" for greenhouse gases. The Solicitor General joins issue on both points sbut evidently regards the second as more important; he informs us that "anyway" sources account for roughly 83% of American stationary-source greenhouse-gas emissions, compared to just 3% for the additional, non-"anyway" sources EPA sought to regulate at Steps 2 and 3 of the Tailoring Rule. Tr. of Oral Arg. 52.

We review EPA's interpretations of the Clean Air Act using the standard set forth in *Chevron U.S.A. Inc. v. Natural Resources Defense Council, Inc.*, 467 U. S. 837, 842–843 (1984) * * *.

A. The PSD and Title V Triggers

We first decide whether EPA permissibly interpreted the statute to provide that a source may be required to obtain a PSD or Title V permit on the sole basis of its potential greenhouse-gas emissions.

1

EPA thought its conclusion that a source's greenhouse-gas emissions may necessitate a PSD or Title V permit followed from the Act's unambiguous language. The Court of Appeals agreed and held that the statute "compelled" EPA's interpretation. 684 F. 3d, at 134. We disagree. The statute compelled EPA's greenhouse-gas-inclusive interpretation with respect to neither the PSD program nor Title V.

The Court of Appeals reasoned by way of a flawed syllogism: Under *Massachusetts*, the general, Act-wide definition of "air pollutant" includes greenhouse gases; the Act requires permits for major emitters of "any air pollutant"; therefore, the Act requires permits for major emitters of greenhouse gases. The conclusion follows from the premises only if the air pollutants referred to in the permit-requiring provisions (the minor premise) are the same air pollutants encompassed by the Act-wide definition as interpreted in *Massachusetts* (the major premise). Yet no one—least of all EPA—endorses that proposition, and it is obviously untenable.

The Act-wide definition says that an air pollutant is "any air pollution agent or combination of such agents, including any physical, chemical, biological, [or] radioactive . . . substance or matter which is emitted into or otherwise enters the ambient air." § 7602(g). In *Massachusetts*, the Court held that the Act-wide definition includes greenhouse gases because it is all-encompassing; it "embraces all airborne compounds of whatever stripe." 549 U. S., at 529. But where the term "air pollutant" appears in the Act's operative provisions, EPA has routinely given it a narrower, context-appropriate meaning.

That is certainly true of the provisions that require PSD and Title V permitting for major emitters of "any air pollutant." Since 1978, EPA's regulations have interpreted "air pollutant" in the PSD permitting trigger as limited to regulated air pollutants, 43 Fed. Reg. 26403, codified, as amended, 40 CFR § 52.21(b)(1)–(2), (50)—a class much narrower than *Massachusetts*' " all airborne compounds of whatever stripe," 549 U. S., at 529. And since 1993 EPA has informally taken the same position with regard to the Title V permitting trigger, a position the Agency ultimately incorporated into some of the regulations at issue here. Those interpretations were appropriate: It is plain as day that the Act does not envision an elaborate, burdensome permitting process for major emitters of steam, oxygen, or other harmless airborne substances. It takes some cheek for EPA to insist that it cannot possibly give "air pollutant" a reasonable, context-appropriate meaning in the PSD and Title V contexts when it has been doing precisely that for decades.

Nor are those the only places in the Act where EPA has inferred from statutory context that a generic reference to air pollutants does not encompass every substance falling within the Act-wide definition * * *.

* * *

To be sure, Congress's profligate use of "air pollutant" where what is meant is obviously narrower than the Act-wide definition is not conducive to clarity. One ordinarily assumes that " 'identical words used in different parts of the same act are intended to have the same meaning.' " *Environmental Defense v. Duke Energy Corp.,* 549 U.S. 561, 574, 127 S.Ct. 1423, 167 L.Ed.2d 295 (2007). In this respect (as in countless others), the Act is far from a *chef d'oevure* of legislative draftsmanship. But we, and EPA, must do our best * * *. As we reiterated the same day we decided *Massachusetts*, the presumption of consistent usage " 'readily yields' " to context, and a statutory term—even one defined in the statute—"may take on distinct characters from association with distinct statutory objects calling for different implementation strategies." *Duke Energy, supra*, at 574, 127 S.Ct. 1423.

We need not, and do not, pass on the validity of all the limiting constructions EPA has given the term "air pollutant" throughout the Act. We merely observe that taken together, they belie EPA's rigid insistence that when interpreting the PSD and Title V permitting requirements it is bound by the Act-wide definition's inclusion of greenhouse gases, no matter how incompatible that inclusion is with those programs' regulatory structure.

In sum, there is no insuperable textual barrier to EPA's interpreting "any air pollutant" in the permitting triggers of PSD and Title V to encompass only pollutants emitted in quantities that enable them to be sensibly regulated at the statutory thresholds, and to exclude those atypical pollutants that, like greenhouse gases, are emitted in such vast quantities that their inclusion would radically transform those programs and render them unworkable as written.

2

Having determined that EPA was mistaken in thinking the Act *compelled* a greenhouse-gas-inclusive interpretation of the PSD and Title V triggers, we next consider the Agency's alternative position that its interpretation was justified as an exercise of its "discretion" to adopt "a reasonable construction of the statute." Tailoring Rule 31517. We conclude that EPA's interpretation is not permissible.

Even under *Chevron's* deferential framework, agencies must operate "within the bounds of reasonable interpretation." *Arlington*, 569 U. S., at ___ (slip op., at 5). And reasonable statutory interpretation must account for both "the specific context in which . . . language is used" and "the broader context of the statute as a whole." *Robinson v. Shell Oil Co.*, 519 U. S. 337, 341 (1997) * * *. Thus, an agency interpretation that is "inconsisten[t] with the design and structure of the statute as a whole," *University of Tex. Southwestern Medical Center v. Nassar*, 570 U.S. ___, ___ (2013) (slip op., at 13), does not merit deference.

EPA itself has repeatedly acknowledged that applying the PSD and Title V permitting requirements to greenhouse gases would be inconsistent with—in fact, would overthrow—the Act's structure and design. In the Tailoring Rule, EPA described the calamitous consequences of interpreting the Act in that way. Under the PSD program, annual permit applications would jump from about 800 to nearly 82,000; annual administrative costs would swell from $12 million to over $1.5 billion; and decade-long delays in issuing permits would become common, causing construction projects to grind to a halt nationwide. Tailoring Rule 31557. The picture under Title V was equally bleak: The number of sources required to have permits would jump from fewer than 15,000 to about 6.1 million; annual administrative costs would balloon from $62 million to $21 billion; and collectively the newly covered sources would face permitting costs of $147 billion. *Id.*, at 31562–31563. Moreover, "the great majority of additional sources brought into the PSD and title V programs would be small sources that Congress did not expect would need to undergo permitting." *Id.*, at 31533. EPA stated that these results would be so "contrary to congressional intent," and would so "severely undermine what Congress sought to accomplish," that they necessitated as much as a 1,000-fold increase in the permitting thresholds set forth in the statute. *Id.*, at 31554, 31562.

Like EPA, we think it beyond reasonable debate that requiring permits for sources based solely on their emission of greenhouse gases at the 100- and 250-tons-per-year levels set forth in the statute would be "incompatible" with "the substance of Congress' regulatory scheme." *Brown & Williamson*, 529 U. S., at 156. A brief review of the relevant statutory provisions leaves no doubt that the PSD program and Title V are designed to apply to, and cannot rationally be extended beyond, a relative handful of large sources capable of shouldering heavy substantive and procedural burdens.

* * * EPA acknowledges that PSD review is a "complicated, resource-intensive, time-consuming, and sometimes contentious process" suitable for "hundreds of larger sources," not "tens of thousands of smaller sources." 74 Fed. Reg. 55304, 55321–55322.

* * * As EPA wrote, Title V is "finely crafted for thousands," not millions, of sources. Tailoring Rule 31563.

The fact that EPA's greenhouse-gas-inclusive interpretation of the PSD and Title V triggers would place plainly excessive demands on limited governmental resources is alone a good reason for rejecting it; but that is not the only reason. EPA's interpretation is also unreasonable because it would bring about an enormous and transformative expansion in EPA's regulatory authority without clear congressional authorization * * *. The power to require permits for the construction and modification of tens of thousands, and the operation of millions, of small sources nationwide falls comfortably within the class of authorizations that we have been reluctant to read into ambiguous statutory text. Moreover, in EPA's assertion of that authority, we confront a singular situation: an agency laying claim to extravagant statutory power over the national economy while at the same time strenuously asserting that the authority claimed would render the statute "unrecognizable to the Congress that designed" it. Tailoring Rule 31555. Since, as we hold above, the statute does not compel EPA's interpretation, it would be patently unreasonable—not to say outrageous—for EPA to insist on seizing expansive power that it admits the statute is not designed to grant.

3

EPA thought that despite the foregoing problems, it could make its interpretation reasonable by adjusting the levels at which a source's greenhouse-gas emissions would oblige it to undergo PSD and Title V permitting. Although the Act, in no uncertain terms, requires permits for sources with the potential to emit more than 100 or 250 tons per year of a relevant pollutant, EPA in its Tailoring Rule wrote a new threshold of 100,000 tons per year for greenhouse gases * * *.

We conclude that EPA's rewriting of the statutory thresholds was impermissible and therefore could not validate the Agency's interpretation of the triggering provisions. An agency has no power to "tailor" legislation to bureaucratic policy goals by rewriting unambiguous statutory terms. Agencies exercise discretion only in the interstices created by statutory silence or ambiguity; they must always " 'give effect to the unambiguously expressed intent of Congress.' " *National Assn. of Home Builders v. Defenders of Wildlife*, 551 U. S. 644, 665 (2007) (quoting *Chevron*, 467 U. S., at 843). It is hard to imagine a statutory term less ambiguous than the precise numerical thresholds at which the Act requires PSD and Title V permitting * * *.

* * *

In the Tailoring Rule, EPA asserts newfound authority to regulate millions of small sources—including retail stores, offices, apartment buildings, shopping centers, schools, and churches—and to decide, on an ongoing basis and without regard for the thresholds prescribed by Congress, how many of those sources to regulate. We are not willing to stand on the dock and wave goodbye as EPA embarks on this multiyear voyage of discovery. We reaffirm the core administrative-law principle that an agency may not rewrite clear statutory terms to suit its own sense of how the statute should operate. EPA therefore lacked authority to "tailor" the Act's unambiguous numerical thresholds to accommodate its greenhouse-gas-inclusive interpretation of the permitting triggers. Instead, the need to rewrite clear provisions of the statute should have alerted EPA that it had taken a wrong interpretive turn * * *.

B.   BACT for "Anyway" Sources

For the reasons we have given, EPA overstepped its statutory authority when it decided that a source could become subject to PSD or Title V permitting by reason of its greenhouse-gas emissions. But what about "anyway" sources, those that would need permits based on their emissions of more conventional pollutants (such as particulate matter)? We now consider whether EPA reasonably interpreted the Act to require those sources to comply with "best available control technology" emission standards for greenhouse gases.

1

To obtain a PSD permit, a source must be "subject to the best available control technology" for "each pollutant subject to regulation under [the Act]" that it emits. § 7475(a)(4). The Act defines BACT as "an emission limitation based on the maximum degree of reduction of each pollutant subject to regulation" that is "achievable . . . through application of production processes and available methods, systems, and techniques, including fuel cleaning, clean fuels, or treatment or innovative fuel combustion techniques." § 7479(3). BACT is determined "on a case-by-case basis, taking into account energy, environmental, and economic impacts and other costs." *Ibid.*

* * *

2

The question before us is whether EPA's decision to require BACT for greenhouse gases emitted by sources otherwise subject to PSD review is, as a general matter, a permissible interpretation of the statute under *Chevron*. We conclude that it is.

The text of the BACT provision is far less open-ended than the text of the PSD and Title V permitting triggers. It states that BACT is required "for each pollutant subject to regulation under this chapter" (i.e., the entire Act), § 7475(a)(4), a phrase that—as the D. C. Circuit wrote 35 years ago— "would not seem readily susceptible [of] misinterpretation." *Alabama Power Co. v. Costle*, 636 F. 2d 323, 404 (1979). Whereas the dubious breadth of "any air pollutant" in the permitting triggers suggests a role for agency judgment in identifying the subset of pollutants covered by the particular regulatory program at issue, the more specific phrasing of the BACT provision suggests that the necessary judgment has already been made by Congress. The wider statutory context likewise does not suggest that the BACT provision can bear a narrowing construction: There is no indication that the Act elsewhere uses, or that EPA has interpreted, "each pollutant subject to regulation under this chapter" to mean anything other than what it says.

Even if the text were not clear, applying BACT to greenhouse gases is not so disastrously unworkable, and need not result in such a dramatic expansion of agency authority, as to convince us that EPA's interpretation is unreasonable. We are not talking about extending EPA jurisdiction over millions of previously unregulated entities, but about moderately increasing the demands EPA (or a state permitting authority) can make of entities already subject to its regulation. And it is not yet clear that EPA's demands will be of a significantly different character from those traditionally associated with PSD review. In short, the record before us does not establish that the BACT provision as written is incapable of being sensibly applied to greenhouse gases.

We acknowledge the potential for greenhouse-gas BACT to lead to an unreasonable and unanticipated degree of regulation, and our decision should not be taken as an endorsement of all aspects of EPA's current approach, nor as a free rein for any future regulatory application of BACT in this distinct context. Our narrow holding is that nothing in the statute categorically prohibits EPA from interpreting the BACT provision to apply to greenhouse gases emitted by "anyway" sources.

* * *

To sum up: We hold that EPA exceeded its statutory authority when it interpreted the Clean Air Act to require PSD and Title V permitting for stationary sources based on their greenhouse-gas emissions. Specifically, the Agency may not treat greenhouse gases as a pollutant for purposes of defining a "major emitting facility" (or a "modification" thereof) in the PSD context or a "major source" in the Title V context. To the extent its regulations purport to do so, they are invalid. EPA may, however, continue to treat greenhouse gases as a "pollutant subject to regulation under this chapter" for purposes of requiring BACT for "anyway" sources.

The judgment of the Court of Appeals is affirmed in part and reversed in part.

It is so ordered.

JUSTICE BREYER, with whom JUSTICE GINSBURG, JUSTICE SOTOMAYOR, and JUSTICE KAGAN join, concurring in part and dissenting in part.

* * *

These cases take as a given our decision in *Massachusetts* that the Act's general definition of "air pollutant" includes greenhouse gases. One of the questions posed by these cases is whether those gases fall within the scope of the phrase "any air pollutant" as that phrase is used in the more specific provisions of the Act here at issue. The Court's answer is "no." I disagree.

* * *

These cases concern the definitions of "major emitting facility" and "major source," each of which is defined to mean any stationary source that emits more than a threshold quantity of "any air pollutant." See § 7479(1) ("major emitting facility"); §§ 7602(j), 7661(2)(B) ("major source"). To simplify the exposition, I will refer only to the PSD program and its definition of "major emitting facility"; a parallel analysis applies to Title V.

As it is used in the PSD provisions,

"[t]he term 'major emitting facility' means any of [a list of specific categories of] stationary sources of air pollutants which emit, or have the potential to emit, one hundred tons per year or more of any air pollutant . . . . Such term also includes any other source with the potential to emit two hundred and fifty tons per year or more of any air pollutant." § 7479(1).

To simplify further, I will ignore the reference to specific types of source that emit at least 100 tons per year (tpy) of any air pollutant. In effect, we are dealing with a statute that says that the PSD program's regulatory requirements must be applied to

"any stationary source that has the potential to emit two hundred fifty tons per year or more of any air pollutant."

The interpretive difficulty in these cases arises out of the definition's use of the phrase "two hundred fifty tons per year or more," which I will call the "250 tpy threshold." When applied to greenhouse gases, 250 tpy is far too low a threshold. As the Court explains, tens of thousands of stationary sources emit large quantities of one greenhouse gas, carbon dioxide. To apply the programs at issue here to all those sources would be extremely expensive and burdensome, counterproductive, and perhaps impossible; it would also contravene Congress's intent that the programs' coverage be limited to those large sources whose emissions are substantial enough to justify the regulatory burdens. The EPA recognized as much, and it addressed the problem by issuing a regulation—the Tailoring Rule—that purports to raise the coverage threshold for greenhouse gases from the statutory figure of 250 tpy to 100,000 tpy in order to keep the programs' coverage limited to "a relatively small number of large industrial sources." 75 Fed. Reg. 31514, 31555 (2010).

The Tailoring Rule solves the practical problems that would have been caused by the 250 tpy threshold. But what are we to do about the statute's language? The statute specifies a definite number—250, not 100,000—and it says that facilities that are covered by that number must meet the program's requirements. The statute says nothing about agency discretion to change that number. What is to be done? How, given the statute's language, can the EPA exempt from regulation sources that emit more than 250 but less than 100,000 tpy of greenhouse gases (and that also do not emit other regulated pollutants at threshold levels)?

The Court answers by (1) pointing out that regulation at the 250 tpy threshold would produce absurd results, (2) refusing to read the statute as compelling such results, and (3) consequently interpreting the phrase "*any* air pollutant" as containing an implicit exception for greenhouse gases. (Emphasis added.) Put differently, the Court reads the statute as defining "major emitting facility" to mean "stationary sources that have the potential to emit two hundred fifty tons per year or more of any air pollutant except for those air pollutants, such as carbon dioxide, with respect to which regulation at that threshold would be impractical or absurd or would sweep in smaller sources that Congress did not mean to cover."

I agree with the Court that the word "any," when used in a statute, does not normally mean "any in the universe." * * *

The law has long recognized that terms such as "any" admit of unwritten limitations and exceptions * * *.

* * *

But I do not agree with the Court that the only way to avoid an absurd or otherwise impermissible result in these cases is to create an atextual greenhouse gas exception to the phrase "any air pollutant." After all, the word "any" makes an earlier appearance in the definitional provision, which defines "major emitting facility" to mean "*any* . . . source with the potential to emit two hundred and fifty tons per year or more of any air pollutant." § 7479(1) (emphasis added). As a linguistic matter, one can just as easily read an implicit exception for small-scale greenhouse gas emissions into the phrase "any source" as into the phrase "any air pollutant." And given the purposes of the PSD program and the Act as a whole, as well as the specific roles of the different parts of the statutory definition, finding flexibility in "any source" is far more sensible than the Court's route of finding it in "any air pollutant."

The implicit exception I propose reads almost word for word the same as the Court's, except that the location of the exception has shifted. To repeat, the Court reads the definition of "major emitting facility" as if it referred to "any source with the potential to emit two hundred fifty tons per year or more of any air pollutant *except for those air pollutants, such as carbon dioxide, with respect to which regulation at that threshold would be impractical or absurd or would sweep in smaller sources that Congress did not mean to cover.*" I would simply move the implicit exception, which I've italicized, so that it applies to "source" rather than "air pollutant": "any source with the potential to emit two hundred fifty tons per year or more of any air pollutant *except for those sources, such as those emitting unmanageably small amounts of greenhouse gases, with respect to which regulation at that threshold would be impractical or absurd or would sweep in smaller sources that Congress did not mean to cover.*"

From a legal, administrative, and functional perspective—that is, from a perspective that assumes that Congress was not merely trying to arrange words on paper but was seeking to achieve a real-world *purpose*—my way of reading the statute is the more sensible one. For one thing, my reading is consistent with the specific purpose underlying the 250 tpy threshold specified by the statute. The purpose of that number was not to prevent the regulation of dangerous air pollutants that cannot be sensibly regulated at that particular threshold, though that is the effect that the Court's reading gives the threshold. Rather, the purpose was to limit the PSD program's obligations to larger sources while exempting the many small sources whose emissions are low enough that imposing burdensome regulatory requirements on them would be senseless.

* * *

An implicit source-related exception would serve this statutory purpose while going no further. The implicit exception that the Court reads into the phrase "any air pollutant," by contrast, goes well beyond the limited congressional objective. Nothing in the statutory text, the legislative history, or common sense suggests that Congress, when it imposed the 250 tpy threshold, was trying to undermine its own deliberate decision to use the broad language "any air pollutant" by removing some substances (rather than some facilities) from the PSD program's coverage.

* * *

I agree with the Court's holding that stationary sources that are subject to the PSD program because they emit other (non-greenhouse-gas) pollutants in quantities above the statutory threshold—those facilities that the Court refers to as "anyway" sources—must meet the "best available control technology" requirement of § 7475(a)(4) with respect to greenhouse gas emissions. I therefore join Part II-B-2 of the Court's opinion. But as for the Court's holding that the EPA cannot interpret the language at issue here to cover facilities that emit more than 100,000 tpy of greenhouse gases by virtue of those emissions, I respectfully dissent.

JUSTICE ALITO, with whom JUSTICE THOMAS joins, concurring in part and dissenting in part.

In *Massachusetts v. EPA*, 549 U. S. 497 (2007), this Court considered whether greenhouse gases fall within the Clean Air Act's general definition of an air "pollutant." Id., at 528–529. The Environmental Protection Agency cautioned us that "key provisions of the [Act] cannot cogently be applied to [greenhouse gas] emissions," Brief for Federal Respondent in *Massachusetts v. EPA*, O. T. 2006, No. 05–1120, p. 22, but the Court brushed the warning aside and had "little trouble" concluding that the Act's "sweeping definition" of a pollutant encompasses greenhouse gases. 549 U. S., at 528–529. I believed *Massachusetts v. EPA* was wrongly decided at the time, and these cases further expose the flaws with that decision.

* * *

As the present cases now show, trying to fit greenhouse gases into "key provisions" of the Clean Air Act involves more than a "little trouble." These cases concern the provisions of the Act relating to the "Prevention of Significant Deterioration" (PSD), 42 U. S. C. §§ 7470–7492, as well as Title V of the Act, § 7661. And in order to make those provisions apply to greenhouse gases in a way that does not produce absurd results, the EPA effectively amended the Act. The Act contains specific emissions thresholds that trigger PSD and Title V coverage, but the EPA crossed out the figures enacted by Congress and substituted figures of its own.

I agree with the Court that the EPA is neither required nor permitted to take this extraordinary step, and I therefore join Parts I and II-A of the Court's opinion.

* * *

I do not agree, however, with the Court's conclusion that what it terms "anyway sources," i.e., sources that are subject to PSD and Title V permitting as the result of the emission of conventional pollutants, must install "best available control technology" (BACT) for greenhouse gases. As is the case with the PSD and Title V thresholds, trying to fit greenhouse gases into the BACT analysis badly distorts the scheme that Congress adopted.

* * *

NOTES

If you are having trouble seeing the step-two problem in *Utility Air Regulatory Group*, perhaps it is because there may not actually be one lurking anywhere, despite the characterization of the case in step-two terms by the former administrative law professors who authored both the majority and dissenting opinions. The case really involves two distinct step-one problems, with a step-two issue playing a rather minor role.

Building on the 2005 decision in *Massachusetts v. EPA,* which construed the word "pollutant" in one portion of the Clean Air Act to include CO_2, the EPA claimed that the plain meaning of "pollutant" mandated that the term receive the same meaning throughout the statute and specifically in the permitting provisions at issue in *Utility Air Regulatory Group.* Said the agency: We will lose at *Chevron* step one if we do not construe the term "pollutant" in the permitting provision to have the same meaning as the term "pollutant" in the provision at issue in *Massachusetts v. EPA.* Said the majority: No, you will not lose at step one if you fail to construe the statute that way. It is not at all clear at step one that the word "pollutant" carries exactly the same meaning in every provision of the Clean Air Act. It would be step-two reasonable, the majority claims, to construe the word "pollutant" in the statute's permitting provision to include CO_2, but it would also be step-two reasonable to read the permitting section to have a narrower meaning of "pollutant" that does not include CO_2. So the agency's inclusive interpretation of "pollutant" in the permitting provision is permissible but not compelled. That resolves the first step one issue—and seems to resolve the only relevant step-two issue squarely in favor of the agency.

The second step-one issue is a bit subtler, because the majority does not identify it as a step-one issue, but: Putting aside for the moment the meaning of the word "pollutant," can 100 tons be read as 100,000 tons instead? Although the majority casts this as part of its step-two inquiry, doesn't the case obviously yield a step-one holding that no such interpretation is permissible? That then leaves the agency with a choice. It is free, after this decision, to choose to construe the permitting provisions to include CO_2, which will be upheld under step two as reasonable, but then the agency must get ready to deal with several million permit applications from small sources that produce more than 100 tons of CO_2 annually. Alternatively, the agency could choose to construe the statute (per the decision's first step-one holding) to exclude CO_2 from the permitting provision, and that determination would be upheld as reasonable as well. Choose, says the Court.

One can agree or disagree with either of the Court's step-one (as your editor has characterized them) determinations, but in no circumstance does the decision say much of interest about step two of *Chevron.* Perhaps the lesson in all of this is that the seemingly sharp distinction between *Chevron's* two steps is an illusion. The author of the majority opinion in *Utility Air Regulatory Group* definitely thought so, *see supra* page 605 n.17, though other jurists strongly defend a harder line between step one and step two. *See Waterkeeper*

Alliance v. EPA, 853 F.3d 527, 539 (D.C.Cir.2017) (Brown, J., concurring) ("Truncating the *Chevron* two-step into a one-step 'reasonableness' inquiry lets the judiciary leave its statutory escort to blow on an agency's dice * * *. If a court could purport fealty to *Chevron* while subjugating statutory clarity to agency 'reasonableness,' textualism will be trivialized.").

The nature of the agency's step-two error was a bit clearer—at least to the five Justices in the majority—in *Michigan v. EPA*, 576 U.S. ___, 135 S.Ct. 2699 (2015). The hazardous air-pollutant program under the Clean Air Act applies to fossil-fuel-fired power plants if the Environmental Protection Agency determines that such regulation is "appropriate and necessary." 42 U.S.C. § 7412(n)(1)(A) (2012). After finding potential health dangers from, *inter alia,* mercury emissions from power plants, the EPA made such an "appropriate and necessary" determination while specifically indicating that costs—whether of compliance with the regulatory program or of other kinds— were not to be considered in the threshold determination of the appropriateness of regulation, though the agency did not foreclose consideration of costs at other stages of the regulatory process, such as the prescription of specific emissions standards or the creation of regulatory categories for different kinds of power plants.

In a 5–4 decision, the Supreme Court held that it was unreasonable to interpret the statute to exclude consideration of costs from the initial decision whether regulation was "appropriate":

> EPA's decision to regulate power plants under § 7412 allowed the Agency to reduce power plants' emissions of hazardous air pollutants and thus to improve public health and the environment. But the decision also ultimately cost power plants, according to the Agency's own estimate, nearly $10 billion a year. EPA refused to consider whether the costs of its decision outweighed the benefits. The Agency gave cost no thought *at all*, because it considered cost irrelevant to its initial decision to regulate.

> EPA's disregard of cost rested on its interpretation of § 7412(n)(1)(A), which, to repeat, directs the Agency to regulate power plants if it "finds such regulation is appropriate and necessary." The Agency accepts that it *could* have interpreted this provision to mean that cost is relevant to the decision to add power plants to the program. Tr. of Oral Arg. 44. But it chose to read the statute to mean that cost makes no difference to the initial decision to regulate. See 76 Fed. Reg. 24988 (2011) ("We further interpret the term 'appropriate' to not allow for the consideration of costs"); 77 Fed. Reg. 9327 ("Cost does not have to be read into the definition of 'appropriate' ").

> We review this interpretation under the standard set out in *Chevron U. S. A. Inc. v. Natural Resources Defense Council, Inc.*, 467 U. S. 837 (1984). *Chevron* directs courts to accept an agency's reasonable resolution of an ambiguity in a statute that the agency

administers. *Id.,* at 842–843. Even under this deferential standard, however, "agencies must operate within the bounds of reasonable interpretation." *Utility Air Regulatory Group* v. *EPA*, 573 U.S. ___, ___ (2014) (slip op., at 16) (internal quotation marks omitted). EPA strayed far beyond those bounds when it read § 7412(n)(1) to mean that it could ignore cost when deciding whether to regulate power plants.

A

* * * Congress instructed EPA to add power plants to the [hazardous emissions] program if (but only if) the Agency finds regulation "appropriate and necessary." § 7412(n)(1)(A) * * *. Read naturally in the present context, the phrase "appropriate and necessary" requires at least some attention to cost. One would not say that it is even rational, never mind "appropriate," to impose billions of dollars in economic costs in return for a few dollars in health or environmental benefits. In addition, "cost" includes more than the expense of complying with regulations; any disadvantage could be termed a cost. EPA's interpretation precludes the Agency from considering *any* type of cost— including, for instance, harms that regulation might do to human health or the environment. The Government concedes that if the Agency were to find that emissions from power plants do damage to human health, but that the technologies needed to eliminate these emissions do even more damage to human health, it would *still* deem regulation appropriate. See Tr. of Oral Arg. 70. No regulation is "appropriate" if it does significantly more harm than good.

There are undoubtedly settings in which the phrase "appropriate and necessary" does not encompass cost. But this is not one of them. Section 7412(n)(1)(A) directs EPA to determine whether "*regulation* is appropriate and necessary." (Emphasis added.) Agencies have long treated cost as a centrally relevant factor when deciding whether to regulate. Consideration of cost reflects the understanding that reasonable regulation ordinarily requires paying attention to the advantages *and* the disadvantages of agency decisions. It also reflects the reality that "too much wasteful expenditure devoted to one problem may well mean considerably fewer resources available to deal effectively with other (perhaps more serious) problems." *Entergy Corp.* v. *Riverkeeper, Inc.*, 556 U. S. 208, 233 (2009) (Breyer, J., concurring in part and dissenting in part). Against the backdrop of this established administrative practice, it is unreasonable to read an instruction to an administrative agency to determine whether "regulation is appropriate and necessary" as an invitation to ignore cost.

* * *

* * * EPA argues that it need not consider cost when first deciding *whether* to regulate power plants because it can consider cost later when deciding *how much* to regulate them. The question before us, however, is the meaning of the "appropriate and necessary" standard that governs the initial decision to regulate. And as we have discussed, context establishes that this expansive standard encompasses cost. Cost may become relevant again at a later stage of the regulatory process, but that possibility does not establish its irrelevance at *this* stage. In addition, once the Agency decides to regulate power plants, it must promulgate certain minimum or floor standards no matter the cost (here, nearly $10 billion a year); the Agency may consider cost only when imposing regulations *beyond* these minimum standards. By EPA's logic, someone could decide whether it is "appropriate" to buy a Ferrari without thinking about cost, because he plans to think about cost later when deciding whether to upgrade the sound system.

135 S.Ct. at 2706–09.

The four dissenting Justices agreed that consideration of costs was an essential part of the statutory structure, but they argued, at much greater length and depth than can be presented here, that such consideration at later stages of the regulatory process sufficed to sustain the initial decision to regulate:

I agree with the majority—let there be no doubt about this—that EPA's power plant regulation would be unreasonable if "[t]he Agency gave cost no thought *at all*." *Ante*, at 5 (emphasis in original). But that is just not what happened here. Over more than a decade, EPA took costs into account at multiple stages and through multiple means as it set emissions limits for power plants. And when making its initial "appropriate and necessary" finding, EPA knew it would do exactly that—knew it would thoroughly consider the cost-effectiveness of emissions standards later on. That context matters. The Agency acted well within its authority in declining to consider costs at the opening bell of the regulatory process given that it would do so in every round thereafter—and given that the emissions limits finally issued would depend crucially on those accountings. Indeed, EPA could not have measured costs at the process's initial stage with any accuracy * * *.

* * *

The only issue in these cases, then, is whether EPA acted reasonably * * * in making its "appropriate and necessary finding" based on pollution's harmful effects and channeling cost considerations to phases of the rulemaking in which emission levels are actually set. Said otherwise, the question is not whether EPA can reasonably find it "appropriate" to regulate without thinking about costs, full stop. It cannot, and it did not. Rather, the question is whether EPA can reasonably find it "appropriate" to trigger the regulatory process based on harms (and technological feasibility) alone, given that costs will come into play, in multiple ways and at multiple stages, before any emission limit goes into effect.

In considering that question, the very nature of the word "appropriate" matters. "[T]he word 'appropriate,'" this Court has recognized, "is inherently context-dependent": Giving it content requires paying attention to the surrounding circumstances. And here that means considering the place of the "appropriate and necessary" finding in the broader regulatory scheme—as a triggering mechanism that gets a complex rulemaking going * * *. The statutory language, in other words, is a directive to remove one's blinders and view things whole—to consider what it is fitting to do at the threshold stage given what will happen at every other.

135 S.Ct. at 2714–15, 2717–18 (Kagan, J., dissenting). The majority responded that "[t]his line of reasoning contradicts the foundational principle of administrative law that a court may uphold agency action only on the grounds that the agency invoked when it took the action. *SEC v. Chenery Corp.*, 318 U. S. 13. When it deemed regulation of power plants appropriate, EPA said that cost was *irrelevant* to that determination—not that cost-benefit analysis would be deferred until later. Much *less* did it say (what the dissent now concludes) that the consideration of cost at subsequent stages will ensure that the costs are not disproportionate to the benefits. What it said is that cost is irrelevant to the decision to regulate." 135 S.Ct. at 2710. The dissent sur-responded: "The 'costs of controls,' the Agency promised, 'will be examined' as 'a part of developing a regulation.' 65 Fed. Reg. 79830. Tellingly, these words appear nowhere in the majority's opinion. But what are they other than a statement that cost concerns, contra the majority, are *not* "irrelevant," *ante*, at 13 (without citation)—that they are simply going to come in later?" 135 S.Ct. at 2725. Is this a dispute about the reasonableness of an agency's interpretation of a statute or about the reasonableness of an agency's policy-making process? Does that difference matter?

The discussion thus far has generally assumed that an interpretation's reasonableness depends in some way on its "fit" with the relevant statute—much as the substantial evidence test measures a conclusion's "fit" with the relevant evidence. Does that exhaust the meaning of reasonableness in the context of *Chevron*? What if the agency reached its conclusion by putting substantively reasonable interpretations into a hat and pulling one out at random? Is the reasonableness of the *process* by which the agency reached its conclusion relevant to step two of *Chevron*? *See Catskill Mountains Chapter of Trout Unlimited, Inc. v. EPA*, 846 F.3d 492, 521 (2d Cir.2017) ("An agency interpretation would surely be 'arbitrary' or 'capricious' if it were picked out of a hat, or arrived at with no explanation, even if it might otherwise be deemed reasonable on some unstated ground."). (Your editor has been using the random-drawing-from-a-hat example for several editions of this book. He does not know whether to be happy or crushed to be upstaged by higher authority.)

The agency's *reasoning process* is generally regulated by a separate doctrine, which we will encounter later in this chapter. *See infra* pages 748–851. The law concerning the relationship between this other doctrine and *Chevron* is just starting to be fleshed out by the courts, and a discussion of this topic requires some analytical tools that we have not yet developed. Accordingly, we will significantly revisit the step two problem later in this chapter.

If *Chevron* step two seems fuzzy, there is reason for that. The lack of articulation in judicial decisions of what step two actually entails leads to very thin doctrine, hard-to-follow reasoning, and a good deal of ad hoc decisionmaking. As with much of administrative law, the only real way to get a handle on what is happening—and that handle is likely to be slippery at best—is to read a *lot* of cases and try to get a "feel" for the general thrust of doctrine. That is obviously not practical in a law school course.

See if the following case makes you feel better, worse, or neither about your understanding of *Chevron* step two. Pay attention to the interpretative methodologies applied in this decision and to the kinds of Supreme Court authorities that the opinion chooses to cite. Is it relevant that all three members of the panel in this case would self-identify as "conservative" judges? Would the case come out differently—or would the opinion have been written any differently—if the issues were viewed through the lens of other interpretative methodologies that also have prominent adherents on the federal bench?

VAN HOLLEN, JR. V. FEC

United States Court of Appeals, District of Columbia Circuit, 2016.
811 F.3d 486.

Before BROWN, CIRCUIT JUDGE, and SENTELLE and RANDOLPH, SENIOR CIRCUIT JUDGES.

BROWN, CIRCUIT JUDGE:

The arc of campaign finance law has been ambivalent, bending toward speech and disclosure. Indeed what has made this area of election law so challenging is that these two values exist in unmistakable tension. Disclosure chills speech. Speech without disclosure risks corruption. And the Supreme Court's track record of expanding who may speak while simultaneously blessing robust disclosure rules has set these two values on an ineluctable collision course.

That tension is on full display in this appeal. At issue is whether to uphold the FEC's rule requiring corporations and labor organizations to disclose only those donations "made for the purpose of furthering electioneering communications" or whether the Bipartisan Campaign Reform Act requires disclosure of *all* donations irrespective of donative purpose. Christopher Van Hollen, Jr.—a member of the United States House of Representatives—challenged this rule under the familiar *Chevron* and *State Farm* frameworks. In a previous judgment, we reversed the district court and held the rule survived *Chevron* Step One. We now consider whether the rule survives Step Two and *State Farm's* "arbitrary and capricious" test. We hold that it does.

I

* * *

* * * Congress passed the Bipartisan Campaign Reform Act (BCRA) in 2002. BCRA recognized and regulated a new category of political advertising called "electioneering communications," defined as communications that "refer[ ] to a clearly identified candidate" "made within" sixty days of a general election or thirty days of a primary election. 2 U.S.C. § 434(f)(3)(A)(i) (2002) * * *. It required any person making an expenditure (referred to as a "disbursement") totaling more than $10,000 to disclose "all persons sharing the costs of the disbursement." Id. §§ 434(f)(2)(A), (B), and (D). BCRA also went one step further: it altogether banned corporations and unions from using their general treasuries to fund electioneering communications. *Id.* § 441b(b)(2). These provisions were upheld [against a First Amendment challenge] by a sharply divided Court in *McConnell v. FEC*, 540 U.S. 93, 124 S.Ct. 619, 157 L.Ed.2d 491 (2003).

In BCRA's wake, the FEC promulgated several rules to enforce the various reforms, two of which are relevant to today's appeal. First, the FEC promulgated a rule enforcing BCRA's ban on corporate and union expenditures for electioneering communications. Electioneering Communications, 67 Fed.Reg. 65190, 65190 (Oct. 23, 2002). Second, the FEC promulgated a rule to enforce BCRA's requirement for disclosure of "the names and addresses of all contributors who contributed an aggregate amount of $1,000 or more to the person making the disbursement." 52 U.S.C. 434(f)(2)(E)–(F). The FEC's rule mirrored this language almost identically but replaced the words "contributor" and "contributed" with "donor" and "donated." Bipartisan Campaign Reform Act of 2002 Reporting, 68 Fed.Reg. 404, 420 (Jan. 3, 2003). Whatever the import of that choice, it is clear that as of 2003, (1) corporations and unions could not fund electioneering communications out of their general treasuries, and (2) with certain exceptions not relevant to this opinion, persons making disbursements for electioneering communications had to disclose the names of anyone who donated $1,000 or more to them.

But the Supreme Court would soon deliver a heavy blow to BCRA's attempt to regulate electioneering communications. With its ruling in *FEC v. Wisconsin Right to Life, Inc.*, 551 U.S. 449, 127 S.Ct. 2652, 168 L.Ed.2d 329 (2007), another sharply divided decision, and this time without even a majority opinion, the Court held corporations and unions could not be barred from electioneering communications unless they are "the functional equivalent of express advocacy." *Id.* at 465, 127 S.Ct. 2652. And an ad is only the functional equivalent of express advocacy, the Court said, when it "is susceptible of no reasonable interpretation other than as an appeal to vote for or against a specific candidate." *Id.* at 469–70, 127 S.Ct. 2652 * * *.

The FEC was now left to decide how BCRA's disclosure requirements should apply to a class of speakers Congress never expected would have anything to disclose. The FEC published a Notice of Proposed Rulemaking (NPRM) and requested comments on proposed rules that "would implement the Supreme Court's decision in *Wisconsin Right to Life*." 72 Fed.Reg. 50261, 50262 (Aug. 31, 2007). That NPRM advanced two proposals for applying BCRA's disclosure provisions to corporations and unions. Under the first, the FEC would simply apply the existing disclosure requirements for individuals and qualified nonprofit corporations (QNCs) to corporations and unions, which would require disclosure of all $1,000 contributors. Under the second, the FEC proposed to exempt corporations and unions from the disclosure requirements altogether.

The FEC received twenty-seven comments and held a two-day hearing. Rather than embracing either of the NPRM's proposals, it adopted a middle path. See Electioneering Communications, 72 Fed.Reg. 72899, 72900 (Dec. 26, 2007). Corporations and unions would not be altogether exempted, but neither would they be required to disclose every donation totaling $1,000 or more. Rather, corporations and unions would be required to disclose all donations totaling $1,000 or more that were "made for the purpose of furthering electioneering communications." *Id.* at 72911. This new "purpose requirement" set corporate and union electioneering communications apart from communications funded by other persons, who were still required to disclose all donations regardless of purpose.

Representative Christopher Van Hollen challenged the FEC's new purpose requirement and persuaded the district court that it violated BCRA's text. That decision was appealed to and reversed by a panel of this court, which concluded BCRA's disclosure provisions were ambiguous, and the FEC's rule cleared Chevron Step One. *Ctr. for Individual Freedom v. Van Hollen*, 694 F.3d 108, 111 (D.C.Cir.2012). Congress's use of the terms "contributors" and "contributed," the panel said, is "anything but clear." *Id.* The panel did "not agree with the District Court that the[se] words . . . cannot be construed to include a 'purpose' requirement." *Id.* However, it concluded that it was "in no position to assess the parties' arguments on whether § 104.20(c)(9) is reasonable, and thus entitled to deference under Chevron Step Two, or whether the regulation survives arbitrary and capricious review." *Id.* at 112. The panel sent the case back to the district court to sort these questions out.

On remand, the district court concluded that the FEC's rule failed at both the *Chevron* Step Two and arbitrary and capricious stages * * *.We review the FEC's action de novo, according no particular deference to the district court's judgment. *Fox v. Clinton*, 684 F.3d 67, 74 (D.C.Cir.2012).

II

Our analysis of Van Hollen's challenge picks up where our prior judgment left off. Van Hollen argues the FEC's disclosure rule is both an impermissible construction of BCRA and an arbitrary and capricious use of the FEC's regulatory authority, and the district court agreed on both scores. For the reasons outlined below, we do not.

A

We are first asked to decide whether the FEC's purpose requirement is "based on a permissible construction of [BCRA] in light of its language, structure, and purpose." *Nat'l Treasury Emp. Union v. FLRA*, 754 F.3d 1031, 1042 (D.C.Cir.2014). This inquiry, often called *Chevron* Step Two, "does not require the best interpretation, only a reasonable one." *Am. Forest and Paper Ass'n v. FERC*, 550 F.3d 1179, 1183 (D.C.Cir.2008). "We are bound to uphold agency interpretations . . . regardless whether there may be other reasonable, or even more reasonable, views." *Gentiva Healthcare Corp. v. Sebelius*, 723 F.3d 292, 296 (D.C.Cir.2013). In this case, BCRA is ambiguous, and the FEC's construction of it is reasonable. We defer accordingly.

The starting place for any *Chevron* Step Two inquiry is the text of the statute. BCRA states, in relevant part:

> "Every person who makes a disbursement for the direct costs of producing and airing electioneering communications in an aggregate amount in excess of $10,000 during any calendar year shall . . . file with the Commission a statement containing . . . the names and addresses of all contributors who contributed an aggregate amount of $1,000 or more to the person making the disbursement."

52 U.S.C. § 30104(f) (emphasis added). This provision directs the disclosure of "all contributors" and omits any explicit mention of a purpose requirement. By contrast, the neighboring section governing express advocacy directs disclosure of "each person who made a contribution . . . for the purpose of furthering an independent expenditure." *Id.* § 30104(c)(2)(C). The nonparallel nature of these two related provisions, Van Hollen contends, renders impermissible the FEC's purpose requirement. At the same time, FECA elsewhere defines "contribution," a term derived from the same root as the words in the challenged section, as a donation "by any person *for the purpose of influencing any election for Federal office.*" 52 U.S.C. § 30101(8)(A)(i) (emphasis added). And the FEC intentionally drew upon the express advocacy purpose requirement as precedent for resolving the ambiguity in the electioneering communications provision. See 72 Fed.Reg. at 72911 n. 22. Our question, then, is this: Does BCRA's text permit the FEC's purpose requirement?

To answer this, we must first remember what we've already settled. In our previous ruling, we concluded Congress did not have "an intention on the precise question" whether a purpose requirement is permissible as "it is doubtful that . . . Congress even anticipated the circumstances that the FEC faced when it promulgated [this regulation]." *Ctr. for Individual Freedom*, 694 F.3d at 111. We noted "it was due to the complicated situation that confronted the agency in 2007 and the absence of plain meaning in the statute that the FEC acted . . . to fill 'a gap' in the statute." *Id.* But while we might have stopped there, our analysis went beyond merely highlighting BCRA's ambiguity. We also weighed in on the precise interpretive question relevant to Step Two. We disagreed with the district court "that the words 'contributors' and 'contributed' . . . cannot be construed to include a 'purpose' requirement" and cited multiple dictionaries that "define 'contribute' in a way that is consistent with the regulation." *Id.* at 110–11. In other words, we held that whether corporations and unions should be required to disclose every person who gave $1,000 or more or only those who gave for the purpose of influencing electioneering communications was an open policy question, one Congress left for the FEC to decide.

That decision largely foreordains our *Chevron* Step Two answer. In deciding the Step One question, we did not limit our analysis to whether BCRA is ambiguous; we specifically concluded the FEC's interpretation of "contributors" was within the range of linguistically permissible constructions. Having thus already concluded section 30104(f) *could* be construed to include a purpose requirement, it would be odd for us to reverse course now and declare it *could not*.

But even setting aside that we all but answered the Step Two question last time around, the FEC's purpose requirement is more than just a permissible construction of BCRA; it's a persuasive one. For one, as suggested above, the FEC's purpose requirement is consistent with the purpose-laden definition of "contribution" set forth in FECA's very own definitional section. *See* 52 U.S.C. § 30101(8)(A)(i) (defining "contribution" as "anything of value made . . . for the purpose of influencing [a federal] election").

Moreover, the FEC's purpose requirement regulates electioneering communication disclosures in precisely the same way BCRA itself regulates express advocacy disclosures. In a neighboring provision, BCRA requires a person making an express advocacy expenditure to disclose only those "person[s] who made a contribution . . . for the purpose of furthering an independent expenditure." *Id.* § 30104(c)(2)(C). Thus, to resolve the ambiguity it faced in *Wisconsin Right to Life's* wake, the FEC simply opted for an approach already endorsed by Congress in a related context. That "Congress codified the very approach" the FEC now adopts in a similar context is "highly persuasive in demonstrating" the FEC's construction of BCRA "does not reflect an unreasonable interpretation of the statute." *Public Citizen v. Carlin*, 184 F.3d 900, 906 (D.C.Cir.1999).

Van Hollen counters this point, arguing Congress's failure to include a purpose requirement in the electioneering communication context— which it included for express advocacy—textually precludes the FEC from later doing so. This is a classic invocation of the *expressio unius* canon of construction, and if we were interpreting this statute directly rather than filtered through an agency's construction, Van Hollen's argument would have serious bite. However, as is usually the case, the procedural posture matters. The *expressio unius* canon operates differently in our review of agency action than it does when we are directly interpreting a statute. *See Tex. Rural Legal Aid, Inc. v. Legal Servs. Corp.*, 940 F.2d 685, 694 (D.C.Cir.1991) ("[T]his canon has little force in the administrative setting."); *Cheney R.R. Co. v. ICC*, 902 F.2d 66, 69 (D.C.Cir.1990) ("Whatever [*expressio unius's*] general force, we think it an especially feeble helper in an administrative setting, where Congress is presumed to have left to reasonable agency discretion questions that it has not directly resolved."). In scenarios of precisely this ilk, "we have consistently recognized that a congressional mandate in one section and silence in another often suggests not a prohibition but simply a decision not to mandate any solution in the second context, i.e., to leave the question to agency discretion." *Catawba Cnty., N.C. v. EPA*, 571 F.3d 20, 36

(D.C.Cir.2009). This approach dovetails appropriately with the wide latitude we afford agencies when interpreting statutes: we do not demand the best interpretation, only a reasonable one.

Nor do Van Hollen's other arguments persuade us that the FEC's purpose requirement was an impermissible construction of BCRA. Van Hollen contends the requirement "frustrate[s] the policy that Congress sought to implement" and therefore must be rejected. *See Shays v. FEC*, 528 F.3d 914, 919 (D.C.Cir.2008). Specifically, he asserts the FEC's rule violates BCRA's primary purpose of "improv[ing] disclosure" and "curtail[ing] circumvention of campaign finance rules," allowing contributors to "avoid reporting altogether" by simply "transmitting funds but remaining silent about their intended use." Van Hollen Br. at 27–28. And here, his invocation of our *Shays* decision does lend a measure of credibility. A panel of this court invalidated a regulation allowing "candidates to evade—almost completely—BCRA's restrictions on the use of soft money" because it "frustrate[d] Congress's goal of prohibiting soft money" in federal elections. 528 F.3d at 925. According to Van Hollen (and the district court), since "the legislative history of the BCRA makes it clear that the purpose behind the disclosure requirements was to enable voters to be informed about who was trying to influence their decisions," the purpose requirement's "limiting language" similarly frustrates BCRA. *Van Hollen v. Federal Election Commission*, 74 F.Supp.3d 407, 433–34 (D.D.C.2014).

But the art of statutory construction has moved beyond this particularly results-oriented brand of purposivism. Just because *one* of BCRA's purposes (even *chief* purposes) was broader disclosure does not mean that anything less than maximal disclosure is subversive. Statutes are hardly, if ever, singular in purpose. Rather, most laws seek to achieve a variety of ends in a way that reflects the give-and-take of the legislative process. *See Patel v. USCIS*, 732 F.3d 633, 636 (6th Cir.2013) ("[I]t is folly to talk about 'the purpose' of the statute when the statute reflects a compromise between multiple purposes."). That BCRA seeks more robust disclosure does not mean Congress wasn't also concerned with, say, the conflicting privacy interests that hang in the balance. In fact, Congress "took great care in crafting . . . language to avoid violating the important p[ ]rinciples in the First Amendment." 147 CONG. REC. S3033 (daily ed. Mar. 28, 2001) (statement of Sen. Jeffords). *Chevron* demands our deference when an agency's interpretation is "a reasonable accommodation of conflicting policies that were committed to the agency's care by the statute." 467 U.S. at 845, 104 S.Ct. 2778.

Moreover, the district court's invocation of such a sweeping disclosure purpose contradicts the very statute whose purposes it purports to protect. BCRA does not require disclosure at all costs; it *limits* disclosure in a number of ways. For example, for electioneering communications under

$10,000, no disclosures are necessary, *see* 52 U.S.C. § 30104(f)(1), and for those over $10,000, BCRA does not require disclosure of those who contribute $999 or less, *see id.* § 30104(f)(2)(E). These disclosure limitations suggest Congress's purposes were far more nuanced than the district court's characterization concedes.

To be sure, a statute's purpose is *relevant* to *Chevron's* Step Two inquiry. *See UC Health v. NLRB*, 803 F.3d 669, 675 (D.C.Cir.2015) (requiring deference so long as an agency construction is "reasonable and consistent with the statute's purpose"). But we are judges, not legislators, and it behooves us to maintain a healthy sense of modesty regarding our ability to discern the scope and priority of purposes the BCRA Congress pursued. "What judges believe Congress 'meant' (apart from the text) has a disturbing but entirely unsurprising tendency to be whatever judges think Congress must have meant, i.e., *should* have meant." *Zuni Pub. Sch. Dist. No. 89 v. Dep't of Educ.*, 550 U.S. 81, 117, 127 S.Ct. 1534, 167 L.Ed.2d 449 (2007) (Scalia, J., dissenting). What matters here is that Congress left the meaning of "contributor" ambiguous. Congressional silence of this sort is, in *Chevron* terms, "an implicit delegation from Congress to the agency to fill in the statutory gaps." *FDA v. Brown & Williamson Tobacco Corp.*, 529 U.S. 120, 159, 120 S.Ct. 1291, 146 L.Ed.2d 121 (2000) (emphasis added). It is a transfer of authority to the FEC, whose task it then became "not to find the best meaning of the text, but to formulate legally binding rules to fill in gaps based on policy judgments made *by the agency rather than Congress.*" *Michigan v. EPA*, ___ U.S. ___, 135 S.Ct. 2699, 2713, 192 L.Ed.2d 674 (2015) (Thomas, J., concurring) (emphasis added). The FEC did precisely that, deciding to fill the gap left in BCRA with the same purpose-requirement Congress adopted in related contexts. We are loathe to upset such a policy judgment based on nothing more than highly generalized overtures to BCRA's "primary purpose."

Because the FEC's purpose requirement is consistent with BCRA's text, history, and purposes, it easily clears the Chevron Step Two hurdle.

6.   HOW FAR DOES THIS GO?

When a court reviews an agency interpretation under *Chevron*, what does it actually decide? If it reverses the agency, the court is saying either that the statute has a clear meaning that is different from the one given by the agency or that the statute does not necessarily have a clear meaning but that the agency's interpretation is outside the realm of reasonable interpretations. But what if the court affirms the agency? The court might affirm the agency because the statute has a clear meaning and the agency nailed that meaning. Or it might affirm in the absence of any clear meaning if the agency's interpretation meets the step two reasonableness standard. In the latter case, can the agency change its mind? Suppose an agency interpretation of a concededly ambiguous statute is affirmed by the federal courts under step two of *Chevron*. We now know that the agency's interpretation was a reasonable resolution of the underlying ambiguity. In all likelihood, it was not the *only* reasonable resolution of that ambiguity; ambiguity by its nature can often be reasonably resolved in several, possibly conflicting, fashions. What if the agency, after savoring its judicial victory for a while, decides that it really should have resolved the ambiguity in a different manner. Is it now free to adopt a totally different (and let us stipulate equally "reasonable") interpretation from the one that it initially defended in court? Pure *Chevron* theory would suggest "yes," because to say on appellate review that the agency was reasonable is *not* to say that a different agency action would be *unreasonable*. Traditions of judicial review would suggest "no," because once the court has spoken, the judicial decision is thought to fix the statute's meaning.

This problem arose in the early years of *Chevron*, and it splintered the en banc Ninth Circuit. *See Mesa Verde Constr. Co. v. Northern Cal. Dist. Council of Laborers*, 861 F.2d 1124 (9th Cir.1988) (en banc). After staying under the rug for a long time, a variant of that problem resurfaced in a major way in 2005—and then again in 2012.

NATIONAL CABLE & TELECOMMUNICATIONS ASS'N V. BRAND X INTERNET SERVICES

Supreme Court of the United States, 2005.
545 U.S. 967, 125 S.Ct. 2688, 162 L.Ed.2d 820.

JUSTICE THOMAS delivered the opinion of the Court.

Title II of the Communications Act of 1934, 48 Stat. 1064, as amended, 47 U.S.C. § 151 *et seq.*, subjects all providers of "telecommunications servic[e]" to mandatory common-carrier regulation. In the order under review, the Federal Communications Commission concluded that cable companies that sell broadband Internet service do not provide "telecommunications servic[e]" as the Communications Act defines that term, and hence are exempt from mandatory common-carrier regulation under Title II. We must decide whether that conclusion is a lawful construction of the Communications Act under *Chevron U.S.A., Inc. v. Natural Resources Defense Council, Inc.*, 467 U.S. 837, 104 S.Ct. 2778, 81 L.Ed.2d 694 (1984), and the Administrative Procedure Act. We hold that it is.

I

The traditional means by which consumers in the United States access the network of interconnected computers that make up the Internet is through "dial-up" connections provided over local telephone facilities. See 345 F.3d 1120, 1123–24 (C.A.9 2003 (cases below)); *In re Inquiry Concerning High-Speed Access to the Internet Over Cable and Other Facilities*, 17 FCC Rcd. 4798, 4802–4803, ¶ 9, 2002 WL 407567 (2002) (hereinafter *Declaratory Ruling*). Using these connections, consumers access the Internet by making calls with computer modems through the telephone wires owned by local phone companies. Internet service providers (ISPs), in turn, link those calls to the Internet network, not only by providing a physical connection, but also by offering consumers the ability to translate raw Internet data into information they may both view on their personal computers and transmit to other computers connected to the Internet. Technological limitations of local telephone wires, however, retard the speed at which data from the Internet may be transmitted through end users' dial-up connections. Dial-up connections are therefore known as "narrowband," or slower speed, connections.

"Broadband" Internet service, by contrast, transmits data at much higher speeds. There are two principal kinds of broadband Internet service: cable modem service and Digital Subscriber Line (DSL) service. Cable modem service transmits data between the Internet and users' computers via the network of television cable lines owned by cable companies. DSL service provides high-speed access using the local telephone wires owned by local telephone companies. Cable companies and telephone companies can either provide Internet access directly to consumers, thus acting as ISPs themselves, or can lease their transmission facilities to independent ISPs that then use the facilities to provide consumers with Internet access. Other ways of transmitting high-speed Internet data into homes, including terrestrial-and satellite-based wireless networks, are also emerging.

II

At issue in these cases is the proper regulatory classification under the Communications Act of broadband cable Internet service. The Act, as amended by the Telecommunications Act of 1996, 110 Stat. 56, defines two categories of regulated entities relevant to these cases: telecommunications carriers and information-service providers. The Act regulates telecommunications carriers, but not information-service providers, as common carriers. Telecommunications carriers, for example, must charge just and reasonable, nondiscriminatory rates to their customers, 47 U.S.C. §§ 201–209, design their systems so that other carriers can interconnect with their communications networks, § 251(a)(1), and contribute to the federal "universal service" fund, § 254(d). These provisions are mandatory, but the Commission must forbear from applying them if it determines that the public interest requires it. §§ 160(a), (b). Information-service providers, by contrast, are not subject to mandatory common-carrier regulation under Title II, though the Commission has jurisdiction to impose additional regulatory obligations under its Title I ancillary jurisdiction to regulate interstate and foreign communications, see §§ 151–161.

* * *

The definitions of the terms "telecommunications service" and "information service" [are] established by the 1996 Act * * *. "Telecommunications service" * * * is "the offering of telecommunications for a fee directly to the public . . . regardless of the facilities used." 47 U.S.C. § 153(46). "Telecommunications" is "the transmission, between or among points specified by the user, of information of the user's choosing, without change in the form or content of the information as sent and received." § 153(43). "Telecommunications carrier[s]"—those subjected to mandatory Title II common-carrier regulation—are defined as "provider[s] of telecommunications services." § 153(44). And "information service" * * * is "the offering of a capability for generating, acquiring, storing, transforming, processing, retrieving, utilizing, or making available information via telecommunications . . ." § 153(20).

In September 2000, the Commission initiated a rulemaking proceeding to, among other things, apply these classifications to cable companies that offer broadband Internet service directly to consumers. In March 2002, that rulemaking culminated in the *Declaratory Ruling* under review in these cases. In the *Declaratory Ruling,* the Commission concluded that broadband Internet service provided by cable companies is an "information service" but not a "telecommunications service" under the Act, and therefore not subject to mandatory Title II common-carrier regulation. In support of this conclusion, the Commission relied heavily on its *Universal Service Report* [13 FCC Rcd. 11501, 1998 WL 166178 (1998)] [which] classified "non-facilities-based" ISPs—those that do not own the transmission facilities they use to connect the end user to the Internet— solely as information-service providers. Unlike those ISPs, cable companies own the cable lines they use to provide Internet access. Nevertheless, in the *Declaratory Ruling,* the Commission found no basis in the statutory definitions for treating cable companies differently from non-facilities-based ISPs: Both offer "a single, integrated service that enables the subscriber to utilize Internet access service . . . and to realize the benefits of a comprehensive service offering." *Declaratory Ruling* 4823, ¶ 38. Because Internet access provides a capability for manipulating and storing information, the Commission concluded that it was an information service.

The integrated nature of Internet access and the high-speed wire used to provide Internet access led the Commission to conclude that cable companies providing Internet access are not telecommunications providers. The [*1998 Universal Service*] *Report* had concluded that, though Internet service "involves data transport elements" because "an Internet access provider must enable the movement of information between customers' own computers and distant computers with which those customers seek to interact," it also "offers end users information-service capabilities inextricably intertwined with data transport." ISPs, therefore, were not "offering . . . telecommunications . . . directly to the public," and so were not properly classified as telecommunications carriers * * *.

The Commission applied this same reasoning to cable companies offering broadband Internet access. Its logic was that, like non-facilities-based ISPs, cable companies do not "offe[r] telecommunications service to the end user, but rather . . . merely us[e] telecommunications to provide end users with cable modem service." *Declaratory Ruling* 4824, ¶ 41. Though the Commission declined to apply mandatory Title II common-carrier regulation to cable companies, it invited comment on whether under its Title I jurisdiction it should require cable companies to offer other ISPs access to their facilities on common-carrier terms * * *.

The [Ninth Circuit] Court of Appeals * * * vacated the ruling to the extent it concluded that cable modem service was not "telecommunications service" under the Communications Act. It held that the Commission could not permissibly construe the Communications Act to exempt cable companies providing Internet service from Title II regulation. Rather than analyzing the permissibility of that construction under the deferential framework of *Chevron,* however, the Court of Appeals grounded its holding in the *stare decisis* effect of *AT & T Corp. v. Portland*, 216 F.3d 871 (C.A.9 2000). *Portland* held that cable modem service was a "telecommunications service," though the court in that case was not reviewing an administrative proceeding and the Commission was not a party to the case. Nevertheless, *Portland's* holding, the Court of Appeals reasoned, overrode the contrary interpretation reached by the Commission in the *Declaratory Ruling*.

We granted certiorari to settle the important questions of federal law that these cases present.

III

We first consider whether we should apply *Chevron's* framework to the Commission's interpretation of the term "telecommunications service." We conclude that we should. We also conclude that the Court of Appeals should have done the same, instead of following the contrary construction it adopted in *Portland*.

A

* * *

The *Chevron* framework governs our review of the Commission's construction. Congress has delegated to the Commission the authority to "execute and enforce" the Communications Act, § 151, and to "prescribe such rules and regulations as may be necessary in the public interest to carry out the provisions" of the Act, § 201(b). These provisions give the Commission the authority to promulgate binding legal rules; the Commission issued the order under review in the exercise of that authority;

and no one questions that the order is within the Commission's jurisdiction * * *.

* * *

B

The Court of Appeals declined to apply *Chevron* because it thought the Commission's interpretation of the Communications Act foreclosed by the conflicting construction of the Act it had adopted in *Portland* * * *. That reasoning was incorrect.

A court's prior judicial construction of a statute trumps an agency construction otherwise entitled to *Chevron* deference only if the prior court decision holds that its construction follows from the unambiguous terms of the statute and thus leaves no room for agency discretion * * *. [A]llowing a judicial precedent to foreclose an agency from interpreting an ambiguous statute, as the Court of Appeals assumed it could, would allow a court's interpretation to override an agency's. *Chevron's* premise is that it is for agencies, not courts, to fill statutory gaps. The better rule is to hold judicial interpretations contained in precedents to the same demanding *Chevron* step one standard that applies if the court is reviewing the agency's construction on a blank slate: Only a judicial precedent holding that the statute unambiguously forecloses the agency's interpretation, and therefore contains no gap for the agency to fill, displaces a conflicting agency construction.

A contrary rule would produce anomalous results. It would mean that whether an agency's interpretation of an ambiguous statute is entitled to *Chevron* deference would turn on the order in which the interpretations issue: If the court's construction came first, its construction would prevail, whereas if the agency's came first, the agency's construction would command *Chevron* deference. Yet whether Congress has delegated to an agency the authority to interpret a statute does not depend on the order in which the judicial and administrative constructions occur * * *.

The dissent answers that allowing an agency to override what a court believes to be the best interpretation of a statute makes "judicial decisions subject to reversal by Executive officers." It does not. Since *Chevron* teaches that a court's opinion as to the best reading of an ambiguous statute an agency is charged with administering is not authoritative, the agency's decision to construe that statute differently from a court does not say that the court's holding was legally wrong. Instead, the agency may, consistent with the court's holding, choose a different construction, since the agency remains the authoritative interpreter (within the limits of reason) of such statutes. In all other respects, the court's prior ruling remains binding law (for example, as to agency interpretations to which *Chevron* is inapplicable). The precedent has not been "reversed" by the agency, any more than a federal court's interpretation of a State's law can be said to have been "reversed" by a state court that adopts a conflicting (yet authoritative) interpretation of state law.

The Court of Appeals derived a contrary rule from a mistaken reading of this Court's decisions. [*See*] *Neal v. United States*, 516 U.S. 284, 116 S.Ct. 763, 133 L.Ed.2d 709 (1996) * * * ; *Maislin Industries, U.S., Inc. v. Primary Steel, Inc.*, 497 U.S. 116, 131, 110 S.Ct. 2759, 111 L.Ed.2d 94 (1990). Those decisions allow a court's prior interpretation of a statute to override an agency's interpretation only if the relevant court decision held the statute unambiguous.

Against this background, the Court of Appeals erred in refusing to apply *Chevron* to the Commission's interpretation of the definition of "telecommunications service." Its prior decision in *Portland* held only that the *best* reading of § 153(46) was that cable modem service was a "telecommunications service," not that it was the *only permissible* reading of the statute * * *. Before a judicial construction of a statute, whether contained in a precedent or not, may trump an agency's, the court must hold that the statute unambiguously requires the court's construction. *Portland* did not do so.

* * *

[The Court found the statute ambiguous and the agency's interpretation reasonable, and it upheld the agency decision.]

JUSTICE STEVENS, concurring. [Omitted]

JUSTICE BREYER, concurring. [Omitted.]

JUSTICE SCALIA, with whom JUSTICE SOUTER and JUSTICE GINSBURG join as to Part I, dissenting.

* * *

I

[This part of the dissent concluded that it was "perfectly clear that someone who sells cable-modem service is 'offering' telecommunications" and accordingly would have found the agency interpretation invalid under *Chevron* step one.]

II

* * *

Imagine the following sequence of events: FCC action is challenged as ultra vires under the governing statute; the litigation reaches all the way to the Supreme Court of the United States. The Solicitor General sets forth the FCC's official position (approved by the Commission) regarding interpretation of the statute. Applying *Mead*, however, the Court denies the agency position *Chevron* deference, finds that the *best* interpretation of the statute contradicts the agency's position, and holds the challenged agency action unlawful. The agency promptly conducts a rulemaking, and adopts a rule that comports with its earlier position—in effect disagreeing with the Supreme Court concerning the best interpretation of the statute. According to today's opinion, the agency is thereupon free to take the action that the Supreme Court found unlawful.

This is not only bizarre. It is probably unconstitutional * * *. Article III courts do not sit to render decisions that can be reversed or ignored by Executive officers * * *.

* * * A court's interpretation is conclusive, the Court says, only if it holds that interpretation to be "the *only permissible* reading of the statute," and not if it merely holds it to be "the *best* reading." Does this mean that in future statutory-construction cases involving agency-administered statutes courts must specify (presumably in dictum) which of the two they are holding? And what of the many cases decided in the past, before this dictum's requirement was established? Apparently, silence on the point means that the court's decision is subject to agency reversal: "Before a judicial construction of a statute, whether contained in a precedent or not, may trump an agency's, the court must hold that the statute unambiguously requires the court's construction." (I have not made, and as far as I know the Court has not made, any calculation of how many hundreds of past statutory decisions are now agency-reversible because of failure to include an "unambiguous" finding. I suspect the number is very large.) How much extra work will it entail for each court confronted with an agency-administered statute to determine whether it has reached, not only the right ("best") result, but "the only permissible" result? Is the standard for "unambiguous" under the Court's new agency-reversal rule the same as the standard for "unambiguous" under step one of *Chevron*? (If so, of course, every case that reaches step two of *Chevron* will be agency-reversible.) Does the "unambiguous" dictum produce *stare decisis* effect even when a court is *affirming,* rather than *reversing,* agency action-so that in the future the agency *must adhere* to that affirmed interpretation? If so, does the victorious agency have the right to appeal a Court of Appeals judgment in its favor, on the ground that the text in question is in fact not (as the Court of Appeals held) unambiguous, so the agency should be able to change its view in the future?

It is indeed a wonderful new world that the Court creates, one full of promise for administrative-law professors in need of tenure articles and, of course, for litigators * * *.

UNITED STATES V. HOME CONCRETE & SUPPLY, LLC

Supreme Court of the United States, 2012.
566 U.S. 478, 132 S.Ct. 1836, 182 L.Ed.2d 746.

JUSTICE BREYER delivered the opinion of the Court, except as to Part IV-C.

Ordinarily, the Government must assess a deficiency against a taxpayer within "3 years after the return was filed." 26 U.S.C. § 6501(a) (2000 ed.). The 3-year period is extended to 6 years, however, when a taxpayer " *omits from gross income an amount properly includible therein* which is in excess of 25 percent of the amount of gross income stated in the return." § 6501(e)(1)(A) (emphasis added). The question before us is whether this latter provision applies (and extends the ordinary 3-year limitations period) when the taxpayer *overstates his basis* in property that he has sold, thereby *understating the gain* that he received from its sale. Following *Colony, Inc. v. Commissioner,* 357 U.S. 28, 78 S.Ct. 1033, 2 L.Ed.2d 1119 (1958), we hold that the provision does not apply to an overstatement of basis. Hence the 6-year period does not apply.

* * *

II

In *Colony* this Court interpreted a provision of the Internal Revenue Code of 1939, the operative language of which is identical to the language now before us. The Commissioner there had determined

> "that the taxpayer had understated the gross profits on the sales of certain lots of land for residential purposes as a result of having overstated the 'basis' of such lots by erroneously including in their cost certain unallowable items of development expense." *Id.*, at 30, 78 S.Ct. 1033.

The Commissioner's assessment came after the ordinary 3-year limitations period had run. And, it was consequently timely only if the taxpayer, in the words of the 1939 Code, had "omit[ted] from gross income an amount properly includible therein which is in excess of 25 per centum of the amount of gross income stated in the return. The Code provision applicable to this case, adopted in 1954, contains materially indistinguishable language.

In *Colony* this Court held that taxpayer misstatements, overstating the basis in property, do not fall within the scope of the statute. But the Court recognized the Commissioner's contrary argument for inclusion. 357 U.S. at 32, 788 S.Ct. 1033. Then as now, the Code itself defined "gross income" in this context as the difference between gross revenue (often the amount the taxpayer received upon selling the property) and basis (often the amount the taxpayer paid for the property). And, the Commissioner pointed out, an overstatement of basis can diminish the "amount" of the gain just as leaving the item entirely off the return might do. Either way, the error wrongly understates the taxpayer's income.

But, the Court added, the Commissioner's argument did not fully account for the provision's language, in particular the word "omit." The key phrase says " *omits* . . . an amount." The word "omits" (unlike, say, "reduces" or "understates") means " '[t]o leave out or unmentioned; not to insert, include, or name.' " *Ibid.* (quoting Webster's New International Dictionary (2d ed. 1939)). Thus, taken literally, "omit" limits the statute's scope to situations in which specific receipts or accruals of income are *left out* of the computation of gross income; to inflate the basis, however, is not to "omit" a specific item, not even of profit.

While finding this latter interpretation of the language the "more plausibl[e]," the Court also noted that the language was not "unambiguous." *Colony*, 357 U.S., at 33, 78 S.Ct. 1033. It then examined various congressional Reports discussing the relevant statutory language. It found in those Reports

> "persuasive indications that Congress merely had in mind failures to report particular income receipts and accruals, and did not intend the [extended] limitation to apply whenever gross income was understated. . ." *Id.*, at 35, 78 S.Ct. 1033.

This "history," the Court said, "shows . . . that the Congress intended an exception to the usual three-year statute of limitations only in the restricted type of situation already described," a situation that did not include overstatements of basis. *Id.* at 36, 78 S.Ct. 1033.

The Court wrote that Congress, in enacting the provision,

> "manifested no broader purpose than to give the Commissioner an additional two [now three] years to investigate tax returns in cases where, because of a taxpayer's omission to report some taxable item, the Commissioner is at a special disadvantage . . . [because] the return on its face provides no clue to the existence of the omitted item. . . [W]hen, *as here* [*i.e.,* where the overstatement of basis is at issue], the understatement of a tax arises from an error in reporting an item disclosed on the face of the return the Commissioner is at no such disadvantage . . . whether the error be one affecting 'gross income' or one, such as overstated deductions, affecting other parts of the return." *Ibid.* (emphasis added).

Finally, the Court noted that Congress had recently enacted the Internal Revenue Code of 1954. And the Court observed that "the conclusion we reach is in harmony with the unambiguous language of § 6501(e)(1)(A)," *id.*, at 37, 78 S.Ct. 1033, *i.e.,* the provision relevant in this present case.

III

In our view, *Colony* determines the outcome in this case. The provision before us is a 1954 reenactment of the 1939 provision that *Colony* interpreted. The operative language is identical. It would be difficult, perhaps impossible, to give the same language here a different interpretation without effectively overruling *Colony* * * *.

The Government, in an effort to convince us to interpret the operative language before us differently, points to differences in other nearby parts of the 1954 Code. It suggests that these differences counsel in favor of a different interpretation than the one adopted in *Colony* * * *.

* * *

In our view, these points are too fragile to bear the significant argumentative weight the Government seeks to place upon them * * *.

IV

A

Finally, the Government points to Treasury Regulation § 301.6501(e)–1, which was promulgated in final form in December 2010. The regulation, as relevant here, departs from *Colony* and interprets the operative language of the statute in the Government's favor. The regulation says that "an understated amount of gross income resulting from an overstatement of unrecovered cost or other basis constitutes an omission from gross income." § 301.6501(e)–1(a)(1)(iii). In the Government's view this new regulation in effect overturns *Colony*'s interpretation of this statute.

The Government points out that the Treasury Regulation constitutes "an agency's construction of a statute which it administers." *Chevron, U.S.A. Inc. v. Natural Resources Defense Council, Inc.*, 467 U.S. 837, 842, 104 S.Ct. 2778, 81 L.Ed.2d 694 (1984). The Court has written that a "court's prior judicial construction of a statute trumps an agency construction otherwise entitled to *Chevron* deference only if the prior court decision holds that its construction follows from the *unambiguous* terms of the statute. . ." *National Cable & Telecommunications Assn. v. Brand X Internet Services*, 545 U.S. 967, 982, 125 S.Ct. 2688,162 L.Ed.2d 820 (2005) (emphasis added). And, as the Government notes, in *Colony* itself the Court wrote that "it cannot be said that the language is unambiguous." 357 U.S., at 33, 78 S.Ct. 1033. Hence, the Government concludes, *Colony* cannot govern the outcome in this case. The question, rather, is whether the agency's construction is a "permissible construction of the statute." *Chevron, supra*, at 843, 104 S.Ct. 2778. And, since the Government argues that the regulation embodies a reasonable, hence permissible, construction of the statute, the Government believes it must win.

B

We do not accept this argument. In our view, *Colony* has already interpreted the statute, and there is no longer any different construction that is consistent with *Colony* and available for adoption by the agency.

C

The fatal flaw in the Government's contrary argument is that it overlooks the *reason why Brand X* held that a "prior judicial construction," unless reflecting an "unambiguous" statute, does not trump a different agency construction of that statute. 545 U.S., at 982, 125 S.Ct. 2688. The Court reveals that reason when it points out that "it is for agencies, not courts, to fill statutory gaps." *Ibid.* The fact that a statute is unambiguous means that there is "no gap for the agency to fill" and thus "no room for agency discretion." *Id.* at 982–983, 125 S.Ct. 2688.

In so stating, the Court sought to encapsulate what earlier opinions, including *Chevron*, made clear. Those opinions identify the underlying interpretive problem as that of deciding whether, or when, a particular statute in effect delegates to an agency the power to fill a gap, thereby implicitly taking from a court the power to void a reasonable gap-filling interpretation * * *.

Chevron and later cases find in unambiguous language a clear sign that Congress did *not* delegate gap-filling authority to an agency; and they find in ambiguous language at least a presumptive indication that Congress did delegate that gap-filling authority * * *.

As the Government points out, the Court in *Colony* stated that the statutory language at issue is not "unambiguous." 357 U.S., at 33, 78 S.Ct. 1033. But the Court decided that case nearly 30 years before it decided *Chevron*. There is no reason to believe that the linguistic ambiguity noted by *Colony* reflects a post-*Chevron* conclusion that Congress had delegated gap-filling power to the agency. At the same time, there is every reason to believe that the Court thought that Congress had "directly spoken to the question at hand," and thus left "[no] gap for the agency to fill." *Chevron, supra,* at 842–843, 104 S.Ct. 2778.

For one thing, the Court said that the taxpayer had the better side of the textual argument. *Colony*, 357 U.S., at 33, 78 S.Ct. 1033. For another, its examination of legislative history led it to believe that Congress had decided the question definitively, leaving no room for the agency to reach a contrary result. It found in that history "persuasive indications" that Congress intended overstatements of basis to fall outside the statute's scope, and it said that it was satisfied that Congress "intended an exception . . . only in the restricted type of situation" it had already described. *Id.* at 35–36, 78 S.Ct. 1033. Further, it thought that the Commissioner's interpretation (the interpretation once again advanced here) would "create a patent incongruity in the tax law." *Id.* at 36–37, 78 S.Ct. 1033. And it reached this conclusion despite the fact that, in the years leading up to *Colony*, the Commissioner had consistently advocated the opposite in the circuit courts. Thus, the Court was aware it was rejecting the expert opinion of the Commissioner of Internal Revenue. And finally, after completing its analysis, *Colony* found its interpretation of the 1939 Code "in harmony with the [now] unambiguous language" of the 1954 Code, which at a minimum suggests that the Court saw nothing in the 1954 Code as inconsistent with its conclusion. 357 U.S., at 37, 78 S.Ct. 1033.

It may be that judges today would use other methods to determine whether Congress left a gap to fill. But that is beside the point. The question is whether the Court in *Colony* concluded that the statute left such a gap. And, in our view, the opinion (written by Justice Harlan for the Court) makes clear that it did not.

Given principles of *stare decisis,* we must follow that interpretation. And there being no gap to fill, the Government's gap-filling regulation cannot change *Colony*'s interpretation of the statute. We agree with the taxpayer that overstatements of basis, and the resulting understatement of gross income, do not trigger the extended limitations period of § 6501(e)(1)(A). The Court of Appeals reached the same conclusion. See 634 F.3d 249 (C.A.4 2011). And its judgment is affirmed.

It is so ordered.

JUSTICE SCALIA, concurring in part and concurring in the judgment.

It would be reasonable, I think, to deny all precedential effect to *Colony, Inc. v. Commissioner,* 357 U.S. 28, 78 S.Ct. 1033, 2 L.Ed.2d 1119 (1958)—to overrule its holding as obviously contrary to our later law that agency resolutions of ambiguities are to be accorded deference. Because of justifiable taxpayer reliance I would not take that course—and neither does the Court's opinion, which says that "*Colony* determines the outcome in this case." That should be the end of the matter.

The plurality, however, goes on to address the Government's argument that Treasury Regulation § 301.6501(e)–1 effectively overturned *Colony*. In my view, that cannot be: "Once a court has decided upon its *de novo* construction of the statute, there no longer is a different construction that is consistent with the court's holding and available for adoption by the agency." *National Cable & Telecommunications Assn. v. Brand X Internet Services,* 545 U.S. 967, 1018 n. 12, 125 S.Ct. 2688, 162 L.Ed.2d 820 (2005) (SCALIA, J., dissenting) (citation and internal quotation marks omitted). That view, of course, did not carry the day in *Brand X*, and the Government quite reasonably relies on the *Brand X* majority's innovative pronouncement that a "court's prior judicial construction of a statute trumps an agency construction otherwise entitled to *Chevron* deference only if the prior court decision holds that its construction follows from the unambiguous terms of the statute." *Id.* at 982, 125 S.Ct. 2688.

In cases decided pre-*Brand X*, the Court had no inkling that it *must* utter the magic words "ambiguous" or "unambiguous" in order to (poof!) expand or abridge executive power, and (poof!) enable or disable administrative contradiction of the Supreme Court. Indeed, the Court was unaware of even the utility (much less the necessity) of making the ambiguous/nonambiguous determination in cases decided pre-*Chevron*, before that opinion made the so-called "Step 1" determination of ambiguity *vel non* a customary (though hardly mandatory[1]) part of judicial-review analysis. For many of those earlier cases, therefore, it will be incredibly difficult to determine whether the decision purported to be giving meaning to an ambiguous, or rather an unambiguous, statute.

Thus, one would have thought that the *Brand X* majority would breathe a sigh of relief in the present case, involving a pre-*Chevron* opinion that (*mirabile dictu*) makes it *inescapably clear* that the Court thought the statute ambiguous: "It *cannot* be said that the language is *unambiguous*." *Colony, supra,* at 33, 78 S.Ct. 1033 (emphasis added). As today's plurality opinion explains, *Colony* "said that the taxpayer had the *better* side of the textual argument," *ante,* at 1844 (emphasis added)—not what *Brand X* requires to foreclose administrative revision of our decisions: "the *only permissible* reading of the statute." 545 U.S., at 984, 125 S.Ct. 2688. Thus, having decided to stand by *Colony* and to stand by *Brand X* as well, the plurality should have found—in order to reach the decision it did—that the Treasury Department's current interpretation was unreasonable.

Instead of doing what *Brand X* would require, however, the plurality manages to sustain the justifiable reliance of taxpayers by revising *yet again* the meaning of *Chevron*—and revising it *yet again* in a direction that will create confusion and uncertainty * * *. To trigger the *Brand X* power of an authorized "gap-filling" agency to give content to an ambiguous text, a pre-*Chevron* determination that language is ambiguous does not alone suffice; the pre-*Chevron* Court must in addition have found that Congress wanted *the particular ambiguity in question* to be resolved by the agency. And here, today's plurality opinion finds, "[t]here is no reason to believe that the linguistic ambiguity noted by *Colony* reflects a post-*Chevron* conclusion that Congress had delegated gap-filling power to the agency." The notion, seemingly, is that post-*Chevron* a finding of ambiguity is

---

[1] "Step 1" has never been an essential part of *Chevron* analysis. Whether a particular statute is ambiguous makes no difference if the interpretation adopted by the agency is clearly reasonable—and it would be a waste of time to conduct that inquiry. See *Entergy Corp. v. Riverkeeper, Inc.,* 556 U.S. 208, 218, and n. 4, 129 S.Ct. 1498, 173 L.Ed.2d 369 (2009). The same would be true if the agency interpretation is clearly beyond the scope of any conceivable ambiguity. It does not matter whether the word "yellow" is ambiguous when the agency has interpreted it to mean "purple." See Stephenson & Vermeule, *Chevron Has Only One Step,* 95 Va. L. Rev. 597, 599 (2009).

accompanied by a finding of agency authority to resolve the ambiguity, but pre-*Chevron* that was not so. The premise is false. Post-*Chevron* cases do not "conclude" that Congress wanted the particular ambiguity resolved by the agency; that is simply the *legal effect* of ambiguity—a legal effect that should obtain whenever the language is in fact (as *Colony* found) ambiguous.

* * *

Perhaps sensing the fragility of its new approach, the plurality opinion then pivots (as the *à la mode* vernacular has it)—from focusing on whether *Colony* concluded that there was gap-filling authority to focusing on whether *Colony* concluded that there was any gap to be filled: "The question is whether the Court in *Colony* concluded that the statute left such a gap. And, in our view, the opinion . . . makes clear that it did not." How does the plurality know this? Because Justice Harlan's opinion "said that the taxpayer had the better side of the textual argument"; because it found that legislative history indicated "that Congress intended overstatements of basis to fall outside the statute's scope"; because it concluded that the Commissioner's interpretation would "create a patent incongruity in the tax law"; and because it found its interpretation "in harmony with the [now] unambiguous language" of the 1954 Code. But these are the sorts of arguments that courts *always* use in *resolving* ambiguities. They do not prove that no ambiguity existed, unless one believes that an ambiguity resolved is an ambiguity that never existed in the first place. *Colony* said unambiguously that the text was ambiguous, and that should be an end of the matter—unless one wants simply to deny *stare decisis* effect to *Colony* as a pre-*Chevron* decision.

Rather than making our judicial-review jurisprudence curiouser and curiouser, the Court should abandon the opinion that produces these contortions, *Brand X*. I join the judgment announced by the Court because it is indisputable that *Colony* resolved the construction of the statutory language at issue here, and that construction must therefore control. And I join the Court's opinion except for Part IV-C.

* * *

I must add a word about the peroration of the dissent, which asserts that "[o]ur legal system presumes there will be continuing dialogue among the three branches of Government on questions of statutory interpretation and application," and that the "constructive discourse," " 'convers[ations],' " and "instructive exchanges" would be "foreclosed by an insistence on adhering to earlier interpretations of a statute even in light of new, relevant statutory amendments." ([O]pinion of KENNEDY, J.). This passage is reminiscent of Professor K.C. Davis's vision that administrative procedure is developed by "a partnership between legislators and judges," who "working [as] partners produce better law than legislators alone could possibly produce." That romantic, judge-empowering image was obliterated by this Court in *Vermont Yankee Nuclear Power Corp. v. Natural Resources Defense Council, Inc.*, 435 U.S. 519, 98 S.Ct. 1197, 55 L.Ed.2d 460 (1978), which held that Congress prescribes and we obey, with no discretion to add to the administrative procedures that Congress has created. It seems to me that the dissent's vision of a troika partnership (legislative-executive-judicial) is a similar mirage. The discourse, conversation, and exchange that the dissent perceives is peculiarly one-sided. Congress prescribes; and where Congress's prescription is ambiguous the Executive can (within the scope of the ambiguity) clarify that prescription; and if the product is constitutional the courts obey. I hardly think it amounts to a "discourse" that Congress or (as this Court would allow in its *Brand X* decision) the Executive can change its prescription so as to render our prior holding irrelevant. What is needed for the system to work is that Congress, the Executive, and the private parties subject to their dispositions, be able to predict the meaning that the courts will give to their instructions. That goal would be obstructed if the judicially established meaning of a technical legal term used in a very specific context could be overturned on the basis of statutory indications as feeble as those asserted here.

JUSTICE KENNEDY, with whom JUSTICE GINSBURG, JUSTICE SOTOMAYOR, and JUSTICE KAGAN join, dissenting.

* * *

In *Colony* there was no need to decide whether the meaning of the provision changed when Congress reenacted it as part of the 1954 revision of the Tax Code. Although the main text of the statute remained the same, Congress added new provisions leading to the permissible conclusion that it would have a different meaning going forward. The *Colony* decision reserved judgment on this issue. In my view, the amended statute leaves room for the Department's reading * * *.

* * *

In the instant case the Court concludes these statutory changes are "too fragile to bear the significant argumentative weight the Government seeks to place upon them." But in this context, the changes are meaningful. *Colony* made clear that the text of the earlier version of the statute could not be described as unambiguous, although it ultimately concluded that an overstatement of basis was not an omission from gross income. The [1954] statutory revisions, which were not considered in *Colony*, may not compel the opposite conclusion under the new statute; but they strongly favor it. As a result, there was room for the Treasury Department to interpret the new provision in that manner.

In an earlier case, and in an unrelated controversy not implicating the Internal Revenue Code, the Court held that a judicial construction of an ambiguous statute did not foreclose an agency's later, inconsistent interpretation of the same provision. *National Cable & Telecommunications Assn. v. Brand X Internet Services*, 545 U.S. 967, 982–983, 125 S.Ct. 2688, 162 L.Ed.2d 820 (2005) ("Only a judicial precedent holding that the statute unambiguously forecloses the agency's interpretation, and therefore contains no gap for the agency to fill, displaces a conflicting agency construction"). This general rule recognizes that filling gaps left by ambiguities in a statute "involves difficult policy choices that agencies are better equipped to make than courts." *Id.* at 980, 125 S.Ct. 2688. There has been no opportunity to decide whether the analysis would be any different if an agency sought to interpret an ambiguous statute in a way that was inconsistent with this Court's own, earlier reading of the law.

These issues are not implicated here. In *Colony* the Court did interpret the same phrase that must be interpreted in this case. The language was in a predecessor statute, however, and Congress has added new language that, in my view, controls the analysis and should instruct the Court to reach a different outcome today. The Treasury Department's regulations were promulgated in light of these statutory revisions, which were not at issue in *Colony*. There is a serious difficulty to insisting, as the Court does today, that an ambiguous provision must continue to be read the same way even after it has been reenacted with additional language suggesting Congress would permit a different interpretation. Agencies with the responsibility and expertise necessary to administer ongoing regulatory schemes should have the latitude and discretion to implement their interpretation of provisions reenacted in a new statutory framework. And this is especially so when the new language enacted by Congress seems to favor the very interpretation at issue * * *.

Our legal system presumes there will be continuing dialogue among the three branches of Government on questions of statutory interpretation and application. In some cases Congress will set out a general principle, to be administered in more detail by an agency in the exercise of its discretion. The agency may be in a proper position to evaluate the best means of implementing the statute in its practical application. Where the agency exceeds its authority, of course, courts must invalidate the regulation. And agency interpretations that lead to unjust or unfair consequences can be corrected, much like disfavored judicial interpretations, by congressional action. These instructive exchanges would be foreclosed by an insistence on adhering to earlier interpretations of a statute even in light of new, relevant statutory amendments. Courts instead should be open to an agency's adoption of a different interpretation where, as here, Congress has given new instruction by an amended statute.

* * *

For these reasons, and with respect, I dissent.

a. The Ongoing Debate

Chevron is without a doubt the most controversial doctrine in modern administrative law. The scholarly literature on *Chevron*, both pro and con, is voluminous. The excerpts that follow are illustrative, not representative, of this scholarship.[20]

RICHARD J. PIERCE, JR., *CHEVRON* AND ITS AFTERMATH: JUDICIAL REVIEW OF AGENCY INTERPRETATIONS OF STATUTORY PROVISIONS
41 Vand. L. Rev. 301 (1988).

* * *

The forceful criticisms of *Chevron* and the attempts to limit or redefine the *Chevron* test are predicated on a misunderstanding of the nature of the statutory interpretation issues that agencies and courts frequently must resolve. Historically, interpretation of terms used in a regulatory statute has been characterized as an issue of law. Thus, some commentators distinguish between the proper scope of judicial review of issues of law, including all agency interpretations of statutory provisions, and judicial review of issues of policy. Professor Sunstein argues that *Chevron* is inconsistent both with *Marbury v. Madison* and the Administrative Procedure Act because courts possess the exclusive responsibility to decide issues of law.

This characterization of *Chevron* is based on a serious misunderstanding of the legislative process and the nature of the issue before a court when it reviews an agency's interpretation of a provision in a regulatory statute. Many instances of statutory interpretation require an agency to resolve policy issues, rather than legal issues. Viewed in this light, the first step in the *Chevron* test requires a court to determine whether the issue of statutory interpretation in question is an issue of law or an issue of policy. If the court determines that it is reviewing an agency's resolution of a policy issue, the court then moves to the second part of the test and affirms the agency's interpretation of the statutory provision—and

---

[20] In addition to the articles excerpted here, other articles that make (in your editor's judgment) especially important contributions to a theoretical understanding of *Chevron* include Aditya Bamzai, *The Origins of Judicial Deference to Executive Interpretation*, 126 Yale L.J. 908 (2017); Kent Barnett & Christopher J. Walker, Chevron *in the Circuit Courts*, 116 Mich. L. Rev. 1 (2017); John F. Duffy, *Administrative Common Law in Judicial Review*, 77 Tex. L. Rev. 113 (1998); Cynthia Farina, *Statutory Interpretation and the Balance of Power in the Administrative State*, 89 Colum. L. Rev. 452 (1989); Jonathan T. Molot, *The Judicial Perspective in the Administrative State: Reconciling Modern Doctrines of Deference with the Judiciary's Structural Role*, 53 Stanford L. Rev. 1 (2000); and Mark Seidenfeld, *A Syncopated* Chevron: *Emphasizing Reasoned Decisionmaking in Reviewing Agency Interpretations of Statutes*, 73 Tex. L. Rev. 83 (1994).

its resolution of the policy issue—if the agency's interpretation is "reasonable."

In determining whether an agency's interpretation of a statute involves an issue of law or policy, it is useful to analyze and characterize the issue prior to Congress' enactment of the statute in question. For example, in *Chevron* most would agree that, prior to the enactment of the Clean Air Act, the question of whether to limit emissions at the plant level or the level of each piece of combustion equipment is a pure question of policy. This question is but one of hundreds of policy issues that some institution of government must resolve in order to implement any regulatory program to reduce air pollution. In the process of enacting the Clean Air Act, or any other regulatory statute, Congress invariably resolves some policy issues but leaves to some other institution of government the task of resolving many other policy issues.

As the Court recognized in *Chevron*, Congress declines to resolve policy issues for many different reasons: Congress simply may have neglected to consider the issue; Congress may have believed that the agency was in a better position to resolve the issue; or finally, Congress may not have been able to forge a coalition or simply may have lacked the political courage necessary to resolve the issue, given that a resolution either way might damage the political future of many members of Congress. The general proposition that Congress cannot and does not resolve all the policy issues raised by its creation of a regulatory scheme probably is not at all controversial.

A more controversial point, however, may be that Congress resolves very few issues when it enacts a statute empowering an agency to regulate. Rather, Congress typically leaves the vast majority of policy issues, including many of the most important issues, for resolution by some other institution of government. Congress accomplishes this through several different statutory drafting techniques, including the use of empty standards, lists of unranked decisional goals, and contradictory standards. Thus, Congress declines to resolve many policy issues by using statutory language that is incapable of meaningful definition and application.

When a court "interprets" imprecise, ambiguous, or conflicting statutory language in a particular manner, the court is resolving a policy issue. Courts frequently resolve policy issues through a process that purports to be statutory interpretation but which, in fact, is not. For lack of a better term, this process will be referred to as "creative" interpretation * * *.

As long as courts follow a process of reasoned decision making, judicial policy making through creative interpretation and application of ambiguous statutory provisions is generally appropriate. The function of a court is to resolve cases or controversies. By enacting a statute that raises but does not resolve myriad policy issues, and by permitting parties to bring judicial actions pursuant to that statute, Congress has created a large number of cases or controversies that courts have no choice but to resolve through a process that can only be characterized as judicial policy making * * *.

* * * Occasionally courts interpret statutory provisions through lengthy discussions of congressional goals and legislative history. In some cases, this analysis undoubtedly is an exercise in what may be termed "real" statutory interpretation; the judge is honestly convinced from reading the language of the statute and its legislative history that Congress resolved a policy issue in a particular manner. When Congress has resolved a policy issue, the court is dealing with an issue of law, in which case the court's role is limited to implementing congressional intent.

In a high proportion of cases, however, an honest analysis of the language, the congressional goals, and the legislative history of the statute will not support a holding that Congress actually resolved the policy issue presented to the court * * *.

In many cases in which a search for congressional intent is futile, courts nevertheless purport to resolve conflicts concerning the meaning of specific provisions in a statute through the process of statutory interpretation. In actuality, however, these courts are resolving a policy issue that Congress raised but declined to resolve * * *.

* * *

Once a court realizes that it is reviewing an agency's resolution of a policy issue, rather than an issue of law, comparative institutional analysis demonstrates that the agency is a more appropriate institution than a court to resolve the controversy. Because agencies are more accountable to the electorate than courts, agencies should have the dominant role in policy making when the choice is between agencies and courts. A court's function in reviewing a policy decision made by an agency should be the same whether the agency policy decision is made by interpreting an ambiguous statutory provision or by any other means of agency policy making. The court should affirm the agency's policy decision, and hence its statutory interpretation, if the policy is "reasonable" * * *. Of course, in deciding whether the agency's policy decision is "reasonable," the court should review the agency's decision making process by which the agency determined that its choice of policy was consistent with statutory goals and the contextual facts of the controversy in question.

* * *

In the process of applying *Chevron*'s first step, the court should refrain from teasing meaning from the statute's ambiguous or conflicting language and legislative history; it should eschew the process of "creative" statutory interpretation that is otherwise essential and appropriate in judicial decision making. Creative statutory interpretation is not appropriate in the administrative law context because creative statutory interpretation permits judges to make policy decisions that should be made instead by agencies. If the process of "real" statutory interpretation does not produce a determination that Congress resolved the specific issue, the court is dealing with a policy decision made by an agency. Although the court still must insure that the agency made its policy decision through a process of reasoned decision making, the court's role should be influenced greatly by the recognition that it is reviewing a policy decision made by another branch of government.

* * *

The conceptual framework established by *Chevron* will not eliminate all difficult cases; nor will it eliminate completely the influence of each judge's personal political philosophy on the process of judicial review of agency actions. Those goals are unattainable through any means. They are important goals, however, and the *Chevron* framework provides a means to further those goals incrementally. The *Chevron* framework can reduce the number of difficult cases that courts must face and limit the influence of each judge's personal political philosophy on the process of policy making in the modern administrative state.

ANTONIN SCALIA, JUDICIAL DEFERENCE TO ADMINISTRATIVE INTERPRETATIONS OF LAW
1989 Duke L.J. 511.

* * *

It is not immediately apparent why a court should ever accept the judgment of an executive agency on a question of law. Indeed, on its face the suggestion seems quite incompatible with Marshall's aphorism that "[i]t is emphatically the province and duty of the judicial department to say what the law is." Surely the law, that immutable product of Congress, is what it is, and its content—ultimately to be decided by the courts—cannot be altered or affected by what the Executive thinks about it. I suppose it is harmless enough to speak about "giving deference to the views of the Executive" "concerning the meaning of a statute, just as we speak of 'giving deference to the views of the Congress' concerning the constitutionality of particular legislation—the mealy-mouthed word 'deference' not necessarily meaning anything more than considering those views with attentiveness and profound respect, before we reject them. But to say that those views, if at least reasonable, will ever be *binding*—that is, seemingly, a striking abdication of judicial responsibility."

This deep-rooted feeling that it is the judges who must say what the law is accounts, I have no doubt, for the stubborn refusal of lawyers, and even of Congress, to admit that courts ever accept executive interpretation * * *. [O]ne provision of the Administrative Procedure Act (APA) itself seems to have been based upon the quite mistaken assumption that questions of law would always be decided de novo by the courts. You may have wondered why the APA's required notice-and-comment procedures for rulemaking—probably the most significant innovation of the legislation—contain an exception for "interpretative rules." One of the reasons given in the 1945 Senate Print is as follows: " '[I]nterpretative' rules—as merely interpretations of statutory provisions—are subject to plenary judicial review. . ." That is not true today, and it was not categorically true in 1945.

What, then, is the theoretical justification for allowing reasonable administrative interpretations to govern? The cases, old and new, that accept administrative interpretations, often refer to the "expertise" of the agencies in question, their intense familiarity with the history and purposes of the legislation at issue, their practical knowledge of what will best effectuate those purposes. In other words, they are more likely than the courts to reach the correct result. That is, if true, a good practical reason for accepting the agency's views, but hardly a valid theoretical justification for doing so. If I had been sitting on the Supreme Court when Learned Hand was still alive, it would similarly have been, as a practical matter, desirable for me to accept his views in all of his cases under review, on the basis that he is a lot wiser than I, and more likely to get it right. But that would hardly have been theoretically valid. Even if Hand would have been *de facto* superior, I would have been *ex officio* so. So also with judicial acceptance of the agencies' views. If it is, as we have always believed, the constitutional duty of the courts to say what the law is, we must search for something beyond relative competence as a basis for ignoring that principle when agency action is at issue.

One possible validating rationale that has been suggested in some recent articles—and that can perhaps even be derived from some of the language of *Chevron* itself—is that the constitutional principle of separation of powers requires *Chevron*. The argument goes something like this: When, in a statute to be implemented by an executive agency, Congress leaves an ambiguity that cannot be resolved by text or legislative history, the "traditional tools of statutory construction," the resolution of that ambiguity necessarily involves policy judgment. Under our democratic system, policy judgments are not for the courts but for the political branches; Congress having left the policy question open, it must be answered by the Executive.

Now there is no one more fond of our system of separation of powers than I am, but even I cannot agree with this approach. To begin with, it seems to me that the "traditional tools of statutory construction" include not merely text and legislative history but also, quite specifically, the consideration of policy consequences. Indeed, that tool is so traditional that it has been enshrined in Latin: "*Ratio est legis anima; mutata legis ratione mutatur et lex.*" ("The reason for the law is its soul; when the reason for the law changes, the law changes as well.") Surely one of the most frequent justifications courts give for choosing a particular construction is that the alternative interpretation would produce "absurd" results, or results less compatible with the reason or purpose of the statute. This, it seems to me, unquestionably involves judicial consideration and evaluation of competing policies, and for precisely the same purpose for which (in the context we are discussing here) *agencies* consider and evaluate them—to determine which one will best effectuate the statutory purpose. Policy evaluation is, in other words, part of the traditional judicial tool-kit that is used in applying the first step of *Chevron*—the step that determines, *before* deferring to agency judgment, whether the law is indeed ambiguous. Only when the court concludes that the policy furthered by *neither* textually possible interpretation will be clearly "better" (in the sense of achieving what Congress apparently wished to achieve) will it, pursuant to *Chevron*, yield to the agency's choice. But the reason it yields is assuredly not that it has no constitutional competence to consider and evaluate policy.

The separation-of-powers justification can be rejected even more painlessly by asking one simple question: If, in the statute at issue in *Chevron*, Congress had specified that in all suits involving interpretation or application of the Clean Air Act the courts were to give no deference to the agency's views, but were to determine the issue de novo, would the Supreme Court nonetheless have acquiesced in the agency's views? I think the answer is clearly no, which means that it is not any constitutional impediment to "policy-making" that explains *Chevron*.

In my view, the theoretical justification for *Chevron* is no different from the theoretical justification for those pre-*Chevron* cases that sometimes deferred to agency legal determinations. As the D.C. Circuit, quoting the First Circuit, expressed it: "The extent to which courts should defer to agency interpretations of law is ultimately 'a function of Congress' intent on the subject as revealed in the particular statutory scheme at issue.'" An ambiguity in a statute committed to agency implementation can be attributed to either of two congressional desires: (1) Congress intended a particular result, but was not clear about it; or (2) Congress had no particular intent on the subject, but meant to leave its resolution to the agency. When the former is the case, what we have is genuinely a question of law, properly to be resolved by the courts. When the latter is the case, what we have is the conferral of discretion upon the agency, and the only question of law presented to the courts is whether the agency has acted within the scope of its discretion—i.e., whether its resolution of the ambiguity is reasonable. As I read the history of developments in this field, the pre-*Chevron* decisions sought to choose between (1) and (2) on a statute-by-statute basis. Hence the relevance of such frequently mentioned factors as the degree of the agency's expertise, the complexity of the question at issue, and the existence of rulemaking authority within the agency. All these factors make an intent to confer discretion upon the agency more likely. *Chevron*, however, if it is to be believed, replaced this statute-by-statute evaluation (which was assuredly a font of uncertainty and litigation) with an across-the-board presumption that, in the case of ambiguity, agency discretion is meant.

It is beyond the scope of these remarks to defend that presumption (I was not on the court, after all, when *Chevron* was decided). Surely, however, it is a more rational presumption today than it would have been thirty years ago—which explains the change in the law. Broad delegation to the Executive is the hallmark of the modern administrative state; agency rulemaking powers are the rule rather than, as they once were, the exception; and as the sheer number of modern departments and agencies suggests, we are awash in agency "expertise." If the *Chevron* rule is not a 100% accurate estimation of modern congressional intent, the prior case-by-case evaluation was not so either—and was becoming less and less so, as the sheer volume of modern dockets made it less and less possible for the Supreme Court to police diverse application of an ineffable rule. And to tell the truth, the quest for the "genuine" legislative intent is probably a wild-goose chase anyway. In the vast majority of cases I expect that Congress neither (1) intended a single result, nor (2) meant to confer discretion upon the agency, but rather (3) didn't think about the matter at all. If I am correct in that, then any rule adopted in this field represents merely a fictional, presumed intent, and operates principally as a background rule of law against which Congress can legislate.

If that is the principal function to be served, *Chevron* is unquestionably better than what preceded it. Congress now knows that the ambiguities it creates, whether intentionally or unintentionally, will be resolved, within the bounds of permissible interpretation, not by the courts but by a particular agency, whose policy biases will ordinarily be known. The legislative process becomes less of a sporting event when those supporting and opposing a particular disposition do not have to gamble upon whether, if they say nothing about it in the statute, the ultimate answer will be provided by the courts or rather by the Department of Labor.

THOMAS W. MERRILL, JUDICIAL DEFERENCE TO EXECUTIVE PRECEDENT
101 Yale L.J. 969 (1992).

Reprinted by permission of The Yale Law Journal Company and Fred B. Rothman & Company from The Yale Law Journal, Vol. 101, pages 969–1014.

Chevron's adoption of a general theoretical framework for structuring the choice between independent judgment and deference was an important advance over the formlessness of the previous era. Unfortunately, evidence is mounting that the Court picked the wrong framework * * *.

* * *

Chevron raises issues that go the heart of our understanding of the judicial role under a system of separation of powers. In terms of formal separation of powers theory, interpretation of law is often said to be the exclusive province of the judiciary. This raises the "*Marbury* problem": if it is the role of courts to "to say what the law is," then how can courts defer to the views of another branch of government on the meaning of the law? In terms of a functional theory of separation of powers, the purpose of an independent judiciary is often described in terms of its capacity for checking arbitrariness and aggrandizement by the other branches of government. This raises the problem of agency accountability: how can we structure judicial review of agency action so that agencies have enough discretion to implement complex regulatory programs, and yet assure that they do not become a tyrannical "Fourth Branch" of government, immune from popular control?

One of the strengths of the *Chevron* doctrine is that it offers, if only implicitly, answers to the *Marbury* and agency accountability problems. The answers it provides, however, are radically different from those that were put forth in the past, and are difficult to square with other, more enduring commitments about the proper role of the courts in a system of separated powers.

In the early days of modern administrative law, the *Marbury* and agency accountability dilemmas were usually resolved by borrowing from longstanding notions about the relationship between judges and juries. Courts would defer to agency findings of fact, but would decide all questions of law de novo. Under such a division of labor, courts would clearly retain final authority to "say what the law is." And by independently ascertaining the meaning of the agency's statutory authority in all cases, courts would provide a powerful constraint against arbitrariness and aggrandizement.

This solution was short lived, however. The comparative advantage of agencies is not limited to finding facts (or applying the law of facts), but extends to resolving many questions of law as well. And if courts decide all questions of law de novo—even where the meaning of the law is uncertain—then the price of containing agency aggrandizement is very likely to be judicial aggrandizement. In response to these shortcomings, the Court abandoned the judge-jury model soon after the Administrative Procedure Act was enacted, gradually developing the multifactored contextual approach that * * * dominated the pre-*Chevron* era.

Chevron in effect advances a third solution to the *Marbury* and agency accountability problems. The *Marbury* problem is resolved by a theory of congressionally mandated deference. Courts reconcile their duty to "say what the law is" with the practice of deferring to agency interpretations of law by positing that Congress, in conferring authority on an agency to administer a statute, has implicitly directed courts to defer to the agency's legal views. Accountability is achieved under *Chevron* by reducing the role of judicial review and relying instead on Presidential oversight.

Both halves of the *Chevron* solution are problematic at best. The mandatory deference solution to the *Marbury* problem rests entirely on the presumption that when Congress delegates the authority to administer a statute to an agency, it wants courts to defer to that agency's interpretations of law. The evidence that would support such a presumption is weak. Congress has never enacted a statute that contains a general delegation of interpretative authority to agencies. The very practice of enacting specific delegations of interpretative authority suggests that Congress understands that no such general authority exists. Moreover, the one general statute on point, the Administrative Procedure Act, directs reviewing courts to "decide *all* relevant questions of law." If anything, this suggests that Congress contemplated courts would always apply independent judgment on questions of law, reserving deference for administrative findings of fact or determinations of policy.

* * *

Chevron's solution to the agency accountability problem is also unsatisfactory. Unlike previous discussions of the accountability problem, which tended to assume that popular control comes about only through the election of representatives who pass statutes that are then enforced by courts, *Chevron* perceives a dual channel of popular control: one operating through the election of representatives who pass statutes; the other through the election of the President who directs the agents who implement those statutes. The Court sought to forge a formula that would allow both channels of popular control to operate by limiting courts to the enforcement of unambiguous legislative directives, leaving all discretionary decisions to be disciplined by Presidential oversight.

The Court's perception that there is a dual channel of control is an important insight. But Presidential oversight has inherent limitations. Many administrative entities—including the "independent" regulatory agencies and "legislative" or Article I courts—enjoy various degrees of statutory immunity from direct Presidential control. Several prominent separation of powers decisions handed down since *Chevron* have legitimized these immunities, diluting the power of the President to assure overall direction of those agents who administer the law. But even without the Court's sanction for these immunities, it is simply unrealistic, given the vastness of the federal bureaucracy, to expect that the President or his principal lieutenants can effectively monitor the policymaking activities of all federal agencies. Nor does it seem wise or appropriate to leave control of agency behavior to congressional oversight hearings. In the end, the primary protection against arbitrary or aggrandizing action by agencies must remain the fundamental constitutional limitation on all executive action—that it "comport with the terms set in legislative directives." And the only effective institutional mechanism for preserving this constraint is judicial review.

To be sure, *Chevron* does not eliminate all judicial enforcement of legal limitations on executive action. But by restricting courts to enforcement of "specific intentions" or "clear and unambiguous" statutory directives, it seriously weakens the primary check on agency abuses while offering no adequate alternative in its place. Of particular concern here is the matter of enforcing boundary limitations. Over the years, the Supreme Court has permitted increasingly broad delegations of discretionary authority to agencies, but only on the understanding that the exercise of this delegated authority would be subject to independent judicial review. To the extent that broad delegations are often ambiguous, *Chevron* undermines this understanding by suggesting that courts must defer to an agency's interpretation of the scope of its own authority * * *.

JACK M. BEERMANN, END THE FAILED *CHEVRON* EXPERIMENT NOW: HOW CHEVRON HAS FAILED AND WHY IT CAN AND SHOULD BE OVERRULED

42 Conn. L. Rev. 779, 782–85 (2010).

* * * *Chevron* should be overruled for the following overlapping sets of reasons

    1.   *Chevron* is contrary to the statute that governs judicial review of statutory interpretation, 5 U.S.C. § 706, so much so that the Court actually found it necessary to rephrase the statutory standard in the opinion to make the statute appear more deferential than the language passed by Congress.

    2.   *Chevron* has no adequate theoretical foundation. It was built on a faulty premise concerning congressional intent and was (and is) contrary to established traditions concerning the distribution of authority in statutory interpretation cases, at least

as embodied in many of the cases decided after the passage of the Administrative Procedure Act ("APA").

3.   The *Chevron* opinion was poorly constructed and unclear on basic issues such as the proper role of interpretation, legislative history, and policy arguments. It is still not clear whether *Chevron* concerns review of statutory interpretation or review of policy decisions.

4.   A short time after establishing the *Chevron* doctrine, the Court created a new version of Step One, which allows the reviewing court to employ the "traditional tools of statutory interpretation" to determine whether Congress's intent is clear. This threw the doctrine into disarray and spawned three competing versions of Step One, leading to conflicting lines of cases. Currently, the application of the *Chevron* doctrine is highly unpredictable, and the decision itself is cited for opposing propositions.

5.   For a variety of reasons, *Chevron* apparently has not had the desired effect of significantly increasing deference to agencies. The reasons for this failure are not altogether clear, but include: first, that *Chevron* is so pliable that courts applying it can still reach any desired result; second, that agencies may have become more adventurous in their statutory interpretation, leading to increased likelihood of rejection on judicial review; and third, that judges may be simply unwilling to defer to interpretations with which they disagree.

6.   The Supreme Court does not even cite *Chevron* in a high proportion of the cases in which it arguably applies. Something is amiss when the Court does not find it necessary to employ the test that it created to govern a class of cases.

7.   The *Chevron* decision created uncertainty about when it applies, making it necessary for the Court to construct a doctrine to determine just that. This doctrine, referred to as *Chevron* Step Zero, is even more uncertain than the *Chevron* doctrine itself.

8.   All of the uncertainty, noted above, surrounding the application of *Chevron* and when it applies has forced the Justices and parties to expend inordinate resources arguing over the *Chevron* doctrine instead of what they should be arguing about, Congress's intent and the rationality of agency policy in the particular case. In short, the litigation costs surrounding *Chevron* appear to outweigh any benefits the doctrine may have created.

9.   *Chevron* encourages irresponsible agency and judicial behavior. Agencies expecting that their interpretive decisions will

be reviewed under a deferential version of *Chevron* are free to disregard congressional intent and impose their own policy views even when it is possible to have at least a good sense of how Congress would have wanted the agency to act. Reviewing courts can brush off serious challenges to agency decisions by invoking *Chevron* without engaging whether the agency is thwarting imperfectly expressed congressional intent.

10. Consensus on the proper understanding and application of the *Chevron* framework is unlikely in the foreseeable future. In addition to the reasons for the indeterminacy of the *Chevron* doctrine discussed above, the unlikelihood of this changing is evidenced by the fact that, despite appearances, there is no stable constituency on the Court for *Chevron* deference and the scholarly commentary on *Chevron* has not come to consensus on basic issues surrounding *Chevron*. In short, after twenty-five years of instability, there is no reason to believe that the *Chevron* framework is likely to become a stable decisionmaking process.

MICHIGAN V. EPA
Supreme Court of the United States, 2015.
576 U.S. ___, 135 S.Ct. 2699.

THOMAS, J., concurring.

* * *

Chevron deference is premised on "a presumption that Congress, when it left ambiguity in a statute meant for implementation by an agency, understood that the ambiguity would be resolved, first and foremost, by the agency, and desired the agency (rather than the courts) to possess whatever degree of discretion the ambiguity allows." *Smiley* v. *Citibank (South Dakota), N. A.,* 517 U. S. 735, 740–741 (1996). We most often describe Congress' supposed choice to leave matters to agency discretion as an allocation of interpretive authority. But we sometimes treat that discretion as though it were a form of legislative power. See, *e.g., United States* v. *Mead Corp.,* 533 U. S. 218, 229 (2001) (noting that the agency "speak[s] with the force of law when it addresses ambiguity in the statute or fills a space in the enacted law" even when " 'Congress did not actually have an intent' as to a particular result"). Either way, *Chevron* deference raises serious separation-of-powers questions.

As I have explained elsewhere, "[T]he judicial power, as originally understood, requires a court to exercise its independent judgment in interpreting and expounding upon the laws." *Perez* v. *Mortgage Bankers Assn.,* 575 U. S. ___, ___ (2015) (opinion concurring in judgment) (slip op., at 8). Interpreting federal statutes—including ambiguous ones administered by an agency—"calls for that exercise of independent judgment." *Id.,* at ___ (slip op., at 12). *Chevron* deference precludes judges from exercising that judgment, forcing them to abandon what they believe is "the best reading of an ambiguous statute" in favor of an agency's construction. It thus wrests from Courts the ultimate interpretative authority to "say what the law is," *Marbury* v. *Madison,* 1 Cranch 137, 177 (1803), and hands it over to the Executive. Such a transfer is in tension with Article III's Vesting Clause, which vests the judicial power exclusively in Article III courts, not administrative agencies. U. S. Const., Art. III, § 1.

In reality * * *, agencies "interpreting" ambiguous statutes typically are not engaged in acts of interpretation at all. Instead, as *Chevron* itself acknowledged, they are engaged in the " 'formulation of policy.' " 467 U. S., at 843. Statutory ambiguity thus becomes an implicit delegation of rule-making authority, and that authority is used not to find the best meaning of the text, but to formulate legally binding rules to fill in gaps based on policy judgments made by the agency rather than Congress.

Although acknowledging this fact might allow us to escape the jaws of Article III's Vesting Clause, it runs headlong into the teeth of Article I's, which vests "[a]ll legislative Powers herein granted" in Congress. U. S. Const., Art I., § 1. For if we give the "force of law" to agency pronouncements on matters of private conduct as to which " 'Congress did not actually have an intent,' " *Mead, supra,* at 229, we permit a body other than Congress to perform a function that requires an exercise of the legislative power.

These cases bring into bold relief the scope of the potentially unconstitutional delegations we have come to countenance in the name of *Chevron* deference. What EPA claims for itself here is not the power to make political judgments in implementing Congress' policies, nor even the power to make tradeoffs between competing policy goals set by Congress. It is the power to decide—without any particular fidelity to the text—which policy goals EPA wishes to pursue. Should EPA wield its vast powers over electric utilities to protect public health? A pristine environment? Economic security? We are told that the breadth of the word "appropriate" authorizes EPA to decide for itself how to answer that question.

Perhaps there is some unique historical justification for deferring to federal agencies, but these cases reveal how paltry an effort we have made to understand it or to confine ourselves to its boundaries. Although we hold today that EPA exceeded even the extremely permissive limits on agency power set by our precedents, we should be alarmed that it felt sufficiently emboldened by those precedents to make the bid for deference that it did here. As in other areas of our jurisprudence concerning administrative agencies, we seem to be straying further and further from the Constitution without so much as pausing to ask why. We should stop to consider that document before blithely giving the force of law to any other agency "interpretations" of federal statutes.

E. REVIEW OF AGENCY DISCRETION AND POLICYMAKING

Many agency determinations cannot be categorized as either findings of fact or conclusions of law. Some determinations involve exercises of discretionary authority that cannot wholly be reduced to questions of fact or law. For example: For most agencies, an ideal set of rules would probably change frequently over time to keep pace with events and changed circumstances. But agencies with finite resources must constantly choose between revisiting and updating old rules or issuing new rules or adjudicatory orders as part of a positive regulatory (or deregulatory) agenda. Organic statutes typically do not specify the portion of resources that agencies must devote to reconsidering old rules rather than studying or issuing new ones. The proper degree of emphasis on the past *vis-a-vis* the present or future is therefore not a question of law that can be resolved by careful statutory interpretation. Nor is it a question of fact, though it may involve ancillary factfinding to determine whether and how much circumstances have changed, how many resources are available to the agency, etc. Rather, agencies generally have a measure of *discretion* to allocate their resources.

Other agency determinations can only be described as determinations of *policy* that cannot be reduced entirely to determinations of fact or law. For example, how should the Occupational Safety and Health Administration draw the dose-response curve for benzene at low levels of exposure for purposes of administering § 6(b)(5) of the OSH Act? The correct shape of the curve is a fact, but that "fact" is unavailable to the agency (and to anyone else), as there is no reliable data from which a curve can scientifically be derived. Nor does the statute tell the agency how to draw the curve—by, for instance, instructing the agency to assume that dose-response curves for toxic substances are always linear unless there is solid evidence to the contrary. Nonetheless, the agency must make some assumption about the shape of the curve in order to carry out its mission. The agency's choice of a curve—and other choices that it makes to resolve scientific and legal uncertainty—is essentially a choice about regulatory *policy*.

To the extent that discretionary or policy determinations implicate or rest on factual or legal determinations, the principles of review for questions of fact or law fully apply. But those principles are, by their terms, inapplicable to those portions of the agency decisionmaking process that cannot be reduced to questions of fact or law.

Section 706 of the APA contains a provision that speaks directly to these nonfactual, nonlegal determinations:

> The reviewing court shall * * * (2) hold unlawful and set aside agency action, findings, and conclusions found to be—(A) arbitrary, capricious, an abuse of discretion, or otherwise not in accordance with law * * *.

5 U.S.C. § 706(2)(A) (2012). We have already seen that this provision imposes a requirement of evidentiary support on agency factual determinations to which the substantial evidence test of § 706(2)(E) does not apply (and for which the agency's organic statute provides no standard of review). But § 706(2)(A) sweeps much more broadly. It potentially applies to *all* agency action—including action that is also subject to other standards of review. No agency action that is subject to § 706 may be "arbitrary, capricious, an abuse of discretion, or otherwise not in accordance with law."

But what does this phrase—generally known as the "arbitrary or capricious" or "arbitrary and capricious" standard—mean in concrete contexts? In particular, how does one determine whether an agency's policy determination is arbitrary or capricious? (We will address later how this provision applies to agency exercises of discretionary authority.)

1. THE GREAT DEBATE: REVIEW OF OUTCOMES VS. REVIEW OF PROCEDURE[21]

Consider the substantive issue in *Industrial Union Department, AFL-CIO v. American Petroleum Institute*, 448 U.S. 607, 100 S.Ct. 2844, 65 L.Ed.2d 1010 (1980):[22] how should the agency regulate low-level exposure to benzene in the workplace in order to assure, "to the maximum extent feasible, on the basis of the best available evidence, that no employee will suffer material impairment of health or functional capacity," 29 U.S.C. § 655(b)(5) (2000), even from regular exposure?

Recall that the agency had very strong factual evidence that high doses of benzene are associated with various blood disorders. The agency, however, had no reliable evidence concerning the health effects of benzene at the low levels of exposure that are typical in workplaces. Thus, many different conclusions about the health effects of low-level benzene exposure are equally consistent with the available factual data. An agency faced with this data must nonetheless choose a standard to impose on low-level benzene exposure. Even a decision to regulate only high-level exposure

---

[21] The following discussion is based on material from Gary Lawson, *Outcome, Procedure, and Process: Agency Duties of Explanation for Legal Conclusions*, 48 Rutgers L. Rev. 313, 320–25 (1996).

[22] *See supra* pages 127–154.

must be justified as consistent with the statutory mandate to protect employee health.

It is possible that health risks at high levels of benzene exposure signal health risks at low levels of exposure, so that the dose-response curve for benzene will always show negative health effects (of some unknown magnitude) at positive exposure levels. It is also possible, however, that below a certain threshold benzene exposure is harmless, so that no inference about low-level exposure can be drawn from evidence concerning high-level exposure. It is even possible that low-level exposure to benzene is affirmatively beneficial. Numerous substances are harmful at high levels of exposure but beneficial at lower levels: Vitamin A is certainly one such substance, and radiation is probably another. If, as we have assumed, the agency does not have any theoretical or factual grounds on which to base a conclusion about the shape of benzene's dose-response curve at low exposure levels, then no scientific method can determine which standard will best protect employee health. Nor can a standard be chosen on the basis of some theory of risk aversion. The question is not whether employees should receive the maximal possible protection, as the statute already mandates such a goal, but rather which standard will provide such maximal protection. A rigorous standard that reduces benzene exposure to zero or near-zero fails to protect employee health best if benzene behaves like Vitamin A or radiation. In that instance, the best standard may well be one that *requires* workplaces to ensure some low-level exposure to benzene.

The agency, in short, has no scientific way to demonstrate that any single decision is the only, or even the best, decision under the terms of the statute. The agency must therefore choose its standard based on considerations external to the evidence and the statute.

A court reviewing the agency's benzene standard faces the same problems as did the agency. The court by hypothesis has no better scientific or statutory ground for selecting an appropriate dose-response curve than does the agency. So how does a court go about determining whether the agency's benzene standard is "arbitrary, capricious, an abuse of discretion, or otherwise not in accordance with law"?

The court has a number of moves available. First, it could say that, because one cannot evaluate the agency's choice of a standard by reference to either objective facts or the organic statute, the choice of a standard is essentially a legislative act, and the statute is therefore an unconstitutional delegation of legislative power. There is accordingly no agency action to review, as there is no valid statute to authorize the action. This may well be the correct answer as a matter of first principles, but, as Chapter 2 illustrates, it is foreclosed by modern constitutional doctrine. In the modern administrative state, agencies routinely make important policy decisions that cannot be reduced to traditional questions of fact or law. The validity of this agency policymaking power is not currently an open question.

Second, the reviewing court could say that its review of an agency's legislative-like policy judgments, such as the choice of a benzene standard in the face of genuine factual uncertainty and statutory silence, is limited to a very minimal rationality review, akin to the kind of review provided to economic legislation under modern substantive due process doctrine. It could choose, in other words, to uphold any agency decision that is not completely ridiculous on its face. There is a good argument that this is precisely the result that was contemplated by the APA in 1946. The language of § 706(2)(A)—"arbitrary, capricious, an abuse of discretion"—is very strong, suggesting an extraordinary level of deference to agencies. Moreover, it has been argued that the provision was intended to codify pre-existing law, *see* United States Dep't of Justice, Attorney General's Manual on the Administrative Procedure Act 108 (1947), which consistently interpreted the phrase "arbitrary or capricious" to permit only the most minimal judicial review of agency decisions. *See, e.g., National Broadcasting Co. v. United States*, 319 U.S. 190, 63 S.Ct. 997, 87 L.Ed. 1344 (1943); *Madison Park Corp. v. Bowles*, 140 F.2d 316, 324 (Em.Ct.App.1943). *See also Wickard v. Filburn*, 317 U.S. 111, 63 S.Ct. 82, 87 L.Ed. 122 (1942) (expressly linking "arbitrary or capricious" review to the standards for reviewing economic legislation under the Due Process Clause); Martin Shapiro, *APA: Past, Present, Future*, 72 Va. L. Rev. 447, 454 (1986) (suggesting that the APA's arbitrary or capricious standard originally called for overturning decisions only when "the agency had acted like a lunatic"). To be sure, the phrase "abuse of discretion," which is familiar from the law in other contexts, suggests a standard of review a bit more rigorous than rational basis review. But whether or not some kind of super-deferential rational basis review can be grounded in the text of the APA, it is a possible judicial strategy for dealing with agency policymaking.

This highly deferential conception of the arbitrary or capricious standard, however, could not survive modern changes in thinking about agency behavior. Someone who believes, with Joseph Eastman and James Landis in the 1920s and 1930s, that agencies are staffed by selfless public servants who are far more trustworthy than courts will find the "rational basis" conception of the original understanding of § 706(2)(A) very congenial. But someone who believes, with Roger Noll in the 1970s, that agencies are frequently subject to special-interest "capture" or various other pathologies identified by public-choice scholars is unlikely to be attracted to a doctrine that gives agencies free reign within the broad range of policymaking permitted by the modern nondelegation doctrine. And indeed, as theories of agency behavior evolved, so did theories of § 706(2)(A). By the 1960s and 1970s, the "rational basis" understanding of the arbitrary or capricious standard was no longer acceptable to courts. The search was on for an interpretation of § 706(2)(A) that permitted a greater degree of judicial control of agency policymaking.

Third, in keeping with this new conception of agency behavior, a court could engage in exacting scrutiny of the agency's decisions. Instead of testing those decisions for rationality, courts could simply determine whether the agency's policy choices are appropriate or correct. More modestly, one could scrutinize agency policy choices with some measure of deference, but substantially less than is given to legislatures in comparable circumstances. This approach, however, has several problems. Even in its more modest guise, it seems wholly inconsistent with commonly held understandings about the judicial role in administrative review. Modern doctrine accepts broad delegations of policymaking to agencies, not to courts. If rubber-stamping of agency decisions is unthinkable today, so is placing judges openly in the role of policymakers. Moreover, this approach assumes that judges are capable of distinguishing better and worse policy choices. Especially in fields that require a high degree of specialized expertise—which includes a fair percentage of modern regulatory activity—courts are unlikely to be able to make fine distinctions among plausible policy options.

Fourth, one could turn instead to agency *procedures*. Courts may not be very good at making policy choices, but they are supposedly experts in determining appropriate decisionmaking procedures. An advocate of this approach might reason that perhaps courts can improve the decisionmaking process of (presumptively untrustworthy) agencies by requiring them to employ extensive procedures that give affected individuals an important role in the decisionmaking process. Good procedures, of course, do not guarantee good decisions, but they may be better than nothing.

These third and fourth moves had powerful advocates on the D.C. Circuit in the 1970s. Judge Harold Leventhal was a forceful advocate of moderately deferential but careful judicial scrutiny of agency decisions, while Judge David Bazelon strongly urged strict court supervision of agency procedures.[23] They extensively debated their respective views in law reviews and in judicial opinions. Their disagreement was aired most famously, and perhaps most sharply, in 1975 in *Ethyl Corp. v. EPA*, 541 F.2d 1 (D.C.Cir.1976) (en banc), in which the en banc D.C. Circuit reviewed EPA regulations concerning the lead content of gasoline. The five separate opinions in the case consumed a total of 111 pages of the Federal Reporter.

---

[23] Other judges on the court in the 1968–78 period also took sides in this debate, though less explicitly and less consistently. Judge Malcolm Wilkey, at least through his actions, agreed with Judge Leventhal in principle, though they often sharply disagreed on the merits of many policy questions. Judge Carl McGowan was generally an ally of Judge Bazelon. Judge J. Skelly Wright played both sides of the fence—which, as we shall see, is by no means an inconsistent or incoherent position.

A majority of the court (reversing Judge Wilkey's panel opinion) upheld the regulations under § 706(2)(A). The majority opinion by Judge Wright and the dissenting opinion by Judge Wilkey both conducted extensive analyses of the evidence considered by the agency. In the face of that discussion, Judges Bazelon (joined by McGowan) and Leventhal issued concurring statements that powerfully expressed their views of the proper understanding of the role of courts in reviewing agency policymaking:

BAZELON, CHIEF JUDGE, with whom MCGOWAN, CIRCUIT JUDGE, joins (concurring):

I concur in Judge Wright's opinion for the court, and wish only to further elucidate certain matters.

I agree with the court's construction of the statute that the Administrator is called upon to make "essentially legislative policy judgments" in assessing risks to public health. But I cannot agree that this automatically relieves the Administrator's decision from the "procedural . . . rigor proper for questions of fact." Quite the contrary, this case strengthens my view that[4]

> . . . in cases of great technological complexity, the best way for courts to guard against unreasonable or erroneous administrative decisions is not for the judges themselves to scrutinize the technical merits of each decision. Rather, it is to establish a decision-making process that assures a reasoned decision that can be held up to the scrutiny of the scientific community and the public.

This record provides vivid demonstration of the dangers implicit in the contrary view, ably espoused by Judge Leventhal, which would have judges "steeping" themselves "in technical matters to determine whether the agency 'has exercised a reasoned discretion'".[5] It is one thing for judges to scrutinize FCC judgments concerning diversification of media ownership to determine if they are rational. But I doubt judges contribute much to improving the quality of the difficult decisions which must be made in highly technical areas when they take it upon themselves to decide, as did the panel in this case, that "in assessing the scientific and medical data the Administrator made clear errors of judgment." The process [of] making a de novo evaluation of the scientific evidence inevitably invites judges of opposing views to make plausible-sounding, but simplistic, judgments of the relative weight to be afforded various pieces of technical data.

---

[4] *International Harvester Co. v. Ruckelshaus*, 478 F.2d 615, 652 (1973) (Bazelon, C.J., concurring).

[5] *Portland Cement Ass'n v. Ruckelshaus*, 158 U.S.App.D.C. 308, 335, 486 F.2d 375, 402 (1973) * * *.

It is true that, where, as here, a panel has reached the result of invalidating agency action by undue involvement in the uncertainties of the typical informal rulemaking record, the court *en banc* will be tempted to justify its affirmation of the agency by confronting the panel on its own terms. But this is a temptation which, if not resisted, will not only impose severe strains upon the energies and resources of the court but also compound the error of the panel in making legislative policy determinations alien to its true function * * *.

Because substantive review of mathematical and scientific evidence by technically illiterate judges is dangerously unreliable, I continue to believe we will do more to improve administrative decision-making by concentrating our efforts on strengthening administrative procedures:[9]

> When administrators provide a framework for principled decision-making, the result will be to diminish the importance of judicial review by enhancing the integrity of the administrative process, and to improve the quality of judicial review in those cases where judicial review is sought.

It does not follow that courts may never properly find that an administrative decision in a scientific area is irrational. But I do believe that in highly technical areas, where our understanding of the import of the evidence is attenuated, our readiness to review evidentiary support for decisions must be correspondingly restrained.

As I read the court's opinion, it severely limits judicial weighing of the evidence by construing the Administrator's decision to be a matter of "legislative policy," and consequently not subject to review with the "substantive rigor proper for questions of fact." Since this result would bar the panel's close analysis of the evidence, it satisfies my concerns.

* * *

Statement of CIRCUIT JUDGE LEVENTHAL:

I concur without reservation in the excellent opinion for the court.

I write an additional word only because of observations in the concurring opinion authored by Chief Judge Bazelon. I would not have thought they required airing today, since they in no way relate, so far as I can see, to the court's en banc opinion. But since

---

[9] *Environmental Defense Fund, Inc. v. Ruckelshaus*, 142 U.S.App.D.C. 74, 88, 439 F.2d 584, 598 (1971), (Bazelon, C. J.).

they have been floated I propose to bring them to earth, though I can here present only the highlights of analysis.

What does and should a reviewing court do when it considers a challenge to technical administrative decision-making? In my view, the panel opinion in this case overstepped the bounds of proper judicial supervision in its willingness to substitute its own scientific judgments for that of the EPA. In an effort to refute that approach convincingly the panel dissent may have over-reacted and responded too much in kind. In a kind of surrebuttal against such overzealousness, Judge Bazelon has also over-reacted. His opinion if I read it right advocates engaging in no substantive review at all, whenever the substantive issues at stake involve technical matters that the judges involved consider beyond their individual technical competence.

If he is not saying that, if he agrees there must be some substantive review, then I am at a loss to discern its significance. Certainly it does not help those seeking enlightenment to recognize when the difference in degree of substantive review becomes a difference in kind.

Taking the opinion in its fair implication, as a signal to judges to abstain from any substantive review, it is my view that while giving up is the easier course, it is not legitimately open to us at present. In the case of legislative enactments, the sole responsibility of the courts is constitutional due process review. In the case of agency decision-making the courts have an additional responsibility set by Congress. Congress has been willing to delegate its legislative powers broadly and courts have upheld such delegation because there is court review to assure that the agency exercises the delegated power within statutory limits, and that it fleshes out objectives within those limits by an administration that is not irrational or discriminatory * * *. Nor is that envisioned judicial role ephemeral, as *Overton Park*[2] makes clear.

Our present system of review assumes judges will acquire whatever technical knowledge is necessary as background for decision of the legal questions. It may be that some judges are not initially equipped for this role, just as they may not be technically equipped initially to decide issues of obviousness and infringement in patent cases. If technical difficulties loom large,

---

[2]   401 U.S. 402, 91 S.Ct. 814, 28 L.Ed.2d 136 (1971). *Citizens to Preserve Overton Park v. Volpe* requires the reviewing court to scrutinize the facts and consider whether the agency decision was "based on a consideration of the relevant factors" in the context of nonformalized, discretionary executive decisionmaking. A fortiori, at least that rigor of review should apply to more formal decisionmaking processes like informal rulemaking.

Congress may push to establish specialized courts. Thus far, it has proceeded on the assumption that we can both have the important values secured by generalist judges and rely on them to acquire whatever technical background is necessary.

The aim of the judges is not to exercise expertise or decide technical questions, but simply to gain sufficient background orientation. Our obligation is not to be jettisoned because our initial technical understanding may be meagre when compared to our initial grasp of FCC or freedom of speech questions. When called upon to make de novo decisions, individual judges have had to acquire the learning pertinent to complex technical questions in such fields as economics, science, technology and psychology. Our role is not as demanding when we are engaged in review of agency decisions, where we exercise restraint, and affirm even if we would have decided otherwise so long as the agency's decisionmaking is not irrational or discriminatory.

The substantive review of administrative action is modest, but it cannot be carried out in a vacuum of understanding. Better no judicial review at all than a charade that gives the imprimatur without the substance of judicial confirmation that the agency is not acting unreasonably. Once the presumption of regularity in agency action is challenged with a factual submission, and even to determine whether such a challenge has been made, the agency's record and reasoning has to be looked at. If there is some factual support for the challenge, there must be either evidence or judicial notice available explicating the agency's result, or a remand to supply the gap.

Mistakes may mar the exercise of any judicial function. While in this case the panel made such a mistake, it did not stem from judicial incompetence to deal with technical issues, but from confusion about the proper stance for substantive review of agency action in an area where the state of current knowledge does not generate customary definitiveness and certainty. In other cases the court has dealt ably with these problems, without either abandoning substantive review or ousting the agency's action for lack of factual underpinning.

On issues of substantive review, on conformance to statutory standards and requirements of rationality, the judges must act with restraint. Restraint, yes, abdication, no.

541 F.2d at 66–69.

Vermont Yankee was something of a rebuke to, if not quite a rejection of, Judge Bazelon's position. But are extensive scrutiny of agency outcomes or the requirement of extra-statutory procedures the only ways to extend the reach of judicial review of agency policy decisions? Could there be another approach that Judges Bazelon and Leventhal could both endorse (even while, perhaps, urging a still further extension of judicial review in their favored directions)?

2. THE GREAT COMPROMISE: REVIEW OF DECISIONMAKING PROCESSES

GARY LAWSON, OUTCOME, PROCEDURE, AND PROCESS: AGENCY DUTIES OF EXPLANATION FOR LEGAL CONCLUSIONS
48 Rutgers L. Rev. 313, 316–19 (1996).

A court reviewing an agency decision can evaluate at least three aspects of the decision: the agency's decisionmaking *outcome*, the agency's decisionmaking *procedure*, and the agency's decisionmaking *process*. A defect in the outcome, the procedure or the process can be an independently sufficient ground to prevent affirmance of the agency decision.

A classic example of an outcome test is the "substantial evidence" test used to review factual conclusions in formal agency proceedings. Whatever may be the appropriate quantum of evidence needed to satisfy the substantial evidence test, application of the test does not require one to know anything about the conclusion under review *other than the conclusion itself*. A judge applying the substantial evidence test need not know *how* or *why* the agency generated the conclusion; rather, the judge need only consider whether that conclusion satisfies a certain threshold of consistency with the record. The conclusion either has the requisite "fit" with the record evidence or it does not. The substantial evidence test judges the *outcome* of the agency proceeding, not the methods by which that outcome was generated.

Although the "how" and "why" of the agency's factual conclusions are irrelevant to the substantial evidence test, they are not necessarily irrelevant to the judicial review process. Suppose that a judge determines, upon examination of an agency factual conclusion and a specified record, that the conclusion has the requisite "fit" with that record to satisfy the substantial evidence test (or any other applicable outcome test). Further suppose that the judge concludes that the agency, in the course of reaching its conclusion, failed to provide a legally required public hearing. The agency decision will be reversed or remanded, not because the outcome is unsupported by substantial evidence, but because the decision is *procedurally* defective. Procedural error—the failure to jump through all of the hoops prescribed by law—is a distinct form of error that is independent of the substantive merits of the agency's outcome. Outcome tests focus on *what* the agency concluded, while procedural tests focus on *how* the agency reached and issued its conclusion. A substantively flawless outcome can fail a procedural test, and a procedurally flawless decision can fail an outcome test.

Suppose now that an agency factual conclusion satisfies the relevant outcome and procedural tests, but the agency reached its conclusion by consulting astrological charts. While the agency's outcome may correspond to the record evidence closely enough to satisfy the substantial evidence or other applicable outcome test, and the agency may have complied with every legally required procedure, the reviewing court will still reject the decision. The law independently requires that the agency's decisionmaking *process*—the chain of reasoning employed by the agency to reach its conclusion once all applicable procedures have been followed—satisfy a minimum standard of rationality. Process tests, which perhaps should be called *reasoning process* or *decisionmaking process* tests to distinguish them clearly from *procedural tests*, concern *why* the agency reached the conclusion that it did.

The Administrative Procedure Act requires reviewing courts to reject agency decisions that are, inter alia, "arbitrary, capricious, an abuse of discretion, or otherwise not in accordance with law." In some contexts, this provision serves as an outcome test; it requires, for example, that an adequate quantum of evidence support factual conclusions in informal proceedings, to which the substantial evidence test generally does not apply. It can also serve as a source of *procedural requirements* if an agency's failure to afford to a party procedures that are permitted, but not otherwise required, by law would be "arbitrary," "capricious" or "an abuse of discretion." Finally, the "arbitrary or capricious" test regulates an agency's *decisionmaking process* by ensuring that the agency reaches its conclusions through a rational decisionmaking mechanism. Astrological divination is not a rational decisionmaking process, and inferences from planetary or stellar positions generally are not rational reasons for adopting a conclusion. Even if the agency's astrological speculations coincidentally yield an outcome that passes the relevant outcome test, the agency decision cannot stand because the agency is obliged to reach its conclusions through a rational reasoning process.

At a minimum, the "arbitrary or capricious" test prohibits decisionmaking processes that are starkly irrational, such as reliance on astrology. At a maximum, it imposes a far more rigorous requirement of explanation. Whenever an agency has legal discretion, the "arbitrary or capricious" test requires the agency to exercise that discretion rationally. Where such discretion involves an issue of policy significance, well-settled principles of administrative review typically impose a substantial duty of explanation on the agency * * *.

NOTES

Judge Leventhal stated the case for careful scrutiny of agency decisionmaking processes in 1970 in *Greater Boston Television Corp. v. FCC*, 444 F.2d 841 (D.C.Cir.1970). By that time, the "agency capture" model had captured the thinking of most of the administrative law community. Judge Leventhal sought to restate the appropriate principles of judicial review of agency action in light of that deeply distrustful conception of agency behavior.

Assuming consistency with law and the legislative mandate, the agency has latitude not merely to find facts and make judgments, but also to select the policies deemed in the public interest. The function of the court is to assure that the agency has given reasoned consideration to all the material facts and issues. This calls for insistence that the agency articulate with reasonable clarity its reasons for decision, and identify the significance of the crucial facts, a course that tends to assure that the agency's policies effectuate general standards, applied without unreasonable discrimination * * *.

Its supervisory function calls on the court to intervene not merely in case of procedural inadequacies, or bypassing of the mandate in the legislative charter, but more broadly if the court becomes aware, especially from a combination of danger signals, that the agency has not really taken a "hard look" at the salient problems, and has not genuinely engaged in reasoned decision-making. If the agency has not shirked this fundamental task, however, the court exercises restraint and affirms the agency's action even though the court would on its own account have made different findings or adopted different standards. Nor will the court upset a decision because of errors that are not material, there being room for the doctrine of harmless error. If satisfied that the agency has taken a hard look at the issues with the use of reasons and standards, the court will uphold its findings, though of less than ideal clarity, if the agency's path may reasonably be discerned, though of course the court must not be left to guess as to the agency's findings or reasons.

The process thus combines judicial supervision with a salutary principle of judicial restraint, an awareness that agencies and courts together constitute a "partnership" in furtherance of the public interest, and are "collaborative instrumentalities of justice." The court is in a real sense part of the total administrative process, and not a hostile stranger to the office of first instance. This collaborative spirit does not undercut, it rather underlines the court's rigorous insistence on the need for conjunction of articulated standards and reflective findings, in furtherance of evenhanded application of law, rather than impermissible whim, improper influence, or misplaced zeal. Reasoned decision-making promotes results in the public interest by requiring the agency to focus on the values served by its decision, and hence releasing the clutch of unconscious preference and irrelevant prejudice. It furthers the broad public interest of enabling the public to repose confidence in the process as well as the judgments of its decision-makers.

There was once a day when a court upheld the "sensible judgments" of a board, say of tax assessors, on the ground that they "express an intuition of experience which outruns analysis." There may still exist narrow areas where this approach persists, partly for historic reasons.

Generally, however, the applicable doctrine that has evolved with the enormous growth and significance of administrative determination in the past forty or fifty years has insisted on reasoned decision-making * * *.

Judicial vigilance to enforce the Rule of Law in the administrative process is particularly called upon where, as here, the area under consideration is one wherein the Commission's policies are in flux. An agency's view of what is in the public interest may change, either with or without a change in circumstances. But an agency changing its course must supply a reasoned analysis indicating that prior policies and standards are being deliberately changed, not casually ignored, and if an agency glosses over or swerves from prior precedents without discussion it may cross the line from the tolerably terse to the intolerably mute.

444 F.2d at 851–52. This conception of judicial review is sometimes called the "hard look doctrine" because of its focus on insuring that agencies have looked carefully and thoughtfully—have taken a "hard look"—at the problems under consideration.

By the early 1970s, this process-oriented review had become a settled part of administrative law, and it remains a bedrock of the modern system of federal judicial review of administrative action. It is very difficult to describe this kind of review in the abstract; it really needs to be seen in action in a variety of contexts. The following five cases, one from each of the past five decades, illustrate some of the ways in which the hard look doctrine—the requirement of reasoned agency decisionmaking—has developed in the modern era.

INDUSTRIAL UNION DEP'T, AFL-CIO v. HODGSON
United States Court of Appeals, District of Columbia Circuit, 1974.
499 F.2d 467.

Before MCGOWAN, LEVENTHAL and MACKINNON, CIRCUIT JUDGES.

MCGOWAN, CIRCUIT JUDGE.

This direct review proceeding presents a classic case of what Judge Friendly has aptly termed "a new form of uneasy partnership" between agency and court that results whenever Congress delegates decision

making of a legislative character to the one, subject to review by the other
* * *.

The petition before us seeks review of standards promulgated by the Secretary of Labor under the Occupational Safety and Health Act of 1970, 29 U.S.C. § 651 et seq., (hereinafter OSHA). The standards in question regulate the atmospheric concentrations of asbestos dust in industrial workplaces. Petitioners are unions whose members are affected by the health hazards of asbestos dust. They challenge the timetable established by the standards for the achievement of permissible levels of concentration, and object to portions of the standards concerning methods of compliance, monitoring intervals and techniques, cautionary labels and notices, and medical examinations and records. We remand two of such issues to the Secretary for further consideration. In all other respects, the petition is denied.

* * *

B. *Asbestos*

Asbestos is a generic term applicable to a number of fibrous, inorganic, silicate minerals that are incombustible in air. Its commercial value is high * * *, and, for many purposes, it cannot easily be replaced with other substances.

Unfortunately, asbestos is as hazardous to health as it is useful to industry. During its production and use, tiny asbestos fibers are released as a dust in the air, and, over the course of this century, thousands of workers have been killed or disabled by the effects of inhaling these fibers * * *.

C. *Proceedings before the Secretary*

Within a few months of the effective date of OSHA, petitioners requested the Secretary to establish an emergency standard to control concentrations of asbestos dust. The Secretary promptly issued a temporary standard and set in motion the procedure for establishment of a permanent standard. Notice of the proposed rulemaking was published, and interested persons were invited to submit their views * * *. On the basis of * * * a formidable record of documents and oral testimony, including highly technical statements by expert witnesses, the Secretary established the standards in question. His statement of reasons covers some four and one-half pages of the Federal Register.

Petitioners allege no procedural errors in the promulgation of these standards, but they characterize them as inadequate to protect the health of employees as required by the Act. They attack the Secretary's interpretation of OSHA in certain particulars, as well as the enforcement measures he has selected.

II

OSHA is a self-contained statute in the sense that it does not depend upon reference to the Administrative Procedure Act for specification of the procedures to be followed. It prescribes that the process of promulgating a standard is to be initiated by the publication of a proposed rule. Interested persons are given a period of 30 days thereafter within which to submit written data or comments. Within this period any interested person may submit written objections, and may request a public hearing thereon. In such event, the Secretary shall publish a notice specifying the particular standard involved and stating the time and place of the hearing. Within 60 days after the completion of such hearing, the Secretary shall make his decision. Judicial review by the courts of appeals is provided.[11]

* * *

* * * [I]n a statute like OSHA where the decision making vested in the Secretary is legislative in character, there are areas where explicit factual findings are not possible, and the act of decision is essentially a prediction based upon pure legislative judgment, as when a Congressman decides to vote for or against a particular bill.

OSHA sets forth general policy objectives and establishes the basic procedural framework for the promulgation of standards, but the formulation of specific substantive provisions is left largely to the Secretary. The Secretary's task thus contains "elements of both a legislative policy determination and an adjudicative resolution of disputed facts." Mobil Oil Corp. v. FPC, 157 U.S.App.D.C. 235, 254, 483 F.2d 1238, 1257 (1973). Although in practice these elements may so intertwine as to be virtually inseparable, they are conceptually distinct and can only be regarded as such by a reviewing court.

From extensive and often conflicting evidence, the Secretary in this case made numerous factual determinations. With respect to some of those questions, the evidence was such that the task consisted primarily of evaluating the data and drawing conclusions from it. The court can review that data in the record and determine whether it reflects substantial support for the Secretary's findings. But some of the questions involved in the promulgation of these standards are on the frontiers of scientific knowledge, and consequently as to them insufficient data is presently available to make a fully informed factual determination. Decision making must in that circumstance depend to a greater extent upon policy judgments and less upon purely factual analysis. Thus, in addition to currently unresolved factual issues, the formulation of standards involves choices that by their nature require basic policy determinations rather than resolution of factual controversies. Judicial review of inherently

---

[11] 29 U.S.C. § 655(f) reads in relevant part: "The determinations of the Secretary shall be conclusive if supported by substantial evidence in the record considered as a whole."

legislative decisions of this sort is obviously an undertaking of different dimensions.

For example, in this case the evidence indicated that reliable data is not currently available with respect to the precisely predictable health effects of various levels of exposure to asbestos dust; nevertheless, the Secretary was obligated to establish some specific level as the maximum permissible exposure. After considering all the conflicting evidence, the Secretary explained his decision to adopt, over strong employer objection, a relatively low limit in terms of the severe health consequences which could result from over-exposure. Inasmuch as the protection of the health of employees is the overriding concern of OSHA, this choice is doubtless sound, but it rests in the final analysis on an essentially legislative policy judgment, rather than a factual determination, concerning the relative risks of underprotection as compared to overprotection.

Regardless of the manner in which the task of judicial review is articulated, policy choices of this sort are not susceptible to the same type of verification or refutation by reference to the record as are some factual questions. Consequently, the court's approach must necessarily be different no matter how the standards of review are labeled * * *.

* * *

What we are entitled to at all events is a careful identification by the Secretary, when his proposed standards are challenged, of the reasons why he chooses to follow one course rather than another. Where that choice purports to be based on the existence of certain determinable facts, the Secretary must, in form as well as substance, find those facts from evidence in the record. By the same token, when the Secretary is obliged to make policy judgments where no factual certainties exist or where facts alone do not provide the answer, he should so state and go on to identify the considerations he found persuasive.

* * *

1. Effective Date for the Two Fiber Standard

The most important aspect of setting the standards was the determination of an acceptable dust concentration level. Under the emergency standards, the eight hour time-weighted average airborne concentration of asbestos dust had been limited to five fibers greater than five microns in length per milliliter of air (hereinafter "the five fiber standard"). A principal issue at the hearings on the permanent standards was whether the standard should remain at five fibers or be lowered to two. Proponents of standards ranging from zero to twelve fibers appeared, and it is fair to say that the evidence did not establish any one position as clearly correct. The Secretary decided to resolve this doubt in favor of greater protection of the health of employees, and established the two fiber standard * * *.

Industry representatives testified that they simply could not reduce concentrations to the two fiber level in the foreseeable future * * *. The Secretary decided to retain the five fiber standard for approximately four years (July 1, 1976) before requiring the reduction to two fibers, in order to give employers time to prepare for the lower limit. Petitioners assert that the four year delay permitted by the Secretary is too long because (1) the health of employees is endangered thereby, and (2) employers do not need that much time.

a. Health Hazards Occasioned by the Delay

The Secretary solicited the views of several experts on the question of the predictable health effects of maintaining a five fiber standard until 1976. The experts differed sharply in some of their opinions, but their responses are generally cautious and reflect deficiencies in available data concerning the relationship between exposure to asbestos dust and the likelihood of disease. The record indicates that no precise prediction of increased harm can be made at this time.

The Secretary must establish those standards that most adequately insure that no employee will suffer material impairment of health. We cannot say, on the basis of the conflicting testimony in the record, that the Secretary erred in his prediction of the health effect of the four year delay, but neither can we say that employees are not exposed to some additional risk of disease because of greater exposure. In view of the Act's express allowance for problems of feasibility, the Secretary's decision to allow a four year delay is not irrational with regard to those industries that require that long to meet the standard. It is appropriate to allow sufficient time to permit an orderly industry-wide transition since, in those cases, the indeterminate degree of risk involved is counterbalanced by considerations of feasibility; it is not, however, a risk to which employees should be needlessly exposed.

b. Industrial Compliance Capability

The evidence indicates that significant inter-industry, as well as intra-industry, differences exist concerning the time needed by employers to meet a two fiber standard. Within particular industries the concentration levels at some plants, usually newer ones, are much lower than at others. More importantly, some industries could implement a two fiber standard more quickly than others * * *.

Despite * * * the evidence of these differences, the Secretary issued a single uniform effective date for all employers in all industries. He explained this decision as follows:

It is concluded there should be one minimum standard of exposure to asbestos applicable to all workplaces exposed to any kind of mixture of kinds of asbestos. Reasons of practical administration preclude a variety of standards for different kinds of asbestos and of workplaces.

We cannot say on this record that an attempt to assign differing effective dates to employers *within* an industry based on the time needed by each employer to alter his plant would be practicable. However, insofar as inter-industry differences are concerned, those reasons of practical administration are neither explained nor readily apparent.

* * *

It may be that the task of devising categories and classifying employers by industry would be unmanageable in view of the many diverse uses of asbestos. However, there is no evidence to that effect in the record, and it is not for the court to guess at the Secretary's reasoning or to supply justifications for his action. We have noted his cryptic reference to "reasons of practical administration," but, insofar as inter-industry distinctions are concerned, those reasons are not self-evident. Therefore, we remand this aspect of the standards to the Secretary for clarification or reconsideration.

* * *

b. *Records of Exposure Levels Detected by Monitoring*

The three year retention period for the monitoring records seems surprisingly short in comparison to the twenty years requirement for medical records—especially in view of their respective functions. Whereas the medical records of primary importance may be those beginning with the first manifestations of a disorder, a complete record of an employee's history of exposure to asbestos prior to the development of disease would be important to research. At this point in time, relatively little is known about the causal relationship between exposure to asbestos dust and various diseases. Persons manifesting disorders are being studied, but that research is hindered by the lack of information concerning the exposure levels at industrial workplaces in the past * * *.

* * *

The Secretary has provided no explanation of the relatively short retention period for monitoring results, and we find no adequate assurance in the record that the requirement as promulgated will provide the date needed for research into the causes and prevention of asbestos related disease. Consequently, we remand the recordkeeping requirements to the Secretary for such modification or clarification as may be necessary to insure that the statutory objectives will be fulfilled.

* * *

What, in our view, differentiates the two provisions we have remanded from those we have left untouched is that the record, examined closely in relation to the relevant concerns of the Act, leaves nagging questions—even for the inexpert observer—as to the reason and rationale for the Secretary's particular choices. However the statutory standard for our review may be characterized, we consider that our dispositions fall within it.

NOTES

Observe that the statutory provision authorizing judicial review cited by the court in *Hodgson* referred only to overturning agency decisions unsupported by "substantial evidence." In an earlier excerpt in this chapter, your editor opined that substantial evidence review of agency fact-finding, strictly understood, "does not require one to know anything about the conclusion under review *other than the conclusion itself.* A judge applying the substantial evidence test need not know *how* or *why* the agency generated the conclusion; rather, the judge need only consider whether that conclusion satisfies a certain threshold of consistency with the record." Your editor believes that your editor was correct in so stating. So from where did the court in *Hodgson* get its requirement that the agency explain its reasoning process?

There are two possible sources of legal grounding for such a requirement. The most obvious source is the APA's mandate that agency decisions not be "arbitrary, capricious, an abuse of discretion, or otherwise not in accordance with law." That provision applies to review of decisions by OSHA unless the Occupational Safety and Health Act expressly declares the provision inapplicable. *See* 5 U.S.C. § 559 (2012) ("Subsequent statute may not be held to supersede or modify this subchapter * * * [or] chapter 7 [containing the arbitrary or capricious standard] * * * except to the extent that it does so expressly"). While the OSH Act expressly preempts application of the APA's rulemaking provisions to emergency standards promulgated by OSHA, *see* 29 U.S.C. § 655(a) (2012), it does not expressly preempt application of the arbitrary or capricious standard of review, and nothing prevents non-conflicting scope of review provisions from operating cumulatively. Indeed, that is their normal mode of operation; the same agency decision can be subject to multiple standards of review for different aspects of the decision. But while there are some court decisions that locate the source of OSHA's obligation of explanation in the APA, *see, e.g., Texas Independent Ginners Ass'n v. OSHA,* 630 F.2d 398, 405 (5th Cir. 1980), *Hodgson* did not directly invoke the arbitrary or capricious standard (although, in a portion of the opinion omitted here, the *government* invoked it on the working, though likely false, assumption that arbitrary or capricious review would be more deferential than substantial evidence review).

Another potential source of an obligation of explanation is the OSH Act itself. The Act requires that "[w]henever the Secretary promulgates any standard * * * under this chapter, he shall include a statement of the reasons for such action, which shall be published in the Federal Register." 29 U.S.C.

§ 655(e) (2012). Since, as Judge (and former Administrative Law professor) McGowan explained at length in *Hodgson,* it does not make sense to review the adequacy of such a statement of reasons for "substantial evidence" in accordance with the traditional, outcome-based, review-of-facts understanding of such review, it is quite sensible to read the application of the OSH Act's "substantial evidence" review provision to agency *policymaking,* as opposed to agency *factfinding,* in much the way that the *Hodgson* court applied it. In other words, when Congress enacted a "substantial evidence" standard of review in the OSH Act, it may have had in mind a broader conception of review than a simple check of factual conclusions against a record. The words "substantial evidence," read in that specific context, might best be understood to import an entire range of review standards applicable to a variety of agency decisions— much as is true of the arbitrary or capricious standard itself.

Such a broad understanding of statutorily prescribed "substantial evidence" review lies behind the decision in *T-Mobile South, LLC v. City of Roswell, Ga.,* 574 U.S. ___, 135 S.Ct. 808 (2015). The case concerned obligations imposed by Congress on local governments, to whom the APA—and therefore the APA's arbitrary or capricious standard of review—does not apply. The Telecommunications Act of 1996 provides that when state or local governments deny requests to erect cell towers, their decisions must "be in writing and supported by substantial evidence contained in a written record." 47 U.S.C. § 332(c)(7)(B)(iii) (2012). Does this provision require that the written decision contain a statement of reasons, and are those reasons subject to a kind of "substantial evidence" review similar to that outlined in *Hodgson?*

The Supreme Court said yes to both questions, finding such a requirement implicit in the statutory provision for substantial evidence review:

> Our conclusion follows from the provisions of the Telecommunications Act * * *. In order to determine whether a locality's denial was supported by substantial evidence, as Congress directed, courts must be able to identify the reason or reasons why the locality denied the application.

> * * *

> This conclusion is not just commonsensical, but flows directly from Congress' use of the term "substantial evidence." The statutory phrase "substantial evidence" is a "term of art" in administrative law that describes how "an administrative record is to be judged by a reviewing court." There is no reason discernible from the text of the Act to think that Congress meant to use the phrase in a different way * * *.

> By employing the term "substantial evidence," Congress thus invoked, among other things, our recognition that "the orderly functioning of the process of [substantial-evidence] review requires that the grounds upon which the administrative agency acted be clearly disclosed," and that "courts cannot exercise their duty of

[substantial-evidence] review unless they are advised of the considerations underlying the action under review." *SEC v. Chenery Corp.*, 318 U.S. 80, 94, 63 S.Ct. 454, 87 L.Ed.2d 626 (1943).

135 S.Ct. at 814–15.

It is actually flatly false rather than "commonsensical" to think that effective substantial evidence review requires a statement of reasons, at least in the traditional setting of review of findings of fact. One needs only the findings and a record (or world) against which to check them. But as soon as judicial review extends to matters that cannot be reduced to traditional factual terms, including perhaps many policy-based considerations that enter into cell tower siting decisions, then an articulation of reasons does become essential to effective review, if that review is to be anything other than either a rubber stamp or a substitute of judicial for agency judgment. The Court thus might well be right that by prescribing "substantial evidence" review, both in the OSH Act and in the Telecommunications Act, Congress was doing more than just telling courts how to review traditional factual findings. It might well have been importing an entire framework of judicial review, part of which treats a "substantial evidence" requirement as at least presumptively calling for reasoned explanation of policy decisions.

If a requirement of judicially reviewable reasons is as fundamental to modern administrative law as this all suggests, then it is quite important to know what kinds of reasons have to be put forth by agencies and how those reasons will be assessed by courts. The remaining cases and materials in this unit try to illuminate (though, as we will see, not necessarily answer) those questions.

MOTOR VEHICLE MANUFACTURERS ASS'N OF THE UNITED STATES v. STATE FARM MUTUAL AUTOMOBILE INS. CO.

Supreme Court of the United States, 1983.
463 U.S. 29, 103 S.Ct. 2856, 77 L.Ed.2d 443.

JUSTICE WHITE delivered the opinion of the Court.

The development of the automobile gave Americans unprecedented freedom to travel, but exacted a high price for enhanced mobility * * *. In 1982, 46,300 Americans died in motor vehicle accidents and hundreds of thousands more were maimed and injured. While a consensus exists that the current loss of life on our highways is unacceptably high, improving safety does not admit to easy solution. In 1966, Congress decided that at least part of the answer lies in improving the design and safety features of the vehicle itself. But much of the technology for building safer cars was undeveloped or untested. Before changes in automobile design could be mandated, the effectiveness of these changes had to be studied, their costs examined, and public acceptance considered. This task called for considerable expertise and Congress responded by enacting the National Traffic and Motor Vehicle Safety Act of 1966, (Act), 15 U.S.C. §§ 1381 *et* *seq.* The Act, created for the purpose of "reduc[ing] traffic accidents and deaths and injuries to persons resulting from traffic accidents," 15 U.S.C. § 1381, directs the Secretary of Transportation or his delegate to issue motor vehicle safety standards that "shall be practicable, shall meet the need for motor vehicle safety, and shall be stated in objective terms." 15 U.S.C. § 1392(a). In issuing these standards, the Secretary is directed to consider "relevant available motor vehicle safety data," whether the proposed standard "is reasonable, practicable and appropriate" for the particular type of motor vehicle, and the "extent to which such standards will contribute to carrying out the purposes" of the Act. 15 U.S.C. § 1392(f)(1), (3), (4).[3]

The Act also authorizes judicial review under the provisions of the Administrative Procedure Act (APA) of all "orders establishing, amending, or revoking a Federal motor vehicle safety standard," 15 U.S.C. § 1392(b). Under this authority, we review today whether NHTSA acted arbitrarily and capriciously in revoking the requirement in Motor Vehicle Safety Standard 208 that new motor vehicles produced after September 1982 be equipped with passive restraints to protect the safety of the occupants of the vehicle in the event of a collision. Briefly summarized, we hold that the agency failed to present an adequate basis and explanation for rescinding the passive restraint requirement and that the agency must either consider the matter further or adhere to or amend Standard 208 along lines which its analysis supports.

I

The regulation whose rescission is at issue bears a complex and convoluted history. Over the course of approximately 60 rulemaking notices, the requirement has been imposed, amended, rescinded, reimposed, and now rescinded again.

As originally issued by the Department of Transportation in 1967, Standard 208 simply required the installation of seatbelts in all automobiles. It soon became apparent that the level of seatbelt use was too low to reduce traffic injuries to an acceptable level. The Department therefore began consideration of "passive occupant restraint systems"— devices that do not depend for their effectiveness upon any action taken by the occupant except that necessary to operate the vehicle. Two types of automatic crash protection emerged: automatic seatbelts and airbags. The automatic seatbelt is a traditional safety belt, which when fastened to the interior of the door remains attached without impeding entry or exit from the vehicle, and deploys automatically without any action on the part of

---

[3]   The Secretary's general authority to promulgate safety standards under the Act has been delegated to the Administrator of the National Highway Traffic Safety Administration (NHTSA). This opinion will use the terms NHTSA and agency interchangeably when referring to the National Highway Traffic Safety Administration, the Department of Transportation, and the Secretary of Transportation.

the passenger. The airbag is an inflatable device concealed in the dashboard and steering column. It automatically inflates when a sensor indicates that deceleration forces from an accident have exceeded a preset minimum, then rapidly deflates to dissipate those forces. The life-saving potential of these devices was immediately recognized, and in 1977, after substantial on-the-road experience with both devices, it was estimated by NHTSA that passive restraints could prevent approximately 12,000 deaths and over 100,000 serious injuries annually.

In 1969, the Department formally proposed a standard requiring the installation of passive restraints, thereby commencing a lengthy series of proceedings. In 1970, the agency revised Standard 208 to include passive protection requirements, and in 1972, the agency amended the standard to require full passive protection for all front seat occupants of vehicles manufactured after August 15, 1975. In the interim, vehicles built between August 1973 and August 1975 were to carry either passive restraints or lap and shoulder belts coupled with an "ignition interlock" that would prevent starting the vehicle if the belts were not connected. On review, the agency's decision to require passive restraints was found to be supported by "substantial evidence" and upheld. *Chrysler Corp. v. Dep't of Transportation*, 472 F.2d 659 (C.A.6 1972).

In preparing for the upcoming model year, most car makers chose the "ignition interlock" option, a decision which was highly unpopular, and led Congress to amend the Act to prohibit a motor vehicle safety standard from requiring or permitting compliance by means of an ignition interlock or a continuous buzzer designed to indicate that safety belts were not in use. Motor Vehicle and Schoolbus Safety Amendments of 1974, Pub.L. 93–492, § 109, 88 Stat. 1482, 15 U.S.C. § 1410b(b) * * *.

The effective date for mandatory passive restraint systems was extended for a year until August 31, 1976. But in June 1976, Secretary of Transportation William Coleman initiated a new rulemaking on the issue. After hearing testimony and reviewing written comments, Coleman extended the optional alternatives indefinitely and suspended the passive restraint requirement. Although he found passive restraints technologically and economically feasible, the Secretary based his decision on the expectation that there would be widespread public resistance to the new systems. He instead proposed a demonstration project involving up to 500,000 cars installed with passive restraints, in order to smooth the way for public acceptance of mandatory passive restraints at a later date.

Coleman's successor as Secretary of Transportation disagreed. Within months of assuming office, Secretary Brock Adams decided that the demonstration project was unnecessary. He issued a new mandatory passive restraint regulation, known as Modified Standard 208. The Modified Standard mandated the phasing in of passive restraints beginning with large cars in model year 1982 and extending to all cars by model year 1984. The two principal systems that would satisfy the Standard were airbags and passive belts; the choice of which system to install was left to the manufacturers * * *.

Over the next several years, the automobile industry geared up to comply with Modified Standard 208. As late as July, 1980, NHTSA reported:

"On the road experience in thousands of vehicles equipped with airbags and automatic safety belts has confirmed agency estimates of the life-saving and injury-preventing benefits of such systems. When all cars are equipped with automatic crash protection systems, each year an estimated 9,000 more lives will be saved and tens of thousands of serious injuries will be prevented."

In February 1981, however, Secretary of Transportation Andrew Lewis reopened the rulemaking due to changed economic circumstances and, in particular, the difficulties of the automobile industry. Two months later, the agency ordered a one-year delay in the application of the standard to large cars, extending the deadline to September 1982, and at the same time, proposed the possible rescission of the entire standard. After receiving written comments and holding public hearings, NHTSA issued a final rule (Notice 25) that rescinded the passive restraint requirement contained in Modified Standard 208.

II

In a statement explaining the rescission, NHTSA maintained that it was no longer able to find, as it had in 1977, that the automatic restraint requirement would produce significant safety benefits. This judgment reflected not a change of opinion on the effectiveness of the technology, but a change in plans by the automobile industry. In 1977, the agency had assumed that airbags would be installed in 60% of all new cars and automatic seatbelts in 40%. By 1981 it became apparent that automobile manufacturers planned to install the automatic seatbelts in approximately 99% of the new cars. For this reason, the life-saving potential of airbags would not be realized. Moreover, it now appeared that the overwhelming majority of passive belts planned to be installed by manufacturers could be detached easily and left that way permanently * * *. For this reason, the agency concluded that there was no longer a basis for reliably predicting that the standard would lead to any significant increased usage of restraints at all.

In view of the possibly minimal safety benefits, the automatic restraint requirement no longer was reasonable or practicable in the agency's view. The requirement would require approximately $1 billion to implement and the agency did not believe it would be reasonable to impose such substantial costs on manufacturers and consumers without more adequate assurance that sufficient safety benefits would accrue. In addition, NHTSA concluded that automatic restraints might have an adverse effect on the public's attitude toward safety. Given the high expense and limited benefits of detachable belts, NHTSA feared that many consumers would regard the standard as an instance of ineffective regulation, adversely affecting the public's view of safety regulation and, in particular, "poisoning . . . popular sentiment toward efforts to improve occupant restraint systems in the future."

State Farm Mutual Automobile Insurance Co. and the National Association of Independent Insurers filed [successful] petitions for review of NHTSA's rescission of the passive restraint standard [in the D.C. Circuit] * * *.

* * *

III

Unlike the Court of Appeals, we do not find the appropriate scope of judicial review to be the "most troublesome question" in the case. Both the Motor Vehicle Safety Act and the 1974 Amendments concerning occupant crash protection standards indicate that motor vehicle safety standards are to be promulgated under the informal rulemaking procedures of § 553 of the Administrative Procedure Act. The agency's action in promulgating such standards therefore may be set aside if found to be "arbitrary, capricious, an abuse of discretion, or otherwise not in accordance with law." 5 U.S.C. § 706(2)(A); *Citizens to Preserve Overton Park v. Volpe*, 401 U.S. 402, 414 (1971); *Bowman Transportation, Inc. v. Arkansas-Best Freight System, Inc.*, 419 U.S. 281 (1974). We believe that the rescission or modification of an occupant protection standard is subject to the same test. Section 103(b) of the Motor Vehicle Safety Act, 15 U.S.C. § 1392(b), states that the procedural and judicial review provisions of the Administrative Procedure Act "shall apply to all orders establishing, amending, or revoking a Federal motor vehicle safety standard," and suggests no difference in the scope of judicial review depending upon the nature of the agency's action.

Petitioner Motor Vehicle Manufacturers Association (MVMA) disagrees, contending that the rescission of an agency rule should be judged by the same standard a court would use to judge an agency's refusal to promulgate a rule in the first place—a standard Petitioner believes considerably narrower than the traditional arbitrary and capricious test and "close to the borderline of nonreviewability." We reject this view. The Motor Vehicle Safety Act expressly equates orders "revoking" and "establishing" safety standards; neither that Act nor the APA suggests that revocations are to be treated as refusals to promulgate standards. Petitioner's view would render meaningless Congress' authorization for judicial review of orders revoking safety rules. Moreover, the revocation of an extant regulation is substantially different than a failure to act. Revocation constitutes a reversal of the agency's former views as to the proper course. A "settled course of behavior embodies the agency's informed judgment that, by pursuing that course, it will carry out the policies committed to it by Congress. There is, then, at least a presumption that those policies will be carried out best if the settled rule is adhered to." *Atchison, T. & S.F.R. Co. v. Wichita Bd. of Trade,* 412 U.S. 800, 807–808, 93 S.Ct. 2367, 2374–2375, 37 L.Ed.2d 350 (1973). Accordingly, an agency changing its course by rescinding a rule is obligated to supply a reasoned analysis for the change beyond that which may be required when an agency does not act in the first instance.

In so holding, we fully recognize that * * * an agency must be given ample latitude to "adapt their rules and policies to the demands of changing circumstances." *Permian Basin Area Rate Cases,* 390 U.S. 747, 784, 88 S.Ct. 1344, 1368–1369, 20 L.Ed.2d 312 (1968). But the forces of change do not always or necessarily point in the direction of deregulation. In the abstract, there is no more reason to presume that changing circumstances require the rescission of prior action, instead of a revision in or even the extension of current regulation. If Congress established a presumption from which judicial review should start, that presumption—contrary to petitioners' views—is not *against* safety regulation, but *against* changes in current policy that are not justified by the rulemaking record. While the removal of a regulation may not entail the monetary expenditures and other costs of enacting a new standard, and accordingly, it may be easier for an agency to justify a deregulatory action, the direction in which an agency chooses to move does not alter the standard of judicial review established by law.

The Department of Transportation accepts the applicability of the "arbitrary and capricious" standard. It argues that under this standard, a reviewing court may not set aside an agency rule that is rational, based on consideration of the relevant factors and within the scope of the authority delegated to the agency by the statute. We do not disagree with this formulation.[9] The scope of review under the "arbitrary and capricious" standard is narrow and a court is not to substitute its judgment for that of the agency. Nevertheless, the agency must examine the relevant data and articulate a satisfactory explanation for its action including a "rational connection between the facts found and the choice made." *Burlington Truck Lines v. United States,* 371 U.S. 156, 168, 83 S.Ct. 239, 245–246, 9 L.Ed.2d 207 (1962). In reviewing that explanation, we must "consider whether the

---

[9] The Department of Transportation suggests that the arbitrary and capricious standard requires no more than the minimum rationality a statute must bear in order to withstand analysis under the Due Process Clause. We do not view as equivalent the presumption of constitutionality afforded legislation drafted by Congress and the presumption of regularity afforded an agency in fulfilling its statutory mandate.

decision was based on a consideration of the relevant factors and whether there has been a clear error of judgment." *Bowman Transp. Inc. v. Arkansas-Best Freight System, supra,* 419 U.S., at 285, 95 S.Ct., at 442; *Citizens to Preserve Overton Park v. Volpe, supra,* 401 U.S., at 416, 91 S.Ct., at 823. Normally, an agency rule would be arbitrary and capricious if the agency has relied on factors which Congress has not intended it to consider, entirely failed to consider an important aspect of the problem, offered an explanation for its decision that runs counter to the evidence before the agency, or is so implausible that it could not be ascribed to a difference in view or the product of agency expertise. The reviewing court should not attempt itself to make up for such deficiencies: "We may not supply a reasoned basis for the agency's action that the agency itself has not given." *SEC v. Chenery Corp.,* 332 U.S. 194, 196, 67 S.Ct. 1575, 1577, 91 L.Ed. 1995 (1947). We will, however, "uphold a decision of less than ideal clarity if the agency's path may reasonably be discerned." *Bowman Transp., Inc. v. Arkansas-Best Freight System, supra,* 419 U.S., at 286, 95 S.Ct., at 442. For purposes of this case, it is also relevant that Congress required a record of the rulemaking proceedings to be compiled and submitted to a reviewing court, 15 U.S.C. § 1394, and intended that agency findings under the Motor Vehicle Safety Act would be supported by "substantial evidence on the record considered as a whole." S.Rep. No. 1301, 89th Cong., 2d Sess. p. 8 (1966); H.R.Rep. No. 1776, 89th Cong., 2d Sess. p. 21 (1966).

* * *

V

The ultimate question before us is whether NHTSA's rescission of the passive restraint requirement of Standard 208 was arbitrary and capricious. We conclude, as did the Court of Appeals, that it was. We also conclude, but for somewhat different reasons, that further consideration of the issue by the agency is therefore required. We deal separately with the rescission as it applies to airbags and as it applies to seatbelts.

A

The first and most obvious reason for finding the rescission arbitrary and capricious is that NHTSA apparently gave no consideration whatever to modifying the Standard to require that airbag technology be utilized. Standard 208 sought to achieve automatic crash protection by requiring automobile manufacturers to install either of two passive restraint devices: airbags or automatic seatbelts. There was no suggestion in the long rulemaking process that led to Standard 208 that if only one of these options were feasible, no passive restraint standard should be promulgated. Indeed, the agency's original proposed standard contemplated the installation of inflatable restraints in all cars. Automatic belts were added as a means of complying with the standard because they were believed to be as effective as airbags in achieving the goal of occupant crash protection. At that time, the passive belt approved by the agency could not be detached. Only later, at a manufacturer's behest, did the agency approve of the detachability feature—and only after assurances that the feature would not compromise the safety benefits of the restraint. Although it was then foreseen that 60% of the new cars would contain airbags and 40% would have automatic seatbelts, the ratio between the two was not significant as long as the passive belt would also assure greater passenger safety.

The agency has now determined that the detachable automatic belts will not attain anticipated safety benefits because so many individuals will detach the mechanism. Even if this conclusion were acceptable in its entirety, standing alone it would not justify any more than an amendment of Standard 208 to disallow compliance by means of the one technology which will not provide effective passenger protection. It does not cast doubt on the need for a passive restraint standard or upon the efficacy of airbag technology. In its most recent rule-making, the agency again acknowledged the life-saving potential of the airbag:

> "The agency has no basis at this time for changing its earlier conclusions in 1976 and 1977 that basic airbag technology is sound and has been sufficiently demonstrated to be effective in those vehicles in current use. . ." NHTSA final regulatory impact analysis (RIA) at XI-4.

Given the effectiveness ascribed to airbag technology by the agency, the mandate of the Safety Act to achieve traffic safety would suggest that the logical response to the faults of detachable seatbelts would be to require the installation of airbags. At the very least this alternative way of achieving the objectives of the Act should have been addressed and adequate reasons given for its abandonment. But the agency not only did not require compliance through airbags, it did not even consider the possibility in its 1981 rulemaking. Not one sentence of its rulemaking statement discusses the airbags-only option * * *. We have frequently reiterated that an agency must cogently explain why it has exercised its discretion in a given manner, and we reaffirm this principle again today.

* * *

Although the agency did not address the mandatory airbags option and the Court of Appeals noted that "airbags seem to have none of the problems that NHTSA identified in passive seatbelts," petitioners recite a number of difficulties that they believe would be posed by a mandatory airbag standard. These range from questions concerning the installation of airbags in small cars to that of adverse public reaction. But these are not the agency's reasons for rejecting a mandatory airbag standard. Not having discussed the possibility, the agency submitted no reasons at all. The short—and sufficient—answer to petitioners' submission is that the courts may not accept appellate counsel's *post hoc* rationalizations for agency action. *Burlington Truck Lines v. United States, supra,* 371 U.S., at 168, 83 S.Ct., at 245. It is well-established that an agency's action must be upheld, if at all, on the basis articulated by the agency itself. *Ibid.; SEC v. Chenery,* 332 U.S. 194, 196, 67 S.Ct. 1575, 1577, 91 L.Ed. 1995 (1947).

* * * We hold only that given the judgment made in 1977 that airbags are an effective and cost-beneficial life-saving technology, the mandatory passive-restraint rule may not be abandoned without any consideration whatsoever of an airbags-only requirement.

B

Although the issue is closer, we also find that the agency was too quick to dismiss the safety benefits of automatic seatbelts. NHTSA's critical finding was that, in light of the industry's plans to install readily detachable passive belts, it could not reliably predict "even a 5 percentage point increase as the minimum level of expected usage increase." The Court of Appeals rejected this finding because there is "not one iota" of evidence that Modified Standard 208 will fail to increase nationwide seatbelt use by at least 13 percentage points, the level of increased usage necessary for the standard to justify its cost. Given the lack of probative evidence, the court held that "only a well-justified refusal to seek more evidence could render rescission non-arbitrary."

Petitioners object to this conclusion. In their view, "substantial uncertainty" that a regulation will accomplish its intended purpose is sufficient reason, without more, to rescind a regulation. We agree with petitioners that just as an agency reasonably may decline to issue a safety standard if it is uncertain about its efficacy, an agency may also revoke a standard on the basis of serious uncertainties if supported by the record and reasonably explained. Rescission of the passive restraint requirement would not be arbitrary and capricious simply because there was no evidence in direct support of the agency's conclusion. It is not infrequent that the available data does not settle a regulatory issue and the agency must then exercise its judgment in moving from the facts and probabilities on the record to a policy conclusion. Recognizing that policymaking in a complex society must account for uncertainty, however, does not imply that it is sufficient for an agency to merely recite the terms "substantial uncertainty" as a justification for its actions. The agency must explain the evidence which is available, and must offer a "rational connection between the facts found and the choice made." *Burlington Truck Lines, Inc. v. United States, supra,* 371 U.S., at 168, 83 S.Ct., at 246. Generally, one aspect of that explanation would be a justification for rescinding the regulation before engaging in a search for further evidence.

In this case, the agency's explanation for rescission of the passive restraint requirement is *not* sufficient to enable us to conclude that the rescission was the product of reasoned decisionmaking. To reach this conclusion, we do not upset the agency's view of the facts, but we do appreciate the limitations of this record in supporting the agency's decision. We start with the accepted ground that if used, seatbelts unquestionably would save many thousands of lives and would prevent tens of thousands of crippling injuries * * *. [T]he safety benefits of wearing seatbelts are not in doubt and it is not challenged that were those benefits to accrue, the monetary costs of implementing the standard would be easily justified. We move next to the fact that there is no direct evidence in support of the agency's finding that detachable automatic belts cannot be predicted to yield a substantial increase in usage. The empirical evidence on the record, consisting of surveys of drivers of automobiles equipped with passive belts, reveals more than a doubling of the usage rate experienced with manual belts. Much of the agency's rulemaking statement—and much of the controversy in this case—centers on the conclusions that should be drawn from these studies. The agency maintained that the doubling of seatbelt usage in these studies could not be extrapolated to an across-the-board mandatory standard because the passive seatbelts were guarded by ignition interlocks and purchasers of the tested cars are somewhat atypical. Respondents insist these studies demonstrate that Modified Standard 208 will substantially increase seatbelt usage. We believe that it is within the agency's discretion to pass upon the generalizability of these field studies. This is precisely the type of issue which rests within the expertise of NHTSA, and upon which a reviewing court must be most hesitant to intrude.

But accepting the agency's view of the field tests on passive restraints indicates only that there is no reliable real-world experience that usage rates will substantially increase. To be sure, NHTSA opines that "it cannot reliably predict even a 5 percentage point increase as the minimum level of increased usage." But this and other statements that passive belts will not yield substantial increases in seatbelt usage apparently take no account of the critical difference between detachable automatic belts and current manual belts. A detached passive belt does require an affirmative act to reconnect it, but—unlike a manual seat belt—the passive belt, once reattached, will continue to function automatically unless again disconnected. Thus, inertia—a factor which the agency's own studies have found significant in explaining the current low usage rates for seatbelts—works in favor of, not against, use of the protective device. Since 20 to 50% of motorists currently wear seatbelts on some occasions, there would seem to be grounds to believe that seatbelt use by occasional users will be substantially increased by the detachable passive belts. Whether this is in fact the case is a matter for the agency to decide, but it must bring its expertise to bear on the question.

* * *

The agency also failed to articulate a basis for not requiring nondetachable belts under Standard 208. It is argued that the concern of the agency with the easy detachability of the currently favored design would be readily solved by a continuous passive belt, which allows the occupant to "spool out" the belt and create the necessary slack for easy extrication from the vehicle. The agency did not separately consider the continuous belt option, but treated it together with the ignition interlock device in a category it titled "option of use-compelling features." The agency was concerned that use-compelling devices would "complicate extrication of [a]n occupant from his or her car." "To require that passive belts contain use-compelling features," the agency observed, "could be counterproductive [given] . . . widespread, latent and irrational fear in many members of the public that they could be trapped by the seat belt after a crash." In addition, based on the experience with the ignition interlock, the agency feared that use-compelling features might trigger adverse public reaction.

By failing to analyze the continuous seatbelts in its own right, the agency has failed to offer the rational connection between facts and judgment required to pass muster under the arbitrary and capricious standard. We agree with the Court of Appeals that NHTSA did not suggest that the emergency release mechanisms used in nondetachable belts are any less effective for emergency egress than the buckle release system used in detachable belts. In 1978, when General Motors obtained the agency's approval to install a continuous passive belt, it assured the agency that nondetachable belts with spool releases were as safe as detachable belts with buckle releases. NHTSA was satisfied that this belt design assured easy extricability * * *. While the agency is entitled to change its view on the acceptability of continuous passive belts, it is obligated to explain its reasons for doing so.

The agency also failed to offer any explanation why a continuous passive belt would engender the same adverse public reaction as the ignition interlock * * *. We see no basis for equating the two devices: the continuous belt, unlike the ignition interlock, does not interfere with the operation of the vehicle. More importantly, it is the agency's responsibility, not this Court's, to explain its decision.

VI

"An agency's view of what is in the public interest may change, either with or without a change in circumstances. But an agency changing its course must supply a reasoned analysis . . ." *Greater Boston Television Corp. v. FCC*, 444 F.2d 841, 852 (C.A.D.C.), *cert. denied*, 403 U.S. 923, 91 S.Ct. 2233, 29 L.Ed.2d 701 (1971). We do not accept all of the reasoning of the Court of Appeals but we do conclude that the agency has failed to supply the requisite "reasoned analysis" in this case. Accordingly, we vacate the judgment of the Court of Appeals and remand the case to that court with directions to remand the matter to the NHTSA for further consideration consistent with this opinion.

So ordered.

JUSTICE REHNQUIST, with whom the CHIEF JUSTICE, JUSTICE POWELL, and JUSTICE O'CONNOR join, concurring in part and dissenting in part.

I join parts I, II, III, IV, and V-A of the Court's opinion. In particular, I agree that, since the airbag and continuous spool automatic seatbelt were explicitly approved in the standard the agency was rescinding, the agency should explain why it declined to leave those requirements intact. In this case, the agency gave no explanation at all. Of course, if the agency can provide a rational explanation, it may adhere to its decision to rescind the entire standard.

I do not believe, however, that NHTSA's view of detachable automatic seatbelts was arbitrary and capricious. The agency adequately explained its decision to rescind the standard insofar as it was satisfied by detachable belts.

* * * The Court rejects the agency's explanation for its conclusion that there is substantial uncertainty whether requiring installation of detachable automatic belts would substantially increase seatbelt usage. The agency chose not to rely on a study showing a substantial increase in seatbelt usage in cars equipped with automatic seatbelts and an ignition interlock to prevent the car from being operated when the belts were not in place and which were voluntarily purchased with this equipment by consumers. It is reasonable for the agency to decide that this study does not support any conclusion concerning the effect of automatic seatbelts that are installed in all cars whether the consumer wants them or not and are not linked to an ignition interlock system.

The Court rejects this explanation because "there would seem to be grounds to believe that seatbelt use by occasional users will be substantially increased by the detachable passive belts," and the agency did not adequately explain its rejection of these grounds. It seems to me that the agency's explanation, while by no means a model, is adequate. The agency acknowledged that there would probably be some increase in belt usage, but concluded that the increase would be small and not worth the cost of mandatory detachable automatic belts. The agency's obligation is to articulate a "rational connection between the facts found and the choice made." I believe it has met this standard.

* * *

The agency's changed view of the standard seems to be related to the election of a new President of a different political party. It is readily apparent that the responsible members of one administration may consider public resistance and uncertainties to be more important than do their counterparts in a previous administration. A change in administration brought about by the people casting their votes is a perfectly reasonable basis for an executive agency's reappraisal of the costs and benefits of its programs and regulations. As long as the agency remains within the bounds established by Congress, it is entitled to assess administrative records and evaluate priorities in light of the philosophy of the administration.

PUERTO RICO SUN OIL CO. v. UNITED STATES EPA
United States Court of Appeals, First Circuit, 1993.
8 F.3d 73.

Before SELYA, CYR and BOUDIN, CIRCUIT JUDGES.

BOUDIN, CIRCUIT JUDGE.

In August 1990, the Environmental Protection Agency issued a pollution discharge permit to Puerto Rico Sun Oil Company ("the Company"). In doing so EPA complied with the substantive requirements of the governing statute and the procedures set forth in the statute and EPA regulations. Only the result gives cause for concern, and that concern is not allayed by the agency's explanation for its decision. In our judgment, the result is so odd that either the EPA has abused its discretion or it has explained itself so poorly as to require further justification. On either view, we must vacate the agency's order adopting the permit and remand for further proceedings.

I.   THE FACTS

The Clean Water Act, 33 U.S.C. § 1251, *et seq.*, prohibits the discharge into protected waters of any pollutant by any person unless a discharge permit has been secured from EPA. The permitting regime is a hybrid one in which both EPA and the counterpart state agency play a role. The precise role depends on whether EPA has delegated permit issuing authority to the state; but no such delegation is present here. Puerto Rico is treated as a state for purposes of the Clean Water Act, and its local agency is the Environmental Quality Board ("EQB").

To obtain a permit, the applicant must satisfy a variety of substantive requirements under the Clean Water Act but, in addition, no EPA permit can issue unless the state in which the discharge will occur gives its own approval (called "certification") or waives its right to do so. Further, the state certification may impose discharge limitations or requirements more stringent than federal law requires, and those more stringent obligations are incorporated into the federal permit as a matter of course. What lies at the heart of this case is EQB's effort to impose, and then back away from, such more stringent obligations.

For some years before this case began, the Company held a discharge permit for its oil refining facility at Yabucoa Bay, Puerto Rico, where it discharges pollutants from two different sources. On May 27, 1988, the Company submitted to EPA an application to renew the permit for its facility. On October 31, 1988, EPA forwarded the application to EQB, requesting that a *draft* certification be prepared promptly. EPA also warned EQB that under EPA regulations, Puerto Rico's right to impose obligations by certification would be waived if a final certification were not received within 60 days after EPA sent a copy of a (yet to be prepared) draft permit to EQB.

On January 25, 1989, EQB released a tentative certification—essentially a draft document that facilitates public comment on the proposed state certification and proposed federal permit. The draft certification in this case probably came as a surprise to the Company. The earlier permit had employed a "mixing zone" analysis in setting the pollution limitations for the Company's discharged effluent; the draft certificate did not include a mixing zone analysis. The difference, which is central to this case, needs a word of explanation.

A discharge permit under the Clean Water Act may include several types of requirements. One set concerns the technology used to limit pollution; another, pertinent here, requires that the amount of specified pollutants not exceed certain percentage levels. In theory, the percentage levels could be measured in the effluent itself—such as storm runoff or waste water—just as it drains into the stream, river or bay which is protected by the Clean Water Act; alternatively, it could be measured at the *edge* of a defined area of the receiving body of water after the pollutant has been diluted by that water.

Such a defined area is called a mixing zone, and it appears that measuring pollutants at the edge of the mixing zone is widespread in the application of the Clean Water Act. According to an EPA publication, "[w]hether to establish such a mixing zone policy is a matter of State discretion." Practically every state and Puerto Rico have adopted mixing zone criteria, although the criteria appear to differ widely * * *.

When in January 1989 EQB issued its draft certification for the Company's requested permit, the EQB was reformulating its mixing zone criteria. EQB's draft certification for the Company neither continued in force the old mixing zone criteria temporarily nor made the certificate subject to the new criteria still under development. Instead, the draft certification simply set further pollutant limitations which, absent the mixing zone analysis, apply directly to the effluent as it enters the receiving waters.

The next event was EPA's release on August 11, 1989, of a draft permit and request for public comment. The draft permit incorporated the requirements of the draft certification issued by EQB and therefore used no mixing zone analysis. Although issuance of the draft permit meant that final EQB certification was now due in 60 days, EQB apparently paid no attention to the deadline or to EPA's earlier warning that failure to meet the deadline would waive Puerto Rico's right to certify. Nevertheless, in October 1989 EPA told the Company's attorneys that it was extending the comment period on the draft permit "indefinitely" while awaiting the EQB's final certification. When the certification arrived, said EPA, it would set a "prompt" close to the comment period.

On July 24, 1990, almost a year after receiving the draft permit, EQB issued what it called its "final" water quality certification for the Company, again eschewing a mixing zone analysis. Both the timing and substance of this action are puzzling because, only four days before, on July 20, 1990, EQB had promulgated new regulations to be effective on August 20, 1990, adopting a new method of determining mixing zones. But if EQB's behavior was slothful and careless, EPA's reaction was even stranger.

At this point the EQB's final certification must have appeared a probable candidate for administrative or judicial revision in Puerto Rico. EQB had used a mixing zone analysis in the past and was proposing to do so in the future, and the use of such an analysis was likely to be significant; indeed, the Company later represented, and EPA has not disputed the claim, that its refinery cannot operate if forced to meet the pollution standards without the help of a mixing zone analysis. Yet just as the Company moved to correct the EQB certification, EPA moved even more swiftly to adopt a final permit based on the EQB certificate that omitted a mixing zone analysis.

The chronology can be compressed. On August 17, 1990, the Company asked EQB to reconsider its certification and include a mixing zone analysis. On August 21, 1990, EPA published a new draft permit incorporating EQB's final certification requirements, and it offered 30 days to submit comments. On September 7, 1990, EQB wrote to EPA saying that it was evaluating the Company's comments on reconsideration and that it might alter its certification. On September 10 and on September 21, 1990, the Company asked EPA to delay action on the permit to allow the EQB to complete its reconsideration. On September 28, 1990, EPA issued a final permit, based on the then July 1990 EQB certification and without provision for a mixing zone.

On November 7, 1990, the Company sought administrative review within EPA, an action that automatically stayed the new permit and left the old one in force on a temporary basis. On November 28, 1990, EQB adopted a resolution staying its certification pending reconsideration and announcing, for the benefit of EPA, that the certificate was "not to become final" until the reconsideration was completed. In February 1991, EQB wrote formally to EPA stating that the certificate should be treated as not final and urging EPA to leave the Company's previous permit in effect for the time being. In June 1992 EPA's regional administrator issued a decision reaffirming the new permit without a mixing zone provision but continuing the stay of the new permit pending a further administrative appeal.

In July 1992, the Company duly appealed the regional administrator's decision to EPA's Environmental Appeals Board, urging a number of the arguments discussed below, and making one further contention of note: the Company said that unless EPA modified the permit on direct review, the Company would likely be unable get the mixing zone analysis incorporated into the permit through subsequent proceedings. The reason, said the Company, was "the probable application of the anti-backsliding policy" of the Clean Water Act, 33 U.S.C. § 1342(o). On October 26, 1992, the EPA Environmental Appeals Board issued a lengthy decision refusing further review. The Company's appeal to this court followed.

II. DISCUSSION

Faced with what may be a disastrous outcome from its standpoint, the Company has offered this court a variety of procedural challenges to EPA. They range from a broad claim that EQB's final certification was ineffective (because Puerto Rico's time to certify had expired) to a trivial complaint that the EPA did not allow a 15-day extension to the comment period at one phase of the proceeding. We think virtually all of the procedural claims fail and, while addressing them at the close of the opinion, we prefer to begin by discussing EPA's central error.

EPA's action in adopting the permit in this case is not flawed by procedural mistake. On the contrary, EPA did a commendable job of dotting i's and crossing t's. Nor is there any violation of substantive provisions of the Clean Water Act; for example, nothing in that statute explicitly requires EPA to use mixing zone analyses in its permits. The problem with EPA's decision is simply that the outcome appears on its face to make no sense. We say "appears" because we cannot rule out the possibility that some further explanation could shore up the EPA's result. Either way, the EPA's present action cannot stand.

It may come as a surprise that agency decisions must make sense to reviewing courts. Agencies, after all, are normally entitled to substantial deference so long as their decisions do not collide directly with substantive statutory commands and so long as procedural corners are squarely turned. This deference is especially marked in technical areas. But in the end an agency decision must also be rational—technically speaking, it must not be "arbitrary or capricious," Administrative Procedure Act, 5 U.S.C. § 706(2)(A)—and that requirement exists even in technical areas of regulation. The requirement is not very hard to meet, but it has not been met here.

The "arbitrary or capricious" concept, needless to say, is not easy to encapsulate in a single list of rubrics because it embraces a myriad of possible faults and depends heavily upon the circumstances of the case. Still, there are rules of thumb. In addressing individual aspects of EPA's decision, we cite to those requirements—discussion of relevant issues, consistency with past practice, avoidance of unexplained discrimination— that are pertinent to EPA's decision in this case.

On the surface of the administrative record, the following scene presents itself. EQB, having used a mixing zone analysis in past cases, neglected to include such a provision in its latest certification for this facility. EQB had previously used a mixing zone analysis for this very facility; and far from abandoning the concept, EQB was in the process of revising its regulations to prescribe such an analysis at the very time it was preparing the Company's certification. Four days before it issued the final certification in this case, omitting a mixing zone provision, it formally promulgated its new mixing zone regulations.

It is not clear whether in August 1990 EPA appreciated that EQB had probably misstepped. The Company's brief implies that the EPA, having obtained EQB's final certification, then proceeded with sinister speed— surely a rare accusation in administrative law—to mousetrap the Company by issuing a final permit before EQB's certification could be revised. An alternative explanation, to us entirely plausible, is that the EPA's patience with EQB had been exhausted and it wanted, as it had warned almost a year before, simply to get done with the permit as soon as it had EQB's final certification.

However this may be, both the Company and EQB made clear to the EPA at once, and before the final permit issued, that reconsideration was under way. EPA published its new draft permit for comment in August 1990; and in September 1990, *before* the EPA issued the final permit on September 28, 1990, EQB advised EPA (on September 7) that it was reconsidering its certification and might alter it, and the Company wrote letters (on September 10 and 21) begging the EPA to defer final action until the EQB acted. The EPA nevertheless proceeded to issue the final permit with no explanation for its refusal to wait.

Even at this stage, it appears that EPA was free to correct the problem on administrative review. There being no fixed timetable, the regional administrator presumably had discretion to defer action until EQB acted on the Company's reconsideration request and, if a mixing zone analysis were adopted by EQB in a revised certification, then to incorporate this revision into the new permit. One of EPA's regulations * * * seems to contemplate just such a situation. During this same period EQB made crystal clear, by its resolution of November 28, 1990, and its formal letter of February 25, 1991, that it was planning to reexamine its certification and did not want the certification treated as final. Once again, EPA proceeded to reject the pleas and reaffirm the permit, sans mixing zone.

EPA has now explained its position at least three times administratively and for a fourth time in this court. Each time EPA deals deftly with the Company's procedural objections by showing why some regulation allowed EPA to await EQB's final certification, but to refuse to await EQB's attempt to repair the certification, and allowed EPA to adopt EQB's certification, but to reject EQB's retroactive attempt to brand it as non-final. The only thing that is missing, among this array of finely wrought explanations, is any reason *why* the EPA should want to frustrate the EQB's clumsy, long-delayed but increasingly evident desire to reconsider a mixing zone analysis for this permit.

Assuredly, some explanation is called for. The mixing zone analysis is not some freakish idea or whim of the Puerto Rico authorities. According to EPA's *Mixing Zones* publication, it is available for use in at least 49 states in varying situations; and the Company said that the refinery in question cannot operate if the permit limitations are applied, without a mixing zone analysis, at the point that the effluent enters the water. Patently, these considerations of history and practical effect would, in a rational decision, warrant at least some discussion.

At oral argument, we inquired of counsel representing the EPA whether there were other situations in which EPA had refused to use a mixing zone analysis despite a state's desire that such an analysis be used. Yes, we were told, counsel for EPA knew of several such instances. On rebuttal, the Company's counsel responded that there were indeed other instances but they were limited to EPA's issuance of permits in Puerto Rico, in the same time frame as this case and to other applicants whose situations paralleled that of the Company. If this is the situation (counsel for EPA made no later effort to respond), then EPA's current posture is in some measure at odds with precedent. *Cf. Atchison, T & S.F. Ry. v. Wichita Bd. of Trade*, 412 U.S. 800, 808, 93 S.Ct. 2367, 2375, 37 L.Ed.2d 350 (1973) ("departure from prior norms" must be explained).

The point is not that EPA has some overriding obligation under the Clean Water Act to do whatever it is that the state wants to do. On the contrary, EPA was entirely free, once Puerto Rico had ignored the clear deadlines for a final certification, to treat the Commonwealth as an interested bystander with no further veto authority. What is beyond explanation, or at least wholly unexplained, is why EPA should be intent on adopting half of what the Commonwealth wanted while systematically frustrating its attempt to secure the other half. The obligation, we repeat, is not one of deference to local authorities but of making sense.

* * *

Perhaps there is some explanation for EPA's action other than a mechanical desire to reach a rapid conclusion without regard to whether the result is sound. Indeed, we suspect that there is an explanation. As noted, the Company insinuates that EPA deliberately took advantage of EQB's carelessness to mousetrap the Company into standards that could not later be relaxed because of the anti-backsliding provisions previously mentioned. Such a result would at least explain what happened, although it is doubtful that the explanation, if adopted by EPA, would commend itself to a reviewing court.

Or, there may be more benign reasons for EPA's action. Perhaps the Company's science is faulty and very slight adjustments in technology would permit it to meet the pollution limitations, and improve the environment to boot, without any mixing zone analysis. In all events, until EPA emerges from its fortress of procedural-rule citations and adopts a rationale for its action, any speculations are beside the point: the agency's decision cannot be supported on reasoning that the agency has not yet adopted. *See SEC v. Chenery Corp.*, 332 U.S. 194, 196, 67 S.Ct. 1575, 1577, 91 L.Ed. 1995 (1947).

* * *

All that we hold here is that EPA's decision to issue a permit in September 1990, adopting EQB's certification but refusing to await EQB's decision on reconsideration, produces a result that on the present record appears manifestly arbitrary and capricious. If legitimate reasons exist for such an outcome, then EPA is free to provide them and re-adopt the present permit (and the Company in turn is free to challenge those reasons and that action by petitioning again for judicial review). EPA, EQB, and the Company may find it possible to chart a more constructive course and make further litigation unnecessary.

The EPA order adopting the permit at issue in this case is *vacated* and the matter is *remanded* to EPA for further proceedings in accordance with this opinion. Costs are taxed in favor of the petitioner.

F.C.C. v. FOX TELEVISION STATIONS, INC.

Supreme Court of the United States, 2009.
556 U.S. 502, 129 S.Ct. 1800, 173 L.Ed.2d 738.

JUSTICE SCALIA delivered the opinion of the Court, except as to Part III-E.

Federal law prohibits the broadcasting of "any . . . indecent . . . language," 18 U.S.C. § 1464, which includes expletives referring to sexual or excretory activity or organs, see *FCC v. Pacifica Foundation,* 438 U.S. 726, 98 S.Ct. 3026, 57 L.Ed.2d 1073 (1978). This case concerns the adequacy of the Federal Communications Commission's explanation of its decision that this sometimes forbids the broadcasting of indecent expletives even when the offensive words are not repeated.

I. Statutory and Regulatory Background

The Communications Act of 1934, 47 U.S.C. § 151 *et seq.*, established a system of limited-term broadcast licenses subject to various "conditions" designed "to maintain the control of the United States over all the channels of radio transmission" * * *.

One of the burdens that licensees shoulder is the indecency ban—the statutory proscription against "utter[ing] any obscene, indecent, or profane language by means of radio communication," 18 U.S.C. § 1464—which Congress has instructed the Commission to enforce between the hours of 6 a.m. and 10 p.m. Public Telecommunications Act of 1992, § 16(a), 106 Stat. 954, note following 47 U.S.C. § 303. Congress has given the Commission various means of enforcing the indecency ban, including civil fines and license revocations or the denial of license renewals.

The Commission first invoked the statutory ban on indecent broadcasts in 1975, declaring a daytime broadcast of George Carlin's "Filthy Words" monologue actionably indecent. *In re Citizen's Complains Against Pacifica Foundation Station WBAI (PM),* 56 F.C.C.2d 94, 1975 WL 29897. At that time, the Commission announced the definition of indecent speech that it uses to this day, prohibiting "language that describes, in terms patently offensive as measured by contemporary community standards for the broadcast medium, sexual or excretory activities and organs, at times of the day when there is a reasonable risk that children may be in the audience." *Id.,* at 98.

In *FCC v. Pacifica Foundation, supra,* we upheld the Commission's order against statutory and constitutional challenge. We rejected the broadcasters' argument that the statutory proscription applied only to speech appealing to the prurient interest, noting that "the normal definition of 'indecent' merely refers to nonconformance with accepted standards of morality." *Id.,* at 740, 98 S.Ct. 3026. And we held that the First Amendment allowed Carlin's monologue to be banned in light of the "uniquely pervasive presence" of the medium and the fact that broadcast programming is "uniquely accessible to children." *Id.,* at 748–749, 98 S.Ct. 3026.

In the ensuing years, the Commission took a cautious, but gradually expanding, approach to enforcing the statutory prohibition against indecent broadcasts. Shortly after *Pacifica,* the Commission expressed its "inten[tion] strictly to observe the narrowness of the *Pacifica* holding," which "relied in part on the repetitive occurrence of the 'indecent' words" contained in Carlin's monologue. *In re Application of WGBH Educ. Foundation,* 69 F.C.C.2d 1250, 1254, ¶ 10, 1978 WL 36042 (1978). When the full Commission next considered its indecency standard, however, it repudiated the view that its enforcement power was limited to "deliberate, repetitive use of the seven words actually contained in the George Carlin monologue." *In re Pacifica Foundation, Inc.,* 2 FCC Rcd. 2698, 2699, ¶ 12, 1987 WL 345577 (1987). The Commission determined that such a "highly restricted enforcement standard . . . was unduly narrow as a matter of law and inconsistent with [the Commission's] enforcement responsibilities under Section 1464." *In re Infinity Broadcasting Corp. of Pa.,* 3 FCC Rcd. 930, ¶ 5, 1987 WL 345514 (1987) * * *.

Although the Commission had expanded its enforcement beyond the "repetitive use of specific words or phrases," it preserved a distinction between literal and nonliteral (or "expletive") uses of evocative language. *In re Pacifica Foundation, Inc.,* 2 FCC Rcd., at 2699, ¶ 13. The Commission explained that each literal "description or depiction of sexual or excretory functions must be examined in context to determine whether it is patently offensive," but that "deliberate and repetitive use . . . is a requisite to a finding of indecency" when a complaint focuses solely on the use of nonliteral expletives. *Ibid.*

Over a decade later, the Commission emphasized that the "full context" in which particular materials appear is "critically important," but that a few "principal" factors guide the inquiry, such as the "explicitness or graphic nature" of the material, the extent to which the material "dwells on or repeats" the offensive material, and the extent to which the material was presented to "pander," to "titillate," or to "shock." *In re Industry Guidance on Commission's Case Law Interpreting 18 U.S.C. § 1464 and Enforcement Policies Regarding Broadcast Indecency,* 16 FCC Rcd. 7999, 8002, ¶ 9, 8003, ¶ 10, 2001 WL 332787 (2001) (emphasis deleted). "No single factor," the Commission said, "generally provides the basis for an indecency finding," but "where sexual or excretory references have been made once or have been passing or fleeting in nature, this characteristic has tended to weigh against a finding of indecency." *Id.,* at 8003, ¶ 10, 8008, ¶ 17.

In 2004, the Commission took one step further by declaring for the first time that a nonliteral (expletive) use of the F- and S-Words could be actionably indecent, even when the word is used only once. The first order to this effect dealt with an NBC broadcast of the Golden Globe Awards, in which the performer Bono commented, " '[T]his is really, really, f* * *ing brilliant.' " *In re Complaints Against Various Broadcast Licensees Regarding Their Airing of "Golden Globe Awards" Program,* 19 FCC Rcd. 4975, 4976, n. 4, 2004 WL 540339 (2004) *(Golden Globes Order).* Although the Commission had received numerous complaints directed at the broadcast, its enforcement bureau had concluded that the material was not indecent because "Bono did not describe, in context, sexual or excretory organs or activities and . . . the utterance was fleeting and isolated." *Id.,* at

4975–4976, ¶ 3. The full Commission reviewed and reversed the staff ruling.

The Commission * * * determined * * * that the broadcast was "patently offensive" because the F-Word "is one of the most vulgar, graphic and explicit descriptions of sexual activity in the English language," because "[i]ts use invariably invokes a coarse sexual image," and because Bono's use of the word was entirely "shocking and gratuitous." *Id.*, at 4979, ¶ 9.

The Commission observed that categorically exempting such language from enforcement actions would "likely lead to more widespread use." *Ibid.* Commission action was necessary to "safeguard the well-being of the nation's children from the most objectionable, most offensive language." *Ibid.* The order noted that technological advances have made it far easier to delete ("bleep out") a "single and gratuitous use of a vulgar expletive," without adulterating the content of a broadcast. *Id.*, at 4980, ¶ 11.

The order acknowledged that "prior Commission and staff action [has] indicated that isolated or fleeting broadcasts of the 'F-Word' . . . are not indecent or would not be acted upon." It explicitly ruled that "any such interpretation is no longer good law." *Ibid.*, ¶ 12. It "clarif[ied] . . . that the mere fact that specific words or phrases are not sustained or repeated does not mandate a finding that material that is otherwise patently offensive to the broadcast medium is not indecent." *Ibid.* Because, however, "existing precedent would have permitted this broadcast," the Commission determined that "NBC and its affiliates necessarily did not have the requisite notice to justify a penalty." *Id.*, at 4981–4982, ¶ 15.

II. The Present Case

This case concerns utterances in two live broadcasts aired by Fox Television Stations, Inc., and its affiliates prior to the Commission's *Golden Globes Order*. The first occurred during the 2002 Billboard Music Awards, when the singer Cher exclaimed, "I've also had critics for the last 40 years saying that I was on my way out every year. Right. So f* * * 'em." Brief for Petitioners 9. The second involved a segment of the 2003 Billboard Music Awards, during the presentation of an award by Nicole Richie and Paris Hilton, principals in a Fox television series called "The Simple Life." Ms. Hilton began their interchange by reminding Ms. Richie to "watch the bad language," but Ms. Richie proceeded to ask the audience, "Why do they even call it 'The Simple Life?' Have you ever tried to get cow s* * * out of a Prada purse? It's not so f* * *ing simple." *Id.*, at 9–10. Following each of these broadcasts, the Commission received numerous complaints from parents whose children were exposed to the language.

On March 15, 2006, the Commission released "Notices of Apparent Liability" for a number of broadcasts that the Commission deemed actionably indecent, including the two described above. *In re Complaints*

Regarding Various Television Broadcasts Between Feb. 2, 2002 and Mar. 8, 2005, 21 FCC Rcd. 2664, 2006 WL 656783 (2006) * * *. The Commission's order on remand upheld the indecency findings for the broadcasts described above. See *In re Complaints Regarding Various Television Broadcasts Between Feb. 2, 2002, and Mar. 8, 2005,* 21 FCC Rcd. 13299, 2006 WL 3207085 (2006) *(Remand Order).*

The order first explained that both broadcasts fell comfortably within the subject-matter scope of the Commission's indecency test * * *. The order relied upon the " 'critically important' " context of the utterances, *id.,* at 13304, ¶ 15, noting that they were aired during prime-time awards shows "designed to draw a large nationwide audience that could be expected to include many children interested in seeing their favorite music stars," *id.,* at 13305, ¶ 18, 13324, ¶ 59. Indeed, approximately 2.5 million minors witnessed each of the broadcasts. *Id.,* at 13306, ¶ 18, 13326, ¶ 65.

The order asserted that both broadcasts under review would have been actionably indecent under the staff rulings and Commission dicta in effect prior to the *Golden Globes Order*—the 2003 broadcast because it involved a literal description of excrement, rather than a mere expletive, because it used more than one offensive word, and because it was planned, 21 FCC Rcd., at 13307, ¶ 22; and the 2002 broadcast because Cher used the F-Word not as a mere intensifier, but as a description of the sexual act to express hostility to her critics, *id.,* at 13324, ¶ 60. The order stated, however, that the pre-*Golden Globes* regime of immunity for isolated indecent expletives rested only upon staff rulings and Commission dicta, and that the Commission itself had never held "that the isolated use of an expletive . . . was not indecent or could not be indecent," 21 FCC Rcd., at 13307, ¶ 21. In any event, the order made clear, the *Golden Globes Order* eliminated any doubt that fleeting expletives could be actionably indecent, 21 FCC Rcd., at 13308, ¶ 23, 13325, ¶ 61, and the Commission disavowed the bureau-level decisions and its own dicta that had said otherwise, *id.,* at 13306–13307, ¶¶ 20, 21. Under the new policy, a lack of repetition "weigh[s] against a finding of indecency," *id.,* at 13325, ¶ 61, but is not a safe harbor.

The order explained that the Commission's prior "strict dichotomy between 'expletives' and 'descriptions or depictions of sexual or excretory functions' is artificial and does not make sense in light of the fact that an 'expletive's' power to offend derives from its sexual or excretory meaning." *Id.,* at 13308, ¶ 23. In the Commission's view, "granting an automatic exemption for 'isolated or fleeting' expletives unfairly forces viewers (including children)" to take " 'the first blow' " and would allow broadcasters "to air expletives at all hours of a day so long as they did so one at a time." *Id.,* at 13309, ¶ 25. Although the Commission determined that Fox encouraged the offensive language by using suggestive scripting in the 2003 broadcast, and unreasonably failed to take adequate precautions in both broadcasts, *id.,* at 13311–13314, ¶¶ 31–37, the order again declined to impose any forfeiture or other sanction for either of the broadcasts, *id.,* at 13321, ¶ 53, 13326, ¶ 66.

* * * The Court of Appeals reversed the agency's orders, finding the Commission's reasoning inadequate under the Administrative Procedure Act * * *.

III. Analysis

A. Governing Principles

The Administrative Procedure Act * * * permits (insofar as relevant here) the setting aside of agency action that is "arbitrary" or "capricious," 5 U.S.C. § 706(2)(A). Under what we have called this "narrow" standard of review, we insist that an agency "examine the relevant data and articulate a satisfactory explanation for its action." *Motor Vehicle Mfrs. Assn. of United States, Inc. v. State Farm Mut. Automobile Ins. Co.,* 463 U.S. 29, 43, 103 S.Ct. 2856, 77 L.Ed.2d 443 (1983). We have made clear, however, that "a court is not to substitute its judgment for that of the agency," *ibid.,* and should "uphold a decision of less than ideal clarity if the agency's path may reasonably be discerned," *Bowman Transp., Inc. v. Arkansas-Best Freight System, Inc.,* 419 U.S. 281, 286, 95 S.Ct. 438, 42 L.Ed.2d 447 (1974).

In overturning the Commission's judgment, the Court of Appeals here relied in part on Circuit precedent requiring a more substantial explanation for agency action that changes prior policy. The Second Circuit has interpreted the Administrative Procedure Act and our opinion in *State Farm* as requiring agencies to make clear " 'why the original reasons for adopting the [displaced] rule or policy are no longer dispositive' " as well as " 'why the new rule effectuates the statute as well as or better than the old rule.' " 489 F.3d, at 456–457 (quoting *New York Council, Assn. of Civilian Technicians v. FLRA,* 757 F.2d 502, 508 (C.A.2 1985); emphasis deleted). The Court of Appeals for the District of Columbia Circuit has similarly indicated that a court's standard of review is "heightened somewhat" when an agency reverses course. *NAACP v. FCC,* 682 F.2d 993, 998 (1982).

We find no basis in the Administrative Procedure Act or in our opinions for a requirement that all agency change be subjected to more searching review. The Act mentions no such heightened standard. And our opinion in *State Farm* neither held nor implied that every agency action representing a policy change must be justified by reasons more substantial than those required to adopt a policy in the first instance. That case, which involved the rescission of a prior regulation, said only that such action requires "a reasoned analysis for the change beyond that which may be required when an agency *does not act* in the first instance." 463 U.S., at 42, 103 S.Ct. 2856 (emphasis added). Treating failures to act and rescissions of prior action differently for purposes of the standard of review makes good sense, and has basis in the text of the statute, which likewise treats the two separately. It instructs a reviewing court to "compel agency action unlawfully withheld or unreasonably delayed," 5 U.S.C. § 706(1), and to "hold unlawful and set aside agency action, findings, and conclusions found to be [among other things] . . . arbitrary [or] capricious," § 706(2)(A). The statute makes no distinction, however, between initial agency action and subsequent agency action undoing or revising that action.

To be sure, the requirement that an agency provide reasoned explanation for its action would ordinarily demand that it display awareness that it *is* changing position. An agency may not, for example, depart from a prior policy *sub silentio* or simply disregard rules that are still on the books. And of course the agency must show that there are good reasons for the new policy. But it need not demonstrate to a court's satisfaction that the reasons for the new policy are *better* than the reasons for the old one; it suffices that the new policy is permissible under the statute, that there are good reasons for it, and that the agency *believes* it to be better, which the conscious change of course adequately indicates. This means that the agency need not always provide a more detailed justification than what would suffice for a new policy created on a blank slate. Sometimes it must—when, for example, its new policy rests upon factual findings that contradict those which underlay its prior policy; or when its prior policy has engendered serious reliance interests that must be taken into account. It would be arbitrary or capricious to ignore such matters. In such cases it is not that further justification is demanded by the mere fact of policy change; but that a reasoned explanation is needed for disregarding facts and circumstances that underlay or were engendered by the prior policy.

* * *

B.   Application to This Case

Judged under the above described standards, the Commission's new enforcement policy and its order finding the broadcasts actionably indecent were neither arbitrary nor capricious. First, the Commission forthrightly acknowledged that its recent actions have broken new ground, taking account of inconsistent "prior Commission and staff action" and explicitly disavowing them as "no longer good law." *Golden Globes Order,* 19 FCC Rcd., at 4980, ¶ 12 * * *. There is no doubt that the Commission knew it was making a change. That is why it declined to assess penalties; and it relied on the *Golden Globes Order* as removing any lingering doubt. *Remand Order,* 21 FCC Rcd., at 13308, ¶ 23, 13325, ¶ 61.

Moreover, the agency's reasons for expanding the scope of its enforcement activity were entirely rational. It was certainly reasonable to determine that it made no sense to distinguish between literal and nonliteral uses of offensive words, requiring repetitive use to render only the latter indecent * * *. Even isolated utterances can be made in "pander[ing,] . . . vulgar and shocking" manners, *Remand Order,* 21 FCC

Rcd., at 13305, ¶ 17, and can constitute harmful " 'first blow[s]' " to children, *id.,* at 13309, ¶ 25. It is surely rational (if not inescapable) to believe that a safe harbor for single words would "likely lead to more widespread use of the offensive language," *Golden Globes Order, supra,* at 4979, ¶ 9.

* * *

The fact that technological advances have made it easier for broadcasters to bleep out offending words further supports the Commission's stepped-up enforcement policy. *Golden Globes Order, supra,* at 4980, ¶ 11. And the agency's decision not to impose any forfeiture or other sanction precludes any argument that it is arbitrarily punishing parties without notice of the potential consequences of their action.

C.   The Court of Appeals' Reasoning

The Court of Appeals found the Commission's action arbitrary and capricious on three grounds. First, the court criticized the Commission for failing to explain why it had not previously banned fleeting expletives as "harmful 'first blow[s].' " 489 F.3d, at 458. In the majority's view, without "evidence that suggests a fleeting expletive is harmful [and] . . . serious enough to warrant government regulation," the agency could not regulate more broadly. *Id.,* at 461. As explained above, the fact that an agency had a prior stance does not alone prevent it from changing its view or create a higher hurdle for doing so. And it is not the Commission, but Congress that has proscribed "any . . . indecent . . . language." 18 U.S.C. § 1464.

There are some propositions for which scant empirical evidence can be marshaled, and the harmful effect of broadcast profanity on children is one of them. One cannot demand a multiyear controlled study, in which some children are intentionally exposed to indecent broadcasts (and insulated from all other indecency), and others are shielded from all indecency. It is one thing to set aside agency action under the Administrative Procedure Act because of failure to adduce empirical data that can readily be obtained. See, *e.g., State Farm,* 463 U.S., at 46–56, 103 S.Ct. 2856 (addressing the costs and benefits of mandatory passive restraints for automobiles). It is something else to insist upon obtaining the unobtainable. Here it suffices to know that children mimic the behavior they observe—or at least the behavior that is presented to them as normal and appropriate. Programming replete with one-word indecent expletives will tend to produce children who use (at least) one-word indecent expletives. Congress has made the determination that indecent material is harmful to children, and has left enforcement of the ban to the Commission. If enforcement had to be supported by empirical data, the ban would effectively be a nullity.

* * *

The court's second objection is that fidelity to the agency's "first blow" theory of harm would require a categorical ban on *all* broadcasts of expletives; the Commission's failure to go to this extreme thus undermined the coherence of its rationale. 489 F.3d, at 458–459 * * *

* * * [T]he agency's decision to consider the patent offensiveness of isolated expletives on a case-by-case basis is not arbitrary or capricious. "Even a prime-time recitation of Geoffrey Chaucer's Miller's Tale," we have explained, "would not be likely to command the attention of many children who are both old enough to understand and young enough to be adversely affected." *Pacifica, supra,* at 750, n. 29, 98 S.Ct. 3026. The same rationale could support the Commission's finding that a broadcast of the film Saving Private Ryan was not indecent—a finding to which the broadcasters point as supposed evidence of the Commission's inconsistency. The frightening suspense and the graphic violence in the movie could well dissuade the most vulnerable from watching and would put parents on notice of potentially objectionable material. See *In re Complaints Against Various Television Licensees Regarding Their Broadcast on Nov. 11, 2004 of ABC Television Network's *521 Presentation of Film "Saving Private Ryan,"* 20 FCC Rcd. 4507, 4513, ¶ 15, 2005 WL 474210 (2005) (noting that the broadcast was not "intended as family entertainment"). The agency's decision to retain some discretion does not render arbitrary or capricious its regulation of the deliberate and shocking uses of offensive language at the award shows under review—shows that were expected to (and did) draw the attention of millions of children.

Finally, the Court of Appeals found unconvincing the agency's prediction (without any evidence) that a *per se* exemption for fleeting expletives would lead to increased use of expletives one at a time. 489 F.3d, at 460. But even in the absence of evidence, the agency's predictive judgment (which merits deference) makes entire sense. To predict that complete immunity for fleeting expletives, ardently desired by broadcasters, will lead to a substantial increase in fleeting expletives seems to us an exercise in logic rather than clairvoyance. The Court of Appeals was perhaps correct that the Commission's prior policy had not yet caused broadcasters to "barrag[e] the airwaves with expletives," *ibid.* That may have been because its prior permissive policy had been confirmed (save in dicta) only at the staff level. In any event, as the *Golden Globes* order demonstrated, it did produce more expletives than the Commission (which has the first call in this matter) deemed in conformity with the statute.

D.   Respondents' Arguments

* * *

* * * [T]he broadcasters claim that the Commission's repeated appeal to "context" is simply a smokescreen for a standardless regime of unbridled

discretion. But we have previously approved Commission regulation based "on a nuisance rationale under which context is all-important," *Pacifica, supra,* at 750, 98 S.Ct. 3026, and we find no basis in the Administrative Procedure Act for mandating anything different.

E. The Dissents' Arguments

Justice BREYER * * * claims that the FCC's status as an "independent" agency sheltered from political oversight requires courts to be "all the more" vigilant in ensuring "that major policy decisions be based upon articulable reasons." *Ibid.* Not so. The independent agencies are sheltered not from politics but from the President, and it has often been observed that their freedom from Presidential oversight (and protection) has simply been replaced by increased subservience to congressional direction. Indeed, the precise policy change at issue here was spurred by significant political pressure from Congress.

* * *

Regardless, it is assuredly not "applicable law" that rulemaking by independent regulatory agencies is subject to heightened scrutiny. The Administrative Procedure Act, which provides judicial review, makes no distinction between independent and other agencies, neither in its definition of agency, 5 U.S.C. § 701(b)(1), nor in the standards for reviewing agency action, § 706. Nor does any case of ours express or reflect the "heightened scrutiny" Justice BREYER and Justice STEVENS would impose. Indeed, it is hard to imagine any closer scrutiny than that we have given to the Environmental Protection Agency, which is not an independent agency. See *Massachusetts v. EPA,* 549 U.S. 497, 533–535, 127 S.Ct. 1438, 167 L.Ed.2d 248 (2007); *Whitman v. American Trucking Assns., Inc.,* 531 U.S. 457, 481–486, 121 S.Ct. 903, 149 L.Ed.2d 1 (2001). There is no reason to magnify the separation-of-powers dilemma posed by the headless Fourth Branch, see *Freytag v. Commissioner,* 501 U.S. 868, 921, 111 S.Ct. 2631, 115 L.Ed.2d 764 (1991) (SCALIA, J., concurring in part and concurring in judgment), by letting Article III judges—like jackals stealing the lion's kill—expropriate some of the power that Congress has wrested from the unitary Executive.

Justice BREYER and Justice STEVENS * * * both claim that the Commission failed adequately to explain its consideration of the constitutional issues inherent in its regulation * * *. According to Justice BREYER, the agency said "next to nothing about the relation between the change it made in its prior 'fleeting expletive' policy and the First-Amendment-related need to avoid 'censorship,'" *post,* at 1832–1833. The *Remand Order* does, however, devote four full pages of small-type, single-spaced text (over 1,300 words not counting the footnotes) to explaining why the Commission believes that its indecency-enforcement regime (which includes its change in policy) is consistent with the First Amendment—and therefore not censorship as the term is understood * * *.

Second, Justice BREYER looks over the vast field of particular factual scenarios unaddressed by the FCC's 35-page *Remand Order* and finds one that is fatal: the plight of the small local broadcaster who cannot afford the new technology that enables the screening of live broadcasts for indecent utterances. Cf. *post*, at 1834–1838. The Commission has failed to address the fate of this unfortunate, who will, he believes, be subject to sanction.

We doubt, to begin with, that small-town broadcasters run a heightened risk of liability for indecent utterances. In programming that they originate, their down-home local guests probably employ vulgarity less than big-city folks; and small-town stations generally cannot afford or cannot attract foul-mouthed glitteratae from Hollywood. Their main exposure with regard to self-originated programming is live coverage of news and public affairs. But the *Remand Order* went out of its way to note that the case at hand did not involve "breaking news coverage," and that "it may be inequitable to hold a licensee responsible for airing offensive speech during live coverage of a public event," 21 FCC Rcd., at 13311, ¶ 33. As for the programming that small stations receive on a network "feed": This *will* be cleansed by the expensive technology small stations (by Justice BREYER's hypothesis) cannot afford.

But never mind the detail of whether small broadcasters are uniquely subject to a great risk of punishment for fleeting expletives. The fundamental fallacy of Justice BREYER's small-broadcaster gloomy scenario is its demonstrably false assumption that the *Remand Order* makes no provision for the avoidance of unfairness—that the single-utterance prohibition will be invoked uniformly, in all situations. The *Remand Order* made very clear that this is not the case. It said that in determining "what, if any, remedy is appropriate" the Commission would consider the facts of each individual case, such as the "possibility of human error in using delay equipment," *id.*, at 13313, ¶ 35. Thus, the fact that the agency believed that Fox (a large broadcaster that used suggestive scripting and a deficient delay system to air a prime-time awards show aimed at millions of children) "fail[ed] to exercise 'reasonable judgment, responsibility and sensitivity,'" *id.*, at 13311, ¶ 33, and n. 91 (quoting *Pacifica Foundation, Inc.*, 2 FCC Rcd., at 2700, ¶ 18), says little about how the Commission would treat smaller broadcasters who cannot afford screening equipment. Indeed, that they would not be punished for failing to purchase equipment they cannot afford is positively suggested by the *Remand Order*'s statement that "[h]olding Fox responsible for airing indecent material in this case does not . . . impose undue burdens on broadcasters." 21 FCC Rcd., at 13313, ¶ 36.

There was, in sum, no need for the Commission to compose a special treatise on local broadcasters. And Justice BREYER can safely defer his concern for those yeomen of the airwaves until we have before us a case that involves one.

* * *

JUSTICE THOMAS concurring (omitted).

JUSTICE KENNEDY, concurring in part and concurring in the judgment.

I join Parts I, II, III-A through III-D, and IV of the opinion of the Court and agree that the judgment must be reversed. This separate writing is to underscore certain background principles for the conclusion that an agency's decision to change course may be arbitrary and capricious if the agency sets a new course that reverses an earlier determination but does not provide a reasoned explanation for doing so. In those circumstances I agree with the dissenting opinion of Justice BREYER that the agency must explain why "it now reject[s] the considerations that led it to adopt that initial policy." *Post,* at 1831.

The question whether a change in policy requires an agency to provide a more reasoned explanation than when the original policy was first announced is not susceptible, in my view, to an answer that applies in all cases. There may be instances when it becomes apparent to an agency that the reasons for a longstanding policy have been altered by discoveries in science, advances in technology, or by any of the other forces at work in a dynamic society. If an agency seeks to respond to new circumstances by modifying its earlier policy, the agency may have a substantial body of data and experience that can shape and inform the new rule. In other cases the altered circumstances may be so new that the agency must make predictive judgments that are as difficult now as when the agency's earlier policy was first announced. Reliance interests in the prior policy may also have weight in the analysis.

The question in each case is whether the agency's reasons for the change, when viewed in light of the data available to it, and when informed by the experience and expertise of the agency, suffice to demonstrate that the new policy rests upon principles that are rational, neutral, and in accord with the agency's proper understanding of its authority. That showing may be required if the agency is to demonstrate that its action is not "arbitrary, capricious, an abuse of discretion, or otherwise not in accordance with law." 5 U.S.C. § 706(2)(A). And, of course, the agency action must not be "in excess of statutory jurisdiction, authority, or limitations, or short of statutory right." § 706(2)(C).

* * *

Where there is a policy change the record may be much more developed because the agency based its prior policy on factual findings. In that instance, an agency's decision to change course may be arbitrary and capricious if the agency ignores or countermands its earlier factual findings without reasoned explanation for doing so. An agency cannot simply disregard contrary or inconvenient factual determinations that it made in the past, any more than it can ignore inconvenient facts when it writes on a blank slate.

This is the principle followed in the Court's opinion in *Motor Vehicle Mfrs. Assn. of United States, Inc. v. State Farm Mut. Automobile Ins. Co.,* 463 U.S. 29, 103 S.Ct. 2856, 77 L.Ed.2d 443 (1983) * * *. This Court found the agency's rescission arbitrary and capricious because the agency did not address its prior factual findings. See *id.,* at 49–51, 103 S.Ct. 2856.

The present case does not raise the concerns addressed in *State Farm* * * *. The FCC did not base its prior policy on factual findings.

The FCC's *Remand Order* explains that the agency has changed its reading of *Pacifica.* The reasons the agency announces for this change are not so precise, detailed, or elaborate as to be a model for agency explanation. But, as the opinion for the Court well explains, the FCC's reasons for its action were the sort of reasons an agency may consider and act upon. The Court's careful and complete analysis—both with respect to the procedural history of the FCC's indecency policies, and the reasons the agency has given to support them—is quite sufficient to sustain the FCC's change of course against respondents' claim that the agency acted in an arbitrary or capricious fashion.

* * *

JUSTICE STEVENS, dissenting (omitted).

JUSTICE GINSBURG, dissenting (omitted).

JUSTICE BREYER, with whom JUSTICE STEVENS, JUSTICE SOUTER, and JUSTICE GINSBURG join, dissenting.

In my view, the Federal Communications Commission failed adequately to explain *why* it *changed* its indecency policy from a policy permitting a single "fleeting use" of an expletive, to a policy that made no such exception. Its explanation fails to discuss two critical factors, at least one of which directly underlay its original policy decision. Its explanation instead discussed several factors well known to it the first time around, which by themselves provide no significant justification for a *change* of policy. Consequently, the FCC decision is "arbitrary, capricious, an abuse of discretion" * * *.

I

I begin with applicable law. That law grants those in charge of independent administrative agencies broad authority to determine relevant policy. But it does not permit them to make policy choices for purely political reasons nor to rest them primarily upon unexplained policy preferences. Federal Communications Commissioners have fixed terms of office; they are not directly responsible to the voters; and they enjoy an independence expressly designed to insulate them, to a degree, from " 'the exercise of political oversight.' " *Freytag v. Commissioner,* 501 U.S. 868, 916, 111 S.Ct. 2631, 115 L.Ed.2d 764 (1991) (SCALIA, J., concurring in part and concurring in judgment); see also *Morrison v. Olson,* 487 U.S. 654, 691, n. 30, 108 S.Ct. 2597, 101 L.Ed.2d 569 (1988). That insulation helps to secure important governmental objectives, such as the constitutionally related objective of maintaining broadcast regulation that does not bend too readily before the political winds. But that agency's comparative freedom from ballot-box control makes it all the more important that courts review its decisionmaking to assure compliance with applicable provisions of the law—including law requiring that major policy decisions be based upon articulable reasons.

The statutory provision applicable here is the Administrative Procedure Act's (APA) prohibition of agency action that is "arbitrary, capricious, [or] an abuse of discretion," 5 U.S.C. § 706(2)(A). This legal requirement helps assure agency decisionmaking based upon more than the personal preferences of the decisionmakers * * *.

The law has also recognized that it is not so much a particular set of substantive commands but rather it is a *process,* a process of learning through reasoned argument, that is the antithesis of the "arbitrary." This means agencies must follow a "logical and rational" decisionmaking "process." *Allentown Mack Sales & Service, Inc. v. NLRB,* 522 U.S. 359, 374, 118 S.Ct. 818, 139 L.Ed.2d 797 (1998). An agency's policy decisions must reflect the reasoned exercise of expert judgment. See *Burlington Truck Lines, supra,* at 167, 83 S.Ct. 239 (decision must reflect basis on which agency "exercised its expert discretion"); see also *Humphrey's Executor v. United States,* 295 U.S. 602, 624, 55 S.Ct. 869, 79 L.Ed. 1611 (1935) (independent agencies "exercise . . . trained judgment . . . 'informed by experience' ") * * *. And when an agency seeks to change those rules, it must focus on the fact of change and explain the basis for that change. See, *e.g., National Cable & Telecommunications Assn. v. Brand X Internet Services,* 545 U.S. 967, 981, 125 S.Ct. 2688, 162 L.Ed.2d 820 (2005) ("*Unexplained* inconsistency is" a "reason for holding an interpretation to be an arbitrary and capricious change from agency practice" (emphasis added)).

To explain a change requires more than setting forth reasons why the new policy is a good one. It also requires the agency to answer the question, "Why did you change?" And a rational answer to this question typically requires a more complete explanation than would prove satisfactory were change itself not at issue. An (imaginary) administrator explaining why he chose a policy that requires driving on the right side, rather than the left side, of the road might say, "Well, one side seemed as good as the other, so I flipped a coin." But even assuming the rationality of that explanation for an *initial* choice, that explanation is not at all rational if offered to explain why the administrator *changed* driving practice, from right side to left side, 25 years later.

* * *

* * * Thus, the agency must explain *why* it has come to the conclusion that it should now change direction. Why does it now reject the considerations that led it to adopt that initial policy? What has changed in the world that offers justification for the change? What other good reasons are there for departing from the earlier policy?

Contrary to the majority's characterization of this dissent, it would not (and *State Farm* does not) require a *"heightened standard"* of review. *Ante,* at 1810–1811 (emphasis added). Rather, the law requires application of the *same standard* of review to different circumstances, namely, circumstances characterized by the fact that *change* is at issue. It requires the agency to focus upon the fact of change where change is relevant, just as it must focus upon any other relevant circumstance. It requires the agency here to focus upon the reasons that led the agency to adopt the initial policy, and to explain why it now comes to a new judgment.

* * * I recognize that *sometimes* the ultimate explanation for a change may have to be, "We now weigh the relevant considerations differently." But at other times, an agency can and should say more. Where, for example, the agency rested its previous policy on particular factual findings, see *ante,* at 1823–1824 (KENNEDY, J., concurring in part and concurring in judgment); or where an agency rested its prior policy on its view of the governing law, see *infra,* at 1832–1835 or where an agency rested its previous policy on, say, a special need to coordinate with another agency, one would normally expect the agency to focus upon those earlier views of fact, of law, or of policy and explain why they are no longer controlling. Regardless, to say that the agency here must answer the question "why change" is not to require the agency to provide a justification that is "*better* than the reasons for the old [policy]." *Ante,* at 1834–1835 (majority opinion). It is only to recognize the obvious fact that *change* is sometimes (not always) a relevant background feature that sometimes (not always) requires focus (upon prior justifications) and explanation lest the adoption of the new policy (in that circumstance) be "arbitrary, capricious, an abuse of discretion."

* * * After all, if it is *always* legally sufficient for the agency to reply to the question "why change?" with the answer "we prefer the new policy" (even when the agency *has not considered* the major factors that led it to adopt its old policy), then why bother asking the agency to focus on the fact of change? More to the point, *why* would the law exempt this and no other aspect of an agency decision from "arbitrary, capricious" review? Where does, and why would, the APA grant agencies the freedom to change major policies on the basis of nothing more than political considerations or even personal whim?

* * *

II

We here must apply the general standards set forth in *State Farm* and *Overton Park* to an agency decision that changes a 25-year-old "fleeting expletive" policy from (1) the old policy that would normally permit broadcasters to transmit a single, fleeting use of an expletive to (2) a new policy that would threaten broadcasters with large fines for transmitting even a single use (including its use by a member of the public) of such an expletive, alone with nothing more. The question is whether that decision satisfies the minimal standards necessary to assure a reviewing court that such a change of policy is not "arbitrary, capricious, [or] an abuse of discretion," 5 U.S.C. § 706(2)(A), particularly as set forth in, *e.g., State Farm* and *Overton Park, supra,* at 1829–1832. The decision, in my view, does not satisfy those standards.

Consider the requirement that an agency at least minimally "consider . . . important aspect[s] of the problem." *State Farm, supra,* at 43, 103 S.Ct. 2856. The FCC failed to satisfy this requirement, for it failed to consider two critically important aspects of the problem that underlay its initial policy judgment (one of which directly, the other of which indirectly). First, the FCC said next to nothing about the relation between the change it made in its prior "fleeting expletive" policy and the First-Amendment-related need to avoid "censorship," a matter as closely related to broadcasting regulation as is health to that of the environment. The reason that discussion of the matter is particularly important here is that the FCC had *explicitly* rested its prior policy in large part upon the need to avoid treading too close to the constitutional line * * *.

* * *

The FCC thus repeatedly made clear that it based its "fleeting expletive" policy upon the need to avoid treading too close to the constitutional line as set forth in Justice Powell's *Pacifica* concurrence. What then did it say, when it changed its policy, about *why* it abandoned this Constitution-based reasoning? The FCC devoted "four full pages of small-type, single-spaced text," *ante,* at 1817–1818 (majority opinion), responding to industry arguments that, *e.g.,* changes in the nature of the broadcast industry made *all* indecency regulation, *i.e.,* 18 U.S.C. § 1464, unconstitutional. In doing so it repeatedly *reaffirmed* its view that *Pacifica* remains good law. *In re Complaints Regarding Various Television Broadcasts Between Feb. 2, 2002, and Mar. 8, 2005,* 21 FCC Rcd. 13299,

13317–13321, ¶¶ 43–52, 2006 WL 3207085 (2006) *(Remand Order)*. All the more surprising then that, in respect to *why* it abandoned its prior view about the critical relation between its prior fleeting expletive policy and Justice Powell's *Pacifica* concurrence, it says no more than the following: "[O]ur decision is not inconsistent with the Supreme Court ruling in *Pacifica*. The Court explicitly left open the issue of whether an occasional expletive could be considered indecent." *In re Complaints Against Various Broadcast Licensees Regarding Their Airing of the "Golden Globe Awards" Program,* 19 FCC Rcd. 4975, 4982, ¶ 16, 2004 WL 540339 (2004) *(Golden Globe Order)*. And (repeating what it already had said), "*[Pacifica]* specifically reserved the question of 'an occasional expletive' and noted that it addressed only the 'particular broadcast' at issue in that case." *Remand Order, supra,* at 13308–13309, ¶ 24.

These two sentences are not a summary of the FCC's discussion about why it abandoned its prior understanding of *Pacifica*. They *are* the discussion. These 28 words (repeated in two opinions) do not acknowledge that an entirely different understanding of *Pacifica* underlay the FCC's earlier policy; they do not explain why the agency changed its mind about the line that *Pacifica* draws or its policy's relation to that line; and they tell us nothing at all about what happened to the FCC's earlier determination to search for "compelling interests" and "less restrictive alternatives." They do not explain the transformation of what the FCC had long thought an insurmountable obstacle into an open door. The result is not simply *Hamlet* without the prince, but *Hamlet* with a prince who, in midplay and without explanation, just disappears.

* * *

Second, the FCC failed to consider the potential impact of its new policy upon local broadcasting coverage. This "aspect of the problem" is particularly important because the FCC explicitly took account of potential broadcasting impact. *Golden Globe Order, supra,* at 4980, ¶ 11 ("The ease with which broadcasters today can block even fleeting words in a live broadcast is an element in our decision"). Indeed, in setting forth "bleeping" technology changes (presumably lowering bleeping costs) as justifying the policy change, it implicitly reasoned that lower costs, making it easier for broadcasters to install bleeping equipment, made it less likely that the new policy would lead broadcasters to reduce coverage, say, by canceling coverage of public events.

What then did the FCC say about the likelihood that smaller independent broadcasters, including many public service broadcasters, still would not be able to afford "bleeping" technology and, as a consequence, would reduce local coverage, indeed cancel coverage, of many public events? It said nothing at all.

* * *

The plurality acknowledges that the Commission entirely failed to discuss this aspect of the regulatory problem. But it sees "no need" for discussion in light of its, *i.e.,* the plurality's, own "doubt[s]" that "small-town broadcasters run a heightened risk of liability for indecent utterances" as a result of the change of policy. *Ante,* at 1818–1819. The plurality's "doubt[s]" rest upon its views (1) that vulgar expression is less prevalent (at least among broadcast guests) in smaller towns, *ibid.,* at 1818; (2) that the greatest risk the new policy poses for "small-town broadcasters" arises when they broadcast local "news and public affairs," *ibid.*; and (3) that the *Remand Order* says "little about how the Commission would treat smaller broadcasters who cannot afford screening equipment," while also pointing out that the new policy " 'does not . . . impose undue burdens on broadcasters' " and emphasizing that the case before it did not involve " 'breaking news,' " *ante,* at 1818–1819.

As to the first point, about the prevalence of vulgarity in small towns, I confess ignorance. But I do know that there are independent stations in many large and medium sized cities. See Television & Cable Factbook, Directory of Television Stations in Operation 2008. As to the second point, I too believe that coverage of local public events, if not news, lies at the heart of the problem.

I cannot agree with the plurality, however, about the critical third point, namely, that the new policy obviously provides smaller independent broadcasters with adequate assurance that they will not be fined. The new policy removes the "fleeting expletive" exception, an exception that assured smaller independent stations that they would not be fined should someone swear at a public event. In its place, it puts a policy that places all broadcasters at risk when they broadcast fleeting expletives, including expletives uttered at public events. The *Remand Order* says that there "is *no outright news exemption from our indecency rules.*" 21 FCC Rcd., at 13327, ¶ 71 (emphasis added). The best it can provide by way of assurance is to say that "it *may* be inequitable to hold a licensee responsible for airing offensive speech during live coverage of a public event *under some circumstances.*" *Id.,* at 13311, ¶ 33 (emphasis added). It does list those circumstances as including the "possibility of human error in using delay equipment." *Id.,* at 13313, ¶ 35. But it says *nothing* about a station's *inability to afford* delay equipment (a matter that in individual cases could itself prove debatable). All the FCC had to do was to *consider* this matter and either grant an exemption or explain why it did not grant an exemption. But it did not. And the result is a rule that may well chill coverage—the kind of consequence that the law has considered important for decades, to which the broadcasters pointed in their arguments before the FCC, and which the FCC nowhere discusses.

* * *

III

* * *

Third, the FCC said that "perhaps" its "most importan[t]" justification for the new policy lay in the fact that its new "contextual" approach to fleeting expletives is better and more "[c]onsistent with" the agency's "general approach to indecency" than was its previous "categorica[l]" approach, which offered broadcasters virtual immunity for the broadcast of fleeting expletives. *Remand Order,* 21 FCC Rcd., at 13308, ¶ 23. This justification, however, offers no support for the change without an understanding of *why, i.e., in what way,* the FCC considered the new approach better or more consistent with the agency's general approach * * *.

In fact, the FCC found that the new policy was better in part because, in its view, the new policy better protects children against what it described as " 'the first blow' " of broadcast indecency that results from the " 'pervasive' " nature of broadcast media. It wrote that its former policy of "granting an automatic exemption for 'isolated or fleeting' expletives unfairly forces viewers (including children) to take 'the first blow.' " *Remand Order, supra,* at 13309, ¶ 25.

The difficulty with this argument, however, is that it does not explain the *change.* The FCC has long used the theory of the "first blow" to justify its regulation of broadcast indecency. See, *e.g., In re Enforcement of Prohibitions Against Broadcast Indecency in 18 U.S.C. § 1464,* 5 FCC Rcd. 5297, 5301–5302, ¶¶ 34–35 (1990). Yet the FCC has also long followed its original "fleeting expletives" policy. Nor was the FCC ever unaware of the fact to which the majority points, namely, that children's surroundings influence their behavior. See, *e.g., In re Enforcement of Prohibitions Against Broadcast Indecency in 18 U.S.C. § 1464,* 8 FCC Rcd. 704, 705–706, ¶ 11, 1993 WL 756823 (1993). So, to repeat the question: What, in respect to the "first blow," has changed?

The FCC points to no empirical (or other) evidence to demonstrate that it previously understated the importance of avoiding the "first blow." Like the majority, I do not believe that an agency must always conduct full empirical studies of such matters. *Ante,* at 1813–1814. But the FCC could have referred to, and explained, relevant empirical studies that suggest the contrary. One review of the empirical evidence, for example, reports that "[i]t is doubtful that children under the age of 12 understand sexual language and innuendo; therefore it is unlikely that vulgarities have any negative effects." Kaye & Sapolsky, Watch Your Mouth! An Analysis of Profanity Uttered by Children on Prime-Time Television, 2004 Mass Communication & Soc'y 429, 433 (Vol.7) (citing two studies). The Commission need not have accepted this conclusion. But its failure to discuss this or any other such evidence, while providing no empirical evidence at all that favors its position, must weaken the logical force of its conclusion. See *State Farm, supra,* at 43, 103 S.Ct. 2856 (explaining that an agency's failure to "examine the relevant data" is a factor in determining whether the decision is "arbitrary").

The FCC also found the new policy better because it believed that its prior policy "would as a matter of logic permit broadcasters to air expletives at all hours of a day so long as they did so one at a time." *Remand Order,* 21 FCC Rcd., at 13309, ¶ 25. This statement, however, raises an obvious question: Did that happen? The FCC's initial "fleeting expletives" policy was in effect for 25 years. Had broadcasters during those 25 years aired a series of expletives "one at a time"? If so, it should not be difficult to find evidence of that fact. But the FCC refers to none. Indeed, the FCC did not even claim that a change had taken place in this respect. It spoke only of the pure "logic" of the initial policy "permitting" such a practice. That logic would have been apparent to anyone, including the FCC, in 1978 when the FCC set forth its initial policy.

Finally, the FCC made certain statements that suggest it did not believe it was changing prior policy in any major way. It referred to that prior policy as based on "staff letters and dicta" and it said that at least one of the instances before it (namely, the Cher broadcast) would have been actionably indecent under that prior policy. Id., at 13306–13307, 13324, ¶¶ 20–21, 60. As we all agree, however, in fact the FCC did change its policy in a major way. See *ante,* at 1812 (majority opinion). To the extent that the FCC minimized that fact when considering the change, it did not fully focus on the fact of change. And any such failure would make its decision still less supportable. See *National Cable,* 545 U.S., at 981, 125 S.Ct. 2688.

* * *

V

In sum, the FCC's explanation of its change leaves out two critically important matters underlying its earlier policy, namely, *Pacifica* and local broadcasting coverage. Its explanation rests upon three considerations previously known to the agency ("coarseness," the "first blow," and running single expletives all day, one at a time). With one exception, it provides no empirical or other information explaining why those considerations, which did not justify its new policy before, justify it now. Its discussion of the one exception (technological advances in bleeping/delay systems), failing to take account of local broadcast coverage, is seriously incomplete.

I need not decide whether one or two of these features, standing alone, would require us to remand the case. Here all come together. And taken together they suggest that the FCC's answer to the question, "Why change?" is, "We like the new policy better." This kind of answer, might be perfectly satisfactory were it given by an elected official. But when given by an agency, in respect to a major change of an important policy where much more might be said, it is not sufficient. *State Farm,* 463 U.S., at 41–42, 103 S.Ct. 2856 * * *.

JUDULANG V. HOLDER

Supreme Court of the United States, 2011.
565 U.S. 42, 132 S.Ct. 476, 181 L.Ed.2d 449.

JUSTICE KAGAN delivered the opinion of the Court.

This case concerns the Board of Immigration Appeals' (BIA or Board) policy for deciding when resident aliens may apply to the Attorney General for relief from deportation under a now-repealed provision of the immigration laws. We hold that the BIA's approach is arbitrary and capricious.

The legal background of this case is complex, but the principle guiding our decision is anything but. When an administrative agency sets policy, it must provide a reasoned explanation for its action. That is not a high bar, but it is an unwavering one. Here, the BIA has failed to meet it.

I

A

Federal immigration law governs both the exclusion of aliens from admission to this country and the deportation of aliens previously admitted. Before 1996, these two kinds of action occurred in different procedural settings, with an alien seeking entry (whether for the first time or upon return from a trip abroad) placed in an "exclusion proceeding" and an alien already here channeled to a "deportation proceeding. Since that time, the Government has used a unified procedure, known as a "removal proceeding," for exclusions and deportations alike. See 8 U.S.C. §§ 1229, 1229a. But the statutory bases for excluding and deporting aliens have always varied. Now, as before, the immigration laws provide two separate lists of substantive grounds, principally involving criminal offenses, for these two actions. One list specifies what kinds of crime render an alien excludable (or in the term the statute now uses, "inadmissible"), see § 1182(a) (2006 ed., Supp. IV), while another—sometimes overlapping and sometimes divergent—list specifies what kinds of crime render an alien deportable from the country, see § 1227(a).

An additional, historic difference between exclusion and deportation cases involved the ability of the Attorney General to grant an alien discretionary relief. Until repealed in 1996, § 212(c) of the Immigration and Nationality Act, 66 Stat. 187, 8 U.S.C. 1182(c) (1994 ed.), authorized the Attorney General to admit certain excludable aliens. The Attorney General could order this relief when the alien had lawfully resided in the United

States for at least seven years before temporarily leaving the country, unless the alien was excludable on one of two specified grounds. But by its terms, § 212(c) did not apply when an alien was being deported.

This discrepancy threatened to produce an odd result in a case called *Matter of L-*, 1 I. & N. Dec. 1 (1940), leading to the first-ever grant of discretionary relief in a deportation case. L- was a permanent resident of the United States who had been convicted of larceny. Although L-'s crime made him inadmissible, he traveled abroad and then returned to the United States without any immigration official's preventing his entry. A few months later, the Government caught up with L- and initiated a deportation action based on his larceny conviction. Had the Government apprehended L- at the border a short while earlier, he would have been placed in an exclusion proceeding where he could have applied for discretionary relief. But because L- was instead in a deportation proceeding, no such relief was available. Responding to this apparent anomaly, Attorney General Robert Jackson (on referral of the case from the BIA) determined that L- could receive a waiver: L- Jackson said, "should be permitted to make the same appeal to discretion that he could have made if denied admission" when returning from his recent trip. *Id.* at 6. In accord with this decision, the BIA adopted a policy of allowing aliens in deportation proceedings to apply for discretionary relief under § 212(c) whenever they had left and reentered the country after becoming deportable. See *Matter of S-* 6 I. & N. Dec. 392, 394–396 (1954).

But this approach created another peculiar asymmetry: Deportable aliens who had traveled abroad and returned could receive § 212(c) relief, while those who had never left could not. In *Fracis v. INS*, 532 F.2d 268 (1976), the Court of Appeals for the Second Circuit concluded that this disparity violated equal protection. The BIA acquiesced in the Second Circuit's decision, thus applying § 212(c) in deportation proceedings regardless of an alien's travel history.

All this might have become academic when Congress repealed § 212(c) in 1996 and substituted a new discretionary remedy, known as "cancellation of removal," which is available in a narrow range of circumstances to excludable and deportable aliens alike. See 8 U.S.C. § 1229b. But in *INS v. St. Cyr*, 533 U.S. 289, 326, 121 S.Ct. 2271, 150 L.Ed.2d 347 (2001), this Court concluded that the broader relief afforded by § 212(c) must remain available, on the same terms as before, to an alien whose removal is based on a guilty plea entered before § 212(c)'s repeal. We reasoned that aliens had agreed to those pleas with the possibility of discretionary relief in mind and that eliminating this prospect would ill comport with " 'familiar considerations of fair notice, reasonable reliance, and settled expectations.' " *Id.* at 323, 121 S.Ct. 2271. Accordingly, § 212(c) has had an afterlife for resident aliens with old criminal convictions.

When the BIA is deciding whether to *exclude* such an alien, applying § 212(c) is an easy matter. The Board first checks the statutory ground that the Department of Homeland Security (DHS) has identified as the basis for exclusion; the Board may note, for example, that DHS has charged the alien with previously committing a "crime involving moral turpitude," see 8 U.S.C. § 1182(a)(2)(A)(i)(I). Unless the charged ground is one of the pair falling outside § 212(c)'s scope, the alien is eligible for discretionary relief. The Board then determines whether to grant that relief based on such factors as "the seriousness of the offense, evidence of either rehabilitation or recidivism, the duration of the alien's residence, the impact of deportation on the family, the number of citizens in the family, and the character of any service in the Armed Forces." *St. Cyr*, 533 U.S., at 296, n. 5, 121 S.Ct. 2271.

By contrast, when the BIA is deciding whether to *deport* an alien, applying § 212(c) becomes a tricky business. Recall that § 212(c) applies on its face only to exclusion decisions. So the question arises: How is the BIA to determine when an alien should receive § 212(c) relief in the deportation context?

One approach that the BIA formerly used considered how the alien would fare in an exclusion proceeding. To perform this analysis, the Board would first determine whether the criminal conviction making the alien deportable fell within a statutory ground for exclusion. Almost all convictions did so, largely because the "crime involving moral turpitude" ground encompasses so many offenses. Assuming that threshold inquiry were met, the Board would mimic its approach in exclusion cases—first making sure the statutory ground at issue was not excepted from § 212(c) and then conducting the multi-factor analysis.

A second approach is the one challenged here; definitively adopted in 2005 (after decades of occasional use), it often is called the "comparable-grounds" rule. That approach evaluates whether the ground for deportation charged in a case has a close analogue in the statute's list of exclusion grounds. If the deportation ground consists of a set of crimes "substantially equivalent" to the set of offenses making up an exclusion ground, then the alien can seek § 212(c) relief. But if the deportation ground charged covers significantly different or more or fewer offenses than any exclusion ground, the alien is not eligible for a waiver. Such a divergence makes § 212(c) inapplicable even if the particular offense committed by the alien falls within an exclusion ground.

Two contrasting examples from the BIA's cases may help to illustrate this approach. Take first an alien convicted of conspiring to distribute cocaine, whom DHS seeks to deport on the ground that he has committed an "aggravated felony" involving "illicit trafficking in a controlled substance." 8 U.S.C. §§ 1101(a)(43)(B), 1227(a)(2)(A)(iii). Under the comparable-grounds rule, the immigration judge would look to see if that deportation ground covers substantially the same offenses as an exclusion ground. And according to the BIA in *Matter of Meza*, 20 I. & N. Dec. 257 (1991), the judge would find an adequate match—the exclusion ground applicable to aliens who have committed offenses "relating to a controlled substance," 8 U.S.C. §§ 1182(a)(2)(A)(i)(II) and (a)(2)(C).

Now consider an alien convicted of first-degree sexual abuse of a child, whom DHS wishes to deport on the ground that he has committed an "aggravated felony" involving "sexual abuse of a minor." §§ 1101(a)(43)(A), 1227(a)(2)(A)(iii). May this alien seek § 212(c) relief? According to the BIA, he may not do so—not because his crime is too serious (that is irrelevant to the analysis), but instead because no statutory ground of exclusion covers substantially the same offenses. To be sure, the alien's own offense is a "crime involving moral turpitude," 8 U.S.C. § 1182(a)(2)(A)(i)(I), and so fits within an exclusion ground. Indeed, that will be true of most or all offenses included in this deportation category. But on the BIA's view, the "moral turpitude" exclusion ground "addresses a distinctly different and much broader category of offenses than the aggravated felony sexual abuse of a minor charge." And the much greater sweep of the exclusion ground prevents the alien from seeking discretionary relief from deportation.

Those mathematically inclined might think of the comparable-grounds approach as employing Venn diagrams. Within one circle are all the criminal offenses composing the particular ground of deportation charged. Within other circles are the offenses composing the various exclusion grounds. When, but only when, the "deportation circle" sufficiently corresponds to one of the "exclusion circles" may an alien apply for § 212(c) relief.

B

Petitioner Joel Judulang is a native of the Philippines who entered the United States in 1974 at the age of eight. Since that time, he has lived continuously in this country as a lawful permanent resident. In 1988, Judulang took part in a fight in which another person shot and killed someone. Judulang was charged as an accessory and eventually pleaded guilty to voluntary manslaughter. He received a 6-year suspended sentence and was released on probation immediately after his plea.

In 2005, after Judulang pleaded guilty to another criminal offense (this one involving theft), DHS commenced an action to deport him. DHS charged Judulang with having committed an "aggravated felony" involving "a crime of violence," based on his old manslaughter conviction. The Immigration Judge ordered Judulang's deportation, and the BIA affirmed. As part of its decision, the BIA considered whether Judulang could apply for § 212(c) relief. It held that he could not do so because the "crime of violence" deportation ground is not comparable to any exclusion ground, including the one for crimes involving moral turpitude. The Court of Appeals for the Ninth Circuit denied Judulang's petition for review in reliance on circuit precedent upholding the BIA's comparable-grounds approach.

We granted certiorari to resolve a circuit split on the approach's validity. We now reverse.

II

This case requires us to decide whether the BIA's policy for applying § 212(c) in deportation cases is "arbitrary [or] capricious" under the Administrative Procedure Act (APA). The scope of our review under this standard is "narrow"; as we have often recognized, "a court is not to substitute its judgment for that of the agency." *Motor Vehicle Mfrs. Assn. of United States, Inc. v. State Farm Mut. Automibile Ins. Co.*, 463 U.S. 29, 43, 103 S.Ct. 2856, 77 L.Ed.2d 443 (1983). Agencies, the BIA among them, have expertise and experience in administering their statutes that no court can properly ignore. But courts retain a role, and an important one, in ensuring that agencies have engaged in reasoned decisionmaking * * *. That task involves examining the reasons for agency decisions—or, as the case may be, the absence of such reasons.

The BIA has flunked that test here. By hinging a deportable alien's eligibility for discretionary relief on the chance correspondence between statutory categories—a matter irrelevant to the alien's fitness to reside in this country—the BIA has failed to exercise its discretion in a reasoned manner.

A

* * *

* * * The BIA may well have legitimate reasons for limiting § 212(c)'s scope in deportation cases. But still, it must do so in some rational way. If the BIA proposed to narrow the class of deportable aliens eligible to seek § 212(c) relief by flipping a coin—heads an alien may apply for relief, tails he may not—we would reverse the policy in an instant. That is because agency action must be based on non-arbitrary, " 'relevant factors,' which here means that the BIA's approach must be tied, even if loosely, to the purposes of the immigration laws or the appropriate operation of the immigration system. A method for disfavoring deportable aliens that bears no relation to these matters—that neither focuses on nor relates to an alien's fitness to remain in the country—is arbitrary and capricious. And that is true regardless whether the BIA might have acted to limit the class of deportable aliens eligible for § 212(c) relief on other, more rational bases.

The problem with the comparable-grounds policy is that it does not impose such a reasonable limitation. Rather than considering factors that might be thought germane to the deportation decision, that policy hinges

§ 212(c) eligibility on an irrelevant comparison between statutory provisions. Recall that the BIA asks whether the set of offenses in a particular deportation ground lines up with the set in an exclusion ground. But so what if it does? Does an alien charged with a particular deportation ground become more worthy of relief because that ground happens to match up with another? Or less worthy of relief because the ground does not? The comparison in no way changes the alien's prior offense or his other attributes and circumstances. So it is difficult to see why that comparison should matter. Each of these statutory grounds contains a slew of offenses. Whether each contains the same slew has nothing to do with whether a deportable alien whose prior conviction falls within both grounds merits the ability to seek a waiver.

This case well illustrates the point. In commencing Judulang's deportation proceeding, the Government charged him with an "aggravated felony" involving a "crime of violence" based on his prior manslaughter conviction. That made him ineligible for § 212(c) relief because the "crime of violence" deportation ground does not sufficiently overlap with the most similar exclusion ground, for "crime[s] involving moral turpitude." The problem, according to the BIA, is that the "crime of violence" ground includes a few offenses—simple assault, minor burglary, and unauthorized use of a vehicle—that the "moral turpitude" ground does not. But this statutory difference in no way relates to Judulang—or to most other aliens charged with committing a "crime of violence." Perhaps aliens like Judulang should be eligible for § 212(c) relief, or perhaps they should not. But that determination is not sensibly made by establishing that simple assaults and minor burglaries fall outside a ground for exclusion. That fact is as extraneous to the merits of the case as a coin flip would be. It makes Judulang no less deserving of the opportunity to seek discretionary relief— just as its converse (the inclusion of simple assaults and burglaries in the "moral turpitude" exclusion ground) would make him no more so.

* * *

And underneath this layer of arbitrariness lies yet another, because the outcome of the Board's comparable-grounds analysis itself may rest on the happenstance of an immigration official's charging decision. This problem arises because an alien's prior conviction may fall within a number of deportation grounds, only one of which corresponds to an exclusion ground. Consider, for example, an alien who entered the country in 1984 and committed voluntary manslaughter in 1988. That person could be charged (as Judulang was) with an "aggravated felony" involving a "crime of violence." If so, the alien could not seek a waiver because of the absence of a comparable exclusion ground. But the alien also could be charged with "a crime involving moral turpitude committed within five years . . . after the date of admission." And if that were the deportation charge, the alien *could* apply for relief, because the ground corresponds to the "moral turpitude" ground used in exclusion cases. So everything hangs on the charge. And the Government has provided no reason to think that immigration officials must adhere to any set scheme in deciding what charges to bring, or that those officials are exercising their charging discretion with § 212(c) in mind. So at base everything hangs on the fortuity of an individual official's decision. An alien appearing before one official may suffer deportation; an identically situated alien appearing before another may gain the right to stay in this country.

* * * The comparable-grounds approach does not rest on any factors relevant to whether an alien (or any group of aliens) should be deported. It instead distinguishes among aliens—decides who should be eligible for discretionary relief and who should not—solely by comparing the metes and bounds of diverse statutory categories into which an alien falls. The resulting Venn diagrams have no connection to the goals of the deportation process or the rational operation of the immigration laws * * *.

B

The Government makes three arguments in defense of the comparable-grounds rule—the first based on statutory text, the next on history, the last on cost. We find none of them persuasive.

1

The Government initially contends that the comparable-grounds approach is more faithful to "the statute's language," Brief for Respondent 21—or otherwise said, that "lifting that limit 'would take immigration practice even further from the statutory text,'" *id.*, at 22 (quoting *Matter of Hernandez-Casillas*, 20 I. & N. Dec. 262, 287 (1990)). In the Government's view, § 212(c) is "phrased in terms of waiving statutorily specified grounds of exclusion"; that phrasing, says the Government, counsels a comparative analysis of grounds when applying § 212(c) in the deportation context. Brief for Respondent 21; see Tr. of Oral Arg. 34 ("[T]he reason [the comparable-grounds approach] makes sense is because the statute only provides for relief from grounds of . . . exclusion").

The first difficulty with this argument is that it is based on an inaccurate description of the statute * * *. [B]ecause § 212(c)'s text is *not* "phrased in terms of waiving statutorily specified grounds of exclusion," Brief for Respondent 21, it cannot counsel a search for corresponding grounds of deportation.

More fundamentally, the comparable-grounds approach would not follow from § 212(c) even were the Government right about the section's phrasing. That is because § 212(c) simply has nothing to do with deportation: The provision was not meant to interact with the statutory grounds for deportation, any more than those grounds were designed to interact with the provision. Rather, § 212(c) refers solely to exclusion decisions; its extension to deportation cases arose from the agency's extra-textual view that some similar relief should be available in that context to avoid unreasonable distinctions. Accordingly, the text of § 212(c), whether or not phrased in terms of "waiving grounds of exclusion," cannot support the BIA's use of the comparable-grounds rule—or, for that matter, any other method for extending discretionary relief to deportation cases. We well understand the difficulties of operating in such a text-free zone; indeed, we appreciate the Government's yearning for a textual anchor. But § 212(c), no matter how many times read or parsed, does not provide one.

2

In disputing Judulang's contentions, the Government also emphasizes the comparable-grounds rule's vintage. See Brief for Respondent 22–23, 30–43. As an initial matter, we think this a slender reed to support a significant government policy. Arbitrary agency action becomes no less so by simple dint of repetition. (To use a prior analogy, flipping coins to determine § 212(c) eligibility would remain as arbitrary on the thousandth try as on the first.) And longstanding capriciousness receives no special exemption from the APA. In any event, we cannot detect the consistency that the BIA claims has marked its approach to this issue. To the contrary, the BIA has repeatedly vacillated in its method for applying § 212(c) to deportable aliens.

* * *

3

The Government finally argues that the comparable-grounds rule saves time and money. The Government claims that comparing deportation grounds to exclusion grounds can be accomplished in just a few "precedential decision[s]," which then can govern broad swaths of cases. See Brief for Respondent 46. By contrast, the Government argues, Judulang's approach would force it to determine whether each and every crime of conviction falls within an exclusion ground. Further, the Government contends that Judulang's approach would grant eligibility to a greater number of deportable aliens, which in turn would force the Government to make additional individualized assessments of whether to actually grant relief. *Id.*, at 47.

Once again, the Government's rationale comes up short. Cost is an important factor for agencies to consider in many contexts. But cheapness alone cannot save an arbitrary agency policy. (If it could, flipping coins would be a valid way to determine an alien's eligibility for a waiver.) * * * And Judulang's proposal may not be the only alternative to the comparable-grounds rule. In rejecting that rule, we do not preclude the BIA from trying to devise another, equally economical policy respecting eligibility for § 212(c) relief, so long as it comports with everything held in both this decision and *St. Cyr.*

III

We must reverse an agency policy when we cannot discern a reason for it. That is the trouble in this case. The BIA's comparable-grounds rule is unmoored from the purposes and concerns of the immigration laws. It allows an irrelevant comparison between statutory provisions to govern a matter of the utmost importance—whether lawful resident aliens with longstanding ties to this country may stay here. And contrary to the Government's protestations, it is not supported by text or practice or cost considerations. The BIA's approach therefore cannot pass muster under ordinary principles of administrative law.

The judgment of the Ninth Circuit is hereby reversed, and the case is remanded for further proceedings consistent with this opinion.

It is so ordered.

3. THE GREAT CONVERGENCE: SUBSTANTIVE REVIEW AND PROCEDURAL ADEQUACY

The Supreme Court aptly summed up the essence of hard look review in explaining its affirmance of the Federal Energy Regulatory Commission ("FERC") in *FERC v. Electric Power Supply Ass'n*, 136 S.Ct. 760, 784, 193 L.Ed.2d 661 (2016):

> The Commission, not this or any other court, regulates electricity rates. The disputed question here involves both technical understanding and policy judgment. The Commission addressed that issue seriously and carefully, providing reasons in support of its position and responding to the principal alternative advanced. In upholding that action, we do not discount the cogency of EPSA's arguments * * *. Nor do we say that * * * FERC made the better call. It is not our job to render that judgment, on which reasonable minds can differ. Our important but limited role is to ensure that the Commission engaged in reasoned decisionmaking—that it weighed competing views, selected a compensation formula with adequate support in the record, and intelligibly explained the reasons for making that choice. FERC satisfied that standard.

The hard look doctrine raises many questions: How much explanation do agencies have to provide? What kinds of reasons count as good reasons in support of agency action? Do those reasons have to be expressed in a particular form? In a rulemaking setting, how does the requirement of reasoned explanation relate to the procedural requirement, imposed by § 553, that agency rules be accompanied by a "concise general statement of their basis and purpose"? And how do technically inexpert courts evaluate the validity of agency explanations? How can courts avoid being "snowed" either by agencies or by the lawyers and experts for parties opposing agency action?

The materials in this chapter cannot possibly answer in a satisfactory fashion these and the many other questions raised by hard look review. But they can—and will—at least point the way towards an understanding of this central feature of modern administrative law.

Recall from the prior materials on *Vermont Yankee* and its aftermath that *Vermont Yankee*'s sweeping, powerful language has never been taken to repudiate a substantial portion of the D.C. Circuit's pre-1978 procedural innovations for informal rulemaking. In particular, the modern notice of proposed rulemaking is generally required to disclose all significant data that is available to agencies at the time that they are proposing rules for consideration, and the statement of basis and purpose is generally required to explain in great detail the agency's reasoning, including a response to important comments filed during the comment period. We can now begin to see why.

The hard look doctrine requires the court as well as the agency to take a hard look at the problem under consideration. That is because the court cannot tell whether the agency has thoroughly considered the important aspects of a problem unless the court knows enough about the problem to identify those aspects that are important, and a court cannot assess the plausibility of an agency's reasoning unless the court is conversant enough with the technical subject under discussion to distinguish plausible from implausible reasoning. If courts are going to do anything other than rubber-stamp agency decisions in complex cases (and a good percentage of modern regulatory decisions present complex cases), courts must be prepared to immerse themselves in the technical details of the issues facing the agency.

Given the enormous caseloads of the federal bench, this is a hopeless task. Judges hear appeals from many agencies on many different subjects. Judges are not, and cannot be, expert enough in even a fraction of these subjects to review agency decisions from the ground up. Accordingly, judges need help if they are going to attempt any kind of serious scrutiny of agency decisionmaking in complex regulatory areas. The two obvious places to look for help are: the agencies and the parties appearing before the agencies.

The modern procedural requirements in rulemaking—extensive notices of proposed rulemaking and statements of basis and purpose—are designed to give courts the material they need to conduct serious substantive review of agency decisions. By requiring agencies to present their evidence and reasoning at the front end of the rulemaking process, either in their notices of proposed rulemaking or in some other publicly available form, courts make it possible for parties challenging the agency decision to expose potential flaws in the agencies' reasoning. The comment period then becomes a vehicle through which the technically expert agencies and parties can identify their disagreements. By requiring agencies to produce elaborate statements of basis and purpose, courts force agencies to address the concerns of parties who may know as much (or more) than the agency about the issues involved in the case.[24] Modern *procedural* requirements are therefore driven largely by concerns about *substantive* review. And that is why *Vermont Yankee* has not resulted in a return to the original meaning of § 553: courts cannot carry out the kind of substantive review of rulemaking demanded by modern theories of agency behavior unless agencies are forced to employ procedures that focus the issues for judicial review.

Accordingly, there is a substantial convergence between procedural review and substantive review. If an agency in an informal rulemaking fails to address an important aspect of a problem, one could view that as a *substantive* defect in the agency's decisionmaking process (an absence of reasoned decisionmaking) or as a *procedural* defect in the agency's statement of basis and purpose (an inadequate "concise and general statement"). Similarly, a failure to give interested parties an opportunity to examine and comment upon important evidence relied on by the agency could be seen either as a failure of the substantive decisionmaking process or as a procedural defect in the notice of proposed rulemaking. As a general matter, when faced with a choice between declaring an agency's policy substantively irrational or procedurally defective, courts opt for the latter.

UNITED STATES v. NOVA SCOTIA FOOD PRODUCTS CORP.
United States Court of Appeals, Second Circuit, 1977.
568 F.2d 240.

Before WATERMAN and GURFEIN, CIRCUIT JUDGES, and BLUMENFELD, DISTRICT JUDGE.

GURFEIN, CIRCUIT JUDGE:

This appeal involving a regulation of the Food and Drug Administration is not here upon a direct review of agency action. It is an appeal from a judgment of the District Court for the Eastern District of New York (Hon. John J. Dooling, Judge) enjoining the appellants, after a hearing, from processing hot smoked whitefish except in accordance with time-temperature-salinity (T-T-S) regulations contained in 21 C.F.R. Part 122 (1977) * * *.

---

[24] The *Chenery* doctrine ensures that all of an agency's reasons for action are presented in the statement of basis and purpose.

The injunction was sought and granted on the ground that smoked whitefish which has been processed in violation of the T-T-S regulation is "adulterated."

Appellant Nova Scotia receives frozen or iced whitefish in interstate commerce which it processes by brining, smoking and cooking. The fish are then sold as smoked whitefish.

The regulations cited above require that hot-process smoked fish be heated by a controlled heat process that provides a monitoring system positioned in as many strategic locations in the oven as necessary to assure a continuous temperature through each fish of not less than 180 F. for a minimum of 30 minutes for fish which have been brined to contain 3.5% Water phase salt or at 150 F. for a minimum of 30 minutes if the salinity was at 5% Water phase. Since each fish must meet these requirements, it is necessary to heat an entire batch of fish to even higher temperatures so that the lowest temperature for any fish will meet the minimum requirements.

Government inspection of appellants' plant established without question that the minimum T-T-S requirements were not being met. There is no substantial claim that the plant was processing whitefish under "insanitary conditions" in any other material respect. Appellants, on their part, do not defend on the ground that they were in compliance, but rather that the requirements could not be met if a marketable whitefish was to be produced * * *. We reject the contention that the regulation is beyond the authority delegated by the statute, but we find serious inadequacies in the procedure followed in the promulgation of the regulation and hold it to be invalid as applied to the appellants herein.

The hazard which the FDA sought to minimize was the outgrowth and toxin formation of Clostridium botulinum Type E spores of the bacteria which sometimes inhabit fish. There had been an occurrence of several cases of botulism traced to consumption of fish from inland waters in 1960 and 1963 which stimulated considerable bacteriological research. These bacteria can be present in the soil and water of various regions. They can invade fish in their natural habitat and can be further disseminated in the course of evisceration and preparation of the fish for cooking. A failure to destroy such spores through an adequate brining, thermal, and refrigeration process was found to be dangerous to public health.

The Commissioner of Food and Drugs ("Commissioner"), employing informal "notice-and-comment" procedures under 21 U.S.C. § 371(a), issued a proposal for the control of C. botulinum bacteria Type E in fish * * *.

Similar guidelines for smoking fish had been suggested by the FDA several years earlier, and were generally made known to people in the industry. At that stage, however, they were merely guidelines without substantive effect as law. Responding to the Commissioner's invitation in the notice of proposed rulemaking, members of the industry, including appellants and the intervenor-appellant, submitted comments on the proposed regulation.

The Commissioner thereafter issued the final regulations in which he adopted certain suggestions made in the comments, including a suggestion by the National Fisheries Institute, Inc. ("the Institute"), the intervenor herein. The original proposal provided that the fish would have to be cooked to a temperature of 180 F. for at least 30 minutes, if the fish have been brined to contain 3.5% Water phase salt, with no alternative. In the final regulation, an alternative suggested by the intervenor "that the parameter of 150 F. for 30 minutes and 5% Salt in the water phase be established as an alternate procedure to that stated in the proposed regulation for an interim period until specific parameters can be established" was accepted, but as a permanent part of the regulation rather than for an interim period.

The intervenor suggested that "specific parameters" be established. This referred to particular processing parameters for different species of fish on a "species by species" basis. Such "species by species" determination was proposed not only by the intervenor but also by the Bureau of Commercial Fisheries of the Department of the Interior. That Bureau objected to the general application of the T-T-S requirement proposed by the FDA on the ground that application of the regulation to all species of fish being smoked was not commercially feasible, and that the regulation should therefore specify time-temperature-salinity requirements, as developed by research and study, on a species-by-species basis. The Bureau suggested that "wholesomeness considerations could be more practically and adequately realized by reducing processing temperature and using suitable concentrations of nitrite and salt." The Commissioner took cognizance of the suggestion, but decided, nevertheless, to impose the T-T-S requirement on *all* species of fish (except chub, which were regulated by 21 C.F.R. 172.177 (1977) (dealing with food additives)).

He did acknowledge, however, in his "basis and purpose" statement required by the Administrative Procedure Act ("APA"), 5 U.S.C. § 553(c), that "adequate times, temperatures and salt concentrations have not been demonstrated for each individual species of fish presently smoked". The Commissioner concluded, nevertheless, that "the processing requirements of the proposed regulations are the safest now known to prevent the outgrowth and toxin formation of C. botulinum Type E". He determined that "the conditions of current good manufacturing practice for this industry should be established without further delay."

The Commissioner did not answer the suggestion by the Bureau of Fisheries that nitrite and salt as additives could safely lower the high temperature otherwise required, a solution which the FDA had accepted in the case of chub. Nor did the Commissioner respond to the claim of Nova Scotia through its trade association, the Association of Smoked Fish Processors, Inc., Technical Center that "(t)he proposed process requirements suggested by the FDA for hot processed smoked fish are neither commercially feasible nor based on sound scientific evidence obtained with the variety of smoked fish products to be included under this regulation."

Nova Scotia, in its own comment, wrote to the Commissioner that "the heating of certain types of fish to high temperatures will completely destroy the product". It suggested, as an alternative, that "specific processing procedures could be established for each species after adequate work and experimention [sic] has been done but not before." We have noted above that the response given by the Commissioner was in general terms. He did not specifically aver that the T-T-S requirements as applied to whitefish were, in fact, commercially feasible.

When, after several inspections and warnings, Nova Scotia failed to comply with the regulation, an action by the United States Attorney for injunctive relief was filed on April 7, 1976, six years later, and resulted in the judgment here on appeal. The District Court denied a stay pending appeal, and no application for a stay was made to this court.

* * *

B

1.

The History of Botulism in Whitefish

The history of botulism occurrence in whitefish, as established in the trial record, which we must assume was available to the FDA in 1970, is as follows. Between 1899 and 1964 there were only eight cases of botulism reported as attributable to hot-smoked whitefish. In all eight instances, vacuum-packed whitefish was involved. All of the eight cases occurred in 1960 and 1963. The industry has abandoned vacuum-packing, and there has not been a single case of botulism associated with commercially prepared whitefish since 1963, though 2,750,000 pounds of whitefish are processed annually. Thus, in the seven-year period from 1964 through 1970, 17.25 million pounds of whitefish have been commercially processed in the United States without a single reported case of botulism. The evidence also disclosed that defendant Nova Scotia has been in business some 56 years, and that there has never been a case of botulism illness from the whitefish processed by it.

2.

The Scientific Data

Interested parties were not informed of the scientific data, or at least of a selection of such data deemed important by the agency, so that comments could be addressed to the data. Appellants argue that unless the scientific data relied upon by the agency are spread upon the public records, criticism of the methodology used or the meaning to be inferred from the data is rendered impossible.

We agree with appellants in this case, for although we recognize that an agency may resort to its own expertise outside the record in an informal rulemaking procedure, we do not believe that when the pertinent research material is readily available and the agency has no special expertise on the precise parameters involved, there is any reason to conceal the scientific data relied upon from the interested parties. As Judge Leventhal said in *Portland Cement Ass'n v. Ruckelshaus*, 158 U.S.App.D.C. 308, 326, 486 F.2d 375, 393 (1973): "It is not consonant with the purpose of a rulemaking proceeding to promulgate rules on the basis of inadequate data, or on data that (in) critical degree, *is known only to the agency*." (Emphasis added.) This is not a case where the agency methodology was based on material supplied by the interested parties themselves. Here all the scientific research was collected by the agency, and none of it was disclosed to interested parties as the material upon which the proposed rule would be fashioned * * *.

* * *

If the failure to notify interested persons of the scientific research upon which the agency was relying actually prevented the presentation of relevant comment, the agency may be held not to have considered all "the relevant factors." We can think of no sound reasons for secrecy or reluctance to expose to public view (with an exception for trade secrets or national security) the ingredients of the deliberative process. Indeed, the FDA's own regulations now specifically require that every notice of proposed rulemaking contain "references to all data and information on which the Commissioner relies for the proposal (copies or a full list of which shall be a part of the administrative file on the matter . . .)." 21 C.F.R. § 10.40(b) (1) (1977). And this is, undoubtedly, the trend.

We think that the scientific data should have been disclosed to focus on the proper interpretation of "insanitary conditions." When the basis for a proposed rule is a scientific decision, the scientific material which is believed to support the rule should be exposed to the view of interested parties for their comment. One cannot ask for comment on a scientific paper without allowing the participants to read the paper. Scientific research is sometimes rejected for diverse inadequacies of methodology;

and statistical results are sometimes rebutted because of a lack of adequate gathering technique or of supportable extrapolation. Such is the stuff of scientific debate. To suppress meaningful comment by failure to disclose the basic data relied upon is akin to rejecting comment altogether. For unless there is common ground, the comments are unlikely to be of a quality that might impress a careful agency. The inadequacy of comment in turn leads in the direction of arbitrary decision-making. We do not speak of findings of fact, for such are not technically required in the informal rulemaking procedures. We speak rather of what the agency should make known so as to elicit comments that probe the fundamentals. Informal rulemaking does not lend itself to a rigid pattern. Especially, in the circumstance of our broad reading of statutory authority in support of the agency, we conclude that the failure to disclose to interested persons the scientific data upon which the FDA relied was procedurally erroneous. Moreover, the burden was upon the agency to articulate rationally why the rule should apply to a large and diverse class, with the same T-T-S parameters made applicable to *all* species.

C

Appellants additionally attack the "concise general statement" required by APA, 5 U.S.C. § 553, as inadequate. We think that, in the circumstances, it was less than adequate. It is not in keeping with the rational process to leave vital questions, raised by comments which are of cogent materiality, completely unanswered. The agencies certainly have a good deal of discretion in expressing the basis of a rule, but the agencies do not have quite the prerogative of obscurantism reserved to legislatures * * *.

* * *

The Secretary was squarely faced with the question whether it was necessary to formulate a rule with specific parameters that applied to all species of fish, and particularly whether lower temperatures with the addition of nitrite and salt would not be sufficient. Though this alternative was suggested by an agency of the federal government, its suggestion, though acknowledged, was never answered.

Moreover, the comment that to apply the proposed T-T-S requirements to whitefish would destroy the commercial product was neither discussed nor answered. We think that to sanction silence in the face of such vital questions would be to make the statutory requirement of a "concise general statement" less than an adequate safeguard against arbitrary decision-making.

* * *

When the District Court held the regulation to be valid, it properly exercised its discretion to grant the injunction. In view of our conclusion to the contrary, we must reverse the grant of the injunction and direct that the complaint be dismissed.

NOTES

The choice to emphasize procedure over substance can produce significant consequences for judicial review: Substantive decisions by agencies are normally reviewed under some deferential standard, while agency procedural decisions are normally reviewed de novo. *See Kern County Farm Bureau v. Allen*, 450 F.3d 1072, 1076 (9th Cir.2006); *Iowa League of Cities v. EPA*, 711 F.3d 844, 872–73 (8th Cir.2013) (discussing at length how and why review of agency procedural compliance is de novo rather than deferential). Be warned, however, that courts are sometimes very loose with the language of procedure and substance. A failure of explanation under arbitrary or capricious review is obviously a substantive rather than procedural defect in an agency decision, but it is very easy to describe the lack of explanation as a "procedural" problem when writing an opinion. *See, e.g., Encino Motorcars, LLC v. Navarro*, 136 S.Ct. 2117, 2125 (2016) ("One of the basic procedural requirements of administrative rulemaking is that an agency must give adequate reasons for its decisions."). But since no court will defer to an agency's view about whether the agency's explanation is adequate, this particular terminological gaffe surely makes no difference for scope of review. Nonetheless, it is good practice to try to keep clear in one's own mind whether a claimed defect in an agency decision goes to procedure or to substance.

When all is said and done, didn't Judge Bazelon and Judge Leventhal both really win?

4.   DEFINING THE "RECORD" IN INFORMAL PROCEEDINGS

In a formal rulemaking or adjudication, "[t]he transcript of testimony and exhibits, together with all papers and requests filed in the proceeding, constitutes the exclusive record for decision * * *." 5 U.S.C. § 556(e) (2012). Any agency decision in such proceedings must be justified solely by reference to material contained in the record.

Informal proceedings typically do not have testimony, exhibits, documentary requests, or the other materials that comprise the record in formal proceedings. Nonetheless, in *Overton Park* in 1971, in a case involving informal adjudication, the Supreme Court thought it obvious that "there is an administrative record that allows the full, prompt review of the Secretary's action that is sought," and it ordered that subsequent judicial review "be based on the full administrative record that was before the Secretary at the time he made his decision." This assumes that informal proceedings generate a well-defined "record" that can form the basis for decision. But while formal procedures automatically generate such a "record," informal procedures do not; there is no requirement in informal proceedings, for example, that the agency decision be based solely on material that is admitted into evidence in an adversary setting. So what exactly do courts review in informal proceedings? Where do they look to determine whether agency factual determinations have adequate evidentiary support or whether agency policy determinations were based on reasoned decisionmaking?

The problems of defining a "record" for review in informal proceedings were perceptively analyzed in an important and influential article in 1975 by former EPA attorney William Pedersen.

WILLIAM F. PEDERSEN JR., FORMAL RECORDS AND INFORMAL RULEMAKING

85 Yale L.J. 38, 62–65 (1975).

The generally accepted standard of review of informal agency rulemaking—the "arbitrary or capricious" test—makes no reference to the role of a record * * *.

Yet there is a record. Rule 17 of the Federal Rules of Appellate Procedure states that when review of a regulation is sought in a court of appeals, "[t]he agency shall file the record with the clerk of the court . . . within 40 days after service . . . of the petition for review. . ." The only guidance on what the record must contain is given in Rule 16 which states that "[t]he order sought to be reviewed or enforced, the findings or report on which it is based, and the pleadings, evidence and proceedings before the agency shall constitute the record on review in proceedings to review or enforce the order of an agency" * * *. Plainly this language was drawn up with adjudicatory proceedings in mind. It does not address how the record in an informal rulemaking case should be assembled.

1. "HISTORICAL" RECORDS AND "PROCEDURAL" RECORDS

In the review of agency actions less formal than full-scale adjudication, the guidelines followed in recent years have been those laid down in the *Overton Park* case * * *. The *Overton* Court said that judicial review of the Secretary of Transportation's decision would have to be based "on the full administrative record that was before the Secretary at the time he made his decision." Since the Court recognized a few pages earlier that there was no formal agency proceeding in decisions of this type for generating a record, the Court must have meant that the documents actually presented to the Secretary for his consideration would constitute the record. But this is based on the false assumption that all documents critical in reaching a given agency decision are in fact placed "before" the head of the agency, and that the internal procedures of the agency are firmly enough established and well enough observed to make location of these documents a rather ministerial act. Since these assumptions are not true, the only way to assemble a record that gives the court a picture of what the agency actually thought and considered is through an ad hoc effort to reconstruct what happened in a particular case. To do this, the documents that have passed through the formal internal procedures of the agency must be examined. But since these *formal* procedures are scarcely the exclusive vehicles for considering issues within an agency, much else must be included as well. I call this effort at post hoc reconstruction of what actually happened a "historical" approach to compiling a record.

Courts and commentators have often endorsed a historical approach. It does not correspond, however, to the way records for decision and judicial review are generated in trial courts and agency adjudication * * *. [A] record is normally defined as the material which has been accepted under a given obligatory set of procedures. I call this a "procedural" approach to compiling the record. A trial court record is "procedural" since it consists of everything that has been properly placed in evidence under defined rules of admissibility during the course of the trial.

2. THE RECOMMENDATIONS OF THE ADMINISTRATIVE CONFERENCE

Unfortunately, the most authoritative recent statement on what rulemaking records should contain completely fails to grasp the distinction between a "procedural" and a "historical" approach * * *. The Administrative Conference of the United States has recommended that the record for judicial review of informal rulemaking should consist of (1) the notice of proposed rulemaking and any documents referred to in it; (2) the comments and documents submitted by interested persons; (3) the transcripts of any hearings held in the course of the rulemaking; (4) reports of any advisory committees; (5) the agency's concise general statement or final order and any documents referred to in it; *and* (6) other factual information "not included in the foregoing that was considered by the authority responsible for promulgation of the rule or that is proffered by the agency as pertinent to the rule."

The first five items cause no difficulty. Both under a historical approach to the record and under a procedural approach, they would certainly be included. But the first clause of the sixth recommendation comes down squarely on the side of the historical approach by explicitly recognizing the agency's right to include in the record whatever documents it "considered"—even if they arose outside the APA notice and comment procedures. In addition, in defining the record as what was considered by the "authority responsible for promulgation of the rule," the Administrative Conference misstates the nature of rulemaking. Only a very few, highly controversial issues can hope to receive detailed personal attention from the administrator of a busy agency, be he or she ever so competent. In all other cases, no single authority passes judgment on the rule. Different parts of the agency work on different parts of the rule, or on the same part from different angles—and the rule emerges. It follows from the lack of any meaningful central "authority" that the phrase "considered by the authority" also loses meaning, and sets no clear boundary to the size or content of the record. Given the diffuse nature of rulemaking, it will be a rare document that cannot claim to have been considered somewhere to some extent by someone in connection with the rulemaking, and a document almost as rare that will have received the personal attention of the administrator.

The other test suggested by the Administrative Conference for including documents in the record—whether they are "proffered by the agency as pertinent to the rule"—is even worse. It breaks free of the restriction implicit even in the historical approach that the record certified to the court should reflect what the agency *actually* weighed and evaluated in some manner at the time of the rulemaking. Indeed, it would apparently allow the agency to include whatever it thinks would help support its actions once litigation has begun.

NOTES

One commentator writing contemporaneously with Mr. Pedersen concluded that the record in informal proceedings indeed consisted of "whatever the agency produces on review." Paul Verkuil, *Judicial Review of Informal Rulemaking*, 60 Va. L. Rev. 185, 204 (1974). To some extent, that is still the current ordinary practice, but with two important qualifications.

First, courts have not formally adopted a procedural approach to defining the record for review in informal proceedings, and any such effort would likely run afoul of *Vermont Yankee*. Nor have courts devised any reliable methods to establish whether agencies "actually" considered particular documents during their rulemakings, and any such effort would likely run afoul of a long-established prohibition against examining the mental states of agency officials. *See United States v. Morgan*, 313 U.S. 409, 61 S.Ct. 999, 85 L.Ed. 1429 (1941). Courts have, however, developed one important constraint on the kind of materials that agencies can advance on appeal in support of their rules. Under the still-vibrant doctrine of *Portland Cement Ass'n v. Ruckelshaus*, 486 F.2d 375 (D.C.Cir.1973), all important documents in the agency's possession, and all important premises that the agency is acting upon, must be disclosed to the public for comment. Does this effectively impose a "procedural" requirement on the content of the record? It might, but for the fact that an agency can sometimes rely on information that was not submitted to the public for comment as long as that information is either not so important that *Portland Cement* required its disclosure, *see Air Transport Ass'n of America v. FAA*, 169 F.3d 1, 7 (D.C.Cir.1999), or first appeared during the rulemaking proceeding but merely reinforces the agency's prior evidence. *See supra* pages 380–381, 407–413.

Second, it is not entirely clear that the agency has, or should have, full control over what counts as an administrative "record" in informal proceedings. The issue is starkly raised by the (as of 2018) ongoing litigation over the Deferred Action for Child Arrivals program, which gives various rights to children who were brought to the United States illegally as minors. The Trump Administration sought to terminate the program effective March 15, 2018, and a lawsuit was brought claiming that the termination was illegal (just as lawsuits were brought claiming that the program itself was illegal). A district court in California required the government to provide substantial additional documentation about the program and the decision to terminate it, in addition to the materials voluntarily provided by the government, in order to complete the administrative record. Specifically, the court ordered disclosure of

> all materials actually seen or considered, however briefly, by Acting Secretary [Elaine] Duke in connection with the potential or actual decision to rescind DACA * * *, (2) all DACA-related materials considered by persons (anywhere in the government) who thereafter provided Acting Secretary Duke with written advice or input regarding the actual or potential rescission of DACA, (3) all DACA-related materials considered by persons (anywhere in the government) who thereafter provided Acting Secretary Duke with verbal input regarding the actual or potential rescission of DACA, (4) all comments and questions propounded by Acting Secretary Duke to advisors or subordinates or others regarding the actual or potential rescission of DACA and their responses, and (5) all materials directly or indirectly considered by former Secretary of DHS John Kelly leading to his February 2017 memorandum not to rescind DACA.

Regents of Univ. of Cal. v. United States Dep't of Homeland Security, 2017 WL 4642324, at *8 (N.D.Cal.2017). The government sought a writ of mandamus in the Supreme Court to block enforcement of the document production order. On December 8, 2017, the Court, by a 5–4 vote, granted a stay pending disposition of the government's motion, which had the effect of nullifying the district court's orders for the time being. *In re United States,* 138 S.Ct. 371, 199 L.Ed.2d 417 (2017). Four Justices dissented from the decision to grant the stay:

> The Government's primary argument is that "the district court plainly erred by . . . ordering the government to 'complete' the administrative record with materials beyond those presented by the agency to the court," because a reviewing court's sole task under the APA is to "determine whether the agency's action may be upheld on the basis of the reasons the agency provides and 'the record the agency presents to the reviewing court.'" Pet. for Mandamus 19, 24. The Government thus contends that review of its decision terminating DACA must be based exclusively on the documents that the Government itself unilaterally selected for submission to the

District Court. I am not aware of any precedent supporting the Government's position.

The APA is clear that a court reviewing agency action must review "the whole record" to determine whether that action is lawful. 5 U.S.C. § 706. The basic question here is what constitutes "the whole record" that the court must review. We held in *Citizens to Preserve Overton Park, Inc. v. Volpe*, 401 U.S. 402, 420, 91 S.Ct. 814, 28 L.Ed.2d 136 (1971), that the "whole record" means "the full administrative record that was before the Secretary at the time he made his decision." *Ibid.* Neither this Court nor the lower courts has ever read *Overton Park* to limit the "full administrative record" to those materials that the agency unilaterally decides should be considered by the reviewing court.

Indeed, judicial review cannot function if the agency is permitted to decide unilaterally what documents it submits to the reviewing court as the administrative record. Effective review depends upon the administrative record containing all relevant materials presented to the agency, including not only materials supportive of the government's decision but also materials contrary to the government's decision. See *Motor Vehicle Mfrs. Assn. of United States, Inc. v. State Farm Mut. Automobile Ins. Co.*, 463 U.S. 29, 43–44, 103 S.Ct. 2856, 77 L.Ed.2d 443 (1983). Otherwise, the reviewing court cannot engage in the "thorough, probing, in-depth review" that the APA requires. *Overton Park*, 401 U.S., at 415–416, 91 S.Ct. 814. A court deprived of a full administrative record could not consider, for example, whether the decision was based on the consideration of irrelevant factors, *id.*, at 411–412, 91 S.Ct. 814; whether it considered the relevant factors, *id.*, at 416, 91 S.Ct. 814; whether the decision was "arbitrary, capricious, an abuse of discretion, or otherwise not in accordance with the law," § 706(2)(A); or whether the decision was unlawful for some other reason.

Perhaps for this reason, the lower courts seem to have unanimously rejected the Government's position that the agency may unilaterally determine the contents of the administrative record that a court may review * * *.

Id. at 371–72 (Breyer, J. dissenting from grant of stay). The full Court subsequently, and unanimously, held that the lower courts should determine certain threshold issues of jurisdiction before entering orders regarding document production; if the government's decision is unreviewable, the composition of the administrative record is irrelevant. *See In re United States*, 138 S.Ct. 443, 199 L.Ed.2d 351 (2017).

If the initial stay by the Court was based on those jurisdictional concerns, the case has no larger significance for administrative law. But if the stay was truly based on the idea that the government's submissions fully define the "administrative record," that would be a holding of some magnitude. If the government, under *Chenery I*, can choose the reasons for an agency decision that it wants a court to consider, does that entail that it can also choose the materials that the court can examine in order to evaluate those reasons? If a court knows that material exists that was not produced, can a court, as an evidentiary matter, assume that those materials are unfavorable to the government's position?

Matters are complicated by the *Morgan* case mentioned above, in which a trial court had allowed parties challenging an order of the Secretary of Agriculture to depose the Secretary about his decision-making process. The Supreme Court said that "the Secretary should never have been subjected to this examination * * *. We have explicitly held in this very litigation that 'it was not the function of the court to probe the mental processes of the Secretary'. 304 U.S. 1, 18, 58 S.Ct. 773, 776, 82 L.Ed. 1129." 313 U.S. at 422, 61 S.Ct. at 1004. This doctrine is sometimes generalized to the proposition that "inquiry into the mental processes of administrative decisionmakers is usually to be avoided." *Citizens to Preserve Overton Park v. Volpe*, 401 U.S. 402, 420, 91 S.Ct. 814, 825, 28 L.Ed.2d 136 (1971). If taken to its extreme, it could prevent courts from questioning the government's assertions about the bases for its decisions. But the *Morgan* case was decided a quarter-century before the development of hard-look review. Given the requirements of hard-look review, can the *Morgan* rule today mean anything more than a general injunction against deposing agency officials? Aren't the reasons for an agency decision at the very heart of modern judicial review? For a thoughtful critique of the so-called *Morgan* rule, see Lisa Heinzerling, *The FDA's Plan B Fiasco: Lessons for Administrative Law,* 102 Geo. L.J. 927, 980–83 (2014).

5. HARD LOOK REVIEW IN PRACTICE: VARIATIONS ON A THEME

LEMOYNE-OWEN COLLEGE V. NLRB

United States Court of Appeals, District of Columbia Circuit, 2004.
357 F.3d 55.

Before: GINSBURG, CHIEF JUDGE, and GARLAND and ROBERTS, CIRCUIT JUDGES.

ROBERTS, CIRCUIT JUDGE:

Petitioner LeMoyne-Owen College is a historically black college in Memphis, Tennessee that traces its roots to a school founded in 1862. The College's full-time faculty (numbering approximately sixty members) sought to unionize in the spring of 2002 to negotiate with management, but the College argued that the faculty members *were* management—that is, managerial employees not entitled to the protection of the National Labor Relations Act (NLRA). *See NLRB v. Bell Aerospace Co.*, 416 U.S. 267, 283, 94 S.Ct. 1757, 1766, 40 L.Ed.2d 134 (1974) (managerial employees, though not specifically excluded from NLRA coverage, were "regarded as so clearly outside the Act that no specific exclusionary provision was thought necessary"). The National Labor Relations Board sided with the faculty, ordering the College to recognize and bargain with the faculty's representative. The College petitioned for review in this court, and the Board filed a cross-application to enforce its order.

The College relies primarily on *NLRB v. Yeshiva University*, 444 U.S. 672, 100 S.Ct. 856, 63 L.Ed.2d 115 (1980), the Supreme Court's leading (because only) case on determining the managerial status of an academic faculty. In *Yeshiva,* a union of the university's faculty sought certification to represent the faculty in collective bargaining with the administration. The NLRB granted the union's petition, but the Supreme Court held that the faculty were managerial employees and thus not covered by the NLRA. The Court drew its definition of managerial employees from *Bell Aerospace,* which held that managers are those who " 'formulate and effectuate management policies by expressing and making operative the decisions of their employer.' " 416 U.S. at 288, 94 S.Ct. at 1767–68. *See Yeshiva,* 444 U.S. at 682, 100 S.Ct. at 862. The Court explained that the exception for "managerial employees," like the express statutory exception for "supervisors," derived from a recognition "[t]hat an employer is entitled to the undivided loyalty of its representatives." *Id.*

Recognizing that the governance structures of academic institutions differ from the standard industry model for which the NLRA was designed, the Court declined to adopt a *per se* rule on the managerial status of faculty members. Instead, the Court emphasized a number of factors that supported its conclusion that Yeshiva University's faculty were beyond the scope of the NLRA:

> The controlling consideration in this case is that the faculty . . . exercise authority which in any other context unquestionably would be managerial. Their authority in academic matters is absolute. They decide what courses will be offered, when they will be scheduled, and to whom they will be taught. They debate and determine teaching methods, grading policies, and matriculation standards. They effectively decide which students will be admitted, retained, and graduated. On occasion their views have determined the size of the student body, the tuition to be charged, and the location of a school.

Id. at 686, 100 S.Ct. at 864 * * *. The Court rejected the suggestion that the faculty's role was merely advisory because some of its decisions could be overturned by the university administration or board of trustees. "[T]he fact that the administration holds a rarely exercised veto power does not diminish the faculty's effective power in decisionmaking and implementation," the Court found; "the relevant consideration is effective recommendation or control rather than final authority." *Id.* at 683 n. 17, 100 S.Ct. at 863.

As might be expected given such a long list of relevant factors and the exquisite variety of academic institutions across the country, the Board has developed a substantial body of cases that explicate and develop the *Yeshiva* standard. In *American International College*, 282 N.L.R.B. 189 (1986), for example, the Board held the approximately ninety faculty members to be managerial employees, noting the authority of faculty standing committees in such areas as admissions, curriculum issues, and graduation requirements. Although there were some instances in which the administration had vetoed faculty proposals, the NLRB said that "they are not substantial or predominant and do not show a pattern of unilateral action by the administration." *Id.* at 202.

In *Livingstone College*, 286 N.L.R.B. 1308 (1987), the NLRB reached the same outcome, even though the faculty exercised their authority through standing committees of mixed membership—including administrators and students. The faculty's "substantial authority" in the development and implementation of policies in the academic sphere, *id.* at 1314, outweighed the lack of faculty input into budget decisions or the tenure process. *Id.* ("[W]e do not believe that lack of participation in [budgeting, tenure decisions, or setting tuition] precludes a finding that the faculty are managerial employees.").

The Board again found faculty members to be managerial employees in *Lewis and Clark College*, 300 N.L.R.B. 155 (1990). Faculty workload policies at the college were set by the administration, but committees (composed predominantly of faculty) made effective recommendations in areas such as admissions requirements and curriculum. The Board rejected a Regional Director's view that "umbrella committees" on which the faculty were a minority, addressing financial issues and long-term planning, negated the faculty's managerial status. As the Board found, "[t]here is . . . nothing inconsistent with the faculty members' having authority over one level of policy (e.g., academics), and the administration (including the board of trustees), having control over another (e.g., financial viability and long-term planning)." *Id.* at 162. The Board further explained:

> The board of trustees and others in the administration are entrusted with the ultimate policy-making and fiduciary responsibility for the College, not the faculty. But, even as to those areas in which the administration has exercised its own managerial decision-making authority, high-level implementation of those decisions is performed by the faculty.

Id.

In *Elmira College*, 309 N.L.R.B. 842 (1992), the Board upheld, without comment, a Regional Director's conclusion that "[w]ithout more, the nature of faculty involvement with respect to academic matters conclusively establishes their status as managerial employees." *Id.,* app. at 849 (Regional Director decision). Under the college by-laws, the faculty had authority over admissions, courses, graduation requirements, the nature of available degrees, and related procedural matters. The Regional Director noted that some factors supported a lack of managerial status: "the college faculty does not participate in promotion decisions exclusive of tenure and, in a few instances, has been overruled in hiring decisions. Also, the faculty has only a limited voice in administrative decisions involving salary or benefits or the budget process." *Id.* at 850. He did not find these factors controlling, because they "fall outside the crucial matters of academic governance considered dispositive by the Supreme Court in *Yeshiva." Id.*

When the faculty of LeMoyne-Owen College petitioned the NLRB for recognition as a bargaining unit, the College responded by contending that "[t]he instant case bears strong similarity to cases in which the Board, utilizing the principles set forth in *Yeshiva,* found that faculty members were managerial employees. . ." Employer's Br. to Regional Dir. at 16 (citing, *inter alia, American International College, Livingstone College,* and *Elmira College*). The College pointed to significant factual parallels between LeMoyne-Owen and the other institutions at which faculty members were deemed managerial employees—particularly when the comparison focuses primarily on academic matters and on "effective recommendation or control rather than final authority." *Yeshiva,* 444 U.S. at 683 n.17, 100 S.Ct. at 863. For example, the LeMoyne-Owen faculty have, according to the *Faculty Handbook,* "policy and procedural authority" over a range of academic areas, including admissions standards, the curriculum, general education requirements, graduation requirements, standards for grading, candidates for graduation, and conditions of academic standing, suspension, and dismissal. *Faculty Handbook* § 3.00.

* * *

Faculty recommendations on academic policies and other matters, such as tenure, often require the approval of the president and ultimately of the College's board of trustees. But the president testified that he had never, in six years as president, failed to approve a faculty recommendation on degree requirements or other matters related to the courses taught at the College. He also stated that he had forwarded all Faculty Assembly recommendations on curricular changes to the trustees, without exception, and that the trustees had never rejected any of those recommendations.

The Regional Director determined, however, that the faculty at LeMoyne-Owen were not managerial employees, and certified a bargaining unit consisting of all full-time faculty members. Decision and Direction of Election, NLRB Case No. 25-RC-10120 (Aug. 6, 2002), at 2–3 (Certification Decision). The Regional Director distinguished the College's faculty from the faculty at Yeshiva University, stating that "the faculty of LeMoyne-Owen College neither possess absolute control over any facet of the school's operations, nor 'effectively' recommend policies affecting its administration. They neither establish new policy nor effectively recommend changes to existing policy." *Id.* at 11. In support of this conclusion, the Regional Director noted that committee recommendations at the College are "subject to multiple levels of review, and subject to change by higher levels of authority." *Id.* The existence of such multiple levels of authority, he stated, makes it less likely that faculty recommendations will be effective, because the recommendations can be altered on their way up the hierarchy. *Id.* at 12. The Regional Director * * * also stated that the faculty play "a limited role in the selection of applicants for hire, [and] no role in the decision to dismiss staff or faculty," and cited specific instances such as the firing of secretaries during a financial crunch at the College in 2000 and the hiring of a professor as a full-time faculty member despite a faculty recommendation that she be hired only as a visiting professor. *Id.*

In reaching his determination, the Regional Director did not discuss any of the cases the College had cited. Instead, he relied primarily on *Florida Memorial College*, 263 N.L.R.B. 1248 (1982); *Kendall School of Design*, 279 N.L.R.B. 281 (1986); and *University of Great Falls*, 325 N.L.R.B. 83 (1997). Each of these post-*Yeshiva* cases held that an academic institution's faculty were not managerial employees. The College, however, contends that the facts of these cases are distinguishable in significant respects from the facts in the LeMoyne-Owen record. There was no tenure system at Florida Memorial College, and teaching contracts were generally only for a single year. Nor was there evidence of any effective faculty input into the college's curriculum; faculty members seeking to introduce new courses had to seek approval directly from the president and the dean of academic affairs. The school had an open admissions policy (precluding a faculty role in admission standards), and the administration established continuation requirements and approved students for graduation. Noting that the administration had "systematically and independently reviewed" faculty proposals and "consistently substituted its own judgment for that of the faculty," the Board found that the faculty's authority did not satisfy the *Yeshiva* standard. *Id.* at 1254.

At the Kendall School of Design, meetings of the full faculty were held only twice per semester, and votes of the full faculty were never taken; a refocusing of the school's curriculum took place under the direction of the academic dean, who gave the faculty curriculum committee only the broad outlines of the revisions and then demanded a simple up-or-down vote. Faculty members played no role in other academic matters such as matriculation standards and graduation requirements. *University of Great Falls* involved an institution where the dean of faculty had on several occasions refused to let faculty use the textbooks of their choice, and the deans—not the faculty—were responsible for approving students for graduation. In addition, the Board found that, unlike in *Elmira College* and *Lewis and Clark College,* there was no "clear evidence that faculty recommendations were generally followed." 325 N.L.R.B. at 83 & n. 8.

LeMoyne-Owen requested that the Board review the Regional Director's decision, challenging the Regional Director's reliance on these cases and renewing its argument that other cases, such as *American International College* and *Lewis and Clark College,* were controlling precedent. The Board denied the request by a 2–1 vote, declaring in a one-sentence order that the College had "raised no substantial issues warranting review." After the faculty voted to accept their bargaining representative, the Regional Director issued a formal certification of that representative and the College again sought the review of the Board. As it had before, the College argued that the LeMoyne-Owen faculty exercise authority comparable to that of the faculty members in *American International College* and the analogous post-*Yeshiva* cases. The Board again issued a terse order denying review, again with no discussion of the precedents. The College refused to bargain with the faculty, and the Board ultimately deemed the College guilty of unfair labor practices and ordered it to bargain. The matter is before this court on the College's petition for review of the order and the Board's cross-application for enforcement. The College's challenge brings the entire NLRB proceeding—including the Regional Director's underlying decision to certify the full-time faculty as a bargaining unit—before this court for review.

We accord deference to the Board's exercise of its authority * * * to certify appropriate bargaining units. *See, e.g., BB & L, Inc. v. NLRB,* 52 F.3d 366, 369 (D.C. Cir. 1995). That deference is subject to certain limits, however, and one of those limits is that the Board "cannot ignore its own relevant precedent but must explain why it is not controlling." *Id.; see also International Union of Operating Eng'rs v. NLRB,* 294 F.3d 186, 188 (D.C.Cir.2002) ("The Board has an obligation to engage in reasoned decisionmaking, which . . . requires it to give a reasoned explanation when it departs from its own precedent."). In this case, the Board has not provided any explanation—let alone an adequate one—of how its disposition is consistent with its contrary holdings in the post-*Yeshiva* cases that appear to have presented similar facts. The only opinion is that of the Regional Director, which did not discuss or even mention a single one of the precedents on which the College relied.

An agency is by no means required to distinguish every precedent cited to it by an aggrieved party. But where, as here, a party makes a significant showing that analogous cases have been decided differently, the agency must do more than simply ignore that argument * * *. Emerson's advice to preachers—"emphasize your choice by utter ignoring of all that you reject,"

Ralph Waldo Emerson, *The Preacher, reprinted in* 10 Lectures and Biographical Sketches 215, 235 (1904)—will not do for administrative agencies.

The need for an explanation is particularly acute when an agency is applying a multi-factor test through case-by-case adjudication. The "open-ended rough-and-tumble of factors" on which *Yeshiva* launched the Board and higher education, *see Yeshiva*, 444 U.S. at 690 n. 31, 100 S.Ct. at 866, n. 31 (Court's analysis "is a starting point only, and . . . other factors not present here may enter into the analysis in other contexts"), can lead to predictability and intelligibility only to the extent the Board explains, in applying the test to varied fact situations, which factors are significant and which less so, and why * * *. In the absence of an explanation, the "totality of the circumstances" can become simply a cloak for agency whim—or worse.

A court reviewing an *ipse dixit* outcome that seems inconsistent with proffered precedent is left to attempt to discern for itself which factual differences might have been determinative, without guidance from the agency, and to assess whether making such distinctions controlling is rational or arbitrary, again without any agency explanation of why particular factors make a difference. The court really has no way of knowing if the rationale it discerns is in fact that of the agency, or one of the court's own devise. Yet only the former can provide a legitimate basis for sustaining agency action. *SEC v. Chenery Corp.*, 318 U.S. 80, 87–88, 63 S.Ct. 454, 459, 87 L.Ed. 626 (1943). Requiring an adequate explanation of apparent departures from precedent thus not only serves the purpose of ensuring like treatment under like circumstances, but also facilitates judicial review of agency action in a manner that protects the agency's predominant role in applying the authority delegated to it by Congress.

The NLRB may have an adequate explanation for the result it reached in this case. We cannot, however, assume that such an explanation exists until we see it * * *.

UNITED STATES DEPARTMENT OF THE TREASURY, BUREAU OF ENGRAVING AND PRINTING v. FLRA

United States Court of Appeals, District of Columbia Circuit, 1993.
995 F.2d 301.

Before SILBERMAN, BUCKLEY and WILLIAMS, CIRCUIT JUDGES.

STEPHEN F. WILLIAMS, CIRCUIT JUDGE:

The Federal Service Labor Management Relations Statute gives federal employees the right to bargain collectively with government employer units over their "conditions of employment". 5 U.S.C. § 7102. Matters "specifically provided for" by federal statute, however, are excepted from bargaining. 5 U.S.C. § 7103(a)(14)(C). We here address the Federal Labor Relations Authority's analysis of that exception as applied to the wages of so-called "prevailing rate" employees. Because the Authority has acted inconsistently with its own prior decisions, and has offered no intelligible explanation of its shift, we reverse and remand.

* * *

In March 1991 unions representing six bargaining units at the Bureau of Engraving and Printing submitted a variety of negotiating proposals to the Bureau and announced that they sought to negotiate the "method by which wage rates of their respective crafts are set, adjusted and maintained insofar as permitted by law." The Bureau promptly responded that it would not bargain over the proposals, invoking both the "management rights" exception of 5 U.S.C. § 7106(a)(1) and the exception for matters "specifically provided for" by statute. The unions appealed to the FLRA, which found the unions' proposals negotiable. The Bureau now appeals to this court, relying only on the "specifically provided for" exception.

The statute governing the wages of Bureau employees, 5 U.S.C. § 5349(a), uses a two-factor formula that looks to the "prevailing rates" of similar private-sector employees and to the demands of the "public interest":

> The pay of employees . . . in [various agencies, including the Bureau of Engraving and Printing] *shall be fixed and adjusted from time to time as nearly as is consistent with the public interest in accordance with prevailing rates . . .* as the pay-fixing authority of each such agency may determine.

5 U.S.C. § 5349(a) (emphasis added).

In a recent case, *National Association of Government Employees, Local R4–26 and Department of the Air Force, Langley Air Force Base, Virginia* ("*Langley*"), 40 FLRA 118 (1991), the Authority held that wages under a related section of the Prevailing Rate Systems Act, 5 U.S.C. § 5343, met the terms of the "specifically provided for" exception. That provision also states that:

> The pay of prevailing rate employees *shall be fixed and adjusted from time to time as nearly as is consistent with the public interest in accordance with prevailing rates. . .*

5 U.S.C. § 5343(a) (emphasis added). The emphasized portions of the provisions are, obviously, identical. Citing a prior FLRA opinion, *American Federation of Government Employees, AFL-CIO and Department of Defense, Department of the Army and Air Force, Headquarters, Army and Air Force Exchange Service, Dallas, Texas* ("*Dallas*"), 32 FLRA 591, 59 9–600 (1988) (Member McKee, concurring), the Authority in *Langley* declared

that "all aspects of pay-setting under the prevailing rate system are specifically provided for by law and, therefore, are excluded from the definition of conditions of employment under section 7103(a)(14)(C)." 40 FLRA at 141.

To come out as it did in the present case, therefore, the Authority had either to distinguish *Langley* and *Dallas* or to reject them and explain the rejection. See *Greater Boston Television Corp. v. FCC*, 444 F.2d 841, 852 (D.C.Cir.1970). It tried to distinguish the precedents, but its distinction does not add up.

The heart of the Authority's distinction was an assertion that § 5343 " 'fix[ed]' wages by prescribing . . . the process of determining wages," whereas § 5349 left " 'fixing' to the Agency, within the general parameters of prevailing rates and [the] public interest." Therefore, the Authority concluded, § 5349(a) gave the Bureau "broad discretion to establish and maintain wage rates."

This treatment of § 5349(a) and § 5343 ignores the fact that both statutes direct the wage-setting agency, in identical language, to look to "prevailing rates" and the "public interest". Although § 5343 spells out more detail of the *process* by which a prevailing rate is to be determined, it does not appear that the detail in § 5343 is likely to affect the substantive determination of "prevailing rate" materially. Section 5343(a)(1)(A), for example, requires a definition of the boundaries of "local wage areas" for employees having "regular wage schedules" and a similar definition for those having "special wage schedules". One would suppose that whatever substantive factors render an employee "regular" or "special" for these purposes would similarly affect any calculation under § 5349(a).

Likewise, while it is perfectly true that the "public interest" criterion of § 5349 gives the agency considerable discretion to override the "prevailing rate" outcome, that discretion appears indistinguishable from the public interest discretion afforded by § 5343. In fact, the cases discussing public interest discretion under various prevailing rate statutes seem to cite each other more or less interchangeably * * *. Given the statutes' uniform and careful repetition of the language that we have quoted from §§ 5343 and 5349 (and which identically appears in § 5348), this interchangeability is hardly surprising. Thus there appears nothing in the public interest discretion under § 5349(a) that differs from that under § 5343. Given the apparent lack of a legally significant distinction here between the prevailing rate aspects of §§ 5349(a) and 5343, the Authority's effort to distinguish the two statutes from each other, and this case from *Langley* and *Dallas*, falls apart.

On remand, the Authority may of course wish to jettison *Langley* and *Dallas* * * *.

* * *

We reverse and remand the case to the FLRA for a more reasoned examination of its precedent and the statutory provisions at issue.

So ordered.

CENTER FOR AUTO SAFETY V. FEDERAL HIGHWAY ADMIN.

United States Court of Appeals, District of Columbia Circuit, 1992.
956 F.2d 309.

Before EDWARDS and RUTH BADER GINSBURG, CIRCUIT JUDGES, and THOMAS, CIRCUIT JUSTICE.

Opinion for the Court filed by CIRCUIT JUSTICE THOMAS.

THOMAS, CIRCUIT JUSTICE.

Before 1988, regulations provided without exception that the states must inspect their respective highway bridges at least every two years. The Federal Highway Administration then amended the regulations (1) to authorize less frequent inspections in certain limited circumstances and (2) to require the inspection of bridges' underwater supports at least every five years. The appellants here, two individuals and an organization devoted to the cause of highway safety, challenged both provisions. The questions presented are whether the FHWA has violated its statutory obligation to "establish" by regulation a "maximum time period between inspections," 23 U.S.C. § 151(b)(2) (1988), and whether the agency acted arbitrarily and capriciously in promulgating either amendment.

I

Title 23 U.S.C. § 151(a) requires the Secretary of Transportation to establish "national bridge inspection standards" to provide for "the proper safety inspection and evaluation of all highway bridges." Section 151(b) imposes various minimum requirements that the inspection standards must satisfy. Section 151(b)(2), the focus of much of this controversy, provides that the standards must "establish the maximum time period between inspections." The Secretary has delegated his section 151 responsibilities, among others, to the Federal Highway Administration. See 23 C.F.R. § 1.37 (1991).

In 1971, the FHWA promulgated the bridge inspection standards required under section 151. As codified, section 650.305(a) of the standards declares categorically that "[e]ach bridge is to be inspected at regular intervals not to exceed 2 years." 23 C.F.R. § 650.305(a). Between 1971 and 1988, all bridges subject to the program were inspected at least every two years, but few states inspected their bridges' underwater supports.

In 1988, the FHWA amended the bridge inspection standards in two respects relevant here. First, it promulgated a new section 650.305(c), which permits the states to apply for, and the agency to approve, bridge-specific exemptions from the two-year inspection rule. Section 650.305(c) provides:

> The maximum inspection interval may be increased for certain types or groups of bridges where past inspection reports and favorable experience and analysis justifies [sic] the increased interval of inspection. If a State proposes to inspect some bridges at greater than the specified 2-year interval, the State shall submit a detailed proposal and supporting data to the Federal Highway Administrator for approval.

23 C.F.R. § 650.305(c).

In its notice of proposed rulemaking, the FHWA justified section 650.305(c) as a means of providing the states "greater flexibility with which to utilize available inspection resources in a cost-effective manner." Savings in bridge inspection costs, the agency reasoned, could be redirected into equally important bridge replacement programs. The FHWA acknowledged no safety tradeoff between less frequent inspections and more frequent replacements; instead, it asserted that the two-year inspection interval "can be increased for some categories of bridges with only a minimal or negligible increase in risk to the public." This reasoning reflected a change in policy since 1984, when the FHWA had concluded that the safety benefits of a strict two-year rule "far outweigh" the potential economic benefits of less frequent inspections. In justifying the change, the FHWA cited with scant elaboration its "further review and analysis since April of 1984."

The 1988 amendments also added to section 650.303 a new subsection (e), which now provides special inspection procedures for certain categories of bridges. In particular, for bridges with "underwater members," it requires that "[t]hese members" be inspected at least every five years. See 23 C.F.R. § 650.303(e)(2). This five-year rule for underwater inspections codifies the interval suggested by the American Association of State Highway and Transportation Officials (AASHTO), an organization that has developed a wide range of suggested highway safety standards. The FHWA explained:

> [T]he collective best judgment of professional bridge, hydraulic and geotechnical engineers as expressed by the current AASHTO Guide for Bridge Maintenance Inspection and comments received regarding this rulemaking procedure is that strong underwater inspection programs which encompass all bridges over waterways are currently needed. The 5 year maximum between underwater inspections is appropriate until a sufficient national data base to alter the period is established and evaluated.

53 Fed.Reg. at 32,614.

Unhappy with both provisions, two of the current appellants (among others) petitioned the FHWA for reconsideration. The FHWA denied the petition. In explaining its decision with respect to section 650.305(c), the agency stated that its post-1984 review had included consideration of two recent draft studies on the deterioration rates of various bridges. Neither of these drafts, however, was entered into the formal record maintained by the agency during the rulemaking.

The appellants sought declaratory and injunctive relief in the district court. They raised three claims: first, that the availability of temporally unbounded exemptions from the general two-year inspection rule violates 23 U.S.C. § 151(b)(2); second and third, that both the exemption provision and the five-year rule for underwater inspections were promulgated arbitrarily and capriciously, in violation of section 10(e)(2)(A) of the Administrative Procedure Act, 5 U.S.C. § 706(2)(A).

The parties disputed the subsidiary question of what constitutes the administrative record subject to review. The FHWA filed with the district court the two drafts cited in its denial of reconsideration, together with a draft of a third bridge deterioration study. Attached to the studies was a declaration asserting that the agency had considered all of them during the rulemaking. The FHWA also filed a declaration explaining how it typically maintains its rulemaking records. According to that declaration, the "formal Administrative Record" includes materials such as notices published and comments received, but it excludes less formal materials such as "draft reports."

The parties filed cross-motions for summary judgment. The district court denied the plaintiffs' motion and granted the agency's, rejecting each of the plaintiffs' claims and upholding both of the challenged provisions. The plaintiffs renew their claims on appeal.

II

* * *

Under well-settled administrative law principles, the district court was obliged to afford the challenged agency actions a fair degree of deference, as are we. In reviewing a regulation challenged under a statute that the promulgating agency is entrusted to administer, we must accept any reasonable interpretation of the statute, *see, e.g., Chevron, U.S.A., Inc. v. Natural Resources Defense Council*, 467 U.S. 837, 842–45, 104 S.Ct. 2778, 2781–83, 81 L.Ed.2d 694 (1984), or the regulation, *see, e.g., Martin v. Occupational Safety & Health Review Comm'n*, 499 U.S. 144, 111 S.Ct. 1171, 1175–76, 113 L.Ed.2d 117 (1991), put forth by the agency in support of the regulation. In reviewing an action challenged as arbitrary and capricious, our task is to determine whether the agency has articulated a rational connection between its factual judgments and its ultimate policy choice, *see, e.g., Motor Vehicle Mfrs. Ass'n v. State Farm Mut. Auto. Ins. Co.,* 463 U.S. 29, 43, 103 S.Ct. 2856, 2866, 77 L.Ed.2d 443 (1983), and whether the underlying factual judgments are supported by substantial evidence, *see, e.g., Association of Data Processing Serv. Orgs. v. Board of Governors,* 745 F.2d 677, 683–84 (D.C.Cir.1984) [hereinafter *ADAPSO*].

A

The regulations cannot be reconciled with 23 U.S.C. § 151(b)(2). Section 650.305(c) authorizes the FHWA to grant permission for states "to inspect some bridges at greater than the [maximum] 2-year interval" established under section 650.305(a). With respect to bridges that qualify for this special treatment, however, the regulations on their face fail to "establish" any "maximum time period between inspections," as required by section 151(b)(2). Section 650.305(c) merely defines the circumstances when a bridge may be exempted from the two-year rule—if a state submits a "detailed proposal" and "supporting data" to the FHWA, and if the FHWA finds that "past inspection reports" and "favorable experience and analysis" justify the proposal. It says absolutely nothing about how frequently a bridge must be inspected once it has qualified for the exemption.

* * *

Nothing we say today prevents the FHWA from establishing different inspection intervals for bridges posing different risks of collapse. Nonetheless, if the agency exempts a certain category of bridges from the two-year rule, the agency must also "establish" by regulation an appropriately longer "maximum time period between inspections" applicable to that category. Because section 650.305(c) fails to do this, we hold it fatally inconsistent with 23 U.S.C. § 151(b)(2).

B

We need not address the appellants' alternative contention that section 650.305(c) was promulgated arbitrarily and capriciously. This claim will likely resurface, however, for the FHWA can readily repair the defect we have identified by qualifying the regulation with any "maximum time period" of its choice. We therefore offer a few comments on the arbitrary and capricious challenge, with the hope that our discussion will obviate the need for another remand.

An agency action is arbitrary and capricious if it rests upon a factual premise that is unsupported by substantial evidence. *See ADAPSO,* 745 F.2d at 683–84. In this case, the FHWA's justification for section 650.305(c) rests primarily on the factual premise that "the [two-year] inspection interval can be increased for some categories of bridges with only a minimal or negligible increase in risk to the public." 52 Fed.Reg. at 11,094. In support of this premise, the FHWA now cites the three draft bridge deterioration studies. The appellants contend that the studies cannot presently be considered because the FHWA never formally introduced them into the administrative record. We agree.

The APA provides that a court reviewing agency action shall consider "the whole record or those parts of it cited by a party." 5 U.S.C. § 706. Interpreting this provision, the Supreme Court in *Citizens to Preserve Overton Park, Inc. v. Volpe*, 401 U.S. 402, 91 S.Ct. 814, 28 L.Ed.2d 136 (1971), stated that "review is to be based on the full administrative record that was before the [agency] at the time [it] made [its] decision." *Id.* at 420, 91 S.Ct. at 825; *see also Camp v. Pitts*, 411 U.S. 138, 142, 93 S.Ct. 1241, 1244, 36 L.Ed.2d 106 (1973) ("[T]he focal point for judicial review should be the administrative record already in existence, not some new record made initially in the reviewing court."). This requirement applies even in the context of informal agency action.

A "record" is simply "everything . . . properly placed in evidence under defined rules of admissibility." Pedersen, *Formal Records and Informal Rulemaking*, 85 Yale L.J. 38, 64 (1975). According to the FHWA's own testimony, the agency follows a defined, if informal, rule under which "draft reports" are not admitted into the "formal Administrative Record" maintained by the agency. Of course the agency could have maintained less strict evidentiary rules, consistent with the forgiving requirements of notice-and-comment rulemaking procedures, under which the draft studies would have been admitted. But having chosen, for whatever reason, to exclude the three draft bridge deterioration studies at the administrative stage, the FHWA cannot now rely on those same studies to provide the requisite evidentiary support during judicial review. This is a straightforward attempt to create "some new record made initially in the reviewing court," *Camp v. Pitts*, 411 U.S. at 142, 93 S.Ct. at 1244, which the record requirement prohibits.[8]

C

Finally, the appellants, who desire bridges' underwater supports to be inspected at least every two years, contend that the FHWA acted arbitrarily and capriciously in requiring only that these inspections occur at least every five years * * *.

* * *

* * * [T]hey assert that the agency failed to develop a sufficient factual basis from which to conclude that a five-year interval would ensure an appropriate level of safety. We reject this line of argument because it fails to view the agency's decision in light of the available data.

---

[8] Nothing we say today prevents the FHWA from changing its rules, if it should desire, in order to admit informal drafts into its administrative records. Whatever materials the agency admits, however, it must supply to the appropriate reviewing court. Whatever materials the agency excludes, it cannot rely upon for support during judicial review.

At the time of this rulemaking, several recent accidents had highlighted "the need for evaluation of the underwater components of many bridges." 52 Fed.Reg. at 11,094. Nonetheless, because underwater inspections had been done so rarely, the FHWA found itself without the sort of "national data base," 53 Fed.Reg. at 32,614, that might have enabled it to calibrate a finely measured response to the problem. In short, the agency faced a known risk of unknown degree—a common predicament for those charged with developing appropriate safety standards. Given "insufficient data" from which to make "a fully informed factual determination," the FHWA was forced, in selecting an appropriate standard, to rely primarily on policy considerations rather than factual ones.

An agency confronted with such uncertainty need not predicate its initial response upon a finding that any more vigorous response would be unwarranted. To so hold would impose a dilemma between an obviously disproportionate response (for example, requiring underwater inspections at least every two weeks) and no response at all—at least until enough accidents had occurred to provide substantial evidence regarding an optimal level of response. Instead, an agency has some leeway reasonably to resolve uncertainty, as a policy matter, in favor of more regulation or less. With this principle in mind, we consider the agency's asserted justification for the five-year rule.

As mentioned above, the FHWA recognized both the need for requiring underwater inspections beginning immediately and the impossibility, given the data available to it, of determining an optimal minimum frequency between those inspections. Following its frequent practice of drawing upon the expertise of the AASHTO, the FHWA decided to adopt as a preliminary measure the relevant AASHTO standard, which it characterized as the "collective best judgment of professional bridge, hydraulic and geotechnical engineers." 53 Fed.Reg. at 32,614. Finally, the FHWA promised to educate itself, and to refine the standards, as more data becomes available. The appellants do not contend that the agency willfully (or even negligently) ignored information available to it, and they do not question the prominence of the AASHTO in matters of highway safety. They offer no attack against the five-year rule, which enjoys support among safety experts outside the AASHTO, except to assert that the agency was required, as a matter of law, to resolve all doubts in favor of more stringent regulation. It was not.

In short, the FHWA both "examine[d] the relevant data"—what little there was—and "articulate[d] a satisfactory explanation for its action." *State Farm*, 463 U.S. at 43, 103 S.Ct. at 2867. The agency did the best it could with the little information it had, and the arbitrary and capricious standard requires no more than that.

III

We agree with the district court that this case is properly resolved on summary judgment. We conclude that the court erred insofar as it failed to declare section 650.305(c) inconsistent with 23 U.S.C. § 151(b)(2) and to enjoin its application on that ground. We also conclude that the court correctly upheld section 650.303(e)(2) against challenge as arbitrary and capricious. Accordingly, we affirm in part, reverse in part, and remand the case to the district court with instructions to remand to the FHWA for further proceedings consistent with this opinion. The agency remains free, of course, to close its rulemaking docket forthwith. But if the agency attempts to cure section 650.305(c), it should make clear what materials will constitute the administrative record, and it must include any necessary evidentiary support within those materials.

It is so ordered.

NOTES

While agencies generally must follow valid regulations until they are repealed, *see Erie Blvd. Hydropower, LP v. FERC,* 878 F.3d 258, 269 (D.C.Cir.2017) ("if an agency action fails to comply with its regulations, that action may be set aside as arbitrary and capricious"), agencies are under no strict obligation to adhere to prior adjudicatory precedents. They must, however, acknowledge and account for those precedents in adjudications, either by following them, overruling them, distinguishing them, or articulating some other non-arbitrary reason for departing from them. *See NBCUniversal Media, LLC v. NLRB,* 815 F.3d 821, 834 (D.C.Cir.2016) ("Because we cannot discern how the *Clarification Decision* applies relevant Board precedent to the facts of this case, we are constrained to remand the case to the Board. On remand, the Board must explain both the principles embodied in the relevant precedent and how application of those principles to the facts here supports its resolution of the parties' dispute.").

This might not seem like a very difficult burden, *see, e.g., W & M Properties of Connecticut, Inc. v. NLRB,* 514 F.3d 1341, 1346–47 (D.C.Cir.2008), but cases in which agencies utterly ignore or fail adequately to distinguish prior precedents are legion. *See, e.g., Noranda Alumina, LLC v. Perez,* 841 F.3d 661, 666–68 (5th Cir.2016); *NLRB v. Southwest Regional Council of Carpenters,* 826 F.3d 460 (D.C.Cir.2016); *Lone Mountain Processing, Inc. v. Secretary of Labor,* 709 F.3d 1161, 1163–64 (D.C.Cir.2013); *Trump Plaza Associates v. NLRB,* 679 F.3d 822, 830–31 (D.C.Cir.2012); *Republic Airline, Inc. v. United States Dep't of Transportation,* 669 F.3d 296, 301–02 (D.C.Cir.2012); *Dillmon v. NTSB,* 588 F.3d 1085, 1089–95 (D.C.Cir.2009). Given that an agency that is unhappy with its precedents can always overrule them, why might agencies so often choose to ignore or weakly distinguish precedents?

It is commonplace for reviewing courts to say that "[a] court generally must be 'at its most deferential' when reviewing scientific judgments and technical analyses within the agency's expertise." *Tri-Valley Cares v. United States Dep't of Energy*, 671 F.3d 1113, 1124 (9th Cir.2012) (quoting *Baltimore Gas & Electric Co. v. NRDC, Inc.*, 462 U.S. 87, 103, 103 S.Ct. 2246, 76 L.Ed.2d 437 (1983)). *See also Center for Biological Diversity v. EPA*, 749 F.3d 1079, 1087–88 (D.C.Cir.2014) (string-citing cases on "super-deference" to agencies on technical matters). Are those the kinds of questions where it is the least important or the most important for agencies to be made to explain their reasoning clearly? For an argument that such extreme deference on technical matters undermines some of the accountability-enhancing benefits of judicial review, see Emily Hammond Meazell, *Super Deference, the Science Obsession, and Judicial Review as Translation of Agency Science*, 109 Mich. L. Rev. 733 (2011).

The most common reason for agencies to lose on arbitrary or capricious review is failure of explanation: There is some seemingly important point (as in *Puerto Rico Sun Oil*) that the agency simply ignores altogether or mentions in a casual or conclusory fashion. For example, in 2011 the Department of Labor changed its mind about whether automotive service advisors (the people who meet with you when you take your car in for repairs at a dealership) are subject to the maximum-hours and overtime provisions of the Fair Labor Standards Act. In 1978, the agency had concluded that such persons were not subject to that law; three decades later, the agency shifted positions.

> The Department said that, in reaching its decision, it had "carefully considered all of the comments, analyses, and arguments made for and against the proposed changes." 76 Fed.Reg. 18832. And it noted that, since 1978, it had treated service advisors as exempt in certain circumstances. *Id.*, at 18838. It also noted the comment from the National Automobile Dealers Association stating that the industry had relied on that interpretation. *Ibid.*

> But when it came to explaining the "good reasons for the new policy," the Department said almost nothing. It stated only that it would not treat service advisors as exempt because "the statute does not include such positions and the Department recognizes that there are circumstances under which the requirements for the exemption would not be met." 76 Fed.Reg. 18838. It continued that it "believes that this interpretation is reasonable" and "sets forth the appropriate approach." *Ibid* . . . . [T]he Department did not analyze or explain why the statute should be interpreted to exempt dealership employees who sell vehicles but not dealership employees who sell services (that is, service advisors). And though several public comments supported the Department's reading of the statute, the Department did not explain what (if anything) it found persuasive in those comments beyond the few statements above.

It is not the role of the courts to speculate on reasons that might have supported an agency's decision . . . . Whatever potential reasons the Department might have given, the agency in fact gave almost no reasons at all. In light of the serious reliance interests at stake, the Department's conclusory statements do not suffice to explain its decision.

Encino Motorcars, LLC v. Navarro, 136 S.Ct. 2117, 2126–27, 195 L.Ed.2d 382 (2016).

6. A HARD LOOK AT STEP TWO OF *CHEVRON*

Step two of *Chevron* requires courts to affirm reasonable agency interpretations of statutes administered by the agencies. What does it mean for an interpretation to be "reasonable"? Does that term describe an outcome test, so that reasonableness simply concerns the degree of "fit" between the agency's interpretation and a correct interpretation of the statute? Or does *Chevron*'s reasonableness requirement apply as well to the agency's decisionmaking *process*, so that a substantively reasonable interpretation that is reached through inappropriate means would fail on review at step two? And if the latter view is correct, how does *Chevron*'s step two differ, if at all, from the hard look doctrine?

Until relatively recently, very little judicial or scholarly attention was paid to the relationship between step two of *Chevron* and § 706(2)(A)'s arbitrary or capricious standard. Courts effectively treated *Chevron*'s step two as an outcome test in which the agency was almost predestined to win, and no one seemed to consider whether the arbitrary or capricious standard independently applied to the process by which agencies formulated interpretations of statutes.

Judge Laurence Silberman of the D.C. Circuit was one of the first judges (and scholars) expressly to discuss the relationship between *Chevron* and the arbitrary or capricious test. In a 1990 law review article, Judge Silberman suggested that step two of *Chevron*

> is not all that different analytically from the APA's arbitrary and capricious review. In either the second step of *Chevron* or in arbitrary and capricious review, the court often asks itself whether the agency considered and weighed the factors Congress wished the agency to bring to bear on its decision. If the agency did so, that the court would have struck the balance somewhat differently cannot be grounds to overturn the agency's action.

Laurence H. Silberman, Chevron—*The Intersection of Law and Policy*, 58 Geo. Wash. L. Rev. 821, 827–28 (1990). This view had been reflected in a small number of cases in the D.C. Circuit up to that point. *See, e.g., General American Transp. Corp. v. ICC*, 872 F.2d 1048, 1053 (D.C.Cir.1989) ("the questions posed—has the Commission adopted an impermissible construction of the Act and is its * * * policy arbitrary and capricious—are quite similar. Both questions require us to determine whether the Commission, in effecting a reconciliation of competing statutory aims, has rationally considered the factors deemed relevant by the Act."). For the most part, however, *Chevron* and the arbitrary or capricious test went their separate ways; agency interpretations of statutes were generally analyzed exclusively under *Chevron*.

In 1994, two events happened that upset the equilibrium. First, Judge Silberman's law review article became a judicial opinion. In *National Ass'n of Regulatory Utility Commissioners v. ICC*, 41 F.3d 721 (D.C.Cir.1994) ("*NARUC*"), Judge Silberman declared that "the inquiry at the second step of *Chevron* overlaps analytically with a court's task under the Administrative Procedure Act (APA) in determining whether agency action is arbitrary and capricious (unreasonable)." *Id.* at 726. As noted above, other decisions had previously made the same identification of the two tests, but none had done so as self-consciously as *NARUC*. The *NARUC* decision made it very difficult to continue to sweep the relationship between *Chevron* and arbitrary or capricious review under the table.

Second, Professor Mark Seidenfeld published the first major law review article that focussed on the meaning of *Chevron*'s step two. *See* Mark Seidenfeld, *A Syncopated* Chevron: *Emphasizing Reasoned Decisionmaking in Reviewing Agency Interpretations of Statutes*, 73 Tex. L. Rev. 83 (1994). Drawing largely on civic republican political theory, Professor Seidenfeld concluded that courts should invigorate *Chevron*'s step two to encompass a review of agency statutory interpretation expressly modelled after the familiar hard look review of agency policymaking:

> Thus, in reviewing an agency's interpretation, courts should require the agency to identify the concerns that the statute addresses and explain how the agency's interpretation took these concerns into account. In addition, the agency should explain why it emphasized certain interests instead of others. In other words, the agency must reveal what led it to balance the statutory aims as it did. The agency should also respond to any likely contentions that its interpretation will have deleterious implications. In short, to satisfy the second step of the syncopated *Chevron*, the agency should explain why its interpretation is good policy in light of the purposes and concerns underlying the statutory scheme.

Id. at 129.

In the ensuing years, the issue of the relationship between *Chevron* and arbitrary or capricious review has become a hot topic in both the law reviews and the federal reporters. The D.C. Circuit has noted the issue with increasing regularity, though without reaching much of a resolution. *See*

Arent v. Shalala, 70 F.3d 610, 614–16 (D.C.Cir.1995) (acknowledging that *Chevron* and arbitrary or capricious review "overlap at the margins," but attempting to carve out separate spheres based on whether the relevant inquiry "is rooted in statutory analysis and is focused on discerning the boundaries of Congress' delegation of authority to the agency"); *Independent Petroleum Ass'n of America v. Babbitt*, 92 F.3d 1248, 1258 (D.C.Cir.1996) (noting in dictum that "[t]he two analytic frameworks in this case produce the same result"); *Animal Legal Defense Fund, Inc. v. Glickman*, 204 F.3d 229, 235 (D.C.Cir.2000) ("The explanation that renders the Secretary's interpretation of the statute reasonable also serves to establish that the final rule was not arbitrary and capricious"); *American Petroleum Inst. v. United States EPA*, 216 F.3d 50, 57 (D.C.Cir.2000) (stating that "the second step of *Chevron* analysis and *State Farm* arbitrary and capricious review overlap, but are not identical" and finding the agency's explanation for its conclusion deficient); *National Mining Ass'n v. Kempthorne*, 512 F.3d 702, 710 (D.C.Cir.2008) (noting "the overlap between step-two *Chevron* review and * * * arbitrary-and-capricious review" and treating the court's *Chevron* step two analysis affirming the agency as sufficient to dispose of an arbitrary or capricious claim as well); *South Coast Air Quality Management District v. EPA*, 554 F.3d 1076, 1080 (D.C.Cir.2009) (petitioners' arbitrary or capricious argument "not surprisingly, reprises the petitioners' statutory argument; when a statute affords an agency substantial discretion * * * the *Chevron* inquiry overlaps analytically with the determination whether the agency acted arbitrarily"). Meanwhile, two law review articles in the late 1990s urged an explicit merger of the two tests—with one article urging that *Chevron*'s step two be held to incorporate the hard look analysis of the arbitrary or capricious test, *see* Ronald A. Levin, *The Anatomy of* Chevron: *Step Two Reconsidered*, 72 Chi.-Kent L. Rev. 1253 (1997), and the other urging that the hard look analysis be superimposed as a "process test" over *Chevron* step two's "outcome test." *See* Gary Lawson, *Outcome, Procedure, and Process: Agency Duties of Explanation for Legal Conclusions*, 48 Rutgers L. Rev. 313 (1996); *see also* Catherine M. Sharkey, *Cutting in on the* Chevron *Two-Step,* 86 Fordham L. Rev. 2359 (2018) (making an argument similar to your editor's). Your editor subsequently conceded that Professor Levin's approach is more sensible, *see* Gary Lawson, *Reconceptualizing* Chevron *and Discretion: A Comment on Levin and Rubin*, 72 Chi.-Kent L. Rev. 1377 (1997), but he is no longer sure that this was a smart concession. At least one circuit has expressly adopted the view that the two forms of review are distinct in precisely this "process vs. outcome" fashion. *See Texas Office of Public Utility Counsel v. FCC,* 183 F.3d 393, 410 (5th Cir.1999) (" 'Arbitrary and capricious' review under the APA differs from *Chevron* step-two review, because it focuses on the reasonability of the agency's decision-making processes rather than on the reasonability of its interpretation"). The D.C. Circuit, as noted above, has been more equivocal about the proper relationship between *Chevron* step two and arbitrary or capricious review. *See, e.g., Wedgewood Village Pharmacy v. DEA*, 509 F.3d 541 (D.C.Cir.2007) (using the language from *State Farm* regarding arbitrary or capricious review as a description of *Chevron* step two and rejecting an agency's interpretation of a statute as inadequately explained); *United States Telecom Ass'n v. FCC*, 227 F.3d 450 (D.C.Cir.2000) (same). The Supreme Court has finally taken notice of the issue in passing, suggesting that *Chevron* step two and the arbitrary or capricious test are essentially equivalent. *See Judulang v. Holder*, 565 U.S. 42, 52 n.7, 132 S.Ct. 476, 483 n.7, 181 L.Ed.2d 449 (2011).

Taking notice in passing and making sense, however, are two very different things. Judicial discussions of the relationship between *Chevron* and arbitrary or capricious review often remain somewhat mysterious. Sometimes judges disagree among themselves about whether *Chevron* or arbitrary or capricious review is the appropriate framework for review. *Cf., e.g., Echostar Satellite, L.L.C. v. FCC*, 704 F.3d 992, 996–97 (D.C.Cir.2013) (applying *Chevron*) *with id.* at 1001–02 (Edwards, J., concurring) (employing arbitrary or capricious review). Sometimes courts seem to change gears in midstream. *See, e.g., Christ the King Manor, Inc. v. Secretary, United States Dep't of Health and Human Services*, 730 F.3d 291, 305–07, 308–09 (3d Cir.2013) (seeming to change gears—several times—in midstream). Sometimes judges blend step one, step two, and arbitrary or capricious review into one large goulash. *See, e.g., White Stallion Energy Center, L.L.C. v. EPA*, 748 F.3d 1222, 1261, 1266 (D.C.Cir.2014) (Kavanaugh, J., concurring in part and dissenting in part), *rev'd, Michigan v. EPA*, 576 U.S. ___, 135 S.Ct. 2699 (2015).

In any event, there is increasing recognition that agencies, on whatever doctrinal basis, must explain how and why they interpret statutes the way that they do. *See Village of Barrington, Ill. v. Surface Transportation Board*, 636 F.3d 650, 660 (D.C.Cir.2011) ("At *Chevron* step two we defer to the agency's permissible interpretation, but only if the agency has offered a reasoned explanation for why it chose that interpretation."). *See* Kent Barnett & Christopher J. Walker, Chevron *Step Two's Domain*, 93 Notre Dame L. Rev. 1441 (2018) (collecting cases that evaluate the agency's reasoning process at step two).

The enhanced awareness of the need to integrate *Chevron* and hard look review makes it likely that the issue will reach some kind of resolution fairly soon (though concededly this book has made such a prediction to no avail for the past several editions). It is unlikely, however, that any such resolution will address all of the problems posed by subjecting agency statutory interpretation to hard look review.

GARY LAWSON, RECONCEPTUALIZING *CHEVRON* AND DISCRETION: A COMMENT ON LEVIN AND RUBIN

72 Chicago-Kent L. Rev. 1377 (1997).

* * * [O]ne critical problem * * * faces all of us who insist—whether we rely on *Chevron*, section 706(2)(A) of the APA, or both—that agencies must explain and justify their choices among permissible interpretations of ambiguous statutes. Under Professor Levin's formulation, an agency survives step one of *Chevron* if its interpretation is a reasonable reading of the statute, taking into consideration all factors that legitimately enter into the interpretative process. Step two then applies traditional arbitrary-or-capricious review, which includes the requirement that agencies articulate reasons for exercising their discretion in one way rather than another. In the *Chevron* context, this would require agencies to explain why they chose their particular interpretation of an ambiguous statute from among the universe of available choices that would also have passed step one if they had been selected. As Professor Levin puts it, "asking for a reasoned explanation of the agency's choice is precisely what step two is about."

But defining what counts as a "reasoned explanation" for choosing from among a range of permissible interpretations of a statute is a bit more complicated than it seems. Agencies make many important decisions that cannot, in any realistic way, be traced to the statutes that they administer. Nothing in the Occupational Safety and Health Act, for example, tells OSHA how to draw a dose-response curve for toxic substances in the absence of any data concerning low-level exposure. The agency's choice of a curve is a *legislative* choice that must be explained (justified) by reference to efficiency, fairness, administrative convenience, and a host of other considerations that courts accept as legitimate tools of policymaking * * *. The kinds of reasons that courts generally accept as legitimate for agency policy choices are not necessarily the kinds of reasons that courts should accept for agency interpretations of statutes. Instead, agencies should have to justify their choices of statutory interpretations, in the first instance, by reference to theories of statutory interpretation.

An example * * * illustrates the point. The substantial evidence test for factfinding gives considerable deference to agencies; courts are obliged to affirm agency decisions even when the court thinks, on balance, that the agency is wrong. But the substantial evidence test is a standard of proof for appellate courts to apply on review; it is not the standard of proof that the agency should be expected to employ in its initial decision. It would not be proper for an agency to say, "We think that the facts, on balance, support a decision for X. But we have policy reasons for wanting Y to win, and although the weight of the evidence supports X, there is enough in the record on Y's behalf to survive substantial evidence review. Accordingly, we will rule in favor of Y." Agencies may in fact do this all the time, but it is not a proper exercise of agency authority. Standards of appellate review are deferential for reasons of efficiency, economy, and fairness. They presuppose that there has already been a full and fair opportunity for the parties to win before a previous tribunal. It would be a perversion of those standards of review to allow the initial decisionmakers to treat them as licenses to reach, with legitimacy (as opposed to impunity), any results that will survive appellate review. If a reviewing court knows that an agency deliberately let the weaker factual argument defeat the stronger, even if the weaker argument survives the substantial evidence test, the agency decision should be reversed as arbitrary or capricious.

The same principles hold true when agencies are interpreting statutes. *Chevron* instructs courts to give agencies some leeway by affirming interpretations that the courts think are wrong but not too egregiously wrong. That does not, however, relieve the agencies of their obligation to try to get the right answer in the first instance. An agency does not do its job simply by concluding that an interpretation that it favors on policy grounds will survive *Chevron* step one review on appeal. The agency must conclude that its chosen interpretation is, all things considered (and policy concerns may be part of that mixture), the best available interpretation of the relevant statute. Accordingly, when an agency explains why it chose a particular interpretation of a statute, the first reasons out of its mouth should be framed in terms of conventional criteria of statutory interpretation. Traditional arbitrary-or-capricious review, framed in the language of policymaking, will be applicable only if (and this will sometimes happen) traditional tools of statutory interpretation do not yield even a best resolution to the question of statutory meaning. Professor Levin's step two and traditional arbitrary-or-capricious review therefore merge only when there is a "false-*Chevron*" issue: that is, where at first glance the statute seems to say something meaningful about the problem, but on further inquiry, the problem turns out to be one of pure policymaking.

In order to make the scheme of review favored by Professor Levin (and by me) work, courts must therefore ensure that agencies have made a good-faith effort to interpret statutes correctly. (The agencies in fact have an obligation to do their very best to interpret statutes correctly, but the deferential standard of review means that appellate courts enforce a somewhat lesser obligation.) That task, however, requires courts to have some idea what a good-faith effort would look like. And that is not as simple a task as it seems.

The embarrassing fact is that our legal system has no governing theory of statutory interpretation * * *.

* * * There is no consensus in our legal system about the appropriate significance or weight to be given to the many considerations that can plausibly be thought relevant to statutory interpretation.

Our legal system has dealt with this problem by burying it very deep beneath the ground. Apart from some occasional outbursts from Justice Scalia, judges say very little about interpretative methodology. And when they do speak, clarity and consistency are not often their hallmarks. Most judicial statutory interpretation takes place without *explicit* articulation of the governing norms of admissibility and significance.

Explicit articulation, however, is the focal point of arbitrary-or-capricious review in the modern administrative state. Professor Levin and I would effectively have courts force agencies to be clear about the considerations that drove their interpretative process. And courts would accordingly have to be clear about their own rules of admissibility and significance for determining statutory meaning—at least to the extent of determining whether the agencies have relied on inadmissible considerations or have clearly assigned an inappropriate weight to admissible evidence of statutory meaning.

Perhaps it would be good for the legal system to bring these issues out into the open. Maybe we need some explicit judicial articulation of the rules of evidence for proving statutory meaning. Then again, considering the likely outcome of such a process, maybe the whole matter is best left buried, and Professor Levin and I should both just shut up about *Chevron*.

NOTES

The courts do not always conform to what your editor regards as best practices by requiring agency statutory interpretations to be justified by reference to theories of statutory interpretation. It is not uncommon for courts to uphold agency interpretations of statutes at step two of *Chevron* solely by reference to the reasonableness of the policy represented by the interpretation. *See, e.g., Animal Legal Defense Fund v. U.S. Dept' of Agriculture*, 789 F.3d 1206, 1223–24 (D.C.Cir.2015). If a statute is so vacuous that it would probably violate the nondelegation doctrine if that doctrine was enforced, is there really any other option?

Nor do agencies always conform to what your editor regards as best practices. Agencies often invoke *Chevron* as a justification for interpreting a statute in a particular way. *See* Kent Barnett & Christopher J. Walker, Chevron *Step Two's Domain*, 93 Notre Dame L. Rev. 1441 (2018). As noted in the article excerpted above, this makes no sense. *Chevron* is a doctrine of judicial review, not a theory of statutory meaning. For an impassioned rant against this prevalent agency practice of misemploying *Chevron* at the stage of initial statutory interpretation, *see* Gary Lawson, *Dirty Dancing—The FDA Stumbles with the* Chevron *Two-Step*, 93 Cornell L. Rev. 927 (2008).

7. CROSSROADS

If one believes that arbitrary or capricious review for policymaking is in any respect different from review under *Chevron*, one must be able to define the proper domain of each standard. Given that many modern statutes say little or nothing of substance, how does one tell whether one is facing a problem of statutory interpretation subject to *Chevron* or a problem of policymaking under hard look review? Put another way, how does one tell a question of law from a question of policy?

Consider, for example, the D.C. Circuit's decision in *Comcast Corp. v. FCC*, 600 F.3d 642 (D.C.Cir.2010). The FCC had sought to regulate Comcast's blocking of certain file-sharing practices by some users that, in Comcast's view, used up too much bandwidth. *See* http://www.msnbc.msn.com/id/21376597/. Comcast maintained that the FCC had no jurisdiction to regulate its network management practices. We saw in *Brand X*, pages 719–725 that the FCC has determined (reasonably in the Court's view) that cable internet service is neither "telecommunications services" nor "cable service" and thus does not fall within the agency's direct regulatory authority. The FCC, however, argued that it could regulate Comcast's actions under § 4(i) of the Communications Act of 1934, which authorizes the Commission to "perform any and all acts, make such rules and regulations, and issue such orders, not inconsistent with this chapter, as may be necessary in the execution of its functions." 47 U.S.C. § 154(i) (2012). The Commission came up with six different statutory provisions to which it claimed its authority over Comcast was properly "ancillary" (as § 4(i) jurisdiction has come to be described). The D.C. Circuit concluded that regulating the network management practices of an internet service provider was not ancillary to any of the agency's statutory functions. *See* 600 F.3d at 661. The court's opinion made no mention of *Chevron*. Should it have? There is no question that the FCC administers the provisions of the Communications Act. Was the FCC making determinations of law regarding those provisions, in which case *Chevron* would seem to apply, or was it in reality doing something else, such as making policy? What happens when the FCC decides that granting a particular broadcast license will not serve "public convenience, interest, or necessity," 47 U.S.C. § 307 (2012)? Is the agency interpreting a statute? Did the EPA do something materially different, in any significant legal sense, when it said that a "stationary source" of pollution could (or, in previous decisions, could not) include an entire factory with multiple smokestacks?

The Supreme Court may have done the same thing in reverse in *Cuozzo Speed Technologies, LLC v. Lee*, 136 S .Ct. 2131, 195 L.Ed.2d 423 (2016). The Patent Office has general rulemaking authority to implement a program for review of the validity of certain patents, under a provision that gives it power to "prescribe regulations . . . establishing and governing inter partes review under this chapter." 35 U.S.C. § 316(a)(4). The agency used that authority to promulgate a regulation that would give patents challenged under this program their broadest reasonable construction (which makes it easier for challengers to raise questions about the validity of those patents than would a narrower construction of the patents). The Court framed the inquiry in terms of *Chevron:*

> We interpret Congress' grant of rulemaking authority in light of our decision in *Chevron*. Where a statute is clear, the agency must follow the statute. But where a statute leaves a "gap" or is "ambigu[ous]," we typically interpret it as granting the agency leeway to enact rules that are reasonable in light of the text, nature, and purpose of the statute. The statute contains such a gap: No statutory provision unambiguously directs the agency to use one standard or the other * * *. Indeed, the statute allows the Patent Office to issue rules "governing inter partes review," § 316(a)(4), and the broadest reasonable construction regulation is a rule that governs inter partes review.

Id. at 2142. Was the agency really "interpreting" its general rulemaking provision? (If so, which words in that provision was it interpreting?) Or was it just making policy under a straightforward delegation of lawmaking authority? The Court's analysis, as opposed to its framing of the issue, suggests the latter, *see id.* at 2144–46, as Justice Thomas pointed out in concurrence:

> The Court invokes *Chevron* * * * to resolve one of the questions presented in this case. But today's decision does not rest on *Chevron's* fiction that ambiguity in a statutory term is best construed as an implicit delegation of power to an administrative agency to determine the bounds of the law * * *. [B]y asking whether the Patent Office's preferred rule is reasonable, the Court effectively asks whether the rulemaking was "arbitrary, capricious, an abuse of discretion, or otherwise not in accordance with law," in conformity with the Administrative Procedure Act, 5 U.S.C. § 706(2)(A). I therefore join the Court's opinion in full.

Id. at 2148 (Thomas, J., concurring).

Over a very large range of cases, the distinction between questions of law and questions of policy is difficult or impossible to maintain—which is no doubt why modern courts often sweep the problem under the rug by announcing that the standards of review "overlap," so that disposition of a *Chevron* claim also disposes of an arbitrary or capricious claim with respect to the same agency action (and vice versa). *See, e.g., Nat'l Ass'n of Broadcasters v. FCC*, 789 F.3d 165, 176 (D.C.Cir.2015) ("We thus reject petitioners' argument that the Commission's decision * * * amounts to an unreasonable interpretation of the Spectrum Act at *Chevron* step two. Our analysis also suffices to dispense of petitioners' arbitrary-and-capricious arguments to the same effect."). Indeed, a meta-problem with the entire scheme of administrative review is that it assumes a distinction among questions of fact, questions of law, and questions of policy that is very difficult to articulate. The problem is not unique to administrative law, and one could spend a good portion of an introductory course on jurisprudence exploring it. Suffice it for now to say that most of the time, the proper characterization of questions seems obvious, so that no one spends time arguing about it, and when that is not the case, there is no clear theoretical (or practical) methodology for classifying issues without controversy. Indeed, even the distinction between fact and policy, which seems clear in the abstract, can cause difficulties and splinter courts.

NLRB v. CURTIN MATHESON SCIENTIFIC, INC.

Supreme Court of the United States, 1990.
494 U.S. 775, 110 S.Ct. 1542, 108 L.Ed.2d 801.

JUSTICE MARSHALL delivered the opinion of the Court.

This case presents the question whether the National Labor Relations Board (NLRB or Board), in evaluating an employer's claim that it had a reasonable basis for doubting a union's majority support, *must* presume that striker replacements oppose the union. We hold that the Board acted within its discretion in refusing to adopt a presumption of replacement opposition to the union and therefore reverse the judgment of the Court of Appeals.

I

Upon certification by the NLRB as the exclusive bargaining agent for a unit of employees, a union enjoys an irrebuttable presumption of majority support for one year. During that time, an employer's refusal to bargain with the union is *per se* an unfair labor practice under §§ 8(a)(1) and 8(a)(5) of the National Labor Relations Act (NLRA), 29 U.S.C. §§ 158(a)(1), 158(a)(5). After the first year, the presumption continues but is rebuttable. Under the Board's longstanding approach, an employer may rebut that presumption by showing that, at the time of the refusal to bargain, either (1) the union did not *in fact* enjoy majority support, or (2) the employer had a "good-faith" doubt, founded on a sufficient objective basis, of the union's majority support. *Station KKHI*, 284 N.L.R.B. 1339 (1987), enf'd, 891 F.2d 230 (CA9 1989). The question presented in this case is whether the Board must, in determining whether an employer has presented sufficient objective evidence of a good-faith doubt, presume that striker replacements oppose the union.[2]

---

[2]   JUSTICE SCALIA's assertion [in dissent] that the question presented is whether "substantial evidence" supported the Board's "factual finding" that a good-faith doubt was not established in this case misconstrues the issue. The question on which we granted the Board's petition for certiorari is whether, in *assessing* whether a particular employer possessed a good-faith doubt, the Board must adopt a general presumption of replacement opposition to the union. See Pet. for Cert. I. Whether the Board permissibly refused to adopt a general presumption applicable to all cases of this type is not an evidentiary question concerning the facts of this particular case. The substantial evidence standard is therefore inapplicable to the issue before us. Rather, we must determine whether the Board's refusal to adopt the presumption is rational and consistent with

The Board has long presumed that new employees hired in nonstrike circumstances support the incumbent union in the same proportion as the employees they replace. The Board's approach to evaluating the union sentiments of employees hired to replace strikers, however, has not been so consistent. Initially, the Board appeared to assume that replacements did not support the union.

A 1974 decision * * * held that "it was not unreasonable for [the employer] to infer that the degree of union support among these employees who had chosen to ignore a Union-sponsored picket line might well be somewhat weaker than the support offered by those who had vigorously engaged in concerted activity on behalf on [sic] Union-sponsored objectives." *Ibid.*

A year later, in *Cutten Supermarket*, 220 N.L.R.B. 507 (1975), the Board reversed course completely, stating that striker replacements, like new employees generally, are presumed to *support* the union in the same ratio as the strikers they replaced * * *.

In 1987, after several Courts of Appeals rejected the Board's approach, the Board determined that no universal generalizations could be made about replacements' union sentiments that would justify a presumption either of support for or of opposition to the union. *Station KKHI*, 284 N.L.R.B. 1339 (1987). On the one hand, the Board found that the prounion presumption lacked empirical foundation because "incumbent unions and strikers sometimes have shown hostility toward the permanent replacements," and "replacements are typically aware of the union's primary concern for the striker's welfare, rather than that of the replacements." *Id.* at 1344. On the other hand, the Board found that an antiunion presumption was "equally unsupportable" factually. *Ibid.* The Board observed that a striker replacement "may be forced to work for financial reasons, or may disapprove of the strike in question but still desire union representation and would support other union initiatives." *Ibid.* Moreover, the Board found as a matter of policy that adoption of an antiunion presumption would "substantially impair the employees' right to strike by adding to the risk of replacement the risk of loss of the bargaining representative as soon as replacements equal in number to the strikers are willing to cross the picket line." *Ibid.* Accordingly, the Board held that it would not apply any presumption regarding striker replacements' union sentiments, but would determine their views on a case-by-case basis.

II

We now turn to the Board's application of its *Station KKHI* no-presumption approach in this case. Respondent Curtin Matheson

---

the Act. Whether substantial evidence supports the Board's finding that respondent did not possess an objectively reasonable doubt is a question for the Court of Appeals to consider, without applying any presumption about replacements' views, on remand.

Scientific, Inc., buys and sells laboratory instruments and supplies. In 1970, the Board certified Teamsters Local 968, General Drivers, Warehousemen and Helpers (hereinafter Union) as the collective-bargaining agent for respondent's production and maintenance employees. On May 21, 1979, the most recent bargaining agreement between respondent and the Union expired. Respondent made its final offer for a new agreement on May 25, but the Union rejected that offer. Respondent then locked out the 27 bargaining-unit employees. On June 12, respondent renewed its May 25 offer, but the Union again rejected it. The Union then commenced an economic strike. The record contains no evidence of any strike-related violence or threats of violence.

Five employees immediately crossed the picket line and reported for work. On June 25, while the strike was still in effect, respondent hired 29 permanent replacement employees to replace the 22 strikers. The Union ended its strike on July 16, offering to accept unconditionally respondent's May 25 contract offer. On July 20, respondent informed the Union that the May 25 offer was no longer available. In addition, respondent withdrew recognition from the Union and refused to bargain further, stating that it doubted that the Union was supported by a majority of the employees in the unit. Respondent subsequently refused to provide the Union with information it had requested concerning the total number of bargaining-unit employees on the payroll, and the job classification and seniority of each employee. As of July 20, the bargaining unit consisted of 19 strikers, 25 permanent replacements, and the 5 employees who had crossed the picket line at the strike's inception.

On July 30, the Union filed an unfair labor practice charge with the Board. Following an investigation, the General Counsel issued a complaint, * * *. In its defense to the charge, respondent claimed that it had a reasonably based, good-faith doubt of the Union's majority status. The Administrative Law Judge agreed with respondent and dismissed the complaint. The Board, however, reversed, holding that respondent lacked sufficient objective basis to doubt the Union's majority support. 287 N.L.R.B. 350 (1987).

* * *

* * * [R]egarding respondent's hiring of striker replacements, the Board stated that, in accordance with the *Station KKHI* approach, it would "not use any presumptions with respect to [the replacements'] union sentiments," but would instead "take a case-by-case approach [and] require additional evidence of a lack of union support on the replacements' part in evaluating the significance of this factor in the employer's showing of good-faith doubt." 287 N.L.R.B., at 352. The Board noted that respondent's only evidence of the replacements' attitudes toward the Union was its employee relations director's account of a conversation with one of the replacements.

The replacement employee reportedly told her that he had worked in union and nonunion workplaces and did not see any need for a union as long as the company treated him well; in addition, he said that he did not think the Union in this case represented the employees. The Board did not determine whether this statement indicated the replacement employee's repudiation of the Union, but found that the statement was, in any event, an insufficient basis for "inferring the union sentiments of the replacement employees as a group." 287 N.L.R.B., at 353.

The Board therefore concluded that "the evidence [was] insufficient to rebut the presumption of the Union's continuing majority status." *Ibid.* Accordingly, the Board held that respondent had violated §§ 8(a)(1) and 8(a)(5) by withdrawing recognition from the Union, failing to furnish the requested information, and refusing to execute a contract embodying the terms respondent had offered on May 25, 1979. The Board ordered respondent to bargain with the Union on request, provide the requisite information, execute an agreement, and make the bargaining-unit employees whole for whatever losses they had suffered from respondent's failure to execute a contract.

The Court of Appeals, in a divided opinion, refused to enforce the Board's order, holding that respondent was justified in doubting the Union's majority support * * *.

III

A

This Court has emphasized often that the NLRB has the primary responsibility for developing and applying national labor policy * * *. This Court therefore has accorded Board rules considerable deference. We will uphold a Board rule as long as it is rational and consistent with the Act, even if we would have formulated a different rule had we sat on the Board. Furthermore, a Board rule is entitled to deference even if it represents a departure from the Board's prior policy. See *NLRB v. J. Weingarten, Inc.*, 420 U.S. 251, 265–66, 95 S.Ct. 959, 967–68, 43 L.Ed.2d 171 (1975) ("The use by an administrative agency of the evolutional approach is particularly fitting. To hold that the Board's earlier decisions froze the development of this important aspect of the national labor law would misconceive the nature of administrative decisionmaking").

B

* * * [T]he starting point for the Board's analysis is the basic presumption that the union is supported by a majority of bargaining-unit employees. The employer bears the burden of rebutting that presumption, after the certification year, either by showing that the union in fact lacks majority support or by demonstrating a sufficient objective basis for doubting the union's majority status. Respondent here urges that in

evaluating an employer's claim of a good-faith doubt, the Board must adopt a second, subsidiary presumption-that replacement employees oppose the union. Under this approach, if a majority of employees in the bargaining unit were striker replacements, the employer would not need to offer *any* objective evidence of the employees' union sentiments to rebut the presumption of the union's continuing majority status. The presumption of the replacements' opposition to the union would, in effect, override the presumption of continuing majority status. In contrast, under its no-presumption approach, the Board "take[s] into account the particular circumstances surrounding each strike and the hiring of replacements, while retaining the long-standing requirement that the employer must come forth with some objective evidence to substantiate his doubt of continuing majority status."

C

We find the Board's no-presumption approach rational as an empirical matter * * *. Although replacements often may not favor the incumbent union, the Board reasonably concluded, in light of its long experience in addressing these issues, that replacements may in some circumstances desire union representation despite their willingness to cross the picket line. Economic concerns, for instance, may force a replacement employee to work for a struck employer even though he otherwise supports the union and wants the benefits of union representation. In this sense the replacement worker is no different from a striker who, feeling the financial heat of the strike on himself and his family, is forced to abandon the picket line and go back to work. In addition, a replacement, like a nonstriker or a strike crossover, may disagree with the purpose or strategy of the particular strike and refuse to support that strike, while still wanting that union's representation at the bargaining table.

Respondent insists that the interests of strikers and replacements are diametrically opposed and that unions inevitably side with the strikers. For instance, respondent argues, picket-line violence often stems directly from the hiring of replacements. Furthermore, unions often negotiate with employers for strike settlements that would return the strikers to their jobs, thereby displacing some or all of the replacements. Respondent asserts that replacements, aware of the union's loyalty to the strikers, most likely would not support the union. See, *e.g., Leveld Wholesale, Inc.*, 218 N.L.R.B. 1344, 1350 (1975) ("Strike replacements can reasonably foresee that, if the union is successful, the strikers will return to work and the strike replacements will be out of a job"). In a related argument, respondent contends that the Board's no-presumption approach is irreconcilable with the Board's decisions holding that employers have no duty to bargain with a striking union over replacements' employment terms because the "inherent conflict" between strikers and replacements renders the union incapable of "bargain[ing] simultaneously in the best interests of both strikers and their replacements." *Service Electric Co.*, 281 N.L.R.B. 633, 641 (1986); see also *Leveld Wholesale, supra*, at 1350.

These arguments do not persuade us that the Board's position is irrational. Unions do not inevitably demand displacement of all strike replacements * * *. The extent to which a union demands displacement of permanent replacement workers logically will depend on the union's bargaining power * * *. [A]n employer is not required to discharge permanent replacements at the conclusion of an economic strike to make room for returning strikers; rather, the employer must only reinstate strikers as vacancies arise. The strikers' only chance for immediate reinstatement, then, lies in the union's ability to force the employer to discharge the replacements as a condition for the union's ending the strike. Unions' leverage to compel such a strike settlement will vary greatly from strike to strike * * *. A union with little bargaining leverage is unlikely to press the employer-at least not very forcefully or for very long-to discharge the replacements and reinstate all the strikers. Cognizant of the union's weak position, many if not all of the replacements justifiably may not fear that they will lose their jobs at the end of the strike. They may still want that union's representation after the strike, though, despite the union's lack of bargaining strength during the strike, because of the union's role in processing grievances, monitoring the employer's actions, and performing other nonstrike roles. Because the circumstances of each strike and the leverage of each union will vary greatly, it was not irrational for the Board to reject the antiunion presumption and adopt a case-by-case approach in determining replacements' union sentiments.

Moreover, even if the interests of strikers and replacements conflict *during* the strike, those interests may converge *after* the strike, once job rights have been resolved. Thus, while the strike continues, a replacement worker whose job appears relatively secure might well want the union to continue to represent the unit regardless of the union's bargaining posture during the strike. Surely replacement workers are capable of looking past the strike in considering whether or not they desire representation by the union. For these reasons, the Board's refusal to adopt an antiunion presumption is not irreconcilable with its position in *Service Electric, supra,* and *Leveld Wholesale,* 218 N.L.R.A. 1344 (1975), regarding an employer's obligation to bargain with a striking union over replacements' employment terms.

* * *

In sum, the Board recognized that the circumstances surrounding each strike and replacements' reasons for crossing a picket line vary greatly. Even if replacements often do not support the union, then, it was not irrational for the Board to conclude that the probability of replacement opposition to the union is insufficient to justify an antiunion presumption.

D

The Board's refusal to adopt an antiunion presumption is also consistent with the Act's "overriding policy" of achieving "'industrial peace.'" [T]he presumption of continuing majority support for a union "further[s] this policy by 'promot[ing] stability in collective-bargaining relationships, without impairing the free choice of employees.'" 482 U.S. at 38, 107 S.Ct. at 2233 * * *.

Furthermore, it was reasonable for the Board to decide that the antiunion presumption might chill employees' exercise of their statutory right to engage in "concerted activities," including the right to strike. If an employer could remove a union merely by hiring a sufficient number of replacements, employees considering a strike would face not only the prospect of being permanently replaced, but also a greater risk that they would lose their bargaining representative, thereby diminishing their chance of obtaining reinstatement through a strike settlement * * *.[13]

* * *

IV

We hold that the Board's refusal to adopt a presumption that striker replacements oppose the Union is rational and consistent with the Act. We therefore reverse the judgment of the Court of Appeals and remand for further proceedings consistent with this opinion.

It is so ordered.

CHIEF JUSTICE REHNQUIST, concurring.

The Board's "no-presumption" rule seems to me to press to the limit the deference to which the Board is entitled in assessing industrial reality, but for the reasons stated in the opinion of the Court I agree that limit is not exceeded. The Court of Appeals did not consider, free from the use of any presumption, whether there was substantial evidence on the record as a whole to support the Board's determination here, and I believe that is a question best left for the Court of Appeals on remand.

* * *

---

[13] JUSTICE SCALIA entirely ignores the Board's policy considerations, apparently on the rationale that policy is an illegitimate factor in the Board's decision. This argument is founded on the premise that the issue before us is the factual question whether substantial evidence supports the Board's finding that respondent lacked a good-faith doubt. As stated earlier, however, the real question is whether the Board must, in assessing the objective reasonableness of an employer's doubt, adopt a particular presumption. Certainly the Board is entitled to consider *both* whether the presumption is factually justified *and* whether that presumption would disserve the Act's policies * * *.

JUSTICE BLACKMUN, dissenting.

I agree with much that JUSTICE SCALIA says in his dissent * * *.

* * *

Perhaps the difference between my approach and that of JUSTICE SCALIA is one only of emphasis, but I think that the difference is worth noting. Rarely will a court feel so certain of the wrongness of an agency's empirical judgment that it will be justified in substituting its own view of the facts. But courts can and should review agency decisionmaking closely to ensure that an agency has adequately explained the bases for its conclusions, that the various components of its policy form an internally consistent whole, and that any apparent contradictions are acknowledged and addressed. This emphasis upon the decisionmaking *process* allows the reviewing court to exercise meaningful control over unelected officials without second-guessing the sort of expert judgments that a court may be ill equipped to make. Such an approach also affords the agency a broad range of discretion. Confronted with a court's conclusion that two of its policy pronouncements are inconsistent, the agency may choose for itself which path to follow, or it may attempt to explain why no contradiction actually exists.

* * * The Board may not assert in one line of cases that the interests of a striking union and replacement workers are irreconcilably in conflict, and proclaim in a different line of decisions that no meaningful generalizations can be made about the union sentiments of the replacement employees. I therefore conclude that the judgment of the Court of Appeals should be affirmed.

I respectfully dissent.

JUSTICE SCALIA, with whom JUSTICE O'CONNOR and JUSTICE KENNEDY join, dissenting.

The Court makes heavy weather out of what is, under well-established principles of administrative law, a straightforward case. The National Labor Relations Board (NLRB or Board) has established as one of the central factual determinations to be made in § 8(a)(5) unfair-labor-practice adjudications, whether the employer had a reasonable, good-faith doubt concerning the majority status of the union at the time it requested to bargain. The Board held in the present case that such a doubt was not established by a record showing that at the time of the union's request a majority of the bargaining unit were strike replacements, and containing no affirmative evidence that any of those replacements supported the union. The question presented is whether that factual finding is supported by substantial evidence. Since the principal employment-related interest of strike replacements (to retain their jobs) is almost invariably opposed to the principal interest of the striking union (to replace them with its striking members) it seems to me impossible to conclude on this record that the employer did not have a reasonable, good-faith doubt regarding the union's majority status. The Board's factual finding being unsupported by substantial evidence, it cannot stand * * *.

I

* * *

II

* * *

The Board's factual finding challenged in the present case is that there was no " 'sufficient objective basis for a reasonable doubt of the union's majority status at the time of the employer refused to bargain.' " 287 N.L.R.B., at 352 * * *. The precise question presented is whether there was substantial evidence to support this factual finding. There plainly was not.

* * * [O]f the 49 employees in the bargaining unit at the time of respondent's refusal to bargain, a majority (25) were strike replacements, and another 5 were former employees who had crossed the union's picket line. It may well be doubtful whether the latter group could be thought to support the union, but it suffices to focus upon the 25 strike replacements, who must be thought to oppose the union if the Board's own policies are to be believed. There was a deep and inherent conflict between the interests of these employees and the interests of the union. As the Board's cases have explained:

> "Strike replacements can reasonably foresee that, if the union is successful, the strikers will return to work and the strike replacements will be out of a job. It is understandable that unions do not look with favor on persons who cross their picket lines and perform the work of strikers." *Leveld Wholesale, Inc.*, 218 N.L.R.B. 1344, 1350 (1975).

> "The Union had been bargaining agent for those discharged employees and there can be no question that the Union's loyalty lay with these employees. The interests of the discharged employees were diametrically opposed to those of the strike replacements. If the discharged employees returned to work, the strike replacements would lose their jobs." *Beacon Upholstery Co.*, 226 N.L.R.B. 1360, 1368 (1976) (footnote omitted).

The Board relies upon this reality of "diametrically opposed" interests as the basis for two of its rules: First, that an employer does not commit an unfair labor practice by refusing to negotiate with the incumbent union regarding the terms and conditions of the replacements' employment. See *Service Electric Co.*, 281 N.L.R.B. 633, 641 (1986). Second, that the union's duty of fair representation does not require it to negotiate in the best interests of the strike replacements regarding the terms and conditions of their employment-in other words, that the union may propose "negotiations leading to replacements being terminated to make way for returning strikers," *ibid.*

The respondent in this case, therefore, had an employee bargaining unit a majority of whose members (1) were not entitled to have their best interests considered by the complainant union, (2) would have been foolish to *expect* their best interests to be considered by that union, and indeed (3) in light of their status as breakers of that union's strike, would have been foolish not to expect their best interests to be subverted by that union wherever possible. There was, moreover, not a shred of affirmative evidence that any strike replacement supported, or had reason to support, the union. On those facts, any reasonable factfinder must conclude that the respondent possessed, not necessarily a certainty, but at least a reasonable, good-faith doubt, that the union did not have majority support * * *.

In making its no-reasonable-doubt finding, the Board relied upon its decision in *Station KKHI,* which stated:

> "[T]he hiring of permanent replacements who cross a picket line, in itself, does not support an inference that the replacements repudiate the union as collective-bargaining representative. . . In this regard, an employee may be forced to work for financial reasons, or may disapprove of the strike in question but still desire union representation and would support other union initiatives. The presumption of union disfavor is therefore not factually compelling." 284 N.L.R.B. at 1344).

The Court finds this reasoning persuasive: "Economic concerns, for instance, may force a replacement employee to work for a struck employer even though he otherwise supports the union and wants the benefits of union representation." *Ante,* at 1550. These responses are entirely inadequate. The question is not whether replacement employees accept employment for economic reasons. Undoubtedly they do-the same economic reasons that would lead them to oppose the union that will likely seek to terminate their employment. Nor is the question whether replacements would like to be represented by *a* union. Some perhaps would. But what the employer is required to have a good-faith doubt about is majority support, not for "union representation" in the abstract, but for representation *by this particular complainant union, at the time the employer withdrew recognition from the union.*

* * *

The Court mentions only as an afterthought the fundamental conflict of interests that is at the center of this case:

"Moreover, even if the interests of strikers and replacements conflict *during* the strike, those interests may converge *after* the strike, once job rights have been resolved. Thus, while the strike continues, a replacement worker whose job appears relatively secure might well want the union to continue to represent the unit regardless of the union's bargaining posture during the strike." *Ante,* at 1552 (emphasis in original).

The trouble with this is that it posits a species of replacement worker that will rarely exist unless and until the union has agreed (as it had not in this case) to accept the replacements' employment status-*i.e.,* until "job rights have been resolved." How can there be "a replacement worker whose job appears relatively secure" when the employer agrees to negotiate in good faith with a union that will surely seek the reinstatement of all its strikers? * * *

The Court's only response to this is that the union's ability to achieve displacement of the strike replacements will depend upon its bargaining power. Its bargaining power could conceivably be so weak, and a strike replacement might conceivably so prefer *this* union over other alternatives, that he would be willing to take the chance that the union will try to oust him. *Ibid.* I suppose so. It might also be that one of the strike replacements hopes the union will continue as the bargaining representative because, as the employer knows, the union president is his son-in-law. The Board Counsel is entirely free to introduce such special circumstances. But unless they appear in the record, the reasonableness of the employer's doubt must be determined on the basis of how a reasonable person would assess the probabilities-and it is overwhelmingly improbable that a strikebreaking replacement so much prefers the incumbent union to some other union, or to no union at all, that he will bet his job the union is not strong enough to replace him. The wager is particularly bad because it is so unnecessary, since he and his fellow replacements could achieve the same objective, without risking their jobs in the least, by simply voting for that union, after the strike is over, in a new certification election.

I reiterate that the burden upon the employer here was not to demonstrate 100% assurance that a majority of the bargaining unit did not support the union, but merely "reasonable doubt" that they did so. It seems to me absurd to deny that it sustained that burden.

III

The Court never directly addresses the question whether there was substantial evidence to support the Board's conclusion that respondent had not established a reasonable good-faith doubt of the union's majority status. Indeed, it asserts that that question is not even at issue, since "[t]he question on which we granted the Board's petition for certiorari is whether, in *assessing* whether a particular employer possessed a good-faith doubt, the Board must adopt a general presumption of replacement opposition to the union." *Ante,* at 1545, n. 2. That is the equivalent of characterizing the appeal of a criminal conviction, in which the defendant asserts that the indictment should have been dismissed because all the evidence demonstrated that he was not at the scene of the crime, as involving, not the adequacy of the evidence, but rather the question whether the jury was required to adopt the general presumption that a person cannot be in two places at the same time. No more in administrative law than in criminal law is the underlying question altered by characterizing factual probabilities as presumptions * * *. The Board's framing of the question presented, like its opinion in this case, invites us to confuse factfinding with policymaking. The Court should not so readily have accepted the invitation.

* * *

It is the proper business of the Board, as of most agencies, to deal in both presumptions (*i.e.,* presumptions of law) and inferences (presumptions of fact). The former it may create and apply *in the teeth of the facts,* as means of implementing authorized law or policy in the course of adjudication. An example is the virtually irrebuttable presumption of majority support for the union during the year following the union's certification by the Board. The latter, however—inferences (or presumptions of fact)—are not creatures of the Board but its masters, representing the dictates of reason and logic that must be applied in making adjudicatory factual determinations. Whenever an agency's action is reversed in court for lack of "substantial evidence," the reason is that the agency has ignored inferences that reasonably must be drawn, or has drawn inferences that reasonably cannot be. As I have discussed above, that is what happened here.

Of course the Board may choose to implement authorized law or policy in adjudication by *forbidding* a *rational* inference, just as it may do so by *requiring* a *nonrational* one (which is what a presumption of law is). And perhaps it could lawfully have reached the outcome it did here in that fashion-saying that *even though* it must reasonably be inferred that an employer has good-faith doubt of majority status when more than half of the bargaining unit are strike replacements whose job rights have not been resolved, we will not permit that inference to be made. (This would produce an effect close to a rule of law eliminating the good-faith doubt defense except for cases in which the employer can demonstrate, by employee statements, lack of support for the union.) But that is not what the agency did here. It relied on the reasoning of *Station KKHI,* which rested upon the conclusion that, *as a matter of logic and reasoning,* "the hiring of permanent replacements who cross a picket line, in itself, does not support an inference that the replacements repudiate the union as collective-bargaining representative." *Id.,* at 1344. That is simply false. It is bad factfinding, and must be reversed under the "substantial evidence" test.

* * *

NOTES

The line between fact and policy was also blurry, and badly split the en banc Ninth Circuit, in *Organized Village of Kake v. U.S. Dep't of Agriculture*, 795 F.3d 956 (9th Cir.2015). In early 2001, as the Clinton Administration was leaving office, the Department of Agriculture prohibited timber harvesting and road construction in so-called "roadless" national forest lands. *See Special Areas; Roadless Area Conservation*, 66 Fed. Reg. 3244 (2001). The agency specifically declined to exempt the Tongass National Forest in Alaska from this rule, notwithstanding the significant economic impact that would result from application of the rule, saying that such an exemption would "risk the loss of important roadless area values," *id.* at 3254, and that "[i]mportant roadless area values would be lost or diminished." *Id.* at 3266. Two years later, after a change in presidential administrations, the agency changed its mind and exempted Tongass from the "roadless rule." *See Special Areas; Roadless Conservation; Applicability to the Tongass National Forest, Alaska*, 68 Fed. Reg. 75,136 (2003). The agency in its 2003 Record of Decision (ROD) did not conduct any new environmental analyses; it explicitly said that it was acting on essentially the same information that was available in 2001. *See id.* at 75,141 ("the overall decisionmaking picture is not substantially different from what it was in November 2000"). Rather, the agency claimed that it was reconsidering the balance between economic and environmental concerns:

> The agency also recognized the unique situation on the Tongass during the development of the roadless rule, and proposed treating the Tongass differently from other national forests until the final rule was adopted in January 2001. At that time, the Department decided that ensuring lasting protection of roadless values on the Tongass outweighed the attendant socioeconomic losses to local communities. The Department now believes that, considered together, the abundance of roadless values on the Tongass, the protection of roadless values included in the Tongass Forest Plan, and the socioeconomic costs to local communities of applying the roadless rule's prohibitions to the Tongass, all warrant treating the Tongass differently from the national forests outside of Alaska.

Id. at 75,139.

A majority of the en banc Ninth Circuit concluded that the agency had not adequately explained its rejection of what the court characterized as factual findings from its 2001 decision:

> We do not question that the Department was entitled in 2003 to give more weight to socioeconomic concerns than it had in 2001, even on precisely the same record * * *. There was a change in presidential administrations just days after the Roadless Rule was promulgated in 2001. Elections have policy consequences. But, *State Farm* teaches

that even when reversing a policy after an election, an agency may not simply discard prior factual findings without a reasoned explanation.

That is precisely what happened here. The 2003 ROD did not simply rebalance old facts to arrive at the new policy. Rather, it made factual findings directly contrary to the 2001 ROD and expressly relied on those findings to justify the policy change. The 2001 ROD explicitly found that wholly exempting the Tongass from the Roadless Rule and returning it to management under the Tongass Forest Plan "would risk the loss of important roadless area values," 66 Fed. Reg. at 3254, and that roadless values would be "lost or diminished" even by a limited exemption, *id.* at 3266. The 2003 ROD found in direct contradiction that the Roadless Rule was "unnecessary to maintain the roadless values," 68 Fed. Reg. at 75,137, and "the roadless values in the Tongass are sufficiently protected under the Tongass Forest Plan," *id.* at 75,138.

There can be no doubt that the 2003 finding was a critical underpinning of the Tongass Exemption. The 2003 ROD states that "[t]he Department has concluded that the social and economic hardships to Southeast Alaska outweigh the potential long-term ecological benefits *because* the Tongass Forest Plan adequately provides for the ecological sustainability of the Tongass." *Id.* at 75,141–42 (emphasis added). The 2003 ROD also makes plain that "[t]his decision reflects the facts . . . that roadless values are plentiful on the Tongass and are well protected by the Tongass Forest Plan. The minor risk of the loss of such values is outweighed by the by the more certain socioeconomic costs of applying the roadless rule's prohibitions to the Tongass." *Id.* at 75,144.

Thus, contrary to the contentions of both Alaska and dissenting colleagues, this is not a case in which the Department—or a new Executive—merely decided that it valued socioeconomic concerns more highly than environmental protection. Rather, the 2003 ROD rests on the express finding that the Tongass Forest Plan poses only "minor" risks to roadless values; this is a direct, and entirely unexplained, contradiction of the Department's finding in the 2001 ROD that continued forest management under precisely the same plan was unacceptable because it posed a high risk to the "extraordinary ecological values of the Tongass." 66 Fed. Reg. at 3254 * * *. The Department was required to provide a "reasoned explanation. . . for disregarding" the "facts and circumstances" that underlay its previous decision. It did not.

795 F.3d at 968. The five dissenting judges characterized the case quite differently.

This case involves a clash between the policies of the outgoing Clinton administration and those of the incoming George W. Bush administration. The two presidents viewed how certain aspects of the laws governing national forests should be implemented very differently * * *.

* * *

Without acknowledging that the factual findings in the 2003 Record of Decision (ROD) rest on different policy views than those in the 2001 ROD, the majority argues that "[t]he Tongass Exemption thus plainly 'rests upon factual findings that contradict those which underlay [the agency's] prior policy.'" This conclusion is simply incorrect. The agency, following the policy instructions of the new president, weighed some of the facts in the existing record differently than had the previous administration, and emphasized other facts in the record that the previous administration had not. Stated differently, the two administrations looked at some of the same facts, and reached different conclusions about the meaning of what they saw. The second administration simply concluded that the facts called for different regulations than those proposed by the previous administration.

There is little dispute that the underlying facts analyzed by the USDA had not changed meaningfully between November 2000, when the USDA completed the original rule's Final Environmental Impact Statement (FEIS), and 2003 * * *.

Nor had the facts underlying the USDA's assessment of the socioeconomic impact of the Tongass Exemption changed meaningfully by 2003; the USDA simply prioritized different aspects of the same socioeconomic data that it had considered in 2000. In the original Roadless Rule, the USDA had found that "[c]ommunities with significant economic activities in these sectors could be adversely impacted. However, the effects on national social and economic systems are minor * * *." 66 Fed.Reg. at 3261. In the 2003 ROD, on the other hand, the USDA assigned greater importance to the adverse socioeconomic impact of the Roadless Rule: "This decision reflects the facts * * * that roadless values are plentiful in the Tongass and are well protected by the Tongass Forest Plan. The minor risk of the loss of such values is outweighed by the more certain socioeconomic costs of applying the roadless rule's prohibitions to the Tongass. Imposing those costs on the local communities of Southeast Alaska is unwarranted." 68 Fed.Reg. at 75,144. In 2003, then, the USDA concluded that it was important to give greater weight to *some* adverse socioeconomic effects than was done when the original Roadless Rule was promulgated.

Given the substantial similarity between the facts the USDA weighed in the 2003 ROD and those it weighed in the 2001 ROD, it is abundantly clear that the differences between the two are the result of a shift in policy. After analyzing essentially the same facts, the

USDA changed policy course at the direction of the new president, prioritizing some outcomes over others.

795 F.3d at 980–982. Was the agency in 2003 finding new facts, making new policy, or both? What kind of explanation was the agency obliged to give?

8. ABUSE OF DISCRETION

Hard look review is, or at least can be, a vigorous form of judicial review. In terms of the intensity of review, it is certainly no more, and probably a good deal less, deferential than the substantial evidence standard. Courts are generally quite exacting in their demands for reasoned explanations, and they are often quite skillful at detecting flaws in agency presentations. *See, e.g., Business Roundtable v. SEC*, 647 F.3d 1144 (D.C.Cir.2011).

That does not mean, however, that every application of the arbitrary or capricious standard is equally intense. Hard look review is a species of arbitrary or capricious review that developed as a means of controlling agency policymaking discretion. There are many agency decisions involving discretion that do not involve significant questions of legislative policy, such as how to allocate agency resources, whether to reopen closed proceedings because of new evidence or changed circumstances, or whether to initiate a rulemaking. For the most part, these discretionary decisions are reviewed (if at all) on a highly deferential basis that fairly closely approximates the APA's original understanding of the phrase "arbitrary, capricious, an abuse of discretion, or otherwise not in accordance with law." *See, e.g., ICC v. Brotherhood of Locomotive Engineers*, 482 U.S. 270, 278, 107 S.Ct. 2360, 2365, 96 L.Ed.2d 222 (1987) (stating that courts should overturn an agency's refusal to reopen a proceeding only upon a showing of the "clearest abuse of discretion"); *WWHT, Inc. v. FCC*, 656 F.2d 807, 809 (D.C.Cir.1981) ("[T]he decision to institute rulemaking is one that is largely committed to the discretion of the agency, and * * * the scope of review of such a determination must, of necessity, be very narrow."). To be sure, the Supreme Court's decision in *Massachusetts v. EPA*, 549 U.S. 547, 127 S.Ct. 1438, 167 L.Ed.2d 248 (2007), reviewed a denial of a petition for rulemaking with uncommon vigor, but that case appears to be a one-off, such that denials of petitions for rulemaking remain " 'at the high end of the range of levels of deference we give to agency action under our arbitrary and capricious review.' " *Electronic Privacy Information Center v. United States Dep't of Homeland Security*, 653 F.3d 1, 5 (D.C.Cir.2011) (quoting *Defenders of Wildlife v. Gutierrez*, 532 F.3d 913, 919 (D.C.Cir.2008)). *See also, e.g., Safari Club Int'l v. Zinke,* 878 F.3d 316, 330–31 (D.C.Cir.2017); *Gulf Restoration Network v. McCarthy,* 783 F.3d 227 (5th Cir.2015); *Wildearth Guardians v. U.S. EPA*, 751 F.3d 649 (D.C.Cir.2014). Accordingly, one must always be exceedingly careful when applying the arbitrary or capricious test to identify the precise agency action that is being challenged. The meaning of the arbitrary or capricious test varies dramatically with the context.

9.   REVIEWING AGENCY INACTION

When an agency denies a petition for rulemaking, it is acting by failing to act, just as happens when an agency refuses to initiate an enforcement proceeding or fails to regulate something within its jurisdiction. At least some of these instances of agency inaction—those that constitute nonenforcement decisions that are analogous to the exercise of prosecutorial discretion—are presumptively unreviewable by courts, as we will see in Chapter 6. *See infra* pages 1038–1055. But the APA, which authorizes judicial review of "final agency action," § 704, specifically defines "agency action" to include "the whole or a part of an agency rule, order, license, sanction, relief, or the equivalent, *or denial thereof, or failure to act.*" *Id.* § 551(13) (emphasis added). Section 706 tells reviewing courts to "compel agency action unlawfully withheld or unreasonably delayed." *Id.* § 706(1). If an agency has a statutory duty to act, courts are instructed to enforce that duty.

The general contours of the judicial role in policing agency inaction were described by the Supreme Court in a unanimous decision in 2004:

> Sections 702, 704, and 706(1) [of the APA] all insist upon an "agency action," either as the action complained of (in §§ 702 and 704) or as the action to be compelled (in § 706(1)). The definition of that term begins with a list of five categories of decisions made or outcomes implemented by an agency—"agency rule, order, license, sanction [or] relief." § 551(13). All of those categories involve circumscribed, discrete agency actions, as their definitions make clear: "an agency statement of . . . future effect designed to implement, interpret, or prescribe law or policy" (rule); "a final disposition . . . in a matter other than rule making" (order); a "permit . . . or other form of permission" (license); a "prohibition . . . or . . . taking [of] other compulsory or restrictive action" (sanction); or a "grant of money, assistance, license, authority," etc., or "recognition of a claim, right, immunity," etc., or "taking of other action on the application or petition of, and beneficial to, a person" (relief). §§ 551(4), (6), (8), (10), (11).

> The terms following those five categories of agency action are not defined in the APA: "or the equivalent or denial thereof, or failure to act." § 551(13). But an "equivalent . . . thereof" must also be discrete (or it would not be equivalent), and a "denial thereof" must be the denial of a discrete listed action (and perhaps denial of a discrete equivalent).

> The final term in the definition, "failure to act," is in our view properly understood as a failure to take an *agency action*—that is, a failure to take one of the agency actions (including their equivalents) earlier defined in § 551(13). Moreover, even without

this equation of "act" with "agency action" the interpretive canon of *ejusdem generis* would attribute to the last item ("failure to act") the same characteristic of discreteness shared by all the preceding items. A "failure to act" is not the same thing as a "denial." The latter is the agency's act of saying no to a request; the former is simply the omission of an action without formally rejecting a request—for example, the failure to promulgate a rule or take some decision by a statutory deadline. The important point is that a "failure to act" is properly understood to be limited, as are the other items in § 551(13), to a *discrete* action.

A second point central to the analysis of the present case is that the only agency action that can be compelled under the APA is action legally *required*. This limitation appears in § 706(1)'s authorization for courts to "compel agency action *unlawfully* withheld." (Emphasis added.) In this regard the APA carried forward the traditional practice prior to its passage, when judicial review was achieved through use of the so-called prerogative writs—principally writs of mandamus under the All Writs Act, now codified at 28 U.S.C. § 1651(a). The mandamus remedy was normally limited to enforcement of "a specific, unequivocal command," *ICC v. New York, N.H. & H.R. Co.,* 287 U.S. 178, 204, 53 S.Ct. 106, 77 L.Ed. 248 (1932), the ordering of a " 'precise, definite act . . . about which [an official] had no discretion whatever,' " *United States ex rel. Dunlap v. Black,* 128 U.S. 40, 46, 9 S.Ct. 12, 32 L.Ed. 354 (1888) (quoting *Kendall v. United States ex rel. Stokes,* 12 Pet. 524, 613, 9 L.Ed. 1181 (1838)) * * *.

Thus, a claim under § 706(1) can proceed only where a plaintiff asserts that an agency failed to take a *discrete* agency action that it is *required to take.* These limitations rule out several kinds of challenges. The limitation to discrete agency action precludes the kind of broad programmatic attack we rejected in *Lujan v. National Wildlife Federation,* 497 U.S. 871, 110 S.Ct. 3177, 111 L.Ed.2d 695 (1990). There we considered a challenge to BLM's land withdrawal review program, couched as unlawful agency "action" that the plaintiffs wished to have "set aside" under § 706(2). We concluded that the program was not an "agency action":

> "[R]espondent cannot seek *wholesale* improvement of this program by court decree, rather than in the offices of the Department or the halls of Congress, where programmatic improvements are normally made. Under the terms of the APA, respondent must direct its attack against some particular 'agency action' that causes it harm." *Id.,* at 891, 110 S.Ct. 3177 (emphasis in original).

The plaintiffs in *National Wildlife Federation* would have fared no better if they had characterized the agency's alleged "failure to revise land use plans in proper fashion" and "failure to consider multiple use," *ibid.*, in terms of "agency action unlawfully withheld" under § 706(1), rather than agency action "not in accordance with law" under § 706(2).

The limitation to *required* agency action rules out judicial direction of even discrete agency action that is not demanded by law (which includes, of course, agency regulations that have the force of law). Thus, when an agency is compelled by law to act within a certain time period, but the manner of its action is left to the agency's discretion, a court can compel the agency to act, but has no power to specify what the action must be. For example, 47 U.S.C. § 251(d)(1), which required the Federal Communications Commission "to establish regulations to implement" interconnection requirements "[w]ithin 6 months" of the date of enactment of the Telecommunications Act of 1996, would have supported a judicial decree under the APA requiring the prompt issuance of regulations, but not a judicial decree setting forth the content of those regulations.

Norton v. So. Utah Wilderness Alliance, 542 U.S. 55, 62–65, 124 S.Ct. 2373, 2378–80, 159 L.Ed.2d 137 (2004). Applying these principles, the Court rejected a claim that the Bureau of Land Management (BLM) had insufficiently protected public lands in Utah, known as wilderness study areas (WSAs), from damage from off-road vehicles (ORVs).

* * * SUWA[ ] * * * claim[s]* * * that by permitting ORV use in certain WSAs, BLM violated its mandate to "continue to manage [WSAs] . . . in a manner so as not to impair the suitability of such areas for preservation as wilderness," 43 U.S.C. § 1782(c) * * *.

Section 1782(c) is mandatory as to the object to be achieved, but it leaves BLM a great deal of discretion in deciding how to achieve it. It assuredly does not mandate, with the clarity necessary to support judicial action under § 706(1), the total exclusion of ORV use.

SUWA argues that § 1782 *does* contain a categorical imperative, namely, the command to comply with the nonimpairment mandate. It contends that a federal court could simply enter a general order compelling compliance with that mandate, without suggesting any particular manner of compliance * * *.

The principal purpose of the APA limitations we have discussed—and of the traditional limitations upon mandamus from which they were derived—is to protect agencies from undue judicial interference with their lawful discretion, and to avoid judicial entanglement in abstract policy disagreements which courts lack both expertise and information to resolve. If courts were empowered to enter general orders compelling compliance with broad statutory mandates, they would necessarily be empowered, as well, to determine whether compliance was achieved-which would mean that it would ultimately become the task of the supervising court, rather than the agency, to work out compliance with the broad statutory mandate, injecting the judge into day-to-day agency management. To take just a few examples from federal resources management, a plaintiff might allege that the Secretary had failed to" manage wild free-roaming horses and burros in a manner that is designed to achieve and maintain a thriving natural ecological balance," or to "manage the [New Orleans Jazz National] [H]istorical [P]ark in such a manner as will preserve and perpetuate knowledge and understanding of the history of jazz," or to "manage the [Steens Mountain] Cooperative Management and Protection Area for the benefit of present and future generations." 16 U.S.C. §§ 1333(a), 410bbb–2(a)(1), 460nnn–12(b). The prospect of pervasive oversight by federal courts over the manner and pace of agency compliance with such congressional directives is not contemplated by the APA.

542 U.S. at 65–67, 124 S.Ct. at 2380–81. The Court also declined to find binding obligations that could be enforced under § 706(1) in statements of regulatory intentions in the BLM's land use plans. For § 706(1) to apply, the agency's legal duty to act—a legal duty tied to a discrete action rather than a broad programmatic mandate—must be relatively clear.

CHAPTER 5

CONSTITUTIONAL CONSTRAINTS ON AGENCY PROCEDURE

■ ■ ■

The Fifth Amendment to the United States Constitution provides, inter alia, that "[n]o person shall * * * be deprived of life, liberty, or property, without due process of law" by the federal government. Section one of the Fourteenth Amendment similarly provides with respect to the states that "[n]o State shall * * * deprive any person of life, liberty, or property, without due process of law."

These due process clauses are two of the centerpieces of modern constitutional law. This development would have startled earlier generations. The Supreme Court did not even decide a due process case until 1856. Many factors are responsible for the contemporary importance of the due process clauses, but three bear special mention.

First, the due process clauses are the Supreme Court's chosen vehicles for the so-called "incorporation doctrine," which makes most (though not quite all) of the provisions of the bill of rights applicable to the states,[1] and the "reverse incorporation doctrine," which effectively makes the Fourteenth Amendment's Equal Protection Clause applicable to the federal government. These applications of the due process clauses, especially the extension of most of the bill of rights' criminal procedure provisions to the states, account for a substantial percentage of modern constitutional doctrine.

Second, the rise of substantive due process—initially to protect slavery, then to protect economic liberty from progressive legislation, and more recently to protect other interests more in favor with the nation's elites—places the due process clauses at the center of many of the "hot button" issues of constitutional law, such as abortion, euthanasia, and marriage.

Finally, the rise of the administrative state has led to an expanded role for the due process clauses as checks on the procedures employed by the administrative arms of government. Many procedural requirements for agency action are imposed by legislatures or the agencies themselves, but

---

[1] As of 2018, the Court has yet to incorporate the Third Amendment's prohibition on the quartering of soldiers in peacetime, the Fifth Amendment's requirement of indictment by grand jury in criminal cases, and the Seventh Amendment's guarantee of the civil jury.

some procedural requirements stem directly from the Constitution. This constitutional requirement of "procedural due process" with regard to agency action is the subject of this chapter. The rest of modern due process jurisprudence is left, for the most part, to courses on constitutional law and criminal procedure.

A. DUE PROCESS: AN OVERVIEW

1. POSITIVE THEORIES OF DUE PROCESS

There are two due process clauses in the Constitution: one in the Fifth Amendment that is applicable to the federal government and one in the Fourteenth Amendment that is applicable to the states. The clauses use the same operative language, and although they were ratified 77 years apart, courts have always (though by no means inevitably) construed the two clauses to impose exactly the same procedural requirements on federal and state agencies. (The Supreme Court at one point hinted at different applications to the federal and state governments but immediately backed off from that hint. *See French v. Barber Asphalt Paving Co.*, 181 U.S. 324, 328–29, 21 S.Ct. 625, 626–27, 45 L.Ed. 879 (1901).) Accordingly, although this book generally confines itself to federal administrative law, the law of procedural due process does not distinguish between state and federal actors. Cases imposing constitutional procedural requirements on state agencies apply fully to cases involving federal agencies and vice versa.

It would be hasty, however, to conclude that we therefore have a single, unitary law of procedural due process. Rather, the appropriate description of modern procedural due process jurisprudence—and indeed whether it even makes sense to speak of such a thing as modern procedural due process jurisprudence—is a subject of considerable controversy. There are three principal theories that seek to explain contemporary procedural due process doctrine, which in their most extreme forms one might label nihilist, compartmentalist, and doctrinalist.

The nihilist account says, in essence, that there is nothing that deserves to be called the "law" of procedural due process, if "law" implies regularities that can be described by a comprehensible set of principles. On this theory, modern due process cases simply reflect the policy preferences of shifting (and frequently bare) majorities of justices, who then employ transparently vacuous formulations to justify their outcomes. If this description sounds like a caricature of Thrasymachus in a bad mood, try to keep an open mind about whether a body of case law could ever justify such an extreme degree of cynicism. Be warned that even the most ardent doctrinalists—of whom your editor is one—generally view the Supreme Court's due process cases as among the law's most vigorous challenges to their faith.

The compartmentalist account of modern due process jurisprudence insists that there is indeed law to be found, but not at the level of generality that is suggested by speaking of "the law of due process." This view maintains that instead of a single, unitary body of procedural law, there are discrete bodies of law governing different governmental activities. There is the law of due process for prisons, the law of due process for public schools, the law of due process for public employment, the law of due process for welfare, the law of due process for government licenses, etc.; and each body of law (such as "prison cases" or "school cases") stands more or less on its own. This compartmentalist position finds strong support in the practices of the Supreme Court—in some instances overtly, in other instances more subtly through selective citation of authorities. Outside of the nihilist camp, there is a wide consensus that this account has considerable explanatory power.

The doctrinalist account contends that there are enough principles in the cases that cross subject-matter boundaries to warrant speaking of a general "law of due process." No one disputes that this "law" is often fluid, uncertain, and highly unpredictable,[2] but advocates of this account maintain that one gains more understanding than one loses (even if only barely) from treating the various procedural due process cases as parts of a single body of doctrine.

Your editor endorses this doctrinalist account, though without a great deal of enthusiasm. Accordingly, the materials in this chapter are largely organized around the concepts contained in the text of the due process clauses. The cases exploring each concept are presented more or less chronologically to reflect the development of doctrine within each area. A sense of history is invaluable for understanding this material—as indeed it is invaluable for understanding most of administrative law. In the end, however, the only way to get a handle on modern due process jurisprudence is simply to read the leading cases, and probably many more besides. You will find in this chapter—perhaps to your frustration—that your editor has generally chosen to let the Supreme Court speak for itself[3] and to let you make up your own mind about the best account of the Court's work product.

2. A ROADMAP FOR DUE PROCESS PROBLEMS

Both due process clauses—in the Fourteenth Amendment expressly and the Fifth Amendment impliedly—speak only to the actions of *government*. Private citizens who are not acting pursuant to any governmental authority cannot violate the due process clauses. Of course,

---

[2] Many would add "disreputable" to this list.

[3] As you have no doubt seen by now, oftentimes the D.C. Circuit rather than the Supreme Court plays the leading role in developing administrative law doctrine. As a species of constitutional law, however, the law of procedural due process revolves primarily around Supreme Court cases.

it can sometimes be difficult to tell whether nominally private conduct should really be attributed to the government. In an era in which privatization of governmental services is increasingly popular, drawing the line between state and private action has become both more important and more difficult. The Supreme Court has generally been very reluctant to classify nominally private conduct as "state action" in the administration of government programs, *see, e.g., American Manufacturers Mutual Insurance v. Sullivan,* 526 U.S. 40, 119 S.Ct. 977, 143 L.Ed.2d 130 (1999); *Blum v. Yaretsky,* 457 U.S. 991, 102 S.Ct. 2777, 73 L.Ed.2d 534 (1982), though some decisions push strongly in the other direction towards a broad view of state action. *See Brentwood Academy v. Tennessee Secondary School Athletic Ass'n,* 531 U.S. 288, 121 S.Ct. 924, 148 L.Ed.2d 807 (2001). Usually, however, it is obvious whether a governmental agency is involved, and this book will therefore not concern itself with the delicate problem of separating the private from the public spheres (though you will be very well served if your instructor chooses to pursue the issue).

The due process clauses forbid government from "depriv[ing] any person" of "life, liberty, or property" "without due process of law." Most of the attention in the case law, and in this chapter, is devoted to the last two quoted phrases, but a few words about the first phrase are appropriate. It may seem obvious what it means to "deprive" a person of something: if they once had it and now don't because of something you have done, you have arguably "deprived" them of that item. But does it matter whether you *intend* to effect a deprivation? If I negligently knock a cup out of your hand, can I be said to have "deprived" you of the cup, or does that word connote some state of mind in which your loss is part of my design? This question did not become an issue in due process law until the 1980s; you will see the outcome(s) of that issue later in this chapter. It may also seem obvious what it means to be a "person" whose interests are protected by the due process clauses. Living people and juridical entities, such as partnerships and corporations, are generally thought of as legal "persons" in most contexts, and there is no reason to doubt that these normal understandings govern the law of due process. Indeed, no significant procedural due process case turns on the meaning of the word "person."

The voluminous modern case law on procedural due process is almost exclusively concerned with defining the phrases "life, liberty, and property" and "without due process of law." The first phrase describes the class of legal interests that are subject to protection under the due process clauses, while the second describes the kind of protection provided. If an interest does not constitute "life, liberty, or property" within the meaning of the due process clauses, then the government can deprive you of it with no procedures at all without violating the due process requirement (though there may be statutory, regulatory, or common law procedural requirements governing the relevant agency action). If an interest does constitute "life, liberty, or property," the procedural aspect of the due process clauses still permits the government to deprive you of that interest if the deprivation is effected through procedures that constitute "due process of law."[4]

It is thus possible to think of the due process clauses as containing three on-off switches: "deprive," "person," and "life, liberty, or property." If the government action in question is not a deprivation, or does not affect a person, or does not involve life, liberty, or property, then the due process clauses, by their terms, require no particular procedures. The clauses simply do not apply to that kind of governmental action. If, however, all three of those requirements are satisfied—if all three switches are "on"—then the due process clauses apply and require the government to act in accordance with principles of "due process of law."

Due process jurisprudence with regard to administrative action has developed one additional on-off switch that must always be kept in mind. In Chapter 1, you encountered *Londoner v. City and County of Denver*, 210 U.S. 373, 28 S.Ct. 708, 52 L.Ed. 1103 (1908), and *Bi-Metallic Investment Co. v. State Board of Equalization*, 239 U.S. 441, 36 S.Ct. 141, 60 L.Ed. 372 (1915). The two cases have come to stand for the proposition that agencies are bound by due process requirements only when they are engaged in adjudicatory functions involving a relatively small number of persons; due process imposes no procedural requirements at all when agencies are acting in a legislative-like capacity affecting large communities. This is commonly expressed by saying that procedural due process applies only to agency adjudication, not to agency rulemaking. This is a fair statement of the law *provided* that one keeps in mind that the relevant definitions of adjudication and rulemaking are matters of constitutional law; statutory definitions, such as those contained in the Administrative Procedure Act, are not controlling in this context. It is possible (even if unlikely) for an agency proceeding to be classified as rulemaking for purposes of the APA and adjudication for purposes of procedural due process.

B. THE ORIGINAL UNDERSTANDING

1. THE ORIGINS OF THE DUE PROCESS CLAUSES

Article 39 of the Magna Carta proclaimed in 1215 that "[n]o free man shall be taken or imprisoned or disseised or outlawed or exiled or in any way ruined, nor will we go or send against him, except by the lawful judgment of his peers or by the law of the land." This meant that the King could only impose certain punishments or disabilities on freemen in accordance with the lawful judgment of the defendants' peers, meaning

---

[4]   Other statutory or constitutional doctrines, such as the doctrine of substantive due process, may forbid the deprivation altogether, regardless of the procedures employed.

trial by jury, or with "the law of the land," meaning preexisting statutory or common law rules. This is an important principle, often called the *principle of legality*, which was understood to prohibit arbitrary action by the King: the executive could only act in accordance with statutory and customary law. If "due process of law" traces its lineage to the principle of legality, then, perhaps counterintuitively, the concept is about substance rather than procedure. The principle of legality says that government can only deprive people of legally protected interests (what an earlier time might call "vested rights") via pre-existing law. If that is what due process of law is about, then in this context "procedural due process" is an oxymoron. If there is no pre-existing law validating a deprivation, no amount of procedures can justify the deprivation. "[T]he principle of legality, at least in its executive guise, is substantive rather than procedural. It concerns what the 'executive Power' can do, not how or by what procedures it can do it." Gary Lawson, *Take the Fifth . . . Please! The Original Insignificance of the Fifth Amendment's Due Process of Law Clause*, 2107 B.Y.U. L. Rev. 611, 626.

The exact phrase "due process of law" also made an early appearance in English law, but with a very narrow, technical meaning. As reflected in its first usage, in a statute of 1354,[5] the phrase "due process of law" initially concerned the procedures of courts—a requirement of "due process of law" meaning specifically that judgments could only issue when the defendant was personally given the opportunity to appear in court pursuant to an appropriate writ. The phrase retained this technical meaning at English law into the eighteenth century. *See* Keith Jurow, *Untimely Thoughts: A Reconsideration of the Origins of Due Process of Law*, 19 Am. J. Leg. Hist. 265, 267 (1975).

At the time of the drafting of the bill of rights, at least eight state constitutions contained clauses restraining government from depriving persons of life, liberty, or property except pursuant to the law of the land. The Fifth Amendment, which otherwise tracked the form of these state provisions, used the phrase "due process of law" instead of "law of the land." The reasons for this change in terminology are not known for certain, but the best guess is that the drafters were misled by some seventeenth-century statements of Lord Coke, whose *Institutes on the Law of England* were widely read and influential in the American colonies. Coke had declared—wrongly, in the judgment of modern historians—that the phrases "law of the land" and "due process of law" were essentially equivalent. Accordingly, the American tradition of due process almost certainly has its roots in the principle of legality expressed in the Magna

---

⁵   28 Ed. III, ch. 3 (1354) ("That no man of what Estate or Condition that he be, shall be put out of land or Tenement, nor taken, nor imprisoned, nor disinherited, nor put to death, without being brought in answer by due process of law.").

Carta rather than in the technical, writ-based meaning of "due process of law" as it was understood in early English law.

The due process clauses require that certain kinds of deprivations—of "life, liberty, or property"—be accompanied by due process of law. The negative implication is that deprivations of interests that do not fall into this listing need not be accompanied by due process of law. The meanings of "life" and "liberty," at least, were well understood in 1791, when the Fifth Amendment's Due Process Clause was ratified. "Life" referred to physical life, and probably as well to certain other interests that William Blackstone, another English legal scholar widely read in the framing generation, lumped together as rights to personal security: "a person's legal and uninterrupted enjoyment of his life, his limbs, his body, his health, and his reputation." 1 William Blackstone, Commentaries on the Laws of England 125 (1765). The right to "liberty" was understood, in accordance with Blackstone, to mean "the power of loco-motion, of changing situation, or removing one's person to whatsoever place one's own inclination may direct; without imprisonment or restraint, unless by due course of law." *Id.* at 130. "Property" probably did not have quite as certain a meaning—it could have referred to land, to anything of exchangeable value, or (most likely) to whatever interests common law courts would recognize as property entitled to legal protection. Government benefits, including government jobs, almost certainly were not "property" in this sense; no one had a common law right to continued receipt of benefits or continued government employment (though one would certainly have a right to benefits already paid or salaries already received or earned). The law distinguished sharply between property rights and mere privileges that the government could continue or terminate at its pleasure.

So understood, the Due Process Clause had a very narrow operation: it ensured that the federal government deprived people of certain important rights only in accordance with preexisting laws and established judicial principles of fair adjudication. It did not apply at all to most actions of legislatures, as legislative action constituted precisely "the law of the land" (or the "due process of law") that was a precondition to legitimate executive or judicial deprivations of life, liberty, or property. At most, the clause limited the legislature's power to effect deprivations directly or to alter the traditional procedural forms of executive and judicial action.

The clause was understood in this narrow fashion for a very long time. The Supreme Court did not decide a case involving the Due Process Clause until 1856. In *Murray's Lessee v. Hoboken Land & Improvement Co.*, 59 U.S. (18 How.) 272, 15 L.Ed. 372 (1856), the Court rejected a constitutional challenge to a procedure in which the government collected deficiencies from tax collectors without first having a court determine whether the tax collector really owed the government the amount in question. The Court found a long tradition in English and American law of such procedures for

auditing tax collectors and accordingly upheld the practice. In the course
of its decision, the Court gave its first interpretation of the meaning of the
phrase "due process of law":

> The words, "due process of law," were undoubtedly intended
> to convey the same meaning as the words, "by the law of the land,"
> in *Magna Charta*. Lord Coke, in his commentary on those words,
> (2 Inst. 50,) says they mean due process of law. The constitutions
> which had been adopted by the several States before the formation
> of the federal constitution, following the language of the great
> charter more closely, generally contained the words, "but by the
> judgment of his peers, or the law of the land." The ordinance of
> congress of July 13, 1787, for the government of the territory of
> the United States northwest of the river Ohio, used the same
> words.

> The constitution of the United States, as adopted, contained
> the provision, that "the trial of all crimes, except in cases of
> impeachment, shall be by jury." When the fifth article of
> amendment containing the words now in question was made, the
> trial by jury in criminal cases had thus already been provided for.
> By the sixth and seventh articles of amendment, further special
> provisions were separately made for that mode of trial in civil and
> criminal cases. To have followed, as in the state constitutions, and
> in the ordinance of 1787, the words of *Magna Charta*, and declared
> that no person shall be deprived of his life, liberty, or property but
> by the judgment of his peers or the law of the land, would have
> been in part superfluous and inappropriate. To have taken the
> clause, "law of the land," without its immediate context, might
> possibly have given rise to doubts, which would be effectually
> dispelled by using those words which the great commentator on
> *Magna Charta* had declared to be the true meaning of the phrase,
> "law of the land," in that instrument, and which were undoubtedly
> then received as their true meaning.

> That the warrant now in question is legal process, is not
> denied. It was issued in conformity with an act of Congress. But
> is it "due process of law"? The constitution contains no description
> of those processes which it was intended to allow or forbid. It does
> not even declare what principles are to be applied to ascertain
> whether it be due process. It is manifest that it was not left to the
> legislative power to enact any process which might be devised.
> The article is a restraint on the legislative as well as on the
> executive and judicial powers of the government, and cannot be so
> construed as to leave congress free to make any process "due
> process of law," by its mere will. To what principles, then, are we
> to resort to ascertain whether this process, enacted by congress, is

due process? To this the answer must be twofold. We must examine the constitution itself, to see whether this process be in conflict with any of its provisions. If not found to be so, we must look to those settled usages and modes of proceeding existing in the common and statute law of England, before the emigration of our ancestors, and which are shown not to have been unsuited to their civil and political condition by having been acted on by them after the settlement of this country.

59 U.S. (18 How.) at 276–77.

Twelve years later, the Fourteenth Amendment made applicable to the states a due process clause that is almost identical to the Fifth Amendment's Due Process Clause. It is possible to argue that understandings of due process had changed between 1791 and 1868, so that the original meaning of the Fifth and Fourteenth Amendments' due process clauses might be different, *see* Ryan C. Williams, *The One and Only Substantive Due Process Clause*, 120 Yale L.J. 408 (2010), but courts have not shown any receptivity to such an argument.

While there is an originalist case for the proposition that "due process of law" in the Fifth Amendment, understood as an embodiment of the principle of legality, is really about keeping the legislative, executive, and judicial departments of the federal government in their proper roles, *see* Nathan S. Chapman and Michael W. McConnell, *Due Process as Separation of Powers*, 121 Yale L.J. 1672 (2012), it is very hard to conceive of the Fourteenth Amendment's due process of law clause as imposing a federal-like separation of powers regime on the states. The Supreme Court long ago rejected any such conception. *See Dreyer v. Illinois*, 187 U.S. 71, 84, 23 S.Ct. 28, 32, 47 L.Ed. 79 (1902) ("Whether the legislative, executive, and judicial powers of a state shall be kept altogether distinct and separate, or whether persons or collections of persons belonging to one department may, in respect to some matters, exert powers which, strictly speaking, pertain to another department of government, is for the determination of the state. And its determination one way or the other cannot be an element in the inquiry, whether the due process of law prescribed by the 14th Amendment has been respected by the state or its representatives when dealing with matters involving life or liberty"). Accordingly, once the Court had to decide how to apply the idea of due process of law to state governments, it locked onto the character of the *procedures* necessary for state actors, especially state executive actors such as administrative agencies, to deprive people of constitutionally protected interests. *See, e.g., Spencer v. Merchant*, 125 U.S. 345, 356, 8 S.Ct. 921, 927, 31 L.Ed. 763 (1888). And once the decision was made to have due process doctrine about state agencies track precisely onto the law for federal agencies, the result was the law of the last century and a half that tries to spell out the constitutionally appropriate procedures for executive deprivations of rights—on the assumption that those deprivations are permissible if the proper procedures are followed. While that assumption is likely wrong as an original matter, at least with respect to the federal government, it is deeply ingrained in modern law; in the words of Eddie Cornelius: "It's too late to turn back now." Our doctrinal story in this chapter is thus all about due process of law as due procedures; hence the label "procedural due process."

2. RIGHTS AND REMEDIES

NORTH AMERICAN COLD STORAGE CO. v. CITY OF CHICAGO

Supreme Court of the United States, 1908.
211 U.S. 306, 29 S.Ct. 101, 53 L.Ed. 195.

The bill of complaint in this case * * * was filed against the city of Chicago and the various individual defendants in their official capacities— Commissioner of Health of the city of Chicago, Secretary of the Department of Health, Chief Food Inspector of the Department of Health and inspectors of that department, and policemen of the city—for the purpose of obtaining an injunction under the circumstances set forth in the bill. It was therein alleged that the complainant was a cold storage company, having a cold storage plant in the city of Chicago; and that it received, for the purpose of keeping in cold storage, food products and goods as bailee for hire; that on an average it received $20,000 worth of goods per day, and returned a like amount to its customers, daily, and that it had on an average in storage about two million dollars' worth of goods; that it received some forty-seven barrels of poultry on or about October 2, 1906, from a wholesale dealer in due course of business, to be kept by it and returned to such dealer on demand; that the poultry was, when received, in good condition and wholesome for human food, and had been so maintained by it in cold storage from that time, and it would remain so, if undisturbed, for three months; that on October 2, 1906, the individual defendants appeared at complainant's place of business and demanded of it that it forthwith deliver the forty-seven barrels of poultry for the purpose of being by them destroyed, the defendants alleging that the poultry had become putrid, decayed, poisonous or infected in such a manner as to render it unsafe or unwholesome for human food. The demand was made under § 1161 of the Revised Municipal Code of the city of Chicago for 1905, which reads as follows:

> "Every person being the owner, lessee or occupant of any room, stall, freight house, cold storage house or other place, other than a private dwelling, where any meat, fish, poultry, game, vegetables, fruit, or other perishable article adapted or designed to be used for human food, shall be stored or kept, whether temporarily or otherwise, and every person having charge of, or

being interested or engaged, whether as principal or agent, in the care of or in respect to the custody or sale of any such article of food supply, shall put, preserve and keep such article of food supply in a clean and wholesome condition, and shall not allow the same, nor any part thereof, to become putrid, decayed, poisoned, infected, or in any other manner rendered or made unsafe or unwholesome for human food; and it shall be the duty of the meat and food inspectors and other duly authorized employees of the health department of the city to enter any and all such premises above specified at any time of any day, and to forthwith seize, condemn and destroy any such putrid, decayed, poisoned and infected food, which any such inspector may find in and upon said premises."

The complainant refused to deliver up the poultry, on the ground that the section above quoted of the Municipal Code of Chicago, in so far as it allows the city or its agents to seize, condemn or destroy food or other food products, was in conflict with that portion of the Fourteenth Amendment which provides that no State shall deprive any person of life, liberty or property without due process of law; nor deny to any person within its jurisdiction the equal protection of the laws.

After the refusal of the complainant to deliver the poultry the defendants stated that they would not permit the complainant's business to be further conducted until it complied with the demand of the defendants and delivered up the poultry, nor would they permit any more goods to be received into the warehouse or taken from the same, and that they would arrest and imprison any person who attempted to do so, until complainant complied with their demand and delivered up the poultry. Since that time the complainant's business has been stopped and the complainant has been unable to deliver any goods from its plant or receive the same.

The bill averred that the attempt to seize, condemn and destroy the poultry, without a judicial determination of the fact that the same was putrid, decayed, poisonous or infected was illegal, and it asked that the defendants, and each of them, might be enjoined from taking or removing the poultry from the warehouse, or from destroying the same, and that they also be enjoined from preventing complainant delivering its goods and receiving from its customers in due course of business the goods committed to its care for storage.

In an amendment to the bill the complainant further stated that the defendants are now threatening to summarily destroy, from time to time, pursuant to the provisions of the above-mentioned section, any and all food products which may be deemed by them, or either of them, as being putrid, decayed, poisonous or infected in such manner as to be unfit for human food, without any judicial determination of the fact that such food products are in such condition.

The defendants demurred to the bill on the ground, among others, that the court had no jurisdiction of the action. The injunction was not issued, but upon argument of the case upon the demurrer the bill was dismissed by the Circuit Court for want of jurisdiction, as already stated.

* * *

MR. JUSTICE PECKHAM, after making the foregoing statement, delivered the opinion of the court.

In this case the ordinance in question is to be regarded as in effect a statute of the State, adopted under a power granted it by the state legislature, and hence it is an act of the State within the Fourteenth Amendment * * *.

* * *

* * * The action of the defendants, which is admitted by the demurrer, in refusing to permit the complainant to carry on its ordinary business until it delivered the poultry, would seem to have been arbitrary and wholly indefensible. Counsel for the complainant, however, for the purpose of obtaining a decision in regard to the constitutional question as to the right to seize and destroy property without a prior hearing, states that he will lay no stress here upon that portion of the bill which alleges the unlawful and forcible taking possession of complainant's business by the defendants * * *.

* * *

The general power of the State to legislate upon the subject embraced in the above ordinance of the city of Chicago, counsel does not deny. Nor does he deny the right to seize and destroy unwholesome or putrid food, provided that notice and opportunity to be heard be given the owner or custodian of the property before it is destroyed. We are of opinion, however, that provision for a hearing before seizure and condemnation and destruction of food which is unwholesome and unfit for use, is not necessary. The right to so seize is based upon the right and duty of the State to protect and guard, as far as possible, the lives and health of its inhabitants, and that it is proper to provide that food which is unfit for human consumption should be summarily seized and destroyed to prevent the danger which would arise from eating it. The right to so seize and destroy is, of course, based upon the fact that the food is not fit to be eaten. Food that is in such a condition, if kept for sale or in danger of being sold, is in itself a nuisance, and a nuisance of the most dangerous kind, involving, as it does, the health, if not the lives, of persons who may eat it. A determination on the part of the seizing officers that food is in an unfit condition to be eaten is not a decision which concludes the owner. The *ex parte* finding of the health officers as to the fact is not in any way binding upon those who own or claim the right to sell the food. If a party cannot get his hearing in advance of the seizure and destruction he has the right to have it afterward, which right may be claimed upon the trial in an action brought for the destruction of his property, and in that action those who destroyed it can only successfully defend if the jury shall find the fact of unwholesomeness as claimed by them * * *.

* * *

Complainant, however, contends that there was no emergency requiring speedy action for the destruction of the poultry in order to protect the public health from danger resulting from consumption of such poultry. It is said that the food was in cold storage, and that it would continue in the same condition it then was for three months, if properly stored, and that therefore the defendants had ample time in which to give notice to complainant or the owner and have a hearing of the question as to the condition of the poultry, and as the ordinance provided for no hearing, it was void. But we think this is not required. The power of the legislature to enact laws in relation to the public health being conceded, as it must be, it is to a great extent within legislative discretion as to whether any hearing need be given before the destruction of unwholesome food which is unfit for human consumption. If a hearing were to be always necessary, even under the circumstances of this case, the question at once arises as to what is to be done with the food in the meantime. Is it to remain with the cold storage company, and if so under what security that it will not be removed? To be sure that it will not be removed during the time necessary for the hearing, which might frequently be indefinitely prolonged, some guard would probably have to be placed over the subject-matter of investigation, which would involve expense, and might not even then prove effectual. What is the emergency which would render a hearing unnecessary? We think when the question is one regarding the destruction of food which is not fit for human use the emergency must be one which would fairly appeal to the reasonable discretion of the legislature as to the necessity for a prior hearing, and in that case its decision would not be a subject for review by the courts. As the owner of the food or its custodian is amply protected against the party seizing the food, who must in a subsequent action against him show as a fact that it was within the statute, we think that due process of law is not denied the owner or custodian by the destruction of the food alleged to be unwholesome and unfit for human food without a preliminary hearing * * *.

* * *

PHILLIPS V. COMMISSIONER OF INTERNAL REVENUE

Supreme Court of the United States, 1931.
283 U.S. 589, 51 S.Ct. 608, 75 L.Ed. 1289.

MR. JUSTICE BRANDEIS delivered the opinion of the Court.

In 1919, the Coombe Garment Company, a Pennsylvania corporation, distributed all of its assets among its stockholders, and then dissolved. Thereafter, the Commissioner of Internal Revenue made deficiency assessments against it for income and profits taxes for the years 1918 and 1919. A small part of these assessments was collected leaving an unpaid balance of $9,306.36. I. L. Phillips of New York City, had owned one-fourth of the company's stock and had received $17,139.61 as his distributive dividend. Pursuant to § 280(a)(1) of the Revenue Act of 1926, the Commissioner sent due notice that he proposed to assess against, and collect from, Phillips the entire remaining amount of the deficiencies * * *. Upon petition by Phillips' executors for a redetermination, the Board of Tax Appeals held that the estate was liable for the full amount. Its order was affirmed by the United States Circuit Court of Appeals for the Second Circuit. Because of conflict in the decisions of the lower courts a writ of certiorari was granted.

Stockholders who have received the assets of a dissolved corporation may confessedly be compelled, in an appropriate proceeding, to discharge unpaid corporate taxes. Before the enactment of § 280(a)(1), such payment by the stockholders could be enforced only by bill in equity or action at law. Section 280(a)(1) provides that the liability of the transferee for such taxes may be enforced in the same manner as that of any delinquent taxpayer. [This procedure permits an administrative determination of liability, and the use of summary collection procedures, without a prior judicial determination of taxpayer liability.]

* * *

First. The contention mainly urged is that the summary procedure permitted by the section violates the Constitution because it does not provide for a judicial determination of the transferee's liability at the outset * * *.

* * *

The right of the United States to collect its internal revenue by summary administrative proceedings has long been settled. Where, as here, adequate opportunity is afforded for a later judicial determination of the legal rights, summary proceedings to secure prompt performance of pecuniary obligations to the government have been consistently sustained. Property rights must yield provisionally to governmental need. Thus, while protection of life and liberty from administrative action alleged to be illegal, may be obtained promptly by the writ of habeas corpus, the statutory prohibition of any "suit for the purpose of restraining the assessment or collection of any tax" postpones redress for the alleged invasion of property rights if the exaction is made under color of their offices by revenue officers charged with the general authority to assess and collect the revenue. This prohibition of injunctive relief is applicable in the case of summary proceedings against a transferee. Proceedings more summary in character than that provided in § 280, and involving less directly the obligation of the taxpayer, were sustained in *Murray's Lessee v. Hoboken Land & Improvement Co.*, 18 How. 272. It is urged that the decision in the *Murray* case was based upon the peculiar relationship of a collector of revenue to his government. The underlying principle in that case was not such relation, but the need of the government promptly to secure its revenues.

Where only property rights are involved, mere postponement of the judicial enquiry is not a denial of due process, if the opportunity given for the ultimate judicial determination of the liability is adequate. Delay in the judicial determination of property rights is not uncommon where it is essential that governmental needs be immediately satisfied. For the protection of public health, a State may order the summary destruction of property by administrative authorities without antecedent notice or hearing. Compare *North American Cold Storage Co. v. Chicago*, 211 U.S. 306 * * *. Because of the public necessity, the property of citizens may be summarily seized in war-time. And at any time, the United States may acquire property by eminent domain, without paying, or determining the amount of the compensation before the taking.

The procedure provided in § 280(a)(1) satisfies the requirements of due process because two alternative methods of eventual judicial review are available to the transferee. He may contest his liability by bringing an action, either against the United States or the collector, to recover the amount paid. This remedy is available where the transferee does not appeal from the determination of the Commissioner, and the latter makes an assessment and enforces payment by distraint; or where the transferee voluntarily pays the tax and is thereafter denied administrative relief. Or the transferee may avail himself of the provisions for immediate redetermination of the liability by the Board of Tax Appeals, since all provisions governing this mode of review are made applicable by § 280. Thus within sixty days after the Commissioner determines that the transferee is liable for an unpaid deficiency, and gives due notice thereof, the latter may file a petition with the Board of Tax Appeals. Formal notice of the tax liability is thus given; the Commissioner is required to answer; and there is a complete hearing *de novo* according to the rules of evidence applicable in courts of equity of the District of Columbia * * *.

It is argued that such review by the Board of Tax Appeals and Circuit Court of Appeals is constitutionally inadequate because of the conditions and limitations imposed. Specific objection is made * * * to the rule under which the Board's findings of fact are treated by that court as final if there is any evidence to support them * * *. It has long been settled that determinations of fact for ordinary administrative purposes are not subject to review. Save as there may be an exception for issues presenting claims of constitutional right, such administrative findings on issues of fact are accepted by the court as conclusive if the evidence was legally sufficient to sustain them and there was no irregularity in the proceedings * * *. The alternative judicial review provided is adequate in both cases.

* * *

NOTES

North American and *Phillips* are recognized today as good authorities for the proposition that government emergencies can sometimes justify deprivations without any prior hearings, provided that adequate procedures for assessing the legality of the deprivations are available after the fact. In 1988, the Supreme Court cited *North American* for the claim that "[a]n important government interest, accompanied by a substantial assurance that the deprivation is not baseless or unwarranted, may in limited cases demanding prompt action justify postponing the opportunity to be heard until after the initial deprivation." *FDIC v. Mallen*, 486 U.S. 230, 240, 108 S.Ct. 1780, 1787, 100 L.Ed.2d 265 (1988).

Does this mean that, in ordinary, non-emergency circumstances, the government must provide some kind of procedure *before* it deprives someone of an interest protected by the due process clauses? The short answer is "mostly yes"; the long answer, which defines "ordinary circumstances" and explains what kinds of procedures are necessary at different stages of the administrative process, will consume much of this chapter.

For now, the short answer is enough to emphasize a crucial feature of procedural due process law, and indeed of non-constitutional procedural law as well: *when* you receive procedures is often as important, or even more important, than *what* procedures you receive. Consider the plaintiff's case in *North American*. The Court made clear that the plaintiff was free to bring a common-law tort action (probably for trespass and conversion) against the offending government officials. Such a tort suit would involve a full-dress judicial trial, complete with jury. Not even the most elaborate and formal agency hearing procedures will measure up to the procedures of an honest-to-goodness jury trial. Nonetheless, the plaintiff fell all over itself trying to establish a right to a pre-deprivation agency hearing—to the point of giving away an easy win in the case by not raising the defendants' clearly illegal blockade of the plaintiff's warehouse. The reason for this strategy is clear: in all future cases of this sort, the plaintiff would much rather have chickens in its warehouse than a lawsuit for the value of lost chickens. If a pre-deprivation hearing, even a procedurally informal hearing, can significantly reduce the likelihood that healthy chickens will be mistakenly seized and destroyed, the plaintiff would almost always prefer a relatively informal pre-deprivation hearing to any level of post-deprivation formality. The desirability, and the constitutional adequacy, of procedures is always a function both of the kinds of procedures at issue and of the point in the administrative process at which those procedures are provided. Precisely the same procedures can be constitutionally adequate at time A and inadequate at time B.

North American spent a great deal of energy explaining that the plaintiffs had a tort suit against the offending government officials. The Court's discussion assumes that such officials can be sued on the same basis as private citizens, subject only to the affirmative defense of valid legal authorization.[6] That assumption was true in 1908, but is no longer true today. As is discussed in more detail in Chapter 6,[7] until the last half of the twentieth century, executive officials were generally liable, in their personal capacities, for tortious activity that was not authorized by a valid statute or regulation. The mere *status* of being a government official conferred no immunity from suit for common law torts. Courts soon enough carved out an exception for themselves, granting absolute immunity for all actions performed in a judicial capacity, *see Bradley v. Fisher*, 80 U.S. (13 Wall.) 335, 347, 20 L.Ed. 646 (1871), including actions by jurors, clerks, prosecutors, and witnesses. But executive officials (other than prosecutors in judicial proceedings) could claim no immunity for their actions except authorization by law.

This doctrine did not survive the rise of the administrative state. Beginning in 1959, *see Barr v. Matteo*, 360 U.S. 564, 79 S.Ct. 1335, 3 L.Ed.2d 1434 (1959), the courts began extending some form of immunity to government officials. Today, government officials can generally be sued in tort only when they violate *clearly established* legal norms. *See Harlow v. Fitzgerald*, 457 U.S. 800, 102 S.Ct. 2727, 73 L.Ed.2d 396 (1982). Reasonable conduct cannot be the basis for a tort suit, even if the conduct is in fact unlawful. Hence, the remedial structure contemplated by *North American*, in which the legality of government deprivations of life, liberty, and property could be tried after the fact by a jury, no longer exists. As you read the modern cases, consider whether due process law was, in any relevant respect, better in 1908 than it is today.

C. "LIFE, LIBERTY, OR PROPERTY"

1. A TALE OF TWO MODELS

The Constitution identifies "life, liberty, or property" as the class of interests subject to due process protection. How should the precise contours of those interests be specified? Should one seek to give independent content to each specific term in the list? Or should one instead treat the list as a generalized reference to any matters that people reasonably regard as

---

[6] In *North American*, the relevant ordinance authorized only the seizure and destruction of unwholesome chickens. If the chickens in question were in fact healthy, then the government officials acted without legal authorization. And an ordinance that authorized the seizure and destruction of healthy chickens would be of questionable constitutional validity, especially in 1908 when the doctrine of economic due process was still vibrant.

[7] *See infra* pages 1007–1017.

important in their lives? Put more bluntly, is the phrase "life, liberty, or property" an enumeration or a metaphor?

As you read the three cases to follow, all of which were decided between 1950 and 1961, and all of which are important precursors to modern law, consider which approach to defining "life, liberty, or property" animates the various opinions in these cases. Consider also how self-consciously the opinions address the problem of giving content to the constitutional language.

BAILEY V. RICHARDSON

United States Court of Appeals, District of Columbia Circuit, 1950.
182 F.2d 46, aff'd by an equally divided Court, 341 U.S. 918, 71 S.Ct. 669,
95 L.Ed. 1352 (1951).

Before EDGERTON, PRETTYMAN, and PROCTOR, CIRCUIT JUDGES.

PRETTYMAN, J.

This is a civil action brought in the United States District Court for the District of Columbia for a declaratory judgment and for an order directing plaintiff-appellant's reinstatement in Government employ. The defendants-appellees are the Administrator of the Federal Security Agency, the members of the Civil Service Commission, members of its Loyalty Review Board, and members of its Loyalty Board of the Fourth Civil Service Region. Answer to the complaint was made by the defendants-appellees, and affidavits were filed. Both plaintiff and defendants made motions for summary judgment. The District Court granted the motion of the defendants. This appeal followed. Upon motion filed in this court by the appellant, the Secretary of Labor was added as party appellee.

THE FACTS

Appellant Bailey was employed in the classified civil service of the United States Government from August 19, 1939, to June 28, 1947. Upon the latter date she was separated from the service due to reduction in force. On March 25, 1948, she was given a temporary appointment, and on May 28, 1948, she was reinstated under circumstances to be related.

The regulations of the Civil Service Commission in effect at the time of appellant's reinstatement made reinstatements subject to the condition that removal might be ordered by the Commission if investigation of the individual's qualifications, made within eighteen months, disclosed disqualification. The regulations listed as a disqualification:

"(7) On all the evidence, reasonable grounds exist for belief that the person involved is disloyal to the Government of the United States."

On July 31, 1948, two months after her reinstatement, Miss Bailey received from the Regional Loyalty Board of the Commission a letter and an enclosed interrogatory * * *. [The interrogatory stated, inter alia, that the Commission had received information—from unnamed, unidentified sources—that Bailey had associations with various Communist or allegedly Communist-associated groups.]

Miss Bailey answered the interrogatories directly and specifically, denying each item of information recited therein as having been received by the Commission, except that she admitted past membership for a short time in the American League for Peace and Democracy. She vigorously asserted her loyalty to the United States. She requested an administrative hearing. A hearing was held before the Regional Board. She appeared and testified and presented other witnesses and numerous affidavits. No person other than those presented by her testified.

On November 1, 1948, the Regional Board advised the Federal Security Agency, in which Miss Bailey was employed, that:

"As a result of such investigation and after a hearing before this Board, it was found that, on all the evidence, reasonable grounds exist for belief that Miss Bailey is disloyal to the Government of the United States.

"Therefore, she has been rated ineligible for Federal employment; she has been barred from competing in civil service examinations for a period of three years, and your office is instructed to separate her from the service."

* * *

Miss Bailey appealed to the Loyalty Review Board and requested a hearing. Hearing was held before a panel of that Board. Miss Bailey appeared, testified, and presented affidavits. No person other than Miss Bailey testified, and no affidavits other than hers were presented on the record.

On February 9, 1949, the Chairman of the Loyalty Review Board advised the Federal Security Agency that the finding of the Regional Board was sustained, and he requested that the Agency remove Miss Bailey's name from the rolls. Notice to that effect was sent to counsel for Miss Bailey on the same day. The full Board subsequently declined to review the conclusions of its panel * * *.

* * *

THE QUESTION

* * *

The case presented for Miss Bailey is undoubtedly appealing. She was denied reinstatement in her former employment because Government officials found reasonable ground to believe her disloyal. She was not given a trial in any sense of the word, and she does not know who informed upon her. Thus viewed, her situation appeals powerfully to our sense of the fair and the just. But the case must be placed in context and in perspective.

The Constitution placed upon the President and the Congress, and upon them alone, responsibility for the welfare of this country in the arena of world affairs. It so happens that we are presently in an adversary position to a government whose most successful recent method of contest is the infiltration of a government service by its sympathizers. This is the context of Miss Bailey's question.

The essence of her complaint is not that she was denied reinstatement; the complaint is that she was denied reinstatement without revelation by the Government of the names of those who informed against her and of the method by which her alleged activities were detected. So the question actually posed by the case is whether the President is faced with an inescapable dilemma, either to continue in Government employment a person whose loyalty he reasonably suspects or else to reveal publicly the methods by which he detects disloyalty and the names of any persons who may venture to assist him.

Even in normal times and as a matter of ordinary internal operation, the ability, integrity and loyalty of purely executive employees is exclusively for the executive branch of Government to determine, except in so far as the Congress has a constitutional voice in the matter. All such employees hold office at the pleasure of the appointing authority; again except only for statutory limitations. Never in our history * * * has a Government employee been entitled as a right to the sort of hearing Miss Bailey demands in respect to dismissal from office. These well-established principles give perspective to the present problem.

The presentation of appellant's contentions is impressive. Each detail of the trial which she unquestionably did not get is depicted separately, in a mounting cumulation into analogies to the Dreyfus case and the Nazi judicial process. Thus, a picture of a simple black-and-white fact—that appellant did not get a trial in the judicial sense—is drawn in bold and appealing colors. But the question is not whether she had a trial. The question is whether she should have had one.

[The Court held, after lengthy discussion, that Bailey's dismissal did not violate relevant executive orders or statutes, but that the Board's order barring Bailey from federal employment for three years was invalid because it constituted punishment for purposes of the Sixth Amendment and thus required compliance with constitutional procedures for criminal punishment. The Court further held, however, that Bailey's dismissal from employment did not implicate the Sixth Amendment.]

* * *

It is next said on behalf of appellant that the due process clause of the Fifth Amendment requires that she be afforded a hearing of the quasi-judicial type before being dismissed. The due process clause provides: "No person shall * * * be deprived of life, liberty, or property, without due process of law; * * *." It has been held repeatedly and consistently that Government employ is not "property" and that in this particular it is not a contract. We are unable to perceive how it could be held to be "liberty". Certainly it is not "life". So much that is clear would seem to dispose of the point. In terms the due process clause does not apply to the holding of a Government office.

* * *

In the absence of statute or ancient custom to the contrary, executive offices are held at the will of the appointing authority, not for life or for fixed terms. If removal be at will, of what purpose would process be? To hold office at the will of a superior and to be removable therefrom only by constitutional due process of law are opposite and inherently conflicting ideas. Due process of law is not applicable unless one is being deprived of something to which he has a right.

* * *

We hold that the due process of law clause of the Fifth Amendment does not restrict the President's discretion or the prescriptive power of Congress in respect to executive personnel.

* * *

[In a lengthy discussion, the Court rejected claims that Bailey's dismissal violated her First Amendment rights, that permitting dismissal for suspected disloyalty exceeds the powers of Congress or the President, or that dismissal for "disloyalty" requires special treatment because of the potential harm to the individual associated with that label.]

EDGERTON, CIRCUIT JUDGE, dissenting.

[Judge Edgerton's dissent was based on his view that Bailey's dismissal violated a relevant executive order and Bailey's First and Sixth Amendment rights; it did not address her claims under the Fifth Amendment.]

JOINT ANTI-FASCIST REFUGEE COMMITTEE V. MCGRATH

Supreme Court of the United States, 1951.
341 U.S. 123, 71 S.Ct. 624, 95 L.Ed. 817.

MR. JUSTICE BURTON announced the judgment of the Court and delivered the following opinion, in which MR. JUSTICE DOUGLAS joins:

In each of these cases the same issue is raised by the dismissal of a complaint for its failure to state a claim upon which relief can be granted. That issue is whether, in the face of the facts alleged in the complaint and therefore admitted by the motion to dismiss, the Attorney General of the United States has authority to include the complaining organization in a list of organizations designated by him as Communist and furnished by him to the Loyalty Review Board of the United States Civil Service Commission. He claims to derive authority to do this from [provisions of an executive order issued by the President on March 21] * * *.

The respective complaints describe the complaining organizations as engaged in charitable or civic activities or in the business of fraternal insurance. Each implies an attitude of cooperation and helpfulness, rather than one of hostility or disloyalty, on the part of the organization toward the United States * * *.

* * *

If, upon the allegations in any of these complaints, it had appeared that the acts of the respondents, from which relief was sought, were authorized by the President under his Executive Order No. 9835, the case would have bristled with constitutional issues. On that basis the complaint would have raised questions as to the justiciability and merit of claims based upon the First, Fifth, Ninth and Tenth Amendments to the Constitution. It is our obligation, however, not to reach those issues unless the allegations before us squarely present them.

The Executive Order contains no express or implied attempt to confer power on anyone to act arbitrarily or capriciously—even assuming a constitutional power to do so. The order includes in the purposes of the President's program not only the protection of the United States against disloyal employees but the "equal protection" of loyal employees against unfounded accusations of disloyalty * * *. Obviously it would be contrary to the purpose of that order to place on a list to be disseminated under the Loyalty Program any designation of an organization that was patently arbitrary and contrary to the uncontroverted material facts * * *.

* * *

For these reasons, we find it necessary * * * to remand the case * * * with instructions to deny respondent's motion that the complaint be dismissed for failure to state a claim upon which relief can be granted.

MR. JUSTICE CLARK took no part in the consideration or decision of any of these cases.

MR. JUSTICE BLACK, concurring. [omitted]

MR. JUSTICE FRANKFURTER, concurring.

The more issues of law are inescapably entangled in political controversies, especially those that touch the passions of the day, the more the Court is under duty to dispose of a controversy within the narrowest confines that intellectual integrity permits. And so I sympathize with the endeavor of my brother Burton to decide these cases on a ground as limited as that which has commended itself to him. Unfortunately, I am unable to read the pleadings as he does. Therefore I must face up to larger issues * * *.

* * *

* * * Petitioners are organizations which, on the face of the record, are engaged solely in charitable or insurance activities. They have been designated "communist" by the Attorney General of the United States. This designation imposes no legal sanction on these organizations other than that it serves as evidence in ridding the Government of persons reasonably suspected of disloyalty. It would be blindness, however, not to recognize that in the conditions of our time such designation drastically restricts the organizations, if it does not proscribe them. Potential members, contributors or beneficiaries of listed organizations may well be influenced by use of the designation, for instance, as ground for rejection of applications for commissions in the armed forces or for permits for meetings in the auditoriums of public housing projects. Yet, designation has been made without notice, without disclosure of any reasons justifying it, without opportunity to meet the undisclosed evidence or suspicion on which designation may have been based, and without opportunity to establish affirmatively that the aims and acts of the organization are innocent. It is claimed that thus to maim or decapitate, on the mere say-so of the Attorney General, an organization to all outward-seeming engaged in lawful objectives is so devoid of fundamental fairness as to offend the Due Process Clause of the Fifth Amendment.

Fairness of procedure is "due process in the primary sense." *Brinkerhoff-Faris Co. v. Hill*, 281 U.S. 673, 681. It is ingrained in our national traditions and is designed to maintain them. In a variety of situations the Court has enforced this requirement by checking attempts of executives, legislatures, and lower courts to disregard the deep-rooted demands of fair play enshrined in the Constitution * * *.

The requirement of "due process" is not a fair-weather or timid assurance. It must be respected in periods of calm and in times of trouble; it protects aliens as well as citizens. But "due process," unlike some legal rules, is not a technical conception with a fixed content unrelated to time, place and circumstances. Expressing as it does in its ultimate analysis respect enforced by law for that feeling of just treatment which has been evolved through centuries of Anglo-American constitutional history and civilization, "due process" cannot be imprisoned within the treacherous limits of any formula. Representing a profound attitude of fairness between man and man, and more particularly between the individual and government, "due process" is compounded of history, reason, the past course of decisions, and stout confidence in the strength of the democratic faith which we profess. Due process is not a mechanical instrument. It is not a yardstick. It is a process. It is a delicate process of adjustment inescapably involving the exercise of judgment by those whom the Constitution entrusted with the unfolding of the process.

* * *

It may fairly be said that, barring only occasional and temporary lapses, this Court has not sought unduly to confine those who have the responsibility of governing by giving the great concept of due process doctrinaire scope. The Court has responded to the infinite variety and perplexity of the tasks of government by recognizing that what is unfair in one situation may be fair in another. Whether the *ex parte* procedure to which the petitioners were subjected duly observed "the rudiments of fair play," *Chicago, M. & St. P. R. Co. v. Polt*, 232 U.S. 165, 168, cannot, therefore, be tested by mere generalities or sentiments abstractly appealing. The precise nature of the interest that has been adversely affected, the manner in which this was done, the reasons for doing it, the available alternatives to the procedure that was followed, the protection implicit in the office of the functionary whose conduct is challenged, the balance of hurt complained of and good accomplished—these are some of the considerations that must enter into the judicial judgment.

Applying them to the immediate situation, we note that publicly designating an organization as within the proscribed categories of the Loyalty Order does not directly deprive anyone of liberty or property. Weight must also be given to the fact that such designation is not made by a minor official but by the highest law officer of the Government. Again, it is fair to emphasize that the individual's interest is here to be weighed against a claim of the greatest of all public interests, that of national security. In striking the balance the relevant considerations must be fairly, which means coolly, weighed with due regard to the fact that this Court is not exercising a primary judgment but is sitting in judgment upon those who also have taken the oath to observe the Constitution and who have the responsibility for carrying on government.

But the significance we attach to general principles may turn the scale when competing claims appeal for supremacy * * *. It is noteworthy that procedural safeguards constitute the major portion of our Bill of Rights. And so, no one now doubts that in the criminal law a "person's right to reasonable notice of a charge against him, and an opportunity to be heard in his defense—a right to his day in court—are basic in our system of jurisprudence." *In re Oliver*, 333 U.S. 257, 273 * * *. Nor is there doubt that notice and hearing are prerequisite to due process in civil proceedings. Only the narrowest exceptions, justified by history become part of the habits of our people or by obvious necessity, are tolerated.

* * *

This Court is not alone in recognizing that the right to be heard before being condemned to suffer grievous loss of any kind, even though it may not involve the stigma and hardships of a criminal conviction, is a principle basic to our society. Regard for this principle has guided Congress and the Executive. Congress has often entrusted, as it may, protection of interests which it has created to administrative agencies rather than to the courts. But rarely has it authorized such agencies to act without those essential safeguards for fair judgment which in the course of centuries have come to be associated with due process. And when Congress has given an administrative agency discretion to determine its own procedure, the agency has rarely chosen to dispose of the rights of individuals without a hearing, however informal.

* * *

The strength and significance of these considerations—considerations which go to the very ethos of the scheme of our society—give a ready answer to the problem before us. That a hearing has been thought indispensable in so many other situations, leaving the cases of denial exceptional, does not of itself prove that it must be found essential here. But it does place upon the Attorney General the burden of showing weighty reason for departing in this instance from a rule so deeply imbedded in history and in the demands of justice. Nothing in the Loyalty Order requires him to deny organizations opportunity to present their case * * *.

We are not here dealing with the grant of Government largess. We have not before us the measured action of Congress, with the pause that is properly engendered when the validity of legislation is assailed. The Attorney General is certainly not immune from the historic requirements of fairness merely because he acts, however conscientiously, in the name of security. Nor does he obtain immunity on the ground that designation is not an "adjudication" or a "regulation" in the conventional use of those terms. Due process is not confined in its scope to the particular forms in which rights have heretofore been found to have been curtailed for want of procedural fairness. Due process is perhaps the most majestic concept in our whole constitutional system. While it contains the garnered wisdom of the past in assuring fundamental justice, it is also a living principle not confined to past instances.

Therefore the petitioners did set forth causes of action which the District Court should have entertained.

MR. JUSTICE DOUGLAS, concurring.

[In footnote 3 of a long, rambling opinion that does not discuss the technical requirements of a Fifth Amendment claim, Justice Douglas states, "As MR. JUSTICE FRANKFURTER points out, due process requires no less. But apart from due process in the constitutional sense is the power of the Court to prescribe standards of conduct and procedure for inferior federal courts and agencies."]

MR. JUSTICE JACKSON, concurring.

* * *

Ordinary dismissals from government service which violate no fixed tenure concern only the Executive branch, and courts will not review such discretionary action. However, these are not discretionary discharges but discharges pursuant to an order having force of law. Administrative machinery is publicly set up to comb the whole government service to discharge persons or to declare them ineligible for employment upon an incontestable finding, made without hearing, that some organization is subversive. To be deprived not only of present government employment but of future opportunity for it certainly is no small injury when government employment so dominates the field of opportunity.

The fact that one may not have a legal right to get or keep a government post does not mean that he can be adjudged ineligible illegally.

* * *

MR. JUSTICE REED, with whom the CHIEF JUSTICE and MR. JUSTICE MINTON join, dissenting.

* * *

The absence of any provision in the Order or rules for notice to suspected organizations, for hearings with privilege to the organizations to confront witnesses, cross-examine, produce evidence and have representation of counsel or judicial review of the conclusion reached by the Attorney General is urged by the petitioners, as a procedure so fundamentally unfair and restrictive of personal freedoms as to violate the Federal Constitution, specifically the Due Process Clause and the First Amendment. No opportunity was allowed by the Attorney General for petitioners to offer proof of the legality of their purposes or to disprove charges of subversive operations. This is the real gravamen of each complaint, the basis upon which the determination of unconstitutionality is sought.

* * *

Does due process require notice and hearing for the Department of Justice investigation under Executive Order No. 9835, Part III, § 3, preliminary to listing? As a standard for due process one cannot do better than to accept as a measure that no one may be deprived of liberty or property without such reasonable notice and hearing as fairness requires. This is my understanding of the meaning of the opinions upon due process cited in the concurring opinions. We are not here concerned with the rightfulness of the extent of participation in the investigations that might be claimed by petitioners. They were given no chance to take part. Their claim is that the listing resulted in a deprivation of liberty or property contrary to the procedure required by the Fifth Amendment.

The contention can be answered summarily by saying that there is no deprivation of any property or liberty of any listed organization by the Attorney General's designation. It may be assumed that the listing is hurtful to their prestige, reputation and earning power. It may be such an injury as would entitle organizations to damages in a tort action against persons not protected by privilege. This designation, however, does not prohibit any business of the organizations, subject them to any punishment or deprive them of liberty of speech or other freedom. The cases relied upon in the briefs and opinions of the majority as requiring notice and hearing before valid action can be taken by administrative officers are where complainant will lose some property or enforceable civil or statutory right by the action taken or proposed. "[A] mere abstract declaration" by an administrator regarding the character of an organization, without the effect of forbidding or compelling conduct on the part of complainant, ought not to be subject to judicial interference. *Rochester Telephone Corp. v. United States*, 307 U.S. 125, 129, 143. That is, it does not require notice and hearing.

These petitioners are not ordered to do anything and are not punished for anything. Their position may be analogized to that of persons under grand jury investigation. Such persons have no right to notice by and hearing before a grand jury; only a right to defend the charge at trial * * *.

* * *

CAFETERIA & RESTAURANT WORKERS UNION, LOCAL 473, AFL–CIO v. McELROY

Supreme Court of the United States, 1961.
367 U.S. 886, 81 S.Ct. 1743, 6 L.Ed.2d 1230.

MR. JUSTICE STEWART delivered the opinion of the Court.

In 1956 the petitioner Rachel Brawner was a short-order cook at a cafeteria operated by her employer, M & M Restaurants, Inc., on the premises of the Naval Gun Factory in the city of Washington. She had worked there for more than six years, and from her employer's point of view her record was entirely satisfactory.

The Gun Factory was engaged in designing, producing, and inspecting naval ordnance, including the development of weapons systems of a highly classified nature. Located on property owned by the United States, the installation was under the command of Rear Admiral D. M. Tyree, Superintendent. Access to it was restricted, and guards were posted at all points of entry. Identification badges were issued to persons authorized to enter the premises by the Security Officer, a naval officer subordinate to the Superintendent. In 1956 the Security Officer was Lieutenant Commander H. C. Williams. Rachel Brawner had been issued such a badge.

* * *

On November 15, 1956, Mrs. Brawner was required to turn in her identification badge because of Lieutenant Commander Williams' determination that she had failed to meet the security requirements of the installation. The Security Officer's determination was subsequently approved by Admiral Tyree * * *. At the request of the petitioner Union, which represented the employees at the cafeteria, M & M sought to arrange a meeting with officials of the Gun Factory "for the purpose of a hearing regarding the denial of admittance to the Naval Gun Factory of Rachel Brawner." This request was denied by Admiral Tyree on the ground that such a meeting would "serve no useful purpose."

Since the day her identification badge was withdrawn Mrs. Brawner has not been permitted to enter the Gun Factory. M & M offered to employ her in another restaurant which the company operated in the suburban Washington area, but she refused on the ground that the location was inconvenient.

The petitioners brought this action in the District Court against the Secretary of Defense, Admiral Tyree, and Lieutenant Commander Williams, in their individual and official capacities, seeking, among other things, to compel the return to Mrs. Brawner of her identification badge, so that she might be permitted to enter the Gun Factory and resume her former employment * * *.

As the case comes here, two basic questions are presented. Was the commanding officer of the Gun Factory authorized to deny Rachel Brawner access to the installation in the way he did? If he was so authorized, did his action in excluding her operate to deprive her of any right secured to her by the Constitution?

* * *

[The Court answers the first question in the affirmative.]

The question remains whether Admiral Tyree's action in summarily denying Rachel Brawner access to the site of her former employment violated the requirements of the Due Process Clause of the Fifth Amendment. This question cannot be answered by easy assertion that, because she had no constitutional right to be there in the first place, she was not deprived of liberty or property by the Superintendent's action. "One may not have a constitutional right to go to Baghdad, but the Government may not prohibit one from going there unless by means consonant with due process of law." *Homer v. Richmond*, 110 U. S. App. D. C. 226, 229, 292 F.2d 719, 722. It is the petitioners' claim that due process in this case required that Rachel Brawner be advised of the specific grounds for her exclusion and be accorded a hearing at which she might refute them. We are satisfied, however, that under the circumstances of this case such a procedure was not constitutionally required.

The Fifth Amendment does not require a trial-type hearing in every conceivable case of government impairment of private interest. "For, though 'due process of law' generally implies and includes actor, reus, judex, regular allegations, opportunity to answer, and a trial according to some settled course of judicial proceedings, . . . yet, this is not universally true." *Murray's Lessee v. Hoboken Land and Improvement Co.*, 18 How. 272, 280. The very nature of due process negates any concept of inflexible procedures universally applicable to every imaginable situation * * *.

* * * [C]onsideration of what procedures due process may require under any given set of circumstances must begin with a determination of the precise nature of the government function involved as well as of the private interest that has been affected by governmental action. Where it has been possible to characterize that private interest (perhaps in oversimplification) as a mere privilege subject to the Executive's plenary power, it has traditionally been held that notice and hearing are not constitutionally required.

What, then, was the private interest affected by Admiral Tyree's action in the present case? It most assuredly was not the right to follow a chosen trade or profession. Rachel Brawner remained entirely free to obtain employment as a short-order cook or to get any other job, either with M &

M or with any other employer. All that was denied her was the opportunity to work at one isolated and specific military installation.

Moreover, the governmental function operating here was not the power to regulate or license, as lawmaker, an entire trade or profession, or to control an entire branch of private business, but, rather, as proprietor, to manage the internal operation of an important federal military establishment. In that proprietary military capacity, the Federal Government, as has been pointed out, has traditionally exercised unfettered control.

* * * The Court has consistently recognized that an interest closely analogous to Rachel Brawner's, the interest of a government employee in retaining his job, can be summarily denied. It has become a settled principle that government employment, in the absence of legislation, can be revoked at the will of the appointing officer * * *.

* * *

* * * [T]he state and federal governments, even in the exercise of their internal operations, do not constitutionally have the complete freedom of action enjoyed by a private employer. But to acknowledge that there exist constitutional restraints upon state and federal governments in dealing with their employees is not to say that all such employees have a constitutional right to notice and a hearing before they can be removed. We may assume that Rachel Brawner could not constitutionally have been excluded from the Gun Factory if the announced grounds for her exclusion had been patently arbitrary or discriminatory—that she could not have been kept out because she was a Democrat or a Methodist. It does not follow, however, that she was entitled to notice and a hearing when the reason advanced for her exclusion was, as here, entirely rational and in accord with the contract with M & M.

Finally, it is to be noted that this is not a case where government action has operated to bestow a badge of disloyalty or infamy, with an attendant foreclosure from other employment opportunity. All this record shows is that, in the opinion of the Security Officer of the Gun Factory, concurred in by the Superintendent, Rachel Brawner failed to meet the particular security requirements of that specific military installation. There is nothing to indicate that this determination would in any way impair Rachel Brawner's employment opportunities anywhere else * * *. For all that appears, the Security Officer and the Superintendent may have simply thought that Rachel Brawner was garrulous, or careless with her identification badge.

For these reasons, we conclude that the Due Process Clause of the Fifth Amendment was not violated in this case.

MR. JUSTICE BRENNAN, with whom the CHIEF JUSTICE, MR. JUSTICE BLACK and MR. JUSTICE DOUGLAS join, dissenting.

* * *

I read the Court's opinion to acknowledge that petitioner's status as an employee at the Gun Factory was an interest of sufficient definiteness to be protected by the Federal Constitution from some kinds of governmental injury * * *. In other words, if petitioner Brawner's badge had been lifted avowedly on grounds of her race, religion, or political opinions, the Court would concede that some constitutionally protected interest—whether "liberty" or "property" it is unnecessary to state—had been injured. But, as the Court says, there has been no such open discrimination here. The expressed ground of exclusion was the obscuring formulation that petitioner failed to meet the "security requirements" of the naval installation where she worked. I assume for present purposes that separation as a "security risk," if the charge is properly established, is not unconstitutional. But the Court goes beyond that. It holds that the mere assertion by government that exclusion is for a valid reason forecloses further inquiry. That is, unless the government official is foolish enough to admit what he is doing—and few will be so foolish after today's decision— he may employ "security requirements" as a blind behind which to dismiss at will for the most discriminatory of causes.

Such a result in effect nullifies the substantive right—not to be arbitrarily injured by Government—which the Court purports to recognize. What sort of right is it which enjoys absolutely no procedural protection? I do not mean to imply that petitioner could not have been excluded from the installation without the full procedural panoply of first having been subjected to a trial, with cross-examination and confrontation of accusers, and proof of guilt beyond a reasonable doubt. I need not go so far in this case. For under today's holding petitioner is entitled to no process at all. She is not told what she did wrong; she is not given a chance to defend herself. She may be the victim of the basest calumny, perhaps even the caprice of the government officials in whose power her status rested completely. In such a case, I cannot believe that she is not entitled to some procedures. "The right to be heard before being condemned to suffer grievous loss of any kind, even though it may not involve the stigma and hardships of a criminal conviction, is a principle basic to our society." *Joint Anti-Fascist Refugee Comm. v. McGrath*, 341 U.S. 123, 168 (1951) (concurring opinion.) In sum, the Court holds that petitioner has a right not to have her identification badge taken away for an "arbitrary" reason, but no right to be told in detail what the reason is, or to defend her own innocence, in order to show, perhaps, that the true reason for deprivation was one forbidden by the Constitution. That is an internal contradiction to which I cannot subscribe.

2. LIFELIBERTYPROPERTY

The view of Justice Frankfurter (and perhaps Justice Jackson) in *JAFRC* and of the four dissenters in *McElroy* that a "grievous loss of any kind" is a constitutionally protected interest essentially treats the phrase "life, liberty, and property" as a shorthand reference to "any matters that are reasonably important in a person's life." It treats the phrase, in other words, as a single concept rather than three separate concepts with independent meanings—as "lifelibertyproperty" rather than "life, liberty, or property."

By 1971, this model had entirely supplanted the traditional model of *Bailey v. Richardson* as the Court's chosen approach for determining the scope of constitutionally protected interests. The following three cases, which include the Court's most famous (though by no means most influential) procedural due process case, graphically illustrate the Court's change in thinking about "life, liberty, and property"—and the potential consequences of that change for administrative law.

GOLDBERG v. KELLY

Supreme Court of the United States, 1970.
397 U.S. 254, 90 S.Ct. 1011, 25 L.Ed.2d 287.

MR. JUSTICE BRENNAN delivered the opinion of the Court.

The question for decision is whether a State that terminates public assistance payments to a particular recipient without affording him the opportunity for an evidentiary hearing prior to termination denies the recipient procedural due process in violation of the Due Process Clause of the Fourteenth Amendment.

This action was brought in the District Court for the Southern District of New York by residents of New York City receiving financial aid under the federally assisted program of Aid to Families with Dependent Children (AFDC) or under New York State's general Home Relief program.[1] Their complaint alleged that the New York State and New York City officials administering these programs terminated, or were about to terminate, such aid without prior notice and hearing, thereby denying them due process of law. At the time the suits were filed there was no requirement of prior notice or hearing of any kind before termination of financial aid. However, the State and city adopted procedures for notice and hearing after the suits were brought, and the plaintiffs, appellees here, then challenged the constitutional adequacy of those procedures.

---

[1] AFDC * * * is a categorical assistance program supported by federal grants-in-aid but administered by the States according to regulations of the Secretary of Health, Education, and Welfare * * *. Home Relief is a general assistance program financed and administered solely by New York state and local governments. It assists any person unable to support himself or to secure support from other sources.

The State Commissioner of Social Services amended the State Department of Social Services' Official Regulations to require that local social services officials proposing to discontinue or suspend a recipient's financial aid do so according to a procedure that conforms to either subdivision (a) or subdivision (b) of § 351.26 of the regulations as amended. The City of New York elected to promulgate a local procedure according to subdivision (b). That subdivision, so far as here pertinent, provides that the local procedure must include the giving of notice to the recipient of the reasons for a proposed discontinuance or suspension at least seven days prior to its effective date, with notice also that upon request the recipient may have the proposal reviewed by a local welfare official holding a position superior to that of the supervisor who approved the proposed discontinuance or suspension, and, further, that the recipient may submit, for purposes of the review, a written statement to demonstrate why his grant should not be discontinued or suspended. The decision by the reviewing official whether to discontinue or suspend aid must be made expeditiously, with written notice of the decision to the recipient. The section further expressly provides that "[a]ssistance shall not be discontinued or suspended prior to the date such notice of decision is sent to the recipient and his representative, if any, or prior to the proposed effective date of discontinuance or suspension, whichever occurs later."

Pursuant to subdivision (b), the New York City Department of Social Services promulgated Procedure No. 68–18. A caseworker who has doubts about the recipient's continued eligibility must first discuss them with the recipient. If the caseworker concludes that the recipient is no longer eligible, he recommends termination of aid to a unit supervisor. If the latter concurs, he sends the recipient a letter stating the reasons for proposing to terminate aid and notifying him that within seven days he may request that a higher official review the record, and may support the request with a written statement prepared personally or with the aid of an attorney or other person. If the reviewing official affirms the determination of ineligibility, aid is stopped immediately and the recipient is informed by letter of the reasons for the action. Appellees' challenge to this procedure emphasizes the absence of any provisions for the personal appearance of the recipient before the reviewing official, for oral presentation of evidence, and for confrontation and cross-examination of adverse witnesses. However, the letter does inform the recipient that he may request a post-termination "fair hearing." This is a proceeding before an independent state hearing officer at which the recipient may appear personally, offer oral evidence, confront and cross-examine the witnesses against him, and have a record made of the hearing. If the recipient prevails at the "fair hearing" he is paid all funds erroneously withheld. A recipient whose aid is not restored by a "fair hearing" decision may have judicial review. The recipient is so notified.

I

The constitutional issue to be decided, therefore, is the narrow one whether the Due Process Clause requires that the recipient be afforded an evidentiary hearing *before* the termination of benefits.[7] The District Court held that only a pre-termination evidentiary hearing would satisfy the constitutional command, and rejected the argument of the state and city officials that the combination of the post-termination "fair hearing" with the informal pre-termination review disposed of all due process claims. The court said: "While post-termination review is relevant, there is one overpowering fact which controls here. By hypothesis, a welfare recipient is destitute, without funds or assets. . . . Suffice it to say that to cut off a welfare recipient in the face of . . . 'brutal need' without a prior hearing of some sort is unconscionable, unless overwhelming considerations justify it." *Kelly v. Wyman*, 294 F.Supp. 893, 899, 900 (1968). The court rejected the argument that the need to protect the public's tax revenues supplied the requisite "overwhelming consideration." "Against the justified desire to protect public funds must be weighed the individual's overpowering need in this unique situation not to be wrongfully deprived of assistance. . . . While the problem of additional expense must be kept in mind, it does not justify denying a hearing meeting the ordinary standards of due process. Under all the circumstances, we hold that due process requires an adequate hearing before termination of welfare benefits, and the fact that there is a later constitutionally fair proceeding does not alter the result." *Id.*, at 901. Although state officials were party defendants in the action, only the Commissioner of Social Services of the City of New York appealed * * *.

Appellant does not contend that procedural due process is not applicable to the termination of welfare benefits. Such benefits are a matter of statutory entitlement for persons qualified to receive them.[8] Their termination involves state action that adjudicates important rights. The constitutional challenge cannot be answered by an argument that

---

[7]   Appellant does not question the recipient's due process right to evidentiary review *after* termination * * *.

[8]   It may be realistic today to regard welfare entitlements as more like "property" than a "gratuity." Much of the existing wealth in this country takes the form of rights that do not fall within traditional common-law concepts of property. It has been aptly noted that

"[s]ociety today is built around entitlement. The automobile dealer has his franchise, the doctor and lawyer their professional licenses, the worker his union membership, contract, and pension rights, the executive his contract and stock options; all are devices to aid security and independence. Many of the most important of these entitlements now flow from government: subsidies to farmers and businessmen, routes for airlines and channels for television stations; long term contracts for defense, space, and education; social security pensions for individuals. Such sources of security, whether private or public, are no longer regarded as luxuries or gratuities; to the recipients they are essentials, fully deserved, and in no sense a form of charity. It is only the poor whose entitlements, although recognized by public policy, have not been effectively enforced."

Reich, *Individual Rights and Social Welfare: The Emerging Legal Issues*, 74 Yale L.J. 1245, 1255 (1965). See also Reich, *The New Property*, 73 Yale L.J. 733 (1964).

public assistance benefits are "a 'privilege' and not a 'right.'" *Shapiro v. Thompson*, 394 U.S. 618, 627 n. 6, 89 S.Ct. 1322, 1327 (1969). Relevant constitutional restraints apply as much to the withdrawal of public assistance benefits as to disqualification for unemployment compensation, *Sherbert v. Verner*, 374 U.S. 398, 83 S.Ct. 1790, 10 L.Ed.2d 965 (1963); or to denial of a tax exemption, *Speiser v. Randall*, 357 U.S. 513, 78 S.Ct. 1332, 2 L.Ed.2d 1460 (1958); or to discharge from public employment, *Slochower v. Board of Higher Education*, 350 U.S. 551, 76 S.Ct. 637, 100 L.Ed. 692 (1956). The extent to which procedural due process must be afforded the recipient is influenced by the extent to which he may be "condemned to suffer grievous loss," *Joint Anti-Fascist Refugee Committee v. McGrath*, 341 U.S. 123, 168, 71 S.Ct. 624, 647, 95 L.Ed. 817 (1951) (Frankfurter, J., concurring), and depends upon whether the recipient's interest in avoiding that loss outweighs the governmental interest in summary adjudication. Accordingly, as we said in *Cafeteria & Restaurant Workers Union, etc. v. McElroy*, 367 U.S. 886, 895, 81 S.Ct. 1743, 1748–1749, 6 L.Ed.2d 1230 (1961), "consideration of what procedures due process may require under any given set of circumstances must begin with a determination of the precise nature of the government function involved as well as of the private interest that has been affected by governmental action."

It is true, of course, that some governmental benefits may be administratively terminated without affording the recipient a pre-termination evidentiary hearing. But we agree with the District Court that when welfare is discontinued, only a pre-termination evidentiary hearing provides the recipient with procedural due process. For qualified recipients, welfare provides the means to obtain essential food, clothing, housing, and medical care. Thus the crucial factor in this context—a factor not present in the case of the blacklisted government contractor, the discharged government employee, the taxpayer denied a tax exemption, or virtually anyone else whose governmental entitlements are ended—is that termination of aid pending resolution of a controversy over eligibility may deprive an *eligible* recipient of the very means by which to live while he waits. Since he lacks independent resources, his situation becomes immediately desperate. His need to concentrate upon finding the means for daily subsistence, in turn, adversely affects his ability to seek redress from the welfare bureaucracy.

Moreover, important governmental interests are promoted by affording recipients a pre-termination evidentiary hearing. From its founding the Nation's basic commitment has been to foster the dignity and well-being of all persons within its borders. We have come to recognize that forces not within the control of the poor contribute to their poverty. This perception, against the background of our traditions, has significantly influenced the development of the contemporary public assistance system.

Welfare, by meeting the basic demands of subsistence, can help bring within the reach of the poor the same opportunities that are available to others to participate meaningfully in the life of the community. At the same time, welfare guards against the societal malaise that may flow from a widespread sense of unjustified frustration and insecurity. Public assistance, then, is not mere charity, but a means to "promote the general Welfare, and secure the Blessings of Liberty to ourselves and our Posterity." The same governmental interests that counsel the provision of welfare, counsel as well its uninterrupted provision to those eligible to receive it; pre-termination evidentiary hearings are indispensable to that end.

Appellant does not challenge the force of these considerations but argues that they are outweighed by countervailing governmental interests in conserving fiscal and administrative resources. These interests, the argument goes, justify the delay of any evidentiary hearing until after discontinuance of the grants. Summary adjudication protects the public fisc by stopping payments promptly upon discovery of reason to believe that a recipient is no longer eligible. Since most terminations are accepted without challenge, summary adjudication also conserves both the fisc and administrative time and energy by reducing the number of evidentiary hearings actually held.

We agree with the District Court, however, that these governmental interests are not overriding in the welfare context. The requirement of a prior hearing doubtless involves some greater expense, and the benefits paid to ineligible recipients pending decision at the hearing probably cannot be recouped, since these recipients are likely to be judgment-proof. But the State is not without weapons to minimize these increased costs. Much of the drain on fiscal and administrative resources can be reduced by developing procedures for prompt pre-termination hearings and by skillful use of personnel and facilities. Indeed, the very provision for a post-termination evidentiary hearing in New York's Home Relief program is itself cogent evidence that the State recognizes the primacy of the public interest in correct eligibility determinations and therefore in the provision of procedural safeguards. Thus, the interest of the eligible recipient in uninterrupted receipt of public assistance, coupled with the State's interest that his payments not be erroneously terminated, clearly outweighs the State's competing concern to prevent any increase in its fiscal and administrative burdens. As the District Court correctly concluded, "[t]he stakes are simply too high for the welfare recipient, and the possibility for honest error or irritable misjudgment too great, to allow termination of aid without giving the recipient a chance, if he so desires, to be fully informed of the case against him so that he may contest its basis and produce evidence in rebuttal." 294 F.Supp., at 904–905.

II

We also agree with the District Court, however, that the pre-termination hearing need not take the form of a judicial or quasi-judicial trial. We bear in mind that the statutory "fair hearing" will provide the recipient with a full administrative review. Accordingly, the pre-termination hearing has one function only: to produce an initial determination of the validity of the welfare department's grounds for discontinuance of payments in order to protect a recipient against an erroneous termination of his benefits. Thus, a complete record and a comprehensive opinion, which would serve primarily to facilitate judicial review and to guide future decisions, need not be provided at the pre-termination stage. We recognize, too, that both welfare authorities and recipients have an interest in relatively speedy resolution of questions of eligibility, that they are used to dealing with one another informally, and that some welfare departments have very burdensome caseloads. These considerations justify the limitation of the pre-termination hearing to minimum procedural safeguards, adapted to the particular characteristics of welfare recipients, and to the limited nature of the controversies to be resolved. We wish to add that we, no less than the dissenters, recognize the importance of not imposing upon the States or the Federal Government in this developing field of law any procedural requirements beyond those demanded by rudimentary due process.

"The fundamental requisite of due process of law is the opportunity to be heard." *Grannis v. Ordean*, 234 U.S. 385, 394, 34 S.Ct. 779, 783, 58 L.Ed. 1363 (1914). The hearing must be "at a meaningful time and in a meaningful manner." *Armstrong v. Manzo*, 380 U.S. 545, 552, 85 S.Ct. 1187, 1191, 14 L.Ed.2d 62 (1965). In the present context these principles require that a recipient have timely and adequate notice detailing the reasons for a proposed termination, and an effective opportunity to defend by confronting any adverse witnesses and by presenting his own arguments and evidence orally. These rights are important in cases such as those before us, where recipients have challenged proposed terminations as resting on incorrect or misleading factual premises or on misapplication of rules or policies to the facts of particular cases.

We are not prepared to say that the seven-day notice currently provided by New York City is constitutionally insufficient *per se*, although there may be cases where fairness would require that a longer time be given. Nor do we see any constitutional deficiency in the content or form of the notice. New York employs both a letter and a personal conference with a caseworker to inform a recipient of the precise questions raised about his continued eligibility. Evidently the recipient is told the legal and factual bases for the Department's doubts. This combination is probably the most effective method of communicating with recipients.

The city's procedures presently do not permit recipients to appear personally with or without counsel before the official who finally determines continued eligibility. Thus a recipient is not permitted to present evidence to that official orally, or to confront or cross-examine adverse witnesses. These omissions are fatal to the constitutional adequacy of the procedures.

The opportunity to be heard must be tailored to the capacities and circumstances of those who are to be heard. It is not enough that a welfare recipient may present his position to the decision maker in writing or second-hand through his caseworker. Written submissions are an unrealistic option for most recipients, who lack the educational attainment necessary to write effectively and who cannot obtain professional assistance. Moreover, written submissions do not afford the flexibility of oral presentations; they do not permit the recipient to mold his argument to the issues the decision maker appears to regard as important. Particularly where credibility and veracity are at issue, as they must be in many termination proceedings, written submissions are a wholly unsatisfactory basis for decision. The second-hand presentation to the decisionmaker by the caseworker has its own deficiencies; since the caseworker usually gathers the facts upon which the charge of ineligibility rests, the presentation of the recipient's side of the controversy cannot safely be left to him. Therefore a recipient must be allowed to state his position orally. Informal procedures will suffice; in this context due process does not require a particular order of proof or mode of offering evidence.

In almost every setting where important decisions turn on questions of fact, due process requires an opportunity to confront and cross-examine adverse witnesses * * *. Welfare recipients must therefore be given an opportunity to confront and cross-examine the witnesses relied on by the department.

"The right to be heard would be, in many cases, of little avail if it did not comprehend the right to be heard by counsel." *Powell v. Alabama*, 287 U.S. 45, 68–69, 53 S.Ct. 55, 64, 77 L.Ed. 158 (1932). We do not say that counsel must be provided at the pre-termination hearing, but only that the recipient must be allowed to retain an attorney if he so desires. Counsel can help delineate the issues, present the factual contentions in an orderly manner, conduct cross-examination, and generally safeguard the interests of the recipient. We do not anticipate that this assistance will unduly prolong or otherwise encumber the hearing * * *.

Finally, the decisionmaker's conclusion as to a recipient's eligibility must rest solely on the legal rules and evidence adduced at the hearing. To demonstrate compliance with this elementary requirement, the decision maker should state the reasons for his determination and indicate the evidence he relied on, though his statement need not amount to a full opinion or even formal findings of fact and conclusions of law. And, of course, an impartial decision maker is essential. We agree with the District Court that prior involvement in some aspects of a case will not necessarily bar a welfare official from acting as a decision maker. He should not, however, have participated in making the determination under review.

Affirmed.

MR. JUSTICE BLACK, dissenting.

* * *

The more than a million names on the relief rolls in New York, and the more than nine million names on the rolls of all the 50 States were not put there at random. The names are there because state welfare officials believed that those people were eligible for assistance. Probably in the officials' haste to make out the lists many names were put there erroneously in order to alleviate immediate suffering, and undoubtedly some people are drawing relief who are not entitled under the law to do so. Doubtless some draw relief checks from time to time who know they are not eligible, either because they are not actually in need or for some other reason. Many of those who thus draw undeserved gratuities are without sufficient property to enable the government to collect back from them any money they wrongfully receive. But the Court today holds that it would violate the Due Process Clause of the Fourteenth Amendment to stop paying those people weekly or monthly allowances unless the government first affords them a full "evidentiary hearing" even though welfare officials are persuaded that the recipients are not rightfully entitled to receive a penny under the law. In other words, although some recipients might be on the lists for payment wholly because of deliberate fraud on their part, the Court holds that the government is helpless and must continue, until after an evidentiary hearing, to pay money that it does not owe, never has owed, and never could owe. I do not believe there is any provision in our Constitution that should thus paralyze the government's efforts to protect itself against making payments to people who are not entitled to them.

* * *

The Court apparently feels that this decision will benefit the poor and needy. In my judgment the eventual result will be just the opposite. While today's decision requires only an administrative, evidentiary hearing, the inevitable logic of the approach taken will lead to constitutionally imposed, time-consuming delays of a full adversary process of administrative and judicial review * * *. [T]he end result of today's decision may well be that the government, once it decides to give welfare benefits, cannot reverse that decision until the recipient has had the benefits of full administrative and judicial review, including, of course, the opportunity to present his case to this Court. Since this process will usually entail a delay of several years, the inevitable result of such a constitutionally imposed burden will be that the government will not put a claimant on the rolls initially until it has made an exhaustive investigation to determine his eligibility. While this Court will perhaps have insured that no needy person will be taken off the rolls without a full "due process" proceeding, it will also have insured that many will never get on the rolls, or at least that they will remain destitute during the lengthy proceedings followed to determine initial eligibility.

* * *

[CHIEF JUSTICE BURGER and JUSTICE STEWART also dissented in *Goldberg* and the companion case of *Wheeler v. Montgomery*, 397 U.S. 280, 90 S.Ct. 1026, 25 L.Ed.2d 307 (1970).]

WISCONSIN V. CONSTANTINEAU
Supreme Court of the United States, 1971.
400 U.S. 433, 91 S.Ct. 507, 27 L.Ed.2d 515.

MR. JUSTICE DOUGLAS delivered the opinion of the Court.

Appellee is an adult resident of Hartford, Wis. She brought suit in a federal district court in Wisconsin to have a Wisconsin statute declared unconstitutional * * *.

The Act, Wis. Stat. § 176.26 (1967), provides that designated persons may in writing forbid the sale or gift of intoxicating liquors to one who "by excessive drinking" produces described conditions or exhibits specified traits, such as exposing himself or family "to want" or becoming "dangerous to the peace" of the community.

The chief of police of Hartford, without notice or hearing to appellee, caused to be posted a notice in all retail liquor outlets in Hartford that sales or gifts of liquors to appellee were forbidden for one year. Thereupon this suit was brought against the chief of police claiming damages and asking for injunctive relief * * *.

We have no doubt as to the power of a State to deal with the evils described in the Act. The police power of the States over intoxicating liquors was extremely broad even prior to the Twenty-first Amendment. The only issue present here is whether the label or characterization given a person by "posting," though a mark of serious illness to some, is to others such a stigma or badge of disgrace that procedural due process requires notice and an opportunity to be heard. We agree with the District Court that the private interest is such that those requirements of procedural due process must be met.

It is significant that most of the provisions of the Bill of Rights are procedural, for it is procedure that marks much of the difference between rule by law and rule by fiat.

We reviewed in *Cafeteria Workers v. McElroy*, 367 U.S. 886, 895, the nature of the various "private interest[s]" that have fallen on one side or the other of the line. Generalizations are hazardous as some state and federal administrative procedures are summary by reason of necessity or history. Yet certainly where the State attaches "a badge of infamy" to the citizen, due process comes into play. "The right to be heard before being condemned to suffer grievous loss of any kind, even though it may not involve the stigma and hardships of a criminal conviction, is a principle basic to our society." *Anti-Fascist Refugee Committee v. McGrath*, 341 U.S. 123, 168 (Frankfurter, J., concurring).

Where a person's good name, reputation, honor, or integrity is at stake because of what the government is doing to him, notice and an opportunity to be heard are essential. "Posting" under the Wisconsin Act may to some be merely the mark of illness, to others it is a stigma, an official branding of a person. The label is a degrading one. Under the Wisconsin Act, a resident of Hartford is given no process at all. This appellee was not afforded a chance to defend herself. She may have been the victim of an official's caprice. Only when the whole proceedings leading to the pinning of an unsavory label on a person are aired can oppressive results be prevented.

* * *

[CHIEF JUSTICE BURGER, JUSTICE BLACK, and JUSTICE BLACKMUN dissented on grounds unrelated to the Court's due process discussion.]

BELL V. BURSON

Supreme Court of the United States, 1971.
402 U.S. 535, 91 S.Ct. 1586, 29 L.Ed.2d 90.

MR. JUSTICE BRENNAN delivered the opinion of the Court.

Georgia's Motor Vehicle Safety Responsibility Act provides that the motor vehicle registration and driver's license of an uninsured motorist involved in an accident shall be suspended unless he posts security to cover the amount of damages claimed by aggrieved parties in reports of the accident. The administrative hearing conducted prior to the suspension excludes consideration of the motorist's fault or liability for the accident. The Georgia Court of Appeals rejected petitioner's contention that the State's statutory scheme, in failing before suspending the licenses to afford him a hearing on the question of his fault or liability, denied him due process in violation of the Fourteenth Amendment: the court held that " 'Fault' or 'innocence' are completely irrelevant factors." 121 Ga. App. 418, 420, 174 S. E. 2d 235, 236 (1970). The Georgia Supreme Court denied review. We granted certiorari. We reverse.

Petitioner is a clergyman whose ministry requires him to travel by car to cover three rural Georgia communities. On Sunday afternoon, November 24, 1968, petitioner was involved in an accident when five-year-old Sherry Capes rode her bicycle into the side of his automobile. The child's parents filed an accident report with the Director of the Georgia Department of Public Safety indicating that their daughter had suffered substantial injuries for which they claimed damages of $5,000. Petitioner was thereafter informed by the Director that unless he was covered by a liability insurance policy in effect at the time of the accident he must file a bond or cash security deposit of $5,000 or present a notarized release from liability, plus proof of future financial responsibility, or suffer the suspension of his driver's license and vehicle registration. Petitioner requested an administrative hearing before the Director asserting that he was not liable as the accident was unavoidable, and stating also that he would be severely handicapped in the performance of his ministerial duties by a suspension of his licenses. A hearing was scheduled but the Director informed petitioner that "[t]he only evidence that the Department can accept and consider is: (a) was the petitioner or his vehicle involved in the accident; (b) has petitioner complied with the provisions of the Law as provided; or (c) does petitioner come within any of the exceptions of the Law." At the administrative hearing the Director rejected petitioner's proffer of evidence on liability, ascertained that petitioner was not within any of the statutory exceptions, and gave petitioner 30 days to comply with the security requirements or suffer suspension. Petitioner then exercised his statutory right to an appeal *de novo* in the Superior Court. At that hearing, the court permitted petitioner to present his evidence on liability, and, although the claimants were neither parties nor witnesses, found petitioner free from fault. As a result, the Superior Court ordered "that the petitioner's driver's license not be suspended . . . [until] suit is filed against petitioner for the purpose of recovering damages for the injuries sustained by the child. . ." This order was reversed by the Georgia Court of Appeals in overruling petitioner's constitutional contention.

If the statute barred the issuance of licenses to all motorists who did not carry liability insurance or who did not post security, the statute would not, under our cases, violate the Fourteenth Amendment. It does not follow, however, that the amendment also permits the Georgia statutory scheme where not all motorists, but rather only motorists involved in accidents, are required to post security under penalty of loss of the licenses. Once licenses are issued, as in petitioner's case, their continued possession may become essential in the pursuit of a livelihood. Suspension of issued licenses thus involves state action that adjudicates important interests of the licensees. In such cases the licenses are not to be taken away without that procedural due process required by the Fourteenth Amendment. This is but an application of the general proposition that relevant constitutional restraints limit state power to terminate an entitlement whether the entitlement is denominated a "right" or a "privilege."

We turn then to the nature of the procedural due process which must be afforded the licensee on the question of his fault or liability for the accident. A procedural rule that may satisfy due process in one context may not necessarily satisfy procedural due process in every case. Thus, procedures adequate to determine a welfare claim may not suffice to try a felony charge. Clearly, however, the inquiry into fault or liability requisite to afford the licensee due process need not take the form of a full adjudication of the question of liability. That adjudication can only be made in litigation between the parties involved in the accident. Since the only purpose of the provisions before us is to obtain security from which to pay any judgments against the licensee resulting from the accident, we hold that procedural due process will be satisfied by an inquiry limited to the determination whether there is a reasonable possibility of judgments in the amounts claimed being rendered against the licensee.

* * *

* * * [W]e reject Georgia's argument that if it must afford the licensee an inquiry into the question of liability, that determination, unlike the determination of the matters presently considered at the administrative hearing, need not be made prior to the suspension of the licenses. While "[m]any controversies have raged about . . . the Due Process Clause," it is fundamental that except in emergency situations (and this is not one) due process requires that when a State seeks to terminate an interest such as that here involved, it must afford "notice and opportunity for hearing appropriate to the nature of the case" before the termination becomes effective.

* * *

THE CHIEF JUSTICE, MR. JUSTICE BLACK, and MR. JUSTICE BLACKMUN concur in the result.

3. THE THIRD WAY: THE RISE OF ENTITLEMENT THEORY

After *Constantineau* and *Bell*, one could be forgiven for thinking that the debate concerning the meaning of "life, liberty, or property" was over. Justice Frankfurter's "grievous loss of any kind" formulation seemed to have carried the day with surprisingly little resistance. In 1972, however, the Court took a good, hard look at where its due process jurisprudence was headed and introduced a third model into the mix. The two cases to follow, and the model for identifying constitutionally protected interests that they introduced, continue to be among the cornerstones of modern due process law.

BOARD OF REGENTS OF STATE COLLEGES V. ROTH

Supreme Court of the United States, 1972.
408 U.S. 564, 92 S.Ct. 2701, 33 L.Ed.2d 548.

MR. JUSTICE STEWART delivered the opinion of the Court.

In 1968 the respondent, David Roth, was hired for his first teaching job as assistant professor of political science at Wisconsin State University-Oshkosh. He was hired for a fixed term of one academic year. The notice of his faculty appointment specified that his employment would begin on September 1, 1968, and would end on June 30, 1969.[1] The respondent completed that term. But he was informed that he would not be rehired for the next academic year.

The respondent had no tenure rights to continued employment. Under Wisconsin statutory law a state university teacher can acquire tenure as a "permanent" employee only after four years of year-to-year employment. Having acquired tenure, a teacher is entitled to continued employment "during efficiency and good behavior." A relatively new teacher without tenure, however, is under Wisconsin law entitled to nothing beyond his one-year appointment. There are no statutory or administrative standards defining eligibility for re-employment. State law thus clearly leaves the decision whether to rehire a nontenured teacher for another year to the unfettered discretion of university officials.

The procedural protection afforded a Wisconsin State University teacher before he is separated from the University corresponds to his job security. As a matter of statutory law, a tenured teacher cannot be "discharged except for cause upon written charges" and pursuant to certain procedures. A nontenured teacher, similarly, is protected to some extent during his one-year term. Rules promulgated by the Board of Regents provide that a nontenured teacher "dismissed" before the end of the year may have some opportunity for review of the "dismissal." But the Rules provide no real protection for a nontenured teacher who simply is not re-employed for the next year. He must be informed by February 1 "concerning retention or non-retention for the ensuing year." But "no reason for non-retention need be given. No review or appeal is provided in such case."

In conformance with these Rules, the President of Wisconsin State University-Oshkosh informed the respondent before February 1, 1969, that he would not be rehired for the 1969–1970 academic year. He gave the respondent no reason for the decision and no opportunity to challenge it at any sort of hearing.

---

[1] The respondent had no contract of employment. Rather, his formal notice of appointment was the equivalent of an employment contract * * *.

The respondent then brought this action in Federal District Court alleging that the decision not to rehire him for the next year infringed his Fourteenth Amendment rights. He attacked the decision both in substance and procedure. First, he alleged that the true reason for the decision was to punish him for certain statements critical of the University administration, and that it therefore violated his right to freedom of speech.[5] Second, he alleged that the failure of University officials to give him notice of any reason for nonretention and an opportunity for a hearing violated his right to procedural due process of law.

The District Court granted summary judgment for the respondent on the procedural issue, ordering the University officials to provide him with reasons and a hearing. The Court of Appeals, with one judge dissenting, affirmed this partial summary judgment. We granted certiorari. The only question presented to us at this stage in the case is whether the respondent had a constitutional right to a statement of reasons and a hearing on the University's decision not to rehire him for another year. We hold that he did not.

I

The requirements of procedural due process apply only to the deprivation of interests encompassed by the Fourteenth Amendment's protection of liberty and property. When protected interests are implicated, the right to some kind of prior hearing is paramount.[7] But the range of interests protected by procedural due process is not infinite.

The District Court decided that procedural due process guarantees apply in this case by assessing and balancing the weights of the particular interests involved. It concluded that the respondent's interest in re-employment at Wisconsin State University-Oshkosh outweighed the University's interest in denying him re-employment summarily. Undeniably, the respondent's re-employment prospects were of major concern to him—concern that we surely cannot say was insignificant. And a weighing process has long been a part of any determination of the *form* of hearing required in particular situations by procedural due process. But,

---

[5]   While the respondent alleged that he was not rehired because of his exercise of free speech, the petitioners insisted that the non-retention decision was based on other, constitutionally valid grounds. The District Court came to no conclusion whatever regarding the true reason for the University President's decision. "In the present case," it stated, "it appears that a determination as to the actual bases of (the) decision must await amplification of the facts at trial. . . . Summary judgment is inappropriate." 310 F.Supp. 972, 982.

[7]   Before a person is deprived of a protected interest, he must be afforded opportunity for some kind of a hearing, "except for extraordinary situations where some valid governmental interest is at stake that justifies postponing the hearing until after the event." *Boddie v. Connecticut*, 401 U.S. 371, 379, 91 S.Ct. 780, 786, 28 L.Ed.2d 113 * * *. For the rare and extraordinary situations in which we have held that deprivation of a protected interest need not be preceded by opportunity for some kind of hearing, see, *e.g.*, *Central Union Trust Co. v. Garvan*, 254 U.S. 554, 566, 41 S.Ct. 214, 215, 65 L.Ed. 403; *Phillips v. Commissioner of Internal Revenue*, 283 U.S. 589, 597, 51 S.Ct. 608, 611, 75 L.Ed. 1289; *Ewing v. Mytinger & Casselberry, Inc.*, 339 U.S. 594, 70 S.Ct. 870, 94 L.Ed. 1088.

to determine whether due process requirements apply in the first place, we must look not to the "weight" but to the *nature* of the interest at stake. We must look to see if the interest is within the Fourteenth Amendment's protection of liberty and property.

"Liberty" and "property" are broad and majestic terms. They are among the "[g]reat [constitutional] concepts ... purposely left to gather meaning from experience. . . [T]hey relate to the whole domain of social and economic fact, and the statesmen who founded this Nation knew too well that only a stagnant society remains unchanged." *National Mutual Ins. Co. v. Tidewater Transfer Co.*, 337 U.S. 582, 646, 69 S.Ct. 1173, 1195, 93 L.Ed. 1556 (Frankfurter, J., dissenting). For that reason, the Court has fully and finally rejected the wooden distinction between "rights" and "privileges" that once seemed to govern the applicability of procedural due process rights.[9] The Court has also made clear that the property interests protected by procedural due process extend well beyond actual ownership of real estate, chattels, or money.[10] By the same token, the Court has required due process protection for deprivations of liberty beyond the sort of formal constraints imposed by the criminal process.[11]

Yet, while the Court has eschewed rigid or formalistic limitations on the protection of procedural due process, it has at the same time observed certain boundaries. For the words "liberty" and "property" in the Due Process Clause of the Fourteenth Amendment must be given some meaning.

II

"While this court has not attempted to define with exactness the liberty ... guaranteed [by the Fourteenth Amendment], the term has received much consideration and some of the included things have been definitely stated. Without doubt, it denotes not merely freedom from bodily restraint but also the right of the individual to contract, to engage in any of the common occupations of life, to acquire useful knowledge, to marry, establish a home and bring up children, to worship God according to the dictates of his own conscience, and generally to enjoy those privileges long recognized ... as essential to the orderly pursuit of happiness by free men." *Meyer v. Nebraska*, 262 U.S. 390, 399, 43 S.Ct. 625, 626, 67 L.Ed. 1042. In

---

[9]   In a leading case decided many years ago, the Court of Appeals for the District of Columbia Circuit held that public employment in general was a "privilege," not a "right," and that procedural due process guarantees therefore were inapplicable. *Bailey v. Richardson*, 86 U.S.App.D.C. 248, 182 F.2d 46, aff'd by an equally divided *Court*, 341 U.S. 918, 71 S.Ct. 669, 95 L.Ed. 1352. The basis of this holding has been thoroughly undermined in the ensuing years * * *.

[10]   *See, e.g., Connell v. Higginbotham*, 403 U.S. 207, 208, 91 S.Ct. 1772, 1773, 29 L.Ed.2d 418; *Bell v. Burson, supra; Goldberg v. Kelly, supra.*

[11]   "Although the Court has not assumed to define 'liberty' (in the Fifth Amendment's Due Process Clause) with any great precision, that term is not confined to mere freedom from bodily restraint." *Bolling v. Sharpe*, 347 U.S. 497, 499, 74 S.Ct. 693, 694, 98 L.Ed. 884. See, *e.g., Stanley v. Illinois*, 405 U.S. 645, 92 S.Ct. 1208, 31 L.Ed.2d 551.

a Constitution for a free people, there can be no doubt that the meaning of "liberty" must be broad indeed.

There might be cases in which a State refused to re-employ a person under such circumstances that interests in liberty would be implicated. But this is not such a case.

The State, in declining to rehire the respondent, did not make any charge against him that might seriously damage his standing and associations in his community. It did not base the nonrenewal of his contract on a charge, for example, that he had been guilty of dishonesty, or immorality. Had it done so, this would be a different case. For "[w]here a person's good name, reputation, honor, or integrity is at stake because of what the government is doing to him, notice and an opportunity to be heard are essential." *Wisconsin v. Constantineau*, 400 U.S. 433, 437, 91 S.Ct. 507, 510, 27 L.Ed.2d 515. In such a case, due process would accord an opportunity to refute the charge before University officials.[12] In the present case, however, there is no suggestion whatever that the respondent's "good name, reputation, honor, or integrity" is at stake.

Similarly, there is no suggestion that the State, in declining to re-employ the respondent, imposed on him a stigma or other disability that foreclosed his freedom to take advantage of other employment opportunities. The State, for example, did not invoke any regulations to bar the respondent from all other public employment in state universities. Had it done so, this, again, would be a different case * * *. The Court has held, for example, that a State, in regulating eligibility for a type of professional employment, cannot foreclose a range of opportunities "in a manner . . . that contravene[s] . . . Due Process," *Schware v. Board of Bar Examiners*, 353 U.S. 232, 238, 77 S.Ct. 752, 756, 1 L.Ed.2d 796, and, specifically, in a manner that denies the right to a full prior hearing. *Willner v. Committee on Character*, 373 U.S. 96, 103, 83 S.Ct. 1175, 1180, 10 L.Ed.2d 224. In the present case, however, this principle does not come into play.[13]

To be sure, the respondent has alleged that the nonrenewal of his contract was based on his exercise of his right to freedom of speech. But

---

[12] The purpose of such notice and hearing is to provide the person an opportunity to clear his name. Once a person has cleared his name at a hearing, his employer, of course, may remain free to deny him future employment for other reasons.

[13] The District Court made an *assumption* "that non-retention by one university or college creates concrete and practical difficulties for a professor in his subsequent academic career." 310 F.Supp., at 979. And the Court of Appeals based its affirmance of the summary judgment largely on the premise that "the substantial adverse effect non-retention is likely to have upon the career interests of an individual professor" amounts to a limitation on future employment opportunities sufficient invoke procedural due process guarantees. 446 F.2d, at 809. But even assuming, *arguendo*, that such a "substantial adverse effect" under these circumstances would constitute a state-imposed restriction on liberty, the record contains no support for these assumptions. There is no suggestion of how nonretention might affect the respondent's future employment prospects. Mere proof, for example, that his record of nonretention in one job, taken alone, might make him somewhat less attractive to some other employers would hardly establish the kind of foreclosure of opportunities amounting to a deprivation of "liberty."

this allegation is not now before us. The District Court stayed proceedings on this issue, and the respondent has yet to prove that the decision not to rehire him was, in fact, based on his free speech activities.

Hence, on the record before us, all that clearly appears is that the respondent was not rehired for one year at one university. It stretches the concept too far to suggest that a person is deprived of "liberty" when he simply is not rehired in one job but remains as free as before to seek another.

III

The Fourteenth Amendment's procedural protection of property is a safeguard of the security of interests that a person has already acquired in specific benefits. These interests—property interests—may take many forms.

Thus, the Court has held that a person receiving welfare benefits under statutory and administrative standards defining eligibility for them has an interest in continued receipt of those benefits that is safeguarded by procedural due process. *Goldberg v. Kelly*, 397 U.S. 254, 90 S.Ct. 1011, 25 L.Ed.2d 287. Similarly, in the area of public employment, the Court has held that a public college professor dismissed from an office held under tenure provisions, *Slochower v. Board of Higher Education*, 350 U.S. 551, 76 S.Ct. 637, 100 L.Ed. 692, and college professors and staff members dismissed during the terms of their contracts, *Wieman v. Updegraff*, 344 U.S. 183, 73 S.Ct. 215, 97 L.Ed. 216, have interests in continued employment that are safeguarded by due process. Only last year, the Court held that this principle "proscribing summary dismissal from public employment without hearing or inquiry required by due process" also applied to a teacher recently hired without tenure or a formal contract, but nonetheless with a clearly implied promise of continued employment. *Connell v. Higginbotham*, 403 U.S. 207, 208, 91 S.Ct. 1772, 1773, 29 L.Ed.2d 418.

Certain attributes of "property" interests protected by procedural due process emerge from these decisions. To have a property interest in a benefit, a person clearly must have more than an abstract need or desire for it. He must have more than a unilateral expectation of it. He must, instead, have a legitimate claim of entitlement to it. It is a purpose of the ancient institution of property to protect those claims upon which people rely in their daily lives, reliance that must not be arbitrarily undermined. It is a purpose of the constitutional right to a hearing to provide an opportunity for a person to vindicate those claims.

Property interests, of course, are not created by the Constitution. Rather they are created and their dimensions are defined by existing rules or understandings that stem from an independent source such as state law—rules or understandings that secure certain benefits and that support claims of entitlement to those benefits. Thus, the welfare recipients in *Goldberg v. Kelly, supra,* had a claim of entitlement to welfare payments that was grounded in the statute defining eligibility for them. The recipients had not yet shown that they were, in fact, within the statutory terms of eligibility. But we held that they had a right to a hearing at which they might attempt to do so.

Just as the welfare recipients' "property" interest in welfare payments was created and defined by statutory terms, so the respondent's "property" interest in employment at Wisconsin State University-Oshkosh was created and defined by the terms of his appointment. Those terms secured his interest in employment up to June 30, 1969. But the important fact in this case is that they specifically provided that the respondent's employment was to terminate on June 30. They did not provide for contract renewal absent "sufficient cause." Indeed, they made no provision for renewal whatsoever.

Thus, the terms of the respondent's appointment secured absolutely no interest in re-employment for the next year. They supported absolutely no possible claim of entitlement to re-employment. Nor, significantly, was there any state statute or University rule or policy that secured his interest in re-employment or that created any legitimate claim to it.[16] In these circumstances, the respondent surely had an abstract concern in being rehired, but he did not have a *property* interest sufficient to require the University authorities to give him a hearing when they declined to renew his contract of employment.

IV

Our analysis of the respondent's constitutional rights in this case in no way indicates a view that an opportunity for a hearing or a statement of reasons for nonretention would, or would not, be appropriate or wise in public colleges and universities. For it is a written Constitution that we apply. Our role is confined to interpretation of that Constitution.

We must conclude that the summary judgment for the respondent should not have been granted, since the respondent has not shown that he was deprived of liberty or property protected by the Fourteenth Amendment. The judgment of the Court of Appeals, accordingly, is reversed and the case is remanded for further proceedings consistent with this opinion.

It is so ordered.

---

[16] To be sure, the respondent does suggest that most teachers hired on a year-to-year basis by Wisconsin State University-Oshkosh are, in fact, rehired. But the District Court has not found that there is anything approaching a "common law" of re-employment so strong as to require University officials to give the respondent a statement of reasons and a hearing on their decision not to rehire him.

MR. JUSTICE POWELL took no part in the decision of this case.

* * *

[CHIEF JUSTICE BURGER's concurrence and JUSTICE BRENNAN's dissent, which essentially agreed with JUSTICE MARSHALL's opinion below, are omitted.]

MR. JUSTICE DOUGLAS, dissenting.

[Justice Douglas' rambling dissent focussed on First Amendment considerations. But it included the following statement: "Moreover, where 'important interests' of the citizen are implicated (*Bell v. Burson*, 402 U.S. 535, 539, 91 S.Ct. 1586, 1589, 29 L.Ed.2d 90) they are not to be denied or taken away without due process. *Bell v. Burson* involved a driver's license. But also included are disqualification for unemployment compensation, discharge from public employment, denial of tax exemption, and withdrawal of welfare benefits. We should now add that nonrenewal of a teacher's contract, whether or not he has tenure, is an entitlement of the same importance and dignity."]

MR. JUSTICE MARSHALL, dissenting.

* * *

While I agree with Part I of the Court's opinion, setting forth the proper framework for consideration of the issue presented, and also with those portions of Parts II and III of the Court's opinion that assert that a public employee is entitled to procedural due process whenever a State stigmatizes him by denying employment, or injures his future employment prospects severely, or whenever the State deprives him of a property interest, I would go further than the Court does in defining the terms "liberty" and "property."

* * *

In my view, every citizen who applies for a government job is entitled to it unless the government can establish some reason for denying the employment. This is the "property" right that I believe is protected by the Fourteenth Amendment and that cannot be denied "without due process of law." And it is also liberty—liberty to work—which is the "very essence of the personal freedom and opportunity" secured by the Fourteenth Amendment.

* * *

It may be argued that to provide procedural due process to all public employees or prospective employees would place an intolerable burden on the machinery of government. The short answer to that argument is that it is not burdensome to give reasons when reasons exist. Whenever an application for employment is denied, an employee is discharged, or a decision not to rehire an employee is made, there should be some reason for the decision. It can scarcely be argued that government would be crippled by a requirement that the reason be communicated to the person most directly affected by the government's action.

Where there are numerous applicants for jobs, it is likely that few will choose to demand reasons for not being hired. But, if the demand for reasons is exceptionally great, summary procedures can be devised that would provide fair and adequate information to all persons. As long as the government has a good reason for its actions it need not fear disclosure. It is only where the government acts improperly that procedural due process is truly burdensome. And that is precisely when it is most necessary.

It might also be argued that to require a hearing and a statement of reasons is to require a useless act, because a government bent on denying employment to one or more persons will do so regardless of the procedural hurdles that are placed in its path. Perhaps this is so, but a requirement of procedural regularity at least renders arbitrary action more difficult. Moreover, proper procedures will surely eliminate some of the arbitrariness that results, not from malice, but from innocent error * * *.

* * *

PERRY v. SINDERMANN

Supreme Court of the United States, 1972.
408 U.S. 593, 92 S.Ct. 2694, 33 L.Ed.2d 570.

MR. JUSTICE STEWART delivered the opinion of the Court.

From 1959 to 1969 the respondent, Robert Sindermann, was a teacher in the state college system of the State of Texas. After teaching for two years at the University of Texas and for four years at San Antonio Junior College, he became a professor of Government and Social Science at Odessa Junior College in 1965. He was employed at the college for four successive years, under a series of one-year contracts. He was successful enough to be appointed, for a time, the cochairman of his department.

During the 1968–1969 academic year, however, controversy arose between the respondent and the college administration. The respondent was elected president of the Texas Junior College Teachers Association. In this capacity, he left his teaching duties on several occasions to testify before committees of the Texas Legislature, and he became involved in public disagreements with the policies of the college's Board of Regents. In particular, he aligned himself with a group advocating the elevation of the college to four-year status—a change opposed by the Regents. And, on one occasion, a newspaper advertisement appeared over his name that was highly critical of the Regents.

Finally, in May 1969, the respondent's one-year employment contract terminated and the Board of Regents voted not to offer him a new contract for the next academic year. The Regents issued a press release setting forth allegations of the respondent's insubordination.[1] But they provided him no official statement of the reasons for the nonrenewal of his contract. And they allowed him no opportunity for a hearing to challenge the basis of the nonrenewal.

The respondent then brought this action in Federal District Court. He alleged primarily that the Regents' decision not to rehire him was based on his public criticism of the policies of the college administration and thus infringed his right to freedom of speech. He also alleged that their failure to provide him an opportunity for a hearing violated the Fourteenth Amendment's guarantee of procedural due process. The petitioners— members of the Board of Regents and the president of the college—denied that their decision was made in retaliation for the respondent's public criticism and argued that they had no obligation to provide a hearing * * *.

* * *

I

The first question presented is whether the respondent's lack of a contractual or tenure right to re-employment, taken alone, defeats his claim that the nonrenewal of his contract violated the First and Fourteenth Amendments. We hold that it does not.

For at least a quarter-century, this Court has made clear that even though a person has no "right" to a valuable governmental benefit and even though the government may deny him the benefit for any number of reasons, there are some reasons upon which the government may not rely. It may not deny a benefit to a person on a basis that infringes his constitutionally protected interests—especially, his interest in freedom of speech. For if the government could deny a benefit to a person because of his constitutionally protected speech or associations, his exercise of those freedoms would in effect be penalized and inhibited. This would allow the government to "produce a result which [it] could not command directly." *Speiser v. Randall*, 357 U.S. 513, 526, 78 S.Ct. 1332, 1342, 2 L.Ed.2d 1460. Such interference with constitutional rights is impermissible.

* * *

Thus, the respondent's lack of a contractual or tenure "right" to re-employment for the 1969–1970 academic year is immaterial to his free speech claim * * *.

---

[1] The press release stated, for example, that the respondent had defied his superiors by attending legislative committee meetings when college officials had specifically refused to permit him to leave his classes for that purpose.

In this case, of course, the respondent has yet to show that the decision not to renew his contract was, in fact, made in retaliation for his exercise of the constitutional right of free speech. The District Court foreclosed any opportunity to make this showing when it granted summary judgment. Hence, we cannot now hold that the Board of Regents' action was invalid.

But we agree with the Court of Appeals that there is a genuine dispute as to "whether the college refused to renew the teaching contract on an impermissible basis—as a reprisal for the exercise of constitutionally protected rights." 430 F.2d, at 943. The respondent has alleged that his nonretention was based on his testimony before legislative committees and his other public statements critical of the Regents' policies. And he has alleged that this public criticism was within the First and Fourteenth Amendments' protection of freedom of speech. Plainly, these allegations present a bona fide constitutional claim. For this Court has held that a teacher's public criticism of his superiors on matters of public concern may be constitutionally protected and may, therefore, be an impermissible basis for termination of his employment.

For this reason we hold that the grant of summary judgment against the respondent, without full exploration of this issue, was improper.

II

The respondent's lack of formal contractual or tenure security in continued employment at Odessa Junior College, though irrelevant to his free speech claim, is highly relevant to his procedural due process claim. But it may not be entirely dispositive.

We have held today in *Board of Regents v. Roth*, 408 U.S. 564, 92 S.Ct. 2701, that the Constitution does not require opportunity for a hearing before the nonrenewal of a nontenured teacher's contract, unless he can show that the decision not to rehire him somehow deprived him of an interest in "liberty" or that he had a "property" interest in continued employment, despite the lack of tenure or a formal contract. In *Roth* the teacher had not made a showing on either point to justify summary judgment in his favor.

Similarly, the respondent here has yet to show that he has been deprived of an interest that could invoke procedural due process protection. As in *Roth*, the mere showing that he was not rehired in one particular job, without more, did not amount to a showing of a loss of liberty. Nor did it amount to a showing of a loss of property.

But the respondent's allegations—which we must construe most favorably to the respondent at this stage of the litigation—do raise a genuine issue as to his interest in continued employment at Odessa Junior College. He alleged that this interest, though not secured by a formal contractual tenure provision, was secured by a no less binding understanding fostered by the college administration. In particular, the respondent alleged that the college had a *de facto* tenure program, and that he had tenure under that program. He claimed that he and others legitimately relied upon an unusual provision that had been in the college's official Faculty Guide for many years:

> "*Teacher Tenure*: Odessa College has no tenure system. The Administration of the College wishes the faculty member to feel that he has permanent tenure as long as his teaching services are satisfactory and as long as he displays a cooperative attitude toward his co-workers and his superiors, and as long as he is happy in his work."

Moreover, the respondent claimed legitimate reliance upon guidelines promulgated by the Coordinating Board of the Texas College and University System that provided that a person, like himself, who had been employed as a teacher in the state college and university system for seven years or more has some form of job tenure. Thus, the respondent offered to prove that a teacher with his long period of service at this particular State College had no less a "property" interest in continued employment than a formally tenured teacher at other colleges, and had no less a procedural due process right to a statement of reasons and a hearing before college officials upon their decision not to retain him.

We have made clear in *Roth* that "property" interests subject to procedural due process protection are not limited by a few rigid, technical forms. Rather, "property" denotes a broad range of interests that are secured by "existing rules or understandings." *Id.*, at 577, 92 S.Ct., at 2709. A person's interest in a benefit is a "property" interest for due process purposes if there are such rules or mutually explicit understandings that support his claim of entitlement to the benefit and that he may invoke at a hearing.

A written contract with an explicit tenure provision clearly is evidence of a formal understanding that supports a teacher's claim of entitlement to continued employment unless sufficient "cause" is shown. Yet absence of such an explicit contractual provision may not always foreclose the possibility that a teacher has a "property" interest in reemployment. For example, the law of contracts in most, if not all, jurisdictions long has employed a process by which agreements, though not formalized in writing, may be "implied." 3 A. Corbin on Contracts §§ 561–572A (1960). Explicit contractual provisions may be supplemented by other agreements implied from "the promisor's words and conduct in the light of the surrounding circumstances." *Id.*, at § 562. And, "[t]he meaning of [the promisor's] words and acts is found by relating them to the usage of the past." *Ibid.*

A teacher, like the respondent, who has held his position for a number of years, might be able to show from the circumstances of this service—and from other relevant facts—that he has a legitimate claim of entitlement to job tenure. Just as this Court has found there to be a "common law of a particular industry or of a particular plant" that may supplement a collective-bargaining agreement, *United Steelworkers v. Warrior & Gulf Nav. Co.*, 363 U.S. 574, 579, 80 S.Ct. 1347, 1351, 4 L.Ed.2d 1409, so there may be an unwritten "common law" in a particular university that certain employees shall have the equivalent of tenure. This is particularly likely in a college or university, like Odessa Junior College, that has no explicit tenure system even for senior members of its faculty, but that nonetheless may have created such a system in practice.[7]

In this case, the respondent has alleged the existence of rules and understandings, promulgated and fostered by state officials, that may justify his legitimate claim of entitlement to continued employment absent "sufficient cause" * * *. Proof of such a property interest would not, of course, entitle him to reinstatement. But such proof would obligate college officials to grant a hearing at his request, where he could be informed of the grounds for his nonretention and challenge their sufficiency.

* * *

MR. JUSTICE POWELL took no part in the decision of this case.

MR. JUSTICE MARSHALL, dissenting in part.

* * *

I agree with Part I of the Court's opinion holding that respondent has presented a bona fide First Amendment claim that should be considered fully by the District Court. But, for the reasons stated in my dissenting opinion in *Board of Regents v. Roth*, 408 U.S. 564, at 587, 92 S.Ct. 2701, at 2714, 33 L.Ed.2d 548, I would modify the judgment of the Court of Appeals to direct the District Court to enter summary judgment for respondent entitling him to a statement of reasons why his contract was not renewed and a hearing on disputed issues of fact.

4. THE MECHANICS OF ENTITLEMENT THEORY: CRITERIA, CONNECTIONS, AND CONSTITUTIONAL CORES

Much of modern due process law consists of elaboration on the framework for identifying protected interests set forth in *Roth* and *Sindermann*. The framework unquestionably requires considerable

---

[7]   We do not now hold that the respondent has any such legitimate claim of entitlement to job tenure. For "[p]roperty interests . . . are not created by the Constitution. Rather, they are created and their dimensions are defined by existing rules or understandings that stem from an independent source such as state law. . . ." *Board of Regents v. Roth, supra,* 408 U.S., at 577, 92 S.Ct., at 2709. If it is the law of Texas that a teacher in the respondent's position has no contractual or other claim to job tenure, the respondent's claim would be defeated.

elaboration. How does one tell when statutes or regulations do or do not create "entitlements"? And what are the limits, if any, on the legislature's power to define the scope of constitutionally protected interests? Is there a "core" constitutional meaning to the terms "life, liberty, and property" that legislatures cannot alter by statute, and if so, how large is that core?

Obviously, there are some interests that fall within the compass of the due process clauses regardless of what any state or federal laws might say. If the government tries to execute you, it is trying to deprive you of "life" in the constitutional sense even if a statute perversely says otherwise. If the government tries to put you in jail, it is trying to deprive you of "liberty" regardless of what statutes or regulations might say. *Roth,* quoting one of the leading cases from the pre-New Deal substantive due process era, made clear that the irreducible "core" of constitutionally protected liberty interests encompasses "not merely freedom from bodily restraint but also the right of the individual to contract, to engage in any of the common occupations of life, to acquire useful knowledge, to marry, establish a home and bring up children, to worship God according to the dictates of his own conscience, and generally to enjoy those privileges long recognized * * * as essential to the orderly pursuit of happiness by free men." *Meyer v. Nebraska,* 262 U.S. 390, 399, 43 S.Ct. 625, 67 L.Ed. 1042 (1923). This "core" idea of "liberty" has been held to be implicated by corporal punishment in schools, *see Ingraham v. Wright,* 430 U.S. 651, 97 S.Ct. 1401, 51 L.Ed.2d 711 (1977), and by assignment of prisoners to (at least some) supermaximum security prison facilities. *See Wilkinson v. Austin,* 545 U.S. 209, 125 S.Ct. 2384, 162 L.Ed.2d 174 (2005). Lower courts have split on what kinds of changes in conditions of confinement, such as placing prisoners in administrative segregation or in special "communications management units" in which their contact with the outside world is sharply limited, might also fall within this "core" of liberty interests. *See Aref v. Lynch,* 833 F.3d 242, 253–58 (D.C.Cir.2016) (surveying the various decisions).

Cases prior to *Roth* suggested that, in Justice Frankfurter's words, a "grievous loss of any kind" was sufficient to trigger due process protections. *Roth* roundly rejected that notion, and subsequent cases roundly reinforced that rejection, *see Meachum v. Fano,* 427 U.S. 215, 224, 96 S.Ct. 2532, 49 L.Ed.2d 451 (1976) ("We reject at the outset the notion that *any* grievous loss visited upon a person by the State is sufficient to invoke the procedural protections of the Due Process Clause")—though not entirely without protest. *See id.* at 235 (Stevens, J., joined by Brennan, J., and Marshall, J., dissenting) (identifying the touchstone of a constitutionally protected interest as a "grievous loss"). Does the open-ended character of the range of constitutional liberty interests essentially reintroduce the "grievous loss" test? Is there anything of significance to a reasonable person that cannot be slotted into the *Roth/Meyer* list of constitutional liberty interests?

While the precise contours of the core of constitutional "liberty" under modern law have not been—and probably never will be—precisely drawn, the Court's decisions identify a number of seemingly quite important interests that do not make the cut. Most obviously, Roth's prospects for re-employment at a public university do not count. Similarly, the Court has made clear that many things of great concern to incarcerated prisoners do not fall within the constitutionally predetermined zone of liberty. There is, for example, no irreducible constitutional right to good-time credits for well-behaved prisoners, *see Wolff v. McDonnell*, 418 U.S. 539, 94 S.Ct. 2963, 41 L.Ed.2d 935 (1974), nor is a prisoner necessarily deprived of constitutional "liberty" by being transferred from a more desirable to a less desirable prison. *See Meachum v. Fano*, 427 U.S. 215, 96 S.Ct. 2532, 49 L.Ed.2d 451 (1976). And the Court in 2015 sharply divided, with no majority opinion, on whether American citizens have an irreducible constitutional "liberty" interest in living in the United States with their non-citizen spouses, which would entitle citizens to due process of law when the government denies visas to their alien spouses. Four Justices, writing in dissent, said that a claimant's "freedom to live together with her husband in the United States * * * easily satisfies" the standards for recognition as a constitutional liberty interest. *Kerry v. Din*, 576 U.S. ___, 135 S.Ct. 2128, 2142 (2015) (Breyer, J., joined by Justices Ginsburg, Sotomayor, and Kagan). Three Justices, in a plurality opinion, flatly declared that "[t]here is no such constitutional right." 135 S.Ct. at 2131 (Scalia, J., joined by Chief Justice Roberts and Justice Thomas). Justices Kennedy and Alito stayed out of the fray, finding that due process was satisfied in the case even if a liberty interest existed, so that there was no occasion to decide whether such an interest should be recognized. *See id.* at 2139 (Kennedy, J., concurring in the judgment).

One of the more intriguing modern omissions from the list of constitutionally protected interests is *reputation*. Many of the cases presented thus far in this chapter involved reputational claims of some sort. Cases such as *Roth* and *Constantineau* clearly contemplated that reputation could be, in some circumstances, a constitutional interest of some sort. *Roth* observed, for example, that a liberty interest might be involved if the government, "in declining to re-employ the respondent, imposed on him a stigma or other disability that foreclosed his freedom to take advantage of other employment opportunities." The Framers of the due process clauses likely would have had no difficulty fitting reputation into the phrase "life, liberty, or property"—though not necessarily where modern observers would expect it to fit. Recall that in the eighteenth century, William Blackstone defined the right to *life* as including "a person's legal and uninterrupted enjoyment of his life, his limbs, his body, his health, *and his reputation*." Given Blackstone's wide influence in the founding generation, there is a good argument that reputation falls squarely within the original meaning of the word "life" in the phrase "life, liberty, and property." For whatever reason, however, courts have never paid serious attention to the possibility that the term "life" in the due process clauses might mean something more than physical existence. And reputation does not seem like a very good fit with either "liberty" or "property." Nonetheless, the pre-1976 due process cases continually hinted at a significant, even if not clearly defined, role for reputation in the constitutional world.

That understanding was flatly rejected in *Paul v. Davis,* 424 U.S. 693, 96 S.Ct. 1155, 47 L.Ed.2d 405 (1976). A 5–4 majority in *Paul* categorically declared that a deprivation of reputation, standing alone, does not implicate an interest of any kind protected by the due process clauses. *See* 424 U.S. at 712, 96 S.Ct. 1155. Given the case law prior to *Paul*, this took some doing. *Wisconsin v. Constantineau,* for example, in the context of a statute forbidding the sale of liquor to designated excessive drinkers, stated that due process protections applied "[w]here a person's good name, reputation, honor, or integrity is at stake because of what the government is doing to him." *Paul* distinguished this case, and other prior cases, by reasoning that loss of reputation is constitutionally cognizable only when it is conjoined with the loss of some other interest, such as a job or the right to purchase liquor. This doctrine, which has come to be known as "reputation-plus," was well described in *O'Donnell v. Barry*, 148 F.3d 1126, 1140 (D.C.Cir.1998):

> "For a defamation to give rise to a right to procedural due process, it is necessary—we need not say when it is sufficient—that the defamation be accompanied by a discharge from government employment or at least a demotion in rank and pay." *Mosrie v. Barry*, 718 F.2d 1151, 1161 (D.C.Cir.1983). Although the conceptual basis for reputation-plus claims is not fully clear, it presumably rests on the fact that official criticism will carry much more weight if the person criticized is at the same time demoted or fired. Requiring a demotion or firing to trigger a defamation claim also helps to limit the scope of permissible due process claims to a small set of truly serious claims, thus limiting the constitutionalization of tort law.

Notwithstanding *Paul*, modern doctrine continues to recognize the (remote) theoretical possibility that, in extreme cases, harm to reputation could foreclose so many employment and social opportunities that it would constitute a deprivation of constitutional liberty. The problems of proving a stigma broad enough to implicate a liberty interest, however, are close to insurmountable. *See Crooks v. Mabus,* 845 F.3d 412, 420–22 (D.C.Cir.2016).

Is there also a "core" to the concept of property that is not subject to legislative alteration? If the Supreme Judicial Court of Massachusetts held that land was not "property" under Massachusetts law, would that mean that Massachusetts could deprive persons of land without implicating the Due Process Clause? No Supreme Court due process case directly addresses this precise question, but an answer might be implicit in *Nelson v. Colorado,* 137 S.Ct. 1249, 197 L.Ed.2d 611 (2017). Nelson and Madden, in separate cases, were convicted of various crimes, and their sentences included court costs, fines, and restitution. The convictions were all overturned on appeal. Under Colorado law, in order to get back the money that had been taken in fees, fines, and restitution, Nelson and Madden had to go through an administrative procedure that required them to prove, by "clear and convincing evidence," that they were actually innocent of the charged crimes. The Supreme Court held that it violated due process of law to require the defendants to prove their innocence in order to get back their money once the convictions that formed the basis for the monetary penalties were invalidated. *See id.* at 1255–58. As Justice Thomas pointed out in his lone dissent, this assumes that the money in question belonged to the defendants rather than to the state. *See id.* at 1263 (Thomas, J, dissenting). Colorado law appeared to say that the money belongs to the state even after the convictions are vacated. *See id.* at 1264–65. The majority must therefore have assumed that some interests are property for constitutional purposes regardless of the government's positive law characterization of those interests.

The same issue arose more directly in *Webb's Fabulous Pharmacies, Inc. v. Beckwith,* 449 U.S. 155, 101 S.Ct. 446, 66 L.Ed.2d 358 (1980), which involved the takings clause of the Fifth Amendment.[8] The strong suggestion is that "property" as well as "liberty" has a constitutional core.

When an insolvent corporation sells its assets, the purchasers want to ensure that the transferred assets are acquired free of any creditors' claims, while the creditors want to make sure that the sale does not worsen their position. A Florida statute permitted purchasers to acquire assets free of all creditors' claims by depositing the purchase price with the court and filing an action that interpleads the creditors. The creditors then file claims with the court, and the claims are satisfied out of the deposited funds. A Florida statute enacted in 1973 directed the clerk of the court to place the deposited funds in interest-bearing accounts while creditors' claims were pending. *See* Fla. Stat. § 28.33 (1977). The statute further provided that "[a]ll interest accruing from moneys deposited shall be deemed income of the office of the clerk of the circuit court investing such moneys and shall be deposited in the same accounts as are other fees and commissions of the clerk's office." *Id.* § 28.33. A separate statute provided

---

[8] The Fifth Amendment contains five distinct clauses, including the Due Process Clause. The last such clause says, "nor shall private property be taken for public use, without just compensation." In 1897, the Supreme Court held that the Fourteenth Amendment made the principles of this clause applicable to the states. *See* Chicago, B. & Q. R. Co. v. Chicago, 166 U.S. 226, 239, 17 S.Ct. 581, 585, 41 L.Ed. 979 (1897).

for payment of fees to the clerk of the court for the service of receiving funds into the court registry. *See id.* § 28.24(14).

In 1976, most of the assets of Webb's Fabulous Pharmacies, Inc., were purchased for nearly $2 million. The money was deposited with the clerk of the court. By the time a receiver was appointed to evaluate and pay the claims of Webb's creditors, the deposited money had earned more than $90,000.00 in interest. The creditors insisted that they should get the interest. Florida insisted, and the Florida Supreme Court held, that the interest was state property rather than private property by virtue of the Florida statute defining the interest as belonging to the clerk of the court.

A unanimous Supreme Court reversed, holding that the Florida statute was an unconstitutional taking of private property without just compensation. Florida pointed to the statement in *Roth* that constitutionally protected property interests "are created and their dimensions are defined by existing rules or understandings that stem from an independent source such as state law." 408 U.S. at 577, 92 S.Ct. at 2709. It insisted that its statutory scheme made the deposited funds public money until the time of distribution to creditors. The Court was not impressed:

> The usual and general rule is that any interest on an interpleaded and deposited fund follows the principal and is to be allocated to those who are ultimately to be the owners of that principal [citing cases from two circuits and five states].

> The Florida Supreme Court, in ruling contrary to this long established general rule, relied on the words of § 28.33 and then proceeded on the theory that without the statute the clerk would have no authority to invest money held in the registry, that in some way the fund assumes temporarily the status of "public money" from the time it is deposited until it leaves the account, and that the statute "takes only what it creates." Then follows the conclusion that the interest "is not private property." 374 So.2d, at 952–953.

* * *

> Neither the Florida Legislature by statute, nor the Florida courts by judicial decree, may accomplish the result the county seeks simply by recharacterizing the principal as "public money" because it is held temporarily by the court. The earnings of a fund are incidents of ownership of the fund itself and are property just as the fund itself is property. The state statute has the practical effect of appropriating for the county the value of the use of the fund for the period in which it is held in the registry.

To put it another way: a State, by *ipse dixit*, may not transform private property into public property without compensation, even for the limited duration of the deposit in court. This is the very kind of thing that the Taking Clause of the Fifth Amendment was meant to prevent. That Clause stands as a shield against the arbitrary use of governmental power.

* * *

We hold that under the narrow circumstances of this case—where there is a separate and distinct state statute authorizing a clerk's fee "for services rendered" based upon the amount of principal deposited; where the deposited fund itself concededly is private; and where the deposit in the court's registry is required by state statute in order for the depositor to avail itself of statutory protection from claims of creditors and others—Seminole County's taking unto itself * * * the interest earned on the interpleader fund while it was in the registry of the court was a taking violative of the Fifth and Fourteenth Amendments. We express no view as to the constitutionality of a statute that prescribes a county's retention of interest earned, where the interest would be the only return to the county for services it renders.

449 U.S. at 162–65, 101 S.Ct. at 451–52.

If an interest is not within the constitutional "core" of life, liberty, or property, it can still receive constitutional protection under *Roth* if state or federal statutes or regulations make it an entitlement. In order to qualify as an entitlement (as Roth discovered to his displeasure), the relevant statutes or regulations must provide adequate *criteria* and *connections*. That is, they must specify identifiable criteria that can be used to determine whether someone is eligible for the benefit that he or she seeks, and they must draw a direct causal link between satisfaction of those criteria and receipt of the benefit. If that seems unhelpfully abstract, consider whether the following three cases—a tiny sample of the voluminous case law—shed any light on the methodology to be employed in making these determinations.

KENTUCKY DEP'T OF CORRECTIONS V. THOMPSON

Supreme Court of the United States, 1989.
490 U.S. 454, 109 S.Ct. 1904, 104 L.Ed.2d 506.

JUSTICE BLACKMUN delivered the opinion of the Court.

In this case we consider whether Kentucky prison regulations give state inmates, for purposes of the Fourteenth Amendment, a liberty interest in receiving certain visitors.

I

* * *

The Commonwealth [of Kentucky] in 1981 issued "Corrections Policies and Procedures" governing general prison visitation, including a nonexhaustive list of visitors who may be excluded.[1] Four years later, the * * * [Kentucky State Reformatory] issued its own more detailed "Procedures Memorandum" on the subject of "Visiting Regulations." The memorandum * * * state[s] that a visitor may be denied entry if his or her presence would constitute a "clear and probable danger to the safety and security of the institution or would interfere with the orderly operation of the institution." A nonexhaustive list of nine specific reasons for excluding visitors is set forth.[2] The memorandum also states that the decision

---

[1]   The relevant provision states:

"Certain visitors who are either a threat to the security or order of the institution or nonconducive to the successful re-entry of the inmate to the community may be excluded. These are, but not restricted to:

"A.   The visitor's presence in the institution would constitute a clear and probable danger to the institution's security or interfere with the orderly operation of the institution.

"B.   The visitor has a past record of disruptive conduct.

"C.   The visitor is under the influence of alcohol or drugs.

"D.   The visitor refuses to submit to search, if requested to do so, or show proper identification.

"E.   The visitor is directly related to the inmate's criminal behavior.

"F.   The visitor is currently on probation or parole and does not have special written permission from both his or her Probation or Parole Officer and the institutional Superintendent." Commonwealth of Kentucky Corrections Policies and Procedures § 403.06 (issued Aug. 28, 1981, effective Sept. 28, 1981).

[2]   The memorandum reads in relevant part:

"K. *Visitor Refused Admittance*

"1.   A visitor may be denied a visit at any time if one or more of the following exists or there are reasonable grounds to believe that:

"a.   The visitor's presence in the institution would constitute a clear and probable danger to the safety and security of the institution or would interfere with the orderly operation of the institution, including, but not limited to:

"(1)   The visitor has a past record of disruptive conduct.

"(2)   The visitor is under the influence of alcohol or drugs.

"(3)   The visitor refuses to submit to search or show proper identification upon request.

"(4)   The visitor is directly related to the inmate's criminal behavior.

"(5)   The visit will be detrimental to the inmate's rehabilitation.

"(6)   The visitor is a former resident currently on parole who does not have the approval of his Parole Officer or the Warden.

"(7)   The visitor is a former resident who has left by maximum expiration of sentence and does not have the prior approval of the Warden.

"(8)   The visitor has previously violated institutional visiting policies.

"(9)   Former employees of the Kentucky State Reformatory will not be allowed to visit inmates unless they have authorization from the Warden prior to the time of the visit.

"2.   A master log will be kept at the Visiting Desk of all visitors who have been denied a visit for any of the reasons listed above. A visitor who is denied a visit will not be allowed to visit an inmate for up to six (6) months following the incident. Persons who bring dangerous drugs or contraband into the institution may be denied visits indefinitely, until permission is granted by the Warden. The Duty Officer has the responsibility of denying a visit for the above reasons.

whether to exclude a visitor rests with the duty officer, who is to be consulted by any staff member who "feels a visitor should not be allowed admittance."

This particular litigation was prompted in large part by two incidents when applicants were denied the opportunity to visit an inmate at the reformatory. The mother of one inmate was denied visitation for six months because she brought to the reformatory a person who had been barred for smuggling contraband. Another inmate's mother and woman friend were denied visitation for a limited time when the inmate was found with contraband after a visit by the two women. In both instances the visitation privileges were suspended without a hearing. The inmates were not prevented from receiving other visitors.

* * *

* * * [T]he District Court found * * * that, under the standards articulated by this Court in *Hewitt v. Helms*, 459 U.S. 460, 103 S.Ct. 864, 74 L.Ed.2d 675 (1983), respondents "possess a liberty interest in open visitation." The District Court directed petitioners to develop "minimal due process procedures," including "an informal, nonadversary review in which a prisoner receives notice of and reasons for" any decision to exclude a visitor, as well as an opportunity to respond * * *.

The United States Court of Appeals for the Sixth Circuit affirmed * * *.

Because this case appeared to raise important issues relevant to general prison administration, we granted certiorari.

II

The Fourteenth Amendment reads in part: "nor shall any State deprive any person of life, liberty, or property, without due process of law," and protects "the individual against arbitrary action of government," *Wolff v. McDonnell*, 418 U.S. 539, 558, 94 S.Ct. 2963, 2975, 41 L.Ed.2d 935 (1974). We examine procedural due process questions in two steps: the first asks whether there exists a liberty or property interest which has been interfered with by the State; the second examines whether the procedures attendant upon that deprivation were constitutionally sufficient. The types of interests that constitute "liberty" and "property" for Fourteenth Amendment purposes are not unlimited; the interest must rise to more than "an abstract need or desire," *Board of Regents v. Roth*, 408 U.S., at 577, 92 S.Ct., at 2709, and must be based on more than "a unilateral hope,"

"a. The master log will be furnished to all institutions and updated as required.

"3. Any time a staff member feels a visitor should not be allowed admittance for any of the reasons above, the Shift Supervisor and the Duty Officer shall be notified. The final decision will be with the Duty Officer. All decisions will be documented. If it is felt that the individual presents a serious threat of danger to himself or others the Kentucky State Police will be advised of the situation so they may make a decision on whether their intervention is needed." Kentucky State Reformatory Procedures Memorandum, No. KSR 16–00–01 (issued and effective Sept. 30, 1985).

Connecticut Board of Pardons v. Dumschat, 452 U.S. 458, 465, 101 S.Ct. 2460, 2464, 69 L.Ed.2d 158 (1981). Rather, an individual claiming a protected interest must have a legitimate claim of entitlement to it. Protected liberty interests "may arise from two sources—the Due Process Clause itself and the laws of the States." *Hewitt v. Helms*, 459 U.S., at 466, 103 S.Ct., at 868.

Respondents do not argue—nor can it seriously be contended, in light of our prior cases—that an inmate's interest in unfettered visitation is guaranteed directly by the Due Process Clause * * *.

We have held, however, that state law may create enforceable liberty interests in the prison setting. We have found, for example, that certain regulations granted inmates a protected interest in parole, *Board of Pardons v. Allen*, 482 U.S. 369, 107 S.Ct. 2415, 96 L.Ed.2d 303 (1987); *Greenholtz v. Nebraska Penal Inmates*, 442 U.S. 1, 99 S.Ct. 2100, 60 L.Ed.2d 668 (1979), in good-time credits, *Wolff v. McDonnell*, 418 U.S., at 556–572, 94 S.Ct., at 2974–2982, in freedom from involuntary transfer to a mental hospital, *Vitek v. Jones*, 445 U.S., at 487–494, 100 S.Ct., at 1260–1264, and in freedom from more restrictive forms of confinement within the prison, *Hewitt v. Helms, supra*. In contrast, we have found that certain state statutes and regulations did not create a protected liberty interest in transfer to another prison. *Meachum v. Fano*, 427 U.S., at 225, 96 S.Ct., at 2538 (intrastate transfer); *Olim v. Wakinekona*, [461 U.S. 238 (1983),] (interstate transfer). The fact that certain state-created liberty interests have been found to be entitled to due process protection, while others have not, is not the result of this Court's judgment as to what interests are more significant than others; rather, our method of inquiry in these cases always has been to examine closely the language of the relevant statutes and regulations.[3]

Stated simply, "a State creates a protected liberty interest by placing substantive limitations on official discretion." *Olim v. Wakinekona*, 461 U.S., at 249, 103 S.Ct., at 1747. A State may do this in a number of ways. Neither the drafting of regulations nor their interpretation can be reduced to an exact science. Our past decisions suggest, however, that the most common manner in which a State creates a liberty interest is by establishing "substantive predicates" to govern official decision-making, *Hewitt v. Helms*, 459 U.S., at 472, 103 S.Ct., at 871, and, further, by

---

[3] Petitioners and their *amici* urge us to adopt a rule that prison regulations, regardless of the mandatory character of their language or the extent to which they limit official discretion, "do not create an entitlement protected by the Due Process Clause when they do not affect the duration or release from confinement, or the very nature of confinement." They argue that this bright line would allow prison officials to issue guidelines to prison staff to govern minor decisions, without thereby transforming the details of prison life into "liberty interests" with accompanying procedural rights. Inasmuch as a "bright line" of this kind is not necessary for a ruling in favor of petitioners, we refrain from considering it at this time. We express no view on the proposal and leave its resolution for another day.

mandating the outcome to be reached upon a finding that the relevant criteria have been met.

Most of our procedural due process cases in the prison context have turned on the presence or absence of language creating "substantive predicates" to guide discretion. For example, the failure of a Connecticut statute governing commutation of sentences to provide "particularized standards or criteria [to] guide the State's decisionmakers," *Connecticut Board of Pardons v. Dumschat*, 452 U.S., at 467, 101 S.Ct., at 2465 (BRENNAN, J., concurring), defeated an inmate's claim that the State had created a liberty interest. See also *Olim v. Wakinekona*, 461 U.S., at 249–250, 103 S.Ct., at 1748 (interstate prison transfer left to "completely unfettered" discretion of administrator); *Meachum v. Fano*, 427 U.S., at 228, 96 S.Ct., at 2540 (intrastate prison transfer at discretion of officials); *Montanye v. Haymes*, 427 U.S., at 243, 96 S.Ct., at 2547 (same). In other instances, we have found that prison regulations or statutes do provide decisionmaking criteria which serve to limit discretion. See, *e.g.*, *Hewitt v. Helms*, 459 U.S., at 472, 103 S.Ct., at 871 (administrative segregation not proper absent particular substantive predicates); *Board of Pardons v. Allen*, 482 U.S., at 381, 107 S.Ct., at 2422 (parole granted unless certain standards met, even though the decision is " 'necessarily subjective . . . and predictive' ").

We have also articulated a requirement, implicit in our earlier decisions, that the regulations contain "explicitly mandatory language," *i.e.*, specific directives to the decisionmaker that if the regulations' substantive predicates are present, a particular outcome must follow, in order to create a liberty interest. See *Hewitt v. Helms*, 459 U.S., at 471–472, 103 S.Ct., at 871–72. The regulations at issue in *Hewitt* mandated that certain procedures be followed, and "that administrative segregation will not occur absent specified substantive predicates." *Id.*, at 472, 103 S.Ct., at 871. In *Board of Pardons v. Allen, supra*, the relevant statute "use[d] mandatory language ('shall') to 'creat[e] a presumption that parole release will be granted' when the designated findings are made," 482 U.S., at 377–378, 107 S.Ct., at 2420–2421, quoting *Greenholtz v. Nebraska Penal Inmates*, 442 U.S., at 12, 99 S.Ct., at 2106. In sum, the use of "explicitly mandatory language," in connection with the establishment of "specified substantive predicates" to limit discretion, forces a conclusion that the State has created a liberty interest. *Hewitt v. Helms*, 459 U.S., at 472, 103 S.Ct., at 871.

III

The regulations and procedures at issue in this case do provide certain "substantive predicates" to guide the decisionmaker. The state procedures provide that a visitor "may be excluded" when, *inter alia*, officials find reasonable grounds to believe that the "visitor's presence in the institution would constitute a clear and probable danger to the institution's security or interfere with [its] orderly operation." Among the more specific reasons listed for denying visitation are the visitor's connection to the inmate's criminal behavior, the visitor's past disruptive behavior or refusal to submit to a search or show proper identification, and the visitor's being under the influence of alcohol or drugs. The reformatory procedures are nearly identical, and include a prohibition on a visit from a former reformatory inmate, without the prior approval of the warden. These regulations and procedures contain standards to be applied by a staff member in determining whether to refer a situation to the duty officer for resolution, and require the staff member to notify the duty officer if the staff member feels that a visitor should not be allowed admittance. The same "substantive predicates" undoubtedly are intended to guide the duty officer's discretion in making the ultimate decision.

The regulations at issue here, however, lack the requisite relevant mandatory language. They stop short of requiring that a particular result is to be reached upon a finding that the substantive predicates are met.[4] The Reformatory Procedures Memorandum begins with the caveat that "administrative staff reserves the right to allow or disallow visits," and goes on to note that "it is the policy" of the reformatory "to respect the right of inmates to have visits." This language is not mandatory. Visitors *may* be excluded if they fall within one of the described categories, but they need not be. Nor need visitors fall within one of the described categories in order to be excluded. The overall effect of the regulations is not such that an inmate can reasonably form an objective expectation that a visit would necessarily be allowed absent the occurrence of one of the listed conditions. Or, to state it differently, the regulations are not worded in such a way that an inmate could reasonably expect to enforce them against the prison officials.

Because the regulations at issue here do not establish a liberty interest entitled to the protections of the Due Process Clause, the judgment of the Court of Appeals is reversed.

It is so ordered.

---

[4] It should be obvious that the mandatory language requirement is not an invitation to courts to search regulations for *any* imperative that might be found. The search is for *relevant* mandatory language that expressly requires the decisionmaker to apply certain substantive predicates in determining whether an inmate may be deprived of the particular interest in question. Thus, one of the examples of mandatory language relied upon by the Court of Appeals is unavailing, that is, the statement that an inmate "is allowed three (3) separate visits in the Visiting Building per week." This directive says nothing about whether any *particular* visitor must be admitted, and thus has no direct relevance to the decision whether to exclude a particular visitor, which is what is at issue here. Another example of irrelevant mandatory language is the following: "A visitor who is denied a visit *will not* be allowed to visit an inmate for up to six (6) months following the incident." (Emphasis added.) This language refers only to the penalty to be imposed once an individual is found to be unfit to visit, and has no role to play in guiding prison officials' discretion in deciding whether to exclude a visitor in the first instance.

JUSTICE KENNEDY, concurring. [omitted]

JUSTICE MARSHALL, with whom JUSTICE BRENNAN and JUSTICE STEVENS join, dissenting.

As a result of today's decision, correctional authorities at the Kentucky State Reformatory are free to deny prisoners visits from parents, spouses, children, clergy members, and close friends for any reason whatsoever, or for no reason at all. Prisoners will not even be entitled to learn the reason, if any, why a visitor has been turned away. In my view, the exercise of such unbridled governmental power over the basic human need to see family members and friends strikes at the heart of the liberty protected by the Due Process Clause of the Fourteenth Amendment * * *.

* * *

I have previously stated that, when prison authorities alter a prisoner's conditions of confinement, the relevant question should be whether the prisoner has suffered "a sufficiently 'grievous loss' to trigger the protection of due process." *Olim v. Wakinekona*, 461 U.S. 238, 252, 103 S.Ct. 1741, 1749, 75 L.Ed.2d 813 (1983) (MARSHALL, J., dissenting), quoting *Vitek v. Jones*, 445 U.S. 480, 488, 100 S.Ct. 1254, 1261, 63 L.Ed.2d 552 (1980). The answer depends not only on the nature and gravity of the change, but also on whether the prisoner has been singled out arbitrarily for disparate treatment * * *. Put another way, the retained liberty interest protected by the Constitution encompasses the right to be free from arbitrary governmental action affecting significant personal interests.

* * *

Even if I believed that visit denials did not implicate a prisoner's retained liberty interest, I would nonetheless find that a liberty interest has been "created" by the Commonwealth's visitation regulations and policies * * *.

As an initial matter, I fail to see why mandatory language always is an essential element of a state-created liberty interest. Once it is clear that a State has imposed substantive criteria in statutes or regulations to guide or limit official discretion, there is no reason to assume—as the majority does—that officials applying the statutes or regulations are likely to ignore the criteria if there is not some undefined quantity of the words "shall" or "must." Drafters of statutes or regulations do not ordinarily view the criteria they establish as mere surplusage. Absent concrete evidence that state officials routinely ignore substantive criteria set forth in statutes or regulations (and there is no such evidence here), it is only proper to assume that the criteria are regularly employed in practice, thereby creating legitimate expectations worthy of protection by the Due Process Clause. Common sense suggests that expectations stem from practice as well as from the language of statutes or regulations * * *.

Even if I thought it proper to rely on the presence or absence of mandatory language, I would still disagree with the majority's determination that the regulations here lack such language * * *.

* * *

SANDIN V. CONNER

Supreme Court of the United States, 1995.
515 U.S. 472, 115 S.Ct. 2293, 132 L.Ed.2d 418.

CHIEF JUSTICE REHNQUIST delivered the opinion of the Court.

We granted certiorari to reexamine the circumstances under which state prison regulations afford inmates a liberty interest protected by the Due Process Clause.

I

DeMont Conner was convicted of numerous state crimes, including murder, kidnapping, robbery, and burglary, for which he is currently serving an indeterminate sentence of 30 years to life in a Hawaii prison. He was confined in the Halawa Correctional Facility, a maximum security prison in central Oahu. In August 1987, a prison officer escorted him from his cell to the module program area. The officer subjected Conner to a strip search, complete with an inspection of the rectal area. Conner retorted with angry and foul language directed at the officer. Eleven days later he received notice that he had been charged with disciplinary infractions. The notice charged Conner with "high misconduct" for using physical interference to impair a correctional function, and "low moderate misconduct" for using abusive or obscene language and for harassing employees.

Conner appeared before an adjustment committee on August 28, 1987. The committee refused Conner's request to present witnesses at the hearing, stating that "[w]itnesses were unavailable due to move [sic] to the medium facility and being short staffed on the modules." At the conclusion of proceedings, the committee determined that Conner was guilty of the alleged misconduct. It sentenced him to 30 days disciplinary segregation in the Special Holding Unit for the physical obstruction charge, and four hours segregation for each of the other two charges to be served concurrent with the 30 days. Conner's segregation began August 31, 1987, and ended September 29, 1987.

Conner sought administrative review within 14 days of receiving the committee's decision. Nine months later, the deputy administrator found the high misconduct charge unsupported and expunged Conner's disciplinary record with respect to that charge. But before the Deputy Administrator decided the appeal, Conner had brought this suit against the adjustment committee chair and other prison officials in the United

States District Court for the District of Hawaii * * *. His amended complaint prayed for injunctive relief, declaratory relief and damages for, among other things, a deprivation of procedural due process in connection with the disciplinary hearing. The District Court granted summary judgment in favor of the prison officials.

The Court of Appeals for the Ninth Circuit reversed the judgment. It concluded that Conner had a liberty interest in remaining free from disciplinary segregation and that there was a disputed question of fact with respect to whether Conner received all of the process due under this Court's pronouncement in *Wolff v. McDonnell*, 418 U.S. 539, 94 S.Ct. 2963, 41 L.Ed.2d 935 (1974). The Court of Appeals based its conclusion on a prison regulation that instructs the committee to find guilt when a charge of misconduct is supported by substantial evidence.[3] The Court of Appeals reasoned from *Kentucky Department of Corrections v. Thompson*, 490 U.S. 454, 109 S.Ct. 1904, 104 L.Ed.2d 506 (1989), that the committee's duty to find guilt was nondiscretionary. From the language of the regulation, it drew a negative inference that the committee may not impose segregation if it does not find substantial evidence of misconduct. It viewed this as a state-created liberty interest, and therefore held that respondent was entitled to call witnesses by virtue of our opinion in *Wolff, supra*. We granted the State's petition for certiorari, and now reverse.

II

Our due process analysis begins with *Wolff*. There, Nebraska inmates challenged the decision of prison officials to revoke good time credits without adequate procedures. Inmates earned good time credits under a state statute that bestowed mandatory sentence reductions for good behavior, revocable only for " 'flagrant or serious misconduct.' " We held that the Due Process Clause itself does not create a liberty interest in credit for good behavior, but that the statutory provision created a liberty interest in a "shortened prison sentence" which resulted from good time credits, credits which were revocable only if the prisoner was guilty of serious misconduct. The Court characterized this liberty interest as one of "real substance," and articulated minimum procedures necessary to reach a "mutual accommodation between institutional needs and objectives and the provisions of the Constitution." Much of *Wolff*'s contribution to the landscape of prisoners' due process derived not from its description of

---

[3]   The full text of the regulation reads as follows:

"Upon completion of the hearing, the committee may take the matter under advisement and render a decision based upon evidence presented at the hearing to which the individual had an opportunity to respond or any cumulative evidence which may subsequently come to light may be used as a permissible inference of guilt, although disciplinary action shall be based upon more than mere silence. *A finding of guilt shall be made where*:

"(1)   The inmate or ward admits the violation or pleads guilty.

"(2)   *The charge is supported by substantial evidence*." Haw. Admin. Rule § 17–201–18(b)(2) (1983) (emphasis added).

liberty interests, but rather from its intricate balancing of prison management concerns with prisoners' liberty in determining the amount of process due. Its short discussion of the definition of a liberty interest, *Wolff, supra*, at 556–558, 94 S.Ct., at 2974–2976, led to a more thorough treatment of the issue in *Meachum v. Fano*, 427 U.S. 215, 96 S.Ct. 2532, 49 L.Ed.2d 451 (1976).

Inmates in *Meachum* sought injunctive relief, declaratory relief and damages by reason of transfers from a Massachusetts medium security prison to a maximum security facility with substantially less favorable conditions. The transfers were ordered in the aftermath of arson incidents for which the transferred inmates were thought to be responsible, and did not entail a loss of good time credits or any period of disciplinary confinement. The Court began with the proposition that the Due Process Clause does not protect every change in the conditions of confinement having a substantial adverse impact on the prisoner. It then held that the Due Process Clause did not itself create a liberty interest in prisoners to be free from intrastate prison transfers. It reasoned that transfer to a maximum security facility, albeit one with more burdensome conditions, was "within the normal limits or range of custody which the conviction has authorized the State to impose." The Court distinguished *Wolff* by noting that there the protected liberty interest in good time credit had been created by state law; here no comparable Massachusetts law stripped officials of the discretion to transfer prisoners to alternate facilities "for whatever reason or for no reason at all." *Meachum, supra*, at 228, 96 S.Ct., at 2540.[4]

Shortly after *Meachum*, the Court embarked on a different approach to defining state-created liberty interests. Because dictum in *Meachum* distinguished *Wolff* by focusing on whether state action was mandatory or discretionary, the Court in later cases laid ever greater emphasis on this somewhat mechanical dichotomy * * *.

* * *

As this methodology took hold, no longer did inmates need to rely on a showing that they had suffered a " 'grievous loss' " of liberty retained even after sentenced to terms of imprisonment. *Morrissey v. Brewer*, 408 U.S. 471, 481, 92 S.Ct. 2593, 2600, 33 L.Ed.2d 484 (1972) (citation omitted). For

---

[4]   Later cases, such as *Vitek v. Jones*, 445 U.S. 480, 100 S.Ct. 1254, 63 L.Ed.2d 552 (1980), found that the Due Process Clause itself confers a liberty interest in certain situations. In *Vitek*, a prisoner was to be transferred involuntarily to a state mental hospital for treatment of a mental disease or defect; the Court held that his right to be free from such transfer was a liberty interest irrespective of state regulation; it was "qualitatively different" from the punishment characteristically suffered by a person convicted of crime, and had "stigmatizing consequences." *Id.*, at 493–494, 100 S.Ct., at 1264. *Washington v. Harper*, 494 U.S. 210, 221–222, 110 S.Ct. 1028, 1036–1037, 108 L.Ed.2d 178 (1990), likewise concluded that, independent of any state regulation, an inmate had a liberty interest in being protected from the involuntary administration of psychotropic drugs.

the Court had ceased to examine the "nature" of the interest with respect to interests allegedly created by the State. *See ibid.*; *Board of Regents of State Colleges v. Roth*, 408 U.S. 564, 571, 92 S.Ct. 2701, 2706, 33 L.Ed.2d 548 (1972). In a series of cases * * *, the Court has wrestled with the language of intricate, often rather routine prison guidelines to determine whether mandatory language and substantive predicates created an enforceable expectation that the state would produce a particular outcome with respect to the prisoner's conditions of confinement.

In *Olim v. Wakinekona*, 461 U.S. 238, 103 S.Ct. 1741, 75 L.Ed.2d 813 (1983), the claimants identified prison regulations that required a particular kind of hearing before the prison administrator could, in his discretion, effect an interstate transfer to another prison. Parsing the language of the regulation led the Court to hold that the discretionary nature of the transfer decision negated any state-created liberty interest. *Id.*, at 249–250, 103 S.Ct., at 1747–1748. *Kentucky Department of Corrections v. Thompson*, 490 U.S. 454, 109 S.Ct. 1904, 104 L.Ed.2d 506 (1989), dealt with regulations governing the visitation privileges of inmates. Asserting that a regulation created an absolute right to visitors absent a finding of certain substantive predicates, the inmates sought review of the adequacy of the procedures. As in *Wakinekona*, the Court determined the regulation left visitor exclusion to the discretion of the officials, and refused to elevate such expectations to the level of a liberty interest. 490 U.S., at 464–465, 109 S.Ct., at 1910–1911.

By shifting the focus of the liberty interest inquiry to one based on the language of a particular regulation, and not the nature of the deprivation, the Court encouraged prisoners to comb regulations in search of mandatory language on which to base entitlements to various state-conferred privileges. Courts have, in response, and not altogether illogically, drawn negative inferences from mandatory language in the text of prison regulations. The Court of Appeals' approach in this case is typical: it inferred from the mandatory directive that a finding of guilt "shall" be imposed under certain conditions the conclusion that the absence of such conditions prevents a finding of guilt.

Such a conclusion may be entirely sensible in the ordinary task of construing a statute defining rights and remedies available to the general public. It is a good deal less sensible in the case of a prison regulation primarily designed to guide correctional officials in the administration of a prison. Not only are such regulations not designed to confer rights on inmates, but the result of the negative implication jurisprudence is not to require the prison officials to follow the negative implication drawn from the regulation, but is instead to attach procedural protections that may be of quite a different nature. Here, for example, the Court of Appeals did not hold that a finding of guilt could *not* be made in the *absence* of substantial evidence. Instead, it held that the "liberty interest" created by the regulation entitled the inmate to the procedural protections set forth in *Wolff*.

[This approach] * * * has produced at least two undesirable effects. First, it creates disincentives for States to codify prison management procedures in the interest of uniform treatment. Prison administrators need be concerned with the safety of the staff and inmate population. Ensuring that welfare often leads prison administrators to curb the discretion of staff on the front line who daily encounter prisoners hostile to the authoritarian structure of the prison environment. Such guidelines are not set forth solely to benefit the prisoner. They also aspire to instruct subordinate employees how to exercise discretion vested by the State in the warden, and to confine the authority of prison personnel in order to avoid widely different treatment of similar incidents. The approach embraced by * * * [cases subsequent to *Wolff*] discourages this desirable development: States may avoid creation of "liberty" interests by having scarcely any regulations, or by conferring standardless discretion on correctional personnel.

Second, [this] * * * approach has led to the involvement of federal courts in the day-to-day management of prisons, often squandering judicial resources with little offsetting benefit to anyone. In so doing, it has run counter to the view expressed in several of our cases that federal courts ought to afford appropriate deference and flexibility to state officials trying to manage a volatile environment. Such flexibility is especially warranted in the fine-tuning of the ordinary incidents of prison life, a common subject of prisoner claims * * *. *See, e.g., Klos v. Haskell*, 48 F.3d 81 (C.A.2 1995) (claiming liberty interest in right to participate in "shock program"—a type of boot camp for inmates); *Segal v. Biller*, No. 94–35448, 1994 WL 594705 (C.A.9 Oct.31, 1994) (claiming liberty interest in a waiver of the travel limit imposed on prison furloughs); *Burgin v. Nix*, 899 F.2d 733, 735 (C.A.8 1990) (claiming liberty interest in receiving a tray lunch rather than a sack lunch); *Spruytte v. Walters*, 753 F.2d 498, 506–508 (C.A.6 1985) (finding liberty interest in receiving a paperback dictionary due to a rule that states a prisoner " 'may receive any book . . . which does not present a threat to the order or security of the institution' ") (citation omitted); *Lyon v. Farrier*, 727 F.2d 766, 768–769 (C.A.8 1984) (claiming liberty interest in freedom from transfer to a smaller cell without electrical outlets for televisions and liberty interest in a prison job); *United States v. Michigan*, 680 F.Supp. 270, 277 (W.D.Mich.1988) (finding liberty interest in not being placed on food loaf diet).

In light of the above discussion, we believe that the search for a negative implication from mandatory language in prisoner regulations has strayed from the real concerns undergirding the liberty protected by the Due Process Clause. The time has come to return to the due process principles we believe were correctly established and applied in *Wolff* and

Meachum.[5] Following *Wolff*, we recognize that States may under certain circumstances create liberty interests which are protected by the Due Process Clause. But these interests will be generally limited to freedom from restraint which, while not exceeding the sentence in such an unexpected manner as to give rise to protection by the Due Process Clause of its own force, see, *e.g.*, *Vitek*, 445 U.S., at 493, 100 S.Ct., at 1263–1264 (transfer to mental hospital), and *Washington*, 494 U.S., at 221–222, 110 S.Ct., at 1036–1037 (involuntary administration of psychotropic drugs), nonetheless imposes atypical and significant hardship on the inmate in relation to the ordinary incidents of prison life.

* * *

This case, though concededly punitive, does not present a dramatic departure from the basic conditions of Conner's indeterminate sentence. Although Conner points to dicta in cases implying that solitary confinement automatically triggers due process protection, this Court has not had the opportunity to address in an argued case the question whether disciplinary confinement of inmates itself implicates constitutional liberty interests. We hold that Conner's discipline in segregated confinement did not present the type of atypical, significant deprivation in which a state might conceivably create a liberty interest. The record shows that, at the time of Conner's punishment, disciplinary segregation, with insignificant exceptions, mirrored those conditions imposed upon inmates in administrative segregation and protective custody. We note also that the State expunged Conner's disciplinary record with respect to the "high misconduct" charge 9 months after Conner served time in segregation. Thus, Conner's confinement did not exceed similar, but totally discretionary confinement in either duration or degree of restriction. Indeed, the conditions at Halawa involve significant amounts of "lockdown time" even for inmates in the general population. Based on a comparison between inmates inside and outside disciplinary segregation, the State's actions in placing him there for 30 days did not work a major disruption in his environment.

Nor does Conner's situation present a case where the State's action will inevitably affect the duration of his sentence. Nothing in Hawaii's code requires the parole board to deny parole in the face of a misconduct record or to grant parole in its absence, even though misconduct is by regulation a relevant consideration. The decision to release a prisoner rests on a myriad of considerations. And, the prisoner is afforded procedural protection at his parole hearing in order to explain the circumstances behind his misconduct record. The chance that a finding of misconduct will

---

[5] Such abandonment * * * does not technically require us to overrule any holding of this Court * * *. Our decision today only abandons an approach that in practice is difficult to administer and which produces anomalous results.

alter the balance is simply too attenuated to invoke the procedural guarantees of the Due Process Clause * * *.

We hold, therefore, that neither the Hawaii prison regulation in question, nor the Due Process Clause itself, afforded Conner a protected liberty interest that would entitle him to the procedural protections set forth in *Wolff.* The regime to which he was subjected as a result of the misconduct hearing was within the range of confinement to be normally expected for one serving an indeterminate term of 30 years to life.

The judgment of the Court of Appeals is accordingly

Reversed.

JUSTICE GINSBURG, with whom JUSTICE STEVENS joins, dissenting.

* * *

Unlike the Court, I conclude that Conner had a liberty interest, protected by the Fourteenth Amendment's Due Process Clause, in avoiding the disciplinary confinement he endured. As JUSTICE BREYER details, Conner's prison punishment effected a severe alteration in the conditions of his incarceration. Disciplinary confinement as punishment for "high misconduct" not only deprives prisoners of privileges for protracted periods; unlike administrative segregation and protective custody, disciplinary confinement also stigmatizes them and diminishes parole prospects. Those immediate and lingering consequences should suffice to qualify such confinement as liberty-depriving for purposes of Due Process Clause protection.[1]

I see the Due Process Clause itself, not Hawaii's prison code, as the wellspring of the protection due Conner. Deriving protected liberty interests from mandatory language in local prison codes would make of the fundamental right something more in certain States, something less in others. Liberty that may vary from Ossining, New York, to San Quentin, California, does not resemble the "Liberty" enshrined among "unalienable Rights" with which all persons are "endowed by their Creator." Declaration of Independence; *see Meachum,* 427 U.S., at 230, 96 S.Ct., at 2541 (STEVENS, J., dissenting) ("[T]he Due Process Clause protects [the unalienable liberty recognized in the Declaration of Independence] rather

---

[1]   The Court reasons that Conner's disciplinary confinement, "with insignificant exceptions, mirrored th[e] conditions imposed upon inmates in administrative segregation and protective custody," and therefore implicated no constitutional liberty interest. But discipline means punishment for misconduct; it rests on a finding of wrongdoing that can adversely affect an inmate's parole prospects. Disciplinary confinement therefore cannot be bracketed with administrative segregation and protective custody, both measures that carry no long-term consequences. The Court notes, however, that the State eventually expunged Conner's disciplinary record as a result of his successful administrative appeal. But hindsight cannot tell us whether a liberty interest existed at the outset. One must, of course, know at the start the character of the interest at stake in order to determine *then* what process, if any, is constitutionally due. "All's well that ends well" cannot be the measure here.

than the particular rights or privileges conferred by specific laws or regulations.").[2]

* * *

JUSTICE BREYER, with whom JUSTICE SOUTER joins, dissenting.

* * *

The Fourteenth Amendment says that a State shall not "deprive any person of life, liberty, or property, without due process of law." U.S. Const., Amdt. 14, § 1. In determining whether state officials have deprived an inmate, such as Conner, of a procedurally protected "liberty," this Court traditionally has looked either (1) to the nature of the deprivation (how severe, in degree or kind) or (2) to the State's rules governing the imposition of that deprivation (whether they, in effect, give the inmate a "right" to avoid it). Thus, this Court has said that certain changes in conditions may be so severe or so different from ordinary conditions of confinement that, whether or not state law gives state authorities broad discretionary power to impose them, the state authorities may not do so "without complying with minimum requirements of due process." *Vitek v. Jones*, 445 U.S. 480, 491–494, 100 S.Ct. 1254, 1263, 63 L.Ed.2d 552 (1980) ("involuntary commitment to a mental hospital"); *Washington v. Harper*, 494 U.S. 210, 221–222, 110 S.Ct. 1028, 1036–1037, 108 L.Ed.2d 178 (1990) ("unwanted administration of antipsychotic drugs"). The Court has also said that deprivations that are less severe or more closely related to the original terms of confinement nonetheless will amount to deprivations of procedurally protected liberty, provided that state law (including prison regulations) narrowly cabins the legal power of authorities to impose the deprivation (thereby giving the inmate a kind of right to avoid it).

If we apply these general pre-existing principles to the relevant facts before us, it seems fairly clear, as the Ninth Circuit found, that the prison punishment here at issue deprived Conner of constitutionally protected "liberty." For one thing, the punishment worked a fairly major change in Conner's conditions. In the absence of the punishment, Conner, like other inmates in Halawa's general prison population would have left his cell and worked, taken classes, or mingled with others for eight *hours* each day. As a result of disciplinary segregation, however, Conner, for 30 days, had to spend his entire time alone in his cell (with the exception of 50 *minutes* each day on average for brief exercise and shower periods, during which he

---

[2] The Court describes a category of liberty interest that is something less than the one the Due Process Clause itself shields, something more than anything a prison code provides. The State may create a liberty interest, the Court tells us, when "atypical and significant hardship [would be borne by] the inmate in relation to the ordinary incidents of prison life." What design lies beneath these key words? The Court ventures no examples, leaving consumers of the Court's work at sea, unable to fathom what would constitute an "atypical, significant deprivation," and yet not trigger protection under the Due Process Clause directly.

nonetheless remained isolated from other inmates and was constrained by leg irons and waist chains).

Moreover, irrespective of whether this punishment amounts to a deprivation of liberty independent of state law, here the prison's own disciplinary rules severely cabin the authority of prison officials to impose this kind of punishment * * *.

* * *

* * * Prison, by design, restricts the inmates' freedom. And, one cannot properly view unimportant matters that happen to be the subject of prison regulations as substantially aggravating a loss that has already occurred. Indeed, a regulation about a minor matter, for example, a regulation that seems to cabin the discretionary power of a prison administrator to deprive an inmate of, say, a certain kind of lunch, may amount simply to an instruction to the administrator about how to do his job, rather than a guarantee to the inmate of a "right" to the status quo. Thus, this Court has never held that comparatively unimportant prisoner "deprivations" fall within the scope of the Due Process Clause even if local law limits the authority of prison administrators to impose such minor deprivations. And, in my view, it should now simply specify that they do not.

I recognize that, as a consequence, courts must separate the unimportant from the potentially significant, without the help of the more objective "discretion-cabining" test. Yet, making that judicial judgment seems no more difficult than many other judicial tasks. It seems to me possible to separate less significant matters such as television privileges, "sack" versus "tray" lunches, playing the state lottery, attending an ex-stepfather's funeral, or the limits of travel when on prison furlough from more significant matters, such as the solitary confinement at issue here. Indeed, prison regulations themselves may help in this respect, such as the regulations here which separate (from more serious matters) "low moderate" and "minor" misconduct * * *.

NOTES

Sandin immediately suggests two questions. First, if the entitlement approach creates perverse incentives for prison administrators by discouraging them from cabining the discretion of government officials through binding rules or policies, why isn't the same true in all other contexts? And second, if the entitlement approach continues to govern outside the context of minor prison matters, as the majority opinion indicates, why would any rational government administrator ever draft regulations that create entitlements?

By its terms, *Sandin* applies only to prison regulations. Outside of that context, the constraint-on-discretion analysis exemplified by *Kentucky v. Thompson* still governs. *See Rodriguez v. McLoughlin*, 214 F.3d 328 (2d Cir.2000). Despite its seemingly narrow compass, however, *Sandin* has already had a huge influence on due process litigation; a significant percentage of due process cases in recent years have involved precisely the kind of prison regulations at issue in *Sandin*. A WESTLAW search of all federal cases in June 2012 turned up "10000" citations to *Sandin*. Nonetheless, *Sandin* has not entirely eliminated the need carefully to consult the language of statutes and regulations even in the prison context. Lower courts have held, for example, that *Sandin* does not apply to state action affecting parole determinations. *See, e.g., Ellis v. District of Columbia*, 84 F.3d 1413 (D.C.Cir.1996). Nor does it apply to pre-trial detainees. *See Fuentes v. Wagner*, 206 F.3d 335 (3d Cir.2000); *Mitchell v. Dupnik*, 75 F.3d 517 (9th Cir.1996).

How does the following case resemble or differ from *Sandin*?

TOWN OF CASTLE ROCK, COLORADO V. GONZALES

Supreme Court of the United States, 2005.
545 U.S. 748, 125 S.Ct. 2796, 162 L.Ed.2d 658.

JUSTICE SCALIA delivered the opinion of the Court.

* * *

* * * Respondent alleges that petitioner, the town of Castle Rock, Colorado, violated the Due Process Clause of the Fourteenth Amendment to the United States Constitution when its police officers, acting pursuant to official policy or custom, failed to respond properly to her repeated reports that her estranged husband was violating the terms of a restraining order.

The restraining order had been issued by a state trial court several weeks earlier in conjunction with respondent's divorce proceedings. The original form order * * *, issued on May 21, 1999, and served on respondent's husband on June 4, 1999, commanded him not to "molest or disturb the peace of [respondent] or of any child," and to remain at least 100 yards from the family home at all times. The bottom of the pre-printed form noted that the reverse side contained "IMPORTANT NOTICES FOR RESTRAINED PARTIES AND LAW ENFORCEMENT OFFICIALS." The preprinted text on the back of the form included the following "**WARNING**":

> "**A KNOWING VIOLATION OF A RESTRAINING ORDER IS A CRIME.**.. A VIOLATION WILL ALSO CONSTITUTE CONTEMPT OF COURT. **YOU MAY BE ARRESTED** WITHOUT NOTICE IF A LAW ENFORCEMENT OFFICER HAS PROBABLE CAUSE TO BELIEVE THAT YOU HAVE KNOWINGLY VIOLATED THIS ORDER."

The preprinted text on the back of the form also included a "**NOTICE TO LAW ENFORCEMENT OFFICIALS**," which read in part:

"YOU SHALL USE EVERY REASONABLE MEANS TO
ENFORCE THIS RESTRAINING ORDER. YOU SHALL
ARREST, OR, IF AN ARREST WOULD BE IMPRACTICAL
UNDER THE CIRCUMSTANCES, SEEK A WARRANT FOR
THE ARREST OF THE RESTRAINED PERSON WHEN YOU
HAVE INFORMATION AMOUNTING TO PROBABLE CAUSE
THAT THE RESTRAINED PERSON HAS VIOLATED OR
ATTEMPTED TO VIOLATE ANY PROVISION OF THIS ORDER
AND THE RESTRAINED PERSON HAS BEEN PROPERLY
SERVED WITH A COPY OF THIS ORDER OR HAS RECEIVED
ACTUAL NOTICE OF THE EXISTENCE OF THIS ORDER."

On June 4, 1999, the state trial court modified the terms of the restraining order and made it permanent. The modified order gave respondent's husband the right to spend time with his three daughters (ages 10, 9, and 7) on alternate weekends, for two weeks during the summer, and, " 'upon reasonable notice,' " for a mid-week dinner visit " 'arranged by the parties' "; the modified order also allowed him to visit the home to collect the children for such "parenting time."

According to the complaint, at about 5 or 5:30 p.m. on Tuesday, June 22, 1999, respondent's husband took the three daughters while they were playing outside the family home. No advance arrangements had been made for him to see the daughters that evening. When respondent noticed the children were missing, she suspected her husband had taken them. At about 7:30 p.m., she called the Castle Rock Police Department, which dispatched two officers. The complaint continues: "When [the officers] arrived . . . , she showed them a copy of the TRO and requested that it be enforced and the three children be returned to her immediately. [The officers] stated that there was nothing they could do about the TRO and suggested that [respondent] call the Police Department again if the three children did not return home by 10:00 p.m."

At approximately 8:30 p.m., respondent talked to her husband on his cellular telephone. He told her "he had the three children [at an] amusement park in Denver." She called the police again and asked them to "have someone check for" her husband or his vehicle at the amusement park and "put out an [all points bulletin]" for her husband, but the officer with whom she spoke "refused to do so," again telling her to "wait until 10:00 p.m. and see if" her husband returned the girls.

At approximately 10:10 p.m., respondent called the police and said her children were still missing, but she was now told to wait until midnight. She called at midnight and told the dispatcher her children were still missing. She went to her husband's apartment and, finding nobody there, called the police at 12:10 a.m.; she was told to wait for an officer to arrive. When none came, she went to the police station at 12:50 a.m. and submitted an incident report. The officer who took the report "made no reasonable effort to enforce the TRO or locate the three children. Instead, he went to dinner."

At approximately 3:20 a.m., respondent's husband arrived at the police station and opened fire with a semiautomatic handgun he had purchased earlier that evening. Police shot back, killing him. Inside the cab of his pickup truck, they found the bodies of all three daughters, whom he had already murdered.

On the basis of the foregoing factual allegations, respondent brought an action under 42 U.S.C. § 1983, claiming that the town violated the Due Process Clause because its police department had "an official policy or custom of failing to respond properly to complaints of restraining order violations" and "tolerate[d] the non-enforcement of restraining orders by its police officers." The complaint also alleged that the town's actions "were taken either willfully, recklessly or with such gross negligence as to indicate wanton disregard and deliberate indifference to" respondent's civil rights.

* * *

* * * [The en banc Tenth Circuit Court of Appeals concluded] that respondent had a "protected property interest in the enforcement of the terms of her restraining order" and that the town had deprived her of due process because "the police never 'heard' nor seriously entertained her request to enforce and protect her interests in the restraining order." We granted certiorari.

II

* * *

* * * The procedural component of the Due Process Clause does not protect everything that might be described as a "benefit": "To have a property interest in a benefit, a person clearly must have more than an abstract need or desire" and "more than a unilateral expectation of it. He must, instead, have a legitimate claim of entitlement to it." *Board of Regents of State Colleges v. Roth,* 408 U.S. 564, 577, 92 S.Ct. 2701, 33 L.Ed.2d 548 (1972). Such entitlements are " 'of course, . . . not created by the Constitution. Rather, they are created and their dimensions are defined by existing rules or understandings that stem from an independent source such as state law.' " *Paul v. Davis,* 424 U.S. 693, 709, 96 S.Ct. 1155, 47 L.Ed.2d 405 (1976) (quoting *Roth*).

A

Our cases recognize that a benefit is not a protected entitlement if government officials may grant or deny it in their discretion. See, *e.g., Kentucky Dept. of Corrections v. Thompson,* 490 U.S. 454, 462–463, 109

S.Ct. 1904, 104 L.Ed.2d 506 (1989). The Court of Appeals in this case determined that Colorado law created an entitlement to enforcement of the restraining order because the "court-issued restraining order . . . specifically dictated that its terms must be enforced" and a "state statute command[ed]" enforcement of the order when certain objective conditions were met (probable cause to believe that the order had been violated and that the object of the order had received notice of its existence). Respondent contends that we are obliged "to give deference to the Tenth Circuit's analysis of Colorado law on" whether she had an entitlement to enforcement of the restraining order. Tr. of Oral Arg. 52.

We will not, of course, defer to the Tenth Circuit on the ultimate issue: whether what Colorado law has given respondent constitutes a property interest for purposes of the Fourteenth Amendment. That determination, despite its state-law underpinnings, is ultimately one of federal constitutional law. "Although the underlying substantive interest is created by 'an independent source such as state law,' *federal constitutional law* determines whether that interest rises to the level of a 'legitimate claim of entitlement' protected by the Due Process Clause." *Memphis Light, Gas & Water Div. v. Craft,* 436 U.S. 1, 9, 98 S.Ct. 1554, 56 L.Ed.2d 30 (1978) (emphasis added). Resolution of the federal issue begins, however, with a determination of what it is that state law provides. In the context of the present case, the central state-law question is whether Colorado law gave respondent a right to police enforcement of the restraining order. It is on this point that respondent's call for deference to the Tenth Circuit is relevant.

We have said that a "presumption of deference [is] given the views of a federal court as to the law of a State within its jurisdiction." That presumption can be overcome, however, and we think deference inappropriate here. The Tenth Circuit's opinion, which reversed the Colorado District Judge, did not draw upon a deep well of state-specific expertise, but consisted primarily of quoting language from the restraining order, the statutory text, and a state-legislative-hearing transcript. These texts, moreover, say nothing distinctive to Colorado, but use mandatory language that (as we shall discuss) appears in many state and federal statutes. As for case law: the only state-law cases about restraining orders that the Court of Appeals relied upon were decisions of Federal District Courts in Ohio and Pennsylvania and state courts in New Jersey, Oregon, and Tennessee * * *.[5]

---

[5] In something of an anyone-but-us approach, the dissent simultaneously (and thus unpersuasively) contends not only that this Court should certify a question to the Colorado Supreme Court, but also that it should defer to the Tenth Circuit (which itself did not certify any such question). No party in this case has requested certification, even as an alternative disposition.

B

The critical language in the restraining order came not from any part of the order itself (which was signed by the state-court trial judge and directed to the restrained party, respondent's husband), but from the preprinted notice to law-enforcement personnel that appeared on the back of the order. That notice effectively restated the statutory provision describing "peace officers' duties" related to the crime of violation of a restraining order. At the time of the conduct at issue in this case, that provision read as follows:

"(a) Whenever a restraining order is issued, the protected person shall be provided with a copy of such order. *A peace officer shall use every reasonable means to enforce a restraining order.*

"(b) *A peace officer shall arrest, or, if an arrest would be impractical under the circumstances, seek a warrant for the arrest of a restrained person* when the peace officer has information amounting to probable cause that:

"(I) The restrained person has violated or attempted to violate any provision of a restraining order; and

"(II) The restrained person has been properly served with a copy of the restraining order or the restrained person has received actual notice of the existence and substance of such order.

"(c) In making the probable cause determination described in paragraph (b) of this subsection (3), a peace officer shall assume that the information received from the registry is accurate. *A peace officer shall enforce a valid restraining order whether or not there is a record of the restraining order in the registry.*" Colo. Rev. Stat. § 18–6–805.5(3) (emphases added).

The Court of Appeals concluded that this statutory provision * * * established the Colorado Legislature's clear intent "to alter the fact that the police were not enforcing domestic abuse retraining orders," and thus its intent "that the recipient of a domestic abuse restraining order have an entitlement to its enforcement" * * *.

* * *

We do not believe that these provisions of Colorado law truly made enforcement of restraining orders *mandatory.* A well established tradition of police discretion has long coexisted with apparently mandatory arrest statutes.

"In each and every state there are long-standing statutes that, by their terms, seem to preclude nonenforcement by the police... However, for a number of reasons, including their legislative history, insufficient resources, and sheer physical impossibility, it has been recognized that such statutes cannot be interpreted literally. . . . [T]hey clearly do not mean that a police officer may not lawfully decline to make an arrest. As to third parties in these states, the full-enforcement statutes simply have no effect, and their significance is further diminished." 1 ABA Standards for Criminal Justice 1–4.5, commentary, pp. 1–124 to 1–125 (2d ed.1980) (footnotes omitted).

The deep-rooted nature of law-enforcement discretion, even in the presence of seemingly mandatory legislative commands, is illustrated by *Chicago v. Morales*, 527 U.S. 41, 119 S.Ct. 1849, 144 L.Ed.2d 67 (1999), which involved an ordinance that said a police officer " 'shall order' " persons to disperse in certain circumstances. This Court rejected out of hand the possibility that "the mandatory language of the ordinance . . . afford[ed] the police *no* discretion." *Id.* at 62, n.32, 119 S.Ct. 1849. It is, the Court proclaimed, simply "common sense that *all* police officers must use some discretion in deciding when and where to enforce city ordinances." *Ibid.* (emphasis added).

Against that backdrop, a true mandate of police action would require some stronger indication from the Colorado Legislature than "shall use every reasonable means to enforce a restraining order" (or even "shall arrest . . . or . . . seek a warrant"). That language is not perceptibly more mandatory than the Colorado statute which has long told municipal chiefs of police that they "shall pursue and arrest any person fleeing from justice in any part of the state" and that they "shall apprehend any person in the act of committing any offense . . . and, forthwith and without any warrant, bring such person before a . . . competent authority for examination and trial." Colo.Rev.Stat. § 31–4–112. It is hard to imagine that a Colorado peace officer would not have some discretion to determine that—despite probable cause to believe a restraining order has been violated—the circumstances of the violation or the competing duties of that officer or his agency counsel decisively against enforcement in a particular instance. The practical necessity for discretion is particularly apparent in a case such as this one, where the suspected violator is not actually present and his whereabouts are unknown.

The dissent correctly points out that, in the specific context of domestic violence, mandatory-arrest statutes have been found in some States to be more mandatory than traditional mandatory-arrest statutes * * *. Even in the domestic-violence context, however, it is unclear how the mandatory-arrest paradigm applies to cases in which the offender is not present to be arrested * * *. [M]uch of the impetus for mandatory-arrest statutes and policies derived from the idea that it is better for police officers to arrest the aggressor in a domestic-violence incident than to attempt to mediate the dispute or merely to ask the offender to leave the scene. Those other options are only available, of course, when the offender is present at the scene.

* * *

Respondent does not specify the precise means of enforcement that the Colorado restraining-order statute assertedly mandated—whether her interest lay in having police arrest her husband, having them seek a warrant for his arrest, or having them "use every reasonable means, up to and including arrest, to enforce the order's terms," Brief for Respondent 29–30. Such indeterminacy is not the hallmark of a duty that is mandatory. Nor can someone be safely deemed "entitled" to something when the identity of the alleged entitlement is vague. The dissent, after suggesting various formulations of the entitlement in question, ultimately contends that the obligations under the statute were quite precise: either make an arrest or (if that is impractical) seek an arrest warrant. The problem with this is that the seeking of an arrest warrant would be an entitlement to nothing but procedure—which we have held inadequate even to support standing; much less can it be the basis for a property interest. See *post,* at 2812–2813 (SOUTER, J., concurring). After the warrant is sought, it remains within the discretion of a judge whether to grant it, and after it is granted, it remains within the discretion of the police whether and when to execute it. Respondent would have been assured nothing but the seeking of a warrant. This is not the sort of "entitlement" out of which a property interest is created.

Even if the statute could be said to have made enforcement of restraining orders "mandatory" because of the domestic-violence context of the underlying statute, that would not necessarily mean that state law gave *respondent* an entitlement to *enforcement* of the mandate. Making the actions of government employees obligatory can serve various legitimate ends other than the conferral of a benefit on a specific class of people. The serving of public rather than private ends is the normal course of the criminal law * * *. This principle underlies, for example, a Colorado district attorney's discretion to prosecute a domestic assault, even though the victim withdraws her charge.

* * *

The creation of a personal entitlement to something as vague and novel as enforcement of restraining orders cannot "simply g[o] without saying." *Post,* at 2821, n. 16 (STEVENS, J., dissenting). We conclude that Colorado has not created such an entitlement.

C

Even if we were to think otherwise concerning the creation of an entitlement by Colorado, it is by no means clear that an individual entitlement to enforcement of a restraining order could constitute a "property" interest for purposes of the Due Process Clause. Such a right would not, of course, resemble any traditional conception of property. Although that alone does not disqualify it from due process protection, as *Roth* and its progeny show, the right to have a restraining order enforced does not "have some ascertainable monetary value," as even our "*Roth*-type property-as-entitlement" cases have implicitly required. Merrill, The Landscape of Constitutional Property, 86 Va. L. Rev. 885, 964 (2000). Perhaps most radically, the alleged property interest here arises *incidentally,* not out of some new species of government benefit or service, but out of a function that government actors have always performed—to wit, arresting people who they have probable cause to believe have committed a criminal offense.

The indirect nature of a benefit was fatal to the due process claim of the nursing-home residents in *O'Bannon v. Town Court Nursing Center*, 447 U.S. 773, 100 S.Ct. 2467, 65 L.Ed.2d 506 (1980). We held that, while the withdrawal of "direct benefits" (financial payments under Medicaid for certain medical services) triggered due process protections, the same was not true for the "indirect benefit[s]" conferred on Medicaid patients when the Government enforced "minimum standards of care" for nursing-home facilities, *id.,* at 787. "[A]n indirect and incidental result of the Government's enforcement action . . . does not amount to a deprivation of any interest in life, liberty, or property." *Ibid.* In this case, as in *O'Bannon,* "[t]he simple distinction between government action that directly affects a citizen's legal rights . . . and action that is directed against a third party and affects the citizen only indirectly or incidentally, provides a sufficient answer to" respondent's reliance on cases that found government-provided services to be entitlements. *Id.,* at 788 * * *.

III

We conclude, therefore, that respondent did not, for purposes of the Due Process Clause, have a property interest in police enforcement of the restraining order against her husband * * *.

* * *

The judgment of the Court of Appeals is

Reversed.

JUSTICE SOUTER, with whom JUSTICE BREYER joins, concurring.

* * *

* * * [I]n every instance of property recognized by this Court as calling for federal procedural protection, the property has been distinguishable from the procedural obligations imposed on state officials to protect it. Whether welfare benefits, *Goldberg v. Kelly*, 397 U.S. 254, 90 S.Ct. 1011, 25 L.Ed.2d 287 (1970), attendance at public schools, *Goss v. Lopez*, 419 U.S.

565, 95 S.Ct. 729, 42 L.Ed.2d 725 (1975), utility services, *Memphis Light, Gas & Water Div. v. Craft*, 436 U.S. 1, 98 S.Ct. 1554, 56 L.Ed.2d 30 (1978), public employment, *Perry v. Sindermann*, 408 U.S. 593, 92 S.Ct. 2694, 33 L.Ed.2d 570 (1972), professional licenses, *Barry v. Barchi*, 443 U.S. 55, 99 S.Ct. 2642, 61 L.Ed.2d 365 (1979), and so on, the property interest recognized in our cases has always existed apart from state procedural protection before the Court has recognized a constitutional claim to protection by federal process. To accede to Gonzales's argument would therefore work a sea change in the scope of federal due process, for she seeks federal process as a substitute simply for state process. (And she seeks damages under 42 U.S.C. § 1983 for denial of process to which she claimed a federal right.) There is no articulable distinction between the object of Gonzales's asserted entitlement and the process she desires in order to protect her entitlement; both amount to certain steps to be taken by the police to protect her family and herself. Gonzales's claim would thus take us beyond *Roth* or any other recognized theory of Fourteenth Amendment due process, by collapsing the distinction between property protected and the process that protects it, and would federalize every mandatory state-law direction to executive officers whose performance on the job can be vitally significant to individuals affected.

The procedural directions involved here are just that. They presuppose no enforceable substantive entitlement, and *Roth* does not raise them to federally enforceable status in the name of due process.

JUSTICE STEVENS, with whom JUSTICE GINSBURG joins, dissenting.

* * *

* * * Respondent certainly could have entered into a contract with a private security firm, obligating the firm to provide protection to respondent's family; respondent's interest in such a contract would unquestionably constitute "property" within the meaning of the Due Process Clause. If a Colorado statute enacted for her benefit, or a valid order entered by a Colorado judge, created the functional equivalent of such a private contract by granting respondent an entitlement to mandatory individual protection by the local police force, that state-created right would also qualify as "property" entitled to constitutional protection.

* * *

The central question in this case is therefore whether, as a matter of Colorado law, respondent had a right to police assistance comparable to the right she would have possessed to any other service the government or a private firm might have undertaken to provide.

* * *

I

The majority's decision to plunge ahead with its own analysis of Colorado law imprudently departs from this Court's longstanding policy of paying "deference [to] the views of a federal court as to the law of a State within its jurisdiction." *Phillips v. Washington Legal Foundation*, 524 U.S. 156, 167, 118 S.Ct. 1925, 141 L.Ed.2d 174 (1998); see also *Bishop v. Wood*, 426 U.S. 341, 346, and n. 10, 96 S.Ct. 2074, 48 L.Ed.2d 684 (1976) (collecting cases) * * *. [W]e have declined to show deference only in rare cases in which the court of appeal's resolution of state law was "clearly wrong" or otherwise seriously deficient.

Unfortunately, the Court does not even attempt to demonstrate that the six-judge en banc majority was "clearly wrong" in its interpretation of Colorado's domestic restraining order statute; nor could such a showing be made * * *. Far from overlooking the traditional presumption of police discretion * * *, the Court of Appeals' diligent analysis of the statute's text, purpose, and history led it to conclude that the Colorado Legislature intended precisely to abrogate that presumption in the specific context of domestic restraining orders. That conclusion is eminently reasonable and, I believe, worthy of our deference.[2]

II

Even if the Court had good reason to doubt the Court of Appeals' determination of state law, it would, in my judgment, be a far wiser course to certify the question to the Colorado Supreme Court * * *. After all, the Colorado Supreme Court is the ultimate authority on the meaning of Colorado law, and if in later litigation it should disagree with this Court's provisional state-law holding, our efforts will have been wasted and respondent will have been deprived of the opportunity to have her claims heard under the authoritative view of Colorado law * * *.

III

Three flaws in the Court's rather superficial analysis of the merits highlight the unwisdom of its decision to answer the state-law question *de novo*. First, the Court places undue weight on the various statutes throughout the country that seemingly mandate police enforcement but are generally understood to preserve police discretion. As a result, the Court gives short shrift to the unique case of "mandatory arrest" statutes in the domestic violence context; States passed a wave of these statutes in the 1980's and 1990's with the unmistakable goal of eliminating police discretion in this area. Second, the Court's formalistic analysis fails to take

---

[2] The Court declines to show deference for the odd reason that, in its view, the Court of Appeals did not "draw upon a deep well of state-specific expertise," but rather examined the statute's text and legislative history and distinguished arguably relevant Colorado case law. This rationale makes a mockery of our traditional practice, for it is precisely when there is no state law on point that the presumption that circuits have local expertise plays any useful role * * *.

seriously the fact that the Colorado statute at issue in this case was enacted for the benefit of the narrow class of persons who are beneficiaries of domestic restraining orders, and that the order at issue in this case was specifically intended to provide protection to respondent and her children. Finally, the Court is simply wrong to assert that a citizen's interest in the government's commitment to provide police enforcement in certain defined circumstances does not resemble any "traditional conception of property"; in fact, a citizen's property interest in such a commitment is just as concrete and worthy of protection as her interest in any other important service the government or a private firm has undertaken to provide.

In 1994, the Colorado General Assembly passed omnibus legislation targeting domestic violence. The part of the legislation at issue in this case mandates enforcement of a domestic restraining order upon probable cause of a violation, while another part directs that police officers "shall, without undue delay, arrest" a suspect upon "probable cause to believe that a crime or offense of domestic violence has been committed." In adopting this legislation, the Colorado General Assembly joined a nationwide movement of States that took aim at the crisis of police underenforcement in the domestic violence sphere by implementing "mandatory arrest" statutes * * *.

Thus, when Colorado passed its statute in 1994, it joined the ranks of 15 States that mandated arrest for domestic violence offenses and 19 States that mandated arrest for domestic restraining order violations.

Given the specific purpose of these statutes, there can be no doubt that the Colorado Legislature used the term "shall" advisedly in its domestic restraining order statute. While "shall" is probably best read to mean "may" in other Colorado statutes that seemingly mandate enforcement, cf. Colo.Rev.Stat. § 31–4–112 (police "*shall suppress* all riots, disturbances or breaches of the peace, *shall apprehend* all disorderly persons in the city . . ."(emphases added)), it is clear that the elimination of police discretion was integral to Colorado and its fellow States' solution to the problem of underenforcement in domestic violence cases. Since the text of Colorado's statute perfectly captures this legislative purpose, it is hard to imagine what the Court has in mind when it insists on "some stronger indication from the Colorado Legislature."

* * *

Indeed, the Court fails to come to terms with the wave of domestic violence statutes that provides the crucial context for understanding Colorado's law * * *. Before this wave of statutes, the legal rule was one of discretion; as the Court shows, the "traditional," general mandatory arrest statutes have always been understood to be "mandatory" in name only. The innovation of the domestic violence statutes was to make police enforcement, not "more mandatory," but simply *mandatory*. If, as the Court says, the existence of a protected "entitlement" turns on whether "government officials may grant or deny it in their discretion," the new mandatory statutes undeniably create an entitlement to police enforcement of restraining orders.

* * * Regardless of whether the enforcement called for in this case was arrest or the seeking of an arrest warrant (the answer to that question probably changed over the course of the night as the respondent gave the police more information about the husband's whereabouts), the crucial point is that, under the statute, the police were *required* to provide enforcement; *they lacked the discretion to do nothing* * * *.

* * *

IV

Given that Colorado law has quite clearly eliminated the police's discretion to deny enforcement, respondent is correct that she had much more than a "unilateral expectation" that the restraining order would be enforced; rather, she had a "legitimate claim of entitlement" to enforcement. Recognizing respondent's property interest in the enforcement of her restraining order is fully consistent with our precedent * * *.

5. ENTITLED TO WHAT?

In all of the cases presented thus far, the plaintiffs suffered termination of something—whether benefits, jobs, or prison conditions—that they already had. Even the plaintiffs in *Roth* and *Sindermann,* who were not being terminated as such but were simply not being re-employed, were facing nonrenewal of existing interests. What about an initial applicant for a job or benefit? Does that applicant have a right to a hearing on whether he or she qualifies under the applicable criteria if a terminated beneficiary would have such a right? Under the strict logic of entitlement theory, the answer would seem to be an obvious "yes." If the relevant statutory and regulatory criteria are enough to create a property interest, the difference between termination and denial of an initial application could perhaps affect the degree of procedures required, but it is hard to see why that should affect whether a property interest has been created.

Nonetheless, the Supreme Court has carefully reserved judgment on whether applicants for benefits can ever have due process rights. As the Court pointedly stated in *Lyng v. Payne,* 476 U.S. 926, 106 S.Ct. 2333, 90 L.Ed.2d 921 (1986), "[w]e have never held that applicants for benefits, as distinct from those already receiving them, have a legitimate claim of entitlement protected by the Due Process Clauses of the Fifth or Fourteenth Amendment." *Id.* at 942, 106 S.Ct. at 2343. *See also American Manufacturers Mutual Ins. Co. v. Sullivan,* 526 U.S. 40, 61 n.13, 119 S.Ct.

977, 990 n.13, 143 L.Ed.2d 130 (1999) (noting that the question remains open).

In *Gregory v. Town of Pittsfield*, 479 A.2d 1304 (1984), the Maine Supreme Judicial Court held that an applicant for state general assistance benefits does not have a constitutionally protected interest in such benefits until the applicant has been ruled eligible. "Without this determination, an applicant, no matter what his financial status, has no more than an abstract expectancy of benefits, which in no case can rise to the level of a constitutionally protected property right." 479 A.2d, at 1308. The Supreme Court denied certiorari, with Justices O'Connor, Brennan, and Marshall dissenting. 470 U.S. 1018, 105 S.Ct. 1380, 84 L.Ed.2d 399 (1985). The dissenters reasoned:

> The conclusion of the Supreme Judicial Court that an applicant for general assistance does not have an interest protected by the Due Process Clause is unsettling in its implication that less fortunate persons in our society may arbitrarily be denied benefits that a State has granted as a matter of right. There is no dispute that Mrs. Gregory was entitled under Maine law to the general assistance benefits denied to her in April 1982. We have held that state statutes or regulations prescribing the substantive predicates for state action may create liberty interests protected by due process. One would think that where state law creates an entitlement to general assistance based on certain substantive conditions, there similarly results a property interest that warrants at least some procedural safeguards.

470 U.S. at 1021. Is the full Court's reluctance to take this step grounded in the logic of due process doctrine or in consideration of the potential consequences of requiring due process hearings for every disappointed applicant of every program that creates entitlements? Is there such a thing as "the logic of due process doctrine" apart from consideration of such consequences?

D. "DUE PROCESS OF LAW"

1. THE DUE PROCESS CALCULUS

Some of the cases already presented in this book have discussed the procedures that are constitutionally necessary once a particular constitutionally protected interest is identified. Almost a century ago, for example, the Court held in *Londoner v. Denver*, 210 U.S. 373, 28 S.Ct. 708, 52 L.Ed. 1103 (1908), that affected landowners were entitled to an informal opportunity to present their views orally to the local board before a special assessment was levied:

If it is enough that, under such circumstances, an opportunity is given to submit in writing all objections to and complaints of the tax to the board, then there was a hearing afforded in the case at bar. But we think that something more than that, even in proceedings for taxation, is required by due process of law. Many requirements essential in strictly judicial proceedings may be dispensed with in proceedings of this nature. But even here a hearing in its very essence demands that he who is entitled to it shall have the right to support his allegations by argument however brief, and, if need be, by proof, however informal.

210 U.S. at 386, 28 S.Ct. at 714. Justice Frankfurter's influential concurring opinion in *Joint Anti-Fascist Refugee Committee v. McGrath*, 341 U.S. 123, 71 S.Ct. 624, 95 L.Ed. 817 (1951), went on at great length about the procedures required by due process of law. An oft-quoted paragraph stated:

But "due process," unlike some legal rules, is not a technical conception with a fixed content unrelated to time, place and circumstances. Expressing as it does in its ultimate analysis respect enforced by law for that feeling of just treatment which has been evolved through centuries of Anglo-American constitutional history and civilization, "due process" cannot be imprisoned within the treacherous limits of any formula. Representing a profound attitude of fairness between man and man, and more particularly between the individual and government, "due process" is compounded of history, reason, the past course of decisions, and stout confidence in the strength of the democratic faith which we profess. Due process is not a mechanical instrument. It is not a yardstick. It is a process. It is a delicate process of adjustment inescapably involving the exercise of judgment by those whom the Constitution entrusted with the unfolding of the process.

341 U.S. at 162–63, 71 S.Ct. at 643–44 (Frankfurter, J., concurring). The majority opinion in *Cafeteria & Restaurant Workers Union, Local 473, AFL-CIO v. McElroy*, 367 U.S. 886, 81 S.Ct. 1743, 6 L.Ed.2d 1230 (1961), expressed a similar view, declaring that "[t]he very nature of due process negates any concept of inflexible procedures universally applicable to every imaginable situation," *id.* at 895, 81 S.Ct. at 1748, and suggesting that "consideration of what procedures due process may require under any given set of circumstances must begin with a determination of the precise nature of the government function involved as well as of the precise nature of the private interest that has been affected by governmental action." *Id.* And *Goldberg v. Kelly*, 397 U.S. 254, 90 S.Ct. 1011, 25 L.Ed.2d 287 (1970), held that highly formal procedures were required before a person could be terminated from the New York state welfare program, but it provided no

methodology for reaching that conclusion. None of these cases *systematically* addressed the question of what procedures are encompassed by "due process of law." Indeed, their language seems to counsel strongly against any attempt at systematization.

This reluctance to prescribe a specific methodology for determining what procedures are due has a distinguished pedigree. The Supreme Court's first procedural due process case noted that "[t]he constitution contains no description of those processes which it was intended to allow or forbid. It does not even declare what principles are to be applied to ascertain whether it be due process." *Murray's Lessee v. Hoboken Land & Improvement Co.*, 59 U.S. (18 How.) 272, 276, 15 L.Ed. 372 (1856). The Court said that "we must look to those settled usages and modes of proceeding existing in the common and statute law of England, before the emigration of our ancestors, and which are shown not to have been unsuited to their civil and political condition by having been acted on by them after the settlement of this country." *Id.* Those "settled usages and modes of proceeding," or traditions, afford some clear answers to some easy cases. A criminal defendant can only be permanently deprived of life, liberty, or property after a full-dress trial, complete with a neutral judge and a jury if the defendant wishes one.[9] At the other extreme, deprivations effected by legislation require only the procedures specified by the relevant state or federal constitution for valid legislative action, such as bicameralism and presentment in the federal system; they do not require prior notice, opportunities for hearings, or other procedural devices familiar from the judicial context.

When the deprivation results from administrative action, which is neither judicial nor legislative, the easy paradigms do not apply. What then?

One of the Supreme Court's earliest pronouncements on procedural due process opined that "there is wisdom, we think, in * * * the gradual process of judicial inclusion and exclusion, as the cases presented for decision shall require." *Davidson v. City of New Orleans*, 96 U.S. 97, 104, 24 L.Ed. 616 (1877). Shortly thereafter, the Court explained that "by 'due process' is meant one which, following the forms of law, is appropriate to the case, and just to the parties to be affected." *Hagar v. Reclamation Dist. No. 108*, 111 U.S. 701, 708, 4 S.Ct. 663, 28 L.Ed. 569 (1884). Five years after *Londoner*, the Court declared that the due process clauses forbid procedures that are "inadequate or manifestly unfair." *ICC v. Louisville & Nashville R.R. Co.*, 227 U.S. 88, 91, 33 S.Ct. 185, 57 L.Ed. 431 (1913). The cases that you have read thus far in this chapter are part of an unbroken line of decisions stretching through the early 1970s that did not try to set

---

[9]   For more than a century, this sweeping principle has been subject to an exception for so-called petty crimes, where the penalty involves fewer than six months imprisonment. *See* Eugene Volokh, *Crime Severity and Constitutional Line-Drawing*, 90 Va. L. Rev. 1957, 1971–72 (2004).

forth any clear or determinative methodology for determining constitutionally appropriate procedures. The law of procedural due process entered the last quarter of the twentieth century much where it had been a hundred years before: the ultimate inquiry remained, as it had always been, a search for what procedures are fair under the circumstances of each particular case.

George Eldridge was surely aware of none of this history on June 8, 1968 when he was awarded Social Security disability benefits by a hearing examiner in Virginia. Nor could he, or anyone else, have suspected that his modest benefits claim would ultimately revolutionize constitutional law.

GARY LAWSON, KATHARINE FERGUSON & GUILLERMO MONTERO, "OH LORD, PLEASE DON'T LET ME BE MISUNDERSTOOD!": REDISCOVERING THE *MATHEWS V. ELDRIDGE* AND *PENN CENTRAL* FRAMEWORKS

Vol. 81 Notre Dame Law Review, Page 1, 15–19 (2005).

Reprinted with permission by *Notre Dame Law Review*, University of Notre Dame[10]

Nearly four years * * * [after Eldridge was awarded his benefits], the state agency that administered the Social Security disability program in Virginia determined that Eldridge had medically improved, was able to work, and was no longer entitled to disability benefits. The Federal Bureau of Disability Insurance of the Social Security Administration affirmed the state's decision, and Eldridge's benefits ceased after July 1972.

The state review process involved notice to Eldridge, receipt and review of evidence of Eldridge's medical condition, and several opportunities for Eldridge to provide written material that he considered relevant to his case. Eldridge challenged the constitutional adequacy of these procedures on the ground that, as with the plaintiffs in *Goldberg [v. Kelly]*, he should have been granted a full evidentiary hearing, complete with oral participation and cross-examination of witnesses, prior to the termination of his benefits. The United States countered that Social Security disability benefits were different enough from benefits under the Aid to Families with Dependent Children program (AFDC) at issue in *Goldberg* (and the Old Age Assistance program at issue in a companion case to *Goldberg*) to require different procedures for termination. In the district court, the government asserted three basic differences between Eldridge's situation and the situation of the plaintiffs in *Goldberg*: AFDC benefits are based on need while Social Security disability benefits are not, so that deprivation of the latter is less serious than deprivation of the former; Social Security disability benefits decisions are based on objective

---

[10] The publisher bears responsibility for any errors which have occurred in reprinting or editing.

medical evidence rather than the " 'rumor and gossip' " that might form the basis for an adverse AFDC decision, so that oral hearings were therefore less useful in disability benefits cases; and the massive Social Security disability system would be seriously disrupted if pre-termination hearings were generally required.

The district court responded in detail to each of the government's proferred distinctions, rejected all of them, and held that a pre-termination evidentiary hearing was constitutionally required. The Fourth Circuit Court of Appeals affirmed in a brief order that simply adopted the reasoning of the district court. The United States sought certiorari, which the Supreme Court granted.

The Solicitor General's merits brief in the Supreme Court acknowledged that the ultimate due process inquiry focused on fairness:

> The procedures for terminating Social Security disability benefits provide an adequate and fair opportunity for a beneficiary to submit all relevant information necessary to enable the Social Security Administration to make an informed and reliable judgment whether the disability has ceased * * *. The procedures by which disability benefits are now terminated are fair and they work.

The government also acknowledged the flexible and multifaceted character of the basis fairness inquiry. But in order to structure the inquiry for purposes of legal argumentation, the government offered the following observation:

> The Court has identified three general interests that must be asserted in determining the constitutional sufficiency of procedures for denying or terminating constitutionally-protected interests. They are: first, the nature of the property (or liberty) interest of which a person is assertedly being deprived; second, the risk of an erroneous deprivation of such interest through the procedures used; and third, the administrative burdens and costs that particular procedural requirements would entail.

The bulk of the government's argument elaborated upon the application of the specific interests identified in this passage [of its brief] to Eldridge's circumstances.

* * *

* * * [T]he government's brief gives every indication that it is simply trying to describe, in lawyerly language, the considerations that the Court's prior opinions had identified as relevant for assessing the ultimate fairness of procedures in a given context. Each of the factors is traced to a prior Court decision, and the more elaborate discussion that follows in the brief further tracks each factor through antecedent decisions.

* * * [T]he amicus brief of the AFL-CIO filed on behalf of Eldridge agreed entirely with the Solicitor General's account of the proper structure for due process inquiry * * *. No one in *Mathews* argued that the Solicitor General had somehow misrepresented the applicable law * * *.

* * * [T]he three factors identified as relevant by the Solicitor General tracked precisely the three considerations that the government believed supported its case in *Mathews*. As was made clear by the district court opinion in *Mathews*, the government sought to distinguish Eldridge's situation from that of the plaintiffs in *Goldberg* on the basis of the alleged lower value of the private interest at stake, the character of the evidence at issue in *Mathews*, and the disruption to the massive Social Security disability program that would result from excessive proceduralism. The government's articulation of the considerations relevant to the due process analysis in its brief in *Mathews* was clearly dictated by the government's specific litigating interest in that case. Put as simply as possible: the Solicitor General in *Mathews* was not trying to shape, or re-shape, due process law. He was trying to win a case.

* * *[T]he government identified "the risk of an erroneous deprivation of such interest through the procedures used" as the principle value of procedures because it thought that it could establish that oral hearings would contribute little to the accuracy of Social Security disability determinations, given the character of the evidence that is normally at issue in such cases. Put simply, the government emphasized decisional accuracy because it was confident that focus on decisional accuracy would lead to a favorable result on the specific facts of *Mathews*.

MATHEWS V. ELDRIDGE
Supreme Court of the United States, 1976.
424 U.S. 319, 96 S.Ct. 893, 47 L.Ed.2d 18.

MR. JUSTICE POWELL delivered the opinion of the Court.

The issue in this case is whether the Due Process Clause of the Fifth Amendment requires that prior to the termination of Social Security disability benefit payments the recipient be afforded an opportunity for an evidentiary hearing.

I

Cash benefits are provided to workers during periods in which they are completely disabled under the disability insurance benefits program created by the 1956 amendments to Title II of the Social Security Act. Respondent Eldridge was first awarded benefits in June 1968. In March 1972, he received a questionnaire from the state agency charged with monitoring his medical condition. Eldridge completed the questionnaire, indicating that his condition had not improved and identifying the medical sources, including physicians, from whom he had received treatment recently. The state agency then obtained reports from his physician and a psychiatric consultant. After considering these reports and other information in his file the agency informed Eldridge by letter that it had made a tentative determination that his disability had ceased in May 1972. The letter included a statement of reasons for the proposed termination of benefits, and advised Eldridge that he might request reasonable time in which to obtain and submit additional information pertaining to his condition.

In his written response, Eldridge disputed one characterization of his medical condition and indicated that the agency already had enough evidence to establish his disability.[2] The state agency then made its final determination that he had ceased to be disabled in May 1972. This determination was accepted by the Social Security Administration (SSA), which notified Eldridge in July that his benefits would terminate after that month. The notification also advised him of his right to seek reconsideration by the state agency of this initial determination within six months.

Instead of requesting reconsideration Eldridge commenced this action challenging the constitutional validity of the administrative procedures established by the Secretary of Health, Education, and Welfare for assessing whether there exists a continuing disability. He sought an immediate reinstatement of benefits pending a hearing on the issue of his disability. The Secretary moved to dismiss on the grounds that Eldridge's benefits had been terminated in accordance with valid administrative regulations and procedures and that he had failed to exhaust available remedies. In support of his contention that due process requires a pretermination hearing, Eldridge relied exclusively upon this Court's decision in *Goldberg v. Kelly*, 397 U.S. 254, 90 S.Ct. 1011, 25 L.Ed.2d 287 (1970), which established a right to an "evidentiary hearing" prior to termination of welfare benefits.[4] The Secretary contended that *Goldberg* was not controlling since eligibility for disability benefits, unlike eligibility

---

[2] Eldridge originally was disabled due to chronic anxiety and back strain. He subsequently was found to have diabetes. The tentative determination letter indicated that aid would be terminated because available medical evidence indicated that his diabetes was under control, that there existed no limitations on his back movements which would impose severe functional restrictions, and that he no longer suffered emotional problems that would preclude him from all work for which he was qualified. In his reply letter he claimed to have arthritis of the spine rather than a strained back.

[4] In *Goldberg* the Court held that the pretermination hearing must include the following elements: (1) "timely and adequate notice detailing the reasons for a proposed termination"; (2) "an effective opportunity (for the recipient) to defend by confronting any adverse witnesses and by presenting his own arguments and evidence orally"; (3) retained counsel, if desired; (4) an "impartial" decisionmaker; (5) a decision resting "solely on the legal rules and evidence adduced at the hearing"; (6) a statement of reasons for the decision and the evidence relied on. 397 U.S., at 266–271, 90 S.Ct., at 1019–1022. In this opinion the term "evidentiary hearing" refers to a hearing generally of the type required in *Goldberg*.

for welfare benefits, is not based on financial need and since issues of credibility and veracity do not play a significant role in the disability entitlement decision, which turns primarily on medical evidence.

The District Court concluded that the administrative procedures pursuant to which the Secretary had terminated Eldridge's benefits abridged his right to procedural due process. The court viewed the interest of the disability recipient in uninterrupted benefits as indistinguishable from that of the welfare recipient in *Goldberg* * * *. Reasoning that disability determinations may involve subjective judgments based on conflicting medical and nonmedical evidence, the District Court held that prior to termination of benefits Eldridge had to be afforded an evidentiary hearing * * *. Relying entirely upon the District Court's opinion, the Court of Appeals for the Fourth Circuit affirmed * * *. We reverse.

* * *

A

Procedural due process imposes constraints on governmental decisions which deprive individuals of "liberty" or "property" interests within the meaning of the Due Process Clause of the Fifth or Fourteenth Amendment. The Secretary does not contend that procedural due process is inapplicable to terminations of Social Security disability benefits. He recognizes * * * that the interest of an individual in continued receipt of these benefits is a statutorily created "property" interest protected by the Fifth Amendment. Rather, the Secretary contends that the existing administrative procedures, detailed below, provide all the process that is constitutionally due before a recipient can be deprived of that interest.

This Court consistently has held that some form of hearing is required before an individual is finally deprived of a property interest * * *. Eldridge agrees that the review procedures available to a claimant before the initial determination of ineligibility becomes final would be adequate if disability benefits were not terminated until after the evidentiary hearing stage of the administrative process. The dispute centers upon what process is due prior to the initial termination of benefits, pending review.

In recent years this Court increasingly has had occasion to consider the extent to which due process requires an evidentiary hearing prior to the deprivation of some type of property interest even if such a hearing is provided thereafter. In only one case, *Goldberg v. Kelly*, has the Court held that a hearing closely approximating a judicial trial is necessary. In other cases requiring some type of pretermination hearing as a matter of constitutional right the Court has spoken sparingly about the requisite procedures * * *.

These decisions underscore the truism that " '[d]ue process,' unlike some legal rules, is not a technical conception with a fixed content unrelated to time, place and circumstances." *Cafeteria Workers v. McElroy*, 367 U.S. 886, 895, 81 S.Ct. 1743, 1748, 6 L.Ed.2d 1230 (1961). "[D]ue process is flexible and calls for such procedural protections as the particular situation demands." *Morrissey v. Brewer*, 408 U.S. 471, 481, 92 S.Ct. 2593, 2600, 33 L.Ed.2d 484 (1972). Accordingly, resolution of the issue whether the administrative procedures provided here are constitutionally sufficient requires analysis of the governmental and private interests that are affected. More precisely, our prior decisions indicate that identification of the specific dictates of due process generally requires consideration of three distinct factors: First, the private interest that will be affected by the official action; second, the risk of an erroneous deprivation of such interest through the procedures used, and the probable value, if any, of additional or substitute procedural safeguards; and finally, the Government's interest, including the function involved and the fiscal and administrative burdens that the additional or substitute procedural requirement would entail.

We turn first to a description of the procedures for the termination of Social Security disability benefits and thereafter consider the factors bearing upon the constitutional adequacy of these procedures.

B

The disability insurance program is administered jointly by state and federal agencies. State agencies make the initial determination whether a disability exists, when it began, and when it ceased. The standards applied and the procedures followed are prescribed by the Secretary, who has delegated his responsibilities and powers under the Act to the SSA.

In order to establish initial and continued entitlement to disability benefits a worker must demonstrate that he is unable

> "to engage in any substantial gainful activity by reason of any medically determinable physical or mental impairment which can be expected to result in death or which has lasted or can be expected to last for a continuous period of not less than 12 months. . ." 42 U.S.C. § 423(d)(1)(A).

To satisfy this test the worker bears a continuing burden of showing, by means of "medically acceptable clinical and laboratory diagnostic techniques," § 423(d)(3), that he has a physical or mental impairment of such severity that

> "he is not only unable to do his previous work but cannot, considering his age, education, and work experience, engage in any other kind of substantial gainful work which exists in the national economy, regardless of whether such work exists in the immediate area in which he lives, or whether a specific job

vacancy exists for him, or whether he would be hired if he applied for work." § 423(d)(2)(A).

The principal reasons for benefits terminations are that the worker is no longer disabled or has returned to work. As Eldridge's benefits were terminated because he was determined to be no longer disabled, we consider only the sufficiency of the procedures involved in such cases.

The continuing-eligibility investigation is made by a state agency acting through a "team" consisting of a physician and a nonmedical person trained in disability evaluation. The agency periodically communicates with the disabled worker, usually by mail in which case he is sent a detailed questionnaire or by telephone, and requests information concerning his present condition, including current medical restrictions and sources of treatment, and any additional information that he considers relevant to his continued entitlement to benefits.

Information regarding the recipient's current condition is also obtained from his sources of medical treatment. If there is a conflict between the information provided by the beneficiary and that obtained from medical sources such as his physician, or between two sources of treatment, the agency may arrange for an examination by an independent consulting physician. Whenever the agency's tentative assessment of the beneficiary's condition differs from his own assessment, the beneficiary is informed that benefits may be terminated, provided a summary of the evidence upon which the proposed determination to terminate is based, and afforded an opportunity to review the medical reports and other evidence in his case file. He also may respond in writing and submit additional evidence.

The state agency then makes its final determination, which is reviewed by an examiner in the SSA Bureau of Disability Insurance. If, as is usually the case, the SSA accepts the agency determination it notifies the recipient in writing, informing him of the reasons for the decision, and of his right to seek de novo reconsideration by the state agency. Upon acceptance by the SSA, benefits are terminated effective two months after the month in which medical recovery is found to have occurred.

If the recipient seeks reconsideration by the state agency and the determination is adverse, the SSA reviews the reconsideration determination and notifies the recipient of the decision. He then has a right to an evidentiary hearing before an SSA administrative law judge. The hearing is nonadversary, and the SSA is not represented by counsel. As at all prior and subsequent stages of the administrative process, however, the claimant may be represented by counsel or other spokesmen. If this hearing results in an adverse decision, the claimant is entitled to request discretionary review by the SSA Appeals Council, and finally may obtain judicial review.

Should it be determined at any point after termination of benefits, that the claimant's disability extended beyond the date of cessation initially established, the worker is entitled to retroactive payments. If, on the other hand, a beneficiary receives any payments to which he is later determined not to be entitled, the statute authorizes the Secretary to attempt to recoup these funds in specified circumstances.

C

Despite the elaborate character of the administrative procedures provided by the Secretary, the courts below held them to be constitutionally inadequate, concluding that due process requires an evidentiary hearing prior to termination. In light of the private and governmental interests at stake here and the nature of the existing procedures, we think this was error.

Since a recipient whose benefits are terminated is awarded full retroactive relief if he ultimately prevails, his sole interest is in the uninterrupted receipt of this source of income pending final administrative decision on his claim. His potential injury is thus similar in nature to that of the welfare recipient in *Goldberg* * * *.

Only in *Goldberg* has the Court held that due process requires an evidentiary hearing prior to a temporary deprivation. It was emphasized there that welfare assistance is given to persons on the very margin of subsistence:

> "The crucial factor in this context a factor not present in the case of . . . virtually anyone else whose governmental entitlements are ended is that termination of aid pending resolution of a controversy over eligibility may deprive an *eligible* recipient of the very means by which to live while he waits." 397 U.S., at 264, 90 S.Ct., at 1018 (emphasis in original).

Eligibility for disability benefits, in contrast, is not based upon financial need.[24] Indeed, it is wholly unrelated to the worker's income or support from many other sources, such as earnings of other family members, workmen's compensation awards, tort claims awards, savings, private insurance, public or private pensions, veterans' benefits, food stamps, public assistance, or the "many other important programs, both public and private, which contain provisions for disability payments affecting a substantial portion of the work force. . ." *Richardson v. Belcher*, 404 U.S., at 85–87, 92 S.Ct., at 259 (Douglas, J., dissenting).

As *Goldberg* illustrates, the degree of potential deprivation that may be created by a particular decision is a factor to be considered in assessing the validity of any administrative decisionmaking process. The potential

---

[24] The level of benefits is determined by the worker's average monthly earnings during the period prior to disability, his age, and other factors not directly related to financial need * * *.

deprivation here is generally likely to be less than in *Goldberg*, although the degree of difference can be overstated. As the District Court emphasized, to remain eligible for benefits a recipient must be "unable to engage in substantial gainful activity." 42 U.S.C. § 423; 361 F.Supp., at 523. Thus, in contrast to the discharged federal employee in *Arnett*, there is little possibility that the terminated recipient will be able to find even temporary employment to ameliorate the interim loss.

As we recognized last Term in *Fusari v. Steinberg*, 419 U.S. 379, 389, 95 S.Ct. 533, 540, 42 L.Ed.2d 521 (1975), "the possible length of wrongful deprivation of . . . benefits [also] is an important factor in assessing the impact of official action on the private interests." The Secretary concedes that the delay between a request for a hearing before an administrative law judge and a decision on the claim is currently between 10 and 11 months. Since a terminated recipient must first obtain a reconsideration decision as a prerequisite to invoking his right to an evidentiary hearing, the delay between the actual cutoff of benefits and final decision after a hearing exceeds one year.

In view of the torpidity of this administrative review process, and the typically modest resources of the family unit of the physically disabled worker, the hardship imposed upon the erroneously terminated disability recipient may be significant. Still, the disabled worker's need is likely to be less than that of a welfare recipient. In addition to the possibility of access to private resources, other forms of government assistance will become available where the termination of disability benefits places a worker or his family below the subsistence level. In view of these potential sources of temporary income, there is less reason here than in *Goldberg* to depart from the ordinary principle, established by our decisions, that something less than an evidentiary hearing is sufficient prior to adverse administrative action.

D

An additional factor to be considered here is the fairness and reliability of the existing pretermination procedures, and the probable value, if any, of additional procedural safeguards. Central to the evaluation of any administrative process is the nature of the relevant inquiry. In order to remain eligible for benefits the disabled worker must demonstrate by means of "medically acceptable clinical and laboratory diagnostic techniques," 42 U.S.C. § 423(d)(3), that he is unable "to engage in any substantial gainful activity by reason of any *medically determinable* physical or mental impairment. . ." § 423(d)(1)(A) (emphasis supplied). In short, a medical assessment of the worker's physical or mental condition is required. This is a more sharply focused and easily documented decision than the typical determination of welfare entitlement. In the latter case, a wide variety of information may be deemed relevant, and issues of witness credibility and veracity often are critical to the decisionmaking process. *Goldberg* noted that in such circumstances "written submissions are a wholly unsatisfactory basis for decision." 397 U.S., at 269, 90 S.Ct., at 1021.

By contrast, the decision whether to discontinue disability benefits will turn, in most cases, upon "routine, standard, and unbiased medical reports by physician specialists," *Richardson v. Perales*, 402 U.S., at 404, 91 S.Ct., at 1428, concerning a subject whom they have personally examined.[28] In *Richardson* the Court recognized the "reliability and probative worth of written medical reports," emphasizing that while there may be "professional disagreement with the medical conclusions" the "specter of questionable credibility and veracity is not present." *Id.*, at 405, 407, 91 S.Ct., at 1428, 1430. To be sure, credibility and veracity may be a factor in the ultimate disability assessment in some cases. But procedural due process rules are shaped by the risk of error inherent in the truthfinding process as applied to the generality of cases, not the rare exceptions. The potential value of an evidentiary hearing, or even oral presentation to the decisionmaker, is substantially less in this context than in *Goldberg*.

The decision in *Goldberg* also was based on the Court's conclusion that written submissions were an inadequate substitute for oral presentation because they did not provide an effective means for the recipient to communicate his case to the decisionmaker. Written submissions were viewed as an unrealistic option, for most recipients lacked the "educational attainment necessary to write effectively" and could not afford professional assistance. In addition, such submissions would not provide the "flexibility of oral presentations" or "permit the recipient to mold his argument to the issues the decision maker appears to regard as important." 397 U.S., at 269, 90 S.Ct., at 1021. In the context of the disability-benefits-entitlement assessment the administrative procedures under review here fully answer these objections.

The detailed questionnaire which the state agency periodically sends the recipient identifies with particularity the information relevant to the entitlement decision, and the recipient is invited to obtain assistance from the local SSA office in completing the questionnaire. More important, the information critical to the entitlement decision usually is derived from medical sources, such as the treating physician. Such sources are likely to

---

[28] The decision is not purely a question of the accuracy of a medical diagnosis since the ultimate issue which the state agency must resolve is whether in light of the particular worker's "age, education, and work experience" he cannot "engage in any . . . substantial gainful work which exists in the national economy. . . ." 42 U.S.C. § 423(d)(2)(A). Yet information concerning each of these worker characteristics is amenable to effective written presentation. The value of an evidentiary hearing, or even a limited oral presentation, to an accurate presentation of those factors to the decisionmaker does not appear substantial. Similarly, resolution of the inquiry as to the types of employment opportunities that exist in the national economy for a physically impaired worker with a particular set of skills would not necessarily be advanced by an evidentiary hearing. The statistical information relevant to this judgment is more amenable to written than to oral presentation.

be able to communicate more effectively through written documents than are welfare recipients or the lay witnesses supporting their cause. The conclusions of physicians often are supported by X-rays and the results of clinical or laboratory tests, information typically more amenable to written than to oral presentation.

A further safeguard against mistake is the policy of allowing the disability recipient's representative full access to all information relied upon by the state agency. In addition, prior to the cutoff of benefits the agency informs the recipient of its tentative assessment, the reasons therefor, and provides a summary of the evidence that it considers most relevant. Opportunity is then afforded the recipient to submit additional evidence or arguments, enabling him to challenge directly the accuracy of information in his file as well as the correctness of the agency's tentative conclusions. These procedures, again as contrasted with those before the Court in *Goldberg*, enable the recipient to "mold" his argument to respond to the precise issues which the decisionmaker regards as crucial.

* * *

E

In striking the appropriate due process balance the final factor to be assessed is the public interest. This includes the administrative burden and other societal costs that would be associated with requiring, as a matter of constitutional right, an evidentiary hearing upon demand in all cases prior to the termination of disability benefits. The most visible burden would be the incremental cost resulting from the increased number of hearings and the expense of providing benefits to ineligible recipients pending decision. No one can predict the extent of the increase, but the fact that full benefits would continue until after such hearings would assure the exhaustion in most cases of this attractive option. Nor would the theoretical right of the Secretary to recover undeserved benefits result, as a practical matter, in any substantial offset to the added outlay of public funds. The parties submit widely varying estimates of the probable additional financial cost. We only need say that experience with the constitutionalizing of government procedures suggests that the ultimate additional cost in terms of money and administrative burden would not be insubstantial.

Financial cost alone is not a controlling weight in determining whether due process requires a particular procedural safeguard prior to some administrative decision. But the Government's interest, and hence that of the public, in conserving scarce fiscal and administrative resources is a factor that must be weighed. At some point the benefit of an additional safeguard to the individual affected by the administrative action and to society in terms of increased assurance that the action is just, may be outweighed by the cost. Significantly, the cost of protecting those whom the preliminary administrative process has identified as likely to be found undeserving may in the end come out of the pockets of the deserving since resources available for any particular program of social welfare are not unlimited.

But more is implicated in cases of this type than ad hoc weighing of fiscal and administrative burdens against the interests of a particular category of claimants. The ultimate balance involves a determination as to when, under our constitutional system, judicial-type procedures must be imposed upon administrative action to assure fairness. We reiterate the wise admonishment of Mr. Justice Frankfurter that differences in the origin and function of administrative agencies "preclude wholesale transplantation of the rules of procedure, trial and review which have evolved from the history and experience of courts." *FCC v. Pottsville Broadcasting Co.*, 309 U.S. 134, 143, 60 S.Ct. 437, 441, 84 L.Ed. 656 (1940). The judicial model of an evidentiary hearing is neither a required, nor even the most effective, method of decisionmaking in all circumstances * * *. All that is necessary is that the procedures be tailored, in light of the decision to be made, to "the capacities and circumstances of those who are to be heard," *Goldberg v. Kelly*, 397 U.S., at 268–269, 90 S.Ct., at 1021, to insure that they are given a meaningful opportunity to present their case. In assessing what process is due in this case, substantial weight must be given to the good-faith judgments of the individuals charged by Congress with the administration of social welfare programs that the procedures they have provided assure fair consideration of the entitlement claims of individuals. This is especially so where, as here, the prescribed procedures not only provide the claimant with an effective process for asserting his claim prior to any administrative action, but also assure a right to an evidentiary hearing, as well as to subsequent judicial review, before the denial of his claim becomes final.

We conclude that an evidentiary hearing is not required prior to the termination of disability benefits and that the present administrative procedures fully comport with due process.

The judgment of the Court of Appeals is

Reversed.

MR. JUSTICE STEVENS took no part in the consideration or decision of this case.

MR. JUSTICE BRENNAN, with whom MR. JUSTICE MARSHALL concurs, dissenting.

* * * I agree with the District Court and the Court of Appeals that, prior to termination of benefits, Eldridge must be afforded an evidentiary hearing of the type required for welfare beneficiaries under Title IV of the Social Security Act. I would add that the Court's consideration that a

discontinuance of disability benefits may cause the recipient to suffer only a limited deprivation is no argument. It is speculative. Moreover, the very legislative determination to provide disability benefits, without any prerequisite determination of need in fact, presumes a need by the recipient which is not this Court's function to denigrate. Indeed, in the present case, it is indicated that because disability benefits were terminated there was a foreclosure upon the Eldridge home and the family's furniture was repossessed, forcing Eldridge, his wife, and their children to sleep in one bed. Finally, it is also no argument that a worker, who has been placed in the untenable position of having been denied disability benefits, may still seek other forms of public assistance.

NOTES

"Early Supreme Court decisions after *Mathews* (properly) identified the three-factor framework as merely a useful tool of analysis. It did not take long, however, before the Court began describing, and using, the *Mathews* framework as a 'test'—that is, as a tool for reaching decisions rather than simply for expressing in legal language the rationale for decisions reached through an assessment of basic fairness." Gary Lawson, Katharine Ferguson & Guillermo Montero, *"Oh Lord, Please Don't Let Me Be Misunderstood!": Rediscovering the* Mathews v. Eldridge *and* Penn Central *Frameworks*, 81 Notre Dame L. Rev. 1, 21 (2005). In 1979, for example, the Court noted that "[t]he parties agree that our prior holdings have set out a general approach for testing challenged state procedures under a due process claim." *Parham v. J.R.*, 442 U.S. 584, 599, 99 S.Ct. 2493, 61 L.Ed.2d 101 (1979). Two years later, the Court explained: "The case of *Mathews v. Eldridge* propounds three elements to be evaluated in deciding what due process requires * * *. We must balance these elements against each other, and then set their net weight in the scales * * *." *Lassiter v. Department of Social Services*, 452 U.S. 18, 27, 101 S.Ct. 2153, 68 L.Ed.2d 640 (1981). Application of the three *Mathews* factors has ever since been a ubiquitous part of due process analysis.

Once *Mathews* was understood as a decisionmaking tool rather than simply a way to organize and focus an inquiry into the basic fairness of procedures, criticism of it became a cottage industry. Long-established case law clearly supports the view that the natures of the private and governmental interests at stake are important elements in a due process calculus. More problematic is the Court's (and Solicitor General's) second factor: the likelihood that the procedures in question will improve decisional accuracy. Is that really the only measure of the value of procedures? Many scholars have argued that procedures can be an important way to uphold so-called "dignitary" interests of citizens: they claim that treating people well, and ensuring that people feel that they have been treated well, is itself an important constitutional objective. *See, e.g.,* Jerry Mashaw, *The Supreme Court's Due Process Calculus for Administrative Adjudication in* Mathews v. Eldridge: *Three Factors in Search of a Theory of Value*, 44 U. Chi. L. Rev. 28 (1976). These dignitarian theorists, however, differ substantially on the appropriate source of the governing conception of human dignity. *See, e.g.*, William J. Brennan, Jr., *Reason, Passion, and "The Progress of the Law"*, 10 Cardozo L. Rev. 3, 20 (1988) ("passion * * *, in the sense of attention to the concrete human realities at stake"); Cynthia Farina, *Conceiving Due Process*, 3 Yale J.L. & Feminism 189 (1991) (feminist theories of relation); Richard B. Saphire, *Specifying Due Process Values: Toward a More Responsive Approach to Procedural Protection*, 127 U. Pa. L. Rev. 111 (1978) (history and philosophy). Does this dissensus among dignitarian theorists explain and/or justify a purely instrumentalist account of the value of procedures? And, more fundamentally, if *Mathews* was merely trying to synthesize the existing case law, rather than to construct an ideal normative structure for due process questions, are dignitarian criticisms of *Mathews* misplaced? Is it relevant to an assessment of *Mathews* that the three-factor inquiry employed by the Court was lifted directly out of the brief of the United States and was endorsed, as an accurate description of governing law, by the principal *amicus* on behalf of Eldridge?

More to the point, it seems fairly clear that neither the government's brief in *Mathews* nor the *Mathews* decision itself meant to say that the due process inquiry must always be limited solely to the specific considerations at issue in *Mathews*; those were simply the considerations that seemed most pertinent (at least to the government) in that particular case. Nonetheless, rote application of the *"Mathews* factors" has become something of a mantra in due process jurisprudence over the past few decades, and it is now very difficult to interject other considerations into the due process conversation. For example, in *Turner v. Rogers*, 564 U.S. 431, 131 S.Ct 2507, 180 L.Ed.2d 452 (2011), the Court held that states need not always provide appointed counsel to defendants in civil contempt proceedings to enforce child support obligations, with the majority opinion relying upon "the 'distinct factors' that this Court has previously found useful in deciding what specific safeguards the Constitution's Due Process Clause requires in order to make a civil proceeding fundamentally fair." 131 S.C. at 2517. Justices Thomas and Scalia reached that same conclusion (while dissenting from the Court's judgment on a different aspect of the state's procedures), but they found the *Mathews* framework inapt: "That test weighs an individual's interest against that of the Government. It does not account for the interests of the child and custodial parent * * *. But their interests are the very reason for the child support obligation and the civil contempt proceedings that enforce it." 131 S.Ct. at 2525 (Thomas, J., dissenting). Does the *Mathews* inquiry have to be construed to exclude consideration of such matters? *Cf.* 131 S.Ct. at 2517–18 (noting that "[a]s relevant here, those *[Mathews]* factors *include*" the nature of the private interest, the relative risk of erroneous deprivations with and without the requested procedures, and any countervailing interests) (emphasis added).

The *Mathews* framework dominates due process law, but it does not govern in every context. The adequacy of procedures in criminal trials (or at least of procedures in criminal trials that are not mandated by specific constitutional provisions) is generally assessed under *Medina v. California*,

505 U.S. 437, 112 S.Ct. 2572, 120 L.Ed.2d 353 (1992), rather than under *Mathews*, *see* 505 U.S. at 442–46, 112 S.Ct. at 2576–77. The *Medina* inquiry focuses on whether the procedures are fundamentally fair, and this is understood to be an approach that is "far less intrusive than that approved in *Mathews*." *Id.* at 446, S.Ct. at 2577. And the adequacy of methods of notice is assessed under *Mullane v. Central Hanover Bank & Trust Co.*, 339 U.S. 306, 70 S.Ct. 652, 94 L.Ed. 865 (1950), which asks whether notice is "reasonably calculated, under all the circumstances, to apprise interested parties of the pendency of the action and afford them an opportunity to present their objections." *Id.* at 314, 70 S.Ct. at 657. *See Dusenberry v. United States*, 534 U.S. 161, 167–68, 122 S.Ct. 694, 699, 151 L.Ed.2d 597 (2002):

> We think *Mullane* supplies the appropriate analytical framework. The *Mathews* balancing test was first conceived in the context of a due process challenge to the adequacy of administrative procedures used to terminate Social Security disability benefits. Although we have since invoked *Mathews* to evaluate due process claims in other contexts, we have never viewed *Mathews* as announcing an all-embracing test for deciding due process claims. Since *Mullane* was decided, we have regularly turned to it when confronted with questions regarding the adequacy of the method used to give notice.

For most administrative law purposes, however, it is *Mathews* all the way down.

The modern (mis?)understanding of *Mathews* as a seemingly mandatory and relatively rigid decisional tool presents three factors for courts and litigants to consider, but it gives no indication of how those factors are to be weighed in any given case. Nor does it provide any metric for measuring the strength of a private or governmental interest or the likely contribution of a procedure to decisional accuracy. Given those facts, is the three-part structure really an advance over pre-1976 law, in which courts identified procedures that seemed fair under the circumstances, more or less on a "we-know-it-when-we-see-it" basis?

CLEVELAND BOARD OF EDUCATION V. LOUDERMILL

Supreme Court of the United States, 1985.
470 U.S. 532, 105 S.Ct. 1487, 84 L.Ed.2d 494.

JUSTICE WHITE delivered the opinion of the Court.

In these cases we consider what pretermination process must be accorded a public employee who can be discharged only for cause.

I

In 1979 the Cleveland Board of Education hired respondent James Loudermill as a security guard. On his job application, Loudermill stated that he had never been convicted of a felony. Eleven months later, as part of a routine examination of his employment records, the Board discovered that in fact Loudermill had been convicted of grand larceny in 1968. By letter dated November 3, 1980, the Board's Business Manager informed Loudermill that he had been dismissed because of his dishonesty in filling out the employment application. Loudermill was not afforded an opportunity to respond to the charge of dishonesty or to challenge his dismissal. On November 13, the Board adopted a resolution officially approving the discharge.

Under Ohio law, Loudermill was a "classified civil servant." Ohio Rev. Code Ann. § 124.11 (1984). Such employees can be terminated only for cause, and may obtain administrative review if discharged. § 124.34. Pursuant to this provision, Loudermill filed an appeal with the Cleveland Civil Service Commission on November 12. The Commission appointed a referee, who held a hearing on January 29, 1981. Loudermill argued that he had thought that his 1968 larceny conviction was for a misdemeanor rather than a felony. The referee recommended reinstatement. On July 20, 1981, the full Commission heard argument and orally announced that it would uphold the dismissal. Proposed findings of fact and conclusions of law followed on August 10, and Loudermill's attorneys were advised of the result by mail on August 21.

Although the Commission's decision was subject to judicial review in the state courts, Loudermill instead brought the present suit in the Federal District Court for the Northern District of Ohio. The complaint alleged that § 124.34 was unconstitutional on its face because it did not provide the employee an opportunity to respond to the charges against him prior to removal. As a result, discharged employees were deprived of liberty and property without due process. The complaint also alleged that the provision was unconstitutional as applied because discharged employees were not given sufficiently prompt postremoval hearings.

Before a responsive pleading was filed, the District Court dismissed for failure to state a claim on which relief could be granted. It held that because the very statute that created the property right in continued employment also specified the procedures for discharge, and because those procedures were followed, Loudermill was, by definition, afforded all the process due. The post-termination hearing also adequately protected Loudermill's liberty interests. Finally, the District Court concluded that, in light of the Commission's crowded docket, the delay in processing Loudermill's administrative appeal was constitutionally acceptable.

* * *

[Another case before the Court, concerning respondent Donnelly, involved "similar facts and followed a similar course" and was joined with the Loudermill case for appeal.]

* * * A divided panel of the Court of Appeals * * * found that both respondents had been deprived of due process * * *.

* * *

II

Respondents' federal constitutional claim depends on their having had a property right in continued employment. If they did, the State could not deprive them of this property without due process.

Property interests are not created by the Constitution, "they are created and their dimensions are defined by existing rules or understandings that stem from an independent source such as state law. . ." *Board of Regents v. Roth*, 408 U.S., at 577, 92 S.Ct., at 2709. The Ohio statute plainly creates such an interest. Respondents were "classified civil service employees," Ohio Rev.Code Ann. § 124.11 (1984), entitled to retain their positions "during good behavior and efficient service," who could not be dismissed "except . . . for . . . misfeasance, malfeasance, or nonfeasance in office," § 124.34.[4] The statute plainly supports the conclusion, reached by both lower courts, that respondents possessed property rights in continued employment. Indeed, this question does not seem to have been disputed below.

The * * * Board argues, however, that the property right is defined by, and conditioned on, the legislature's choice of procedures for its deprivation. The Board stresses that in addition to specifying the grounds for termination, the statute sets out procedures by which termination may take place.[6] The procedures were adhered to in these cases. According to petitioner, "[t]o require additional procedures would in effect expand the scope of the property interest itself."

This argument, which was accepted by the District Court, has its genesis in the plurality opinion in *Arnett v. Kennedy*, 416 U.S. 134, 94 S.Ct. 1633, 40 L.Ed.2d 15 (1974). *Arnett* involved a challenge by a former federal employee to the procedures by which he was dismissed. The plurality reasoned that where the legislation conferring the substantive right also

---

    [4] The relevant portion of § 124.34 provides that no classified civil servant may be removed except "for incompetency, inefficiency, dishonesty, drunkenness, immoral conduct, insubordination, discourteous treatment of the public, neglect of duty, violation of such sections or the rules of the director of administrative services or the commission, or any other failure of good behavior, or any other acts of misfeasance, malfeasance, or nonfeasance in office."

    [6] After providing for dismissal only for cause, § 124.34 states that the dismissed employee is to be provided with a copy of the order of removal giving the reasons therefor. Within 10 days of the filing of the order with the Director of Administrative Services, the employee may file a written appeal with the State Personnel Board of Review or the Commission. "In the event such an appeal is filed, the board or commission shall forthwith notify the appointing authority and shall hear, or appoint a trial board to hear, such appeal within thirty days from and after its filing with the board or commission, and it may affirm, disaffirm, or modify the judgment of the appointing authority." Either side may obtain review of the Commission's decision in the State Court of Common Pleas.

sets out the procedural mechanism for enforcing that right, the two cannot be separated:

"The employee's statutorily defined right is not a guarantee against removal without cause in the abstract, but such a guarantee as enforced by the procedures which Congress has designated for the determination of cause.

. . .

"[W]here the grant of a substantive right is inextricably intertwined with the limitations on the procedures which are to be employed in determining that right, a litigant in the position of appellee must take the bitter with the sweet." *Id.*, at 152–154, 94 S.Ct., at 1643–1644.

This view garnered three votes in *Arnett*, but was specifically rejected by the other six Justices. Since then, this theory has at times seemed to gather some additional support. See *Bishop v. Wood,* 426 U.S. 341, 355–361, 96 S.Ct. 2074, 2082–2085, 48 L.Ed.2d 684 (1976) (WHITE, J., dissenting). More recently, however, the Court has clearly rejected it. In *Vitek v. Jones,* 445 U.S. 480, 491, 100 S.Ct. 1254, 1263, 63 L.Ed.2d 552 (1980), we pointed out that "minimum [procedural] requirements [are] a matter of federal law, they are not diminished by the fact that the State may have specified its own procedures that it may deem adequate for determining the preconditions to adverse official action." This conclusion was reiterated in *Logan v. Zimmerman Brush Co.,* 455 U.S. 422, 432, 102 S.Ct. 1148, 1155, 71 L.Ed.2d 265 (1982), where we reversed the lower court's holding that because the entitlement arose from a state statute, the legislature had the prerogative to define the procedures to be followed to protect that entitlement.

In light of these holdings, it is settled that the "bitter with the sweet" approach misconceives the constitutional guarantee. If a clearer holding is needed, we provide it today. The point is straightforward: the Due Process Clause provides that certain substantive rights—life, liberty, and property—cannot be deprived except pursuant to constitutionally adequate procedures. The categories of substance and procedure are distinct. Were the rule otherwise, the Clause would be reduced to a mere tautology. "Property" cannot be defined by the procedures provided for its deprivation any more than can life or liberty. The right to due process "is conferred, not by legislative grace, but by constitutional guarantee. While the legislature may elect not to confer a property interest in [public] employment, it may not constitutionally authorize the deprivation of such an interest, once conferred, without appropriate procedural safeguards." *Arnett v. Kennedy, supra,* 416 U.S., at 167, 94 S.Ct., at 1650 (POWELL, J., concurring in part and concurring in result in part).

In short, once it is determined that the Due Process Clause applies, "the question remains what process is due." *Morrissey v. Brewer*, 408 U.S. 471, 481, 92 S.Ct. 2593, 2600, 33 L.Ed.2d 484 (1972). The answer to that question is not to be found in the Ohio statute.

III

An essential principle of due process is that a deprivation of life, liberty, or property "be preceded by notice and opportunity for hearing appropriate to the nature of the case." *Mullane v. Central Hanover Bank & Trust Co.*, 339 U.S. 306, 313, 70 S.Ct. 652, 656, 94 L.Ed. 865 (1950). We have described "the root requirement" of the Due Process Clause as being "that an individual be given an opportunity for a hearing *before* he is deprived of any significant property interest."[7] *Boddie v. Connecticut*, 401 U.S. 371, 379, 91 S.Ct. 780, 786, 28 L.Ed.2d 113 (1971) (emphasis in original); see *Bell v. Burson*, 402 U.S. 535, 542, 91 S.Ct. 1586, 1591, 29 L.Ed.2d 90 (1971) * * *. Even decisions finding no constitutional violation in termination procedures have relied on the existence of some pretermination opportunity to respond. For example, in *Arnett* six Justices found constitutional minima satisfied where the employee had access to the material upon which the charge was based and could respond orally and in writing and present rebuttal affidavits.

The need for some form of pretermination hearing, recognized in these cases, is evident from a balancing of the competing interests at stake. These are the private interests in retaining employment, the governmental interest in the expeditious removal of unsatisfactory employees and the avoidance of administrative burdens, and the risk of an erroneous termination. See *Mathews v. Eldridge*, 424 U.S. 319, 335, 96 S.Ct. 893, 903, 47 L.Ed.2d 18 (1976).

First, the significance of the private interest in retaining employment cannot be gainsaid. We have frequently recognized the severity of depriving a person of the means of livelihood. While a fired worker may find employment elsewhere, doing so will take some time and is likely to be burdened by the questionable circumstances under which he left his previous job.

Second, some opportunity for the employee to present his side of the case is recurringly of obvious value in reaching an accurate decision. Dismissals for cause will often involve factual disputes. Even where the facts are clear, the appropriateness or necessity of the discharge may not be; in such cases, the only meaningful opportunity to invoke the discretion of the decisionmaker is likely to be before the termination takes effect.

---

[7] There are, of course, some situations in which a postdeprivation hearing will satisfy due process requirements. See *Ewing v. Mytinger & Casselberry, Inc.*, 339 U.S. 594, 70 S.Ct. 870, 94 L.Ed. 1088 (1950); *North American Cold Storage Co. v. Chicago*, 211 U.S. 306, 29 S.Ct. 101, 53 L.Ed. 195 (1908).

The cases before us illustrate these considerations. Both respondents had plausible arguments to make that might have prevented their discharge. The fact that the Commission saw fit to reinstate Donnelly suggests that an error might have been avoided had he been provided an opportunity to make his case to the Board. As for Loudermill, given the Commission's ruling we cannot say that the discharge was mistaken. Nonetheless, in light of the referee's recommendation, neither can we say that a fully informed decisionmaker might not have exercised its discretion and decided not to dismiss him, notwithstanding its authority to do so. In any event, the termination involved arguable issues,[9] and the right to a hearing does not depend on a demonstration of certain success.

The governmental interest in immediate termination does not outweigh these interests. As we shall explain, affording the employee an opportunity to respond prior to termination would impose neither a significant administrative burden nor intolerable delays. Furthermore, the employer shares the employee's interest in avoiding disruption and erroneous decisions; and until the matter is settled, the employer would continue to receive the benefit of the employee's labors. It is preferable to keep a qualified employee on than to train a new one. A governmental employer also has an interest in keeping citizens usefully employed rather than taking the possibly erroneous and counterproductive step of forcing its employees onto the welfare rolls. Finally, in those situations where the employer perceives a significant hazard in keeping the employee on the job, it can avoid the problem by suspending with pay.

IV

The foregoing considerations indicate that the pretermination "hearing," though necessary, need not be elaborate. We have pointed out that "[t]he formality and procedural requisites for the hearing can vary, depending upon the importance of the interests involved and the nature of the subsequent proceedings." *Boddie v. Connecticut*, 401 U.S., at 378, 91 S.Ct., at 786. See *Cafeteria Workers v. McElroy*, 367 U.S. 886, 894–895, 81 S.Ct. 1743, 1748, 6 L.Ed.2d 1230 (1961). In general, "something less" than a full evidentiary hearing is sufficient prior to adverse administrative action. *Mathews v. Eldridge*, 424 U.S., at 343, 96 S.Ct., at 907. Under state law, respondents were later entitled to a full administrative hearing and judicial review. The only question is what steps were required before the termination took effect.

In only one case, *Goldberg v. Kelly*, 397 U.S. 254, 90 S.Ct. 1011, 25 L.Ed.2d 287 (1970), has the Court required a full adversarial evidentiary hearing prior to adverse governmental action. However, as the *Goldberg*

---

[9] Loudermill's dismissal turned not on the objective fact that he was an ex-felon or the inaccuracy of his statement to the contrary, but on the subjective question whether he had lied on his application form. His explanation for the false statement is plausible in light of the fact that he received only a suspended 6-month sentence and a fine on the grand larceny conviction.

Court itself pointed out, that case presented significantly different considerations than are present in the context of public employment. Here, the pretermination hearing need not definitively resolve the propriety of the discharge. It should be an initial check against mistaken decisions— essentially, a determination of whether there are reasonable grounds to believe that the charges against the employee are true and support the proposed action.

The essential requirements of due process, and all that respondents seek or the Court of Appeals required, are notice and an opportunity to respond. The opportunity to present reasons, either in person or in writing, why proposed action should not be taken is a fundamental due process requirement. The tenured public employee is entitled to oral or written notice of the charges against him, an explanation of the employer's evidence, and an opportunity to present his side of the story. To require more than this prior to termination would intrude to an unwarranted extent on the government's interest in quickly removing an unsatisfactory employee.

V

Our holding rests in part on the provisions in Ohio law for a full post-termination hearing. In his cross-petition Loudermill asserts, as a separate constitutional violation, that his administrative proceedings took too long.[11] The Court of Appeals held otherwise, and we agree * * *. At some point, a delay in the post-termination hearing would become a constitutional violation. In the present case, however, the complaint merely recites the course of proceedings and concludes that the denial of a "speedy resolution" violated due process. This reveals nothing about the delay except that it stemmed in part from the thoroughness of the procedures. A 9-month adjudication is not, of course, unconstitutionally lengthy *per se*. Yet Loudermill offers no indication that his wait was unreasonably prolonged other than the fact that it took nine months. The chronology of the proceedings set out in the complaint, coupled with the assertion that nine months is too long to wait, does not state a claim of a constitutional deprivation.

VI

We conclude that all the process that is due is provided by a pretermination opportunity to respond, coupled with post-termination administrative procedures as provided by the Ohio statute. Because respondents allege in their complaints that they had no chance to respond, the District Court erred in dismissing for failure to state a claim. The

---

[11] Loudermill's hearing before the referee occurred two and one-half months after he filed his appeal. The Commission issued its written decision six and one-half months after that * * *.

judgment of the Court of Appeals is affirmed, and the case is remanded for further proceedings consistent with this opinion.

So ordered.

JUSTICE MARSHALL, concurring in part and concurring in the judgment.

* * *

I write separately * * * to reaffirm my belief that public employees who may be discharged only for cause are entitled, under the Due Process Clause of the Fourteenth Amendment, to more than respondents sought in this case. I continue to believe that *before the decision is made to terminate an employee's wages*, the employee is entitled to an opportunity to test the strength of the evidence "by confronting and cross-examining adverse witnesses and by presenting witnesses on his own behalf, whenever there are substantial disputes in testimonial evidence," *Arnett v. Kennedy*, 416 U.S. 134, 214, 94 S.Ct. 1633, 1674, 40 L.Ed.2d 15 (1974) (MARSHALL, J., dissenting). Because the Court suggests that even in this situation due process requires no more than notice and an opportunity to be heard before wages are cut off, I am not able to join the Court's opinion in its entirety.

* * *

JUSTICE BRENNAN, concurring in part and dissenting in part.

* * *

* * * I concur in Parts I-IV of the Court's opinion * * *.

* * *

Recognizing the limited scope of the holding in Part V, I must still dissent from its result, because the record in this case is insufficiently developed to permit an informed judgment on the issue of overlong delay * * *.

JUSTICE REHNQUIST, dissenting.

In *Arnett v. Kennedy*, 416 U.S. 134, 94 S.Ct. 1633, 40 L.Ed.2d 15 (1974), six Members of this Court agreed that a public employee could be dismissed for misconduct without a full hearing prior to termination. A plurality of Justices agreed that the employee was entitled to exactly what Congress gave him, and no more. The CHIEF JUSTICE, Justice Stewart, and I said:

> "Here appellee did have a statutory expectancy that he not be removed other than for 'such cause as will promote the efficiency of [the] service.' But the very section of the statute which granted him that right, a right which had previously existed only by virtue of administrative regulation, expressly provided also for the

procedure by which 'cause' was to be determined, and expressly omitted the procedural guarantees which appellee insists are mandated by the Constitution. Only by bifurcating the very sentence of the Act of Congress which conferred upon appellee the right not to be removed save for cause could it be said that he had an expectancy of that substantive right without the procedural limitations which Congress attached to it. In the area of federal regulation of government employees, where in the absence of statutory limitation the governmental employer has had virtually uncontrolled latitude in decisions as to hiring and firing, *Cafeteria Workers v. McElroy*, 367 U.S. 886, 896–897, 81 S.Ct. 1743, 1749–1750, 6 L.Ed.2d 1230 (1961), we do not believe that a statutory enactment such as the Lloyd-La Follette act may be parsed as discretely as appellee urges. Congress was obviously intent on according a measure of statutory job security to governmental employees which they had not previously enjoyed, but was likewise intent on excluding more elaborate procedural requirements which it felt would make the operation of the new scheme unnecessarily burdensome in practice. Where the focus of legislation was thus strongly on the procedural mechanism for enforcing the substantive right which was simultaneously conferred, we decline to conclude that the substantive right may be viewed wholly apart from the procedure provided for its enforcement. The employee's statutorily defined right is not a guarantee against removal without cause in the abstract, but such a guarantee as enforced by the procedures which Congress has designated for the determination of cause." *Id.*, at 151–152, 94 S.Ct., at 1643.

In these cases, the relevant Ohio statute provides in its first paragraph that

"[t]he tenure of every officer or employee in the classified service of the state and the counties, civil service townships, cities, city health districts, general health districts, and city school districts thereof, holding a position under this chapter of the Revised Code, shall be during good behavior and efficient service and no such officer or employee shall be reduced in pay or position, suspended, or removed, except . . . for incompetency, inefficiency, dishonesty, drunkenness, immoral conduct, insubordination, discourteous treatment of the public, neglect of duty, violation of such sections or the rules of the director of administrative services or the commission, or any other failure of good behavior, or any other acts of misfeasance, malfeasance, or nonfeasance in office." Ohio Rev.Code Ann. § 124.34 (1984).

The very next paragraph of this section of the Ohio Revised Code provides that in the event of suspension of more than three days or removal the appointing authority shall furnish the employee with the stated reasons for his removal. The next paragraph provides that within 10 days following the receipt of such a statement, the employee may appeal in writing to the State Personnel Board of Review or the Commission, such appeal shall be heard within 30 days from the time of its filing, and the Board may affirm, disaffirm, or modify the judgment of the appointing authority.

Thus in one legislative breath Ohio has conferred upon civil service employees such as respondents in these cases a limited form of tenure during good behavior, and prescribed the procedures by which that tenure may be terminated. Here, as in *Arnett*, "[t]he employee's statutorily defined right is not a guarantee against removal without cause in the abstract, but such a guarantee as enforced by the procedures which [the Ohio Legislature] has designated for the determination of cause." 416 U.S., at 152, 94 S.Ct., at 1643 (opinion of REHNQUIST, J.). We stated in *Board of Regents v. Roth*, 408 U.S. 564, 577, 92 S.Ct. 2701, 2709, 33 L.Ed.2d 548 (1972):

> "Property interests, of course, are not created by the Constitution. Rather, they are created and their dimensions are defined by existing rules or understandings that stem from an independent source such as state law—rules or understandings that secure certain benefits and that support claims of entitlement to those benefits."

We ought to recognize the totality of the State's definition of the property right in question, and not merely seize upon one of several paragraphs in a unitary statute to proclaim that in that paragraph the State has inexorably conferred upon a civil service employee something which it is powerless under the United States Constitution to qualify in the next paragraph of the statute. This practice ignores our duty under *Roth* to rely on state law as the source of property interests for purposes of applying the Due Process Clause of the Fourteenth Amendment. While it does not impose a federal definition of property, the Court departs from the full breadth of the holding in *Roth* by its selective choice from among the sentences the Ohio Legislature chooses to use in establishing and qualifying a right.

Having concluded by this somewhat tortured reasoning that Ohio has created a property right in the respondents in these cases, the Court naturally proceeds to inquire what process is "due" before the respondents may be divested of that right. This customary "balancing" inquiry conducted by the Court in these cases reaches a result that is quite unobjectionable, but it seems to me that it is devoid of any principles which will either instruct or endure. The balance is simply an ad hoc weighing which depends to a great extent upon how the Court subjectively views the underlying interests at stake. The results in previous cases and in these cases have been quite unpredictable. To paraphrase Justice Black, today's balancing act requires a "pretermination opportunity to respond" but there is nothing that indicates what tomorrow's will be. *Goldberg v. Kelly*, 397 U.S. 254, 276, 90 S.Ct. 1011, 1024, 25 L.Ed.2d 287 (1970) (Black, J., dissenting). The results from today's balance certainly do not jibe with the result in *Goldberg* or *Mathews v. Eldridge*, 424 U.S. 319, 96 S.Ct. 893, 47 L.Ed.2d 18 (1976). The lack of any principled standards in this area means that these procedural due process cases will recur time and again. Every different set of facts will present a new issue on what process was due and when. One way to avoid this subjective and varying interpretation of the Due Process Clause in cases such as these is to hold that one who avails himself of government entitlements accepts the grant of tenure along with its inherent limitations.

Because I believe that the Fourteenth Amendment of the United States Constitution does not support the conclusion that Ohio's effort to confer a limited form of tenure upon respondents resulted in the creation of a "property right" in their employment, I dissent.

NOTES

The weight of scholarly commentary supports the *Loudermill* majority's rejection of Justice Rehnquist's view that the statutory procedures for terminating an entitlement are part of the entitlement's definition.[11] *See, e.g.*, Henry Monaghan, *Of "Liberty" and "Property,"* 62 Cornell L. Rev. 405, 439 (1977) (stating that "our legal traditions strongly oppose" the conflation of procedural and substantive rights); Laurence H. Tribe, *Structural Due Process*, 10 Harv. C.R.C.L.L. Rev. 269 (1975) (arguing that people are more likely to rely on governmental definitions of substantive rights than on definitions of procedural rights). *But see* Frank Easterbrook, *Substance and Due Process*, 1982 Sup. Ct. Rev. 85, 112 ("Procedural rules usually are just a measure of how much the substantive entitlements are worth, of what we are willing to sacrifice to see a given goal attained. The body that creates a substantive rule is the logical judge of how much should be spent to avoid errors in the process of disposing of claims to that right."). Doesn't Justice Rehnquist's view essentially do away with entitlement theory and return us to the model of *Bailey v. Richardson*? Is that a strength or a weakness of his approach?

---

[11] Justice Rehnquist's position is often called the "bitter with the sweet" theory, because his plurality opinion in *Arnett* said: "where the grant of a substantive right is inextricably intertwined with the limitations on the procedures which are to be employed in determining that right, a litigant * * * must take the bitter with the sweet." 416 U.S. at 153–54.

GILBERT V. HOMAR

Supreme Court of the United States, 1997.
520 U.S. 924, 117 S.Ct. 1807, 138 L.Ed.2d 120.

JUSTICE SCALIA delivered the opinion of the Court.

This case presents the question whether a State violates the Due Process Clause of the Fourteenth Amendment by failing to provide notice and a hearing before suspending a tenured public employee without pay.

I

Respondent Richard J. Homar was employed as a police officer at East Stroudsburg University (ESU), a branch of Pennsylvania's State System of Higher Education. On August 26, 1992, when respondent was at the home of a family friend, he was arrested by the Pennsylvania State Police in a drug raid. Later that day, the state police filed a criminal complaint charging respondent with possession of marijuana, possession with intent to deliver, and criminal conspiracy to violate the controlled substance law, which is a felony. The state police notified respondent's supervisor, University Police Chief David Marazas, of the arrest and charges. Chief Marazas in turn informed Gerald Levanowitz, ESU's Director of Human Resources, to whom ESU President James Gilbert had delegated authority to discipline ESU employees. Levanowitz suspended respondent without pay effective immediately. Respondent failed to report to work on the day of his arrest, and learned of his suspension the next day, when he called Chief Marazas to inquire whether he had been suspended. That same day, respondent received a letter from Levanowitz confirming that he had been suspended effective August 26 pending an investigation into the criminal charges filed against him. The letter explained that any action taken by ESU would not necessarily coincide with the disposition of the criminal charges.

Although the criminal charges were dismissed on September 1, respondent's suspension remained in effect while ESU continued with its own investigation. On September 18, Levanowitz and Chief Marazas met with respondent in order to give him an opportunity to tell his side of the story. Respondent was informed at the meeting that the state police had given ESU information that was "very serious in nature," Record, Doc. No. 26, p. 48, but he was not informed that that included a report of an alleged confession he had made on the day of his arrest; he was consequently unable to respond to damaging statements attributed to him in the police report.

In a letter dated September 23, Levanowitz notified respondent that he was being demoted to the position of groundskeeper effective the next day, and that he would receive backpay from the date the suspension took effect at the rate of pay of a groundskeeper. (Respondent eventually received backpay for the period of his suspension at the rate of pay of a university police officer.) The letter maintained that the demotion was being imposed "as a result of admissions made by yourself to the Pennsylvania State Police on August 26, 1992 that you maintained associations with individuals whom you knew were dealing in large quantities of marijuana and that you obtained marijuana from one of those individuals for your own use. Your actions constitute a clear and flagrant violation of Sections 200 and 200.2 of the [ESU] Police Department Manual." App. 82a. Upon receipt of this letter, the president of respondent's union requested a meeting with President Gilbert. The requested meeting took place on September 24, at which point respondent had received and read the police report containing the alleged confession. After providing respondent with an opportunity to respond to the charges, Gilbert sustained the demotion.

Respondent filed this suit under 42 U.S.C. § 1983, in the United States District Court for the Middle District of Pennsylvania against President Gilbert, Chief Marazas, Levanowitz, and a Vice President of ESU, Curtis English, all in both their individual and official capacities. He contended, *inter alia*, that petitioners' failure to provide him with notice and an opportunity to be heard before suspending him without pay violated due process. The District Court entered summary judgment for petitioners. A divided Court of Appeals reversed the District Court's determination that it was permissible for ESU to suspend respondent without pay without first providing a hearing. 89 F.3d 1009 (C.A.3 1996). We granted certiorari.

II

The protections of the Due Process Clause apply to government deprivation of those perquisites of government employment in which the employee has a constitutionally protected "property" interest. Although we have previously held that public employees who can be discharged only for cause have a constitutionally protected property interest in their tenure and cannot be fired without due process, see *Board of Regents of State Colleges v. Roth*, 408 U.S. 564, 578, 92 S.Ct. 2701, 2709–2710, 33 L.Ed.2d 548 (1972); *Perry v. Sindermann*, 408 U.S. 593, 602–603, 92 S.Ct. 2694, 2700–2701, 33 L.Ed.2d 570 (1972), we have not had occasion to decide whether the protections of the Due Process Clause extend to discipline of tenured public employees short of termination. Petitioners, however, do not contest this preliminary point, and so without deciding it we will, like the District Court, "[a]ssum[e] that the suspension infringed a protected property interest," and turn at once to petitioners' contention that respondent received all the process he was due.

A

In *Cleveland Bd. of Ed. v. Loudermill*, 470 U.S. 532, 105 S.Ct. 1487, 84 L.Ed.2d 494 (1985), we concluded that a public employee dismissible only for cause was entitled to a very limited hearing prior to his termination, to be followed by a more comprehensive post-termination hearing. Stressing that the pretermination hearing "should be an initial check against mistaken decisions—essentially, a determination of whether there are reasonable grounds to believe that the charges against the employee are true and support the proposed action," *id.*, at 545–546, 105 S.Ct., at 1495, we held that pretermination process need only include oral or written notice of the charges, an explanation of the employer's evidence, and an opportunity for the employee to tell his side of the story, *id.*, at 546, 105 S.Ct., at 1495. In the course of our assessment of the governmental interest in immediate termination of a tenured employee, we observed that "in those situations where the employer perceives a significant hazard in keeping the employee on the job, it can avoid the problem by suspending *with pay.*" *Id.*, at 544–545, 105 S.Ct., at 1495 (emphasis added).

Relying on this dictum, which it read as "strongly suggest[ing] that suspension without pay must be preceded by notice and an opportunity to be heard *in all instances,*" 89 F.3d, at 1015 (emphasis added), and determining on its own that such a rule would be "eminently sensible," *id.*, at 1016, the Court of Appeals adopted a categorical prohibition: "[A] governmental employer may not suspend an employee without pay unless that suspension is preceded by some kind of pre-suspension hearing, providing the employee with notice and an opportunity to be heard." *Ibid.* Respondent (as well as most of his *amici*) makes no attempt to defend this absolute rule, which spans all types of government employment and all types of unpaid suspensions. Brief for Respondent 8, 12–13. This is eminently wise, since under our precedents such an absolute rule is indefensible.

It is by now well established that " 'due process,' unlike some legal rules, is not a technical conception with a fixed content unrelated to time, place and circumstances." *Cafeteria & Restaurant Workers v. McElroy*, 367 U.S. 886, 895, 81 S.Ct. 1743, 1748, 6 L.Ed.2d 1230 (1961). "[D]ue process is flexible and calls for such procedural protections as the particular situation demands." *Morrissey v. Brewer*, 408 U.S. 471, 481, 92 S.Ct. 2593, 2600, 33 L.Ed.2d 484 (1972). This Court has recognized, on many occasions, that where a State must act quickly, or where it would be impractical to provide predeprivation process, postdeprivation process satisfies the requirements of the Due Process Clause * * *. [I]n *FDIC v. Mallen*, 486 U.S. 230, 108 S.Ct. 1780, 100 L.Ed.2d 265 (1988), where we unanimously approved the Federal Deposit Insurance Corporation's (FDIC's) suspension, without prior hearing, of an indicted private bank employee, we said: "An important government interest, accompanied by a substantial assurance that the deprivation is not baseless or unwarranted, may in limited cases demanding prompt action justify postponing the opportunity to be heard until after the initial deprivation." *Id.*, at 240, 108 S.Ct., at 1787–1788.

The dictum in *Loudermill* relied upon by the Court of Appeals is of course not inconsistent with these precedents. To say that when the government employer perceives a hazard in leaving the employee on the job it "can avoid the problem by suspending with pay" is not to say that that is the only way of avoiding the problem. Whatever implication the phrase "with pay" might have conveyed is far outweighed by the clarity of our precedents which emphasize the flexibility of due process as contrasted with the sweeping and categorical rule adopted by the Court of Appeals.

B

To determine what process is constitutionally due, we have generally balanced three distinct factors:

"First, the private interest that will be affected by the official action; second, the risk of an erroneous deprivation of such interest through the procedures used, and the probable value, if any, of additional or substitute procedural safeguards; and finally, the Government's interest." *Mathews v. Eldridge*, 424 U.S. 319, 335, 96 S.Ct. 893, 903, 47 L.Ed.2d 18 (1976).

Respondent contends that he has a significant private interest in the uninterrupted receipt of his paycheck. But while our opinions have recognized the severity of depriving someone of the means of his livelihood, they have also emphasized that in determining what process is due, account must be taken of "the *length*" and "*finality* of the deprivation." Unlike the employee in *Loudermill*, who faced *termination*, respondent faced only a *temporary suspension* without pay. So long as the suspended employee receives a sufficiently prompt postsuspension hearing, the lost income is relatively insubstantial (compared with termination), and fringe benefits such as health and life insurance are often not affected at all.

On the other side of the balance, the State has a significant interest in immediately suspending, when felony charges are filed against them, employees who occupy positions of great public trust and high public visibility, such as police officers. Respondent contends that this interest in maintaining public confidence could have been accommodated by suspending him *with* pay until he had a hearing. We think, however, that the government does not have to give an employee charged with a felony a paid leave at taxpayer expense. If his services to the government are no longer useful once the felony charge has been filed, the Constitution does not require the government to bear the added expense of hiring a replacement while still paying him * * *.

The last factor in the *Mathews* balancing, and the factor most important to resolution of this case, is the risk of erroneous deprivation and the likely value of any additional procedures * * *. We noted in *Loudermill* that the purpose of a pre-*termination* hearing is to determine "whether there are reasonable grounds to believe that the charges against the employee are true and support the proposed action." 470 U.S., at 545–546, 105 S.Ct., at 1495. By parity of reasoning, the purpose of any pre-*suspension* hearing would be to assure that there are reasonable grounds to support the suspension without pay. But here that has already been assured by the arrest and the filing of charges.

In *Mallen*, we concluded that an "*ex parte* finding of probable cause" such as a grand jury indictment provides adequate assurance that the suspension is not unjustified. *Id.*, at 240–241, 108 S.Ct., at 1787–1788. The same is true when an employee is arrested and then formally charged with a felony. First, as with an indictment, the arrest and formal charges imposed upon respondent "by an independent body demonstrat[e] that the suspension is not arbitrary." *Id.*, at 244, 108 S.Ct., at 1790. Second, like an indictment, the imposition of felony charges "itself is an objective fact that will in most cases raise serious public concern." *Id.*, at 244–245, 108 S.Ct., at 1790. It is true, as respondent argues, that there is more reason to believe an employee has committed a felony when he is indicted rather than merely arrested and formally charged; but for present purposes arrest and charge give reason enough. They serve to assure that the state employer's decision to suspend the employee is not "baseless or unwarranted," *id.*, at 240, 108 S.Ct., at 1788, in that an independent third party has determined that there is probable cause to believe the employee committed a serious crime.

Respondent further contends that since (as we have agreed to assume) Levanowitz had discretion *not* to suspend despite the arrest and filing of charges, he had to be given an opportunity to persuade Levanowitz of his innocence before the decision was made. We disagree. In *Mallen*, despite the fact that the FDIC had *discretion* whether to suspend an indicted bank employee, we nevertheless did not believe that a presuspension hearing was necessary to protect the private interest. Unlike in the case of a termination, where we have recognized that "the only meaningful opportunity to invoke the discretion of the decisionmaker is likely to be before the termination takes effect," *Loudermill, supra*, at 543, 105 S.Ct., at 1494, in the case of a suspension there will be ample opportunity to invoke discretion later—and a short delay actually benefits the employee by allowing state officials to obtain more accurate information about the arrest and charges. Respondent "has an interest in seeing that a decision concerning his or her continued suspension is not made with excessive haste." *Mallen*, 486 U.S., at 243, 108 S.Ct., at 1789. If the State is forced to act too quickly, the decisionmaker "may give greater weight to the public interest and leave the suspension in place." *Ibid.*

C

Much of respondent's argument is dedicated to the proposition that he had a due process right to a presuspension hearing because the suspension was open-ended and he "theoretically may not have had the opportunity to be heard for weeks, months, or even years after his initial suspension without pay." Brief for Respondent 23. But, as respondent himself asserts in his attempt to downplay the governmental interest, "[b]ecause the employee is entitled, in any event, to a prompt post-suspension opportunity to be heard, the period of the suspension should be short and the amount of pay during the suspension minimal." *Id.*, at 24–25.

Whether respondent was provided an adequately prompt *post-suspension* hearing in the present case is a separate question. Although the charges against respondent were dropped on September 1 (petitioners apparently learned of this on September 2), he did not receive any sort of hearing until September 18. Once the charges were dropped, the risk of erroneous deprivation increased substantially, and, as petitioners conceded at oral argument, there was likely value in holding a prompt hearing, Tr. of Oral Arg. 19. Cf. *Mallen, supra,* at 243, 108 S.Ct., at 1789 (holding that 90 days before the agency hears and decides the propriety of a suspension does not exceed the permissible limits where coupled with factors that minimize the risk of an erroneous deprivation). Because neither the Court of Appeals nor the District Court addressed whether, under the particular facts of this case, petitioners violated due process by failing to provide a sufficiently prompt postsuspension hearing, we will not consider this issue in the first instance, but remand for consideration by the Court of Appeals.

* * *

The judgment of the Court of Appeals is reversed, and the case is remanded for further proceedings consistent with this opinion.

NOTES

Loudermill and *Homar* both involve claims to relatively modest predeprivation procedures. The main arguments in both cases were not about full-fledged, on-the-record evidentiary hearings, as in *Goldberg*, but about informal "give-and-take" hearings whose most important feature is the opportunity for an oral presentation to the governmental agency. The idea is that an oral hearing, even without any other trappings of procedural formality, can often significantly reduce the risk of error at a fairly low cost. Hearings of this kind are often called "*Goss* hearings," because of the holding in *Goss v. Lopez*, 419 U.S. 565, 95 S.Ct. 729, 42 L.Ed.2d 725 (1975), that public schoolchildren must generally receive such an informal hearing before being suspended. Of course, the idea that a hearing of this kind might constitute due process of law in some circumstances did not originate with *Goss*, or even with the modern due process revolution: the affected landowners in *Londoner v. Denver* were held entitled to a "*Goss* hearing" in 1908, two-thirds of a century before *Goss* was decided.

Given the *Mathews* framework, which balances the private interest, the efficacy of the requested procedures, and the cost to the government, it is obviously easier to convince a court to award you a *Goss* hearing—or, if one prefers,[12] a *Londoner* hearing—than a trial-type evidentiary hearing. Due process litigants are thus well advised to keep their procedural requests to the minimum necessary to accomplish their ends.

2. THE ADEQUACY OF POST-DEPRIVATION HEARINGS

North American Cold Storage in 1908 held that the appropriate "process" in connection with seizures of potentially unwholesome food was a common-law tort suit against the individual government officials. Such a suit would have as much procedural formality as American law ever provides—a jury trial—but would provide procedures only *after* the plaintiff had been deprived of a property interest by government action. The cause of action would arise under state tort law, and the suit would ordinarily take place in state court.[13]

This remedy is still available in principle today. If the actions of government officials would constitute a tort if committed by private citizens, one can ordinarily sue the government officials, in their personal capacities, in state court.[14] In practice, however, modern law typically gives government officials immunity for all but the most egregious conduct committed in their official capacities. Moreover, not all offending conduct by government officials fits neatly into the categories of common-law torts, so there simply may not be an applicable cause of action for certain alleged governmental wrongs. In addition, state courts may not be the most hospitable forums for claims against their own states' officials. Finally, under the so-called "American rule," each party in a lawsuit ordinarily bears its own costs of litigation, including attorneys fees. Unless the damages caused by government action are substantial, the attorneys fees may well exceed the value of the suit. For these and other reasons, the tort law remedy contemplated by the Court in *North American* is not as attractive as the Court seemed to suggest.

State law tort suits, however, are not the only vehicles for seeking judicial redress from governmental action. In 1971, the Supreme Court recognized the possibility of federal causes of action for damages against federal officials brought directly under provisions of the Constitution, such as the Fourth Amendment, without need for a federal statute to provide a

---

[12] I do.

[13] If the suit was against federal officials, they would probably seek to remove the case to federal court, though the underlying cause of action would remain a state-law tort.

[14] Bringing suit against the government itself often runs into problems of sovereign immunity.

cause of action.[15] Most of the modern cases in this chapter, though, have involved *federal* court lawsuits against *state* officials. The vehicle for these lawsuits is an important federal statute that reads:

> Every person who, under color of any statute, ordinance, regulation, custom, or usage, of any State or Territory or the District of Columbia, subjects, or causes to be subjected, any citizen of the United States or other person within the jurisdiction thereof to the deprivation of any rights, privileges, or immunities secured by the Constitution and laws, shall be liable to the party injured in an action at law, suit in equity, or other proper proceeding for redress.

42 U.S.C. § 1983 (2012). This statute was enacted in 1871, following the Civil War, as a mechanism for enforcing the Fourteenth Amendment and the post-Civil War congressional effort to secure equality for blacks. State law tort suits brought by southern blacks in southern courts, with all-white benches and juries, were not likely to be an effective remedy against racial oppression. Accordingly, section 1983 (as it is popularly called) authorized a direct federal cause of action, heard in federal court,[16] against state officials who violate federally protected civil rights. For nearly a century, the statute was understood to apply almost exclusively in the civil rights context. After all, the Constitution, even as altered by the post-Civil War amendments, secures relatively few "rights, privileges, or immunities" against the states, and the reference in section 1983 to rights secured by "laws" was long read to mean only laws protecting the civil rights of blacks. A number of modern developments, however, have dramatically expanded the scope of this statute.

First, the incorporation of most of the provisions of the bill of rights through the Fourteenth Amendment, coupled with modern decisions greatly expanding the substantive scope of many of these provisions, has exponentially increased the range of state conduct that can plausibly be said to implicate "rights, privileges, or immunities" secured against the states by the Constitution. Second, the Supreme Court has held that section 1983's reference to "laws" that secure federal rights is not limited to civil rights laws, as that term is traditionally understood. *See Maine v. Thiboutot*, 448 U.S. 1, 100 S.Ct. 2502, 65 L.Ed.2d 555 (1980). Third, the Supreme Court has made clear that section 1983 is an alternative remedy to any available state law remedies; one need not "exhaust" available state avenues of relief before invoking the federal statute. *See Monroe v. Pape*,

---

[15] *See* Bivens v. Six Unknown Named Agents of the Federal Bureau of Narcotics, 403 U.S. 388, 91 S.Ct. 1999, 29 L.Ed.2d 619 (1971). The ebb and flow—in recent years primarily ebb—of this cause of action is a story in itself. For a useful introduction, see Susan Bandes, *Reinventing* Bivens: *The Self-Executing Constitution*, 68 So. Cal. L. Rev. 289 (1995).

[16] Federal jurisdiction over section 1983 actions, and other actions involving federal civil rights statutes, was provided by a companion statute, now codified as 42 U.S.C. § 1343 (2012).

365 U.S. 167, 81 S.Ct. 473, 5 L.Ed.2d 492 (1961). Fourth, a variety of forces, ranging from relative backlogs to relative competence to relative objectivity, often make federal courts a preferred forum when plaintiffs have a choice between state and federal court. Fifth, although states cannot be sued directly under section 1983, and local government bodies cannot be sued under a respondeat superior theory, state agencies such as municipal governments, with their potentially deep pockets, are permissible defendants in section 1983 cases. Sixth, and finally, a series of decisions construing 42 U.S.C. § 1988 (2012), the statute that provides the package of remedies for section 1983 and other federal civil rights statutes, makes it very likely that winning plaintiffs (and very, very unlikely that winning defendants) in section 1983 suits will recover their attorneys' fees and other costs. There is accordingly strong incentive for plaintiffs' attorneys to make every effort to fit lawsuits within section 1983 if it is at all possible.

The result of these forces is that "section 1983 litigation" has become a distinct, recognizable subset of federal court cases. Because of its serious implications for federalism, and for the overall workload of the federal courts, the rise of section 1983 litigation has been a major topic of judicial and academic attention in the last few decades. In many ways, the story of modern due process jurisprudence is the story of section 1983.

To see why, consider a municipal delivery truck driver who hops the curb and crosses your yard, destroying your flower garden. Depending on the vagaries of local laws, you may well have a state-law tort action against the offending driver or the municipality. But even if you have a valid cause of action, you will have to pay your own attorneys' fees. Is there any way you can fit your case within section 1983 and take advantage of its generous array of remedies, including the enticing promise of attorneys fees? One of the rights secured against state action by the federal Constitution, and thus within the scope of section 1983, is the guarantee against deprivations of life, liberty, or property without due process of law. You have arguably been deprived of property: your flowers are clearly property, and you no longer have them. You received no prior hearing before the truck wreaked its havoc on your begonias. The Supreme Court held in *Monroe v. Pape* that the availability of a state remedy is no bar to a federal action under section 1983. Is there any reason why you do not have a valid section 1983 cause of action?

This seemingly absurd hypothetical is in fact very real, as was graphically illustrated in 1981 in *Parratt v. Taylor*, 451 U.S. 527, 101 S.Ct. 1908, 68 L.Ed.2d 420 (1981). Employees in a Nebraska prison mailroom negligently lost $23.50 worth of hobby materials ordered by an inmate. The inmate could have sued in tort in Nebraska state court, but chose instead to bring a section 1983 action in federal court alleging a deprivation of his property without due process of law. He won easily in the lower courts: the hobby materials were clearly property, the prison employees seemingly deprived him of that property by losing it, and the prison employees held no hearings before negligently losing his goods. What could more clearly constitute a deprivation of property without due process of law?

The Supreme Court reversed. The Court agreed that the hobby materials were "property." It also agreed that negligent action could constitute a deprivation within the meaning of the Fourteenth Amendment. But it held that the absence of any procedures before the negligent deprivation did not violate "due process of law" because Nebraska's tort remedy—a procedure that is available *after* the deprivation occurs—was a constitutionally adequate procedure:

> This Court has never directly addressed the question of what process is due a person when an employee of a State negligently takes his property * * *.

> We have, however, recognized that postdeprivation remedies made available by the State can satisfy the Due Process Clause. In such cases, the normal predeprivation notice and opportunity to be heard is pretermitted if the State provides a postdeprivation remedy * * *. These cases recognize that either the necessity of quick action by the State or the impracticality of providing any meaningful predeprivation process, when coupled with the availability of some meaningful means by which to assess the propriety of the State's action at some time after the initial taking, can satisfy the requirements of procedural due process * * *.

> * * *

> The justifications which we have found sufficient to uphold takings of property without any predeprivation process are applicable to a situation such as the present one involving a tortious loss of a prisoner's property as a result of a random and unauthorized act by a state employee. In such a case, the loss is not a result of some established state procedure and the State cannot predict precisely when the loss will occur. It is difficult to conceive of how the State could provide a meaningful hearing before the deprivation takes place. The loss of property, although attributable to the State as action under "color of law," is in almost all cases beyond the control of the State. Indeed, in most cases it is not only impracticable, but impossible, to provide a meaningful hearing before the deprivation. That does not mean, of course, that the State can take property without providing a meaningful postdeprivation hearing. The prior cases which have excused the prior-hearing requirement have rested in part on the availability of some meaningful opportunity subsequent to the initial taking for a determination of rights and liabilities.

* * *

Application of the principles recited above to this case leads us to conclude the respondent has not alleged a violation of the Due Process Clause of the Fourteenth Amendment. Although he has been deprived of property under color of state law, the deprivation did not occur as a result of some established state procedure. Indeed, the deprivation occurred as a result of the unauthorized failure of agents of the State to follow established state procedure. There is no contention that the procedures themselves are inadequate nor is there any contention that it was practicable for the State to provide a predeprivation hearing * * *.

* * * To accept respondent's argument that the conduct of the state officials in this case constituted a violation of the Fourteenth Amendment would almost necessarily result in turning every alleged injury which may have been inflicted by a state official acting under "color of law" into a violation of the Fourteenth Amendment cognizable under § 1983. It is hard to perceive any logical stopping place to such a line of reasoning. Presumably, under this rationale any party who is involved in nothing more than an automobile accident with a state official could allege a constitutional violation under § 1983. Such reasoning "would make of the Fourteenth Amendment a font of tort law to be superimposed upon whatever systems may already be administered by the States." *Paul v. Davis*, 424 U.S. 693, 701, 96 S.Ct. 1155, 1160, 47 L.Ed.2d 405 (1976). We do not think that the drafters of the Fourteenth Amendment intended the Amendment to play such a role in our society.

451 U.S. at 537, 541, 543–44, 101 S.Ct. at 1914, 1916–17. Justice Powell concurred in the judgment: he maintained that losses caused by negligent rather than deliberate conduct simply were not deprivations within the meaning of the Constitution. *Id.* at 548–52, 101 S.Ct. at 1919–21 (Powell, J., concurring in the result).

Justice Blackmun joined the majority opinion in *Parratt,* but he wrote separately to express doubts whether a post-deprivation remedy would normally be adequate for *intentional* rather than *negligent* acts by government officials. *Id.* at 545–46, 101 S.Ct. at 1918 (Blackmun, J., concurring). Nonetheless, in *Hudson v. Palmer*, 468 U.S. 517, 104 S.Ct. 3194, 82 L.Ed.2d 393 (1984), the Court extended *Parratt* to hold that deprivations caused by intentional but officially unauthorized government action require only post-deprivation procedures, such as the availability of a tort remedy, to satisfy due process. The Court explained, "The state can no more anticipate and control in advance the random and unauthorized intentional conduct of its employees than it can anticipate similar negligent conduct." 468 U.S. at 533, 104 S.Ct. at 3203.

What if, by reason of sovereign immunity or a substantive gap in state law, there is no post-deprivation tort remedy for a loss inflicted by a state official's negligence? The Supreme Court took up that question in 1986 in *Daniels v. Williams,* 474 U.S. 327, 106 S.Ct. 662, 88 L.Ed.2d 662 (1986). The Court's answer, which remains the law today, was that Justice Powell had been right all along that negligently inflicted losses do not constitute deprivations of property within the meaning of the due process clauses: "injuries inflicted by governmental negligence are not addressed by the United States Constitution * * *." 474 U.S. at 333, 106 S.Ct. at 666.

These cases yield the following scheme: In order for the absence of predeprivation procedures to constitute a violation of the Fourteenth Amendment's Due Process Clause, and hence a violation of section 1983, a plaintiff must prove a loss that results from intentional (or, by the overwhelming weight of lower court authority, reckless) governmental action pursuant to an official governmental policy or established set of procedures. If the loss results from unauthorized conduct by government officials, meaning conduct that does not carry out authoritatively-defined governmental policies, post-deprivation remedies are constitutionally adequate.

Alas, application of that seemingly settled scheme can be nightmarishly complicated and unpredictable. Details are best left for specialized courses in civil rights law or section 1983 (which abound in law schools). For an especially perplexing case that split the Court 5–4, see *Zinermon v. Burch,* 494 U.S. 113, 110 S.Ct. 975, 108 L.Ed.2d 100 (1990).

CHAPTER 6

TIMING AND AVAILABILITY OF JUDICIAL REVIEW

■ ■ ■

The material in Chapters 2–5 deals largely with the manner in which courts review agency decisions. That discussion assumes away the answers to a great many questions: <u>Is judicial review of the relevant agency decision in fact available</u>? Is it available to a particular plaintiff? Against a particular defendant? In a particular court? At a particular moment in time? In the particular form in which the suit is brought?

Full answers to these questions would consume this entire course—as well as much of several other courses in constitutional law, federal jurisdiction, and civil procedure. The materials in this chapter hit the highlights but leave many of the details unaddressed. Unfortunately, mastery of the law is often mastery of details, so do not expect to emerge from this course with anything resembling a full understanding of the law governing the availability, timing, and form of judicial review of agency action. Indeed, you should expect this chapter to generate more than its share of frustration. If frustration ever threatens to turn into panic, take some heart in the fact that judges and administrative lawyers often struggle with this material too. It is without a doubt the most difficult aspect of federal administrative law.

Most (though not quite all) of the relevant questions concerning the timing and availability of judicial review of agency action can be summed up as the five "Ws": whether, whom, what, where, and when—*whether* judicial review of a specific agency action is available, for (and against) *whom* such review is available, *what* form the action for judicial review must take, *where* an action for judicial review must be brought, and *when* an action for judicial review is appropriate. As usual, the primary sources of answers to these questions are the APA and organic statutes—with the Constitution, agency regulations, and judicial creativity playing strong supporting roles. Also as usual, the answers today are often very different from the answers that would have been given sixty years ago, but one must often understand the past in order to get a good handle on the present.

The issues raised by each of the five "Ws" often overlap, which accounts for much of the doctrinal confusion that you are about to experience. Nonetheless, if you try to keep the different questions clear in your own mind, you will be ahead of the game—and in all likelihood ahead of the courts.

A.   "WHAT" AND "WHERE"?: AN INTRODUCTION TO JUDICIAL REVIEW OF FEDERAL AGENCY ACTION

1.   NONSTATUTORY REVIEW

a.   Tort Actions

A federal agency has taken action that damages you—for example, by entering your warehouse and seizing and destroying some of your chickens on the ground that they are adulterated in violation of federal poultry marketing standards.[1] You believe that the action is illegal, either because it exceeds the agency's statutory authority or because the action is putatively authorized by a statute that you believe is unconstitutional.[2] What do you do?

If the party that injured you was a private entity, you would probably invoke your local jurisdiction's tort law and bring an action for trespass, conversion, or any other appropriate tort. Most likely, you would sue the private party in state court; and even if you sued in federal court (based on diversity of citizenship), the underlying cause of action would be grounded in state law, and the federal court would decide the case in accordance with local law.

Does it matter that the party that injured you is the federal government or an agent thereof? Indeed it does. On the positive side, there are certain special avenues of judicial relief that are available only when the defendant is a governmental entity; these are discussed in the next two subsections and consume most of the rest of this chapter. On the much larger negative side, however, there are other avenues that are not available, or are available only under very limited circumstances, when the defendant is governmental rather than private.

Consider your tort action for trespass and conversion based on the government's allegedly illegal destruction of your chickens. Suppose that you want to sue the United States itself, reasoning that it has the deepest pocket of any defendant that you are likely to find. You will immediately run headlong into the doctrine of sovereign immunity: you cannot sue the

---

[1]   This is an adaption of the facts in *North American Cold Storage Co. v. Chicago*, 211 U.S. 306, 29 S.Ct. 101, 53 L.Ed. 195 (1908). *See supra* pages 884–887.

[2]   If you are harmed by agency action that is authorized by a constitutional statute, you obviously have no expectation of a legal remedy, though it is possible that a legislature could choose to provide one.

United States, for any reason or for any form of relief, unless Congress has *expressly* consented by statute to be sued.

Does this mean that the United States government can ransack your house, bulldoze your farm, destroy your business, and break contracts with you, and you cannot sue for any kind of redress unless Congress deigns to permit such suit? That is precisely what it means. Sovereign immunity is a complete bar to any lawsuit against the government that is not specifically authorized by statute. Although the doctrine of federal sovereign immunity has a somewhat mysterious—and, in the judgment of many observers, highly dubious—origin,[3] it is a firm feature of the modern legal landscape.

Accordingly, your first task is to determine whether there is any statute that permits you to sue the government for the destruction of your chickens. Prior to the late nineteenth century, the answer would very clearly have been no. Your only recourse against the federal government for damage caused by its agents, whether due to the breach of a contract or a tortious invasion of your property, was to seek special legislation from Congress, called a private bill, providing for compensation.

Private bills remain important today as sources of relief. In modern times, however, there are also a number of statutes to be found. After the Civil War, Congress began forming special tribunals to determine the validity of monetary claims against the government, in large measure because Congress simply got tired of dealing with a large volume of requests for private bills. In 1887, this procedure was formalized with the passage of the Tucker Act, which remains (with some important amendments) on the statute books today. *See* 28 U.S.C. §§ 1346(a)(2), 1491 (2012). This statute authorizes suit against the United States for certain monetary claims. If the amount in question is less than $10,000, suit may be brought either in a federal district court or in the Court of Federal Claims, which is an Article I court situated in the District of Columbia whose judges do not have constitutional tenure or salary guarantees (and which does not use the services of a jury). If the amount in question is more than $10,000, the suit *must* be brought in the Court of Federal Claims. Appeals from adverse decisions on these claims must be taken to the Article III Court of Appeals for the Federal Circuit and from there on certiorari to the Supreme Court.

The Tucker Act, however, will not help you get compensation for your lost chickens, because the statute only authorizes suit for claims "founded either upon the Constitution, or any Act of Congress or any regulation of an executive department, or upon any express or implied contract with the

---

[3] At least two Supreme Court Justices, writing 200 years apart, have harshly criticized the doctrine of sovereign immunity. *See* Chisholm v. Georgia, 2 U.S. (2 Dall.) 419, 456–65, 1 L.Ed. 440 (1793) (Wilson, J.); John Paul Stevens, *Is Justice Irrelevant?*, 87 Nw. U.L. Rev. 1121 (1993).

United States, or for liquidated or unliquidated damages in cases *not sounding in tort*." 28 U.S.C. § 1491 (2012) (emphasis added). This statute waives sovereign immunity for, *inter alia*, breach of contract actions and claims alleging takings of property without just compensation, but it does not contemplate suits against the government based on ordinary torts.

Another statute, however, seems directly suited to this task: the Federal Tort Claims Act (FTCA). 28 U.S.C. §§ 1346, 2671–80 (2012). This statute was enacted in 1946 to fill at least part of the gap left by the Tucker Act by providing an avenue of judicial relief for damages caused by governmental torts. It proclaims that "[t]he United States shall be liable, respecting the provisions of this title relating to tort claims, in the same manner and to the same extent as a private individual under like circumstances, but shall not be liable for interest prior to judgment or for punitive damages." *Id.* § 2674. Despite this broad language, however, the statute is very limited in scope.[4] There is no liability for damages caused by, *inter alia*, postal services, tax collection, monetary policy, or (helped along by generous judicial construction) military functions. *See id.* § 2680; *Feres v. United States*, 340 U.S. 135, 71 S.Ct. 153, 95 L.Ed. 152 (1950). There is generally no liability for "[a]ny claim arising out of assault, battery, false imprisonment, false arrest, malicious prosecution, abuse of process, libel, slander, misrepresentation, deceit, or interference with contract rights," *id.* § 2680(h), although some of these torts are actionable if committed by law enforcement personnel. *Id.* Most importantly, the statute does not encompass "[a]ny claim based upon an act or omission of an employee of the Government, exercising due care, in the execution of a statute or regulation, whether or not such statute or regulation be valid, or based upon the exercise or performance or the failure to exercise or perform a discretionary function or duty on the part of a federal agency or employee of the Government, whether or not the discretion involved be abused." *Id.* § 2680(a). The first part of this provision makes clear that the FTCA is not a vehicle for challenging the validity of statutes or regulations; the faithful execution of an invalid statute or regulation cannot be grounds for governmental liability under the FTCA. The second part of this provision is even more sweeping: there is no liability for exercises of discretion, including abuses of discretion, in the execution of government functions. The courts have construed this provision to exempt the government from liability for any actions that are "based on considerations of public policy." *Berkovitz v. United States*, 486 U.S. 531, 537, 108 S.Ct. 1954, 1958, 100 L.Ed.2d 531 (1988). Such actions can include seemingly routine,

---

[4] It also presents some procedural obstacles to litigants—for example, it requires presentation of the claim to the appropriate government agency before a judicial action is brought, and it does not provide for trial by jury. How can the government avoid the Seventh Amendment's guarantee of a jury in civil actions? The courts reason that because Congress does not have to permit suit against the United States at all, it is capable of placing any (germane) conditions that it thinks appropriate on suits that it chooses to allow through a waiver of sovereign immunity.

operational activities if those activities require choices that are not mandated by statute or regulation and are driven by policy considerations. The government is not liable under the FTCA, for example, for the actions of federal bank regulators who involve themselves in a bank's affairs by making hiring recommendations, consulting on legal matters, and advising on salary disputes, bankruptcy filings, and chartering decisions. *See United States v. Gaubert*, 499 U.S. 315, 111 S.Ct. 1267, 113 L.Ed.2d 335 (1991). This last exception in § 2680(a)—the so-called "discretionary function" exception—will surely doom our hypothetical claim for damages for lost chickens. Enforcement decisions classically involve policy-laden exercises of discretion, and the FTCA fails to authorize liability even for abuses of such discretion. Unless we can find some other statute that waives the government's sovereign immunity for claims of this kind (and we cannot), we cannot recover damages from the United States government.

Can we avoid the bar of sovereign immunity by naming the agency rather than the United States as the defendant? Clearly not—or there would be no such thing as sovereign immunity. The agency is part of the United States, and suit against the agency therefore requires a congressional waiver of sovereign immunity.

What about suing the government officials who entered the warehouse and took the chickens? They probably do not have the world's deepest pockets, but perhaps they have bank accounts that can be attached or real property that can be sold at judicial auction to pay a judgment. Can we sue them in their *personal* capacities, just as we could sue our neighbor if he or she broke into our warehouse and destroyed our chickens?

In principle, the answer is (perhaps surprisingly) "Yes." A person is not immunized from legal liability simply by accepting employment with the federal government. That is clear enough when the conduct generating liability takes place when the employee is off-duty; a person's mere status as a government official does not provide any defense to a lawsuit. But what if the government employee is performing official governmental functions? If his or her action would be tortious if committed by a private party, does its official context immunize it from suit?

For nearly two centuries, the clear answer was (perhaps surprisingly) "No"—at least when the official in question was an executive official.[5] The rule was very simple: if an executive official's conduct was in fact authorized by a valid statute or regulation, then it could not be the basis for civil liability. But if there was no valid authorization, the official could

---

[5]   Legislative officials have *constitutional immunity* for their official acts. *See* U.S. Const. art. I, § 6, cl. 1. Federal judicial officials have traditionally enjoyed some degree of immunity for their official conduct, though the precise scope of that immunity was uncertain until 1871, when the Supreme Court crafted a sweeping rule of absolute judicial immunity from civil liability even for "malice and corruption in their action whilst exercising their judicial functions within the general scope of their jurisdiction." Bradley v. Fisher, 80 U.S. (13 Wall.) 335, 354, 20 L.Ed. 646 (1871).

be held liable even for a good-faith attempt to follow the law. A tort suit against the official was thus an excellent vehicle—and indeed the primary vehicle—for obtaining judicial review of the legality of agency action. In our hypothetical case of chicken destruction, for example, one would bring a state-law tort action for trespass and conversion against the agency officials who entered the warehouse, just as one would sue any thug who came onto one's property and carted away or destroyed chickens. The officials would respond, "We are not thugs; we are duly authorized agents of the United States government," and would introduce as proof the relevant statutes and regulations that purportedly authorized their conduct. The court would then have to determine whether the statutes or regulations, properly interpreted, in fact authorized the conduct in question. If the court determined that no statute or regulation actually authorized their conduct, then the government officials would stand before the law as private citizens. They could draw immunity from actual legal authorization, but not from status or position. Good faith would be a defense only if it was generally a defense to the applicable tort action.[6] And if the court concluded that there was actual statutory or regulatory authorization, the plaintiff could seek to "strip away" that authorization by arguing that the relevant statute or regulation was *unconstitutional*. If, for example, the government officials relied for their authorization on a statute that said, "Agents enforcing the poultry laws may conduct unreasonable searches and seizures," one could respond that the statute is in fact no authorization at all, because it is unconstitutional under the Fourth Amendment. An unconstitutional statute must be disregarded by a court, leaving the defendants with no authorization. In this fashion, a common-law tort suit could be the vehicle—and for many decades was the primary vehicle—for resolving important statutory and constitutional questions of agency authority. This form of review of agency action is aptly named "nonstatutory review," because the underlying cause of action against the agency official does not stem from a federal statute. It stems, rather, from state common law, or perhaps from a state statute establishing the applicable tort law. Federal statutes may well be involved in the case, especially if the agency officials offer legal authorization as a defense to the action, but the plaintiff in such a case does not rely on a federal statute as the basis for suit.[7]

But what about government officials who acted pursuant to ambiguous or invalid statutory authority? What if they acted in complete good faith? Indeed, what if their superiors ordered them to take action that turned out, in retrospect, to be unauthorized? Did they really have to choose between disobeying orders—including orders that people quite reasonably, even if

---

[6] Trespass and conversion are generally strict liability offenses, so the defendant's state of mind would be irrelevant in such actions.

[7] As we shall soon see, there are other forms of judicial review that are also, albeit less aptly, called "nonstatutory." *See infra* pages 1017–1018.

mistakenly, could readily have believed were justified—or risking personal liability in tort? The following remarkable case illustrates the answer that until very recently held sway.

LITTLE V. BARREME

Supreme Court of the United States, 1804.
6 U.S. (2 Cranch) 170, 2 L.Ed. 243.

* * *

MR. CHIEF JUSTICE MARSHALL delivered the opinion of the court.

The Flying Fish, a Danish vessel, having on board Danish and neutral property, was captured on the 2d of December 1799, on a voyage from Jeremie to St. Thomas's, by the United States frigate Boston, commanded by Captain Little, and brought into the port of Boston, where she was libelled as an American vessel that had violated the non-intercourse law.

The judge before whom the cause was tried, directed a restoration of the vessel and cargo as neutral property, but refused to award damages for the capture and detention, because, in his opinion, there was probable cause to suspect the vessel to be American.

On an appeal to the circuit court this sentence was reversed, because the Flying Fish was on a voyage from, not to, a French port, and was therefore, had she even been an American vessel, not liable to capture on the high seas.

During the hostilities between the United States and France, an act for the suspension of all intercourse between the two nations was annually passed. That under which the Flying Fish was condemned, declared every vessel, owned, hired or employed wholly or in part by an American, which should be employed in any traffic or commerce with or for any person resident within the jurisdiction or under the authority of the French Republic, to be forfeited together with her cargo; the one half to accrue to the United States, and the other to any person or persons, citizens of the United States, who will inform and prosecute for the same.

The fifth section of this act authorizes the president of the United States, to instruct the commanders of armed vessels, "to stop and examine any ship or vessel of the United States on the high sea, which there may be reason to suspect to be engaged in any traffic or commerce contrary to the true tenor of the act, and if upon examination it should appear that such ship or vessel is bound or sailing to any or place within the territory of the French republic or her dependencies, it is rendered lawful to seize such vessel, and send her into the United States for adjudication."

It is by no means clear that the president of the United States, whose high duty it is to "take care that the laws be faithfully executed," and who is commander in chief of the armies and navies of the United States, might not, without any special authority for that purpose, in the then existing state of things, have empowered the officers commanding the armed vessels of the United States, to seize and send into port for adjudication, American vessels which were forfeited by being engaged in this illicit commerce. But when it is observed that the general clause of the first section of the "act, which declares that such vessels may be seized, and may be prosecuted in any district or circuit court, which shall be holden within or for the district where the seizure shall be made," obviously contemplates a seizure within the United States; and that the fifth section gives a special authority to seize on the high seas, and limits that authority to the seizure of vessels bound or sailing to a French port, the legislature seem to have prescribed that the manner in which this law shall be carried into execution, was to exclude a seizure of any vessel not bound to a French port. Of consequence, however, strong the circumstances might be, which induced captain Little to suspect the Flying Fish to be an American vessel, they could not excuse the detention of her, since he would not have been authorized to detain her had she been really American.

It was so obvious, that if only vessels sailing to a French port could be seized on the high seas, that the law would be very often evaded, that this act of congress appears to have received a different construction from the executive of the United States; a construction much better calculated to give it effect.

A copy of this act was transmitted by the secretary of the navy to the captains of the armed vessels, who were ordered to consider the fifth section as a part of their instructions. The same letter contained the following clause. "A proper discharge of the important duties enjoined on you, arising out of this act, will require the exercise of a sound and an impartial judgment. You are not only to do all that in you lies, to prevent all intercourse, whether direct or circuitous, between the ports of the United States and those of France or her dependencies, where the vessels are apparently as well as really American, and protected by American papers only, but you are to be vigilant that vessels or cargoes really American, but covered by Danish or other foreign papers, and bound to or from French ports, do not escape you."

These orders, given by the executive under the construction of the act of congress made by the department to which its execution was assigned, enjoin the seizure of American vessels sailing from a French port. Is the officer who obeys them liable for damages sustained by this misconstruction of the act, or will his orders excuse him? If his instructions afford him no protection, then the law must take its course, and he must pay such damages as are legally awarded against him; if they excuse an act not otherwise excusable, it would then be necessary to inquire whether this is a case in which the probable cause which existed to induce a suspicion that the vessel was American, would excuse the captor from damages when the vessel appeared in fact to be neutral.

I confess the first bias of my mind was very strong in favour of the opinion that though the instructions of the executive could not give a right, they might yet excuse from damages. I was much inclined to think that a distinction ought to be taken between acts of civil and those of military officers; and between proceedings within the body of the country and those on the high seas. That implicit obedience which military men usually pay to the orders of their superiors, which indeed is indispensably necessary to every military system, appeared to me strongly to imply the principle that those orders, if not to perform a prohibited act, ought to justify the person whose general duty it is to obey them, and who is placed by the laws of his country in a situation which in general requires that he should obey them. I was strongly inclined to think that where, in consequence of orders from the legitimate authority, a vessel is seized with pure intention, the claim of the injured party for damages would be against that government from which the orders proceeded, and would be a proper subject for negotiation. But I have been convinced that I was mistaken, and I have receded from this first opinion. I acquiesce in that of my brethren, which is, that the instructions cannot change the nature of the transaction, or legalize an act which without those instructions would have been a plain trespass.

It becomes therefore unnecessary to inquire whether the probable cause afforded by the conduct of the Flying Fish to suspect her of being an American, would excuse Captain Little from damages for having seized and sent her into port, since had she actually been an American, the seizure would have been unlawful.

Captain Little then must be answerable in damages to the owner of this neutral vessel, and as the account taken by order of the circuit court is not objectionable on its face, and has not been excepted to by counsel before the proper tribunal, this court can receive no objection to it.

There appears then to be no error in the judgment of the circuit court, and it must be affirmed with costs.

NOTES

The doctrine of *Little v. Barreme* considerably softened the impact of sovereign immunity: the government itself could not be sued, but the offending government officials were liable as ordinary tortfeasors in the absence of valid legal authorization. In other words, under *Little* there might have been substantial *sovereign* immunity, but there was no *official* immunity. As long as the government conduct in question fell under a common-law cause of action and was not actually authorized, judicial relief (and, if raised, review of the legality of the agency action) was available.

So did Captain Little really have to pay damages out of his own pocket for obeying the orders of his commander in chief? The answer would have been "yes" if Congress had not bailed him out by passing a private bill indemnifying him for the damages. *See* Act for the Relief of George Little, ch. 4, 6 Stat. 63 (1807). Thus, despite the bar of sovereign immunity, Congress chose to let the United States government foot the bill. This kind of case-by-case indemnification by private bill was very common in the founding era. *See* James E. Pfander & Jonathan L. Hunt, *Public Wrongs and Private Bills: Indemnification and Government Accountability in the Early Republic*, 85 N.Y.U.L. Rev. 1862 (2010).

Several modern developments have almost totally transformed this remedial scheme. One development has already been sketched above: the federal government has waived its sovereign immunity in some important respects, so that an action is now available in some circumstances against the government. In addition to the Tucker Act and the FTCA, a 1976 amendment to the APA provides:

> An action in a court of the United States seeking relief other than money damages and stating a claim that an agency or an officer or employee thereof acted or failed to act in an official capacity or under color of legal authority shall not be dismissed nor relief therein be denied on the ground that it is against the United States or that the United States is an indispensable party. The United States may be named as a defendant in any such action, and a judgment or decree may be entered against the United States: Provided, That any mandatory or injunctive decree shall specify the Federal officer or officers (by name or by title), and their successors in office, personally responsible for compliance. Nothing herein (1) affects other limitations on judicial review or the power or duty of the court to dismiss any action or deny relief on any other appropriate legal or equitable ground; or (2) confers authority to grant relief if any other statute that grants consent to suit expressly or impliedly forbids the relief which is sought.

5 U.S.C. § 702 (2012).[8] Thus, as long as you are not seeking monetary relief, sovereign immunity is no longer generally a barrier to judicial review of federal agency action.[9] Because plaintiffs are often interested primarily in preventing

---

[8]   The statute's waiver of sovereign immunity does not serve also as a grant of jurisdiction to federal courts. One must still find a distinct statutory grant of jurisdiction for one's claim in order to bring it in federal court, but once jurisdiction is established, § 702 abolishes the government's (jurisdictional) defense of sovereign immunity.

[9]   Suppose that you seek to challenge the actions of an agency that administers a grant program. Your claim is that the agency has failed to comply with applicable statutes and regulations in denying your grant, and you seek a mandatory injunction ordering the agency to conduct its affairs in accordance with applicable law. Is this a claim for nonmonetary relief under § 702, or is it really a claim for money damages "founded * * * upon * * * any Act of Congress or any regulation" within the meaning of the Tucker Act? The answer determines, among other things, the forum in which suit must be brought: if the amount in controversy is more than $10,000, a Tucker Act suit must be brought in the Article I Court of Federal Claims, while a suit for nonmonetary relief will be brought in an Article III court.

or compelling certain kinds of agency action rather than in obtaining monetary redress for past harms, § 702 of the APA is the most important waiver of sovereign immunity for administrative lawyers.[10]

A second important development is the rise (and, to some extent, fall) of so-called *Bivens* actions against federal government officials. Civil damages actions against *state* officials for violations of federal constitutional rights are expressly authorized by 42 U.S.C. § 1983 (2012), but no comparable statute authorizes civil suits against *federal* officials for constitutional violations. Instead, the traditional avenue of relief was the common law tort action. Constitutional issues would arise only if the defendant raised legal authorization as a defense to the tort action. If the purportedly authorizing statute or regulation was unconstitutional, then the defense of legal authorization would fail.

The scope of modern constitutional protection, however, can exceed the reach of state tort law. For example, one can imagine action by federal law enforcement personnel that constitutes an unreasonable search or seizure under the Fourth Amendment but which does not constitute a trespass under local tort law (perhaps because there is a common law or statutory exception for law enforcement officials in the particular jurisdiction). In such a circumstance, can one bring a cause of action for damages directly under the Constitution, bypassing state tort law altogether as a source of liability? In 1971, in *Bivens v. Six Unknown Named Agents of the Federal Bureau of Narcotics*, 403 U.S. 388, 91 S.Ct. 1999, 29 L.Ed.2d 619 (1971), the Supreme Court held that a violation of the Fourth Amendment could itself constitute a valid cause of action for damages. Subsequent cases in the 1970s and early 1980s extended this doctrine to violations of the Fifth and Eighth Amendments. *See Carlson v. Green*, 446 U.S. 14, 100 S.Ct. 1468, 64 L.Ed.2d 15 (1980) (permitting *Bivens* actions under the Eighth Amendment's Cruel and Unusual Punishment Clause); *Davis v. Passman*, 442 U.S. 228, 99 S.Ct. 2264, 60 L.Ed.2d 846 (1979) (permitting *Bivens* actions under the Fifth Amendment's Due Process Clause). Thus, where agency action raises constitutional

---

Prior to 1988, it would have been very clear that this was an action under the Tucker Act. That year, however, the Supreme Court held (over a ferocious four-Justice dissent) in *Bowen v. Massachusetts*, 487 U.S. 879, 108 S.Ct. 2722, 101 L.Ed.2d 749 (1988), that the State of Massachusetts could sue the Department of Health and Human Services for Medicaid payments under § 702's waiver of sovereign immunity. If taken seriously, this decision could have substantially undermined traditional understandings about the allocation of jurisdiction between the Court of Federal Claims and the Article III courts. Suffice it to say that lower courts have not taken this decision very seriously. If money is involved, it is almost certain that the suit will be held to fall (if at all) under the Tucker Act's waiver of sovereign immunity rather than § 702's.

[10] Prior to 1976, one could often get around the sovereign immunity barrier in suits for nonmonetary relief by suing the official rather than the agency for an injunction. As long as the official's actions were not authorized, one could plausibly argue that one was not seeking to enjoin "the government" (which would raise sovereign immunity problems), but was merely seeking to enjoin the actions of a private citizen who happened also to work for the government. This led to immensely complicated arguments about what it means for an action to be "authorized" and when a suit against an official is "really" a suit against the government. *See* Antonin Scalia, *Sovereign Immunity and Nonstatutory Review of Federal Administrative Action: Some Conclusions from the Public-Lands Cases*, 68 Mich. L. Rev. 867 (1970). The 1976 amendment to § 702 mercifully did away with most of these machinations.

questions, one can, under *Bivens*, raise those questions directly in a federal damages action without having to find an applicable state-law cause of action.

The last four-plus decades, however, have seen a substantial narrowing of the *Bivens* doctrine. Justice Brennan's majority opinion in *Bivens* suggested (in dictum that he no doubt subsequently regretted) that a direct cause of action under the Constitution might be inappropriate if there were "special factors counselling hesitation in the absence of affirmative action by Congress," 403 U.S. at 396, 91 S.Ct. at 2004, or an "explicit congressional declaration that persons injured by a federal officer's violation * * * may not recover money damages from the agents, but must instead be remitted to another remedy, equally effective in the view of Congress," *id.* at 397, 91 S.Ct. at 2005. Both statements have blossomed into significant limitations on the scope of *Bivens* actions. The Supreme Court has found "special factors counselling hesitation" in virtually all circumstances involving the military, *see Chappell v. Wallace*, 462 U.S. 296, 103 S.Ct. 2362, 76 L.Ed.2d 586 (1983); *United States v. Stanley*, 483 U.S. 669, 107 S.Ct. 3054, 97 L.Ed.2d 550 (1987); and the Court has been adept at finding congressionally-prescribed alternatives to *Bivens* actions even when those alternatives were surely not viewed by Congress as "equally effective" remedies. *See, e.g., Schweiker v. Chilicky*, 487 U.S. 412, 108 S.Ct. 2460, 101 L.Ed.2d 370 (1988); *Bush v. Lucas*, 462 U.S. 367, 103 S.Ct. 2404, 76 L.Ed.2d 648 (1983). Despite these limitations, *Bivens* actions remain a potential avenue of judicial relief against unconstitutional agency action.

The third, and most important, modern development that has transformed the world of nonstatutory review is the rise of official immunity. *Little* described a world in which executive officials were immune from personal liability for their official actions only when there was actual legal authorization for their conduct. That regime began to erode slowly in the late nineteenth and early twentieth centuries. In *Bradley v. Fisher*, 80 U.S. (13 Wall.) 335, 20 L.Ed. 646 (1871), the Court crafted a rule of absolute immunity for judges acting within the scope of their jurisdiction. That absolute immunity was then extended to prosecutors and other executive officials for their participation in judicial proceedings. *See Yaselli v. Goff*, 275 U.S. 503, 48 S.Ct. 155, 72 L.Ed. 395 (1927) (summary affirmance). In addition, the Court held in *Spalding v. Vilas*, 161 U.S. 483, 16 S.Ct. 631, 40 L.Ed. 780 (1896), that the Postmaster General could not be sued for allegedly malicious use of his authorized powers. This result was not inevitable; a court could have said that every statutory authorization implicitly requires that exercises of authority not be malicious, so that malicious abuse of power would always be unauthorized within the meaning of *Little*. That was clearly the view of founding-era English administrative law, which assumed that all statutory grants of power came with an implicit requirement of reasonableness in execution. *See* Gary Lawson & Guy I. Seidman, *Necessity, Propriety, and Reasonableness, in* Gary Lawson, Geoffrey P. Miller, Robert G. Natelson & Guy I. Seidman, The Origins of the Necessary and Proper Clause 120, 121–25 (2010).

The definitive beginning of the end for the rule of *Little v. Barreme*, however, came in 1959. In *Barr v. Matteo*, 360 U.S. 564, 79 S.Ct. 1335, 3

L.Ed.2d 1434 (1959), the Court (albeit with no majority opinion) broadly immunized federal officials from suit for actions within the "outer perimeter" of their duties. The precise scope of the decision was unclear, but the terms of the debate had clearly changed. The issue was no longer *whether* to provide some level of immunity for government officials, but *how much* immunity to provide.

Through a story too long to tell here, modern law has (at least for now) finally settled on what is typically called *qualified immunity* as the norm for government officials performing executive functions (with absolute immunity applying to executive officials in the performance of judicial or judicial-like functions). As the Court explained in its leading decision on the subject:

> Even if they cannot establish that their official functions require absolute immunity, petitioners assert that public policy at least mandates an application of the qualified immunity standard that would permit the defeat of insubstantial claims without resort to trial. We agree.

A

The resolution of immunity questions inherently requires a balance between the evils inevitable in any available alternative. In situations of abuse of office, an action for damages may offer the only realistic avenue for vindication of constitutional guarantees. It is this recognition that has required the denial of absolute immunity to most public officers. At the same time, however, it cannot be disputed seriously that claims frequently run against the innocent as well as the guilty—at a cost not only to the defendant officials, but to society as a whole. These social costs include the expenses of litigation, the diversion of official energy from pressing public issues, and the deterrence of able citizens from acceptance of public office. Finally, there is the danger that fear of being sued will "dampen the ardor of all but the most resolute, or the most irresponsible [public officials], in the unflinching discharge of their duties." *Gregoire v. Biddle*, 177 F.2d 579, 581 (C.A.2 1949), cert. denied, 339 U.S. 949, 70 S.Ct. 803, 94 L.Ed. 1363 (1950).

* * *

B

Qualified or "good faith" immunity is an affirmative defense that must be pleaded by a defendant official. Decisions of this Court have established that the "good faith" defense has both an "objective" and a "subjective" aspect. The objective element involves a presumptive knowledge of and respect for "basic, unquestioned constitutional rights." *Wood v. Strickland*, 420 U.S. 308, 322, 95 S.Ct. 992, 1001, 43 L.Ed.2d 214 (1975). The subjective component refers to "permissible intentions." *Ibid*. Characteristically the Court has defined these elements by identifying the circumstances in which qualified immunity would not be available. Referring both to the objective and subjective elements, we have held that qualified immunity would be defeated if an official *"knew or reasonably should have known* that the action he took within his sphere of official responsibility would violate the constitutional rights of the [plaintiff], *or* if he took the action *with the malicious intention* to cause a deprivation of constitutional rights or other injury. . ." *Ibid.* (emphasis added).

The subjective element of the good-faith defense frequently has proved incompatible with our admonition in *Butz* [*v. Economou*, 438 U.S. 478 (1978),] that insubstantial claims should not proceed to trial. Rule 56 of the Federal Rules of Civil Procedure provides that disputed questions of fact ordinarily may not be decided on motions for summary judgment. And an official's subjective good faith has been considered to be a question of fact that some courts have regarded as inherently requiring resolution by a jury.

In the context of *Butz'* attempted balancing of competing values, it now is clear that substantial costs attend the litigation of the subjective good faith of government officials. Not only are there the general costs of subjecting officials to the risks of trial—distraction of officials from their governmental duties, inhibition of discretionary action, and deterrence of able people from public service. There are special costs to "subjective" inquiries of this kind. Immunity generally is available only to officials performing discretionary functions. In contrast with the thought processes accompanying "ministerial" tasks, the judgments surrounding discretionary action almost inevitably are influenced by the decisionmaker's experiences, values, and emotions. These variables explain in part why questions of subjective intent so rarely can be decided by summary judgment. Yet they also frame a background in which there often is no clear end to the relevant evidence. Judicial inquiry into subjective motivation therefore may entail broad-ranging discovery and the deposing of numerous persons, including an official's professional colleagues. Inquiries of this kind can be peculiarly disruptive of effective government.

Consistently with the balance at which we aimed in *Butz*, we conclude today that bare allegations of malice should not suffice to subject government officials either to the costs of trial or to the burdens of broad-reaching discovery. We therefore hold that government officials performing discretionary functions generally are shielded from liability for civil damages insofar as their conduct does not violate clearly established statutory or constitutional rights of which a reasonable person would have known.

Reliance on the objective reasonableness of an official's conduct, as measured by reference to clearly established law, should avoid excessive disruption of government and permit the resolution of many insubstantial claims on summary judgment. On summary judgment, the judge appropriately may determine, not only the currently applicable law, but whether that law was clearly established at the time an action occurred. If the law at that time was not clearly established, an official could not reasonably be expected to anticipate subsequent legal developments, nor could he fairly be said to "know" that the law forbade conduct not previously identified as unlawful. Until this threshold immunity question is resolved, discovery should not be allowed. If the law was clearly established, the immunity defense ordinarily should fail, since a reasonably competent public official should know the law governing his conduct. Nevertheless, if the official pleading the defense claims extraordinary circumstances and can prove that he neither knew nor should have known of the relevant legal standard, the defense should be sustained. But again, the defense would turn primarily on objective factors.

Harlow v. Fitzgerald, 457 U.S. 800, 813–19, 102 S.Ct. 2727, 2735–39, 73 L.Ed.2d 396 (1982).

Harlow is obviously a far distance from *Little v. Barreme*. Modern immunity doctrines do not, of course, eliminate tort actions as a vehicle for judicial review of agency action, but they do make them far less effective than is often desired. After all, courts will generally decide only whether the defendant violated "clearly established" law; this frequently will neither require nor entail determination of whether the agency action in question was or was not actually unlawful. *See, e.g., Reichle v. Howards*, 566 U.S. 658, 132 S.Ct. 2088, 182 L.Ed.2d 985 (2012).

There is one respect in which executive officials enjoy a form of absolute immunity from tort liability. By virtue of a federal statute enacted in 1988, common law tort actions can no longer be brought against federal employees in their individual capacities. Instead, an action against the United States under the FTCA is the exclusive remedy. *See* 28 U.S.C. § 2679(b)(1) (2012).[11]

b. Statutory "Nonstatutory" Review

A variety of mechanisms for obtaining judicial review generally go under the heading of "nonstatutory" review even though they are grounded firmly in federal statutes. These mechanisms most notably include requests for actions in the nature of mandamus, *see id.* § 1361,[12] for declaratory judgments, *see id.* § 2201, for writs of habeas corpus, *see id.*

---

[11] Does the statute bar a common law tort action against the individual officer even if the tort comes within one of the exceptions to the FTCA, so that an action against the United States is not in fact available? The Supreme Court says yes. *See* United States v. Smith, 499 U.S. 160, 111 S.Ct. 1180, 113 L.Ed.2d 134 (1991).

[12] The awkward formulation "action in the nature of mandamus" is necessary because the Federal Rules of Civil Procedure formally abolished the writ of mandamus. See Fed. R. Civ. Proc. 81(b). The "action in the nature of mandamus," however, generally follows the legal rules that previously governed actions for mandamus.

§§ 2241–55, and for injunctions. Although these actions are generally based on statutes,[13] the relevant statutes are not targeted specifically at review of federal agency action but instead govern the operation of federal courts in general. Accordingly, administrative lawyers typically describe them (occasionally with a mildly apologetic tone) as forms of "nonstatutory" review. There is authority suggesting that such review is available only when agencies have very clearly exceeded their authority. *See Trudeau v. FTC*, 456 F.3d 178, 189–90 (D.C.Cir.2006).

2. GENERAL STATUTORY REVIEW

Federal courts, unlike many of their state counterparts, are courts of limited jurisdiction. No lower federal court can hear a case unless (1) the Constitution brings the case within the jurisdictional competence of the federal courts as a whole, *see* U.S. Const. art. III, § 2, and (2) Congress has passed a statute authorizing the court in question to hear the case, *see Sheldon v. Sill*, 49 U.S. (8 How.) 441, 12 L.Ed. 1147 (1850). Because challenges to federal agency action almost always involve construction of at least one statute or constitutional provision, there is an obvious route past this jurisdictional threshold: the Constitution extends the federal judicial power to "all Cases, in Law and Equity, arising under the Constitution, the Laws of the United States, and Treaties made, or which shall be made, under their Authority," U.S. Const. art. III, § 2, cl. 1, and Congress has vested the federal district courts with jurisdiction over "all civil actions arising under the Constitution, laws or treaties of the United States." 28 U.S.C. § 1331 (2012). Accordingly, one possible form of judicial review of federal agency action is a civil action in district court pursuant to 1331—provided only that we can find an applicable cause of action.

Such an action is provided in very general terms by the APA. Section 704 of the APA provides that "[a]gency action made reviewable by statute and final agency action for which there is no other adequate remedy in a court are subject to judicial review." 5 U.S.C. § 704 (2012). The APA thus provides a residual action for judicial review of agency action: if no other source of law authorizes a judicial remedy, § 704 fills the gap. Section 704, however, merely creates a cause of action. It does not waive sovereign immunity or otherwise confer jurisdiction on federal courts. A suit under § 704 can be maintained only if another statute—most likely 28 U.S.C. § 1331—provides jurisdiction in a federal court and if yet another statute— most likely 5 U.S.C. § 702—waives sovereign immunity to permit suit.

The APA also prescribes the form and venue of suits for judicial review of agency action:

---

[13] The question whether actions for injunction similarly must be grounded in statute is best left to courses in Remedies or Federal Courts. For the leading case involving this form of review, see *American School of Magnetic Healing v. McAnnulty*, 187 U.S. 94, 23 S.Ct. 33, 47 L.Ed. 90 (1902).

> The form of proceeding for judicial review is the special statutory review proceeding relevant to the subject matter in a court specified by statute or, in the absence or inadequacy thereof, any applicable form of legal action, including actions for declaratory judgments or writs of prohibitory or mandatory injunction or habeas corpus, in a court of competent jurisdiction. If no special statutory review proceeding is applicable, the action for judicial review may be brought against the United States, the agency by its official title, or the appropriate officer. Except to the extent that prior, adequate, and exclusive opportunity for judicial review is provided by law, agency action is subject to judicial review in civil or criminal proceedings for judicial enforcement.

5 U.S.C. § 703 (2012). In other words: use whatever works. If the "applicable form of legal action" is an action for review under § 704, such action can be brought in any "court of competent jurisdiction." Because the jurisdictional basis for such an action will almost always be 28 U.S.C. § 1331, this means that § 704 actions will normally be brought in federal district court. Proper venue is determined by the general venue provisions of 28 U.S.C. § 1391. And if the agency invokes court processes to enforce its decisions, judicial review is normally available in those enforcement proceedings.[14]

Judicial review under § 704 is typically called "general statutory review," because it is authorized by a statute that is targeted at agency action but applies generally to all agency action that is not handled by other sources of law.

3. SPECIAL STATUTORY REVIEW

Section 703 of the APA provides for general statutory review of agency action only in the event of the "absence or inadequacy" of any "special statutory review proceeding relevant to the subject matter in a court specified by statute * * *." 5 U.S.C. § 703 (2012). What is a "special statutory review proceeding"?

Quite simply, it is any statutory provision authorizing judicial review of agency action that is targeted specifically at a particular agency or subject matter. Most modern organic statutes contain special review provisions (which are usually called "special review statutes," even though they are normally part of a larger statutory scheme rather than stand-alone statutes), in which Congress specifies the precise form and timing of judicial review of particular kinds of agency action. For example, section 6 of the Occupational Safety and Health Act of 1970 (OSH Act), which was

---

[14] For the special problems that arise when statutes seek to cut off this avenue of judicial review, *see infra* pages 1188–1191.

at issue in the *Industrial Union* case that is presented in Chapter 2,[15] provides with respect to standards for workplace exposure to toxic substances:

> Any person who may be adversely affected by a standard issued under this section may at any time prior to the sixtieth day after such standard is promulgated file a petition challenging the validity of such standard with the United States court of appeals for the circuit wherein such person resides or has his principal place of business, for a judicial review of such standard. A copy of the petition shall be forthwith transmitted by the clerk of the court to the Secretary. The filing of such petition shall not, unless otherwise ordered by the court, operate as a stay of the standard. The determinations of the Secretary shall be conclusive if supported by substantial evidence in the record considered as a whole.

29 U.S.C. § 655(f) (2012). This provision is typical of modern special review statutes in at least two important respects. First, it provides that petitions for review must be made "prior to the sixtieth day after such standard is promulgated." This requirement that review actions be brought within a relatively short time frame after promulgation of a challenged agency rule is a common feature in today's world and is discussed in more detail later in this chapter.[16] Second, the statute calls for review in an appropriate "United States court of appeals" rather than in a district court. This too is a common, though not universal, feature of modern administrative review: review of most important agency action, especially rulemaking action, takes place initially in a court of appeals.[17]

The OSH Act identifies as well the appropriate venue for challenges to standards promulgated under § 6(b)(5): "the circuit wherein such person resides or has his principal place of business." Suppose, however, that a manufacturer whose principal place of business is in Chicago and a union headquartered in Denver both object to an OSHA standard for toxic substances—the employer because the standard is too strict and the union because the standard is too lenient. Suppose further that the manufacturer and union both believe that the Seventh Circuit will be more hospitable to the industry's challenge than will the Tenth Circuit. Within sixty days after promulgation of the standard, the manufacturer petitions for review in the Seventh Circuit and the union petitions for review in the Tenth Circuit. Which court will hear the case?

---

[15] *See supra* pages 127–154.

[16] *See infra* pages 1188–1191.

[17] A good deal of agency adjudication is reviewed initially in a court of appeals as well, though much adjudication, especially by the Social Security Administration, is initially appealed to district courts. *See* 42 U.S.C. §§ 405(g), 421(d) (2012).

Until fairly recently, venue in such cases was determined by a "first filing" rule: whichever court first received a valid petition for review would have exclusive jurisdiction over the appeal. This often led to a "race to the courthouse," as litigants who thought that various courts would be more favorably inclined to their interests scrambled to insure that review of important agency action took place in a "friendly" forum. For a near-comical illustration of the lengths to which parties would sometimes go to secure a desired forum, see *City of Gallup v. FERC*, 702 F.2d 1116 (D.C.Cir.1983). In 1988, Congress amended the venue statute, 28 U.S.C. § 2112(a) (2012), to avoid any "race to the courthouse" shenanigans. Section 2112(a) now provides that jurisdiction will be determined by random lot among all courts in which valid petitions were filed within ten days of the issuance of the agency decision in question.

One unique statute straddles the line between general and special review. The Administrative Orders Review Act, 28 U.S.C. §§ 2341–51 (2012), popularly known as the Hobbs Act, specifies in considerable detail the form, timing, and venue of appeals from certain decisions of a selected group of agencies.[18] Those agencies' organic statutes may also contain special review provisions that supplement the Hobbs Act.

B. "WHETHER": PRECLUSION OF JUDICIAL REVIEW

Some form of judicial review of agency action—whether pursuant to special statutory, general statutory, or nonstatutory review doctrines—will almost always be available. The APA notes, however, that its provisions on judicial review do not apply "to the extent that—(1) statutes preclude judicial review; or (2) agency action is committed to agency discretion by law." 5 U.S.C. § 701(a) (2012). There are some circumstances, in other words, in which judicial review of particular agency action will be unavailable.

1. EXPRESS PRECLUSION

Section 701(a)(1)'s reference to circumstances in which "statutes preclude judicial review" seems straightforward: if Congress provides by

---

[18] An "agency" under the statute is:

"(A)   the Commission, when the order sought to be reviewed was entered by the Federal Communications Commission, the Federal Maritime Commission, or the Atomic Energy Commission [now called the Nuclear Regulatory Commission], as the case may be;

"(B)   the Secretary, when the order was entered by the Secretary of Agriculture or the Secretary of Transportation;

"(C)   the Administration, when the order was entered by the Maritime Administration;

"(D)   the Secretary, when the order is under section 812 of the Fair Housing Act; and

"(E)   the Board, when the order was entered by the Surface Transportation Board."

28 U.S.C. § 2341 (2012).

statute that judicial review is unavailable, that is the end of the matter. In principle, one must merely read the relevant statutes to see whether they indeed instruct courts to keep their hands off the administrative enterprise. In practice, things are much messier.

Consider, for example, a 1952 statute providing that deportation orders of the Attorney General shall be "final." A 1917 version of the same statute, employing exactly the same language, had been construed by the Supreme Court to preclude judicial review of deportation orders through any means other than habeas corpus. *See Heikkila v. Barber*, 345 U.S. 229, 73 S.Ct. 603, 97 L.Ed. 972 (1953). Nonetheless, in 1955 the Supreme Court held that the language of this statute was insufficient to preclude judicial review of deportation orders under the APA. *See Shaughnessy v. Pedreiro*, 349 U.S. 48, 75 S.Ct. 591, 99 L.Ed. 868 (1955). The Court reasoned that "[s]uch a restrictive construction of the finality provision" would be inconsistent with the APA's "purpose * * * to remove obstacles to judicial review of agency action under subsequently enacted statutes like the 1952 Immigration Act." Accordingly, the Court held, "[i]t is more in harmony with the generous review provisions of the Administrative Procedure Act to construe the ambiguous word 'final' in the 1952 Immigration Act as referring to finality in administrative procedure rather than as cutting off the right of judicial review in whole or in part. And it would certainly not be in keeping with either of these Acts to require a person ordered deported to go to jail in order to obtain review by a court." *Id.* at 51, 75 S.Ct. at 594.

The philosophy expressed in *Pedreiro* has generally prevailed to this day. Cases have repeatedly emphasized that the APA embodies a "presumption of judicial review" that is overcome only when there is "persuasive reason to believe that such was the purpose of Congress." *Abbott Laboratories v. Gardner*, 387 U.S. 136, 140, 87 S.Ct. 1507, 1510, 18 L.Ed.2d 681 (1967).

Nothing better illustrates this principle than the strange saga of the veterans benefits statutes. An extensive set of statutes, administered by the Department of Veterans' Affairs (formerly known as the Veterans' Administration), provides benefits to military veterans under often elaborate eligibility criteria. Congress envisioned the Department of Veterans' Affairs as an ally, not an adversary, of veterans seeking benefits and thus sought to "dejudicialize" the process as much as possible. For example, from 1864 until 1988, Congress prohibited any attorney, under pain of criminal penalties, from receiving a fee of more than $10 for representing veterans in claims proceedings before the Department of Veterans' Affairs.[19] In keeping with this "dejudicialization" philosophy,

---

[19] This provision was upheld against a due process challenge in 1985. *See* Walters v. National Ass'n of Radiation Survivors, 473 U.S. 305, 105 S.Ct. 3180, 87 L.Ed.2d 220 (1985). In 1988, the statute was amended to permit reasonable fees that cannot exceed 20 percent of the amount recovered. *See* 38 U.S.C. § 5904(c), (d) (2012).

Congress sought to minimize the involvement of the federal courts in veterans benefits decisions. Perhaps aware of the fate awaiting statutes declaring merely that administrative decisions are "final," Congress in 1957 (drawing on similar statutes dating back to 1933) specified that

> the decisions of the Administrator on any question of law or fact concerning a claim for benefits or payments under any law administered by the Veterans' Administration shall be final and conclusive and no other official or any court of the United States shall have power or jurisdiction to review any such decision.

38 U.S.C. § 211(a) (1964).

Before you conclude that this language was needless overkill, consider that almost immediately after § 211(a)'s enactment, the D.C. Circuit construed it to preclude review only of attempts by veterans to *obtain* benefits and not of decisions by the Veterans' Administration to *terminate* previously-granted benefits. *See Wellman v. Whittier*, 259 F.2d 163 (D.C.Cir.1958). As a subsequent D.C. Circuit decision deadpanned, "[i]f Congress had intended § 211(a) to apply to termination of previously awarded benefits, as well as to claims, it could easily have so provided." *Tracy v. Gleason*, 379 F.2d 469, 473 (D.C.Cir.1967).

Congress took the hint and so provided. In 1970, § 211(a) was amended to read:

> the decisions of the Administrator on any question of law or fact under any law administered by the Veterans' Administration providing benefits for veterans and their dependents or survivors shall be final and conclusive and no other official or any court of the United States shall have power or jurisdiction to review any such decision by an action in the nature of mandamus or otherwise.

38 U.S.C. § 211(a) (1970).

The seeds of destruction for this amendment, however, were sown in 1974 in *Johnson v. Robison*, 415 U.S. 361, 94 S.Ct. 1160, 39 L.Ed.2d 389 (1974). Military draftees who claim conscientious objector status and satisfy their draft obligations through civilian service are (unambiguously) declared ineligible for veterans benefits by the applicable statutes. *See* 38 U.S.C. §§ 1652(a)(1), 1661(a) (2012). Robison was denied benefits for this reason and sought to challenge the statutory classification on various constitutional grounds. The Court held that § 211(a) did not bar federal court review of the constitutionality of the veterans benefits statutes.

> We consider first appellants' contention that § 211(a) bars federal courts from deciding the constitutionality of veterans' benefits legislation. Such a construction would, of course, raise serious questions concerning the constitutionality of § 211(a), and

in such case "it is a cardinal principle that this Court will first ascertain whether a construction of the statute is fairly possible by which the [constitutional] question[s] may be avoided." *United States v. Thirty-Seven (37) Photographs*, 402 U.S. 363, 369, 91 S.Ct. 1400, 1404, 28 L.Ed.2d 822 (1971).

Plainly, no explicit provision of § 211(a) bars judicial consideration of appellee's constitutional claims * * *. The prohibitions would appear to be aimed at review only of those decisions of law or fact that arise in the *administration* by the Veterans' Administration of a *statute* providing benefits for veterans. A decision of law or fact "under" a statute is made by the Administrator in the interpretation or application of a particular provision of the statute to a particular set of facts. Appellee's constitutional challenge is not to any such decision of the *Administrator*, but rather to a decision of *Congress* to create a statutory class entitled to benefits that does not include I—O conscientious objectors who performed alternative civilian service * * *.

This construction is also supported by the administrative practice of the Veterans' Administration * * * [which] accepts and follows the principle that "[a]djudication of the constitutionality of congressional enactments has generally been thought beyond the jurisdiction of administrative agencies." *Oestereich v. Selective Service Board*, 393 U.S. 233, 242, 89 S.Ct. 414, 419, 21 L.Ed.2d 402 (1968) (Harlan, J., concurring in result).

Nor does the legislative history accompanying the 1970 amendment of § 211(a) demonstrate a congressional intention to bar judicial review even of constitutional questions. No-review clauses similar to § 211(a) have been a part of veterans' benefits legislation since 1933. While the legislative history accompanying these precursor no-review clauses is almost nonexistent, the Administrator, in a letter written in 1952 in connection with a revision of the clause under consideration by the Subcommittee of the House Committee on Veterans' Affairs, comprehensively explained the policies necessitating the no-review clause and identified two primary purposes: (1) to insure that veterans' benefits claims will not burden the courts and the Veterans' Administration with expensive and time-consuming litigation, and (2) to insure that the technical and complex determinations and applications of Veterans' Administration policy connected with veterans' benefits decisions will be adequately and uniformly made.

* * *

* * * Nothing whatever in the legislative history of the 1970 amendment, or predecessor no-review clauses, suggests any congressional intent to preclude judicial cognizance of constitutional challenges to veterans' benefits legislation. Such challenges obviously do not contravene the purposes of the no-review clause, for they cannot be expected to burden the courts by their volume, nor do they involve technical considerations of Veterans' Administration policy. We therefore conclude * * * [that] neither the text nor the scant legislative history of § 211(a) provides the "clear and convincing" evidence of congressional intent required by this Court before a statute will be construed to restrict access to judicial review.

415 U.S. at 366–70, 373–74, 94 S.Ct. at 1165–67, 1168–69. *Robison*'s reasoning is quite persuasive, even without invoking any presumptions (constitutionally based or otherwise) in favor of judicial review: it is difficult to classify as a "decision[ ] of the Administrator" something that the Administrator openly says that he or she has no power to decide. A great many lower courts, however, took *Robison* to stand for the much broader proposition that § 211(a) applied only to "interpretation or application of a particular provision of the statute to a particular set of facts," that is, to agency adjudications. Accordingly, these courts almost uniformly held that § 211(a) did not bar judicial consideration of the validity of agency *regulations* issued under the veterans statutes. Indeed, only one federal court held that § 211(a) precluded judicial review of Veterans' Administration regulations. Ironically, it was the D.C. Circuit, in an opinion authored by then-Judge Scalia. *See Gott v. Walters*, 756 F.2d 902 (D.C.Cir.1985). Even this holding was short-lived: The en banc court voted to vacate the panel opinion and rehear the case, but the suit was dismissed on a joint motion of the parties before a decision on the scope of § 211(a) could issue. *See Gott v. Walters*, 791 F.2d 172 (D.C.Cir.1985).

The saga ended in 1988. First, the Supreme Court held in *Traynor v. Turnage*, 485 U.S. 535, 108 S.Ct. 1372, 99 L.Ed.2d 618 (1988), that § 211(a) did not bar judicial consideration of whether Veterans' Administration regulations violated the Rehabilitation Act of 1973. Then, Congress once more amended the veterans' benefits statutes—this time surrendering to the inevitable. The 1988 statute created an Article I Court of Veterans Appeals to hear appeals from decisions of the (now re-named) Department of Veterans Affairs, with limited review available in the Federal Circuit (which also has power directly to review Department of Veterans Affairs regulations).

The moral of this story is that preclusion of review is not as simple a matter as it might seem. The saga of the veterans' benefits statutes is extreme, but not entirely atypical; courts will often strain mightily to avoid giving preclusive statutes their full effect. For example, the statute governing benefits decisions by the Secretary of Labor under the Federal Employees Compensation Act provides that the Secretary's decisions are "(1) final and conclusive for all purposes and with respect to all questions of law and fact; and (2) not subject to review by another official of the United States or by a court by mandamus or otherwise." 5 U.S.C. § 8128(b) (2012). A panel of the D.C. Circuit held that this statute did not preclude review of constitutional issues raised by benefits decisions. *See Lepre v. Department of Labor*, 275 F.3d 59, 64–68 (D.C.Cir.2001). Judge Silberman concurred in the judgment only because he "doubt[ed] that the Supreme Court has left us any principled ground upon which a Court of Appeals judge can honor a congressional preclusion of review of a constitutional claim." *See id.* at 75 (Silberman, J., concurring).

As *Lepre* suggests, overhanging the issue of preclusion are serious doubts whether the Constitution permits Congress entirely to preclude consideration of claims, especially constitutional claims. Even when courts give seemingly straightforward effect to preclusion statutes (as they do on occasion), they carve out exceptions for constitutional claims. *See, e.g., Cuozzo Speed Technologies, LLC v. Lee*, 136 S.Ct. 2131, 2141, 195 L.Ed.2d 423 (2016).

2.   IMPLIED PRECLUSION

One might think that if courts are reluctant to give effect to statutes that *expressly* preclude judicial review, they would never, or almost never, find that statutes *implicitly* preclude review. And indeed, for many years the category of "implied preclusion of review" was virtually an empty set. The lone significant exception was *Switchmen's Union v. National Mediation Board*, 320 U.S. 297, 64 S.Ct. 95, 88 L.Ed. 61 (1943)—a case whose context (contentious disputes about which union was the proper representative of employees) and timing (the very height of post-New Deal judicial deference to agencies) made it something of a purple cow. The Court's oft-repeated requirement that one must find "clear and convincing" evidence of congressional intent to preclude review made implied preclusion almost impossible by definition.

And so it was until 1984.

BLOCK v. COMMUNITY NUTRITION INST.

Supreme Court of the United States, 1984.
467 U.S. 340, 104 S.Ct. 2450, 81 L.Ed.2d 270.

JUSTICE O'CONNOR delivered the opinion of the Court.

This case presents the question whether ultimate consumers of dairy products may obtain judicial review of milk market orders issued by the Secretary of Agriculture (Secretary) under the authority of the Agricultural Marketing Agreement Act of 1937 (Act), ch. 296, 50 Stat. 246, as amended,

7 U.S.C. § 601 *et seq.* We conclude that consumers may not obtain judicial review of such orders.

I

A

In the early 1900's, dairy farmers engaged in intense competition in the production of fluid milk products. To bring this destabilizing competition under control, the 1937 Act authorizes the Secretary to issue milk market orders setting the minimum prices that handlers (those who process dairy products) must pay to producers (dairy farmers) for their milk products. The "essential purpose [of this milk market order scheme is] to raise producer prices," S.Rep. No. 1011, 74th Cong., 1st Sess., 3 (1935), and thereby to ensure that the benefits and burdens of the milk market are fairly and proportionately shared by all dairy farmers.

Under the scheme established by Congress, the Secretary must conduct an appropriate rulemaking proceeding before issuing a milk market order * * *. Moreover, before any market order may become effective, it must be approved by the handlers of at least 50% of the volume of milk covered by the proposed order and at least two-thirds of the affected dairy producers in the region. 7 U.S.C. §§ 608c(8), 608c(5)(B)(i). If the handlers withhold their consent, the Secretary may nevertheless impose the order. But the Secretary's power to do so is conditioned upon at least two-thirds of the producers consenting to its promulgation and upon his making an administrative determination that the order is "the only practical means of advancing the interests of the producers." 7 U.S.C. § 608c(9)(B).

The Secretary currently has some 45 milk market orders in effect. Each order covers a different region of the country, and collectively they cover most, though not all, of the United States. The orders divide dairy products into separately priced classes based on the uses to which raw milk is put. Raw milk that is processed and bottled for fluid consumption is termed "Class I" milk. Raw milk that is used to produce milk products such as butter, cheese, or dry milk powder is termed "Class II" milk.

For a variety of economic reasons, fluid milk products would command a higher price than surplus milk products in a perfectly functioning market. Accordingly, the Secretary's milk market orders require handlers to pay a higher order price for Class I products than for Class II products. To discourage destabilizing competition among producers for the more desirable fluid milk sales, the orders also require handlers to submit their payments for either class of milk to a regional pool. Administrators of these regional pools are then charged with distributing to dairy farmers a weighted average price for each milk product they have produced, irrespective of its use.

In particular, the Secretary has regulated the price of "reconstituted milk"—that is, milk manufactured by mixing milk powder with water—since 1964. The Secretary's orders assume that handlers will use reconstituted milk to manufacture surplus milk products. Handlers are therefore required to pay only the lower Class II minimum price. However, handlers are required to make a "compensatory payment" on any portion of the reconstituted milk that their records show has not been used to manufacture surplus milk products. The compensatory payment is equal to the difference between the Class I and Class II milk product prices. Handlers make these payments to the regional pool, from which moneys are then distributed to producers of fresh fluid milk in the region where the reconstituted milk was manufactured and sold.

B

In December 1980, respondents brought suit in District Court, contending that the compensatory payment requirement makes reconstituted milk uneconomical for handlers to process.[2] Respondents, as plaintiffs in the District Court, included three individual consumers of fluid dairy products, a handler regulated by the market orders, and a nonprofit organization. The District Court concluded that the consumers and the nonprofit organization did not have standing to challenge the market orders. In addition, it found that Congress had intended by the Act to preclude such persons from obtaining judicial review * * *.

The Court of Appeals * * * agreed that the milk handler and the nonprofit organization had been properly dismissed by the District Court. But the court concluded that the individual consumers had standing * * * [and] that the statutory structure and purposes of the Act did not reveal "the type of clear and convincing evidence of congressional intent needed to overcome the presumption in favor of judicial review" * * *.

* * *

II

Respondents filed this suit under the Administrative Procedure Act (APA), 5 U.S.C. § 701 et seq. The APA confers a general cause of action upon persons "adversely affected or aggrieved by agency action within the meaning of a relevant statute," 5 U.S.C. § 702, but withdraws that cause of

---

[2] Prior to filing suit, respondents petitioned the Secretary to hold a rulemaking hearing to amend the market orders so that reconstituted milk would no longer be subject to the compensatory payment rule. See 44 Fed.Reg. 65989 (1979). The Secretary published a Notice of Request and asked for comments. *Ibid.* Subsequently, the Secretary published a preliminary impact analysis of the proposal and invited comments. See 45 Fed.Reg. 75956 (1980). In April 1981, after respondents had filed suit in the District Court, the Secretary determined not to hold a rulemaking hearing because respondents' proposal would not further the purposes of the Act. See App. 5763. The portion of respondents' complaint challenging the Secretary's inaction on their rulemaking request was held moot by the Court of Appeals. 225 U.S.App.D.C. 387, 403, and n. 93, 698 F.2d 1239, 1255, and n. 93 (1983). Respondents did not cross-petition for certiorari review of this issue, and we therefore have no occasion to consider it.

action to the extent the relevant statute "preclude[s] judicial review," 5 U.S.C. § 701(a)(1). Whether and to what extent a particular statute precludes judicial review is determined not only from its express language, but also from the structure of the statutory scheme, its objectives, its legislative history, and the nature of the administrative action involved * * *.

It is clear that Congress did not intend to strip the judiciary of all authority to review the Secretary's milk market orders * * *. Section 608c(15) requires [dairy] handlers first to exhaust the administrative remedies made available by the Secretary. After these formal administrative remedies have been exhausted, handlers may obtain judicial review of the Secretary's ruling in the federal district court in any district "in which [they are] inhabitant[s], or ha[ve their] principal place[s] of business." 7 U.S.C. § 608c(15)(B). These provisions for handler-initiated review make evident Congress' desire that *some* persons be able to obtain judicial review of the Secretary's market orders.

The remainder of the statutory scheme, however, makes equally clear Congress' intention to limit the classes entitled to participate in the development of market orders. The Act contemplates a cooperative venture among the Secretary, handlers, and producers the principal purposes of which are to raise the price of agricultural products and to establish an orderly system for marketing them. Handlers and producers—but not consumers—are entitled to participate in the adoption and retention of market orders. The Act provides for agreements among the Secretary, producers, and handlers, for hearings among them, and for votes by producers and handlers. Nowhere in the Act, however, is there an express provision for participation by consumers in any proceeding. In a complex scheme of this type, the omission of such a provision is sufficient reason to believe that Congress intended to foreclose consumer participation in the regulatory process.

* * *

Respondents would have us believe that, while Congress unequivocally directed handlers first to complain to the Secretary that the prices set by milk market orders are too high, it was nevertheless the legislative judgment that the same challenge, if advanced by consumers, does not require initial administrative scrutiny * * *. Had Congress intended to allow consumers to attack provisions of marketing orders, it surely would have required them to pursue the administrative remedies provided in § 608c(15)(A) as well. The restriction of the administrative remedy to handlers strongly suggests that Congress intended a similar restriction of judicial review of market orders.

Allowing consumers to sue the Secretary would severely disrupt this complex and delicate administrative scheme. It would provide handlers with a convenient device for evading the statutory requirement that they first exhaust their administrative remedies. A handler may also be a consumer and, as such, could sue in that capacity. Alternatively, a handler would need only to find a consumer who is willing to join in or initiate an action in the district court. The consumer or consumer-handler could then raise precisely the same exceptions that the handler must raise administratively * * *. For these reasons, we think it clear that Congress intended that judicial review of market orders issued under the Act ordinarily be confined to suits brought by handlers in accordance with 7 U.S.C. § 608c(15).

III

The Court of Appeals viewed the preclusion issue from a somewhat different perspective. First, it recited the presumption in favor of judicial review of administrative action that this Court usually employs. It then noted that the Act has been interpreted to authorize producer challenges to the administration of market order settlement funds, and that no legislative history or statutory language directly and specifically supported the preclusion of consumer suits. In these circumstances, the Court of Appeals reasoned that the Act could not fairly be interpreted to overcome the presumption favoring judicial review and to leave consumers without a judicial remedy. We disagree with the Court of Appeals' analysis.

The presumption favoring judicial review of administrative action is just that—a presumption. This presumption, like all presumptions used in interpreting statutes, may be overcome by specific language or specific legislative history that is a reliable indicator of congressional intent. The congressional intent necessary to overcome the presumption may also be inferred from contemporaneous judicial construction barring review and the congressional acquiescence in it or from the collective import of legislative and judicial history behind a particular statute. More important for purposes of this case, the presumption favoring judicial review of administrative action may be overcome by inferences of intent drawn from the statutory scheme as a whole * * *.

* * *

In this case, the Court of Appeals did not take * * * [a] balanced approach to statutory construction * * *. Rather, it recited this Court's oft-quoted statement that "only upon a showing of 'clear and convincing evidence' of a contrary legislative intent should the courts restrict access to judicial review." *Abbott Laboratories v. Gardner*, 387 U.S. 136, 141, 87 S.Ct. 1507, 1511, 18 L.Ed.2d 681 (1967). According to the Court of Appeals, the "clear and convincing evidence" standard required it to find unambiguous proof, in the traditional evidentiary sense, of a congressional intent to preclude judicial review at the consumers' behest. Since direct statutory language or legislative history on this issue could not be found, the Court of Appeals found the presumption favoring judicial review to be controlling.

This Court has, however, never applied the "clear and convincing evidence" standard in the strict evidentiary sense the Court of Appeals thought necessary in this case. Rather, the Court has found the standard met, and the presumption favoring judicial review overcome, whenever the congressional intent to preclude judicial review is "fairly discernible in the statutory scheme." In the context of preclusion analysis, the "clear and convincing evidence" standard is not a rigid evidentiary test but a useful reminder to courts that, where substantial doubt about the congressional intent exists, the general presumption favoring judicial review of administrative action is controlling. That presumption does not control in cases such as this one, however, since the congressional intent to preclude judicial review is "fairly discernible" in the detail of the legislative scheme. Congress simply did not intend for consumers to be relied upon to challenge agency disregard of the law.

* * *

JUSTICE STEVENS took no part in the decision of this case.

NOTES

Block was a bombshell—not because of the result, which was unsurprising, but because of its reliance on and discussion of the implied preclusion doctrine. The court of appeals had devoted only a single footnote in a very lengthy opinion to a backhanded dismissal of the implied preclusion argument. *See Community Nutrition Inst. v. Block*, 698 F.2d 1239, 1252 n.75 (D.C.Cir.1983). The argument in the lower court, and in the Supreme Court, was primarily about the *standing* of consumers under the statute, and the expectation was that the Court would decide the case on the same basis. It was surprising to most observers that the Court even mentioned, much less resuscitated, the implied preclusion doctrine.

Two years after *Block*, the Court again took up the implied preclusion issue.

BOWEN V. MICHIGAN ACADEMY OF FAMILY PHYSICIANS

Supreme Court of the United States, 1986.
476 U.S. 667, 106 S.Ct. 2133, 90 L.Ed.2d 623.

JUSTICE STEVENS delivered the opinion of the Court.

The question presented in this case is whether Congress, in either § 1395ff or § 1395ii of Title 42 of the United States Code, barred judicial review of regulations promulgated under Part B of the Medicare program.

Respondents, who include an association of family physicians and several individual doctors, filed suit to challenge the validity of 42 CFR

§ 405.504(b) (1985), which authorizes the payment of benefits in different amounts for similar physicians' services. The District Court held that the regulation contravened several provisions of the statute governing the Medicare program * * *. The Court of Appeals agreed with the District Court * * *.

The Secretary of Health and Human Services has not sought review of the decision on the merits invalidating the regulation. Instead, he renews the contention, rejected by both the District Court and the Court of Appeals, that Congress has forbidden judicial review of all questions affecting the amount of benefits payable under Part B of the Medicare program. Because the question is important and has divided the Courts of Appeals, we granted the petition for a writ of certiorari. We now affirm.

I

We begin with the strong presumption that Congress intends judicial review of administrative action. From the beginning "our cases [have established] that judicial review of a final agency action by an aggrieved person will not be cut off unless there is persuasive reason to believe that such was the purpose of Congress." *Abbott Laboratories v. Gardner*, 387 U.S. 136, 140, 87 S.Ct. 1507, 1510, 18 L.Ed.2d 681 (1967) (citing cases) * * *. This standard has been invoked time and again when considering whether the Secretary has discharged "the heavy burden of overcoming the strong presumption that Congress did not mean to prohibit all judicial review of his decision," *Dunlop v. Bachowski*, 421 U.S. 560, 567, 95 S.Ct. 1851, 1857, 44 L.Ed.2d 377 (1975).

Subject to constitutional constraints, Congress can, of course, make exceptions to the historic practice whereby courts review agency action. The presumption of judicial review is, after all, a presumption, and "like all presumptions used in interpreting statutes, may be overcome by," inter alia, "specific language or specific legislative history that is a reliable indicator of congressional intent," or a specific congressional intent to preclude judicial review that is " 'fairly discernible' in the detail of the legislative scheme." *Block v. Community Nutrition Institute*, 467 U.S. 340, 349, 351, 104 S.Ct. 2450, 2456, 2457, 81 L.Ed.2d 270 (1984).

In this case, the Government asserts that two statutory provisions remove the Secretary's regulation from review under the grant of general federal-question jurisdiction found in 28 U.S.C. § 1331. First, the Government contends that 42 U.S.C. § 1395ff(b), which authorizes "Appeal by individuals," impliedly forecloses administrative or judicial review of any action taken under Part B of the Medicare program by failing to authorize such review while simultaneously authorizing administrative and judicial review of "any determination . . . as to . . . the amount of benefits under part A," § 1395ff(b)(1)(C). Second, the Government asserts that 42 U.S.C. § 1395ii, which makes applicable 42 U.S.C. § 405(h), of the

Social Security Act to the Medicare program, expressly precludes all administrative or judicial review not otherwise provided in that statute. We find neither argument persuasive.

II

Section 1395ff on its face is an explicit authorization of judicial review, not a bar[5] * * *.

In the Medicare program, however, the situation is somewhat more complex. Under Part B of that program, which is at issue here, the Secretary contracts with private health insurance carriers to provide benefits for which individuals voluntarily remit premiums. This optional coverage, which is federally subsidized, supplements the mandatory institutional health benefits (such as coverage for hospital expenses) provided by Part A. Subject to an amount-in-controversy requirement, individuals aggrieved by delayed or insufficient payment with respect to benefits payable under Part B are afforded an "opportunity for a fair hearing by the *carrier*," 42 U.S.C. § 1395u(b)(3)(C) (emphasis added); in comparison, and subject to a like amount-in-controversy requirement, a similarly aggrieved individual under Part A is entitled "to a hearing thereon by the *Secretary* . . . and to judicial review," 42 U.S.C. §§ 1395ff(b)(1)(C), (b)(2). "In the context of the statute's precisely drawn provisions," we held in *United States v. Erika, Inc.*, 456 U.S. 201, 208, 102 S.Ct. 1650, 1654, 72 L.Ed.2d 12 (1982), that the failure "to authorize further review for determinations of the amount of Part B awards . . . provides persuasive evidence that Congress deliberately intended to foreclose further review of such claims." Not limiting our consideration to the statutory text, we investigated the legislative history which "confirm[ed] this view," and disclosed a purpose to " 'avoid overloading the courts' " with " 'trivial matters,' " a consequence which would " 'unduly

---

[5] The pertinent text of § 1395ff reads as follows:

"(a)   Entitlement to and amount of benefits

"The determination of whether an individual is entitled to benefits under part A or part B, and the determination of the amount of benefits under part A, shall be made by the Secretary in accordance with regulations prescribed by him.

"(b)   Appeal by individuals

"(1)   Any individual dissatisfied with any determination under subsection (a) of this section as to—

"(A)   whether he meets the conditions of section 426 or section 426a of this title [which set forth eligibility requirements to be satisfied before an individual is permitted to participate in Part A of the Medicare program], or

"(B)   whether he is eligible to enroll and has enrolled pursuant to the provisions of part B of [the Medicare program] . . . , or

"(C)   the amount of the benefits under part A (including a determination where such amount is determined to be zero)

shall be entitled to a hearing thereon by the Secretary to the same extent as is provided in section 405(b) of this title and to judicial review of the Secretary's final decision after such hearing as is provided in section 405(g) of this title."

ta[x]' " the federal court system with " 'little real value' " to be derived by participants in the program.

Respondents' federal-court challenge to the validity of the Secretary's regulation is not foreclosed by § 1395ff as we construed that provision in *Erika*. The reticulated statutory scheme, which carefully details the forum and limits of review of "any determination . . . of . . . the amount of benefits under part A," 42 U.S.C. § 1395ff(b)(1)(C), and of the "amount of . . . payment" of benefits under Part B, 42 U.S.C. § 1395u(b)(3)(C), simply does not speak to challenges mounted against the *method* by which such amounts are to be determined rather than the *determinations* themselves. As the Secretary has made clear, "the legality, constitutional or otherwise, of any provision of the Act or regulations relevant to the Medicare Program" is not considered in a "fair hearing" held by a carrier to resolve a grievance related to a determination of the amount of a Part B award. As a result, an attack on the validity of a regulation is not the kind of administrative action that we described in *Erika* as an "amount determination" which decides "the amount of the Medicare payment to be made on a particular claim" and with respect to which the Act impliedly denies judicial review. 456 U.S., at 208, 102 S.Ct., at 1654.

That Congress did not preclude review of the method by which Part B awards are computed (as opposed to the computation) is borne out by the very legislative history we found persuasive in *Erika* * * *.

Careful analysis of the governing statutory provisions and their legislative history thus reveals that Congress intended to bar judicial review only of determinations of the amount of benefits to be awarded under Part B. Congress delegated this task to carriers who would finally determine such matters in conformity with the regulations and instructions of the Secretary. We conclude, therefore, that those matters which Congress did not leave to be determined in a "fair hearing" conducted by the carrier—including challenges to the validity of the Secretary's instructions and regulations—are not impliedly insulated from judicial review by 42 U.S.C. § 1395ff.

III

In light of Congress' express provision for carrier review of millions of what it characterized as "trivial" claims, it is implausible to think it intended that there be no forum to adjudicate statutory and constitutional challenges to regulations promulgated by the Secretary. The Government nevertheless maintains that this is precisely what Congress intended to accomplish in 42 U.S.C. § 1395ii. That section states that 42 U.S.C. § 405(h), along with a string citation of 10 other provisions of Title II of the Social Security Act, "shall also apply with respect to this subchapter to the same extent as they are applicable with respect to subchapter II of this chapter." Section 405(h), in turn, reads in full as follows:

"(h) Finality of Secretary's decision

"The findings and decision of the Secretary after a hearing shall be binding upon all individuals who were parties to such hearing. No findings of fact or decision of the Secretary shall be reviewed by any person, tribunal, or governmental agency except as herein provided. No action against the United States, the Secretary, or any officer or employee thereof shall be brought under section 1331 or 1346 of title 28 to recover on any claim arising under this subchapter."

The Government contends that the third sentence of § 405(h) by its terms prevents any resort to the grant of general federal-question jurisdiction contained in 28 U.S.C. § 1331. It finds support for this construction in *Weinberger v. Salfi*, 422 U.S. 749, 756–762, 95 S.Ct. 2457, 2462–2465, 45 L.Ed.2d 522 (1975), and *Heckler v. Ringer,* 466 U.S. 602, 614–616, 620–626, 104 S.Ct. 2013, 2021, 2022, 80 L.Ed.2d 622 (1984). Respondents counter that the dispositions in these two cases are consistent with the view that Congress' purpose was to make clear that whatever specific procedures it provided for judicial review of final action by the Secretary were exclusive, and could not be circumvented by resort to the general jurisdiction of the federal courts.

Whichever may be the better reading of *Salfi* and *Ringer*, we need not pass on the meaning of § 405(h) in the abstract to resolve this case. Section 405(h) does not apply on its own terms to Part B of the Medicare program, but is instead incorporated mutatis mutandis by § 1395ii. The legislative history of both the statute establishing the Medicare program and the 1972 amendments thereto provides specific evidence of Congress' intent to foreclose review only of "amount determinations"—i.e., those "quite minor matters," 118 Cong.Rec. 33992 (1972) (remarks of Sen. Bennett), remitted finally and exclusively to adjudication by private insurance carriers in a "fair hearing." By the same token, matters which Congress did not delegate to private carriers, such as challenges to the validity of the Secretary's instructions and regulations, are cognizable in courts of law. In the face of this persuasive evidence of legislative intent, we will not indulge the Government's assumption that Congress contemplated review by carriers of "trivial" monetary claims, but intended no review at all of substantial statutory and constitutional challenges to the Secretary's administration of Part B of the Medicare program. This is an extreme position, and one we would be most reluctant to adopt without "a showing of 'clear and convincing evidence,'" *Abbott Laboratories v. Gardner*, 387 U.S., at 141, 87 S.Ct., at 1511, to overcome the "strong presumption that Congress did not mean to prohibit all judicial review" of executive action, *Dunlop v. Bachowski*, 421 U.S., at 567, 95 S.Ct., at 1857. We ordinarily presume that Congress intends the executive to obey its statutory commands and, accordingly, that it expects the courts to grant relief when an executive agency violates such a command. That presumption has not been surmounted here.[12]

The judgment of the Court of Appeals is

Affirmed.

JUSTICE REHNQUIST took no part in the consideration or decision of this case.

NOTES

Block and *Michigan Academy* were both unanimous decisions. In *Shalala v. Illinois Council on Long Term Care, Inc.*, 529 U.S. 1, 120 S.Ct. 1084, 146 L.Ed.2d 1 (2000), however, a 5–4 Supreme Court limited *Michigan Academy's* holding on preclusion by construing it to force actions for judicial review under the Medicare Act through the specialized Medicare review statutes unless doing so would cut off judicial review altogether. *See Council for Urological Interests v. Sebelius*, 668 F.3d 704 (D.C.Cir.2011) (describing the scheme of review established by *Michigan Academy* and *Illinois Council*). None of the opinions in *Illinois Council*, or in any other cases since *Michigan Academy*, significantly refines the standard for determining implied preclusion. Consider, for example, a subsequent Supreme Court entry into the field. The Clean Water Act authorizes the Environmental Protection Agency to issue "compliance orders" to people who it believes are violating the Act and to enforce those compliance orders through civil actions. Those agency-initiated suits are obviously apt vehicles for challenging the legality of the agency's actions; if the agency action is unlawful, the court will not enforce the relevant compliance order. But the penalties for violating the Clean Water Act can be draconian—up to $75,000 per day. Can a citizen avoid the accumulation of potentially staggering penalties by challenging the legality of a compliance order without waiting for the EPA to bring an enforcement action?

> Nothing in the Clean Water Act *expressly* precludes judicial review under the APA or otherwise. But in determining "[w]hether and to what extent a particular statute precludes judicial review," we do not look "only [to] its express language." *Block v. Community Nutrition Institute*, 467 U.S. 340, 345, 104 S.Ct. 2450, 81 L.Ed.2d 270 (1984). The APA, we have said, creates a "presumption favoring judicial review of administrative action," but as with most presumptions, this one "may be overcome by inferences of intent drawn from the statutory scheme as a whole." *Id.* at 349, 104 S.Ct. 2450. The Government offers several reasons why the statutory scheme of the Clean Water Act precludes review.

> The Government first points to 33 U.S.C. § 1319(a)(3), which provides that, when the EPA "finds that any person is in violation" of

---

[12] Our disposition avoids the "serious constitutional question" that would arise if we construed § 1395ii to deny a judicial forum for constitutional claims arising under Part B of the Medicare program * * *.

certain portions of the Act, the agency "shall issue an order requiring such person to comply with [the Act], or . . . shall bring a civil action [to enforce the Act]." The Government argues that, because Congress gave the EPA the choice between a judicial proceeding and an administrative action, it would undermine the Act to allow judicial review of the latter. But that argument rests on the question-begging premise that the relevant difference between a compliance order and an enforcement proceeding is that only the latter is subject to judicial review. There are eminently sound reasons other than insulation from judicial review why compliance orders are useful. The Government itself suggests that they "provid[e] a means of notifying recipients of potential violations and quickly resolving the issues through voluntary compliance." Brief for Respondents 39. It is entirely consistent with this function to allow judicial review when the recipient does not choose "voluntary compliance." The Act does not guarantee the EPA that issuing a compliance order will always be the most effective choice.

* * *

The Government further urges us to consider that Congress expressly provided for prompt judicial review, on the administrative record, when the EPA assesses administrative penalties after a hearing, see § 1319(g)(8), but did not expressly provide for review of compliance orders. But if the express provision of judicial review in one section of a long and complicated statute were alone enough to overcome the APA's presumption of reviewability for all final agency action, it would not be much of a presumption at all.

The cases on which the Government relies simply are not analogous. In *Block v. Community Nutrition Institute, supra,* we held that the Agricultural Marketing Agreement Act of 1937, which expressly allowed milk handlers to obtain judicial review of milk market orders, precluded review of milk market orders in suits brought by milk *consumers.* Where a statute provides that particular agency action is reviewable at the instance of one party, who must first exhaust administrative remedies, the inference that it is not reviewable at the instance of other parties, who are not *subject* to the administrative process, is strong. In *United States v. Erika, Inc.,* 456 U.S. 201, 102 S.Ct. 1650, 72 L.Ed.2d 12 (1982), we held that the Medicare statute, which expressly provided for judicial review of awards under Part A, precluded review of awards under Part B. The strong parallel between the award provisions in Part A and Part B of the Medicare statute does not exist between the issuance of a compliance order and the assessment of administrative penalties under the Clean Water Act. And in *United States v. Fausto,* 484 U.S. 439, 108 S.Ct. 668, 98 L.Ed.2d 830 (1988), we held that the Civil Service Reform Act, which expressly excluded certain "nonpreference" employees from the statute's review scheme, precluded review at the instance of those employees in a separate Claims Court action. Here, there is no suggestion that Congress has sought to exclude compliance-order recipients from the Act's review scheme; quite to the contrary, the Government's case is premised on the notion that the Act's primary review mechanisms are open to the Sacketts.

Finally, the Government notes that Congress passed the Clean Water Act in large part to respond to the inefficiency of then-existing remedies for water pollution. Compliance orders, as noted above, can obtain quick remediation through voluntary compliance. The Government warns that the EPA is less likely to use the orders if they are subject to judicial review. That may be true—but it will be true for all agency actions subjected to judicial review. The APA's presumption of judicial review is a repudiation of the principle that efficiency of regulation conquers all. And there is no reason to think that the Clean Water Act was uniquely designed to enable the strong-arming of regulated parties into "voluntary compliance" without the opportunity for judicial review—even judicial review of the question whether the regulated party is within the EPA's jurisdiction. Compliance orders will remain an effective means of securing prompt voluntary compliance in those many cases where there is no substantial basis to question their validity.

* * *

We conclude that the compliance order in this case is final agency action for which there is no adequate remedy other than APA review, and that the Clean Water Act does not preclude that review. We therefore reverse the judgment of the Court of Appeals and remand the case for further proceedings consistent with this opinion.

Sackett v. EPA, 566 U.S. 120, 132 S.Ct. 1367, 182 L.Ed.2d 367 (2012).

If you were a lower court judge, how would you resolve implied preclusion claims?[20]

3. "COMMITTED TO AGENCY DISCRETION BY LAW"

Section 701(a)(2) of the APA indicates that judicial review is unavailable to the extent that "agency action is committed to agency discretion by law." What does this mean, especially in view of the fact that courts often review agency decisions, under § 706(2)(A) of the APA, for "abuse of discretion"?

The case law under this section is as confusing as any body of doctrine in administrative law—which is saying quite a lot. A good way to get a very

---

[20] If your answer is "Cite everything and hope for the best," please step up to the bench. *See, e.g.,* Kirby Corp. v. Pena, 109 F.3d 258 (5th Cir.1997).

strong headache is to read, in one sitting, three or four lower court decisions attempting to apply the "committed to agency discretion by law" doctrine.

Problems began with the Supreme Court's first important interpretation of § 701(a)(2) in *Citizens to Preserve Overton Park, Inc. v. Volpe*, 401 U.S. 402, 91 S.Ct. 814, 28 L.Ed.2d 136 (1971). That case, you will recall,[21] concerned a decision by the Secretary of Transportation to release federal highway funds for purchase of parkland under a statute that prohibited such use of funds "unless (1) there is no feasible and prudent alternative to the use of such land, and (2) such program includes all possible planning to minimize harm to such park * * *." The Secretary urged that judicial review was precluded by § 701(a)(2). The Court disagreed:

> [T]he Secretary's decision here does not fall within the exception for action "committed to agency discretion." This is a very narrow exception. The legislative history of the Administrative Procedure Act indicates that it is applicable in those rare instances where "statutes are drawn in such broad terms that in a given case there is no law to apply." S.Rep. No. 752, 79th Cong., 1st Sess., 26 (1945).

> Section 4(f) of the Department of Transportation Act and § 138 of the Federal-Aid Highway Act are clear and specific directives. Both * * * provide that the Secretary "shall not approve any program or project" that requires the use of any public parkland "unless (1) there is no feasible and prudent alternative to the use of such land, and (2) such program includes all possible planning to minimize harm to such park * * *." This language is a plain and explicit bar to the use of federal funds for construction of highways through parks—only the most unusual situations are exempted.

* * *

> Plainly, there is "law to apply" and thus the exemption for action "committed to agency discretion" is inapplicable * * *.

Overton Park's use of the "no law to apply" standard quickly became a mantra. Courts repeatedly stated that § 701(a)(2) precluded review only where statutes conferred such enormous discretion on agencies that judicial review was literally impossible. Thus, while "normal" grants of discretion to agencies would lead to review for abuse of discretion under § 706(2)(A), extraordinary grants of discretion would cut off judicial review altogether.

---

[21] Other portions of *Overton Park* are provided at pages 485–491, *supra*.

The "no law to apply" formulation, however, fails to capture at least some forms of agency action that the Court has squarely held to be within the scope of § 701(a)(2). Moreover, the Court does not apply the formulation faithfully. There are very few circumstances—fewer even than the Court acknowledges—in which one can fairly say that it is impossible to craft manageable standards for judicial review. "Even a broad statutory mandate, which gives an agency wide latitude to strike a balance among varied public policy factors, can have teeth when a litigant alleges that the agency failed to take the prescribed factors into account." Ronald M. Levin, *Understanding Unreviewability in Administrative Law*, 74 Minn. L. Rev. 689, 735 (1990). Furthermore, the "no law to apply" formulation generates the following well-known conundrum: § 706(2)(A) authorizes review of "abuse of discretion." So how can a statute that commits discretion to an agency be unreviewable when the APA specifically contemplates review of agency discretion?

Consider how those issues were addressed in 1985 in perhaps the Court's most famous treatment of § 701(a)(2).

HECKLER V. CHANEY

Supreme Court of the United States, 1985.
470 U.S. 821, 105 S.Ct. 1649, 84 L.Ed.2d 714.

JUSTICE REHNQUIST delivered the opinion of the Court.

This case presents the question of the extent to which a decision of an administrative agency to exercise its "discretion" not to undertake certain enforcement actions is subject to judicial review under the Administrative Procedure Act. Respondents are several prison inmates convicted of capital offenses and sentenced to death by lethal injection of drugs. They petitioned the Food and Drug Administration (FDA) alleging that under the circumstances the use of these drugs for capital punishment violated the Federal Food, Drug, and Cosmetic Act and requesting that the FDA take various enforcement actions to prevent these violations. The FDA refused their request. We review here a decision of the Court of Appeals for the District of Columbia Circuit, Justice which held the FDA's refusal to take enforcement actions both reviewable and an abuse of discretion * * *.

Respondents have been sentenced to death by lethal injection of drugs under the laws of the States of Oklahoma and Texas. Those States, and several others, have recently adopted this method for carrying out the capital sentence. Respondents first petitioned the FDA, claiming that the drugs used by the States for this purpose, although approved by the FDA for the medical purposes stated on their labels, were not approved for use in human executions. They alleged that the drugs had not been tested for the purpose for which they were to be used, and that, given that the drugs would likely be administered by untrained personnel, it was also likely that the drugs would not induce the quick and painless death intended. They urged that use of these drugs for human execution was the "unapproved use of an approved drug" and constituted a violation of the Act's prohibitions against "misbranding." They also suggested that the FDCA's requirements for approval of "new drugs" applied, since these drugs were now being used for a new purpose. Accordingly, respondents claimed that the FDA was required to approve the drugs as "safe and effective" for human execution before they could be distributed in interstate commerce. They therefore requested the FDA to take various investigatory and enforcement actions to prevent these perceived violations * * *.

"unapproved" use of the drug

FDA had to approve as "safe + effective"

The FDA Commissioner responded, refusing to take the requested actions. The Commissioner first detailed his disagreement with respondents' understanding of the scope of FDA jurisdiction over the unapproved use of approved drugs for human execution, concluding that FDA jurisdiction in the area was generally unclear but in any event should not be exercised to interfere with this particular aspect of state criminal justice systems. He went on to state:

FDA's decision

> "Were FDA clearly to have jurisdiction in the area, moreover, we believe we would be authorized to decline to exercise it under our inherent discretion to decline to pursue certain enforcement matters. The unapproved use of approved drugs is an area in which the case law is far from uniform. Generally, enforcement proceedings in this area are initiated only when there is a serious danger to the public health or a blatant scheme to defraud. We cannot conclude that those dangers are present under State lethal injection laws, which are duly authorized statutory enactments in furtherance of proper State functions. . . ."

* * * [R]eview of the agency action was sought under the judicial review provisions of the APA, 5 U.S.C. §§ 701–706 * * *.

review sought under APA

A divided panel of the Court of Appeals for the District of Columbia Circuit * * * noted that the APA only precludes judicial review of final agency action—including refusals to act—when review is precluded by statute, or "committed to agency discretion by law." Citing this Court's opinions in *Dunlop v. Bachowski*, 421 U.S. 560, 95 S.Ct. 1851, 144 L.Ed.2d 377 (1975), and *Citizens to Preserve Overton Park v. Volpe*, 401 U.S. 402, 91 S.Ct. 814, 28 L.Ed.2d 136 (1971), for the view that these exceptions should be narrowly construed, the court held that the "committed to agency discretion by law" exception of § 701(a)(2) should be invoked only where the substantive statute left the courts with "no law to apply." The court cited *Dunlop* as holding that this presumption "applies with no less force to review of . . . agency decisions to refrain from enforcement action."

The court found "law to apply" in the form of a FDA policy statement which indicated that the agency was "obligated" to investigate the

DC circ. reasoning

unapproved use of an approved drug when such use became "widespread" or "endanger[ed] the public health." The court held that this policy statement constituted a "rule" and was considered binding by the FDA. Given the policy statement indicating that the FDA should take enforcement action in this area, and the strong presumption that all agency action is subject to judicial review, the court concluded that review of the agency's refusal was not foreclosed. It then proceeded to assess whether the agency's decision not to act was "arbitrary, capricious, or an abuse of discretion." * * * [T]he court found that the FDA's refusal * * * was irrational, and that respondents' evidence that use of the drugs could lead to a cruel and protracted death was entitled to more searching consideration. The court therefore remanded the case to the District Court, to order the FDA "to fulfill its statutory function."

The dissenting judge expressed the view that an agency's decision not to institute enforcement action generally is unreviewable, and that such exercises of "prosecutorial discretion" presumptively fall within the APA's exception for agency actions "committed to agency discretion by law" * * *.

* * *

* * * [S]ection [701(a)(2)] provides that the chapter on judicial review "applies, according to the provisions thereof, except to the extent that—(1) statutes preclude judicial review; or (2) agency action is committed to agency discretion by law." Petitioner urges that the decision of the FDA to refuse enforcement is an action "committed to agency discretion by law" under § 701(a)(2).

This Court has not had occasion to interpret this second exception in § 701(a)(2) in any great detail. On its face, the section does not obviously lend itself to any particular construction; indeed, one might wonder what difference exists between § (a)(1) and § (a)(2). The former section seems easy in application; it requires construction of the substantive statute involved to determine whether Congress intended to preclude judicial review of certain decisions * * *. But one could read the language "committed to agency discretion *by law*" in § (a)(2) to require a similar inquiry. In addition, commentators have pointed out that construction of § (a)(2) is further complicated by the tension between a literal reading of § (a)(2), which exempts from judicial review those decisions committed to agency "discretion," and the primary scope of review prescribed by § 706(2)(A)—whether the agency's action was "arbitrary, capricious, or an *abuse of discretion.*" How is it, they ask, that an action committed to agency discretion can be unreviewable and yet courts still can review agency actions for abuse of that discretion? The APA's legislative history provides little help on this score * * *. [W]e think there is a proper construction of § (a)(2) which satisfies each of these concerns.

This Court first discussed § (a)(2) in *Citizens to Preserve Overton Park v. Volpe.* That case dealt with the Secretary of Transportation's approval of the building of an interstate highway through a park in Memphis, Tennessee * * *. This Court first addressed the "threshold question" of whether the agency's action was at all reviewable * * *:

> "In this case, there is no indication that Congress sought to prohibit judicial review and there is most certainly no 'showing of "clear and convincing evidence" of a . . . legislative intent' to restrict access to judicial review.

> "Similarly, the Secretary's decision here does not fall within the exception for action 'committed to agency discretion.' This is a very narrow exception. . . . The legislative history of the Administrative Procedure Act indicates that it is applicable in those rare instances where 'statutes are drawn in such broad terms that in a given case there is no law to apply.' S.Rep. No. 752, 79th Cong., 1st Sess., 26 (1945)."

The above quote answers several of the questions raised by the language of § 701(a), although it raises others. First, it clearly separates the exception provided by § (a)(1) from the § (a)(2) exception. The former applies when Congress has expressed an intent to preclude judicial review. The latter applies in different circumstances; even where Congress has not affirmatively precluded review, review is not to be had if the statute is drawn so that a court would have no meaningful standard against which to judge the agency's exercise of discretion. In such a case, the statute ("law") can be taken to have "committed" the decisionmaking to the agency's judgment absolutely. This construction avoids conflict with the "abuse of discretion" standard of review in § 706—if no judicially manageable standards are available for judging how and when an agency should exercise its discretion, then it is impossible to evaluate agency action for "abuse of discretion." In addition, this construction * * * [identifies] a separate class of cases to which § 701(a)(2) applies.

To this point our analysis does not differ significantly from that of the Court of Appeals. That court purported to apply the "no law to apply" standard of *Overton Park.* We disagree, however, with that court's insistence that the "narrow construction" of § (a)(2) required application of a presumption of reviewability even to an agency's decision not to undertake certain enforcement actions. Here we think the Court of Appeals broke with tradition, case law, and sound reasoning.

Overton Park did not involve an agency's refusal to take requested enforcement action. It involved an affirmative act of approval under a statute that set clear guidelines for determining when such approval should be given. Refusals to take enforcement steps generally involve precisely the opposite situation, and in that situation we think the presumption is that judicial review is not available. This Court has recognized on several occasions over many years that an agency's decision not to prosecute or enforce, whether through civil or criminal process, is a decision generally committed to an agency's absolute discretion. See *United States v. Batchelder*, 442 U.S. 114, 123–124, 99 S.Ct. 2198, 2203–2204, 60 L.Ed.2d 755 (1979); *United States v. Nixon*, 418 U.S. 683, 693, 94 S.Ct. 3090, 3100, 41 L.Ed.2d 1039 (1974); *Vaca v. Sipes,* 386 U.S. 171, 182, 87 S.Ct. 903, 912, 17 L.Ed.2d 842 (1967); *Confiscation Cases*, 7 Wall. 454, 19 L.Ed. 196 (1869). This recognition of the existence of discretion is attributable in no small part to the general unsuitability for judicial review of agency decisions to refuse enforcement.

The reasons for this general unsuitability are many * * *. [A]n agency decision not to enforce often involves a complicated balancing of a number of factors which are peculiarly within its expertise * * *. The agency is far better equipped than the courts to deal with the many variables involved in the proper ordering of its priorities * * *.

* * * [A]n agency's refusal to institute proceedings shares to some extent the characteristics of the decision of a prosecutor in the Executive Branch not to indict—a decision which has long been regarded as the special province of the Executive Branch, inasmuch as it is the Executive who is charged by the Constitution to "take Care that the Laws be faithfully executed."

We of course only list the above concerns to facilitate understanding of our conclusion that an agency's decision not to take enforcement action should be presumed immune from judicial review under § 701(a)(2). For good reasons, such a decision has traditionally been "committed to agency discretion," and we believe that the Congress enacting the APA did not intend to alter that tradition. In so stating, we emphasize that the decision is only presumptively unreviewable; the presumption may be rebutted where the substantive statute has provided guidelines for the agency to follow in exercising its enforcement powers.[4] Thus, in establishing this presumption in the APA, Congress did not set agencies free to disregard legislative direction in the statutory scheme that the agency administers. Congress may limit an agency's exercise of enforcement power if it wishes, either by setting substantive priorities, or by otherwise circumscribing an agency's power to discriminate among issues or cases it will pursue. How

---

4   We do not have in this case a refusal by the agency to institute proceedings based solely on the belief that it lacks jurisdiction. Nor do we have a situation where it could justifiably be found that the agency has "consciously and expressly adopted a general policy" that is so extreme as to amount to an abdication of its statutory responsibilities. See, *e.g., Adams v. Richardson*, 156 U.S.App.D.C. 267, 480 F.2d 1159 (1973) (en banc). Although we express no opinion on whether such decisions would be unreviewable under § 701(a)(2), we note that in those situations the statute conferring authority on the agency might indicate that such decisions were not "committed to agency discretion."

to determine when Congress has done so is the question left open by
Overton Park.

Dunlop v. Bachowski, relied upon heavily by respondents and the
majority in the Court of Appeals, presents an example of statutory
language which supplied sufficient standards to rebut the presumption of
unreviewability. *Dunlop* involved a suit by a union employee, under the
Labor-Management Reporting and Disclosure Act, (LMRDA), asking the
Secretary of Labor to investigate and file suit to set aside a union election.
Section 482 provided that, upon filing of a complaint by a union member,
"[t]he Secretary shall investigate such complaint and, if he finds probable
cause to believe that a violation . . . has occurred . . . he shall . . . bring a
civil action. . . ." After investigating the plaintiff's claims the Secretary of
Labor declined to file suit, and the plaintiff sought judicial review under
the APA. This Court held that review was available. It rejected the
Secretary's argument that the statute precluded judicial review, and in a
footnote it stated its agreement with the conclusion of the Court of Appeals
that the decision was not "an unreviewable exercise of prosecutorial
discretion." 421 U.S., at 567, n.7, 95 S.Ct., at 1858, n.7. Our textual
references to the "strong presumption" of reviewability in *Dunlop* were
addressed only to the § (a)(1) exception; we were content to rely on the
Court of Appeals' opinion to hold that the § (a)(2) exception did not apply.
The Court of Appeals, in turn, had found the "principle of absolute
prosecutorial discretion" inapplicable, because the language of the LMRDA
indicated that the Secretary was required to file suit if certain "clearly
defined" factors were present * * *.

Dunlop is thus consistent with a general presumption of
unreviewability of decisions not to enforce. The statute being administered
quite clearly withdrew discretion from the agency and provided guidelines
for exercise of its enforcement power * * *. [W]e therefore turn to the FDCA
to determine whether in this case Congress has provided us with "law to
apply" * * *.

To enforce the various substantive prohibitions contained in the
FDCA, the Act provides for injunctions, criminal sanctions, and seizure of
any offending food, drug, or cosmetic article. The Act's general provision for
enforcement provides only that "[t]he Secretary is authorized to conduct
examinations and investigations . . ." (emphasis added). Unlike the statute
at issue in *Dunlop* * * *, [the FDCA] gives no indication of when an
injunction should be sought * * *. The section on criminal sanctions states
baldly that any person who violates the Act's substantive prohibitions
"shall be imprisoned . . . or fined." Respondents argue that this statement
mandates criminal prosecution of every violator of the Act but they adduce
no indication in case law or legislative history that such was Congress'
intention in using this language, which is commonly found in the criminal
provisions of Title 18 of the United States Code. We are unwilling to

attribute such a sweeping meaning to this language, particularly since the Act charges the Secretary only with recommending prosecution; any criminal prosecutions must be instituted by the Attorney General. The Act's enforcement provisions thus commit complete discretion to the Secretary to decide how and when they should be exercised.

* * * [W]e reject respondents' argument that the Act's substantive prohibitions of "misbranding" and the introduction of "new drugs" absent agency approval supply us with "law to apply." These provisions are simply irrelevant to the agency's discretion to refuse to initiate proceedings.

We also find singularly unhelpful the agency "policy statement" on which the Court of Appeals placed great reliance. We would have difficulty with this statement's vague language even if it were a properly adopted agency rule. Although the statement indicates that the agency considered itself "obligated" to take certain investigative actions, that language did not arise in the course of discussing the agency's discretion to exercise its enforcement power, but rather in the context of describing agency policy with respect to unapproved uses of approved drugs by physicians * * *. Whatever force such a statement might have, and leaving to one side the problem of whether an agency's rules might under certain circumstances provide courts with adequate guidelines for informed judicial review of decisions not to enforce, we do not think the language of the agency's "policy statement" can plausibly be read to override the agency's express assertion of unreviewable discretion * * *.

Respondents' third argument, based upon § 306 of the FDCA, merits only slightly more consideration. That section provides:

> "Nothing in this chapter shall be construed as requiring the Secretary to report for prosecution, or for the institution of libel or injunction proceedings, minor violations of this chapter whenever he believes that the public interest will be adequately served by a suitable written notice or ruling." 21 U.S.C. § 336.

Respondents seek to draw from this section the negative implication that the Secretary is *required* to report for prosecution all "major" violations of the Act, however those might be defined, and that it therefore supplies the needed indication of an intent to limit agency enforcement discretion. We think that this section simply does not give rise to the negative implication which respondents seek to draw from it. The section is not addressed to agency proceedings designed to discover the existence of violations, but applies only to a situation where a violation has already been established to the satisfaction of the agency. We do not believe the section speaks to the criteria which shall be used by the agency for investigating *possible* violations of the Act.

We therefore conclude that the presumption that agency decisions not to institute proceedings are unreviewable under 5 U.S.C. § 701(a)(2) is not overcome by the enforcement provisions of the FDCA. The FDA's decision not to take the enforcement actions requested by respondents is therefore not subject to judicial review under the APA. The general exception to reviewability provided by § 701(a)(2) for action "committed to agency discretion" remains a narrow one, but within that exception are included agency refusals to institute investigative or enforcement proceedings, unless Congress has indicated otherwise. In so holding, we essentially leave to Congress, and not to the courts, the decision as to whether an agency's refusal to institute proceedings should be judicially reviewable. No colorable claim is made in this case that the agency's refusal to institute proceedings violated any constitutional rights of respondents, and we do not address the issue that would be raised in such a case. The fact that the drugs involved in this case are ultimately to be used in imposing the death penalty must not lead this Court or other courts to import profound differences of opinion over the meaning of the Eighth Amendment to the United States Constitution into the domain of administrative law.

The judgment of the Court of Appeals is

Reversed.

JUSTICE BRENNAN, concurring [omitted].

JUSTICE MARSHALL, concurring in the judgment.

Easy cases at times produce bad law, for in the rush to reach a clearly ordained result, courts may offer up principles, doctrines, and statements that calmer reflection, and a fuller understanding of their implications in concrete settings, would eschew. In my view, the "presumption of unreviewability" announced today is a product of that lack of discipline that easy cases make all too easy. The majority, eager to reverse what it goes out of its way to label as an "implausible result," *ante,* at 1654, not only does reverse, as I agree it should, but along the way creates out of whole cloth the notion that agency decisions not to take "enforcement action" are unreviewable unless Congress has rather specifically indicated otherwise. Because this "presumption of unreviewability" is fundamentally at odds with rule-of-law principles firmly embedded in our jurisprudence, because it seeks to truncate an emerging line of judicial authority subjecting enforcement discretion to rational and principled constraint, and because, in the end, the presumption may well be indecipherable, one can only hope that it will come to be understood as a relic of a particular factual setting in which the full implications of such a presumption were neither confronted nor understood.

I write separately to argue for a different basis of decision: that refusals to enforce, like other agency actions, are reviewable in the absence of a "clear and convincing" congressional intent to the contrary, but that such refusals warrant deference when, as in this case, there is nothing to suggest that an agency with enforcement discretion has abused that discretion.

* * *

NOTES

The dissenting judge in the Court of Appeals in *Chaney* was then-Judge Scalia. A few years later, Judge Scalia had the opportunity to express his views on § 701(a)(2) in another dissenting opinion in a different forum.

Section 102(c) of the National Security Act of 1947 provided that the director of the Central Intelligence Agency "may, in his discretion, terminate the employment of any officer or employee of the Agency whenever he shall deem such termination necessary or advisable in the interests of the United States." 50 U.S.C. § 403(c) (1988). In *Webster v. Doe,* 486 U.S. 592, 108 S.Ct. 2047, 100 L.Ed.2d 632 (1988), the Supreme Court unanimously held that termination decisions under this statute are "committed to agency discretion by law" and thus not subject to judicial review—but then added, over the dissents of Justices O'Connor and Justice Scalia, that review is not foreclosed under § 701(a)(2) when the underlying claim of unlawfulness is founded on the Constitution:

> [T]he section does commit employment termination decisions to the Director's discretion, and precludes challenges to these decisions based upon the statutory language of § 102(c). A discharged employee thus cannot complain that his termination was not "necessary or advisable in the interests of the United States," since that assessment is the Director's alone. Subsections (a)(1) and (a)(2) of § 701, however, remove from judicial review only those determinations specifically identified by Congress or "committed to agency discretion by law." Nothing in § 102(c) persuades us that Congress meant to preclude consideration of colorable constitutional claims arising out of the actions of the Director pursuant to that section; we believe that a constitutional claim based on an individual discharge may be reviewed by the District Court.

486 U.S. at 603–04, 108 S.Ct. at 2054. Justice Scalia agreed with the result regarding § 102(c), but disagreed with some aspects of the majority's reasoning. The majority emphasized that § 102(c) was drawn in such broad terms that there was "no law to apply." Justice Scalia thought this too narrow a conception of the circumstances that could constitute commitment of a decision to agency discretion by law:

> * * * The "no law to apply" test can account for the nonreviewability of certain issues, but falls far short of explaining the full scope of the areas from which the courts are excluded. For the fact is that there is no governmental decision that is not subject to a fair number of legal constraints precise enough to be susceptible of judicial application—beginning with the fundamental constraint that

[handwritten margin notes:] Webster v. Doe → review is not foreclosed where there are constitutional claims

Scalia's dissent

the decision must be taken in order to further a public purpose rather than a purely private interest; yet there are many governmental decisions that are not at all subject to judicial review. A United States Attorney's decision to prosecute, for example, will not be reviewed on the claim that it was prompted by personal animosity. Thus, "no law to apply" provides much less than the full answer to whether § 701(a)(2) applies.

The key to understanding the "committed to agency discretion *by law*" provision of § 701(a)(2) lies in contrasting it with the "*statutes* preclude judicial review" provision of § 701(a)(1). Why "statutes" for preclusion, but the much more general term "law" for commission to agency discretion? The answer is, as we implied in *Chaney*, that the latter was intended to refer to "the 'common law' of judicial review of agency action," 470 U.S., at 832, 105 S.Ct. at 1656—a body of jurisprudence that had marked out, with more or less precision, certain issues and certain areas that were beyond the range of judicial review. That jurisprudence included principles ranging from the "political question" doctrine, to sovereign immunity (including doctrines determining when a suit against an officer would be deemed to be a suit against the sovereign), to official immunity, to prudential limitations upon the courts' equitable powers, to what can be described no more precisely than a traditional respect for the functions of the other branches * * *. Only if all that "common law" were embraced within § 701(a)(2) could it have been true that, as was generally understood, "[t]he intended result of [§ 701(a)] is to restate the existing law as to the area of reviewable agency action." Attorney General's Manual on the Administrative Procedure Act 94 (1947). Because that is the meaning of the provision, we have continued to take into account for purposes of determining reviewability, post-APA as before, not only the text and structure of the statute under which the agency acts, but such factors as whether the decision involves "a sensitive and inherently discretionary judgment call," *Department of Navy v. Egan*, 484 U.S. 518, 527, 108 S.Ct. 818, 824, 98 L.Ed.2d 918 (1988), whether it is the sort of decision that has traditionally been nonreviewable, *ICC v. Locomotive Engineers*, 482 U.S. 270, 282, 107 S.Ct. 2360, 2367, 96 L.Ed.2d 222 (1987); *Chaney, supra*, 470 U.S., at 832, 105 S.Ct. at 1656 and whether review would have "disruptive practical consequences," *see Southern R. Co. v. Seaboard Allied Milling Corp.*, 442 U.S. 444, 457, 99 S.Ct. 2388, 2395, 60 L.Ed.2d 1017 (1979). This explains the seeming contradiction between § 701(a)(2)'s disallowance of review to the extent that action is "committed to agency discretion," and § 706's injunction that a court shall set aside agency action that constitutes "an abuse of discretion." Since, in the former provision, "committed to agency discretion by law" means "of the sort that is traditionally unreviewable," it operates to keep certain categories of agency action out of the courts; but when agency action is appropriately in the courts, abuse of discretion is of course grounds for reversal.

All this law, shaped over the course of centuries and still developing in its application to new contexts, cannot possibly be contained within the phrase "no law to apply." It is not surprising, then, that although the Court recites the test it does not really apply it * * *. The standard set forth in § 102(c) of the National Security Act of 1947, 50 U.S.C. § 403(c), "necessary or advisable in the interests of the United States," at least excludes dismissal out of personal vindictiveness, or because the Director wants to give the job to his cousin. Why, on the Court's theory, is respondent not entitled to assert the presence of such excesses, under the "abuse of discretion" standard of § 706?

486 U.S. at 608–10, 108 S.Ct. at 2056–57 (Scalia, J., dissenting). Justice Scalia dissented from the conclusion that constitutional claims pertaining to dismissals of intelligence officers were reviewable and thus dissented from the Court's judgment.

How much of Justice Scalia's position prevailed in the following case?

reallocation of $ for Indian Children's program

LINCOLN V. VIGIL

Supreme Court of the United States, 1993.
508 U.S. 182, 113 S.Ct. 2024, 124 L.Ed.2d 101.

JUSTICE SOUTER delivered the opinion of the Court.

For several years in the late 1970's and early 1980's, the Indian Health Service provided diagnostic and treatment services, referred to collectively as the Indian Children's Program (Program), to handicapped Indian children in the Southwest. In 1985, the Service decided to reallocate the Program's resources to a nationwide effort to assist such children. We hold that the Service's decision to discontinue the Program was "committed to agency discretion by law" and therefore not subject to judicial review under the Administrative Procedure Act, 5 U.S.C. § 701(a)(2) * * *.

HOLDING

I

The Indian Health Service, an agency within the Public Health Service of the Department of Health and Human Services, provides health care for some 1.5 million American Indian and Alaska Native people. The Service receives yearly lump-sum appropriations from Congress and expends the funds under authority of the Snyder Act, 42 Stat. 208, as amended, 25 U.S.C. § 13, and the Indian Health Care Improvement Act, 90 Stat. 1400, as amended, 25 U.S.C. § 1601 et seq. So far as it concerns us here, the Snyder Act authorizes the Service to "expend such moneys as Congress may from time to time appropriate, for the benefit, care, and assistance of the Indians," for the "relief of distress and conservation of health." 25 U.S.C. § 13. The Improvement Act authorizes expenditures for, *inter alia,*

Snyder Act

Indian mental-health care, and specifically for "therapeutic and residential treatment centers." § 1621(a)(4)(D).

The Service employs roughly 12,000 people and operates more than 500 health-care facilities in the continental United States and Alaska. This case concerns a collection of related services, commonly known as the Indian Children's Program, that the Service provided from 1978 to 1985. In the words of the Court of Appeals, a "clou[d] [of] bureaucratic haze" obscures the history of the Program, *Vigil v. Rhoades*, 953 F.2d 1225, 1226 (C.A.10 1992), which seems to have grown out of a plan "to establish therapeutic and residential treatment centers for disturbed Indian children." H.R.Rep. No. 94–1026, pt. 1, p. 80 (1976) (prepared in conjunction with enactment of the Improvement Act). These centers were to be established under a "major cooperative care agreement" between the Service and the Bureau of Indian Affairs, *id.*, at 81, and would have provided such children "with intensive care in a residential setting." *Id.*, at 80.

Congress <u>never expressly appropriated funds for these centers</u>. In 1978, however, the <u>Service</u> allocated approximately $292,000 from its fiscal year 1978 appropriation to its office in Albuquerque, New Mexico, for the planning and development of a pilot project for handicapped Indian children, which became known as the Indian Children's Program. The pilot project apparently convinced the Service that a building was needed, and, in 1979, the Service requested $3.5 million from Congress to construct a diagnostic and treatment center for handicapped Indian children. The appropriation for fiscal year 1980 did not expressly provide the requested funds, however, and legislative reports indicated only that Congress had increased the Service's funding by $300,000 for nationwide expansion and development of the Program in coordination with the Bureau.

Plans for a national program to be managed jointly by the Service and the Bureau were never fulfilled, however, and the Program continued simply as an offering of the Service's Albuquerque office, from which the Program's staff of 11 to 16 employees would make monthly visits to Indian communities in New Mexico and southern Colorado and on the Navajo and Hopi Reservations * * *. <u>Congress never authorized or appropriated moneys expressly</u> for the Program, and the Service continued to pay for its regional activities out of annual lump-sum appropriations from 1980 to 1985, during which period the Service repeatedly apprised Congress of the Program's continuing operation.

Nevertheless, the Service had not abandoned the proposal for a nationwide treatment program * * *. In August 1985, the Service determined that Program staff hitherto assigned to provide direct clinical services should be reassigned as consultants to other nationwide Service programs and discontinued the direct clinical services to Indian children in

[handwritten margin notes:] no express appropriation of funds ↑ just based on the Service's allocation of its general budget

reassigned staff + discontinued direct services

the Southwest. The Service announced its decision in a memorandum, dated August 21, 1985, addressed to Service offices and Program referral sources * * *.

Respondents, handicapped Indian children eligible to receive services through the Program, subsequently brought this action for declaratory and injunctive relief against petitioners, the Director of the Service and others (collectively, the Service), in the United States District Court for the District of New Mexico. Respondents alleged, *inter alia*, that the Service's decision to discontinue direct clinical services violated the federal trust responsibility to Indians, the Snyder Act, the Improvement Act, the Administrative Procedure Act, various agency regulations, and the Fifth Amendment's Due Process Clause.

The District Court granted summary judgment for respondents * * *.

The Court of Appeals affirmed. Like the District Court, it rejected the Service's argument that the decision to discontinue the Program was committed to agency discretion under the APA. Although the court concededly could identify no statute or regulation even mentioning the Program, it believed that the repeated references to it in the legislative history of the annual appropriations Acts, "in combination with the special relationship between the Indian people and the federal government," provided a basis for judicial review * * *.

II

First is the question whether it was error for the Court of Appeals to hold the substance of the Service's decision to terminate the Program reviewable under the APA * * *. [W]e have read the APA as embodying a "basic presumption of judicial review," *Abbott Laboratories v. Gardner*, 387 U.S. 136, 140, 87 S.Ct. 1507, 1511, 18 L.Ed.2d 681 (1967). This is "just" a presumption, however, *Block v. Community Nutrition Institute*, 467 U.S. 340, 349, 104 S.Ct. 2450, 2455, 81 L.Ed.2d 270 (1984), and under § 701(a)(2) agency action is not subject to judicial review "to the extent that" such action "is committed to agency discretion by law." As we explained in *Heckler v. Chaney*, 470 U.S. 821, 830, 105 S.Ct. 1649, 1655, 84 L.Ed.2d 714 (1985), § 701(a)(2) makes it clear that "review is not to be had" in those rare circumstances where the relevant statute "is drawn so that a court would have no meaningful standard against which to judge the agency's exercise of discretion." See also *Webster v. Doe*, 486 U.S. 592, 599–600, 108 S.Ct. 2047, 2052, 100 L.Ed.2d 632 (1988); *Citizens to Preserve Overton Park, Inc. v. Volpe*, 401 U.S. 402, 410, 91 S.Ct. 814, 820–821, 28 L.Ed.2d 136 (1971). "In such a case, the statute ('law') can be taken to have 'committed' the decisionmaking to the agency's judgment absolutely." *Heckler, supra*, at 830, 105 S.Ct. at 1655.

Over the years, we have read § 701(a)(2) to preclude judicial review of certain categories of administrative decisions that courts traditionally have regarded as "committed to agency discretion." See *Franklin v. Massachusetts*, 505 U.S. 788, 817, 112 S.Ct. 2767, 2783, 120 L.Ed.2d 636 (1992) (STEVENS, J., concurring in part and concurring in judgment); *Webster, supra*, at 609, 108 S.Ct., at 2056–2057 (SCALIA, J., dissenting). In *Heckler* itself, we held an agency's decision not to institute enforcement proceedings to be presumptively unreviewable under § 701(a)(2). 470 U.S., at 831, 105 S.Ct., at 1655–1656. An agency's "decision not to enforce often involves a complicated balancing of a number of factors which are peculiarly within its expertise," *ibid.*, and for this and other good reasons, we concluded, "such a decision has traditionally been 'committed to agency discretion,'" *id.*, at 832, 105 S.Ct., at 1656. Similarly, in *ICC v. Locomotive Engineers*, 482 U.S. 270, 282, 107 S.Ct. 2360, 2368, 96 L.Ed.2d 222 (1987), we held that § 701(a)(2) precludes judicial review of another type of administrative decision traditionally left to agency discretion, an agency's refusal to grant reconsideration of an action because of material error. In so holding, we emphasized "the impossibility of devising an adequate standard of review for such agency action." *Ibid.* Finally, in *Webster, supra*, at 599–601, 108 S.Ct., at 2051–2053, we held that § 701(a)(2) precludes judicial review of a decision by the Director of Central Intelligence to terminate an employee in the interests of national security, an area of executive action "in which courts have long been hesitant to intrude." *Franklin, supra*, 505 U.S. at 819, 112 S.Ct. at 2785 (STEVENS, J., concurring in part and concurring in judgment).

The allocation of funds from a lump-sum appropriation is another administrative decision traditionally regarded as committed to agency discretion. After all, the very point of a lump-sum appropriation is to give an agency the capacity to adapt to changing circumstances and meet its statutory responsibilities in what it sees as the most effective or desirable way. See *International Union, United Automobile, Aerospace & Agricultural Implement Workers of America v. Donovan*, 241 U.S.App.D.C. 122, 128, 746 F.2d 855, 861 (1984) (Scalia, J.) ("A lump-sum appropriation leaves it to the recipient agency (as a matter of law, at least) to distribute the funds among some or all of the permissible objects as it sees fit"); 2 United States General Accounting Office, Principles of Federal Appropriations Law, p. 6–159 (2d ed. 1992). For this reason, a fundamental principle of appropriations law is that where "Congress merely appropriates lump-sum amounts without statutorily restricting what can be done with those funds, a clear inference arises that it does not intend to impose legally binding restrictions, and indicia in committee reports and other legislative history as to how the funds should or are expected to be spent do not establish any legal requirements on" the agency. *LTV Aerospace Corp.*, 55 Comp.Gen. 307, 319 (1975). Put another way, a lump-sum appropriation reflects a congressional recognition that an agency must be allowed "flexibility to shift . . . funds within a particular . . . appropriation account so that" the agency "can make necessary adjustments for 'unforeseen developments'" and "'changing requirements.'" *LTV Aerospace Corp.*, *supra*, at 318 (citation omitted).

Like the decision against instituting enforcement proceedings, then, an agency's allocation of funds from a lump-sum appropriation requires "a complicated balancing of a number of factors which are peculiarly within its expertise": whether its "resources are best spent" on one program or another; whether it "is likely to succeed" in fulfilling its statutory mandate; whether a particular program "best fits the agency's overall policies"; and, "indeed, whether the agency has enough resources" to fund a program "at all." *Heckler*, 470 U.S., at 831, 105 S.Ct., at 1655. As in *Heckler*, so here, the "agency is far better equipped than the courts to deal with the many variables involved in the proper ordering of its priorities." *Id.*, at 831–832, 105 S.Ct., at 1656. Of course, an agency is not free simply to disregard statutory responsibilities: Congress may always circumscribe agency discretion to allocate resources by putting restrictions in the operative statutes (though not, as we have seen, just in the legislative history). And, of course, we hardly need to note that an agency's decision to ignore congressional expectations may expose it to grave political consequences. But as long as the agency allocates funds from a lump-sum appropriation to meet permissible statutory objectives, § 701(a)(2) gives the courts no leave to intrude. "[T]o [that] extent," the decision to allocate funds "is committed to agency discretion by law." § 701(a)(2).

The Service's decision to discontinue the Program is accordingly unreviewable under § 701(a)(2). As the Court of Appeals recognized, the appropriations Acts for the relevant period do not so much as mention the Program, and both the Snyder Act and the Improvement Act likewise speak about Indian health only in general terms. It is true that the Service repeatedly apprised Congress of the Program's continued operation, but, as we have explained, these representations do not translate through the medium of legislative history into legally binding obligations. The reallocation of agency resources to assist handicapped Indian children nationwide clearly falls within the Service's statutory mandate to provide health care to Indian people, and respondents, indeed, do not seriously contend otherwise. The decision to terminate the Program was committed to the Service's discretion.

The Court of Appeals saw a separate limitation on the Service's discretion in the special trust relationship existing between Indian people and the Federal Government. We have often spoken of this relationship, see, e.g., *Cherokee Nation v. Georgia*, 30 U.S. (5 Pet.) 1, 17, 8 L.Ed. 25 (1831) (Marshall, C.J.) (Indians' "relation to the United States resembles that of a ward to his guardian"), and the law is "well established that the Government in its dealings with Indian tribal property acts in a fiduciary capacity." *United States v. Cherokee Nation of Okla.*, 480 U.S. 700, 707, 107 S.Ct. 1487, 1491, 94 L.Ed.2d 704 (1987). Whatever the contours of that relationship, though, it could not limit the Service's discretion to reorder its priorities from serving a subgroup of beneficiaries to serving the broader class of all Indians nationwide.

One final note: although respondents claimed in the District Court that the Service's termination of the Program violated their rights under the Fifth Amendment's Due Process Clause, that court expressly declined to address respondents' constitutional arguments, as did the Court of Appeals. Thus, while the APA contemplates, in the absence of a clear expression of contrary congressional intent, that judicial review will be available for colorable constitutional claims, see *Webster*, 486 U.S., at 603–604, 108 S.Ct., at 2054, the record at this stage does not allow mature consideration of constitutional issues, which we leave for the Court of Appeals on remand.

C. "WHOM": THE PROBLEM OF STANDING

As *Block v. Community Nutrition Inst., see supra* pages 1026–1031, well illustrates, judicial review can be available to some parties but not others. This concept is not unique to administrative law: an action for breach of contract can be brought only by an aggrieved party to the contract (or a third-party beneficiary), not by random bystanders who feel strongly about the importance of contractual obligations. In other words, to say that judicial review is not precluded, under either the express preclusion, implied preclusion, or committed to agency discretion by law doctrines, is merely to say that judicial review is available to some class of plaintiffs. One must still determine whether any particular plaintiff is a member of that class for whom review is available. Such determinations generally go under the heading of *standing to sue.*[22]

There are two dimensions to the standing inquiry in federal administrative law. One dimension is constitutional: there are certain minimum requirements that any plaintiff, in any federal lawsuit, must satisfy in order to bring an action in federal court. Another dimension is statutory: plaintiffs who satisfy the constitutional minima for challenges to agency action must *additionally* be appropriate plaintiffs under the governing statutes.

Each dimension, considered alone, is a doctrinal disaster area. Together, they make a detailed study of the Rule against Perpetuities look appealing. But because standing is potentially a threshold issue in every case, the administrative lawyer cannot escape it.

---

[22] As *Block* illustrates, however, it is sometimes difficult, or impossible, to draw a sharp line between inquiries about standing and inquiries about partial preclusion. A determination that review is precluded for a certain class of plaintiffs is functionally, and to some extent conceptually, indistinguishable from a determination that the class in question has no standing to sue.

1. CONSTITUTIONAL STANDING

As indicated above, the law has always distinguished proper from improper plaintiffs. A person's legal violation—whether by tort, breach of contract, or disregard of an applicable statute—is not by itself grounds for suit. The plaintiff must demonstrate that he or she has suffered some injury beyond mere distress at the thought of lawbreakers going unpunished. Only in the twentieth century, however, has the doctrine of standing acquired an explicit constitutional dimension.

Frothingham v. Mellon

The seminal case is *Frothingham v. Mellon*, 262 U.S. 447, 43 S.Ct. 597, 67 L.Ed. 1078 (1923). The plaintiff was a taxpayer who sued to enjoin implementation of a spending measure that was allegedly beyond Congress' constitutional powers. The claimed injury was "that the effect of the appropriations complained of will be to increase the burden of future taxation * * *." The Court held that this injury was insufficient to sustain a lawsuit.

> [A taxpayer's] interest in the moneys of the treasury—partly realized from taxation and partly from other sources—is shared with millions of others, is comparatively minute and indeterminable, and the effect upon future taxation, of any payment out of the funds, so remote, fluctuating and uncertain, that no basis is afforded for an appeal to the preventive powers of a court of equity.
>
> The administration of any statute, likely to produce additional taxation to be imposed upon a vast number of taxpayers, the extent of whose several liability is indefinite and constantly changing, is essentially a matter of public and not of individual concern. If one taxpayer may champion and litigate such a cause, then every other taxpayer may do the same, not only in respect of the statute here under review, but also in respect of every other appropriation act and statute whose administration requires the outlay of public money, and whose validity may be questioned. The bare suggestion of such a result, with its attendant inconveniences, goes far to sustain the conclusion which we have reached, that a suit of this character cannot be maintained. It is of much significance that no precedent sustaining the right to maintain suits like this has been called to our attention, although, since the formation of the government, as an examination of the acts of Congress will disclose, a large number of statutes appropriating or involving the expenditure of moneys for nonfederal purposes have been enacted and carried into effect.
>
> * * * We have no power *per se* to review and annul acts of Congress on the ground that they are unconstitutional. That

question may be considered only when the justification for some direct injury suffered or threatened, presenting a justiciable issue, is made to rest upon such an act. Then the power exercised is that of ascertaining and declaring the law applicable to the controversy. It amounts to little more than the negative power to disregard an unconstitutional enactment, which otherwise would stand in the way of the enforcement of a legal right. The party who invokes the power must be able to show, not only that the statute is invalid, but that he has sustained or is immediately in danger of sustaining some direct injury as the result of its enforcement, and not merely that he suffers in some indefinite way in common with people generally. If a case for preventive relief be presented, the court enjoins, in effect, not the execution of the statute, but the acts of the official, the statute notwithstanding. Here the parties plaintiff have no such case. Looking through forms of words to the substance of their complaint, it is merely that officials of the executive department of the government are executing and will execute an act of Congress asserted to be unconstitutional; and this we are asked to prevent. To do so would be, not to decide a judicial controversy, but to assume a position of authority over the governmental acts of another and coequal department, an authority which plainly we do not possess.

262 U.S. at 487–89, 43 S.Ct. at 601. From these humble beginnings have sprung, primarily in the past half century, one of the most complex, confusing, and controversial bodies of doctrine the Supreme Court has ever produced. The underlying rationale of *Frothingham*—that courts deciding constitutional (and statutory) cases merely decide whether certain sources of law are relevant to the adjudications before them—has all but disappeared from modern public law. Its place has been taken by an elaborate, multi-part analysis for determining which claims are cognizable in the federal courts. The roots of that modern analysis are difficult to trace, and its precise contours are defended by no one.[23] A full treatment of the contemporary law of standing is best left to courses on constitutional law and federal jurisdiction. The doctrine's basic elements, however, and its specific implications for administrative law can at least be gleaned from examining some of the Supreme Court's entries into the field.

---

[23] Scholars vigorously disagree about precisely what features of modern standing law are mistaken, in what respect those features are mistaken, and who is to blame for the muddled state of the case law, but your editor knows of no one, on any side of any relevant spectrum, who finds the existing body of doctrine satisfactory.

handwritten: Lujan V. Defenders of Wildlife

LUJAN V. DEFENDERS OF WILDLIFE

handwritten: interp of End. Spec. Act that makes it only applic. → actions w/in US (or high seas)

Supreme Court of the United States, 1992.
504 U.S. 555, 112 S.Ct. 2130, 119 L.Ed.2d 351.

JUSTICE SCALIA delivered the opinion of the Court with respect to Parts I, II, III-A, and IV, and an opinion with respect to Part III-B, in which THE CHIEF JUSTICE, JUSTICE WHITE, and JUSTICE THOMAS join.

This case involves a challenge to a rule promulgated by the Secretary of the Interior interpreting § 7 of the Endangered Species Act of 1973 (ESA), 87 Stat. 884, 892, as amended, 16 U.S.C. § 1536, in such fashion as to render it applicable only to actions within the United States or on the high seas. The preliminary issue, and the only one we reach, is whether respondents here, plaintiffs below, have standing to seek judicial review of the rule.

handwritten: ISSUE = standing

I

The ESA seeks to protect species of animals against threats to their continuing existence caused by man. The ESA instructs the Secretary of the Interior to promulgate by regulation a list of those species which are either endangered or threatened under enumerated criteria, and to define the critical habitat of these species. Section 7(a)(2) of the Act then provides, in pertinent part:

> "Each Federal agency shall, in consultation with and with the assistance of the Secretary [of the Interior], insure that any action authorized, funded, or carried out by such agency . . . is not likely to jeopardize the continued existence of any endangered species or threatened species or result in the destruction or adverse modification of habitat of such species which is determined by the Secretary, after consultation as appropriate with affected States, to be critical." 16 U.S.C. § 1536(a)(2).

In 1978, the Fish and Wildlife Service (FWS) and the National Marine Fisheries Service (NMFS), on behalf of the Secretary of the Interior and the Secretary of Commerce respectively, promulgated a joint regulation stating that the obligations imposed by § 7(a)(2) extend to actions taken in foreign nations. The next year, however, the Interior Department began to reexamine its position. A revised joint regulation, reinterpreting § 7(a)(2) to require consultation only for actions taken in the United States or on the high seas, was proposed in 1983 and promulgated in 1986.

handwritten: FWS reg that ESA applied → actions in foreign nations ↑ then revised + made ESA only applic → US

Shortly thereafter, respondents, organizations dedicated to wildlife conservation and other environmental causes, filed this action against the Secretary of the Interior, seeking a declaratory judgment that the new regulation is in error as to the geographic scope of § 7(a)(2) and an injunction requiring the Secretary to promulgate a new regulation restoring the initial interpretation * * *.

II

While the Constitution of the United States divides all power conferred upon the Federal Government into "legislative Powers," Art. I, § 1, "[t]he executive Power," Art. II, § 1, and "[t]he judicial Power," Art. III, § 1, it does not attempt to define those terms. To be sure, it limits the jurisdiction of federal courts to "Cases" and "Controversies," but an executive inquiry can bear the name "case" (the Hoffa case) and a legislative dispute can bear the name "controversy" (the Smoot-Hawley controversy). Obviously, then, the Constitution's central mechanism of separation of powers depends largely upon common understanding of what activities are appropriate to legislatures, to executives, and to courts. In The Federalist No. 48, Madison expressed the view that "[i]t is not infrequently a question of real nicety in legislative bodies whether the operation of a particular measure will, or will not, extend beyond the legislative sphere," whereas "the executive power [is] restrained within a narrower compass and . . . more simple in its nature," and "the judiciary [is] described by landmarks still less uncertain." The Federalist No. 48, p. 256 (Carey and McClellan eds. 1990). One of those landmarks, setting apart the "Cases" and "Controversies" that are of the justiciable sort referred to in Article III—"serv[ing] to identify those disputes which are appropriately resolved through the judicial process," *Whitmore v. Arkansas*, 495 U.S. 149, 155, 110 S.Ct. 1717, 1722, 109 L.Ed.2d 135 (1990)—is the doctrine of standing. Though some of its elements express merely prudential considerations that are part of judicial self-government, the core component of standing is an essential and unchanging part of the case-or-controversy requirement of Article III. See, e.g., *Allen v. Wright*, 468 U.S. 737, 751, 104 S.Ct. 3315, 3324, 82 L.Ed.2d 556 (1984).

Over the years, our cases have established that the irreducible constitutional minimum of standing contains three elements. First, the plaintiff must have suffered an "injury in fact"—an invasion of a legally protected interest which is (a) concrete and particularized, see *id.*, at 756, 104 S.Ct., at 3327,[1] and (b) "actual or imminent, not 'conjectural' or 'hypothetical,'" *Whitmore*, *supra*, 495 U.S., at 155, 110 S.Ct., at 1723 (quoting *Los Angeles v. Lyons*, 461 U.S. 95, 102, 103 S.Ct. 1660, 1665, 75 L.Ed.2d 675 (1983)). Second, there must be a causal connection between the injury and the conduct complained of—the injury has to be "fairly . . . trace[able] to the challenged action of the defendant, and not . . . th[e] result [of] the independent action of some third party not before the court." *Simon v. Eastern Ky. Welfare Rights Organization*, 426 U.S. 26, 41–42, 96 S.Ct. 1917, 1926, 48 L.Ed.2d 450 (1976). Third, it must be "likely," as opposed to merely "speculative," that the injury will be "redressed by a favorable decision." *Id.*, at 38, 43, 96 S.Ct., at 1924, 1926.

---

[1] By particularized, we mean that the injury must affect the plaintiff in a personal and individual way.

The party invoking federal jurisdiction bears the burden of establishing these elements. Since they are not mere pleading requirements but rather an indispensable part of the plaintiff's case, each element must be supported in the same way as any other matter on which the plaintiff bears the burden of proof, *i.e.*, with the manner and degree of evidence required at the successive stages of the litigation. At the pleading stage, general factual allegations of injury resulting from the defendant's conduct may suffice, for on a motion to dismiss we "presum[e] that general allegations embrace those specific facts that are necessary to support the claim." In response to a summary judgment motion, however, the plaintiff can no longer rest on such "mere allegations," but must "set forth" by affidavit or other evidence "specific facts," Fed.Rule Civ.Proc. 56(e), which for purposes of the summary judgment motion will be taken to be true. And at the final stage, those facts (if controverted) must be "supported adequately by the evidence adduced at trial."

When the suit is one challenging the legality of government action or inaction, the nature and extent of facts that must be averred (at the summary judgment stage) or proved (at the trial stage) in order to establish standing depends considerably upon whether the plaintiff is himself an object of the action (or forgone action) at issue. If he is, there is ordinarily little question that the action or inaction has caused him injury, and that a judgment preventing or requiring the action will redress it. When, however, as in this case, a plaintiff's asserted injury arises from the government's allegedly unlawful regulation (or lack of regulation) of *someone else*, much more is needed. In that circumstance, causation and redressability ordinarily hinge on the response of the regulated (or regulable) third party to the government action or inaction—and perhaps on the response of others as well. The existence of one or more of the essential elements of standing "depends on the unfettered choices made by independent actors not before the courts and whose exercise of broad and legitimate discretion the courts cannot presume either to control or to predict," *ASARCO Inc. v. Kadish*, 490 U.S. 605, 109 S.Ct. 2037, 104 L.Ed.2d 696 (1989) (opinion of KENNEDY, J.); and it becomes the burden of the plaintiff to adduce facts showing that those choices have been or will be made in such manner as to produce causation and permit redressability of injury. Thus, when the plaintiff is not himself the object of the government action or inaction he challenges, standing is not precluded, but it is ordinarily "substantially more difficult" to establish. *Allen, supra*, 468 U.S., at 758, 104 S.Ct., at 3328.

III

* * * Respondents had not made the requisite demonstration of (at least) injury and redressability.

A

Respondents' claim to injury is that the lack of consultation with respect to certain funded activities abroad "increas[es] the rate of extinction of endangered and threatened species." Complaint ¶ 5. Of course, the[desire to use or observe an animal species,]even for purely esthetic purposes, is undeniably a cognizable interest for purpose of standing. See, *e.g., Sierra Club v. Morton*, 405 U.S., at 734, 92 S.Ct., at 1366. "But the 'injury in fact' test requires more than an injury to a cognizable interest. It requires that the party seeking review be himself among the injured." *Id.*, at 734–735, 92 S.Ct., at 1366. To survive the Secretary's summary judgment motion, respondents had to submit affidavits or other evidence showing, through specific facts, not only that listed species were in fact being threatened by funded activities abroad, but also that one or more of respondents' members would thereby be "directly" affected apart from their " 'special interest' in th[e] subject." *Id.*, at 735, 739, 92 S.Ct., at 1366, 1368.

With respect to this aspect of the case, the Court of Appeals focused on the affidavits of two Defenders' members—Joyce Kelly and Amy Skilbred. Ms. Kelly stated that she traveled to Egypt in 1986 and "observed the traditional habitat of the endangered nile crocodile there and intend[s] to do so again, and hope[s] to observe the crocodile directly," and that she "will suffer harm in fact as the result of [the] American . . . role . . . in overseeing the rehabilitation of the Aswan High Dam on the Nile . . . and [in] develop [ing] . . . Egypt's . . . Master Water Plan." Ms. Skilbred averred that she traveled to Sri Lanka in 1981 and "observed th[e] habitat" of "endangered species such as the Asian elephant and the leopard" at what is now the site of the Mahaweli project funded by the Agency for International Development (AID), although she "was unable to see any of the endangered species"; "this development project," she continued, "will seriously reduce endangered, threatened, and endemic species habitat including areas that I visited . . . [, which] may severely shorten the future of these species"; that threat, she concluded, harmed her because she "intend[s] to return to Sri Lanka in the future and hope[s] to be more fortunate in spotting at least the endangered elephant and leopard." When Ms. Skilbred was asked at a subsequent deposition if and when she had any plans to return to Sri Lanka, she reiterated that "I intend to go back to Sri Lanka," but confessed that she had no current plans: "I don't know [when]. There is a civil war going on right now. I don't know. Not next year, I will say. In the future."

We shall assume for the sake of argument that these affidavits contain facts showing that certain agency-funded projects threaten listed species—though that is questionable. They plainly contain no facts, however, showing how damage to the species will produce "imminent" injury to Mses. Kelly and Skilbred. That the women "had visited" the areas of the projects before the projects commenced proves nothing * * *. And the affiants' profession of an "inten[t]" to return to the places they had visited before—where they will presumably, this time, be deprived of the opportunity to observe animals of the endangered species—is simply not enough. Such "some day" intentions—without any description of concrete plans, or indeed even any specification of when the some day will be—do not support a finding of the "actual or imminent" injury that our cases require.[2]

Besides relying upon the Kelly and Skilbred affidavits, respondents propose a series of novel standing theories. The first, inelegantly styled "ecosystem nexus," proposes that any person who uses *any part* of a "contiguous ecosystem" adversely affected by a funded activity has standing even if the activity is located a great distance away. This approach, as the Court of Appeals correctly observed, is inconsistent with our opinion in * * * [*Lujan v. National Wildlife Federation*, 497 U.S. 871, 110 S.Ct. 3177, 111 L.Ed.2d 695 (1990)], which held that a plaintiff claiming injury from environmental damage must use the area affected by the challenged activity and not an area roughly "in the vicinity" of it. 497 U.S., at 887–889, 110 S.Ct., at 3188–3189 * * *.

Respondents' other theories are called, alas, the "animal nexus" approach, whereby anyone who has an interest in studying or seeing the endangered animals anywhere on the globe has standing; and the "vocational nexus" approach, under which anyone with a professional interest in such animals can sue. Under these theories, anyone who goes to see Asian elephants in the Bronx Zoo, and anyone who is a keeper of Asian elephants in the Bronx Zoo, has standing to sue because the Director of the Agency for International Development (AID) did not consult with the Secretary regarding the AID-funded project in Sri Lanka. This is beyond all reason. Standing is not "an ingenious academic exercise in the conceivable," *United States v. Students Challenging Regulatory Agency Procedures (SCRAP)*, 412 U.S. 669, 688, 93 S.Ct. 2405, 2416, 37 L.Ed.2d 254 (1973), but as we have said requires, at the summary judgment stage, a factual showing of perceptible harm. It is clear that the person who observes or works with a particular animal threatened by a federal decision is facing perceptible harm, since the very subject of his interest will no

---

[2]   The dissent acknowledges the settled requirement that the injury complained of be, if not actual, then at least imminent, but it contends that respondents could get past summary judgment because "a reasonable finder of fact could conclude . . . that . . . Kelly or Skilbred will soon return to the project sites." This analysis suffers either from a factual or from a legal defect, depending on what the "soon" is supposed to mean. If "soon" refers to the standard mandated by our precedents—that the injury be "imminent"—we are at a loss to see how, as a factual matter, the standard can be met by respondents' mere profession of an intent, some day, to return. But if, as we suspect, "soon" means nothing more than "in this lifetime," then the dissent has undertaken quite a departure from our precedents. Although "imminence" is concededly a somewhat elastic concept, it cannot be stretched beyond its purpose, which is to ensure that the alleged injury is not too speculative for Article III purposes * * *. It has been stretched beyond the breaking point when, as here, the plaintiff alleges only an injury at some indefinite future time, and the acts necessary to make the injury happen are at least partly within the plaintiff's own control * * *.

      * * *

longer exist. It is even plausible—though it goes to the outermost limit of plausibility—to think that a person who observes or works with animals of a particular species in the very area of the world where that species is threatened by a federal decision is facing such harm, since some animals that might have been the subject of his interest will no longer exist. It goes beyond the limit, however, and into pure speculation and fantasy, to say that anyone who observes or works with an endangered species, anywhere in the world, is appreciably harmed by a single project affecting some portion of that species with which he has no more specific connection.

B

Redressability

Besides failing to show injury, respondents failed to demonstrate redressability. Instead of attacking the separate decisions to fund particular projects allegedly causing them harm, respondents chose to challenge a more generalized level of Government action (rules regarding consultation), the invalidation of which would affect all overseas projects. This programmatic approach has obvious practical advantages, but also obvious difficulties insofar as proof of causation or redressability is concerned * * *.

R took generalized approach here

The most obvious problem in the present case is redressability. Since the agencies funding the projects were not parties to the case, the District Court could accord relief only against the Secretary: He could be ordered to revise his regulation to require consultation for foreign projects. But this would not remedy respondents' alleged injury unless the funding agencies were bound by the Secretary's regulation, which is very much an open question * * *. When the Secretary promulgated the regulation at issue here, he thought it was binding on the agencies. The Solicitor General, however, has repudiated that position here, and the agencies themselves apparently deny the Secretary's authority * * *.

agencies funding the projects ≠ parties to this case

↑ open Q as to whether specific agencies would be bound by Secr. revising reg.

Respondents assert that this legal uncertainty did not affect redressability (and hence standing) because the District Court itself could resolve the issue of the Secretary's authority as a necessary part of its standing inquiry. Assuming that it is appropriate to resolve an issue of law such as this in connection with a threshold standing inquiry, resolution by the District Court would not have remedied respondents' alleged injury anyway, because it would not have been binding upon the agencies. They were not parties to the suit, and there is no reason they should be obliged to honor an incidental legal determination the suit produced * * *.

would NOT have been binding

A further impediment to redressability is the fact that the agencies generally supply only a fraction of the funding for a foreign project. AID, for example, has provided less than 10% of the funding for the Mahaweli project. Respondents have produced nothing to indicate that the projects they have named will either be suspended, or do less harm to listed species, if that fraction is eliminated. As in *Simon*, 426 U.S., at 43–44, 96 S.Ct., at

ALSO, agencies provide only a fraction of the project funding

1926–1927, it is entirely conjectural whether the nonagency activity that affects respondents will be altered or affected by the agency activity they seek to achieve. There is no standing.

No STANDING here

IV

CoA reasoning
↑
"procedural injury"

The Court of Appeals found that respondents had standing for an additional reason: because they had suffered a "procedural injury." The so-called "citizen-suit" provision of the ESA provides, in pertinent part, that "any person may commence a civil suit on his own behalf (A) to enjoin any person, including the United States and any other governmental instrumentality or agency . . . who is alleged to be in violation of any provision of this chapter." 16 U.S.C. § 1540(g). The court held that, because § 7(a)(2) requires interagency consultation, the citizen-suit provision creates a "procedural righ[t]" to consultation in all "persons"—so that anyone can file suit in federal court to challenge the Secretary's (or presumably any other official's) failure to follow the assertedly correct consultative procedure, notwithstanding his or her inability to allege any discrete injury flowing from that failure. To understand the remarkable nature of this holding one must be clear about what it does not rest upon: This is not a case where plaintiffs are seeking to enforce a procedural requirement the disregard of which could impair a separate concrete interest of theirs (*e.g.*, the procedural requirement for a hearing prior to denial of their license application, or the procedural requirement for an environmental impact statement before a federal facility is constructed next door to them).[7] Nor is it simply a case where concrete injury has been suffered by many persons, as in mass fraud or mass tort situations. Nor, finally, is it the unusual case in which Congress has created a concrete private interest in the outcome of a suit against a private party for the government's benefit, by providing a cash bounty for the victorious plaintiff. Rather, the court held that the injury-in-fact requirement had been satisfied by congressional conferral upon *all* persons of an abstract, self-contained, noninstrumental "right" to have the Executive observe the procedures required by law. We reject this view.

We have consistently held that a plaintiff raising only a generally available grievance about government—claiming only harm to his and

---

[7]   There is this much truth to the assertion that "procedural rights" are special: The person who has been accorded a procedural right to protect his concrete interests can assert that right without meeting all the normal standards for redressability and immediacy. Thus, under our case law, one living adjacent to the site for proposed construction of a federally licensed dam has standing to challenge the licensing agency's failure to prepare an environmental impact statement, even though he cannot establish with any certainty that the statement will cause the license to be withheld or altered, and even though the dam will not be completed for many years. (That is why we do not rely, in the present case, upon the Government's argument that, *even* if the other agencies were obliged to consult with the Secretary, they might not have followed his advice.) What respondents' "procedural rights" argument seeks, however, is quite different from this: standing for persons who have no concrete interests affected—persons who live (and propose to live) at the other end of the country from the dam.

every citizen's interest in proper application of the Constitution and laws, and seeking relief that no more directly and tangibly benefits him than it does the public at large—does not state an Article III case or controversy * * *.

* * *

* * * The question presented here is whether the public interest in proper administration of the laws (specifically, in agencies' observance of a particular, statutorily prescribed procedure) can be converted into an individual right by a statute that denominates it as such, and that permits all citizens (or, for that matter, a subclass of citizens who suffer no distinctive concrete harm) to sue. If the concrete injury requirement has the separation-of-powers significance we have always said, the answer must be obvious: To permit Congress to convert the undifferentiated public interest in executive officers' compliance with the law into an "individual right" vindicable in the courts is to permit Congress to transfer from the President to the courts the Chief Executive's most important constitutional duty, to "take Care that the Laws be faithfully executed," Art. II, § 3. It would enable the courts, with the permission of Congress, "to assume a position of authority over the governmental acts of another and co-equal department," *Massachusetts v. Mellon*, 262 U.S., at 489, 43 S.Ct., at 601, and to become " 'virtually continuing monitors of the wisdom and soundness of Executive action.' " *Allen, supra*, 468 U.S., at 760, 104 S.Ct., at 3329 (quoting *Laird v. Tatum*, 408 U.S. 1, 15, 92 S.Ct. 2318, 2326, 33 L.Ed.2d 154 (1972)). We have always rejected that vision of our role * * *.

[margin note: separation of powers issue]

* * *

JUSTICE KENNEDY, with whom JUSTICE SOUTER joins, concurring in part and concurring in the judgment.

[margin note: concurrence]

Although I agree with the essential parts of the Court's analysis, I write separately to make several observations.

I agree with the Court's conclusion in Part III-A that, on the record before us, respondents have failed to demonstrate that they themselves are "among the injured." *Sierra Club v. Morton*, 405 U.S. 727, 735, 92 S.Ct. 1361, 1366, 31 L.Ed.2d 636 (1972) * * *.

[margin note: agrees that p has failed to demonstrate injury]

While it may seem trivial to require that Mses. Kelly and Skilbred acquire airline tickets to the project sites or announce a date certain upon which they will return, this is not a case where it is reasonable to assume that the affiants will be using the sites on a regular basis, nor do the affiants claim to have visited the sites since the projects commenced. With respect to the Court's discussion of respondents' "ecosystem nexus," "animal nexus," and "vocational nexus" theories, I agree that on this record respondents' showing is insufficient to establish standing on any of these bases. I am not willing to foreclose the possibility, however, that in different

[margin note: possible that one of the nexus theories could support standing on diff. facts]

circumstances a nexus theory similar to those proffered here might support a claim to standing.

In light of the conclusion that respondents have not demonstrated a concrete injury here sufficient to support standing under our precedents, I would not reach the issue of redressability that is discussed by the plurality in Part III-B.

I also join Part IV of the Court's opinion with the following observations. As Government programs and policies become more complex and farreaching, we must be sensitive to the articulation of new rights of action that do not have clear analogs in our common-law tradition. Modern litigation has progressed far from the paradigm of Marbury suing Madison to get his commission, *Marbury v. Madison,* 5 U.S. (1 Cranch) 137, 2 L.Ed. 60 (1803), or Ogden seeking an injunction to halt Gibbons' steamboat operations, *Gibbons v. Ogden,* 22 U.S. (9 Wheat.) 1, 6 L.Ed. 23 (1824). In my view, Congress has the power to define injuries and articulate chains of causation that will give rise to a case or controversy where none existed before, and I do not read the Court's opinion to suggest a contrary view. In exercising this power, however, Congress must at the very least identify the injury it seeks to vindicate and relate the injury to the class of persons entitled to bring suit. The citizen-suit provision of the Endangered Species Act does not meet these minimal requirements, because while the statute purports to confer a right on "any person . . . to enjoin . . . the United States and any other governmental instrumentality or agency . . . who is alleged to be in violation of any provision of this chapter," it does not of its own force establish that there is an injury in "any person" by virtue of any "violation." 16 U.S.C. § 1540(g)(1)(A).

* * *

[margin note: concurrence]

JUSTICE STEVENS, concurring in the judgment.

[margin note: R loses on merits, but disagrees that they lack standing]

Because I am not persuaded that Congress intended the consultation requirement in § 7(a)(2) of the Endangered Species Act of 1973 (ESA), 16 U.S.C. § 1536(a)(2), to apply to activities in foreign countries, I concur in the judgment of reversal. I do not, however, agree with the Court's conclusion that respondents lack standing * * *.

In my opinion a person who has visited the critical habitat of an endangered species, has a professional interest in preserving the species and its habitat, and intends to revisit them in the future has standing to challenge agency action that threatens their destruction * * *. Indeed, this Court has often held that injuries to such interests are sufficient to confer standing, and the Court reiterates that holding today.

The Court nevertheless concludes that respondents have not suffered "injury in fact" because they have not shown that the harm to the endangered species will produce "imminent" injury to them. I disagree. An injury to an individual's interest in studying or enjoying a species and its natural habitat occurs when someone (whether it be the Government or a private party) takes action that harms that species and habitat. In my judgment, therefore, the "imminence" of such an injury should be measured by the timing and likelihood of the threatened environmental harm, rather than—as the Court seems to suggest—by the time that might elapse between the present and the time when the individuals would visit the area if no such injury should occur.

* * *

* * * If respondents are genuinely interested in the preservation of the endangered species and intend to study or observe these animals in the future, their injury will occur as soon as the animals are destroyed. Thus the only potential source of "speculation" in this case is whether respondents' intent to study or observe the animals is genuine. In my view, Joyce Kelly and Amy Skilbred have introduced sufficient evidence to negate petitioner's contention that their claims of injury are "speculative" or "conjectural" * * *.

* * *

[JUSTICE STEVENS further argued that the plaintiffs satisfied the "redressability" prong of standing analysis because a ruling by the Supreme Court that the Secretary of the Interior's regulations bound other agencies would effectively resolve the issue regardless of whether the other agencies were formally parties to the lawsuit. The plurality responded that standing, as with other aspects of federal jurisdiction, must be determined at the time of the lawsuit, so that the relevant inquiry is whether a *district court* determination of the Secretary's power would resolve the issue.]* * *

JUSTICE BLACKMUN, with whom JUSTICE O'CONNOR joins, dissenting.

I part company with the Court in this case in two respects. First, I believe that respondents have raised genuine issues of fact—sufficient to survive summary judgment—both as to injury and as to redressability. Second, I question the Court's breadth of language in rejecting standing for "procedural" injuries. I fear the Court seeks to impose fresh limitations on the constitutional authority of Congress to allow citizen suits in the federal courts for injuries deemed "procedural" in nature. I dissent.

I

* * *

A

To survive petitioner's motion for summary judgment on standing, respondents need not prove that they are actually or imminently harmed. They need show only a "genuine issue" of material fact as to standing. Fed.Rule Civ.Proc. 56(c). This is not a heavy burden. A "genuine issue" exists so long as "the evidence is such that a reasonable jury could return a verdict for the nonmoving party [respondents]." *Anderson v. Liberty Lobby, Inc.*, 477 U.S. 242, 248, 106 S.Ct. 2505, 2510, 91 L.Ed.2d 202 (1986) * * *.

* * *

1

Were the Court to apply the proper standard for summary judgment, I believe it would conclude that the sworn affidavits and deposition testimony of Joyce Kelly and Amy Skilbred advance sufficient facts to create a genuine issue for trial concerning whether one or both would be imminently harmed by the Aswan and Mahaweli projects * * *.

I think a reasonable finder of fact could conclude from the information in the affidavits and deposition testimony that either Kelly or Skilbred will soon return to the project sites, thereby satisfying the "actual or imminent" injury standard * * *. Contrary to the Court's contention that Kelly's and Skilbred's past visits "prov[e] nothing," the fact of their past visits could demonstrate to a reasonable factfinder that Kelly and Skilbred have the requisite resources and personal interest in the preservation of the species endangered by the Aswan and Mahaweli projects to make good on their intention to return again * * *.

* * *

2

The Court also concludes that injury is lacking, because respondents' allegations of "ecosystem nexus" failed to demonstrate sufficient proximity to the site of the environmental harm * * *. Many environmental injuries, however, cause harm distant from the area immediately affected by the challenged action. Environmental destruction may affect animals traveling over vast geographical ranges or rivers running long geographical courses. It cannot seriously be contended that a litigant's failure to use the precise or exact site where animals are slaughtered or where toxic waste is dumped into a river means he or she cannot show injury.

* * *

B

A plurality of the Court suggests that respondents have not demonstrated redressability: a likelihood that a court ruling in their favor would remedy their injury * * *.

* * *

[After a lengthy analysis, to which the plurality offers a lengthy response, Justice Blackmun concludes that the plurality's redressability analysis is based "on its invitation of executive lawlessness, ignorance of principles of collateral estoppel, unfounded assumptions about causation, and erroneous conclusions about what the record does not say."]

II

The Court concludes that any "procedural injury" suffered by respondents is insufficient to confer standing. It rejects the view that the "injury-in-fact requirement [is] satisfied by congressional conferral upon *all* persons of an abstract, self-contained, noninstrumental 'right' to have the Executive observe the procedures required by law." Whatever the Court might mean with that very broad language, it cannot be saying that "procedural injuries" *as a class* are necessarily insufficient for purposes of Article III standing.

Most governmental conduct can be classified as "procedural." Many injuries caused by governmental conduct, therefore, are categorizable at some level of generality as "procedural" injuries. Yet, these injuries are not categorically beyond the pale of redress by the federal courts. When the Government, for example, "procedurally" issues a pollution permit, those affected by the permittee's pollutants are not without standing to sue. Only later cases will tell just what the Court means by its intimation that "procedural" injuries are not constitutionally cognizable injuries. In the meantime, I have the greatest of sympathy for the courts across the country that will struggle to understand the Court's standardless exposition of this concept today.

* * *

NOTES

The "injury in fact" prong of the standing inquiry has provoked the most discord, though the "redressability" element has generated its share of differences as well. Consider how well *Lujan* coheres with the following case.

FRIENDS OF THE EARTH, INC. v. LAIDLAW ENVIRONMENTAL SERVICES (TOC), INC.

Supreme Court of the United States, 2000.
528 U.S. 167, 120 S.Ct. 693, 145 L.Ed.2d 610.

Friends of the Earth v. Laidlaw

JUSTICE GINSBURG delivered the opinion of the Court.

* * *

I

A

In 1972, Congress enacted the Clean Water Act (Act), also known as the Federal Water Pollution Control Act, 86 Stat. 816, as amended, 33 U.S.C. § 251 et *seq.* Section 402 of the Act, 33 U.S.C. § 342, provides for the

Clean Water Act

issuance, by the Administrator of the Environmental Protection Agency (EPA) or by authorized States, of National Pollutant Discharge Elimination System (NPDES) permits. NPDES permits impose limitations on the discharge of pollutants, and establish related monitoring and reporting requirements, in order to improve the cleanliness and safety of the Nation's waters. Noncompliance with a permit constitutes a violation of the Act.

Under § 505(a) of the Act, a suit to enforce any limitation in an NPDES permit may be brought by any "citizen," defined as "a person or persons having an interest which is or may be adversely affected." 33 U.S.C. §§ 1365(a), (g) * * *.

B

In 1986, defendant-respondent Laidlaw Environmental Services (TOC), Inc., bought a hazardous waste incinerator facility in Roebuck, South Carolina, that included a wastewater treatment plant * * *. Shortly after Laidlaw acquired the facility, the South Carolina Department of Health and Environmental Control (DHEC), acting under 33 U.S.C. § 1342(a)(1), granted Laidlaw an NPDES permit authorizing the company to discharge treated water into the North Tyger River. The permit, which became effective on January 1, 1987, placed limits on Laidlaw's discharge of several pollutants into the river, including—of particular relevance to this case—mercury, an extremely toxic pollutant. The permit also regulated the flow, temperature, toxicity, and pH of the effluent from the facility, and imposed monitoring and reporting obligations.

Once it received its permit, Laidlaw began to discharge various pollutants into the waterway; repeatedly, Laidlaw's discharges exceeded the limits set by the permit. In particular, despite experimenting with several technological fixes, Laidlaw consistently failed to meet the permit's stringent 1.3 ppb (parts per billion) daily average limit on mercury discharges. The District Court later found that Laidlaw had violated the mercury limits on 489 occasions between 1987 and 1995.

* * *

On June 12, 1992, FOE filed this citizen suit against Laidlaw under § 505(a) of the Act, alleging noncompliance with the NPDES permit and seeking declaratory and injunctive relief and an award of civil penalties. Laidlaw moved for summary judgment on the ground that FOE had failed to present evidence demonstrating injury in fact, and therefore lacked Article III standing to bring the lawsuit * * *. [T]he District Court denied Laidlaw's summary judgment motion, finding—albeit "by the very slimmest of margins"—that FOE had standing to bring the suit.

* * *

On July 16, 1998, the Court of Appeals for the Fourth Circuit issued its judgment. 149 F.3d 303. The Court of Appeals assumed without deciding that FOE initially had standing to bring the action, *id.*, at 306, n. 3, but went on to hold that the case had become moot * * *.

[handwritten margin note: CoA found case was moot]

* * *

We granted certiorari * * *.

II

A

* * *

Laidlaw contends first that FOE lacked standing from the outset even to seek injunctive relief, because the plaintiff organizations failed to show that any of their members had sustained or faced the threat of any "injury in fact" from Laidlaw's activities. In support of this contention Laidlaw points to the District Court's finding, made in the course of setting the penalty amount [of $405,800], that there had been "no demonstrated proof of harm to the environment" from Laidlaw's mercury discharge violations. 956 F.Supp., at 602; see also *ibid.* ("[T]he NPDES permit violations at issue in this citizen suit did not result in any health risk or environmental harm.").

[handwritten margin note: injury in fact]

[handwritten margin note: Laidlaw claims "no demonstr. proof of harm → enviro"]

The relevant showing for purposes of Article III standing, however, is not injury to the environment but injury to the plaintiff. To insist upon the former rather than the latter as part of the standing inquiry (as the dissent in essence does) is to raise the standing hurdle higher than the necessary showing for success on the merits in an action alleging noncompliance with an NPDES permit. Focusing properly on injury to the plaintiff, the District Court found that FOE had demonstrated sufficient injury to establish standing. For example, FOE member Kenneth Lee Curtis averred in affidavits that he lived a half-mile from Laidlaw's facility; that he occasionally drove over the North Tyger River, and that it looked and smelled polluted; and that he would like to fish, camp, swim, and picnic in and near the river between 3 and 15 miles downstream from the facility, as he did when he was a teenager, but would not do so because he was concerned that the water was polluted by Laidlaw's discharges. Curtis reaffirmed these statements in extensive deposition testimony. For example, he testified that he would like to fish in the river at a specific spot he used as a boy, but that he would not do so now because of his concerns about Laidlaw's discharges.

[handwritten margin note: BUT relevant injury = to P, not to enviro]

[handwritten margin note: eg. aesthetic + recreational injuries in affidavits]

[handwritten margin note: "concern" that water was polluted]

Other members presented evidence to similar effect. CLEAN member Angela Patterson attested that she lived two miles from the facility; that before Laidlaw operated the facility, she picnicked, walked, birdwatched, and waded in and along the North Tyger River because of the natural beauty of the area; that she no longer engaged in these activities in or near the river because she was concerned about harmful effects from discharged pollutants; and that she and her husband would like to purchase a home near the river but did not intend to do so, in part because of Laidlaw's discharges. CLEAN member Judy Pruitt averred that she lived one-quarter mile from Laidlaw's facility and would like to fish, hike, and picnic along the North Tyger River, but has refrained from those activities because of the discharges. FOE member Linda Moore attested that she lived 20 miles from Roebuck, and would use the North Tyger River south of Roebuck and the land surrounding it for recreational purposes were she not concerned that the water contained harmful pollutants. In her deposition, Moore testified at length that she would hike, picnic, camp, swim, boat, and drive near or in the river were it not for her concerns about illegal discharges. CLEAN member Gail Lee attested that her home, which is near Laidlaw's facility, had a lower value than similar homes located further from the facility, and that she believed the pollutant discharges accounted for some of the discrepancy. Sierra Club member Norman Sharp averred that he had canoed approximately 40 miles downstream of the Laidlaw facility and would like to canoe in the North Tyger River closer to Laidlaw's discharge point, but did not do so because he was concerned that the water contained harmful pollutants.

[handwritten: these affidavits adequately show injury in fact] These sworn statements, as the District Court determined, adequately documented injury in fact. We have held that environmental plaintiffs adequately allege injury in fact when they aver that they use the affected area and are persons "for whom the aesthetic and recreational values of the area will be lessened" by the challenged activity. *Sierra Club v. Morton*, 405 U.S. 727, 735, 92 S.Ct. 1361, 31 L.Ed.2d 636 (1972).

[handwritten: Lujan v. Natl. Wildlife Federation] Our decision in *Lujan v. National Wildlife Federation*, 497 U.S. 871, 110 S.Ct. 3177, 111 L.Ed.2d 695 (1990), is not to the contrary. In that case * * * [w]e held that the plaintiff could not survive the summary judgment motion merely by offering "averments which state only that one of [the organization's] members uses unspecified portions of an immense tract of territory, on some portions of which mining activity has occurred or probably will occur by virtue of the governmental action." 497 U.S., at 889, 110 S.Ct. 3177.

In contrast, the affidavits and testimony presented by FOE in this case assert that Laidlaw's discharges, and the affiant members' reasonable concerns about the effects of those discharges, directly affected those affiants' recreational, aesthetic, and economic interests. These submissions present dispositively more than the mere "general averments" and "conclusory allegations" found inadequate in *National Wildlife Federation*. *Id.*, at 888, 110 S.Ct. 3177. Nor can the affiants' conditional statements—that they would use the nearby North Tyger River for recreation if Laidlaw were not discharging pollutants into it—be equated with the speculative *[handwritten: Lujan v. Defenders of Wildlife]* "'some day' intentions" to visit endangered species halfway around the world that we held insufficient to show injury in fact in *Defenders of Wildlife*. 504 U.S., at 564, 112 S.Ct. 2130.

Los Angeles v. Lyons, 461 U.S. 95, 103 S.Ct. 1660, 75 L.Ed.2d 675 (1983), relied on by the dissent, does not weigh against standing in this case. In *Lyons*, we held that a plaintiff lacked standing to seek an injunction against the enforcement of a police chokehold policy because he could not credibly allege that he faced a realistic threat from the policy. 461 U.S., at 107, n. 7, 103 S.Ct. 1660 * * *. Unlike the dissent, we see nothing "improbable" about the proposition that a company's continuous and pervasive illegal discharges of pollutants into a river would cause nearby residents to curtail their recreational use of that waterway and would subject them to other economic and aesthetic harms. The proposition is entirely reasonable, the District Court found it was true in this case, and that is enough for injury in fact.

Laidlaw argues next that even if FOE had standing to seek injunctive relief, it lacked standing to seek civil penalties. Here the asserted defect is not injury but redressability. Civil penalties offer no redress to private plaintiffs, Laidlaw argues, because they are paid to the government, and therefore a citizen plaintiff can never have standing to seek them.

Laidlaw is right to insist that a plaintiff must demonstrate standing separately for each form of relief sought. But it is wrong to maintain that citizen plaintiffs facing ongoing violations never have standing to seek civil penalties.

* * *

It can scarcely be doubted that, for a plaintiff who is injured or faces the threat of future injury due to illegal conduct ongoing at the time of suit, a sanction that effectively abates that conduct and prevents its recurrence provides a form of redress. Civil penalties can fit that description. To the extent that they encourage defendants to discontinue current violations and deter them from committing future ones, they afford redress to citizen plaintiffs who are injured or threatened with injury as a consequence of ongoing unlawful conduct.

The dissent argues that it is the *availability* rather than the *imposition* of civil penalties that deters any particular polluter from continuing to pollute. This argument misses the mark in two ways. First, it overlooks the interdependence of the availability and the imposition; a threat has no deterrent value unless it is credible that it will be carried out. Second, it is reasonable for Congress to conclude that an actual award of civil penalties does in fact bring with it a significant quantum of deterrence over and above what is achieved by the mere prospect of such penalties. A would-be polluter may or may not be dissuaded by the existence of a remedy on the books, but a defendant once hit in its pocketbook will surely think twice before polluting again.

We recognize that there may be a point at which the deterrent effect of a claim for civil penalties becomes so insubstantial or so remote that it cannot support citizen standing * * *. In this case we need not explore the outer limits of the principle that civil penalties provide sufficient deterrence to support redressability. Here, the civil penalties sought by FOE carried with them a deterrent effect that made it likely, as opposed to merely speculative, that the penalties would redress FOE's injuries by abating current violations and preventing future ones—as the District Court reasonably found when it assessed a penalty of $405,800. 956 F.Supp., at 610–611.

* * *

[Concurring opinions by JUSTICE STEVENS and JUSTICE KENNEDY are omitted.]

JUSTICE SCALIA, with whom JUSTICE THOMAS joins, dissenting.

* * *

Typically, an environmental plaintiff claiming injury due to discharges in violation of the Clean Water Act argues that the discharges harm the environment, and that the harm to the environment injures him. This route to injury is barred in the present case, however, since the District Court concluded after considering all the evidence that there had been "no demonstrated proof of harm to the environment," 956 F.Supp. 588, 602 (D.S.C.1997) * * *.

The Court finds these conclusions unproblematic for standing, because "[t]he relevant showing for purposes of Article III standing . . . is not injury to the environment but injury to the plaintiff." This statement is correct, as far as it goes. We have certainly held that a demonstration of harm to the environment is not *enough* to satisfy the injury-in-fact requirement unless the plaintiff can demonstrate how he personally was harmed. In the normal course, however, a lack of demonstrable harm to the environment will translate, as it plainly does here, into a lack of demonstrable harm to citizen plaintiffs. While it is perhaps possible that a plaintiff could be harmed even though the environment was not, such a plaintiff would have the burden of articulating and demonstrating the nature of that injury. Ongoing "concerns" about the environment are not enough, for "[i]t is the *reality* of the threat of repeated injury that is relevant to the standing inquiry, not the plaintiff's subjective apprehensions," *Los Angeles v. Lyons*, 461 U.S. 95, 107, n. 8, 103 S.Ct. 1660, 75 L.Ed.2d 675 (1983). At the very least, in the present case, one would expect to see evidence supporting the affidavits' bald assertions regarding decreasing recreational usage and declining home values, as well as evidence for the improbable proposition that Laidlaw's violations, even though harmless to the environment, are somehow responsible for these effects. Plaintiffs here have made no attempt at such a showing, but rely entirely upon unsupported and unexplained affidavit allegations of "concern."

Indeed, every one of the affiants deposed by Laidlaw cast into doubt the (in any event inadequate) proposition that subjective "concerns" actually affected their conduct. Linda Moore, for example, said in her affidavit that she would use the affected waterways for recreation if it were not for her concern about pollution. Yet she testified in her deposition that she had been to the river only twice, once in 1980 (when she visited someone who lived by the river) and once after this suit was filed. Similarly, Kenneth Lee Curtis, who claimed he was injured by being deprived of recreational activity at the river, admitted that he had not been to the river since he was "a kid," and when asked whether the reason he stopped visiting the river was because of pollution, answered "no." As to Curtis's claim that the river "looke[d] and smell[ed] polluted," this condition, if present, was surely not caused by Laidlaw's discharges, which according to the District Court "did not result in any health risk or environmental harm." 956 F.Supp., at 602. The other affiants cited by the Court were not deposed, but their affidavits state either that they *would* use the river if it were not polluted or harmful (as the court subsequently found it is not), or said that the river looks polluted (which is also incompatible with the court's findings). These affiants have established nothing but "subjective apprehensions."

* * *

* * * By accepting plaintiffs' vague, contradictory, and unsubstantiated allegations of "concern" about the environment as adequate to prove injury in fact, and accepting them even in the face of a finding that the environment was not demonstrably harmed, the Court makes the injury-in-fact requirement a sham. If there are permit violations, and a member of a plaintiff environmental organization lives near the offending plant, it would be difficult not to satisfy today's lenient standard.

II

* * *

* * * The Court recognizes, of course, that to satisfy Article III, it must be "likely," as opposed to "merely speculative," that a favorable decision will redress plaintiffs' injury, Lujan, *supra*, at 561, 112 S.Ct. 2130 * * *.

redressability

* * *

If the Court had undertaken the necessary inquiry into whether significant deterrence of the plaintiffs' feared injury was "likely," it would have had to reason something like this: Strictly speaking, no polluter is deterred by a penalty for past pollution; he is deterred by the *fear* of a penalty for *future* pollution. That fear will be virtually nonexistent if the prospective polluter knows that all emissions violators are given a free pass; it will be substantial under an emissions program such as the federal scheme here, which is regularly and notoriously enforced; it will be even higher when a prospective polluter subject to such a regularly enforced program has, as here, been the object of public charges of pollution and a suit for injunction; and it will surely be near the top of the graph when, as here, the prospective polluter has already been subjected to *state* penalties for the past pollution. The deterrence on which the plaintiffs must rely for standing in the present case is the marginal increase in Laidlaw's fear of future penalties that will be achieved by adding federal penalties for Laidlaw's past conduct.

* * *

* * * [I]f this case is, as the Court suggests, within the central core of "deterrence" standing, it is impossible to imagine what the "outer limits" could possibly be. The Court's expressed reluctance to define those "outer limits" serves only to disguise the fact that it has promulgated a revolutionary new doctrine of standing that will permit the entire body of public civil penalties to be handed over to enforcement by private interests.

* * *

NOTES

Summers v. Earth Island Institute

Just in case you have not had your fill of split decisions involving the standing of environmental groups, consider *Summers v. Earth Island Institute*, 555 U.S. 488, 129 S.Ct. 1142, 173 L.Ed.2d 1 (2009). The Forest Service is generally required by statute to provide notice, comment, and appeal procedures for proposed actions that implement resource management plans. The Service enacted regulations that exempted from these procedures "fire-rehabilitation activities on areas of less than 4,200 acres, and salvage-timber sales of 250 acres or less * * *." 129 S.Ct. at 1147. Petitioners challenged the validity of the these procedural regulations and the Forest Service's application of those regulations (and resultant failure to provide for notice, comment, and appeal) to one specific project known as the Burnt Ridge Project. The claims involving Burnt Ridge—for which everyone agreed standing was appropriate—were settled after the district granted a preliminary injunction for the petitioners, but even after that claim was resolved, the district court imposed a nationwide injunction against application of the regulations in future cases. A five-justice majority, in an opinion by Justice Scalia, held that petitioners had no standing:

> It is common ground that the respondent organizations can assert the standing of their members. To establish the concrete and particularized injury that standing requires, respondents point to their members' recreational interests in the National Forests * * *.

Affidavits submitted to the District Court alleged that organization member Ara Marderosian had repeatedly visited the Burnt Ridge site, that he had imminent plans to do so again, and that his interests in viewing the flora and fauna of the area would be harmed if the Burnt Ridge Project went forward without incorporation of the ideas he would have suggested if the Forest Service had provided him an opportunity to comment. The Government concedes that this was sufficient to establish Article III standing with respect to Burnt Ridge * * *. After the District Court had issued a preliminary injunction, however, the parties settled their differences on that score * * *.

Respondents have identified no other application of the invalidated regulations that threatens imminent and concrete harm to the interests of their members. The only other affidavit relied on was that of Jim Bensman. He asserted, first, that he had suffered injury in the past from development on Forest Service land. That does not suffice for several reasons: because it was not tied to application of the challenged regulations, because it does not identify any particular site, and because it relates to past injury rather than imminent future injury that is sought to be enjoined.

Bensman's affidavit further asserts that he has visited many National Forests and plans to visit several unnamed National Forests in the future * * *. The National Forests occupy more than 190 million acres, an area larger than Texas. There may be a chance, but it hardly a likelihood, that Bensman's wanderings will bring him to a parcel about to be affected by a project unlawfully subject to the regulations. Indeed, without further specification, it is impossible to tell *which* projects are (in respondents' view) unlawfully subject to the regulations * * *. Here we are asked to assume not only that Bensman will stumble across a project tract unlawfully subject to the regulations, but also that the tract is about to be developed by the Forest Service in a way that harms his recreational, and that he would have commented on the project but for the regulation * * *.

The Bensman affidavit does refer specifically to a series of projects in the Allegheny National Forest that are subject to the challenged regulations. It does not assert, however, any firm intention to visit their locations, saying only that Bensman " 'want[s] to' " go there. This vague desire to return is insufficient to satisfy the requirement of imminent injury * * *.

555 U.S. at 494–96, 129 S.Ct. at 1149–51. Four justices, led by Justice Breyer, strongly dissented:

How can the majority credibly claim that salvage-timber sales, and similar projects, are unlikely to harm the asserted interests of the members of these environmental groups? The majority apparently does so in part by arguing that the Forest Service actions are not "imminent" * * *. I concede that the Court has sometimes used the word "imminent" in the context of constitutional standing. But it has done so primarily to emphasize that the harm in question—the harm that was not "imminent"—was merely "conjectural" or "hypothetical" or otherwise speculative. Where the Court has directly focused on the matter, *i.e.*, where, as here, a plaintiff has *already* been subject to the injury it wishes to challenge, the Court has asked whether there is a *realistic likelihood* that the challenged future conduct will, in fact, recur and harm the plaintiff * * *.

* * *

* * * [A] threat of future harm may be realistic even where the plaintiff cannot specify precise times, dates, and GPS coordinates * * *.

The Forest Service admits that it intends to conduct thousands of further salvage-timber sales and other projects exempted under the challenged regulations "in the reasonably near future." How then can the Court deny that the plaintiffs have shown a "realistic" threat that the Forest Service will continue to authorize (without the procedures claimed necessary) salvage-timber sales and other Forest Service projects, that adversely affect the recreational, aesthetic, and environmental interests of the plaintiffs' members?

* * *

The Bensman affidavit does not say *which particular* sites will be affected by future Forest Service projects, but the Service itself has conceded that it will conduct thousands of exempted projects in the future. Why is more specificity needed to show a "realistic" threat that a project will impact land Bensman uses? To know, virtually for certain, that snow will fall in New England this winter is not to know the name of each particular town where it is bound to arrive.

555 U.S. at 505–08, 129 S.Ct. at 1155–57.

2. STATUTORY STANDING AND THE "ZONE OF INTERESTS" TEST

a. The Original Understanding

A plaintiff who satisfies constitutional standing requirements—and most plaintiffs in administrative law cases satisfy constitutional standing requirements—must also satisfy whatever requirements for standing are specified by Congress for particular actions. Section 702 of the APA identifies the class of persons that is entitled to judicial review of agency action: "A person suffering legal wrong because of agency action, or adversely affected or aggrieved by agency action within the meaning of a relevant statute, is entitled to judicial review thereof." 5 U.S.C. § 702 (2012).

In 1946, the meaning of this provision was clear. Consider first the clause conferring standing on "[a] person suffering legal wrong because of agency action." A "legal wrong" was simply any kind of injury that was traditionally cognizable by courts. A person whose freedom of movement was restricted, or whose contract was breached, or whose chickens were seized and destroyed could assert a "legal wrong," but Mrs. Frothingham, who alleged only the possibility that her taxes would increase if Congress was permitted to exceed its constitutional spending powers, could not.

Two propositions about the scope of the term "legal wrong" in 1946 are especially important. First, it plainly did not include generalized assertions of distress at the prospect of government lawbreaking. Second, it plainly did not include freedom from lawful competition. This latter point is crucial to a grasp of modern standing law and warrants a brief detour.

Suppose that you operate a grocery store. Another party acquires the land across the street and opens a competing store. They have the temerity to offer better products at lower prices. There is no question that their actions cause you damage (and certainly enough damage to satisfy the constitutional "injury in fact" requirement), but assuming that your competitor competes fairly and without violating applicable antitrust laws, the damage is not a legal wrong. Modern courts will not accept damage, even serious damage, from lawful competition as a legally cognizable injury.

Suppose you discover, however, that the competing grocery store owner acquired your neighbor's land through fraud. Can you enjoin operation of the grocery store on the ground that the land on which the store is operated was acquired illegally? The answer is no. The defrauded seller has standing to raise the issue of fraud, but you do not. Even though the store is, in one sense, operating illegally, that illegality is not yours to raise. As long as the store's competitive activities are lawful, your damage from loss of customers remains unredressable. In other words, at common law, lawful competition is not a legal wrong even when the competition is made possible by an underlying illegal act.

Assume now that all grocery stores in your jurisdiction must obtain licenses from an administrative agency. Suppose that the competing store obtained a license illegally—the governing statutes would not warrant the grant of a license, but the agency ignored or misconstrued the relevant statutes. Can you enjoin the operation of the competing store because of the underlying governmental illegality?

The common law's answer was no—just as an underlying fraud in the purchase of land would not sustain an action against otherwise lawful competition. A disappointed applicant for the license, who was turned down in favor of your competitor, might well have had standing to object to the government's illegal conduct, but you as a mere competitor would not.

Thus, as clearly understood in 1946, competitive injury was not a "legal wrong" unless the *competitive acts* themselves were illegal. Competitors did not, at common law, have standing to challenge underlying illegal acts, including governmental acts, that made the lawful competition possible in the first place.

If a legal wrong is a prerequisite to standing to challenge agency action, this common law regime would effectively insulate a large amount of governmental activity from judicial review. Consider, for example, the actions of the Federal Communications Commission in granting radio broadcast licenses. There is a limited number of licenses in each geographic area because of the limited number of available broadcast frequencies. Suppose—not at all unrealistically—that there are dozens of valid applications for a particular broadcast license that, once granted, will permit competition with an existing licensed radio station. And suppose that the Commission *wrongly* grants the license to a particular applicant. Any of the disappointed applicants clearly have standing to sue, but they may not have the incentive. After all, if one of them sues successfully, it will assure only that the Commission must regrant the license; it will not assure that the Commission must regrant the license to the successful litigant. It is possible that one of the applicants will nonetheless incur the expense of a lawsuit in pursuit of a one-in-dozens chance at the license, but it is also possible that each of the disappointed applicants will conclude that the costs of litigation outweigh the highly uncertain potential benefits.

In settings like this, the *existing station owner* with whom the new licensee will compete is the person with the most incentive to challenge the agency's action, if only to delay the onset of competition a bit longer by forcing a new licensing proceeding (or to hope for a weaker competitor to emerge with the license). The existing station clearly has *constitutional* standing—competition will decrease profits, the lost profits are attributable to the government's illegal action, and revocation of the illegally granted license will redress the injury—but not all persons who meet constitutional standing requirements also suffer a "legal wrong" within the meaning of the common law's "legal interest" test (as it is generally called). One can therefore imagine that Congress might wish to expand the range of potential litigants beyond those persons who suffer a "legal wrong" at common law. Congress might, for instance, pass a statute authorizing review of agency action by any person "adversely affected or aggrieved by agency action." Obviously, such a statute could not authorize standing for someone who fails the constitutional requirement, but it could authorize standing for competitors who meet constitutional requirements but do not suffer deprivation of a legally protected interest.

In the years before enactment of the APA, Congress enacted a number of statutes aimed precisely at expanding the range of persons who could challenge agency action to include, *inter alia*, competitors of government licensees. These statutes used a number of formulations to describe the class of permissible plaintiffs, the most common of which was something to the effect of "all persons adversely affected or aggrieved by agency action." These statutes were the obvious referents of the second clause in § 702: persons "adversely affected or aggrieved by agency action within the meaning of a relevant statute." In other words, it was very clear in 1946 that a "relevant statute" within the meaning of § 702 was a *special review statute* that expanded the class of plaintiffs beyond the common-law legal interest test. Of course, not every agency organic act contained a special review statute, and not every special review statute contained a provision broadening the class of plaintiffs. In the absence of a special review statute that contained language expanding the right to sue, § 702 of the APA, as originally understood, would require all plaintiffs to satisfy the common law legal interest test. And even special review statutes that expanded the right to sue would not do so limitlessly. A statute authorizing suit by "any person adversely affected or aggrieved by agency action" is not necessarily intended by Congress to authorize suit by any person who meets the constitutional minima for standing. It was clear, for example, that a person who felt mental anguish at the prospect of agency lawbreaking would not be "adversely affected or aggrieved" within the meaning of the special review statutes that used that language at the time of enactment of the APA. Congress meant for these statutes to permit suit by some parties who would be denied standing at common law, but careful analysis of each statute's language, purpose, and legislative history would no doubt disclose some limits to the class of statutorily authorized plaintiffs.

The original understanding of § 702 was well described by the following leading case from 1955.

KANSAS CITY POWER & LIGHT CO. V. MCKAY

United States Court of Appeals District of Columbia Circuit, 1955.
225 F.2d 924.

Before PRETTYMAN, BAZELON and WASHINGTON, CIRCUIT JUDGES.

WASHINGTON, CIRCUIT JUDGE.

This case involves the question whether utility companies which claim they are in competition with a federally-supported power program can obtain the aid of the courts in challenging the validity of that program.

Plaintiffs-appellants, electric utility companies operating in Kansas, Missouri and Arkansas, ask for relief under the Declaratory Judgment Act, 28 U.S.C. §§ 2201–2202, against the Secretaries of the Interior, Agriculture and the Treasury and the Administrators of the Southwestern Power

Administration ("SPA") and of the Rural Electrification Administration ("REA") as defendants: (1) enjoining them from lending or disbursing funds of the United States to SPA or to certain federated power cooperatives for the construction by the latter of electric generating and transmission facilities and for the sale and purchase of electric power to and from them by SPA; (2) enjoining them from doing anything in furtherance of an alleged plan by which SPA would in effect construct and acquire control of these generating and transmission facilities contrary to law; and (3) declaring that they have no right, power or authority to carry out the alleged plan.

Defendants moved to dismiss the complaint for the reason, among others, that plaintiffs did not have the capacity and did not show any injury or interest entitling them, to maintain the suit * * *.

Defendants SPA and REA have made contracts with five federated cooperatives [providing loans for constructing power generating plants] * * *.

Plaintiffs are electric power utilities, supplying electric service to a large number of customers in Missouri, Kansas and Arkansas, including rural electric distribution cooperatives to whom central station service is rendered. None of them has exclusive franchises to supply electric power. They have programs, in various stages of planning or execution, to expand their facilities to meet estimated increases in demand for electric energy from all of these consumers and customers. They claim that the contractual arrangements made by REA and SPA with the federated cooperatives will thwart their plans and duplicate their facilities (existing, under construction, or authorized), which are or will be available to serve the federated cooperatives' demand for central station service. They contend that the contracts violate the loan standards of the Rural Electrification Act of 1936; that SPA's power rates are uneconomical, and that the congressionally-imposed restrictions on SPA's activities have been violated, contrary to the provisions of the Flood Control Act of 1944; that the contracts enable the federated cooperatives to engage in destructive federally-subsidized competition with plaintiffs; and that the defendants (other than the Secretary of the Treasury) are misusing the lending powers of REA to obtain for SPA control or ownership of the large steam generating plants and transmission lines built by the federated cooperatives, contrary to the intent of Congress, the Constitution and the laws above referred to.

It is indisputable that the essence of plaintiffs' complaint is the competition which they will suffer if the Government's contracts are carried out. They can claim no other interest or injury. The defendants have not undertaken to regulate them in any way. They have not been ordered to abandon any of their activities or to forego the expansion programs planned by them. They have not been subjected to any obligation or duty. Their sole interest and objective is to eliminate the competition which they fear. Controlling decisions of the Supreme Court, dealing with other electric power contracts of the Federal Government, establish that an interest of this kind is not sufficient to enable them to sue to enjoin execution of the power contracts and program of the Government.

* * * The Court * * * [in *Alabama Power Co. v. Ickes*, 302 U.S. 464, 58 S.Ct. 300, 82 L.Ed. 374 (1938)] made it clear that one whose only injury will result from lawful competition has no standing to question whether the contracts with the municipalities were authorized by statute and thus legal * * *.

* * *

Neither the Rural Electrification Act, the Flood Control Act of 1944 nor the "continuing fund" and other appropriation acts referred to in these proceedings provides for judicial, or indeed even administrative, review of action taken by the respective agencies. These statutes differ sharply from the Transportation Act, 1920, which specifically authorized suits for injunction by any "party in interest". 49 U.S.C.A. § 647. Thus cases arising under that statute * * *, upon which appellants rely, have no relevance here * * *.

Appellants seek, finally, to base their right to bring this action on their alleged status as persons "suffering legal wrong" or "adversely affected or aggrieved" within the meaning of Section 10(a) of the Administrative Procedure Act. 5 U.S.C.A. § 1009(a) * * *.

* * *

Section 10(a) is for the benefit of "any person suffering legal wrong", that is, one whose legal rights have been violated. As we have seen, these plaintiffs cannot effectively make such a claim. Nor are we confronted with any relevant statute within the meaning of which the plaintiffs are "adversely affected or aggrieved." Plaintiffs-appellants cite and rely on the view expressed in *American President Lines v. Federal Maritime Board*, D.C.D.C.1953, 112 F.Supp. 346, at page 349, which would in effect delete from Section 10(a) the phrase "within the meaning of any relevant statute". That view cannot, of course, be accepted.

* * *

[Judge Prettyman, in dissent, read the complaint to allege that petitioners would face not merely competition but the total destruction of their business from the allegedly illegal government contracts, which he thought was a sufficient allegation to constitute a legal wrong within the meaning of § 702.]

b.   Cracks in the Foundation

The original understanding of § 702 leaves a fair number of agency decisions effectively unreviewable—or at least unreviewable by the parties with the most direct and powerful interest in seeking review. We have seen that in the absence of a special review statute that expands the permissible class of plaintiffs in a given case, the common law legal interest test denies standing to plaintiffs whose sole injury is competitive harm. The legal interest test similarly denies standing to plaintiffs whose primary interests are ideological or aesthetic. Suppose that a federal agency illegally grants a license to construct a dam. People who regard the dam as unsightly clearly have not suffered a "legal wrong," nor have people who allege that the dam will harm indigenous plant or animal life (unless they have a cognizable property interest in the damaged flora or fauna). Indeed, it is entirely possible that *no one* who has any real interest in challenging the dam will have standing under the legal interest test to object to an illegal licensing proceeding. And even if Congress had passed a special review statute conferring standing on any person "adversely affected or aggrieved" by the licensing agency's action, it was highly doubtful in 1946 that such language intended to grant standing to plaintiffs with aesthetic or ideological concerns.

If one believes, with James Landis, that judicial involvement in the administrative process is something to be avoided, one will see nothing wrong (and much right) with a system of judicial review that leaves large classes of agency activity unreviewable by any likely plaintiff. But if one believes instead that agencies are readily subject to "capture" by special interests, especially industry interests, the standing regime established by § 702 will seem less satisfactory. That dissatisfaction will dramatically increase as the aesthetic and ideological concerns that are seemingly excluded from the standing inquiry under § 702 grow in importance in the judicial mind. This was especially pertinent during the 1960s, with the rise of interest among the intellectual classes in the environmental and civil rights movements.

Two famous circuit court decisions from the mid-1960s illustrate the changing judicial attitude towards standing—and towards the role of courts in the administrative process. In *Scenic Hudson Preservation Conference v. FPC*, 354 F.2d 608 (2d Cir.1965), the Federal Power Commission had granted a license for construction of a dam near Storm King Mountain in New York. The project was opposed by the Scenic Hudson Preservation Conference, "an unincorporated association consisting of a number of non-profit, conservationist organizations," *id.* at 611, and three local communities, on the ground that the agency had failed to take adequate account of the project's impact on recreational and aesthetic values. After a lengthy discussion of the importance of such values under the Federal Power Act and of the likely impact of the project on those values, the court addressed petitioners' standing:

> Respondent argues that "petitioners do not have standing to obtain review" because they "make no claim of any personal economic injury resulting from the Commission's action."

> Section 313(b) of the Federal Power Act, 16 U.S.C. § 825l(b), reads:

> > "(b)   Any party to a proceeding under this chapter aggrieved by an order issued by the Commission in such proceeding may obtain a review of such order in the United States Court of Appeals for any circuit wherein the licensee or public utility to which the order relates is located * * *."

> * * *

> * * * The Federal Power Act seeks to protect non-economic as well as economic interests * * *.

> In order to insure that the Federal Power Commission will adequately protect the public interest in the aesthetic, conservational, and recreational aspects of power development, those who by their activities and conduct have exhibited a special interest in such areas, must be held to be included in the class of "aggrieved" parties under § 313(b). We hold that the Federal Power Act gives petitioners a legal right to protect their special interests.

> * * *

> Moreover, petitioners have sufficient economic interest to establish their standing. The New York-New Jersey Trail Conference, one of the two conservation groups that organized Scenic Hudson, has some seventeen miles of trailways in the area of Storm King Mountain. Portions of these trails would be inundated by the construction of the project's reservoir.

> The primary transmission lines are an integral part of the Storm King project. The towns that are co-petitioners with Scenic Hudson have standing because the transmission lines would cause a decrease in the proprietary value of publicly held land, reduce tax revenues collected from privately held land, and significantly interfere with long-range community planning * * *.

Id. at 615–16.

In *Office of Communication of the United Church of Christ v. FCC*, 359 F.2d 994 (D.C.Cir.1966), the court faced a challenge brought by viewers of a Mississippi television station to a decision by the Federal

Communications Commission to relicense the station (albeit on a probationary basis). The petitioners alleged that the station had persistently engaged in racially and religiously discriminatory programming.[24] The Commission argued, with considerable caselaw support, that the viewers had no standing to sue as persons "adversely affected or aggrieved" under the relevant special review statute[25] because the statute granted standing only to persons complaining of economic injury or electrical interference from an improperly licensed facility. The court disagreed:

> Up to this time, the courts have granted standing to intervene only to those alleging electrical interference or alleging some economic injury * * *.

> What the Commission apparently fails to see in the present case is that the courts have resolved questions of standing as they arose and have at no time manifested an intent to make economic interest and electrical interference the exclusive grounds for standing * * *.

> * * *

> The Commission's rigid adherence to a requirement of direct economic injury in the commercial sense operates to give standing to an electronics manufacturer who competes with the owner of a radio-television station only in the sale of appliances, while it denies standing to spokesmen for the listeners, who are most directly concerned with and intimately affected by the performance of a licensee. Since the concept of standing is a practical and functional one designed to insure that only those with a genuine and legitimate interest can participate in a proceeding, we can see no reason to exclude those with such an obvious and acute concern as the listening audience. This much seems essential to insure that the holders of broadcasting licenses be responsive to the needs of the audience, without which the broadcaster could not exist.

Id. at 1000–02.

Although the *Scenic Hudson* and *United Church of Christ* decisions gave expansive readings to special review statutes, those decisions nonetheless operated within the traditional framework of § 702: in the

---

[24] "[T]he first complaints go back to 1955 when it was claimed that WLBT had deliberately cut off a network program about race relations problems on which the General Counsel of the NAACP was appearing and had flashed on the viewers' screens a 'Sorry, Cable Trouble' sign. In 1957 another complaint was made to the Commission that WLBT had presented a program urging the maintenance of racial segregation and had refused requests for time to present the opposing viewpoint. Since then numerous other complaints have been made." *Id.* at 998.

[25] The viewers clearly had no legal interest at common law.

absence of special review statutes for the courts to (mis?)construe, it is doubtful whether the courts would have found the hikers and viewers to have suffered "legal wrongs" by virtue of the agencies' actions. In 1970, however, the traditional framework simply vanished.

c. An Earth-Shattering Kaboom

ASSOCIATION OF DATA PROCESSING SERVICE ORGANIZATIONS, INC. V. CAMP
Supreme Court of the United States, 1970.
397 U.S. 150, 90 S.Ct. 827, 25 L.Ed.2d 184.

MR. JUSTICE DOUGLAS delivered the opinion of the Court.

Petitioners sell data processing services to businesses generally. In this suit they seek to challenge a ruling by respondent Comptroller of the Currency that, as an incident to their banking services, national banks, including respondent American National Bank & Trust Company, may make data processing services available to other banks and to bank customers. The District Court dismissed the complaint for lack of standing of petitioners to bring the suit. The Court of Appeals affirmed. The case is here on a petition for writ of certiorari which we granted.

Generalizations about standing to sue are largely worthless as such. One generalization is, however, necessary and that is that the question of standing in the federal courts is to be considered in the framework of Article III which restricts judicial power to "cases" and "controversies" * * *.

The first question is whether the plaintiff alleges that the challenged action has caused him injury in fact, economic or otherwise. There can be no doubt but that petitioners have satisfied this test. The petitioners not only allege that competition by national banks in the business of providing data processing services might entail some future loss of profits for the petitioners, they also allege that respondent American National Bank & Trust Company was performing or preparing to perform such services for two customers for whom petitioner Data Systems, Inc., had previously agreed or negotiated to perform such services. The petitioners' suit was brought not only against the American National Bank & Trust Company, but also against the Comptroller of the Currency. The Comptroller was alleged to have caused petitioners injury in fact by his 1966 ruling which stated:

> "Incidental to its banking services, a national bank may make available its data processing equipment or perform data processing services on such equipment for other banks and bank customers." Comptroller's Manual for National Banks 3500 (October 15, 1966).

The Court of Appeals viewed the matter differently, stating:

> "(A) Plaintiff may challenge alleged illegal competition when as complainant it pursues (1) a legal interest by reason of public charter or contract, . . . (2) a legal interest by reason of statutory protection, . . . or (3) a 'public interest' in which congress has recognized the need for review of administrative action and plaintiff is significantly involved to have standing to represent the public . . ." 406 F.2d, at 842–843.[1]

Those tests were based on prior decisions of this Court, such as *Tennessee Electric Power Co. v. TVA*, 306 U.S. 118, 59 S.Ct. 366, 83 L.Ed. 543, where private power companies sought to enjoin TVA from operating, claiming that the statutory plan under which it was created was unconstitutional. The Court denied the competitors' standing, holding that they did not have that status "unless the right invaded is a legal right,— one of property, one arising out of contract, one protected against tortious invasion, or one founded on a statute which confers a privilege." *Id.*, at 137– 138, 59 S.Ct. at 369.

The "legal interest" test goes to the merits. The question of standing is different. It concerns, apart from the "case" or "controversy" test, the question whether the interest sought to be protected by the complainant is arguably within the zone of interests to be protected or regulated by the statute or constitutional guarantee in question. Thus the Administrative Procedure Act grants standing to a person "aggrieved by agency action within the meaning of a relevant statute." 5 U.S.C. § 702. That interest, at times, may reflect "aesthetic, conservational, and recreational" as well as economic values. *Scenic Hudson Preservation Conference v. FPC*, 2 Cir., 354 F.2d 608, 616; *Office of Communication of United Church of Christ v. FCC*, 123 U.S.App.D.C. 328, 334–340, 359 F.2d 994, 1000–1006 * * *. We mention these noneconomic values to emphasize that standing may stem from them as well as from the economic injury in which petitioners rely here * * *.

* * *

Where statutes are concerned, the trend is toward enlargement of the class of people who may protest administrative action. The whole drive for enlarging the category of aggrieved "persons" is symptomatic of that trend. In a closely analogous case we held that an existing entrepreneur had standing to challenge the legality of the entrance of a newcomer into the business, because the established business was allegedly protected by a

---

[1]   The first two tests applied by the Court of Appeals required a showing of a "legal interest." But the existence or non-existence of a "legal interest" is a matter quite distinct from the problem of standing. The third test mentioned by the Court of Appeals, which rests on an explicit provision in a regulatory statute conferring standing and is commonly referred to in terms of allowing suits by "private attorneys general," is inapplicable to the present case.

valid city ordinance that protected it from unlawful competition. *Chicago v. Atchison, T. & S.F.R. Co.,* 357 U.S. 77, 83–84, 78 S.Ct. 1063, 1066–1068, 2 L.Ed.2d 1174. In that tradition was *Hardin v. Kentucky Utilities Co.,* 390 U.S. 1, 88 S.Ct. 651, 19 L.Ed.2d 787, which involved a section of the TVA Act designed primarily to protect, through area limitations, private utilities against TVA competition. We held that no explicit statutory provision was necessary to confer standing, since the private utility bringing suit was within the class of persons that the statutory provision was designed to protect.

* * *

We find no evidence that Congress in either the Bank Service Corporation Act or the National Bank Act sought to preclude judicial review of administrative rulings by the Comptroller as to the legitimate scope of activities available to national banks under those statutes. Both Acts are clearly "relevant" statutes within the meaning of § 702. The Acts do not in terms protect a specified group. But their general policy is apparent; and those whose interests are directly affected by a broad or narrow interpretation of the Acts are easily identifiable. It is clear that petitioners, as competitors of national banks which are engaging in data processing services, are within that class of "aggrieved" persons who, under § 702, are entitled to judicial review of "agency action."

Whether anything in the Bank Service Corporation Act or the National Bank Act gives petitioners a "legal interest" that protects them against violations of those Acts, and whether the actions of respondents did in fact violate either of those Acts, are questions which go to the merits and remain to be decided below.

We hold that petitioners have standing to sue and that the case should be remanded for a hearing on the merits.

Reversed and remanded.

NOTES

The *Data Processing* decision was accompanied by *Barlow v. Collins,* 397 U.S. 159, 90 S.Ct. 832, 25 L.Ed.2d 192 (1970), in which the Court held that tenant farmers could seek review of a Department of Agriculture regulation concerning the terms on which federal crop payments could be assigned to landlords. The Court reasoned that the farmers were within the "zone of interests" of the relevant substantive provisions of the Food and Agriculture Act of 1965. Within the next year, the Court decided two more standing cases under its new "zone of interests" standard. *See Arnold Tours, Inc. v. Camp,* 400 U.S. 45, 91 S.Ct. 158, 27 L.Ed.2d 179 (1970) (travel agents have standing to challenge the Comptroller of the Currency's ruling that national banks can provide travel services); *Investment Co. Institute v. Camp,* 401 U.S. 617, 91 S.Ct. 1091, 28 L.Ed.2d 367 (1971) (investment companies have standing to challenge the Comptroller's decision to allow national banks to operate mutual funds). All of these decisions granted standing to plaintiffs who clearly would not have had standing under the traditional interpretation of § 702.[26] All of these decisions construed § 702's reference to a "relevant statute" to mean the *substantive* terms of the agency's organic statute rather than the terms of any *special review* provisions targeted specifically at standing. All of these decisions required plaintiffs to be "arguably within the zone of interests" protected by those substantive statutes. And none of these decisions said anything useful to lower courts about how this new "zone of interests" standing test was to be applied. The only elaboration of the zone of interests test came in the brief per curiam decision in *Arnold Tours*, which made clear that a class of plaintiffs could be within a statute's "zone of interests" even if the class was not specifically mentioned in the statute's legislative history. *See* 400 U.S. at 46, 91 S.Ct. at 159.

The only objections on the Court to the new "zone of interests" formulation came from Justices who thought that it was *too restrictive*. Justice Brennan, joined by Justice White, concurred in the results in *Data Processing* and *Barlow* but rejected the Court's rationale. Their position, quite flatly, was that § 702 should not be read to impose any standing requirements beyond the minimum constitutional requirement of injury in fact. *See* 397 U.S. at 168–69, 90 S.Ct. at 838–39.

After announcing, without elaboration, a new test for standing, the Supreme Court vanished from the scene for 16 years. Lower courts thus had to resolve standing questions, which arise more than occasionally in administrative law,[27] with virtually no guidance from the Supreme Court other than a clear message not to apply traditional standing doctrine. The results were aptly summarized by the D.C. Circuit in 1981, in a case whose tone was not untypical of lower court decisions attempting to apply the zone of interests test:

> The zone of interests test made its initial appearances in four cases decided by the Supreme Court in 1970 and 1971.

> * * *

> In these four cases the Supreme Court discarded the outdated legal interest criterion and interposed a new zone of interests test more compatible with the perceived trend toward the enlargement of the class of persons entitled to protest administrative action. This new test was starkly stated, however, without accompanying

---

[26] The plaintiffs in the three banking cases suffered only competitive harm, and the plaintiffs in *Barlow* merely failed to receive as favorable a regulation as they desired, none of which constitutes a "legal wrong" at common law. Nor were the plaintiffs in any of the four cases "persons adversely affected or aggrieved" within the meaning of a relevant special review statute, because neither the National Banking Act nor the Food and Agriculture Act of 1965 contained a special review statute.

[27] Because it goes to the jurisdiction of the reviewing court, standing is potentially an issue in every case, whether or not the parties choose to raise it. Most of the time, however, the plaintiff's entitlement to standing is obvious, even under the vague zone of interests test.

expression of the methods to be utilized in its application. Moreover, the Court's own applications of the fledgling standard were generally conclusory in nature, and consequently failed to provide the desired clarification.

Despite the difficulties engendered by this lack of guidance, the Court has not attempted to develop, in the years since *Data Processing* and its immediate progeny, a more mature zone of interests standard. In that time the Court has specified no guidelines for the test's application nor has it even undertaken to apply the zone test in a standing inquiry. At least one commentator has suggested that this neglect indicates the Court's implicit abandonment of the zone standard. The Court's express reaffirmation of the test's existence, albeit in summary fashion, requires us to assume, however, the test's continued role as a prudential limitation. We must, therefore, apply the test despite the Court's failure to provide more specific guidance.

* * *

* * * We turn, therefore, to the case law of the federal courts for help in making a principled application of that [zone of interests] standard.

A survey of this law reveals, however, more variety than uniformity among the approaches to the zone test. Some courts, reacting strongly to the Supreme Court's vague formulation of the test, have expressed disagreement with the standard,[16] clearly misapplied it,[17] or virtually ignored it.[18] Other courts, taking a more active approach, have attempted to refine the test into a workable standard. As a result of these efforts, it is generally recognized that in applying the zone test a court must discern whether the interest asserted by a party in the particular instance is one intended by Congress to be protected or regulated by the statute under which suit is brought. Most courts also acknowledge that the sources pertinent to this examination are the language of the relevant statutory provisions and their legislative history.

Control Data Corp. v. Baldrige, 655 F.2d 283, 289, 291, 293–94 (D.C.Cir.1981).

---

[16] *See*, e. g., *Park View Heights Corp. v. City of Black Jack*, 467 F.2d 1208 (8th Cir.1972). In this case the court recorded its "preference for simplifying the 'law on standing.' We think that all that is required for a plaintiff to have standing to sue for a constitutional or statutory violation is a showing of 'injury in fact.' " *Id.* at 1212 n. 4.

[17] *See Upper Pecos Ass'n v. Stans*, 452 F.2d 1233, 1235 (10th Cir.1971), vacated on other grounds, 409 U.S. 1021, 93 S.Ct. 458, 34 L.Ed.2d 313 (1972), and *Izaak Walton League of America v. St. Clair*, 313 F.Supp. 1312, 1316–17 (D.Minn.1970). *See also Gibson & Perin Co. v. City of Cincinnati*, 480 F.2d 936 (6th Cir.), *cert. denied*, 414 U.S. 1068, 94 S.Ct. 577, 38 L.Ed.2d 473 (1973).

[18] *See*, e. g., *Florida v. Weinberger*, 492 F.2d 488, 494 (5th Cir.1974) (grant of standing to the state plaintiff solely on the basis of its "clear interest . . . in the manner in which the Medicaid program is administered vis-a-vis its citizens and in being spared the reconstitution of its statutory program. . . ."); *William F. Wilke, Inc. v. Department of Army of United States*, 485 F.2d 180 (4th

d.   Clearing the Rubble

Finally, in 1987, for the first time since 1971 the Supreme Court decided a case involving the zone of interests test. Was the Court now prepared, at long last, to clarify the test's meaning?

CLARKE v. SECURITIES INDUSTRY ASS'N

Supreme Court of the United States, 1987.
479 U.S. 388, 107 S.Ct. 750, 93 L.Ed.2d 757.

JUSTICE WHITE delivered the opinion of the Court.

In these cases, we review an application of the so-called "zone of interest" standing test that was first articulated in *Association of Data Processing Service Organizations, Inc. v. Camp*, 397 U.S. 150, 90 S.Ct. 827, 25 L.Ed.2d 184 (1970) * * *.

I

In 1982, two national banks, Union Planters National Bank of Memphis (Union Planters) and petitioner Security Pacific National Bank of Los Angeles (Security Pacific), applied to the Comptroller of the Currency for permission to open offices that would offer discount brokerage services to the public. Union Planters proposed to acquire an existing discount brokerage operation, and Security Pacific sought to establish an affiliate named Discount Brokerage. Both banks proposed to offer discount brokerage services not only at their branch offices but also at other locations inside and outside of their home States.

In passing on Security Pacific's application, the Comptroller was faced with the question whether the operation of Discount Brokerage would violate the National Bank Act's branching provisions. Those limitations, enacted as §§ 7 and 8 of the McFadden Act, 44 Stat. 1228, as amended, are codified at 12 U.S.C. § 36 and 12 U.S.C. § 81. Section 81 limits "the general business" of a national bank to its headquarters and any "branches" permitted by § 36. Section 36(c) provides that a national bank is permitted to branch only in its home State and only to the extent that a bank of the same State is permitted to branch under state law. The term "branch" is defined at 12 U.S.C. § 36(f) "to include any branch bank, branch office, branch agency, additional office, or any branch place of business . . . at which deposits are received, or checks paid, or money lent."

The Comptroller concluded that "the non-chartered offices at which Discount Brokerage will offer its services will not constitute branches under the McFadden Act because none of the statutory branching functions will be performed there." He explained that although Discount Brokerage

---

Cir.1973) (grant of standing to a disappointed bidder for a government contract without mentioning the zone standard).

would serve as an intermediary for margin lending, loan approval would take place at chartered Security Pacific offices, so that Discount Brokerage offices would not be lending money within the meaning of § 36(f). Likewise, although Discount Brokerage would maintain, and pay interest on, customer balances created as an incident of its brokerage business, the Comptroller concluded that these accounts differ sufficiently in nature from ordinary bank accounts that Discount Brokerage would not be engaged in receiving deposits. He further observed that treating offices conducting brokerage activities as branches under § 36(f) would be inconsistent with the "long-standing and widespread" practice of banks' operating nonbranch offices dealing in United States Government or municipal securities. Accordingly, the Comptroller approved Security Pacific's application.[3]

Respondent, a trade association representing securities brokers, underwriters, and investment bankers, brought this action in the United States District Court for the District of Columbia. Among other things, respondent contended that bank discount brokerage offices are branches within the meaning of § 36(f) and thus are subject to the geographical restrictions imposed by § 36(c). The Comptroller disputed this position on the merits and also argued that respondent lacks standing because it is not within the zone of interests protected by the McFadden Act. The Comptroller contended that Congress passed the McFadden Act not to protect securities dealers but to establish competitive equality between state and national banks.

The District Court, relying on *Association of Data Processing Service Organizations, Inc. v. Camp*, 397 U.S. 150, 90 S.Ct. 827, 25 L.Ed.2d 184 (1970), held that respondent has standing and rejected the Comptroller's submission that national banks may offer discount brokerage services at nonbranch locations. A divided panel of the Court of Appeals affirmed in a brief per curiam opinion,[6] and rehearing en banc was denied, with three judges dissenting.

* * *

II

In *Association of Data Processing Service Organizations, Inc. v. Camp*, *supra*, the association challenged a ruling by the Comptroller allowing national banks, as part of their incidental powers under 12 U.S.C. § 24

---

[3] A month later, the Comptroller approved without comment the application of Union Planters to acquire an existing brokerage firm.

[6] The dissenting judge argued that there was no standing, as he did in dissenting, with two other judges, from the denial of en banc rehearing. In his view, the purpose of the McFadden Act is to establish competitive equality between national and state banks as regards branching, and while "state banks (and state banking commissions) are obviously within the zone of interests protected by the statute, . . . the brokerage houses suing in the present case are no more within it than are businesses competing for the parking spaces that an unlawful branch may occupy" * * *.

Seventh, to make data-processing services available to other banks and to bank customers. There was no serious question that the data processors had sustained an injury in fact by virtue of the Comptroller's action. Rather, the question, which the Court described as one of standing, was whether the data processors should be heard to complain of that injury. The matter was basically one of interpreting congressional intent, and the Court looked to § 10 of the Administrative Procedure Act (APA), 5 U.S.C. § 702, which "grants standing to a person 'aggrieved by agency action within the meaning of a relevant statute.'" 397 U.S., at 153, 90 S.Ct., at 829. The Court of Appeals had interpreted § 702 as requiring either the showing of a "legal interest," as that term had been narrowly construed in our earlier cases, or alternatively as requiring an explicit provision in the relevant statute permitting suit by any party "adversely affected or aggrieved."[8] This Court was unwilling to take so narrow a view of the APA's "'generous review provisions,'" 397 U.S., at 156, 90 S.Ct., at 831 (quoting *Shaughnessy v. Pedreiro*, 349 U.S. 48, 51, 75 S.Ct. 591, 593, 99 L.Ed. 868 (1955)), and stated that in accordance with previous decisions the Act should be construed "not grudgingly but as serving a broadly remedial purpose." Accordingly, the data processors could be "within that class of 'aggrieved' persons who, under § 702, are entitled to judicial review of 'agency action,'" 397 U.S., at 157, 90 S.Ct., at 831, even though the National Bank Act itself has no reference to aggrieved persons, and, for that matter, no review provision whatsoever. It was thought, however, that Congress, in enacting § 702, had not intended to allow suit by every person suffering injury in fact. What was needed was a gloss on the meaning of § 702. The Court supplied this gloss by adding to the requirement that the complainant be "adversely affected or aggrieved," *i.e.*, injured in fact, the additional requirement that "the interest sought to be protected by the complainant [be] arguably within the zone of interests to be protected or regulated by the statute or constitutional guarantee in question." *Id.*, at 153, 90 S.Ct., at 829.

The Court concluded that the data processors were arguably within the zone of interests established by § 4 of the Bank Service Corporation Act of 1962 * * *. The data processors were therefore permitted to litigate the validity of the Comptroller's ruling.

The "zone of interest" formula in *Data Processing* has not proved self-explanatory,[11] but significant guidance can nonetheless be drawn from that opinion. *First.* The Court interpreted the phrase "a relevant statute" in § 702 broadly; the data processors were alleging violations of 12 U.S.C. § 24 Seventh, yet the Court relied on the legislative history of a much later

---

[8]   Section 402(b) of the Communications Act of 1934, as amended, 47 U.S.C. § 402(b), is an example of a statute granting an explicit right of review to all persons adversely affected or aggrieved by particular agency actions (there, licensing actions by the Federal Communications Commission).

[11]   The zone test has also been the subject of considerable scholarly writing, much of it critical.

statute, § 4 of the Bank Service Corporation Act of 1962, in holding that the data processors satisfied the "zone of interest" test. *Second.* The Court approved the "trend . . . toward [the] enlargement of the class of people who may protest administrative action." 397 U.S., at 154, 90 S.Ct., at 830. At the same time, the Court implicitly recognized the potential for disruption inherent in allowing every party adversely affected by agency action to seek judicial review. The Court struck the balance in a manner favoring review, but excluding those would-be plaintiffs not even "arguably within the zone of interests to be protected or regulated by the statute. . ." Id., at 153, 90 S.Ct., at 829.

* * *

The "zone of interest" test is a guide for deciding whether, in view of Congress' evident intent to make agency action presumptively reviewable, a particular plaintiff should be heard to complain of a particular agency decision. In cases where the plaintiff is not itself the subject of the contested regulatory action, the test denies a right of review if the plaintiff's interests are so marginally related to or inconsistent with the purposes implicit in the statute that it cannot reasonably be assumed that Congress intended to permit the suit. The test is not meant to be especially demanding; in particular, there need be no indication of congressional purpose to benefit the would-be plaintiff.[15]

* * *

In considering whether the "zone of interest" test provides or denies standing in these cases, we first observe that the Comptroller's argument focuses too narrowly on 12 U.S.C. § 36, and does not adequately place § 36 in the overall context of the National Bank Act. As *Data Processing* demonstrates, we are not limited to considering the statute under which respondents sued, but may consider any provision that helps us to understand Congress' overall purposes in the National Bank Act.

Section 36 is a limited exception to the otherwise applicable requirement of § 81 that "the general business of each national banking association shall be transacted in the place specified in its organization certificate. . ." Prior to the enactment of § 36, § 81 had been construed to prevent branching by national banks * * *. [In enacting § 36] Congress rejected attempts to allow national banks to branch without regard to state law. There were many expressions of concern about the effects of branching among those who supported the McFadden Act, as well as among its opponents. Allusion was made to the danger that national banks might obtain monopoly control over credit and money if permitted to branch * * *.

---

[15] Insofar as lower court decisions suggest otherwise, see, *e.g.*, *Control Data Corp. v. Baldrige*, 210 U.S.App.D.C. 170, 180–181, 655 F.2d 283, 293–294, cert. denied, 454 U.S. 881, 102 S.Ct. 363, 70 L.Ed.2d 190 (1981), they are inconsistent with our understanding of the "zone of interest" test, as now formulated.

In short, Congress was concerned not only with equalizing the status of state and federal banks, but also with preventing the perceived dangers of unlimited branching.

The interest respondent asserts has a plausible relationship to the policies underlying §§ 36 and 81 of the National Bank Act. Congress has shown a concern to keep national banks from gaining a monopoly control over credit and money through unlimited branching. Respondent's members compete with banks in providing discount brokerage services—activities which give banks access to more money, in the form of credit balances, and enhanced opportunities to lend money, viz., for margin purchases * * *.

These cases can be analogized to *Data Processing* and *Investment Company Institute*. In those cases the question was what activities banks could engage in at all; here, the question is what activities banks can engage in without regard to the limitations imposed by state branching law. In both cases, competitors who allege an injury that implicates the policies of the National Bank Act are very reasonable candidates to seek review of the Comptroller's rulings * * *. We conclude, therefore, that respondent was a proper party to bring this lawsuit, and we now turn to the merits.

[The Court held, in an early application of the *Chevron* doctrine, that the Comptroller's interpretation of the law was reasonable.]

* * *

JUSTICE SCALIA took no part in the consideration or decision of these cases.

JUSTICE STEVENS, with whom the CHIEF JUSTICE and JUSTICE O'CONNOR join, concurring in part and concurring in the judgment.

Analysis of the purposes of the branching limitations on national banks demonstrates that respondent is well within the "zone of interest" as that test has been applied in our prior decisions. Because I believe that these cases call for no more than a straightforward application of those prior precedents, I do not join Part II of the Court's opinion, which, in my view, engages in a wholly unnecessary exegesis on the "zone of interest" test * * *.

* * * [T]he McFadden Act was in large part a compromise in which Congress started from a general antibranching rule and created a limited exception just large enough to allow national banks to compete effectively with state banks, but also narrow enough to continue to serve the policy of exercising control on the financial power of national banks. The general policy against branching was based in part on a concern about the national banks' potential for becoming massive financial institutions that would establish monopolies on financial services. Petitioners' zone of interest

argument is therefore predicated on too narrow a reading of the statutory purposes, and hence too narrow a view of the applicable "zone of interest" that the broad legislative scheme sought to protect.

* * *

Because I would decide the standing issue on this ground alone, I decline to join the Court's sweeping discussion of the "zone of interest" test. There will be time enough to deal with the broad issues surrounding that test when a case requires us to do so.

NOTES

It is fair to say that *Clarke,* in the ensuing four years, had little appreciable effect on the lower courts' applications of the zone of interests test, though such things are impossible to measure. Lower courts generally continued to look for evidence of congressional intent to benefit particular plaintiffs and to see whether plaintiffs were arguably within the zone of interests of the specific statutory provisions under which they were suing.

We did not have to wait 16 years for another Supreme Court decision. In 1991, the Court again took up the zone of interests test. And for the first time in history, a zone-of-interests plaintiff lost the standing issue in the Supreme Court.

AIR COURIER CONFERENCE OF AMERICA V. AMERICAN POSTAL WORKERS UNION, AFL-CIO

Supreme Court of the United States, 1991.
498 U.S. 517, 111 S.Ct. 913, 112 L.Ed.2d 1125.

CHIEF JUSTICE REHNQUIST delivered the opinion of the Court.

This case requires us to decide whether postal employees are within the "zone of interests" of the group of statutes known as the Private Express Statutes (PES), so that they may challenge the action of the United States Postal Service in suspending the operation of the PES with respect to a practice of private courier services called "international remailing." We hold that they are not.

Since its establishment, the United States Postal Service has exercised a monopoly over the carriage of letters in and from the United States. The postal monopoly is codified in the PES, 18 U.S.C. §§ 1693–1699 and 39 U.S.C. §§ 601–606. The monopoly was created by Congress as a revenue protection measure for the Postal Service to enable it to fulfill its mission. It prevents private competitors from offering service on low-cost routes at prices below those of the Postal Service, while leaving the Service with high-cost routes and insufficient means to fulfill its mandate of providing uniform rates and service to patrons in all areas, including those that are remote or less populated.

A provision of the PES allows the Postal Service to "suspend [the PES restrictions] upon any mail route where the public interest requires the suspension." 39 U.S.C. § 601(b). In 1979, the Postal Service suspended the PES restrictions for "extremely urgent letters," thereby allowing overnight delivery of letters by private courier services. Private courier services, including members of petitioner-intervenor Air Courier Conference of America, relied on that suspension to engage in a practice called "international remailing." This entails bypassing the Postal Service and using private courier systems to deposit with foreign postal systems letters destined for foreign addresses. Believing this international remailing was a misuse of the urgent-letter suspension, the Postal Service issued a proposed modification and clarification of its regulation in order to make clear that the suspension for extremely urgent letters did not cover this practice. The comments received in response to the proposed rule were overwhelmingly negative and focused on the perceived benefits of international remailing: Lower cost, faster delivery, greater reliability, and enhanced ability of United States companies to remain competitive in the international market. Because of the vigorous opposition to the proposed rule, the Postal Service agreed to reconsider its position and instituted a rulemaking "to remove the cloud" over the validity of the international remailing services. After receiving additional comments and holding a public meeting on the subject, on June 17, 1986, the Postal Service issued a proposal to suspend operation of the PES for international remailing. Additional comments were received, and after consideration of the record it had compiled, the Postal Service issued a final rule suspending the operation of the PES with respect to international remailing.

Respondents, the American Postal Workers Union, AFL-CIO, and the National Association of Letter Carriers, AFL-CIO (Unions), sued in the United States District Court for the District of Columbia, challenging the international remailing regulation pursuant to the judicial review provisions of the Administrative Procedure Act (APA), 5 U.S.C. § 702. They claimed that the rulemaking record was inadequate to support a finding that the suspension of the PES for international remailing was in the public interest. Petitioner Air Courier Conference of America (ACCA) intervened. On December 20, 1988, the District Court granted summary judgment in favor of the Postal Service and ACCA. The Unions appealed to the Court of Appeals for the District of Columbia Circuit, and that court vacated the grant of summary judgment. It held that the Unions satisfied the zone-of-interests requirement for APA review under *Clarke v. Securities Industry Ass'n.*, 479 U.S. 388, 107 S.Ct. 750, 93 L.Ed.2d 757 (1987) * * *. In determining that the Unions' interest in employment opportunities was protected by the PES, the Court of Appeals noted that the PES were reenacted as part of the Postal Reorganization Act (PRA), Pub.L. 91–375, 84 Stat. 719, codified at 39 U.S.C. § 101 et seq. The Court of Appeals found that a "key impetus" and "principal purpose" of the PRA was "to implement various labor reforms that would improve pay, working conditions and labor-management relations for postal employees." Reasoning that "[t]he Unions' asserted interest is embraced directly by the labor reform provisions of the PRA," and that "[t]he PES constitute the linchpin in a statutory scheme concerned with maintaining an effective, financially viable Postal Service," the court concluded that "[t]he interplay between the PES and the entire PRA persuades us that there is an 'arguable' or 'plausible' relationship between the purposes of the PES and the interests of the Union[s]." The Court of Appeals also held that "the revenue protective purposes of the PES, standing alone, plausibly relate to the Unions' interest in preventing the reduction of employment opportunities," since "postal workers benefit from the PES's function in ensuring a sufficient revenue base" for the Postal Service's activities.

* * *

To establish standing to sue under the APA, respondents must establish that they have suffered a legal wrong because of the challenged agency action, or are adversely affected or "aggrieved by agency action within the meaning of a relevant statute." 5 U.S.C. § 702. Once they have shown that they are adversely affected, *i.e.*, have suffered an "injury in fact," see *Allen v. Wright*, 468 U.S. 737, 751, 104 S.Ct. 3315, 3324, 82 L.Ed.2d 556 (1984), the Unions must show that they are within the zone of interests sought to be protected through the PES * * *.

The District Court found that the Unions had satisfied the injury-in-fact test because increased competition through international remailing services might have an adverse effect on employment opportunities of postal workers. This finding of injury in fact was not appealed. The question before us, then, is whether the adverse effect on the employment opportunities of postal workers resulting from the suspension is within the zone of interests encompassed by the PES—the statutes which the Unions assert the Postal Service has violated in promulgating the international remailing rule.

The Court of Appeals found that the Unions had standing because "the revenue protective purposes of the PES, standing alone, plausibly relate to the Unions' interest in preventing the reduction of employment opportunities." This view is mistaken, for it conflates the zone-of-interests test with injury in fact. In *Lujan* [*v. National Wildlife Federation*, 497 U.S. 871 (1990)], this Court gave the following example illustrating how injury in fact does not necessarily mean one is within the zone of interests to be protected by a given statute:

> "[T]he failure of an agency to comply with a statutory provision requiring 'on the record' hearings would assuredly have an adverse effect upon the company that has the contract to record and transcribe the agency's proceedings; but since the provision

was obviously enacted to protect the interests of the parties to the proceedings and not those of the reporters, that company would not be 'adversely affected within the meaning' of the statute." 497 U.S., at 883, 110 S.Ct., at 3186.

We must inquire then, as to Congress' intent in enacting the PES in order to determine whether postal workers were meant to be within the zone of interests protected by those statutes. The particular language of the statutes provides no support for respondents' assertion that Congress intended to protect jobs with the Postal Service. In fact, the provisions of 18 U.S.C. § 1696(c), allowing private conveyance of letters if done on a one-time basis or without compensation, and 39 U.S.C. § 601(a), allowing letters to be carried out of the mails if certain procedures are followed, indicate that the congressional concern was not with opportunities for postal workers but with the receipt of necessary revenues for the Postal Service.

Nor does the history of this legislation—such as it is—indicate that the PES were intended for the benefit of postal workers. When the first statutes limiting private carriage of letters on post roads were enacted in 1792, the Post Office offered no pickup or delivery services. Statutory authority to employ letter carriers was not enacted until two years later and was largely ignored until the late 1820's. The 1792 restrictions on private carriage protected the Government's capital investment in the post roads, not the jobs of as yet virtually nonexistent postal employees. In 1825 and 1827, Acts were passed prohibiting the private carriage of letters through the use of stages or other vehicles, packet boats, or other vessels, and foot and horse posts. Postal employees cannot have been within the zone of interests of either the 1824 or 1827 Acts; those Acts targeted transportation of mail which even then was contracted out to private carriers.

Congress' consideration of the 1845 Act was the only occasion on which the postal monopoly was the subject of substantial debate. The 1845 statute, entitled "An Act to reduce the rates of postage, to limit the use and correct the abuse of the franking privilege, and for the prevention of frauds on the revenues of the Post Office Department," 5 Stat. 732, was the result of three circumstances, none of which involved the interests of postal employees. First, the Post Office Department continued to run substantial deficits in spite of high postage rates. Second, high postal rates enabled private expresses to make substantial inroads into the domestic market for delivery of letters and the 1825 and 1827 Acts proved unsuccessful in prosecuting them. Third, inauguration of the "penny post" in England quadrupled use of the mails, and it was thought that a substantial reduction in American postal rates would have the dual virtues of driving private expresses out of business and increasing mail volume of the Post Office. This, in turn, would help reduce the Post Office's deficit.

The legislative history of the sections of the Act limiting private carriage of letters shows a two-fold purpose. First, the Postmaster General and the States most distant from the commercial centers of the Northeast believed that the postal monopoly was necessary to prevent users of faster private expresses from taking advantage of early market intelligence and news of international affairs that had not yet reached the general populace through the slower mails. Second, it was thought to be the duty of the Government to serve outlying, frontier areas, even if it meant doing so below cost. Thus, the revenue protection provisions were not seen as an end in themselves, nor in any sense as a means of ensuring certain levels of public employment, but rather were seen as the means to achieve national integration and to ensure that all areas of the Nation were equally served by the Postal Service.

The PES enable the Postal Service to fulfill its responsibility to provide service to all communities at a uniform rate by preventing private courier services from competing selectively with the Postal Service on its most profitable routes. If competitors could serve the lower cost segment of the market, leaving the Postal Service to handle the high-cost services, the Service would lose lucrative portions of its business, thereby increasing its average unit cost and requiring higher prices to all users. The postal monopoly, therefore, exists to ensure that postal services will be provided to the citizenry at large, and not to secure employment for postal workers.

The Unions' claim on the merits is that the Postal Service has failed to comply with the mandate of 39 U.S.C. § 601(b) that the PES be suspended only if the public interest requires. The foregoing discussion has demonstrated that the PES were not designed to protect postal employment or further postal job opportunities, but the Unions argue that the courts should look beyond the PES to the entire 1970 PRA in applying the zone-of-interests test. The Unions argue that because one of the purposes of the labor-management provisions of the PRA was to stabilize labor-management relations within the Postal Service, and because the PES is the "linchpin" of the Postal Service, employment opportunities of postal workers are arguably within the zone of interests covered by the PES. The Unions rely upon our opinion in *Clarke v. Securities Industry Ass'n.*, 479 U.S. 388, 107 S.Ct. 750, 93 L.Ed.2d 757 (1987), to support this contention.

Clarke is the most recent in a series of cases in which we have held that competitors of regulated entities have standing to challenge regulations. In *Clarke*, we said that "we are not limited to considering the statute under which respondents sued, but may consider any provision that helps us to understand Congress' overall purposes in the National Bank Act." 479 U.S., at 401, 107 S.Ct., at 758. This statement, like all others in our opinions, must be taken in the context in which it was made. In the next paragraph of the opinion, the Court pointed out that 12 U.S.C. § 36, which the plaintiffs in that case claimed had been misinterpreted by the Comptroller, was itself "a limited exception to the otherwise applicable requirement of [12 U.S.C.] § 81," limiting the places at which a national bank could transact business to its headquarters and any "branches" permitted by § 36. Thus the zone-of-interests test was to be applied not merely in the light of § 36, which was the basis of the plaintiffs' claim on the merits, but also in the light of § 81, to which § 36 was an exception.

The situation in the present case is quite different. The only relationship between the PES, upon which the Unions rely for their claim on the merits, and the labor-management provisions of the PRA, upon which the Unions rely for their standing, is that both were included in the general codification of postal statutes embraced in the PRA. The statutory provisions enacted and reenacted in the PRA are spread over some 65 pages in the United States Code and take up an entire title of that volume. We said in *Lujan* that "the relevant statute [under the APA] of course, is the statute whose violation is the gravamen of the complaint." 497 U.S., at 886, 110 S.Ct., at 3187. To adopt the unions' contention would require us to hold that the "relevant statute" in this case is the PRA, with all of its various provisions united only by the fact that they deal with the Postal Service. But to accept this level of generality in defining the "relevant statute" could deprive the zone-of-interests test of virtually all meaning.

Unlike the two sections of the National Bank Act discussed in *Clarke*, *supra*, none of the provisions of the PES have any integral relationship with the labor-management provisions of the PRA * * *.

None of the documents constituting the PRA legislative history suggest that those concerned with postal reforms saw any connection between the PES and the provisions of the PRA dealing with labor-management relations. The Senate and House Reports simply note that the proposed bills continue existing law without change and require the Postal Service to conduct a study of the PES. The Court of Appeals referred to the PES as the "linchpin" of the Postal Service, which it may well be; but it stretches the zone-of-interests test too far to say that because of that fact those who a different part of the PRA was designed to benefit may challenge a violation of the PES.

It would be a substantial extension of our holdings in *Clarke*, *supra*, *Data Processing*, *supra*, and *Investment Co. Institute*, *supra*, to allow the Unions in this case to leapfrog from their asserted protection under the labor-management provisions of the PRA to their claim on the merits under the PES. We decline to make that extension, and hold that the Unions do not have standing to challenge the Postal Service's suspension of the PES to permit private couriers to engage in international remailing. We therefore do not reach the merits of the Unions' claim that the suspension was not in the public interest. The judgment of the Court of Appeals is

Reversed.

JUSTICE STEVENS, with whom JUSTICE MARSHALL and JUSTICE BLACKMUN join, concurring in the judgment.

[The concurring Justices found judicial review unavailable because of 39 U.S.C. § 410(a), which expressly provides that the APA's judicial review provisions do not apply to the Postal Service. They did not reach the question of standing.]

NOTES

In 1997, in *Bennett v. Spear*, 520 U.S. 154, 117 S.Ct. 1154, 137 L.Ed.2d 281 (1997), the Court again briefly addressed the zone of interests test to hold that commercial users of water have standing to challenge decisions under the Endangered Species Act (ESA) that would affect access to water sources.

> In determining whether the petitioners have standing under the zone-of-interests test to bring their APA claims, we look not to the terms of the ESA's citizen-suit provision, but to the substantive provisions of the ESA, the alleged violations of which serve as the gravamen of the complaint * * *. The Court of Appeals concluded that this test was not met here, since petitioners are neither directly regulated by the ESA nor seek to vindicate its overarching purpose of species preservation. That conclusion was error.

> Whether a plaintiff's interest is "arguably . . . protected . . . by the statute" within the meaning of the zone-of-interests test is to be determined not by reference to the overall purpose of the Act in question (here, species preservation), but by reference to the particular provision of law upon which the plaintiff relies * * *. As we said with the utmost clarity in *National Wildlife Federation*, "the plaintiff must establish that the injury he complains of . . . falls within the 'zone of interests' sought to be protected *by the statutory provision whose violation forms the legal basis for his complaint.*" *National Wildlife Federation*, *supra*, at 883, 110 S.Ct., at 3186 (emphasis added). See also *Air Courier Conference v. Postal Workers*, 498 U.S. 517, 523–524, 111 S.Ct. 913, 917–918, 112 L.Ed.2d 1125 (1991) (same).

520 U.S. at 175–76, 117 S.Ct. at 1167–68.

Does the following case make the law of standing any clearer?

NATIONAL CREDIT UNION ADMINISTRATION V. FIRST NATIONAL BANK & TRUST CO.

Supreme Court of the United States, 1998.
522 U.S. 479, 118 S.Ct. 927, 140 L.Ed.2d 1.

JUSTICE THOMAS delivered the opinion of the Court, except as to footnote 6.*

Section 109 of the Federal Credit Union Act (FCUA), 48 Stat. 1219, 12 U.S.C. § 1759, provides that "[f]ederal credit union membership shall be limited to groups having a common bond of occupation or association, or to groups within a well-defined neighborhood, community, or rural district." Since 1982, the National Credit Union Administration (NCUA), the agency charged with administering the FCUA, has interpreted § 109 to permit federal credit unions to be composed of multiple unrelated employer groups, each having its own common bond of occupation. In this action, respondents, five banks and the American Bankers Association, have challenged this interpretation on the ground that § 109 unambiguously requires that the same common bond of occupation unite every member of an occupationally defined federal credit union * * *.

I

A

In 1934, during the Great Depression, Congress enacted the FCUA, which authorizes the chartering of credit unions at the national level and provides that federal credit unions may, as a general matter, offer banking services only to their members. Section 109 of the FCUA, which has remained virtually unaltered since the FCUA's enactment, expressly restricts membership in federal credit unions. In relevant part, it provides:

> "Federal credit union membership shall consist of the incorporators and such other persons and incorporated and unincorporated organizations, to the extent permitted by rules and regulations prescribed by the Board, as may be elected to membership and as such shall each, subscribe to at least one share of its stock and pay the initial installment thereon and a uniform entrance fee if required by the board of directors; except that Federal credit union membership shall be limited to groups having a common bond of occupation or association, or to groups within a well-defined neighborhood, community, or rural district."
> 12 U.S.C. § 1759 (emphasis added).

Until 1982, the NCUA and its predecessors consistently interpreted § 109 to require that the same common bond of occupation unite every member of an occupationally defined federal credit union. In 1982, however, the NCUA reversed its longstanding policy in order to permit

---

* JUSTICE SCALIA joins this opinion, except as to footnote 6.

credit unions to be composed of multiple unrelated employer groups. It thus interpreted § 109's common bond requirement to apply only to each employer group in a multiple-group credit union, rather than to every member of that credit union. Under the NCUA's new interpretation, all of the employer groups in a multiple-group credit union had to be located "within a well-defined area," but the NCUA later revised this requirement to provide that each employer group could be located within "an area surrounding the [credit union's] home or a branch office that can be reasonably served by the [credit union] as determined by NCUA." Since 1982, therefore, the NCUA has permitted federal credit unions to be composed of wholly unrelated employer groups, each having its own distinct common bond.

B

After the NCUA revised its interpretation of § 109, petitioner AT & T Family Federal Credit Union (ATTF) expanded its operations considerably by adding unrelated employer groups to its membership. As a result, ATTF now has approximately 110,000 members nationwide, only 35% of whom are employees of AT & T and its affiliates. The remaining members are employees of such diverse companies as the Lee Apparel Company, the Coca-Cola Bottling Company, the Ciba-Geigy Corporation, the Duke Power Company, and the American Tobacco Company.

In 1990, after the NCUA approved a series of amendments to ATTF's charter that added several such unrelated employer groups to ATTF's membership, respondents brought this action. Invoking the judicial review provisions of the Administrative Procedure Act (APA), 5 U.S.C. § 702, respondents claimed that the NCUA's approval of the charter amendments was contrary to law because the members of the new groups did not share a common bond of occupation with ATTF's existing members, as respondents alleged § 109 required. ATTF and petitioner Credit Union National Association were permitted to intervene in the action as defendants.

The District Court * * * held that respondents lacked prudential standing to challenge the NCUA's chartering decision because their interests were not within the "zone of interests" to be protected by § 109 * * *.

The Court of Appeals for the District of Columbia Circuit reversed * * *.

* * *

* * * Because of the importance of the issues presented, we granted certiorari.

II

Respondents claim a right to judicial review of the NCUA's chartering decision under § 10(a) of the APA, which provides:

> "A person suffering legal wrong because of agency action, or adversely affected or aggrieved by agency action within the meaning of a relevant statute, is entitled to judicial review thereof." 5 U.S.C. § 702.

We have interpreted § 10(a) of the APA to impose a prudential standing requirement in addition to the requirement, imposed by Article III of the Constitution, that a plaintiff have suffered a sufficient injury in fact * * *.

* * *

* * * The proper inquiry is simply "whether the interest sought to be protected by the complainant is *arguably* within the zone of interests to be protected . . . by the statute." *Data Processing*, 397 U.S., at 153, 90 S.Ct., at 830 (emphasis added). Hence in applying the "zone of interests" test, we do not ask whether, in enacting the statutory provision at issue, Congress specifically intended to benefit the plaintiff. Instead, we first discern the interests "arguably . . . to be protected" by the statutory provision at issue; we then inquire whether the plaintiff's interests affected by the agency action in question are among them.

Section 109 provides that "[f]ederal credit union membership shall be limited to groups having a common bond of occupation or association, or to groups within a well-defined neighborhood, community, or rural district." 12 U.S.C. § 1759. By its express terms, § 109 limits membership in every federal credit union to members of definable "groups." Because federal credit unions may, as a general matter, offer banking services only to members, see, *e.g.*, 12 U.S.C. §§ 1757(5)–(6), § 109 also restricts the markets that every federal credit union can serve. Although these markets need not be small, they unquestionably are limited. The link between § 109's regulation of federal credit union membership and its limitation on the markets that federal credit unions can serve is unmistakable. Thus, even if it cannot be said that Congress had the specific purpose of benefiting commercial banks, one of the interests "arguably . . . to be protected" by § 109 is an interest in limiting the markets that federal credit unions can serve.[6] This interest is precisely the interest of respondents affected by the NCUA's interpretation of § 109. As competitors of federal credit unions, respondents certainly have an interest in limiting the markets that federal

---

[6]   The legislative history of § 109, upon which petitioners so heavily rely, supports this conclusion * * *.

credit unions can serve, and the NCUA's interpretation has affected that interest by allowing federal credit unions to increase their customer base.[7]

Section 109 cannot be distinguished from the statutory provisions at issue in *Clarke, ICI, Arnold Tours*, and *Data Processing* * * *.

* * *

Petitioners attempt to distinguish this action principally on the ground that there is no evidence that Congress, when it enacted the FCUA, was at all concerned with the competitive interests of commercial banks, or indeed at all concerned with competition. See Brief for Petitioner ATTF 21–22. Indeed, petitioners contend that the very reason Congress passed the FCUA was that "[b]anks were simply not in the picture" as far as small borrowers were concerned, and thus Congress believed it necessary to create a new source of credit for people of modest means. See *id.*, at 25.

The difficulty with this argument is that similar arguments were made unsuccessfully in each of *Data Processing, Arnold Tours, ICI*, and *Clarke* * * *.

* * *

In each case, we declined to accept the Comptroller's argument. In *Data Processing*, we considered it irrelevant that the statutes in question "d[id] not in terms protect a specified group," because "their general policy [was] apparent[,] and those whose interests [were] directly affected by a broad or narrow interpretation of [the statutes] [were] easily identifiable." 397 U.S., at 157, 90 S.Ct., at 832. In *Arnold Tours*, we similarly believed it irrelevant that Congress had shown no concern for the competitive position of travel agents in enacting the statutes in question. See 400 U.S., at 46, 91 S.Ct., at 159. In *ICI*, we were unmoved by Justice Harlan's comment in dissent that the Glass-Steagall Act was passed *in spite* of its positive effects on the competitive position of investment banks. See 401 U.S., at 640, 91 S.Ct., at 1103–1104. And in *Clarke*, we did not debate whether the Congress that enacted the McFadden Act was concerned about the competitive position of securities dealers. See 479 U.S., at 403, 107 S.Ct., at 759. The provisions at issue in each of these cases, moreover, could be said merely to be safety-and-soundness provisions, enacted only to protect

---

[7]   Contrary to the dissent's contentions, our formulation does not "eviscerat[e]" or "abolis[h]" the zone of interests requirement. Nor can it be read to imply that, in order to have standing under the APA, a plaintiff must merely have an interest in enforcing the statute in question. The test we have articulated—discerning the interests "arguably . . . to be protected" by the statutory provision at issue and inquiring whether the plaintiff's interests affected by the agency action in question are among them—differs only as a matter of semantics from the formulation that the dissent has accused us of "eviscerating" or "abolishing."

Our only disagreement with the dissent lies in the application of the "zone of interests" test. Because of the unmistakable link between § 109's express restriction on credit union membership and the limitation on the markets that federal credit unions can serve * * *, respondents are more than merely incidental beneficiaries of § 109's effects on competition.

national banks and their depositors and without a concern for competitive effects. We nonetheless did not hesitate to find standing.

We therefore cannot accept petitioners' argument that respondents do not have standing because there is no evidence that the Congress that enacted § 109 was concerned with the competitive interests of commercial banks. To accept that argument, we would have to reformulate the "zone of interests" test to require that Congress have specifically intended to benefit a particular class of plaintiffs before a plaintiff from that class could have standing under the APA to sue. We have refused to do this in our prior cases, and we refuse to do so today.

Petitioners also mistakenly rely on our decision in *Air Courier Conference v. Postal Workers*, 498 U.S. 517, 111 S.Ct. 913, 112 L.Ed.2d 1125 (1991). In *Air Courier*, we held that the interest of Postal Service employees in maximizing employment opportunities was not within the "zone of interests" to be protected by the postal monopoly statutes, and hence those employees did not have standing under the APA to challenge a Postal Service regulation suspending its monopoly over certain international operations. We stated that the purposes of the statute were solely to increase the revenues of the Post Office and to ensure that postal services were provided in a manner consistent with the public interest Only those interests, therefore, and not the interests of Postal Service employees in their employment, were "arguably within the zone of interests to be protected" by the statute. We further noted that although the statute in question regulated competition, the interests of the plaintiff employees had nothing to do with competition. See *Air Courier, supra*, at 528, n. 5, 111 S.Ct., at 920, n. 5 (stating that "[e]mployees have generally been denied standing to enforce competition laws because they lack competitive and direct injury"). In this action, not only do respondents have "competitive and direct injury," but, as the foregoing discussion makes clear, they possess an interest that is "arguably . . . to be protected" by § 109.

* * *

JUSTICE O'CONNOR, with whom JUSTICE STEVENS, JUSTICE SOUTER, and JUSTICE BREYER join, dissenting.

In determining that respondents have standing under the zone-of-interests test to challenge the National Credit Union Administration's (NCUA's) interpretation of the "common bond" provision of the Federal Credit Union Act (FCUA), 12 U.S.C. § 1759, the Court applies the test in a manner that is contrary to our decisions and, more importantly, that all but eviscerates the zone-of-interests requirement * * *.

* * *

The "injury respondents complain of," as the Court explains, is that the NCUA's interpretation of the common bond provision "allows persons who might otherwise be their customers to be . . . customers" of petitioner AT & T Family Federal Credit Union. Put another way, the injury is a loss of respondents' customer base to a competing entity, or more generally, an injury to respondents' commercial interest as a competitor. The relevant question under the zone-of-interests test, then, is whether injury to respondents' commercial interest as a competitor "falls within the zone of interests sought to be protected by the [common bond] provision" * * *.

* * *

In each of the competitor standing cases * * *, we found that Congress had enacted an "anti-competition limitation," see *Bennett*, 520 U.S., at 176, 117 S.Ct., at 1167 (discussing *Data Processing*), or, alternatively, that Congress had "legislated against . . . competition," see *Clarke*, *supra*, at 403, 107 S.Ct. at 759; *ICI*, *supra*, at 620–621, 91 S.Ct., at 1094, and accordingly, that the plaintiff-competitor's "commercial interest was sought to be protected by the anti-competition limitation" at issue, *Bennett*, *supra*, at 176, 117 S.Ct., at 1167. We determined, in other words, that "the injury [the plaintiff] complain[ed] of . . . [fell] within the zone of interests sought to be protected by the [relevant] statutory provision." *National Wildlife Federation*, 497 U.S., at 883, 110 S.Ct., at 3186. The Court fails to undertake that analysis here.

* * *

Applying the proper zone-of-interests inquiry to this action, I would find that competitive injury to respondents' commercial interests does not arguably fall within the zone of interests sought to be protected by the common bond provision. The terms of the statute do not suggest a concern with protecting the business interests of competitors * * *.

Nor is there any nontextual indication to that effect * * *.

* * *

The circumstances surrounding the enactment of the FCUA also indicate that Congress did not intend to legislate against competition through the common bond provision * * *.

* * *

In this light, I read our decisions as establishing that there must at least be *some* indication in the statute, beyond the mere fact that its enforcement has the effect of incidentally benefiting the plaintiff, from which one can draw an inference that the plaintiff's injury arguably falls within the zone of interests sought to be protected by that statute. The provisions we construed in *Clarke*, *ICI*, and *Data Processing* allowed such an inference: Where Congress legislates against competition, one can properly infer that the statute is at least arguably intended to protect competitors from injury to their commercial interest, even if that is not the statute's principal objective. Accordingly, "[t]here [was] sound reason to infer" in those cases "that Congress intended [the] class [of plaintiffs] to be relied upon to challenge agency disregard of the law." *Clarke, supra,* at 403, 107 S.Ct. at 759 (internal quotation marks omitted).

The same cannot be said of respondents in this action, because neither the terms of the common bond provision, nor the way in which the provision operates, nor the circumstances surrounding its enactment, evince a congressional desire to legislate against competition. This, then, is an action "the plaintiff's interests are so marginally related to or inconsistent with the purposes implicit in the statute that it cannot reasonably be assumed that Congress intended to permit the suit." 479 U.S., at 399, 107 S.Ct., at 757 * * *.

* * *

NOTES

Add to the mix *Match-E-Be-Nash-She-Wish Band of Pottawatomi Indians v. Patchak,* 567 U.S. 209, 132 S.Ct. 2199, 183 L.Ed.2d 211 (2012). The Indian Reorganization Act ("IRA") of 1934 authorizes the Secretary of the Interior to acquire property "for the purpose of providing land for Indians." 25 U.S.C. § 465 (2012). The Secretary acquired some land in Michigan to be used for a tribal casino, and a local resident challenged the acquisition on the ground that the IRA only allowed acquisition of property for tribes that were federally recognized in 1934 when the statute was enacted; the Match-E-Be-Nash-She-Wish Band of Pottawatomi Indians was not recognized until 1999. Patchak's complaint alleged that a casino "would 'destroy the lifestyle he has enjoyed' by causing 'increased traffic,' increased crime,' 'decreased property values,' 'an irreversible change in the rural character of the area,' and 'other aesthetic, socioeconomic, and environmental problems.' " The government challenged his standing to sue.

> * * * This Court has long held that a person suing under the APA must satisfy not only Article III's standing requirements, but an additional test: The interest he asserts must be "arguably within the zone of interests to be protected or regulated by the statute" that he says was violated. *Association of Data Process Service Organizations, Inc. v. Camp,* 397 U.S. 150, 153, 90 S.Ct. 827, 25 L.Ed.2d 184 (1970). Here, Patchak asserts that in taking title to the Bradley Property, the Secretary exceeded her authority under § 465, which authorizes the acquisition of property "for the purpose of providing land for Indians." And he alleges that this statutory violation will cause him economic, environmental, and aesthetic harm as a nearby property owner. The Government and Band argue that the relationship between § 465 and Patchak's asserted interests is insufficient. That is so, they contend, because the statute focuses on land *acquisition,*

whereas Patchak's interests relate to the land's *use* as a casino. We find this argument unpersuasive.

The prudential standing test Patchak must meet "is not meant to be especially demanding." *Clarke v. Security Industries Ass'n.*, 479 U.S. 388, 399, 107 S.Ct. 750, 93 L.Ed.2d 757 (1987). We apply the test in keeping with Congress's "evident intent" when enacting the APA "to make agency action presumptively reviewable." *Ibid.* We do not require any "indication of congressional purpose to benefit the would-be plaintiff." *Id.* at 399–400, 107 S.Ct. 750. And we have always conspicuously included the word "arguably" in the test to indicate that the benefit of any doubt goes to the plaintiff. The test forecloses suit only when a plaintiff's "interests are so marginally related to or inconsistent with the purposes implicit in the statute that it cannot reasonably be assumed that Congress intended to permit the suit." *Id.* at 399, 107 S.Ct. 750.

Patchak's suit satisfies that standard, because § 465 has far more to do with land use than the Government and Band acknowledge. Start with what we and others have said about § 465's context and purpose. As the leading treatise on federal Indian law notes, § 465 is "the capstone" of the IRA's land provisions. F. Cohen, Handbook of Federal Indian Law § 15.07[1][a], p. 1010 (2005 ed.) (hereinafter Cohen). And those provisions play a key role in the IRA's overall effort "to rehabilitate the Indian's economic life," *Mescalero Apache Tribe v. Jones*, 411 U.S. 145, 152, 93 S.Ct. 1267, 36 L.Ed.2d 114 (1973) (internal quotation marks omitted). "Land forms the basis" of that "economic life," providing the foundation for "tourism, manufacturing, mining, logging, . . . and gaming." Cohen § 15.01, at 965. Section 465 thus functions as a primary mechanism to foster Indian tribes' economic development * * *. So when the Secretary obtains land for Indians under § 465, she does not do so in a vacuum. Rather, she takes title to properties with at least one eye directed toward how tribes will use those lands to support economic development.

* * *

The Secretary's acquisition of the Bradley Property is a case in point. The Band's application to the Secretary highlighted its plan to use the land for gaming purposes. See App. 41 ("[T]rust status for this Property is requested in order for the Tribe to acquire property on which it plans to conduct gaming"); *id.*, at 61–62 ("The Tribe intends to . . . renovate the existing . . . building into a gaming facility. . . to offer Class II and/or Class III gaming"). Similarly, DOI's notice of intent to take the land into trust announced that the land would "be used for the purpose of construction and operation of a gaming facility," which the Department had already determined would meet the Indian Gaming Regulatory Act's requirements. 70 Fed.Reg.

25596. So from start to finish, the decision whether to acquire the Bradley Property under § 465 involved questions of land use.

> And because § 465's implementation encompasses these issues, the interests Patchak raises—at least arguably—fall "within the zone . . . protected or regulated by the statute." If the Government had violated a statute specifically addressing how federal land can be used, no one would doubt that a neighboring landowner would have prudential standing to bring suit to enforce the statute's limits. The difference here, as the Government and Band point out, is that § 465 specifically addresses only land acquisition. But for the reasons already given, decisions under the statute are closely enough and often enough entwined with considerations of land use to make that difference immaterial. As in this very case, the Secretary will typically acquire land with its eventual use in mind, after assessing potential conflicts that use might create. See 25 CFR §§ 151.10(c), 151.10(f), 151.11(a). And so neighbors to the use (like Patchak) are reasonable—indeed, predictable—challengers of the Secretary's decisions: Their interests, whether economic, environmental, or aesthetic, come within § 465's regulatory ambit.

132 S.Ct. 2199. *See also Bank of America Corp. v. City of Miami*, 137 S.Ct. 1296, 197 L.Ed.2d 678 (2017) (holding, by a 5–3 vote, that the City of Miami had zone-of-interests standing to sue banks under the Fair Housing Act for discriminatory lending policies that, so the City argued, reduced city tax revenues and led to more municipal spending on social services).

Match-E-Be-Nash-She-Wish, as with many zone-of-interests standing cases, described the inquiry as involving "prudential standing." The term was meant to distinguish zone-of-interests standing from the irreducible injury/causation/redressability requirements of Article III, but it carried the connotation—not actually reflected in practice—that application of the zone-of-interests test was somehow discretionary or free-standing. That was never true: The zone-of-interests inquiry was always about discerning the class of persons protected by a *statute*, which required consideration of the statute's terms and purposes. If the statute authorizes suit in this fashion, the Court has no discretion to refuse to hear the case (and no discretion to hear it if the statute does not in fact authorize suit).

This understanding of the zone-of-interests test was made explicit in *Lexmark Int'l, Inc. v. Static Control Components, Inc.*, 572 U.S. 118, 134 S.Ct. 1377, 188 L.Ed.2d 392 (2014):

> Although we admittedly have placed that [zone-of-interests] test under the "prudential" rubric in the past, it does not belong there * * *. Whether a plaintiff comes within "the 'zone of interests'" is an issue that requires us to determine, using traditional tools of statutory interpretation, whether a legislatively conferred cause of action encompasses a particular plaintiff's claim. As Judge Silberman of the D.C. Circuit recently observed, "'prudential standing' is a

misnomer" as applied to the zone-of-interests analysis, which asks whether "this particular class of persons ha[s] a right to sue under this substantive statute." *Association of Battery Recyclers, Inc. v. EPA*, 716 F.3d 667, 675–676 (2013) (concurring opinion).

In sum, the question this case presents is whether Static Control falls within the class of plaintiffs whom Congress has authorized to sue under * * * [a provision of the Lanham Act prohibiting false advertising in connection with a trademark]. In other words, we ask whether Static Control has a cause of action under the statute. That question requires us to determine the meaning of the congressionally enacted provision creating a cause of action. In doing so, we apply traditional principles of statutory interpretation. We do not ask whether in our judgment Congress should have authorized Static Control's suit, but whether Congress in fact did so. Just as a court cannot apply its independent policy judgment to recognize a cause of action that Congress has denied, see *Alexander v. Sandoval*, 532 U.S. 275, 286–287, 121 S.Ct. 1511, 149 L.Ed.2d 517 (2001), it cannot limit a cause of action that Congress has created merely because "prudence" dictates.

134 S.Ct. at 1387–88.

If you were a lower court judge, how would you resolve zone-of-interests standing claims?[28]

e. Standing and Special Review Statutes

Under the zone of interests test, the statutes that are "relevant" for the standing inquiry are the agency's substantive statutes, not the special review provisions originally contemplated by § 702. Do those special review statutes still play any role in the standing inquiry?

They can, though in a very different way than they would have done pre-1970. A special review provision can provide standing even when a zone-of-interests inquiry that looks only to the relevant substantive statutory provisions would deny it. The Court's opinion in *Bennett v. Spear* is illustrative:

> * * * The first question in the present case is whether the ESA's citizen-suit provision, set forth in pertinent part in the margin,[2] negates the zone-of-interests test (or, perhaps more

---

[28] If your answer is "Cite everything and hope for the best," please step up to the bench. *See, e.g.*, Federation for American Immigration Reform, Inc. v. Reno, 93 F.3d 897 (D.C.Cir.1996).

[2] "(1) Except as provided in paragraph (2) of this subsection any person may commence a civil suit on his own behalf—

"(A)   to enjoin any person, including the United States and any other governmental instrumentality or agency (to the extent permitted by the eleventh amendment to the Constitution), who is alleged to be in violation of any provision of this chapter or regulation issued under the authority thereof; or

. . . .

accurately, expands the zone of interests). We think it does. The first operative portion of the provision says that "any person may commence a civil suit"—an authorization of remarkable breadth when compared with the language Congress ordinarily uses. Even in some other environmental statutes, Congress has used more restrictive formulations, such as "[any person] having an interest which is or may be adversely affected," 33 U.S.C. § 1365(g) (Clean Water Act); see also 30 U.S.C. § 1270(a) (Surface Mining Control and Reclamation Act) (same); "[a]ny person suffering legal wrong," 15 U.S.C. § 797(b)(5) (Energy Supply and Environmental Coordination Act); or "any person having a valid legal interest which is or may be adversely affected . . . whenever such action constitutes a case or controversy," 42 U.S.C. § 9124(a) (Ocean Thermal Energy Conversion Act). And in contexts other than the environment, Congress has often been even more restrictive. In statutes concerning unfair trade practices and other commercial matters, for example, it has authorized suit only by "[a]ny person injured in his business or property," 7 U.S.C. § 2305(c); see also 15 U.S.C. § 72 (same), or only by "competitors, customers, or subsequent purchasers," § 298(b).

Our readiness to take the term "any person" at face value is greatly augmented by two interrelated considerations: that the overall subject matter of this legislation is the environment (a matter in which it is common to think all persons have an interest) and that the obvious purpose of the particular provision in question is to encourage enforcement by so-called "private attorneys general"—evidenced by its elimination of the usual amount-in-controversy and diversity-of-citizenship requirements, its provision for recovery of the costs of litigation (including even expert witness fees), and its reservation to the Government of a right of first refusal to pursue the action initially and a right to intervene later. Given these factors, we think the conclusion of expanded standing follows *a fortiori* from our decision in *Trafficante v. Metropolitan Life Ins. Co.*, 409 U.S. 205, 93 S.Ct. 364, 34 L.Ed.2d 415 (1972), which held that standing was expanded to the full extent permitted under Article III by a provision of the Civil Rights Act of 1968 that authorized "[a]ny person who claims to have been injured by a discriminatory

---

"(C)   against the Secretary where there is alleged a failure of the Secretary to perform any act or duty under section 1533 of this title which is not discretionary with the Secretary. The district courts shall have jurisdiction, without regard to the amount in controversy or the citizenship of the parties, to enforce any such provision or regulation, or to order the Secretary to perform such act or duty, as the case may be. . . ."

* * *

16 U.S.C. § 1540(g).

housing practice" to sue for violations of the Act. There also we relied on textual evidence of a statutory scheme to rely on private litigation to ensure compliance with the Act. The statutory language here is even clearer, and the subject of the legislation makes the intent to permit enforcement by everyman even more plausible.

It is true that the plaintiffs here are seeking to prevent application of environmental restrictions rather than to implement them. But the "any person" formulation applies to all the causes of action authorized by § 1540(g)—not only to actions against private violators of environmental restrictions, and not only to actions against the Secretary asserting underenforcement under § 1533, but also to actions against the Secretary asserting overenforcement under § 1533 * * *. [T]he citizen-suit provision does favor environmentalists in that it covers all private violations of the Act but not all failures of the Secretary to meet his administrative responsibilities; but there is no textual basis for saying that its expansion of standing requirements applies to environmentalists alone. The Court of Appeals therefore erred in concluding that petitioners lacked standing under the zone-of-interests test to bring their claims under the ESA's citizen-suit provision.

520 U.S. at 164–66, 117 S.Ct. at 1162–63.

D. "WHEN": THE TIMING OF JUDICIAL REVIEW

If a plaintiff has standing to challenge a particular agency action, and judicial review of that action is not precluded, the plaintiff will eventually get to court. But the plaintiff must get to court *at the right time*: neither too early nor too late.

Identifying the proper time for judicial review is one of the most difficult tasks facing the administrative lawyer. There are a number of overlapping doctrines to consider, and all of those doctrines are complex and ill-understood, even (and perhaps especially) by courts.

Four principal doctrines determine whether an action for judicial review of agency action is premature: exhaustion, finality, ripeness, and primary jurisdiction. The lines separating these doctrines are often very fine, if indeed they can be found at all. Nonetheless, each doctrine has an identifiable core that gives it some measure of independent existence. But if at times, when you read cases, you get the impression that ripeness is slipping into finality at a time when the court ought to be discussing exhaustion—you are probably right.

1.   EXHAUSTION

Exhaustion is, in principle, the simplest timing doctrine in administrative law. An exhaustion requirement tells you to present—or perhaps re-present—your argument to the agency before you bring it before a court. Exhaustion requirements come from two sources: statutes and judicial common law.

a.   Statutory Exhaustion

Congress will sometimes require parties to present arguments to an agency, occasionally more than once, before those arguments can form the basis of a judicial action. For example, the special review statute governing decisions of the Federal Energy Regulatory Commission provides:

(a) Orders

* * *

(2) Rehearing

Any person aggrieved by any order issued by the Commission in a proceeding under this chapter to which such person is a party may apply for a rehearing within 30 days after the issuance of such order. Any application for rehearing shall set forth the specific ground upon which such application is based. Upon the filing of such application, the Commission may grant or deny the requested rehearing or modify the original order without further hearing. Unless the Commission acts upon such application for rehearing within 30 days after it is filed, such application shall be deemed to have been denied. No person may bring an action under this section to obtain judicial review of any order of the Commission unless—

(A) such person shall have made application to the Commission for a rehearing under this subsection; and

(B) the Commission shall have finally acted with respect to such application.

For purposes of this section, if the Commission fails to act within 30 days after the filing of such application, such failure to act shall be deemed final agency action with respect to such application.

* * *

(4) Judicial review

Any person who is a party to a proceeding under this chapter aggrieved by any final order issued by the Commission in such proceeding may obtain review of such order in the United States

Court of Appeals for any circuit in which the party to which such order relates is located or has its principal place of business, or in the United States Court of Appeals for the District of Columbia circuit. Review shall be obtained by filing a written petition, requesting that such order be modified or set aside in whole or in part, in such Court of Appeals within 60 days after the final action of the Commission on the application for rehearing required under paragraph (2) * * *. No objection to such order of the Commission shall be considered by the court if such objection was not urged before the Commission in the application for rehearing unless there was reasonable ground for the failure to do so * * *.

15 U.S.C. §§ 3416(a)(2), 3416(a)(4) (2012). Section (a)(2) makes the filing of a rehearing petition to the agency a prerequisite to judicial review. Even if the agency has already rejected your position and you have no real expectation that the agency will change its mind, you must nonetheless seek rehearing before bringing your challenge to court. The statute does not specify any grounds that might excuse a party's failure to seek rehearing before asking the court for relief.[29] Section (a)(4) then extends the rehearing requirement to preclude the court from considering any argument on appeal that "was not urged before the Commission in the application for rehearing unless there was reasonable ground for the failure to do so." Thus, not only must you seek an agency rehearing before coming to court, but you must raise in that rehearing petition *any arguments* that you ultimately plan to raise in court. Unlike § (a)(2), however, § (a)(4) contemplates some circumstances in which a failure to raise an argument before the agency will not bar subsequent presentation to the court: if there was "reasonable ground" for failing to raise the issue in a rehearing petition.

Other statutes contain similar rehearing requirements. *See* 15 U.S.C. § 717r (2012); 16 U.S.C. § 8251 (2012); 29 U.S.C. § 160(e) (2012). Statutory exhaustion is thus a matter of reading the relevant special review statutes to see whether and how they make appeals to agencies a prerequisite to judicial review. A recurring question is whether statutory exhaustion requirements are jurisdictional requirements for federal court action—meaning that courts and parties cannot waive the requirements even if

---

[29] That does not mean that no such grounds can ever be found. Suppose that the Commission issues an order that you reasonably believe does not affect your business. Two years later, the Commission "interprets" its original order to apply to you. Are you prevented from seeking judicial review because you failed to seek rehearing of the original order? Clearly not. Courts will reason that you were not "aggrieved" by the original order, but only by the Commission's subsequent (unreasonable) re-interpretation of that order. As long as you promptly seek rehearing of the new order, you will be granted judicial review. *See* Sam Rayburn Dam Electric Cooperative v. FPC, 515 F.2d 998, 1006–07 (D.C.Cir.1975). But this doctrine only applies if *no reasonable person* would have determined that he or she was "aggrieved" by the original order. The test is objective, and it has teeth. *See* Interstate Natural Gas Ass'n of America v. FERC, 716 F.2d 1, 15 (D.C.Cir.1983) (refusing to excuse a party's failure to seek rehearing of an ambiguous order when other parties with similar interests had sought rehearing).

they all agree that it is a good idea to do so—or affirmative defenses that agencies can choose not to raise if they want the court to reach the merits of a case. The general rule is that courts will not construe exhaustion requirements to be jurisdictional unless Congress has expressly indicated the jurisdictional nature of the requirement. *See Hettinga v. United States,* 560 F.3d 498, 503 (D.C.Cir.2009). This requires a careful analysis of the language and structure of each particular statute, and courts will not always agree on the outcome. *See Forest Guardians v. United States Forest Service,* 579 F.3d 1114, 1121 (10th Cir.2009) (noting a circuit split concerning whether the exhaustion requirement in 7 U.S.C. § 6912(e) (2012) is jurisdictional).

b.   Common Law Exhaustion

For many years, both before and after enactment of the APA, courts would routinely require litigants to exhaust available administrative remedies even in the absence of statutory exhaustion requirements. That is, if an agency provided an internal review or rehearing procedure, courts would generally insist that litigants employ those procedures before coming to court, whether or not Congress made use of those procedures a statutory prerequisite to judicial review. *See Myers v. Bethlehem Shipbuilding Corp.,* 303 U.S. 41, 58 S.Ct. 459, 82 L.Ed. 638 (1938). Courts also evolved an elaborate set of exceptions to this generally applicable exhaustion requirement. The rationales for, and exceptions to, the judicially created exhaustion doctrine were well described by the Court in a leading decision.

McCARTHY V. MADIGAN
Supreme Court of the United States, 1992.
503 U.S. 140, 112 S.Ct. 1081, 117 L.Ed.2d 291.

JUSTICE BLACKMUN delivered the opinion of the Court.

The issue in this case is whether a federal prisoner must resort to the internal grievance procedure promulgated by the Federal Bureau of Prisons before he may initiate a suit, pursuant to the authority of *Bivens v. Six Unknown Fed. Narcotics Agents,* 403 U.S. 388, 91 S.Ct. 1999, 29 L.Ed.2d 619 (1971), solely for money damages * * *.

I

While he was a prisoner in the federal penitentiary at Leavenworth, petitioner John J. McCarthy filed a pro se complaint in the United States District Court for the District of Kansas against four prison employees: the hospital administrator, the chief psychologist, another psychologist, and a physician. McCarthy alleged that respondents had violated his constitutional rights under the Eighth Amendment by their deliberate indifference to his needs and medical condition resulting from a back operation and a history of psychiatric problems. On the first page of his complaint, he wrote: "This Complaint seeks Money Damages Only."

The District Court dismissed the complaint on the ground that petitioner had failed to exhaust prison administrative remedies. Under 28 CFR pt. 542 (1991), setting forth the general "Administrative Remedy Procedure for Inmates" at federal correctional institutions, a prisoner may "seek formal review of a complaint which relates to any aspect of his imprisonment." § 542.10. When an inmate files a complaint or appeal, the responsible officials are directed to acknowledge the filing with a "signed receipt" which is returned to the inmate, to "[c]onduct an investigation," and to "[r]espond to and sign all complaints or appeals." §§ 542.11(a)(2) to (4). The general grievance regulations do not provide for any kind of hearing or for the granting of any particular type of relief.

[handwritten margin note: DC dismissed for failure to exhaust]

To promote efficient dispute resolution, the procedure includes rapid filing and response timetables. An inmate first seeks informal resolution of his claim by consulting prison personnel. § 542.13(a). If this informal effort fails, the prisoner "may file a formal written complaint on the appropriate form, within fifteen (15) calendar days of the date on which the basis of the complaint occurred." § 542.13(b). Should the warden fail to respond to the inmate's satisfaction within 15 days, the inmate has 20 days to appeal to the Bureau's Regional Director, who has 30 days to respond. If the inmate still remains unsatisfied, he has 30 days to make a final appeal to the Bureau's general counsel, who has another 30 days to respond. §§ 542.14 and 542.15. If the inmate can demonstrate a "valid reason for delay," he "shall be allowed" an extension of any of these time periods for filing. § 542.13(b).

[handwritten margin note: informal resolution ↓ formal written complaint ↓ Bureau's Regional Director ↓ final appeal to Bureau's general counsel]

Petitioner McCarthy filed with the District Court a motion for reconsideration under Federal Rule of Civil Procedure 60(b), arguing that he was not required to exhaust his administrative remedies, because he sought only money damages which, he claimed, the Bureau could not provide. The court denied the motion.

[handwritten margin note: DC denied motion]

The Court of Appeals, in affirming, observed that because *Bivens* actions are a creation of the judiciary, the courts may impose reasonable conditions upon their filing. The exhaustion rule, the court reasoned, "is not keyed to the type of relief sought, but to the need for preliminary fact-finding" to determine "whether there is a possible *Bivens* cause of action." Accordingly, " '[a]lthough the administrative apparatus could not award money damages . . . , administrative consideration of the possibility of corrective action and a record would have aided a court in measuring liability and determining the *extent* of the damages.' " (emphasis in original). Exhaustion of the general grievance procedure was required notwithstanding the fact that McCarthy's request was solely for money damages.

[handwritten margin note: CoA aff'd ↳ Bivens = judicial creation (so cts can impose reasonable conditions)]

II

The doctrine of exhaustion of administrative remedies is one among related doctrines—including abstention, finality, and ripeness—that govern the timing of federal-court decisionmaking. Of "paramount importance" to any exhaustion inquiry is congressional intent. Where Congress specifically mandates, exhaustion is required. But [where Congress has not clearly required exhaustion, sound judicial discretion governs.] Nevertheless, even in this field of judicial discretion, appropriate deference to Congress' power to prescribe the basic procedural scheme under which a claim may be heard in a federal court requires fashioning of exhaustion principles in a manner consistent with congressional intent and any applicable statutory scheme.

A

This Court long has acknowledged the general rule that parties exhaust prescribed administrative remedies before seeking relief from the federal courts. See, *e.g., Myers v. Bethlehem Shipbuilding Corp.*, 303 U.S. 41, 50–51, and n. 9, 58 S.Ct. 459, 463–464, and n. 9 (1938) (discussing cases as far back as 1898). Exhaustion is required because it serves the twin purposes of protecting administrative agency authority and promoting judicial efficiency.

As to the first of these purposes, the exhaustion doctrine recognizes the notion, grounded in deference to Congress' delegation of authority to coordinate branches of Government, that agencies, not the courts, ought to have primary responsibility for the programs that Congress has charged them to administer. Exhaustion concerns apply with particular force when the action under review involves exercise of the agency's discretionary power or when the agency proceedings in question allow the agency to apply its special expertise. *McKart v. United States*, 395 U.S. 185, 194, 89 S.Ct. 1657, 1662, 23 L.Ed.2d 194 (1969). The exhaustion doctrine also acknowledges the commonsense notion of dispute resolution that an agency ought to have an opportunity to correct its own mistakes with respect to the programs it administers before it is haled into federal court. Correlatively, exhaustion principles apply with special force when "frequent and deliberate flouting of administrative processes" could weaken an agency's effectiveness by encouraging disregard of its procedures. 395 U.S., at 195, 89 S.Ct., at 1663.

As to the second of the purposes, exhaustion promotes judicial efficiency in at least two ways. When an agency has the opportunity to correct its own errors, a judicial controversy may well be mooted, or at least piecemeal appeals may be avoided. And even where a controversy survives administrative review, exhaustion of the administrative procedure may produce a useful record for subsequent judicial consideration, especially in a complex or technical factual context.

B

Notwithstanding these substantial institutional interests, federal courts are vested with a "virtually unflagging obligation" to exercise the jurisdiction given them. *Colorado River Water Conservation Dist. v. United States*, 424 U.S. 800, 817–818, 96 S.Ct. 1236, 1246–1247, 47 L.Ed.2d 483 (1976). "We have no more right to decline the exercise of jurisdiction which is given, than to usurp that which is not given." *Cohens v. Virginia*, 6 Wheat. 264, 404, 5 L.Ed. 257 (1821). Accordingly, this Court has declined to require exhaustion in some circumstances even where administrative and judicial interests would counsel otherwise. In determining whether exhaustion is required, federal courts must balance the interest of the individual in retaining prompt access to a federal judicial forum against countervailing institutional interests favoring exhaustion. "[A]dministrative remedies need not be pursued if the litigant's interests in immediate judicial review outweigh the government's interests in the efficiency or administrative autonomy that the exhaustion doctrine is designed to further." *West v. Bergland*, 611 F.2d 710, 715 (C.A.8 1979), cert. denied, 449 U.S. 821, 101 S.Ct. 79, 66 L.Ed.2d 23 (1980). Application of this balancing principle is "intensely practical," because attention is directed to both the nature of the claim presented and the characteristics of the particular administrative procedure provided.

C

This Court's precedents have recognized at least three broad sets of circumstances in which the interests of the individual weigh heavily against requiring administrative exhaustion. First, requiring resort to the administrative remedy may occasion undue prejudice to subsequent assertion of a court action. Such prejudice may result, for example, from an unreasonable or indefinite timeframe for administrative action. Even where the administrative decisionmaking schedule is otherwise reasonable and definite, a particular plaintiff may suffer irreparable harm if unable to secure immediate judicial consideration of his claim. By the same token, exhaustion principles apply with less force when an individual's failure to exhaust may preclude a defense to criminal liability.

Second, an administrative remedy may be inadequate "because of some doubt as to whether the agency was empowered to grant effective relief." *Gibson v. Berryhill*, 411 U.S., at 575, n. 14, 93 S.Ct., at 1696, n. 14. For example, an agency, as a preliminary matter, may be unable to consider whether to grant relief because it lacks institutional competence to resolve the particular type of issue presented, such as the constitutionality of a statute. In a similar vein, exhaustion has not been required where the challenge is to the adequacy of the agency procedure itself, such that " 'the question of the adequacy of the administrative remedy . . . [is] for all practical purposes identical with the merits of [the plaintiff's] lawsuit.'" *Barry v. Barchi*, 443 U.S. 55, 63, n. 10, 99 S.Ct. 2642, 2648, n. 10, 61 L.Ed.2d 365 (1979) (quoting *Gibson v. Berryhill*, 411 U.S., at 575, 93 S.Ct., at 1696). Alternatively, an agency may be competent to adjudicate the issue presented, but still lack authority to grant the type of relief requested.

Third, an administrative remedy may be inadequate where the administrative body is shown to be biased or has otherwise predetermined the issue before it.

III

In light of these general principles, we conclude that petitioner McCarthy need not have exhausted his constitutional claim for money damages. As a preliminary matter, we find that Congress has not meaningfully addressed the appropriateness of requiring exhaustion in this context. Although respondents' interests are significant, we are left with a firm conviction that, given the type of claim McCarthy raises and the particular characteristics of the Bureau's general grievance procedure, McCarthy's individual interests outweigh countervailing institutional interests favoring exhaustion.

A

Turning first to congressional intent, we note that the general grievance procedure was neither enacted nor mandated by Congress. Respondents, however, urge that Congress, in effect, has acted to require exhaustion by delegating power to the Attorney General and the Bureau of Prisons to control and manage the federal prison system. We think respondents confuse what Congress could be claimed to allow by implication with what Congress affirmatively has requested or required. By delegating authority, in the most general of terms, to the Bureau to administer the federal prison system, Congress cannot be said to have spoken to the particular issue whether prisoners in the custody of the Bureau should have direct access to the federal courts.

* * *

B

Because Congress has not *required* exhaustion of a federal prisoner's *Bivens* claim, we turn to an evaluation of the individual and institutional interests at stake in this case. The general grievance procedure heavily burdens the individual interests of the petitioning inmate in two ways. First, the procedure imposes short, successive filing deadlines that create a high risk of forfeiture of a claim for failure to comply. Second, the administrative "remedy" does not authorize an award of monetary damages—the only relief requested by McCarthy in this action. The combination of these features means that the prisoner seeking only money damages has everything to lose and nothing to gain from being required to exhaust his claim under the internal grievance procedure.

The filing deadlines for the grievance procedure require an inmate, within 15 days of the precipitating incident, not only to attempt to resolve his grievance informally but also to file a formal written complaint with the prison warden. Then, he must successively hurdle 20-day and 30-day deadlines to advance to the end of the grievance process. Other than the Bureau's general and quite proper interest in having early notice of any claim, we have not been apprised of any urgency or exigency justifying this timetable. As a practical matter, the filing deadlines, of course, may pose little difficulty for the knowledgeable inmate accustomed to grievances and court actions. But they are a likely trap for the inexperienced and unwary inmate, ordinarily indigent and unrepresented by counsel, with a substantial claim.

* * *

As we have noted, the grievance procedure does not include any mention of the award of monetary relief. Respondents argue that this should not matter, because "in most cases there are other things that the inmate wants." This may be true in some instances. But we cannot presume, as a general matter, that when a litigant has deliberately forgone any claim for injunctive relief and has singled out discrete past wrongs, specifically requesting monetary compensation only, that he is likely interested in "other things." The Bureau, in any case, is always free to offer an inmate administrative relief in return for withdrawal of his lawsuit. We conclude that the absence of any monetary remedy in the grievance procedure also weighs heavily against imposing an exhaustion requirement.

* * *

We do not find the interests of the Bureau of Prisons to weigh heavily in favor of exhaustion in view of the remedial scheme and particular claim presented here. To be sure, the Bureau has a substantial interest in encouraging internal resolution of grievances and in preventing the undermining of its authority by unnecessary resort by prisoners to the federal courts. But other institutional concerns relevant to exhaustion analysis appear to weigh in hardly at all. The Bureau's alleged failure to render medical care implicates only tangentially its authority to carry out the control and management of the federal prisons. Furthermore, the Bureau does not bring to bear any special expertise on the type of issue presented for resolution here. *[Bureau's interests]*

The interests of judicial economy do not stand to be advanced substantially by the general grievance procedure. No formal factfindings are made. The paperwork generated by the grievance process might assist *[judicial interests]* a court somewhat in ascertaining the facts underlying a prisoner's claim more quickly than if it has only a prisoner's complaint to review. But the grievance procedure does not create a formal factual record of the type that can be relied on conclusively by a court for disposition of a prisoner's claim on the pleadings or at summary judgment without the aid of affidavits.

C

In conclusion, we are struck by the absence of supporting material in the regulations, the record, or the briefs that the general grievance procedure here was crafted with any thought toward the principles of exhaustion of claims for money damages. The Attorney General's professed concern for internal dispute resolution has not translated itself into a more effective grievance procedure that might encourage the filing of an administrative complaint as opposed to a court action. Congress, of course, is free to design or require an appropriate administrative procedure for a prisoner to exhaust his claim for money damages. Even without further action by Congress, we do not foreclose the possibility that the Bureau itself may adopt an appropriate administrative procedure consistent with congressional intent.

The judgment of the Court of Appeals is reversed.

It is so ordered.

Concurrence

CHIEF JUSTICE REHNQUIST, with whom JUSTICE SCALIA and JUSTICE THOMAS join, concurring in the judgment.

I agree with the Court's holding that a federal prisoner need not exhaust the procedures promulgated by the Federal Bureau of Prisons. My view, however, is based entirely on the fact that the grievance procedure at issue does not provide for any award of monetary damages. As a result, in cases such as this one where prisoners seek monetary relief, the Bureau's administrative remedy furnishes no effective remedy at all, and it is therefore improper to impose an exhaustion requirement.

Because I would base the decision on this ground, I do not join the Court's extensive discussion of the general principles of exhaustion, nor do I agree with the implication that those general principles apply without modification in the context of a *Bivens* claim. In particular, I disagree with the Court's reliance on the grievance procedure's filing deadlines as a basis for excusing exhaustion * * *.

NOTES

Until 1993, the common-law scheme described in *McCarthy* was routinely applied by courts in cases involving the APA. (*McCarthy* was a *Bivens* action, in which the cause of action arose directly under the Constitution rather than under the APA.) Section 704 of the APA, however, seems to prohibit a judicially-crafted exhaustion requirement in cases founded upon the APA. Section 704 provides:

> Except as otherwise expressly required by statute, agency action otherwise final is final for purposes of this section [authorizing review of final agency action] whether or not there has been presented or determined an application for a declaratory order, for any form of reconsideration, or, unless the agency otherwise requires by rule and provides that the action meanwhile is inoperative, for an appeal to superior agency authority.

5 U.S.C. § 704 (2012). In 1993, 47 years after enactment of the APA, the Supreme Court considered whether the long-established, routine practice of the federal courts of requiring litigants to exhaust administrative remedies was forbidden by the APA.

[handwritten margin note: whether cts can req exhaustion under the APA]

DARBY V. CISNEROS

Supreme Court of the United States, 1993.
509 U.S. 137, 113 S.Ct. 2539, 125 L.Ed.2d 113.

[handwritten margin note: Darby v. Cisneros]

JUSTICE BLACKMUN delivered the opinion of the Court.*

This case presents the question whether federal courts have the authority to require that a plaintiff exhaust available administrative remedies before seeking judicial review under the Administrative Procedure Act (APA), 5 U.S.C. § 701 et seq., where neither the statute nor agency rules specifically mandate exhaustion as a prerequisite to judicial review. At issue is the relationship between the judicially created doctrine of exhaustion of administrative remedies and the statutory requirements of § 10(c) of the APA.[1]

[handwritten margin note: ← ISSUE]

I

Petitioner R. Gordon Darby is a self-employed South Carolina real estate developer who specializes in the development and management of multifamily rental projects. In the early 1980s, he began working with Lonnie Garvin, Jr., a mortgage banker, who had developed a plan to enable

---

* The CHIEF JUSTICE, JUSTICE SCALIA, and JUSTICE THOMAS join all but Part III of this opinion.

[1] Section 10(c), 80 Stat. 392–393, 5 U.S.C. § 704, provides:

"Agency action made reviewable by statute and final agency action for which there is no other adequate remedy in a court are subject to judicial review. A preliminary, procedural, or intermediate agency action or ruling not directly reviewable is subject to review on the review of the final agency action. Except as otherwise expressly required by statute, agency action otherwise final is final for the purposes of this section whether or not there has been presented or determined an application for a declaratory order, for any form of reconsideration, or, unless the agency otherwise requires by rule and provides that the action meanwhile is inoperative, for an appeal to superior agency authority."

We note that the statute as codified in the United States Code refers to "any form of reconsiderations," with the last word being in the plural. The version of § 10(c) as currently enacted, however, uses the singular "reconsideration." We quote the text as enacted in the Statutes at Large.

multifamily developers to obtain single-family mortgage insurance from respondent Department of Housing and Urban Development (HUD). Respondent Secretary of HUD (Secretary) is authorized to provide single-family mortgage insurance under § 203(b) of the National Housing Act, 48 Stat. 1249, as amended, 12 U.S.C. § 1709(b). Although HUD also provides mortgage insurance for multifamily projects under § 207 of the National Housing Act, 12 U.S.C. § 1713, the greater degree of oversight and control over such projects makes it less attractive for investors than the single-family mortgage insurance option.

The principal advantage of Garvin's plan was that it promised to avoid HUD's "Rule of Seven." This rule prevented rental properties from receiving single-family mortgage insurance if the mortgagor already had financial interests in seven or more similar rental properties in the same project or subdivision. Under Garvin's plan, a person seeking financing would use straw purchasers as mortgage insurance applicants. Once the loans were closed, the straw purchasers would transfer title back to the development company. Because no single purchaser at the time of purchase would own more than seven rental properties within the same project, the Rule of Seven appeared not to be violated. HUD employees in South Carolina apparently assured Garvin that his plan was lawful and that he thereby would avoid the limitation of the Rule of Seven.

Darby obtained financing for three separate multiunit projects, and, through Garvin's plan, Darby obtained single-family mortgage insurance from HUD. Although Darby successfully rented the units, a combination of low rents, falling interest rates, and a generally depressed rental market forced him into default in 1988. HUD became responsible for the payment of over $6.6 million in insurance claims.

HUD had become suspicious of Garvin's financing plan as far back as 1983. In 1986, HUD initiated an audit but concluded that neither Darby nor Garvin had done anything wrong or misled HUD personnel. Nevertheless, in June 1989, HUD issued a limited denial of participation (LDP) that prohibited petitioners for one year from participating in any program in South Carolina administered by respondent Assistant Secretary of Housing. Two months later, the Assistant Secretary notified petitioners that HUD was also proposing to debar them from further participation in all HUD procurement contracts and in any nonprocurement transaction with any federal agency.

Petitioners' appeals of the LDP and of the proposed debarment were consolidated, and an Administrative Law Judge (ALJ) conducted a hearing on the consolidated appeals in December 1989. The judge issued an "Initial Decision and Order" in April 1990, finding that the financing method used by petitioners was "a sham which improperly circumvented the Rule of Seven." The ALJ concluded, however, that most of the relevant facts had been disclosed to local HUD employees, that petitioners lacked criminal intent, and that Darby himself "genuinely cooperated with HUD to try [to] work out his financial dilemma and avoid foreclosure." In light of these mitigating factors, the ALJ concluded that an indefinite debarment would be punitive and that it would serve no legitimate purpose; good cause existed, however, to debar petitioners for a period of 18 months.

> Under HUD regulations,
>
> "The hearing officer's determination shall be final unless, pursuant to 24 CFR part 26, the Secretary or the Secretary's designee, within 30 days of receipt of a request decides as a matter of discretion to review the finding of the hearing officer. The 30 day period for deciding whether to review a determination may be extended upon written notice of such extension by the Secretary or his designee. Any party may request such a review in writing within 15 days of receipt of the hearing officer's determination." 24 CFR § 24.314(c) (1992).

Neither petitioners nor respondents sought further administrative review of the ALJ's "Initial Decision and Order."

On May 31, 1990, petitioners filed suit in the United States District Court for the District of South Carolina. They sought an injunction and a declaration that the administrative sanctions were imposed for purposes of punishment, in violation of HUD's own debarment regulations, and therefore were "not in accordance with law" within the meaning of § 10(e)(B)(1) of the APA, 5 U.S.C. § 706(2)(A).

Respondents moved to dismiss the complaint on the ground that petitioners, by forgoing the option to seek review by the Secretary, had failed to exhaust administrative remedies. The District Court denied respondents' motion to dismiss, reasoning that the administrative remedy was inadequate and that resort to that remedy would have been futile. In a subsequent opinion, the District Court granted petitioners' motion for summary judgment, concluding that the "imposition of debarment in this case encroached too heavily on the punitive side of the line, and for those reasons was an abuse of discretion and not in accordance with the law."

The Court of Appeals for the Fourth Circuit reversed. It recognized that neither the National Housing Act nor HUD regulations expressly mandate exhaustion of administrative remedies prior to filing suit. The court concluded, however, that the District Court had erred in denying respondents' motion to dismiss, because there was no evidence to suggest that further review would have been futile or that the Secretary would have abused his discretion by indefinitely extending the time limitations for review.

* * *

II

Section 10(c) of the APA bears the caption "Actions reviewable." It provides in its first two sentences that judicial review is available for "final agency action for which there is no other adequate remedy in a court," and that "preliminary, procedural, or intermediate agency action . . . is subject to review on the review of the final agency action." The last sentence of § 10(c) reads:

> "Except as otherwise expressly required by statute, agency action otherwise final is final for the purposes of this section whether or not there has been presented or determined an application for a declaratory order, for any form of reconsideration * * *, or, unless the agency otherwise requires by rule and provides that the action meanwhile is inoperative, for an appeal to superior agency authority." 80 Stat. 392–393, 5 U.S.C. § 704.

P's argmt: Petitioners argue that this provision means that a litigant seeking judicial review of a final agency action under the APA need not exhaust available administrative remedies unless such exhaustion is expressly required by statute or agency rule. According to petitioners, since § 10(c) contains an explicit exhaustion provision, federal courts are not free to require further exhaustion as a matter of judicial discretion.

R's argmt: Respondents contend that § 10(c) is concerned solely with timing, that is, when agency actions become "final," and that Congress had no intention to interfere with the courts' ability to impose conditions on the timing of their exercise of jurisdiction to review final agency actions. Respondents concede that petitioners' claim is "final" under § 10(c), for neither the National Housing Act nor applicable HUD regulations require that a litigant pursue further administrative appeals prior to seeking judicial review. However, even though nothing in § 10(c) precludes judicial review of petitioners' claim, respondents argue that federal courts remain free under the APA to impose appropriate exhaustion requirements.

We have recognized that the judicial doctrine of exhaustion of administrative remedies is conceptually distinct from the doctrine of finality:

> "[T]he finality requirement is concerned with whether the initial decisionmaker has arrived at a definitive position on the issue that inflicts an actual, concrete injury; the exhaustion requirement generally refers to administrative and judicial procedures by which an injured party may seek review of an adverse decision and obtain a remedy if the decision is found to be unlawful or otherwise inappropriate." *Williamson County Regional Planning Comm'n v. Hamilton Bank of Johnson City*, 473 U.S. 172, 193, 105 S.Ct. 3108, 3119, 87 L.Ed.2d 126 (1985).

Whether courts are free to impose an exhaustion requirement as a matter of judicial discretion depends, at least in part, on whether Congress has provided otherwise, for "[o]f 'paramount importance' to any exhaustion inquiry is congressional intent," *McCarthy v. Madigan*, 503 U.S. 140, 144, 112 S.Ct. 1081, 1086, 117 L.Ed.2d 291 (1992). We therefore must consider whether § 10(c), by providing the conditions under which agency action becomes "final for the purposes of" judicial review, limits the authority of courts to impose additional exhaustion requirements as a prerequisite to judicial review.

It perhaps is surprising that it has taken over 45 years since the passage of the APA for this Court definitively to address this question. Professor Davis noted in 1958 that § 10(c) had been almost completely ignored in judicial opinions, see 3 K. Davis, Administrative Law Treatise § 20.08, p. 101 (1958); he reiterated that observation 25 years later, noting that the "provision is relevant in hundreds of cases and is customarily overlooked." 4 K. Davis, Administrative Law Treatise § 26.12, pp. 468–469 (2d ed. 1983). Only a handful of opinions in the Courts of Appeals have considered the effect of § 10(c) on the general exhaustion doctrine.

This Court has had occasion, however, to consider § 10(c) in other contexts * * *.

* * *

While some dicta in these cases might be claimed to lend support to respondents' interpretation of § 10(c), the text of the APA leaves little doubt that petitioners are correct. Under § 10(a) of the APA, "[a] person suffering legal wrong because of agency action, or adversely affected or aggrieved by agency action within the meaning of a relevant statute, *is entitled to judicial review thereof.*" 5 U.S.C. § 702 (emphasis added). Although § 10(a) provides the general right to judicial review of agency actions under the APA, § 10(c) establishes when such review is available. When an aggrieved party has exhausted all administrative remedies expressly prescribed by statute or agency rule, the agency action is "final for the purposes of this section" and therefore "subject to judicial review" under the first sentence. While federal courts may be free to apply, where appropriate, other prudential doctrines of judicial administration to limit the scope and timing of judicial review, § 10(c), by its very terms, has limited the availability of the doctrine of exhaustion of administrative remedies to that which the statute or rule clearly mandates.

[margin note: text of APA leaves little doubt that Ps = correct]

[margin note: exhaustion limited to where clearly mandated by statute/rule]

The last sentence of § 10(c) refers explicitly to "any form of reconsideration" and "an appeal to superior agency authority." Congress clearly was concerned with making the exhaustion requirement unambiguous so that aggrieved parties would know precisely what administrative steps were required before judicial review would be available. If courts were able to impose additional exhaustion requirements beyond those provided by Congress or the agency, the last sentence of § 10(c) would make no sense * * *. Section 10(c) explicitly requires exhaustion of all intra-agency appeals mandated either by statute or by agency rule; it would be inconsistent with the plain language of § 10(c) for courts to require litigants to exhaust optional appeals as well.

III

[handwritten: no need to look → leg. history]

Recourse to the legislative history of § 10(c) is unnecessary in light of the plain meaning of the statutory text. Nevertheless, we consider that history briefly because both sides have spent much of their time arguing about its implications * * *.

* * *

[After extensive discussion, the Court concludes that the APA's legislative history does not contradict the plain language of the text.]

IV

We noted just last Term in a non-APA case that

"appropriate deference to Congress' power to prescribe the basic procedural scheme under which a claim may be heard in a federal court requires fashioning of exhaustion principles in a manner consistent with congressional intent and any applicable statutory scheme." *McCarthy v. Madigan*, 503 U.S., at 144, 112 S.Ct., at 1086.

[handwritten: exhaustion = matter of judicial discr. in cases not governed by APA]

Appropriate deference in this case requires the recognition that, with respect to actions brought under the APA, Congress effectively codified the doctrine of exhaustion of administrative remedies in § 10(c). Of course, the exhaustion doctrine continues to apply as a matter of judicial discretion in cases not governed by the APA. But where the APA applies, an appeal to "superior agency authority" is a prerequisite to judicial review only when expressly required by statute or when an agency rule requires appeal before review and the administrative action is made inoperative pending that review. Courts are not free to impose an exhaustion requirement as a rule of judicial administration where the agency action has already become "final" under § 10(c).

The judgment of the Court of Appeals is reversed, and the case is remanded for further proceedings consistent with this opinion.

It is so ordered.

NOTES

One hundred years of practice are not so easily dislodged from the judicial mind, and courts that are accustomed to the traditional exhaustion analysis are sometimes slow to change their ways. *See, e.g., Howell v. INS*, 72 F.3d 288 (2d Cir.1995) ((mis)reading *Darby* as requiring exhaustion whenever the agency has regulations in place for internal appeals, even if those regulations do not necessarily stay the effectiveness of the agency's decision while the appeal is pending). Even the D.C. Circuit has sometimes had difficulty processing *Darby*. In *CSX Transportation, Inc. v. Surface Transportation Board.*, 568 F.3d 236, 247 (D.C.Cir.2009), the court held that, notwithstanding *Darby*, parties had to give the agency at least one chance to rule on all challenges to final agency orders before bringing those challenges in court. On rehearing, the panel gracefully agreed that it had construed *Darby* too narrowly and that courts have no power to require parties to seek reconsideration of final agency orders unless a statute requires reconsideration. *CSX Transportation, Inc., v. Surface Transportation Board*, 584 F.3d 1076, 1079 (D.C.Cir.2009). For the most part, however, courts have taken *Darby* at face value, *see DSE, Inc. v. United States*, 169 F.3d 21 (D.C.Cir.1999); *Young v. Reno*, 114 F.3d 879 (9th Cir.1997), and one should be reluctant to rely on *Howell* even in the Second Circuit.

Even under the broadest reading of *Darby*, the traditional exhaustion doctrine continues to be of great importance. *Darby* is an interpretation of § 704 of the APA. As *Darby* acknowledges, "the exhaustion doctrine continues to apply as a matter of judicial discretion in cases not governed by the APA," which includes cases brought under nonstatutory review, special review statutes, *see Tesoro Refining & Marketing Co. v. FERC*, 552 F.3d 868, 872–75 (D.C.Cir.2009), or directly under the Constitution via *Bivens* actions.

When special review statutes or regulations prescribe an exhaustion requirement, do the traditional common-law exceptions to exhaustion apply to exhaustion? Strangely enough, the matter appears to be unresolved. *See Marine Mammal Conservancy v. Department of Agriculture*, 134 F.3d 409 (D.C.Cir.1998) (noting but not resolving the question); *Sousa v. INS*, 226 F.3d 28 (1st Cir.2000) (same). If the real issue is whether the statute or regulation in question implicitly contains such exceptions, there may be no general resolution because the answer will depend upon the proper interpretation of each statute or regulation.

2. FINALITY

Section 704 declares that judicial review is available for "[a]gency action made reviewable by statute and final agency action for which there is no other adequate remedy in a court * * *." Thus, in the absence of an applicable special review statute, § 704 creates a cause of action for review of *final* agency action. Nonfinal agency action is therefore not reviewable under this provision. In addition, special review statutes uniformly authorize review only of final agency action.[30] Through one route or

---

[30] There is nothing to prevent Congress from authorizing review of nonfinal agency action through a special review statute, but your editor knows of no statute that clearly does so. Even when the occasional statute makes no express mention of finality, *see, e.g.*, 49 U.S.C. § 46110(a) (2012) (authorizing judicial review of "an order issued by the Secretary of Transportation (or the Under Secretary of Transportation for Security with respect to security duties and powers designated to be carried out by the Under Secretary or the Administrator of the Federal Aviation

another, finality of agency action is therefore a prerequisite to all judicial review in the federal system.

In principle, the meaning of finality could vary from statute to statute. In practice, courts have evolved a uniform meaning for the term that Congress is presumed to adopt unless it says otherwise. *See, e.g., John Doe, Inc. v. DEA*, 484 F.3d 561, 566 n.4 (D.C.Cir.2007) ("We see no reason, however, that the word 'final' in § 877 should be interpreted differently than the word 'final' in the APA").

FTC v. STANDARD OIL CO. OF CALIFORNIA
Supreme Court of the United States, 1980.
449 U.S. 232, 101 S.Ct. 488, 66 L.Ed.2d 416.

JUSTICE POWELL delivered the opinion of the Court.

This case presents the question whether the issuance of a complaint by the Federal Trade Commission is "final agency action" subject to judicial review before administrative adjudication concludes.

I

On July 18, 1973, the Federal Trade Commission issued and served upon eight major oil companies, including Standard Oil Company of California (Socal), a complaint averring that the Commission had "reason to believe" that the companies were violating § 5 of the Federal Trade Commission Act, 38 Stat. 719, as amended, 15 U.S.C. § 45,[2] and stating the Commission's charges in that respect. The Commission issued the complaint under authority of § 5(b) of the Act, 15 U.S.C. § 45(b), which provides:

> "Whenever the Commission shall have reason to believe that any . . . person, partnership, or corporation has been or is using any unfair method of competition or unfair or deceptive act or practice in or affecting commerce, and if it shall appear to the Commission that a proceeding by it in respect thereof would be to the interest of the public, it shall issue and serve upon such person, partnership, or corporation a complaint stating its charges in that respect and containing a notice of a hearing. . ."

An adjudication of the complaint's charges began soon thereafter before an Administrative Law Judge, and is still pending.

Administration with respect to aviation duties and powers designated to be carried out by the Administrator)"), courts read a finality requirement into the statute. *See* Flytenow, Inc. v. FAA, 808 F.3d 882, 888–89 (D.C.Cir.2015).

2   Section 5 of the Act, as set forth in 15 U.S.C. § 45, provides in pertinent part:

"(a) . . . (1) Unfair methods of competition in or affecting commerce, and unfair or deceptive acts or practices in or affecting commerce, are declared unlawful."

On May 1, 1975, Socal filed a complaint against the Commission in the District Court for the Northern District of California, alleging that the Commission had issued its complaint without having "reason to believe" that Socal was violating the Act. Socal sought an order declaring that the issuance of the complaint was unlawful and requiring that the complaint be withdrawn. Socal had sought this relief from the Commission and been denied. In support of its allegation and request, Socal recited a series of events that preceded the issuance of the complaint and several events that followed. In Socal's estimation, the only inference to be drawn from these events was that the Commission lacked sufficient evidence when it issued the complaint to warrant a belief that Socal was violating the Act.

The gist of Socal's recitation of events preceding the issuance of the complaint is that political pressure for a public explanation of the gasoline shortages of 1973 forced the Commission to issue a complaint against the major oil companies despite insufficient investigation * * *.

* * *

The District Court dismissed Socal's complaint on the ground that "a review of preliminary decisions made by administrative agencies, except under most unusual circumstances, would be productive of nothing more than chaos." The Court of Appeals for the Ninth Circuit reversed. It held the Commission's determination whether evidence before it provided the requisite reason to believe is "committed to agency discretion" and therefore is unreviewable according to § 10 of the Administrative Procedure Act (APA), 5 U.S.C. § 701(a)(2). The Court of Appeals held, however, that the District Court could inquire whether the Commission *in fact* had made the determination that it had reason to believe that Socal was violating the Act. If the District Court were to find upon remand that the Commission had issued the complaint "solely because of outside pressure or with complete absence of a 'reason to believe' determination," then it was to order the Commission to dismiss the complaint. The Court of Appeals further held that the issuance of the complaint was "final agency action" under § 10(c) of the APA, 5 U.S.C. § 704.

We granted the Commission's petition for a writ of certiorari because of the importance of the questions raised by Socal's request for judicial review of the complaint before the conclusion of the adjudication. We now reverse.

II

The Commission averred in its complaint that it had reason to believe that Socal was violating the Act. That averment is subject to judicial review before the conclusion of administrative adjudication only if the issuance of the complaint was "final agency action" or otherwise was "directly reviewable" under § 10(c) of the APA, 5 U.S.C. § 704. We conclude that the issuance of the complaint was neither.

A

The Commission's issuance of its complaint was not "final agency action." The Court observed in *Abbott Laboratories v. Gardner*, 387 U.S. 136, 149, 87 S.Ct. 1507, 1516, 18 L.Ed.2d 681 (1967), that "[t]he cases dealing with judicial review of administrative actions have interpreted the 'finality' element in a pragmatic way." In *Abbott Laboratories*, for example, the publication of certain regulations by the Commissioner of Food and Drugs was held to be final agency action subject to judicial review in an action for declaratory judgment brought prior to any Government action for enforcement. The regulations required manufacturers of prescription drugs to print certain information on drug labels and advertisements. The regulations were "definitive" statements of the Commission's position, *id.*, at 151, 87 S.Ct., at 1516, and had a "direct and immediate . . . effect on the day-to-day business" of the complaining parties. *Id.*, at 152, 87 S.Ct., at 1517. They had "the status of law" and "immediate compliance with their terms was expected." *Ibid.* * * *.

By its terms, the Commission's averment of "reason to believe" that Socal was violating the Act is not a definitive statement of position. It represents a threshold determination that further inquiry is warranted and that a complaint should initiate proceedings. To be sure, the issuance of the complaint is definitive on the question whether the Commission avers reason to believe that the respondent to the complaint is violating the Act. But the extent to which the respondent may challenge the complaint and its charges proves that the averment of reason to believe is not "definitive" in a comparable manner to the regulations in *Abbott Laboratories* and the cases it discussed.

Section 5 of the Act, 15 U.S.C. § 45(b), in conjunction with Commission regulations, 16 CFR §§ 3.41–3.46 (1980), and § 5 of the APA, 5 U.S.C. § 554, requires that the complaint contain a notice of hearing at which the respondent may present evidence and testimony before an administrative law judge to refute the Commission's charges. Either party to the adjudication may appeal an adverse decision of the administrative law judge to the full Commission, which then may dismiss the complaint. If instead the Commission enters an order requiring the respondent to cease and desist from engaging in the challenged practice the respondent still is not bound by the Commission's decision until judicial review is complete or the opportunity to seek review has lapsed. Thus, the averment of reason to believe is a prerequisite to a definitive agency position on the question whether Socal violated the Act, but itself is a determination only that adjudicatory proceedings will commence.

Serving only to initiate the proceedings, the issuance of the complaint averring reason to believe has no legal force comparable to that of the regulation at issue in *Abbott Laboratories*, nor any comparable effect upon Socal's daily business. The regulations in *Abbott Laboratories* forced manufacturers to "risk serious criminal and civil penalties" for noncompliance, 387 U.S., at 153, 87 S.Ct., at 1517, or "change all their labels, advertisements, and promotional materials; . . . destroy stocks of printed matter; and . . . invest heavily in new printing type and new supplies." *Id.*, at 152, 87 S.Ct., at 1517. Socal does not contend that the issuance of the complaint had any such legal or practical effect, except to impose upon Socal the burden of responding to the charges made against it. Although this burden certainly is substantial, it is different in kind and legal effect from the burdens attending what heretofore has been considered to be final agency action.

In contrast to the complaint's lack of legal or practical effect upon Socal, the effect of the judicial review sought by Socal is likely to be interference with the proper functioning of the agency and a burden for the courts. Judicial intervention into the agency process denies the agency an opportunity to correct its own mistakes and to apply its expertise. Intervention also leads to piecemeal review which at the least is inefficient and upon completion of the agency process might prove to have been unnecessary. Furthermore, unlike the review in *Abbott Laboratories*, judicial review to determine whether the Commission decided that it had the requisite reason to believe would delay resolution of the ultimate question whether the Act was violated. Finally, every respondent to a Commission complaint could make the claim that Socal had made. Judicial review of the averments in the Commission's complaints should not be a means of turning prosecutor into defendant before adjudication concludes.

In sum, the Commission's issuance of a complaint averring reason to believe that Socal was violating the Act is not a definitive ruling or regulation. It had no legal force or practical effect upon Socal's daily business other than the disruptions that accompany any major litigation. And immediate judicial review would serve neither efficiency nor enforcement of the Act. These pragmatic considerations counsel against the conclusion that the issuance of the complaint was "final agency action."

B

Socal relies, however, upon different considerations than these in contending that the issuance of the complaint is "final agency action."

Socal first contends that it exhausted its administrative remedies by moving in the adjudicatory proceedings for dismissal of the complaint. By thus affording the Commission an opportunity to decide upon the matter, Socal contends that it has satisfied the interests underlying the doctrine of administrative exhaustion. The Court of Appeals agreed. We think, however, that Socal and the Court of Appeals have mistaken exhaustion for finality. By requesting the Commission to withdraw its complaint and by awaiting the Commission's refusal to do so, Socal may well have exhausted its administrative remedy as to the averment of reason to believe. But the Commission's refusal to reconsider its issuance of the complaint does not render the complaint a "definitive" action. The Commission's refusal does not augment the complaint's legal force or practical effect upon Socal. Nor does the refusal diminish the concerns for efficiency and enforcement of the Act.

Socal also contends that it will be irreparably harmed unless the issuance of the complaint is judicially reviewed immediately. Socal argues that the expense and disruption of defending itself in protracted adjudicatory proceedings constitutes irreparable harm. As indicated above, we do not doubt that the burden of defending this proceeding will be substantial. But "the expense and annoyance of litigation is 'part of the social burden of living under government.'" *Petroleum Exploration, Inc. v. Public Service Comm'n*, 304 U.S. 209, 222, 58 S.Ct. 834, 841, 82 L.Ed. 1294 (1938). As we recently reiterated: "Mere litigation expense, even substantial and unrecoupable cost, does not constitute irreparable injury." *Renegotiation Board v. Bannercraft Clothing Co.*, 415 U.S. 1, 24, 94 S.Ct. 1028, 1040, 39 L.Ed.2d 123 (1974).

Socal further contends that its challenge to the Commission's averment of reason to believe can never be reviewed unless it is reviewed before the Commission's adjudication concludes * * *. Socal also suggests that the unlawfulness will be "insulated" because the reviewing court will lack an adequate record and it will address only the question whether substantial evidence supported the cease-and-desist order.

We are not persuaded by this speculation * * *. [T]he APA specifically provides that a "preliminary, procedural, or intermediate agency action or ruling not directly reviewable is subject to review on the review of the final agency action," 5 U.S.C. § 704 * * *. Thus, assuming that the issuance of the complaint is not "committed to agency discretion by law," a court of appeals reviewing a cease-and-desist order has the power to review alleged unlawfulness in the issuance of a complaint. We need not decide what action a court of appeals should take if it finds a cease-and-desist order to be supported by substantial evidence but the complaint to have been issued without the requisite reason to believe. It suffices to hold that the possibility does not affect the application of the finality rule.

* * *

III

Because the Commission's issuance of a complaint averring reason to believe that Socal has violated the Act is not "final agency action" under

§ 10(c) of the APA, it is not judicially reviewable before administrative adjudication concludes. We therefore reverse the Court of Appeals and remand for the dismissal of the complaint.

It is so ordered.

JUSTICE STEWART took no part in the consideration or decision of this case.

JUSTICE STEVENS, concurring in the judgment.

[JUSTICE STEVENS concurred in the result on the ground that initiation of a complaint is not "agency action" within the meaning of 5 U.S.C. § 551(13).]

NOTES

Agency action is final if it is definitive and has legal (and not merely practical) consequences. *See Parsons v. United States Dep't of Justice,* 878 F.3d 162, 167–69 (6th Cir.2017) (report from the National Gang Intelligence Center designating fans of the Insane Clown Posse as a gang is non-final when the report had no direct legal consequence, even though it had many practical consequences as a result of third-party actors relying on the designation). This formulation seems simple—and usually is. Complications arise primarily from disputes about when agency decisions are definitive, *compare Natural Resources Defense Council v. EPA,* 22 F.3d 1125, 1132–33 (D.C.Cir.1994) (agency positions expressed in letters and memoranda rather than formal rules or orders can nonetheless be final if they are sufficiently authoritative) *with Center for Auto Safety v. NHTSA,* 452 F.3d 798 (D.C.Cir.2006) (holding non-final a policy statement expressing the agency's legal views), or when seemingly nonfinal action can nonetheless be reviewed because it violates a clear statutory or constitutional right. *See Ticor Title Ins. Co. v. FTC,* 814 F.2d 731, 749–50 (D.C.Cir.1987) (Williams, J.) (describing the contours of a "clear right" exception to the finality rule).

When the finality requirement stems from the language of special review statutes authorizing review of agency action and serving as the sources of the federal court's jurisdiction, a lack of finality means that federal courts do not have subject matter jurisdiction over the case. Courts are therefore obliged to raise finality concerns even when the parties do not. In principle, courts must also resolve finality issues before addressing nonjurisdictional timing doctrines such as common law exhaustion or ripeness, *see American Train Dispatchers Ass'n v. ICC,* 949 F.2d 413 (D.C.Cir.1991) ("At the threshold, the ICC argues that the Union's petition is barred for want of finality, ripeness, and exhaustion of administrative remedies. Of these three requirements for review, only finality is jurisdictional, and so we are bound to consider it first."), though courts do not always pay attention to such niceties. When review is based on § 704 of the APA, lack of finality means that there is no cause of action (and the plaintiff therefore loses), but it does not go to the jurisdiction of the court, because the court's jurisdiction comes from the general "federal question" statute, 28 U.S.C. § 1331 (2012), rather than from the APA. *See Center for Auto Safety*, 452 F.3d at 805–06; *John Doe, Inc. v. DEA*, 484 F.3d at 565. Again, courts and litigants do not always observe these niceties. *See Minard Run Oil Co. v. United States Forest Service*, 670 F.3d 236, 247 (3d Cir. 2011) (treating APA finality as jurisdictional); *Sierra Club v. Jackson*, 648 F.3d 848, 853–54 (D.C.Cir.2011) (noting the conflicting authorities within the D.C. Circuit on the question).

It is not, of course, always clear whether an agency's action has sufficient consequences to meet the functional test for finality. *See Rhea Lana, Inc. v. Dep't of Labor,* 824 F.3d 1023, 1027 (D.C.Cir.2016) ("The law in this area is hardly crisp. Our finality precedent lacks many 'self-implementing, bright-line rule[s],' given the 'pragmatic' and 'flexible' nature of the inquiry as a whole.").

AIR BRAKE SYSTEMS, INC. V. MINETA
United States Court of Appeals, Sixth Circuit, 2004.
357 F.3d 632.

Before KEITH, MARTIN, and SUTTON, CIRCUIT JUDGES.

SUTTON, CIRCUIT JUDGE.

This case arises from a longstanding dispute between the National Highway Traffic Safety Administration (NHTSA) and Air Brake Systems, Inc. (Air Brake). Air Brake manufactures a "non-electronic" antilock brake system for trucks and trailers, which purports to comply with Federal Motor Vehicle Safety Standard 121, a NHTSA regulation concerning antilock brakes. When an Air Brake customer asked NHTSA whether a vehicle with Air Brake's brake system-the only non-electronic antilock brake system on the market-would comply with Standard 121, NHTSA's Acting Chief Counsel issued two opinion letters stating that the brake system would not satisfy the standard. NHTSA posted the letters on its website (with negative consequences for Air Brake's business), but it did not begin the statutory process for determining whether vehicles carrying such brakes were noncompliant or the statutory process for ordering a recall of vehicles with these brakes.

Soon after NHTSA posted the first of these letters on its website, Air Brake filed this action challenging the Chief Counsel's conclusion as well as the Chief Counsel's authority to issue the letter. The district court granted summary judgment in favor of NHTSA, reasoning that interpretive letters issued by NHTSA's Acting Chief Counsel do not constitute "final agency action" subject to judicial review under the Administrative Procedure Act. We agree that the tentative conclusions reached in the letters, which are based in part on Air Brake's representations about its antilock brake system and which NHTSA acknowledges are neither binding on the industry nor entitled to any administrative deference, do not constitute final agency action regarding the meaning of Standard 121 or Air Brake's compliance with that standard. At the same time, however, the letters *do* reflect final agency action with respect to the distinct question whether the Chief Counsel has authority to issue them, because the practice does not lend itself to further review at the agency level and has legal consequences. Yet because the practice of permitting NHTSA's Chief Counsel to issue advisory opinions in response to inquiries from the public does not exceed the Chief Counsel's authority (and indeed has much to recommend it), we affirm the district court's judgment in favor of the Government.

I.

When Congress enacted the National Traffic and Motor Vehicle Safety Act of 1966, 80 Stat. 718, 49 U.S.C. § 30101 *et seq.,* it directed the Secretary of Transportation to prescribe motor vehicle safety standards. The Secretary in turn delegated this task to NHTSA. The first Federal Motor Vehicle Safety Standard was promulgated in 1967 and NHTSA has promulgated numerous other standards since then, including Standard 121 (codified at 49 C.F.R. § 571.121), which covers the requirements for air brake systems used in heavy vehicles.

In 1995, NHTSA amended Standard 121 to require that trucks, buses and trailers equipped with air brakes have an "antilock brake system." *See* Standard No. 121, Air Brake Systems, 60 Fed.Reg. 13,216 (Mar. 10, 1995). The standard defines "antilock brake system" as

a portion of a service brake system that automatically controls the degree of rotational wheel slip during braking by:

(1) Sensing the rate of angular rotation of the wheels;

(2) Transmitting signals regarding the rate of wheel angular rotation to one or more controlling devices which interpret those signals and generate responsive controlling output signals; and

(3) Transmitting those controlling signals to one or more modulators which adjust brake actuating forces in response to those signals.

49 C.F.R. § 571.121. In accordance with this standard, antilock brakes also must have an electrical circuit capable of signaling a malfunction in the brakes through an external warning light. NHTSA enacted the 1995 amendment amid concerns that only electronic braking systems would satisfy this provision.

One company concerned about the impact of the amended standard was Air Brake Systems, which manufactures braking systems installed on trucks and trailers. After devoting ten years to developing a pneumatic antilock brake system for trucks and trailers, Air Brake patented its new brake system—the "MSQR-5000"—in 1992. The MSQR-5000 is a non-electronic brake or, in the words of Air Brake, is a "non-computerized antilock braking system which is a combination differential pressure regulator/quick release valve that is installed at each braking axle into the service air lines centered between the brake chambers." Air Brake initially sold its non-electronic antilock brakes on the retrofit after-market for used trucks and trailers (which is not subject to Standard 121), but not on the original-equipment market for new trucks and trailers (which is subject to Standard 121).

After NHTSA amended Standard 121, William Washington, the current president of Air Brake, challenged the validity of the rule in federal court. Among other contentions, he claimed that the standard improperly sought to exclude non-electronic antilock brakes from the market and improperly imposed design specifications rather than performance criteria, all in violation of NHTSA's regulatory authority. The Tenth Circuit rejected Washington's challenge. *See Washington v. Dep't of Transp.*, 84 F.3d 1222 (10th Cir. 1996). In doing so, the court noted that a manufacturer "that has devised a new means of obtaining the same or better safety performance" may seek an exemption from a safety standard's requirements, and that "no special exemption would be necessary for a new device *meeting* [an] existing . . . standard[ ]" if the standard is "purely performative," as opposed to one that requires "a particular type of equipment." *Id.* at 1225 & n. 3. Air Brake seized upon this language and at some point began marketing its product as compliant with Standard 121, despite the acknowledged absence of a warning light. Air Brake represented in its Manufacturer's Certification that "[t]he exclusion of a warning light" in its pneumatic antilock brake system "is permissible pursuant to *Washington v. DOT.*" J.A. at 224.

In January 2001, Air Brake tried to sell the MSQR-5000 to MAC Trailer Manufacturing, a manufacturer of vehicles subject to Standard 121. Because Air Brake's product was the only non-electronic antilock brake system on the market, MAC Trailer asked NHTSA (orally) whether the device met the requirements of Standard 121. NHTSA responded (also orally) that it did not.

A month later, William Washington and consultants hired by Air Brake met with NHTSA to explain the operation and features of the MSQR-5000, in an apparent attempt to persuade NHTSA that the braking system complied with the agency's safety standards. During the meeting, NHTSA requested that certain tests be performed on the product and that Air Brake submit the test data to the agency. Air Brake scheduled another meeting with NHTSA for this purpose on June 12, 2001.

On June 4, 2001, eight days before the scheduled meeting, NHTSA's Acting Chief Counsel, John Womack, sent a letter to MAC Trailer in response to its earlier oral inquiry and a subsequent written inquiry as to whether the MSQR-5000 satisfied Standard 121. In the letter, the Chief Counsel noted that NHTSA does not pre-approve equipment, and that the applicable statutes make the vehicle manufacturer, not the parts manufacturer, responsible for ensuring compliance with NHTSA's safety standards. Nonetheless, based on NHTSA's review of Air Brake's promotional materials and the "principles involved in [the braking system's] operation," he noted that "the installation of the MSQR-5000 alone would not allow a vehicle to meet [Standard] 121's [antilock brake system] requirement." J.A. at 172. The Chief Counsel expressed specific concern that (1) "the MSQR-5000 does not seem to have any means of automatically controlling wheel slip during braking by sensing, analyzing, and modulating the rate of angular rotation of the wheel," and (2) "the MSQR-5000 also appears to lack any provision for illuminating a warning light providing notification of an [antilock brake system] malfunction." J.A. at 173. NHTSA posted the letter on its website.

Air Brake met with NHTSA as planned on June 12th. At the meeting NHTSA recommended that Air Brake perform certain tests on the brakes. Air Brake conducted the tests and forwarded the results to NHTSA. At the same time, it asked NHTSA to post a letter from Air Brake's counsel on its website so that Air Brake's views about MSQR-5000 and specifically about the brake system's compliance with Standard 121 could be seen by visitors to NHTSA's website alongside the contrary opinion of NHTSA's Chief Counsel. NHTSA never posted the letter.

On August 29, 2001, Air Brake sued Secretary of Transportation Norman Mineta and NHTSA (collectively, NHTSA), challenging the agency's determination that the MSQR-5000 did not comply with Standard 121 and seeking to enjoin NHTSA from continuing to publish the offending letter on its website. The United States District Court for the Eastern District of Michigan denied Air Brake a temporary restraining order, but took Air Brake's motion for a preliminary injunction under consideration and ordered the parties to take the steps necessary for NHTSA to complete its review of Air Brake's product. As a culmination of these steps and as requested by the district court, NHTSA's Acting Chief Counsel issued a letter on December 10, 2001 to Air Brake containing his interpretation and application of Standard 121 to Air Brake's pneumatic brake system. The letter superceded the June 4th letter and essentially reaffirmed the Chief Counsel's conclusion that the MSQR-5000 braking system would not by itself bring a vehicle into compliance with Standard 121.

NHTSA then moved for summary judgment, which the district court granted on the ground that neither the June 4th letter nor the December 10th letter issued by the Chief Counsel constituted "final agency action" * * *. Air Brake appealed the judgment * * *.

II.

Air Brake raises two essential challenges. It first challenges the merits of "[t]he findings and conclusions contained in the [Chief Counsel's] Letter," including the Chief Counsel's opinion that the MSQR-5000 does not comply with Standard 121. It then challenges the Chief Counsel's authority to issue opinions on whether a product complies with NHTSA safety standards without following the recall process set forth in the Safety Act.

Before reaching the merits of either challenge, we must consider whether the federal courts have jurisdiction over them under the right to review created by § 10 of the Administrative Procedure Act. In accordance with that provision, federal courts may review two types of agency actions: "[1] Agency action made reviewable by statute and [2] final agency action for which there is no other adequate remedy in a court." 5 U.S.C. § 704. In contrast, "[a] preliminary, procedural, or intermediate agency action or ruling [is] not directly reviewable" and may be examined by a federal court only through "review of the final agency action" itself. *Id.* Because no specific statute creates a right to review the agency actions in this case, as the parties agree, the jurisdictional question here is one of statutory interpretation: Do the letters constitute "final" agency action for which no other adequate judicial remedy exists?

"As a general matter," the Supreme Court has instructed, "two conditions must be satisfied for agency action to be 'final': First, the action must mark the consummation of the agency's decisionmaking process . . . [and] must not be of a tentative or interlocutory nature. And second, the action must be one by which rights or obligations have been determined, or from which legal consequences will flow." *Bennett v. Spear*, 520 U.S. 154, 177–78, 117 S.Ct. 1154, 137 L.Ed.2d 281 (1997).

III.

Air Brake claims that we have jurisdiction to review three distinct actions by the agency: (1) the Chief Counsel's statements (in each letter) that Air Brake's product fails to satisfy the general requirements of Standard 121; (2) the Chief Counsel's legal interpretation (in each letter) of Standard 121's warning-light requirement; and (3) the authority of the Chief Counsel to issue the letters in the first place. As each of these issues presents a distinct finality question, we examine them separately.

A.

The essential content of each letter, explaining why Air Brake's product generally does not comply with Standard 121, is not final agency action under § 10 of the APA. First and foremost, "[a]n agency action is not final if it is . . . 'tentative' " in nature. *Franklin v. Massachusetts,* 505 U.S. 788, 797, 112 S.Ct. 2767, 120 L.Ed.2d 636 (1992). And agency letters based on hypothetical facts or facts submitted to the agency, as opposed to factfindings made by the agency, are classically non-final for this reason. *See Nat'l Res. Def. Council v. FAA*, 292 F.3d 875, 882 (D.C.Cir.2002) (holding that an opinion letter issued by the FAA "based on a hypothetical factual situation" presented to the agency by the parties was "not appropriate for review"); *Ass'n of Am. Med. Colls. v. United States*, 217 F.3d 770, 780–81 (9th Cir.2000) (holding that a letter from the general counsel of the Department of Health and Human Services was not final where facts remained to be developed).

Both letters suffer from this defect. By their terms, they state tentative conclusions based on limited information presented to the agency. For example, the June 4th letter states that it "represents our opinion based on the facts presented in [MAC Trailer's] letter, the attachments provided with [MAC Trailer's] letter and agency review of other data obtained from [Air Brake]." J.A. at 172. Later, the letter stresses that "NHTSA's view" about the MSQR-5000 is "based on a review of the promotional materials describing the device and the principles involved in its operation." J.A. at 172; *see* J.A. at 173 ("The MSQR-5000 *appears* to lack one or more features that an ABS must have to meet [Standard] 121. *Based on the literature provided to us,* the MSQR-5000 does not *seem* to have any means of automatically controlling wheel slip during braking by sensing, analyzing, and modulating the rate of angular rotation of a wheel or wheels.") (emphasis added); *id.* ("In addition, the MSQR-5000 also *appears* to lack any provision for illuminating a warning light providing notification of an ABS malfunction.") (emphasis added). The December 10th letter, too, relies on "materials received or obtained since June 4, as well as those that we had previously obtained," J.A. at 192, and disclaims any intent to adjudicate factual issues. *See* J.A. at 194 ("[I]t is not the function of an interpretive letter to adjudicate factual issues. . .."). In this respect, the second letter also expresses an opinion based on "[t]he test data and information provided by [Air Brake]," not based upon any factfinding by the agency. J.A. at 198.

By itself, the conditional nature of the Chief Counsel's advice-conditioned on the untested factual submissions of the parties-suggests that it is non-final and non-reviewable. But the regulatory context in which the issue arises makes that conclusion all the more appropriate. In the world of vehicle safety requirements, fact-specific conclusions about whether a product complies with NHTSA's regulations generally come at the end of a recall proceeding, not before the process for initiating a recall has begun. As the applicable statutes explain, the Secretary generally must follow a carefully-delineated process for reaching a conclusion of non-compliance that has the force of law. The Secretary must make an "initial decision" that a product does not comply. *See* 49 U.S.C. § 30118(a). After that, the Secretary follows a specific process for making "a final decision" about compliance. *See id.* § 30118(b)(1). Then, if appropriate, the Secretary may order non-complying manufacturers to remedy the problem through notice to the vehicle owners and a recall (or other remedy). *See id.* § 30118(b)(2). This systematic method for making a fact-based determination whether a given product satisfies the agency's safety regulations is a far cry from the informal answers provided by NHTSA's Chief Counsel to questions from Air Brake's potential customer.

Besides being conditional and tentative and besides arising outside of the customary setting for determining safety compliance, the main body of each letter contains a related flaw: "An agency action is not final if it is only 'the ruling of a subordinate official.'" *Franklin*, 505 U.S. at 797, 112 S.Ct. 2767. While NHTSA's Chief Counsel has considerable authority over purely legal interpretations of pertinent statutes and regulations, the Secretary has not delegated authority to the Chief Counsel to make final fact-bound determinations of compliance with NHTSA's safety standards * * *.

B.

A different analysis, but a similar conclusion, applies to the legal interpretation in each letter of Standard 121's warning-light requirement. While the letters in the main address fact-specific issues based upon the materials presented to the agency by the parties requesting the opinion, they also appear to contain a statement of general applicability designed to interpret the law-namely, that Standard 121 requires all antilock brake systems, even non-electronic ones, to include a warning light.

One cannot lightly dismiss this legal interpretation of Standard 121 as either tentative or as the view of a subordinate agency official. There is nothing provisional about this interpretation of the standard: Either it requires a warning light or it does not. And there is nothing hypothetical or intricately fact dependent about the inquiry: Either Air Brake's product has these features or it does not. Neither are these the views of a subordinate official, at least when it comes to this purely-legal interpretation. The Secretary of Transportation has delegated to NHTSA's Chief Counsel responsibility to "[i]ssue authoritative interpretations of the statutes administered by NHTSA and the regulations [*i.e.,* Safety Standards] issued by the agency." 49 C.F.R. § 501.8(d)(5). So unlike his general take on compliance, the Chief Counsel's views about purely legal questions—does, for example, Standard 121 require a warning light?—may constitute the final word within the agency. Bolstering the point, NHTSA's website states that the Chief Counsel's legal interpretation letters "represent the definitive view of the agency on the question addressed and may be relied upon." In view of the Secretary's delegation of authority to the Chief Counsel over legal issues and in view of NHTSA's public use of that authority through its website, an interpretive letter like this one (or at least partially like this one) may indeed represent the "consummation" of the agency's process as to purely legal questions.

To say that a legal interpretation is final because it is not subject to further review within the agency, however, is not to say that it is "final" in the sense that § 10 of the APA requires it to be. If the interpretation nonetheless (1) does not "determine rights or obligations" or (2) does not have "legal consequences," it remains non-final for purposes of review under the APA. *See Bennett*, 520 U.S. at 178, 117 S.Ct. 1154. Neither measure of finality is availing to Air Brake here. An agency's determination of "rights or obligations" generally stems from an agency action that is directly binding on the party seeking review, such as an administrative adjudication (like a recall proceeding) or legislative rulemaking, both of which did not happen here.

The harder question is whether the letters, while not directly binding on Air Brake, occasion sufficient "legal consequences" to make them reviewable. One reliable indicator that an agency interpretation still has the requisite legal consequence, we have held, is whether the agency may claim *Chevron* deference for it. *See Franklin Fed. Sav. Bank v. Dir., Office of Thrift Supervision*, 927 F.2d 1332, 1337 (6th Cir. 1991) ("When an agency has acted so definitively that its actions are defended based on *Chevron*, we believe that its action should be treated as final.").

Decisions from other courts also have looked to the eligibility for administrative deference as a sufficient legal consequence for finality purposes * * *.

* * *

Air Brake, however, cannot rely upon this principle because the Chief Counsel's legal interpretations have no claim to deference of any sort. For one reason, they are too informal. Congress does not generally expect agencies to make law through general counsel opinion letters [citing, *inter alia*, *Christensen* and *Mead*].

For another reason, the letters interpret a regulation (Standard 121), not the statute that the agency is charged with enforcing (the Safety Act). *Chevron* does not apply in this setting.

Other administrative-law doctrines do not advance Air Brake's cause either. Under *Skidmore v. Swift & Co.*, 323 U.S. 134, 65 S.Ct. 161, 89 L.Ed. 124 (1944), federal courts give respectful consideration to authoritative interpretations that lack the force of law, but that nonetheless have the "power to persuade." Unlike *Chevron* deference, however, *Skidmore* respect is not the kind of "legal consequence[ ]" that may make an interpretation final for purposes of direct review: *Skidmore* permits courts to give consideration to an agency's expertise and ability to persuade, not its ability to speak with legal effect. Put another way, *Chevron* allows the agency to make law, which is what gives the agency's views "legal consequences," while courts still determine the meaning of a law under *Skidmore*. *Skidmore* thus permits an agency to *earn* the weight given to it by the courts, while *Chevron* gives reasonable agency interpretations controlling weight as *a matter of right*. The result is that "legal consequences" do not flow from the *Skidmore* doctrine, and accordingly its application does not assist a court in determining that an agency's action is final under the APA.

The better candidate for finding the requisite "legal consequences" is still another administrative-law doctrine—*Seminole Rock* deference—the "controlling weight" that federal courts generally give an agency's interpretation of its own ambiguous regulation. *See Bowles v. Seminole Rock & Sand Co.*, 325 U.S. 410, 414, 65 S.Ct. 1215, 89 L.Ed. 1700 (1945) (an agency's interpretation of its own regulation is entitled to "controlling weight unless it is plainly erroneous or inconsistent with the regulation"). The controlling nature of *Seminole Rock* deference, moreover, would seem to have the requisite legal consequences for APA finality purposes.

Nonetheless, the doctrine does not apply here. In this case, the Department of Justice emphatically denies that the opinion letters issued by NHTSA's Chief Counsel are authoritative views entitled to *any* deference. While that position is supported by dicta from at least one case from this court, *see Fisher v. Ford Motor Co.*, 224 F.3d 570, 575 (6th Cir. 2000) ("[T]he General Counsel [of NHTSA's] opinion [interpreting Standard 208] is not legally binding on the courts."), cases from other circuits (dealing with general counsel letters from different agencies) appear to reach a different conclusion. Either way, as this case suggests, it is one thing for an agency's general counsel to have authority to issue definitive interpretations on behalf of the agency; it is another for the general counsel to invoke that authority. We accept the Government's acknowledgment that the opinion letters here are not entitled to any deference in the federal courts—whether under *Chevron* or *Seminole Rock*—and thus do not have legal consequences. Having no direct, binding effect on Air Brake and having no legal consequences for Air Brake by virtue of the deference courts might give to them, the Chief Counsel's letters are not "final" agency action under the APA.

C.

Air Brake offers several arguments in favor of reviewing the compliance and legal interpretations in the letters, all unpersuasive * * *. Air Brake urges [that] the views expressed in the letters have devastated its business, effectively foreclosing it from selling the MSQR-5000 to vehicle manufacturers regulated by NHTSA, none of which appears willing to run the risk of a government-ordered recall. While this may be so, adverse economic effects accompany many forms of indisputably non-final government action. Initiating an enforcement proceeding against a company, for example, may have a devastating effect on the company's business, but that does not make the agency's action final.

Contrary to Air Brake's assertion, moreover, this approach does not place the company in a "Catch-22" position. In Air Brake's view, no manufacturer will ever put the MSQR-5000 on its new vehicles given the risks of a recall. No recall, as a result, will ever occur, making NHTSA's views about Air Brake's product (and, worse, the Chief Counsel's views on the subject) effectively unreviewable—because only the results of a recall proceeding would be final and reviewable. Even if this were true, which it turns out it is not, this development would stem from the market's weighing of the costs (one of which is the possibility of government action) and benefits of purchasing Air Brake's product, not the government's tentative response to an inquiry posed by a potential Air Brake customer.

In all events, Air Brake errs in suggesting it has no other options. The company remains free to show the market its confidence in the product by agreeing to indemnify a prospective manufacturer against the costs of defending any potential NHTSA action. And more importantly (and perhaps more realistically for smaller companies), the company remains free to petition NHTSA to alter Standard 121 under the agency's rulemaking powers. 49 C.F.R. § 552.3(a) ("Any interested party may file with the Administrator a petition requesting him . . . [t]o commence a proceeding respecting the issuance, amendment or revocation of a motor vehicle safety standard."). The denial of such a petition, notably, *would be* a final reviewable order.

* * *

D.

Although the letters do not constitute final agency action with respect to the opinions expressed in them, they do represent final agency action in another respect—namely, as to whether the Chief Counsel has authority to issue advisory opinions in the first instance. In contrast to the contents of the letters, all of the finality factors point to the conclusion that the agency's view regarding the Chief Counsel's authority to issue them is "final" agency action under the APA.

First, there is nothing tentative or fact dependent about the authority to issue the letters. The Secretary has delegated this power to the Chief Counsel in concrete and unconditional terms, and the issue is purely a legal one. Second, as the head of the Department of Transportation, the Secretary is anything but a subordinate official for these purposes. Third, this decision would receive deference from the federal courts as an interpretation of the agency's regulations under *Seminole Rock,* and (in contrast to the letters) the agency has not disclaimed deference regarding this position * * *.

* * *

IV.

Because we have jurisdiction to review the Chief Counsel's authority to issue these letters, we must decide whether this was a permissible exercise of power. Like the district court before us, we conclude that it was * * *.

NOTES

As *Standard Oil* made clear, agency action is not "final" for purposes of judicial review simply because it has some kind of adverse effect on people. Those adverse effects must result from some *legal* consequence that stems from the agency decision. Thus, interpretative rules, guidances, and other forms of non-binding "advice" either to the public or to agency personnel are generally not final agency action. *See American Tort Reform Ass'n v. OSHA*, 738 F.3d 387, 395 (D.C.Cir.2013). But what about preliminary determinations that an agency has jurisdiction over a particular subject matter? Suppose that the Environmental Protection Agency and/or the Army Corps of Engineers, both of which share responsibility for ensuring that nothing enters the waters of the United States without a proper permit, determines that certain land that is within the vicinity of waters of the United States but that does not appear itself to contain such waters is subject to the statutory permitting requirements? The substantive law governing what does and does not constitute navigable waters of the United States subject to federal jurisdiction is evolving, complicated, and at times incomprehensible even to the Supreme Court:

> In *United States v. Riverside Bayview Homes, Inc.,* 474 U.S. 121, 106 S.Ct. 455, 88 L.Ed.2d 419 (1985), we upheld a regulation that construed "the navigable waters" to include "freshwater wetlands," themselves not actually navigable, that were adjacent to navigable-in-fact waters. Later, in *Solid Waste Agency of Northern Cook Cty. v. Army Corps of Engineers*, 531 U.S. 159, 121 S.Ct. 674, 148 L.Ed.2d 576 (2001), we held that an abandoned sand and gravel pit, which "seasonally ponded" but which was not adjacent to open water, was not part of the navigable waters. Then most recently, in *Rapanos v. United States*, 547 U.S. 715, 126 S.Ct. 2208, 165 L.Ed.2d 159 (2006), we considered whether a wetland not adjacent to navigable-in-fact waters fell within the scope of the Act. Our answer was no, but no one rationale commanded a majority of the Court.

Sackett v. EPA, 566 U.S. 120, 123–24, 132 S.Ct. 1367, 1370, 182 L.Ed.2d 367 (2012). *See also id.* at 1375 (Alito, J., concurring) ("The reach of the Clean Water Act is notoriously unclear"). If the landowner gets it wrong, the consequences are dire: "If the EPA determines that any person is in violation of this restriction, the Act directs the agency either to issue a compliance order or to initiate a civil enforcement action. When the EPA prevails in a civil action, the Act provides for 'a civil penalty not to exceed [$37,500] per day for each violation.' And according to the Government, when the EPA prevails against any person who has been issued a compliance order but has failed to comply, that amount is increased to $75,000—up to $37,500 for the statutory violation and up to an additional $37,500 for violating the compliance order." *Id.*

In *Sackett*, the EPA issued a compliance order to homeowners who filled in part of their 2/3 acre lot, which is near a navigable lake but separated from the lake by several other lots. If the Sacketts' lot constituted navigable waters within the meaning of the statute (and, as noted above, it is actually quite easy for dry land to be considered "navigable waters" under the Clean Water Act), then the Sacketts were in plain violation of the law and faced stiff penalties if they did not obey the strict, and expensive, compliance order. The Sacketts challenged the compliance order in court, only to have the district court and the Ninth Circuit dismiss their suit on the ground that the EPA compliance order was not "final" agency action. According to the lower courts—and this was the view of essentially all lower courts to consider similar matters—judicial review was not available until the EPA sought to enforce the compliance order. At that point, the landowners could bring their challenges to the EPA's authority—while facing the prospect of $75,000/day penalties for the privilege of the challenge if they lost. The Supreme Court unanimously disagreed with the lower courts and found the compliance order reviewable:

> We consider first whether the compliance order is final agency action * * *. It has all of the hallmarks of APA finality that our opinions establish * * *. By reason of the order, the Sacketts have the legal obligation to "restore" their property according to an agency-approved Restoration Work Plan, and must give the EPA access to their property and to "records and documentation related to the conditions at the Site." Also, " 'legal consequences * * * flow' " from issuance of the order. For one, according to the Government's current litigating position, the order exposes the Sacketts to double penalties in a future enforcement proceeding. It also severely limits the Sacketts' ability to obtain a permit for their fill from the Army Corps of Engineers. The Corps' regulations provide that, once the EPA has issued a compliance order with respect to certain property, the Corps will not process a permit application for that property unless doing so "is clearly appropriate."

566 U.S. at 126, 132 S.Ct. at 1371–72.

Does the following case apply *Sackett*, misapply *Sackett*, or extend it?

U.S. ARMY CORPS OF ENGINEERS V. HAWKES CO., INC.

Supreme Court of the United States, 2016.
136 S.Ct. 1807, 195 L.Ed.2d 77.

CHIEF JUSTICE ROBERTS delivered the opinion of the Court.

The Clean Water Act regulates the discharge of pollutants into "the waters of the United States." 33 U.S.C. §§ 1311(a), 1362(7), (12). Because it can be difficult to determine whether a particular parcel of property contains such waters, the U.S. Army Corps of Engineers will issue to property owners an "approved jurisdictional determination" stating the agency's definitive view on that matter. See 33 CFR § 331.2 and pt. 331, App. C (2015). The question presented is whether that determination is final agency action judicially reviewable under the Administrative Procedure Act, 5 U.S.C. § 704.

I

A

The Clean Water Act prohibits "the discharge of any pollutant" without a permit into "navigable waters," which it defines, in turn, as "the waters of the United States." 33 U.S.C. §§ 1311(a), 1362(7), (12). During the time period relevant to this case, the U.S. Army Corps of Engineers defined the waters of the United States to include land areas occasionally or regularly saturated with water—such as "mudflats, sandflats, wetlands, sloughs, prairie potholes, wet meadows, [and] playa lakes"—the "use, degradation or destruction of which could affect interstate or foreign commerce." 33 CFR § 328.3(a)(3) (2012). The Corps has applied that definition to assert jurisdiction over "270-to-300 million acres of swampy lands in the United States—including half of Alaska and an area the size of California in the lower 48 States." *Rapanos v. United States*, 547 U.S. 715, 722, 126 S.Ct. 2208, 165 L.Ed.2d 159 (2006) (plurality opinion).

It is often difficult to determine whether a particular piece of property contains waters of the United States, but there are important consequences if it does. The Clean Water Act imposes substantial criminal and civil penalties for discharging any pollutant into waters covered by the Act without a permit from the Corps. The costs of obtaining such a permit are significant. For a specialized "individual" permit of the sort at issue in this case, for example, one study found that the average applicant "spends 788 days and $271,596 in completing the process," without "counting costs of mitigation or design changes." *Rapanos*, 547 U.S., at 721, 126 S.Ct. 2208. Even more readily available "general" permits took applicants, on average, 313 days and $28,915 to complete. *Ibid.* See generally 33 CFR § 323.2(h) (limiting "general" permits to activities that "cause only minimal individual and cumulative environmental impacts").

The Corps specifies whether particular property contains "waters of the United States" by issuing "jurisdictional determinations" (JDs) on a case-by-case basis. § 331.2. JDs come in two varieties: "preliminary" and "approved." While preliminary JDs merely advise a property owner "that there *may* be waters of the United States on a parcel," approved JDs definitively "stat[e] the presence or absence" of such waters. *Ibid.* (emphasis added). Unlike preliminary JDs, approved JDs can be administratively appealed and are defined by regulation to "constitute a Corps final agency action." §§ 320.1(a)(6), 331.2. They are binding for five years on both the Corps and the Environmental Protection Agency, which share authority to enforce the Clean Water Act. See 33 U.S.C. §§ 1319, 1344(s); 33 CFR pt. 331, App. C; EPA, Memorandum of Agreement: Exemptions Under Section 404(F) of the Clean Water Act § VI–A (1989) (Memorandum of Agreement).

B

Respondents are three companies engaged in mining peat in Marshall County, Minnesota. Peat is an organic material that forms in waterlogged grounds, such as wetlands and bogs. It is widely used for soil improvement and burned as fuel. It can also be used to provide structural support and moisture for smooth, stable greens that leave golfers with no one to blame but themselves for errant putts. At the same time, peat mining can have significant environmental and ecological impacts, and therefore is regulated by both federal and state environmental protection agencies, see, e.g., Minn.Stat. § 103G.231 (2014).

Respondents own a 530-acre tract near their existing mining operations. The tract includes wetlands, which respondents believe contain sufficient high quality peat, suitable for use in golf greens, to extend their mining operations for 10 to 15 years.

In December 2010, respondents applied to the Corps for a Section 404 permit for the property. A Section 404 permit authorizes "the discharge of dredged or fill material into the navigable waters at specified disposal sites." 33 U.S.C. § 1344(a). Over the course of several communications with respondents, Corps officials signaled that the permitting process would be very expensive and take years to complete. The Corps also advised respondents that, if they wished to pursue their application, they would have to submit numerous assessments of various features of the property, which respondents estimate would cost more than $100,000.

In February 2012, in connection with the permitting process, the Corps issued an approved JD stating that the property contained "water of the United States" because its wetlands had a "significant nexus" to the Red River of the North, located some 120 miles away. Respondents appealed the JD to the Corps' Mississippi Valley Division Commander, who remanded for further factfinding. On remand, the Corps reaffirmed its original conclusion and issued a revised JD to that effect.

Respondents then sought judicial review of the revised JD under the Administrative Procedure Act (APA), 5 U.S.C. § 500 et seq. The District Court dismissed for want of subject matter jurisdiction, holding that the revised JD was not "final agency action for which there is no other adequate remedy in a court," as required by the APA prior to judicial review, 5 U.S.C. § 704. 963 F.Supp.2d 868, 872, 878 (Minn.2013). The Court of Appeals for the Eighth Circuit reversed, 782 F.3d 994, 1002 (2015), and we granted certiorari.

II

* * *

A

In *Bennett v. Spear*, 520 U.S. 154, 117 S.Ct. 1154, 137 L.Ed.2d 281 (1997), we distilled from our precedents two conditions that generally must be satisfied for agency action to be "final" under the APA. First, the action must mark the consummation of the agency's decisionmaking process—it must not be of a merely tentative or interlocutory nature. And second, the action must be one by which rights or obligations have been determined, or from which legal consequences will flow." *Id.*, at 177–178, 117 S.Ct. 1154 (internal quotation marks and citation omitted).

The Corps does not dispute that an approved JD satisfies the first Bennett condition. Unlike preliminary JDs—which are "advisory in nature" and simply indicate that "there may be waters of the United States" on a parcel of property, 33 CFR § 331.2—an approved JD clearly "mark[s] the consummation" of the Corps' decisionmaking process on that question. It is issued after extensive factfinding by the Corps regarding the physical and hydrological characteristics of the property, and is typically not revisited if the permitting process moves forward. Indeed, the Corps itself describes approved JDs as "final agency action," see 33 CFR § 320.1(a)(6), and specifies that an approved JD "will remain valid for a period of five years," Corps, Regulatory Guidance Letter No. 05–02, § 1(a), p. 1 (June 14, 2005) (2005 Guidance Letter); see also 33 CFR pt. 331, App. C.

* * *

The definitive nature of approved JDs also gives rise to "direct and appreciable legal consequences," thereby satisfying the second prong of *Bennett*. Consider the effect of an approved JD stating that a party's property does not contain jurisdictional waters—a "negative" JD, in Corps parlance. As noted, such a JD will generally bind the Corps for five years. Under a longstanding memorandum of agreement between the Corps and EPA, it will also be "binding on the Government and represent the

Government's position in any subsequent Federal action or litigation concerning that final determination." Memorandum of Agreement §§ IV–C–2, VI–A. A negative JD thus binds the two agencies authorized to bring civil enforcement proceedings under the Clean Water Act, creating a five-year safe harbor from such proceedings for a property owner. Additionally, although the property owner may still face a citizen suit under the Act, such a suit—unlike actions brought by the Government—cannot impose civil liability for wholly past violations. See §§ 1319(d), 1365(a); *Gwaltney of Smithfield, Ltd. v. Chesapeake Bay Foundation, Inc.*, 484 U.S. 49, 58–59, 108 S.Ct. 376, 98 L.Ed.2d 306 (1987). In other words, a negative JD both narrows the field of potential plaintiffs and limits the potential liability a landowner faces for discharging pollutants without a permit. Each of those effects is a "legal consequence[ ]" satisfying the second *Bennett* prong.

[handwritten: 5 years of safe harbor]

It follows that affirmative JDs have legal consequences as well: They represent the denial of the safe harbor that negative JDs afford. See 5 U.S.C. § 551(13) (defining "agency action" to include an agency "rule, order, license, sanction, relief, or the equivalent," or the "denial thereof"). Because "legal consequences . . . flow" from approved JDs, they constitute final agency action.

This conclusion tracks the "pragmatic" approach we have long taken to finality. *Abbott Laboratories v. Gardner*, 387 U.S. 136, 149, 87 S.Ct. 1507, 18 L.Ed.2d 681 (1967). For example, in *Frozen Food Express v. United States*, 351 U.S. 40, 76 S.Ct. 569, 100 L.Ed. 910 (1956), we considered the finality of an order specifying which commodities the Interstate Commerce Commission believed were exempt by statute from regulation, and which it believed were not. Although the order "had no authority except to give notice of how the Commission interpreted" the relevant statute, and "would have effect only if and when a particular action was brought against a particular carrier," *Abbott*, 387 U.S., at 150, 87 S.Ct. 1507 we held that the order was nonetheless immediately reviewable, *Frozen Food*, 351 U.S., at 44–45, 76 S.Ct. 569. The order, we explained, "warns every carrier, who does not have authority from the Commission to transport those commodities, that it does so at the risk of incurring criminal penalties." *Id.*, at 44, 76 S.Ct. 569. So too here, while no administrative or criminal proceeding can be brought for failure to conform to the approved JD itself, that final agency determination not only deprives respondents of a five-year safe harbor from liability under the Act, but warns that if they discharge pollutants onto their property without obtaining a permit from the Corps, they do so at the risk of significant criminal and civil penalties.

[handwritten: conclusion reflects "pragmatic" approach]

[handwritten: warns of risk of signif. crim + civ. penalty]

B

Even if final, an agency action is reviewable under the APA only if there are no adequate alternatives to APA review in court. 5 U.S.C. § 704. The Corps contends that respondents have two such alternatives: either discharge fill material without a permit, risking an EPA enforcement action during which they can argue that no permit was required, or apply for a permit and seek judicial review if dissatisfied with the results.

no adequate alternative

Neither alternative is adequate. As we have long held, parties need not await enforcement proceedings before challenging final agency action where such proceedings carry the risk of "serious criminal and civil penalties." *Abbott*, 387 U.S., at 153, 87 S.Ct. 1507. If respondents discharged fill material without a permit, in the mistaken belief that their property did not contain jurisdictional waters, they would expose themselves to civil penalties of up to $37,500 for each day they violated the Act, to say nothing of potential criminal liability. See 33 U.S.C. §§ 1319(c), (d); *Sackett*, 566 U.S., at ___, n. 1, 132 S.Ct., at 1370, n. 1 (citing 74 Fed.Reg. 626, 627 (2009)). Respondents need not assume such risks while waiting for EPA to "drop the hammer" in order to have their day in court. *Sackett*, 566 U.S., at ___, 132 S.Ct., at 1372.

Nor is it an adequate alternative to APA review for a landowner to apply for a permit and then seek judicial review in the event of an unfavorable decision. As Corps officials indicated in their discussions with respondents, the permitting process can be arduous, expensive, and long. On top of the standard permit application that respondents were required to submit, see 33 CFR § 325.1(d) (detailing contents of permit application), the Corps demanded that they undertake, among other things, a "hydrogeologic assessment of the rich fen system including the mineral/nutrient composition and pH of the groundwater; groundwater flow spatially and vertically; discharge and recharge areas"; a "functional/resource assessment of the site including a vegetation survey and identification of native fen plan communities across the site"; an "inventory of similar wetlands in the general area (watershed), including some analysis of their quality"; and an "inventory of rich fen plant communities that are within sites of High and Outstanding Biodiversity Significance in the area." App. 33–34. Respondents estimate that undertaking these analyses alone would cost more than $100,000. And whatever pertinence all this might have to the issuance of a permit, none of it will alter the finality of the approved JD, or affect its suitability for judicial review. The permitting process adds nothing to the JD.

The Corps nevertheless argues that Congress made the "evident [ ]" decision in the Clean Water Act that a coverage determination would be made "as part of the permitting process, and that the property owner would obtain any necessary judicial review of that determination at the conclusion of that process." Brief for Petitioner 46. But * * * given "the APA's presumption of reviewability for all final agency action," *Sackett*, 566 U.S., at ___, 132 S.Ct., at 1373, "[t]he mere fact" that permitting decisions are "reviewable should not suffice to support an implication of exclusion as to other[ ]" agency actions, such as approved JDs, *Abbott*, 387 U.S., at 141,

87 S.Ct. 1507 (internal quotation marks omitted); see also *Sackett*, 566 U.S., at ___, 132 S.Ct., at 1373 ("[I]f the express provision of judicial review in one section of a long and complicated statute were alone enough to overcome the APA's presumption of reviewability . . . , it would not be much of a presumption at all").

Finally, the Corps emphasizes that seeking review in an enforcement action or at the end of the permitting process would be the only available avenues for obtaining review "[i]f the Corps had never adopted its practice of issuing standalone jurisdictional determinations upon request." Reply Brief 3; see also *id.* at 4, 23. True enough. But such a "count your blessings" argument is not an adequate rejoinder to the assertion of a right to judicial review under the APA.

* * *

[Concurring opinions by JUSTICES KENNEDY, KAGAN, and GINSBURG are omitted.]

NOTES

Does it seem to you that *Frozen Food Express* was correctly decided? If so, does it mean that all interpretative rules are final? Does that, in turn, mean that "final" interpretative rules have the force of law for purposes of *Chevron* and *Mead?* Is *Frozen Food Express* at all necessary to support the Court's decision in *Hawkes*, given the Court's premise that the JD in *Hawkes* removed a safe harbor from litigation? And on that score, what happens if the agencies in this case, the Army Corps of Engineers and the EPA, change their minds and revoke their Memorandum of Agreement (or even just choose to ignore it)? Can federal agencies really bind themselves not to enforce the law simply by exchanging memos? *Cf. id.* at 1817 (Ginsburg, J., concurring in part and concurring in the judgment) ("I join the Court's opinion, save for its reliance upon the Memorandum of Agreement between the Army Corps of Engineers and the Environmental Protection Agency") *with id.* (Kagan, J., concurring) ("I write separately to note that for me, unlike for Justice Ginsburg, the memorandum of agreement between the Army Corps of Engineers and the Environmental Protection Agency is central to the disposition of this case.").

The cases thus far have focused on what it means for agency action to have legal consequences. But the Supreme Court in *Bennett v. Spear*, 520 U.S. 154, 117 S.Ct. 1154, 137 L.Ed.2d 281 (1997), emphasized that a final decision must also "mark the 'consummation' of the agency's decisionmaking process, *Chicago & Southern Air Lines, Inc. v. Waterman S.S. Corp.*, 333 U.S. 103, 113, 68 S.Ct. 431, 437, 92 L.Ed. 568 (1948)—it must not be of a merely tentative or interlocutory nature." 520 U.S. at 177–78, 117 S.Ct. at 1168. How does one tell when the agency process has come to an end, especially when the agency says that it hasn't?

FRIEDMAN V. FAA

United States Court of Appeals, District of Columbia Circuit, 2016.
841 F.3d 537.

Before ROGERS, BROWN, and PILLARD, CIRCUIT JUDGES.

BROWN, CIRCUIT JUDGE:

* * *

[handwritten margin note: request for commercial airline pilot's license]

Petitioner Eric Friedman ("Friedman"), a commercial airline pilot, claims Respondent Federal Aviation Administration ("the FAA" or "the Agency") has behaved in an arbitrary and capricious manner in assessing his request for a commercial airline pilot's license. Friedman has been diagnosed with Insulin Treated Diabetes Mellitus ("ITDM"), and although he holds a *third* class medical certificate authorizing him to pilot non-commercial flights in the United States, he seeks the *first* class certificate necessary to serve as a commercial airline pilot. He argues the FAA has impermissibly conditioned issuance of a first class license on ninety days of continuous blood glucose monitoring, a costly and invasive procedure not medically necessary for his care. Since we believe the Agency's unwavering position constitutes final action, we remand to the FAA to provide reasons for its denial.

I.

Congress has granted the FAA broad authority to regulate those "practices, methods, and procedure[s] the Administrator finds necessary for safety in air commerce and national security." 49 U.S.C. § 44701(a)(5). Accordingly, the FAA issues airman certificates to pilots who are "qualified for, and physically able to perform the duties related to, the position." *Id.* § 44703(a). The Agency has also established rules requiring pilots to hold both a medical certificate and a pilot certificate. *See, e.g.,* 14 C.F.R. § 61.3(a) & (c). The FAA lists a number of conditions generally disqualifying for any class of medical certification, among them a "medical history or clinical diagnosis of diabetes mellitus that requires insulin or any other hypoglycemic drug for control," otherwise known as ITDM. 14 C.F.R. §§ 67.113(a), 67.213(a), 67.313(a). While a diagnosis of ITDM generally excludes a pilot from any medical certificate issued by the FAA pursuant to 49 U.S.C. § 44703(a), the FAA has the discretionary authority to grant exceptions to the medical regulations contained in 14 C.F.R. § 67. *See* 49 U.S.C. § 44701(f). An Authorization for Special Issuance of a Medical Certificate may be provided to an applicant with a disqualifying condition "if the person shows to the satisfaction of the Federal Air Surgeon that the duties authorized by the class of medical certificate applied for can be performed without endangering public safety during the period in which the Authorization would be in force." 14 C.F.R. § 67.401(a).

[handwritten margin note: FAA has discretionary authority to grant exceptions]

Regulations require the Federal Air Surgeon ("FAS") to make his determination using standards published for each condition as set forth in the FAA's Guide to Aviation Medical Examiners ("AME Guide"). The process includes a medical examination performed by a member of the community of Aviation Medical Examiners ("AME"s), and it may require pilots to provide additional medical information to the FAA where necessary. Specifically, the FAS must "consider[ ] the need to protect the safety of persons and property in other aircraft and on the ground." *Id.* § 67.401(e).

For much of its history the FAA enforced a blanket ban on the issuance of medical certificates to individuals with ITDM, but in 1996 it reversed course and established criteria for pilots with ITDM to receive a third class medical certificate (but *not* a first class certificate). Since the policy change was adopted, there has been no medically related accident, incident, or inflight incapacitation, from any cause, of any such insulin treated special issuance pilot. In light of the strong record of third class pilots with ITDM, and in reliance on the expert analysis provided by an Expert Panel on Pilots with Insulin Treated Diabetes ("Expert Panel")—convened by the American Diabetes Association ("ADA") at the FAA's request—the FAA amended its AME Guide to broaden the third class ITDM protocol to all classes of medical certificates on April 21, 2015.

On April 27, 2015, Friedman submitted a completed application for a first class license to the FAA. A few days later, on April 30, 2015, the FAA requested supplemental information, including "any and all information that you may have that is relevant to your condition, which may include . . . (if applicable) continuous glucose monitor readings." JA 73. The next month, Friedman inquired as to the FAA's method for evaluating glucose testing results and stated "I do not use a continuous glucose monitor." JA 31–32. Continuous Glucose Monitoring ("CGM"), according to the ADA, is an invasive procedure that "uses a sensor inserted under the skin to check glucose levels in tissue fluid. A transmitter sends information about glucose levels via radio waves from the sensor to a wireless monitor." ADA Amicus Br. 14. This technique provides a "historical record of glucose levels over time" and can "provid[e] helpful information about historic trends in one's blood sugar levels and how those levels have been affected by diet and exercise." *Id.* However, CGM data is not as accurate as other blood glucose measures like fingersticks. *Id.* 15–16. Moreover, CGM is costly and is not covered by insurance unless medically necessary.

On June 17, 2015, just two days after Friedman wrote to the FAA to note the Agency had requested information beyond its own published evaluation protocol, the FAA revised its AME Guide. The newly-minted version provided "[f]irst and second class applicants will be evaluated on a case-by-case basis by the Federal Air Surgeon's Office" and omitted any protocol for evaluation. JA 469. Later, on October 6, 2015, the FAA again requested Friedman provide "any and all information that you may have that is relevant to your condition, which may include . . . [a] report for continuous glucose monitoring (CGM) conducted for a minimum of 90 days." JA 71. The letter informed Friedman his application would be denied if he did not indicate he planned to comply with the request within *sixty* days. JA 72. In response, Friedman again advised the FAA he did not possess any CGM data. This time, however, Friedman also presented letters from his physicians explaining CGM was not medically necessary in his case. The Expert Panel even submitted a letter in support of Friedman's application to explain, "CGM systems have value, [but] they are neither necessary nor appropriate for making decisions on medical certification of pilots with diabetes" and are less accurate than the blood glucose data Friedman had already submitted. JA 65–66. On November 13, 2015, the FAA wrote to Friedman yet *again* to request CGM data and *again* cautioned that failure to respond within *thirty* days with an agreement to supply CGM data would result in denial of his application.

Thereafter, on December 1, 2015, the FAA wrote Friedman to explain it was "unable to proceed with further determination of [his] potential eligibility for special issuance of a first-class airman medical certificate until [the Agency] receive[d] the [CGM] information previously requested. . . ." JA 53. On December 18, 2015, the FAS sent an additional letter informing Friedman his request for a first class certification "remains under consideration" and granting him a third class certificate— the certificate level he already held. JA 47–48. Specifically, the letter noted the FAS had reviewed the information submitted in Friedman's April 27, 2015 application and granted the third class license in response. *Ibid.* It further advised Friedman "should not undergo a new FAA medical examination until advised to do so by the Aerospace Medicine Certification Division (AMCD)." JA 48.

II.

The threshold question in this case is whether the FAA has, either actually or impliedly, issued a final order eligible for judicial review * * *.

Here, the FAA contends it did not issue a final order regarding Friedman's first class medical certificate application; it purportedly ruled solely on his independent request for a third class medical certificate and specifically indicated the first class certificate remained under review. *See* JA 47–48, 53. Accordingly, the Court initially considers whether the Agency's admitted actions nonetheless meet the two-part test of finality:

First, the action must mark the consummation of the agency's decisionmaking process—it must not be of a merely tentative or interlocutory nature. And second, the action must be one by which rights or obligations have been determined, or from which legal consequences will flow * * *.

The specific facts presented here establish a constructive denial of Friedman's application for a first class certificate.

In its October 6, 2015 letter, the FAA first expressly required CGM data from Friedman: the Agency warned it would "deny [his] request for upgrade" to a first class certificate if he did not "reply within 60 days . . . [to] advise [the FAA] of [his] plans" to provide the requested data. JA 72; *see* 14 C.F.R. § 67.413(a) & (b) (noting an applicant "must" provide requested supplemental information and authorizing the FAA to "deny the application for a medical certificate" for those who fail to comply). Friedman refused. Thereafter, on November 13, 2015—about one month after the FAA's countdown clock started—the FAA repeated its demand, and it requested a "reply within 30 days." JA 55. The Agency was clearly counting down towards a denial on December 13, 2015, and yet Friedman continued to explain that he did not possess or intend to procure the requested CGM data. Then, in its December 1, 2015 letter acknowledging communication from Friedman's attorney, the FAA ignored the ticking clock. Instead, it merely noted, "We are unable to proceed with further determination of your potential eligibility for special issuance of a first-class airman medical certificate until we receive the information previously requested in our letter of November 13, 2015. We look forward to reviewing that information when you are able to provide it." JA 53. Thereafter, in its only communication authored after the thirty-day deadline had passed, the FAA acknowledged Friedman's "request for upgrade[d] first-class special issuance medical certification remains under consideration," but it failed to offer an extension of the previously-set deadline or otherwise establish any timetable for denial of Friedman's application for failure to comply. JA 47 (December 18, 2015 letter).

Here, the FAA has issued no formal decision on Friedman's application for a first class certificate. Despite his consistent refusal to provide the requested CGM data, the Agency has placed Friedman in a holding pattern—preventing him from obtaining any explicitly final determination on his application and thwarting the Court's interest in reviewing those agency actions that, in practical effect if not formal acknowledgement, constitute "the consummation of the agency's decisionmaking process" and determine "rights or obligations." *Bennett*, 520 U.S. at 177–78, 117 S.Ct. 1154; *see also* 5 U.S.C. § 551(13) (defining agency "action" to include a "failure to act"). Indeed, this Court has repeatedly noted the applicable test is not whether there are further administrative proceedings available, but rather "whether the impact of the order is sufficiently 'final' to warrant review in the context of the particular case." *Envtl. Def. Fund, Inc. v. Ruckelshaus*, 439 F.2d 584, 591 (D.C. Cir. 1971) (assessing the Federal Insecticide, Fungicide, and Rodenticide Act's provision for judicial review "[i]n a case of actual controversy as to the validity of any order" of the Secretary of Agriculture as articulated in 7 U.S.C. § 135b(d) (1970)); *Ciba-*

Geigy Corp. v. EPA, 801 F.2d 430, 435–37 (D.C. Cir. 1986) (finding final agency action where a letter from the Environmental Protection Agency confirmed its policy with respect to new labeling changes and noting "[o]nce the agency publicly articulates an unequivocal position . . . and expects regulated entities to alter their primary conduct to conform to that position, the agency has voluntarily relinquished the benefit of postponed judicial review"); *Envtl. Def. Fund, Inc. v. Hardin*, 428 F.2d 1093, 1098–99 (D.C. Cir. 1970).

Where an agency has clearly communicated it will not reach a determination on a petitioner's submission due to petitioner's recalcitrance but simultaneously refuses to deny the petitioner's submission on those grounds, it has engaged in final agency action subject to this Court's review. In *Securitypoint Holdings, Inc. v. Transportation Security Administration*, 769 F.3d 1184 (D.C. Cir. 2014), for example, we reviewed as final agency action a letter from the Transportation Security Agency ("TSA") Chief Counsel refusing to lift a contracting requirement newly imposed on TSA airport security checkpoint contractors. SecurityPoint sought to obtain the government contract, but it objected to and refused to sign TSA's new Memorandum of Understanding ("MOU") promising to indemnify TSA for intellectual property claims. *Id.* at 1186. The company wrote to the TSA's Chief Counsel to urge the agency to abandon the MOU, and TSA denied the request by letter. The Court later held that letter represented the consummation of the agency's "decisionmaking process regarding SecurityPoint's contention that it should abandon the challenged alterations of the MOU language." *Id.* at 1187. Here, Friedman refuses to comply with the agency requirement he seeks to challenge, and the Agency has made clear it will not act on his application until he submits. Friedman, for his part, repeatedly asserts that he provided all that is required under the April 2015 AME Guide, and no FAA "regulation or policy require[s] the use of [CGM] for either initial certification or inflight monitoring." JA 41–43. Accordingly, as with the TSA Chief Counsel's letter in *SecurityPoint*, the FAA's communications here represent the agency's rejection of Friedman's argument, its final decision to require CGM data, and its confirmation that it is not now opening the third-class applicants' case-by-case exemption process to first-class applicants.

The government, apparently ignoring the power of the Court to ensure justice in an area of law governed by a "pragmatic and flexible" approach, *Rhea Lana*, 824 F.3d at 1027, is content to distinguish the cases cited by Friedman on their specific facts. *Air One Helicopters, Inc. v. FAA*, 86 F.3d 880 (9th Cir. 1996), the Agency contends, applies only to a scenario where an agency and a private party find themselves at an impasse that neither is empowered to clear. Similarly, the FAA reads *Air Line Pilots Ass'n, International v. Civil Aeronautics Board*, 750 F.2d 81 (D.C. Cir. 1984), to apply only to situations where the private party has done everything in his power to comply with an agency's request but the agency, nonetheless, excessively delays determination of his claims. Finally, the FAA asserts the doctrine of *Environmental Defense Fund, Inc. v. Hardin*, 428 F.2d 1093, 1099 (D.C. Cir. 1970), reviewing "administrative inaction [that] has precisely the same impact on the rights of the parties as denial of relief," does not apply since Friedman is free to trigger a new six-month license validity period at his option. The Agency has missed the forest for the trees. Nothing in our case law suggests the law of final agency action is confined to the specific facts of prior circuit cases.

To the contrary, the doctrine asks whether a particular agency action represents the "consummation of [its] decisionmaking process" and determines "rights or obligations." *Bennett*, 520 U.S. at 177–78, 117 S.Ct. 1154. The standard is met here. As described above, the FAA has set deadlines, counted down towards them, and then allowed them to pass without discussion; its actions suggest the FAA has made up its mind, yet it seeks to avoid judicial review by holding out a vague prospect of reconsideration. And, as a result of the FAA's conduct, Friedman has been unable to resume his job as a commercial airline pilot at American Airlines, a job that requires a first class medical certificate. *See Safe Extensions, Inc. v. FAA*, 509 F.3d 593, 598 (D.C. Cir. 2007) (finding adequate legal consequences where an agency's new test for runway lighting "effectively prohibits airports from buying light bases that fail the new . . . test, and . . . bars manufacturers like Safe Extensions from selling their products to airports").

* * *

The FAA has placed Friedman in administrative limbo—he has neither a first class medical certificate nor an official order denying him the certificate—and the only way out requires capitulation to the very requirement he seeks to challenge. The Agency cannot manipulate its own processes, threatening denial but then refusing to deny or otherwise take definitive action on Friedman's application, in an effort to thwart judicial review.

[On the merits, the court remanded the case to the agency so that the agency could either grant the license or explain the reasons for denial. The agency denied the license, and the denial was upheld. *See Friedman v. FAA*, 890 F.3d 1092 (D.C.Cir.2018).]

3. RIPENESS

The concepts of ripeness and finality are often run together.[31] In many contexts, ripeness is merely an aspect of finality, but in other contexts it

---

[31] Examples abound, including many from the federal bench's most capable administrative lawyers. *See, e.g.*, State of California v. Department of Justice, 114 F.3d 1222, 1225 (D.C.Cir.1997) ("[W]e affirm the district court's dismissal of the appellants' APA claim as unripe. Under the APA,

has independent significance. The best way to understand modern ripeness doctrine is, as is often the case, to examine the doctrine that it has in large measure superseded.

Prior to 1967, agency rules could, in many circumstances, be challenged only if and when those rules were enforced against a party in an adjudication. An attempt to seek judicial review of a rule prior to any enforcement action would often (though not invariably) be dismissed by courts as "unripe." Rather than rule on an abstract challenge to an agency's authority, such courts thought it best to postpone review until an enforcement proceeding (generally involving a formal adjudication) gave a more concrete sense of the agency's position and a more effective record for judicial review. There was, however, little in the case law that specified precisely when pre-enforcement review of rules was appropriate.

In 1967, the Court decided three cases that continue to define the modern ripeness doctrine.

a.   The Revolution (?)

ABBOTT LABORATORIES V. GARDNER

Supreme Court of the United States, 1967.
387 U.S. 136, 87 S.Ct. 1507, 18 L.Ed.2d 681.

MR. JUSTICE HARLAN delivered the opinion of the Court.

In 1962 Congress amended the Federal Food, Drug, and Cosmetic Act 21 U.S.C. § 301 et seq.), to require manufacturers of prescription drugs to print the "established name" of the drug "prominently and in type at least half as large as that used thereon for any proprietary name or designation for such drug," on labels and other printed material, 21 U.S.C. § 352(e)(1)(B). The "established name" is one designated by the Secretary of Health, Education, and Welfare * * * ; the "proprietary name" is usually a trade name under which a particular drug is marketed. The underlying purpose of the 1962 amendment was to bring to the attention of doctors and patients the fact that many of the drugs sold under familiar trade names are actually identical to drugs sold under their "established" or less familiar trade names at significantly lower prices. The Commissioner of Food and Drugs, exercising authority delegated to him by the Secretary, published proposed regulations designed to implement the statute. After inviting and considering comments submitted by interested parties the Commissioner promulgated the following regulation for the "efficient enforcement" of the Act:

---

we review only 'final agency action.' An agency action is final only if it 'imposes an obligation, denies a right, or fixes some legal relationship.' The DOJ had done nothing of that sort as of the time of the district court's decision.").

"If the label or labeling of a prescription drug bears a proprietary name or designation for the drug or any ingredient thereof, the established name, if such there be, corresponding to such proprietary name or designation, shall accompany each appearance of such proprietary name or designation." 21 CFR § 1.104(g)(1).

A similar rule was made applicable to advertisements for prescription drugs.

The present action was brought by a group of 37 individual drug manufacturers and by the Pharmaceutical Manufacturers Association, of which all the petitioner companies are members, and which includes manufacturers of more than 90% of the Nation's supply of prescription drugs. They challenged the regulations on the ground that the Commissioner exceeded his authority under the statute by promulgating an order requiring labels, advertisements, and other printed matter relating to prescription drugs to designate the established name of the particular drug involved every time its trade name is used anywhere in such material.

The District Court * * * granted the declaratory and injunctive relief sought * * *. The Court of Appeals for the Third Circuit reversed without reaching the merits of the case. It held * * * that under the statutory scheme provided by the Federal Food, Drug, and Cosmetic Act pre-enforcement[1] review of these regulations was unauthorized and therefore beyond the jurisdiction of the District Court * * *.

I.

The first question we consider is whether Congress by the Federal Food, Drug, and Cosmetic Act intended to forbid pre-enforcement review of this sort of regulation promulgated by the Commissioner. The question is phrased in terms of "prohibition" rather than "authorization" because a survey of our cases shows that judicial review of a final agency action by an aggrieved person will not be cut off unless there is persuasive reason to believe that such was the purpose of Congress. Early cases in which this type of judicial review was entertained have been reinforced by the enactment of the Administrative Procedure Act, which embodies the basic presumption of judicial review * * *. [O]nly upon a showing of "clear and convincing evidence" of a contrary legislative intent should the courts restrict access to judicial review.

Given this standard, we are wholly unpersuaded that the statutory scheme in the food and drug area excludes this type of action * * *.

---

[1] That is, a suit brought by one before any attempted enforcement of the statute or regulation against him.

* * *

II.

A further inquiry must, however, be made. The injunctive and declaratory judgment remedies are discretionary, and courts traditionally have been reluctant to apply them to administrative determinations unless these arise in the context of a controversy "ripe" for judicial resolution. Without undertaking to survey the intricacies of the ripeness doctrine it is fair to say that its basic rationale is to prevent the courts, through avoidance of premature adjudication, from entangling themselves in abstract disagreements over administrative policies, and also to protect the agencies from judicial interference until an administrative decision has been formalized and its effects felt in a concrete way by the challenging parties. The problem is best seen in a twofold aspect, requiring us to evaluate both the fitness of the issues for judicial decision and the hardship to the parties of withholding court consideration.

As to the former factor, we believe the issues presented are appropriate for judicial resolution at this time. First, all parties agree that the issue tendered is a purely legal one: whether the statute was properly construed by the Commissioner to require the established name of the drug to be used *every time* the proprietary name is employed. Both sides moved for summary judgment in the District Court, and no claim is made here that further administrative proceedings are contemplated. It is suggested that the justification for this rule might vary with different circumstances, and that the expertise of the Commissioner is relevant to passing upon the validity of the regulation. This of course is true, but the suggestion overlooks the fact that both sides have approached this case as one purely of congressional intent, and that the Government made no effort to justify the regulation in factual terms.

Second, the regulations in issue we find to be "final agency action" within the meaning of § 10 of the Administrative Procedure Act, 5 U.S.C. § 704, as construed in judicial decisions * * *.

* * *

* * * The regulation challenged here, promulgated in a formal manner after announcement in the Federal Register and consideration of comments by interested parties is quite clearly definitive. There is no hint that this regulation is informal or only the ruling of a subordinate official or tentative. It was made effective upon publication, and the Assistant General Counsel for Food and Drugs stated in the District Court that compliance was expected.

* * *

This is also a case in which the impact of the regulations upon the petitioners is sufficiently direct and immediate as to render the issue appropriate for judicial review at this stage. These regulations purport to give an authoritative interpretation of a statutory provision that has a direct effect on the day-to-day business of all prescription drug companies; its promulgation puts petitioners in a dilemma that it was the very purpose of the Declaratory Judgment Act to ameliorate. As the District Court found on the basis of uncontested allegations, "Either they must comply with the every time requirement and incur the costs of changing over their promotional material and labeling or they must follow their present course and risk prosecution." The regulations are clear-cut, and were made effective immediately upon publication; as noted earlier the agency's counsel represented to the District Court that immediate compliance with their terms was expected. If petitioners wish to comply they must change all their labels, advertisements, and promotional materials; they must destroy stocks of printed matter; and they must invest heavily in new printing type and new supplies. The alternative to compliance—continued use of material which they believe in good faith meets the statutory requirements, but which clearly does not meet the regulation of the Commissioner—may be even more costly. That course would risk serious criminal and civil penalties for the unlawful distribution of "misbranded" drugs.

It is relevant at this juncture to recognize that petitioners deal in a sensitive industry, in which public confidence in their drug products is especially important. To require them to challenge these regulations only as a defense to an action brought by the Government might harm them severely and unnecessarily. Where the legal issue presented is fit for judicial resolution, and where a regulation requires an immediate and significant change in the plaintiffs' conduct of their affairs with serious penalties attached to noncompliance, access to the courts under the Administrative Procedure Act and the Declaratory Judgment Act must be permitted, absent a statutory bar or some other unusual circumstance, neither of which appears here.

* * *

* * * [T]he Government urges that to permit resort to the courts in this type of case may delay or impede effective enforcement of the Act. We fully recognize the important public interest served by assuring prompt and unimpeded administration of the Pure Food, Drug, and Cosmetic Act, but we do not find the Government's argument convincing. First, in this particular case, a pre-enforcement challenge by nearly all prescription drug manufacturers is calculated to speed enforcement. If the Government prevails, a large part of the industry is bound by the decree; if the Government loses, it can more quickly revise its regulation.

The Government contends, however, that if the Court allows this consolidated suit, then nothing will prevent a multiplicity of suits in various jurisdictions challenging other regulations. The short answer to this contention is that the courts are well equipped to deal with such eventualities. The venue transfer provision, 28 U.S.C. § 1404(a), may be invoked by the Government to consolidate separate actions. Or, actions in all but one jurisdiction might be stayed pending the conclusion of one proceeding. A court may even in its discretion dismiss a declaratory judgment or injunctive suit if the same issue is pending in litigation elsewhere * * *.

Further, the declaratory judgment and injunctive remedies are equitable in nature, and other equitable defenses may be interposed. If a multiplicity of suits are undertaken in order to harass the Government or to delay enforcement, relief can be denied on this ground alone. And courts may even refuse declaratory relief for the nonjoinder of interested parties who are not, technically speaking, indispensable.

In addition to all these safeguards against what the Government fears, it is important to note that the institution of this type of action does not by itself stay the effectiveness of the challenged regulation. There is nothing in the record to indicate that petitioners have sought to stay enforcement of the "every time" regulation pending judicial review. See 5 U.S.C. § 705. If the agency believes that a suit of this type will significantly impede enforcement or will harm the public interest, it need not postpone enforcement of the regulation and may oppose any motion for a judicial stay on the part of those challenging the regulation. It is scarcely to be doubted that a court would refuse to postpone the effective date of an agency action if the Government could show, as it made no effort to do here, that delay would be detrimental to the public health or safety.

* * *

Reversed and remanded.

MR. JUSTICE BRENNAN took no part in the consideration or decision of this case.

TOILET GOODS ASS'N V. GARDNER

Supreme Court of the United States, 1967.
387 U.S. 158, 87 S.Ct. 1520, 18 L.Ed.2d 697.

MR. JUSTICE HARLAN delivered the opinion of the Court.

Petitioners in this case are the Toilet Goods Association, an organization of cosmetics manufacturers accounting for some 90% of annual American sales in this field, and 39 individual cosmetics manufacturers and distributors. They brought this action in the United States District Court for the Southern District of New York seeking declaratory and injunctive relief against the Secretary of Health, Education, and Welfare and the Commissioner of Food and Drugs, on the ground that certain regulations promulgated by the Commissioner exceeded his statutory authority under the Color Additive Amendments to the Federal Food, Drug and Cosmetic Act, 74 Stat. 397, 21 U.S.C. §§ 321–376. The District Court held that the Act did not prohibit this type of pre-enforcement suit, that a case and controversy existed, that the issues presented were justiciable, and that no reasons had been presented by the Government to warrant declining jurisdiction on discretionary grounds * * *. The Court of Appeals affirmed the judgment of the District Court that jurisdiction to hear the suit existed as to three of the challenged regulations, but sustained the Government's contention that judicial review was improper as to a fourth.

* * *

In our decisions reversing the judgment in *Abbott Laboratories*, 387 U.S. 136, 87 S.Ct. 1507, 18 L.Ed.2d 681, and affirming the judgment in *Gardner v. Toilet Goods Ass'n*, 387 U.S. 167, 87 S.Ct. 1526, 18 L.Ed.2d 704, both decided today, we hold that nothing in the Food, Drug, and Cosmetic Act, 52 Stat. 1040, as amended, bars a pre-enforcement suit under the Administrative Procedure Act and the Declaratory Judgment Act. We nevertheless agree with the Court of Appeals that judicial review of this particular regulation in this particular context is inappropriate at this stage because, applying the standards set forth in *Abbott Laboratories v. Gardner*, the controversy is not presently ripe for adjudication.

The regulation in issue here was promulgated under the Color Additive Amendments of 1960, a statute that revised and somewhat broadened the authority of the Commissioner to control the ingredients added to foods, drugs, and cosmetics that impart color to them. The Commissioner of Food and Drugs, exercising power delegated by the Secretary * * *, issued the following regulation * * *:

"(a) When it appears to the Commissioner that a person has:

. . .

"(4) Refused to permit duly authorized employees of the Food and Drug Administration free access to all manufacturing facilities, processes, and formulae involved in the manufacture of color additives and intermediates from which such color additives are derived;

"he may immediately suspend certification service to such person and may continue such suspension until adequate corrective action has been taken."

The petitioners maintain that this regulation is an impermissible exercise of authority, that the FDA has long sought congressional authorization for free access to facilities, processes, and formulae, but that Congress has always denied the agency this power except for prescription drugs. 21 U.S.C. § 374. Framed in this way, we agree with petitioners that a "legal" issue is raised, but nevertheless we are not persuaded that the present suit is properly maintainable.

In determining whether a challenge to an administrative regulation is ripe for review a twofold inquiry must be made: first to determine whether the issues tendered are appropriate for judicial resolution, and second to assess the hardship to the parties if judicial relief is denied at that stage.

As to the first of these factors, we agree with the Court of Appeals that the legal issue as presently framed is not appropriate for judicial resolution. This is not because the regulation is not the agency's considered and formalized determination, for we are in agreement with petitioners that * * * this regulation—promulgated in a formal manner after notice and evaluation of submitted comments—is a "final agency action" under § 10 of the Administrative Procedure Act, 5 U.S.C. § 704. Also, we recognize the force of petitioners' contention that the issue as they have framed it presents a purely legal question: whether the regulation is totally beyond the agency's power under the statute, the type of legal issue that courts have occasionally dealt with without requiring a specific attempt at enforcement or exhaustion of administrative remedies.

These points which support the appropriateness of judicial resolution are, however, outweighed by other considerations. The regulation serves notice only that the Commissioner *may* under certain circumstances order inspection of certain facilities and data, and that further certification of additives *may* be refused to those who decline to permit a duly authorized inspection until they have complied in that regard. At this juncture we have no idea whether or when such an inspection will be ordered and what reasons the Commissioner will give to justify his order. The statutory authority asserted for the regulation is the power to promulgate regulations "for the efficient enforcement" of the Act. Whether the regulation is justified thus depends not only, as petitioners appear to suggest, on whether Congress refused to include a specific section of the Act authorizing such inspections, although this factor is to be sure a highly relevant one, but also on whether the statutory scheme as a whole justified promulgation of the regulation. This will depend not merely on an inquiry into statutory purpose, but concurrently on an understanding of what types of enforcement problems are encountered by the FDA, the need for various sorts of supervision in order to effectuate the goals of the Act, and the safeguards devised to protect legitimate trade secrets. We believe that judicial appraisal of these factors is likely to stand on a much surer footing in the context of a specific application of this regulation than could be the case in the framework of the generalized challenge made here.

We are also led to this result by considerations of the effect on the petitioners of the regulation, for the test of ripeness, as we have noted, depends not only on how adequately a court can deal with the legal issue presented, but also on the degree and nature of the regulation's present effect on those seeking relief * * *.

This is not a situation in which primary conduct is affected—when contracts must be negotiated, ingredients tested or substituted, or special records compiled. This regulation merely states that the Commissioner may authorize inspectors to examine certain processes or formulae * * *. Moreover, no irremediable adverse consequences flow from requiring a later challenge to this regulation by a manufacturer who refuses to allow this type of inspection. Unlike the other regulations challenged in this action, in which seizure of goods, heavy fines, adverse publicity for distributing "adulterated" goods, and possible criminal liability might penalize failure to comply, see *Gardner v. Toilet Goods Ass'n*, 387 U.S. 167, 87 S.Ct. 1526, 18 L.Ed.2d 704, a refusal to admit an inspector here would at most lead only to a suspension of certification services to the particular party, a determination that can then be promptly challenged through an administrative procedure,[2] which in turn is reviewable by a court. Such review will provide an adequate forum for testing the regulation in a concrete situation.

* * *

For these reasons the judgment of the Court of Appeals is affirmed.

Affirmed.

MR. JUSTICE DOUGLAS dissents * * *.

MR. JUSTICE BRENNAN took no part in the consideration or decision of this case.

[In a third case decided the same day as *Abbott Laboratories* and *Toilet Goods*, *Gardner v. Toilet Goods Ass'n*, 387 U.S. 167, 87 S.Ct. 1526, 18 L.Ed.2d 704 (1967), the Court held that the regulations at issue were ripe for review under the authority of *Abbott Laboratories*. Justice Fortas issued a partial dissenting opinion in this case that applied as well to the decision in *Abbott Laboratories*].

---

[2] We recognize that a denial of certification might under certain circumstances cause inconvenience and possibly hardship, depending upon such factors as how large a supply of certified additives the particular manufacturer may have, how rapidly the administrative hearing and judicial review are conducted, and what temporary remedial or protective provisions, such as compliance with a reservation pending litigation, might be available to a manufacturer testing the regulation. In the context of the present case we need only say that such inconvenience is speculative and we have been provided with no information that would support an assumption that much weight should be attached to this possibility.

MR. JUSTICE FORTAS, with whom the CHIEF JUSTICE and MR. JUSTICE CLARK join, concurring in [*Toilet Goods*], and dissenting in [*Abbott Laboratories* and *Gardner*].

I am in agreement with the Court in *Toilet Goods Assn. v. Gardner* * * *.

I am, however, compelled to dissent from the decisions of the Court in *Abbott Laboratories v. Gardner* and *Gardner v. Toilet Goods Assn.* * * *.

* * *

With all respect, I submit that established principles of jurisprudence, solidly rooted in the constitutional structure of our Government, require that the courts should not intervene in the administrative process at this stage, under these facts and in this gross, shotgun fashion * * *. In none of these cases is judicial interference warranted at this stage, in this fashion, and to test—on a gross, free-wheeling basis—whether the content of these regulations is within the statutory intendment. The contrary is dictated by a proper regard for the purpose of the regulatory statute and the requirements of effective administration; and by regard for the salutary rule that courts should pass upon concrete, specific questions in a particularized setting rather than upon a general controversy divorced from particular facts.

The Court, by today's decisions * * *, has opened Pandora's box. Federal injunctions will now threaten programs of vast importance to the public welfare. The Court's holding here strikes at programs for the public health. The dangerous precedent goes even further. It is cold comfort—it is little more than delusion—to read in the Court's opinion that "It is scarcely to be doubted that a court would refuse to postpone the effective date of an agency action if the Government could show * * * that delay would be detrimental to the public health or safety." Experience dictates, on the contrary, that it can hardly be hoped that some federal judge somewhere will not be moved as the Court is here, by the cries of anguish and distress of those regulated, to grant a disruptive injunction.

* * *

I.

Since enactment of the Federal Food, Drug, and Cosmetic Act in 1938, the mechanism for judicial review of agency actions under its provisions has been well understood. Except for specific types of agency regulations and actions * * * [not relevant here], judicial review has been confined to enforcement actions instituted by the Attorney General on recommendation of the agency * * *.

* * *

The present regulations concededly would be reviewable in the course of any of the * * * [statutorily prescribed enforcement] proceedings * * *.

* * *

In effect, the Court says that the Food, Drug, and Cosmetic Act has always authorized threshold injunctions or declaratory judgement relief: that this relief has been available since the enactment of the law in 1938, and that it would have been granted in appropriate cases which are "ripe" for review. I must with respect characterize this as a surprising revelation. Despite the highly controversial nature of many provisions of such regulations under the Act, this possibility has not been realized by ingenious and aggressive counsel for the drug and food and cosmetics industries until this time * * *. The fact of the matter is that, except for * * * [certain regulations not at issue here], the avenue for attack upon the statute and regulations has been by defense to specific enforcement actions by the agency. Congress has been well aware of this for more than a generation that the statute has been in effect.

* * *

II.

* * *

* * * [T]he dilemma [facing the petitioners in *Abbott Laboratories*] is no more than citizens face in connection with countless statutes and with the rules of the SEC, FTC, FCC, ICC, and other regulatory agencies. This has not heretofore been regarded as a basis for injunctive relief unless Congress has so provided * * *. I submit that a much stronger showing is necessary than the expense and trouble of compliance and the risk of defiance. Actually, if the Court refused to permit this shotgun assault, experience and reasonably sophisticated common sense show that there would be orderly compliance without the disaster so dramatically predicted by the industry, reasonable adjustments by the agency in real hardship cases, and where extreme intransigence involving substantial violations occurred, enforcement actions in which legality of the regulation would be tested in specific, concrete situations. I respectfully submit that this would be the correct and appropriate result * * *. The courts cannot properly— and should not—attempt to judge in the abstract and generally whether this regulation is within the statutory scheme. Judgment as to the "every time" regulation should be made only in light of specific situations, and it may differ depending upon whether the FDA seeks to enforce it as to doctors' circulars, pamphlets for patients, labels, etc.

* * * Those challenging the regulations have a remedy and there are no special reasons to relieve them of the necessity of deferring their challenge to the regulations until enforcement is undertaken. In this way, and only in this way, will the administrative process have an opportunity

to function—to iron out differences, to accommodate special problems, to grant exemptions, etc. The courts do not and should not pass on these complex problems in the abstract and the general—because these regulations peculiarly depend for their quality and substance upon the facts of particular situations. We should confine ourselves—as our jurisprudence dictates—to actual, specific, particularized cases and controversies, in substance as well as in technical analysis * * *.

b.   The Aftermath

Abbott Laboratories' two-part ripeness test continues to govern today, and the balance that it strikes has made pre-enforcement review of agency rules the norm rather than the exception. Three Supreme Court Justices have expressly endorsed a presumption in favor of construing statutes to provide for pre-enforcement review. *See Shalala v. Illinois Council on Long Term Care, Inc.*, 529 U.S. 1, 43–52, 120 S.Ct. 1084, 1110–14, 146 L.Ed.2d 1 (2000) (Thomas, J., dissenting). This philosophy has also reached Congress, which routinely in modern special review statutes not only *permits* but affirmatively *requires* pre-enforcement review of rules. *See infra* pages 1189–1191.

Application of the ripeness doctrine often turns on fact-bound determinations concerning the effects on parties of postponing review and the likelihood that further agency proceedings will shed light on the issues before the court. It is therefore hard to make useful generalizations about ripeness. Normally, however,

> a claim that raises purely legal questions is presumptively fit for judicial review so long as "the challenged policy is . . . sufficiently fleshed out to allow the court to see the concrete effects and implications of its decision." *Chamber of Commerce v. Reich*, 57 F.3d 1099, 1100 (D.C.Cir.1995) (internal quotation marks omitted). Thus, "a controversy is ripe if further administrative process will not aid in the development of facts needed by the court to decide the question it is asked to consider." *New York State Ophthalmological Soc'y v. Bowen*, 854 F.2d 1379, 1386 (D.C.Cir.1988).

Time Warner Entertainment Co. v. FCC, 93 F.3d 957, 974 (D.C.Cir.1996). Occasionally, as in *Toilet Goods*, a court will conclude that further agency proceedings are necessary to clear up ambiguities concerning the agency's rules or actions. *See Aulenback, Inc. v. FHA*, 103 F.3d 156, 166–67 (D.C.Cir.1997) (postponing review of an agency policy allegedly contained in a manual until the agency interpreted the manual's disputed provisions in a concrete context).

If this all seems a bit fuzzy, does the following case make you feel better or worse?

OHIO FORESTRY ASS'N, INC. v. SIERRA CLUB

Supreme Court of the United States, 1998.
523 U.S. 726, 118 S.Ct. 1665, 140 L.Ed.2d 921.

Forest Service plan permits too much logging/clearcutting

JUSTICE BREYER delivered the opinion of the Court.

The Sierra Club challenges the lawfulness of a federal land and resource management plan adopted by the United States Forest Service for Ohio's Wayne National Forest on the ground that the plan permits too much logging and too much clearcutting. We conclude that the controversy is not yet ripe for judicial review.

ct: controv. is not yet ripe

I

The National Forest Management Act of 1976 (NFMA) requires the Secretary of Agriculture to "develop, maintain, and, as appropriate, revise land and resource management plans for units of the National Forest System." 90 Stat. 2949, as renumbered and amended, 16 U.S.C. § 1604(a) * * *.

This case focuses upon a plan that the Forest Service has developed for the Wayne National Forest located in southern Ohio. When the Service wrote the plan, the forest consisted of 178,000 federally owned acres (278 sq. mi.) in three forest units that are interspersed among privately owned lands, some of which the Forest Service plans to acquire over time. The Plan permits logging to take place on 126,000 (197 sq. mi.) of the federally owned acres * * *.

Although the Plan sets logging goals, selects the areas of the forest that are suited to timber production, and determines which "probable methods of timber harvest," are appropriate, § 1604(f)(2), it does not itself authorize the cutting of any trees. Before the Forest Service can permit the logging, it must: (a) propose a specific area in which logging will take place and the harvesting methods to be used, (b) ensure that the project is consistent with the Plan, (c) provide those affected by proposed logging notice and an opportunity to be heard, (d) conduct an environmental analysis pursuant to the National Environmental Policy Act of 1969 (NEPA), to evaluate the effects of the specific project and to contemplate alternatives, and (e) subsequently take a final decision to permit logging, which decision affected persons may challenge in an administrative appeals process and in court * * *. Despite the considerable legal distance between the adoption of the Plan and the moment when a tree is cut, the Plan's promulgation nonetheless makes logging more likely in that it is a logging precondition; in its absence logging could not take place.

Plan does not itself authorize cutting of any trees

When the Forest Service first proposed its Plan, the Sierra Club and the Citizens Council on Conservation and Environmental Control each objected. In an effort to bring about the Plan's modification, they (collectively Sierra Club), pursued various administrative remedies. The Sierra Club then brought this lawsuit in federal court * * *.

* * *

DC granted SJ for FS

The District Court reviewed the Plan, decided that the Forest Service had acted lawfully in making the various determinations that the Sierra Club had challenged, and granted summary judgment for the Forest Service. The Sierra Club appealed. The Court of Appeals for the Sixth Circuit held that the dispute was justiciable * * * [and] disagreed with the District Court about the merits * * *. We granted certiorari to determine whether the dispute about the Plan presents a controversy that is justiciable now, and if so, whether the Plan conforms to the statutory and regulatory requirements for a forest plan.

CoA found dispute was justiciable + disagreed w/DC on merits

ISSUE

II

* * *

As this Court has previously pointed out, the ripeness requirement is designed

> "to prevent the courts, through avoidance of premature adjudication, from entangling themselves in abstract disagreements over administrative policies, and also to protect the agencies from judicial interference until an administrative decision has been formalized and its effects felt in a concrete way by the challenging parties." *Abbott Laboratories v. Gardner*, 387 U.S. 136, 148–149, 87 S.Ct. 1507, 1515, 18 L.Ed.2d 681 (1967).

Ripeness:
① fitness for judicial review
② hardship → parties of withholding court consid.

In deciding whether an agency's decision is, or is not, ripe for judicial review, the Court has examined both the "fitness of the issues for judicial decision" and the "hardship" to the parties of withholding court consideration." *Id.*, at 149, 87 S.Ct., at 1515. To do so in this case, we must consider: (1) whether delayed review would cause hardship to the plaintiffs; (2) whether judicial intervention would inappropriately interfere with further administrative action; and (3) whether the courts would benefit from further factual development of the issues presented. These considerations, taken together, foreclose review in the present case.

First, to "withhol[d] court consideration" at present will not cause the parties significant "hardship" as this Court has come to use that term. For one thing, the provisions of the Plan that the Sierra Club challenges do not create adverse effects of a strictly legal kind, that is, effects of a sort that traditionally would have qualified as harm. To paraphrase this Court's language in *United States v. Los Angeles & Salt Lake R. Co.*, 273 U.S. 299, 309–310, 47 S.Ct. 413, 414–415, 71 L.Ed. 651 (1927) (opinion of Brandeis, J.), they do not command anyone to do anything or to refrain from doing anything; they do not grant, withhold, or modify any formal legal license, power, or authority; they do not subject anyone to any civil or criminal liability; they create no legal rights or obligations. Thus, for example, the Plan does not give anyone a legal right to cut trees, nor does it abolish anyone's legal authority to object to trees being cut.

here, Plan creates no legal rights/ obligations

Nor have we found that the Plan now inflicts significant practical harm upon the interests that the Sierra Club advances—an important consideration in light of this Court's modern ripeness cases. As we have pointed out, before the Forest Service can permit logging, it must focus upon a particular site, propose a specific harvesting method, prepare an environmental review, permit the public an opportunity to be heard, and (if challenged) justify the proposal in court. The Sierra Club thus will have ample opportunity later to bring its legal challenge at a time when harm is more imminent and more certain. Any such later challenge might also include a challenge to the lawfulness of the present Plan if (but only if) the present Plan then matters, *i.e.*, if the Plan plays a causal role with respect to the future, then-imminent, harm from logging. Hence we do not find a strong reason why the Sierra Club must bring its challenge now in order to get relief.

no significant practical harm

Nor has the Sierra Club pointed to any other way in which the Plan could now force it to modify its behavior in order to avoid future adverse consequences, as, for example, agency regulations can sometimes force immediate compliance through fear of future sanctions. Cf. *Abbott Laboratories*, *supra*, at 152–153, 87 S.Ct., at 1517–1518 (finding challenge ripe where plaintiffs must comply with Federal Drug Administration labeling rule at once and incur substantial economic costs or risk later serious criminal and civil penalties for unlawful drug distribution); *Columbia Broadcasting System, Inc. v. United States*, 316 U.S. 407, 417–419, 62 S.Ct. 1194, 1200–1201, 86 L.Ed. 1563 (1942) (finding challenge ripe where plaintiffs must comply with burdensome Federal Communications Commission rule at once or risk later loss of license and consequent serious harm).

The Sierra Club does say that it will be easier, and certainly cheaper, to mount one legal challenge against the Plan now, than to pursue many challenges to each site-specific logging decision to which the Plan might eventually lead. It does not explain, however, why one initial site-specific victory (if based on the Plan's unlawfulness) could not, through preclusion principles, effectively carry the day. And, in any event, the Court has not considered this kind of litigation cost-saving sufficient by itself to justify review in a case that would otherwise be unripe * * *.

litigation cost-saving ≠ suffic. by itself

Second, from the agency's perspective, immediate judicial review directed at the lawfulness of logging and clearcutting could hinder agency efforts to refine its policies: (a) through revision of the Plan, *e.g.*, in response to an appropriate proposed site-specific action that is inconsistent with the Plan, or (b) through application of the Plan in practice, *e.g.*, in the

could hinder agency action

form of site-specific proposals, which proposals are subject to review by a court applying purely legal criteria. And, here, the possibility that further consideration will actually occur before the Plan is implemented is not theoretical, but real. Hearing the Sierra Club's challenge now could thus interfere with the system that Congress specified for the agency to reach forest logging decisions.

time-consuming judicial consideration

Third, from the courts' perspective, review of the Sierra Club's claims regarding logging and clearcutting now would require time-consuming judicial consideration of the details of an elaborate, technically based plan, which predicts consequences that may affect many different parcels of land in a variety of ways, and which effects themselves may change over time. That review would have to take place without benefit of the focus that a particular logging proposal could provide. Thus, for example, the court below in evaluating the Sierra Club's claims had to focus upon whether the Plan as a whole was "improperly skewed," rather than focus upon whether the decision to allow clearcutting on a particular site was improper, say, because the site was better suited to another use or logging there would cumulatively result in too many trees' being cut. And, of course, depending upon the agency's future actions to revise the Plan or modify the expected methods of implementation, review now may turn out to have been unnecessary.

This type of review threatens the kind of "abstract disagreements over administrative policies," *Abbott Laboratories*, 387 U.S., at 148, 87 S.Ct., at 1515, that the ripeness doctrine seeks to avoid * * *. All this is to say that further factual development would "significantly advance our ability to deal with the legal issues presented" and would "aid us in their resolution." *Duke Power Co. v. Carolina Environmental Study Group, Inc.*, 438 U.S. 59, 82, 98 S.Ct. 2620, 2635, 57 L.Ed.2d 595 (1978).

Finally, Congress has not provided for pre-implementation judicial review of forest plans * * *.

* * *

For these reasons, we find the respondents' suit not ripe for review * * *.

NOTES

The Court also found a dispute unripe in *National Park Hospitality Ass'n v. Department of the Interior*, 538 U.S. 803, 123 S.Ct. 2026, 155 L.Ed.2d 1017 (2003). The National Park Service promulgated a regulation declaring that contracts with concessioners in national parks were not subject to the Contracts Disputes Act ("CDA"), 41 U.S.C. §§ 601–613 (2012), which provides procedures for resolving disputes between the government and its contractors. *See* 36 C.F.R. § 51.3. The petitioner, a trade association representing concessioners, challenged the validity of the regulation, which the Court concluded was unripe for review. The Park Service did not "administer" the CDA and had no rulemaking authority under that statute, so at most its regulation was a non-binding policy statement indicating its position.

Viewed in this light, § 51.3 does not create "adverse effects of a strictly legal kind," which we have previously required for a showing of hardship. *Ohio Forestry Ass'n, Inc.*, 523 U.S., at 733, 118 S.Ct. 1665 * * *.

Moreover, § 51.3 does not affect a concessioner's primary conduct. Unlike the regulation at issue in *Abbott Laboratories*, which required drug manufacturers to change the labels, advertisements, and promotional materials they used in marketing prescription drugs on pain of criminal and civil penalties, the regulation here leaves a concessioner free to conduct its business as it sees fit.

* * *

Petitioner contends that delaying judicial resolution of this issue will result in real harm because the applicability *vel non* of the CDA is one of the factors a concessioner takes into account when preparing its bid for NPS concession contracts. Petitioner's argument appears to be that mere uncertainty as to the validity of a legal rule constitutes a hardship for purposes of the ripeness analysis. We are not persuaded. If we were to follow petitioner's logic, courts would soon be overwhelmed with requests for what essentially would be advisory opinions because most business transactions could be priced more accurately if even a small portion of existing legal uncertainties were resolved * * *.

We next consider whether the issue in this case is fit for review. Although the question presented here is "a purely legal one" and § 51.3 constitutes "final agency action" * * *, we nevertheless believe that further factual development would "significantly advance our ability to deal with the legal issues presented," *Duke Power Co. v. Carolina Environmental Study Group, Inc.*, 438 U.S. 59, 82, 98 S.Ct. 2620, 57 L.Ed.2d 595 (1978). While the federal respondents generally argue that NPS was correct to conclude that the CDA does not cover concession contracts, they acknowledge that certain types of concession contracts might come under the broad language of the CDA. Similarly, while petitioner and respondent Xanterra Parks & Resorts, LLC, present a facial challenge to § 51.3, both rely on specific characteristics of certain types of concession contracts to support their positions. In light of the foregoing, we conclude that judicial resolution of the question presented here should await a concrete dispute about a particular concession contract.

123 S.Ct. at 2031–32. Justices Stevens, Breyer and O'Connor disagreed. In the view of the latter two Justices, "the case now presents a legal issue—the applicability of the CDA to concession contracts—that is fit for judicial

determination. That issue is a purely legal one demanding for its resolution only use of ordinary judicial interpretive techniques." *Id.* at 2036 (Breyer, J., dissenting). Justice Stevens agreed with this conclusion but would have decided the case on standing rather than ripeness grounds. *See id.* at 2033–34 (Stevens, J., concurring in the judgment) (finding the issue fit for resolution). Justices Breyer and O'Connor would also have found hardship in the higher contract implementation costs likely to be faced by concessioners. *Id.* at 2035, 2037–38 (Breyer, J., dissenting).

If the Park Service regulation did not have any legal effect whatsoever, exactly why was the regulation "final agency action"? And exactly why did anyone have standing to challenge the regulation?

c.   The Consequences

Abbott Laboratories may have had consequences that the Court never imagined or intended. *Abbott Laboratories* was decided in 1967, just as the modern era of informal rulemaking was getting underway. Under a restrictive ripeness regime, parties would generally be unable to challenge agency rules until those rules were applied in an enforcement proceeding. Such enforcement proceedings would almost always be formal adjudications, either by virtue of organic statutes and the APA, constitutional due process requirements (since the enforcement action will certainly be seeking to deprive the defendants of constitutionally protected interests), or both. The formal adjudication, in turn, would produce a thorough *record for review*, so that the case would reach the courts only after full development of the issues through formal adversary proceedings before the agency.

A liberal ripeness regime would produce a very different environment for the review of rulemaking. *Abbott Laboratories* shifted the balance—how much is hard to say—in favor of pre-enforcement review of rules. If that shift was considerable, then after 1967, challenges to rulemakings would normally reach courts as soon as the rules were issued. If the rules were generated through informal rulemaking, the only "record" for review would be the notice of proposed rulemaking, which in 1967 was generally a very sparse document,[32] any comments filed with the agency, and the "concise and general" statement of basis and purpose provided by the agency, which also in 1967 was likely to be a very sparse document. This would be an adequate record for review if courts were content simply to affirm any agency rules that were not absurd on their faces. But by 1967, the rise of agency-capture theories of agency behavior made this standard of review unacceptable to courts that felt strongly about many of the substantive missions entrusted to agencies. The informal rulemaking procedures specified in the APA simply would not generate the record needed for

---

[32]   Review at this point the notices of proposed rulemaking issued by the ICC in 1967 in connection with the *Florida East Coast Ry.* case. *See supra* pages 332–338.

vigorous, hard-look review. An adequate basis for activist review could be provided only if courts restructured the informal rulemaking process to generate the kind of documentary record and adversary interplay that is automatically provided by formal adjudications.

Hence, in 1967, the ripeness regime of *Abbott Laboratories*, the rise of informal rulemaking, the prevalence of agency capture theory, and the dominance of an activist judiciary all seemingly dovetailed to make the procedural revolution in informal rulemaking virtually inevitable.

The only flaw in this elegant story is that it depends on the assumption that *Abbott Labs* substantially liberalized the pre-1967 ripeness regime. That is not at all clear. Justice Harlan certainly did not evince any intention of dramatically changing the law, nor was pre-enforcement review unheard of in the years prior to 1967, as the copious citations that this book deletes from the *Abbott Labs* opinion demonstrate. For a vigorous argument that *Abbott Labs* merely applied settled law concerning pre-enforcement review, see John Duffy, *Administrative Common Law in Judicial Review*, 77 Tex. L. Rev. 113, 173–74 (1998). (More fundamentally, Professor Duffy also argues, quite persuasively, that the real revolution wrought by *Abbott Labs* was the creation of the free-standing ripeness regime itself, unconnected to particular organic statutes. *See id.* at 162–78.)

It is certainly true that pre-enforcement review is today the norm in a way that was not true before the modern era of administrative law. But that merely poses a chicken-and-egg question: did ripeness law change in a way that had ripple effects on substantive and procedural doctrines, or did substantive and procedural law change in a way that had ripple effects on ripeness doctrine? Perhaps pre-enforcement review is more common post-1967 simply because the enhanced agency records generated by the procedural revolution make it more likely that cases will be found fit for judicial review without the need for an adjudicatory record.

d. Variations on a Theme

Ripeness issues generally arise from attempts by parties to challenge regulations that, if enforced, will impose a burden. In *Reno v. Catholic Social Services, Inc.*, 509 U.S. 43, 113 S.Ct. 2485, 125 L.Ed.2d 38 (1993), the Supreme Court addressed ripeness in the context of regulations that confer benefits. The Immigration and Naturalization Service promulgated regulations specifying procedures that must be followed by illegal aliens seeking a change in their status. Compliance with the regulations was a necessary but not a sufficient condition for receiving a change in status. The Court held that challenges to the regulations were unripe:

> The regulations challenged here * * * impose no penalties for violating any newly imposed restriction, but limit access to a

> benefit created by the Reform Act but not automatically bestowed on eligible aliens. Rather, the Act requires each alien desiring the benefit to take further affirmative steps, and to satisfy criteria beyond those addressed by the disputed regulations. It delegates to the INS the task of determining on a case-by-case basis whether each applicant has met all of the Act's conditions, not merely those interpreted by the regulations in question. In these circumstances, the promulgation of the challenged regulations did not itself give each * * * class member a ripe claim; a class member's claim would ripen only once he took the affirmative steps that he could take before the INS blocked his path by applying the regulation to him.

509 U.S. at 58–59, 113 S.Ct. at 2496–97. The Court held, however, that certain plaintiffs might have ripe challenges to the regulations if, as was alleged, the agency on some occasions rejected applications for change of status based solely on documents submitted under the regulations, so that any further action by the applicant would be irrelevant. *See id.* at 61–67, 113 S.Ct. at 2497–2501. Four Justices disagreed with this application of the ripeness doctrine. Justice O'Connor, in particular, concurred in the result but specifically rejected "a categorical rule that would-be beneficiaries cannot challenge benefit-conferring regulations until they apply for benefits." *Id.* at 69, 113 S.Ct. at 2502 (O'Connor, J., concurring in the judgment). Are there any reasons that would justify different reviewability rules for beneficiaries and targets of regulation?

e. State of Confusion

Students who find it difficult to keep clear in their minds the distinctions among exhaustion, finality, and ripeness might be heartened to learn that they are not alone. In *Ticor Title Ins. Co. v. FTC*, 814 F.2d 731 (D.C.Cir.1987), the petitioners, against whom the FTC had filed an administrative complaint, challenged the constitutionality of the Commission's structure on the ground that independent agencies could not validly execute federal laws.[33] The court of appeals panel unanimously concluded that the suit was premature, but no two judges agreed on a rationale. Judge Edwards held that the action was ripe and final but that the petitioners had not exhausted their administrative remedies, Judge Green held that exhaustion and finality were satisfied but that the case was not ripe, and Judge Williams held that the agency action was not final and that the court therefore had no power to consider exhaustion or ripeness. *See also John Doe, Inc. v. DEA*, 484 F.3d 561, 567 (D.C.Cir.2007) ("exhaustion, ripeness, and finality may be difficult to distinguish in some contexts").

---

[33] Their position on the merits was effectively rejected the next year in *Morrison v. Olson*. *See supra* pages 252–256.

f.   Overripeness?

The ripeness doctrine, along with the exhaustion and finality doctrines, operate to prevent judicial review at too early a stage of the administrative process. A party can also seek review, however, at too *late* a stage of the administrative process.

Statutes of limitations—statutory time periods after which even meritorious suits are barred—are standard features of the legal order. They can be especially important in administrative law where agencies and regulated parties need to plan their conduct around a known and settled legal landscape. It is therefore common for Congress to prescribe very short statutes of limitations—measured in months rather than years—for challenges to agency action. The timing provision of the Hobbs Act[34] is typical of this kind of statute: parties aggrieved by a final decision reviewable under that statute "may, within 60 days after its entry, file a petition to review the order in the court of appeals wherein venue lies." 28 U.S.C. § 2344 (2012).[35] The statute's clear implication is that an action for review may not be brought *later* than 60 days after entry of a final order.

One might think that the only question posed by a statute like the Hobbs Act is whether the 60-day period applies only to actions initiated by a party (which are generally called actions for direct review) or also to actions initiated by the agency, in which the agency's decision is challenged as a defense to an enforcement action. The APA specifically addresses this issue, providing that "[e]xcept to the extent that prior, adequate, and exclusive opportunity for judicial review is provided by law, agency action is subject to judicial review in civil or criminal proceedings for enforcement." 5 U.S.C. § 703 (2012). One could plausibly argue under the Hobbs Act either that 60 days means 60 days whether or not there is a subsequent agency enforcement action, and that the statute therefore provides "prior, adequate, and exclusive opportunity for judicial review," or that the Hobbs Act's language, which specifically refers to party-initiated petitions for review, does not *expressly* preclude review in an agency-initiated enforcement action. However one resolves this issue, it is hard to imagine what else there could be to argue about.

The courts, however, have generated an astonishingly complex body of doctrine for determining precisely which kinds of challenges to agency action must be brought within the time limits of statutes such as the Hobbs Act.

---

[34]   For a short discussion of the Hobbs Act, *see supra* page 1021.

[35]   Judicial review statutes frequently use the term "orders," which strictly speaking describes only the products of adjudications, to refer to both rules and orders. You should be very hesitant to conclude that a statute governing review of agency "orders" does not also govern review of agency rules.

NATIONAL LABOR RELATIONS BOARD UNION v. FLRA

United States Court of Appeals, District of Columbia Circuit, 1987.
834 F.2d 191.

Before EDWARDS, STARR and D.H. GINSBURG, CIRCUIT JUDGES.

HARRY T. EDWARDS, CIRCUIT JUDGE:

[In 1980, the Federal Labor Relations Authority, the agency charged with governing the relations between government agencies and employee unions, adopted regulations limiting the remedies available to unions when agencies violate their statutory duty to bargain with the unions. In 1985, the petitioner union asked the agency to amend its regulations on the ground that they were inconsistent with the governing organic statute. The agency refused, and in 1986 the union appealed the agency's refusal to amend its rules.]

* * *

Final orders of the FLRA must be appealed within sixty days. 5 U.S.C. § 7123(a). The FLRA's promulgation of final rules or regulations constitutes a final order marking the commencement of the sixty-day limitations period. The regulations the Union seeks to amend were issued in final form on January 17, 1980 * * *. Because the Union's appeal appears to be an attack on regulations adopted almost seven years before that appeal was filed, the FLRA submits that judicial review should be barred by the sixty-day statute of limitations.

The FLRA's contention ignores the settled law of this circuit. In a long line of cases stretching back to *Functional Music, Inc. v. FCC*, 274 F.2d 543 (D.C.Cir.1958), this court has repeatedly distinguished indirect attacks on the substantive validity of regulations initiated more than sixty days after their promulgation from like attacks on their procedural lineage. It has also noted that the scope of appellate review varies with the nature of the substantive attack. To avoid further confusion on this score, we offer a brief summary of prior holdings.

An agency's regulations may be attacked in two ways once the statutory limitations period has expired. First, a party who possesses standing may challenge regulations directly on the ground that the issuing agency acted in excess of its statutory authority in promulgating them. A challenge of this sort might be raised, for example, by way of defense in an enforcement proceeding. Thus, suppose that the FLRA adopted a regulation prohibiting unions from representing women; suppose, further, that the regulation went unchallenged during the statutory limitations period; finally, suppose that the General Counsel filed ulp [unfair labor practice] charges against a union for failure to execute a negotiated collective bargaining agreement because the employer refused to extend coverage of the agreement to female employees. Under such circumstances, the union could clearly challenge the validity of the regulation on which the employer and the FLRA were relying, even if that regulation went uncontested throughout the applicable statutory limitations period. As this court said in *Functional Music*:

> As applied to rules and regulations, the statutory time limit restricting judicial review of [agency] action is applicable only to cut off review directly from the order promulgating a rule. It does not foreclose subsequent examination of a rule where properly brought before this court for review of further [agency] action applying it. For unlike ordinary adjudicative orders, administrative rules and regulations are capable of continuing application; limiting the right of review of the underlying rule would effectively deny many parties ultimately affected by a rule an opportunity to question its validity.

274 F.2d at 546.

The second method of obtaining judicial review of agency regulations once the limitations period has run is to petition the agency for amendment or rescission of the regulations and then to appeal the agency's decision. We have distinguished three types of challenges on appeal.

(a) A petitioner's contention that a regulation suffers from some *procedural* infirmity, such as an agency's unjustified refusal to allow affected parties to comment on a rule before issuing it in final form, will not be heard outside of the statutory limitations period. This court held in *Natural Resources Defense Council v. NRC*, 666 F.2d 595 (D.C.Cir.1981), that "[w]ith respect to routine procedural challenges made by those against whom the agency is not proceeding to enforce the regulation," *id.* at 603, "[t]he 60 day period for seeking judicial review . . . is jurisdictional in nature and may not be enlarged or altered by the courts." *Id.* at 602. Countenancing such challenges, the court reasoned, would on balance waste administrative resources and unjustifiably impair the reliance interests of those who conformed their conduct to the contested regulation. Hence, the court dismissed as untimely NRDC's procedural objection to the Commission's decision to promulgate final rules without a notice-and-comment period.

(b) A petitioner's claim that a regulation suffers from some *substantive* deficiency *other than the agency's lack of statutory authority* to issue that regulation may be brought by petitioning the agency for amendment or rescission and then appealing the denial of that petition * * *. An appellate court's review in cases of this kind, however, is limited to the "*narrow issues as defined by the denial of the petition for rulemaking*," and does not extend to a challenge of the agency's original action in promulgating the disputed rule. *Professional Drivers Council v. Bureau of Motor Carrier Safety*, 706 F.2d 1216, 1217 n. 2 (D.C.Cir.1983) (emphasis added). Furthermore, review of an agency's decision not to promulgate a rule proposed by the petitioner is extremely limited. *See WWHT, Inc. v. FCC*, 656 F.2d 807, 816–20 (D.C.Cir.1981).

(c) Finally, a petitioner's contention that a regulation should be amended or rescinded because it *conflicts with the statute* from which its authority derives is reviewable outside of a statutory limitations period. *See Natural Resources Defense Council v. NRC*, 666 F.2d at 603–04 * * *.

The Union's charge that * * * [the challenged regulations] are inconsistent with the Statute falls under this third category of indirect challenges, and thus warrants judicial consideration * * *.

* * *

NOTES

An issue not covered by the discussion in *National Labor Relations Board Union* is whether procedural rather than substantive challenges to rules can be raised in enforcement actions outside of statutory time limits. (There is no question under governing law that substantive challenges can be so raised.) The D.C. Circuit took up that question in 1994.

JEM BROADCASTING CO., INC. V. FCC

United States Court of Appeals, District of Columbia Circuit, 1994.
22 F.3d 320.

Before: MIKVA, CHIEF JUDGE, EDWARDS and SILBERMAN, CIRCUIT JUDGES.

Opinion for the Court filed by CIRCUIT JUDGE HARRY T. EDWARDS.

HARRY T. EDWARDS, CIRCUIT JUDGE:

In July 1988, appellant JEM Broadcasting Company, Inc. ("JEM") submitted a license application for a new FM station in Bella Vista, Arkansas. The Federal Communications Commission ("FCC" or "Commission") accepted JEM's application for filing, but determined upon further review that JEM had provided inconsistent geographic coordinates for its proposed transmitter site. Unable to resolve the inconsistency from the application papers, the FCC, acting pursuant to its "hard look" processing rules, dismissed JEM's application without providing JEM an opportunity to correct its error.

[The "hard look" rules at issue provide that certain license applications will be summarily rejected without opportunity for revision or amendment if they fail to provide specified information or if they contain inconsistencies that cannot be resolved on the face of the applications. The rules, which are subject to judicial review under the Hobbs Act, were promulgated and became final on May 13, 1985. JEM's license application and ultimate appeal came three years later.]

JEM * * * contends that the so-called "hard look" rules cannot be applied against it because the rules were promulgated without notice and comment in violation of the Administrative Procedure Act * * *.

* * *

Section 2344 of the Hobbs Act provides that any party "aggrieved" by a "final [agency] order may, within 60 days after its entry, file a petition to review the order in the court of appeals wherein venue lies." 28 U.S.C. § 2344. JEM attempts to avoid the stricture of the limitations period on two grounds. First, while conceding that direct petitions for review of an agency order are governed by the 60-day limitations period, it claims that indirect attacks on a rule's validity in the context of an adjudicatory proceeding are not so governed. Second, JEM urges that it could not have petitioned for direct review of the "hard look" rules within the statutory period because it was not then an aggrieved party. As we explain below, the limitations period applies in this case, and JEM's notice and comment challenge must be rejected as untimely.

JEM is correct in arguing that the statutory limitations period is not a rule of inflexible application. Our cases have identified two variables that may affect its applicability: (1) whether the challenge to a particular rule is substantive or procedural; and (2) whether the challenge arises directly via petition for amendment or rescission of the rule, or whether it arises indirectly as a defense to an agency enforcement action. *See generally NLRB Union v. FLRA*, 834 F.2d 191, 195–97 (D.C.Cir.1987) (summarizing circuit law with respect to various types of challenges). JEM's appeal, however, presents only one of the possible permutations: an attack on the *procedural genesis* of the "hard look" rules in the context of an *enforcement action*. Although both parties point to supportive language in our prior cases, it appears that we have never squarely considered whether the 60-day limitations period bars an attack of this type. We hold today that it does.

The FCC appears to consider dispositive our *NLRB Union* decision, in which, summarizing the law of the circuit, we said that:

> [a] petitioner's contention that a regulation suffers from some *procedural* infirmity, such as an agency's unjustified refusal to allow affected parties to comment on a rule before issuing it in final form, will not be heard outside of the statutory limitations period.

Id. at 196 (emphasis in original). Although not so limited, that statement of the law in *NLRB Union* was cited in connection with a case in which a party sought judicial review by "petition[ing] the agency for amendment or rescission of the regulations and then [appealing] the agency's decision." *Id.* In this respect, *NLRB Union* restated our unequivocal holding in *Natural Resources Defense Council v. NRC*, 666 F.2d 595 (D.C.Cir.1981), to the effect that a party could not

> do indirectly what it is forbidden by statute from doing directly— that is, . . . seek review of the procedure by which the [regulations] were promulgated, even though it could have but did not seek direct review thereof, by simply raising its objections in a petition for rulemaking and seeking direct review of the order denying the petition.

Id. at 601–02 (footnote omitted). Thus, both *Natural Resources Defense Council* and *NLRB Union* speak directly to situations in which a petitioner seeks a "back door" to judicial review via petition for amendment or rescission of the offending regulations after the period for direct review has elapsed. These cases are not directly on point here, but only because JEM has challenged the "hard look" rules as an affirmative defense to the FCC's application of those rules to JEM's detriment. This, however, is a difference without meaning.

Although *NLRB Union* and *Natural Resources Defense Council* arose in a context different from this case, the relevant principle enunciated in those cases carries equal force here. JEM does not meaningfully distinguish this authority, as it relies on an inapposite line of cases to support its argument that its claim is timely. For example, JEM cites *Functional Music, Inc. v. FCC*, 274 F.2d 543, 546 (D.C.Cir.1958), *cert. denied*, 361 U.S. 813, 80 S.Ct. 50, 4 L.Ed.2d 60 (1959), a case in which we allowed a petitioner to challenge the *substantive* validity of an FCC rule in an adjudicatory action brought more than 60 days after the rule's promulgation. But JEM does not claim in this case that the "hard look" rules are unconstitutional, that they exceed the scope of the FCC's substantive authority, or, as was the case in *Functional Music*, that the rules are premised on an erroneous interpretation of a statutory term. Thus, *Functional Music* is inapplicable. "[Since] *Functional Music*, this court has repeatedly distinguished indirect attacks on the substantive validity of regulations initiated more than sixty days after their promulgation from like attacks on their procedural lineage." *NLRB Union*, 834 F.2d at 195 (citation omitted).

We conclude that the aforecited rule stated in *NLRB Union* and *Natural Resources Defense Council* is equally applicable to cases of the type presented here. Thus, challenges to the *procedural lineage of agency regulations*, whether raised by direct appeal, by petition for amendment or rescission of the regulation or as a defense to an agency enforcement proceeding, will not be entertained outside the 60-day period provided by statute. The policies underlying Congress' adoption of the limitations period strongly support this result. As we have noted before, Congress has "determined that the agency's interest generally lies in prompt review of agency regulations," and "[w]e accord heavy weight to that view." *Mountain States Tel. & Tel. Co. v. FCC*, 939 F.2d 1035, 1040 (D.C.Cir.1991) (citation and quotation omitted). We place a high value on finality in administrative processes, for finality "conserv[es] administrative resources and protect[s] the reliance interests of regulatees who conform their conduct to the regulations." *Natural Resources Defense Council*, 666 F.2d at 602. Accordingly, our baseline standard long has been that statutory limitations on petitions for review are "jurisdictional in nature," *id.*, and may be enlarged by this court only in "a limited number of exceptional situations." *Raton Gas Transmission Co. v. FERC*, 852 F.2d 612, 615 (D.C.Cir.1988). A procedural challenge to agency rules does not constitute such an exceptional situation.

In a further effort to circumvent the limitations period, JEM argues that it would have lacked standing to file a timely petition for review because it was not "aggrieved" by the "hard look" rules at the time of their issuance. Indeed, JEM claims that no party could have known whether the rules applied to it, and thus been aggrieved, unless and until the Commission actually dismissed a defective application under the rules. We disagree. Of course, only parties whose license applications actually contain certain errors or omissions will suffer the concrete *effects* of the "hard look" rules, but that does not make the rules any less *applicable* as a general matter to all potential FCC license applicants. By JEM's logic, virtually no agency rules ever could be reviewed by timely petition, since rules, by definition, must have prospective application. Instead, all challenges would have to arise as a defense to an enforcement proceeding, and this clearly is not the law.

Some rules will no doubt defy review upon promulgation for lack of "ripeness." But this does not mean that affected parties will lack standing to challenge a rule upon promulgation. And the possibility that a rule may not be ripe for review does not excuse an untimely petition.

In a case of this sort, neither standing nor ripeness issues are of significant concern. We have held unequivocally that when a party complains of an agency's failure to provide notice and comment prior to acting, it is that failure which causes "injury"; and interested parties are "aggrieved" by the order promulgating the rules. Moreover, the failure to provide notice and comment is a ground for complaint that is or should be fully known to all interested parties at the time the rules are promulgated. Accordingly, we hold that any person or entity within the class affected by the "hard look" rules, *i.e.* actual or potential license applicants, would have been "aggrieved" within the meaning of section 2344 at the time the rules were promulgated, and thus would have had standing to challenge the procedural lineage of the "hard look" rules by direct petition for review thereof. And, had such a challenge been raised in a timely fashion, there is no doubt that the matter would have been ripe for review.

We recognize that as a result of our holdings today, some parties—such as those not yet in existence when a rule is promulgated—never will have the opportunity to challenge the procedural lineage of rules that are applied to their detriment. In our view, the law countenances this result because of the value of repose. "Strict enforcement of the [statutory] time limit is necessary to preserve finality in agency decisionmaking and to protect justifiable reliance on agency rules." *Raton Gas*, 852 F.2d at 615. Of course, under our established law, the result might differ if it could be shown that no party ever had adequate opportunity to challenge a particular agency action. Thus, we have recognized exceptions to the limitations period when agency action fails to put aggrieved parties on reasonable notice of the rule's content, or when such action remains unripe for judicial review throughout the statutory review period. In this instance, however, JEM cannot deny that the FCC's failure to conduct notice and comment rulemaking was an immediately obvious fact that, as we hold, was subject to immediate challenge by any number of then-existing would-be license applicants. The mere fact that JEM, in particular, had no opportunity to challenge the procedural provenance of the "hard look" rules within the statutory period is of no moment. Accordingly, we reject JEM's arguments and hold that the instant challenge to the "hard look" rules is untimely.

NOTES

Suppose, as the court in *JEM* acknowledges is possible, you reasonably believe that your claim will be unripe if it is brought as a pre-enforcement review action within the statutory review period. Must you bring your action within the time period, fully expecting it to be dismissed under the ripeness doctrine? In general, the answer is yes. In *Eagle-Picher Industries v. EPA*, 759 F.2d 905 (D.C.Cir.1985), the D.C. Circuit indicated that it will not normally entertain claims that a late filing is justified because an earlier filing would have been unripe.

> [E]xcept where events occur or information becomes available after the statutory review period expires that essentially create a challenge that did not previously exist, or where a petitioner's claim is, under our precedents, *indisputably* not ripe until the agency takes further action, we will be very reluctant, in order to save a late petitioner from the strictures of a timeliness requirement, to engage in a retrospective determination of whether we would have held the claim ripe had it been brought on time.

Id. at 914. As the court explained, "[i]t is the duty of the court to make the prudential judgment whether a challenge to agency action is ripe; it is the responsibility of petitioners to file for review within the period set by Congress." *Id.* at 912.

The Hobbs Act does not expressly preclude review of agency action in enforcement proceedings. Occasionally, however, Congress does provide for pre-enforcement review of rules that is expressly intended to preclude review even in subsequent criminal enforcement proceedings. The model for such statutes was § 204(d) of the Emergency Price Control Act of January 30, 1942, which governed judicial review of determinations issued by the federal government's World War II price control authorities. Section 203(a) of the statute required review of decisions of the price Administrator to be brought within 60 days of their issuance, and § 204(d) stated that:

> [t]he Emergency Court of Appeals, and the Supreme Court upon review of judgments and orders of the Emergency Court of Appeals, shall have exclusive jurisdiction to determine the validity of any regulation or order * * *, of any price schedule * * *, and of any provision of any such regulation, order, or price schedule [issued by the Administrator]. Except as provided in this section, no court, Federal, State, or Territorial, shall have jurisdiction or power to consider the validity of any such regulation, order, or price schedule, or to stay, restrain, enjoin, or set aside, in whole or in part, any provision of this Act authorizing the issuance of such regulations or orders, or making effective any such price schedule, or any provision of any such regulation, order, or price schedule, or to restrain or enjoin the enforcement of any such provision.

In *Yakus v. United States*, 321 U.S. 414, 64 S.Ct. 660, 88 L.Ed. 834 (1944), the Court held that these provisions foreclosed all review outside of the 60-day period, including review of regulations in criminal enforcement proceedings, and that such preclusion of review was constitutional. Modern statutes, especially in the environmental area, increasingly contain similar provisions for the review of rules.[36]

Can Congress really force you to seek review of agency rules—and to seek the review in the District of Columbia—within a few months after they appear in the Federal Register or forever lose your right to challenge their legality on any ground? *Yakus* suggests that the answer is yes, but *Yakus* was decided in a time and context (in the middle of a war, and at the height of judicial deference to agency decisionmaking) that may cast some doubt on its current vitality. Such, at least, was the view of Justice Powell. In *Adamo Wrecking Co.*

---

[36] For example, section 113(a) of the Comprehensive Environmental Response, Compensation, and Liability Act (popularly known as the "Superfund" statute) provides:

> Review of any regulation promulgated under this chapter may be had upon application by any interested person only in the Circuit Court of Appeals of the United States for the District of Columbia. Any such application shall be made within ninety days from the date of promulgation of such regulations. Any matter with respect to which review could have been obtained under this subsection shall not be subject to judicial review in any civil or criminal proceeding for enforcement or to obtain damages or recovery of response costs.

42 U.S.C. § 9613(a) (2012).

v. United States, 434 U.S. 275, 98 S.Ct. 566, 54 L.Ed.2d 538 (1978), the Court held that a statute that expressly forbids all review, including review in enforcement proceedings, of any "emission standard" beyond 30 days of its promulgation did not bar a criminal defendant's challenge to a regulation that specifies procedures for demolishing buildings but does not establish quantitative limits on emissions of substances. The Court reasoned that the regulation, even though denominated an "emission standard" by the agency, was not in fact an "emission standard" within the meaning of the statute. *Id.* at 286–89, 98 S.Ct. at 573–75. Justice Powell concurred, but wrote separately to emphasize his serious doubts about the constitutionality of this preclusion scheme.

> If the constitutional validity of § 307(b) of the Clean Air Act had been raised by petitioner, I think it would have merited serious consideration. This section limits judicial review to the filing of a petition in the United States Court of Appeals for the District of Columbia Circuit within 30 days from the date of the promulgation by the Administrator of an emission standard. No notice is afforded a party who may be subject to criminal prosecution other than publication of the Administrator's action in the Federal Register. The Act in this respect is similar to the preclusion provisions of the Emergency Price Control Act before the Court in *Yakus v. United States*, 321 U.S. 414, 64 S.Ct. 660, 88 L.Ed. 834 (1944), and petitioner may have thought the decision in that case effectively foreclosed a due process challenge in the present case.

> Although I express no considered judgment, I think *Yakus* is at least arguably distinguishable. The statute there came before the Court during World War II, and it can be viewed as a valid exercise of the war powers of Congress * * *. Although the opinion of Mr. Chief Justice Stone is not free from ambiguity, there is language emphasizing that the price controls imposed by the Congress were a "war emergency measure." Indeed, the Government argued that the statute should be upheld under the war powers authority of Congress. As important as environmental concerns are to the country, they are not comparable—in terms of an emergency justifying the shortcutting of normal due process rights—to the need for national mobilization in wartime of economic as well as military activity.

> The 30-day limitation on judicial review imposed by the Clean Air Act would afford precariously little time for many affected persons even if some adequate method of notice were afforded. It also is totally unrealistic to assume that more than a fraction of the persons and entities affected by a regulation—especially small contractors scattered across the country—would have knowledge of its promulgation or familiarity with or access to the Federal Register * * *.

I join the Court's opinion with the understanding that it implies no view as to the constitutional validity of the preclusion provisions of § 307(b) in the context of a criminal prosecution.

Id. at 289–91, 98 S.Ct. at 575–76 (Powell, J., concurring). No frontal challenge to *Yakus* has since been attempted.

4. PRIMARY JURISDICTION

The exhaustion, finality, and ripeness doctrines concern whether appeals from agency proceedings are appropriate at a particular time. The doctrine of primary jurisdiction concerns whether actions filed directly in court should be referred to an agency for initial consideration. Primary jurisdiction thus does not involve the timing of review of agency action, but it does involve the timing of judicial consideration of issues that are within the scope of agency authority and expertise.

Primary jurisdiction is a twentieth-century invention, and its use by courts has tended to ebb and flow over time. For a fairly typical modern invocation of the doctrine, see *Williams Pipe Line Co. v. Empire Gas Corp.*, 76 F.3d 1491 (10th Cir.1996).

APPENDIX A

THE CONSTITUTION OF THE UNITED STATES

■ ■ ■

We the People of the United States in Order to form a more perfect Union, to establish Justice, insure domestic Tranquility, provide for the common defense, promote the general Welfare, and secure the blessings of Liberty to ourselves and our Posterity, do ordain and establish this Constitution for the United States of America.

ARTICLE I

Section 1

All legislative Powers herein granted shall be vested in a Congress of the United States, which shall consist of a Senate and House of Representatives.

Section 2

[1] The House of Representatives shall be composed of Members chosen every second Year by the People of the several States, and the Electors in each State shall have the Qualifications requisite for Electors of the most numerous Branch of the State Legislature.

[2] No Person shall be a Representative who shall not have attained to the Age of twenty five Years, and been seven Years a Citizen of the United States, and who shall not, when elected, be an Inhabitant of that State in which he shall be chosen.

[3] Representatives and direct Taxes shall be apportioned among the several States which may be included within this Union, according to their respective Numbers, which shall be determined by adding to the whole Number of free Persons, including those bound to Service for a Term of Years, and excluding Indians not taxed, three fifths of all other Persons. The actual Enumeration shall be made within three Years after the first Meeting of the Congress of the United States, and within every subsequent Term of ten Years, in such Manner as they shall by Law direct. The Number of Representatives shall not exceed one for every thirty Thousand, but each State shall have at Least one Representative; and until such enumeration shall be made, the State of New Hampshire shall be entitled to chuse three, Massachusetts eight, Rhode-Island and Providence Plantations one, Connecticut five, New York six, New Jersey four,

Pennsylvania eight, Delaware one, Maryland six, Virginia ten, North Carolina five, South Carolina five, and Georgia three.

[4] When vacancies happen in the Representation from any State, the Executive Authority thereof shall issue Writs of Election to fill such Vacancies.

[5] The House of Representatives shall chuse their Speaker and other Officers; and shall have the sole Power of Impeachment.

Section 3

[1] The Senate of the United States shall be composed of two Senators from each State, chosen by the Legislature thereof, for six Years; and each Senator shall have one Vote.

[2] Immediately after they shall be assembled in Consequence of the first Election, they shall be divided as equally as may be into three Classes. The Seats of the Senators of the first Class shall be vacated at the Expiration of the second Year, of the second Class at the Expiration of the fourth Year, and of the third Class at the Expiration of the sixth Year, so that one third may be chosen every second Year; and if Vacancies happen by Resignation, or otherwise, during the Recess of the Legislature of any State, the Executive thereof may make temporary Appointments until the next Meeting of the Legislature, which shall then fill such Vacancies.

[3] No Person shall be a Senator who shall not have attained to the Age of thirty Years, and been nine Years a Citizen of the United States, and who shall not, when elected, be an Inhabitant of that State for which he shall be chosen.

[4] The Vice President of the United States shall be President of the Senate, but shall have no Vote, unless they be equally divided.

[5] The Senate shall chuse their other Officers, and also a President pro tempore, in the Absence of the Vice President, or when he shall exercise the Office of President of the United States.

[6] The Senate shall have the sole Power to try all Impeachments. When sitting for that Purpose, they shall be on Oath or Affirmation. When the President of the United States is tried, the Chief Justice shall preside: And no Person shall be convicted without the Concurrence of two thirds of the Members present.

[7] Judgment in Cases of Impeachment shall not extend further than to removal from Office, and disqualification to hold and enjoy any Office of honor, Trust or Profit under the United States: but the Party convicted shall nevertheless be liable and subject to Indictment, Trial, Judgment and Punishment, according to Law.

Section 4

[1]   The Times, Places and Manner of holding Elections for Senators and Representatives, shall be prescribed in each State by the Legislature thereof; but the Congress may at any time by Law make or alter such Regulations, except as to the Places of chusing Senators.

[2]   The Congress shall assemble at least once in every Year, and such Meeting shall be on the first Monday in December, unless they shall by Law appoint a different Day.

Section 5

[1]   Each House shall be the Judge of the Elections, Returns and Qualifications of its own Members, and a Majority of each shall constitute a Quorum to do Business; but a smaller Number may adjourn from day to day, and may be authorized to compel the Attendance of absent Members, in such Manner, and under such Penalties as each House may provide.

[2]   Each House may determine the Rules of its Proceedings, punish its Members for disorderly Behaviour, and, with the Concurrence of two thirds, expel a Member.

[3]   Each House shall keep a Journal of its Proceedings, and from time to time publish the same, excepting such Parts as may in their Judgment require Secrecy; and the Yeas and Nays of the Members of either House on any question shall, at the Desire of one fifth of those Present, be entered on the Journal.

[4]   Neither House, during the Session of Congress, shall, without the Consent of the other, adjourn for more than three days, nor to any other Place than that in which the two Houses shall be sitting.

Section 6

[1]   The Senators and Representatives shall receive a Compensation for their Services, to be ascertained by Law, and paid out of the Treasury of the United States. They shall in all Cases, except Treason, Felony and Breach of the Peace, be privileged from Arrest during their Attendance at the Session of their respective Houses, and in going to and returning from the same; and for any Speech or Debate in either House, they shall not be questioned in any other Place.

[2]   No Senator or Representative shall, during the Time for which he was elected, be appointed to any civil Office under the Authority of the United States, which shall have been created, or the Emoluments whereof shall have been encreased during such time; and no Person holding any Office under the United States, shall be a Member of either House during his Continuance in Office.

Section 7

[1] All Bills for raising Revenue shall originate in the House of Representatives; but the Senate may propose or concur with Amendments as on other Bills.

[2] Every Bill which shall have passed the House of Representatives and the Senate, shall, before it become a Law, be presented to the President of the United States; If he approve he shall sign it, but if not he shall return it, with his Objections to that House in which it shall have originated, who shall enter the Objections at large on their Journal, and proceed to reconsider it. If after such Reconsideration two thirds of that House shall agree to pass the Bill, it shall be sent, together with the Objections, to the other House, by which it shall likewise be reconsidered, and if approved by two thirds of that House, it shall become a Law. But in all such Cases the Votes of both Houses shall be determined by yeas and Nays, and the Names of the Persons voting for and against the Bill shall be entered on the Journal of each House respectively. If any Bill shall not be returned by the President within ten Days (Sundays excepted) after it shall have been presented to him, the Same shall be a Law, in like Manner as if he had signed it, unless the Congress by their Adjournment prevent its Return, in which Case it shall not be a Law.

[3] Every Order, Resolution, or Vote to which the Concurrence of the Senate and House of Representatives may be necessary (except on a question of Adjournment) shall be presented to the President of the United States; and before the Same shall take Effect, shall be approved by him, or being disapproved by him, shall be repassed by two thirds of the Senate and House of Representatives, according to the Rules and Limitations prescribed in the Case of a Bill.

Section 8

[1] The Congress shall have Power To lay and collect Taxes, Duties, Imposts and Excises, to pay the Debts and provide for the common Defence and general Welfare of the United States; but all Duties, Imposts and Excises shall be uniform throughout the United States;

[2] To borrow Money on the credit of the United States;

[3] To regulate Commerce with foreign Nations, and among the several States, and with the Indian Tribes;

[4] To establish an uniform Rule of Naturalization, and uniform Laws on the subject of Bankruptcies throughout the United States;

[5] To coin Money, regulate the Value thereof, and of foreign Coin, and fix the Standard of Weights and Measures;

[6] To provide for the Punishment of counterfeiting the Securities and current Coin of the United States;

[7] To establish Post Offices and post Roads;

[8] To promote the Progress of Science and useful Arts, by securing for limited Times to Authors and Inventors the exclusive Right to their respective Writings and Discoveries;

[9] To constitute Tribunals inferior to the supreme Court;

[10] To define and punish Piracies and Felonies committed on the high Seas, and Offences against the Law of Nations;

[11] To declare War, grant Letters of Marque and Reprisal, and make Rules concerning Captures on Land and Water;

[12] To raise and support Armies, but no Appropriation of Money to that Use shall be for a longer Term than two Years;

[13] To provide and maintain a Navy;

[14] To make Rules for the Government and Regulation of the land and naval Forces;

[15] To provide for calling forth the Militia to execute the Laws of the Union, suppress Insurrections and repel Invasions;

[16] To provide for organizing, arming, and disciplining, the Militia, and for governing such Part of them as may be employed in the Service of the United States, reserving to the States respectively, the Appointment of the Officers, and the Authority of training the Militia according to the discipline prescribed by Congress;

[17] To exercise exclusive Legislation in all Cases whatsoever, over such District (not exceeding ten Miles square) as may, by Cession of particular States, and the Acceptance of Congress, become the Seat of the Government of the United States, and to exercise like Authority over all Places purchased by the Consent of the Legislature of the State in which the Same shall be, for the Erection of Forts, Magazines, Arsenals, dock-Yards, and other needful Buildings;—and

[18] To make all Laws which shall be necessary and proper for carrying into Execution the foregoing Powers, and all other Powers vested by this Constitution in the Government of the United States, or in any Department or Officer thereof.

Section 9

[1] The Migration or Importation of such Persons as any of the States now existing shall think proper to admit, shall not be prohibited by the Congress prior to the Year one thousand eight hundred and eight, but a Tax or duty may be imposed on such Importation, not exceeding ten dollars for each Person.

[2] The Privilege of the Writ of Habeas Corpus shall not be suspended, unless when in Cases of Rebellion or Invasion the public Safety may require it.

[3] No Bill of Attainder or ex post facto Law shall be passed.

[4] No Capitation, or other direct, Tax shall be laid, unless in Proportion to the Census or Enumeration herein before directed to be taken.

[5] No Tax or Duty shall be laid on Articles exported from any State.

[6] No Preference shall be given by any Regulation of Commerce or Revenue to the Ports of one State over those of another: nor shall Vessels bound to, or from, one State, be obliged to enter, clear, or pay Duties in another.

[7] No Money shall be drawn from the Treasury, but in Consequence of Appropriations made by Law; and a regular Statement and Account of the Receipts and Expenditures of all public Money shall be published from time to time.

[8] No Title of Nobility shall be granted by the United States: And no Person holding any Office of Profit or Trust under them, shall, without the Consent of the Congress, accept of any present, Emolument, Office, or Title, of any kind whatever, from any King, Prince, or foreign State.

Section 10

[1] No State shall enter into any Treaty, Alliance, or Confederation; grant Letters of Marque and Reprisal; coin Money; emit Bills of Credit; make any Thing but gold and silver Coin a Tender in Payment of Debts; pass any Bill of Attainder, ex post facto Law, or Law impairing the Obligation of Contracts, or grant any Title of Nobility.

[2] No State shall, without the Consent of the Congress, lay any Imposts or Duties on Imports or Exports, except what may be absolutely necessary for executing its inspection Laws: and the net Produce of all Duties and Imposts, laid by any State on Imports or Exports, shall be for the Use of the Treasury of the United States; and all such Laws shall be subject to the Revision and Control of the Congress.

[3] No State shall, without the Consent of Congress, lay any Duty of Tonnage, keep Troops, or Ships of War in time of Peace, enter into any Agreement or Compact with another State, or with a foreign Power, or engage in War, unless actually invaded, or in such imminent Danger as will not admit of delay.

ARTICLE II

Section 1

[1]   The executive Power shall be vested in a President of the United States of America. He shall hold his Office during the Term of four Years, and, together with the Vice President, chosen for the same Term, be elected, as follows:

[2]   Each State shall appoint, in such Manner as the Legislature thereof may direct, a Number of Electors, equal to the whole Number of Senators and Representatives to which the State may be entitled in the Congress: but no Senator or Representative, or Person holding an Office of Trust or Profit under the United States, shall be appointed an Elector.

[3]   The Congress may determine the Time of chusing the Electors, and the Day on which they shall give their Votes; which Day shall be the same throughout the United States. The electors shall meet in their respective States, and vote by ballot for two Persons, of whom one at least shall not be an Inhabitant of the same State with themselves. And they shall make a List of all the Persons voted for, and of the Number of Votes for each; which List they shall sign and certify, and transmit sealed to the Seat of the Government of the United States, directed to the President of the Senate. The President of the Senate shall, in the Presence of the Senate and House of Representatives, open all the Certificates, and the Votes shall then be counted. The Person having the greatest Number of Votes shall be the President, if such Number be a Majority of the whole Number of Electors appointed; and if there be more than one who have such Majority, and have an equal Number of Votes, then the House of Representatives shall immediately chuse by Ballot one of them for President; and if no Person have a Majority, then from the five highest on the List the said House shall in like Manner chuse the President. But in chusing the President, the Votes shall be taken by States, the Representation from each State having one Vote; A quorum for this Purpose shall consist of a Member or Members from two-thirds of the States, and a Majority of all the States shall be necessary to a Choice. In every Case, after the Choice of the President, the Person having the greatest Number of Votes of the Electors shall be the Vice President. But if there should remain two or more who have equal Votes, the Senate shall chuse from them by Ballot the Vice-President.

[4]   No Person except a natural born Citizen, or a Citizen of the United States, at the time of the Adoption of this Constitution, shall be eligible to the Office of President; neither shall any Person be eligible to that Office who shall not have attained to the Age of thirty five Years, and been fourteen Years a Resident within the United States.

[5]   In Case of the Removal of the President from Office, or of his Death, Resignation, or Inability to discharge the Powers and Duties of the

said Office, the Same shall devolve on the Vice President, and the Congress may by Law provide for the Case of Removal, Death, Resignation or Inability, both of the President and Vice President, declaring what Officer shall then act as President, and such Officer shall act accordingly, until the Disability be removed, or a President shall be elected.

[6] The President shall, at stated Times, receive for his Services, a Compensation, which shall neither be encreased nor diminished during the Period for which he shall have been elected, and he shall not receive within that Period any other Emolument from the United States, or any of them.

[7] Before he enter on the Execution of his Office, he shall take the following Oath or Affirmation:—"I do solemnly swear (or affirm) that I will faithfully execute the Office of President of the United States, and will to the best of my Ability, preserve, protect and defend the Constitution of the United States."

Section 2

[1] The President shall be Commander in Chief of the Army and Navy of the United States, and of the Militia of the several States, when called into the actual Service of the United States; he may require the Opinion, in writing, of the principal Officer in each of the executive Departments, upon any Subject relating to the Duties of their respective Offices, and he shall have Power to grant Reprieves and Pardons for Offenses against the United States, except in Cases of Impeachment.

[2] He shall have Power, by and with the Advice and Consent of the Senate, to make Treaties, provided two thirds of the Senators present concur; and he shall nominate, and by and with the Advice and Consent of the Senate, shall appoint Ambassadors, other public Ministers and Consuls, Judges of the supreme Court, and all other Officers of the United States, whose Appointments are not herein otherwise provided for, and which shall be established by Law: but the Congress may by Law vest the Appointment of such inferior Officers, as they think proper, in the President alone, in the Courts of Law, or in the Heads of Departments.

[3] The President shall have Power to fill up all Vacancies that may happen during the Recess of the Senate, by granting Commissions which shall expire at the End of their next Session.

Section 3

He shall from time to time give to the Congress Information of the State of the Union, and recommend to their Consideration such Measures as he shall judge necessary and expedient; he may, on extraordinary Occasions, convene both Houses, or either of them, and in Case of Disagreement between them, with Respect to the Time of Adjournment, he may adjourn them to such Time as he shall think proper; he shall receive Ambassadors and other public Ministers; he shall take Care that the Laws be faithfully executed, and shall Commission all the Officers of the United States.

Section 4

The President, Vice President and all civil Officers of the United States, shall be removed from Office on Impeachment for, and Conviction of, Treason, Bribery, or other high Crimes and Misdemeanors.

ARTICLE III

Section 1

The judicial Power of the United States, shall be vested in one supreme Court, and in such inferior Courts as the Congress may from time to time ordain and establish. The Judges, both of the supreme and inferior Courts, shall hold their Offices during good Behaviour, and shall, at stated Times, receive for their Services, a Compensation, which shall not be diminished during their Continuance in Office.

Section 2

[1] The judicial Power shall extend to all Cases, in Law and Equity, arising under this Constitution, the Laws of the United States, and Treaties made, or which shall be made, under their Authority;—to all Cases affecting Ambassadors, other public Ministers and Consuls;—to all Cases of admiralty and maritime Jurisdiction;—to Controversies to which the United States shall be a Party;—to Controversies between two or more States;—between a State and Citizens of another State;—between Citizens of different States;—between Citizens of the same State claiming Lands under Grants of different States, and between a State, or the Citizens thereof, and foreign States, Citizens or Subjects.

[2] In all Cases affecting Ambassadors, other public Ministers and Consuls, and those in which a State shall be Party, the supreme Court shall have original Jurisdiction. In all the other Cases before mentioned, the supreme Court shall have appellate Jurisdiction, both as to Law and Fact, with such Exceptions, and under such Regulations as the Congress shall make.

[3] The Trial of all Crimes, except in Cases of Impeachment, shall be by Jury; and such Trial shall be held in the State where the said Crimes shall have been committed; but when not committed within any State, the Trial shall be at such Place or Places as the Congress may by Law have directed.

Section 3

[1] Treason against the United States, shall consist only in levying War against them, or in adhering to their Enemies, giving them Aid and Comfort. No Person shall be convicted of Treason unless on the Testimony of two Witnesses to the same overt Act, or on Confession in open Court.

[2] The Congress shall have Power to declare the Punishment of Treason, but no Attainder of Treason shall work Corruption of Blood, or Forfeiture except during the Life of the Person attainted.

ARTICLE IV

Section 1

Full Faith and Credit shall be given in each State to the public Acts, Records, and judicial Proceedings of every other State. And the Congress may by general Laws prescribe the Manner in which such Acts, Records and Proceedings shall be proved, and the Effect thereof.

Section 2

[1] The Citizens of each State shall be entitled to all Privileges and Immunities of Citizens in the several States.

[2] A person charged in any State with Treason, Felony, or other Crime, who shall flee from Justice, and be found in another State, shall on Demand of the executive Authority of the State from which he fled, be delivered up, to be removed to the State having Jurisdiction of the Crime.

[3] No Person held to Service or Labour in one State, under the Laws thereof, escaping into another, shall, in Consequence of any Law or Regulation therein, be discharged from such Service or Labour, but shall be delivered up on Claim of the Party to whom such Service or Labour may be due.

Section 3

[1] New States may be admitted by the Congress into this Union; but no new State shall be formed or erected within the Jurisdiction of any other State; nor any State be formed by the Junction of two or more States, or Parts of States, without the Consent of the Legislatures of the States concerned as well as of the Congress.

[2] The Congress shall have Power to dispose of and make all needful Rules and Regulations respecting the Territory or other Property belonging to the United States; and nothing in this Constitution shall be so construed as to Prejudice any Claims of the United States, or of any particular State.

Section 4

The United States shall guarantee to every State in this Union a Republican Form of Government, and shall protect each of them against Invasion; and on Application of the Legislature, or of the Executive (when the Legislature cannot be convened) against domestic Violence.

ARTICLE V

The Congress, whenever two thirds of both Houses shall deem it necessary, shall propose Amendments to this Constitution, or on the

Application of the Legislatures of two thirds of the several States, shall call a Convention for proposing Amendments, which, in either Case, shall be valid to all Intents and Purposes, as Part of this Constitution, when ratified by the Legislatures of three fourths of the several States, or by Conventions in three fourths thereof, as the one or the other Mode of Ratification may be proposed by the Congress; Provided that no Amendment which may be made prior to the Year One thousand eight hundred and eight shall in any Manner affect the first and fourth Clauses in the Ninth Section of the first Article; and that no State, without its Consent, shall be deprived of its equal Suffrage in the Senate.

ARTICLE VI

[1] All Debts contracted and Engagements entered into, before the Adoption of this Constitution, shall be as valid against the United States under this Constitution, as under the Confederation.

[2] This Constitution, and the Laws of the United States which shall be made in Pursuance thereof; and all Treaties made, or which shall be made, under the Authority of the United States, shall be the supreme Law of the Land; and the Judges in every State shall be bound thereby, any Thing in the Constitution or Laws of any State to the Contrary notwithstanding.

[3] The Senators and Representatives before mentioned, and the Members of the several State Legislatures, and all executive and judicial Officers, both of the United States and of the several States, shall be bound by Oath or Affirmation, to support this Constitution; but no religious Test shall ever be required as a Qualification to any Office or public Trust under the United States.

ARTICLE VII

The Ratification of the Conventions of nine States, shall be sufficient for the Establishment of this Constitution between the States so ratifying the Same.

AMENDMENT 1

Congress shall make no law respecting an establishment of religion, or prohibiting the free exercise thereof; or abridging the freedom of speech, or of the press; or the right of the people peaceably to assemble, and to petition the Government for a redress of grievances.

AMENDMENT 2

A well regulated Militia, being necessary to the security of a free State, the right of the people to keep and bear Arms, shall not be infringed.

AMENDMENT 3

No Soldier shall, in time of peace be quartered in any house, without the consent of the Owner, nor in time of war, but in a manner to be prescribed by law.

AMENDMENT 4

The right of the people to be secure in their persons, houses, papers, and effects, against unreasonable searches and seizures, shall not be violated, and no Warrants shall issue, but upon probable cause, supported by Oath or affirmation, and particularly describing the place to be searched, and the persons or things to be seized.

AMENDMENT 5

No person shall be held to answer for a capital, or otherwise infamous crime, unless on a presentment or indictment of a Grand Jury, except in cases arising in the land or naval forces, or in the Militia, when in actual service in time of War or public danger; nor shall any person be subject for the same offence to be twice put in jeopardy of life or limb; nor shall be compelled in any criminal case to be a witness against himself, nor be deprived of life, liberty, or property, without due process of law; nor shall private property be taken for public use, without just compensation.

AMENDMENT 6

In all criminal prosecutions, the accused shall enjoy the right to a speedy and public trial, by an impartial jury of the State and district wherein the crime shall have been committed, which district shall have been previously ascertained by law, and to be informed of the nature and cause of the accusation; to be confronted with the witnesses against him; to have compulsory process for obtaining witnesses in his favor, and to have the Assistance of Counsel for his defence.

AMENDMENT 7

In Suits at common law, where the value in controversy shall exceed twenty dollars, the right of trial by jury shall be preserved, and no fact tried by a jury, shall be otherwise reexamined in any Court of the United States, than according to the rules of the common law.

AMENDMENT 8

Excessive bail shall not be required, nor excessive fines imposed, nor cruel and unusual punishments inflicted.

AMENDMENT 9

The enumeration in the Constitution, of certain rights, shall not be construed to deny or disparage others retained by the people.

AMENDMENT 10

The powers not delegated to the United States by the Constitution, nor prohibited by it to the States, are reserved to the States respectively, or to the people.

AMENDMENT 11

The Judicial power of the United States shall not be construed to extend to any suit in law or equity, commenced or prosecuted against one of the United States by Citizens of another State, or by Citizens or Subjects of any Foreign State.

AMENDMENT 12

The Electors shall meet in their respective states and vote by ballot for President and Vice-President, one of whom, at least, shall not be an inhabitant of the same state with themselves; they shall name in their ballots the person voted for as President, and in distinct ballots the person voted for as Vice-President, and they shall make distinct lists of all persons voted for as President, and of all persons voted for as Vice-President, and of the number of votes for each, which lists they shall sign and certify, and transmit sealed to the seat of the government of the United States, directed to the President of the Senate;—The President of the Senate shall, in the presence of the Senate and House of Representatives, open all the certificates and the votes shall then be counted;—The person having the greatest number of votes for President, shall be the President, if such number be a majority of the whole number of Electors appointed; and if no person have such majority, then from the persons having the highest numbers not exceeding three on the list of those voted for as President, the House of Representatives shall choose immediately, by ballot, the President. But in choosing the President, the votes shall be taken by states, the representation from each state having one vote; a quorum for this purpose shall consist of a member or members from two-thirds of the states, and a majority of all the states shall be necessary to a choice. And if the House of Representatives shall not choose a President whenever the right of choice shall devolve upon them, before the fourth day of March next following, then the Vice-President shall act as President, as in the case of the death or other constitutional disability of the President.—The person having the greatest number of votes as Vice-President, shall be the Vice-President, if such number be a majority of the whole number of Electors appointed, and if no person have a majority, then from the two highest numbers on the list, the Senate shall choose the Vice-President; a quorum for the purpose shall consist of two-thirds of the whole number of Senators, and a majority of the whole number shall be necessary to a choice. But no person constitutionally ineligible to the office of President shall be eligible to that of Vice-President of the United States.

AMENDMENT 13

Section 1

Neither slavery nor involuntary servitude, except as a punishment for crime whereof the party shall have been duly convicted, shall exist within the United States, or any place subject to their jurisdiction.

Section 2

Congress shall have power to enforce this article by appropriate legislation.

AMENDMENT 14

Section 1

All persons born or naturalized in the United States, and subject to the jurisdiction thereof, are citizens of the United States and of the State wherein they reside. No State shall make or enforce any law which shall abridge the privileges or immunities of citizens of the United States; nor shall any State deprive any person of life, liberty, or property, without due process of law; nor deny to any person within its jurisdiction the equal protection of the laws.

Section 2

Representatives shall be apportioned among the several States according to their respective numbers, counting the whole number of persons in each State, excluding Indians not taxed. But when the right to vote at any election for the choice of electors for President and Vice President of the United States, Representatives in Congress, the Executive and Judicial officers of a State, or the members of the Legislature thereof, is denied to any of the male inhabitants of such State, being twenty-one years of age, and citizens of the United States, or in any way abridged, except for participation in rebellion, or other crime, the basis of representation therein shall be reduced in the proportion which the number of such male citizens shall bear to the whole number of male citizens twenty-one years of age in such State.

Section 3

No person shall be a Senator or Representative in Congress, or elector of President and Vice President, or hold any office, civil or military, under the United States, or under any State, who, having previously taken an oath, as a member of Congress, or as an officer of the United States, or as a member of any State legislature, or as an executive or judicial officer of any State, to support the Constitution of the United States, shall have engaged in insurrection or rebellion against the same, or given aid or comfort to the enemies thereof. But Congress may by a vote of two-thirds of each House, remove such disability.

Section 4

The validity of the public debt of the United States, authorized by law, including debts incurred for payment of pensions and bounties for services in suppressing insurrection or rebellion, shall not be questioned. But neither the United States nor any State shall assume or pay any debt or obligation incurred in aid of insurrection or rebellion against the United States, or any claim for the loss or emancipation of any slave; but all such debts, obligations and claims shall be held illegal and void.

Section 5

The Congress shall have power to enforce, by appropriate legislation, the provisions of this article.

AMENDMENT 15

Section 1

The right of citizens of the United States to vote shall not be denied or abridged by the United States or by any State on account of race, color, or previous condition of servitude.

Section 2

The Congress shall have power to enforce this article by appropriate legislation.

AMENDMENT 16

The Congress shall have power to lay and collect taxes on incomes, from whatever source derived, without apportionment among the several States, and without regard to any census or enumeration.

AMENDMENT 17

[1] The Senate of the United States shall be composed of two Senators from each State, elected by the people thereof, for six years; and each Senator shall have one vote. The electors in each State shall have the qualifications requisite for electors of the most numerous branch of the State legislatures.

[2] When vacancies happen in the representation of any State in the Senate, the executive authority of such State shall issue writs of election to fill such vacancies: Provided, That the legislature of any State may empower the executive thereof to make temporary appointments until the people fill the vacancies by election as the legislature may direct.

[3] This amendment shall not be so construed as to affect the election or term of any Senator chosen before it becomes valid as part of the Constitution.

AMENDMENT 18

Section 1

After one year from the ratification of this article the manufacture, sale, or transportation of intoxicating liquors within, the importation thereof into, or the exportation thereof from the United States and all territory subject to the jurisdiction thereof for beverage purposes is hereby prohibited.

Section 2

The Congress and the several States shall have concurrent power to enforce this article by appropriate legislation.

Section 3

This article shall be inoperative unless it shall have been ratified as an amendment to the Constitution by the legislatures of the several States, as provided in the Constitution, within seven years from the date of the submission hereof to the States by the Congress.

AMENDMENT 19

[1] The right of citizens of the United States to vote shall not be denied or abridged by the United States or by any State on account of sex.

[2] Congress shall have power to enforce this article by appropriate legislation.

AMENDMENT 20

Section 1

The terms of the President and Vice President shall end at noon on the 20th day of January, and the terms of Senators and Representatives at noon on the 3d day of January, of the years in which such terms would have ended if this article had not been ratified; and the terms of their successors shall then begin.

Section 2

The Congress shall assemble at least once in every year, and such meeting shall begin at noon on the 3d day of January, unless they shall by law appoint a different day.

Section 3

If, at the time fixed for the beginning of the term of the President, the President elect shall have died, the Vice President elect shall become President. If a President shall not have been chosen before the time fixed for the beginning of his term, or if the President elect shall have failed to qualify, then the Vice President elect shall act as President until a President shall have qualified; and the Congress may by law provide for the case wherein neither a President elect nor a Vice President elect shall have qualified, declaring who shall then act as President, or the manner in which one who is to act shall be selected, and such person shall act accordingly until a President or Vice President shall have qualified.

Section 4

The Congress may by law provide for the case of the death of any of the persons from whom the House of Representatives may choose a President whenever the right of choice shall have devolved upon them, and for the case of the death of any of the persons from whom the Senate may choose a Vice President whenever the right of choice shall have devolved upon them.

Section 5

Sections 1 and 2 shall take effect on the 15th day of October following the ratification of this article.

Section 6

This article shall be inoperative unless it shall have been ratified as an amendment to the Constitution by the legislatures of three-fourths of the several States within seven years from the date of its submission.

AMENDMENT 21

Section 1

The eighteenth article of amendment to the Constitution of the United States is hereby repealed.

Section 2

The transportation or importation into any State, Territory, or possession of the United States for delivery or use therein of intoxicating liquors, in violation of the laws thereof, is hereby prohibited.

Section 3

This article shall be inoperative unless it shall have been ratified as an amendment to the Constitution by conventions in the several States, as provided in the Constitution, within seven years from the date of the submission hereof to the States by the Congress.

AMENDMENT 22

Section 1

No person shall be elected to the office of the President more than twice, and no person who has held the office of President, or acted as President, for more than two years of a term to which some other person was elected President shall be elected to the office of the President more than once. But this Article shall not apply to any person holding the office of President when this Article was proposed by the Congress, and shall not prevent any person who may be holding the office of President, or acting as

President, during the term within which this Article becomes operative from holding the office of President or acting as President during the remainder of such term.

Section 2

This article shall be inoperative unless it shall have been ratified as an amendment to the Constitution by the legislatures of three-fourths of the several States within seven years from the date of its submission to the States by the Congress.

AMENDMENT 23

Section 1

The District constituting the seat of Government of the United States shall appoint in such manner as the Congress may direct:

A number of electors of President and Vice President equal to the whole number of Senators and Representatives in Congress to which the District would be entitled if it were a State, but in no event more than the least populous State; they shall be in addition to those appointed by the States, but they shall be considered, for the purposes of the election of President and Vice President, to be electors appointed by a State; and they shall meet in the District and perform such duties as provided by the twelfth article of amendment.

Section 2

The Congress shall have power to enforce this article by appropriate legislation.

AMENDMENT 24

Section 1

The right of citizens of the United States to vote in any primary or other election for President or Vice President, for electors for President or Vice President, or for Senator or Representative in Congress, shall not be denied or abridged by the United States or any State by reason of failure to pay any poll tax or other tax.

Section 2

The Congress shall have power to enforce this article by appropriate legislation.

AMENDMENT 25

Section 1

In case of the removal of the President from office or of his death or resignation, the Vice President shall become President.

Section 2

Whenever there is a vacancy in the office of the Vice President, the President shall nominate a Vice President who shall take office upon confirmation by a majority vote of both Houses of Congress.

Section 3

Whenever the President transmits to the President pro tempore of the Senate and the Speaker of the House of Representatives his written declaration that he is unable to discharge the powers and duties of his office, and until he transmits to them a written declaration to the contrary, such powers and duties shall be discharged by the Vice President as Acting President.

Section 4

[1] Whenever the Vice President and a majority of either the principal officers of the executive departments or of such other body as Congress may by law provide, transmit to the President pro tempore of the Senate and the Speaker of the House of Representatives their written declaration that the President is unable to discharge the powers and duties of his office, the Vice President shall immediately assume the powers and duties of the office as Acting President.

[2] Thereafter, when the President transmits to the President pro tempore of the Senate and the Speaker of the House of Representatives his written declaration that no inability exists, he shall resume the powers and duties of his office unless the Vice President and a majority of either the principal officers of the executive department or of such other body as Congress may by law provide, transmit within four days to the President pro tempore of the Senate and the Speaker of the House of Representatives their written declaration that the President is unable to discharge the powers and duties of his office. Thereupon Congress shall decide the issue, assembling within forty-eight hours for that purpose if not in session. If the Congress, within twenty-one days after receipt of the latter written declaration, or, if Congress is not in session, within twenty-one days after Congress is required to assemble, determines by two-thirds vote of both Houses that the President is unable to discharge the powers and duties of his office, the Vice President shall continue to discharge the same as Acting President; otherwise, the President shall resume the powers and duties of his office.

AMENDMENT 26

Section 1

The right of citizens of the United States, who are eighteen years of age or older, to vote shall not be denied or abridged by the United States or by any State on account of age.

Section 2

The Congress shall have power to enforce this article by appropriate legislation.

AMENDMENT 27

No law, varying the compensation for the services of the Senators and Representatives, shall take effect, until an election of Representatives shall have intervened.

APPENDIX B

THE ADMINISTRATIVE PROCEDURE ACT

■ ■ ■

THE ADMINISTRATIVE PROCEDURE ACT

5 U.S.C. §§ 551, 553–559, 701–706

§ 551. *Definitions*

For the purpose of this subchapter—

(1) "agency" means each authority of the Government of the United States, whether or not it is within or subject to review by another agency, but does not include—

(A) the Congress;

(B) the courts of the United States;

(C) the governments of the territories or possessions of the United States;

(D) the government of the District of Columbia;

or except as to the requirements of section 552 of this title—

(A) agencies composed of representatives of the parties or of representatives of organizations of the parties to the disputes determined by them;

(B) courts martial and military commissions;

(C) military authority exercised in the field in time of war or in occupied territory; or

(D) functions conferred by sections 1738, 1739, 1743, and 1744 of title 12; chapter 2 of title 41; subchapter II of chapter 471 of title 49; or sections 1884, 1891–1902, and former section 1641(b)(2), of title 50, appendix;

(2) "person" includes an individual, partnership, corporation, association, or public or private organization other than an agency;

(3) "party" includes a person or agency named or admitted as a party, or properly seeking and entitled as of right to be admitted as a party, in an agency proceeding, and a person or agency admitted by an agency as a party for limited purposes;

(4) "rule" means the whole or a part of an agency statement of general or particular applicability and future effect designed to implement, interpret, or prescribe law or policy or describing the organization, procedure, or practice requirements of an agency and includes the approval or prescription for the future of rates, wages, corporate or financial structures or reorganizations thereof, prices, facilities, appliances, services or allowances therefor or of valuations, costs, or accounting, or practices bearing on any of the foregoing;

(5) "rule making" means agency process for formulating, amending, or repealing a rule;

(6) "order" means the whole or a part of a final disposition, whether affirmative, negative, injunctive, or declaratory in form, of an agency in a matter other than rule making but including licensing;

(7) "adjudication" means agency process for the formulation of an order;

(8) "license" includes the whole or a part of an agency permit, certificate, approval, registration, charter, membership, statutory exemption or other form of permission;

(9) "licensing" includes agency process respecting the grant, renewal, denial, revocation, suspension, annulment, withdrawal, limitation, amendment, modification, or conditioning of a license;

(10) "sanction" includes the whole or a part of an agency—

(A) prohibition, requirement, limitation, or other condition affecting the freedom of a person;

(B) withholding of relief;

(C) imposition of penalty or fine;

(D) destruction, taking, seizure, or withholding of property;

(E) assessment of damages, reimbursement, restitution, compensation, costs, charges, or fees;

(F) requirement, revocation, or suspension of a license; or

(G) taking other compulsory or restrictive action;

(11) "relief" includes the whole or a part of an agency—

(A) grant of money, assistance, license, authority, exemption, exception, privilege, or remedy;

(B) recognition of a claim, right, immunity, privilege, exemption, or exception; or

(C) taking of other action on the application or petition of, and beneficial to, a person;

(12) "agency proceeding" means an agency process as defined by paragraphs (5), (7), and (9) of this section;

(13) "agency action" includes the whole or a part of an agency rule, order, license, sanction, relief, or the equivalent or denial thereof, or failure to act; and

(14) "ex parte communication" means an oral or written communication not on the public record with respect to which reasonable prior notice to all parties is not given, but it shall not include requests for status reports on any matter or proceeding covered by this subchapter.

[Section 552 appears in Appendix C; Sections 552a and 552b are omitted.]

§ 553. *Rule making*

(a) This section applies, according to the provisions thereof, except to the extent that there is involved—

(1) a military or foreign affairs function of the United States; or

(2) a matter relating to agency management or personnel or to public property, loans, grants, benefits, or contracts.

(b) General notice of proposed rule making shall be published in the Federal Register, unless persons subject thereto are named and either personally served or otherwise have actual notice thereof in accordance with law. The notice shall include—

(1) a statement of the time, place, and nature of public rule making proceedings;

(2) reference to the legal authority under which the rule is proposed; and

(3) either the terms or substance of the proposed rule or a description of the subjects and issues involved.

Except when notice or hearing is required by statute, this subsection does not apply—

(A) to interpretative rules, general statements of policy, or rules of agency organization, procedure, or practice; or

(B) when the agency for good cause finds (and incorporates the finding and a brief statement of reasons therefor in the rules issued) that notice and public procedure thereon are impracticable, unnecessary, or contrary to the public interest.

(c) After notice required by this section, the agency shall give interested persons an opportunity to participate in the rule making through submission of written data, views, or arguments with or without opportunity for oral presentation. After consideration of the relevant matter presented, the agency shall incorporate in the rules adopted a concise general statement of their basis and purpose. When rules are required by statute to be made on the record after opportunity for an agency hearing, sections 556 and 557 of this title apply instead of this subsection.

(d) The required publication or service of a substantive rule shall be made not less than 30 days before its effective date, except—

(1) a substantive rule which grants or recognizes an exemption or relieves a restriction;

(2) interpretative rules and statements of policy; or

(3) as otherwise provided by the agency for good cause found and published with the rule.

(e) Each agency shall give an interested person the right to petition for the issuance, amendment, or repeal of a rule.

§ 554. *Adjudications*

(a) This section applies, according to the provisions thereof, in every case of adjudication required by statute to be determined on the record after opportunity for an agency hearing, except to the extent that there is involved—

(1) a matter subject to a subsequent trial of the law and the facts de novo in a court;

(2) the selection or tenure of an employee, except a administrative law judge appointed under section 3105 of this title;

(3) proceedings in which decisions rest solely on inspections, tests, or elections;

(4) the conduct of military or foreign affairs functions;

(5) cases in which an agency is acting as an agent for a court; or

(6) the certification of worker representatives.

(b) Persons entitled to notice of an agency hearing shall be timely informed of—

(1) the time, place, and nature of the hearing;

(2) the legal authority and jurisdiction under which the hearing is to be held; and

(3) the matters of fact and law asserted.

When private persons are the moving parties, other parties to the proceeding shall give prompt notice of issues controverted in fact or law; and in other instances agencies may by rule require responsive pleading. In fixing the time and place for hearings, due regard shall be had for the convenience and necessity of the parties or their representatives.

(c)   The agency shall give all interested parties opportunity for—

(1)   the submission and consideration of facts, arguments, offers of settlement, or proposals of adjustment when time, the nature of the proceeding, and the public interest permit; and

(2)   to the extent that the parties are unable so to determine a controversy by consent, hearing and decision on notice and in accordance with sections 556 and 557 of this title.

(d)   The employee who presides at the reception of evidence pursuant to section 556 of this title shall make the recommended decision or initial decision required by section 557 of this title, unless he becomes unavailable to the agency. Except to the extent required for the disposition of ex parte matters as authorized by law, such an employee may not—

(1)   consult a person or party on a fact in issue, unless on notice and opportunity for all parties to participate; or

(2)   be responsible to or subject to the supervision or direction of an employee or agent engaged in the performance of investigative or prosecuting functions for an agency.

An employee or agent engaged in the performance of investigative or prosecuting functions for an agency in a case may not, in that or a factually related case, participate or advise in the decision, recommended decision, or agency review pursuant to section 557 of this title, except as witness or counsel in public proceedings. This subsection does not apply—

(A)   in determining applications for initial licenses;

(B)   to proceedings involving the validity or application of rates, facilities, or practices of public utilities or carriers; or

(C)   to the agency or a member or members of the body comprising the agency.

(e)   The agency, with like effect as in the case of other orders, and in its sound discretion, may issue a declaratory order to terminate a controversy or remove uncertainty.

§ 555. *Ancillary matters*

(a)   This section applies, according to the provisions thereof, except as otherwise provided by this subchapter.

(b)   A person compelled to appear in person before an agency or representative thereof is entitled to be accompanied, represented, and advised by counsel or, if permitted by the agency, by other qualified representative. A party is entitled to appear in person or by or with counsel or other duly qualified representative in an agency proceeding. So far as the orderly conduct of public business permits, an interested person may appear before an agency or its responsible employees for the presentation, adjustment, or determination of an issue, request, or controversy in a proceeding, whether interlocutory, summary, or otherwise, or in connection with an agency function. With due regard for the convenience and necessity of the parties or their representatives and within a reasonable time, each agency shall proceed to conclude a matter presented to it. This subsection does not grant or deny a person who is not a lawyer the right to appear for or represent others before an agency or in an agency proceeding.

(c) Process, requirement of a report, inspection, or other investigative act or demand may not be issued, made, or enforced except as authorized by law. A person compelled to submit data or evidence is entitled to retain or, on payment of lawfully prescribed costs, procure a copy or transcript thereof, except that in a nonpublic investigatory proceeding the witness may for good cause be limited to inspection of the official transcript of his testimony.

(d) Agency subpenas authorized by law shall be issued to a party on request and, when required by rules of procedure, on a statement or showing of general relevance and reasonable scope of the evidence sought. On contest, the court shall sustain the subpena or similar process or demand to the extent that it is found to be in accordance with law. In a proceeding for enforcement, the court shall issue an order requiring the appearance of the witness or the production of the evidence or data within a reasonable time under penalty of punishment for contempt in case of contumacious failure to comply.

(e) Prompt notice shall be given of the denial in whole or in part of a written application, petition, or other request of an interested person made in connection with any agency proceeding. Except in affirming a prior denial or when the denial is self-explanatory, the notice shall be accompanied by a brief statement of the grounds for denial.

§ 556. *Hearings; presiding employees; powers and duties; burden of proof; evidence; record as basis of decision*

(a) This section applies, according to the provisions thereof, to hearings required by section 553 or 554 of this title to be conducted in accordance with this section.

(b) There shall preside at the taking of evidence—

(1) the agency;

(2) one or more members of the body which comprises the agency; or

(3) one or more administrative law judges appointed under section 3105 of this title.

This subchapter does not supersede the conduct of specified classes of proceedings, in whole or in part, by or before boards or other employees specially provided for by or designated under statute. The functions of presiding employees and of employees participating in decisions in accordance with section 557 of this title shall be conducted in an impartial manner. A presiding or participating employee may at any time disqualify himself. On the filing in good faith of a timely and sufficient affidavit of personal bias or other disqualification of a presiding or participating employee, the agency shall determine the matter as a part of the record and decision in the case.

(c)   Subject to published rules of the agency and within its powers, employees presiding at hearings may—

(1)   administer oaths and affirmations;

(2)   issue subpenas authorized by law;

(3)   rule on offers of proof and receive relevant evidence;

(4)   take depositions or have depositions taken when the ends of justice would be served;

(5)   regulate the course of the hearing;

(6)   hold conferences for the settlement or simplification of the issues by consent of the parties or by the use of alternative means of dispute resolution as provided in subchapter IV of this chapter;

(7)   inform the parties as to the availability of one or more alternative means of dispute resolution, and encourage use of such methods;

(8)   require the attendance at any conference held pursuant to paragraph (6) of at least one representative of each party who has authority to negotiate concerning resolution of issues in controversy;

(9)   dispose of procedural requests or similar matters;

(10) make or recommend decisions in accordance with section 557 of this title; and

(11) take other action authorized by agency rule consistent with this subchapter.

(d)   Except as otherwise provided by statute, the proponent of a rule or order has the burden of proof. Any oral or documentary evidence may be received, but the agency as a matter of policy shall provide for the exclusion of irrelevant, immaterial, or unduly repetitious evidence. A sanction may not be imposed or rule or order issued except on consideration of the whole record or those parts thereof cited by a party and supported by and in accordance with the reliable, probative, and substantial evidence. The agency may, to the extent consistent with the interests of justice and the policy of the underlying statutes administered by the agency, consider a violation of section 557(d) of this title sufficient grounds for a decision adverse to a party who has knowingly committed such violation or knowingly caused such violation to occur. A party is entitled to present his case or defense by oral or documentary evidence, to submit rebuttal evidence, and to conduct such cross-examination as may be required for a full and true disclosure of the facts. In rule making or determining claims for money or benefits or applications for initial licenses an agency may, when a party will not be prejudiced thereby, adopt procedures for the submission of all or part of the evidence in written form.

(e) The transcript of testimony and exhibits, together with all papers and requests filed in the proceeding, constitutes the exclusive record for decision in accordance with section 557 of this title and, on payment of lawfully prescribed costs, shall be made available to the parties. When an agency decision rests on official notice of a material fact not appearing in the evidence in the record, a party is entitled, on timely request, to an opportunity to show the contrary.

§ 557. *Initial decisions; conclusiveness; review by agency; submissions by parties; contents of decisions; record*

(a) This section applies, according to the provisions thereof, when a hearing is required to be conducted in accordance with section 556 of this title.

(b) When the agency did not preside at the reception of the evidence, the presiding employee or, in cases not subject to section 554(d) of this title, an employee qualified to preside at hearings pursuant to section 556 of this title, shall initially decide the case unless the agency requires, either in specific cases or by general rule, the entire record to be certified to it for decision. When the presiding employee makes an initial decision, that decision then becomes the decision of the agency without further proceedings unless there is an appeal to, or review on motion of, the agency within time provided by rule. On appeal from or review of the initial decision, the agency has all the powers which it would have in making the initial decision except as it may limit the issues on notice or by rule. When the agency makes the decision without having presided at the reception of the evidence, the presiding employee or an employee qualified to preside at hearings pursuant to section 556 of this title shall first recommend a decision, except that in rule making or determining applications for initial licenses—

(1) instead thereof the agency may issue a tentative decision or one of its responsible employees may recommend a decision; or

(2) this procedure may be omitted in a case in which the agency finds on the record that due and timely execution of its functions imperatively and unavoidably so requires.

(c) Before a recommended, initial, or tentative decision, or a decision on agency review of the decision of subordinate employees, the parties are entitled to a reasonable opportunity to submit for the consideration of the employees participating in the decisions—

(1) proposed findings and conclusions; or

(2) exceptions to the decisions or recommended decisions of subordinate employees or to tentative agency decisions; and

(3) supporting reasons for the exceptions or proposed findings or conclusions.

The record shall show the ruling on each finding, conclusion, or exception presented. All decisions, including initial, recommended, and tentative decisions, are a part of the record and shall include a statement of—

(A) findings and conclusions, and the reasons or basis therefor, on all the material issues of fact, law, or discretion presented on the record; and

(B) the appropriate rule, order, sanction, relief, or denial thereof.

(d)(1)   In any agency proceeding which is subject to subsection (a) of this section, except to the extent required for the disposition of ex parte matters as authorized by law—

(A) no interested person outside the agency shall make or knowingly cause to be made to any member of the body comprising the agency, administrative law judge, or other employee who is or may reasonably be expected to be involved in the decisional process of the proceeding, an ex parte communication relevant to the merits of the proceeding;

(B) no member of the body comprising the agency, administrative law judge, or other employee who is or may reasonably be expected to be involved in the decisional process of the proceeding, shall make or knowingly cause to be made to any interested person outside the agency an ex parte communication relevant to the merits of the proceeding;

(C) a member of the body comprising the agency, administrative law judge, or other employee who is or may reasonably be expected to be involved in the decisional process of such proceeding who receives, or who makes or knowingly causes to be made, a communication prohibited by this subsection shall place on the public record of the proceeding:

(i)   all such written communications;

(ii) memoranda stating the substance of all such oral communications; and

(iii) all written responses, and memoranda stating the substance of all oral responses, to the materials described in clauses (i) and (ii) of this subparagraph;

(D) upon receipt of a communication knowingly made or knowingly caused to be made by a party in violation of this subsection, the agency, administrative law judge, or other employee presiding at the hearing may, to the extent consistent with the interests of justice and the policy of the underlying statutes, require the party to show cause why his claim or interest in the proceeding should not be dismissed, denied, disregarded, or otherwise adversely affected on account of such violation; and

(E) the prohibitions of this subsection shall apply beginning at such time as the agency may designate, but in no case shall they begin to apply later than the time at which a proceeding is noticed for hearing unless the person responsible for the communication has knowledge that it will be noticed, in which case the prohibitions shall apply beginning at the time of his acquisition of such knowledge.

(2) This subsection does not constitute authority to withhold information from Congress.

§ 558. *Imposition of sanctions; determination of applications for licenses; suspension, revocation, and expiration of licenses*

(a) This section applies, according to the provisions thereof, to the exercise of a power or authority.

(b) A sanction may not be imposed or a substantive rule or order issued except within jurisdiction delegated to the agency and as authorized by law.

(c) When application is made for a license required by law, the agency, with due regard for the rights and privileges of all the interested parties or adversely affected persons and within a reasonable time, shall set and complete proceedings required to be conducted in accordance with sections 556 and 557 of this title or other proceedings required by law and shall make its decision. Except in cases of willfulness or those in which public health, interest, or safety requires otherwise, the withdrawal, suspension, revocation, or annulment of a license is lawful only if, before the institution of agency proceedings therefor, the licensee has been given—

(1) notice by the agency in writing of the facts or conduct which may warrant the action; and

(2) opportunity to demonstrate or achieve compliance with all lawful requirements.

When the licensee has made timely and sufficient application for a renewal or a new license in accordance with agency rules, a license with reference to an activity of a continuing nature does not expire until the application has been finally determined by the agency.

§ 559. *Effect on other laws; effect of subsequent statute*

This subchapter, chapter 7, and sections 1305, 3105, 3344, 4301(2)(E), 5372, and 7521 of this title, and the provisions of section 5335(a)(B) of this title that relate to administrative law judges, do not limit or repeal additional requirements imposed by statute or otherwise recognized by law. Except as otherwise required by law, requirements or privileges relating to evidence or procedure apply equally to agencies and persons. Each agency is granted the authority necessary to comply with the requirements of this subchapter through the issuance of rules or otherwise. Subsequent statute may not be held to supersede or modify this subchapter, chapter 7, sections 1305, 3105, 3344, 4301(2)(E), 5372, or 7521 of this title, or the provisions of section 5335(a)(B) of this title that relate to administrative law judges, except to the extent that it does so expressly.

[Sections 601–12 appear in Appendix D]

§ 701. *Application; definitions*

(a) This chapter applies, according to the provisions thereof, except to the extent that—

(1) statutes preclude judicial review; or

(2) agency action is committed to agency discretion by law.

(b) For the purpose of this chapter—

(1) [the term "agency" for purposes of sections 701–06 has the same definition provided in section 551(1)];

(2) "person", "rule", "order", "license", "sanction", "relief", and "agency action" have the meanings given them by section 551 of this title.

§ 702. *Right of review*

A person suffering legal wrong because of agency action, or adversely affected or aggrieved by agency action within the meaning of a relevant statute, is entitled to judicial review thereof. An action in a court of the United States seeking relief other than money damages and stating a claim that an agency or an officer or employee thereof acted or failed to act in an official capacity or under color of legal authority shall not be dismissed nor relief therein be denied on the ground that it is against the United States or that the United States is an indispensable party. The United States may be named as a defendant in any such action, and a judgment or decree may be entered against the United States: Provided, That any mandatory or injunctive decree shall specify the Federal officer or officers (by name or by title), and their successors in office, personally responsible for compliance. Nothing herein (1) affects other limitations on judicial review or the power or duty of the court to dismiss any action or deny relief on any other appropriate legal or equitable ground; or (2) confers authority to grant relief if any other statute that grants consent to suit expressly or impliedly forbids the relief which is sought.

§ 703. *Form and venue of proceeding*

The form of proceeding for judicial review is the special statutory review proceeding relevant to the subject matter in a court specified by statute or, in the absence or inadequacy thereof, any applicable form of legal action, including actions for declaratory judgments or writs of prohibitory or mandatory injunction or habeas corpus, in a court of competent jurisdiction. If no special statutory review proceeding is applicable, the action for judicial review may be brought against the United States, the agency by its official title, or the appropriate officer. Except to the extent that prior, adequate, and exclusive opportunity for judicial review is provided by law, agency action is subject to judicial review in civil or criminal proceedings for judicial enforcement.

§ 704. *Actions reviewable*

Agency action made reviewable by statute and final agency action for which there is no other adequate remedy in a court are subject to judicial review. A preliminary, procedural, or intermediate agency action or ruling not directly reviewable is subject to review on the review of the final agency action. Except as otherwise expressly required by statute, agency action otherwise final is final for the purposes of this section whether or not there has been presented or determined an application for a declaratory order, for any form of reconsideration, or, unless the agency otherwise requires by rule and provides that the action meanwhile is inoperative, for an appeal to superior agency authority.

§ 705. *Relief pending review*

When an agency finds that justice so requires, it may postpone the effective date of action taken by it, pending judicial review. On such conditions as may be required and to the extent necessary to prevent irreparable injury, the reviewing court, including the court to which a case may be taken on appeal from or on application for certiorari or other writ to a reviewing court, may issue all necessary and appropriate process to postpone the effective date of an agency action or to preserve status or rights pending conclusion of the review proceedings.

§ 706. *Scope of review*

To the extent necessary to decision and when presented, the reviewing court shall decide all relevant questions of law, interpret constitutional and statutory provisions, and determine the meaning or applicability of the terms of an agency action. The reviewing court shall—

(1) compel agency action unlawfully withheld or unreasonably delayed; and

(2) hold unlawful and set aside agency action, findings, and conclusions found to be—

(A) arbitrary, capricious, an abuse of discretion, or otherwise not in accordance with law;

(B) contrary to constitutional right, power, privilege, or immunity;

(C) in excess of statutory jurisdiction, authority, or limitations, or short of statutory right;

(D) without observance of procedure required by law;

(E) unsupported by substantial evidence in a case subject to sections 556 and 557 of this title or otherwise reviewed on the record of an agency hearing provided by statute; or

(F) unwarranted by the facts to the extent that the facts are subject to trial de novo by the reviewing court.

In making the foregoing determinations, the court shall review the whole record or those parts of it cited by a party, and due account shall be taken of the rule of prejudicial error.

APPENDIX C

GOVERNMENT RECORDS AND MEETINGS

■ ■ ■

THE FREEDOM OF INFORMATION ACT
5 U.S.C. § 552

§ 552. *Public information; agency rules, opinions, orders, records, and proceedings*

(a) Each agency shall make available to the public information as follows:

(1) Each agency shall separately state and currently publish in the Federal Register for the guidance of the public—

(A) descriptions of its central and field organization and the established places at which, the employees (and in the case of a uniformed service, the members) from whom, and the methods whereby, the public may obtain information, make submittals or requests, or obtain decisions;

(B) statements of the general course and method by which its functions are channeled and determined, including the nature and requirements of all formal and informal procedures available;

(C) rules of procedure, descriptions of forms available or the places at which forms may be obtained, and instructions as to the scope and contents of all papers, reports, or examinations;

(D) substantive rules of general applicability adopted as authorized by law, and statements of general policy or interpretations of general applicability formulated and adopted by the agency; and

(E) each amendment, revision, or repeal of the foregoing.

Except to the extent that a person has actual and timely notice of the terms thereof, a person may not in any manner be required to resort to, or be adversely affected by, a matter required to be published in the Federal Register and not so published. For the purpose of this paragraph, matter reasonably available to the class of persons affected thereby is deemed published in the Federal Register when incorporated by reference therein with the approval of the Director of the Federal Register.

(2) Each agency, in accordance with published rules, shall make available for public inspection and copying—

(A) final opinions, including concurring and dissenting opinions, as well as orders, made in the adjudication of cases;

(B) those statements of policy and interpretations which have been adopted by the agency and are not published in the Federal Register;

(C) administrative staff manuals and instructions to staff that affect a member of the public;

(D) copies of all records, regardless of form or format, which have been released to any person under paragraph (3) and which, because of the nature of their subject matter, the agency determines have become or are likely to become the subject of subsequent requests for substantially the same records; and

(E) a general index of the records referred to under subparagraph (D);

unless the materials are promptly published and copies offered for sale. For records created on or after November 1, 1996, within one year after such date, each agency shall make such records available, including by computer telecommunications or, if computer telecommunications means have not been established by the agency, by other electronic means. To the extent required to prevent a clearly unwarranted invasion of personal privacy, an agency may delete identifying details when it makes available or publishes an opinion, statement of policy, interpretation, staff manual, instruction, or copies of records referred to in subparagraph (D). However, in each case the justification for the deletion shall be explained fully in writing, and the extent of such deletion shall be indicated on the portion of the record which is made available or published, unless including that indication would harm an interest protected by the exemption in subsection (b) under which the deletion is made. If technically feasible, the extent of the deletion shall be indicated at the place in the record where the deletion was made. Each agency shall also maintain and make available for public inspection and copying current indexes providing identifying information for the public as to any matter issued, adopted, or promulgated after July 4, 1967, and required by this paragraph to be made available or published. Each agency shall promptly publish, quarterly or more frequently, and distribute (by sale or otherwise) copies of each index or supplements thereto unless it determines by order published in the Federal Register that the publication would be unnecessary and impracticable, in which case the agency shall nonetheless provide copies of such index on request at a cost not to exceed the direct cost of duplication. Each agency shall make the index referred to in subparagraph (E) available by computer telecommunications by December 31, 1999. A final order, opinion, statement of policy, interpretation, or staff manual or instruction that affects a member of the public may be relied on, used, or cited as precedent by an agency against a party other than an agency only if—

(i) it has been indexed and either made available or published as provided by this paragraph; or

(ii) the party has actual and timely notice of the terms thereof.

(3)(A) Except with respect to the records made available under paragraphs (1) and (2) of this subsection, each agency, upon any request for records which (i) reasonably describes such records and (ii) is made in accordance with published rules stating the time, place, fees (if any), and procedures to be followed, shall make the records promptly available to any person.

(B) In making any record available to a person under this paragraph, an agency shall provide the record in any form or format requested by the person if the record is readily reproducible by the agency in that form or format. Each agency shall make reasonable efforts to maintain its records in forms or formats that are reproducible for purposes of this section.

(C) In responding under this paragraph to a request for records, an agency shall make reasonable efforts to search for the records in electronic form or format, except when such efforts would significantly interfere with the operation of the agency's automated information system.

(D) For purposes of this paragraph, the term "search" means to review, manually or by automated means, agency records for the purpose of locating those records which are responsive to a request.

(4)(A)(i) In order to carry out the provisions of this section, each agency shall promulgate regulations, pursuant to notice and receipt of public comment, specifying the schedule of fees applicable to the processing of requests under this section and establishing procedures and guidelines for determining when such fees should be waived or reduced. Such schedule shall conform to the guidelines which shall be promulgated, pursuant to notice and receipt of public comment, by the Director of the Office of Management and Budget and which shall provide for a uniform schedule of fees for all agencies.

(ii) Such agency regulations shall provide that—

(I) fees shall be limited to reasonable standard charges for document search, duplication, and review, when records are requested for commercial use;

(II) fees shall be limited to reasonable standard charges for document duplication when records are not sought for commercial use and the request is made by an educational or noncommercial scientific institution, whose purpose is scholarly or scientific research; or a representative of the news media; and

(III) for any request not described in (I) or (II), fees shall be limited to reasonable standard charges for document search and duplication.

(iii) Documents shall be furnished without any charge or at a charge reduced below the fees established under clause (ii) if disclosure of the information is in the public interest because it is likely to contribute significantly to public understanding of the operations or activities of the government and is not primarily in the commercial interest of the requester.

(iv) Fee schedules shall provide for the recovery of only the direct costs of search, duplication, or review. Review costs shall include only the direct costs incurred during the initial examination of a document for the purposes of determining whether the documents must be disclosed under this section and for the purposes of withholding any portions exempt from disclosure under this section. Review costs may not include any costs incurred in resolving issues of law or policy that may be raised in the course of processing a request under this section. No fee may be charged by any agency under this section—

(I)   if the costs of routine collection and processing of the fee are likely to equal or exceed the amount of the fee; or

(II) for any request described in clause (ii)(II) or (III) of this subparagraph for the first two hours of search time or for the first one hundred pages of duplication.

(v) No agency may require advance payment of any fee unless the requester has previously failed to pay fees in a timely fashion, or the agency has determined that the fee will exceed $250.

(vi) Nothing in this subparagraph shall supersede fees chargeable under a statute specifically providing for setting the level of fees for particular types of records.

(vii) In any action by a requester regarding the waiver of fees under this section, the court shall determine the matter de novo: Provided, That the court's review of the matter shall be limited to the record before the agency.

(B) On complaint, the district court of the United States in the district in which the complainant resides, or has his principal place of business, or in which the agency records are situated, or in the District of Columbia, has jurisdiction to enjoin the agency from withholding agency records and to order the production of any agency records improperly withheld from the complainant. In such a case the court shall determine the matter de novo, and may examine the contents of such agency records in camera to determine whether such records or any part thereof shall be withheld under any of the exemptions set forth in subsection (b) of this section, and the burden is on the agency to sustain its action. In addition to any other matters to which a court accords substantial weight, a court shall accord substantial weight to an affidavit of an agency concerning the agency's determination as to technical feasibility under paragraph (2)(C) and subsection (b) and reproducibility under paragraph (3)(B).

(C) Notwithstanding any other provision of law, the defendant shall serve an answer or otherwise plead to any complaint made under this subsection within thirty days after service upon the defendant of the pleading in which such complaint is made, unless the court otherwise directs for good cause shown.

[(D) Repealed. Pub.L. 98–620, Title IV, § 402(2), Nov. 8, 1984, 98 Stat. 3357].

(E) The court may assess against the United States reasonable attorney fees and other litigation costs reasonably incurred in any case under this section in which the complainant has substantially prevailed.

(F) Whenever the court orders the production of any agency records improperly withheld from the complainant and assesses against the United States reasonable attorney fees and other litigation costs, and the court additionally issues a written finding that the circumstances surrounding the withholding raise questions whether agency personnel acted arbitrarily or capriciously with respect to the withholding, the Special Counsel shall promptly initiate a proceeding to determine whether disciplinary action is warranted against the officer or employee who was primarily responsible for the withholding. The Special Counsel, after investigation and consideration of the evidence submitted, shall submit his findings and recommendations to the administrative authority of the agency concerned and shall send copies of the findings and recommendations to the officer or employee or his representative. The administrative authority shall take the corrective action that the Special Counsel recommends.

(G) In the event of noncompliance with the order of the court, the district court may punish for contempt the responsible employee, and in the case of a uniformed service, the responsible member.

(5) Each agency having more than one member shall maintain and make available for public inspection a record of the final votes of each member in every agency proceeding.

(6)(A) Each agency, upon any request for records made under paragraph (1), (2), or (3) of this subsection, shall—

(i) determine within ten days (excepting Saturdays, Sundays, and legal public holidays) after the receipt of any such request whether to comply with such request and shall immediately notify the person making such request of such determination and the reasons therefor, and of the right of such person to appeal to the head of the agency any adverse determination; and

(ii) make a determination with respect to any appeal within twenty days (excepting Saturdays, Sundays, and legal public holidays) after the receipt of such appeal. If on appeal the denial of the request for records is in whole or in part upheld, the agency shall notify the person making such request of the provisions for judicial review of that determination under paragraph (4) of this subsection.

(B) In unusual circumstances as specified in this subparagraph, the time limits prescribed in either clause (i) or clause (ii) of subparagraph (A) may be extended by written notice to the person making such request setting forth the reasons for such extension and the date on which a determination is expected to be dispatched. No such notice shall specify a date that would result in an extension for more than ten working days. As used in this subparagraph, "unusual circumstances" means, but only to the extent reasonably necessary to the proper processing of the particular request—

(i) the need to search for and collect the requested records from field facilities or other establishments that are separate from the office processing the request;

(ii) the need to search for, collect, and appropriately examine a voluminous amount of separate and distinct records which are demanded in a single request; or

(iii) the need for consultation, which shall be conducted with all practicable speed, with another agency having a substantial interest in the determination of the request or among two or more components of the agency having substantial subject-matter interest therein.

(b) This section does not apply to matters that are—

(1)(A) specifically authorized under criteria established by an Executive order to be kept secret in the interest of national defense or foreign policy and (B) are in fact properly classified pursuant to such Executive order;

(2) related solely to the internal personnel rules and practices of an agency;

(3) specifically exempted from disclosure by statute (other than section 552b of this title), provided that such statute (A) requires that the matters be withheld from the public in such a manner as to leave no discretion on the issue, or (B) establishes particular criteria for withholding or refers to particular types of matters to be withheld;

(4) trade secrets and commercial or financial information obtained from a person and privileged or confidential;

(5) inter-agency or intra-agency memorandums or letters which would not be available by law to a party other than an agency in litigation with the agency;

(6) personnel and medical files and similar files the disclosure of which would constitute a clearly unwarranted invasion of personal privacy;

(7) records or information compiled for law enforcement purposes, but only to the extent that the production of such law enforcement records or information (A) could reasonably be expected to interfere with enforcement proceedings, (B) would deprive a person of a right to a fair trial or an impartial adjudication, (C) could reasonably be expected to constitute an unwarranted invasion of personal privacy, (D) could reasonably be expected to disclose the identity of a confidential source, including a State, local, or foreign agency or authority or any private institution which furnished information on a confidential basis, and, in the case of a record or information compiled by criminal law enforcement authority in the course of a criminal investigation or by an agency conducting a lawful national security intelligence investigation, information furnished by a confidential source, (E) would disclose techniques and procedures for law enforcement investigations or prosecutions, or would disclose guidelines for law enforcement investigations or prosecutions if such disclosure could reasonably be expected to risk circumvention of the law, or (F) could reasonably be expected to endanger the life or physical safety of any individual;

(8) contained in or related to examination, operating, or condition reports prepared by, on behalf of, or for the use of an agency responsible for the regulation or supervision of financial institutions; or

(9) geological and geophysical information and data, including maps, concerning wells.

Any reasonably segregable portion of a record shall be provided to any person requesting such record after deletion of the portions which are exempt under this subsection. The amount of information deleted shall be indicated on the released portion of the record, unless including that indication would harm an interest protected by the exemption in this subsection under which the deletion is made. If technically feasible, the amount of the information shall be indicated at the place in the record where such deletion is made.

(c)(1)   Whenever a request is made which involves access to records described in subsection (b)(7)(A) and—

(A) the investigation or proceeding involves a possible violation of criminal law; and

(B) there is reason to believe that (i) the subject of the investigation or proceeding is not aware of its pendency, and (ii) disclosure of the existence of the records could reasonably be expected to interfere with enforcement proceedings,

the agency may, during only such time as that circumstance continues, treat the records as not subject to the requirements of this section.

(2) Whenever informant records maintained by a criminal law enforcement agency under an informant's name or personal identifier are requested by a third party according to the informant's name or personal identifier, the agency may treat the records as not subject to the requirements of this section unless the informant's status as an informant has been officially confirmed.

(3) Whenever a request is made which involves access to records maintained by the Federal Bureau of Investigation pertaining to foreign intelligence or counterintelligence, or international terrorism, and the existence of the records is classified information as provided in subsection (b)(1), the Bureau may, as long as the existence of the records remains classified information, treat the records as not subject to the requirements of this section.

(d) This section does not authorize withholding of information or limit the availability of records to the public, except as specifically stated in this section. This section is not authority to withhold information from Congress.

(e)(1)   On or before February 1 of each year, each agency shall submit to the Attorney General of the United States a report which shall cover the preceding fiscal year and which shall include—

(A) the number of determinations made by the agency not to comply with requests for records made to such agency under subsection (a) and the reasons for each such determination;

(B)(i)   the number of appeals made by persons under subsection (a)(6), the result of such appeals, and the reason for the action upon each appeal that results in a denial of information; and

(ii) a complete list of all statutes that the agency relies upon to authorize the agency to withhold information under subsection (b)(3), a description of whether a court has upheld the decision of the agency to withhold information under each such statute, and a concise description of the scope of any information withheld;

(C) the number of requests for records pending before the agency as of September 30 of the preceding year, and the median number of days that such requests had been pending before the agency as of that date;

(D) the number of requests for records received by the agency and the number of requests which the agency processed;

(E) the median number of days taken by the agency to process different types of requests;

(F) the total amount of fees collected by the agency for processing requests; and

(G) the number of full-time staff of the agency devoted to processing requests for records under this section, and the total amount expended by the agency for processing such requests.

(2) Each agency shall make each such report available to the public including by computer telecommunications, or if computer telecommunications means have not been established by the agency, by other electronic means.

(3) The Attorney General of the United States shall make each report which has been made available by electronic means available at a single electronic access point. The Attorney General of the United States shall notify the Chairman and ranking minority member of the Committee on Government Reform and Oversight of the House of Representatives and the Chairman and ranking minority member of the Committees on Governmental Affairs and the Judiciary of the Senate, no later than April 1 of the year in which each such report is issued, that such reports are available by electronic means.

(4) The Attorney General of the United States, in consultation with the Director of the Office of Management and Budget, shall develop reporting and performance guidelines in connection with reports required by this subsection by October 1, 1997, and may establish additional requirements for such reports as the Attorney General determines may be useful.

(5) The Attorney General of the United States shall submit an annual report on or before April 1 of each calendar year which shall include for the prior calendar year a listing of the number of cases arising under this section, the exemption involved in each case, the disposition of such case, and the cost, fees, and penalties assessed under subparagraphs (E), (F), and (G) of subsection (a)(4). Such report shall also include a description of the efforts undertaken by the Department of Justice to encourage agency compliance with this section.

(f) For purposes of this section, the term—

(1) "agency" as defined in section 551(1) of this title includes any executive department, military department, Government corporation, Government controlled corporation, or other establishment in the executive branch of the Government (including the Executive Office of the President), or any independent regulatory agency; and

(2) "record" and any other term used in this section in reference to information includes any information that would be an agency record subject to the requirements of this section when maintained by an agency in any format, including an electronic format.

(g) The head of each agency shall prepare and make publicly available upon request, reference material or a guide for requesting records or information from the agency, subject to the exemptions in subsection (b), including—

(1) an index of all major information systems of the agency;

(2) a description of major information and record locator systems maintained by the agency; and

(3) a handbook for obtaining various types and categories of public information from the agency pursuant to chapter 35 of title 44, and under this section.

THE PRIVACY ACT

5 U.S.C. § 552a

[Omitted]

THE GOVERNMENT IN THE SUNSHINE ACT

5 U.S.C. § 552b

[Omitted]

APPENDIX D

EXECUTIVE ORDERS

■ ■ ■

EXECUTIVE ORDER NO. 12291
46 Fed. Reg. 13193, Feb. 17, 1981

By the authority vested in me as President by the Constitution and laws of the United States of America, and in order to reduce the burdens of existing and future regulations, increase agency accountability for regulatory actions, provide for presidential oversight of the regulatory process, minimize duplication and conflict of regulations, and insure well-reasoned regulations, it is hereby ordered as follows:

Sec 1. *Definitions.* For the purposes of this Order:

(a) 'Regulation' or 'rule' means an agency statement of general applicability and future effect designed to implement, interpret, or prescribe law or policy or describing the procedure or practice requirements of an agency, but does not include:

(1) Administrative actions governed by the provisions of Sections 556 and 557 of Title 5 of the United States Code;

(2) Regulations issued with respect to a military or foreign affairs function of the United States; or

(3) Regulations related to agency organization, management, or personnel.

(b) 'Major rule' means any regulation that is likely to result in:

(1) An annual effect on the economy of $100 million or more;

(2) A major increase in costs or prices for consumers, individual industries, Federal, State, or local government agencies, or geographic regions; or

(3) Significant adverse effects on competition, employment, investment, productivity, innovation, or on the ability of United States-based enterprises to compete with foreign-based enterprises in domestic or export markets.

(c) 'Director' means the Director of the Office of Management and Budget.

(d) 'Agency' means any authority of the United States that is an 'agency' under 44 U.S.C. 3502(1), excluding those agencies specified in 44 U.S.C. 3502(10).

(e) 'Task Force' means the Presidential Task Force on Regulatory Relief.

Sec. 2. *General Requirements.* In promulgating new regulations, reviewing existing regulations, and developing legislative proposals concerning regulation, all agencies, to the extent permitted by law, shall adhere to the following requirements:

(a) Administrative decisions shall be based on adequate information concerning the need for and consequences of proposed government action;

(b) Regulatory action shall not be undertaken unless the potential benefits to society for the regulation outweigh the potential costs to society;

(c) Regulatory objectives shall be chosen to maximize the net benefits to society;

(d) Among alternative approaches to any given regulatory objective, the alternative involving the least net cost to society shall be chosen; and

(e) Agencies shall set regulatory priorities with the aim of maximizing the aggregate net benefits to society, taking into account the condition of the particular industries affected by regulations, the condition of the national economy, and other regulatory actions contemplated for the future.

Sec. 3. *Regulatory Impact Analysis and Review.*

(a) In order to implement Section 2 of this Order, each agency shall, in connection with every major rule, prepare, and to the extent permitted by law consider, a Regulatory Impact Analysis. Such Analysis may be combined with any Regulatory Flexibility Analyses performed under 5 U.S.C. 603 and 604.

(b) Each agency shall initially determine whether a rule it intends to propose or to issue is a major rule, *provided that*, the Director, subject to the direction of the Task Force, shall have authority, in accordance with Sections 1(b) and 2 of this Order, to prescribe criteria for making such determinations, to order a rule to be treated as a major rule, and to require any set of related rules to be considered together as a major rule.

(c) Except as provided in Section 8 of this Order, agencies shall prepare Regulatory Impact Analyses of major rules and transmit them, along with all notices of proposed rulemaking and all final rules, to the Director as follows:

(1) If no notice of proposed rulemaking is to be published for a proposed major rule that is not an emergency rule, the agency shall

prepare only a final Regulatory Impact Analysis, which shall be transmitted, along with the proposed rule, to the Director at least 60 days prior to the publication of the major rule as a final rule;

(2) With respect to all other major rules, the agency shall prepare a preliminary Regulatory Impact Analysis, which shall be transmitted, along with a notice of proposed rulemaking, to the Director at least 60 days prior to the publication of a notice of proposed rulemaking, and a final Regulatory Impact Analysis, which shall be transmitted along with the final rule at least 30 days prior to the publication of the major rule as a final rule;

(3) For all rules other than major rules, agencies shall submit to the Director, at least 10 days prior to publication, every notice of proposed rulemaking and final rule.

(d) To permit each proposed major rule to be analyzed in light of the requirements stated in Section 2 of this Order, each preliminary and final Regulatory Impact Analysis shall contain the following information:

(1) A description of the potential benefits of the rule, including any beneficial effects that cannot be quantified in monetary terms, and the identification of those likely to receive the benefits;

(2) A description of the potential costs of the rule, including any adverse effects that cannot be quantified in monetary terms, and the identification of those likely to bear the costs;

(3) A determination of the potential net benefits of the rule, including an evaluation of effects that cannot be quantified in monetary terms;

(4) A description of alternative approaches that could substantially achieve the same regulatory goal at lower cost, together with an analysis of this potential benefit and costs and a brief explanation of the legal reasons why such alternatives, if proposed, could not be adopted; and

(5) Unless covered by the description required under paragraph (4) of this subsection, an explanation of any legal reasons why the rule cannot be based on the requirements set forth in Section 2 of this Order.

(e)(1) The Director, subject to the direction of the Task Force, which shall resolve any issues raised under this Order or ensure that they are presented to the President, is authorized to review any preliminary or final Regulatory Impact Analysis, notice of proposed rulemaking, or final rule based on the requirements of this Order.

(2) The Director shall be deemed to have concluded review unless the Director advises an agency to the contrary under subsection (f) of this Section:

(A) Within 60 days of a submission under subsection (c)(1) or a submission of a preliminary Regulatory Impact Analysis or notice of proposed rulemaking under subsection (c)(2);

(B) Within 30 days of the submission of a final Regulatory Impact Analysis and a final rule under subsection (c)(2); and

(C) Within 10 days of the submission of a notice of proposed rulemaking or final rule under subsection (c)(3).

(f)(1)   Upon the request of the Director, an agency shall consult with the Director concerning the review of a preliminary Regulatory Impact Analysis or notice of proposed rulemaking under this Order, and shall, subject to Section 8(a)(2) of this Order, refrain from publishing its preliminary Regulatory Impact Analysis or notice of proposed rulemaking until such review is concluded.

(2) Upon receiving notice that the Director intends to submit views with respect to any final Regulatory Impact Analysis or final rule, the agency shall, subject to Section 8(a)(2) of this Order, refrain from publishing its final Regulatory Impact Analysis or final rule until the agency has responded to the Director's views, and incorporated those views and the agency's response in the rulemaking file.

(3) Nothing in this subsection shall be construed as displacing the agencies' responsibilities delegated by law.

(g) For every rule for which an agency publishes a notice of proposed rulemaking, the agency shall include in its notice:

(1) A brief statement setting forth the agency's initial determination whether the proposed rule is a major rule, together with the reasons underlying that determination; and

(2) For each proposed major rule, a brief summary of the agency's preliminary Regulatory Impact Analysis.

(h) Agencies shall make their preliminary and final Regulatory Impact Analyses available to the public.

(i) Agencies shall initiate reviews of currently effective rules in accordance with the purposes of this Order, and perform Regulatory Impact Analyses of currently effective major rules. The Director, subject to the direction of the Task Force, may designate currently effective rules for review in accordance with this Order, and establish schedules for reviews and Analyses under this Order.

Sec. 4. *Regulatory Review*. Before approving any final major rule, such agency shall:

(a) Make a determination that the regulation is clearly within the authority delegated by law and consistent with congressional intent, and include in the Federal Register at the time of promulgation a memorandum of law supporting that determination.

(b)   Make a determination that the factual conclusions upon which the rule is based have substantial support in the agency record, viewed as a whole, with full attention to public comments in general and the comments of persons directly affected by the rule in particular.

Sec. 5. *Regulatory Agendas.*

(a)   Each agency shall publish, in October and April of each year, an agenda of proposed regulations that the agency has issued or expects to issue, and currently effective rules that are under agency review pursuant to this Order. These agendas may be incorporated with the agendas published under 5 U.S.C. 602, and must contain at the minimum:

(1)   A summary of the nature of each major rule being considered, the objectives and legal basis for the issuance of the rule, and an approximate schedule for completing action on any major rule for which the agency has issued a notice of proposed rulemaking;

(2)   The name and telephone number of a knowledgeable agency official for each item on the agenda; and

(3)   A list of existing regulations to be reviewed under the terms of this Order, and a brief discussion of each such regulation.

(b)   The Director, subject to the direction of the Task Force, may, to the extent permitted by law:

(1)   Require agencies to provide additional information in an agenda; and

(2)   Require publication of the agenda in any form.

Sec. 6. *The Task Force and Office of Management and Budget.*

(a)   To the extent permitted by law, the Director shall have authority, subject to the direction of the Task Force, to:

(1)   Designate any proposed or existing rule as a major rule in accordance with Section 1(b) of this Order;

(2)   Prepare and promulgate uniform standards for the identification of major rules and the development of Regulatory Impact Analyses;

(3)   Require an agency to obtain and evaluate, in connection with a regulation, any additional relevant data from any appropriate source;

(4)   Waive the requirements of Sections 3, 4, or 7 of this Order with respect to any proposed or existing major rule;

(5)   Identify duplicative, overlapping and conflicting rules, existing or proposed, and existing or proposed rules that are inconsistent with the policies underlying statutes governing agencies other than the issuing

agency or with the purposes of this Order, and, in each such case, require appropriate interagency consultation to minimize or eliminate such duplication, overlap, or conflict;

(6) Develop procedures for estimating the annual benefits and costs of agency regulations, on both an aggregate and economic or industrial sector basis, for purposes of compiling a regulatory budget;

(7) In consultation with interested agencies, prepare for consideration by the President recommendations for changes in the agencies' statutes; and

(8) Monitor agency compliance with the requirements of this Order and advise the President with respect to such compliance.

(b) The Director, subject to the direction of the Task Force, is authorized to establish procedures for the performance of all functions vested in the Director by this Order. The Director shall take appropriate steps to coordinate the implementation of the analysis, transmittal, review, and clearance provisions of this Order with the authorities and requirements provided for or imposed upon the Director and agencies under the Regulatory Flexibility Act, 5 U.S.C. 601 *et seq.*, and the Paperwork Reduction Plan Act of 1980, 44 U.S.C. 3501 *et seq.*

Sec. 7. *Pending Regulations.*

(a) To the extent necessary to permit reconsideration in accordance with this Order, agencies shall, except as provided in Section 8 of this Order, suspend or postpone the effective dates of all major rules that they have promulgated in final form as of the date of this Order, but that have not yet become effective, excluding:

(1) Major rules that cannot legally be postponed or suspended;

(2) Major rules that, for good cause, ought to become effective as final rules without reconsideration. Agencies shall prepare, in accordance with Section 3 of this Order, a final Regulatory Impact Analysis for each major rule that they suspend or postpone.

(b) Agencies shall report to the Director no later than 15 days prior to the effective date of any rule that the agency has promulgated in final form as of the date of this Order, and that has not yet become effective, and that will not be reconsidered under subsection (a) of this Section:

(1) That the rule is excepted from reconsideration under subsection (a), including a brief statement of the legal or other reasons for that determination; or

(2) That the rule is not a major rule.

(c) The Director, subject to the direction of the Task Force, is authorized, to the extent permitted by law, to:

(1) Require reconsideration, in accordance with this Order, of any major rule that an agency has issued in final form as of the date of this Order and that has not become effective; and

(2) Designate a rule that an agency has issued in final form as of the date of this Order and that has not yet become effective as a major rule in accordance with Section 1(b) of this Order.

(d) Agencies may, in accordance with the Administrative Procedure Act and other applicable statutes, permit major rules that they have issued in final form as of the date of this Order, and that have not yet become effective, to take effect as interim rules while they are being reconsidered in accordance with this Order, *provided that*, agencies shall report to the Director, no later than 15 days before any such rule is proposed to take effect as an interim rule, that the rule should appropriately take effect as an interim rule while the rule is under reconsideration.

(e) Except as provided in Section 8 of this Order, agencies shall, to the extent permitted by law, refrain from promulgating as a final rule any proposed major rule that has been published or issued as of the date of this Order until a final Regulatory Impact Analysis, in accordance with Section 3 of this Order, has been prepared for the proposed major rule.

(f) Agencies shall report to the Director, no later than 30 days prior to promulgating as a final rule any proposed rule that the agency has published or issued as of the date of this Order and that has not been considered under the terms of this Order:

(1) That the rule cannot legally be considered in accordance with this Order, together with a brief explanation of the legal reasons barring such consideration; or

(2) That the rule is not a major rule, in which case the agency shall submit to the Director a copy of the proposed rule.

(g) The Director, subject to the direction of the Task Force, is authorized, to the extent permitted by law, to:

(1) Require consideration, in accordance with this Order, of any proposed major rule that the agency has published or issued as of the date of this Order; and

(2) Designate a proposed rule that an agency has published or issued as of the date of this Order, as a major rule in accordance with Section 1(b) of this Order.

(h) The Director shall be deemed to have determined that an agency's report to the Director under subsections (b), (d), or (f) of this Section is consistent with the purposes of this Order, unless the Director advises the agency to the contrary:

(1) Within 15 days of its report, in the case of any report under subsections (b) or (d); or

(2) Within 30 days of its report, in the case of any report under subsection (f).

(i) This Section does not supersede the President's Memorandum of January 29, 1981, entitled 'Postponement of Pending Regulations', which shall remain in effect until March 30, 1981.

(j) In complying with this Section, agencies shall comply with all applicable provisions of the Administrative Procedure Act, and with any other procedural requirements made applicable to the agencies by other statutes.

Sec. 8. *Exemptions.*

(a) The procedures prescribed by this Order shall not apply to:

(1) Any regulation that responds to an emergency situation, *provided that*, any such regulation shall be reported to the Director as soon as is practicable, the agency shall publish in the Federal Register a statement of the reasons why it is impracticable for the agency to follow the procedures of this Order with respect to such a rule, and the agency shall prepare and transmit as soon as is practicable a Regulatory Impact Analysis of any such major rule; and

(2) Any regulation for which consideration or reconsideration under the terms of this Order would conflict with deadlines imposed by statute or by judicial order, *provided that*, any such regulation shall be reported to the Director together with a brief explanation of the conflict, the agency shall publish in the Federal Register a statement of the reasons why it is impracticable for the agency to follow the procedures of this Order with respect to such a rule, and the agency, in consultation with the Director, shall adhere to the requirements of this Order to the extent permitted by statutory or judicial deadlines.

(b) The Director, subject to the direction of the Task Force, may, in accordance with the purposes of this Order, exempt any class or category of regulations from any or all requirements of this Order.

Sec. 9. *Judicial Review.* This Order is intended only to improve the internal management of the Federal government, and is not intended to create any right or benefit, substantive or procedural, enforceable at law by a party against the United States, its agencies, its officers or any person. The determinations made by agencies under Section 4 of this Order, and any Regulatory Impact Analyses for any rule, shall be made part of the whole record of agency action in connection with the rule.

Sec. 10. *Revocations.* Executive Orders No. 12044, as amended, and No. 12174 are revoked.

RONALD REAGAN

EXECUTIVE ORDER NO. 12866

58 Fed. Reg. 51735, Sept. 30, 1993

The American people deserve a regulatory system that works for them, not against them: a regulatory system that protects and improves their health, safety, environment, and well-being and improves the performance of the economy without imposing unacceptable or unreasonable costs on society; regulatory policies that recognize that the private sector and private markets are the best engine for economic growth; regulatory approaches that respect the role of State, local, and tribal governments; and regulations that are effective, consistent, sensible, and understandable. We do not have such a regulatory system today.

With this Executive order, the Federal Government begins a program to reform and make more efficient the regulatory process. The objectives of this Executive order are to enhance planning and coordination with respect to both new and existing regulations; to reaffirm the primacy of Federal agencies in the regulatory decision-making process; to restore the integrity and legitimacy of regulatory review and oversight; and to make the process more accessible and open to the public. In pursuing these objectives, the regulatory process shall be conducted so as to meet applicable statutory requirements and with due regard to the discretion that has been entrusted to the Federal agencies.

Accordingly, by the authority vested in me as President by the Constitution and the laws of the United States of America, it is hereby ordered as follows:

Sec 1. *Statement of Regulatory Philosophy and Principles.*

(a) *The Regulatory Philosophy.* Federal agencies should promulgate only such regulations as are required by law, are necessary to interpret the law, or are made necessary by compelling public need, such as material failures of private markets to protect or improve the health and safety of the public, the environment, or the well-being of the American people. In deciding whether and how to regulate, agencies should assess all costs and benefits of available regulatory alternatives, including the alternative of not regulating. Costs and benefits shall be understood to include both quantifiable measures (to the fullest extent that these can be usefully estimated) and qualitative measures of costs and benefits that are difficult to quantify, but nevertheless essential to consider. Further, in choosing among alternative regulatory approaches, agencies should select those approaches that maximize net benefits (including potential economic, environmental, public health and safety, and other advantages;

distributive impacts; and equity), unless a statute requires another regulatory approach.

(b) *The Principles of Regulation.* To ensure that the agencies' regulatory programs are consistent with the philosophy set forth above, agencies should adhere to the following principles, to the extent permitted by law and where applicable:

(1) Each agency shall identify the problem that it intends to address (including, where applicable, the failures of private markets or public institutions that warrant new agency action) as well as assess the significance of that problem.

(2) Each agency shall examine whether existing regulations (or other law) have created, or contributed to, the problem that a new regulation is intended to correct and whether those regulations (or other law) should be modified to achieve the intended goal of regulation more effectively.

(3) Each agency shall identify and assess available alternatives to direct regulation, including providing economic incentives to encourage the desired behavior, such as user fees or marketable permits, or providing information upon which choices can be made by the public.

(4) In setting regulatory priorities, each agency shall consider, to the extent reasonable, the degree and nature of the risks posed by various substances or activities within its jurisdiction.

(5) When an agency determines that a regulation is the best available method of achieving the regulatory objective, it shall design its regulations in the most cost-effective manner to achieve the regulatory objective. In doing so, each agency shall consider incentives for innovation, consistency, predictability, the costs of enforcement and compliance (to the government, regulated entities, and the public), flexibility, distributive impacts, and equity.

(6) Each agency shall assess both the costs and the benefits of the intended regulation and, recognizing that some costs and benefits are difficult to quantify, propose or adopt a regulation only upon a reasoned determination that the benefits of the intended regulation justify its costs.

(7) Each agency shall base its decisions on the best reasonably obtainable scientific, technical, economic, and other information concerning the need for, and consequences of, the intended regulation.

(8) Each agency shall identify and assess alternative forms of regulation and shall, to the extent feasible, specify performance

objectives, rather than specifying the behavior or manner of compliance that regulated entities must adopt.

(9) Wherever feasible, agencies shall seek views of appropriate State, local, and tribal officials before imposing regulatory requirements that might significantly or uniquely affect those governmental entities. Each agency shall assess the effects of Federal regulations on State, local, and tribal governments, including specifically the availability of resources to carry out those mandates, and seek to minimize those burdens that uniquely or significantly affect such governmental entities, consistent with achieving regulatory objectives. In addition, as appropriate, agencies shall seek to harmonize Federal regulatory actions with related State, local, and tribal regulatory and other governmental functions.

(10) Each agency shall avoid regulations that are inconsistent, incompatible, or duplicative with its other regulations or those of other Federal agencies.

(11) Each agency shall tailor its regulations to impose the least burden on society, including individuals, businesses of differing sizes, and other entities (including small communities and governmental entities), consistent with obtaining the regulatory objectives, taking into account, among other things, and to the extent practicable, the costs of cumulative regulations.

(12) Each agency shall draft its regulations to be simple and easy to understand, with the goal of minimizing the potential for uncertainty and litigation arising from such uncertainty.

Sec. 2. *Organization.* An efficient regulatory planning and review process is vital to ensure that the Federal Government's regulatory system best serves the American people.

(a) *The Agencies.* Because Federal agencies are the repositories of significant substantive expertise and experience, they are responsible for developing regulations and assuring that the regulations are consistent with applicable law, the President's priorities, and the principles set forth in this Executive order.

(b) *The Office of Management and Budget.* Coordinated review of agency rulemaking is necessary to ensure that regulations are consistent with applicable law, the President's priorities, and the principles set forth in this Executive order, and that decisions made by one agency do not conflict with the policies or actions taken or planned by another agency. The Office of Management and Budget (OMB) shall carry out that review function. Within OMB, the Office of Information and Regulatory Affairs (OIRA) is the repository of expertise concerning regulatory issues, including methodologies and procedures that affect more than one agency, this Executive order, and the President's regulatory policies. To the extent permitted by law, OMB shall provide guidance to agencies and assist the President, the Vice President, and other regulatory policy advisors to the President in regulatory planning and shall be the entity that reviews individual regulations, as provided by this Executive order.

(c) *The Vice President.* The Vice President is the principal advisor to the President on, and shall coordinate the development and presentation of recommendations concerning, regulatory policy, planning, and review, as set forth in this Executive order. In fulfilling their responsibilities under this Executive order, the President and the Vice President shall be assisted by the regulatory policy advisors within the Executive Office of the President and by such agency officials and personnel as the President and the Vice President may, from time to time, consult.

Sec. 3. *Definitions.* For purposes of this Executive order: (a) "Advisors" refers to such regulatory policy advisors to the President as the President and Vice President may from time to time consult, including, among others: (1) the Director of OMB; (2) the Chair (or another member) of the Council of Economic Advisers; (3) the Assistant to the President for Economic Policy; (4) the Assistant to the President for Domestic Policy; (5) the Assistant to the President for National Security Affairs; (6) the Assistant to the President for Science and Technology; (7) the Assistant to the President for Intergovernmental Affairs; (8) the Assistant to the President and Staff Secretary; (9) the Assistant to the President and Chief of Staff to the Vice President; (10) the Assistant to the President and Counsel to the President; (11) the Deputy Assistant to the President and Director of the White House Office on Environmental Policy; and (12) the Administrator of OIRA, who also shall coordinate communications relating to this Executive order among the agencies, OMB, the other Advisors, and the Office of the Vice President.

(b) "Agency," unless otherwise indicated, means any authority of the United States that is an "agency" under 44 U.S.C. 3502(1), other than those considered to be independent regulatory agencies, as defined in 44 U.S.C. 3502(10).

(c) "Director" means the Director of OMB.

(d) "Regulation" or "rule" means an agency statement of general applicability and future effect, which the agency intends to have the force and effect of law, that is designed to implement, interpret, or prescribe law or policy or to describe the procedure or practice requirements of an agency. It does not, however, include:

(1) Regulations or rules issued in accordance with the formal rulemaking provisions of 5 U.S.C. 556, 557;

(2) Regulations or rules that pertain to a military or foreign affairs function of the United States, other than procurement regulations and regulations involving the import or export of non-defense articles and services;

(3) Regulations or rules that are limited to agency organization, management, or personnel matters; or

(4) Any other category of regulations exempted by the Administrator of OIRA.

(e) "Regulatory action" means any substantive action by an agency (normally published in the Federal Register) that promulgates or is expected to lead to the promulgation of a final rule or regulation, including notices of inquiry, advance notices of proposed rulemaking, and notices of proposed rulemaking.

(f) "Significant regulatory action" means any regulatory action that is likely to result in a rule that may:

(1) Have an annual effect on the economy of $100 million or more or adversely affect in a material way the economy, a sector of the economy, productivity, competition, jobs, the environment, public health or safety, or State, local, or tribal governments or communities;

(2) Create a serious inconsistency or otherwise interfere with an action taken or planned by another agency;

(3) Materially alter the budgetary impact of entitlements, grants, user fees, or loan programs or the rights and obligations of recipients thereof; or

(4) Raise novel legal or policy issues arising out of legal mandates, the President's priorities, or the principles set forth in this Executive order.

Sec. 4. *Planning Mechanism.* In order to have an effective regulatory program, to provide for coordination of regulations, to maximize consultation and the resolution of potential conflicts at an early stage, to involve the public and its State, local, and tribal officials in regulatory planning, and to ensure that new or revised regulations promote the President's priorities and the principles set forth in this Executive order, these procedures shall be followed, to the extent permitted by law:

(a) *Agencies' Policy Meeting.* Early in each year's planning cycle, the Vice President shall convene a meeting of the Advisors and the heads of agencies to seek a common understanding of priorities and to coordinate regulatory efforts to be accomplished in the upcoming year.

(b) *Unified Regulatory Agenda.* For purposes of this subsection, the term "agency" or "agencies" shall also include those considered to be independent regulatory agencies, as defined in 44 U.S.C. 3502(10). Each agency shall prepare an agenda of all regulations under development or review, at a time and in a manner specified by the Administrator of OIRA. The description of each regulatory action shall contain, at a minimum, a regulation identifier number, a brief summary of the action, the legal authority for the action, any legal deadline for the action, and the name and telephone number of a knowledgeable agency official. Agencies may incorporate the information required under 5 U.S.C. 602 and 41 U.S.C. 402 into these agendas.

(c) *The Regulatory Plan.* For purposes of this subsection, the term "agency" or "agencies" shall also include those considered to be independent regulatory agencies, as defined in 44 U.S.C. 3502(10). (1) As part of the Unified Regulatory Agenda, beginning in 1994, each agency shall prepare a Regulatory Plan (Plan) of the most important significant regulatory actions that the agency reasonably expects to issue in proposed or final form in that fiscal year or thereafter. The Plan shall be approved personally by the agency head and shall contain at a minimum:

(A) A statement of the agency's regulatory objectives and priorities and how they relate to the President's priorities;

(B) A summary of each planned significant regulatory action including, to the extent possible, alternatives to be considered and preliminary estimates of the anticipated costs and benefits;

(C) A summary of the legal basis for each such action, including whether any aspect of the action is required by statute or court order;

(D) A statement of the need for each such action and, if applicable, how the action will reduce risks to public health, safety, or the environment, as well as how the magnitude of the risk addressed by the action relates to other risks within the jurisdiction of the agency;

(E) The agency's schedule for action, including a statement of any applicable statutory or judicial deadlines; and

(F) The name, address, and telephone number of a person the public may contact for additional information about the planned regulatory action.

(2) Each agency shall forward its Plan to OIRA by June 1st of each year.

(3) Within 10 calendar days after OIRA has received an agency's Plan, OIRA shall circulate it to other affected agencies, the Advisors, and the Vice President.

(4) An agency head who believes that a planned regulatory action of another agency may conflict with its own policy or action taken or planned shall promptly notify, in writing, the Administrator of OIRA,

who shall forward that communication to the issuing agency, the Advisors, and the Vice President.

(5) If the Administrator of OIRA believes that a planned regulatory action of an agency may be inconsistent with the President's priorities or the principles set forth in this Executive order or may be in conflict with any policy or action taken or planned by another agency, the Administrator of OIRA shall promptly notify, in writing, the affected agencies, the Advisors, and the Vice President.

(6) The Vice President, with the Advisors' assistance, may consult with the heads of agencies with respect to their Plans and, in appropriate instances, request further consideration or inter-agency coordination.

(7) The Plans developed by the issuing agency shall be published annually in the October publication of the Unified Regulatory Agenda. This publication shall be made available to the Congress; State, local, and tribal governments; and the public. Any views on any aspect of any agency Plan, including whether any planned regulatory action might conflict with any other planned or existing regulation, impose any unintended consequences on the public, or confer any unclaimed benefits on the public, should be directed to the issuing agency, with a copy to OIRA.

(d) *Regulatory Working Group.* Within 30 days of the date of this Executive order, the Administrator of OIRA shall convene a Regulatory Working Group ("Working Group"), which shall consist of representatives of the heads of each agency that the Administrator determines to have significant domestic regulatory responsibility, the Advisors, and the Vice President. The Administrator of OIRA shall chair the Working Group and shall periodically advise the Vice President on the activities of the Working Group. The Working Group shall serve as a forum to assist agencies in identifying and analyzing important regulatory issues (including, among others (1) the development of innovative regulatory techniques, (2) the methods, efficacy, and utility of comparative risk assessment in regulatory decision-making, and (3) the development of short forms and other streamlined regulatory approaches for small businesses and other entities). The Working Group shall meet at least quarterly and may meet as a whole or in subgroups of agencies with an interest in particular issues or subject areas. To inform its discussions, the Working Group may commission analytical studies and reports by OIRA, the Administrative Conference of the United States, or any other agency.

(e) *Conferences.* The Administrator of OIRA shall meet quarterly with representatives of State, local, and tribal governments to identify both existing and proposed regulations that may uniquely or significantly affect those governmental entities. The Administrator of OIRA shall also convene, from time to time, conferences with representatives of businesses, nongovernmental organizations, and the public to discuss regulatory issues of common concern.

Sec. 5. *Existing Regulations.* In order to reduce the regulatory burden on the American people, their families, their communities, their State, local, and tribal governments, and their industries; to determine whether regulations promulgated by the executive branch of the Federal Government have become unjustified or unnecessary as a result of changed circumstances; to confirm that regulations are both compatible with each other and not duplicative or inappropriately burdensome in the aggregate; to ensure that all regulations are consistent with the President's priorities and the principles set forth in this Executive order, within applicable law; and to otherwise improve the effectiveness of existing regulations:

(a) Within 90 days of the date of this Executive order, each agency shall submit to OIRA a program, consistent with its resources and regulatory priorities, under which the agency will periodically review its existing significant regulations to determine whether any such regulations should be modified or eliminated so as to make the agency's regulatory program more effective in achieving the regulatory objectives, less burdensome, or in greater alignment with the President's priorities and the principles set forth in this Executive order. Any significant regulations selected for review shall be included in the agency's annual Plan. The agency shall also identify any legislative mandates that require the agency to promulgate or continue to impose regulations that the agency believes are unnecessary or outdated by reason of changed circumstances.

(b) The Administrator of OIRA shall work with the Regulatory Working Group and other interested entities to pursue the objectives of this section. State, local, and tribal governments are specifically encouraged to assist in the identification of regulations that impose significant or unique burdens on those governmental entities and that appear to have outlived their justification or be otherwise inconsistent with the public interest.

(c) The Vice President, in consultation with the Advisors, may identify for review by the appropriate agency or agencies other existing regulations of an agency or groups of regulations of more than one agency that affect a particular group, industry, or sector of the economy, or may identify legislative mandates that may be appropriate for reconsideration by the Congress.

Sec. 6. *Centralized Review of Regulations.* The guidelines set forth below shall apply to all regulatory actions, for both new and existing regulations, by agencies other than those agencies specifically exempted by the Administrator of OIRA:

(a) *Agency Responsibilities.* (1) Each agency shall (consistent with its own rules, regulations, or procedures) provide the public with meaningful participation in the regulatory process. In particular, before issuing a notice of proposed rulemaking, each agency should, where appropriate, seek the involvement of those who are intended to benefit from and those expected to be burdened by any regulation (including, specifically, State, local, and tribal officials). In addition, each agency should afford the public a meaningful opportunity to comment on any proposed regulation, which in most cases should include a comment period of not less than 60 days. Each agency also is directed to explore and, where appropriate, use consensual mechanisms for developing regulations, including negotiated rulemaking.

(2)   Within 60 days of the date of this Executive order, each agency head shall designate a Regulatory Policy Officer who shall report to the agency head. The Regulatory Policy Officer shall be involved at each stage of the regulatory process to foster the development of effective, innovative, and least burdensome regulations and to further the principles set forth in this Executive order.

(3)   In addition to adhering to its own rules and procedures and to the requirements of the Administrative Procedure Act [sections 551 et seq., 701 et seq. of this title], the Regulatory Flexibility Act [this chapter], the Paperwork Reduction Act [section 3501 et seq. of Title 44, Public Printing and Documents], and other applicable law, each agency shall develop its regulatory actions in a timely fashion and adhere to the following procedures with respect to a regulatory action:

(A)   Each agency shall provide OIRA, at such times and in the manner specified by the Administrator of OIRA, with a list of its planned regulatory actions, indicating those which the agency believes are significant regulatory actions within the meaning of this Executive order. Absent a material change in the development of the planned regulatory action, those not designated as significant will not be subject to review under this section unless, within 10 working days of receipt of the list, the Administrator of OIRA notifies the agency that OIRA has determined that a planned regulation is a significant regulatory action within the meaning of this Executive order. The Administrator of OIRA may waive review of any planned regulatory action designated by the agency as significant, in which case the agency need not further comply with subsection (a)(3)(B) or subsection (a)(3)(C) of this section.

(B)   For each matter identified as, or determined by the Administrator of OIRA to be, a significant regulatory action, the issuing agency shall provide to OIRA:

(i)   The text of the draft regulatory action, together with a reasonably detailed description of the need for the regulatory action and an explanation of how the regulatory action will meet that need; and

(ii) An assessment of the potential costs and benefits of the regulatory action, including an explanation of the manner in which the regulatory action is consistent with a statutory mandate and, to the extent permitted by law, promotes the President's priorities and avoids undue interference with State, local, and tribal governments in the exercise of their governmental functions.

(C) For those matters identified as, or determined by the Administrator of OIRA to be, a significant regulatory action within the scope of section 3(f)(1), the agency shall also provide to OIRA the following additional information developed as part of the agency's decision-making process (unless prohibited by law):

(i) An assessment, including the underlying analysis, of benefits anticipated from the regulatory action (such as, but not limited to, the promotion of the efficient functioning of the economy and private markets, the enhancement of health and safety, the protection of the natural environment, and the elimination or reduction of discrimination or bias) together with, to the extent feasible, a quantification of those benefits;

(ii) An assessment, including the underlying analysis, of costs anticipated from the regulatory action (such as, but not limited to, the direct cost both to the government in administering the regulation and to businesses and others in complying with the regulation, and any adverse effects on the efficient functioning of the economy, private markets (including productivity, employment, and competitiveness), health, safety, and the natural environment), together with, to the extent feasible, a quantification of those costs; and

(iii) An assessment, including the underlying analysis, of costs and benefits of potentially effective and reasonably feasible alternatives to the planned regulation, identified by the agencies or the public (including improving the current regulation and reasonably viable nonregulatory actions), and an explanation why the planned regulatory action is preferable to the identified potential alternatives.

(D) In emergency situations or when an agency is obligated by law to act more quickly than normal review procedures allow, the agency shall notify OIRA as soon as possible and, to the extent practicable, comply with subsections (a)(3)(B) and (C) of this section. For those regulatory actions that are governed by a statutory or court-imposed deadline, the agency shall, to the extent practicable, schedule rulemaking proceedings so as to permit sufficient time for OIRA to conduct its review, as set forth below in subsections (b)(2) through (4) of this section.

(E) After the regulatory action has been published in the Federal Register or otherwise issued to the public, the agency shall:

(i) Make available to the public the information set forth in subsections (a)(3)(B) and (C);

(ii) Identify for the public, in a complete, clear, and simple manner, the substantive changes between the draft submitted to OIRA for review and the action subsequently announced; and

(iii) Identify for the public those changes in the regulatory action that were made at the suggestion or recommendation of OIRA.

(F) All information provided to the public by the agency shall be in plain, understandable language.

(b) *OIRA Responsibilities.* The Administrator of OIRA shall provide meaningful guidance and oversight so that each agency's regulatory actions are consistent with applicable law, the President's priorities, and the principles set forth in this Executive order and do not conflict with the policies or actions of another agency. OIRA shall, to the extent permitted by law, adhere to the following guidelines:

(1) OIRA may review only actions identified by the agency or by OIRA as significant regulatory actions under subsection (a)(3)(A) of this section.

(2) OIRA shall waive review or notify the agency in writing of the results of its review within the following time periods:

(A) For any notices of inquiry, advance notices of proposed rulemaking, or other preliminary regulatory actions prior to a Notice of Proposed Rulemaking, within 10 working days after the date of submission of the draft action to OIRA;

(B) For all other regulatory actions, within 90 calendar days after the date of submission of the information set forth in subsections (a)(3)(B) and (C) of this section, unless OIRA has previously reviewed this information and, since that review, there has been no material change in the facts and circumstances upon which the regulatory action is based, in which case, OIRA shall complete its review within 45 days; and

(C) The review process may be extended (1) once by no more than 30 calendar days upon the written approval of the Director and (2) at the request of the agency head.

(3) For each regulatory action that the Administrator of OIRA returns to an agency for further consideration of some or all of its provisions, the Administrator of OIRA shall provide the issuing agency a written explanation for such return, setting forth the pertinent provision of this Executive order on which OIRA is relying. If the agency head disagrees with some or all of the bases for the return, the agency head shall so inform the Administrator of OIRA in writing.

(4) Except as otherwise provided by law or required by a Court, in order to ensure greater openness, accessibility, and accountability in the regulatory review process, OIRA shall be governed by the following disclosure requirements:

(A) Only the Administrator of OIRA (or a particular designee) shall receive oral communications initiated by persons not employed by the executive branch of the Federal Government regarding the substance of a regulatory action under OIRA review;

(B) All substantive communications between OIRA personnel and persons not employed by the executive branch of the Federal Government regarding a regulatory action under review shall be governed by the following guidelines:

(i) A representative from the issuing agency shall be invited to any meeting between OIRA personnel and such person(s);

(ii) OIRA shall forward to the issuing agency, within 10 working days of receipt of the communication(s), all written communications, regardless of format, between OIRA personnel and any person who is not employed by the executive branch of the Federal Government, and the dates and names of individuals involved in all substantive oral communications (including meetings to which an agency representative was invited, but did not attend, and telephone conversations between OIRA personnel and any such persons); and

(iii) OIRA shall publicly disclose relevant information about such communication(s), as set forth below in subsection (b)(4)(C) of this section.

(C) OIRA shall maintain a publicly available log that shall contain, at a minimum, the following information pertinent to regulatory actions under review:

(i) The status of all regulatory actions, including if (and if so, when and by whom) Vice Presidential and Presidential consideration was requested;

(ii) A notation of all written communications forwarded to an issuing agency under subsection (b)(4)(B)(ii) of this section; and

(iii) The dates and names of individuals involved in all substantive oral communications, including meetings and telephone conversations, between OIRA personnel and any person not employed by the executive branch of the Federal Government, and the subject matter discussed during such communications.

(D) After the regulatory action has been published in the Federal Register or otherwise issued to the public, or after the agency has announced its decision not to publish or issue the regulatory action,

OIRA shall make available to the public all documents exchanged between OIRA and the agency during the review by OIRA under this section.

(5) All information provided to the public by OIRA shall be in plain, understandable language.

Sec. 7. *Resolution of Conflicts.* To the extent permitted by law, disagreements or conflicts between or among agency heads or between OMB and any agency that cannot be resolved by the Administrator of OIRA shall be resolved by the President, or by the Vice President acting at the request of the President, with the relevant agency head (and, as appropriate, other interested government officials). Vice Presidential and Presidential consideration of such disagreements may be initiated only by the Director, by the head of the issuing agency, or by the head of an agency that has a significant interest in the regulatory action at issue. Such review will not be undertaken at the request of other persons, entities, or their agents.

Resolution of such conflicts shall be informed by recommendations developed by the Vice President, after consultation with the Advisors (and other executive branch officials or personnel whose responsibilities to the President include the subject matter at issue). The development of these recommendations shall be concluded within 60 days after review has been requested.

During the Vice Presidential and Presidential review period, communications with any person not employed by the Federal Government relating to the substance of the regulatory action under review and directed to the Advisors or their staffs or to the staff of the Vice President shall be in writing and shall be forwarded by the recipient to the affected agency(ies) for inclusion in the public docket(s). When the communication is not in writing, such Advisors or staff members shall inform the outside party that the matter is under review and that any comments should be submitted in writing.

At the end of this review process, the President, or the Vice President acting at the request of the President, shall notify the affected agency and the Administrator of OIRA of the President's decision with respect to the matter.

Sec. 8. *Publication.* Except to the extent required by law, an agency shall not publish in the Federal Register or otherwise issue to the public any regulatory action that is subject to review under section 6 of this Executive order until (1) the Administrator of OIRA notifies the agency that OIRA has waived its review of the action or has completed its review without any requests for further consideration, or (2) the applicable time period in section 6(b)(2) expires without OIRA having notified the agency that it is returning the regulatory action for further consideration under section 6(b)(3), whichever occurs first. If the terms of the preceding sentence have not been satisfied and an agency wants to publish or otherwise issue a regulatory action, the head of that agency may request Presidential consideration through the Vice President, as provided under section 7 of this order. Upon receipt of this request, the Vice President shall notify OIRA and the Advisors. The guidelines and time period set forth in section 7 shall apply to the publication of regulatory actions for which Presidential consideration has been sought.

Sec. 9. *Agency Authority.* Nothing in this order shall be construed as displacing the agencies' authority or responsibilities, as authorized by law.

Sec. 10. *Judicial Review.* Nothing in this Executive order shall affect any otherwise available judicial review of agency action. This Executive order is intended only to improve the internal management of the Federal Government and does not create any right or benefit, substantive or procedural, enforceable at law or equity by a party against the United States, its agencies or instrumentalities, its officers or employees, or any other person.

Sec. 11. *Revocations.* Executive Orders Nos. 12291 and 12498 [formerly set out as notes under this section]; all amendments to those Executive orders; all guidelines issued under those orders; and any exemptions from those orders heretofore granted for any category of rule are revoked.

WILLIAM J. CLINTON

EXECUTIVE ORDER NO. 13258
67 Fed. Reg. 9385, Feb. 26, 2002

By the authority vested in me as President by the Constitution and the laws of the United States of America, it is hereby ordered that Executive Order 12866, of September 30, 1993, is amended as follows:

Section 1. Section (2)(b) is amended by striking ", the Vice President, and other regulatory policy advisors" and inserting in lieu thereof "and regulatory policy advisors".

Sec. 2. Section (2)(c) is amended by:

(a) striking in the heading the words "The Vice President" and inserting in lieu thereof "Assistance";

(b) striking the sentence that begins "The Vice President is";

(c) striking "In fulfilling their responsibilities" and inserting in lieu thereof "In fulfilling his responsibilities"; and

(d) striking "and the Vice President" both times it appears.

Sec. 3. Section 3(a) is amended by:

(a) striking "and Vice President";

(b) striking "the Assistant to the President for Science and Technology" and inserting in lieu thereof "the Director of the Office of Science and Technology Policy";

(c) striking "the Assistant to the President for Intergovernmental Affairs" and inserting in lieu thereof "the Deputy Assistant to the President and Director for Intergovernmental Affairs";

(d) striking "the Deputy Assistant to the President and Director of the White House Office of Environmental Policy" and inserting in lieu thereof "the Chairman of the Council on Environmental Quality and Director of the Office of Environmental Quality"; and

(e) striking "and (12)" and inserting in lieu thereof "(12) the Assistant to the President for Homeland Security; and (13)".

Sec. 4. Section 4(a) is amended by striking "the Vice President shall convene" and inserting in lieu thereof "the Director shall convene".

Sec. 5. Section 4(c)(3) is amended by striking ", the Advisors, and the Vice President" and inserting in lieu thereof "and the Advisors".

Sec. 6. Section 4(c)(4) is amended by striking ", the Advisors, and the Vice President" and inserting in lieu thereof "and the Advisors".

Sec. 7. Section 4(c)(5) is amended by striking ", the Advisors, and the Vice President" and inserting in lieu thereof "and the Advisors".

Sec. 8. Section 4(c)(6) is amended by striking "Vice President, with the Advisors' assistance," and inserting in lieu thereof "Director".

Sec. 9. Section 4(d) is amended by:

(a) striking ", the Advisors, and the Vice President" and inserting in lieu thereof "and the Advisors"; and

(b) striking "periodically advise the Vice President" and inserting in lieu thereof "periodically advise the Director".

Sec. 10. Section 5(c) is amended by striking "Vice President" and inserting in lieu thereof "Director".

Sec. 11. Section 6(b)(4)(C)(i) is amended by striking "Vice Presidential and".

Sec. 12. Section 7 is amended by:

(a) striking "resolved by the President, or by the Vice President acting at the request of the President" and inserting in lieu thereof "resolved by the President, with the assistance of the Chief of Staff to the President ("Chief of Staff")";

(b) striking "Vice Presidential and Presidential consideration" and inserting in lieu thereof "Presidential consideration";

(c) striking "recommendations developed by the Vice President" and inserting in lieu thereof "recommendations developed by the Chief of Staff";

(d) striking "Vice Presidential and Presidential review period" and inserting in lieu thereof "Presidential review period";

(e) striking "or to the staff of the Vice President" and inserting in lieu thereof "or to the staff of the Chief of Staff";

(f) striking "the President, or the Vice President acting at the request of the President, shall notify" and insert in lieu thereof "the President, or the Chief of Staff acting at the request of the President, shall notify".

Sec. 13. Section 7 is also amended in the first paragraph by inserting the designation "(a)" after the words "Resolution of Conflicts.", and by designating the following three paragraphs as "(b)", "(c)", and "(d)" in order.

Sec. 14. Section 8 is amended by striking "Vice President" both times it appears and inserting in lieu thereof "Director".

GEORGE W. BUSH

EXECUTIVE ORDER NO. 13422

72 Fed. Reg. 2763, Jan. 18, 2007

By the authority vested in me as President by the Constitution and laws of the United States of America, it is hereby ordered that Executive Order 12866 of September 30, 1993, as amended, is further amended as follows:

Section 1. Section 1 is amended as follows:

(a) Section 1(b)(1) is amended to read as follows:

"(1) Each agency shall identify in writing the specific market failure (such as externalities, market power, lack of information) or other specific problem that it intends to address (including, where applicable, the failures of public institutions) that warrant new agency action, as well as assess the significance of that problem, to enable assessment of whether any new regulation is warranted."

(b) by inserting in section 1(b)(7) after "regulation" the words "or guidance document".

(c) by inserting in section 1(b)(10) in both places after "regulations" the words "and guidance documents".

(d) by inserting in section 1(b)(11) after "its regulations" the words "and guidance documents".

(e) by inserting in section 1(b)(12) after "regulations" the words "and guidance documents".

Sec. 2. Section 2 is amended as follows:

(a) by inserting in section 2(a) in both places after "regulations" the words "and guidance documents".

(b) by inserting in section 2(b) in both places after "regulations" the words "and guidance documents".

Sec. 3. Section 3 is amended as follows:

(a) by striking in section 3(d) "or 'rule' " after " 'Regulation' ";

(b) by striking in section 3(d)(1) "or rules" after "Regulations";

(c) by striking in section 3(d)(2) "or rules" after "Regulations";

(d) by striking in section 3(d)(3) "or rules" after "Regulations";

(e) by striking in section 3(e) "rule or" from "final rule or regulation";

(f) by striking in section 3(f) "rule or" from "rule or regulation";

(g) by inserting after section 3(f) the following:

"(g) "Guidance document" means an agency statement of general applicability and future effect, other than a regulatory action, that sets forth a policy on a statutory, regulatory, or technical issue or an interpretation of a statutory or regulatory issue.

(h) "Significant guidance document" –

(1) Means a guidance document disseminated to regulated entities or the general public that, for purposes of this order, may reasonably be anticipated to:

(A) Lead to an annual effect of $100 million or more or adversely affect in a material way the economy, a sector of the economy, productivity, competition, jobs, the environment, public health or safety, or State, local, or tribal governments or communities;

(B) Create a serious inconsistency or otherwise interfere with an action taken or planned by another agency;

(C) Materially alter the budgetary impact of entitlements, grants, user fees, or loan programs or the rights or obligations of recipients thereof; or

(D) Raise novel legal or policy issues arising out of legal mandates, the President's priorities, or the principles set forth in this Executive order; and

(2) Does not include:

(A) Guidance documents on regulations issued in accordance with the formal rulemaking provisions of 5 U.S.C. 556, 557;

(B) Guidance documents that pertain to a military or foreign affairs function of the United States, other than procurement regulations and regulations involving the import or export of non-defense articles and services;

(C) Guidance documents on regulations that are limited to agency organization, management, or personnel matters; or

(D) Any other category of guidance documents exempted by the Administrator of OIRA."

Sec. 4. Section 4 is amended as follows:

(a) Section 4(a) is amended to read as follows: "The Director may convene a meeting of agency heads and other government personnel as appropriate to seek a common understanding of priorities and to coordinate regulatory efforts to be accomplished in the upcoming year."

(b) The last sentence of section 4(c)(1) is amended to read as follows: "Unless specifically authorized by the head of the agency, no rulemaking shall commence nor be included on the Plan without the approval of the agency's Regulatory Policy Office, and the Plan shall contain at a minimum:".

(c) Section 4(c)(1)(B) is amended by inserting "of each rule as well as the agency's best estimate of the combined aggregate costs and benefits of all its regulations planned for that calendar year to assist with the identification of priorities" after "of the anticipated costs and benefits".

(d) Section 4(c)(1)(C) is amended by inserting ", and specific citation to such statute, order, or other legal authority" after "court order".

Sec. 5. Section 6 is amended as follows:

(a) by inserting in section 6(a)(1) "In consultation with OIRA, each agency may also consider whether to utilize formal rulemaking procedures under 5 U.S.C. 556 and 557 for the resolution of complex determinations" after "comment period of not less than 60 days."

(b) by amending the first sentence of section 6(a)(2) to read as follows: "Within 60 days of the date of this Executive order, each agency head shall designate one of the agency's Presidential Appointees to be its Regulatory Policy Officer, advise OMB of such designation, and annually update OMB on the status of this designation."

Sec. 6. Sections 9–11 are redesignated respectively as sections 10–12.

Sec. 7. After section 8, a new section 9 is inserted as follows:

"Sec. 9. *Significant Guidance Documents.* Each agency shall provide OIRA, at such times and in the manner specified by the Administrator of OIRA, with advance notification of any significant guidance documents. Each agency shall take such steps as are necessary for its

Regulatory Policy Officer to ensure the agency's compliance with the requirements of this section. Upon the request of the Administrator, for each matter identified as, or determined by the Administrator to be, a significant guidance document, the issuing agency shall provide to OIRA the content of the draft guidance document, together with a brief explanation of the need for the guidance document and how it will meet that need. The OIRA Administrator shall notify the agency when additional consultation will be required before the issuance of the significant guidance document."

Sec. 8. Newly designated section 10 is amended to read as follows:

"Sec. 10. *Preservation of Agency Authority.* Nothing in this order shall be construed to impair or otherwise affect the authority vested by law in an agency or the head thereof, including the authority of the Attorney General relating to litigation."

GEORGE W. BUSH

EXECUTIVE ORDER NO. 13497

74 Fed. Reg. 6113, Jan. 30, 2009

By the authority vested in me as President by the Constitution and the laws of the United States of America, it is hereby ordered that:

Section 1. Executive Order 13528 of February 26, 2002, and Executive Order 13422 of January 18, 2007, concerning regulatory planning and review, which amended Executive Order 12866 of September 30, 1993, are revoked.

Sec. 2. The Director of the Office of Management and Budget and the heads of executive departments and agencies shall promptly rescind any orders, rules, regulations, guidelines, or policies implementing or enforcing Executive Order 13528 or Executive Order 13422, to the extent consistent with law.

Sec. 3. This order is not intended to, and does not, create any right or benefit, substantive or procedural, enforceable at law or in equity by any party against the United States, its departments, agencies, or entities, its officers, employees, or agents, or any other person.

BARACK OBAMA

EXECUTIVE ORDER NO. 13563

76 Fed. Reg. 3821, Jan. 18, 2011

By the authority vested in me as President by the Constitution and the laws of the United States of America, and in order to improve regulation and regulatory review, it is hereby ordered as follows:

Section 1. *General Principles of Regulation.* (a) Our regulatory system must protect public health, welfare, safety, and our environment while promoting economic growth, innovation, competitiveness, and job creation. It must be based on the best available science. It must allow for public participation and an open exchange of ideas. It must promote predictability and reduce uncertainty. It must identify and use the best, most innovative, and least burdensome tools for achieving regulatory ends. It must take into account benefits and costs, both quantitative and qualitative. It must ensure that regulations are accessible, consistent, written in plain language, and easy to understand. It must measure, and seek to improve, the actual results of regulatory requirements.

(b) This order is supplemental to and reaffirms the principles, structures, and definitions governing contemporary regulatory review that were established in Executive Order 12866 of September 30, 1993. As stated in that Executive Order and to the extent permitted by law, each agency must, among other things: (1) propose or adopt a regulation only upon a reasoned determination that its benefits justify its costs (recognizing that some benefits and costs are difficult to quantify); (2) tailor its regulations to impose the least burden on society, consistent with obtaining regulatory objectives, taking into account, among other things, and to the extent practicable, the costs of cumulative regulations; (3) select, in choosing among alternative regulatory approaches, those approaches that maximize net benefits (including potential economic, environmental, public health and safety, and other advantages; distributive impacts; and equity); (4) to the extent feasible, specify performance objectives, rather than specifying the behavior or manner of compliance that regulated entities must adopt; and (5) identify and assess available alternatives to direct regulation, including providing economic incentives to encourage the desired behavior, such as user fees or marketable permits, or providing information upon which choices can be made by the public.

(c) In applying these principles, each agency is directed to use the best available techniques to quantify anticipated present and future benefits and costs as accurately as possible. Where appropriate and permitted by law, each agency may consider (and discuss qualitatively) values that are difficult or impossible to quantify, including equity, human dignity, fairness, and distributive impacts.

Sec. 2. *Public Participation.*

(a) Regulations shall be adopted through a process that involves public participation. To that end, regulations shall be based, to the extent feasible and consistent with law, on the open exchange of information and perspectives among State, local, and tribal officials, experts in relevant disciplines, affected stakeholders in the private sector, and the public as a whole.

(b) To promote that open exchange, each agency, consistent with Executive Order 12866 and other applicable legal requirements, shall endeavor to provide the public with an opportunity to participate in the regulatory process. To the extent feasible and permitted by law, each agency shall afford the public a meaningful opportunity to comment through the Internet on any proposed regulation, with a comment period that should generally be at least 60 days. To the extent feasible and permitted by law, each agency shall also provide, for both proposed and final rules, timely online access to the rulemaking docket on regulations.gov, including relevant scientific and technical findings, in an open format that can be easily searched and downloaded. For proposed rules, such access shall include, to the extent feasible and permitted by law, an opportunity for public comment on all pertinent parts of the rulemaking docket, including relevant scientific and technical findings.

(c) Before issuing a notice of proposed rulemaking, each agency, where feasible and appropriate, shall seek the views of those who are likely to be affected, including those who are likely to benefit from and those who are potentially subject to such rulemaking.

Sec. 3. *Integration and Innovation.* Some sectors and industries face a significant number of regulatory requirements, some of which may be redundant, inconsistent, or overlapping. Greater coordination across agencies could reduce these requirements, thus reducing costs and simplifying and harmonizing rules. In developing regulatory actions and identifying appropriate approaches, each agency shall attempt to promote such coordination, simplification, and harmonization. Each agency shall also seek to identify, as appropriate, means to achieve regulatory goals that are designed to promote innovation.

Sec. 4. *Flexible Approaches.* Where relevant, feasible, and consistent with regulatory objectives, and to the extent permitted by law, each agency shall identify and consider regulatory approaches that reduce burdens and maintain flexibility and freedom of choice for the public. These approaches include warnings, appropriate default rules, and disclosure requirements as well as provision of information to the public in a form that is clear and intelligible.

Sec. 5. *Science.* Consistent with the President's Memorandum for the Heads of Executive Departments and Agencies, "Scientific Integrity" (March 9, 2009), and its implementing guidance, each agency shall ensure the objectivity of any scientific and technological information and processes used to support the agency's regulatory actions.

Sec. 6. *Retrospective Analyses of Existing Rules.* (a) To facilitate the periodic review of existing significant regulations, agencies shall consider how best to promote retrospective analysis of rules that may be outmoded, ineffective, insufficient, or excessively burdensome, and to modify, streamline, expand, or repeal them in accordance with what has been learned. Such retrospective analyses, including supporting data, should be released online whenever possible.

(b) Within 120 days of the date of this order, each agency shall develop and submit to the Office of Information and Regulatory Affairs a preliminary plan, consistent with law and its resources and regulatory priorities, under which the agency will periodically review its existing significant regulations to determine whether any such regulations should be modified, streamlined, expanded, or repealed so as to make the agency's regulatory program more effective or less burdensome in achieving the regulatory objectives.

Sec. 7. *General Provisions.* (a) For purposes of this order, "agency" shall have the meaning set forth in section 3(b) of Executive Order 12866.

(b) Nothing in this order shall be construed to impair or otherwise affect:

(i) authority granted by law to a department or agency, or the head thereof; or

(ii) functions of the Director of the Office of Management and Budget relating to budgetary, administrative, or legislative proposals.

(c) This order shall be implemented consistent with applicable law and subject to the availability of appropriations.

(d) This order is not intended to, and does not, create any right or benefit, substantive or procedural, enforceable at law or in equity by any party against the United States, its departments, agencies, or entities, its officers, employees, or agents, or any other person.

BARACK OBAMA

EXECUTIVE ORDER No. 13771

82 Fed. Reg. 9339, Feb. 3, 2017

By the authority vested in me as President by the Constitution and the laws of the United States of America, including the Budget and Accounting Act of 1921, as amended (31 U.S.C. 1101 *et seq.*), section 1105 of title 31, United States Code, and section 301 of title 3, United States Code, it is hereby ordered as follows:

Sec. 1. *Purpose.* It is the policy of the executive branch to be prudent and financially responsible in the expenditure of funds, from both public and private sources. In addition to the management of the direct expenditure of taxpayer dollars through the budgeting process, it is essential to manage the costs associated with the governmental imposition of private expenditures required to comply with Federal regulations. Toward that end, it is important that for every one new regulation issued, at least two prior regulations be identified for elimination, and that the cost of planned regulations be prudently managed and controlled through a budgeting process.

Sec. 2. *Regulatory Cap for Fiscal Year 2017.* (a) Unless prohibited by law, whenever an executive department or agency (agency) publicly proposes for notice and comment or otherwise promulgates a new regulation, it shall identify at least two existing regulations to be repealed.

(b) For fiscal year 2017, which is in progress, the heads of all agencies are directed that the total incremental cost of all new regulations, including repealed regulations, to be finalized this year shall be no greater than zero, unless otherwise required by law or consistent with advice provided in writing by the Director of the Office of Management and Budget (Director).

(c) In furtherance of the requirement of subsection (a) of this section, any new incremental costs associated with new regulations shall, to the extent permitted by law, be offset by the elimination of existing costs associated with at least two prior regulations. Any agency eliminating existing costs associated with prior regulations under this subsection shall do so in accordance with the Administrative Procedure Act and other applicable law.

(d) The Director shall provide the heads of agencies with guidance on the implementation of this section. Such guidance shall address, among other things, processes for standardizing the measurement and estimation of regulatory costs; standards for determining what qualifies as new and offsetting regulations; standards for determining the costs of existing regulations that are considered for elimination; processes for accounting for costs in different fiscal years; methods to oversee the issuance of rules with costs offset by savings at different times or different agencies; and emergencies and other circumstances that might justify individual waivers of the requirements of this section. The Director shall consider phasing in and updating these requirements.

Sec. 3. *Annual Regulatory Cost Submissions to the Office of Management and Budget.* (a) Beginning with the Regulatory Plans (required under Executive Order 12866 of September 30, 1993, as amended, or any successor order) for fiscal year 2018, and for each fiscal year thereafter, the head of each agency shall identify, for each regulation that increases incremental cost, the offsetting regulations described in section 2(c) of this order, and provide the agency's best approximation of the total costs or savings associated with each new regulation or repealed regulation.

(b) Each regulation approved by the Director during the Presidential budget process shall be included in the Unified Regulatory Agenda required under Executive Order 12866, as amended, or any successor order.

(c) Unless otherwise required by law, no regulation shall be issued by an agency if it was not included on the most recent version or update of the published Unified Regulatory Agenda as required under Executive Order 12866, as amended, or any successor order, unless the issuance of such regulation was approved in advance in writing by the Director.

(d) During the Presidential budget process, the Director shall identify to agencies a total amount of incremental costs that will be allowed for each agency in issuing new regulations and repealing regulations for the next fiscal year. No regulations exceeding the agency's total incremental cost allowance will be permitted in that fiscal year, unless required by law or approved in writing by the Director. The total incremental cost allowance may allow an increase or require a reduction in total regulatory cost.

(e) The Director shall provide the heads of agencies with guidance on the implementation of the requirements in this section.

Sec. 4. *Definition.* For purposes of this order the term "regulation" or "rule" means an agency statement of general or particular applicability and future effect designed to implement, interpret, or prescribe law or policy or to describe the procedure or practice requirements of an agency, but does not include:

(a) regulations issued with respect to a military, national security, or foreign affairs function of the United States;

(b) regulations related to agency organization, management, or personnel; or

(c) any other category of regulations exempted by the Director.

Sec. 5. *General Provisions.* (a) Nothing in this order shall be construed to impair or otherwise affect:

(i) the authority granted by law to an executive department or agency, or the head thereof; or

(ii) the functions of the Director relating to budgetary, administrative, or legislative proposals.

(b) This order shall be implemented consistent with applicable law and subject to the availability of appropriations.

(c) This order is not intended to, and does not, create any right or benefit, substantive or procedural, enforceable at law or in equity by any party against the United States, its departments, agencies, or entities, its officers, employees, or agents, or any other person.

DONALD J. TRUMP